# Writing in all its forms, inside the classroom and out

**Coverage and support for writing with new media.**

- Updated Chapter 42, "**Making Presentations and Using Multimedia**," explains how and why to use various strategies for effective oral presentations.
- Updated Chapter 45, "**Document and Visual Design**," helps students make effective and ethical uses of visual rhetoric.
- Revised Chapter 46, "**Multimodal Texts and Writing for the Web**," teaches students how to produce effective texts that incorporate not only images but also sound and video.

**A new streamlined, open, functional design.** The book's layout serves to emphasize the most important topics, ideas, and examples to make finding critical information easy. Greater use of open space, full-color images, and illustrations throughout not only enhances interest for students but also conforms to the increased use of visual rhetoric in composition.

**Quick Reference** features offer must-have information and helpful hints to students.

# www.mycomplab.com

Taking the market-leading resources for writing, grammar, and research that users have come to trust, the new Pearson **MyCompLab®** integrates those resources with an online composing space and new assessment tools. The result is a revolutionary application that offers a seamless and flexible teaching and learning environment built specifically for writers.

## ■ Composing

The new **MyCompLab**'s dynamic space for composing, editing, and revising includes a "Writer's Toolkit" that provides students with writing, grammar, research, and tutoring help at their fingertips. Built to look and function like the most popular word processing programs, **MyCompLab**'s composing space will be familiar to students and easy for them to use.

In this space, students can view instructor, peer, and tutor comments on their documents, pulling together all the feedback they will need to produce better writing. The intuitive commenting functionality will save instructors time by allowing them to insert favorite comments and common errors. It also allows instructors to create personalized study plans for students by linking to tutorials and exercises in the Resources section, putting resources in the context of each student's writing.

## ■ Portfolio

Students can create, publish, manage, and share e-portfolios for their composition course, other courses, or for their personal writing. Students create portfolios by dragging and dropping documents written within **MyCompLab** or by uploading documents from their hard drive. Portfolios can be exported as either .pdf or .html files and can contain images and links to other online media.

# Resources

The Resources area offers instruction, multimedia tutorials, and exercises for a wide range of writing, grammar, and research topics. This is where users of the current version of **MyCompLab** will find the assets with which they are familiar.

- **Writing**—guided assistance through each stage of the writing process, practice exercises, and sample documents from across the curriculum.
- **Grammar**—video tutorials for the most common errors, multiple diagnostics, and more than 4,600 exercises.
- **Research**—self-tests, exercises, and step-by-step guidance through the research process, including coverage of evaluating sources, avoiding plagiarism, and citing sources.

# To Do (Instructor)

From their To Do space, instructors create and grade all assignments for their course. **MyCompLab**'s unique assignment builder enables instructors to create and easily post six kinds of assignments. Instructors can copy assignments across courses and share them with colleagues.

# To Do (Student)

In their To Do view, students see all course assignments created by their instructor and a list of recommended topics from the Resources area. With a clear calendar of assignments—listed by date, type, and status—students can more easily manage their course responsibilities. Students can also add their own personal items to their To Do view.

PEARSON
mycomplab

# PEARSON and your writing program: making progress together

**MyCompLab®.** The new MyCompLab® uniquely integrates proven resources and new assessment tools with a student's own writing. This seamless and flexible application, built for writers by writers, will help instructors and students accomplish everyday composition tasks more easily and effectively.

## Pearson Comp Pro Web Site.

www.pearsonhighered.com/comppro
Growing out of Pearson's deep commitment to the discipline of composition and to the people who teach it, this useful site offers an abundance of professional development resources including audio lectures by renowned rhetoricians, access to book consultants for select texts, author workshops on DVD, *Open Words Journal*, and more.

## Trends & Teaching in Composition: A Professional Development DVD.

The first part of this professional development DVD for Composition teachers offers stimulating insights from renowned rhetoricians on seven topics that represent current approaches and issues in the Composition classroom. The second part provides practical teaching advice from experienced adjuncts and graduate teaching assistants. Segments from *Trends & Teaching* could be used during TA or faculty training, in courses on teaching Composition, as discussion starters in faculty development workshops, or on an individual basis by TAs, part-time faculty, or full-time faculty who are interested in learning new ideas they can apply to their Composition courses.

## Professional Development Series in Composition.

This series of books provides insights and ideas for composition professionals of all experience levels, from WPAs to new teaching assistants. Titles include *The Teaching Assistant's Handbook* by Steven Wilhoit, *The Allyn & Bacon Sourcebook for College Writing Teachers* by James C. McDonald, *The Longman Sourcebook for Writing Program Administrators* by Irene Ward & William Carpenter, and *Theory and Practice for Writing Tutors* by J. Paul Johnson and Ethan Krase.

## Other Great Resources.

Your students can receive a dictionary, thesaurus, or pocket reader when these resources are packaged with a Pearson English title. For complete details and ordering information, please contact your local Pearson sales representative.

ANNOTATED INSTRUCTOR'S EDITION

# Simon & Schuster
# Handbook for Writers

NINTH EDITION

**LYNN QUITMAN TROYKA**

**DOUGLAS HESSE**

Upper Saddle River, NJ 07458

VP/Editorial Director: Leah Jewell
Editor in Chief: Craig Campanella
Executive Editor: Kevin Molloy
Project Manager, Editorial: Jessica A. Kupetz
Editorial Assistant: David Nitti
VP/Director of Marketing: Tim Stookesbury
Executive Marketing Manager:
  Megan Galvin-Fak
Senior Marketing Manager: Susan E. Stoudt
Marketing Assistant: Sara Fry
Text Permissions Specialist: Jane Scelta
Development Editor in Chief: Rochelle Diogenes
Development Editor: Paul Sarkis
Permissions Assistant: Peggy Davis
Senior Operations Specialist: Sherry Lewis
Manager, Image Rights and Permissions:
  Zina Arabia

Manager, Visual Research: Beth Brenzel
Image Permissions Coordinator:
  Ang'John Ferreri
Image Researcher: Beth Brenzel
Senior Art Director: Nancy Wells
Art Director: Anne Nieglos
Interior and Cover Designer: Anne DeMarinis
Cover Art:"Mulberry Tree" 1889 by Vincent Van
  Gogh © The Gallery Collection/Corbis
Full-Service Project Management: Karen Berry,
  Pine Tree Composition, Inc.
Copyeditor: Steve Hopkins
Composition: Pine Tree Composition, Inc.
Printer/Binder: Courier Companies
Cover Printer: Phoenix Color Corporation
Text Font: 10/12 Adobe Garamond

Microsoft® and Windows® are registered trademarks of the Microsoft Corporation in the USA and other countries. Screen shots and icons are reprinted with permission from the Microsoft Corporation.

This book is not sponsored or endorsed by or affiliated with the Microsoft Corporation. For permission to use copyrighted material, grateful acknowledgment is made to the copyright holders on pages 907–911, which are considered an extension of this copyright page.

Pearson Education Ltd., London
Pearson Education Singapore, Pte. Ltd
Pearson Education Canada, Inc.
Pearson Education–Japan
Pearson Education Australia PTY, Limited

Pearson Education North Asia, Ltd., Hong Kong
Pearson Educación de Mexico, S.A. de C.V.
Pearson Education Malaysia, Pte. Ltd.
Pearson Education, Upper Saddle River,
  New Jersey

To order student edition, use
ISBN-13: 978-0-13-602860-4
ISBN-10: 0-13-602860-8

10  9  8  7  6  5  4  3  2  1

**Prentice Hall**
is an imprint of

www.pearsonhighered.com

ISBN-13:
978-0-205-62067-8

ISBN-10:
0-205-62067-1

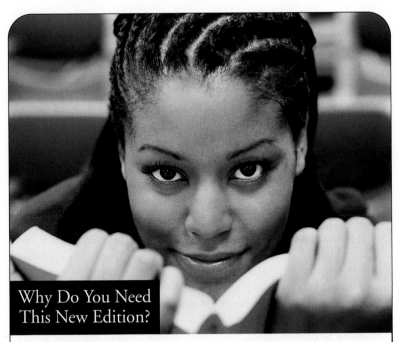

# Why Do You Need This New Edition?

The *Simon & Schuster Handbook for Writers* has been revised to provide more useful instruction and examples for writing students and instructors. Some of the helpful features that you'll find only in the new edition are:

❶ **The most up-to-date coverage of documentation styles:** this ninth edition features the most current standards for MLA and APA documentation, which you'll need in first-year composition as well as in many courses in your field of study.

❷ **New and revised Quick Reference boxes** highlight the most important must-have concepts for easy use. These are key to finding the information you need in the handbook.

❸ New Chapters 2 and 7, **"Essential Processes for Academic Writing"** and **"Strategies for Writing Typical Kinds of College Papers,"** give not only general writing advice but also specific strategies for producing the most common types of academic writing in first-year composition and other courses. (This makes the ninth edition a great resource for any class, not just first-year composition.)

❹ **New** Chapters 43 and 44, **"Business and Professional Writing"** and **"Writing for the Public,"** are great resources for writing outside of your classroom, whether you are creating **resumés, cover letters**, or **personal Web sites.**

❺ The book's **exercises**, which are popular as assignments for many instructors, have been thoroughly revised.

❻ **Coverage and support for writing with new media** includes making oral presentations and using multimedia, document and visual design, and using audio and video.

❼ A **new** Chapter 8, **"Style and Tone in Writing,"** illustrates the importance of *how* you say something in addition to *what* you say.

# HOW TO USE THE SIMON & SCHUSTER HANDBOOK FOR WRITERS

The *Simon & Schuster Handbook for Writers* is designed to help you find what you need to become a better writer. You will find many features intended to highlight key concepts and develop your skills. We are confident that you will find the *Simon & Schuster Handbook for Writers* to be a useful tool for you throughout college and beyond.

- **The detailed Overview of Contents** starting on the inside front cover lists all parts and chapters in the book. Locate the specific topic you need to reference and then turn to the page indicated.
- **MyCompLab®**
- A list of **supplementary material** available with this book can be found in the Preface.
- **Quick Reference boxes**, found throughout the text, highlight some of the most important issues that will come up as you write. You will also find them listed by subject in the Index.
- **Documentation Source Maps** are designed to clearly illustrate the process for citing different types of sources. Annotated replications of original sources are presented along with step-by-step guidelines. Color is used carefully to help students see where information is pulled from a source and then where it is placed in a citation.
- **The Terms Glossary** is an easy way to find the definitions for common writing-related terms. Words and phrases called out in SMALL CAPITAL LETTERS throughout the book can be found in the Terms Glossary.
- **The Index** provides quick and convenient navigation by topic, covering virtually everything in the book. Quick Reference boxes are also listed in the Index according to the topic they refer to.
- **The one-of-a-kind Quick Card** at the end of the book puts some of the most useful information on research and documentation in a portable format. Take the card to class, to the writing lab, or to the library for easy access to invaluable information.
- **A list of Proofreading Marks and Response Symbols** is provided on the inside back cover. Consult this list if your instructor uses revision and proofreading symbols when commenting on your writing.

The sample composite page to the right illustrates features that help you navigate the *Simon & Schuster Handbook for Writers*.

Quick Reference boxes highlight key information.

## Quick Reference 15.7

### Forms of the verbs *do* and *have*

| | | |
|---|---|---|
| SIMPLE FORM | do | have |
| -*S* FORM | does | has |
| PAST TENSE | did | had |
| PRESENT PARTICIPLE | doing | having |
| PAST PARTICIPLE | done | had |

Alerts call attention to important rules and best practices.

**⚠ Alert:** In ACADEMIC WRITING, always use the standard forms for *be, do,* and *have,* as shown in Quick References 15.6 and 15.7.

End of Alert

> The gym **is** [not *be*] a busy place.
> The gym **is** [not *be*] filling with spectators. ●

ESOL icons call out information of particular use for multilingual students.

**🌐 ESOL Tip:** When *be, do,* and *have* function as auxiliary verbs, change their form to agree with a third-person singular subject—and don't add -*s* to the main verb.

End of ESOL Tip

> **NO**   **Does** the library **closes** at 6:00?
>
> **YES**   **Does** the library **close** at 6:00? ●

**EXERCISE 15-4**   Using the auxiliary verbs in the list below, fill in the blanks in the following passage. Use each auxiliary word only once, even if a listed word can fit into more than one blank. For help, consult 15e.

> are   have   may   will   might   can   has

**EXAMPLE**   Completing a marathon <u>can</u> be the highlight of a runner's life.

Exercises for practice and skill-building are offered throughout the text.

(1) The marathon _____ been a challenging and important athletic event since the 19th century. (2) Athletes who _____ training for a marathon _____ use one of the many online training guides. (3) Running with a partner or friend _____ boost confidence and motivation.

Indicates new section of a chapter

## 15f   What are intransitive and transitive verbs?

A verb is **intransitive** when an OBJECT isn't required to complete the verb's meaning: *I sing.* A verb is **transitive** when an object is necessary to complete the verb's meaning: *I need a guitar.* Many verbs have both transitive and intransitive meanings. Some verbs are only transitive: *need, have, like, owe, remember.* Only transitive verbs function in the PASSIVE VOICE. Dictionaries label verbs as transitive (*vt*) or intransitive (*vi*).

Small capitals call out Glossary key terms; these terms are also discussed in depth elsewhere in the text.

For more help with your writing, grammar, and research, go to **www.mycomplab.com**

mycomp**lab**

A wealth of writing resources is available through MyCompLab.

# ESSENTIAL FEATURES OF THE *SIMON & SCHUSTER HANDBOOK FOR WRITERS*

The *Simon & Schuster Handbook for Writers* is an indispensable tool for your composition course, but you'll find that it is full of information that you'll need for writing throughout college and beyond.

**College writing.** New Chapters 2 and 7, "Essential Processes for Academic Writing" and "Strategies for Writing Typical Kinds of College Papers," guide you not only through the writing process but also offer specific instruction for the most common types of academic writing in any of your college courses.

> ### 7e.3 Lab reports and empirical studies
>
> A **lab report** is a specific and formal way of presenting and discussing the results of experiments or laboratory measurements, in fields such as chemistry, biology, physics, engineering, and other sciences. Lab experiments are one kind of **empirical research**, a name that generally refers to attempts to measure something (from physical substances to behaviors) in order to prove or disprove a theory or hypothesis. Disciplines other than the sciences use experiments, too; among them are psychology and other social sciences, some areas of education (for example, "Does this teaching strategy work better than that teaching strategy?"), economics, and so on. However, those disciplines also use sources like surveys or very specific observations to collect data. Both lab reports and other kinds of empirical research studies tend to have the same standard elements.
>
> **Important Sections of Lab Reports and Similar Empirical Studies**
>
> • **Introduction.** State your purpose, present background materials (for example, a review of previous studies), and your hypothesis.

**Writing outside the classroom.** New Chapters 43 and 44, "Business and Professional Writing" and "Writing for the Public," give you essential guidance for resumés and cover letters, memos, and reports.

> ### Quick Reference 43.4
>
> **Guidelines for writing a resumé**
>
> • Place your name, address, e-mail address, and telephone number at the top. If you have a professional Web site or online PORTFOLIO (Chapter 47), include the URL.
> • Make sure you have a professional e-mail address. No employer will be impressed by beermaster@gmail.com or daddyslittlegirl@hotmail.com.
> • Make it easy to read. Label the sections clearly, and target the resumé to the position you want. Help employers see your most significant attributes as quickly and as easily as possible.
> • Adjust your resumé to fit your PURPOSE. For example, if you're applying for a job as a computer programmer, you'll want to emphasize different facts than you would if you're applying for a job selling computers in an electronics store.
> • Use headings to separate blocks of information. Include the following headings, as appropriate: Position Desired or Career Objective; Educa-
> continued >>

**Documentation chapters.** Chapters 36–38 present everything you'll need throughout college when writing any research paper. MLA documentation reflects the anticipated 2009 updates to MLA style as outlined in the third edition of the *MLA Style Manual and Guide to Scholarly Publishing.* APA documentation, used in the social sciences, reflects the latest (2007) guidelines for electronic sources. CSE documentation, for science and engineering, is completely updated to reflect the latest (2006) guidelines.

> **39. Online Version of a Print Magazine Article—MLA**
>
> The example below is for the online version of the same article cited in 25, above. In addition to the print information, include the date you accessed the online version. (If the page numbers from the print version are available, include them, too, before the access date.)
>
> Fallows, James. "The $1.4 Trillion Question." *The Atlantic.com.* Atlantic Monthly Group, Jan.-Feb. 2008. Web. 2 May 2008.
>
> If the article is unsigned, begin with the title.
>
> "Too Smart to Marry." *The Atlantic.com.* Atlantic Monthly Group, 14 Apr. 2005. Web. 7 Mar. 2005.
>
> **40. Online Version of a Print Journal Article—MLA**
>
> Hoge, Charles W., et al. "Mild Traumatic Brain Injury in U.S. Soldiers Returning from Iraq." *New England Journal of Medicine* 358.5 (31 Jan. 2008): 453-63. Web. 10 Sept. 2008.

**Writing with new media.** Chapter 42, "Making Presentations and Using Multimedia," explains how and why to use tools like PowerPoint for presentations, and Chapter 46, "Multimodal Texts and Writing for the Web," teaches you how to create Web sites and other digital texts that incorporate not only images but also sound and video.

**Extensive help for speakers of other languages.** Part 7 is devoted to presenting English to nonnative speakers of English. Going beyond just the basics of grammar, this part of the book will help you understand what your instructors expect from your writing as well as giving you specific help with understanding the many rules of the English language.

**MyCompLab.** The new MyCompLab uniquely integrates proven resources and new assessment tools with a student's own writing. This seamless and flexible application, built for writers by writers, will help instructors and students accomplish everyday composition tasks more easily and effectively.

For more help with your writing, grammar, and research, go to **www.mycomplab.com**

# PREFACE

This ninth edition of the *Simon & Schuster Handbook for Writers* gives you comprehensive access to the information you need about the writing process, from mastering grammar to using correct punctuation, from writing research papers to documenting sources, and from writing for the Web to writing using visuals. The **organizational structure** corresponds to the way that writers actually use the topics and strategies. The newest edition of the *Simon & Schuster Handbook* is carefully designed for usability not just in first-year composition but in other courses outside of English, and beyond the classroom altogether, as illustrated in this Preface.

**New Chapters 2 and 7**, "Essential Processes for Academic Writing" and "Strategies for Writing Typical Kinds of College Papers," guide students not only with general writing advice and processes but also specific strategies for producing the most common types of academic writing in first-year and other courses.

**Emphasizing style as a part of writing effectively**  A new Chapter 8, "Style and Tone in Writing," illustrates for students the importance of *how* they say something in addition to *what* they say.

**A greater focus on writing outside the classroom**  New Chapters 43 and 44, "Business and Professional Writing" and "Writing for the Public," offer students a tangible connection between the concepts they learn in their composition course and the activities they take part in outside the classroom. Both chapters include writing for common genres and writing in new digital environments.

**Coverage and support for writing with new media**

- Updated Chapter 42, "Making Presentations and Using Multimedia," explains how and why to use various strategies for effective oral presentations. This chapter also discusses how to use several types of multimedia and the strategies associated with them.
- Updated Chapter 45, "Document and Visual Design," helps students make effective and ethical uses of visual rhetoric.
- Revised Chapter 46, "Multimodal Texts and Writing for the Web," shows students how to produce effective texts that incorporate not only images but also sound and video, especially in works produced for online audiences.

**Support for multilingual writers integrated throughout**  The *Simon & Schuster Handbook for Writers* is an excellent resource whether English is your native language or you are multilingual. You'll find answers in the *Simon &*

*Schuster Handbook for Writers* to your questions about standard American English grammar, punctuation, and sentence correctness and style. **ESOL Tips** are integrated throughout, and there's a built-in **mini ESOL handbook** (Part 7) devoted to questions of special concern to multilingual students.

**Research and documentation sections that provide applicable strategies and are designed for utility**    We know from talking to instructors and students that the research and documentation sections of a handbook are the most often referenced. Therefore, we have taken great care in designing these sections to be as useful as possible.

- Research chapters emphasize the distinction between scholarly sources (such as those found in libraries and professionally edited databases) and less reliable sources, including strategies for recognizing and integrating credible sources.
- The book emphasizes research as potentially an important component of any writing situation, which teaches students to see the act of researching as valuable beyond designated research papers.
- The use of computer-based research strategies is fully integrated throughout the book.
- Chapter 35, "Using Sources and Avoiding Plagiarism," helps students appreciate the importance of citing sources and provides useful strategies for avoiding plagiarism.

**Completely reorganized MLA documentation, APA documentation, *Chicago Manual* (CM) documentation, and the Council of Science Editors (CSE) documentation**    These sections are designed to help students find the right models quickly and accurately. We have provided updated examples throughout.

**Documentation coverage reflects the most current standards** across the disciplines.

- MLA documentation reflects the anticipated 2009 updates to MLA style as outlined in the third edition of the *MLA Style Manual and Guide to Scholarly Publishing*.
- APA documentation reflects the latest (2007) guidelines for electronic sources.
- CSE documentation is completely updated to reflect the latest version.

**Student and professional writing samples**    The *Simon & Schuster Handbook for Writers* contains eight complete samples of student writing, five of which are new papers, on fresh topics of interest. This book also includes new examples of professional writing. The list on page xi shows just a few of the examples you will find throughout the book.

- Three drafts of a student essay to illustrate drafting and revising strategies (Chapter 2)
- New examples of student writing for several types of academic situations (Chapter 3)
- A new student argument paper that includes research (Chapter 5)
- A student's literature essay (Chapter 40)
- Various examples of business and public writing (Chapter 43 and 44)
- Student-made flyer (Chapter 45) and Web site (Chapter 46)

**A streamlined, open, functional design**   The book's layout serves to emphasize the most important topics, ideas, and examples, making finding critical information easy. Greater use of full-color images and illustrations throughout not only enhances interest for students but also conforms to the increased use of visual rhetoric in composition.

**Boxes** have been revised and reconceived as "Quick Reference" features, offering must-have information and helpful hints to students

## SUPPLEMENTS

The following supplements accompany the ninth edition to aid in teaching and learning:

### For the Instructor

- **Annotated Instructor's Edition (AIE).** Annotations in the margins of the AIE for the *Simon & Schuster Handbook for Writers,* Ninth Edition, offer instructors and teaching assistants teaching tips, annotated bibliographic citations from major journals in composition, thought-provoking quotations about writing, and answers to the in-text exercises.

- **Instructor's Manual.** *Strategies and Resources for Teaching Writing with the Simon & Schuster Handbook for Writers* offers practical, hands-on advice for new and experienced composition instructors for organizing their syllabi, planning, and teaching.

- **Prentice Hall Resources for Writing.** This series is a specially designed set of supplements for the instructor that support timely classroom and composition topics. These supplements are available upon adoption of the *Simon & Schuster Handbook for Writers,* Ninth Edition.

  - *Teaching Writing Across the Curriculum* by Art Young is written for college teachers in all disciplines and provides useful advice on teaching writing across the curriculum.

  - *Teaching Civic Literacy* by Cheryl Duffy offers advice on how to integrate civic literacy into the composition classroom.

- *Teaching Visual Rhetoric* by Susan Loudermilk provides an illustrated look at visual rhetoric and offers guidance on how to incorporate this topic into the classroom.
- *Teaching Writing for ESL Students* by Ruth Spack addresses various strategies that can be employed to teach writing to nonnative speakers.

### For the Instructor and Student

**MyCompLab**    The new MyCompLab uniquely integrates proven resources and new assessment tools with a student's own writing. This seamless and flexible application, built for writers by writers, will help instructors and students accomplish everyday composition tasks more easily and effectively.

**Student Workbook and Answer Key**    *The Simon & Schuster Workbook for Writers* contains hundreds of additional exercises and activities with answers to help improve writing skills.

**Prentice Hall WAC Resources**    A compilation of resources designed to facilitate teaching and learning Writing Across the Curriculum (WAC), which includes *Papers Across the Curriculum* (edited by Judith Ferster), a series of sample student papers, and *A Prentice Hall Pocket Reader: Writing Across the Curriculum* (by Stephen Brown, University of Nevada, Las Vegas). If you would like to put additional emphasis on WAC in your composition course(s), please contact your Pearson sales representative for more information.

**Dictionary, Thesaurus, Writer's Guides, Workbooks, and Pocket Readers**
The following resources can be packaged with the *Simon & Schuster Handbook for Writers,* Ninth Edition. These valuable student resources provide additional depth on specialized topics that may only be touched upon in the text, and allow you to customize the handbook to your specific needs. Contact your local Prentice Hall representative for additional information.

- *The New American Webster Handy College Dictionary*
- *The New American Roget's College Thesaurus*
- *A Writer's Guide to Research and Documentation*
- *A Writer's Guide to Oral Presentations and Writing in the Disciplines*
- *A Writer's Guide to Document and Web Design*
- *A Writer's Guide to Writing About Literature*
- *The Prentice Hall Grammar Workbook*
- *The Prentice Hall ESL Workbook*
- *Applying English to Your Career (Workbook)*

- *A Prentice Hall Pocket Reader: Argument*
- *A Prentice Hall Pocket Reader: Literature*
- *A Prentice Hall Pocket Reader: Patterns*
- *A Prentice Hall Pocket Reader: Themes*
- *A Prentice Hall Pocket Reader: Purposes*
- *A Prentice Hall Pocket Reader: Writing Across the Curriculum*
- *Papers Across the Curriculum*

## ACKNOWLEDGMENTS

With this ninth edition of the *Simon & Schuster Handbook for Writers,* we heartily thank all those students who, to our great luck, have landed in our writing courses. We admire how they and their counterparts in classrooms around the world strive to write skillfully, think critically, and communicate successfully, in college and beyond. We especially thank the individual students who have given us permission to make them "published authors" by including their exemplary writing in this handbook.

Hundreds of students have contacted us by e-mail or letter with their reactions to, and questions about, the *Simon & Schuster Handbook for Writers* or related matters. We deeply appreciate these messages. We take your comments seriously and use them to improve our teaching and this book. Any student now using the *Simon & Schuster Handbook for Writers* is welcome to get in touch with us at <troykalq@nyc.rr.com>, at <dhesse@du.edu>, or c/o Executive English Editor, Pearson Education, One Lake Street, Upper Saddle River, NJ 07458. We promise to answer.

Along with our colleagues at Prentice Hall, we'd like to call special attention to an expert team of advisors and contributors who helped us shape and polish this ninth edition to be a truly great resource for instructors and students alike. We could not have completed this challenging task without the meaningful contributions of this team:

Susan Miller-Cochran, North Carolina State University, provided expert guidance and revisions of sections concerning multilingual writers. Richard Colby and Rebekah Schultz Colby, University of Denver, helped revise sections dealing with design, multimodal writing, and writing with new media. Geoffrey Stacks, University of Denver, skillfully added new exercises throughout the book.

We continue to benefit from expert contributions to earlier editions, including from Melinda Reichelt, University of Toledo; Dorothy Minor, Tulsa Community College; Leslie Leach, College of the Redwoods; and Georgia Newman, Polk Community College, a colleague and dear friend.

For their helpful analytic reviews of the eighth edition of the *Simon & Schuster Handbook for Writers* and drafts of this ninth edition, we sincerely thank Marci Bartolotta, Nova Southeastern University; Jim Baskin, Joliet Junior College; Susan Bussey, University of Science and Arts of Oklahoma; Jason DePolo, North Carolina A&T University; Daren Dean, William Woods University; Cheryl Easly, Central Texas College; John Hodgson, Cameron University; Dawn Hubbell-Staeble, Bowling Green State University; Margaret Loweth, Loyola University of Chicago; Dorothy Minor, Tulsa Community College; Kathryn Nielsen-Dube, Merrimack College; Dawn Pickett, Blinn College; Gavin Richardson, Union University; Sharon Walsh, Loyola University of Chicago; and Pauline Uchmanowitz, SUNY New Paltz.

We're also grateful to past contributors, advisors, and reviewers of this handbook and related projects: Linda de Roche, Wesley College; Andy Anderson, Johnson County Community College; Mailin Barlow, Valencia Community College; Pauline Uchmanowicz, State University of New York, New Paltz; Monroe Lerner, Milwaukee Area Technical College; Carolyn Kinslow, Cameron University; Colleen Lloyd, Cuyahoga Community College; Nate Gordon, Kishwaukee Community College; Muriel Fuqua, Daytona Beach Community College; James McWard, Johnson County Community College; Esther DiMarzio, Kishwaukee Community College; Carolyn Calhoun-Dillahunt, Yakima Valley Community College; Kip Strasma, Illinois Central College; Cy Strom, Colborne Communications Centre in Toronto, Ontario; Mary Angelo, University of South Florida; Martha Bachman, Camden County College; Sandra Barnhill, South Plains College; Nancy Blattner, Longwood University; Brian J. Benson, A&T State University; Ken Claney, Tulsa Community College; Gary Christenson, Elgin Community College; Nita Danko, Purdue University, Calumet; David Elias, Eastern Kentucky University; Diana Grahn, Longview Community College; Jean Harmon, Chemetka Community College; Lola Harmon, Greenville Technical College; Sarah Harrison, Tyler Junior College; Gary Hatch, Brigham Young University; Elaine Kromhout, Indian River Community College; Patrick McMahon, Tallahassee Community College; Dorothy Minor, Tulsa Community College; Catherine C. Olson, Tomball College; Lindee Owens, University of Central Florida; Michael Suwak, College of Southern Maryland; Carolyn West, Daytona Beach Community College; Kathleen Bell, University of Central Florida; Jon Bentley, Albuquerque Technical Vocational Institute; Don Jay Coppersmith, Internet consultant; Jo Ellen Coppersmith, Utah Valley State College; Ann B. Dobie, University of Southwestern Louisiana; David Fear, Valencia Community College; Michael J. Freeman, Director of the Utah Valley State College Library; Kathryn Fitzgerald, University of Utah; Barbara Gaffney, University of New Orleans; D. J. Henry, Daytona Beach Community College; Scott Leonard, Youngstown State University; Dorothy V. Lindman, Brookhaven College; Alice Maclin, DeKalb College; Darlene

Malaska, Youngstown Christian University; Marilyn Middendorf, Embry Riddle University; Patricia Morgan, Louisiana State University; Mary Ruetten, University of New Orleans; Matilda Delgado Saenz; Phillip Sipiora, University of South Florida; Maggy Smith, University of Texas at El Paso; Martha Smith, Brookhaven College; Paulette Smith, Reference Librarian, Valencia Community College; Donnie Yeilding, Central Texas College; Valerie Zimbaro, Valencia Community College; Westrich Baker, Southeast Missouri State University; Marilyn Barry, Alaska Pacific University; Norman Bosley, Ocean Community College; Phyllis Brown, Santa Clara University; Judith A. Burnham, Tulsa Community College; Robert S. Caim, West Virginia University at Parkersburg; Joe R. Christopher, Tarleton State University; Marilyn M. Cleland, Purdue University, Calumet; Thomas Copeland, Youngstown State University; Janet Cutshall, Sussex Community College; Dawn Elmore-McCrary, San Antonio College; Joanne Ferreira, State University of New York at New Paltz and Fordham University; Sheryl Forste-Grupp, Villanova University; Carol L. Gabel, William Paterson College; Joe Glaser, Western Kentucky University; Michael Goodman, Fairleigh Dickinson University; Mary Multer Greene, Tidewater Community College at Virginia Beach; Jimmy Guignard, University of Nevada at Reno; Julie Hagemann, Purdue University, Calumet; John L. Hare, Montgomery College; Kimberly Harrison, Florida International University; Lory Hawkes, DeVry Institute of Technology, Irving; Janet H. Hobbs, Wake Technical Community College; Frank Hubbard, Marquette University; Rebecca Innocent, Southern Methodist University; Ursula Irwin, Mount Hood Community College; Denise Jackson, Southeast Missouri State University; Margo K. Jang, Northern Kentucky University; Peggy Jolly, University of Alabama at Birmingham; Myra Jones, Manatee Community College; Rodney Keller, Brigham Young University, Idaho; Judith C. Kohl, Dutchess Community College; James C. McDonald, University of Southwestern Louisiana; Martha Marinara, University of Central Florida; Michael J. Martin, Illinois State University; Michael Matto, Yeshiva University; Susan J. Miller, Santa Fe Community College; Pamela Mitzelfeld, Oakland University; Rosemary G. Moffett, Elizabethtown Community College; Rhonda Morris, Lake City Community College; Roarck Mulligan, Christopher Newport University; Alyssa O'Brien, Stanford University; Jon F. Patton, University of Toledo; Pamela T. Pittman, University of Central Oklahoma; Nancy B. Porter, West Virginia Wesleyan College; Stephen Prewitt, David Lipscomb University; Kirk Rasmussen, Utah Valley State College; Edward J. Reilly, St. Joseph's College; Mary Anne Reiss, Elizabethtown Community College; Peter Burton Ross, University of the District of Columbia; Eileen Schwartz, Purdue University, Calumet; Lisa Sebti, Central Texas College; Eileen B. Seifert, DePaul University; John S. Shea, Loyola University at Chicago; Tony Silva, Purdue University; Beverly J. Slaughter, Broward Community College; Martha A. Smith, Brookhaven College; Scott R.

Stankey, Anoka Ramsey Community College; Bill M. Stiffler, Harford Community College; Michael Strysick, Wake Forest University; Jack Summers, Central Piedmont Community College; Susan Swartwout, Southeast Missouri State College; Vivian A. Thomlinson, Cameron University; Michael Thro, Tidewater Community College at Virginia Beach; William P. Weiershauser, Iowa Wesleyan College; Joe Wenig, Purdue University; Carolyn West, Daytona Beach Community College; Roseanna B. Whitlow, Southeast Missouri State University; and the late and wildly admired Sally Young, University of Tennessee at Chattanooga.

A project as complicated as the *Simon & Schuster Handbook for Writers* cannot be undertaken without the expertise and dedication of many professionals. We would like to thank the exceptional people at Prentice Hall who facilitated our work on the ninth edition. We're especially grateful for the expertise of Kevin Molloy, Paul Sarkis, Dave Nitti, Jessica Kupetz, Leslie Taggart, Megan Galvin, Joan Foley, Ann Marie McCarthy, Anne Nieglos, Anne DeMarinis, Leah Jewell, Craig Campanella, Rochelle Diogenes, and Yolanda De Rooy. All have worked creatively, tirelessly, and with good cheer.

Doug values Lynn Troyka's vast knowledge, skill, dedication to teaching, and patience. He appreciates the support of all his colleagues at the University of Denver, but most specifically Eliana Schonberg, Amy Kho, Jennifer Karas, and Gregg Kvistad. He further states, "Carol Rutz, Cheryl Glenn, Erika Lindemann and, always, Kathi Yancey have been exemplary professional and personal friends. Dan Graybill, Susan Bellas, and Laurence Bellas are constant sources of support and friendship. My children, Monica, Andrew, and Paige, amaze me with their creativity, as does the best writer I know: Becky Bradway, my wife."

Lynn is especially grateful to her coauthor Doug Hesse for his gentle friendship and invaluable participation in revising the *Simon & Schuster Handbook for Writers* for its eighth edition. Lynn also places on the record her gratitude to Ida Morea, her administrative assistant and special pal, Lynn's central support with her solid expertise and clever problem solving; Kristen Black, along with Dan, Lindsey, and Ryan, the beloved, ever-present joy of her life; Avery Ryan, Lynn's superb friend and "niece," along with Jimmy, Gavin, and Ian, for being irreplaceably woven into the texture of her life; and Edith Klausner, Lynn's sister and grand friend, a vital part of her life. Other exceptional folks include Susan Bartelstone; Florence Bolden; Rita and Hy Cohen; Esther DiMarzio; Alan, Lynne, Adam, and Josh Furman; Edie and Alan Lipp; JoAnn Lavery; Roberta Moore; Betty Renshaw; Magdelena Rogalskaja; Joseph W. Thweatt; Lisa and Nathaniel Wallace; Muriel Wolfe; and extraordinary Douglas Young III and his wife Anna. Principally, Lynn thanks her husband and sweetheart, David Troyka, for being her treasured companion and most discerning critic.

*Lynn Quitman Troyka*
*Doug Hesse*

To David, the love of my life

LYNN QUITMAN TROYKA

To Don and Coral Hesse

DOUG HESSE

■ ■ ■ ■ ■ ■ ■

# Personal Message to Students

## FROM LYNN QUITMAN TROYKA AND DOUG HESSE

As writers, many of you have much in common with both of us. Sure, we've been at it longer, so we've had more practice, and most rules have become cemented in our heads. However, we share with you a common goal: to put ideas into words worthy of someone else's reading time.

We also share the constant desire to become better writers. Given our extensive teaching experience, this probably sounds odd. However, writing is a lifelong enterprise. Just as we did, you'll write not only in composition classes, but also in other courses throughout college. Writing will likely be an important part of your career, of your role as a public citizen, and even of your personal life. It has certainly been central to ours. Whenever we get stuck in an unfamiliar writing situation or while learning new writing technology, we rummage through strategies we've developed over time. We talk to friends and colleagues, in person, by phone, and by e-mail, and they consult us, too.

We offer this book to you, then, as our partners in the process of writing. We hope that its pages help you give voice to your thoughts—now and years from now. We trust you'll find our advice useful in the wide range of writing situations you're bound to encounter in college and in life. You're always welcome to write us at <troykalq@nyc.rr.com> or <ddhesse@du.edu> to share your reactions to this book and your experiences as writers. We promise to answer.

Each of us would like to end this message with a personal story.

*From Doug:* I first glimpsed the power of writing in high school, when I wrote sappy—but apparently successful—love poems. Still, when I went to college, I was surprised to discover all I didn't know about writing. Fortunately, I had good teachers and developed lots of patience. I needed it. I continue to learn from my colleagues, my students, and my coauthor, Lynn.

*From Lynn:* When I was an undergraduate, handbooks for writers weren't common. Questions about writing nagged at me. One day, browsing in the library, I found an incorrectly shelved, dust-covered book whose title included the words *handbook* and *writing.* I read it hungrily and kept checking it out from the library. Back then, I could never have imagined that someday I might write such a book myself. Now that we've completed the ninth edition of the *Simon & Schuster Handbook for Writers,* I'm amazed that I ever had the nerve to begin. This proves to me—and I hope to you—that anyone can write. Students don't always believe that. I hope you will.

With cordial regards,

*Lynn Quitman Troyka*    *Doug Hesse*

# PREFACE: ANNOTATED INSTRUCTOR'S EDITION

In this *Annotated Instructor's Edition (AIE)* to accompany the *Simon & Schuster Handbook for Writers*, Ninth Edition, annotations in the margins provide instructors and teaching assistants with teaching tips, annotated bibliographic citations from major journals in composition, thought-provoking quotations about writing, and answers to the book's exercises, which cite the related subsections in the chapter so that teachers can instantly diagnose each student's exact strengths and weaknesses.

This *AIE* is an invaluable resource for first-time writing teachers and seasoned veterans alike. Indeed, the *AIE* is meant for anyone who prefers a comprehensive handbook that consistently applies up-to-date theory in rhetoric, linguistics, and learning; respects and encourages students' journeys to become increasingly comfortable and skillful writers; and recognizes the benefits of rigor supported by time-tested clearly presented information and an accessible, user-friendly tone.

This AIE was revised and updated, alongside the Ninth Edition of the *Simon & Schuster Handbook for Writers,* with invaluable help and hard work from Elizabeth Clark and Carlos Hernandez.

# Writing Situations and Processes

# 1

# Understanding College and Other Writing Situations

## 1a What is the current scene for writers in college and beyond?

Writing well improves your success in college. That plain fact has been true for decades. However, writing plays an equally key role in your career and your life beyond the classroom. We wrote this book to help you achieve success in all of these settings. As writers and writing teachers, we find it fascinating—and heartening—to witness the current explosion of writing. You might be among the millions of people who regularly compose e-mails and text messages, keep journals or **blogs**, craft stories or poems, create Web sites, or use FaceBook or MySpace to connect with others—all without anyone asking you to do so. Ordinary people write about their favorite television programs, analyze politics, or simply share their experiences and thoughts. The Internet and wireless devices have made it easier for people to share writing, and digital technologies allow them to mix words, images, sounds, and videos. We live in an age when people do more writing than they have at any other time in history.

If you're someone who chooses to write out of personal interest, we offer this book to help you stretch into new types of writing. If you don't very much like to write, we hope that you might discover the satisfaction of putting your thoughts into words—and we hope this book helps ease your way. We've composed these pages because we repeatedly see in our classes that everyone can make the concentrated effort needed to become an effective writer. Certainly, if you spend time and energy working on your writing skills, your efforts can bring you academic, professional, and personal rewards.

Probably your most immediate interest in using this book is the writing you'll do in college. As a student, you can expect to write in almost every course, not just in English or first-year writing. Chapter 2 of this book explains general processes that are useful for most academic writing. Chapter 7 focuses on common types of college papers, while Chapters 39 to 41 give advice for writing in different disciplines.

Writing is also vital in your career. A survey of business leaders by the National Commission on Writing found that "most professional employees are expected to write" and that "individual opportunity in the United States depends critically on

**Figure 1.1** Different varieties and styles of writing

use with your students. Here are a few ways: (1) You could greet the class with a different quotation on the board each day. (2) You could use quotations to begin class discussions about writing issues. (3) You could give students a quotation as a prompt for a journal entry, for freewriting, or for an essay exploring their own views about writing.

**TEACHING TIP**
The concept of a writing situation may be new to many students. In this book, *writing situation* is used as an inclusive term for the combination of topic, purpose, audience, and special requirements such as word or time limits. Each of these variables influences every decision a writer makes. These variables are especially important in narrowing a topic, as demonstrated by the inclusion of writing situations in the examples in Chapter 2.

**QUOTATION: ON WRITING**
Writing teaches us our mysteries.
—Marie de L'Incarnation

**QUOTATION: ON WRITING**
Education is our passport to the future, for tomorrow belongs to the people who prepare for it today.
—Malcolm X

**QUOTATION: ON WRITING**
I shall live badly if I do not write, and I shall write badly if I do not live.
—Françoise Sagan

the ability to present one's thoughts coherently, cogently, and persuasively on paper" (*Writing: A Ticket to Work . . . or a Ticket Out?* College Board, 2004). Recent studies of people in a variety of jobs and professions find that they spend an average of 30 percent of each day writing. We explain business writing in Chapter 43.

## 1b  What is a writing situation?

Think of the following situations: writing a text message to a friend; a research paper for a history class; a job application letter; a Web site for a museum. These situations result in texts widely different in length, format, content, organization, style, and so on. A **writing situation** is the combination of several elements: your topic, your purpose, your audience, your role as a writer, and your context and special requirements.

**TEACHING TIP**

To help students better understand the Elements of a Writing Situation, choose 3–4 different students to be on a panel at the front of the room. Assign each student the same topic and purpose, but a different audience, role, and context. For example, ask students to talk about whether or not file sharing for music should be legal. One student could play a student trying to convince a dean that the college's network should not prohibit file sharing; another student might play a music executive providing testimony in a legal case that file sharing affects profits for artists; still another student might play the role of an artist who, in an interview, explains why she prefers to let her fans download her music for free. For a homework assignment, students might be asked to find "real life" examples of each audience and role and to analyze the elements of the writing situation in each piece.

**BACKGROUND**

*A Theory of Discourse* by James L. Kinneavy (New York: Norton, 1980) is a classic citation in composition and rhetoric. To this day, many theorists, researchers, and practitioners rely on Kinneavy's work. Kinneavy explores the fundamental purposes for which people use language. He explains the centrality of the concept of purpose in writing:

> Purpose in discourse is all important. The aim of a discourse determines everything else in the process of discourse. "What" is talked about, the oral or written medium which is chosen, the words and grammatical patterns used—all of these are largely determined by the purpose of the discourse. (48)

Kinneavy is enthusiastic about the potential for composition as a field of scholarship:

> It is the thesis of this work that the field of composition—or discourse as it will presently be termed—is a rich and fertile discipline with a worthy past which should be consulted before being consigned to oblivion, an exciting present, and a future that seems as limitless as either linguistics or literature. (2)

## Quick Reference 1.1

### Elements of a writing situation

- **Topic:** What subject will you be writing about?
- **Purpose:** What should the writing accomplish? (see 1c)
- **Audience:** Who are your main readers? (see 1d)
- **Role:** How do you want your audience to perceive you?
- **Context and Special Requirements:** When and how will your writing be read? Do you have requirements such as length, type of writing, format, or due dates?

We explain the important concepts of **purpose** and **audience** in sections 1c and 1d, but first we'll define some other elements of the writing situation. You'll often be assigned a topic, the subject you need to write about and, perhaps, the sources (7b) that you'll need to use. Topics can be very general ("Write about poverty") or very specific ("Analyze the factors that led to James Ferguson's poverty"); you'll be more successful if you narrow broad topics (2b.3).

It may surprise you to learn that you can take on different **roles** (personalities or identities) for different writing situations. For example, suppose you're trying to persuade readers to save energy. You might emphasize your concerns as a prospective parent who is personally worried about the future, or you might instead present yourself as an objective and impersonal analyst.

The **context** of your purpose and audience can affect the writing situation. Context refers to the circumstances in which your readers will encounter your writing. For example, persuading people to buy fuel-efficient cars when gas costs $1 per gallon is very different from when it costs well over $4. Informing college students about child-care options when your message will appear on a poster in the student center is different from when that message appears in the campus newspaper.

**Special requirements** are practical matters such as how much time you're given to complete the assignment and the required length of your writing. For example, your reading audience expects more from an assignment that you had a week to complete than from one due overnight. In the second case, your readers realize you had to write in relative haste, though no one ever accepts sloppy or careless work. Your audience expects most from assignments that call for reading or other research, so be sure to build enough time for that process early into your schedule.

Understanding a writing situation guides your writing process and shapes your final draft. A writing process that might be effective in one situation might not be appropriate for another, and the final drafts would have different characteristics. For example, consider the following task: "In a five-page paper for a political science course, describe government restrictions on cigarette advertising." Your INFORMATIVE* purpose would require careful research and an objective, serious style, complete with a list of works cited or references. In contrast, if you were asked to write a 300-word newspaper editorial arguing that "Smoking should (or should not) be banned in all public places," your writing would reflect your PERSUASIVE purpose for a public audience, explain positions more quickly, probably have a more energetic style, and include no list of references. Consider other examples. Writing a history paper in the short, informal style of a text message definitely won't impress a professor. Similarly, texting your friends in long paragraphs will make them impatient (and perhaps wonder who's using your cell phone).

As the above examples show, your writing situation also helps determine the tone of your writing. Tone refers to the attitude conveyed in writing, mostly by the writer's word choice. A tone can be formal, informal, laid back, pompous, sarcastic, concerned, judgmental, sympathetic, and so on. The tone you use greatly affects your readers' sense of the ROLE you've chosen. If you want to come across as a serious, thoughtful writer in an academic situation, but your tone is sarcastic and biting, your readers won't take you seriously. We discuss tone at greater length in section 17d.

**EXERCISE 1-1**    Either in a class discussion or in a short paper, explain how these different situations would result in different kinds of writing: a résumé and cover letter, a research paper for a sociology course, an e-mail to a friend about that sociology paper, a poster for an upcoming concert, a newspaper editorial.

## 1c  What does "purpose" mean for writing?

A writer's purpose motivates what and how he or she writes. Quick Reference 1.2 lists four major purposes for writing.

### 1c.1  What is expressive writing?

**Expressive writing** is writing to express your personal thoughts, feelings, and opinions. Some expressive writing is for the writer's eyes only, such as that in diaries, personal journals, or exploratory drafts. Other people, however, express themselves in e-mails to friends and colleagues or in blogs for all the world to see. A crucial reason for much of this kind of writing is simply for people to make connections with others. Social networking sites like Facebook, for example, do impart information and, occasionally, try to persuade others; however, their main purpose is to establish and deepen human contact. This purpose, which

---

*Words printed in SMALL CAPITAL LETTERS are discussed elsewhere in the text and are defined in the Terms Glossary at the back of this book.

Other modern influential theorists who concentrate on writers' purposes include the highly respected James Britton, who classifies purposes as poetic, expressive, and transactional. More recently, scholars of rhetoric and composition have discussed the problems caused when teachers expect writers always to have a clear purpose in mind before writing. Writers often discover their purpose as they write, and their purpose may change from draft to draft.

**QUOTATION: ON WRITING**
The role of writers is not to say what we can all say, but what we are unable to say.

—Anaïs Nin

**ANSWERS: EXERCISE 1-1**
Answers will vary. You might want to make a chart on the board, with the categories "Resume," "Cover Letter, "Sociology Research Paper," "E-mail to a friend," "Poster," and "Newspaper Editorial." Working as a class, you can solicit ideas from students about the ways in which the discourse changes for each writing situation. The emphasis for this exercise, whether it is completed as a class, in small groups, or individually at home, is for students to understand how the role, purpose, audience, context, and specific requirements of any writing situation affect the writing.

**TEACHING TIP**
One good way to help students understand tone is to select a particularly sarcastic editorial or letter to the editor from a current newspaper and ask students to rewrite the selection in an objective voice with a somewhat formal tone. This assignment adapts well for online classes, for an out-of-class assignment, or for in-class work—whether as a reflective, solo activity or for collaborative group work. When students post their rewrites online or read them in class, they are able to see or hear and evaluate a variety of options.

**BACKGROUND**
Since the 1870s, writing has sometimes been classified according to four modes of discourse: narration, description, exposition, and

argumentation. These modes describe some characteristics of written products. The modes overlap often. A writer might narrate an incident in the service of arguing an opinion; a writer might describe a scene in the service of offering information.

This handbook starts with the purposes for writing. Purposes are familiar territory for instructors used to modes because two of the modes are purposes: People write for the purpose of informing (expositing) and for the purpose of persuading (arguing). The concept of purposes is based on the notion that people write for a reason. Most college writing is done either to inform or to persuade.

**TEACHING TIP**

To begin a course in composition, you might ask students to talk about the kinds of writing they already do. Chapter 1 begins by engaging students with examples like FaceBook, MySpace, blogs, and other forms of personal writing. As you begin the course, you will want to help students transition between these forms of public, personal writing and academic writing. Work with students to make a public list of the kinds of writing they already do. Then, ask students to talk about how these kinds of writing situations are often different from academic writing. What makes these situations different? What makes students feel successful in each kind of writing? Do students write to inform or persuade in these contexts? Would students use the label of "writer" to describe their relationship between writing and keeping a blog? Updating a page on FaceBook? Writing a research paper? Why or why not?

To encourage students to share their experiences, ask them first to jot down some notes and then participate in the discussion. If the group is large, you can divide it into small groups and give each group specific directions (written are more effective than oral) about what to discuss. The directions can have students discuss, in turn, each question listed in the preceding paragraph. After a suitable amount of time, you might ask each group to report to the whole class.

---

## Quick Reference 1.2
■ ■ ■ ■ ■ ■

### Purposes for writing

- To express yourself or build connections with others
- To inform a reader
- To persuade a reader
- To create a literary work

In this handbook, we concentrate on two major purposes for most forms of college writing: to **inform** and to **persuade**. The two remaining purposes listed above are important for contributing to human thought and culture, but they relate less to what most college writing involves.

---

is as old as personal letter writing, has been invigorated by digital communication. For example, Figure 1.2 is part of a blog kept by Doug's friend, Dan.

Still other expressive writing is just to blow off steam. Writing that "Congressman Miller is a total idiot" might make an author feel good, but simply expressing that belief won't change many minds. Finally, some expressive writing for public audiences falls into the category of literary writing. The excerpt here comes from a memoir intended for public reading.

> For much of her life my mother longed, passionately longed, for a decent house. One with a yard that did not have to be cleared with an ax. One with a roof that kept out the rain. One with a floor that you could not fall through. She longed for a beautiful house of wood or stone. Or of red brick, like the houses her many sisters and their husbands had. When I was thirteen she found such a house. Green-shuttered, white-walled. Breezy. With a lawn and a hedge and giant pecan trees. A porch swing. There her gardens flourished in spite of the shade, as did her youngest daughter, for whom she sacrificed her life doing hard labor in someone else's house, in order to afford peace and prettiness for her child, to whose grateful embrace she returned each night.
>
> —Alice Walker, "My Mother's Blue Bowl"

## 1c.2    What is informative writing?

Informative writing seeks to give information to readers and usually to explain it. Another name for this type of writing is expository writing because it expounds on—sets forth in detail—observations, ideas, facts, scientific data, and statistics. You can find informative writing in textbooks, encyclopedias, technical and business reports, manuals, nonfiction books, newspapers, and many magazines.

The essential goal of informative writing is to educate your readers about something. Like all good educators, therefore, you want to present your infor-

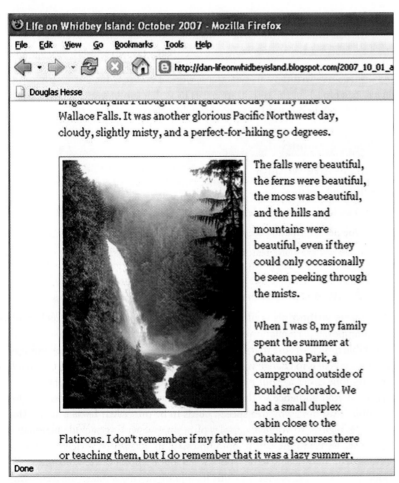

Figure 1.2 A blog written for friends

mation clearly, accurately, completely, and fairly. In Chapter 3 of this handbook, we show you many strategies that writers use for informative writing. These strategies can help you deliver your message, but above all, your success depends on whether your readers can verify your information as accurate. Quick Reference 1.3 gives you a checklist to assess your informative writing. But first, here's a paragraph written to inform.

"Diamonds in the rough" are usually round and greasy looking. But diamond miners are in no need of dark glasses to shield them from the dazzling brilliance of the mines for quite another reason: even in a diamond pipe, there is only one part diamond per 14 million parts of worthless rock.

been writers. They wish they had a book in print.

—James Michener

**TEACHING TIP**

Basic writers feel more confident when they are provided a stimulus, a "springboard into writing," that is immediately accessible—either because it is drawn from personal experience or because it opens the world of the imagination. "A Dangerous Carnival Ride" is one such topic. You may ask your students to discuss how such a topic could be developed as a narrative for teens, as a description for parents, as an informative piece for a board of safety inspectors, as a persuasive letter to the local Better Business Bureau. In the process, students learn how purpose and audience direct their writing.

**QUOTATION: ON WRITING**

The mere imparting of information is not education. Above all things, the effort must result in making a man think and do for himself.

—Carter G. Woodson, 1933

**BACKGROUND**

In "Up Close and Personal: A Real-World Audience Awareness Assignment" (*Teaching English in the Two-Year College,* March 1999: 286–290), Shelley M. Ellis suggests that instructors promote audience awareness by having students analyze and then respond to actual complaint letters. Working with students on audience awareness, particularly in the digital age, is a critical component of classroom writing. You can build on previous conversations with students about the kinds of writing they already do to discuss audience awareness.

**TEACHING TIP**

To help students understand the importance of audience, you may want to ask them to submit sample blogs that they enjoy reading. You can add to that list by choosing some well-written, audience-focused blogs. In your list, make sure that you have a good range of diverse opinions, writing styles, and topics. Divide students into groups and ask them to think about the ways in

Approximately 46,000 pounds of earth must be mined and sifted to produce the half-carat gem you might be wearing. No wonder diamonds are expensive!

—Richard B. Manchester, "Diamonds"

As informative writing, this paragraph works because it focuses clearly on its TOPIC (diamonds in the rough), presents facts that can be verified (who, what, when, where), and is written in a reasonable tone.

---

**Quick Reference 1.3**  ■ ■ ■ ■ ■ ■

**Informative writing**

- Is its information clear?
- Does it present facts, ideas, and observations that can be verified?
- Does its information seem complete and accurate?
- Is the writer's TONE reasonable and free of distortions? (8d)

---

**1c.3    What is persuasive writing?**

**Persuasive writing**, also called *argumentative* writing, seeks to persuade readers to support a particular opinion. When you write to persuade, you deal with debatable topics—those that people can consider from more than one point of view. Your goal is to change your readers' minds—or at least to bring your readers' opinions closer to your point of view. To succeed, you want to evoke a reaction in your audience so that they think beyond their present position (for example, reasoning why free speech needs to be preserved) or take action (for example, register to vote). Examples of persuasive writing include newspaper editorials, letters to the editor, opinion essays in magazines, reviews, sermons, advertising, fund-raising letters, books that argue a point of view, business proposals, and so on. Chapter 5 of this handbook discusses many different ways to write effective arguments.

In general terms, persuasive writing means you need to move beyond merely stating your opinion. You need to give the basis for that opinion. You support your opinion by using specific, illustrative details to back up your **generalizations**, which are usually very broad statements. The first sentences of sections 1c.1, 1c.2, and 1c.3 in this chapter are examples of generalizations.

Quick Reference 1.4 gives you a checklist to assess your persuasive writing. But first, here's a short passage written to persuade.

Our nation's economic and democratic future depends on preparing more students to succeed in college, work and life. We must engage all students in meaningful and rigorous academic work in high school and prepare more of them to succeed in college.

Connecting studies to real-world issues through learning communities is a proven way to get students engaged and motivated. But there is a difference between providing students with good learning environments that include fellow students with similar interests and narrowing students' options by tracking especially less-advantaged students into career-oriented paths in high school.

The fact is that many of the well-paying jobs that today's ninth graders might have 10 years from now do not yet exist—and the technical demands of all jobs are changing so rapidly that narrowing one's academic focus too early won't prepare one well for college and will diminish rather than enhance one's employability over the long term.

The key to success in the global economy is having the broad capacities and knowledge developed by a solid liberal education. In an economy fueled by innovation, these capabilities have, in fact, become America's most valuable economic asset.

—Debra Humphreys, "Give Students Broad
Education, Not Narrow Vocational Tracks"

As persuasive writing, this passage works because it provides factual information on school and work; it expresses a point of view that resides in sound reasoning (American schools should emphasize broad general education and not narrow vocational tracks); it offers evidence (a logical line of reasoning); and it tries to get the reader to agree with the point of view.

## Quick Reference 1.4   ■ ■ ■ ■ ■ ■ ■

### Persuasive writing

- Does it present a point of view about which opinions vary?
- Does it support its point of view with specifics?
- Does it provide sound reasoning and logic?
- Are the parts of its argument clear?
- Does it intend to evoke a reaction from the reader?

**EXERCISE 1-2**   For each paragraph, decide if the dominant purpose is informative, persuasive, or expressive. Then, use the information in section 1c to explain your answers.

A.    Trees are living archives, carrying within their structure a record not only of their age but also of precipitation and temperature for each year in which a ring was formed. The record might also include the marks of forest fires, early frosts and, incorporated into the wood itself, chemical elements the tree removed from its environment. Thus, if we only knew how to unlock its secrets, a tree could tell us a great deal about what was happening in its

which various blogs are addressed to different types of readers. The blogs and the diverse audiences they assume can lead to lively conversations, especially if the class is divided into groups for early discussion and later reconvenes as a whole class. You can also modify this assignment to focus on current publications. Giving students a list of publications popular with varied groups of people will ensure effective contrasts in the articles they find. (The monthly magazine *Writer's Digest* lists publication sources, with a brief description of audiences for many magazines.) In either case, this exercise can help students to understand the idea of audience awareness and the distinctions between a generally educated or specialist audience.

**QUOTATION: ON WRITING**
I have come to feel that "the voice of the text" best describes what actually happens. We all speak one way to grandfather in the nursing home and another to an old acquaintance at a party. We have child voices and parent voices, neighborhood voices and stranger voices, a hundred varieties of work voices, voices for friends and voices for lovers.

—Donald M. Murray

**ANSWERS: EXERCISE 1-2**
**A.** Informative. While the paragraph is written in an interesting and engaging way, Trefil does not take a position on what one should do with the information found there. There is no "call to action." The fact that trees contain precipitation and temperature records is not debatable, but based on scientific research. The point is to inform the reader that trees contain information that is useful to future generations.

**B.** Persuasive. Is physical location a thing of the past? Lanham is writing to persuade the reader that "physicality" does not matter. This is an interesting and debatable argument; therefore, Lanham has to persuade a reader to agree with him.

**C.** Expressive. Although this writing has some factual information about Linda's dog, Littleman, the piece also expresses Linda's personal thoughts and opinions. For example, Simone is "snobby" and Littleman is "friendly." These comments distinguish the piece from an informative piece. Since Linda is not writing to persuade the reader about the dogs, this cannot be categorized as a persuasive piece.

**TEACHING TIP**

Ask students, individually or in groups, to choose something specific about their college or university that they would like to see developed, eliminated, or improved in a particular way. Ask them to jot down notes on the details, including what, when, where, how, and why. Next, ask them to imagine three different audiences: an administrator or professor who might have the power to act on their request; a group of peers whose support they may want to secure; a Board of Regents or Trustees or other formal body to whom they may appeal if their request is not approved by the administration. Allot the students some time to make three-column notes (a column for each audience), responding to the following questions: What and how much detail should be mentioned? What tone should be used? At this point, all can come together in small groups (best) or in one large group. The ensuing discussion should help students connect with the concept that audience differences call for different tones and techniques. Further guided discussion might reveal how audiences themselves are not static, how one member of a board, for example, may have different needs and expectations from another.

**ANSWERS: EXERCISE 1-3**

Answers will vary. The focus is on differences in tone for the same topic. Ask students to consult the Quick References 1.3 and 1.4 to distinguish between informative and persuasive writing.

**BACKGROUND**

The essays in *Public Works: Student Writing as Public Text* (Portsmouth, NH: Boynton/Cook-Heinemann, 2001), edited by Emily J. Isaacs and Phoebe Jackson, offer strategies for having students publish their writings, as well as several

neighborhood from the time of its beginning. Trees can tell us what was happening before written records became available. They also have a great deal to tell us about our future. The records of past climate that they contain can help us to understand the natural forces that produce our weather, and this, in turn, can help us plan.

—James S. Trefil, "Concentric Clues from Growth Rings Unlock the Past"

B.    Actual physical location threatens to evaporate everywhere we look. Information, we are everywhere taught, has annihilated distances. Surgeons can cut you open from a thousand miles away. Facsimile Las Vegas casinos deliver Rome and New York on the same daily walk. You don't have to go to the office to go to the office. You can shop in your kitchen and go to school in your living room. And, sadly enough, when you actually do go out shopping, one mall seems much like another. For what actually matters, physicality doesn't matter anymore. Even with money; now, we are told, information about money is more important than the actual green.

—Richard Lanham, *The Economics of Attention*

C.    Although Littleman, my eleven-year-old poodle, has never been separated from his thirteen-year-old mother, Simone, they are remarkably different. Simone weighs in at about five kilograms with very delicate, sophisticated features and coarse, curly hair. Slightly shorter, Littleman tops the scale at no more than three kilograms and is quite handsome with his teddy-bear features and soft wavy hair. Simone was the first dog in the family and is a pedigreed poodle. In many ways she is the picture of a thoroughbred, with her snobby attitude and nonchalant manners. On the other hand, Littleman came into the family a year later with four other puppies of pure breeding, but they were never registered. Unlike his mother, Littleman is very friendly, almost to the point of being pesty at times.

—Linda Neal, student

**EXERCISE 1-3**    Consulting section 1c, write on each of these topics twice, once to inform and once to persuade your reader: diets, tastes in music, reality television, part-time jobs, road rage. Be prepared to discuss how your two treatments of each topic differ.

# 1d    What does "audience" mean for writing?

Your **audience** consists of everyone who will read your writing, but it especially refers to readers to whom you're most directly aiming your words. For example, anyone can read an issue of *The New England Journal of Medicine* (or at least try), but that publication is aimed at doctors and medical researchers. Thinking about audience means figuring out how to reach your audience in various kinds of situations. For example, papers that you write for a history course differ in form and style from lab reports that you write in biology, and both differ from memos that you write on the job, letters that you write to a newspaper editor, or e-mails that you write to a friend. Effective writers know they need to adjust their writing for different tasks and audiences.

After college, your audiences are likely to be readers of your business, professional, and public writing (Chapters 43–44). In college, you'll surely address a mix of audience types that expect to read ACADEMIC WRITING. Here's a list of categories of those audiences, each of which is detailed in the section listed in parentheses.

- General educated audiences (1d.1)
- Specialist audiences (1d.2)
- Your instructor (who represents your general or specialized readers) (1d.3)
- Your peers (classmates, co-workers, friends, or others like yourself) (6a)

The more specifics you understand about each of your audiences, the better your chances of communicating with them successfully.

🌐 **ESOL Tips:** (1) If you do not share a cultural background with your readers, it may be difficult for you to estimate how much your readers know about your topic. Discussing your topic with friends or classmates might help you decide what background information you need to include in your paper.

(2) As someone from a non-US culture, you might be surprised—even offended—by the directness with which people speak and write in the United States. If so, we hope you'll read our open letter—it introduces Part Seven of this handbook—to multilingual students about honoring their cultures. You may come from a written-language tradition that expects elaborate, formal, or ceremonial language; that reserves the central point of an academic essay for the middle; that requires tactful, indirect discussions (at least in comparison with the US style); and, in some cultures, that accommodates digressions that might, or might not, lead back to the main point. In contrast, US writers and readers expect language and style that are very direct, straightforward, and without embellishment (as compared with the styles of many other cultures). US college instructors expect essays in academic writing to contain a thesis statement (usually at the end of the introductory paragraph). They further expect your writing to contain an organized presentation of information that moves tightly from one paragraph to the next, with generalizations that you always back up with strong supporting details, and with an ending paragraph that presents a logical conclusion to your discussion. Also, for writing in the United States, you need to use so-called edited American English. This means following the rules used by educated speakers. In reality, the United States has a rich mixture of grammar systems, but academic

cautions. You may want to experiment with a "classroom contained" type of public writing—having students publish on a class-specific site on BlackBoard, WebCT, or Angel. This will keep students' writing private within the context of the course, but will emphasize the fact that much of the writing we do in work and academic contexts is public writing. If you are comfortable with digital pedagogy, you might want to ask students to keep blogs—accessible to the general public—as part of your course.

**QUOTATION: ON WRITING**
[Writing is] the sense of being in contact with people who are part of a particular audience that really makes a difference to me.
—Sherley Anne Williams

**QUOTATION: ON WRITING**
Those who trust us educate us.
—George Eliot

**TEACHING TIP**
As a collaborative project, choose a single subject about which your students are likely to have some knowledge (for example, their first experiences at college). Assign each group an audience to whom they will write a letter describing the subject. To get them to think about the different language choices they must use to make a favorable impression on different audiences, it is often very effective to assign groups a comparatively informal, friendly relationship—a parent, a grandparent, a good friend, a sibling, a member of the clergy, a favorite high school teacher. Even without being coached, students will notice the difference that audience makes to word choice, information selection, and tone.

**QUOTATION: ON WRITING**
I started writing because of a terrible feeling of powerlessness: I felt I was drifting and obscure, and I rebelled against that. I didn't see what I could do to change my condition. I wanted to control rather than be controlled, to ordain rather than be ordained, and to relegate rather than be relegated.
—Anita Brookner

**TEACHING TIP**
One way to engage students in thinking about audience (Quick Reference 1.5) is to ask students to prepare a collage on their potential audience, answering all of the questions posed in the Quick Reference.

**TEACHING TIP**
Today's students are apt to be far more technologically savvy than many or most of their instructors. If you are highly experienced with the software programs your students are already using (or with those you want them to learn), be sure to share some of your own "goofs" as well as successes. Students relate more keenly to an expert who admits mistakes. Ask your students to self-identify as to level of expertise with various technologies, and encourage student experts to demonstrate to others what they know. If each student volunteers to share at least one "helpful hint," the classroom (including the "virtual classroom") becomes a more exciting environment. In the process, students see that

writing nevertheless requires edited American English. If you want to hear these forms spoken, listen to the anchors of television and radio news programs. You also need to choose words for your writing that are accurate in meaning and spelled correctly. ●

To analyze your audience, you might ask yourself whatever questions in Quick Reference 1.5 you think will be useful in each situation.

---

**Quick Reference 1.5**                                    ■ ■ ■ ■ ■ ■

### Ways to analyze your audience

**WHAT SETTING ARE THEY READING IN?**
- Academic setting? Specifically, what subject?
- Workplace setting? Specifically, what business area?
- Public setting? Specifically, what form of communication? (newspaper? blog? poster?)

**WHO ARE THEY?**
- Age, gender, economic situation
- Ethnic backgrounds, political philosophies, religious beliefs
- Roles (student, parent, voter, wage earner, property owner, veteran, and others)
- Interests, hobbies

**WHAT DO THEY KNOW?**
- General level of education
- Specific level of knowledge about topic: Do they know less than you about the subject? as much as you about the subject? more than you about the subject?
- Beliefs: Is the audience likely to agree with your point of view? disagree with your point of view? have no opinion about the topic?
- Interests: Is the audience eager to read about the topic? open to the topic? resistant to or not interested in the topic?

**WHAT IS THEIR RELATIONSHIP TO YOU?**
- Distance and formality: Do you know each other personally or not? Does your audience consist of friends, family, or close peers, or are they more remote?
- Authority: Does your reader have the authority to judge or evaluate you (a supervisor at work, a teacher). Do you have the authority to evaluate your reader, or does this not apply?

## 1d.1 What is a general educated audience?

A **general educated audience** is composed of experienced readers who regularly read newspapers, magazines, and books, not only because they have to but because they want to. These readers typically have a general knowledge of many subjects and are likely to understand something about your topic. If your writing contains too many technical details or unusual references, your writing may confuse and alienate these readers. Consequently, for general educated readers you need to avoid using specialized terms without plainly defining them, or referring to uncommon information without explaining it.

General educated readers usually approach a piece of writing expecting to become interested in it, to learn about a new topic, to add to their store of knowledge about a subject, or to see a subject from a perspective other than their own. As a writer, work to fulfill those expectations. While some readers aren't particularly knowledgeable or open to new ideas, your goal in most writing that's not intended for specialized audiences needs to be targeting a general audience, as defined above.

## 1d.2 What is a specialist audience?

A **specialist audience** is composed of readers who have a thorough knowledge of specific subjects or who are particularly committed to certain interests or viewpoints. Many people are experts in their occupational fields, and some become experts in areas that simply interest them, such as astronomy or raising orchids. People from a particular group background (for example, Democrats, Republicans, Catholics, or military veterans) are knowledgeable in those areas.

Specialist readers may also share certain assumptions and beliefs. For example, suppose you're writing for an audience of immigrants to the United States who feel strongly about keeping their cultural traditions alive. You can surely assume your readers know those traditions well, so you won't need to describe and explain the basics. Similarly, if you intend to argue that immigrants should abandon their cultural traditions in favor of US practices, you'll want to write respectfully about their beliefs. Whenever you introduce a concept that might be new to a specialist audience, explain the concept thoroughly rather than assuming the audience will understand it right away.

Examples of specialized audiences include:

- Members of specific academic disciplines (chemistry, political science, art history)
- People in specific professions (finance, education, engineering)
- People with common interests or hobbies (fans of certain television shows, of cooking, of NASCAR)

traditional lines of expertise are blurred and that all benefit when each person in the group contributes her or his own special knowledge and skill.

**BACKGROUND**

In the essay "Online Teaching: Purpose and Methods" (*ejc/rec: The Electronic Journal of Communication/La Revue Electronique de Communication* 9.1, 1999 <http://www.cios.org/www/ejc/v9n199.htm>), Zane Berge (University of Maryland) notes how increasing numbers of adult learners, along with the development of new technologies, are changing the face of postsecondary education, particularly in the demand for distance education. Berge notes the importance of viewing online instruction in the larger context of technology-mediated learning, its goal being to transform students into self-directed, lifelong learners. Reporting the results of research into the design and delivery of online instruction, Berge points to survey data that suggest the importance of discussion, collaboration, authentic learning activities, and self-reflection and self-assessment in the online classroom. More recently, Carmen Luke's 2003 article on "Pedagogy, Connectivity, Multimodality, and Interdisciplinarity" provides a brief look at the ways in which technology-mediated learning can be effective in the classroom because it relies on multiple pedagogical approaches (*Reading Research Quarterly* 38.3(2003): 397–403). "Becoming Literate in the Information Age: Cultural Ecologies and the Literacies of Technology" by Gail E. Hawisher, Cynthia L. Selfe, Brittney Moraski, and Melissa Pearson also provides a powerful argument for the changing nature of the composition classroom (*College Composition and Communication* 55.4 (2004): 642–692). The Spring 2008 online edition of *Computers and Composition* provides an excellent introduction to multimodal composition studies and a plethora of references for additional study on this topic (<http://www.bgsu.edu/cconline/edwelcomesp08.htm>).

- People with common political beliefs (conservatives, liberals, independents) or views (on health care, the environment, immigration)
- People with common experiences (veterans, single parents, athletes)

## 1d.3    What is my instructor's role as audience?

As your audience, your instructor functions in three ways. First, your instructor assumes the role of your target audience by reading and responding to your writing as though he or she is one of your intended general or specific readers. Second, your instructor acts as a coach who is dedicated to helping improve your writing. Third, your instructor evaluates your final drafts.

Although instructors know that few students are experienced writers or experts on the subjects they write about, they expect your writing to reflect your having taken the time to learn something worthwhile about a topic and then to write about it clearly. They can recognize a minimal effort almost immediately.

Instructors are also people whose professional lives center on intellectual endeavors. Therefore, you need to write about topics that contain intellectual interest, and discuss them according to the expectations for academic writing.

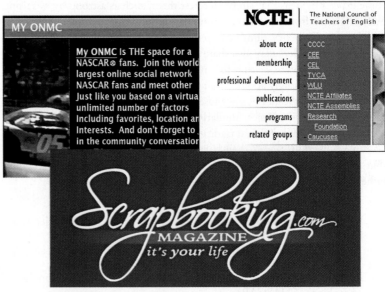

**Figure 1.3** Examples of specialized audience publications

Don't assume that your instructor can mentally fill in what you leave out of your writing. Indeed, you might think that it's wrong, even insulting to your instructor, if you extend your discussion beyond simple statements. Instructors—indeed, all readers—can't be mind readers, and they expect students' writing to fully explore their chosen topic. If you think you might be saying too little, ask your peers to read your writing and tell you if you've developed your topic sufficiently.

# 1e  What should I know about writing in a digital age?

Computers are important tools for creating documents, finding resources, managing work, and communicating with others. Almost all writing projects, whether in college or beyond, require them. Although some instructors make allowances for students with no access to a computer, they clearly prefer word-processed final drafts. If you don't own a computer or live with someone who does, you can usually get access to one on most college campuses (often in libraries and student centers), in public libraries, or in Internet cafés.

## 1e.1  Creating documents

A computer's word-processing software (for example, Microsoft Word or OpenOffice) offers invaluable help at various stages of the WRITING PROCESS. Word processing allows you easily to add, delete, revise, or move around material, even from one document to another. Some writers prefer to print their drafts to revise or edit them by hand and then enter the changes in the computer; other writers do almost all their revising and editing on the screen.

Word processing also allows you to make quick format changes. You can easily shift between single-spacing and double-spacing or put a WORKS CITED page into the correct DOCUMENTATION STYLE (Chapters 36–38). The toolbars typically found at the top of word-processing windows contain numerous formatting options, and exploring how they work can save you time in the long run. At the very least, learn how to set line spacing, margins, and indentations; how to use header and footer options to insert page numbers automatically; how to create footnotes; and how to check spelling and grammar. However, the special aids for writers that are built into word-processing software have limitations.

- **Spell-check tools** alert you when words don't match the dictionary in the software. These programs can be a big help for spotting a misspelled word or a typo, but they won't call your attention to your having typed *form* when you intended to type *from*. Therefore, always remember to read your work carefully after you use a spell-checker.

- **Thesaurus tools** suggest SYNONYMS for words. They can't, however, tell you which ones fit well into your particular sentences. Whenever a suggested

**QUOTATION: ON WRITING**

The faster I write the better my output. If I'm going slow I'm in trouble. It means I'm pushing the words instead of being pulled by them.

—Raymond Chandler

**QUOTATION: ON WRITING**

At the time of writing, I don't write for my friends or myself, either; I write for it, for the pleasure of it.

—Eudora Welty

**QUOTATION: ON WRITING**

Nothing in life is to be feared. It is only to be understood.

—Marie Curie

synonym is unfamiliar, look it up in your dictionary to be sure that it doesn't distort your communication. For example, a synonym for *friend* is *acquaintance,* but these words have different senses.

- **Grammar-** or **style-check tools** check your writing against the software's strict interpretations of rules of grammar, word use, punctuation, and other conventions. Can you always rely on those standards? No. While a tool can call attention to a possible error, the decision to change the usage is yours. Consult this handbook when you're not sure whether you need to deviate from the program's suggestions.

## 1e.2  Finding resources

In addition to helping you produce and revise writing, computers can help you find SOURCES. Nearly all library catalogs and databases are now searchable electronically, both from within the library and remotely through the Internet. Catalogs and databases are large collections of references that experts have gathered and organized. Some of those references exist only in print, but increasingly, they're also available online. Many workplaces also subscribe to database and information services that are useful in their business. Chapter 34 explains how to use catalogs and databases.

Sources on the World Wide Web, which you find using search engines like Google and Yahoo, usually aren't in databases that experts have compiled. Chapter 34 explains how to use the Web—and how to avoid misusing it. Remember that anyone can post anything online and that some of what you find is plain wrong.

Online sources present particular challenges to writers, including the possibility of **plagiarism**, a serious academic offense that occurs when you repre-

**Figure 1.4** A library database

sent someone else's wording or ideas as your own. Chapter 35 describes effective and ethical ways of using sources and avoiding plagiarism.

## 1e.3  Managing your work

Computers allow you to save drafts of your papers and organize your work. For example, you might create a separate folder for each document you write and keep all notes, drafts, and ideas related to that project in the folder. Figure 1.5 shows how one student has started a folder for all the projects in her writing course. In

**Figure 1.5** Using the computer to manage writing projects

the subfolder for project 2, she has ideas, notes, peer comments, and drafts. She created this folder in the "My Documents" directory in Microsoft Windows.

Computers and associated technologies also allow you to store vast quantities of your own writing and research, in forms even more portable than laptops. Storage devices such as flash drives (often called thumb, jump, or keychain drives) allow you cheaply to store hundreds or thousands of megabytes of information, in something small enough to keep in your pocket. Not only can you potentially keep every word you ever write (as a lifelong portfolio), but you can store photos and other images that you might need for a certain writing project, and you can download vast quantities of source materials from databases.

### 1e.4   Communicating with others

E-mail, instant messaging, and similar technologies not only help you communicate with friends but also help you prepare formal writing projects. For example, discussing a topic online with others can generate ideas. Some college instructors organize such discussions in Web-based programs such as WebCT or Blackboard. People in all walks of life often exchange ideas on discussion boards, listservs, and blogs.

Computers allow you to share drafts of your work without physically meeting with others. You can send a draft as an e-mail attachment or save it on a community server or Web site such as Google Docs. That way, classmates or colleagues—or even instructors or supervisors—have access to it and can offer suggestions for revision. If you're working on a collaborative project, the ability to share drafts and to discuss revisions online has many advantages. Chapter 6 explains how to work effectively with others.

🛈 **Alert:** College instructors vary in terms of the amount of input they want students to receive outside of class. A few teachers may not want you to have anyone (not a friend or family member or classmate or tutor) give you advice or feedback. Clarify each instructor's rules about such matters. Pleading ignorance of a law is rarely a sufficient defense. ●

## 1f   What forms of writing do computers enable?

For decades, formal writing has consisted of essays and reports containing only paragraphs of connected words. These forms will always remain essential, and you need to master them. However, computers enable different kinds of writing, both in college and beyond. You can place photographs or illustrations into documents. You can easily create tables and graphs, and you can use different fonts and graphic elements. As a result, writers can more easily produce brochures, pamphlets, or other documents that, in the past, required a graphic artist (see Chapter 45).

**TEACHING TIP**
As you discuss the multimodal possibilities of digital writing in 1f, you might want to point out the technologies you will be using this semester, the technologies your college uses, and the technologies students might want to explore in your course.

Other forms of writing, such as Web pages and blogs, are designed specifically to appear on computers rather than on paper. Sometimes they contain audio or video files, or they contain links to other documents and Web sites. The Web site of the Smithsonian Institution, shown in Figure 1.6, incorporates several images to create a pleasing effect, and it has links to many other pages. Some writing situations may call for you to make a Web page rather than write a traditional paper.

Blogs (short for We**b logs**) allow a writer to post messages that anyone can read on the Internet. Some people create blogs to serve as a diary of their daily experiences, while others write about professions or other matters of interest. Blogs can be very personal, such as those written for an audience of friends and family. They can also be relatively more formal or journalistic. Other blogs have taken on a national readership, as is the case with particular news, political, and author blogs.

A **wiki** is a Web site that allows multiple readers to change its content. Several people can work on the same document from remote places around the globe. Figure 1.7 is an image from Wikipedia, an online encyclopedia. Keep in mind that any Internet user can post an article to Wikipedia, and anyone can revise an article already posted there. You always need to question the accuracy of a wiki article. It can contain incorrect information. Always ask your instructor whether he or she will permit you to use it as a source for scholarly research. Also try to confirm all information you find in Wikipedia in other reliable sources. For more information on using and citing Wikipedia and other Web resources, see Chapters 36–38.

**Figure 1.6** Images add interest to a Web site

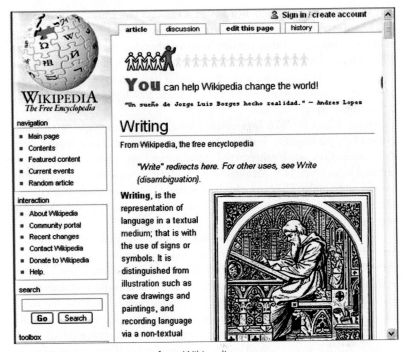

**Figure 1.7** A screen capture from Wikipedia

A **digital portfolio** is a collection of several of your own texts in electronic format that you've chosen to represent the range of your skills and abilities. Unlike regular paper portfolios, digital versions contain links between—and within—individual texts; they can be modified and shared easily and cheaply; and they can be put online for public reading. Figure 1.8 shows the opening screen of one student's digital portfolio for a first semester writing course. Note that all the titles function as links to the papers themselves.

**Presentations**, using software such as PowerPoint, allow you to create visuals to accompany your oral remarks. PowerPoint slides can incorporate both words and images, as well as sounds and video clips. Chapter 42 provides more advice on creating presentations.

**Podcasts** are sound files that can be shared over the Internet. Their name derives from Apple's familiar iPod player. You can download podcasts to a computer or portable device for listening anywhere. What do podcasts have to do with writing? A good number of podcasts are miniature essays or commentaries that their writers have carefully polished and then read, as a script. Podcasts are the oral form of blogs. Figure 1.9 shows one of many podcast directories available on the Internet.

People who click on the button "listen" or "subscribe" get to the listed podcasts; the directory on the right shows other topic categories.

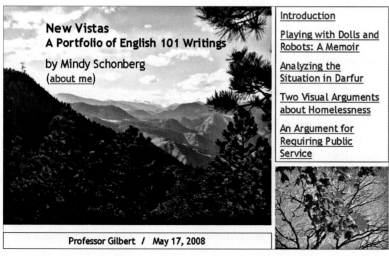

**Figure 1.8** Opening screen of a student's digital portfolio

**Figure 1.9** A screen capture of a podcast directory

**Videos** are motion image files or clips. People increasingly convey some ideas or information through short videos filmed with a camera, edited with computer software, and uploaded to the Internet. Video clips may enhance some presentations. Web sites like YouTube.com demonstrate the ease with which people can produce and upload videos, some of them amazingly good, many of them plain awful. Mainstream professional, educational, and commercial Web sites also frequently contain videos. Some blogs actually take the form of video logs or "vlogs."

What is a discussion of videos doing in a handbook of writing? Similar to podcasts, effective videos are often built around carefully written and narrated scripts, which may contain titles or captions. We discuss visuals in multimedia in Chapter 42. Always check with instructors before integrating audio or visual elements into your writing. And don't worry if your knowledge about producing any of these types of writing is limited. Instructors who require such projects can tell you how to proceed.

## 1g What resources can help me with writing?

Every writer needs access to four essential resources: a dictionary, a thesaurus, a handbook for writers, and a library. The first three are each generally available in electronic form as well as in traditional print, although you may find the book versions more convenient. A **dictionary** is indispensable. Most college bookstores offer a variety of hardback "college dictionaries." Before buying one, browse through a few definitions, check the format and accessories (information in the front and back), and choose the book you like best. Keeping a lightweight paperback abridged dictionary in your book bag can be very handy for checking unknown words on the spot. Also, many dictionaries and other reference books can be downloaded onto a **personal digital assistant (PDA)** for even greater portability.

Unabridged dictionaries list all recognized words in standard use in English. Being comprehensive, they're usually oversized, so the reference section of every library usually stocks one in its reference section. Some college libraries may also maintain an unabridged dictionary online for their students.

Another valuable resource for writers is a **thesaurus**, which is a collection of *synonyms*. The alphabetically arranged ones are the easiest to use. Be sure you check for this feature since some thesauruses are not organized alphabetically. *Roget's 21st Century Thesaurus* is an excellent volume arranged alphabetically.

A **handbook for writers** is also vital for you to own. A handbook—such as the one you're reading—gives you detailed information about rules of grammar and punctuation and about other writing conventions. (Note that this handbook also exists in an online version that can be accessed through a code you received if you bought the book new.) It also offers extensive advice about how to write successfully, whether for college, business, or the public. It shows

**TEACHING TIP**
Students will always appreciate a list of free, online resources to use in their writing. Throughout this text, we will point to a variety of helpful online resources that you may want to share with your students.

you step by step how to write and document research papers. Some handbooks, including this one, contain guidance on how to write for a variety of courses other than English. This resource is an invaluable writing tool in courses other than English, as well as in your career after college, and it will serve you well for years.

**College libraries**, sometimes called *learning resource centers,* are essential for writers. Libraries are fully stocked with all manner of reference books, circulating books, resources for online access, and more. Some resources are available online, in "full text versions," through the library's Web site. It's helpful to know what resources are available at your library so that you can dive right in when you need to get information. Chapter 34 provides extensive advice on using the library.

Finally, you need two other, less tangible resources as a writer: time and confidence. We know that people live incredibly busy lives, juggling work, school, and personal responsibilities. While it may seem obvious (or insensitive) to say that you need time to write effectively, we're simply encouraging you to create and protect time for yourself as a writer. It helps to think of writing as a series of several processes, and you'll need time to pursue them. Confidence may seem just as elusive, especially when you face challenging new writing situations. It might help to remember that countless people like you are steadily developing their writing skills each day. We see them in our classes all the time. We have confidence that your efforts will also bring rewards.

For more help with your writing, grammar, and research, go to **www.mycomplab.com**

# 2

## Essential Processes for Academic Writing

## 2a What processes do academic writers use?

Many people think that professional writers can sit down at their computers, think of ideas, and magically produce a finished draft, word by perfect word. Experienced writers know better. They know that writing is a process, a series of activities that starts the moment they begin thinking about a subject and ends with proofreading the final draft. Experienced writers also know that good writing is rewriting, again and yet again. Their drafts are filled with additions, deletions, rewordings, and rearrangements.

**QUOTATION: ON WRITING**
I write rather quickly. I've come to accept it. For a long time I was ashamed of myself for writing fast because I talked to people and I thought I wasn't taking enough pains or something. But I do write the first draft very quickly, and then I come back and work on it.
—Eilis Ni Dhuibhne

**TEACHING TIP**
Lynn says, "The facsimile of my writing and revising at the opening of this chapter is completely authentic (though the handwriting is not mine because I tend to scrawl illegibly). I have included this draft to show students that most teachers and professional writers evolve a text rather than produce it in one fell swoop. When I do this in my writing classes, the students never fail to be surprised that their instructor's first draft could be so rough. You might also bring in a few examples of your own drafts. A paragraph or two can suffice. And if you write at a computer, as I do, plan ahead and

keep those sentences you love to delete with the press of a key. Interestingly, I have found that a few students sometimes think that my rough drafts are better than their final drafts, which can be discouraging. I try to emphasize that I am not as much of an apprentice writer as the students are. And I am writing from a base of where I am after decades of writing, not from the base where I started in college."

## QUOTATION: ON WRITING

Writers are notorious for using any reason to keep from working: overresearching, retyping, going to meetings, waxing the floors—anything.

—Gloria Steinem

## BACKGROUND

In "Using Principles of Universal Design in College Composition Courses" (*Basic Writing e-Journal* 5.1, Spring 2004 <http://www.asu.edu/clas/english/composition/cbw/BWEspring 2004.html>), Patricia J. McAlexander (University of Georgia) supports the view of other proponents of Universal Design for Learning (UDL) that there is no single best way to teach writing and that students' individual learning strengths and motivation require individual approaches for students—all students, those with and those without physical or learning disabilities. McAlexander suggests some ways that a composition instructor can adapt his or her teaching to individual learners while following a mandated curriculum and engaging students in common classroom activities. These include strategies for (1) providing personally relevant material, (2) offering an appropriate level of challenge, and (3) giving individualized feedback.

**Figure 2.1** Draft and revision of Lynn Troyka's first paragraph in Chapter 2

For example, see in Figure 2.1 how Lynn revised the paragraph you just read. Lynn didn't make all the changes at the same time, even though it looks that way on the example. She went through the paragraph four times before she was satisfied with it. Notice that she deleted two sentences, combined two sentences, added a sentence at the end, and changed wording throughout. For another example, see Figure 2.2 on page 26, an image of revisions Doug made in the opening of Chapter 1.

Writing is an ongoing process of considering alternatives and making choices. Knowing and practicing a few general processes will help you with almost every writing situation in college and beyond. Different assignments may emphasize some techniques more than others, and we'll discuss them in Chapter 7. Here, however, we focus on processes that are essential for nearly all writing.

In this chapter, we discuss each part of the writing process separately. In real life, the steps overlap. They loop back and forth, which is why writing is called a recursive process. Quick Reference 2.1 lists the steps.

Do you like, as we do, to visualize a process? If so, see the drawing in Figure 2.3 on page 27. The arrows show movement. You might move back before going ahead (perhaps as you revise, you realize you need to plan some more); or you might skip a step and come back to it later (perhaps in the middle of revising, you jump into editing for a few minutes because a punctuation or grammar rule affects how you express your point); and so on.

As you work with the writing process, allow yourself to move freely through each step to see what's involved. Notice what works best for you. As you de-

## Quick Reference 2.1

■ ■ ■ ■ ■ ■ ■

### Steps in the writing process

- **Planning** means discovering and compiling ideas for your writing.
- **Shaping** means organizing your material.
- **Drafting** means writing your material into sentences and paragraphs.
- **Revising** means evaluating your draft and then rewriting it by adding, deleting, rewording, and rearranging.
- **Editing** means checking for correct grammar, spelling, punctuation, and mechanics.
- **Proofreading** means reading your final copy to eliminate typing or handwriting errors.

velop a sense of your preferred writing methods, adapt the process to fit each writing situation. No single way exists for applying the writing process.

Our personal advice from one writer to another is this: Most writers struggle some of the time with ideas that are difficult to express, sentences that won't take shape, and words that aren't precise. Be patient with yourself. Don't get discouraged. The more you write, the easier it will become—though writing never happens magically.

## 2b How do I begin a college writing project?

Begin every writing assignment by carefully analyzing the writing situation you're given. Some assignments are very specific. For example, here's an assignment that leaves no room for choice: "In a 500-word article for an audience of seventh graders, explain how oxygen is absorbed in the lungs." Students need to do precisely what's asked, taking care not to wander off the topic. More often, however, writing-class assignments aren't nearly as specific as that one. Often, you'll be expected to select your own topic (2b.1) or even your own purpose and audience.

### 2b.1 Selecting your own topic or purpose

If you have to choose a topic, don't rush. Take time to think through your ideas. Avoid getting so deeply committed to one topic that you cannot change to a more suitable topic in the time allotted.

Not all topics are suitable for ACADEMIC WRITING. Your topic needs to have ideas and issues meaty enough to demonstrate your thinking and writing abilities. Think through potential topics by breaking each one down into its logical

**TEACHING TIP**
Sometimes students are uncomfortable with the idea of drafting and revising their own work. To create a low stakes simulation of the writing process, consider finding a blog post or a newspaper article on a contemporary topic that you think could be better written. Print copies for each student in the class. After students have read the piece, make a list of possible revisions on the board. Then, break students into groups to collaborate on a revision. Have each group annotate the changes they make in the piece. You can refer to this later in the course as you encourage students to do more work with drafting and revision. It is important to begin the course by establishing the writing process you want students to use.

**TEACHING TIP**
Early on in the semester, establish with your students how you will assign writing (handouts, on the board, online, etc.). Also help your students to understand clearly the parameters for *academic writing* in your course. Are there topics that are unacceptable in your course? What level of formality do you expect in their writing? Help students to know the parameters for success right away.

**TEACHING TIP**
To help students understand that writing is a recursive, not a strictly linear, process (even though stages of writing can be represented by a variety of linear and curvilinear models), ask your students to become "metacognitive" as you give them fifteen minutes to write a single paragraph on the topic "A Song I Couldn't Get Out of My Head." As they "watch themselves" think and write, plan, draft, and edit (but not necessarily in that sequence), ask them to make notes about what they are doing during their writing process. Extraverts sometimes dive in, writing in order to think. Introverts are more likely to think first, and then write. Some students will edit a sentence or two before drafting a new sentence; others will write quickly to complete the task before considering options for sentence-combining, phrasing, and the like. Then, ask students to read their notes aloud so that you

can help everyone see that the "right way to write" is whatever process produces the best results for them. They may want to experiment with different approaches to find what works best.

## BACKGROUND

Donald Graves was the first to use the term *rehearsing* to describe the activities that precede a completed draft. His pioneering work, still a central force in composition and rhetoric, began with *Balance the Basics: Let Them Write* (Ford Foundation Papers on Research About Learning, 1978). He discusses the stage of the writing process in which the writer (mentally and on paper) prepares to write, without yet knowing what that writing will be. Drawing conclusions for all writers from his observations of children writing, Graves points out the importance of experimenting with meaning, form, and voices, an attitude of play that is important in making meaning.

## QUOTATION: ON WRITING

The number one reason why any professional writer writes is to pay the bills. This isn't the Lawn Tennis Association where you play just for the thrill of it.

—Jimmy Breslin

## TEACHING TIP

Students may be surprised to learn that all writers find the blank sheet of paper (or blank computer screen) a source of anxiety. The experienced writer knows that the most effective way to move past that feeling is to write something, regardless of its value. Once the clean surface has words on it, other words follow more easily. Unrelated ideas, notes, questions, and examples—all help relieve the writer's discomfort with getting started. A good habit for students to cultivate is to jot down responses and reactions to writing tasks as soon as the tasks are given. These jottings can sometimes be effective, lively catalysts for writing.

## BACKGROUND

In *Composition-Rhetoric: Backgrounds, Theory, and Pedagogy* (Pittsburgh: University of

**1A WHAT IS THE CURRENT SCENE FOR WRITERS IN COLLEGE**

**AND BEYOND?**

Writing well is important to college success. That plain fact has been true for decades. But writing plays an equally key role in your career and life beyond classrooms. In this book, we'd like to help you achieve success in those many roles.

We live in an age when people do more writing than they have at any other time in history. The Internet and wireless devices have made it easier for people to share writing, both formally and informally, and digital technologies allow us to mix words, images, sounds, and videos. As writers and writing teachers, then, we find it fascinating—and heartening—to witness the explosion of writing that people choose to do on their own. You might be among the millions of people who regularly write e-mails and text messages, keep journals, craft stories or poems, create Web sites, use FaceBook to connect with others, or write stuff on blogs or sites (Web logs)—all without anyone asking you to do so. Ordinary people write about their favorite television programs, analyze politics, or simply share their experiences and thoughts.

If you're someone who chooses to write out of personal interest, we respect you and offer this book to help you stretch into less familiar types of writing. If you're someone who doesn't very much like to write, we hope that you might explore the satisfaction of putting your thoughts into words—and we hope this book helps ease your way. We've composed these pages because we repeatedly see in our classes that everyone can make the concentrated effort needed to become an effective writer. Certainly, if you spend some time and energy improving your writing skills, your efforts will bring you academic, professional, and personal rewards.

As a student, you can expect to write in a variety of courses across the curriculum, not just in English. Chapter 2 of this book will explain general processes that are useful for most writing.

2

**Figure 2.2** Doug's revisions of Chapter 1

subsections. Then, make sure you can supply sufficiently specific details to back up each general statement. Conversely, make sure you aren't bogged down with so many details you can't figure out what GENERALIZATIONS they support.

Work toward balance by finding a middle ground. Beware of topics so broad that they lead to well-meaning but vague generalizations (for example, "Educa-

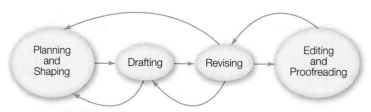

**Figure 2.3** Visualizing the writing process

tion is necessary for success"). Also, beware of topics so narrow that they lead nowhere after a few sentences (for example, "Jessica Max attends Tower College").

Suppose your assignment doesn't indicate a writing purpose—for example, "Write an essay on smoking." Here, you're expected to choose a purpose and think about what you intend to write on the topic. Will you try to explain to a general educated audience why people smoke? Will you try to persuade a specialized audience of smoking parents to quit? Will you summarize the current literature on the costs of smoking in order to inform an audience of economists? Considering different audiences and purposes can help you find a topic angle that engages you.

Most instructors put each assignment in writing, in a handout, on a Web site, or perhaps on the board. But some instructors give assignments orally during class, expecting you to write them down. Try to record every word. Don't hesitate to ask questions if you don't catch all the words or if something isn't clear—and be sure to write down the answers because they often tend to slip from memory. Listen, too, to questions other students ask.

In the rest of this chapter, we present the writing processes of two college students, Sara Cardini and Alex Garcia, as they plan and shape their material. You'll see Cardini's essay evolving through three separate, complete drafts. Later, in Chapter 5, you'll see how Garcia's essay developed. To start, here are the written assignments each student received.

### Sara Cardini received this assignment:

Addressing an educated audience, write an essay of 900 to 1,300 words discussing something you learned outside of a classroom. Your writing purpose can be informative or persuasive. Expect to write three drafts. (1) Your first draft, typed double-spaced, is due two classes from today. (2) Your clean second draft, typed double-spaced, without notes or comments, is due two classes later. Clip to it your first draft showing all notes you made to yourself or from comments your peer-response group made; you can handwrite notes and comments. I'll read your second draft as an "essay in progress" and will make comments to help you toward a third

continued >>

Pittsburgh Press, 1997), Robert J. Connors recounts various notions of invention that have been studied and taught in American colleges since the early nineteenth century.

**QUOTATION: ON WRITING**
The best time for planning . . . is when you're doing the dishes.
—Agatha Christie

**QUOTATION: ON WRITING**
I don't wait to be struck by lightning and don't need certain slants of light in order to write.
—Toni Morrison

**QUOTATION: ON WRITING**
Writing is no trouble: you just jot down ideas as they occur to you. The jotting is simplicity itself—it is the occurring which is difficult.
—Stephen Leacock

**TEACHING TIP**
Some students have difficulty thinking abstractly or linearly when they hear general statements such as "limit the topic" and "broaden or enlarge the topic." These students are often "visual picture" learners, and they, as well as their classmates of other learning styles, are likely to find the task of limiting the topic a bigger challenge than enlarging it. One way for you to help them grasp the concept of limiting is for you first to think of a broad (and fairly dull) topic such as "The environment" and then ask students to limit it by imagining with you something highly specific and concrete, something that can be pictured. Encourage students to think in sensory terms, involving as many of the senses as possible. If no one comes up with an image or something else, perhaps have them close their eyes and think of a lake. Where is it? What is its name? What does it look like? How clean is the water? What wildlife is there? Next, ask the students to zoom in on one aspect of the lake environment they find intriguing or disturbing. Name it. Provide a title: "Eagle Soars at Eagle Lake" or "The Murky Waters of Lake Claire," for example. Now ask the students to

work in groups to repeat the exercise with "Buildings" or perhaps "Big ideas."

**TEACHING TIP**

Some students see little connection between reading and writing, yet a large part of each writing task is to "contribute to the conversation," a natural response to those who read actively and confront new ideas. To help students realize that ideas occur naturally to curious readers, ask them to bring to class (or to share with others online) a current magazine or journal. For in-class work, allow students ten minutes to begin reading any article or essay. Then, allow five minutes for them to jot down on paper or onscreen any images, words and phrases, viewpoints, or questions that caught their attention, stimulated their interest, or invited debate. Ask them what else they would like to discover on the topic. What else might they read? With whom might they speak? What might they view or listen to? The ideas begin to surface!

**QUOTATION: ON WRITING**

It took me fifteen years to discover that I had no talent for writing, but I couldn't give it up because by that time I was too famous.
                                    —Robert Benchley

**TEACHING TIP: ESOL**

An activity that both ESOL students and native speakers enjoy is the exchange journal. ESOL students exchange entries on cultural matters with native speakers in a different class. In the first entry, students introduce themselves to their partners, perhaps including information like age, sex, marital status, place of birth, college major, and hobbies or interests. They then list some topics they're interested in learning about. In each subsequent weekly or biweekly entry, students explain an aspect of their culture: dating, courtship, family structure, food, school, manners, holidays, language, sports, entertainment, and so on. Entries are as long as students want to make them. Instructors rarely read the journals—and certainly never correct them—but instructors may require a report about the experience at the end of the term (and perhaps interim reports). The two

(and final) draft. (3) The third draft, typed double-spaced, is due one week after I return your second draft with my comments.

**Alex Garcia was given this assignment:**

Write an essay of 1,000 to 1,500 words that argues for a particular action on an issue that interests you. Your final draft is due in two weeks.

Cardini's first step was to analyze her writing situation (see Quick Reference 1.1). She looked at the very general topic—explain to an educated audience something you learned outside of a classroom—and she saw that she needed to narrow it considerably. She tentatively decided her purpose would be informative, though she thought she might have to switch to a persuasive purpose as she went along. She knew that she would share her first draft with her peer-response group to help her toward her second draft. She also understood that her instructor would be her final audience. She was aware of the requirements for time and length.

Garcia also read his assignment and analyzed his writing situation. Because the topic was very broad, he knew he would have to spend a good deal of time deciding what he wanted to write about. On the other hand, he understood that his assigned purpose was persuasive. The audience was not specified; he knew that his instructor would be the main audience, but he also decided to write in a way that would address a broader public audience. He kept in mind the requirements for time and length.

## 2b.2 Broadening a narrow topic

You know a topic is too narrow when you realize there's little to say after a few sentences. When faced with a too-narrow topic, think about underlying concepts. For example, suppose you want to write about Oprah Winfrey. If you chose "Oprah Winfrey's television show debuted in 1986," you'd be working with a single fact rather than a topic. To expand beyond such a narrow thought, you could think about the general area that your fact fits into—say, the impact of television shows on American culture. Although that is too broad to be a useful topic, you're headed in the right direction. Next, you might think of a topic that relates to Oprah's influence, such as "What impact has Oprah Winfrey's television show had on American culture since she began broadcasting in 1986?" Depending on your WRITING SITUATION (1b), you might need to narrow your idea further by focusing on Oprah's impact in a single area, such as how her book club influenced publishing and reading habits, how her guests and topics brought certain issues to national visibility, or how the style of her show affected other talk shows.

## 2b.3  Narrowing a broad topic

Narrowing a broad topic calls for you to break the topic down into subtopics. Most broad subjects can be broken down in hundreds of ways, but you need not think of all of them. Settle on a topic that interests you, one narrowed enough—but not too much—from a broad topic. For example, if you're assigned "relationships" as the topic for a 1,000-word essay, you'd be too broad if you chose "What kinds of relationships are there?" You'd be too narrow if you came up with "Alexandra and Gavin have dated for two years." You'd probably be on target with a subtopic such as "In successful relationships, people learn to accept each other's faults." You could use 1,000 words to explain and give concrete examples of typical faults and discuss various reasons why accepting them is important. Here are two more examples.

| | |
|---|---|
| SUBJECT | *music* |
| WRITING SITUATION | freshman composition class<br>informative purpose<br>instructor as audience<br>500 words; one week |
| POSSIBLE TOPICS | "How music affects moods"<br>"The main characteristics of country music"<br>"The types of songs in Disney animations" |
| SUBJECT | *cities* |
| WRITING SITUATION | sociology course<br>persuasive purpose<br>peers and then instructor as audience<br>950 to 1,000 words; ten days |
| POSSIBLE TOPICS | "The importance of public transportation"<br>"Discomforts of city living"<br>"How open spaces enhance the quality of city life" |

Sara Cardini, the student whose essay appears in this chapter, knew that her very general assigned topic—"Explain to an educated audience something you learned outside of a classroom"—was too broad. To narrow it, she used the following structured techniques for discovering and compiling ideas: browsing her journal (2c.1), FREEWRITING (2.c2), and MAPPING (2.c4). They helped her decide that she wanted to discuss how she learned about a culture other than her own. She realized that even her narrower topic "Japanese culture" would still be too broad. She considered "Japanese music" or "Japanese schools." In the end, she chose "Japanese videos" and, even more specifically, a kind of Japanese animation called "anime" (commonly pronounced AN-a-may). Extensive experience had taught her about the topic, and she could think of both

instructors pass the journals back and forth to each other to distribute in classes; they should also arrange for the students to meet and interview each other near the end of the term, if possible. The assignment helps break down stereotypes and develops students' fluency in writing; indeed, some students write considerably better in journals than in compositions.

Note: Using two journals—one from ESOL student to native speaker and one from native speaker to ESOL student—makes it more convenient for students to write their reports. Bluebooks may be used for easy portability; when one is filled, the student can staple another to the back of the previous one.

**TEACHING TIP**

The concept of a writing situation may be new to many students. *Writing situation* is an inclusive term for the combination of topic, purpose, audience, and special requirements such as word or time limits. Each of these variables influences every decision a writer makes. These variables are especially important in narrowing a topic, as demonstrated by the inclusion of writing situation in the examples for narrowing a topic we give in 2b.3.

**QUOTATION: ON WRITING**

People want to know why I do this; why I write such gross stuff. I like to tell them I have the heart of a small boy—and I keep it in a jar on my desk.

—Stephen King, on himself

**TEACHING TIP**

You might want to ask your students to keep a writing log that works this way: At the end of each piece of writing, they note where, when, and how they have worked. The more detailed their notations, the more they will help students draw conclusions about how their best writing takes place. After a series of such notations, the students can write a paragraph evaluating the approaches they used, summarizing the information, reflecting on it, and planning for future writing. Many teachers ask students to use their notes and paragraphs at midterm and at the end of the course to write a long reflection on how their writing has changed as a result of studying writing as a process. Some students have even experimented with making reflective videos, documenting their approaches to writing essays!

## BACKGROUND
In "Digital Mirrors: Multimodal Reflection in the Composition Classroom" (Computers and Composition online, Spring 2008, <http://www.bgsu/cconline/Digital_Mirrors/>), Debra Journet, Tabetha Adkins, Chris Alexander, Patrick Corbett, and Ryan Trauman offer an extensive look at the possibilities for using reflection in the composition classroom.

## TEACHING TIP
Freewriting and journal writing are sometimes unpopular with students at first, but on their end-of-the-semester evaluations of Lynn's classes, students consistently mention these activities as being among the most helpful in the course. Perhaps one of the reasons students resist these techniques at first is that they think freewriting and journal writing will be corrected or graded. Few teachers do that. It is important, however, to respond to students' journals, although instructors should not feel obliged to read and respond to every entry of every journal. In fact, you might tell students that you'll select and read several pages at random. Responses should not be directive or critical but should create an informal dialogue with students that encourages them to discuss their ideas and experiences in greater depth and detail.

## QUOTATION: ON WRITING
We must do the things we think we cannot do.
—Eleanor Roosevelt

## TEACHING TIP
Ask students to evaluate the different strategies for discovering and compiling ideas for writing. They can share what works best for them and inspire other students to try new approaches.

generalizations and specific details to use in her essay. In addition, Cardini knew that if she needed to do research, she could find sources in books and magazines and on the Internet.

Alex Garcia also needed to narrow his topic to suit a 1,000- to 1,500-word essay. To explore several possible topics, he used BRAINSTORMING (2c.3). Once he had chosen a topic (whether buying organic food was worthwhile), he used the "journalist's questions" (2.c4) to compile more ideas and then a subject tree (2e) to check whether he was ready to begin drafting.

## 2c    How can I come up with ideas and information?

If you've ever felt you'll never think of anything to write about, don't despair. Instead, use structured techniques, sometimes called *prewriting strategies* or *invention techniques,* for discovering and compiling ideas. Professional writers use them to uncover hidden resources in their minds. For a list of the techniques, see Quick Reference 2.2.

Try out each one. Experiment to find out which techniques suit your style of thinking. Even if one technique produces good ideas, try another to see what additional possibilities might turn up.

Save all of the ideas you generate as you explore possible topics. You never know when something you have initially rejected might become useful from another point of view. Computers make it easy to keep a folder labeled, for example, "explorations," in which you can store your ideas.

---

### Quick Reference 2.2    ■ ■ ■ ■ ■ ■ ■

#### Ways to discover and compile ideas for writing

* Keep an idea log and a journal (see 2c.1).
* Freewrite (see 2c.2).
* Brainstorm (see 2c.3).
* Ask the "journalist's questions" (see 2c.4).
* Map (see 2c.5).
* Talk it over (see 2c.6).
* Read, browse, or search (see 2c.7).
* Incubate (see 2c.8).

---

⊕ **ESOL Tip:** The structured techniques discussed here aim to let your ideas flow out of you without your judging them right away. If it's difficult for you to implement these techniques using English, consider doing several in your primary language. Then, choose one that seems to have potential for your writing and do it over again in English. ●

## 2c.1  Using an idea log or journal

As you develop the habits of mind and behavior of a writer, your ease with writing will grow. One such habit is keeping an idea log. Professional writers are always on the lookout for ideas to write about and details to develop their ideas. They listen, watch, talk with people, and generally keep an open mind. Because they know that good ideas can evaporate as quickly as they spring to mind, they're always ready to jot down their thoughts and observations. Some carry a pocket-size notepad, while others use a personal digital assistant (PDA) or a laptop. If you use an idea log throughout your college years, you'll see your powers of observation increase dramatically.

Additionally, many professional writers keep a daily writing **journal**. Doing this will allow you to have a conversation in writing with yourself. Your audience is you, so the content and tone can be as personal and informal as you wish. Even fifteen minutes a day can be enough. If you don't have that chunk of time, write in your journal before you go to bed, between classes, or on a bus. Some people find that the feel of pen on paper, perhaps in a bound blank journal, is important to this kind of writing. Others keep journals in computer files or online as BLOGS (short for "Web logs"). For examples of blogs (or to start one of your own), go to http://www.blogger.com.

Unlike a diary, a journal isn't a record of what you do each day. A journal is for your thoughts from your reading, your observations, even your dreams. You can respond to quotations, react to movies or plays, or reflect on your opinions, beliefs, and tastes. Keeping a journal can help you in three ways. First, writing every day gives you the habit of productivity; the more you write and the more you feel words pouring out of you onto paper, the more easily you'll write in all situations. Second, a journal instills the practice of close observation and discovery, two habits of mind that good writers cultivate. Third, a journal is an excellent source of ideas for assignments.

Figure 2.4 shows an excerpt of a journal entry Sara Cardini had made before she got the assignment to write about something she had learned outside the classroom. Even though she hadn't thought of her entry as a potential subject for a later essay, when she read through her journal for ideas, she realized that one of her great interests had started beyond classroom walls.

## 2c.2  Freewriting

**Freewriting** is writing nonstop. You write down whatever comes into your mind without stopping to wonder whether the ideas are good or the spelling is correct. When you freewrite, don't do anything to interrupt the flow. Don't censor any thoughts or flashes of insight. Don't go back and review. Don't delete.

**BACKGROUND**
In "Mediated Texts: A Heuristic for Academic Writing" (*Journal of Basic Writing,* September 1998: 56–72), Eileen Biser, Linda Rubel, and Rose Marie Toscano offer an innovative invention technique that may be particularly valuable for ESOL and basic writers.

**QUOTATION: ON WRITING**
Strategy is better than strength.
—Hausa legend

**QUOTATION: ON WRITING**
When you are looking for obstacles, you can't find opportunities.
—J. C. Bell

**USING COLLABORATION**
Recent research on small-group dynamics suggests that the quality and number of ideas generated by invention can be enhanced by having group members first engage individually in such planning activities as mapping and focused freewriting before coming together for group brainstorming.

Sometimes, the group will decide to narrow its focus to one of the ideas suggested during a brainstorming session. Before the group pursues its topic any further, you might repeat the individual-first, group-second planning process on the new, narrower idea.

**QUOTATION: ON WRITING**
The ideal view for daily writing, hour on hour, is the blank brick wall of a cold-storage warehouse. Failing this, a stretch of sky will do, cloudless if possible.
—Edna Ferber

**QUOTATION: ON WRITING**
I need noise and interruptions and irritation: irritation and discomfort are a great starter. The loneliness of doing it any other way would kill me.
—Anita Brookner

**QUOTATION: ON WRITING**
All you need is a room without any particular interruptions.

—John Dos Passos

**QUOTATION: ON WRITING**
Genius begins great works; labor alone finishes them.

—Joseph Joubert

**TEACHING TIP**
Student writing groups can benefit greatly from group mapping. If you can supply each group with large sheets of plain brown wrapping or butcher paper, they can map out invention topics while seated around a table. If your room has multiple chalkboards or whiteboards, supply each group with enough chalk or markers to map its ideas at one of the boards. If you are in a computer lab or a smart classroom, you might also use mapping software like FreeMind at <http://freemind.sourceforge.net/wiki/index.php/Main_Page>, Pimki at <http://pimki.rubyforge.org/>, or VUE at <http://vue.uit.tufts.edu/index.cfm>. When students map together, they can pool their resources for generating topic ideas and organizational strategies.

**QUOTATION: ON WRITING**
Writing is just having a sheet of paper, a pen and not a shadow of an idea of what you're going to say.

—Françoise Sagan

**QUOTATION: ON WRITING**
My writing is a conscious letter to myself. It's a way for me to hold on to pieces as I grow and change and get on with my life.

—Joan Stein

**QUOTATION: ON WRITING**
There's nothing to writing. All you do is sit down at a typewriter and open a vein.

—Red (Walter Wellesley) Smith

My first visit to an anime club. I see they spend all their time talking about Japan, eating Japanese food, and watching Japanese cartoons. Adults watching cartoons must be a bunch of nerds. But they say these are not like the cartoons made in the US. Better than The Lion King?! But I have gotten hooked on Sailor Moon. I see that fans of anime come from many different backgrounds, races, and ethnicities and watch anime for many different reasons. You can choose robots or samurai, romance, or comedy. There seems to be an anime for everyone. The experience sure opened my eyes.

**Figure 2.4** Excerpt from Sara Cardini's journal

Freewriting helps get you used to the "feel" of your fingers rapidly hitting computer keys or your pen moving across paper. Freewriting works best if you set a goal—perhaps writing for fifteen minutes or filling one or two pages. Keep going until you reach that goal, even if you have to write one word repeatedly until a new word comes to mind. Some days when you read over your freewriting, it might seem mindless, but other days your interesting ideas may startle you.

In **focused freewriting**, you write from a specific starting point—a sentence from your general freewriting, an idea, a quotation, or anything else you choose. Except for this initial focal point, focused freewriting is the same as regular freewriting. Write until you meet your time or page limit, and don't censor yourself. If you go off the topic, that's fine: See where your thoughts take you. Just keep moving forward.

Like a journal, freewriting is a good source of ideas and details. When Sara Cardini thought her growing interest in Japanese animation might qualify for her assignment, she explored the topic through focused freewriting on watching anime (Figure 2.5).

## 2c.3 Brainstorming

**Brainstorming** means listing everything you can think of about a topic. Let your mind roam freely, generating quantities of ideas. Write words, phrases, or sentence fragments—whatever comes to you. If you run out of ideas, ask yourself exploratory questions, such as *What is it? What is it the same as? How is it different? Why or how does it happen? How is it done? What causes it or results*

In watching anime, my eyes were opened to a world I would never have known otherwise. I learned not to be so judgmental about animation (which I always thought was for kids). While anime seemed strange and confusing to me at first, before long I realized the importance of studying art from another country. The more I watched and understood anime, the less strange it seemed, and the more I realized that I had just been judging from my limited American point of view. Somewhere in Japan, there is probably some college student who is learning about America from our movies. Now, if the Japanese student and I ever meet, we will be closer to understanding each other.

**Figure 2.5** Excerpt from Sara Cardini's freewriting

*from it? What does it look, smell, sound, feel, or taste like? Who benefits from it? Who loses?*

After you've compiled a list, go to step two: Look for patterns, ways to group the ideas into categories. You'll probably find several categories. Set aside any items that don't fit into a group. If a category interests you but has only a few items, brainstorm that category alone.

You can brainstorm in one concentrated session or over several days, depending on how much time you have for an assignment. Brainstorming with other writers can be especially fruitful: One person's ideas bounce off the next person's, and collectively more ideas come to mind. Chapter 6 explains strategies for working with others.

When brainstorming or freewriting on a computer, try "invisible writing." Temporarily darken your computer monitor. A blank screen can help you focus on getting the words out without the temptation to stop and criticize, but the computer will still be recording your words. When you can write no more, turn on the monitor to see what you have.

Brainstorming was a technique Alex Garcia used to find his topic about the benefits of organic foods. Brainstorming helped him think through several topics and generate some ideas about the one that most appealed to him (Figure 2.6).

**BACKGROUND**

In "Habits of Mind: Historical Configurations of Textual Ownership in Peer Writing Groups" (*College Composition and Communication*, May 1998: 234–255), Candace Spigelman argues that students' attitudes about authorship and intellectual property rights are evidence of cultural "habits of mind." She examines Western historical ideas that have influenced current concepts of textual ownership.

**QUOTATION: ON WRITING**

The two hardest things to handle in life are failure and success.

—Unknown

**BACKGROUND**

Writers, both amateurs and professionals, tend to devise rituals that help them begin and carry out a piece of writing. Some of these are elaborate; some are relatively simple. They're identifiable by the fact that repeated actions seem to be irrelevant to the task at hand but are in some way helpful to the writer looking for ideas and ways to express them. Some are silly, such as using the same coffee mug each time one writes, or illogical, such as sweeping the front walk before getting started, but the fact is that they're effective in helping a writer make the transition from some other activity to that of composition. In "Writing Rituals" (ERIC ED 295 172), Ann B. Dobie shares the results of her study of students' and professional writers' composing habits. Dobie suggests that an understanding of these rituals can help improve student writing.

Writers who are in the process of devising writing rituals can make their individual habits more productive by being aware of which steps are helpful and which are not. They can begin by asking themselves questions about where, when, and with what they write. Where do they get the most work done? Does it afford them access to materials they need? Is it free from interruptions? Does it make them comfortable but not too relaxed? Can they see well? Do they have room to spread out notes and books? What time of day or night do they usually do their writing? Are they alert and energetic at that time? Does it give them a block of time in which to work? Do they use a typewriter? A legal pad? A word processor? A notebook? What objects, environments, or activities not directly connected with writing provide a sense of well-being during the process?

The answers will vary from one writer to another, but for best results, the process should remain fairly constant with the individual. Rituals are habits that provide structure—reassurance that the writer has done a task this way once before. With each repetition, they become more comfortable, making the writer feel more competent, more at home with the act of writing.

**TEACHING TIP**

The notion of focus in a thesis statement might be new to some students. A useful analogy can be that the topic is the subject but the focus is the predicate. Without predication, sentences make no assertion. As Josephine Miles said in her classic monograph "Working Out Ideas: Predication and Other Uses of Language," "Sentence making is predication, and to predicate is to assert an idea, selecting and treating facts from a point of view." Predication says something, asserts something, answers a question, or takes a position about the topic. It may, for example, define the topic, describe it, evaluate it, compare it to something, explain its purpose, or identify its causes.

**ANSWERS: EXERCISE 2-1**

Answers will vary according to the categories students choose. In this activity, help students to understand how categorization will help them in taking material from a brainstormed list and using it in an essay. Some categories for this assignment might include "Viewer-Driven Advertisement," "Fan-Based Advertisement," "Interviews," and "Advertising."

**QUOTATION: ON WRITING**

There are two literary maladies: writer's cramp and swelled head. The worst of writer's cramp is that it is never cured; the worst of swelled head is that it never kills.

—Coulson Kernahan

--steroids in sports: how much do people care?
--global warming—awfully big
--possibilities for wind energy: argue or explain
--the American diet
--the effects of fast food—do I have anything to add?
--organized sports and young kids, good or bad?
--organic foods: worth it? benefits? costs?

**Figure 2.6** Alex Garcia's brainstorming

**EXERCISE 2-1** Here's a list brainstormed for a writing assignment. The topic was "Ways to promote a new movie." Working individually or in a peer-response group, look over the list and group the ideas. You'll find that some ideas don't fit into a group. Then, add any other ideas you have to the list.

| | |
|---|---|
| coming attractions | suspense |
| TV ads | book the movie was based on |
| provocative | locations |
| movie reviews | Internet trailers |
| how movie was made | adventure |
| sneak previews | newspaper ads |
| word of mouth | stars |
| director | dialogue |
| topical subject | excitement |
| special effects | photography |

## 2c.4 The "journalist's questions"

When journalists report a story, they gather and write about information by asking who did what, when it happened, where it happened, and why and how it happened. The same questions come in handy for writers exploring a topic. The **journalist's questions** are *Who? What? When? Where? Why?* and *How?*

Alex Garcia used the journalist's questions to expand his thinking on the value of eating organic foods. His answers, listed below, showed him that he had enough material for a good essay.

**WHO?**      **Who** benefits from buying or selling organic food?

**WHAT?**      **What** kinds of organic foods are available?

| WHEN? | **When** did the practice of growing organic foods begin? |
| WHERE? | **Where** can I find evidence if organic foods are healthier? |
| WHY? | **Why** do some people doubt the value of organic foods? |
| HOW? | **How** exactly should someone evaluate the evidence? |

## 2c.5  Mapping

**Mapping**, also called *clustering,* is a visual form of brainstorming. Some writers find that they begin to think more creatively if they can actually see ways that their ideas connect. Other writers use mapping to help them check the logical relationships between ideas.

To map, write your topic in the middle of a sheet of paper and draw a circle around it. Now, moving out from the center, use lines and circles to show ideas that are subtopics of the topic in the center circle. Continue to subdivide and add details. At any time, you can move to a blank space on your map and start a new subtopic. Try to keep going without censoring yourself.

Sara Cardini used mapping to prompt herself to discover ideas about Japanese animation. When she finished, she was satisfied that she'd have enough to say in her essay. Figure 2.7 shows part of Sara Cardini's clustering for the second paragraph of her essay about Japanese anime.

**Figure 2.7** Part of Sara Cardini's mapping for her essay on anime

## 2c.6  Talking it over

**Talking it over** is based on the notion that two heads are better than one. When you discuss a topic with someone interested in listening and making suggestions, you often think of new ideas. You can even play roles, having other people pretend they disagree with you or are confused. Answering their questions or challenges can spur new thinking.

People you trust can serve as "sounding boards" and tell you if your ideas are complete and reasonable. If your instructor sets up PEER-RESPONSE GROUPS in your class, you might ask the other members to serve as sounding boards. Otherwise, talk with a good friend or another adult.

Chatting, in the traditional sense, means talking face to face. In a more recent sense, however, chatting also refers to instant messaging, e-mailing, text messaging, or using discussion features in course software like Blackboard. Exchanging ideas online not only stimulates your thinking but also acts as a writing warm-up. Figure 2.8 is an excerpt from instant messaging. Chapter 6 provides more advice on working with others.

## 2c.7  Reading and Browsing

Reading newspapers, magazines, and books can provide a constant source of ideas. While it might sound old-fashioned, academic writers do this all the time. Spending time in the PERIODICALS or new books section of a library or browsing a good bookstore can alert you to fresh topics. Just looking at magazine covers, images, or a table of contents is often productive. If browsing generates a topic, systematic searches will yield more information (Chapter 34).

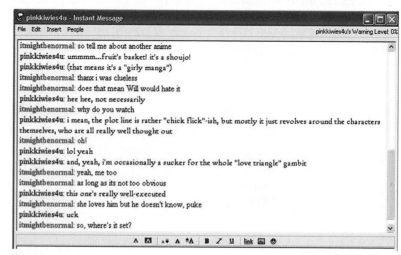

**Figure 2.8** Instant messaging screen capture

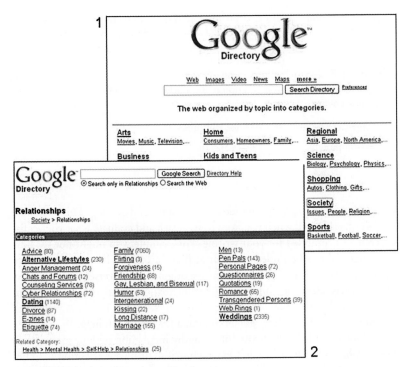

**Figure 2.9** Screen shot of Google directory

Of course, **Internet searches** also help you find topics and locate specific information. Chapter 32 provides extensive guidelines for searching the WORLD WIDE WEB. Briefly, however, access the Yahoo! directory at http://dir.yahoo.com or the Google directory at http://www.google.com/dirhp. You'll see a screen that lists broad subject areas.

On the Google directory, click on the broad subject "Society" to see a number of slightly more specific topics, including one on "Relationships." Note that each of them would be much too broad to write about. However, if you keep clicking on topic headings, you'll move to more and more specific subjects. Under "Relationships," you'll find a heading for "Long Distance Relationships," which might be an idea for writing. Browsing through the layers of topics can help you think of several ideas for your writing. If you know a general topic area, you can type it in the search window of the program and then click on more specific subcategories. Figure 2.9 illustrates this process.

**EXERCISE 2-2**    Go to http://www.google.com/dirhp or http://dir.yahoo.com. Choose one of the headings on the directory. Continue to click on topics under that heading to create a path to a specific possible topic. Be ready

to explain the path you used, what you found, and what you think the strengths
and weaknesses of the topics you identified would be. Finally, go back to the
opening page and repeat the process with a different heading.

**EXERCISE 2-3**  Explore some of the following topics by typing them into
the search window of a search engine. Be ready to explain the sequence of topics you discover.

1. global warming
2. sustainability
3. weightlifting
4. world music
5. disability

## 2c.8  Incubation

**Incubation** refers to giving your ideas time to grow and develop. This technique
works especially well when you need to step back and evaluate what you've discovered and compiled for your writing. For example, you might not see how
your material can be pulled together at first, but if you let it incubate, you
might discover connections you didn't see originally. Conversely, if some parts
of your essay seem too thin in content, incubation gives you distance from
your material so that you can decide what works. Ideally, incubate your ideas
overnight or for a couple of days; but even a few hours can help.

If you don't have the luxury of a lengthy incubation period, some strategies may help you jump-start it. One method is to turn your attention to something entirely unrelated to your writing. Concentrate hard on that other matter
so that you give your conscious mind over to it totally. After a while, relax and
guide your mind back to your writing. Often, you'll see what you've discovered
and compiled for writing in a different way.

**EXERCISE 2-4**  Try each structured technique for discovering and compiling ideas discussed in 2c.1 through 2c.8. Use your own topics or select from the
suggestions below.

1. Professions and job prospects
2. An important personal decision
3. Professional sports
4. Advertisements on television
5. What you want in a life partner

## 2d  What is a thesis statement?

A **thesis statement** is the central message of an essay. The thesis statement presents the TOPIC of your essay, your particular focus on that topic, and your
PURPOSE for writing about that topic. As a writer, you want to write a thesis
statement with great care so that it prepares your readers for what follows.
Quick Reference 2.3 lists the basic requirements for a thesis statement.

## Quick Reference 2.3

■ ■ ■ ■ ■ ■ ■

### Basic requirements for a thesis statement

- It states the essay's subject—the topic that you discuss.
- It conveys the essay's purpose—either informative or persuasive.
- It indicates your focus—the assertion that presents your point of view.
- It uses specific language, not vague words.
- It may briefly state the major subdivisions of the essay's topic.

Some instructors add to these basic requirements for a thesis statement. You might, for example, be asked to put your thesis statement at the end of your introductory paragraph (as in the final draft of Sara Cardini's essay, in section 2l.3). Some instructors require that the thesis statement be contained in one sentence; other instructors permit two sentences if the topic is complex. All requirements, basic and additional, are designed to help you develop a thesis statement that will guide the writing of your essay and help you communicate clearly with your reader. By the way, never confuse the role of a thesis statement with the role of an essay's title (2l.3).

🌐 **ESOL Tip:** A thesis statement, especially in the introductory paragraph, is commonly found in the ACADEMIC WRITING of North American and some other cultures. Readers and writers from some cultures prefer not to state their main idea so bluntly at the beginning of a piece of writing. Because US readers of academic writing generally expect such a statement, using one will probably help your readers better understand your writing. ●

Most writers find that their thesis statement changes somewhat with each successive draft of an essay, so you shouldn't feel locked into your first thesis draft. Still, when you revise its language, be sure to stick to the essential idea you want to communicate. A thesis statement is a guide; it helps you stay on the topic and develop your ideas. To start, make an **assertion**—a sentence stating your topic and the point you want to make about it. This assertion focuses your thinking as you develop a preliminary thesis statement. Next, move toward a final thesis statement that most accurately reflects the content of your essay.

Following is the evolution of Sara Cardini's thesis statement from a simple assertion to the final version in her essay on anime. The final version fulfills all the requirements described in Quick Reference 2.3.

**NO**   I think Japanese animation is interesting. [This assertion is a start, but simply proclaiming something "interesting" is dull.]

**TEACHING TIP**

You may want to ask your students to test their thesis statements by exchanging them with one another. Asking the readers to answer questions about the thesis statements may help the writers discover weaknesses (and strengths) that they didn't see before. Encourage students to turn the requirements for a thesis statement shown in Quick Reference 2.3 into questions such as the following:

**1.** Is the main idea, the central point, clearly stated?

**2.** Is the purpose of the essay clear?

**3.** Is the thesis stated in specific terms? That is, does it avoid overly general, vague language?

**4.** Can the thesis be developed in the time available?

**5.** Can the thesis be developed in an essay of the length planned?

**6.** Is the thesis limited enough for development but general enough to be worth the effort?

## QUOTATION: ON WRITING

I don't know anything about inspiration because I don't know what inspiration is; I've heard about it, but I never saw it.

—William Faulkner

## TEACHING TIP

If your students have trouble organizing an outline, you might suggest that they write each item on a 3-by-5-inch index card. The ability to move the cards around, make piles, and easily eliminate items often facilitates students' work.

## TEACHING TIP

Writers use outlines in a variety of ways. They turn to them, for example, at different stages of the composing process. Some writers find it productive to move from mapping or freewriting directly into a listing of ideas in a particular order, using the outline to plan the drafting process; others use outlines to check the organization of a draft after it is written, testing to see if the paper has order and balance. Some writers find topic outlines helpful; some prefer sentence outlines. Each writer has to find the shaping strategies that prove to be most effective in his or her case.

**NO**    Most people think cartoons are simple entertainments for kids, but there are exceptions to that rule. [This statement draws readers in by promising to show them how their expectations may be inadequate, but it's very broad.]

**NO**    Anime films are sophisticated Japanese cartoons. [This statement is closer to a thesis statement because it's more specific. It promises to show that anime is sophisticated. However, the concept that anime contrasts with American cartoons is an important part of Sara's paper, and that concept is missing here.]

**NO**    The purpose of this paper is to explain Japanese anime and how anime films differ from American cartoons. [This version clearly states a main point of the paper, but it's inappropriate because it blandly announces what the writer is going to do.]

**YES**    Anime has traditions and features that distinguish it from American cartoons and make it sophisticated enough to appeal to adults. [The final version serves as Cardini's thesis statement by effectively conveying the main ideas and point of her essay.]

## THESIS STATEMENTS FOR INFORMATIVE ESSAYS

For essays with an informative purpose (1c.2), here are more examples of thesis statements for 900- to 1,300-word essays. The NO versions are assertions or preliminary thesis statements. The YES versions are good because they fulfill the requirements in Quick Reference 2.3.

**TOPIC**    *Reality television*

**NO**    There are many kinds of reality television shows.

**YES**    A common feature of reality television shows is a villain, a contestant that viewers love to hate.

**TOPIC**    *Women artists*

**NO**    Paintings by women are getting more attention.

**YES**    During the past ten years, the works of the artists Mary Cassatt and Rosa Bonheur have finally gained widespread critical acclaim.

## THESIS STATEMENTS FOR PERSUASIVE ESSAYS

For essays written with a persuasive purpose (1c.3), here are examples of thesis statements written for 900- to 1,300-word essays. Again, the NO versions are assertions or preliminary thesis statements. The YES versions fulfill the requirements in Quick Reference 2.3.

**TOPIC**    *Public transportation*

**NO**    Public transportation has many advantages.

YES  Investing in public transportation pays strong benefits in environmental quality, economic development, and social interactions.

TOPIC  *Deceptive advertising*

NO  Deceptive advertising can cause many problems for consumers.

YES  Deceptive advertising costs consumers not only their money but also their health.

**EXERCISE 2-5**  Each set of sentences below offers several versions of a thesis statement. Within each set, the thesis statements progress from weak to strong. The fourth thesis statement in each set is the best. Referring to requirements listed in Quick Reference 2.3, work individually or with a group to explain why the first three choices in each set are weak and the last is best.

A.  1. Advertising is complex.
    2. Magazine advertisements appeal to readers.
    3. Magazine advertisements must be creative and appealing to all readers.
    4. To appeal to readers, magazine advertisements must skillfully use language, color, and design.

B.  1. Soccer is a widely played sport.
    2. Playing soccer is fun.
    3. Soccer requires various skills.
    4. Playing soccer for fun and exercise requires agility, stamina, and teamwork.

C.  1. *Hamlet* is a play about revenge.
    2. Hamlet must avenge his father's murder.
    3. Some characters in the play *Hamlet* want revenge.
    4. In the play *Hamlet*, Hamlet, Fortinbras, and Laertes all seek revenge.

D.  1. We should pay attention to the environment.
    2. We should worry about air pollution.
    3. Automobile emissions cause air pollution.
    4. Congress should raise emissions standards for passenger cars and SUVs.

E.  1. Cell phones are popular.
    2. People use cell phones in many situations.
    3. The increased use of cell phones causes problems.
    4. Using cell phones while driving should be illegal.

**EXERCISE 2-6**  Here are writing assignments, narrowed topics, and tentative thesis statements. Alone or with a peer-response group, evaluate each thesis statement according to the basic requirements in Quick Reference 2.3.

**ANSWERS: EXERCISE 2-5**

**A.** The fourth thesis statement succeeds because it states a main idea (about magazine advertisements' appeal to readers); it reflects a purpose (to persuade); it has a focus (that magazine advertisements must be skillfully done); and it briefly presents subdivisions (language, color, and design). The first and second thesis statements are too general, showing neither a purpose nor a focus. The third thesis statement shows a persuasive purpose but is still too general and has no focus ("must" isn't explained).

**B.** The fourth thesis statement succeeds because it states a main idea (about playing soccer for fun and exercise); it reflects a purpose (to inform); it has a focus (what is required for playing soccer for fun and exercise); and it briefly presents subdivisions (agility, stamina, and teamwork). The first statement is too general ("widely played" is a very broad term) and shows no purpose or focus. The second statement is also too vague ("fun" is a very broad term when used without a context) and shows no purpose or focus. The third statement reflects an informative purpose but lacks a focus ("various skills" is too vague).

**C.** The fourth thesis statement succeeds because it states a main idea (characters in *Hamlet* seek revenge); it reflects a purpose (to inform); it has a focus (all three characters seek revenge); and it briefly states the major subdivisions (Hamlet, Fortinbras, and Laertes). The first statement is much too general, and though it suggests an informative intent, the statement lacks a focus. The second and third statements reflect an informative purpose but lack a focus ("must" and "want" are vague words here).

**D.** The fourth thesis statement succeeds because it states a main idea (about car emissions standards); it reflects a purpose (to persuade); and it has a focus (the specific action that Congress should take). The first statement uses vague language ("pay attention" and "environment"), and it suggests neither a persuasive nor an informative intent. The second statement reflects a persuasive purpose, but "worry" is vague. The third statement reflects either an informative or a persuasive purpose, but the broad claim is so obvious that it will not lead to an effective paper.

**E.** The fourth thesis statement succeeds because it states a main idea (about cell phone usage); it reflects a purpose (to persuade); and it has a focus (cell phone usage while driving should be illegal). The first statement is too general ("cell phones are popular") has neither a persuasive nor an informative intent and lacks a purpose or focus. The second statement is equally general and lacks a focus. The third statement suggests an informative purpose but lacks a focus.

## ANSWERS: EXERCISE 2-6

**1.** The thesis is good because it reflects the purpose (to persuade), states a main idea, and focuses specifically on logical subdivisions of the topic.

**2.** The thesis suggests that the theater review will do what such reviews should do: evaluate in an attempt to persuade a reader. The words "was very interesting," however, are too vague; they need to be revised to be more specific. A brief indication of subdivisions might help the thesis communicate its message.

**3.** The thesis, though specific and focused, doesn't reflect a careful response to the assignment: The assignment requires an informative report, but this thesis reflects a persuasive purpose not connected to the assignment (DNA testing instead of DNA sequencing).

**4.** This thesis is good because it states a main idea, reflects a purpose (to inform), and includes a focus.

**5.** This thesis doesn't address the assignment adequately because its focus is on training, rather than technology. Here, a better thesis might argue how hand-held computers have changed nursing.

## BACKGROUND

In "Ethical Issues Raised by Students' Personal Writing" (*College English,* March 1998: 318–325), Dan Morgan explores an instructor's responsibility to respond to student writing that is "confessional." He suggests assignment topics that circumvent this problem.

1. **Marketing assignment:** 700- to 800-word persuasive report on a local restaurant. *Audience:* the instructor and the restaurant's owner. *Topic:* increasing business. *Thesis:* The restaurant could attract more students if it changed its menu and redesigned its interior.

2. **Theater assignment:** 300- to 500-word review of a performance. *Audience:* the instructor and other students in the class. *Topic:* a touring production of the musical *Wicked. Thesis:* The recent performance of *Wicked* was very interesting.

3. **Biology assignment:** 800- to 1,000-word informative report about DNA sequencing. *Audience:* the instructor and visiting students and instructors attending a seminar at the state college. *Topic:* people paying to learn their own genetic code. *Thesis:* Scientists should oppose individual DNA tests.

4. **Journalism assignment:** 200- to 300-word article about campus diversity. *Audience:* the instructor, the student body, and the college administration. *Topic:* international students. *Thesis:* There are 279 international students this year at Orwell College.

5. **Nursing assignment:** 400- to 500-word persuasive report about technology changes in nursing. *Audience:* nursing students and professionals. *Topic:* using handheld computers to track patient information. *Thesis:* Hospitals should train nurses more effectively to use handheld computers to enter patient data.

## 2e   How do I plan and organize my ideas?

After you've generated ideas and information, you need to decide the best way to organize it. A plan helps you start drafting. Like a story, an essay needs a beginning, a middle, and an end: a shape. The essay's introduction sets the stage; the essay's body paragraphs provide the substance of your message in a sequence that makes sense; the concluding paragraph ends the essay logically. Each paragraph's length in an informative essay needs to be in proportion to its function. Introductory and concluding paragraphs are usually shorter than body paragraphs. Body paragraphs need to be approximately equal to each other in length. If one body paragraph becomes overly long in relation to the others, consider breaking it into two paragraphs. (We discuss paragraph writing in Chapter 3.) The major elements in an informative essay are listed in Quick Reference 2.4. (For the major elements in a persuasive essay using classical argument, see Quick Reference 5.1 in 5e.)

Shaping an essay takes place on two levels. One is grouping individual ideas or pieces of information into paragraphs. The other is arranging those paragraphs into the best possible order and relationship to each other.

To group your information, look for topics that are related to each other and, within them, search for layers of generality. Which ideas or information can fit under which topics? For example, suppose you're writing a paper about

## Quick Reference 2.4

### Elements in an informative essay

1. **Introductory paragraph:** Leads into the topic of the essay and tries to capture the reader's interest (see 3c).

2. **Thesis statement:** States the central message of the writing. The thesis statement usually appears at the end of the introductory paragraph (2d).

3. **Background information:** Provides a context for understanding the points that a writer wants to make. You can integrate background information into the introductory paragraph. More complex information may require a separate paragraph of information (as in the second paragraph in Sara Cardini's essay, in section 2l).

4. **Points of discussion:** Supports the essay's thesis statement. They're the essential content of the body paragraphs in an essay (3d). Each point of discussion consists of a general statement backed up by specific details.

5. **Concluding paragraph:** Ends the essay smoothly, flowing logically from the rest of the essay (3k).

why the *Wizard of Oz* remains a popular movie. Among the ideas that you've brainstormed are the following:

The settings are spectacular.

Dorothy is a good mixture of innocence and determination.

The munchkin village is imaginative.

The Scarecrow is funny.

Oz appears magical at the end of the poppy field.

The Cowardly Lion is different from our expectations.

The Haunted Forest is truly creepy.

The characters are interesting.

Although the list seems somewhat random, you can see that several of the ideas are about characters, and several are about the setting. You can group the ideas under those generalizations, and you can generate even more specific ideas about each one. For example, more specific details about Dorothy's innocence could include the way she sings "Over the Rainbow," and specific examples of her determination could include her efforts to stay awake in the poppy field. Keep in mind that what separates most good writing from bad is the writer's ability to move back and forth between general statements and specific details.

**QUOTATION: ON WRITING**

I had to make my own living and my own opportunity. . . . Don't sit down and wait for the opportunities to come; you have to get up and make them.

—Madame C. J. Walker

**QUOTATION: ON WRITING**

Writing is a deliberate act; one has to make up one's mind to do it.

—James Britton

**BACKGROUND**

In her essay "The Effects of Computers on Traditional Writing" (*Journal of Electronic Publishing* 8.1, August 2002. <http://quod.lib.umich.edu/cgi/t/text/text-idx?c=jep;view;rgn=main;idno=3336451.0008.104>), Sharmila Pixy Ferris questions the validity of our viewing electronic writing as an extension of traditional writing in print. Although electronic writing often requires writers to learn new technologies, incorporate interactive techniques, and gain expertise in design-related issues of presentation, Ferris notes that most scholars neglect to see that electronic writing generates conventions and standards noticeably different from those of writing in print. To see electronic writing as an extension of orality rather than print, contends Ferris, will help guide the development of new patterns and standards for electronic writing, where the importance of interactivity in particular is emphasized. Does your own experience with academic writing support this point of view? What do you think? E-mail Lynn at <troykalq@nyc.rr.com> or Doug at <ddhesse@ilstu.edu>.

**QUOTATION: ON WRITING**

There is always a point in the writing of a piece when I sit in a room literally papered with false starts and cannot put one word after another and imagine that I have suffered a small stroke, leaving me apparently undamaged but actually aphasic.

—Joan Didion

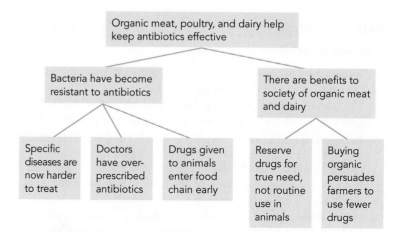

**Figure 2.10**  Alex Garcia's subject tree for the fifth paragraph in his essay

A **subject tree** shows you visually whether you have sufficient content, at varying levels of generality or specificity, to start a first draft of your writing. A subject tree also visually demonstrates whether you have a good balance of general ideas and specific details. If what you have are mostly general ideas—or, the other way around, mostly specific details—go back to techniques for dis-covering and compiling ideas (2c) so that you can come up with the sorts of materials that are missing. Alex Garcia created a subject tree, shown in Figure 2.10, using software tools to help him shape the fifth paragraph in his essay (5n).

Once you've sorted your ideas and information into groups organized by generalizations, you're ready to shape your work at another level. You need to figure out the best order for the sections and paragraphs that you've planned. Of course, like all elements of the writing process, organizing is recursive. Although an initial plan might change considerably as you revise your work, a plan is still helpful for writing your first draft.

## 2f    What is outlining?

An **outline** lays out the relationships among ideas in a piece of writing. Out-lines can lead writers to see how well their writing is organized. Many instruc-tors require outlines either before or with an essay.

Some writers like to outline; others don't. If you don't, but you're required to write one, tackle the job with an open mind. You may be pleasantly surprised at what the rigor of outline writing does to your perception of your essay.

An outline can be *informal* or *formal*. Try outlining at various steps of the WRITING PROCESS: before drafting, to arrange ideas; while you draft, to keep track of your material; while you revise, to check the logical flow of thought or to reveal what information is missing, repeated, or off the topic; or in whatever other ways you find helpful.

## INFORMAL OUTLINES

An **informal outline** is a working plan that lays out the major points of an essay. Because it's informal, it doesn't need to use the numbering and lettering conventions of a formal outline. Complete sentences aren't required; words and phrases are acceptable. Sara Cardini used an informal outline for planning her essay. Here is part of an informal outline for the third paragraph of her essay.

### Sara Cardini's Informal Outline

*Thesis statement:* Anime has traditions and features that distinguish it from American cartoons and make it sophisticated enough to appeal to adults.

qualities of anime

quick movements

jazz and rock music

large eyes for characters

complicated drawings

*Samurai X* as an example

## FORMAL OUTLINES

A traditional **formal outline** follows long-established conventions for using numbers and letters to show relationships among ideas. MLA STYLE (see Chapter 36) doesn't officially endorse using an outline or, indeed, any one outline style. However, many instructors do assign outlines, and they prefer the traditional format shown here. Some instructors prefer a less traditional format for a formal outline, one which includes the content of the introductory and the concluding paragraphs. An example of such an outline appears in section 36e, written by a student whose instructor required that format for an MLA-style research paper. Either of these styles of formal outline—the traditional or the less traditional—can be a sentence outline, composed entirely of complete sentences, or a topic outline, composed only of words and phrases. So that you can compare the two styles of outlines, both examples below outline the third paragraph of Sara Cardini's essay on Japanese anime. Never mix the two styles in one outline.

Writers who use formal outlines say that a sentence outline brings them closer to drafting than a topic outline does. This makes sense because topic outlines contain less information. But you have to find out which type works better for you.

3. If you had peer readers, did you use their suggestions? Did you use all of them? If some of them, which ones? Why?

4. Did you need to make any changes in your introduction or conclusion because of other changes in your text? Explain.

5. Was your title still appropriate? Explain.

6. Where did you add new words, sentences, or paragraphs? Explain.

7. Where did you cut out words, sentences, or paragraphs? Explain.

8. Did you change the sequence of paragraphs? Explain.

9. Did you edit your paper in a single reading, or look for possible errors in a series of readings? Explain.

10. Did you use a checklist, either the one in this chapter or one supplied by your instructor, to examine your writing for grammar, spelling, punctuation, and capitalization problems? How did it help or not help?

### Topic Outline

*Thesis statement:* Anime has traditions and features that distinguish it from American cartoons and make it sophisticated enough to appeal to adults.

I. Anime qualities

   A. Quick images

   B. Jazz and rock soundtracks

   C. Character eyes and features

   D. Colorful, complicated art

     1. *Samurai X* as example

     2. *Samurai X* about nineteenth-century warrior

     3. *Samurai X* art like old Japanese prints

### Sentence Outline

*Thesis statement:* Anime has traditions and features that distinguish it from American cartoons and make it sophisticated enough to appeal to adults.

I. Complex plots are but one of the distinctive features of anime.

   A. Anime images move quickly, with a style often more frantic than in American cartoons.

   B. Their soundtracks frequently use jazz and rock music rather than symphonic music.

   C. Most striking are the large eyes and sharp features of the characters.

   D. The drawing is more colorful, more complicated, and often more abstract than that in most American cartoons.

     1. A TV series called *Samurai X* is one of the most popular anime series with both American and Japanese audiences.

     2. *Samurai X* is set in the nineteenth century and tells the story of one warrior's life.

     3. *Samurai X* art is drawn beautifully to look both like older Japanese art prints and like more contemporary movies such as *Crouching Tiger, Hidden Dragon.*

**EXERCISE 2-7**   Here is a sentence outline. Individually or with your peer-response group, revise it into a topic outline. Then, be ready to explain why you prefer using a topic outline or a sentence outline as a guide to writing.

*Thesis statement:* Taxpayers should demand more investment in public transportation.

I. The current level of public transportation is inadequate everywhere.
   A. Cities need the ability to move lots of residents.
      1. Increased population in large cities causes transportation pressures.
      2. Some cities have responded well.
      3. Most cities have responded poorly.
   B. People need to move easily and cheaply between cities and towns.
      1. Cars are the only way to reach many cities and towns.
      2. It is easier and less expensive to travel in Europe.
II. The lack of public transportation causes many problems.
   A. Driving individual cars increases pollution.
   B. Space for building new roads and highways is limited.
   C. Congestion on city streets limits productivity.
   D. Many people aren't able to drive themselves.
      1. Young or elderly people may not drive.
      2. Many people cannot afford cars.
III. Improving public transportation is possible.
   A. Cities can expand bus services and light rail services.
   B. The United States can develop a wider national rail service.
   C. Although improvements are costly, we can afford them.
      1. We can reallocate money from building new roads.
      2. Building and running transportation creates jobs and adds to our tax base.
      3. Individual savings will offset any tax increases.

## 2g  What can help me write a first draft?

**Drafting** means you get ideas onto paper or into the computer, in sentences and paragraphs. In everyday conversation, people use the word *writing* to talk about drafting, but writing is too broad a term here. The word *drafting* more accurately describes what you do when you write your first attempt—your first *draft*—to generate words.

A **first draft** is the initial version of a piece of writing. Before you begin a first draft, seek out places and times of the day that encourage you to write. You might write best in a quiet corner of the library, or at 4:30 a.m. at the kitchen table before anyone else is awake, or outside alone with nature, or with a steady flow of people walking by. Most experienced writers find they concentrate best when they're alone and won't be interrupted. But individuals differ, and you may prefer background noise—a crowded cafeteria, with the low hum of conversation at the next table or in the next room, for example.

A caution: Don't mislead yourself. You might consider yourself great at multitasking, but academic writing generally demands a higher level of

**ANSWERS: EXERCISE 2-7**
Answers may vary.

Thesis statement: Taxpayers should demand more investment in public transportation.

I. Inadequate public transportation
   A. Cities need to move residents
      1. Increased population
      2. Good responses
      3. Poor responses
   B. People need to move easily and cheaply
      1. Dependent on cars
      2. Cheaper and easier in Europe

II. Lack of public transportation=problems
   A. Cars =pollution
   B. Limited space for new roads and highways
   C. Congestion limits productivity
   D. People cannot drive themselves
      1. Young and old don't drive
      2. Expense of cars

III. Improving public transportation possible
   A. Bus service and light rail
   B. Wider national rail
   C. Even though costly, affordable
      1. Money from new roads
      2. New transportation=jobs=new tax base
      3. Savings offset tax increases

**TEACHING TIP**
Students may find it helpful to know that the strengths and weaknesses in a piece of writing are often easier for the writer to recognize if a "cooling off" period intervenes between the time of writing and the time of revision. If there is an opportunity to put the piece away for a day or so, the writer returns to it not as the composer but as a reader, thus finding it easier to spot confusing passages or awkward statements. Because students are not famous for working far ahead of schedule, they should be encouraged to provide at least a few hours to distance themselves from the writing before trying to revise it. However, if too much time elapses between the draft and the rereading, the writer is likely to lose the sense of purpose and meaning that accompanied the original effort.

## QUOTATION: ON WRITING
One never notices what has been done; one can only see what remains to be done.
—Marie Curie

## QUOTATION: ON TITLES
Were it inquired of an ingenious writer what page of his work had occasioned his most perplexity, he would often point to the title-page. The curiosity which we there would excite, is, however, most fastidious to gratify.

It is too often with the Title of Books, as with those painted representations exhibited by the keepers of wild beasts; where, in general, the picture itself is made more striking and inviting to the eye, than the enclosed animal is always found to be.
—Isaac Disraeli, *Curiosities of Literature*

## TEACHING TIP
To help students become aware of the importance of titles, ask them to experiment with devising alternative titles, both direct and indirect ones, for each other's essays or for short essays that they find in magazines or in their readers. Before doing so, students need to state the thesis of the piece they intend to retitle. After retitling, they can then explain in writing their rationale for the new titles.

## TEACHING TIP
Lynn says, "Many students think that revisers are poor writers. Indeed, I have been scolded more than once by people who have seen me writing in waiting rooms, on the bus, or on a park bench: 'Don't you know not to make a mess when you write?' The tone is always well-meaning, as if the person is trying to help me out of a deep difficulty I seem to be having. I have always been amazed at how forward strangers can be after watching me write while they supposedly stare straight ahead. Some people start to squirm, and the wise ones simply move away. But a few hardy folks want to let me know that I could suddenly become 'a writer' if only I would stop crossing out and drawing arrows on my paper. For a while, the confrontations inhibited me about writing outside my home, but I soon became so interested

concentration than other tasks. You can't produce a useful first draft while talking to friends and stopping only now and then to jot down a sentence. You won't draft smoothly while watching television or being constantly interrupted.

Finally, resist delaying tactics. While you certainly need a computer or a pad of paper and a pencil, you don't need fifteen perfectly sharpened pencils neatly lined up on your desk.

Quick Reference 2.5 offers suggestions for ways to move from planning and shaping into drafting. Experiment to see what works best for you. And be ready to adjust what works according to each WRITING SITUATION.

### Quick Reference 2.5

#### Ways to start drafting

- **Write a discovery draft.** Put aside all your notes from planning and shaping, and write a discovery draft. This means using FOCUSED FREEWRITING to get ideas on paper or onto your computer screen so that you can make connections that spring to mind as you write. Your discovery draft can serve as a first draft or as one more part of your notes when you write a more structured first draft.

- **Work from your notes.** Sort your notes from planning and shaping into groups of subtopics. When you start writing, you can systematically concentrate on each subtopic without having to search repeatedly through your pile of notes. Arrange the subtopics in what seems to be a sensible sequence, knowing you can always go back later and resequence the subtopics. Now, write a first draft by working through your notes on each subtopic. Draft either the entire essay or chunks of a few paragraphs at one time.

- **Use a combination of approaches.** When you know the shape of your material, write according to that structure. When you feel "stuck" and don't know what to say next, switch to writing as you would for a discovery draft.

Now, dive in. Using the planning and shaping you've done as a basis, start writing. The direction of drafting is forward: Keep pressing ahead. If you wonder about the spelling of a word or a point of grammar, don't stop. Use a symbol or other signal to alert you to revisit the question later. Use whatever you like: boldface, underlining, a question mark before and after, an asterisk, or all capital letters. If the exact word you want escapes you while you're drafting, substitute an easy synonym and mark it to go back to later. If you question your sentence style or the order in which you present supporting details, boldface or underline the passage or insert a symbol or the word *Style?* or *Order?* nearby so that you can return to it later. If you begin to run out of ideas, reread what you have written—not to start revising prematurely, but only to propel yourself to keep moving ahead with your first draft. Once you finish your draft, search for marks that you've used to alert yourself to reconsider something. If it's a word, you can use the "Edit > Find" function on your word processing program toolbar.

When drafting on the computer, use your "Save" function often to protect your work, at least every five minutes. (This can be set up as an automatic function.) To prevent losing what you've written, back up your files diligently. Also, print your work regularly—very definitely at the end of each work session—so that you always have a hard copy in case your computer develops problems. Instructors hear so many versions of "I had computer problems" that they've often stopped sorting out which reports are fake and which are real.

A first draft is a preliminary or *rough draft*. Its purpose is to get your ideas onto disk or into computer memory or on paper. Never are first drafts meant to be perfect.

## 2h    How can I overcome writer's block?

If you're afraid or otherwise feel unable to start writing, perhaps you're being stopped by **writer's block**. You want to get started but somehow can't. Often, writer's block occurs because the writer harbors a fear of being wrong. To overcome that fear, or any other cause of your block, first admit it to yourself. Face it honestly so that you can understand whatever is holding you back. Writer's block can strike professional as well as student writers, and a variety of techniques to overcome it have become popular.

The most common cause of writer's block involves a writer's belief in myths about writing.

| | |
|---|---|
| MYTH | Writers are born, not made. |
| TRUTH | Everyone can write. Writers don't expect to "get it right" the first time. Being a good writer means being a patient rewriter. |
| MYTH | Writers have to be "in the mood" to write. |
| TRUTH | If writers always waited for "the mood" to occur, few would write at all. News reporters and other professional writers have deadlines to meet, whether or not they're in the mood to write. |
| MYTH | Writers have to be really good at grammar and spelling. |
| TRUTH | Writers don't let spelling and grammar block them. They write, and when they hear that quiet inner voice saying that a word or sentence isn't quite right, they mark the spot with a symbol or word in all capitals. After they're finished drafting, |

in the reactions that I got caught up in the 'research' of the situations. (Try it sometime—a doctor's office or a barber or beauty shop would be prime territory.) Students are always similarly surprised when they see how messy real writing can be."

**TEACHING TIP**

Many of us have had the experience of reading a student's revision of an essay that we responded to in an earlier draft, only to find that most of our comments have been ignored. The revision turns out to be the original essay with a few spelling errors corrected. Sometimes this happens because students do not know how to respond fully to an instructor's comments.

One way to demystify comments is to have the class respond collectively to the instructor's comments on Sara Cardini's second draft (2l.2). Ask the students to read the instructor's comments on Cardini's essay and decide what Cardini might do in response to each one. You might lead a discussion of the options for resolving each problem. As you come to each comment, allow time for students to draft revisions or to look up the needed information in their handbook. Ask students for their revisions at each comment, and keep students alert to the many good alternatives for responses to the instructor's questions. You might also point out that responses are more likely to be identical to the coded comments of the instructor because those call for corrections of grammar or punctuation.

A useful alternative to the comment-by-comment class discussion is to assign the entire revision as a home or class exercise. Then, students can discuss their thought-through answers and compare their results. As much as possible, try to use copies of the material or overhead transparencies or PowerPoint for the discussion of alternate complete third drafts. Students often cannot follow the discussion if it relies on the memory of various similar versions.

**TEACHING TIP**

At the other end of the spectrum from nonrevisers are overrevisers. Some students are never satisfied with their work and so never hand it in.

This phenomenon is a form of writer's block. Students who suffer from this sort of inhibition often need a little special treatment at first. For example, you might help such students by telling them that for the first few assignments, you will consider their work to be "in progress," even its final version. You might also share with them the words of Eudora Welty:

> I know I can never get it perfect. You just have to know when you've done it the best way. A friend of mine who is a writer said he kept thirteen drafts of a story and put them all in a drawer. Years later he went back, and it was number 7 that was the right one. That taught me a real, true lesson.

## TEACHING TIP

A personal editing checklist, a list of problems that recur from one piece of writing to the next, can help any writer note potential trouble spots. You may want to suggest that students go through returned papers, listing each marked error and grouping those that are similar, such as spelling errors, subject-verb agreement errors, and comma splices. After becoming aware of the kinds of problems and patterns that are most likely to occur, the writer can devise ways of checking new writing to make sure such errors are not present. For example, if the *s* has been left off third-person singular verbs, the student should go through each new paper checking each such construction for agreement.

## QUOTATION: ON WRITING

I praise loudly; I blame softly.
—Catherine II

## QUOTATION: ON WRITING

I don't write easily or rapidly. My first draft usually has only a few elements worth keeping. I have to find out what those are and build from them and throw out what doesn't work, or what simply is not alive.
—Susan Sontag

## BACKGROUND

Online Writing Labs (OWLs) can create global communities by helping writers connect with

they return to those spots and work on them, perhaps using this handbook or a dictionary or thesaurus to check themselves.

MYTH    Writers don't have to revise.

TRUTH    Writers expect to revise—several times. Once words are on paper, writers can see what readers will see. This "revision" helps writers revise.

MYTH    Writing can be done at the last minute.

TRUTH    Drafting and revising take time. Ideas don't leap onto paper in final, polished form.

Quick Reference 2.6 lists reliable strategies writers have developed to overcome writer's block. If you feel blocked, experiment to discover which works best for you. Also, add your own ideas about how to get started. As you use the list in Quick Reference 2.6, suspend judgment of your writing. Let things flow. Don't find fault with what you're keyboarding or writing. Your goal is to get yourself under way. You can evaluate and improve your writing when you're revising it. According to research, premature revision stops many writers cold—and leads to writer's block. Your reward for waiting to revise until after you finish your first draft is the comfort of having a springboard for the revision work in front of you.

---

**Quick Reference 2.6**    ■ ■ ■ ■ ■ ■ ■

### Ways to overcome writer's block

- **Check that one of the myths about writing discussed in section 2h, or one of your own, isn't stopping you.**

- **Avoid staring at a blank page.** Relax and move your hand across the keyboard or page. Write words, scribble, or draw while you think about your topic. The physical act of getting anything on paper can stir up ideas and lead you to begin drafting.

- **Visualize yourself writing.** Many professional writers say that they write more easily if they first picture themselves doing it. Before getting out of bed in the morning or while waiting for a bus or walking to classes, mentally construct a visual image of yourself in the place where you usually write, with the materials you need, busy at work.

- **Picture an image or a scene, or imagine a sound that relates to your topic.** Start writing by describing what you see or hear.

continued >>

## Quick Reference 2.6    (continued)

- **Write about your topic in a letter or e-mail to a friend.** This technique helps you relax and makes drafting nothing more than a chat on paper with someone you feel comfortable with.
- **Write a draft to a different audience.** If it feels intimidating writing for your instructor, imagine you're writing for a roommate or parent or someone much younger.
- **Try writing your material as if you were someone else.** When they take on a role, many writers feel less inhibited about writing. Pretend you're an expert, for example, and imagine that everyone wants to know what you think.
- **Start by writing the middle of your essay.** Skip the introduction and begin with a body paragraph, and write from the center of your essay out, instead of from beginning to end.
- **Use FREEWRITING or FOCUSED FREEWRITING.**
- **Change your method of writing.** If you usually use a computer, try writing by hand. When you write by hand, switch between pencil and pen or ink colors and treat yourself to good-quality paper so that you can enjoy the pleasure of writing on smooth, strong paper. Often that pleasure propels you to keep going.
- **Switch temporarily to writing about a topic that you care about passionately.** Write freely about that topic. Once writing starts to pour out of you, you can often use the momentum to switch back to the topic of your assignment.

## 2i  How do I revise?

**Revising** is rewriting. When you see the word *revision,* break it down to *re-vision,* which means "to see again with fresh eyes." To revise, you evaluate, change, and reevaluate your draft to figure out ways to improve it. To do this, you need to read your writing honestly, without losing confidence or becoming defensive. After all, what's on the page is ink, not ego. As you work, look at whatever you change and evaluate the revision first on its own and then in the context of the surrounding material. Continue until you're satisfied that your essay is the best you can make it, in light of your specific WRITING SITUATION.

Whenever possible within your time frame, distance yourself from each draft. The best way is to leave a chunk of time between finishing a first draft

one another and form supportive networks. However, to do this effectively, argues writing center consultant Beth Godbee ("Community Building in Online Writing Centers," *Praxis: A Writing Center Journal* 3.1, Spring 2005 <http://projects.uwc.utexas.edu/praxis/?q=node/21>), online writing centers need to avoid replicating the one-on-one tutorial of the face-to-face center; nor need they simply transfer a question-and-answer format to a virtual environment. Godbee admonishes instructors to heed the advice of those scholars who are calling for more small-group sessions and larger workshops online. OWLs can provide students and tutors the opportunity to explore various sources together as they meet in online libraries, collaborate on Internet searches, and evaluate sources and propose ideas synchronously. Tutors themselves can work together, sharing their expertise to provide assistance to students in an interactive electronic environment.

**BACKGROUND**
In "Revision and Process: 'Round Robin' Group Writing" (*Teaching English in the Two-Year College,* March 2000: 342), Judith Platz describes a group drafting assignment that encourages students to thoughtfully consider organization, structure, and content.

**BACKGROUND**
Recognizing that many instructors come to online courses as novices, with limited or no opportunity for the thorough training provided by a few exceptional programs, educators Beth L. Hewett and Christa Ehmann Powers call for those who have implemented successful programs to provide comprehensive and systematic online support for online instruction ("How Do You Ground Your Training?" *Kairos: Journal of Rhetoric, Technology, and Pedagogy* 10.1, Fall 2005 <http://english.ttu.edu/kairos/10.1/binder.html?praxis/hewett/index.htm>). If clearly stated goals, supportive measures, and a variety of training strategies become a part of the support that instructors in online environments provide for one another, Hewett and Powers argue that all can learn not only the

processes that build success but also the principles that ground these practices.

See also Hewett and Powers, *Preparing Educators for Online Writing Instruction: Principles and Processes* (NCTE, 2004).

**BACKGROUND**

In "The Ill Effects of the Five Paragraph Theme" (*English Journal* 90, September 2000: 57–60), Kimberly Wesley argues that adhering too rigidly to the five-paragraph theme format hinders the development of critical thinking. In contrast, Robert Perrin defends the five-paragraph essay, arguing that the maligned form may actually foster creativity ("10:00 and 2:00: A Ten-Paragraph Defense of the Five-Paragraph Theme," *Teaching English in the Two-Year College,* March 2000: 312–314).

**TEACHING TIP**

Certainly, all of us sometimes feel that we are drowning in student writing. The battle rages constantly: Do I spend twenty minutes on each essay, or do I spend five minutes, thereby responding to more students?

Given the few minutes that we have for each essay, decisions about what to write are important. If you're relatively new to teaching composition and need to use codes (abbreviations, such as *sp* and *agr,* or references to text, such as *15a,* or proofreader's symbols, such as # for *space*), be sure students know what the messages mean. You might review the codes and symbols you ordinarily use as part of the follow-up to their receiving their first piece of writing back from you, or you can refer students to the chart of correction symbols in this handbook. Along with citing errors, symbols send a secondary message: "This matter is important but relatively uninspiring. Fix it quickly (and learn the information) and move on to the more interesting aspects of your essay."

Many issues of substance are impossible to respond to by code. Besides, students like to feel that a real human being is reading their work—and real people ask questions when they are puzzled. Therefore, whenever possible, phrase your reactions as questions. Instead of writing "unclear," ask "How does this relate to

and starting to revise. Doing so helps you develop an objective sense of your work. Student writers often want to hold on to their every word, especially if they had trouble getting started on a first draft. Resist such a feeling vigorously. Put away your draft and allow the rosy glow of authorial pride to dim a bit. The classical writer Horace recommended waiting nine years before revising! You might try to wait a few hours or even thirty minutes. Better yet, take a day or two before going back to look at your work with fresh eyes.

Also, as you're revising, don't start EDITING too soon. Editing comes after revising. Research shows that premature editing distracts writers from dealing with the larger issues that revision involves.

## 2i.1   Goals and activities during revision

Your goal during revision is to improve your draft at three levels: content, organization, and ideas.

To revise successfully, you need to understand that writing is revising. The myth that good writers never have to revise is nonsense. Final drafts evolve from first drafts. Here's how to prepare your mind for revising:

- Shift mentally from suspending judgment (during idea gathering and drafting) to making judgments. Read your draft objectively with "a cold eye" to evaluate it.

- Decide whether to write an entirely new draft or to revise the one you have. Be critical as you evaluate your first draft, but don't be overly harsh. Many early drafts provide sufficient raw material for revision to get under way.

- Be systematic. Don't evaluate at random. Most writers work best when they concentrate on each element sequentially. Start with your draft's overall organization; next, move to its paragraphs, then to its sentences, and finally to its word choice. If you need practice in being systematic, try using a revision checklist, either one supplied by your instructor or the one in this handbook.

You can engage in the activities of revision, listed in Quick Reference 2.7, by hand or on the computer, which allows you to make both large and small changes easily. Use "Cut" and "Paste" to reorder sentences or rearrange paragraphs. For example, you might decide to split up a paragraph, join two paragraphs, or otherwise shuffle them. Similarly, you might reorder the sequence of some sentences or interchange sentences between paragraphs. Sometimes, these experiments won't yield anything useful, but they might reveal a few surprises that help you "re-vision" your work.

As you try various revisions, use the "Save As" function on your computer to save drafts under slightly different names, such as "Animation Draft 1," "Animation Draft 2," and so on. By saving several drafts of your paper, you can al-

> ### Quick Reference 2.7 ∎∎∎∎∎∎
>
> #### Major activities during revision
>
> - **Add:** Insert needed words, sentences, paragraphs, or ideas. If your additions require new content, return to the structured techniques shown in section 2b.
> - **Cut:** Get rid of whatever goes off the topic or repeats what has already been said.
> - **Replace:** As needed, substitute new words, sentences, and paragraphs for what you have cut.
> - **Move:** Change the sequence of paragraphs if the material isn't presented in logical order. Move sentences within paragraphs or to other paragraphs when your PARAGRAPH ARRANGEMENT does not allow the material to flow.

ways return to earlier versions if you later decide you prefer something in one of them. If you want to drop material, resist deleting it instantly. As handbook authors, we save almost everything. Doug, for instance, typically keeps a file named "Junk" for just this purpose. Lynn names her folder of discarded drafts of sentences, paragraphs, and whole essays "Discarded Stuff."

Beware of two temptations when writing with the computer. Because you can rearrange and otherwise revise endlessly, you may need to set limits, or you'll never finish the assignment. The opposite seduction is also possible: A neatly printed page may look like a final draft, but it definitely isn't one.

### 2i.2 The role of a thesis statement in revision

The THESIS STATEMENT of your essay has great organizing power because it controls and limits what your essay can cover. Therefore, as you revise, keep checking the accuracy of your thesis statement. Use the thesis statement's controlling power to bring it and your essay into line with each other. Adjust your thesis if necessary, for example, if revisions have resulted in more interesting or effective ideas—or have even changed your position. When your essay is finished, the thesis statement and what you say in your essay need to match. If they don't, you need to revise either the thesis statement or the essay—or sometimes both.

Every writer's experience with revising a thesis statement varies from essay to essay. Sara Cardini, the student you met earlier in this chapter as she did her planning and shaping, wrote several versions of her thesis statement (shown in 2d) for her drafts. You can read Cardini's three complete drafts, along with comments, at the end of this chapter.

your thesis?" If you do not have time to write many questions, try at least two or three per paper. Psychologically, people can't help but answer questions—at least in their own minds. So, to ask a question is to guarantee an answer. And with the answer in mind, a student can revise. Whenever time permits, a good description deserves more than "nice" scribbled in the margin; you might say, "You really made me see the lake at sundown." If a student tells you about a cooking disaster, you might say, "You had me laughing in sympathy." Such comments validate students' experiences and also demonstrate compassionate reading.

**QUOTATION: ON WRITING**
After making a start, children sometimes decide that it won't do and begin again. The strength of their conviction that a new start must be made, even though the teacher may have no complaints about what has been written, is sometimes remarkable. They are not easily persuaded to reconsider a decision to reject what they have done. Some seem to make a habit of rejecting their beginning, and rarely complete anything. These may be timid children for whom committing themselves to paper at all—"finding a tone to talk with" and "being oneself in talking"—imposes a severe strain.
—James Britton, writing about young writers

**QUOTATION: ON WRITING**
Let your literary compositions be kept from the public eye for nine years at least.
—Horace

**QUOTATION: ON WRITING**
My speed depends on the state of my bank account.
—Mickey Spillane

### 2i.3   The role of a title in revision

Your **title** can also show you what needs revising because it clarifies the overall point of the essay. An effective title sets you on your course and tells your readers what to expect. Some writers like to begin their first drafts with a title at the top of the page to focus their thinking. Then, as they revise drafts, they revise the title. If, however, no title springs to mind, don't be concerned. Often, a good title doesn't surface until after drafting, revising, and even editing. Whatever you do, never tack on a title as an afterthought right before handing in your essay. A suitable title is essential for readers to think about as they begin focusing on your essay.

Titles can be direct or indirect. A **direct title** tells exactly what the essay will be about—for example, "The Characteristics of Japanese Animation." A direct title contains key words under which the essay could be cataloged in a library or an online database. A direct title shouldn't be too broad. For example, Cardini's first and second drafts of a title were "Japanese Videos" and "Japanese Anime" (2l.1 and 2l.2). By her final draft, Cardini had revised the title to "The Appeal of Japanese Animation for Adults" (2l.3). Conversely, a direct title should not be too narrow. "The Graphics of Anime" is too narrow a title for Cardini's essay, given what she discusses in it.

An **indirect title** only hints at the essay's topic. It tries to catch the reader's interest by presenting a puzzle that can be solved by reading the essay. When writing an indirect title, you don't want to be overly obscure or too cute. For example, a satisfactory indirect title for Cardini's final draft might be "More Than Simple Cartoons?" In contrast, the indirect title "Imagining That Walt Disney Had Been Japanese" wouldn't work because it's only remotely related to the point of the essay. Also, "Thanks, *Sailor Moon*" would probably be seen as overly cute for academic writing.

⚠ **Alert:** When you write the title at the top of the page or on a title page, never enclose it in quotation marks or underline it. Let your title stand on its own, without decoration. Where you place it will depend on which DOCUMENTATION STYLE you're using. ●

Whether direct or indirect, your essay title stands on its own. Never does the first sentence of an essay refer to the essay's title. For example, Cardini's essay, titled "The Appeal of Japanese Animation for Adults," would suffer a major blow if the first sentence were "It certainly does have appeals" or "I am the proof." Rather, the first sentence starts the flow of the essay's content.

### 2i.4   The role of unity and coherence

Chapter 3 shows you many techniques for achieving unity and coherence in an essay, but here we need to preview those concepts because they're central concerns as you revise.

An essay has **unity** when all of its parts relate to the THESIS STATEMENT and to one another. Does each paragraph—especially each body paragraph—contain examples, reasons, facts, and details that relate directly to your thesis and contribute to your writing situation? As you revise, do you notice that anything in the essay is off the topic? An essay achieves **coherence** through closely built relationships among ideas and details that are built on word choice, use of TRANSITIONAL EXPRESSIONS, clear use of PRONOUNS, and effective PARALLELISM.

## 2i.5 Using a revision checklist

A revision checklist can focus your attention as you evaluate and revise your writing. Use such a checklist, either one provided by your instructor or one that you compile on your own, based on Quick Reference 2.8.

---

### Quick Reference 2.8    ■ ■ ■ ■ ■ ■ ■

**Revision**

Your goal is to answer *yes* to each question on the following list. If you answer *no,* you need to revise your writing accordingly. The section numbers in parentheses tell you where to look in this handbook for help.

1. Is your essay topic suitable and sufficiently narrow? (2b.3)
2. Does your thesis statement communicate your topic, focus, and purpose? (2d, Quick Reference 2.3)
3. Does your essay show that you are aware of your audience? (Quick Reference 1.5)
4. Have you checked for places where your reader would be confused or need more information?
5. Have you checked for places where a skeptical reader would object to your argument or not be convinced?
6. Is your essay arranged effectively?
7. Have you checked for material that strays off the topic?
8. Does your introduction prepare your reader for the rest of the essay? (3c)
9. Do your body paragraphs express main ideas in topic sentences as needed? (3e) Are your main ideas clearly related to your thesis statement? (2d)
10. Do you provide specific, concrete support for each main idea? (3f)
11. Do you use transitions and other techniques to connect ideas within and between paragraphs? (3j)
12. Does your conclusion give your essay a sense of completion?

🌐 **ESOL Tip:** If you'd like information about issues of English grammar that often affect multilingual students, consult Part Seven in this handbook. Topics include those related to culture and education, as well as linguistic concerns, such as ARTICLES (Chapter 51); WORD ORDER (Chapter 52); PREPOSITIONS (Chapter 53); VERBALS (Chapter 54); and MODAL AUXILIARY VERBS (Chapter 55). ●

## 2j    How do I edit?

**Editing** means checking the sentence-level wording and the technical correctness of your writing. You carefully examine your writing for correct grammar, spelling, punctuation, capitalization, and use of numbers, italics, and abbreviations. You see if you can improve the style of your sentences. Some people use the terms *editing* and *revising* interchangeably, but these terms refer to very different steps in the writing process. Revising refers to making changes that affect the content, meaning, and organization of a paper. In contrast, editing involves fine-tuning the surface features of your writing.

Editing is crucial. No matter how much attention you've paid to planning, shaping, drafting, and revising, you need to edit carefully. Slapdash editing distracts and annoys your reader; lowers that reader's opinion of you and what you say in your essay; and, in a college assignment, usually earns a lower grade.

Our best advice to you about editing is this: Don't rush. Editing takes time. Inexperienced writers sometimes rush editing, eager to "get it over with." Resist any impulse to hurry. Be systematic and patient. Checking grammar and punctuation takes your full concentration, along with time to look up and apply the rules in this handbook.

When do you know you've finished revising and are ready to edit? Ask yourself, "Is there anything else I can do to improve the content, organization, and development of this draft?" If the answer is no, you're ready to edit.

Word-processing programs include editing tools such as a spell-checker, style-checker, thesaurus, and readability analyzer. However, as we explained in Chapter 1, each of these tools has shortcomings serious enough to create new errors. Yet, if you use the tools intelligently, with their shortcomings in mind, they can be useful.

Whenever possible, edit on a paper copy of your writing. It's much easier to spot editing errors on a printed page than on a computer screen. Double-space your paper before printing it for revising or editing. The extra space gives you room to write your changes clearly so that you can read them easily later. After you finish editing, you can transfer your corrections to the computer. If you must edit onscreen, highlight every two or three sentences and read each slowly. By working in small segments, you reduce the tendency to read too quickly and miss errors.

Using an editing checklist—either one provided by your instructor or one based on Quick Reference 2.9 that you tailor to your particular needs—can help you find errors by moving through editing systematically. A time-saving method for editing is to create a personal list of common errors you tend to make repeatedly. For example, if the difference between *its* and *it's* always escapes you, or if you tend to misuse the colon, using your personal list of common errors while you edit can remind you to look carefully for those problems.

---

**Quick Reference 2.9**                           ■ ■ ■ ■ ■ ■ ■

### Editing

Your goal is to answer *yes* to each question below. If you answer *no,* you need to edit. The numbers in parentheses tell you which chapters in this handbook to go to for more information.

1. Are your sentences concise? (Chapter 11)
2. Are your sentences interesting? Do you use parallelism, variety, and emphasis correctly and to increase the impact of your writing? (Chapters 9–10)
3. Have you used exact words? (Chapter 12)
4. Is your usage correct and your language appropriate? (Chapter 13)
5. Have you avoided sexist or stereotypical language? (Chapter 12)
6. Is your grammar correct? (Chapters 14–22)
7. Is your spelling correct? (Chapter 31)
8. Have you used commas correctly? (Chapter 24)
9. Have you used all other punctuation correctly? (Chapters 23 and 25–29)
10. Have you used capital letters, italics, abbreviations, and numbers correctly? (Chapter 30)
11. Have you used the appropriate citation and documentation formats? (Chapters 36–38)

---

## 2k   How do I proofread?

To **proofread**, check your final draft for accuracy and neatness before handing it in. In contrast to editing, which is a check for technical correctness, proofreading is a check for typographical accuracy. This is your last chance to catch typing (or handwriting) errors and to make sure that you hand in a clean transcription of your final draft. You don't want all your hard efforts drafting, revising, and editing to be undercut by your not taking this final step.

When proofreading, read your work carefully line by line, looking for typing errors such as "form" vs. "from," letters or words accidentally omitted, words typed twice in a row, wrong indents to start each paragraph, and similar typos or slips. Then, print out a complete fresh copy. Reprinting just one page is often difficult because of reflowing text. Never expect your instructor to make allowances for handwritten corrections.

Some techniques for proofreading include: (1) using a ruler under each line as you read it to prevent yourself from looking beyond that line; (2) reading backwards, sentence by sentence, to prevent yourself from being distracted by the content of the paper; and (3) proofreading your final draft aloud, to yourself or to a friend, so that you can hear errors that have slipped past your eyes. As with revising and editing, whenever possible, print and proofread a double-spaced paper copy of your writing. Again, it's much easier to spot errors on a printed page than onscreen. If you must proofread onscreen, highlight every two or three sentences and read each slowly. Enlarging the type onscreen is another helpful trick to help you focus word by word.

## **2I**    A student essay in three drafts

The following sections observe Sara Cardini, a student, planning to write on the topic of Japanese animation. Elsewhere in this chapter, you'll find her writing assignment (2b), how she used an entry in her journal (2c.1), mapped her ideas (2c.5), wrote her thesis statement (2d), and outlined (2f).

### **2I.1**    The first draft of a student essay

Here's Cardini's first draft showing her own notes to herself about revisions to make in the second draft. The notes resulted from comments from other students in her peer-response group (6c) and from her personal rereading of her draft.

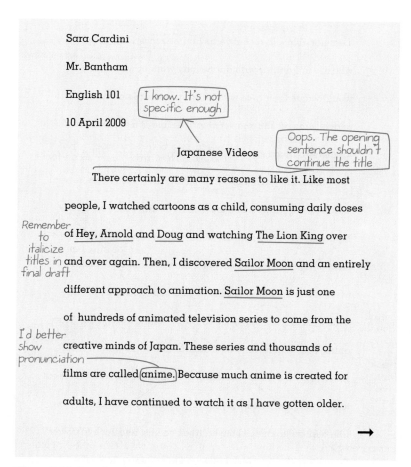

**Figure 2.11** Sara Cardini's first draft, with notes

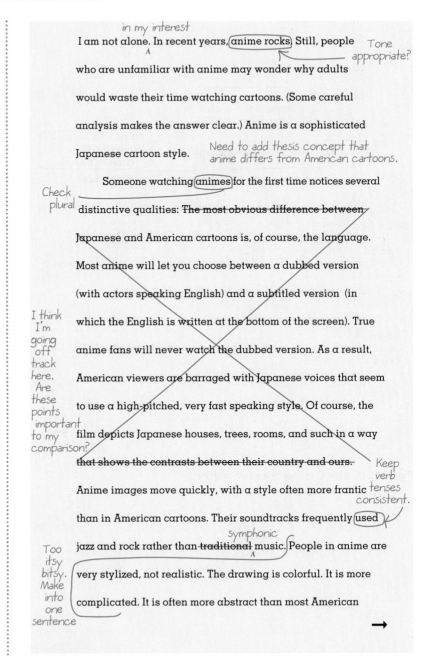

*in my interest*

I am not alone. In recent years, anime rocks. Still, people *Tone appropriate?*

who are unfamiliar with anime may wonder why adults

would waste their time watching cartoons. (Some careful

analysis makes the answer clear.) Anime is a sophisticated

Japanese cartoon style. *Need to add thesis concept that anime differs from American cartoons.*

Someone watching animes for the first time notices several

*Check plural* distinctive qualities: ~~The most obvious difference between~~

~~Japanese and American cartoons is, of course, the language.~~

~~Most anime will let you choose between a dubbed version~~

~~(with actors speaking English) and a subtitled version (in~~

*I think I'm going off track here. Are these points important to my comparison?*

~~which the English is written at the bottom of the screen). True~~

~~anime fans will never watch the dubbed version. As a result,~~

~~American viewers are barraged with Japanese voices that seem~~

~~to use a high-pitched, very fast speaking style. Of course, the~~

~~film depicts Japanese houses, trees, rooms, and such in a way~~

~~that shows the contrasts between their country and ours.~~

*Keep verb tenses consistent.*

Anime images move quickly, with a style often more frantic

than in American cartoons. Their soundtracks frequently used

*symphonic*

*Too itsy bitsy. Make into one sentence* jazz and rock rather than ~~traditional~~ music. People in anime are

very stylized, not realistic. The drawing is colorful. It is more

complicated. It is often more abstract than most American

→

**Figure 2.11** continued

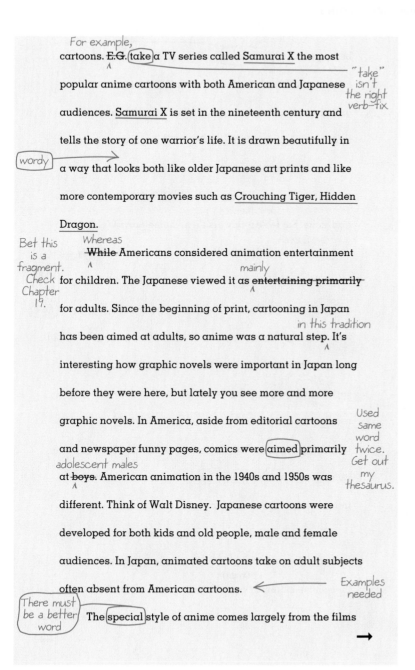

cartoons. ~~E.G.~~ *For example,* (take) a TV series called <u>Samurai X</u> the most

popular anime cartoons with both American and Japanese *"take" isn't the right verb—fix*

audiences. <u>Samurai X</u> is set in the nineteenth century and

tells the story of one warrior's life. It is drawn beautifully in

*wordy* →  a way that looks both like older Japanese art prints and like

more contemporary movies such as <u>Crouching Tiger, Hidden</u>

<u>Dragon.</u>

*Bet this is a fragment. Check Chapter 19.*

*Whereas* ~~While~~ Americans considered animation entertainment

for children. The Japanese viewed it as ~~entertaining primarily~~ *mainly*

for adults. Since the beginning of print, cartooning in Japan

*in this tradition*
has been aimed at adults, so anime was a natural step. It's

interesting how graphic novels were important in Japan long

before they were here, but lately you see more and more

graphic novels. In America, aside from editorial cartoons

*Used same word twice. Get out my thesaurus.*

and newspaper funny pages, comics were (aimed) primarily

*adolescent males*
at ~~boys~~. American animation in the 1940s and 1950s was

different. Think of Walt Disney. Japanese cartoons were

developed for both kids and old people, male and female

audiences. In Japan, animated cartoons take on adult subjects

often absent from American cartoons. ← *Examples needed*

*There must be a better word*
The (special) style of anime comes largely from the films

→

**Figure 2.11** continued

being produced for ~~narrow~~ audiences. The animators were    *Right word?*

creating works only for a Japanese market, at least until

quite recently. Therefore, they did not take into account the

traditions of other cultures. Indeed, US animation was

produced for an international audience, which called for

recognizable themes that came out of familiar European

traditions. For ~~rookie~~ *uninitiated* viewers then, anime provides a crash

course in ~~a~~ *an Eastern* culture quite different from their own. Nearly

all serious anime fans own guides that explain such things    *Add more detail here*

as Japanese social hierarchies. For instance, several anime

feature a *hagoromo* or feathered cloak worn by a mythological

figure known as the *tennyo*. Knowing that this figure has a

certain *symbolic* meaning for a Japanese viewer and is not just a

random decoration or character adds to the depth of a scene

in which it appears. Decoding some of these cultural

references is undoubtedly some of the fun and challenge for

the true *otakon*, or anime fan.

Japanese television has many daily animated series

that vary in terms of sophistication and audience. Some of

these have extremtly ~~complicated~~ *complex* scripts, while others are

bad by nearly any standard. Several of these television series

→

**Figure 2.11** continued

*[Add examples]* now appear in the United States. A wide range of anime

feature films is readily available on DVD, and many have

even found their way into American theaters. For instance,

Akira is a film about life thirty years after a nuclear war.

Probably the most famous theatrical anime in the United   *[Better look at this sentence again!]*

States is Spirited Away. Directed by Hayao Miyasaki, in

which a young girl, Chihiro, is able to free her parents from   *[probably]*

a spell after many magical adventures. The movie will become

a ~~probably~~ classic. Anime appears in all kinds of types and   *[probably ^]*

genres, from childish works like Pokémon to dark science

fiction like Ghost in the Shell.   *[I think I should move this up as the topic sentence for this paragraph.]*

*[Best word?]* One reason [grown-ups] enjoy anime is because they

*[Verb tense ok?]* [missed] a form they loved as children. Anime gives them

*of design, creativity, sophistication and content*

animated art but adds an adult level. While there have   *[^]*

been a few American cartoons aimed at adults (The Simpsons,

South Park), the animation is less detailed and the tone is

usually satiric. There is no such barrier in anime.

By studying anime, I also learned more about Japan.

I met people who took Japanese language classes and had

traveled to cities such as Tokyo and Osaka. I found out about

Japanese popular culture and how much fashion, music, etc.,

→

**Figure 2.11** continued

the Japanese borrow from Americans and how much we

borrow from them. I discovered that while the Japanese are

very different in some traditions, they are very much like us

in terms of their love of movies, TV, and music. For the first

time, I became very interested in how people in another *[Does this para relate directly to my thesis?]*

country live. Now I am considering traveling to Japan

    As Americans come to embrace anime, the form may

*[watered down]*

change. Some fans fear that the art of anime will be ~~wasted~~

in the bid for popularity and profits. Others celebrate the

combination of styles as some American animators borrow

from the Japanese. In this essay I have explained Japanese

animation.  ← *[I shouldn't declare what I have done. My ending needs work.]*

**Figure 2.11**  continued

## 21.2  The second draft of a student essay

For her second draft, Cardini revised by working systematically through the notes she had written on the draft. The notes came from her own thinking as well as from the comments of the peer-response group with which she had shared her paper.

From the assignment (2b), Cardini knew that her instructor would consider this second draft an "essay in progress." Her instructor's responses would help her write a final draft. She expected two types of comments: questions to help her clarify and expand on some of her ideas, and references to some of this handbook's section codes (designated by number-letter combinations) to point out errors. Here is her second draft.

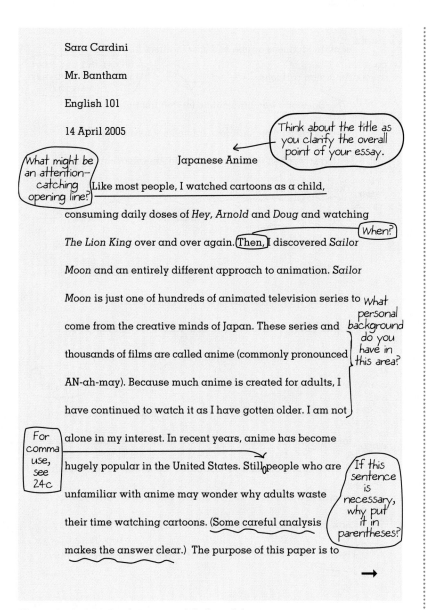

Sara Cardini

Mr. Bantham

English 101

14 April 2005

*Think about the title as you clarify the overall point of your essay.*

Japanese Anime

*What might be an attention-catching opening line?*

Like most people, I watched cartoons as a child,

consuming daily doses of *Hey, Arnold* and *Doug* and watching

*The Lion King* over and over again. Then, I discovered *Sailor*

*When?*

*Moon* and an entirely different approach to animation. *Sailor*

*Moon* is just one of hundreds of animated television series to

come from the creative minds of Japan. These series and

thousands of films are called anime (commonly pronounced

AN-ah-may). Because much anime is created for adults, I

have continued to watch it as I have gotten older. I am not

*What personal background do you have in this area?*

alone in my interest. In recent years, anime has become

*For comma use, see 24c*

hugely popular in the United States. Still, people who are

unfamiliar with anime may wonder why adults waste

their time watching cartoons. (Some careful analysis

*If this sentence is necessary, why put it in parentheses?*

makes the answer clear.) The purpose of this paper is to

→

**Figure 2.12** Sara Cardini's second draft, with her instructor's responses

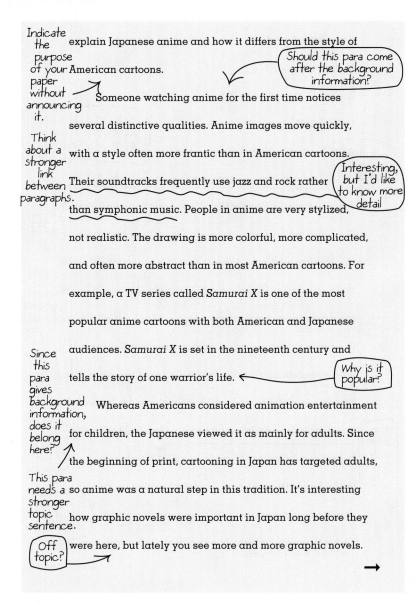

*Indicate the purpose of your paper without announcing it.*

explain Japanese anime and how it differs from the style of American cartoons.

*Should this para come after the background information?*

Someone watching anime for the first time notices several distinctive qualities. Anime images move quickly, with a style often more frantic than in American cartoons.

*Think about a stronger link between paragraphs.*

Their soundtracks frequently use jazz and rock rather than symphonic music.

*Interesting, but I'd like to know more detail*

People in anime are very stylized, not realistic. The drawing is more colorful, more complicated, and often more abstract than in most American cartoons. For example, a TV series called *Samurai X* is one of the most popular anime cartoons with both American and Japanese audiences. *Samurai X* is set in the nineteenth century and tells the story of one warrior's life.

*Why is it popular?*

*Since this para gives background information, does it belong here?*

Whereas Americans considered animation entertainment for children, the Japanese viewed it as mainly for adults. Since the beginning of print, cartooning in Japan has targeted adults, so anime was a natural step in this tradition. It's interesting how graphic novels were important in Japan long before they were here, but lately you see more and more graphic novels.

*This para needs a stronger topic sentence.*

*Off topic?*

**Figure 2.12** continued

In the United States, aside from editorial cartoons and newspaper funny pages, comics were aimed primarily at [A little more guidance, please.] adolescent males. American animation in the 1940s and [From what?] 1950s was (different.) Think of Walt Disney. Japanese cartoons [Off topic?] were developed for both kids and old people, male and female audiences. In Japan, animated cartoons take on adult subjects often absent from American cartoons. These subjects include war, death, sacrifice, love, Japan's historical past [A link to the next para would be welcome here.] and future, and even occasionally sex and violence.

The unique style of anime comes largely from the [Right word?] films being produced for (narrow) audiences. The animators were creating works only for a Japanese market, at least [What does *it* refer to? See 16p] until quite recently. Therefore, (it) did not take into account the traditions of other cultures. (Indeed,) American animation [Right word?] was produced for an international audience, which called for recognizable themes that came out of familiar European traditions. For uninitiated viewers, then, anime provides a crash course in an Eastern culture quite different from their own. Nearly all serious anime fans own guides that explain such

→

**Figure 2.12** continued

things as Japanese social hierarchies, clothing, dining habits, traditions, rituals, and mythology. For instance, several anime *[See next page.]* feature a *hagoromo*, or feathered cloak, worn by a mythological figure known as the *tennyo*. Knowing that this figure has a symbolic meaning for a Japanese viewer and is not just a random decoration or character adds to the depth of a scene in which it appears. Decoding some of these cultural references is undoubetedly some of the fun and challenge for the true *otakon*, or anime fan. *[Excellent point!]*

   Anime appears in all kinds of types and genres, from *[Do you really mean childish?]* childish works like *Pokémon* to dark science fiction like *Ghost in the Shell*. Japanese televison has many daily animated series that vary in terms of sophistication and audience. Some of *[Meaning what?]* these have extremely complex scripts, while others are bad by nearly any standard. Several of these television series now appear in the United States, with some of the best known including *Inuyasha* and *Evangelion*. A wide range of anime feature films are readily available on DVD, and many have even found their way into American theaters.

**Figure 2.12** continued

*See previous page.*

For instance, *Akira* is a film about life thirty years after a nuclear war. Probably the most famous theatrical anime video in the United States is *Spirited Away*, directed by Hayao Miyasaki, in which a young girl, Chihiro, is able to free her parents from a spell after many magical adventures. The movie will probably become a classic.

*More detail would make this vivid.*

One reason American adults enjoy anime is because they miss a form they loved as children. Anime gives them animated art but adds an adult level of design, creativity, sophistication, and content. While there have been a few American cartoons aimed at adults (*The Simpsons*, *South Park*). the animation is less detailed and the tone is usually satiric. There are no such barriers in anime.

*Interesting concluding thoughts*

As Americans come to embrace anime, the form may change. Some fans fear that the art of anime will be watered down in the bid for popularity and profits. Others celebrate the combination of styles as some American animators borrow from the Japanese. In this essay I have proved that anime deserves our attention.

*Bringing in your voice again makes for an effective ending.*

*But avoid making an absolute claim like this.*

**Figure 2.12** continued

Dear Sara,

 You've done yourself proud. And you've inspired me to look up the fascinating subject of Japanese anime.

 As you revise for your final draft, I'd urge you to acquire a little more personal voice. Think about how you feel on this subject and put that in words. Also, think about my questions and the codes that refer you to sections of the Troyka handbook.

 I will enjoy reading your final draft.

         RB

## 21.3   A student's final draft

For her final draft, Cardini worked systematically through her second draft with an eye on her instructor's responses. Also, she revised in places where her instructor hadn't commented. As another check, Cardini referred to the revision checklist (Quick Reference 2.8).

Next, to edit her final draft, Cardini looked up the handbook codes (number-letter combinations) her instructor wrote on her second draft. She also consulted the editing checklist (Quick Reference 2.9). Then, before she started to proofread, she took a break from writing so she could refresh her ability to see typing errors. Distance from her work, she knew, would also help her see it more objectively.

Cardini's final draft appears on the following pages with notes in the margins to point out elements that help the essay succeed. These notes are for you only; don't write any notes on your final drafts.

## Sara Cardini's final draft

Cardini 1

Sara Cardini

Mr. Bantham

English 101

13 April 2008

*Includes name, course information, and date; double-spaced and flush left*

*Header at top right has name and page number*

The Appeal of Japanese Animation for Adults

I confess that I am an animation addict. Like most people, I watched cartoons as a child, consuming daily doses of *Hey, Arnold* and *Doug* and watching *The Lion King* over and over again. Then in junior high, just about the time I was getting tired of cartoons, I discovered *Sailor Moon* and an entirely different approach to animation. *Sailor Moon* is just one of hundreds of animated television series to come from the creative minds of Japan. These series and thousands of films are called *anime* (commonly pronounced AN-ah-may). Because much anime is created for adults, I have continued to watch it as I have gotten older. In fact, my interest has grown so strong that I have studied Japanese, have attended anime conferences, and am now studying filmmaking. I am not alone in my interest. In recent years, anime has become hugely popular in the United States. Still, people who are unfamiliar with anime may wonder why adults would waste their time watching cartoons. Some careful analysis makes the answer clear. Anime has traditions and features that distinguish it from American cartoons and make it sophisticated enough to appeal to adults.

Animation developed differently in Japan and America after World War II. Whereas Americans considered animation

*Centers title*

*Includes attention-getting first line*

*Provides her credentials on this topic*

*Introduces a question*

*Offers a thesis*

*Provides background on topic*

(Proportions shown in this paper are adjusted to fit space limitations of this book. Follow actual dimensions given in this book and your instructor's directions.)

Cardini 2

**Uses comparison and contrast to dvelop paragraph**

entertainment for children, the Japanese viewed it as mainly for adults. Since the beginning of print, cartooning in Japan has targeted adults, so anime was a natural step in this tradition. In America, aside from editorial cartoons and newspaper funny pages, comics were aimed primarily at adolescent males. Therefore, American animation in the 1940s and 1950s was different from the type developed in Japan. The early work of Walt Disney, for example, came from fairy tales, or it featured cute animal characters. In Japan, animated cartoons take on adult subjects often absent from American cartoons. These subjects include war, death, sacrifice, love, Japan's historical past and future, and even occasionally sex and violence. The plot lines are often extremely complex. Stories that would be kept simple in a Disney film to avoid viewer confusion have no such restrictions in Japan.

**Uses specific details to explain anime**

**Provides a concrete example**

Complex plots are but one of the distinctive features of anime. Anime images move quickly, with a style often more frantic than in American cartoons. Their soundtracks frequently use jazz and rock rather than symphonic music. However, perhaps most striking are the large eyes and sharp features of the characters. People in anime are very stylized, not realistic. The drawing is more colorful, more complicated, and often more abstract than most American cartoons. For example, a TV series called *Samurai X* is one of the most popular anime cartoons with both American and Japanese audiences. *Samurai X* is set in the nineteenth century and tells the story of one warrior's life. It is drawn beautifully in a way that looks both like older Japanese art prints and like more contemporary movies such as *Crouching Tiger, Hidden Dragon*.

continued >>

Cardini 3

The unique style of anime comes largely from the films being produced for specific audiences. The animators were creating works only for a Japanese market, at least until quite recently. Therefore, they did not take into account the traditions of other cultures. In contrast, American animation was produced for an international audience, which called for recognizable themes that came out of familiar European traditions. For uninitiated viewers, then, anime provides a crash course in an Eastern culture quite different from their own. Nearly all serious anime fans own guides that explain such things as Japanese social hierarchies, clothing, dining habits, traditions, rituals, and mythology. To cite one small example, several anime feature a *hagoromo*, or feathered cloak, worn by a mythological figure known as the *tennyo*. Knowing that this figure has a symbolic meaning for a Japanese viewer and is not just a random decoration or character adds to the depth of a scene in which it appears. Decoding some of these cultural references is undoubtedly some of the fun and challenge for the true *otakon*, or anime fan.

Anime appears in all kinds of types and genres, from children's works like *Pokémon* to dark science fiction like *Ghost in the Shell*. Japanese television has many daily animated series that vary in terms of sophistication and audience. Some of these have extremely complex scripts, while others are painfully simplistic. Several of these television series now appear in America, with some of the best known including *Inuyasha* and *Evangelion*. A wide range of anime feature films are readily available on DVD in

Uses cause and effect to explain differences

Cites a very specific example

Uses classification to explain types

Provides specific titles as examples

continued >>

Cardini 4

**Focuses at length on one prominent example**

America, and many have even found their way into theaters. For example, *Akira* is a film about life thirty years after a nuclear war. A misfit boy, Tetsuo, accidentally discovers the government experiments that led to that war and then learns that scientists are starting similar experiments once again. Probably the most famous theatrical anime films in the United States are *Howl's Moving Castle* and *Spirited Away*. In the last one, directed by Hayao Miyasaki, a young girl, Chihiro, is able to free her parents from a spell after many magical adventures. The movie will probably become a classic.

**States a reason in the topic sentence**

**Contrasts American cartoons with anime**

One reason American adults enjoy anime is because they miss a form they loved as children. Anime gives them animated art but adds an adult level of design, creativity, sophistication, and content. While there have been a few American cartoons aimed at adults (*The Simpsons*, *South Park*), the animation is not very detailed and the tone is usually satiric. There are no such barriers in anime.

**Speculates about the future in concluding strategy**

**Uses final comment to return to her opening idea**

As Americans come to embrace anime, the form may change. Some fans fear that the art of anime will be watered down in the bid for popularity and profits. Others celebrate the combination of styles as some American animators borrow from the Japanese. As an animation addict, I welcome more American animation for adults. Still, I would be disappointed if the distinctive qualities of anime disappeared. I fervently hope the Japanese animators will maintain their exotic creativity.

# 3

# Writing Paragraphs, Shaping Essays

## 3a How do I shape essays?

A good essay has an effective beginning, middle, and end. The key word is *effective*. Beginnings interest your reader and create expectations for the rest of the essay, usually through a THESIS STATEMENT, your main point. Middles explain or provide arguments for the thesis, usually through a series of statements and supporting details or evidence. Writers organize their main ideas to build a logical and engaging sequence. What separates most good writing from bad is the writer's ability to move back and forth between main ideas and specific details. Endings provide closure. They make readers feel that the writing achieved its purpose and that the writer had a skilled sense of his or her audience to the very end. One key to shaping essays is understanding how paragraphs work.

## 3b How do paragraphs work?

A **paragraph** is a group of sentences that work together to develop a unit of thought. Paragraphing permits writers to divide material into manageable parts. When a group of paragraphs works together in logical sequence, the result is a complete essay or other whole piece of writing.

Paragraphs function differently in different types of writing. In many academic papers, each paragraph is a logical unit that develops a single idea, often expressed as a topic sentence (3e), with each topic sentence contributing to the paper's thesis. In such writings, you might think of individual paragraphs as bricks that form a wall, or as rooms that together form a building. In writings that tell a story or explain a process, there are often few topic sentences. In newspaper or journalistic writings, paragraph breaks frequently occur more for dramatic effect than for logic.

To signal the start of a new paragraph, indent the first line about one-half inch. Skip no extra lines between paragraphs. Business writing (Chapter 43) is an exception: It calls for BLOCK STYLE for paragraphs, which means you do not indent the first line but rather leave a double space between paragraphs.

**BACKGROUND**

Essay paragraphing differs considerably from paragraphing in a newspaper article. Anyone can see at a glance that newspapers frequently have paragraphs of only a sentence or two. Such short paragraphs are rare in essays, except perhaps as transitions. The reason for the difference in the look of essays and newspaper articles is found in the physical design of newspapers and the different rationales behind essays and newspaper articles. The narrow width of newspaper columns makes lengthy paragraphs difficult to read. More significantly, essays attempt to present material in a simultaneously logical and dramatic way. They begin with a hook to grab the reader's interest and then usually proceed from point to point until the end (of the narrative or of the list of causes) is reached. Rarely is the first paragraph used to reveal key information. Essays are written on the assumption that they will be read from beginning to end.

In contrast, newspaper articles (not to be confused with editorial and Op-Ed essays in newspapers) use few such dramatic devices for suspense purposes. Usually, the main hook is the headline. Then, in paragraph 1, the reader gets the *who, what, where, when, why,* and *how.* Subsequent paragraphs reveal additional details, but all the key facts are given in paragraph 1— the opposite of the procedure in the essay's first paragraph. The further one gets into most newspaper articles, the less important the content. In some cases, a reader can get the idea that the piece doesn't conclude so much as trail off. This is because newspaper articles are written on the assumption that they will not be read from beginning to end. Editors may cut off the last few inches of a story to make it fit on a page; readers may go only as far as the first paragraph.

**TEACHING TIP**

The above "background" information suggests the following implications for the writing classroom: First, most newspaper articles and many magazine articles make poor models for paragraphing (unless you are teaching journalism). Be aware that composition textbooks often include some newspaper and magazine articles as model essays. Second, encouraging students to read a newspaper regularly may make them better informed and expose them to new vocabulary, but such reading alone is not likely to help them form subconscious ideas about paragraph structure that can be usefully applied to academic writing. To learn to write essays, the student must—at least part of the time—read essays.

One way to show your students the difference between essay paragraphing and newspaper paragraphing is to give them copies of pieces dealing with the same experience: a newspaper account of a fire and an essay written in response to the event, or a newspaper account of a trial and a magazine essay discussing the case. Ask students to list the differences. At minimum, they will mention differences in length and number of paragraphs and in the presence or absence of personal opinion. They may also notice the lack of a thesis statement and a conclusion in the newspaper article and the presence of both in the essay.

You might also ask students how satisfied they would be if they were given only the first paragraph of the newspaper article and of the essay. The article's introduction will probably be far more satisfying in terms of information but less satisfying in terms of graceful presentation, background, pacing, and the like.

Another way to underscore the difference between the genres is to give students (or assign them to find) a meaty newspaper article—the kind that runs for two pages. Have them rewrite the article as an essay. Before the students write, you might discuss with them the kinds of changes they anticipate making.

**TEACHING TIP**

Students know that first and last impressions are important. For example, they probably want to project a positive image when they meet someone for the first time, and they want to reinforce this image when they leave. You might want to explain that, similarly, an introduction and a conclusion are important parts of any essay. Together they provide the first and last contact students have with their reader.

You might have students look at a story in a literature textbook, an article in a magazine, and a newspaper editorial. Ask them to

We explain later in this chapter the rich variety of paragraph arrangements (3h) and rhetorical patterns (3i) at your disposal for writing paragraphs. But first, let's look at characteristics of paragraphs in general. We start by discussing introductory paragraphs (3c); then, body paragraphs (3d through 3i); and last, concluding paragraphs (3k).

## 3c How can I write effective introductory paragraphs?

An **introductory paragraph** leads the reader to sense what's ahead. It sets the stage. It also, if possible, attempts to arouse a reader's interest in the topic.

A THESIS STATEMENT can be an important component in an introduction. Many instructors require students to place the thesis statement at the end of the opening paragraph. Doing so disciplines students to state early the central point of the essay. If an introduction points in one direction, and the rest of the essay goes off in another, the essay isn't communicating a clear message. Professional writers don't necessarily include a thesis statement in their introductory paragraphs. Most have the skill to maintain a line of thought without overtly stating a main idea. Introductory paragraphs, as well as concluding paragraphs (3k), are often shorter than body paragraphs (3d).

Be careful not to tack on a sloppy introduction at the last minute. The introductory paragraph plays too important a role to be tossed off with merely a few shallow lines. That doesn't mean you have to write an introduction first; you might put down ideas and a thesis to start, then return during the revision process to write an effective, polished introduction. For a list of specific strategies to use and pitfalls to avoid for introductory paragraphs, see Quick Reference 3.1.

### Quick Reference 3.1    ■ ■ ■ ■ ■ ■ ■

#### Introductory paragraphs

**STRATEGIES TO USE**

- Providing relevant background information
- Relating briefly an interesting story or anecdote
- Giving one or more pertinent—perhaps surprising—statistics
- Asking one or more provocative questions
- Using an appropriate quotation
- Defining a KEY TERM
- Presenting one or more brief examples (3i)
- Drawing an ANALOGY (3i)

continued >>

## Quick Reference 3.1    (continued)

### STRATEGIES TO AVOID

- Don't write statements about your purpose, such as "I am going to discuss the causes of falling oil prices."

- Don't apologize, as in "I am not sure this is right, but this is my opinion."

- Don't use overworked expressions, such as "Haste makes waste, as I recently discovered" or "Love is grand" or "According to Webster's dictionary."

Always integrate an introductory device into the paragraph so that it leads smoothly into the thesis statement. Some examples follow. In this chapter, each example paragraph has a number to its left for your easy reference. Here's an introductory paragraph that uses two brief examples to lead into the thesis statement at the end of the paragraph.

1   On seeing another child fall and hurt himself, Hope, just nine months old, stared, tears welling up in her eyes, and crawled to her mother to be comforted—as though she had been hurt, not her friend. When 15-month-old Michael saw his friend Paul crying, Michael fetched his own teddy bear and offered it to Paul; when that didn't stop Paul's tears, Michael brought Paul's security blanket from another room. Such small acts of sympathy and caring, observed in scientific studies, are leading researchers to trace the roots of empathy—the ability to share another's emotions—to infancy, contradicting a long-standing assumption that infants and toddlers were incapable of these feelings.

—Daniel Goleman, "Researchers Trace Empathy's Roots to Infancy"

In paragraph 2, the opening quotation sets up a dramatic contrast with the thesis statement.

2   "Alone one is never lonely," says May Sarton in her essay "The Rewards of Living a Solitary Life." Most people, however, don't share Sarton's opinion: They're terrified of living alone. They're used to living with others—children with parents, roommates with roommates, friends with friends, spouses with spouses. When the statistics catch up with them, therefore, they're rarely prepared. Chances are high that most adult men and women will need to know how to live alone, briefly or longer, at some time in their lives.

—Tara Foster, student

In paragraph 3, the writer asks a direct question, and next puts the reader in a dramatic situation to arouse interest in the topic.

underline a key statement or phrase in the introduction and conclusion of each. What was memorable? Why? If the students were advising the writer, what, if anything, would they change to capture interest at the outset and cement a lasting impression at the end?

### QUOTATION: ON WRITING

Etymologically, *introduction* means "a leading into." The Greek and Latin rhetorical terms for this part carried the same suggestion. The Greek term *proemium* meant "before the song"; the Latin term *exordium* meant "beginning a web"—by mounting a woof or laying a warp. The basic function then of the introduction is to lead the audience into the discourse. Instinctively we feel that an abrupt, immediate entry into the body of our discourse would unsettle and confuse the audience. We sense that in most instances an audience must, as it were, be "eased into" the subject of the discourse.

—Edward P. J. Corbett

### TEACHING TIP

Ask students to locate (or to write themselves) several different types of introductions for an essay on a particular topic. Options may include the following: an interest-getting anecdote; a startling fact or statistic; a rhetorical question; a "quotable quote"; an exaggerated statement. Students often enjoy working collaboratively on this activity, and they certainly learn the value of "baiting" the reader through a lively introduction.

### TEACHING TIP: ESOL

Some ESOL students may attempt to weave every fact included in the body of the paper into their introductions. Unfortunately, this "tapestry" technique usually strikes native speakers as repetitive, even though it demonstrates considerable skill. Instructors might explain that introductions in English are less all-encompassing and more subtle. See Joy Reid's essay for instructors in this book. Also, see Part Seven in the student edition.

**QUOTATION: ON WRITING**

One of the most difficult things is the first paragraph. I have spent many months on a first paragraph, and once I get it, the rest just comes out very easily.

—Gabriel García Márquez

**ANSWERS: EXERCISE 3-1**

Answers will vary. Students may learn more by writing a different type of introduction for a single prompt than they might by writing different introductions for different prompts. If you find yourself short on time—and what instructor doesn't?—have students write multiple kinds of introductions for a single prompt.

**BACKGROUND**

ú·ní·ty (yoo · nə · tē) n. *pl.* -ties (1) The state, property, or product of being united physically, socially, or morally; oneness; opposed to *division, plurality.*

—*Britannica World Language Dictionary*

**QUOTATION: ON WRITING**

I just write, and things come to a crest, and that's how it is. My mind works in this way—it's sort of like a puzzle. I know where the pieces are, but I don't want to fit them for myself or for the reader. I just write.

—Jamaica Kincaid

**EXTRA EXERCISE A**

Provide students with the first sentence and last sentence of an introduction, then ask them to write enough middle sentences to connect the two. Here are two example first and last sentences.

**A.** First sentence: I went shopping at the grocery store today.

Last sentence: This is why it is important for the American government to subsidize agriculture in the United States.

**B.** First Sentence: According to the U.S. Census Bureau, the United States' official poverty rate in 2004 was 12.7 percent, up from 12.5 percent 2003.

**3** What should you do? You're out riding your bike, playing golf, or in the middle of a long run when you look up and suddenly see a jagged streak of light shoot across the sky, followed by a deafening clap of thunder. Unfortunately, most outdoor exercisers don't know whether to stay put or make a dash for shelter when a thunderstorm approaches, and sometimes the consequences are tragic.

—Gerald Secor Couzens, "If Lightning Strikes"

**EXERCISE 3-1**    Write an introduction for each of the three essays informally outlined below. Then, for more practice, write one alternative introduction for each. If you have a peer-response group, share the various written introductions and decide which are most effective. For help, see section 3b.

1. Play at school
   *Thesis statement:* School recesses today differ tremendously from recess a generation ago.
   Body paragraph 1: types of recess activities thirty years ago
   Body paragraph 2: types of games now, including ultimate frisbee
   Body paragraph 3: other activities, including climbing walls and free running

2. Cell phones
   *Thesis statement:* Cell phones have changed how some people behave in public.
   Body paragraph 1: driving
   Body paragraph 2: restaurants
   Body paragraph 3: movies and concerts
   Body paragraph 4: sidewalks, parks, and other casual spaces

3. Identity theft
   *Thesis statement:* Taking some simple precautions can reduce the danger of identity theft.
   Body paragraph 1: discarding junk mail
   Body paragraph 2: watching store purchases
   Body paragraph 3: internet security

# 3d    What are body paragraphs?

In most academic writing, each **body paragraph**, the several paragraphs between an introductory paragraph (3c) and a concluding paragraph (3k), consists of a main idea and support for that idea. To be effective, a body paragraph needs three characteristics: development (3f), unity (3g), and coherence (3g). Quick Reference 3.2 gives an overview of all three characteristics.

## Quick Reference 3.2

### Characteristics of effective body paragraphs

- **Development:** Have you included detailed and sufficient support for the main idea of the paragraph? (3f)
- **Unity:** Have you made a clear connection between the main idea of the paragraph and the sentences that support, develop, or illustrate the main idea? (3g)
- **Coherence:** Have you progressed from one sentence to the next in the paragraph smoothly and logically? (3g)

Paragraph 4 is an example of an effective body paragraph.

4  The Miss Plastic Surgery contest, trumpeted by Chinese promoters as "the world's first pageant for artificial beauties," shows the power of cosmetic surgery in a country that has swung from one extreme to another when it comes to the feminine ideal. In the 10th century, Emperor Li Yu ordered his consort to bind her feet; women practiced the painful ritual for more than 900 years in the belief that small feet were more alluring. In contrast, at the height of the Cultural Revolution in the 1960s and 1970s, Maoist officials condemned any form of personal grooming or beautification as "unrevolutionary" and regularly beat women for owning hairbrushes, wearing blush, or painting their nails.

—Abigail Haworth, "Nothing About These Women Is Real"

Paragraph 4 has UNITY (3g) in that the main idea—the feminine ideal in China has swung from one extreme to another—stated in the TOPIC SENTENCE (3e) is supported by detailed examples. It has COHERENCE (3g) in that the content of every sentence ties into the content of the other sentences. Also, the paragraph *coheres*—sticks together—because of the use of transitional phrases ("In the 10th century" and "In contrast," for example). It has PARAGRAPH DEVELOPMENT (3f) in that the details provide support for the main idea.

## 3e  What are topic sentences?

A **topic sentence** contains the main idea of a paragraph and controls its content. Often, the topic sentence comes at the beginning of a paragraph, though not always. Professional essay writers, because they have the skill to carry the reader along without explicit signposts, sometimes decide not to use topic sentences. However, instructors often require students to use topic sentences. As apprentice writers, students might have more difficulty writing unified paragraphs.

Last sentence: Even if we must pay higher taxes, we need to do more to help the less fortunate in our country.

**Answers to Extra Exercise A**
Answers will vary. The most important criterion for success in this assignment is how seamlessly the students were able to bridge the gap between first and last sentence.

**TEACHING TIP**
The root cause of weak writing is often unclear thinking. You may want to encourage your students to practice writing strong topic sentences at the beginning of their paragraphs as a way to ensure that they have a clear focus and clear direction. Help them to see that only carefully crafted paragraphs can have a legitimately "implied" topic sentence and that most paragraphs will gain coherence through a clearly stated topic sentence. Class or online exercises that allow sharing of the students' own writing provide a good way to reinforce this concept.

**QUOTATION: ON WRITING**
As you begin a sentence, you have to prepare your readers for new and therefore important information. Give your readers a familiar context to help them move from the more familiar to the less familiar, from the known to the unknown.

—Joseph M. Williams, *Style: Toward Clarity and Grace*

**TEACHING TIP**
Regardless of students' interests, virtually any topic, if well written, can capture their imaginations. You can choose to invite students to bring in feature articles of events that intrigue them or case studies of industries that capture their attention. Ideally, ask for writing samples on topics that initially don't seem interesting but which prompt them to dive in and read because of the writing style and delivery. Ask students to pinpoint a paragraph or even a sentence that they especially like.

**QUOTATION: ON WRITING**

That's the purpose of paragraphing: to give the reader a breather by sensibly breaking up the prose. A paragraph is to a writer what a quick intake of breath is to a singer—a little interruption that makes possible refreshed continuation.
—William Safire

**QUOTATION: ON WRITING**

I don't know why I am so helplessly led to condensation in both my fiction and my essays. Some people find it hard to follow my meaning because I don't spell it out, not entirely. My writing is simple but I like to be sort of emphatic and let it go. I remember when I was writing exams in school I'd be the first one finished. All these people writing away. As I look back on it I think I didn't want to tell the teacher what he already knew, but to try to get at things from an angle—nothing very grand, just a little twist.
—Elizabeth Hardwick

**QUOTATION: ON WRITING**

I don't wait for moods. You accomplish nothing if you do that. Your mind must know it has got to get down to work.
—Pearl S. Buck

**QUOTATION: ON WRITING**

You must once and for all give up being worried about successes and failures. Don't let that concern you. It's your duty to go on working steadily day by day, quite steadily, to be prepared for mistakes, which are inevitable, and for failures.
—Anton Chekhov

**QUOTATION: ON WRITING**

There is no pleasure in the world like writing well and going fast. It's like nothing else. It's like a love affair, it goes on and on, and doesn't end in marriage. It's all courtship.
—Tennessee Williams

**TOPIC SENTENCE STARTING A PARAGRAPH**

In ACADEMIC WRITING, most paragraphs begin with a topic sentence so that readers know immediately what to expect. Paragraph 5 is an example.

5    Music patronage was at a turning point when Mozart went to Vienna in the last part of the eighteenth century. Many patrons of music continued to be wealthy aristocrats. Haydn's entire career was funded by a rich prince. Mozart's father and, for a time, Mozart himself were in the employ of another prince. But when Mozart went to Vienna in 1781, he contrived to make a living from a variety of sources. In addition to performances at aristocratic houses and commissions for particular works, Mozart gave piano and composition lessons, put on operas, and gave many public concerts of his own music.

—Jeremy Yudkin, "Composers and Patrons in the Classic Era"

Sometimes, a topic sentence both starts a paragraph and, in different wording, ends the paragraph. Paragraph 6 is an example.

6    Modern science cannot explain why the laws of physics are exactly balanced for animal life to exist. For example, if the big bang had been one-part-in-a-billion more powerful, it would have rushed out too fast for the galaxies to form and for life to begin. If the strong nuclear force were decreased by two percent, atomic nuclei wouldn't hold together. Hydrogen would be the only atom in the universe. If the gravitational force were decreased, stars (including the sun) would not ignite. There are just three of more than 200 physical parameter within the solar system and universe so exact that they cannot be random. Indeed, the lack of a scientific explanation has allowed these facts to be hijacked as a defense of intelligent design.

—Robert Lanza, "A New Theory of the Universe"

**TOPIC SENTENCE ENDING A PARAGRAPH**

Some paragraphs give supporting details first and wait to state the topic sentence at the paragraph's end. This approach is particularly effective for building suspense or for creating a bit of drama. Paragraph 7 is an example.

7    Once the Romans had left, the political situation in Britain deteriorated rapidly. Softened by their dependence on the Roman legions, the Romanized Britons were ill equipped to defend themselves from renewed attacks by the Picts in the north. Then, even as the Britons were trying to cope with their fiercer northern neighbors, a much more calamitous series of events took place: waves of Germanic-speaking people from the Continent began to invade the island. The "English" were coming to England.

—C. M. Millward, "The Arrival of the English"

## TOPIC SENTENCE IMPLIED, NOT STATED

Some paragraphs are a unified whole even without a single sentence that readers can point to as the topic sentence. Yet, most readers can catch the main idea anyway. Paragraph 8 is an example. What do you think might be a straightforward topic sentence for it?

**8**  It is easy to identify with the quest for a secret document, somewhat harder to do so with a heroine whose goal is identifying and understanding the element radium, which is why in dramatic biography writers and directors end up reverting to fiction. To be effective, the dramatic elements must, and finally will, take precedence over any "real" biographical facts. We viewers do not care—if we wanted to know about the element radium, we would read a book on the element radium. When we go to the movies to see *The Story of Marie Curie* we want to find out how her little dog Skipper died.

—David Mamet, *Three Uses of the Knife:
On the Nature and Purpose of Drama*

**EXERCISE 3-2**  Working individually or with a group, identify the topic sentences in the following paragraphs. If the topic sentence is implied, write the point the paragraph conveys. For help, consult section 3e.

**9**  A. A good college program should stress the development of high-level reading, writing, and mathematical skills and should provide you with a broad historical, social, and cultural perspective, no matter what subject you choose as your major. The program should teach you not only the most current knowledge in your field but also—just as important—prepare you to keep learning throughout your life. After all, you'll probably change jobs, and possibly even careers, at least six times, and you'll have other responsibilities, too—perhaps as a spouse and as a parent and certainly as a member of a community whose bounds extend beyond the workplace.

—Frank T. Rhodes, "Let the Student Decide"

**10**  B. The once majestic oak tree crashes to the ground amid the destructive flames, as its panic-stricken inhabitants attempt to flee the fiery tomb. Undergrowth that formerly flourished smolders in ashes. A family of deer darts furiously from one wall of flame to the other, without an emergency exit. On the outskirts of the inferno, firefighters try desperately to stop the destruction. Somewhere at the source of this chaos lies a former campsite containing the cause of this destruction—an untended campfire. This scene is one of many that illustrate how human apathy and carelessness destroy nature.

—Anne Bryson, student

C. Rudeness isn't a distinctive quality of our own time. People today would be shocked by how rudely our ancestors behaved. In the colonial period, a French traveler marveled that "Virginians don't use napkins, tools that are familiar to me and they fit snugly in my hands.

—Natalia Ginzburg

**QUOTATION: ON WRITING**

I have two methods of working. One of them involves tapping the sources of creativity. . . . I might be anywhere when it comes and I could end up writing all over the floor or up the walls and not knowing what is going on. It is like having a fit. . . .

The second method is following a trail made by my words themselves—by sitting down and writing . . . writing anything, fast. The words include the vision. That rush—that vision or high or whatever it is—doesn't last very long. A lot of writing gets done in a very short time, but it's not very good writing. Often it turns out to be just a reminder about how something felt. It has to be reworked.

—Maxine Hong Kingston

but they wear silk cravats, and instead of carrying white handkerchiefs, they blow their noses either with their fingers or with a silk handkerchief that also serves as a cravat, a napkin, and so on." In the 19th century, up to about the 1830s, even very distinguished people routinely put their knives in their mouths. And when people went to the theater, they would not just applaud politely—they would chant, jeer, and shout. So, the notion that there's been a downhill slide in manners ever since time began is just not so.

—"Horizons," *U.S. News & World Report*

## 3f  How can I develop my body paragraphs?

You develop a **body paragraph** by supplying detailed support for the main idea of the paragraph communicated by your TOPIC SENTENCE (3e), whether stated or implied. **Paragraph development** is not merely a repetition, using other words, of the main idea. When this happens, you're merely going around in circles. We've deliberately manipulated paragraph 4 above to create paragraph 12. It is an example of a poorly developed paragraph. It goes nowhere; rather, it restates one idea three times in different words.

**NO**   The Miss Plastic Surgery contest, trumpeted by Chinese promoters as "the world's first pageant for artificial beauties," shows the power of cosmetic surgery in a country that has swung from one extreme to another when it comes to the feminine ideal. In past decades, China did not promote personal grooming. Beautification is a recent development.

To check whether you are providing sufficient detail in a body paragraph, use the RENNS Test. Each letter in the made-up word *RENNS* cues you to remember a different kind of supporting detail at your disposal, as listed in Quick Reference 3.3.

Use the RENNS Test to check the quality of your paragraph development. Of course, not every paragraph needs all five kinds of RENNS details, nor do the supporting details need to occur in the order of the letters in *RENNS*. Paragraph 13 contains three of the five types of RENNS details. Identify the topic sentence and as many RENNS as you can before reading the analysis that follows the paragraph.

U.S. shores are also being inundated by waves of plastic debris. On the sands of the Texas Gulf Coast one day last September, volunteers collected 307 tons of litter, two-thirds of which was plastic, including 31,733 bags, 30,295 bottles, and 15,631 six-pack yokes. Plastic trash is being found far out to sea. On a four-day trip from Maryland to Florida that ranged 100 miles offshore, John Hardy, an Oregon State University marine biologist, spotted "Styrofoam and other plastic on the surface, most of the whole cruise."

—"The Dirty Seas," *Time*

---

## Quick Reference 3.3

### The RENNS Test: Checking for supporting details

**R = Reasons** provide support.

Jules Verne, a nineteenth-century writer of science fiction, amazes readers today **because he imagined inventions impossible to develop until recent years**.

**E = Examples** provide support.

**For example**, he predicted submarines and moon rockets.

**N = Names** provide support.

He forecast that the moon rockets would take off from an area in the **state of Florida**.

**N = Numbers** provide support.

Specifically, he declared as the point of departure **27 degrees North Latitude and 5 degrees West Longitude**.

**S = Senses**—sight, sound, smell, taste, touch—provide support.

Today, space vehicles are **heard blasting off** from Cape Kennedy, only eighty miles from the site Verne chose.

---

In paragraph 13, the first sentence serves as the topic sentence. Supporting details for that main idea include examples, names, and numbers. The writer provides examples of the kinds of litter found washed up on the beach and floating offshore. The writer names many specific things: Texas Gulf Coast, September, bags, bottles, six-pack yokes, Maryland, Florida, John Hardy, Oregon State University, marine biologist, and Styrofoam. And the writer uses specific numbers to describe the volume of litter collected (307 tons), to give counts of specific items (such as 31,733 bags), and to tell how far from shore (100 miles) the litter had traveled.

**EXERCISE 3-3** Working individually or with a peer-response group, look again at the paragraphs in Exercise 3-2. Identify the RENNS in each paragraph. For help, consult 3f.

**ANSWERS: EXERCISE 3-3**

**A.** (paragraph 11). Reasons include learning current knowledge, keeping you learning through life, having a job, and being a spouse, a parent, and a member of the community. Examples include job, spouse, parent, and member of the community. Number named is six.

**B.** (paragraph 12). Names include oak, deer, firefighters. Senses are invoked by sound of crashing oak, sight of flames, "fiery tomb," smoldering in ashes, deer family darting furiously, and the smell (implied) of burning trees.

**C.** (paragraph 13). Examples include colonial Virginians using their cravats as handkerchiefs and people putting their knives in their mouths. Names include the French traveler, distinguished people, and people in the theater. Numbers include the dates—the 1830s and the nineteenth century. Senses include the noise—chants, jeers, and shouts—made by the audience in the theater.

**EXTRA EXERCISE B**

Mark all of the transitional expressions used in the following paragraph. Answers appear in italics.

Edith Newbold Jones was the descendant of wealthy, socially prominent New York families. *As a result,* she made her formal debut before she married Edward Wharton of Boston in 1885. *Soon after* her marriage, she began writing as a therapeutic measure. She *also* used her writing as a means of occupying her free time when her husband was suffering from a mental illness. *Naturally,* much of her writing was concerned with the closed, wealthy New York society she had known as a child. In the 1890s, *as a result* of her "hobby," she published her first short stories in *Scribner's* magazine, using her married name, Edith Wharton. *Subsequently,* she was recognized as one of America's best popular writers. *For example,* in 1924 she became the first woman ever to receive an honorary degree from Yale University. *Equally important,* she was awarded the Pulitzer Prize in 1921 for *The Age of Innocence,* a novel about the unbreakable moral code of Victorian society. Her most famous work, *however*, is *Ethan Frome*, a tragic love story. *Although* she continued to write about American subjects and characters, she spent much of her later life in France, where she had a home. She died there in 1937.

## EXTRA EXERCISE C

Rewrite the following paragraph, using transitional words and phrases to make it more coherent. Combine and rearrange the sentences as you think necessary. Answers will vary.

Americans are beginning to recognize the importance of regular exercise. Jogging gives the heart a good workout. It can damage the runner's ankles and calves. Jogging by itself does little to exercise the upper body. Some people prefer to walk. Bicycling is popular. In a pleasant setting, it provides visual pleasures as well as a way to burn calories. Some people ride a stationary bicycle at home. They can watch television while they rotate the pedals. Swimming involves the upper body as well as the legs. It allows a person to exert as much energy as possible without straining muscles. On a hot summer day, swimming seems more like fun than like exercise.

## QUOTATION: ON WRITING

Images of the world should yield a description that is useful to the viewer and not cluttered by irrelevant information.

—Howard Gardner

## TEACHING TIP

How does mastery of a language enhance a student's ability to write? What is the relationship between language and writing? The following excerpt could be used as the starting point for classroom discussion about the connection between language and writing.

It is commonly thought that at birth the neurons begin to make connections and that these connections increase as we age and acquire experience. However, the opposite appears to be the case: there may be many

# 3g How can I create unity and coherence in paragraphs?

A paragraph has **unity** when the connection between the main idea and its supporting sentences is clear. A paragraph has **coherence** when its sentences relate to each other not only in content but also in choice of words and grammatical structures. Unity emphasizes meaning; coherence emphasizes structure.

Unity is ruined when any sentence in a paragraph "goes off the topic," which means its content doesn't relate to the main idea or to the other sentences in the paragraph. To show you broken unity, in paragraph 14 we've deliberately inserted two sentences (the fourth and the next to last) that go off the topic and ruin a perfectly good paragraph, shown as paragraph 15. (Neither a personal complaint about stress nor hormones produced by men and women during exercise belong in a paragraph defining different kinds of stress.)

**NO**

**14** Stress has long been the subject of psychological and physiological speculation. In fact, more often than not, the word itself is ill defined and overused, meaning different things to different people. Emotional stress, for example, can come about as the result of a family argument or the death of a loved one. Everyone says, "Don't get stressed," but I have no idea how to do that. Environmental stress, such as exposure to excessive heat or cold, is an entirely different phenomenon. Physiologic stress has been described as the outpouring of the steroid hormones from the adrenal glands. During exercise, such as weightlifting, males and females produce different hormones. Whatever its guise, a lack of a firm definition of stress has seriously impeded past research.

**YES**

**15** Stress has long been the subject of psychological and physiological speculation. In fact, more often than not, the word itself is ill defined and overused, meaning different things to different people. Emotional stress, for example, can come about as the result of a family argument or the death of a loved one. Environmental stress, such as exposure to excessive heat or cold, is an entirely different phenomenon. Physiologic stress has been described as the outpouring of the steroid hormones from the adrenal glands. Whatever its guise, a lack of a firm definition of stress has seriously impeded past research.

—Herbert Benson, MD, *The Relaxation Response*

In a coherent paragraph, the sentences follow naturally from one to the next. Techniques for achieving coherence are listed in Quick Reference 3.4; refer to the sections shown in parentheses for complete explanations.

## Quick Reference 3.4 ∎∎∎∎∎∎∎∎

### Techniques for achieving coherence

- Using appropriate transitional expressions (3g.1)
- Using pronouns when possible (3g.2)
- Using deliberate repetition of a key word (3g.3)
- Using parallel structures (3g.4)
- Using coherence techniques to create connections among paragraphs (3g.5)

## 3g.1 Using transitional expressions for coherence

**Transitional expressions** are words and phrases that signal connections among ideas.

**Transitions** are bridges that lead your reader along your line of thought. They offer cues about what follows. Commonly used transitional expressions are listed in Quick Reference 3.5.

## Quick Reference 3.5 ∎∎∎∎∎∎∎∎

### Transitional expressions and the relationships they signal

| | |
|---|---|
| ADDITION | also, in addition, too, moreover, and, besides, furthermore, equally important, then, finally |
| EXAMPLE | for example, for instance, thus, as an illustration, namely, specifically |
| CONTRAST | but, yet, however, nevertheless, nonetheless, conversely, in contrast, still, at the same time, on the one hand, on the other hand |
| COMPARISON | similarly, likewise, in the same way |
| CONCESSION | of course, to be sure, certainly, granted |
| RESULT | therefore, thus, as a result, so, accordingly, consequently |
| SUMMARY | hence, in short, in brief, in summary, in conclusion, finally |
| TIME | first, second, third, next, then, finally, afterward, before, soon, later, meanwhile, subsequently, immediately, eventually, currently |
| PLACE | in the front, in the foreground, in the back, in the background, at the side, adjacent, nearby, in the distance, here, there |

more connections and nerve cells in the brain of an infant than in an elderly adult. Development seems to be more a matter of "pruning" those original connections than of making any new ones. Consider this about infant babbling: in the first weeks of life, a baby utters almost every sound of every known language. Later on, the infant loses the ability to make sounds that are not in the language he has learned to speak. There may be an enormous potential of sound patterns available to us at birth, but we learn only a few of them.

—Robert Ornstein and
Richard F. Thompson

**TEACHING TIP**

Most students will be familiar with the marvelous repetition in the "I Have a Dream" speech by Dr. Martin Luther King Jr. However, you may want your students to listen to the speech again, preferably to the recording of Dr. King's voice. Spend a few moments eliciting student response to questions of how the repetition worked and why it was effective in this speech.

Students are likely also to remember the conclusion of Abraham Lincoln's "Gettysburg Address" ("that a government of the people, by the people, for the people shall not perish from the earth") and a memorable quotation from John F. Kennedy, "Ask not what your country can do for you; ask what you can do for your country." Enjoy watching your students groan when you ask if anyone would have remembered Lincoln's saying "that a government developed by the people, one that was meant to include all the people and that would be led by some of the people, would surely not fail." Nor would anyone have remembered "Ask not what your country can do for you; instead, you need to be raising the question of what you can do for your country." Students may enjoy looking for other examples of memorable repetition or parallelism. Better yet, ask them to experiment with some sentences of their own, especially in their introductions and conclusions.

**TEACHING TIP**
In her paper "The Preliminaries," Esther Di-Marzio of Kishwaukee Community College (in Illinois) extols the power of repetition. She recommends that writers judiciously repeat "a sentence . . . or perhaps refer to the title" of an essay for a "unified effect." Most students are aware that repetition plays a key role in memorization. You might ask students how a writer uses repetition for maximum impact. Perhaps reading to the class a poem that repeats certain words or phrases (such as A. E. Housman's "When I Was One-and-Twenty") can serve to illustrate DiMarzio's point. Housman's poem is available on-line at Bartleby <http://www.bartleby.com/123/13.html>.

**QUOTATION: ON WRITING**
Composing is like an organic process, not an assembly line on which some prefabricated parts are fitted together. . . . The task of the computer is to find the forms that find forms; the structures that guide and encourage growth; the limits by means of which development can be shaped. [Composing] is a way of making meanings by using the forms provided by language to re-present the relationships we see.
                                    —Ann E. Berthoff

**ANOTHER EXAMPLE OF PARALLEL STRUCTURES**
I am not complaining that the brewing and baking were taken over by the men. If they can brew and bake as well as women or better, then by all means let them do it. But they cannot have it both ways. If they are going to adopt the very sound principle that the job should be done by the person who does it best, then that rule must be applied universally. If the women make better office-workers than men, then they must have the office work. If any individual woman is able to make a first-class lawyer, doctor, architect or engineer, then she must be allowed to try her hand at it.
    —Dorothy L. Sayers, "Are Women Human?"

**QUOTATION: ON WRITING**
As writing teachers, we find ourselves under enormous pressure to master a broader range of

**Alert:** In ACADEMIC WRITING, set off a transitional expression with a comma, unless the expression is one short word (24c and 24g). ●

Vary your choices of transitional words. For example, instead of always using *for example,* try *for instance.* Also, when choosing a transitional word, make sure it correctly says what you mean. For instance, don't use *however* in the sense of *on the other hand* if you mean *therefore* in the sense of *as a result.* The three brief examples below demonstrate how to use transitional expressions for each context.

**COHERENCE BY ADDITION**

Woodpeckers use their beaks to find food and to chisel out nests. *In addition,* they claim their territory and signal their desire to mate by using their beaks to drum on trees.

**COHERENCE BY CONTRAST**

Most birds communicate by singing. Woodpeckers, *however,* communicate by the duration and rhythm of the drumming of their beaks.

**COHERENCE BY RESULT**

The woodpecker's strong beak enables it to communicate by drumming on dry branches and tree trunks. *As a result,* woodpeckers can communicate across greater distances than songbirds can.

Paragraph 16 demonstrates how transitional expressions (shown in **bold**) enhance a paragraph's COHERENCE. The TOPIC SENTENCE is the final sentence.

16    Before the days of television, people were entertained by exciting radio shows such as *Superman, Batman,* and "War of the Worlds." **Of course**, the listener was required to pay careful attention to the story if all details were to be comprehended. **Better yet**, while listening to the stories, listeners would form their own images of the actions taking place. When the broadcaster would give brief descriptions of the Martian space ships invading earth, **for example**, every member of the audience would imagine a different space ship. **In contrast**, television's version of "War of the Worlds" will not stir the imagination at all, for everyone can clearly see the actions taking place. All viewers see the same space ship with the same features. Each aspect is clearly defined, and **therefore**, no one will imagine anything different from what is seen. **Thus**, television can't be considered an effective tool for stimulating the imagination.

                              —Tom Paradis, "A Child's Other World"

## 3g.2 Using pronouns for coherence

**Pronouns**—words that refer to nouns or other pronouns—allow readers to follow your train of thought from one sentence to the next without boring repetition. Without pronouns, you would have to repeat nouns over and over. For example, this sentence uses no pronouns and therefore has needless repetition: *The woodpecker scratched the woodpecker's head with the woodpecker's foot.* In contrast, with pronouns the sentence can be *The woodpecker scratched **its** head with **its** foot.* Paragraph 17 illustrates how pronouns (shown in **bold**) contribute to COHERENCE.

> **17** After Gary Hanson, now 56, got laid off from **his** corporate position in 2003, **he, his** wife, Susan, and **his** son, John, now 54 and 27, respectively, wanted to do a spot of cleaning. Though **they** are hard at work, **they** are not scrubbing floors or washing windows. **They** are running **their** very own house-cleaning franchise, *The Maids Home Services,* which **they** opened in February.
>
> —Sara Wilson, "Clean House: Getting Laid Off from His Corporate Job Gave This Franchisee a Fresh Start"

## 3g.3 Using deliberate repetition for coherence

A key word or phrase is central to the main idea of the paragraph. **Repetition** of key words or phrases is a useful way to achieve COHERENCE in a paragraph. The word or phrase usually appears first in the paragraph's TOPIC SENTENCE (3e) and then again throughout the paragraph. The idea of repetition is to keep a concept in front of the reader. Use this technique sparingly to avoid being monotonous. Paragraph 18 contains repeated words and phrases (shown in **bold**) closely tied to the concept of anthropology that make the paragraph more coherent.

> **18** **Anthropology**, broadly defined, is the study of **humanity**, from its evolutionary origins millions of years ago to its present great numbers and worldwide diversity. Many other disciplines, of course, share with **anthropology** a focus on one aspect or another of **humanity**. **Like** sociology, economics, political science, psychology, and other behavioral and social sciences, **anthropology** is concerned with the way people organize their lives and relate to one another in interacting, interconnected groups—societies—that share basic beliefs and practices. **Like** economists, **anthropologists are interested in** society's material foundations—in how people produce and distribute food and other valued goods. **Like** sociologists, **anthropologists are interested in** the way people structure their relations in society—in families, at work, in institutions. **Like** political scientists, **anthropologists are interested in** power and authority: who has them and how they are allocated. And, **like** psychologists, **anthropologists are interested in** individual development and the interaction between society and individual people.
>
> —Nancy Bonvillain, "The Study of Humanity"

communication technologies, which places even greater stress on the already demanding responsibility of teaching writing. Of course, some of that pressure has been felt by everyone in our culture with the growth of the Internet and the proliferation of email and electronic commerce.
—David Blakesley

**QUOTATION: ON WRITING**
The secret to a clear and readable style is in the first five or six words of every sentence.
—Joseph M. Williams, *Style: Toward Clarity and Grace*

**QUOTATION: ON WRITING**
"When *I* use a word," Humpty Dumpty said in a rather scornful tone, "it means just what I choose it to mean—neither more nor less."

"The question is," said Alice, "whether you can make words mean so many different things."

"The question is," said Humpty Dumpty, "which is to be master—that's all."
—Lewis Carroll

**TEACHING TIP**
When they learn new subjects, students may differ in the way they organize the material in their minds. Some students may prefer to consider the broad "big picture" objectives first, with the details following behind. By contrast, other students might like to know the details first so they can fit them into the larger context. Interestingly, students' preferences for how they receive a new assignment may reveal the way they are inclined to write. Some students may like to arrange their paragraphs from general to specific, whereas other students would choose a specific-to-general approach. You might invite students to explain their preferred ways of learning new material and then ask them to think about whether different learning patterns affect how they arrange their paragraphs.

**EXAMPLE OF SPATIAL SEQUENCE**
The wash [low land that is sometimes flooded and at other times nearly dry] looked perfectly

dry in my headlights. I drove down, across, up the other side and on into the night. Glimpses of weird humps of pale rock on either side, like petrified elephants, dinosaurs, stone-age hob-goblins. Now and then something alive scurried across the road: kangaroo mice, a jackrabbit, an animal that looked like a cross between a raccoon and a squirrel—the ringtail cat. Farther on a pair of mule deer started from the brush and bounded obliquely through the beams of my lights, raising puffs of dust which the wind, moving faster than my pickup truck, caught and carried ahead of me out of sight into the dark. The road, narrow and rocky, twisted sharply left and right, dipped in and out of tight ravines, climbing by degrees toward a summit which I would see only in the light of the coming day.

—Edward Abbey, "The Most Beautiful
Place on Earth"

**EXAMPLE: FROM GENERAL
TO SPECIFIC**

We all listen to music according to our separate capacities. But, for the sake of analysis, the whole listening process may become clearer if we break it up into its component parts, so to speak. In a certain sense we all listen to music on three separate planes. For lack of a better terminology, one might name these: (1) the sensuous plane, (2) the expressive plane, (3) the sheerly musical plane.

—Aaron Copland

**TEACHING TIP**

One function that paragraphs serve is to cue readers about shifts in ideas. Paragraphs, then, have an aspect of design to them, however modest. Consider, for example, how pages would look different without the white space breaks provided by paragraphing. Web pages cue readers in other fashions. In pages that were designed specifically for the Web (as opposed to being first written for traditional print, then copied onto the Web), the screen functions in ways parallel to the paragraph. In other words, writers and designers think in terms of what readers and viewers will grasp in one screen, without scrolling down. You might have students look at several documents that are

## 3g.4    Using parallel structures for coherence

**Parallel structures** are created when grammatically equivalent forms are used in series, usually of three or more items, but sometimes only two (see PARALLELISM, Chapter 18). Using parallel structures helps to give a paragraph coherence. The repeated parallel structures reinforce connections among ideas, and they add both tempo and sound to the sentence. Look back to paragraph 18 and the succession of sentences that begin with the word *like*.

In paragraph 19, the authors use several parallel structures (shown in **bold**): a parallel series of words (*the sacred, the secular, the scientific*); parallel phrases (*sometimes smiled at, sometimes frowned upon*); and six parallel clauses (the first being *banish danger with a gesture*).

> **19**   Superstitions are **sometimes smiled at** and **sometimes frowned upon** as observances characteristic of **the old-fashioned**, **the unenlightened**, children, peasants, servants, immigrants, foreigners, or backwoods people. Nevertheless, they give all of us ways of moving back and forth among the different worlds in which we live—**the sacred**, **the secular**, and **the scientific**. They allow us to keep a private world also, where, smiling a little, we can **banish danger with a gesture** and **summon luck with a rhyme**, **make the sun shine in spite of storm clouds**, **force the stranger to do our bidding**, **keep an enemy at bay**, and **straighten the paths of those we love**.
>
> —Margaret Mead and Rhoda Metraux, "New Superstitions for Old"

## 3g.5    Creating coherence among paragraphs

The same techniques for achieving COHERENCE in a paragraph apply to showing connections among paragraphs in a piece of writing. All four techniques help: transitional expressions (3g.1), pronouns (3g.2), deliberate repetition (3g.3), and parallel structures (3g.4).

Example 20 shows two short paragraphs and the start of a third. The writer achieves coherence among the paragraphs by repeating the key word *gratitude* and the related words *grateful, thankful,* and *thank* and by using them as a transition into the next paragraph. The writer also uses PARALLELISM within the paragraphs in this example.

> **20**   To me, gratitude and inner peace go hand in hand. The more genuinely grateful I feel for the gift of my life, the more peaceful I feel. Gratitude, then, is worthy of a little practice.
>
> If you're anything like me, you probably have many people to be thankful for: friends, family members, people from your past, teachers, gurus, people from work, someone who gave you a break, as well as countless others. You may want to thank a higher power for the gift of life itself, or for the beauty of nature.

As you think of people to be grateful for, remember that it can be any-one—someone who held a door open for you, or a physician who saved your life. . . .

**EXERCISE 3-4** Working individually or with a peer-response group, locate the coherence techniques in each paragraph. Look for transitional expressions, pronouns, deliberate repetition, and parallel structures. For help, consult 3g.

A. Kathy sat with her legs dangling over the edge of the side of the hood. The band of her earphones held back strands of straight copper hair that had come loose from two thick braids that hung down her back. She swayed with the music that only she could hear. Her shoulders raised, making cir-
**21** cles in the warm air. Her arms reached out to her side; her open hands reached for the air; her closed hands brought the air back to her. Her arms reached over her head; her opened hands reached for a cloud; her closed hands brought the cloud back to her. Her head moved from side to side; her eyes opened and closed to the tempo of the tunes. Kathy was motion.

—Claire Burke, student

B. Newton's law may have wider application than just the physical world. In the social world, racism, once set into motion, will remain in motion unless acted upon by an outside force. The collective "we" must be the outside force. We must fight racism through education. We must make sure every school has
**22** the resources to do its job. We must present to our children a culturally diverse curriculum that reflects our pluralistic society. This can help students understand that prejudice is learned through contact with prejudiced people, rather than with the people toward whom the prejudice is directed.

—Randolph H. Manning, "Fighting Racism with Inclusion"

C. The snow geese are first, rising off the ponds to breakfast in the sorghum fields up the river. Twenty thousand of them, perhaps more, great white birds with black wing tips rising out of the darkness into the rosy reflected light of dawn. They make a sweeping turn, a cloud of wings rising above the
**23** cottonwoods. But cloud is the wrong word. They don't form a disorderly blackbird rabble but a kaleidoscope of goose formations, always shifting, but always orderly. The light catches them—white against the tan velvet of the hills. Then they're overhead, line after line, layer above layer of formations, and the sky is filled with the clamor of an infinity of geese.

—Tony Hillerman, *Hillerman Country*

**EXERCISE 3-5** Working individually or with a peer-response group, use RENNS (3f) and techniques for achieving coherence (3g) to develop three of the following topic sentences into paragraphs. When finished, list the RENNS and the coherence techniques you used in each paragraph.

designed to be read online and compare the relationship between paragraphs and screens full of the information in those documents.

**ANSWERS: EXERCISE 3-4**
**A.** (paragraph 22). *Pronouns:* her, she. *Deliberate repetition:* Kathy, arms, hands opened, closed. *Parallel structures:* Many parallel clauses, starting with "Her shoulders raised"; open hands reaching out and closed hands bringing back.

**B.** (paragraph 23). *Pronouns:* we, our, whom, this. *Deliberate repetition:* world, we, racism, prejudice. *Parallel structures:* once set in motion, will remain in motion; we must.

**C.** (paragraph 24). *Pronouns:* them, they. *Transitional expressions:* first, but, then. *Deliberate repetition:* cloud, always, line, layer, white. *Parallel structures:* always shifting, but always orderly; line after line; layer above layer.

**QUOTATION: ON WRITING**
We should not only appreciate that standards for literacy achievement keep rising but also examine what is behind that escalation: how games of economic competition—the wins, losses, and draws—destabilize the value of existing literacy skills such that "the literacy crisis" becomes chronic.

—Deborah Brandt

**QUOTATION: ON WRITING**
Writing is a lot like sewing. You bring pieces together and make a quilt.

—Rosario Ferre

**QUOTATION: ON WRITING**
Sometimes you get a line, a phrase, sometimes you're crying, or it's the curve of a chair that hurts you and you don't know why, or sometimes you just want to write a poem, and you don't know what it's about. I will fool around on the typewriter. It might take me ten pages of nothing, of terrible writing, and then I'll get a line, and I'll think, "That's what I mean!" What you're doing is hunting for what you mean, what you're trying to say. You don't know when you start.

—Anne Sexton

## ANSWERS: EXERCISE 3-5

Each paragraph will differ in content, but this exercise should help students see that they need to support general statements with graphic details (developed through RENNS, discussed in 3f) that are smoothly linked by the techniques of coherence discussed in 3g: transitional expressions, pronouns, repetition, and parallel structures.

## QUOTATION: ON WRITING

Purpose and craftsmanship—ends and means—these are the keys to your judgment.
—Marya Mannes

## QUOTATION: ON WRITING

Description, for example, is related to definition. Describing something provides a means of analyzing and identifying it. Defining is a kind of abstract description. Definition, division into parts, and classification share fundamental relationships: to define is to limit or set boundaries to a thing by separating it from other things (division); to define is to put the thing to be defined into a class (classification); to classify is to divide into categories, so classification and division are related categories. Exemplification is related to definition (giving examples is one way of defining), to division in parts (examples are parts of wholes), and to classification (each example is a member of a group or class of persons and things).
—Frank D'Angelo

## QUOTATION: ON WRITING

Like narration, process suggests ongoing movement and continuous action. The emphasis in a process theme, however, is on the how, rather than on the what.
—Frank D'Angelo

## EXTRA EXERCISE D

Using paragraph 34 as an example, have students write a paragraph about a time in their lives when an unplanned encounter has led to a positive consequence. After they have finished, have them share their essays with each other, either aloud or in small groups. Afterwards, ask

1. Video games reflect current concerns in our culture.
2. The content of trash in the United States says a great deal about US culture.
3. Reality shows on television tend to have several common elements.
4. In many respects, our culture is very wasteful.
5. College students face several true challenges.

# 3h   How can I arrange a paragraph?

During DRAFTING, you concentrate on getting ideas onto the page or screen. Later, during REVISION, you can experiment to see how your sentences might be arranged for greatest impact. You may find sometimes that only one possible arrangement can work. For example, if you're explaining how to bake a cake, you want to give the directions in a particular order. At other times, you may find that more than one arrangement is possible. For example, if you're writing about solving a problem and therefore using the problem-to-solution arrangement, you might also use the technique of ordering from least to most important—or its reverse. Quick Reference 3.6 lists the most common ways to arrange a paragraph. More about each arrangement follows in this section.

---

### Quick Reference 3.6   ■ ■ ■ ■ ■ ■ ■

#### Ways to arrange sentences in a paragraph

- By time
- By location
- From general to specific
- From specific to general
- From least to most important
- From problem to solution

---

## ARRANGING BY TIME

In a paragraph arranged according to time, or **chronological order**, events are presented in whatever order they took place. For example, when you tell a story, you write what happened first, then second, then third, and so on. Using a time sequence is a very natural and easy way to organize a paragraph. Paragraph 24 is an example.

**24**   In 1924, The Dawes Plan renegotiated the sums mandated from Germany as reparations and smoothed debt repayments to the United States. The private American capital that then began to flow to Europe (especially to Germany) created a short burst of prosperity for Europeans. In 1928, however, the booming New York stock market began to siphon money away from European investments, and virtually unregulated financial speculation led to Wall Street's crash in October 1929. The crash produced a banking crisis, for U.S. banks had lent their customers large amounts of money to invest in the stock market. The crash made repayments of these loans impossible and caused banks to fail. Little American capital remained for investment in Europe or elsewhere. Credit of all kinds grew scarce, and renewal of loans already made to Europeans became difficult.

—Donald Kagan, "American Investments"

## ARRANGING BY LOCATION

A paragraph arranged according to location, or **spatial order**, leads the reader's attention from one place to another. The movement can be in any direction—from top to bottom, left to right, inside to outside, and so on. Paragraph 25 traces natural disasters across the United States from west to east.

25   In the United States, most natural disasters are confined to specific geographical areas. For example, the West Coast can be hit by damaging earthquakes at any time. Most Southern and Midwestern states can be swept by devastating tornadoes, especially in the spring, summer, and early fall. The Gulf of Mexico and the Atlantic Ocean can experience violent hurricanes in late summer and fall. These different natural disasters, and others as dangerous, teach people one common lesson— advance preparation can mean survival.

—Dawn Seaford, student

## ARRANGING FROM GENERAL TO SPECIFIC

The most common pattern for arranging information is from **general to specific**. Typically, the general statement is the TOPIC SENTENCE, and the supporting details (see RENNS, Quick Reference 3.3) explain the specifics. Paragraph 26 is an example.

26   Memory is something we all know intimately. It is a central and unambiguous part of our commonsense world, its presence as indisputable, if unsteady, as the weather. But when we begin to talk about memory, ambiguities and complexities rapidly emerge. How can we grasp memory itself? It is virtually impossible to imagine memory—what it is, how it works, where it lies—without recourse to metaphor. Is memory a storehouse, a computer, a filing system, an encyclopedia, or a landscape, a cathedral, a city? If it is a kind of narrative, is our model to be Proust or Joyce, Virginia Woolf or Christa Wolf?

—Michael Lambek and Paul Antze, "Forecasting Memory"

## ARRANGING FROM SPECIFIC TO GENERAL

A less common paragraph arrangement moves from **specific to general**. Paragraph 27 is an example. To achieve the greatest impact, the paragraph starts with details that support the topic sentence, which ends the paragraph.

them to think about what essay topics this narrative might fit well.

**QUOTATION: ON WRITING**
You must *write*, not just think you're going to. . . . And you must widen your vocabulary, enjoy words. You just read widely, not in order to copy, but to find your own voice. It's a matter of going through life with all one's senses alive, to be responsive to experience, to other people.

—P. D. James

**QUOTATION: ON WRITING**
Writing is making sense of life.

—Nadine Gordimer

**EXTRA EXERCISE E**
Write a paragraph defining one of the terms listed below. You may find it helpful to begin by determining the class (genus) of the term and the characteristics that distinguish it from other members of the class. In a paragraph of definition, you might find using synonyms, etymological information, and contrasting examples helpful. (Answers will vary.)

1. chemistry
2. extrasensory perception
3. movies
4. weather
5. physical fitness

**EXTRA EXERCISE F**
The sentences below have been jumbled. They are intended to form a paragraph of definition. Indicate which is the topic sentence; then, record the order of the remaining sentences by numbering them.

1. It is the total of all substantive things called economic goods.
2. In other words, wealth is a stock, while income is a flow of economic goods.
3. The wealth of a nation is the stock of economic goods owned by its inhabitants as individuals or as members of the national group.

**4.** Economists use the term *economic goods* to refer to sources of satisfaction that are scarce enough to command a price.

**5.** Wealth differs from income in that wealth is the sum of the goods owned at a particular time, whereas income is derived from the quantity of goods consumed during a specific period.

**Answer to Extra Exercise F**
The order of sentences should be 3, 1, 4, 5, 2.

**EXTRA EXERCISE G**
To practice the principles of classification, arrange the following terms into three groups on the basis of their similarities. Give each group a heading.

1. violin
2. helmet
3. bulb
4. conductor
5. perennial
6. referee
7. concerto
8. touchdown
9. blossom
10. baton
11. Mozart
12. quarterback
13. leaves and stems
14. spectators
15. nursery

**Answers to Extra Exercise G**

*Symphony Orchestra:* violin, conductor, concerto, baton, Mozart

*Football:* helmet, referee, touchdown, quarterback, spectators

*Flowers:* bulb, perennial, blossom, leaves and stems, nursery

Replacing the spark plugs is probably the first thing most home auto mechanics do. But too often, the problem lies elsewhere. In the ignition system, the plug wires, distributor unit, coil, and ignition control unit play just as vital a role as the spark plugs. Moreover, performance problems are by no means limited to the ignition system. The fuel system and emissions control system also contain several components that equal the spark plug in importance. The do-it-yourself mechanic who wants to provide basic care for a car must be able to do more than change the spark plugs.

—Danny Witt, student

**ARRANGING FROM LEAST TO MOST IMPORTANT**

A paragraph arranged from **least to most important** uses **climactic order**, which means that the high point—the climax—comes at the end. For a paragraph to be arranged from least to most important, it has to have at least three items: least, more, most. And remember that the last item always packs the greatest impact and is the most memorable. Paragraph 28 is an example.

For a year, Hal and I worked diligently on that boat. At times, it was a real struggle for me to stay on course: as an 11-year-old, my attentions often wandered and the work was not always exciting. But Hal's dedication profoundly influenced me. By his own example, he taught me important lessons about how to be organized, how to set priorities, and how to be responsible. He also, through working with me on the design of the boat's electronics, played a pivotal role in developing my passion for science.

—Patrick Regan Buckley, "Lessons in Boat-Building—and Life"

**ARRANGING FROM PROBLEM TO SOLUTION**

In some cases, an effective arrangement for a paragraph is **problem to solution**. Usually, the topic sentence presents the problem. The very next sentence presents the main idea of the solution. Then, the rest of the paragraph covers the specifics of the solution. Paragraph 29 is an example.

When I first met them, Sara and Michael were a two-career couple with a home of their own, and a large boat bought with a large loan. What interested them in a concept called voluntary simplicity was the birth of their daughter and a powerful desire to raise her themselves. Neither one of them, it turned out, was willing to restrict what they considered their "real life" into the brief time before work and the tired hours afterward. "A lot of people think that as they have children and things get more expensive, the only answer is to work harder in order to earn more money. It's not the only answer," insists Michael. The couple's decision was to trade two full-time careers for two half-time careers, and to curtail consumption. They decided to spend their money only on things that contributed to their major goal, the construction of a world where family and friendship, work and play, were all of a piece, a world, moreover, which did not make wasteful use of the earth's resources.

—Linda Weltner, "Stripping Down to Bare Happiness"

**EXERCISE 3-6**   Working individually or with a peer-response group, re-arrange the sentences in each paragraph below so that it flows logically. To begin, identify the topic sentence, use it as the paragraph's first sentence, and continue from there. For help, consult 3i.

### PARAGRAPH A

1. Remember, many people who worry about offending others wind up living according to other people's priorities.
2. Learn to decline, tactfully but firmly, every request that doesn't contribute to your goals.
3. Of all the timesaving techniques ever developed, perhaps the most effective is the frequent use of the word *no*.
4. If you point out that your motivation isn't to get out of work but to save your time to do a better job on the really important things, you'll have a good chance of avoiding unproductive tasks.

—Edwin Bliss, "Getting Things Done:
The ABC's of Time Management"

### PARAGRAPH B

1. After a busy day, lens wearers often don't feel like taking time out to clean and disinfect their lenses, and many wearers skip the chore.
2. When buying a pair of glasses, a person deals with just the expense of the glasses themselves.
3. Although contact lenses make the wearer more attractive, glasses are easier and less expensive to care for.
4. However, in addition to the cost of the lenses themselves, contact lens wearers must shoulder the extra expense of cleaning supplies.
5. This inattention creates a danger of infection.
6. In contrast, contact lenses require daily cleaning and weekly enzyming that inconvenience lens wearers.
7. Glasses can be cleaned quickly with water and tissue at the wearer's convenience.

—Heather Martin, student

### PARAGRAPH C

1. The researchers found that the participation of women in sport was a significant indicator of the health and living standards of a country.
2. Today, gradually, women have begun to enter sport with more social acceptance and individual pride.

## ANSWERS: EXERCISE 3-6

Answers may vary; alternative versions that students can defend are acceptable.

**A.** In the original paragraph, the sentences appeared in this order: 3, 2, 4, 1.

**B.** In the original paragraph, the sentences appeared in this order: 3, 7, 6, 1, 5, 2, 4.

**C.** In the original paragraph, the sentences appeared in this order: 4, 3, 1, 2.

## EXTRA EXERCISE H

To practice the skills of comparing and contrasting, list the most important aspects of the following pairs of items. Using that information, write a topic sentence about their relative value or about their similarities and differences.

1. baseball and football
2. Halloween and the Fourth of July
3. small towns and large cities
4. apartments and houses
5. books and television

### Answers to Extra Exercise H

Answers will vary, but the information listed should lead to a topic sentence.

## EXAMPLE OF CAUSE AND EFFECT

It is warm down here on Earth because the Sun shines. If the Sun were somehow turned off, the Earth would rapidly cool. The oceans would freeze, eventually the atmosphere itself would condense out and our planet would be covered everywhere by snowbanks of solid oxygen and nitrogen 10 meters (about 30 feet) high. Only the tiny trickle of heat from the Earth's interior and the faint starlight would save our world from a temperature of absolute zero.

—Carl Sagan

## QUOTATION: ON WRITING

Philosophers sometimes talk about cause-and-effect thinking as "the billiard ball model of the universe." In cause-and-effect reasoning, events are explained in much the same way as a motion on the billiard table. . . . One billiard ball ("the cause") strikes another, which moves ("the effect"). But if the second ball also strikes something, it becomes a cause and the reaction of that something becomes an effect.

—Richard M. Coe

## ANSWERS: EXERCISE 3-7

Students will probably see more than one arrangement in some of these paragraphs.

*Note:* You might also ask students to analyze these paragraphs in light of what was previously discussed in this chapter: the topic sentence (3e), words in topic sentences that create focus and control (3d), development with RENNS (3f), and techniques of coherence (3g).

**A.** (paragraph 31). Topic sentence last; specific to general

**B.** (paragraph 32). Topic sentence last; problem to solution (and perhaps time)

**C.** (paragraph 33). Topic sentence first; least to most important

## EXAMPLE OF CAUSE AND EFFECT

Considering the whole span of earthly time, the opposite effect, in which life actually modifies its surroundings, has been relatively slight. Only within the moment of time represented by the present century has one species—[humans]—acquired significant power to alter the nature of this world.

—Rachel Carson, *The Obligation to Endure*

## USING COLLABORATION

With full class participation, establish a shared text by having students retell a traditional children's story such as "Jack and the Beanstalk" or "Little Red Riding Hood." Divide the class into groups, assigning each group one pattern for developing a paragraph. Ask each group to choose any element in the story and write a paragraph according to the assigned pattern of development. One group might write a detailed *description* of the hen that lays golden eggs. Another might explain the *process* by which Jack climbs the beanstalk. Another might *analyze* the root cause of Jack and his mother's poverty. Have one member of each group read its paragraph aloud, providing you and the class with an opportunity for comment and response. Such entertaining activities can also make the

3.  In 1952, researchers from the Finnish Institute of Occupational Health who conducted an intensive study of the athletes participating in the Olympics in Helsinki predicted, "Women are able to shake off civil disabilities which millennia of prejudice and ignorance have imposed upon them."

4.  Myths die hard, but they do die.

—Marie Hart, "Sport: Women Sit in the Back of the Bus"

**EXERCISE 3-7**    Working individually or with a peer-response group, determine the arrangements in these paragraphs. Choose from time, location, general to specific, specific to general, least to most important, and problem to solution. For help, consult 3h.

A.    A combination of cries from exotic animals and laughter and gasps from children fills the air along with the aroma of popcorn and peanuts. A hungry lion bellows for dinner, his roar breaking through the confusing chatter of other animals. Birds of all kinds chirp endlessly at curious children.

**30**   Monkeys swing from limb to limb, performing gymnastics for gawking onlookers. A comedy routine by orangutans employing old shoes and garments incites squeals of amusement. Reptiles sleep peacefully behind glass windows, yet they send shivers down the spines of those who remember the quick death many of these reptiles can induce. The sights and sounds and smells of the zoo inform and entertain children of all ages.

—Deborah Harris, student

B.    No one even agrees anymore on what "old" is. Not long ago, 30 was middle-aged and 60 was old. Now, more and more people are living into

**31**   their 70s, 80s and beyond—and many of them are living well, without any incapacitating mental or physical decline. Today, old age is defined not simply by chronological years, but by degree of health and well-being.

—Carol Tavris, "Old Age Isn't What It Used to Be"

C.    Lately, bee researchers have been distracted by a new challenge from abroad. It's, of course, the so-called "killer bee" that was imported into Brazil from Africa in the mid-1950s and has been heading our way ever since. The Africanized bee looks like the Italian bee but is more defensive

**32**   and more inclined to attack in force. It consumes much of the honey that it produces, leaving relatively little for anyone who attempts to work with it. It travels fast, competes with local bees and, worse, mates with them. It has ruined the honey industry in Venezuela and now the big question is: Will the same thing happen here?

—Jim Doherty, "The Hobby That Challenges You to Think Like a Bee"

**EXERCISE 3-8**    Working individually or collaborating with others, decide what would be the best arrangement for a paragraph on each topic listed here. Choose one or a combination of time, location, general to specific, specific to general, least to most important, and problem to solution. For help, consult 3h.

1. Qualities of annoying people
2. Romantic comedies
3. How to deliver bad news
4. Teaching someone a new job

## 3i How can rhetorical patterns help me write paragraphs?

**Rhetorical patterns** (sometimes called *rhetorical strategies*) are techniques for presenting ideas clearly and effectively in academic and other situations. You choose a specific rhetorical strategy according to what you want to accomplish. Quick Reference 3.7 lists the common rhetorical strategies at your disposal.

### Quick Reference 3.7

**Common rhetorical patterns of thought (strategies) for paragraphs**

- Narrative
- Description
- Process
- Examples
- Definition
- Analysis
- Classification
- Comparison and contrast
- Analogy
- Cause-and-effect analysis

Often, your TOPIC SENTENCE will steer you toward a particular pattern. For example, if a topic sentence is "Grilling a great hot dog is easy," the implied pattern—or rhetorical strategy—is to explain the process of how to grill a hot dog. Or if a topic sentence is "To see many different styles of architecture in one US city, visit Chicago," the implied pattern—or rhetorical strategy—is to give examples.

Sometimes, you need to use a combination of rhetorical strategies. For example, in a paragraph on types of color blindness, you might use a combination of definition and classification. A paragraph explaining why one brand of house paint is superior to another might call for comparison and contrast combined with description—and, perhaps, also definition and examples.

### NARRATIVE

**Narrative** writing tells a story. A *narration* relates what is happening or what has happened. Paragraph 33 is an example.

writing process seem less onerous to resistant students.

**ANSWERS: EXERCISE 3-8**
Answers will vary according to how each student conceives of each subject. Comparisons of the methods of arrangement can reveal the multiplicity of available choices.

**BACKGROUND**
Many of the conventions followed by contemporary writers did not exist in the ancient world. For example, words were not divided from each other until sometime in the seventh century, and word division was not systematically practiced until the eleventh century. Some marks of punctuation, such as the question mark and the exclamation point, evolved during the Middle Ages. Paragraphs had been indicated since pre-Christian days, first by short horizontal strokes or wedge-shaped signs. Later, they were noted in Latin manuscripts by a new line. At the same time, it became the practice to indicate the beginning of a new paragraph with enlarged letters, sometimes extending the length of the page. Such elaborate figures became the ancestors of our capital letters. The paragraph as it is known today took shape late in the seventeenth century but was not systematically described until the nineteenth century, when Alexander Bain published his *English Composition and Rhetoric* (1866).

**QUOTATION: ON WRITING**
Whatever the method used, the conclusion must exist, in spirit or in fact, in order to save the end of your essay from creating an unpleasant sense of abruptness. Yet it should not be unnecessarily long . . . but should be designed to make a lasting impression on the reader.
—Esther DiMarzio, "The Preliminaries"

**QUOTATION: ON WRITING**
The perfect ending should take the reader slightly by surprise and yet seem exactly right.
—William Zinsser

**QUOTATION: ON WRITING**
In the end is my beginning.
—T. S. Eliot

**33**  Gordon Parks speculates that he might have spent his life as a waiter on the North Coast Limited train if he hadn't strolled into one particular movie house during a stopover in Chicago. It was shortly before World War II began, and on the screen was a hair-raising newsreel of Japanese planes attacking a gunboat. When it was over the camera operator came out on stage and the audience cheered. From that moment on Parks was determined to become a photographer. During his next stopover, in Seattle, he went into a pawnshop and purchased his first camera for $7.50. With that small sum, Parks later proclaimed, "I had bought what was to become my weapon against poverty and racism." Eleven years later, he became the first black photographer at *Life* magazine.

—Susan Howard, "Depth of Field"

### DESCRIPTION

Writing a **description** is a rhetorical strategy that appeals to a reader's senses— sight, sound, smell, taste, and touch. *Descriptive writing* paints a picture in words. Paragraph 34 is an example.

**34**  Walking to the ranch house from the shed, we saw the Northern Lights. They looked like talcum powder fallen from a woman's face. Rouge and blue eye shadow streaked the spires of a white light which exploded, then pulsated, shaking the colors down—like lives—until they faded from sight.

—Gretel Ehrlich, "Other Lives"

### PROCESS

Writing about a **process** reports a sequence of actions or pattern by which something is done or made. A process usually proceeds chronologically—first do this, then do that. A process's complexity dictates the level of detail in the writing. For example, paragraph 35 provides an overview of a complicated process. Paragraph 36, on the other hand, gives explicit step-by-step directions.

**35**  Making chocolate isn't as simple as grinding a bag of beans. The machinery in a chocolate factory towers over you, rumbling and whirring. A huge cleaner first blows the beans away from their accompanying debris—sticks and stones, coins and even bullets can fall among cocoa beans being bagged. Then they go into another machine for roasting. Next comes separation in a winnower, shells sliding out one side, beans falling from the other. Grinding follows, resulting in chocolate liquor. Fermentation, roasting, and "conching" all influence the flavor of chocolate. Chocolate is "conched"—rolled over and over against itself like pebbles in the sea—in enormous circular machines named conches for the shells they once resembled. Climbing a flight of steps to peer into this huge, slow-moving glacier, I was expecting something like molten mud but found myself forced to conclude it resembled nothing so much as chocolate.

—Ruth Mehrtens Galvin, "Sybaritic to Some, Sinful to Others"

Traditionally, oil was extracted by pressing the olives between granite mill-stones. Many nonindustrial mills now use a modern continuous-cycle system. The olives are conveyed up a belt, washed, and cut into pulp. The resulting paste is kneaded and centrifugally "decanted" to separate it into solids, water, and oil.

36

—Lori de Mori, "Making Olive Oil"

### EXAMPLES

A paragraph developed by **examples** presents particular instances of a larger category. For instance, examples of the category "endangered animals" could include the black rhinoceros, South China tiger, Bulmer's fruit bat, and silvery gibbon. Paragraph 37 is an example of this strategy. On the other hand, sometimes one **extended example**, often called an *illustration,* is useful. Paragraph 38 is an example of this technique.

37

It's hard for us to imagine what it must have been like to live in a culture before the advent of printed books or before you could carry around a ball-point pen and paper to jot notes. "In a world of few books, and those mostly in communal libraries, one's education had to be remembered, for one could never depend on having continuing access to specific material," writes Mary Carruthers, author of *The Book of Memory*, a study of the role of memory techniques in medieval culture. "Ancient and medieval people reserved their awe for memory. Their greatest geniuses they describe as people of superior memories." Thirteenth-century theologian Thomas Aquinas, for example, was celebrated for composing his Summa Theologica entirely in his head and dictating it from memory with no more than a few notes. Roman philosopher Seneca the Elder could repeat 2,000 names in the order they'd been given to him. Another Roman named Simplicius could recite Virgil by heart—backward. A strong memory was seen as the greatest of virtues since it represented the internalization of a universe of external knowledge. Indeed, a common theme in the lives of the saints was that they had extraordinary memories.

—Joshua Foer, "Remember This"

38

He was one of the greatest scientists the world has ever known, yet if I had to convey the essence of Albert Einstein in a single word, I would choose *simplicity.* Perhaps an anecdote will help. Once, caught in a downpour, he took off his hat and held it under his coat. Asked why, he explained, with admirable logic, that the rain would damage the hat, but his hair would be none the worse for its wetting. This knack of going instinctively to the heart of the matter was the secret of his major scientific discoveries—this and his extraordinary feeling for beauty.

—Banesh Hoffman, "My Friend, Albert Einstein"

## DEFINITION

When you define something, you give its meaning. **Definition** is often used together with other rhetorical strategies. If, for example, you were explaining how to organize a seashell collection, you'd probably want to define the two main types of shells: bivalve and univalve. You can also develop an entire paragraph by using definition, called an **extended definition**. An extended definition discusses the meaning of a word or concept in more detail than a dictionary definition. If the topic is very abstract, the writer tries to put the definition in concrete terms. Sometimes a definition tells what something is not, as well as what it is, as in paragraph 39.

**39**    Chemistry is that branch of science that has the task of investigating the materials out of which the universe is made. It is not concerned with the forms into which they may be fashioned. Such objects as chairs, tables, vases, bottles, or wires are of no significance in chemistry; but such substances as glass, wool, iron, sulfur, and clay, as the materials out of which they are made, are what it studies. Chemistry is concerned not only with the composition of such substances, but also with their inner structure.

—John Arrend Timm, *General Chemistry*

## ANALYSIS

**Analysis**, sometimes called *division,* divides things up into their parts. It usually starts, often in its topic sentence, by identifying one subject and continues by explaining the subject's distinct parts, as in paragraph 40.

**40**    Jazz is by its very nature inexact, and thus difficult to define with much precision: humble in its roots, yet an avenue to wealth and fame for its stars; improvised anew with each performance, but following a handful of tried-and-true formulas; done by everybody but mastered by an elite few; made by African Americans, but made the definition of its age by white bands—and predominantly white audiences. Jazz is primarily an instrumental idiom, but nearly all jazz is based on songs with words, and there are great jazz singers. "If you have to ask what jazz is," said Louis Armstrong, "you'll never know."

—D. Kern Holoman, "Jazz"

## CLASSIFICATION

**Classification** groups items according to an underlying, shared characteristic. Paragraph 41 groups—classifies—interior violations of building-safety codes.

**41**    A public health student, Marian Glaser, did a detailed analysis of 180 cases of building code violation. Each case represented a single building, almost all of which were multiple-unit dwellings. In these 180 buildings, there were an incredible total of 1,244 different recorded violations—about seven per building. What did the violations consist of? First of all, over one-third of the violations were exterior defects: broken doors and stairways, holes in the walls, sagging roofs, broken chimneys, damaged porches, and so on. Another one-third were interior violations that could scarcely be attributed to the most ingeniously destructive rural southern migrant in America. There were, for example, a total of 160 instances of defective wiring or other electrical hazards, a very common cause of the excessive number of fires and needless tragic deaths in the slums. There were 125 instances of inadequate, defective, or inoperable plumbing or heating. There were 34 instances of serious infestation by rats and roaches.

—William Ryan, "Blaming the Victim"

## COMPARISON AND CONTRAST

A paragraph developed by *comparison* deals with similarities; a paragraph developed by *contrast* deals with differences. **Comparison and contrast** writing is usually organized one of two ways: You can use *point-by-point organization,* which moves back and forth between the items being compared; or you can use *block organization,* which discusses one item completely before discussing the other. Quick Reference 3.8 lays out the two patterns visually.

---

**Quick Reference 3.8**                          ■ ■ ■ ■ ■ ■ ■

### Comparison and contrast

| POINT-BY-POINT STRUCTURE | BLOCK STRUCTURE |
|---|---|
| *Student body:* college A, college B | *College A:* student body, curriculum, location |
| *Curriculum:* college A, college B | *College B:* student body, curriculum, location |
| *Location:* college A, college B | |

---

Paragraph 42 is structured point by point, going back and forth between the two children (whose names are in **boldface**) being compared.

42    My husband and I constantly marvel at the fact that our two sons, born of the same parents and only two years apart in age, are such completely different human beings. The most obvious differences became apparent at their births. Our firstborn, **Mark**, was big and bold—his intense, already wise eyes, broad shoulders, huge and heavy hands, and powerful, chunky legs gave us the impression he could have walked out of the delivery room on his own. Our second son, **Wayne**, was delightfully different. Rather than having the football physique that **Mark** was born with, **Wayne** came into the world with a long, slim, wiry body more suited to running, jumping, and contorting. **Wayne's** eyes, rather than being intense like **Mark's**, were impish and innocent. When **Mark** was delivered, he cried only momentarily, and then seemed to settle into a state of intense concentration, as if trying to absorb everything he could about the strange, new environment he found himself in. Conversely,

**Wayne** screamed from the moment he first appeared. There was nothing helpless or pathetic about his cry either—he was darn angry!

—Rosanne Labonte, student

Paragraph 43 uses the block pattern for comparison and contrast. The writer first discusses games and then business (each key word is in **boldface**).

**43**

**Games** are of limited duration, take place on or in fixed and finite sites, and are governed by openly promulgated rules that are enforced on the spot by neutral professionals. Moreover, they're performed by relatively evenly matched teams that are counseled and led through every move by seasoned hands. Scores are kept, and at the end of the game, a winner is declared. **Business** is usually a little different. In fact, if there is anyone out there who can say that the business is of limited duration, takes place on a fixed site, is governed by openly promulgated rules that are enforced on the spot by neutral professionals, competes only on relatively even terms, and performs in a way that can be measured in runs or points, then that person is either extraordinarily lucky or seriously deluded.

—Warren Bennis, "Time to Hang Up the Old Sports Clichés"

## ANALOGY

An **analogy** is an extended comparison between objects or ideas from different classes—things not normally associated. Analogy is particularly effective in explaining unfamiliar or abstract concepts because a comparison can be drawn between what is familiar and what is not. An analogy often begins with a simile or metaphor (12c), as in paragraph 44.

**44**

Casual dress, like casual speech, tends to be loose, relaxed, and colorful. It often contains what might be called "slang words": blue jeans, sneakers, baseball caps, aprons, flowered cotton housedresses, and the like. These garments could not be worn on a formal occasion without causing disapproval, but in ordinary circumstances, they pass without remark. "Vulgar words" in dress, on the other hand, give emphasis and get immediate attention in almost any circumstances, just as they do in speech. Only the skillful can employ them without some loss of face, and even then, they must be used in the right way. A torn, unbuttoned shirt or wildly uncombed hair can signify strong emotions: passion, grief, rage, despair. They're most effective if people already think of you as being neatly dressed, just as the curses of well-spoken persons count for more than those of the customarily foul-mouthed do.

—Alison Lurie, *The Language of Clothes*

## CAUSE-AND-EFFECT ANALYSIS

**Cause-and-effect analysis** examines outcomes and the reasons for those outcomes. Causes lead to an event or an effect, and effects result from causes. (For a discussion of correct logic for assessing CAUSE AND EFFECT, see 4h.) Paragraph

45 discusses how television (the cause) becomes indispensable (the effect) to parents of young children.

**45**  Once upon a time, flavor research was a matter of asking housewives to munch a few potato chips in the hopes that the company had stumbled on the perfect formula for reconstituting potatoes. But as the science became more sophisticated, and market pressures demanded more novelty and authenticity, flavor scientists had to create new varieties like "Mesquite BBQ" chips to sit alongside regular barbecue flavor. To fill that hungry maw, Dewis and his colleagues work to analyze hundreds of thousands of substances and develop compounds that will please the buying public in four ways—through smell, taste, sensation and emotion. To do so flavor scientists are homing in on molecules, receptors, brain structures and genetic code that will enable them to create flavors tailored to consumers' palates, health condition, demographics, even genotype. The industry doesn't just talk about things tasting good anymore. Now it's about providing an exceptional "flavor experience."

—Tamara Holt, "The Science of Yummy"

**EXERCISE 3-9**   Working individually or with a peer-response group, decide what rhetorical strategies are used in each of paragraphs 46–50. Choose from any one or a combination of narrative, description, process, example, definition, analysis, classification, comparison and contrast, analogy, and cause and effect. For help, consult 3i.

A.   Another way to think about metamessages is that they frame a conversation, much as a picture frame provides a context for the images in the picture.
**46**   Metamessages let you know how to interpret what someone is saying by identifying the activity that is going on. Is this an argument or a chat? Is it helping, advising, or scolding? At the same time, they let you know what position the speaker is assuming in the activity, and what position you are being assigned.

—Deborah Tannen, *You Just Don't Understand*

B.   I retain only one confused impression from my earliest years: it's all red, and black, and warm. Our apartment was red: the upholstery was of red moquette, the Renaissance dining-room was red, the figured silk hangings over the stained-glass doors were red, and the velvet curtains in Papa's
**47**   study were red too. The furniture in this awful sanctum was made of black pear wood; I used to creep into the kneehole under the desk and envelop myself in its dusty glooms; it was dark and warm, and the red of the carpet rejoiced my eyes. That is how I seem to have passed the early days of infancy. Safely ensconced, I watched, I touched, I took stock of the world.

—Simone de Beauvoir, *Memoirs of a Dutiful Daughter*

C.   In the case of wool, very hot water can actually cause some structural changes within the fiber, but the resulting shrinkage is minor. The fundamental cause of shrinkage in wool is felting, in which the fibers scrunch together

**ANSWERS: EXERCISE 3-9**

Some paragraphs can be interpreted to illustrate more than one pattern. This is a basic list only.

**A.** (paragraph 47). Extended definition (or illustration)

**B.** (paragraph 48). Description, narrative, analysis, examples

**C.** (paragraph 49). Cause and effect, definition, analogy

**D.** (paragraph 50). Narration, description

**E.** (paragraph 51). Classification, examples

48   in a tighter bunch, and the yarn, fabric, and garment follow suit. Wool fibers are curly and rough-surfaced, and when squished together under the lubricating influence of water, the fibers wind around each other, like two springs interlocking. Because of their rough surfaces, they stick together and can't be pulled apart.

—James Gorman, "Gadgets"

D.     After our lunch, we drove to the Liverpool public library, where I was scheduled to read. By then, we were forty-five minutes late, and on arrival we saw five middle-aged white women heading away toward an old car across the street. When they recognized me, the women came over and apologized: They were really sorry, they said, but they had to leave or they'd get in trouble on the job. I looked at them. Every one of them was wearing an inexpensive, faded housedress and, over that, a cheap and shapeless cardigan sweater. I felt honored by their open-mindedness in having wanted to come and listen to my poetry. I thought and I said that it was I who should apologize: I was late. It was I who felt, moreover, unprepared: What in my work, to date, deserves the open-minded attention of blue-collar white women terrified by the prospect of overstaying a union-guaranteed hour for lunch?

—June Jordan, "Waiting for a Taxi"

E.     Lacking access to a year-round supermarket, the many species— from ants to wolves—that in the course of evolution have learned the advantages of hoarding must devote a lot of energy and ingenuity to protecting their stashes from marauders. Creatures like beavers and honeybees, for example, hoard food to get them through cold winters. Others, like desert rodents that face food scarcities throughout the year, must take advantage of the short-lived harvests that follow occasional rains. For animals like burying beetles that dine on mice hundreds of times their size, a habit of biting off more than they can chew at the moment forces them to store their leftovers. Still others, like the male MacGregor's bowerbird, stockpile goodies during mating season so they can concentrate on wooing females and defending their arena d'amour.

—Jane Brody, "A Hoarder's Life:
Filling the Cache—and Finding It"

**ANSWERS: EXERCISE 3-10**

**A.** (paragraph 31). Description, examples

**B.** (paragraph 32). Definition

**C.** (paragraph 33). Definition, cause and effect, process, examples

**EXERCISE 3-10**   Working individually or with a peer-response group, reread the paragraphs in Exercise 3-7 and determine the rhetorical strategy (or strategies) being used in each.

## 3j   What is a transitional paragraph?

**Transitional paragraphs** form a bridge between one long discussion on a single topic that requires a number of paragraphs and another discussion, usually lengthy, of another topic. Paragraph 51 is an example of a transitional paragraph that allows the writer to move from a long discussion of the extent and sources of anger in our society to a long discussion of possible remedies.

**51** So is there any hope for you and your anger? Is there any reason to believe that you will be able to survive the afternoon commute without screaming or tailgating or displaying choice fingers?

—Andrew Santella, "All the Rage"

## 3k   What are effective concluding paragraphs?

A **concluding paragraph** ends the discussion smoothly by following logically from the essay's introductory paragraph (3c) and the essay's body paragraphs (3d). Always integrate a concluding device into the final paragraph so that the discussion does not end abruptly. A conclusion that is hurriedly tacked on is a missed opportunity to provide a sense of completion and a finishing touch that adds to the whole essay. Quick Reference 3.9 lists strategies for concluding your essay as well as strategies to avoid.

---

### Quick Reference 3.9   ■ ■ ■ ■ ■ ■ ■

#### Strategies for concluding paragraphs

**STRATEGIES TO TRY**

- A strategy adapted from those used for introductory paragraphs (3c)—but be careful to choose a different strategy for your introduction and conclusion
- Relating a brief concluding interesting story or anecdote
- Giving one or more pertinent—perhaps surprising—concluding statistics
- Asking one or more provocative questions for further thought
- Using an appropriate quotation to sum up the THESIS STATEMENT
- Redefining a key term for emphasis
- An ANALOGY that summarizes the thesis statement
- A SUMMARY of the main points, but only if the piece of writing is longer than three to four pages
- A statement that urges awareness by the readers
- A statement that looks ahead to the future
- A call to readers

continued >>

**TEACHING TIP**

One way to help students succeed with Exercise 3-11 is to talk them through these imaginary essays before they think about the endings and how they might relate to the beginnings they wrote in Exercise 3-1. A class discussion about what details might support the topics of each paragraph can strengthen students' understanding of the importance of evidence. At the same time, it can give students a fuller concept of the essays on which they based their introductory paragraphs and are now basing their concluding paragraphs. When the students write their conclusions, you can alert them to the lists of useful devices and of what to avoid, explained in Quick Reference 3.9 in section 3k.

**ANSWERS: EXERCISE 3-11**

Answers will vary. As suggested before in regards to introductions, students may learn more by writing a different type of conclusion for a single prompt than they might by writing different introductions for different prompts.

---

**Quick Reference 3.9**   (continued)

**STRATEGIES TO AVOID**

- Introducing new ideas or facts that belong in the body of the essay
- Rewording your introduction
- Announcing what you've discussed, as in "In this paper, I have explained why oil prices have dropped."
- Making absolute claims, as in "I have proved that oil prices don't always affect gasoline prices."
- Apologizing, as in "Even though I'm not an expert, I feel my position is correct."

The same writers who wait to write their introductory paragraph until they've drafted their body paragraphs often also wait to write their concluding paragraph until they've drafted their introduction. They do this to coordinate the beginning and end so that they can make sure they don't repeat the same strategy in both places.

Paragraph 52 is a concluding paragraph that summarizes the main points of the essay.

> **52** Now the equivalent to molecule fingerprints, DNA profiles have indeed proven to be valuable investigative tools. As the FBI Laboratory continues to develop innovative technologies and share its expertise with criminal justice professionals worldwide, it takes great strides in bringing offenders to swift and sure justice, while clearing innocent individuals and protecting crime victims.
>
> —"DNA Profiling Advancement: The Use of DNA Profiles in Solving Crimes," *The FBI Law Enforcement Bulletin*

Paragraph 53 is a concluding paragraph from an essay on the potential collapse of public schools. It looks ahead to the future and calls for action that involves taking control of them.

> **53** Our schools provide a key to the future of society. We must take control of them, watch over them, and nurture them if they are to be set right again. To do less is to invite disaster upon ourselves, our children, and our nation.
>
> —John C. Sawhill, "The Collapse of Public Schools"

**EXERCISE 3-11**   Working individually or in a peer-response group, return to Exercise 3-1, in which you wrote introductory paragraphs for three informally outlined essays. Now, write a concluding paragraph for each.

For more help with your writing, grammar, and research, go to **www.mycomplab.com**

# 4

# Thinking Critically About Ideas and Images

## 4a What is critical thinking?

Thinking isn't something you choose to do, any more than a fish chooses to live in water. To be human is to think. But while thinking may come naturally, being deliberate about how you think doesn't.

**Critical thinking** means taking control of your conscious thought processes. If you don't, you risk being controlled by the ideas of others. For example, consider the claim "Because climate change is natural, we shouldn't worry about global warming." It's true that the earth's climate has varied over the millenia, but critical readers won't immediately accept that statement without further thought. They might ask, for example, whether the same conditions that caused climate change in the past are the ones causing change today. They might wonder whether the kinds of change happening today are similar to the changes in the past. They might wonder how most scientists would respond to the assertion. It could be true that we shouldn't worry about global warming (though evidence does support the contrary), so a critical reader might ultimately accept the original claim—but not without careful analysis.

The essence of critical thinking is thinking beyond the obvious—beyond the flash of images on a television screen, the alluring promises of glossy advertisements, the evasive statements by some people in the news, the half-truths of propaganda, or even the punchlines of bumper stickers, as in Figure 4.1. Thinking critically means identifying the weaknesses—and the strengths—of an idea, a text, an image, or a presentation. It means analyzing the quality of evidence and how writers or speakers make their cases. It means interpreting, considering implications, imagining alternatives, connecting information and ideas in one situation to information and ideas in another.

The word *critical* here has a neutral meaning. It doesn't mean taking a negative view or finding fault, as when someone criticizes another person for doing something incorrectly. Rather, the term means examining ideas thoroughly and deeply.

As an example of how critical thinking works, consider how the various elements of Figure 4.2 shape our response to the image. When you look at the

**TEACHING TIP**
A review of the history of critical thinking, beginning in the West with the Socratic method, may help students better understand its value and importance. For a concise history of critical thinking, have your students visit <http://www.criticalthinking.org/aboutCT/briefHistoryCT.cfm>.

**QUOTATION: ON LANGUAGE**
By *opinion,* I mean my own conclusion about the rightness of anything, which I am well aware may not be yours. . . . *Opinion* comes from the Latin *opinari,* "to think."
—William Safire

**QUOTATION: ON THINKING**
Man is but a reed, the weakest in nature, but he is a thinking reed.
—Blaise Pascal

**QUOTATION: ON WRITING**
Thinking is the activity I love best, and writing to me is simply thinking through my fingers. I can write up to 18 hours a day. Typing 90 words a minute, I've done better than 50 pages a day. Nothing interferes with my concentration. You could put on an orgy in my office and I wouldn't look up—well, maybe once.
—Isaac Asimov

**BACKGROUND**
In her thoughtful study *Literacy in American Lives* (New York: Cambridge University Press, 2001), Deborah Brandt concludes one chapter, "The Sacred and the Profane: Reading Versus Writing in Popular Memory" (146–168), with the observation that new relationships may yet develop between reading and writing, literacy activities too often separated in the past in the lived experiences of "ordinary people."

**QUOTATION: ON THINKING**
A man is not idle because he is absorbed in thought. There is a visible labor, and there is an invisible labor.
—Victor Hugo

**BACKGROUND**
In recent years, visual literacy has become increasingly important in composition courses. Diana George, in "From Analysis to Design: Visual Communication in the Teaching of Writing" (*College Composition and Communication* 54.1 (2002): 11–39), provides an extensive review of historical and current theories, research, and pedagogy on visual literacy. Already in the 1940s, composition textbooks pointed out the significance of being able to read pictures as well as words. Calling contemporary culture "aggressively visual," George notes that students today need to be skilled not only as analysts but also as producers of visual rhetoric. Two emphases that have increased the importance of the visual are the cultural studies movement of the 1980s and the way that computers have enabled, even demanded, that writers consider design elements, not just writing elements. For additional background on this topic, see John Berger's *Ways of Seeing* (London: BBC and Penguin, 1977); Lester Faigley's "Material Literacy and Visual Design," in *Rhetorical Bodies: Toward a Material Rhetoric* (Madison: University of Wisconsin Press, 1999: 171–201), edited by Jack Selzer and Sharon Crowley; and Bill Cope and Mary Kalantzi's *Multiliteracies: Literacy Learning and the Design of Social Futures* (London: Routledge, 2000).

**BACKGROUND**
In "Advertising and Interpretive Analysis: Developing Reading, Thinking, and Writing Skills in the Composition Course" (*Teaching English in the Two-Year College* 29.4 (2002): 355–366), Matthew Henry explains how teaching students to analyze advertisements develops broad critical thinking, reading, and writing skills.

**Figure 4.1** Two bumper stickers

obvious, surface content of the photograph, you may simply see a number of people standing in line. However, a closer look shows the deeper message that the photographer seeks to convey. The details in the photograph combine to lead viewers to a negative "close reading" of the scene.

Several elements of the photograph convey the idea that these people aren't gathered for a pleasant experience, such as going to a concert. Their body language is slumped and tired. Some people have crossed arms, and others (for example, the

**Figure 4.2** Photo of people standing in line

man in the striped shirt) have shifted their weight to one leg. It seems as though they've been in this line a long time, and in fact, it's hard to tell from the picture's angle just how long the line stretches. People stare ahead or blankly into space, not interacting with others around them. They aren't here for fun or socializing.

The setting of the image contributes to the sense of unpleasantness. Although it seems to be a very large room, the ceiling appears quite low. Although the ceiling has numerous lights (indeed, the stretch of lights makes you perceive the room as vast), the image is fairly dark. Both of these qualities contribute to a vague sense that the environment is oppressive or controlled. The physical surroundings echo the collective mood.

There are commonalities and differences among the people. There are men and women of different races. People are dressed in jeans and in shorts, in shirts and in jackets. However, notice what the people have in common. While there's some difference in clothing, nothing is very dressy and nothing is very flashy. Everyone wears fairly casual clothes, with sneakers being the most common footwear. Furthermore, the general age range is comparatively narrow. Are there any children, youths, or elderly? Finally, several people are carrying sheets of paper. Perhaps they're turning in a test, an application, or a form.

In fact, this photograph depicts an unemployment line. Someone who wanted to depict waiting on an unemployment line as an optimistic or pleasant event would have created quite a different image. We're not saying that losing a job is ever pleasant—far from it. However, a different image would have shaped a different response. We imagine that a state unemployment agency that wanted to convey its work as efficient and friendly wouldn't be very happy with this image. We'll return to analyzing images in greater detail, in section 4j, below.

## 4b What are the elements of critical thinking?

Quick Reference 4.1 describes the general steps of critical thinking, steps that are just as fluid as those in the WRITING PROCESS. Expect sometimes to combine steps, reverse their order, and return to parts of the process you thought you had completed.

### Quick Reference 4.1

#### Steps in the critical thinking process

1. **Comprehend** or **summarize.** Understand the **literal** meaning: the "plain" meaning on the surface of the material. Be able to extract and restate its main message or central point or to accurately and objectively describe an image, event, or situation. Add nothing. Read "on the lines."

continued >>

**BACKGROUND**

In the essay "Intertextual Composition: The Power of the Digital Pen" (*English Education* 35.1 (2002): 46–65), Meg Callahan (University of Rochester, NY) contends that instructors of English must use technology in literacy not merely to reinforce conventional practices. If language is to be seen as something more than a conduit or technology for information dispersal and retrieval, students must experience the production of multimodal texts and learn how to integrate seamlessly multiple modes of text from multiple sources (such as music, song lyrics, strangers' stories, proverbs, and a variety of visual media). Only through this direct experience can students become viewers, readers, and listeners capable of analyzing texts critically.

**QUOTATION: ON READING**

A room without books is like a body without a soul.

—Cicero

**BACKGROUND**

Two pioneers in research about reading as a process are Robert J. Tierney and P. David Pearson. They have drawn many parallels between the processes of writing and reading. They have found that, like writers, readers plan by determining their purposes for reading a text, assessing what they know about the topic, focusing their goals and topics, and questioning themselves. Each reader's goals and knowledge influence how he or she reads and understands the text. Like writers, when they begin, readers approach the text with particular goals and review what they know about a subject and then discover, revise, and delete goals and call up other knowledge as they read.

Like writers, readers draft, at first trying to discover a lead or hypothesis that will help them make sense of the rest of the text, refining and developing that lead as they read, making connections and filling in gaps in the text with their own inferences and knowledge, and trying to fit all the pieces of the text together into a coherent whole. Readers and writers also both engage in aligning. Readers take a stance (passive, critical, sympathetic, challenging) in relation to the author to help them construct meaning from the text, just as writers take a stance toward their audiences.

Readers and writers both need to revise. Readers need to reflect on and evaluate the meanings they have constructed from the text, rereading the text and questioning and revising their interpretations. Finally, readers and writers need to monitor themselves as they compose, distancing themselves from the meaning they compose and examining their composing activities. Readers and writers should both be in dialogue with their "other self," to determine how well they are accomplishing their purposes.

## BACKGROUND

Noting that explicit instruction in reading is now included in many introductory writing classes, Patricia Harkin (University of Illinois) questions the place of reader-response theory in English studies ("The Reception of Reader-Response Theory," *College Composition and Communication* 56.3 (2005): 410–425). Tracing the popularity of this theory from its inception in the populist, political movements of the 1960s and 1970s through its eventual "de-authorization" in elitist advocacy of "high theory," Harkin laments the absence today of early thinkers who taught not only *that* readers make meaning, but showed also *how* readers make meaning. Harkin calls for risk-takers in composition studies who will dare to return to work begun more than a quarter century ago for the purpose of engaging in the discovery of reading processes that could allow a current professoriate to teach more effectively.

## TEACHING TIP

Read and discuss sections 4c.1 and 4c.2, then have students preview, read, and review section 4d, individually and on paper. Once they have finished, have them exchange papers and evaluate how completely their partners followed the "preview, read, review" process. Get them in the habit of reading this text carefully!

---

**Quick Reference 4.1**    (continued)

2. **Analyze.** Examine the material by breaking it into its component parts. Ask about the nature or meaning of each part and how it contributes to the overall meaning or effect.

3. **Infer.** Read "between the lines" to see what's not stated but implied.

4. **Synthesize.** Connect what you've summarized, analyzed, and inferred with your prior knowledge or experiences, with other ideas or perspectives, or with other readings, texts, or situations.

5. **Evaluate.** Read "beyond the lines." Judge the quality of the material or form your own informed opinion about it. Answer such questions as "Is it reasonable? Fair? Accurate? Convincing? Ethical? Useful? Comprehensive? Important?"

## 4c  How do I read to comprehend?

When you read to comprehend, you try to understand the basic, literal meaning of a text. Your goal is to discover the main ideas, the supporting details, or, in a work of fiction, the central details of plot and character.

### 4c.1  Reading closely and actively

Reading is an active process—a dynamic, meaning-making interaction between the page and your brain. The secret to **reading closely and actively** is to annotate as you read. Annotating means writing notes to yourself in a book or article's margins and using asterisks and other codes to alert you to special material. Some readers start annotating right away, while others wait to annotate after they've previewed the material and read it once. Experiment to determine what works best for you. We recommend your using two different ink colors, one for close reading (blue in the example in Figure 4.3) and one for active reading (black in the example).

**Close reading** means annotating for content. You might, for example, number and briefly list the steps in a process or summarize major points in the margin. When you review, your marginal notes help you glance over the material and quickly recall what it's about.

**Active reading** means annotating to make connections between the material and your own knowledge or experiences. This is your chance to converse on paper with the writer. Consider yourself a partner in the making of meaning, a full participant in the exchange of ideas that characterizes a college education. Active reading is a key to ANALYSIS (section 4d), INFERENCE (4e), SYNTHESIS (4f), and EVALUATION (4g).

If you feel uncomfortable writing in a book—even though the practice of annotating texts dates back to the Middle Ages—create a *double-entry notebook*.

My colleagues and I, along with other researchers, have begun amassing evidence -- both in the laboratory and in the field -- that increased choice can lead to *decreased* well-being. This is especially true for people we have termed maximizers, people whose goal is to get the best possible result when they make decisions. Choice overload is also a problem for people we call "satisficers," people who seek only "good enough" results from their choices, but the problem is greatly magnified for maximizers. Much of the relevant research is summarized in my book, *The Paradox of Choice: Why More Is Less*. Here are some examples:

- Shoppers who confront a display of 30 jams or varieties of gourmet chocolate are less likely to purchase any than when they encounter a display of six.

- Students given 30 topics from which to choose to write an extra-credit essay are less likely to write one than those given six. And if they do write one, it tends to be of lower quality.

- The majority of medical patients do not want the decision authority that the canons of medical ethics have thrust upon them. Responsibility for medical decisions looks better to people in prospect than in actuality: Sixty-five percent of respondents say that if they were to get cancer, they would want to be in charge of treatment decisions, but among those who actually have cancer, only 12 percent want that control and responsibility.

*Handwritten annotations:*
Choice decreases well-being
choice hardest on them
shoppers
students
patients: "let doctors choose" think of grandpa

- but could there be other reasons?
"good enough"
- like when I was buying the GPS
- but in this case, I'd want options

**Figure 4.3** A sample of annotated reading

Draw a line down the center of your notebook page. On one side, write content notes (close reading). On the other, write synthesis notes (active reading). Be sure to write down exactly where in the reading you're referring to. Illustrated in Figure 4.4 is a short example from a double-entry notebook.

| Content Notes | Synthesis Notes |
|---|---|
| --increased wealth and choice hasn't made people happier | |
| --14 million people fewer than in 1974 report being "very happy" | I wonder if people define happiness different today than they did 30-40 years ago |
| --depression and suicide has increased, especially among young people | Scary. There could be lots of causes, and I wonder if wealth and choice are the most important |
| --demand for counseling has increased at colleges | Could it be that more students seek counseling? Maybe need was there before but people didn't act. |

**Figure 4.4** Double entry notebook example

**TEACHING TIP**
Your students are likely to appreciate your using some in-class time to guide them in learning and practicing the "SQ4R" approach to active reading. Here are some instructions you can read to lead your students through the process:

- S = Scan/Survey. Take just a few minutes to glance quickly at headings, subheadings, italics, photos, charts, and graphics in what you are about to read.

- Q = Formulate questions from what is emphasized in your survey findings. For example, from the heading "Reading for literal meaning," you could derive several questions: "What is meant by *literal* reading?" "How can/should I read for literal meaning?" "Why is literal meaning important for me to grasp?"

- R = Read. Note that "reading" is the *third*, not first, step in an active reading process.

- R = Record answers to your questions by taking notes that highlight the key ideas, including answers to the questions you have raised. Underlining or highlighting print text and marking online text with a color font, bold print, or other symbols will help ensure that you are reading thoughtfully.

- R = Recite. Yes, summarize aloud, in your own words, what you have just read. If you cannot restate what you have read, you may need to reread the passage.

- R = Reflect and Review. Reflection is a key component of critical thinking (see 4a). For reading assignments that you will need to recall later (for presentations, extended projects, test-taking, etc.), a review within 24 hours will move into long-term memory those facts, ideas, and details stored initially in short-term memory.

Allow ten minutes for students to apply the first four steps in "SQ4R" to a short passage from this handbook. (Section 4e, "How do

I tell the difference between summary and synthesis," is a particularly good choice for this time limit.) Then, ask students to pair with a partner and take turns telling each other what they have just learned. Students will probably be amazed at how much more effective (and, ultimately, time-saving) their reading becomes when they take the time to "SQ4R" their reading. (*Note:* This process works well, too, for on-line "reading" of both graphic-intensive and text-based Web sites. Students can develop questions from links and photos as well as from regular print text.)

**ANSWERS: EXERCISE 4-1**
Answers will vary. Have students review their results via some kind of communal exercise such as small group discussion. If you have time, encourage students to review answers on the board so that students can visually appreciate the differences between different students' notes.

**QUOTATION: ON READING**
Do not dictate to your author; try to become him. Be his fellow-worker and accomplice. If you hang back, and reserve and criticize at first, you are preventing yourself from getting the fullest possible value from what you read. But if you open your mind as widely as possible, then signs and hints of almost imperceptible fineness, from the twist and turn of the first sentences, will bring you in the presence of a human being unlike any other. Steep yourself in this, acquaint yourself with this, and soon you will find that your author is giving you, or attempting to give you, something far more definite.
—Virginia Woolf

**QUOTATION: ON READING**
We always read for some purpose—unless some sad, bad, mad schoolteacher has got hold of us. There is no such thing as merely reading words; always through the words we are trafficking or trying to traffic with things—things gone by, present, to come or eternal.
—I. A. Richards

**EXERCISE 4-1**    Annotate the rest of the essay by Barry Schwartz, titled "The Tyranny of Choice," on pages 196–198. Depending on your instructor's directions, either follow the annotation example in Figure 4.3, the double-entry example in Figure 4.4, or try both.

**4c.2    Reading systematically**

To **read systematically** is to use a structured plan: **Preview**, **Read**, and **Review**.

1. **Preview:** Before you begin reading, start making predictions. When your mind is reading actively, it is guessing what's coming next, either confirming or revising its prediction, and moving on to new predictions. For example, suppose you're glancing through a magazine and come across the title "The Heartbeat." Your mind begins guessing: Is this a love story? Is this about how the heart pumps blood? Maybe, you say to yourself, it's a story about someone who had a heart attack. Then, as you read the first few sentences, your mind confirms which guess was correct. If you see words like *electrical impulse, muscle fibers,* and *contraction,* you know instantly that you're in the realm of physiology.

   - To preview a book, first look at the table of contents. What topics are included? What seems to be the main emphasis? Which sections will be most important? If there's an introduction or preface, skim it.

   - To preview a particular reading (for example, a chapter or an article), read all the headings, large and small. Note the **boldfaced** words (in darker print), and all visuals and their captions, including photographs, drawings, figures, tables, and boxes.

   - Check for introductory notes about the author and head notes, which often precede individual works in collections of essays or short stories. Read pivotal paragraphs, such as the opening and (unless you're reading for suspense) closing.

   - Jot a few questions that you expect—or hope—the reading will answer.

2. **Read:** Read the material closely and actively (see section 4c.1). Identify the main points and start thinking about how the writer supports them.

3. **Review:** Go back to questions you jotted during previewing. Did the reading answer them? (If not, either your predictions could have been wrong, or you didn't read carefully; reread to determine which.) Also, look at the annotations you made through close and active reading. What do these add up to? Where are places you need to go back? Keep in mind that collaborative learning can reinforce what you learn from reading. Ask a friend or classmate to discuss the material with you and quiz you.

**Alert:** The speed at which you read depends on your purpose for reading. When you're hunting for a particular fact, you can skim the page until you find what you want. When you read about a subject you know well, you might read somewhat rapidly, slowing down when you come to new material. When you're unfamiliar with the subject, you need to work slowly to give your mind time to absorb the new material. ●

---

### Quick Reference 4.2

#### More ways to help your reading comprehension

- **Make associations.** Link new material to what you already know, especially when you're reading about an unfamiliar subject. You may even find it helpful to read an encyclopedia article or an easier book or article on the subject first in order to build your knowledge base.

- **Simplify tough sentences.** If the author's writing style is complex, "unpack" the sentences: Break them into smaller units or reword them in a simpler style.

- **Make it easy for you to focus.** If your mind wanders, do whatever it takes to concentrate. Arrange for silence or music, for being alone or in the library with others who are studying. Try to read at your best time of day.

- **Allot the time you need.** To comprehend new material, you must allow sufficient time to read, reflect, reread, and study. Discipline yourself to balance classes, working, socializing, and family activities. Alas, reading for comprehension takes time.

- **Master the vocabulary.** If you don't understand key terms in your reading, you can't fully understand the concepts. As you encounter new words, try to figure out their meanings from context clues. Also, many textbooks list key terms and their definitions (called a *glossary*) at the end of each chapter or of the book. Of course, nothing replaces having a good dictionary at hand.

---

# 4d  How do I analyze a reading?

To analyze something is to break it into parts, just as a chemist does, for example, in order to figure out the compounds in a particular mixture. However, it's easier to define analysis than to understand and apply it to reading. The key is knowing what parts to examine and how.

**BACKGROUND**

Good readers go beyond awareness of words as they take into account date, aims, and tone of a text as well as organizational features, genre, and other considerations. Although John Peters wrote *Elements of Critical Reading* in 1991, his analysis of reading habits provides good advice even now for readers of print text (New York: MacMillan, 1991). Consider also how Peters's admonitions can be adapted to "readers" of visual and audio "texts" as well:

1. Examine organizational features. "When you first encounter a text of any kind, you should pause to examine its outward features. Depending on the kind of text, those may include cover, title page, table of contents, chapter or section divisions, glossary, notes, bibliography, and other accessories" (13). They will provide a useful first impression of the text.

2. Know when the text was written.

3. Determine apparent aims. "Spot-reading" selected passages (also known as "pre-reading" and "X-raying") "allows you to inspect parts which can give you an idea of the text's aims and audience level" (15). Generally, begin with the preface or the opening paragraphs and, with nonfiction texts, then skip to the conclusion because it often summarizes the main points and purposes of the text. You should also drift a little back and forth through the center of the text, "eyeing those spots where expository writing often focuses its aims" (15–16), such as the first and last paragraphs of a section, the first sentence of each body paragraph, and any visual aids and illustrations.

4. Adapt to the genre. "From nonfiction you should usually expect an orderly discussion such as you might hear at a lecture or business meeting. In general, your relation to nonfiction is that of a student, colleague, or general reader who wants information upon which to base opinions, decisions, or future activity related to the subject—but it's a good idea to be slightly skeptical, aware that a text may have misinformation or raise more questions than it answers" (16–17).

5. Listen to the language. Reading only for the message of the text, ignoring its emotions, tone,

and rhythms, can cause a reader to miss much of what the text offers as well as much of the pleasure in reading.

**6.** Become aware of contrasts. "It is said that there are two sides to everything. As a reader you should become aware of the contrasts within a text. The inner structure is bound to reveal a play of opposites that close reading uncovers" (21).

**7.** Get to the heart of the matter. "For some readers, the heart of a text may be a passage or series of passages that seem to tie everything together and coordinate the flow of ideas throughout the entire work" (23). "The 'heart' can also be viewed as a sort of overall personality that characterizes the text. . . . But on the best occasions and as a result of our patient attentiveness, the heart of a text may reveal itself in the fullness of its meaning, both logical and emotional, and make us feel that we truly know what we've read" (25).

**8.** Sense what may be missing. "Of the many responses that reading can inspire, a few may be strong while plenty of others remain inactive. The intensity of your feelings is important, but so is the absence of those emotions which a text might have brought you but did not. . . . Knowing what a text means to you depends on your sense of what is present or missing in the relationship you've just concluded" (26).

**TEACHING TIP**

Your students may enjoy analyzing the tone of the following two passages. How can they be compared and contrasted?

**A.** I can't eat or drink anything. I can't go anywhere. I have become a victim of the consumer reporter. Ever since Ralph Nader and his pals started investigating, I have gradually become an anorexia nervosa hermit. My friends warn me that I've been taking the news too seriously. But if you read the paper and watch television every night, you begin to get the feeling that if the mugger doesn't kill you—BOTULISM will!

—Joanna Wolper, "A Victim of the Consumer Crusaders"

---

| Quick Reference 4.3 | ▪ ▪ ▪ ▪ ▪ ▪ ▪ |
|---|---|

**Elements of analysis**

1. Separate facts from opinions (4d.1).
2. Identify the evidence (4d.2).
3. Identify cause and effect (4d.3).
4. Describe the tone (4d.4).

## 4d.1   Separating facts from opinions

A helpful step in analyzing a reading is to distinguish **fact** from **opinion**. *Facts* are statements that can be verified. *Opinions* are statements of personal beliefs. While facts can be verified by observation, research, or experimentation, opinions are open to debate. Problems arise when a writer blurs the distinction between fact and opinion. Critical readers will know the difference.

For example, here are two statements, one a fact, the other an opinion.

1. Women can never make good mathematicians.

2. Although fear of math isn't purely a female phenomenon, girls tend to drop out of math classes sooner than boys, and some adult women have an aversion to math and math-related activity that is akin to anxiety.

Reading inferentially, you can see that statement 1 is clearly an opinion. Is it worthy of consideration? Perhaps it could be open to debate, but the word *never* implies that the writer is unwilling to allow for even one exception. Conversely, statement 2 at least seems to be factual, though research would be necessary to confirm or deny the position.

You may find it practical to label key sentences "facts" or "opinions" as part of your analysis. You could put an "F" or "O" in the margin next to those sentences. Or, you could include a brief note to yourself explaining why certain sentences are opinions.

**EXERCISE 4-2**   Working individually or with a collaborative group, decide which of the statements below are facts and which are opinions. When the author and source are provided, explain how that information influenced your judgment. For help, consult section 4c.2.

1. The life of people on earth is better now than it has ever been—certainly much better than it was 500 years ago.

—Peggy Noonan, "Why Are We So Unhappy When We Have It So Good?"

2. The fast food industry pays the minimum wage to a higher proportion of its workers than any other American industry.
—Eric Schlosser, *Fast Food Nation*

3. Grief, when it comes, is nothing we expect it to be.
—Joan Didion, *The Year of Living Dangerously*

4. A mind is a terrible thing to waste.
—United Negro College Fund

5. History is the branch of knowledge that deals systematically with the past.
—*Webster's New World College Dictionary*, Fourth Edition

6. In 1927, F. E. Tylcote, an English physician, reported in the medical journal *Lancet* that in almost every case of lung cancer he had seen or known about, the patient smoked.
—William Ecenbarger, "The Strange History of Tobacco"

7. Trucks that must travel on frozen highways in Alaska for most of the year now sometimes get stuck in the mud as the permafrost thaws.
—Al Gore, *An Inconvenient Truth*

8. You can, Honest Abe notwithstanding, fool most of the people all of the time.
—Stephen Jay Gould, "The Creation Myths of Cooperstown"

9. You change laws by changing lawmakers.
—Sissy Farenthold, political activist, *Bakersfield Californian*

10. A critical task for all of the world's religions and spiritual traditions is to enrich the vision—and the reality—of the sense of community among us.
—Joel D. Beversluis, *A Sourcebook for Earth's Community of Religions*

## 4d.2   Identifying the evidence

For any opinions or claims, you next need to identify and analyze the evidence that the writer provides. **Evidence** consists of facts, examples, the results of formal studies, and the opinions of experts. A helpful step in analysis is to identify the kind of evidence used (or what evidence is missing).

### RECOGNIZING PRIMARY VERSUS SECONDARY SOURCES

**Primary sources** are firsthand evidence based on your own or someone else's original work or direct observation. Primary sources can take the form of experiments, surveys, interviews, memoirs, observations (such as in ETHNOGRAPHIES), original creative works (for example, poems, novels, paintings and other visual art, plays, films, or musical compositions).

**Secondary sources** report, describe, comment on, or analyze the experiences or work of others. Quick Reference 4.4 illustrates the difference.

**B.** Too much of anything—too much music, entertainment, happy snacks, or time spent with one's friends—creates a kind of impotence of living by which one can no longer hear, or taste, or see, or love, or remember. Life is short and precious, and appetite is one of its guardians, and loss of appetite is a sort of death. So if we are to enjoy this short life we should respect the divinity of appetite, and keep it eager and not too much blunted.

It is a long time now since I knew that acute moment of bliss that comes from putting parched lips to a cup of cold water. The springs are still there to be enjoyed—all one needs is the original thirst.
—Laurie Lee, "Appetite"

**ANSWERS: EXERCISE 4-2**

| | | | |
|---|---|---|---|
| 1. opinion | | 6. fact |
| 2. fact | | 7. fact |
| 3. opinion | | 8. opinion |
| 4. opinion | | 9. opinion |
| 5. fact | | 10. opinion |

**TEACHING TIP**
You may want to underscore the importance of evaluating reliability of sources by asking students to identify any area of their own lives in which they claim to have a good measure of expertise (e.g., using spices in cooking, pitching a fastball to the outside corner, getting compliance from a two-year-old, etc.). Ask them to name individuals or types of persons who could be counted on for further reliable information. Then, ask what they would think if *you* used your own opinions as evidence on the topic of their expertise, assuming you had none in the areas they named. Engage them in discussing the benefits and limitations of both primary and secondary sources.

**EXTRA EXERCISE A**
Determine which sentences state facts and which state opinions.

1. Nuclear fusion releases energy.
2. Nuclear fusion is a possible solution to our energy problems.

3. Solar energy has attracted a great deal of public attention over the past decade.

4. Many people hope that it will produce a clean, nonpolluting means of heating our homes and offices.

5. Oil and gas production in the United States has been falling for over a decade.

6. The petroleum industry is shrinking yearly.

7. In the interest of national security, the petroleum industry should be encouraged by government legislation.

8. The early pioneers generated energy from the wind on the frontier.

9. Such nonpolluting means of creating energy should immediately replace those produced by fossil fuels.

10. Because natural gas, methane, is a clean fuel, the government should encourage its use.

### Answers to Extra Exercise A

| | | | |
|---|---|---|---|
| 1. | fact | 6. | fact |
| 2. | opinion | 7. | opinion |
| 3. | fact | 8. | fact |
| 4. | fact | 9. | opinion |
| 5. | fact | 10. | opinion |

---

## Quick Reference 4.4 ■ ■ ■ ■ ■ ■

### Examples of differences between primary and secondary sources

| Primary Source | Secondary Source |
|---|---|
| Professor Fassi interviews thirty single parents and reports his findings in a journal article. | *Time* magazine summarizes Professor Fassi's study in a longer article on single parents. |
| Medical researcher Molly Doran publishes the results of her experiments with a new cancer drug in the *New England Journal of Medicine*. | *The Washington Post* runs an article that summarizes findings from Doran's study. |
| The National Assessment of Educational Progress publishes test results on the reading abilities of ninth graders. | National Public Radio refers to the NAEP study in a story on reading in America. |
| A team of researchers at Bowling Green State University survey 2,259 Ohio citizens about their voting patterns and write an article explaining their findings. | Scholar Maya Dai conducts a study of politics in Colorado; in her review of literature section of her study, she summarizes the Bowling Green study, along with studies in four other states. |
| Rosa Rodriguez writes a memoir about life as a migrant worker. | Writer Phil Gronowski discusses Rodriguez's memoir in his daily blog. |
| Gerhard Richter exhibits his paintings at the Art Institute of Chicago. | The *Chicago Tribune* publishes a review of Richter's exhibition. |

---

Primary sources have the advantage of being "closer" to the subject matter or phenomenon. Of course, that doesn't make them perfect. For example, you can't interview only three sophomores and make claims about all college students everywhere. Furthermore, not all eyewitnesses are reliable, so you must judge which ones to believe. Still, readers often find enhanced credibility in primary research. With secondary sources, there's always a risk that the writer isn't reporting the original material accurately, whether intentionally or not.

For example, suppose a primary source author concluded "It would be a mistake to assume that people's poverty level reflects their intelligence," but a secondary source author represents this as "poverty level is connected to intelligence." Problem! The value of a secondhand account hinges on the reliability of the reporter, which depends on the specificity, accuracy, and authority of his or her observations, as well as where he or she published them. Quick Reference 4.5 provides a checklist for evaluating sources.

---

### Quick Reference 4.5  ■ ■ ■ ■ ■ ■ ■ ■

### Evaluating sources

- **Is the source authoritative?** Did an expert or a person you can expect to write credibly on the subject write it? If it's a memoir or eyewitness account, does it have the kind of detail and perspective that makes the writer credible?

- **Is the source published in a reliable place?** Does the material appear in a reputable publication—a book published by an established publisher, a respected journal or magazine—or on a reliable Internet site?

- **Is the source well known?** Is the source cited elsewhere as you read about the subject? (If so, the authority of the source is probably widely accepted.)

- **Is the tone balanced?** Is the language relatively objective (and therefore more likely to be reliable), or is it slanted (probably not reliable)?

- **Is the source current?** Is the material up-to-date and therefore more likely to be reliable, or has later authoritative and reliable research made it outdated? ("Old" isn't necessarily unreliable. In many fields, classic works of research remain authoritative for decades or even centuries.)

- **Are its findings valid (if a primary source)?** Did the experiment, survey, interview, or study seem to be conducted rigorously? Are the conclusions justified by the data?

- **Is it accurate and complete (if a secondary source)?** Does it accurately summarize and interpret the primary resource? Does it leave out anything important?

---

**EXERCISE 4-3**  Indicate for each of the passages below whether it contains primary or secondary evidence. Then, decide whether the evidence is reliable or not, and explain why or why not. Refer to section 4d.2 for help.

A.  Midland has the kind of air that hits you like a brick. After a few minutes, your throat burns. After a few days, your skin feels powdery, your eyelids stick, your hair feels dusty and rough. The longer you spend there, the more you become a little bit like the land—you dry out and cake and crack. Not until I spent time in Midland did I fully appreciate the fact that the earth has an actual crust, like bread that has been slowly baked. I became convinced that if I stayed for a while, I would develop one, too.

—Susan Orlean, "A Place Called Midland"

---

**BACKGROUND**

In *Society and Solitude,* Ralph Waldo Emerson suggests three practical rules for reading (ed. H. G. Callaway. Lewiston, NY: Edwin Mellen Press, 2008).

1. Never read any book that is not a year old.

2. Never read any but the famed books.

3. Never read any but what you like.

**ANSWERS: EXERCISE 4-3**

Students should debate the reliability of each passage. Here are some general guides.

**A.** Primary evidence. Orlean is describing her own experiences. The language is evocative, even poetic. There is no objective way of knowing how reliable this account is, based solely on the information the paragraph provides.

**B.** Secondary evidence. The paragraph depends on a 2005 report of the International Centre for Prison Studies for its validity. The paragraph reads as a well-supported argument, but its value is dependent on the quality of that report. Should the report from the International Centre for Prison Studies be discredited, the paragraph would lose virtually all of its truth value.

**C.** A mix of primary and secondary evidence. The author of the paragraph, Barker, uses an interview with Eric Dunayer (primary evidence), as well as a summary of the number of calls to the Urbana, Illinois, ASPCA and the content of those calls (secondary evidence). The mix of primary and secondary evidence bolsters Barker's argument.

## QUOTATION: ON READING

I took a course in speed reading and was able to read *War and Peace* in twenty minutes. It's about Russia.

—Woody Allen

## BACKGROUND

In their essay "Reading (and) the Profession" (*Reader: Essays in Reader-Oriented Theory, Criticism, and Pedagogy* 47 (2002): 9–37), Gary Ettari and Heather C. Easterling (at the time, graduate students at the University of Washington) questioned why "making sense . . . of what happens when we read" never became the topic of conversation in their graduate study of English. Considering the view that critical reading is a central activity in English, Ettari and Easterling argue for active discussion of the reading process itself as a key component of English instruction.

## ANSWERS: EXERCISE 4-4

Answers will vary. Whichever thesis they pursue, encourage them to include both primary and secondary sources.

## QUOTATION: ON READING

Literature is no one's private ground, literature is common ground; let us trespass freely and fearlessly and find our own way for ourselves.
—Virginia Woolf

## BACKGROUND

Students entering a first-year composition course probably have experienced college placement and achievement tests in English language skills, with significant emphasis on reading. Recognizing the importance of reading skill for thinking adults, the Conference on English Leadership (CEL) developed its 2005 convention around the theme "Leading and Reading: What Teacher-Leaders Can Do." Points of emphasis for postsecondary educators included how technology and reader-response can enhance students' understanding of texts; how diversity can be honored not only through texts but through context and technology as well; and how collaboration (among readers and

B.     According to a 2005 report of the International Centre for Prison Studies in London, the United States—with 5 percent of the world's population—houses 25 percent of the world's inmates. Our incarceration rate (714 per 100,000 residents) is almost 40 percent greater than those of our nearest competitors (Bermuda, Belarus, and Russia). Other industrial democracies, even those with significant crime problems of their own, are much less punitive: Our incarceration rate is 6.2 times that of Canada, 7.8 times that of France, and 12.3 times that of Japan.

—Glenn C. Loury, "America Incarcerated"

C.     Ordinary human foods can be dangerous to dogs, and the list of potentially hazardous items is growing. Reports from pet owners can prompt an investigation, says Eric Dunayer, senior toxicologist at the ASPCA's Animal Poison Control Center in Urbana, Illinois. In 2006, the center's hotline fielded roughly 116,000 calls. Nearly 200 asked about xylitol, a sugar substitute gaining popularity in baked goods, candy, and gum. "We often see vomiting, followed by weakness, staggering, collapse, and possibly seizures as blood sugar drops," say Dunayer.

—Catherine L. Barker, "Spotting Pet Threats"

**EXERCISE 4-4**    Individually or with a group, choose one of the following thesis statements and list the kinds of primary and secondary sources you might consult to support the thesis (you can guess intelligently, rather than checking to make sure that the sources exist). Then, decide which sources in your list would be primary and which secondary.

**THESIS STATEMENT 1:** People who regularly perform volunteer work lead happier lives than those who don't.

**THESIS STATEMENT 2:** Whether someone regularly performs volunteer work or not ultimately has no effect on their happiness.

## EVALUATING EVIDENCE

You can evaluate evidence by asking the following questions to guide your judgment.

- **Is the evidence sufficient?** To be sufficient, evidence can't be skimpy. As a rule, the more evidence, the better. Readers have more confidence in the results of a survey that draws on a hundred respondents rather than on ten. As a writer, you may convince your reader that violence is a serious problem in high schools on the basis of only two examples, but you'll be more convincing with additional examples.

- **Is the evidence representative?** Evidence is representative if it is typical. As a reader, assess the objectivity and fairness of evidence. Don't trust a claim or conclusion about a group based on only a few members rather than on a truly typical sample. For example, a pollster surveying national political views would not get representative evidence by interviewing people only in Austin, Texas, because that group doesn't represent the regional, racial, political, and ethnic makeup of the entire US electorate.

- **Is the evidence relevant?** Relevant evidence is directly related to the conclusion you're drawing. Determining relevance often demands subtle thinking. Suppose you read that one hundred students who had watched television for more than two hours a day throughout high school earned significantly lower scores on a college entrance exam than one hundred students who had not. Can you conclude that students who watch less television perform better on college entrance exams? Not necessarily. Other differences between the two groups could account for the different scores: geographical region, family background, socioeconomic group, or the quality of schools attended.

- **Is the evidence accurate?** Accurate evidence is correct and complete. To be accurate, evidence must come from a reliable source, whether it is primary or secondary. Equally important, evidence must be presented honestly, not misrepresented or distorted.

- **Is the evidence qualified?** Reasonable evidence doesn't make extreme claims. Claims that use words such as *all, always, never,* and *certainly* are disqualified if even one exception is found. Conclusions are more sensible and believable when qualified with words such as *some, many, may, possibly, often,* and *usually.* Remember that today's "facts" may be revised as time passes and knowledge grows. It's a fact today that no life has been found on Mars; a future space mission could change that, however unlikely it might be.

## 4d.3 Identifying cause and effect

**Cause and effect** describes the relationship between one event (cause) and another event that happens as a result (effect). The relationship also works in reverse: One event (effect) results from another event (cause). Whether you begin with a cause or with an effect, you're using the same basic pattern.

> Cause A → produces → effect B

You may seek to understand the effects of a known cause:

> More studying → produces → ?

Or you may seek to determine the cause or causes of a known effect:

> ? → produces → recurrent headaches

When you're analyzing a reading, look for any claims of cause and effect. (Of course, not all readings will have them.) For any that you find, think

instructors) can enlarge the reading perspectives of all.

**QUOTATION: ON WRITING**
Good writing uses every technique and tool available in order to make its effect.
—Gloria Anzaldua

**QUOTATION: ON READING**
Some books are to be tasted, others to be swallowed, and some few to be chewed and digested. . . .
—Francis Bacon

**QUOTATION: ON READING**
I think of life as a good book. The further you get into it, the more it begins to make sense.
—Harold S. Kushner

**TEACHING TIP**
You may want to ask your students to think about their own experiences, analyzing them for their causes and effects. You might ask your students to diagram these causes and effects and to write some of these diagrams on the board for discussion. The questions that follow can help stimulate students' thinking.

1. How did you get your first job?
2. What did you learn from that job?
3. Whose advice is particularly important to you?
4. How do you reach a decision?
5. What difference do you expect college to make in your life?
6. Why do you have a particular way of doing something?
7. How do you make friends?
8. Who is the most important person in your life? Why?
9. When did you learn to drive a car?
10. What will you be doing in ten years?

**EXTRA EXERCISE B**

Supply answers for the blanks in the sentences that follow, checking each choice by the guidelines for evaluating cause and effect to be sure that it is accurate.

1. Frequently eating food with high sodium content can cause _____.

2. _____ can lead to a traffic violation.

3. Regular exercise produces _____.

4. _____ is a leading cause of _____.

5. Because she _____, she is expected to be named Gourmet of the Year.

6. Her mother refuses to intervene so that _____.

7. If you don't quit _____, you are likely to end up in a lawsuit.

8. She decided to stay in college when she learned that _____.

9. More funding for preschool education is needed in order to _____.

10. _____ has resulted in increased numbers of homeless people in our major cities.

**Answers to Extra Exercise B**

Answers will vary, but here are possible responses:

1. high blood pressure

2. Ignoring a stop sign

3. better health

4. Inattention in class, low grades

5. led a revolt against the school cafeteria

6. the daughter will become more independent

7. telling lies about your neighbor

8. employers in her profession usually hire people with college degrees

9. prepare all children adequately for school

10. Slashing the budget for public housing

**ANSWERS: EXERCISE 4-5**

Answers will vary. Below are some possible additional causes.

carefully through the relationship between cause A and effect B. Just because A happened before B or because A and B are associated with each other doesn't mean A caused B. Consult the guidelines in Quick Reference 4.6.

> ### Quick Reference 4.6    ■ ■ ■ ■ ■ ■ ■
>
> ### Assessing cause and effect
>
> - **Is there a clear relationship between events?** Related causes and effects happen in sequence: A cause occurs before an effect. First the wind blows; then a door slams; then a pane of glass in the door breaks. But CHRONOLOGICAL ORDER merely implies a cause-and-effect relationship. Perhaps someone slammed the door shut. Perhaps someone threw a baseball through the glass pane. A cause-and-effect relationship must be linked by more than chronological sequence. The fact that B happens after A doesn't prove that A causes B.
>
> - **Is there a pattern of repetition?** Scientific proof depends on a pattern of repetition. To establish that A causes B, every time A is present, B must occur. Or, put another way, B never occurs unless A is present. The need for repetition explains why the US Food and Drug Administration (FDA) runs thousands of clinical trials before approving a new medicine.
>
> - **Are there multiple causes and/or effects?** Avoid oversimplification. The basic pattern of cause and effect—single cause, single effect (A causes B)—rarely represents the full picture. Multiple causes and/or effects are more typical of real life. For example, it would be oversimplification to assume that a lower crime rate is strictly due to high employment rates. Similarly, one cause can produce multiple effects. For example, advertisements for a liquid diet drink might focus on the drink's most appealing effect, rapid weight loss, while ignoring less desirable effects such as lost nutrients and a tendency to regain the weight.

**EXERCISE 4-5**    For each of the sentences below, explain how the effect might not be a result of the cause given.

EXAMPLE    The number of shoppers downtown increased because the city planted more trees there.

Of course, planting trees might have made the downtown more attractive and drawn more shoppers. However, perhaps there are other reasons: new stores opening, more parking, a suburban mall closed down, and so on.

1. Attendance at baseball games declined because the team raised prices.

2. Test scores improved because the school instituted a dress code.

3. Because of the Internet, Americans are reading fewer books than they did twenty years ago.

## 4d.4 Describing the tone

**Tone** refers to the attitude conveyed in writing, mostly by the writer's word choice. A tone can be formal, informal, laid back, pompous, sarcastic, concerned, judgmental, sympathetic, and so on. We discuss tone at greater length in section 8d.

For now, however, as a critical reader, be suspicious of a highly emotional tone in writing. If you find it, chances are the writer is trying to manipulate the audience. As a writer, if you find your tone growing emotional, step back and rethink the situation. No matter what point you want to make, your chance of communicating successfully to an audience depends on your using a moderate, reasonable tone. For instance, the exaggerations below in the NO example (*robbing treasures, politicians are murderers*) might hint at the truth of a few cases, but they're too extreme to be taken seriously. The language of the YES version is far more likely to deliver its intended message.

**NO**    Urban renewal must be stopped. Urban redevelopment is ruining this country, and money-hungry capitalists are robbing treasures from law-abiding citizens. Corrupt politicians are murderers, caring nothing about people being thrown out of their homes into the streets.

**YES**    Urban renewal is revitalizing our cities, but it has caused some serious problems. While investors are trying to replace slums with decent housing, they must also remember that they're displacing people who don't want to leave their familiar neighborhoods. Surely, a cooperative effort between government and the private sector can lead to creative solutions.

## 4e How do I draw inferences?

When you read for **inferences**, you're reading to understand what's suggested or implied but not explicitly stated. Here's an example.

> The band finally appeared an hour after the concert was scheduled to start. The lead singer spent the first two songs staring at the stage and mumbling into his microphone, before finally looking at the audience and saying, "It's great to be here in Portland." The only problem was that they were playing in Denver. At that point the crowd was too stunned even to boo. I started texting some friends to see if they had any more interesting prospects for the evening.

—Jenny Shi, student

1. Attendance may have declined because the team started losing; there was unseasonably bad weather; there was competition from other sporting events.

2. Test scores may have improved because the school added more tutoring hours; teachers spent more time in class preparing students for tests; the PTA has encouraged parents to become more involved in helping students study.

3. Many reasons may exist why Americans are reading fewer books: the competition that comes from the many types of media besides the Internet, including movies, television, and video games; Americans are working longer hours and taking less vacation time from work than they did twenty years ago; high school and college curricula may be emphasizing professional educational tracks such as business and nursing rather than degrees in the liberal arts, which would more directly cultivate a love of reading.

**QUOTATION: ON READING**

My education was the liberty I had to read indiscriminately and all the time, with my eyes hanging out.

—Dylan Thomas

**QUOTATION: ON READING**

A book is meant not only to be read, but to haunt you, to importune you like a lover or a parent, to stick in your teeth like a piece of gristle.

—Anatole Broyard

**QUOTATION: ON READING**

No entertainment is so cheap as reading; nor any pleasure so lasting.

—Lady Mary Wortley Montagu

**QUOTATION: ON READING**

No book is really worth reading at the age of ten which is not equally (and often far more) worth reading at the age of fifty and beyond.

—C. S. Lewis

**QUOTATION: ON WRITING**

I've always disliked words like *inspiration*. Writing is probably like a scientist thinking about some scientific problem, or an engineer about an engineering problem.

—Doris Lessing

**QUOTATION: ON READING**

There is no frigate like a book
To take us lands away

—Emily Dickinson

**QUOTATION: ON WRITING**

We have read your manuscript with boundless delight. If we were to publish your paper, it would be impossible for us to publish any work of lower standard. And as it is unthinkable that in the next thousand years we shall see its equal, we are, to our regret, compelled to return your divine composition, and to beg you a thousand times to overlook our short sight and timidity.

—Rejection slip from a Chinese economic journal, quoted in the *Financial Times*

**QUOTATION: ON READING AND WRITING**

Eventually, the books that seemed so distant, those Great Books, would work their way into my curiosity, would influence the way I framed problems and the way I wrote.

—Mike Rose

**QUOTATION: ON READING**

It is absurd to have a hard-and-fast rule about what one should read and what one shouldn't. More than half of modern culture depends on what one shouldn't read.

—Oscar Wilde

**QUOTATION: ON READING AND WRITING**

For me, philosophically, existentially, the fundamental task of human beings should be reading the world, writing the world; reading the words, writing the words. If we did that consciously, with a critical consciousness, of course we would be active, willing, choosing subjects

Literally, this paragraph describes what happened at a concert. But there's clearly more going on. Among the inferential meanings are that (1) the band wasn't very enthusiastic about this concert; and (2) this wasn't a very pleasant experience for Jenny or, probably, others at the event. The writer doesn't say this directly, but it's clear from her choice of details.

Drawing inferences takes practice. Quick Reference 4.7 lists questions to help you read "between the lines." A discussion of each point follows the box.

---

**Quick Reference 4.7**   ■ ■ ■ ■ ■ ■

### Drawing inferences during reading

- What is the point, even if the writer doesn't state it outright?
- How might the writer's position influence his or her perspective?
- Can I detect **bias** in the material?
- What are the implications of the reading?

---

### 4e.1   The writer's position

As a reader, when you can "consider the source"—that is, find out exactly who made a statement—you can open up new perspectives. For example, you would probably read an essay for or against capital punishment differently if you knew the writer was an inmate on death row rather than a noninmate who wished to express an opinion. For example, consider the statement, "Freedom isn't the ability to do what you want but rather the ability to do what you should." If you were told this statement was made by a third-world dictator, you would interpret it differently than if you were told it was made by a leader of the American Legion (which it actually was).

Although considering the source can help you draw inferences, take care that you don't fall prey to ARGUMENT TO THE PERSON (4i). Just because someone you don't respect voices an opinion doesn't mean that the position is necessarily wrong.

### 4e.2   Bias

For inferential reading, you want to detect **bias**, also known as **prejudice**. When writing is distorted by hatred or distrust of individuals, groups of people, or ideas, you as a critical reader want to suspect the accuracy and fairness of the material. Bias can be worded in positive language, but critical readers aren't deceived by such tactics. Similarly, writers can merely imply their bias rather than state it outright. For example, suppose you read, "Poor people like living in crowded conditions because they're used to such surroundings" or "Women are so wonderfully nurturing that they can't succeed in business." As a critical reader, you will immediately detect the bias. Therefore, always question material that rests on a weak foundation of discrimination or narrow-mindedness.

## 4e.3 What are implications of the reading?

An **implication** takes the form, "If this is true (or if this happens), then that might also be true (or that might be the consequence.)" One way to consider implications, especially for readings that contain a proposal, is to ask, "Who might benefit from an action, and who might lose?" For example, consider the following short argument.

> Because parking downtown is so limited, we should require anyone putting up a new building to construct a parking lot or contribute to parking garages.

It doesn't take much to infer who might benefit: people driving downtown who are looking for places to park. With a little more thought, you can see how store owners could benefit if shoppers have an easier time finding parking. Who might lose? Well, having to provide parking will add to building costs, and these may be passed to customers. More room for parking means less room for building, so the downtown could sprawl into neighborhoods. More parking can encourage more driving, which contributes to congestion and pollution.

Now, benefits may outweigh losses—or the other way around. The point is that if you think about the implications of ideas in a reading, you can generate some inferences.

**EXERCISE 4-6** Consider the implications of the following short argument, focusing on who might gain and lose from the following proposal: "In an effort to enhance its prestige, DaVinci College will reduce its enrollment from 10,000 students to 7,000 over the next four years. It will accomplish this reduction by increasing the admissions requirements and more selectively recruiting across the country, not only in the local region."

**EXERCISE 4-7** Read the following passages, then (1) list all literal information, (2) list all implied information, and (3) list the opinions stated. Refer to sections 4c.1 and 4c.2 for help.

EXAMPLE   The study found many complaints against the lawyers were not investigated, seemingly out of a "desire to avoid difficult cases."

—Norman F. Dacey

**Literal information:** Few complaints against lawyers are investigated.

**Implied information:** The term *difficult cases* implies a cover-up: Lawyers, or others in power, hesitate to criticize lawyers for fear of being

of history. Then we could speak freely about our presence in the world.

—Paulo Freire

**ANSWERS: EXERCISE 4-6**
Answers will vary. Students should consider whether a smaller number of students will cause the college's reputation to be enhanced, what other factors go into a college's reputation, any adverse effects that may come from decreasing enrollment, and why a college's reputation is important to begin with (i.e., who stands to gain from an enhanced college reputation).

**ANSWERS: EXERCISE 4-7**
Here are some of the main points from each passage.

**A.** Literal Information: Girls outnumbered in almost half the countries of the world; the number of countries where the gap between the sexes has disappeared has risen by 20 percent since 1991; girls outnumber boys at the university in 83 of 141 countries; in Mongolia and Guyana university education in the past has not been "for everyone" [i.e., for women].

Implied Information: In the majority of countries, boys still outnumber girls by a ratio of 87/171; many countries still have significant gender inequalities at the secondary level; developed countries are more likely to educate women than poorer countries.

Opinions: "[T]he sexual balance of power is changing, slowly but surely." "It is something to celebrate." "The most obvious changes are in education." "They do so not only in the rich world, which is perhaps not surprising. . . ."

**B.** Literal information: De Palma heard Roger Schank speak on National Public Radio; Schank was an early pioneer of Artificial Intelligence who at the time was a professor at Yale; Schank insisted that most people did not need personal computers.

Implied information: We have trouble remembering a time when personal computers weren't an intimate part of our lives; the "need" for a personal computer is in part a marketing scheme perpetrated by Bill Gates and others; "information superhighway" as a phrase has not only lost all meaning but may never had had much to begin with; if Schank did not think we needed personal computers, his opinion as an expert in the field should hold sway; the marketing of personal computers has worked well, since most people own them and regularly purchase upgrades; owning a computer is akin to making a "deal with the devil" ("fiendishly clever"); De Palma is indebted to computers, whatever he thinks of them.

Opinions: We do not need computers nearly as much as marketing has convinced us we do; see "Implied Information" above for more (implied) opinions.

**TEACHING TIP**

You can help "cement" the concepts of summary and synthesis by assigning or allowing class time for a summary and synthesis activity. Ask students to make a short list of three to five songs, movies, or writings on a particular topic or theme. Then, ask them to choose their favorite from the list and summarize it in a single paragraph beginning with any appropriate variation of this topic sentence: "The song/movie/story [*give title*] develops the theme/topic _____." The second part of this activity/assignment invites your students to write a second paragraph stemming from a version of the following topic sentence: "The theme/topic of _____ has worked its way into a number of songs/movies/stories/other media." When students share and compare their paragraphs, most will probably be able to see quite clearly the differences between summaries and syntheses.

**QUOTATION: ON WRITING AND READING**

Read, read, read. Read everything—trash, classics, good and bad, and see how they do it. Just like a carpenter who works as an apprentice and studies the master. Read! You'll absorb it. Then write. If it is good, you'll find out. If it's not, throw it out the window.

—William Faulkner

**QUOTATION: ON WRITING**

The Latin roots of the word *induction* give us a clue as to how this method of arguing works: *in*

sued or for fear of a public outcry if the truth about abuses and errors were revealed.

**Opinions:** No opinions. It reports on a study.

A.  [T]he sexual balance of power in the world is changing, slowly but surely. New evidence can be found in the 2007 World Development Indicators from the World Bank. It is something to celebrate.

The most obvious changes are in education. In 2004 girls outnumbered boys at secondary schools in almost half the countries of the world (84 of 171). The number of countries in which the gap between the sexes has more or less disappeared has risen by a fifth since 1991. At university level, girls do better still, outnumbering boys in 83 of 141 countries. They do so not only in the rich world, which is perhaps not surprising, but also in countries such as Mongolia and Guyana where university education for anyone is not common.

—*The Economist,* "A Man's World?"

B.  In the misty past, before Bill Gates joined the company of the world's richest men, before the mass-marketed personal computer, before the metaphor of an information superhighway had been worn down to a cliché, I heard Roger Schank interviewed on National Public Radio. Then a computer science professor at Yale, Schank was already well known in artificial intelligence circles. Because those circles did not include me, a new programmer at Sperry Univac, I hadn't heard of him. Though I've forgotten the details of the conversation, I have never forgotten Schank's insistence that most people do not need to own computers.

That view, of course, has not prevailed. Either we own a personal computer and fret about upgrades, or we are scheming to own one and fret about the technical marvel yet to come that will render our purchase obsolete. Well, there are worse ways to spend money, I suppose. For all I know, even Schank owns a personal computer. They're fiendishly clever machines, after all, and they've helped keep the wolf from my door for a long time.

—Paul De Palma, "http://www.when_is_enough_enough?.com"

## 4f  How do I synthesize?

To **synthesize** is to put things together. When analysis and inference generate specific ideas, try to put them together with things you know from your experience or previous learning or from other readings. For example, suppose you read an opinion that reminds you of a similar opinion by an expert you respect. Making that connection is an act of critical thinking. It takes you beyond the reading itself. Or suppose that someone provides evidence for a claim, but that some further reading shows you that their facts are incomplete or even inaccurate. This synthesis allows you to read the first source more critically.

Synthesis also happens between a reading and your own experience. Take the following example.

> Probably no time in life is as liberating or stimulating as the college years. Freed from the drudgery of a career and the obligations of family life, college students have the luxury to explore new ideas and pursue new paths of knowledge. College is a joyful time of endless possibility.

If you're a single parent taking classes at night or someone who is working a couple of jobs and worrying about paying back loans, your perspective probably differs from the author's. Synthesizing the reading and your experience would result in a critical evaluation. We discuss synthesis with additional examples in section 7f.4.

## 4g How do I evaluate?

When you read to evaluate, you're judging the writer's work. **Evaluative reading** comes after you've summarized, analyzed, and synthesized the material (see Quick Reference 4.1). Reading "between the lines" is usually concerned with recognizing tone, detecting prejudice, differentiating fact from opinion, and determining the writer's position. Reading to evaluate "beyond the lines" requires an overall assessment of the soundness of the writer's reasoning, evidence, or observations, and the fairness and perceptiveness the writer shows, from accuracy of word choice and tone to the writer's respect for the reader.

Evaluating is the step where you make judgments. Ultimately, should we trust the author or not? Should we accept his or her conclusions and recommendations? An important additional strategy for answering questions like these is assessing reasoning processes.

## 4h How do I assess reasoning processes critically?

To think, read, and write critically, you need to distinguish *sound reasoning* from *faulty reasoning*. **Induction** and **deduction** are two basic reasoning processes, natural thought patterns people use every day to help them think through ideas and make decisions.

### 4h.1 Inductive reasoning

Inductive reasoning moves from particular facts or instances to general principles. Suppose you go to the Registry of Motor Vehicles to renew your driver's license and have to stand in line for two hours. A few months later you return to get new license plates, and once again you have to stand in line for two hours. You mention your annoyance to a couple of friends who say they had exactly the same experience. You conclude that the registry is inefficient and

= intro + *ducere* = to lead—literally, "to lead into." After noting a series of similar phenomena, we draw some conclusion, we make some generalization about all phenomena of that kind. In other words, after observing a number of similar examples of something, we are "led into" a conclusion about all examples of that kind.

—Edward P. J. Corbett

**TEACHING TIP**
Using analogy is a way to think inductively. An analogy compares two dissimilar objects, ideas, or experiences by focusing on what they have in common. For example, some people make an analogy between the role of a teacher and that of a coach. Like coaches, teachers train people in fundamentals through repetition and practice, recommend changes in technique, and try to inspire excellence. However, despite points of similarity, two dissimilar items remain dissimilar.

First, coaches work primarily with the body rather than the mind, developing physical rather than mental skills. Second, team coaches praise the team player, whereas good teachers reward independence and originality. Thus, the analogy between teachers and coaches breaks down at some point.

In the absence of other evidence, an analogy will not prove anything. Nevertheless, although an analogy can always be shown as flawed under close scrutiny, it can still help explain a point and thus help persuade an audience.

**QUOTATION: ON WRITING**
I think the writer ought to help the reader as much as he can without damaging what he wants to say; and I don't think it ever hurts the writer to sort of stand back now and then and look at his stuff as if he were reading it instead of writing it.

—James Jones

**QUOTATION: ON READING**

There is a great deal of difference between an eager man who wants to read a book and a tired man who wants a book to read.

—G. K. Chesterton

**QUOTATION: ON THINKING**

Everything that can be thought at all can be thought clearly.

—John Locke

**QUOTATION: ON READING**

Reading is to the mind what exercise is to the body.

—Joseph Addison and Richard Steele

**TEACHING TIP**

You may want to ask students to bring to class a published review (from a legitimate online source or a popular magazine or newspaper) that critiques a song album, a TV program, an art exhibition, or a book that is well known in popular culture. Instruct students to choose a review of something they have read, viewed, or listened to carefully themselves. Take time in class (or online) for students to share (post) their findings, noting how effectively the reviewer has summarized the material, placed it within a larger context (synthesized it), responded to it in light of the reviewer's prior knowledge and experience, and cited or documented any relevant comparisons or viewpoints from other reviewers.

**TEACHING TIP**

Ask students to find online a contemporary study of political propaganda and compare its findings to those cited in the following report on political propaganda in 1992:

In a 1992 article for *The New York Times*, psychologist Daniel Goleman cited research about the effect of political propaganda on the human psyche. Goleman pointed out that, near election time, candidates often use propaganda techniques to sway voters, sometimes with tactics that work, sometimes with techniques that backfire. One study cited by Goleman showed that attack

indifferent to the needs of its patrons. You've arrived at this conclusion by means of induction. Quick Reference 4.8 shows the features of inductive reasoning.

---

### Quick Reference 4.8

■ ■ ■ ■ ■ ■ ■

#### Inductive reasoning

- **Inductive reasoning moves from the specific to the general.** It begins with specific evidence—facts, observations, or experiences—and moves to a general conclusion.

- **Inductive conclusions are considered reliable or unreliable, not true or false.** Because inductive thinking is based on a sampling of facts, an inductive conclusion indicates probability—the degree to which the conclusion is likely to be true—not certainty.

- **An inductive conclusion is held to be reliable or unreliable in relation to the quantity and quality of the evidence** (4g) on which it's based.

- **Induction leads to new "truths."** It can support statements about the unknown based on what's known.

---

## 4h.2 Deductive reasoning

**Deductive reasoning** is the process of reasoning from general claims to a specific conclusion. Suppose you know that students who don't study for Professor Sanchez's history tests tend to do poorly. If your friend tells you that she didn't study, you can make a reasonable conclusion about her grade. Your reasoning might go something like this:

| | |
|---|---|
| PREMISE 1 | Students who don't study do poorly on Professor Sanchez's exams. |
| PREMISE 2 | My friend didn't study. |
| CONCLUSION | Therefore, my friend probably did poorly on the exam. |

Deductive arguments have three parts: two **premises** and a conclusion. This three-part structure is known as a **syllogism**. The first and second premises of a deductive argument may be statements of fact or assumptions. They lead to a conclusion, which is the point at which you want to think as precisely as possible because you're into the realm of *validity*.

Whether or not an argument is **valid** has to do with its form or structure. Here, the word *valid* isn't the general term people use in conversation to mean "acceptable" or "well grounded." In the context of reading and writing logical arguments, the word *valid* has a very specific meaning. A deductive argument is *valid* when the conclusion logically follows from the premises; a deductive argument is *invalid* when the conclusion doesn't logically follow from the premises. For example:

**VALID DEDUCTIVE ARGUMENT**

PREMISE 1    When it snows, the streets get wet. [fact]

PREMISE 2    It is snowing. [fact]

CONCLUSION    Therefore, the streets are getting wet.

**INVALID DEDUCTIVE ARGUMENT**

PREMISE 1    When it snows, the streets get wet. [fact]

PREMISE 2    The streets are getting wet. [fact]

CONCLUSION    Therefore, it is snowing.

Here's the problem with the invalid deductive argument: It has acceptable premises because they are facts. However, the argument's conclusion is wrong because it ignores other reasons why the streets might be wet. For example, the street could be wet from rain, from street-cleaning trucks that spray water, or from people washing their cars. Therefore, because the conclusion doesn't follow logically from the premises, the argument is invalid.

Another problem in a deductive argument can occur when the premises are implied but not stated—called **unstated assumptions**. An argument can be logically valid even though it is based on wrong assumptions. To show that such an argument is invalid, you need to attack the assumptions, not the conclusion, as wrong. For example, suppose a corporation argues that it can't install pollution-control devices because the cost would cut deeply into its profits. This argument rests on the unstated assumption that a corporation should never do something that would lower its profits. That assumption is wrong, and so is the argument. To show that both are wrong, you need to challenge the assumptions.

Similarly, when a person says that certain information is correct because it's written in the newspaper, that person's deductive reasoning is flawed. The unstated assumption is that everything in a newspaper is correct—which isn't true. Whenever there's an unstated assumption, you need to state it outright and then check that it's true. Quick Reference 4.9 summarizes deductive reasoning.

## Quick Reference 4.9  ■ ■ ■ ■ ■ ■ ■

### Deductive reasoning

- **Deductive reasoning moves from the general to the specific.** The three-part structure that makes up a deductive argument, or SYLLOGISM, includes two premises and a conclusion drawn from them.

continued >>

ads could discourage voters from voting altogether. In a sidebar to this article, Dr. Anthony Pratkanis, a University of California psychologist studying persuasion, outlined several propagandistic distortions, including the powerful "Appeal to Fear." Goleman and others found that voters who were aware of these techniques were more likely to think for themselves and less likely to believe distorted appeals. ("Voters Assailed by Unfair Persuasion" *The New York Times*, Oct. 27, 1992, late ed. sec. C:1).

What differences in findings, if any, are there in the 1992 article and the contemporary study? Applying the five criteria (questions) for "evaluating evidence" cited in 4g.1, conduct a critical evaluation of the new sociological/psychological study. Alternatively, evaluate the "evidence" cited in a recent campaign ad.

**QUOTATION: ON THINKING**
Man can believe the impossible but can never believe the improbable.
—Oscar Wilde

**BACKGROUND**
The *Journal of Consumer Research* reported in a 1998 study that individuals purchasing compact disc players were "influenced more by magazine ads that presented relevant facts and allowed readers to draw their own conclusions than by ads that presented the same facts and then stated the conclusions." Do you think consumers today are similarly motivated?

**QUOTATION: ON TEACHING**
We have this kind of understanding when students are taught to interpret texts, including the texts other students create, or the texts that hang in the air as talk, or those that emerge within us from our experiences and feelings. This is the kind of work that encourages critical thinking.
—Anthony Petrosky

**ANSWERS: EXERCISE 4-8**

**1.** *Invalid.* The shirt's being expensive does not mean that it shares other characteristics of faddish clothing.

**2.** *Valid.* The conclusion follows logically from the premises.

**3.** *Invalid.* Some outstanding literary works have not received a Pulitzer Prize.

**4.** *Invalid.* All states do send representatives, but that does not mean that all representatives come from a state.

**5.** *Invalid.* The first premise does not say that patience alone is sufficient to find a good job.

---

**Quick Reference 4.9**        (continued)

- **A deductive argument is valid if the conclusion logically follows from the premises.**

- **A deductive conclusion may be judged true or false.** If both premises are true, the conclusion is true. If the argument contains an assumption, the writer must prove the truth of the assumption to establish the truth of the argument.

- **Deductive reasoning applies what the writer already knows.** Though it doesn't yield new information, it builds stronger arguments than inductive reasoning because it offers the certainty that a conclusion is either true or false.

---

**EXERCISE 4-8**    Working individually or with a peer-response group, determine whether each conclusion here is valid or invalid. Be ready to explain your answers. For help, consult section 4h.

1. Faddish clothes are expensive.
   This shirt is expensive.
   This shirt must be part of a fad.

2. When a storm is threatening, small-craft warnings are issued.
   A storm is threatening.
   Small-craft warnings will be issued.

3. The Pulitzer Prize is awarded to outstanding literary works.
   *The Great Gatsby* never won a Pulitzer Prize.
   *The Great Gatsby* isn't an outstanding literary work.

4. All states send representatives to the United States Congress.
   Puerto Rico sends a representative to the United States Congress.
   Puerto Rico is a state.

5. Finding a good job requires patience.
   Sherrill is patient.
   Sherrill will find a good job.

**4i**    How can I recognize and avoid logical fallacies?

**Logical fallacies** are flaws in reasoning that lead to illogical statements. Though logical fallacies tend to occur when ideas are argued, they can be found in all types of writing. Interestingly, most logical fallacies masquerade as reasonable statements, but in fact, they're attempts to manipulate readers by appealing to their emotions instead of their intellects, their hearts rather than their heads. The name for each logical fallacy indicates the way that thinking has gone wrong.

## HASTY GENERALIZATION

A **hasty generalization** draws conclusions from inadequate evidence. Suppose someone says, "My hometown is the best place in the state to live," and gives only two examples to support the opinion. That's not enough. And others might not feel the same way, perhaps for many reasons. Therefore, the person who makes such a statement is indulging in a hasty generalization.

**Stereotyping** is another kind of hasty generalization. It happens, for example, when someone says, "Everyone from country X is dishonest." Making such a sweeping claim about all members of a particular ethnic, religious, racial, or political group is an example of stereotyping. Other kinds of stereotyping include **sexism**, and **agism**.

## FALSE ANALOGY

A **false analogy** draws a comparison in which the differences outweigh the similarities or the similarities are irrelevant. For example, "Old Joe Smith would never make a good president because an old dog can't learn new tricks" is a false analogy. Joe Smith isn't a dog. Also, learning the role of a president bears no comparison to a dog's learning tricks. Homespun analogies like this appear to have an air of wisdom about them, but they tend to fall apart when examined closely.

## BEGGING THE QUESTION

**Begging the question**, also called *circular reasoning,* tries to offer proof by simply using another version of the argument itself. For example, the statement "Wrestling is a dangerous sport because it is unsafe" begs the question. Because *unsafe* is a synonym for *dangerous,* the statement goes around in a circle, getting nowhere. Here's another example of circular reasoning but with a different twist: "Wrestling is a dangerous sport because wrestlers get injured." Here, the support given in the second part of the statement, "wrestlers get injured," is the argument made in the first part of the statement. Obviously, wrestling can be safe when undertaken with proper training and practice.

## IRRELEVANT ARGUMENT

An **irrelevant argument** reaches a conclusion that doesn't follow from the premises. Irrelevant argument is also called *non sequitur* (Latin for "it does not follow"). An argument is irrelevant when a conclusion doesn't follow from the premises. Here's an example: "Jane Jones is a forceful speaker, so she'll make a good mayor." You'd be on target if you asked "What does speaking ability have to do with being a good mayor?"

**QUOTATION: ON THINKING**
Most people would sooner die than think; in fact, they do so.
—Bertrand Russell

**QUOTATION: ON TEACHING**
Our first task, it seems to me, is to offer our students assisted invitations to discover the naming and articulating powers of language, to see how language provides the means of making meaning.
—Ann E. Berthoff

**QUOTATION: ON THINKING**
Experimental studies have shown that juries believe more readily in the closing arguments of prosecuting attorneys when they begin by arguing against their own position.
—Daniel Goleman

**QUOTATION: ON WRITING**
Don't expect readers to believe you merely because you say something is the cause: proof is the writer's job.
—Sheena Gillespie

**QUOTATION: ON READING**
Reading is a basic tool in the living of a good life.
—Mortimer J. Adler

**QUOTATION: ON THINKING**
Logic is in the eye of the logician.
—Gloria Steinem

**QUOTATION: ON WRITING**
Comment is free but facts are sacred.
—Charles P. Scott

**OTHER EXAMPLES OF SYLLOGISMS**

**Invalid**
Some round things are bubbles.
Some human heads are round things.
Therefore, some human heads are bubbles.

**Valid**

All mammals are animals.
All whales are mammals.
Therefore, all whales are animals.

**QUOTATION: ON WRITING**

A fact in itself is nothing. It is valuable only for the idea attached to it, or for the proof which it furnishes.

—Claude Bernard

**TEACHING TIP**

You may want to ask students to consider a controversial issue such as whether violent juvenile offenders are promising candidates for rehabilitation. You might choose to engage the class in a discussion on the topic. As you do, compile lists of the different factors to consider. You may want to raise the following questions: What sources would students need to cite or consult to support a position (e.g., child psychologists, probation officers, rehabilitation counselors)? What factors would students weigh in their decision? (A partial list might include the following: age of the offender, degree of remorse, and severity of crime.)

**QUOTATION: ON THINKING**

Logic is the anatomy of thought.

—John Locke

**TEACHING TIP**

Many students enjoy finding and correcting logical fallacies in newspaper editorials and opinion columns, as well as in the work of their peers. You might distribute copies of works containing fallacies, as a spur to class discussion or for revision. A less adept class might benefit from a preliminary lesson based on a list of logical fallacies you can cull from assorted sources (newspapers, political literature, advertisements, student papers); tell the students all the passages are illogical and have them explain why, as a prelude to revision (oral or written, as time allows).

**FALSE CAUSE**

A **false cause** assumes that because two events are related in time, the first caused the second. False cause is also known as *post hoc, ergo propter hoc* (Latin for "after this, therefore because of this"). For example, if someone claims that a new weather satellite launched last week has caused the rain that's been falling ever since, that person is connecting two events that, while related in time, have no causal relationship to each other. The launching didn't cause the rain.

**SELF-CONTRADICTION**

**Self-contradiction** uses two premises that can't both be true at the same time. Here's an example: "Only when nuclear weapons have finally destroyed us will we be convinced of the need to control them." This is self-contradictory because no one would be around to be convinced if everyone has been destroyed.

**RED HERRING**

A **red herring**, also called *ignoring the question,* tries to distract attention from one issue by introducing a second that's unrelated to the first. Here's an example: "Why worry about pandas becoming extinct when we haven't solved the plight of the homeless?" You'd be on target if you asked, "What do homeless people have to do with pandas?" If the argument were to focus on proposing that the money spent to prevent the extinction of pandas should go instead to the homeless, the argument would be logical; however, the original statement is a fallacy. By using an irrelevant issue, a person hopes to distract the audience, just as putting a herring in the path of a bloodhound would distract it from the scent it's been following.

**ARGUMENT TO THE PERSON**

An **argument to the person** means attacking the person making the argument rather than the argument itself. It's also known as the *ad hominem* (Latin for "to the man") attack. When someone criticizes a person's appearance, habits, or character instead of the merits of that person's argument, the attack is a fallacy. Here's an example: "We'd take her position on child abuse seriously if she were not so nasty to her husband." You'd be on target if you were to ask, "What does nastiness to an adult, though not at all nice, have to do with child abuse?"

**GUILT BY ASSOCIATION**

**Guilt by association** means that a person's arguments, ideas, or opinions lack merit because of that person's activities, interests, or companions. Here's an example: "Jack belongs to the International Hill Climbers Association, which declared bankruptcy last month. This makes him unfit to be mayor of our city." The fact that Jack is a member of a group that declared bankruptcy has nothing to do with Jack's ability to be mayor.

## JUMPING ON THE BANDWAGON

**Jumping on the bandwagon** means something is right or permissible because "everyone does it." It's also called *ad populum* (Latin for "to the people"). This fallacy operates in a statement such as "How could snowboarding be dangerous if thousands of people have done it?" Following the crowd in this example doesn't work because research shows that many people who snowboard eventually suffer serious knee injuries.

## FALSE OR IRRELEVANT AUTHORITY

Using **false** or **irrelevant authority** means citing the opinion of someone who has no expertise in the subject at hand. This fallacy attempts to transfer prestige from one area to another. Many advertisements containing celebrity endorsements rely on this tactic—a famous athlete praising a brand of energy drink or a popular movie star lauding a wireless phone service provider.

## CARD-STACKING

**Card-stacking**, also known as *special pleading,* ignores evidence on the other side of a question. From all available facts, people choose only those facts that show the best (or worst) possible case. Many television commercials use this strategy. For example, after three slim, happy consumers praise a diet plan, the announcer adds—in a very low and speedy voice—that results vary. Indeed, even that statement is vague and uninformative.

## THE EITHER-OR FALLACY

The **either-or fallacy,** also called *false dilemma,* offers only two alternatives when more exist. Such fallacies tend to touch on emotional issues, so many people accept them until they analyze the statement. Here's an example: "Either go to college or forget about getting a job." This rigid, two-sided statement ignores the truth that many jobs don't require a college education.

## TAKING SOMETHING OUT OF CONTEXT

**Taking something out of context** deliberately distorts an idea or a fact by removing it from its previously surrounding material. For example, suppose that a newspaper movie critic writes, "The plot was predictable and boring, but the music was sparkling." The next day, an advertisement for the movie claims "critics call it 'sparkling.'" Clearly, the ad has taken the critic's words out of context (only the music was called "sparkling"), and it thereby distorts the original meaning.

## APPEAL TO IGNORANCE

**Appeal to ignorance** tries to make an incorrect argument based on something never having been shown to be false—or, the reverse, never having been shown to be true. Here's an example: "Because it hasn't been proven that eating

Your analytically minded students may be interested in additional logical fallacies:

An *alleged certainty* presents something as certain that is open to debate: "Everyone knows" and "It is obvious that" are typical phrases. This statement is flawed: "It is common knowledge that jobs in Texas pay more than jobs in Idaho"; in contrast, this statement is logical: "A recent government survey revealed that, on the average, workers in the oil fields of Texas are paid more than loggers in the timber industries of Idaho."

A *complex question* (also known as a *loaded question*) contains one or more unproven assumptions: "Are you still spending time with known criminals?" Notice what happens when you try to answer such a question. If you say yes, you are guilty. If you say no, you are still guilty, because you are admitting that you used to spend time with criminals. To correct: Split the question into its parts ("Are you still spending time with those people?" "Are those people criminals?") and deal with each separately.

*Appeal to fear* uses scare tactics instead of legitimate evidence. Such an argument implies danger: "Anyone who stages a protest against the government is a Communist, so we must outlaw all protests."

*Name-calling* attaches an unpleasant label to something or someone. Consider how a label can stop people from thinking: "Jane Jones was once an alcoholic, so she cannot possibly say anything of value about politics."

*Appeal to pity* attempts to arouse sympathy: "He embezzled $1,500 of company money, but after all, his wife recently died and his child needs surgery."

The *genetic fallacy,* a special form of hasty generalization, predicts something about a person on the basis of that person's origins: "Joe Smith is from New York City, so he knows how to deal with street crime." Often, this fallacy involves a person's religion, sex, race, or economic status.

## ANSWERS: EXERCISE 4-9
Answers will vary. Following are possible analyses.

**1.** The letter writer relies heavily on *ad hominem* argument. He attacks the mayor for being wealthy (yet provides no evidence that she is) rather than providing arguments against the proposal. He also uses hasty generalizations by claiming that "everyone knows" the mayor's motives; that "no one I know likes this plan"; and that "if you're working hard" you won't have time for the trail. He provides no evidence for any of these claims, which are also a form of jumping on the bandwagon. He makes an extreme assertion that the mayor would "turn schools into art museums or the park into a golf course," which is a form of false analogy. Finally, the tone of the letter tends to be biased. He characterizes the mayor as wanting a "place to play" and as being part of "the wine and cheese set," and he calls the plan "nonsense." His final statement is confrontational, which implies he is not someone who has examined this issue openly.

**2.** The letter writer begs the question. The claim that "Good recreation facilities are the key to the success of any community" comes without any evidence, and the assertion that building the trail will guarantee success is just that: an assertion, which is debatable. She also uses a false-cause argument. Just because the town of Springfield went into an economic decline after it failed to build a new park does not mean that the absence of the park caused the town's decline. Calling opponents "narrow-minded, selfish, and almost unpatriotic" is an *ad hominem* argument. Quoting John Paul Jones has nothing to do with the issue at hand.

**3.** The letter writer relies on hasty generalizations. He cites some cold days in the winter and summer as evidence that there is no global warming, but this evidence is not nearly comprehensive enough. He cites a false authority when he quotes his dentist, who is hardly an expert on global warming. His assertion that "you can't trust numbers" comes with no evidence; instead, he questions the integrity of "liberal scientists" and goes on to add a further unsubstantiated claim about their motives

food X doesn't cause cancer, we can assume that it does." The statement is a fallacy because the absence of opposing evidence proves nothing. Such appeals can be very persuasive because they prey on people's superstitions or lack of knowledge. Often, they're stated in the fuzzy language of DOUBLE NEGATIVES.

### AMBIGUITY AND EQUIVOCATION

**Ambiguity** and **equivocation** are statements open to more than one interpretation, thus concealing the truth. Here's an example: Suppose a person is asked, "Is she doing a good job?" and the person answers, "She's performing as expected." The answer is a fallacy because it's open to positive or negative interpretation.

**EXERCISE 4-9** Following are letters to the editor of a newspaper. Working alone or with a peer-response group, do a critical analysis of each, paying special attention to logical fallacies.

1. To the Editor:
I am writing to oppose the plan to convert the abandoned railroad tracks into a bicycle trail. Everyone knows that the only reason the mayor wants to do this is so that she and her wealthy friends can have a new place to play. No one I know likes this plan, and if they did, it would probably be because they're part of the wine and cheese set, too. The next thing you know, the mayor will be proposing that we turn the schools into art museums or the park into a golf course. If you're working hard to support a family, you don't have time for this bike trail nonsense. And if you're not working hard, I don't have time for you.

Russell Shields

2. To the Editor:
I encourage everyone to support the bicycle trail project. Good recreation facilities are the key to the success of any community. Since the bike trail will add more recreation opportunities, it will guarantee the success of our town. Remember that several years ago our neighbors over in Springfield decided not to build a new park, and look what happened to their economy, especially that city's high unemployment rate. We can't afford to let the same thing happen to us. People who oppose this plan are narrow-minded, selfish, and almost unpatriotic. As that great patriot John Paul Jones said, "I have not yet begun to fight."

Susan Thompson

3. To the Editor:
I'm tired of all this nonsense about pollution and global warming. We had plenty of cold days last winter, and as my dentist said, "If this is global warming, then I'd sure hate to see global cooling." Plus, there were lots of days this summer when I haven't had to turn on my air conditioner. I know there are statistics that some people say show the climate is changing, but you can't trust numbers, especially when they come from liberal

scientists. These people just aren't happy unless they're giving us something to feel guilty about, whether it's smoking, drinking, or driving SUVs. Maybe if they stopped wasting their time worrying about pollution, they could do something useful, like find a cure for cancer.

Marcus Johnson

# 4j How can I view images with a critical eye?

Our digital age surrounds us with images in publications, on computers, on television, on cell phones. These images shape attitudes and beliefs, often in subtle ways. Consider, for example, how our notions of beauty have been shaped through the years by countless pictures of certain shapes and sizes of people. As a result—and as we suggested in the beginning of this chapter—you need to use critical thinking to analyze images as well as words. Doing so heightens your sensitivity to how others use images and equips you to use them effectively yourself.

You can view images critically in the same way that you can read texts critically by using summary, analysis, synthesis, and evaluation (Quick Reference 4.1) and by using literal, analytic inferential, and evaluative reading (see section 4.c). For example, look at Figure 4.5 with a critical eye.

- *Summarizing* the picture, as well as viewing it literally, you can see—at a minimum—a street full of older houses with modern skyscrapers in the distance.

**Figure 4.5** Photo of houses against a city skyline

(making us feel guilty). The letter concludes with a red herring by turning attention to the unrelated issue of finding a cure for cancer.

**EXTRA EXERCISE C**

Each analogy here can be defended. Like all analogies, each can also be attacked. First, defend each one—give one or more arguments to show that the two parts of the analogy are similar and are relevant to the claim being made. Second, attack each one by pointing out how the two parts of the analogy are not similar. Finally, offer other types of evidence that would help make the claim ultimately more convincing.

**1.** Like warfare, the aim of football is to destroy.

**2.** Don't bother to take your books home over vacation. Vacation is like a "study date"—no studying ever takes place.

**3.** Taking care of a group of young children is like trying to string beads without a knot on the end of the string.

**4.** The atom is like a small solar system, with its own "sun" and its own satellites.

**Answers to Extra Exercise C**

Answers will vary. Answers here are intended to be suggestive.

**1.** *Pro:* Both involve uniformed "teams" inflicting injury on each other in pursuit of territorial gain. *Con:* Football is played according to rules, with clear time limits, for entertainment. *To revise:* Add statistics on actual injuries inflicted on high school, college, and professional football players, as well as evidence of asocial attitudes (if any) developed by players.

**2.** *Pro:* In both cases, serious intentions readily give way to the pursuit of pleasure. *Con:* A study date ostensibly has a serious purpose, whereas vacation, by definition, is unstructured free time. *To revise:* Add eyewitness accounts or reported observations about how time was spent on actual study dates, actual vacations.

**3.** *Pro:* Both are nearly impossible to control. The moment you get one "on the string," the others fall off. *Con:* Beads are much easier to control. *To revise:* Provide eyewitness accounts of baby-sitting experiences.

4. *Pro:* Both have large centers with smaller objects orbiting them. *Con:* The sun is chemically more complex than the nuclei of atoms; planets orbit the sun because of gravity rather than electrical charge. *To revise:* Other than listing additional similarities, the analogy cannot be made stronger—the properties of the solar system and of the atom are what they are.

**QUOTATION: ON THINKING**

The mind has its own logic but does not often let others in on it.

—Bernard Augustine de Voto

**QUOTATION: ON WRITING**

Eloquence is logic on fire.

—Lyman Beecher

**QUOTATION: ON WRITING**

Visuals (be they paintings, films, comic books, or television narratives) were to be studied in the same way as literary texts, as subjects of close analysis—a use of the visual that continues throughout the history of writing instruction.

—Diana George

**QUOTATION: ON IMAGES**

A photograph is usually looked at—seldom looked into.

—Ansel Adams

**BACKGROUND**

In 2002, Diana George argued that "current discussions of visual communication and writing instruction have only tapped the surface of possibilities for the role of visual communication in the composition classroom"(12). She posits the idea that the composition classroom is a place not only for critical analysis of "the visual," but as a site to produce visual arguments. Such production would answer our society's need for "multiliterate" students (13). (*College Composition and Communication* 54.1 (2002):11–39).

- *Analyzing* the picture, as well as viewing it inferentially, you can "read between the lines" to see that it's fairly rich with layers of meaning. You can think about the meanings conveyed by the condition of the houses versus those of the modern buildings or about the lives of the people who live and work in each place. You can focus on the message of the comparative sizes of the houses and skyscrapers; on the contrast between this street and those you imagine at the base of the skyscrapers; on why the photographer chose this perspective; on how different captions might give the picture different meanings. For example, consider the meanings that would be suggested by three different captions: "Progress," "Inequality," or "The Neighborhood." Many possible ideas can come to mind as you study the picture critically.

- *Synthesizing* the picture, you can connect what you've analyzed and inferred to your previous knowledge and experiences, readings, or even other images.

- *Evaluating* the picture is the last step in viewing it critically. Resist evaluating prematurely because your evaluation becomes informed by more than a noncritical personal reaction such as "I do/don't like the picture" only after you go through the earlier steps of thinking and reading critically. In evaluating a visual critically, you can speak of how the visual "struck" you at first glance; how it did or didn't gain depth of meaning as you analyzed it, looking at what could be inferred and/or imagined; and how it lent itself to synthesis within the realms of your personal experience and education.

## Quick Reference 4.10

### Some helpful questions for analyzing visual images

- What does the image show?

- What are its parts? Do the parts belong together (like a lake, trees, and mountains), or do they contrast with one another (such as a woman in a fancy dress sitting on a tractor)? What might be the significance of the relationships among the parts?

- If there is a foreground and a background in the image, what is in each and why?

- If the image is a scene, what seems to be going on? What might be its message? If the image seems to be part of a story, what might have happened before or after?

continued >>

## Quick Reference 4.10     (continued)

- How do the people, if any, seem to be related? For example, do they appear to be friends, acquaintances, or strangers?
- If the image has a variety of shadings, colorings, and focuses, what's sharply in focus, blurry, bright, in shadows, colorful, or drab? How do such differences, or lack of them, call attention to various parts of the image?
- Can you think of any connections between the image and things you've experienced or learned from school, work, or reading; visits to museums or other cultural sites; watching movies, plays, and television; or other aspects of your life?
- From your observations, what is your evaluation of the image?

**EXERCISE 4-10** Working individually or with a peer-response group, use critical thinking to consider one or both of the following photographs: Figure 4.6 and Figure 4.7 on page 134. Write either informal notes or a mini-essay, according to what your instructor requires. Use the questions in Quick Reference 4.10 to generate your summary, analysis, synthesis, and evaluation of the photograph(s).

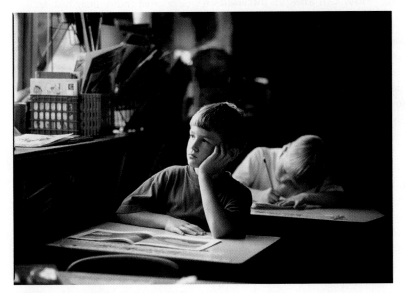

**Figure 4.6** Photo for Exercise 4-10

**QUOTATION: ON IMAGES**
I hate cameras. They are so much more sure than I am about everything.
—John Steinbeck

**QUOTATION: ON IMAGES**
All photos are accurate. None of them is the truth.
—Richard Avedon

**QUOTATION: ON IMAGES**
While there is perhaps a province in which the photograph can tell us nothing more than what we see with our own eyes, there is another in which it proves to us how little our eyes permit us to see.
—Dorothea Lange

**ANSWERS: EXERCISE 4-10**
Answers will vary, depending on which version of the assignment you require. One good technique may be to have students write informal notes on one image and a mini-essay on the other. In this way, you can be sure they understand the ways to read an image critically before they try to do so in essay form.

**QUOTATION: ON IMAGES**
In America, the photographer is not simply the person who records the past, but the one who invents it.
—Susan Sontag

## EXTRA EXERCISE D

Identify the kind of fallacy in each item, then explain why it's a fallacy. If there's no logical flaw in a statement, explain why it isn't a fallacy.

1. Joanna Hayes should write a book about the Central Intelligence Agency. She has starred in three films that show the inner workings of the agency.

2. It is ridiculous to have spent thousands of dollars to rescue those two whales trapped in the Arctic ice. Why, look at all of the people trapped in jobs that they don't like.

3. Every time my roommate has a math test, she becomes extremely nervous. Clearly, she isn't good at math.

4. Plagiarism is deceitful because it is dishonest.

5. The local political coalition to protect the environment would get my support if its leaders did not drive cars that are such gas hogs.

6. UFOs must exist because no reputable studies have proved conclusively that they don't.

7. Water fluoridation affects the brain. Citywide, students' test scores began to drop five months after fluoridation began.

8. Learning to manage a corporation is exactly like learning to ride a bicycle: Once you learn the skills, you never forget how, and you never fall.

9. Medicare is free; the government pays for it from taxes.

10. Reading good literature is the one way to appreciate culture.

### Answers to Extra Exercise D

1. *False authority.* An actor is not an authority on the CIA.

2. *Red herring.* The social issue is introduced to divert attention from the real issue—whether or not money should have been spent to rescue the whales.

**Figure 4.7** Photo for Exercise 4-10

## 4k How can images persuade?

Because they convey lots of information in a small space, and because they can generate powerful emotional responses (*pathos*), images play a strong role in persuasion. (Just think about advertising!) Sometimes persuasion comes through a single well-chosen image: a picture of a bruised child's face demonstrates the cruelty of child abuse; a picture of a grateful civilian hugging a soldier seeks to show that a military action is just and good. In their campaign ads, politicians frequently choose highly unflattering photographs of their opponents, hoping to make them look foolish, incompetent, or unpleasant.

Figure 4.8 is a photograph of a pile of rusted barrels in a beautiful natural setting. The contrast between the barrels and the snow-covered mountains in the background, the lake, and the blue sky is stark and alarming. The barrels stand between viewers and the stunning scenery; they can't be ignored. The photographer has created this juxtaposition to persuade you—but to what purpose? Perhaps this photo makes an argument against pollution. Perhaps it's a statement against industrial development. Perhaps it emphasizes that people can act carelessly. While images can be powerful, they're often more ambiguous than words; images can't state what they mean, although they can move viewers in certain fairly predictable directions. In Figure 4.8, you're aware that the photographer intends to disturb you.

**Figure 4.8** Photo of barrels in a natural setting

Frequently, people use a series of images to persuade. Some magazines use photo essays—two or more pictures meant to be viewed in a specific order to achieve a desired effect. An editorial cartoon might include two or more panels to make its point. More often than not, photo essays and editorials include captions or other words along with the images themselves.

## 4l How can I analyze words combined with images?

Many texts—from Web pages to advertisements, posters, brochures, and so on—are **multimodal** in that they combine words and images. (See section 46a for a further discussion of multimodal texts.) These texts can take advantage of *logos* and *ethos,* in addition to the *pathos* (5g) readily created by pictures alone. Critically analyzing multimodal texts means considering the images (Quick Reference 4.10) and the words separately, and then analyzing how the two elements combine to create a single effect.

Ask yourself, "What is the relationship between the words and the image(s)?" and "Why did the writer choose this particular image for these particular words?"

- Sometimes words and images reinforce one another. A poster with several sentences about poverty, for example, may have a picture of an obviously malnourished person.

- Other times, words and images contrast with one another for effect. Think of a picture of a belching smokestack accompanied by a caption that says, "Everyone deserves fresh air."

3. *Irrelevant argument,* or *non sequitur.* A person can be nervous about something and still be good at it.

4. *Begging the question,* or *circular argument.* "Dishonest" is merely a slightly different term for "deceitful."

5. *Argument to the person,* or *ad hominem.* These people are being attacked for materialism, but they are perhaps serious environmentalists whose cars are irrelevant to their environmental stance.

6. *Appeal to ignorance.* Just because no evidence exists for one side of the argument does not mean that the other side of the argument is valid.

7. *False cause,* or *post hoc, ergo propter hoc.* The sequence of events does not prove any connection between them.

8. *False analogy.* Analogies are dangerous in argument because they equate things that are not the same. Riding a bicycle is much different from learning to run a company, and although the skills for riding a bicycle remain the same, those of running a company may change with the economy and other pressures so that one could "fall" if he or she did not adapt those skills.

9. *Self-contradiction.* Medicare cannot be free if it is paid for.

10. *Either-or fallacy.* Reading good literature is not the only way to appreciate culture.

- Occasionally, a text might contain images simply to add visual interest. A little decoration is sometimes fine, but always be wary of images that seem simply to be thrown in for the sake of including an image. If there isn't a good reason for a particular combination of words and images, chances are that the document or message is weak.

*Document design* is the name given to the overall arrangement of words and visuals in a text. Chapter 45 explains several principles of document design.

**EXERCISE 4-11**    Working individually or with a peer-response group, use critical thinking to analyze either or both of the visual arguments that follow. Write either informal notes or a mini-essay, according to what your instructor requires.

**Figure 4.9**  Photo for Exercise 4-11

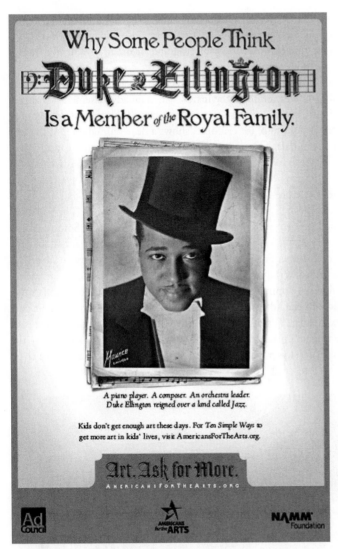

**Figure 4.10** Photo for Exercise 4-11

# 4m What can images add to my writing?

Occasionally, you might be tempted to add images to your writing because you want to add visual interest. That is a laudable goal, as long as the images support or enhance the message your writing is trying to deliver. However, be wary of throwing in one or more images merely for the sake of including an image. Your readers will rightly assume your images are communicating a message related to the text, and if none emerges, your entire document loses credibility. The best rule for inserting a photograph or other type of illustration into an essay is "When in doubt, leave it out."

There are four basic relationships between an image and a text. The image can simply illustrate or reinforce the text, as when an advertisement for apples contains a picture of an apple. The image can extend the text, as when a text about dangers of pollution, for example, shows a dead animal, even if the text doesn't refer to animals. The image can contrast with the text, creating irony. For example, suppose you see a picture of starving children, and the caption says, "What a great time to be alive!" Finally, the image can simply decorate the text, bearing none of the previous four relationships to the words but simply existing to draw attention.

Of course, some types of writing almost require images. Some posters, advertisements and Web sites, for example, would have far less impact if they contained words alone. For example, Figure 4.11 is a public service advertisement by the World Wildlife Fund, an organization dedicated to conservation and sustainable development. You'll notice that the image not only calls stunning attention to the ad, it reinforces the message in the bottom right corner. The text reads, "A single tin of paint can pollute millions of litres of water." The impact of improperly disposed waste is clearly illustrated by the striking image of a skyscraper-sized paint can as the mouth of an urban river.

**Figure 4.11** An advertisement from the World Wildlife Fund

However, sometimes the use of words alone as stylized design elements can emphasize the message the writer is trying to convey. For example, Figure 4.12 is a poster that simply includes some words in various colors and sizes. The result is a powerful visual message about climate change.

As you think about whether to include images in your papers, consult Chapter 45, which discusses DOCUMENT DESIGN, the overall, well-planned arrangement of words and visuals in a text. Also, you may want to consult Chapter 47, which gives advice about MULTIMODAL TEXTS—compositions that extensively combine words, images, and perhaps even more.

> **Ice**
> Glacier  Permafrost
> Ocean Lake River Aquifer
> Harvest  Spring Fall Winter Plenty
> $CO_2$  $H_2SO_4$  CO  $CH_4$ $N_2O$
> Industrial Coal "Bigger is Better" Hummer
> ~~Conservation  Kyoto  Future Children~~
> Ross Ice Shelf, Polar Cap, Tibetan Glacier
> Drought Hunger War
> **Despair**

**Figure 4.12** A poster about global warming

For more help with your writing, grammar, and research, go to **www.mycomplab.com**

# 5

# Writing Arguments

## 5a What is a written argument?

When you write an **argument**, you attempt to convince a reader to agree with you on a topic open to debate. You support your position, proposal, or interpretation with EVIDENCE, reasons, and examples. Some people use the terms *argumentative writing* and *persuasive writing* interchangeably. When people distinguish between them, *persuasive writing* is the broader term. It includes advertisements, letters to editors, and emotional speeches, as well as the kind of formal written arguments expected in college courses and other formal situations.

A written argument consists of two main elements:

- The **claim** states the issue and then takes a position on a debatable topic (the position can be written as a THESIS STATEMENT).
- Facts and logical reasoning provide **support** for the claim (the support needs to be in the form of evidence, reasons, and examples).

In daily life, you might think of an argument as a personal conflict or disagreement, begun in anger and involving emotional confrontations. Many radio programs, Web sites, and BLOGS reinforce this impression by featuring people who seem more interested in pushing their own agendas than in trying to persuade reasonably. For academic writing, as well as business and public writing, however, arguments are ways of demonstrating CRITICAL THINKING, calmly and respectfully. On difficult issues, your goal is to persuade an audience to consider your ideas with an open mind, which means that your audience's viewpoints and values need to influence your decisions about content, organization, and style. The passion that underlies a writer's position comes not from angry words but from the force of a balanced, well-developed, clearly written presentation.

In this chapter, you'll learn how to develop an effective claim, or thesis, how to generate support, and how to organize your argument using two strategies: the classical pattern and the Rogerian pattern. In addition, you'll find information about how to analyze and refute opposing arguments.

# 5b What are common types of arguments?

Many people believe that all writing contains an element of argument. In this view, even seemingly informative pieces like summaries, reports, and analyses attempt to convince readers that the author has done a skillful job and that the result is worth their time and attention. Even if we just concentrate on those writings in which writers are explicitly trying to persuade readers, there are several different types of arguments.

**Definition arguments** persuade readers to interpret a particular term in a particular way. You might think it strange that definitions are a matter for argument; after all, doesn't the dictionary solve all those questions? But consider how people contest terms like "patriot," "sexual harassment," "success," or even "happiness." What some people might label a work of art, others might term pornography. Is assisted suicide "murder" or "a medical procedure"? What are the characteristics a film must have to be called a romantic comedy?

**Evaluation arguments** persuade readers that something is good or bad, worthwhile or a waste of time, better or worse than other things like it, and so on. Common examples are movie, music, or television reviews, but every time we judge a politician or new model of car, we're also evaluating. Evaluation arguments have two elements. They argue that a particular set of criteria are important for measuring a particular class of things (for example, "mysteries must keep the audience guessing until the end"), and they argue that the thing being evaluated meets or doesn't meet those criteria ("because you could figure out very early who was the thief, it was a bad film").

**Cause-and-effect arguments** take one of two different forms. One is to argue that an existing situation results from a particular cause or set of causes. For example, you might take the situation of homelessness and argue that certain causes are most responsible (such as mental illness or minimum wages that are too low). Another is to argue that a cause will result in a certain effect. For example, you might argue that if we built more nuclear power plants, we would reduce global warming. You can see how cause-and-effect arguments are important in making policy decisions.

**Proposal arguments** convince readers that a particular solution to a problem or a particular way of addressing a need is best. Such arguments need to do two things. First, they must prove the existence of a need or problem that is important enough to require attention. Second, they must offer a solution and demonstrate how it will work and will be more feasible and effective than other possibilities. Suppose you want to convince college administrators to build more student parking. You'd be writing a proposal argument.

"freedom," "duty," "intelligence," "success." The discussion that will follow will no doubt give you a clear basis on which to discuss the importance of definition arguments!

**BACKGROUND**

In "Moments of Argument: Agonistic Inquiry and Confrontational Cooperation" (*College Composition and Communication* 48.1 (1997): 61–85), Dennis A. Lynch, Diana George, and Marilyn M. Cooper argue that we need to stimulate students to debate, challenge, and oppose in writing arguments. The authors explain that the approach of cooperation and collaboration in finding common ground does not prepare students for a "bureaucratic world that resists change."

**BACKGROUND**

Chapter 1 of this handbook lists five aspects of writing situations that affect the decisions that the writer makes. They are (1) the topic, (2) the purpose, (3) the audience that will read or hear the written work, (4) the role and the way in which you want the audience to perceive you, and (5) the special requirements that influence every writing situation, such as deadlines and length. For explanations of each aspect, see Quick Reference 1.1 in Chapter 1 for more information.

**QUOTATION: ON WRITING**

A fanatic is one who can't change his mind and won't change the subject.
—Sir Winston Churchill

**BACKGROUND**

In "Tapping the Living Database: A Practical Activity for Writing Classes" (*RhetNet: A CyberJournal for Rhetoric and Writing*, October 1994 <http://wac.colostate.edu/rhetnet/mday_livingdb.html>), Michael Day reminds teachers of composition that the Internet now permits students to access what Howard Rheingold calls a "living database" of people grouped into virtual communities with similar interests. By first monitoring discussion groups on the network, then analyzing the audience and discourse conventions used there, and then posting messages to these groups, students can gain experience writing for real audiences spanning the globe. At the same time, they can gain the type of information for research projects that only human respondents can provide. For other resources from Michael Day, see his Web site <http://www3.niu.edu/~tb0mxd1/>.

**EXTRA EXERCISE A**

Which of the following topics are concerned with fact, and which state a position open to debate?

1. The term *journalism* refers to the business of publishing a regularly recurring text.

2. Television news programs are more influential than they should be.

3. Journalists in the United States operate under the protection of the First Amendment to the Constitution.

4. Most reporters are biased in their descriptions of political figures.

5. The government should not let journalists have access to information dealing with national security.

6. Journalism involves both reporting the news and forming public opinion.

7. Reporters should verify a controversial story with two sources before running it.

8. Weekly newspapers are becoming increasingly popular in large cities.

9. Cartoons are one of the most entertaining features of newspapers.

10. Television commentators should not give their own opinions about political and social matters.

**Answers to Extra Exercise A**

1. fact
2. opinion
3. fact
4. opinion
5. opinion
6. fact
7. opinion

## 5c How do I choose a topic for an argument?

When you choose a topic for written argument, be sure that it's open to debate. Don't confuse matters of information (facts) with matters of debate. An essay becomes an argument when it makes a claim—that is, *takes a position*—about a debatable topic. An effective way to develop a position is to ask two (or more) opposing questions about a topic.

| | |
|---|---|
| **FACT** | Students at Calhoon College must study a foreign language. |
| **DEBATABLE** | Should Calhoon College require students to study a foreign language? |
| **ONE SIDE** | Calhoon College should not require students to study a foreign language. |
| **OTHER SIDE** | Calhoon College should require students to study a foreign language. |

Though you need to select one side of a debatable question to defend in your essay, always keep the other side (or sides) in mind. Devoting some space to state and counter opposing viewpoints shows readers that you're well informed and fair-minded. This effect is even stronger if you always maintain a respectful tone by avoiding insults, abstaining from exaggerations, and resisting sarcasm. If you neglect to mention opposing views, your readers could justifiably assume you're not well informed, fair-minded, or disciplined as a thinker.

Instructors sometimes assign students a topic and even the position to take. In such cases, you need to fulfill the assignment skillfully even if you disagree with the point of view. Indeed, experienced debate teams practice arguing all sides of an issue. Being assigned topics or positions is common beyond college, especially in work settings. Perhaps a manager asks you to develop a persuasive marketing campaign or to negotiate a price break from a supplier. Perhaps you'll be told to convince other workers that a new process will save them time and effort.

If you choose your own topic and position, select one that has sufficient substance for college writing. Readers expect you to take an intelligent, defensible position and to support it reasonably and convincingly. For example, "We should prevent censorship in public libraries" is worthy of a college-level essay; "People should wear yellow baseball caps" is not.

Even if you think that all sides of a debatable topic have merit, you need to choose one of them anyway. Don't become paralyzed from indecision. You're not making a lifetime commitment. Concentrate on the merits of one position, and argue that position as effectively as possible, reserving some space to counter objections. Of course, the more thoroughly you think through all sides of the topic, the broader the perspective you'll bring to your writing, and the more likely it is that your writing will be effective. Finally, however, take a position.

## 5d How do I develop a claim and a thesis statement for my argument?

A CLAIM is a statement that expresses a point of view on a debatable topic. It can be supported by evidence, reasons, and examples (including facts, statistics, names, experiences, and expert testimony). The exact wording of the claim rarely finds its way into the essay, but the claim serves as a focus for your thinking. Later, it serves as the basis for developing your THESIS STATEMENT.

| | |
|---|---|
| TOPIC | Wild animals as domestic pets |
| CLAIM | People should not be allowed to own wild animals. |
| CLAIM | People should be allowed to own wild animals. |

To stimulate your thinking about the topic and decide the claim you'll argue, work with the PLANNING techniques discussed in Chapter 2. Another well-favored strategy is to create a two-column list, labeling one column *Pro* or *For,* the other *Con* or *Against.* If there are more than two opposing sides, label the columns accordingly. The columned list displays the quantity and quality of your material so that you can decide whether you're ready to start DRAFTING.

Alex Garcia, the student who wrote the argument essay that appears in section 5n, chose his own topic for a written argument in a first-year college writing class. Alex was a biology major who was fascinated about genetic engineering, especially of food. While exploring this topic, he became interested in the broader issue of organic food and whether it was really better. As a consumer himself, he had a direct stake in this matter. When he began reading articles he found through library research, he thought they would all come out clearly in favor of organic foods. When he found that not all of them did, he knew that the controversy would make a good topic for his argument. Here's how Alex progressed from topic to claim to thesis statement.

| | |
|---|---|
| TOPIC | Whether organic foods are better than regular ones |
| MY POSITION | I think people should buy organic foods when they can. |
| THESIS STATEMENT (FIRST DRAFT) | It is good for people to buy organic foods. [This is a preliminary thesis statement. It clearly states the writer's position, but the word *good* is vague.] |

8. fact
9. opinion
10. opinion

an author of influential books on rhetorical theory.

### ANSWERS: EXERCISE 5-1

Claims and thesis statements will vary.

### EXTRA EXERCISE C

Rewrite the following paragraph, improving its persuasiveness by defining key terms that may be vague to the reader.

> Some Americans react strongly to actions that show disrespect for our flag. They revere it as a symbol of the values for which the United States is known around the world. They are quick to rise up against those who would use their freedom to desecrate Old Glory, calling them traitors to the Constitution and all it upholds: our rights and our democratic form of government. Calling for a Constitutional amendment, they even want to restrict our freedoms by making it illegal to misuse the flag. Wouldn't such an amendment show disrespect for the freedom the flag represents?

### Answer to Extra Exercise C

Answers will vary. Here is one possible answer.

> Some Americans react strongly to acts that they construe as insulting to our flag. Television news footage showing the flag being burned or torn apart makes them violently angry because they revere our flag as a symbol of the freedom and liberty for which this country is known around the world. They are quick to rise up against fellow citizens who use their freedom to desecrate Old Glory, calling them traitors to the Constitution and its guarantees of legislative representation and civil rights, such as the right of free speech. Calling for a constitutional amendment, they even want to restrict citizens' freedoms by making it illegal to misuse the flag. But what constitutes misuse: Wearing it? Letting it fly outside on a rainy day? Displaying it on a banquet table? A more important question is, Wouldn't such an amendment show disrespect for the freedom the flag represents?

| | |
|---|---|
| **THESIS STATEMENT (SECOND DRAFT)** | In order to achieve health benefits and to improve the quality of the environment, organic foods should be purchased by consumers. [This revised thesis statement is better because it states not only the writer's claim but also a reason for the claim. However, it suffers from a lack of conciseness and from the unnecessary passive construction "should be purchased."] |
| **THESIS STATEMENT (FINAL DRAFT)** | Research shows that the health and environmental benefits of organic foods outweigh their extra costs. [This final version works well because it states the writer's claim clearly and concisely, with verbs all in the active voice. The writer now has a thesis statement suitable for the time and length given in his assignment. Also, it meets the requirements for a thesis statement given in Quick Reference 2.3.] |

**EXERCISE 5-1**    Working individually or with a peer-response group, develop a claim and a thesis statement for each of the topics listed at the end of the exercise. You may choose any defensible position. For help, consult sections 5a through 5c.

EXAMPLE   **TOPIC:** Book censorship in high school

**CLAIM:** Books should not be censored in high school.

**THESIS STATEMENT:** When books are taken off high school library shelves or are dropped from high school curricula because they are considered inappropriate to read, students are denied an open exchange of ideas.

1. Commercials for weight loss pills on television
2. Taxing new cars according to their mileage
3. Athletes' use of steroids and performance drugs
4. Requiring students to undertake volunteer or community service

## 5e    What is the structure of a classical argument?

No single method is best for organizing all arguments, but a frequently used structure is the **classical argument**. The ancient Greeks and Romans developed this six-part structure, which is described in Quick Reference 5.1.

## Quick Reference 5.1

■ ■ ■ ■ ■ ■ ■

### The structure of a classical argument

1. **Introductory paragraph:** Sets the stage for the position argued in the essay. It gains the reader's interest and respect (3c).

2. **Thesis statement:** States the topic and position you want to argue (2d).

3. **Background information:** Gives readers the basic information they need for understanding your thesis and its support. As appropriate, you might include definitions of key terms, historical or social context, prior scholarship, and other related material. You can include this as part of your introductory paragraph, or it can appear in its own paragraph placed immediately after the introduction.

4. **Evidence and reasons:** Supports the position you're arguing on the topic. This is the core of the essay. Each reason or piece of evidence usually consists of a general statement backed up with specific details, including examples and other RENNS (that is, reasons, examples, names, numbers, and senses). (See section 3f.) Evidence needs to meet the standards for critical thinking (Chapter 4). Depending on the length of the essay, you might devote one or two paragraphs to each reason or type of evidence. For organization, you might choose to present the most familiar reasons and evidence first, saving the most unfamiliar for last. Alternatively, you might proceed from the least important to the most important point so that your essay builds to a climax, leaving the most powerful impact for the end.

5. **Response to opposing position:** Sometimes referred to as the *rebuttal* or *refutation*. This material mentions and defends against an opposite point of view. Often this refutation, which can be lengthy or brief according to the overall length of the essay, appears in its own paragraph or paragraphs, usually immediately before the concluding paragraph or immediately following the introductory paragraph, as a bridge to the rest of the essay. If you use the latter structure, you can choose to place your thesis statement either at the end of the introductory paragraph or at the end of the rebuttal paragraph. Yet another choice for structure consists of having each paragraph present one type of evidence or reason and then immediately stating and responding to the opposing position. (See 5l for advice on handling opposing arguments.)

6. **Concluding paragraph:** Ends the essay logically and gracefully— never abruptly. It often summarizes the argument, elaborates its significance, or calls readers to action (3k).

### BACKGROUND

Classical persuasion consisted of six parts that represented six basic functions. Although the writer or orator was granted some flexibility in how and in what order the parts were presented, they provided effective guidelines for presenting an argument. Often used today, the six parts of an argument, according to the classical precept, are as follows:

1. *Exordium,* meaning "beginning a web." As an introduction, the purpose of the exordium is to attract the attention of the audience, indicate the subject, and favorably dispose the audience to what will follow.

2. *Narratio.* In this section, now usually referred to as "statement of fact," the writer defines the issue by stating pertinent facts about the subject. It is, therefore, basically expository.

3. *Partitio.* If the thesis has not yet been identified, it will be presented here, along with an indication of how the rest of the argument will be organized. The purpose of partitio is to prepare the reader or listener for what will follow.

4. *Confirmatio.* Arguments to support the thesis, forming the bulk of the piece, are developed at this point. The question of the order of presentation of arguments is critical to the effectiveness of the confirmation.

5. *Refutatio.* Opposing arguments are considered and rendered ineffective in the refutation section. To ignore them is to risk letting them appear to be more attractive than one's own thesis. The refutation may be placed at various points in the piece, depending on where it will be most effective.

6. *Peroratio.* The classical rhetoricians used a number of terms to indicate the conclusion of a piece; it usually furnished a summary of proofs and refutations, a restatement of the major points, and a re-creation of emotional and ethical appeals.

### BACKGROUND

While this chapter of the handbook presents the most familiar modes of argument, one often sees in postmodern rhetorical practice a blurring of genres and cross-pollination of purposes and forms. A good example of the use of expressive writing embedded within narrative to develop an argument may be seen in *Letters for the Living: Teaching Writing in a Violent Age* (NCTE, 1998). In this work, Michael Blitz (John Jay College of Criminal Justice, CUNY) and C. Mark Hurlbert (Indiana University of Pennsylvania) relate their own teaching experience and share student journaling about violence to point out how instructors of composition can help students, through the use of "private writings," to confront violence and ultimately shape a more peaceful world.

**TEACHING TIP**

Persuasive writing has much in common with argumentation. Both aim to lead the audience to agreement with the opinions of the writer. Persuasion additionally attempts to induce the reader to commit to a particular action. Advertising is probably the form of persuasive writing we encounter most often in the course of our daily lives. Because students enjoy looking at familiar advertisements in an analytical way, you may want to ask them to bring their favorites to class, or perhaps you will prefer to provide some. Helpful background information is available in such publications as *Advertising Age*.

**BACKGROUND**

According to Aristotle's *Rhetoric*, the conclusion of an argument can have as many as four functions. It should create a favorable impression toward the speaker and an unfavorable impression toward the speaker's opponents. It should emphasize the points of the speaker while minimizing the points of the opposition. It should appeal strongly to the audience's emotions. And it should summarize the chief points of the argument.

**TEACHING TIP**

When students write to convince their peers in the classroom or online class, they may find it helpful to submit several key questions for an opinion survey on their topic to be answered by each student in the class. The survey results can help students shape their writing for a real-world audience, an audience that is likely to

## 5f How do I support my argument?

Use reasons, examples, and evidence to support an argument's claim. (See RENNS, Quick Reference 3.3.) One good method for developing reasons for an argument is to ask yourself *why* you believe your claim. When you respond "Because . . .," you offer reasons for your claim. Evidence needs to be sufficient, representative, relevant, accurate, reasonable, and current. Specifically, evidence consists of facts, statistics, expert testimony, personal experience, and so on.

If you consult SOURCES to find supporting evidence, reasons, or examples, be sure to use correct DOCUMENTATION within the text of your essay and in your WORKS CITED or REFERENCES list at the end of your paper (Chapters 36–38). By doing this, you avoid PLAGIARISM, adopting someone else's ideas and trying to pass them off as your own. Plagiarism is a serious offense that can result in your failing a course or even being dismissed from college (Chapter 35).

## 5g What types of appeals can provide support?

An effective argument relies on three types of **persuasive appeals**: logical appeals, emotional appeals, and ethical appeals. The ancient Greeks called these appeals *logos, pathos,* and *ethos.* Quick Reference 5.2 summarizes how to use the appeals.

### Quick Reference 5.2

**Guidelines for persuasive appeals**

- **Be logical:** Use sound reasoning (*logos*).
- **Enlist the emotions of the reader:** Appeal to the values and beliefs of the reader by arousing the reader's "better self" (*pathos*).
- **Establish credibility:** Show that you as the writer can be relied on as a knowledgeable person with good sense (*ethos*).

The **logical appeal** (*logos*) is the most widely used and intellectually solid and sound appeal in arguments. Sound reasoning involves using effective evidence and reasons. When the student writer Alex Garcia argues that certain foods carry health risks, he cites research that points to specific diseases (5n). Logical writers analyze CAUSE AND EFFECT correctly. Also, they use appropriate patterns of INDUCTIVE REASONING and DEDUCTIVE REASONING, and they distinguish clearly between fact and opinion. Finally, sound reasoning means avoiding LOGICAL FALLACIES. One strategy for generating logical appeals is the **Toulmin model**, developed by the philosopher Stephen Toulmin, discussed in 5h.

When you use **emotional appeals** (*pathos*), you try to persuade your readers by appealing to their hearts more than their minds. Such appeals are generally more effective when you combine them with logical appeals. If an employee asks for a raise and gives reasons like "I have a family to support" or "I need to pay medical bills," that person probably won't get very far. The employee needs in addition to prove how his or her contributions have gone well beyond the job description, dramatically increased sales, or created other advantages.

Emotional appeals can use descriptive language and concrete details or examples to create a mental picture for readers, which is an approach that leads them to feel or understand the importance of your claim. Figure 5.1 provides an example of emotional appeals. You want to appeal to your audience's values and beliefs through honest examples and descriptions that add a sense of humanity and reality to the issue you're arguing. You want, however, to avoid

## Sleeping Sickness
## Untreated, It Inevitably Kills

Spread by tsetse flies, this dreaded tropical disease claims more than 66,000 lives a year in 36 African nations. Doctors Without Borders volunteer Rebecca Golden returned from Angola, where a desperate battle against sleeping sickness is being waged after years of war have wrecked that nation's health care system.

"The treatment is a form of arsenic and is extremely painful," says Rebecca. "I was visiting some children receiving their medicine and was amazed at their courage and strength. **When the arsenic entered their bloodstream, they curled their toes, turned their heads, and closed their eyes tightly.** Their choice was to die or take the treatment. They accepted it with such calm. After 20 years of war and lost family members, they seem to accept this as just another part of the survival process."

Your support helps Doctors Without Borders save lives. **In our battle against sleeping sickness and other diseases, your gift can make a vital difference.**

### *Every Dollar Counts*

**$35** – **Supplies a basic suture kit to repair minor shrapnel wounds.**

**$75** – **Provides 1,500 patients with clean water for a week.**

**$100** – **Provides infection-fighting antibiotics to treat nearly 40 wounded children.**

**$200** – **Supplies 40 malnourished children with special high-protein food for a day.**

### Visit www.doctorswithoutborders.org

**Figure 5.1** An argument that appeals to emotions

include a number of different perspectives and needs.

## OTHER EXAMPLES OF APPEALS TO REASON

### Emotional Appeal

A child's world is fresh and new and beautiful, full of wonder and excitement. It is our misfortune that for most of us that clear-eyed vision, that true instinct for what is beautiful and awe-inspiring, is dimmed and even lost before we reach adulthood. If I had influence with the good fairy who is supposed to preside over the christening of all children I should ask that her gift to each child in the world be a sense of wonder so indestructible that it would last throughout life, as an unfailing antidote against the boredom and disenchantments of later years, the sterile preoccupation with things that are artificial, the alienation from the sources of our strength.

I sincerely believe that . . . it is not half so important to know as to feel. If facts are the seeds that later produce knowledge and wisdom, then the emotions and the impressions of the senses are the fertile soil in which the seeds must grow. The years of early childhood are the time to prepare the soil. Once the emotions have been aroused—a sense of the beautiful, the excitement of the new and the unknown, a feeling of sympathy, pity, admiration or love—then we wish for knowledge about the object of our emotional response.

—Rachel Carson, *The Sense of Wonder*

### Ethical Appeal

Our tragedy today is a general and universal physical fear so long sustained by now that we can even bear it. There are no longer problems of the spirit. There is only the question: When will I be blown up? Because of this, the young man or woman writing today has forgotten the problems of the human heart in conflict with itself which alone can make good writing because only this is worth writing about, worth the agony and the sweat.

He must learn them again. He must teach himself that the basest of all things is to be afraid; and, teaching himself that, forget it forever, leaving no room in his workshop for anything but the old verities and truths of the heart, the old universal truths lacking which any story is ephemeral and doomed—love and honor and pity and pride and compassion and sacrifice. Until he does so, he labors under a curse. He writes not of love but of lust, of defeats in which nobody loses anything of value, of victories without hope and, worst of all, without pity or compassion. His griefs grieve on no universal bones, leaving no scars. He writes not of the heart but of the glands.

—William Faulkner,
Nobel Prize acceptance speech

**QUOTATION: ON WRITING**

Aristotle believed that the most important element of persuasion wasn't the logical appeal, or the emotional appeal, but the ethical appeal—by which he meant both the force of the speaker's reputation and the qualities such as fair-mindedness and common sense reflected in the argument itself.

—Sally DeWitt Spurgin

**QUOTATION: ON WRITING**

For Toulmin, argument evaluation is field-dependent. That is, arguments are not judged good or bad on the basis of universal and timeless criteria, but are determined to be solid or defective on the basis of accepted standards of the field in which they are used.

—Richard Fulkerson, *Teaching the Argument in Writing*

manipulating your readers with biased, SLANTED LANGUAGE. Readers see through such tactics and resent them.

When you use **ethical appeals**, or *ethos,* you establish your personal credibility with your audience. Audiences don't trust a writer who states opinions as fact, distorts evidence, or makes claims that can't be supported. They do trust a writer who comes across as honest, knowledgeable, and fair. Ethical appeals can't take the place of logical appeals, but the two work well together. One effective way to make an ethical appeal is to draw on your personal experience. (Some college instructors don't want students to write in the first person, so check with your instructor before you try this technique.) Alex Garcia creates an ethical appeal in his first paragraph when he identifies himself as a shopper with a limited budget who, nonetheless, chooses more expensive options. Another way to make an ethical appeal is to consider a variety of perspectives, reasonably and fairly addressing opposing viewpoints (Quick Reference 5.1). Using reliable SOURCES and a reasonable TONE all communicate that you're being fair-minded.

## 5h  What is the Toulmin model for argument?

One powerful method for generating logical appeals and for analyzing the arguments of others is the Toulmin model. The Toulmin model defines three essential elements in an effective argument: the claim, the support, and the warrants. They describe concepts that you've encountered before (as Quick Reference 5.3 explains). For example, identifying the **warrants** (assumptions that are often unstated) is a good critical thinking strategy.

### Quick Reference 5.3

#### The Toulmin model for argument

- **Claim:** A variation of a thesis statement. If needed, the claim is qualified or limited.

  Alex Garcia makes the following claim in his argument: Health and environmental benefits of organic foods outweigh their extra costs.

- **Support:** REASONS and EVIDENCE, moving from broad reasons to specific data and details, support the claim.

  Alex offers three main reasons: (1) Organic produce is safer for individuals; (2) Organic meats and dairy products are safer for society as a whole; and (3) Organic farming is better for the environment. He then provides evidence for each of those reasons, drawing on source materials.

- **Warrants:** The writer's underlying assumptions, which are often implied rather than stated. Warrants may also need support (also called *backing*).

continued >>

## Quick Reference 5.3 (continued)

Alex's essay has several warrants, among them: (1) We should always make choices that increase our safety; and (2) Preserving the environment enhances our quality of life. (Notice that these warrants are debatable. For example, we routinely make choices that are less safe than their options; going skiing or roller skating is more dangerous than staying at home, for instance. Quality of life is determined by many factors.)

The concept of *warrant* is similar to the concept of *inferences,* a key component of critical thinking (4a). Inferences are not stated outright but are implied "between the lines" of the writing. Similarly, warrants are unspoken underlying assumptions in an argument. Consider the following simple argument: "Johnson should not be elected mayor. She was recently divorced." The *claim* is that Johnson shouldn't be elected. The *support* is that Johnson has been divorced. The unstated *warrant* is "divorced people are not qualified to be mayor." Before they can accept the claim that Johnson shouldn't be elected, readers have to accept this warrant. Of course, a majority of readers would reject the warrant. Thus, this argument is weak. To identify the warrants in an argument, ask "What do I need to assume so that the support is sufficient for establishing each claim?"

The concepts in the Toulmin model can help you write arguments with a critical eye. They can be quite useful on their own as well as applied to the CLASSICAL ARGUMENT structure (Quick Reference 5.1). As you read and revise your own arguments, identify the claim, support, and warrants. If you don't have a clear claim or support, you'll probably have to assume that your argument is weak. Furthermore, make sure that all of your warrants will be convincing to readers. If they aren't, you need to provide backing, or reasons why the warrants are reasonable. For example, consider the following argument: "People should not receive a driver's license until the age of 25 because the accident rate for younger drivers is much higher than for older ones." One of the warrants here is that reducing the number of accidents should have highest priority. Obviously, many 18-to-24-year-old readers will not find that warrant convincing.

**EXERCISE 5-2** Individually or with a peer-response group, discuss these simple arguments. Identify the claim, support, and warrants for each.

EXAMPLE    The college should establish an honor code. Last semester more than fifty students were caught cheating on exams.

    CLAIM:      The college should establish an honor code.

    SUPPORT:   Last semester, more than fifty students were caught cheating on exams.

## ANSWERS: EXERCISE 5-2

1. *Claim:* The college should raise tuition.
   *Support:* The football stadium is in such poor repair that the coach is having trouble recruiting players.
   *Warrants:*

   **A.** Tuition and fees should go toward repairing the football stadium.

   **B.** A football team is important to the college.

   **C.** Repairing the stadium will improve recruiting.

2. *Claim:* People should vote against raising taxes.
   *Support:* In the past two years, we have already had a 2 percent tax increase.
   *Warrants:*

   **A.** Taxes are too high.

   **B.** A 2 percent increase in the past two years is a good reason for not increasing taxes again.

3. *Claim:* The college should require all students to own laptop computers.
   *Support:* Most students will have to use computers in their jobs after graduation.
   *Warrants:*

   **A.** Students have to own computers in order to use them.

   **B.** Owning a computer will help students get and keep a job.

### BACKGROUND

The ideal format of a Rogerian argument, according to experts, is as follows:
   *Introduction.* State the subject as a problem rather than as an issue in order to interest your audience in reading about something with which they disagree.
   *Fair statement of the opposing position.* In this section, the writer states the reader's opposing position in a manner that seems fair and accurate to the reader.
   *Statement of contexts in which that position may be valid.* The writer tries to show readers that he or she understands their position by asserting that it is valid in some contexts.

*Fair statement of the writer's position.* The goal of this section is to get readers to understand the writer's position as fairly and thoroughly as the writer has understood theirs.

*Statement of contexts in which the writer's position is valid.* The writer tries to get readers to look at the problem from new perspectives and in new contexts.

*Statement of how readers would benefit by adopting at least some elements of the writer's position.* The writer appeals to readers' self-interest. In this section, the writer's position turns from a threat to a promise.

**QUOTATION: ON WRITING**

Real communication occurs . . . when we listen with understanding. What does this mean? It means to see the expressed idea and attitude from the other person's point of view, to sense how it feels to him, to achieve his frame of reference in regard to the thing he is talking about.
—Carl Rogers

**QUOTATION: ON WRITING**

Rhetoric may be defined as the faculty of observing in any given case the available means of persuasion.

—Aristotle

**QUOTATION: ON WRITING**

Had I been blessed with even a limited access to my own mind there would have been no reason to write. I write entirely to find out what I'm thinking, what I'm looking at, what I see and what it means.

—Joan Didion

**QUOTATION: ON WRITING**

A prejudice is a vagrant opinion without visible means of support.

—Ambrose Bierce

**EXTRA EXERCISE D**

Analyze the following paragraphs to discover the dominant appeal of each.

**1.** We observe today not a victory of party but a celebration of freedom—symbolizing an end

**WARRANTS:**

A. Enough students cheat on exams that the college should address the problem.

B. Cheating should be prevented.

C. Students would not have cheated if there had been an honor code.

1. The college should raise student tuition and fees. The football stadium is in such poor repair that the coach is having trouble recruiting players.

2. Vote against raising our taxes. In the past two years, we have already had a 2 percent tax increase.

3. The college should require all students to own laptop computers. Most students will have to use computers in their jobs after graduation.

## 5i   What part does audience play in my argument?

The PURPOSE of written argument is to convince your AUDIENCE either to agree with you or to be open to your position. In writing an argument, you want to consider what your readers already know or believe about your topic. Will the audience be hostile or open-minded to your position? Will it resist or adopt your point of view? What values, viewpoints, and assumptions will your audience hold? (See the questions in Quick Reference 1.5 to help you analyze your audience.)

Unfortunately, some members of some audiences can be persuaded by purely sensational or one-sided claims. Witness the effects on some readers of highly charged advertising or of narrowly one-sided ultraconservative or ultraliberal claims. However, such arguments rarely change the minds of people who don't already agree with them. Critical thinking quickly reveals the weaknesses of such arguments, including a frequent use of LOGICAL FALLACIES (4i). That's why academic audiences expect a higher standard and value, above all, logical appeals and appropriate, adequate support.

In many instances, of course, you can't actually expect to change your reader's mind, which means your goal is to demonstrate that your point of view has its own merit. If you think that your audience is likely to read your point of view with hostility, you might consider using Rogerian argument.

## 5j   How can Rogerian argument help me reach opposing audiences?

**Rogerian argument** seeks common ground between points of view. The Rogerian approach is based on the principles of communication developed by the psychologist Carl Rogers. According to Rogers, communication is eased when people find common ground in their points of view. For example, the common ground in a debate over capital punishment might be that serious crimes are increasing in numbers and viciousness. Once both sides agree that this is the problem, they might be more willing to consider opposing opinions. Quick Reference 5.4 explains the structure of a Rogerian argument, which can be an effective alternative to CLASSICAL ARGUMENT structure.

## Quick Reference 5.4

### The structure of a Rogerian argument

1. **Introduction:** Sets the stage for the position that is argued in the essay. It gains the reader's interest and respect (3c).

2. **Thesis statement:** States the topic and position you want to argue (5c and 5d).

3. **Common ground:** Explains the issue, acknowledging that your readers probably don't agree with you. Speculates about and respectfully gives attention to the points of agreement you and your readers might share, especially concerning underlying problems or issues. For example, people on both sides of the gun control issue can share the desire for fewer violent crimes with guns. You might even acknowledge situations in which your reader's position may be desirable. This may take one paragraph or several, depending on the complexity of the issue.

4. **Discussion of your position:** Gives evidence and reasons for your stand on the topic, as in classical argument (see Quick Reference 5.1).

5. **Concluding paragraph:** Summarizes why your position is preferable to your opponent's (3k). You might, for example, explain why a particular situation makes your position desirable.

When it comes to argument, people often "agree to disagree" in the best spirit of intellectual exchange. As you write a Rogerian argument, remember that your audience wants to see how effectively you've reasoned and presented your position. This stance approaches that of a formal oral debate in which all sides are explored with similar intellectual rigor.

## 5k  What is a reasonable tone in an argument?

A reasonable TONE tells your audience that you're being fair-minded. When you anticipate opposing positions and refute them with balanced language and emphasis, you demonstrate that you respect the other side. No matter how strongly you disagree with opposing arguments, never insult the other side. Name-calling reflects poor judgment and a lack of self-control. The saying "It's not what you say but how you say it" needs to be on your mind at all times as

as well as a beginning—signifying renewal as well as change. For I have sworn before you and Almighty God the same solemn oath our forebears prescribed nearly a century and three quarters ago.

The world is very different now. For man holds in his mortal hands the power to abolish all forms of human poverty and all forms of human life. And yet the same revolutionary beliefs for which our forebears fought are still at issue around the globe—the belief that the rights of man come not from the generosity of the state but from the hand of God.

We dare not forget today that we are the heirs of that first revolution. Let the word go forth from this time and place, to friend and foe alike, that the torch has been passed to a new generation of Americans—born in this century, tempered by war; disciplined by a hard and bitter peace, proud of our ancient heritage—and unwilling to witness or permit the slow undoing of those human rights to which this nation has always been committed, and to which we are committed today at home and around the world.

—John F. Kennedy, Inaugural Address

2. Harlem got its first private project, Riverton—which is now, naturally, a slum—about twelve years ago because at that time Negroes were not allowed to live in Stuyvesant Town. Harlem watched Riverton go up, therefore, in the most violent bitterness of spirit, and hated it long before the builders arrived. They began hating it at about the time people began moving out of their condemned houses to make room for this additional proof of how thoroughly the white world despised them. And they had scarcely moved in, naturally, before they began smashing windows, defacing walls, urinating in the elevators, and fornicating in the playgrounds. Liberals, both white and black, were appalled at the spectacle. I was appalled by the liberal innocence—or cynicism, which comes out in practice as much the same thing. Other people were delighted to be able to point to proof positive that nothing could be done to better the lot of the colored people. They were, and are, right in one respect: that nothing can be done as long as they are treated like colored

people. The people in Harlem know they are living there because white people do not think they are good enough to live anywhere else. No amount of "improvement" can sweeten this fact. Whatever money is now being earmarked to improve this, or any other ghetto, might as well be burnt. A ghetto can be improved in one way only: out of existence.

—James Baldwin, "Fifth Avenue Uptown: A Letter from Harlem"

## ANSWERS: EXERCISE 5-3

The e-mail is rich with emotional and ethical appeals. A few examples follow.

*Ethical appeals:*

Author claims she is humble.

Author appears to be sensitive to the reader's concerns, noting possible apprehensions and offering assurances.

Author asserts that she is a Christian and expresses trust in the reader.

Author says "Thank you and God bless."

*Emotional appeals:*

Author claims her father was killed by rebels.

Author portrays herself as unknowledgeable and uncertain (for example, she doesn't know where to invest the money; she needs the help of a "trusted" foreigner).

## Answers to Extra Exercise D

Answers will vary. Here are possible answers.

**1.** In his Inaugural Address, John F. Kennedy makes extensive use of ethical appeal. By referring to the "solemn oath" he has just taken before God and the American people, he calls attention to his commitment to work for what is good and right. When, in reference to the complexity of the modern world, he again invokes the name of God as the source of "the rights of man," he underscores the high moral calling of his office. In the final paragraph, he appeals to the ethical sense of the audience by exhorting citizens to join him in the struggle to make a better world. By using the pronoun *we,* he repledges himself to work with all Americans for the spread and preservation of the beliefs on which this country was founded.

you write an argument. Avoid exaggerating, and never show anger. The more emotionally loaded a topic (for example, abortion or capital punishment), the more tempted you might be to use careless, harsh words. For instance, calling the opposing position "stupid" would say more about you as the writer than it would about the issue.

**EXERCISE 5-3**     Here is the text of a notorious e-mail fraud that has been sent to many people. Hundreds of variations of this e-mail exist, but usually the writer claims to have a large amount of money that he or she wants to transfer to an American bank. The writer wants the recipient's help in making the transfer. This is a complete lie. The writer has no money and is trying to trick people into revealing their bank account numbers to steal their money.

Either alone or in a small group, examine the ways this writer tries to establish emotional and ethical appeals. *Note:* We've reproduced the e-mail with the often incorrect original wording, grammar, and punctuation.

Good day,

It is my humble pleasure to write this letter irrespective of the fact that you do not know me. However, I came to know of you in my private search for a reliable and trustworthy person that can handle a confidential transaction of this nature in respect of this, I got your contact through an uprooted search on the internet. Though I know that a transaction of this magnitude will make any one apprehensive and worried, but I am assuring you that all will be well at the end of the day.

I am Ruth Malcasa, daughter of late Mr. James Malcasa of Somalia, who was killed by the rebel forces on the 24th of December, 2007 in my country Somalia. When he was still alive, he deposited one trunk box containing the sum of USD$10 million dollars in cash (Ten Million dollars). with a private security and safe deposit company here in Lagos Nigeria. This money was made from the sell of Gold and Diamond by my mother and she has already decided to use this money for future investment of the family.

My father instructed me that in the case of his death, that I should look for a trusted foreigner who can assist me to move out this money from Nigeria immediately for investment. Based on this, I solicit for your assistance to transfer this fund into your Account, but I will demand for the following requirement: (1) Could you provide for me a safe Bank Account where this fund will be transferred to in your country after retrieving the box containing the money from the custody of the security company. (2) Could you be able to introduce me to a profitable business venture that would not require much technical expertise in your country where part of this fund will be invested?

I am a Christian and I want you to handle this transaction based on the trust I have established on you. For your assistance in this transaction,

I have decided to compensate you with 10 percent of the total amount at the end of this business. The security of this business is very important to me and as such, I would like you to keep this business very confidential. I shall expect an early response from you. Thank you and God bless. Yours sincerely, Ruth Malcasa.

# 5l  How do I handle opposing arguments?

Dealing with opposing positions is crucial to writing an effective argument. If you don't acknowledge arguments that your opponents might raise and explain why they are faulty or inferior, you create doubts that you have thoroughly explored the issue. You risk seeming narrow-minded.

The next to last paragraph in Alex Garcia's paper (section 5n), which summarizes opposing arguments, strengthens both his *ethos* (credibility) and his *logos* (logic). He's so confident in his own position that not only can he point out research findings that contradict his position but also concede that this research is reasonably solid. Alex does suggest some promising new research that might eventually support him, but the most important thing he does is explain why, even if organic food is not more nutritious, the other reasons he has argued are strong enough to carry his thesis. He had encountered this counterargument while doing his research. When you do research for your own arguments, look for essays, articles, and opinions that oppose your position, not only ones that agree with yours.

If your research doesn't generate opposing arguments, you need to develop them yourself. Imagine that you're debating someone who disagrees with you; what positions would that person take and why? Note that you can ask a classmate or friend to perform this role. Another strategy is to take the opposite side of the argument and try to develop the best reasons you can for that position. (In some formal debating situations, people are expected to prepare both sides of an issue and only learn immediately before the debate which position they are to argue.)

Once you have generated opposing arguments, you need to refute them, which means you want to show why they're weak or undesirable. Imagine that you're writing about national security and individual rights. You believe that the government shouldn't be allowed to monitor a private citizen's e-mail without a court order, and you have developed a number of reasons for your position. To strengthen your paper, you also generate some opposing arguments, including "People will be safer from terrorism if police can monitor e-mail," "Only people who have something to hide have anything to fear," and "It is unpatriotic to oppose the government's plans." How might you refute these or other opposing claims? Following are some suggestions.

**2.** James Baldwin's comments about Riverton seethe with anger, bitterness, and even hatred. The strong emotions that the reader hears and feels emanate not only from phrases such as "violent bitterness of spirit," "hated it," "hating it," and "despised them" but also from the images of destruction that he provides: "smashing windows, defacing walls, urinating in the elevators, and fornicating in the playgrounds." Any positive term that Baldwin uses, such as "improvement," he puts in quotation marks, suggesting its unreality.

## QUOTATION: ON WRITING

To persuade, there are two things which must be carefully studied by the orator. The first is to excite some desire or passion in the hearers; the second is to satisfy their judgment that there is a connection between the action to which he would persuade them and the gratification of the desire or passion he excites.

—George Campbell

## TEACHING TIP

Most newspapers, including campus newspapers, carry numerous pieces of persuasive discourse in the letters to the editor, daily columns, and editorials. You may want to ask students to bring examples to class that can be analyzed in terms of claims and thesis, as well as the order and means of development.

A different kind of experience, but an equally interesting one, can come from analysis of a longer, more sustained argument, such as Henry David Thoreau's essay "Civil Disobedience" or Martin Luther King Jr.'s "Letter from Birmingham Jail."

## TEACHING TIP

An assignment that has caught more than one student off guard but led to powerful results is to ask a class to brainstorm a number of topics that, while not "hot button topics" for most, are yet likely to provoke controversy: animal-testing of cosmetics; building nuclear power plants in heavily populated areas; authorizing government subsidies to rescue a bankrupt airline or automobile company; and the like. Have students sign up for a topic of interest, allowing only two students per topic: one to argue for, one against. When all have signed up for a topic and a position, inform the students that those listed in the "for" column will take the "against" position and vice versa. You will definitely hear groans! However, tell the students that they will be guided in their efforts by their partner who has a feel for (and with luck some knowledge of) the opposite point of view. During the development of this writing project, students meet in pairs (in class or online) to ask each other questions and to get feedback on their tone and their style of presentation. Each can help direct the other to resources beyond those readily found by the researcher. This project helps students to understand the "other" side more fully and to discover what kind and how much evidence the opposition may require to become convinced.

### QUOTATION: ON WRITING
We seldom defend a view that we do not favor and we often assume that any view we favor is true. Hence, when we are constructing arguments in support of our views, it often happens that we simply assume the view we should be proving.

—Alex C. Michalos

### QUOTATION: ON WRITING
Many suffer from the incurable disease of writing, and it becomes chronic in their sick minds.

—Juvenal

### ANSWERS: EXERCISE 5-4
Answers will vary.

### BACKGROUND
In "Teaching Critical Thinking in First-Year Composition: Sometimes More Is More" (*Teaching English in the Two-Year College* 29.2 (2001): 162–171), Ruth Stewart advocates teaching argument by having students analyze primary source materials. In order to make sure that students focus on critical thinking, she provides materials and asks the students to argue positions from them. Stewart details her

- **Examine the evidence for each opposing argument** (4d–4h). Look especially for missing or contradictory facts. In the given example, you might question the evidence that people would be safer from terrorism if police could monitor e-mail.
- **Use the Toulmin model to analyze the opposing argument** (5h). What are the claims, support, and warrants? Often, it's possible to show that the warrants are questionable or weak. For example, a warrant in the counterarguments above is that the promise of increased safety is worth the price of privacy or individual rights. You might show why this warrant is undesirable.
- **Demonstrate that an opposing argument depends on emotion rather than reasoning.** The assertion that it's unpatriotic to oppose the government is primarily an emotional one.
- **Redefine key terms.** The term *patriotism* can be defined in various ways. You might point out, for example, that at the time of the American Revolution, "patriots" were the people who were opposing the British government then in power.
- **Explain the negative consequences of the opposing position.** Imagine that the opposing position actually won out, and explain how the results would be damaging. For example, if everyone knew that government officials might monitor their computer use, consider how this might affect free speech.
- **Concede an opposing point, but explain that doing so doesn't destroy your own argument.** For example, you might decide to concede that governmental monitoring of e-mails could reduce terrorism. However, you might argue that the increase in safety is not worth the threat to privacy and personal freedom.
- **Explain that the costs of the other position are not worth the benefits.**

**EXERCISE 5-4**  Individually or with a peer-response group, practice developing objections to specific arguments and responses to those objections. To do this, choose a debatable topic and brainstorm a list of points on that topic, some on one side of the topic, some on another. Following are some arguments to get you started. If you're part of a group, work together to assign the different positions for each topic to different sets of students. Then, conduct a brief debate on which side has more merit, with each side taking turns. At the end, your group can vote for the side that is more convincing.

1. It should be legal/illegal to ride motorcycles without a helmet.
2. Political candidates should/should not use negative advertising.
3. Students should/should not be required to take certain courses in order to graduate.
4. Paid public service (for example, the military or social work) should/should not be required of all 18-to-20-year-olds.

# 5m How did one student draft and revise his argument essay?

In his first draft, Alex focused on how organic farming would benefit the environment, and he found lots of studies of how traditional farming practices affect water and soil quality. However, he realized that this argument alone might seem remote to many readers, so he explored how agricultural chemicals affect consumers. Extensive research resulted in a second draft that included not only immediate concerns for individuals but also society at large. While doing that research, he was surprised to encounter evidence that organic foods weren't necessarily more nutritious. Initially, Alex wanted just to ignore it, but then he decided his paper would be stronger if he included and dealt with this opposing viewpoint in his third draft. That draft also was where he developed his introductory paragraph, which until this point he had just sketched generally. Throughout the process, he found the need to check facts and sources in library databases. Before completing the paper, he looked carefully at his use of *pathos* and *ethos* and consulted the revision checklist (see Quick Reference 2.8). Finally, he referred to the special checklist for revising written arguments in Quick Reference 5.5.

---

## Quick Reference 5.5 ■ ■ ■ ■ ■ ■ ■

### Revising written arguments

- Is the thesis statement about a debatable topic? (5c and 5d)
- Do the reasons or evidence support the thesis statement? Are the generalizations supported by specific details? (5d)
- Does the argument deal with reader needs and concerns? (5i)
- Does the argument appeal chiefly to reason? Is it supported by an ethical appeal? If it uses an emotional appeal, is the appeal restrained? (5g)
- Is the tone reasonable? (5k)
- Is the opposing position stated and refuted? (5l)

---

**EXERCISE 5-5** Working individually or with a peer-response group, choose a topic from this list. Then, plan an essay that argues a debatable position on the topic. Apply all the principles you've learned in this chapter.

1. Animal experimentation
2. Genetically engineered food
3. Cloning of human beings
4. Taxpayer support for public colleges
5. Home schooling

approach by explaining how her students used documents from the 1763 Conestoga Massacre.

**QUOTATION: ON WRITING**
You must now draw up a timetable and stick to it. When you'll write and at what rate you'll write at are a matter of individual capacity and circumstance, but I suggest that three two-hourly sessions a week are quite enough. It is essential that you record the number of words written each session. This has a valuable psychological effect. Whether you're pleased with what you've written or not, you have before you the proof that you're achieving something, that you actually are working.

—John Braine

**QUOTATION: ON WRITING**
I work four hours a day and then usually early in the evening I read over what I've written during the day and I do a lot of changing and shifting around. See, I write in longhand and I do two versions of whatever I'm doing. I write first on yellow paper and then I write on white paper and then when I finally have it more or less settled the way I want, then I type it. When I'm typing it, that's when I do my final rewrite. I almost never change a word after that.

—Truman Capote

**QUOTATION: ON WRITING**
The exigence of the situation provides the motivation to write about the issue in the first place. Issues often emerge from real-life events that signal something is wrong.

—Nancy V. Wood

**ANSWERS: EXERCISE 5-5**
Answers will vary.

**BACKGROUND**
Andrea Greenbaum's book *Emancipatory Movements in Composition: The Rhetoric of Possibility* (Albany: SUNY Press, 2002) argues that first-year writing instructors should help students develop abilities to think and argue clearly as citizens in a democracy. Greenbaum synthesizes recent developments in rhetorical theory.

**QUOTATION: ON WRITING**

No one can write decently who is distrustful of the reader's intelligence, or whose attitude is patronizing.

—E. B. White

**QUOTATION: ON WRITING**

I find the process of writing very difficult, and often painful, but I love to revise. For me, this involves polishing, listening to the rhythm of sentences and making sure I've heard them right, cutting out excess words, varying sentence structure, eliminating repetition.

—Susan Allen Toth

**QUOTATION: ON WRITING**

I write double-spaced to leave plenty of room for the inevitable revisions and I never write on both sides of the paper. I write on a right-hand page, leaving the facing page blank for insertions and revisions. Then I leave the following double-page blank.

—Len Deighton

**QUOTATION: ON WRITING**

The art of writing has for backbone some fierce attachment to an idea.

—Virginia Woolf

**QUOTATION: ON WRITING**

I think of my first draft as a beautiful piece of marble. That is what is given; it is the gift that is given. But the hard work—how I earn the gift—is what I make out of it.

—Julia Alvarez

**QUOTATION: ON WRITING**

Dr. King prepared a text for the march on Washington address during the early morning hours of August 28, 1963. Several of his close advisers worked with him for many hours, passing revisions back and forth.

—D. Louise Cook

## 5n  Final draft of a student's argument essay in MLA style

Garcia 1

Alex Garcia

WRIT 1122

Professor Brosnahan

4 May 2008

Why Organic Foods are Worth the Extra Money

A small decision confronts me every time I walk into the grocery store. I see a display of enticing apples for around $1.79 per pound. Next to them is a similar display of the same kind of apples, perhaps just a little smaller and just a little less perfect. These sell for $2.29 per pound. The difference between the two is the tiny sticker that reads "organic." Are those apples worth the extra money, especially when my budget is tight and the other ones appear just fine? Millions of shoppers face this same decision whenever they decide whether to buy organic food, and the right answer seems complicated, especially when the US Department of Agriculture "makes no claims that organically produced food is safer or more nutritious than conventionally produced food" (National). However, current research shows that the health and environmental benefits of organic foods outweigh their extra costs.

Organic foods are produced without using most chemical pesticides, without artificial fertilizers, without genetic engineering, and without radiation (National). In the case of organic meat, poultry, eggs, and dairy products, the animals are raised without antibiotics or growth hormones. As a result, people sometimes use the term "natural" instead of organic,

continued >>

Garcia 2

but "natural" is less precise. Before 2002, people could never be quite sure what they were getting when they bought supposedly organic food, unless they bought it directly from a farmer they knew personally. In 2002, the US Department of Agriculture established standards that food must meet in order to be labeled and sold as organic.

According to environmental scientist Craig Minowa, organic foods tend to cost about 15 percent more than nonorganic, mainly because they are currently more difficult to mass-produce (Minowa). Farmers who apply pesticides often get larger crops from the same amount of land because there is less insect damage. Artificial fertilizers tend to increase the yield, size, and uniformity of fruits and vegetables, and herbicides kill weeds that compete with desirable crops for sun, nutrients, and moisture. Animals who routinely receive antibiotics and growth hormones tend to grow more quickly and produce more milk and eggs. In contrast, organic farmers have lower yields and, therefore, higher costs. These get passed along as higher prices to consumers.

Still, the extra cost is certainly worthwhile in terms of health benefits. Numerous studies have shown the dangers of pesticides for humans. An extensive review of research by the Ontario College of Family physicians concludes that "Exposure to all the commonly used pesticides . . . has shown positive associations with adverse health effects" (Sanborn 173). The risks include cancer, psychiatric effects, difficulties becoming pregnant, miscarriages, and dermatitis. Carefully washing fruits and vegetables can remove some of these dangerous chemicals, but according to the prestigious journal

continued >>

Fig. 1. A display of organic foods.

*Nature*, even this does not remove all of them (Giles 797).
Certainly, if there's a way to prevent these poisons entering our
bodies, we should take advantage of it. The few cents saved on
cheaper food can quickly disappear in doctor's bills needed to
treat conditions caused or worsened by chemicals.

Organic meat, poultry, and dairy products can address
another health concern: the diminishing effectiveness of
antibiotics. In the past decades, many kinds of bacteria have
become resistant to drugs, making it extremely difficult to treat
some kinds of tuberculosis, pneumonia, staphylococcus
infections, and less serious diseases (Dangerous 1). True, this
has happened mainly because doctors overly prescribed
antibiotics to patients who expect a pill for every illness.
However, routinely giving antibiotics to all cows and chickens

continued >>

Garcia 4

means that these drugs enter our food chain early, giving bacteria lots of chances to develop resistance. A person who switches to organic meats won't suddenly experience better results from antibiotics; the benefit is a more gradual one for society as a whole. However, if we want to be able to fight infections with effective drugs, we need to reserve antibiotics for true cases of need and discourage their routine use in animals raised for food. Buying organic is a way to persuade more farmers to adopt this practice.

Another benefit of organic foods is also a societal one: Organic farming is better for the environment. In his review of several studies, Colin Macilwain concluded that organic farms nurture larger numbers and more diverse kinds of plants and animals than regular farms (797). Organic farms also don't release pesticides and herbicides that can harm wildlife and run into our water supply, with implications for people's health, too. Macilwain notes that those farms also can generate less carbon dioxide, which will help with global warming; also, many scientists believe that organic farming is more sustainable because it results in better soil quality (798). Once again, these benefits are not ones that you will personally experience right away. However, a better natural environment means a better quality of living for everyone and for future generations.

Some critics point out that organic products aren't more nutritious than regular ones. Physician Sanjay Gupta, for example, finds the medical evidence for nutritional advantages is "thin" (60). The *Tufts University Health and Nutrition Letter* also reports that the research on nutritional benefits is mixed, with one important study showing "no

continued >>

Garcia 5

Fig. 2. Organic farming betters the environment.

overall differences" ("Is Organic" 8). Nutritional value, which includes qualities such as vitamins and other beneficial substances, is a different measure than food safety. At this point, it seems that nutrition alone is not a sufficient reason to buy organic foods. Perhaps future research will prove otherwise; a 2007 study, for example, showed that organically raised tomatoes have higher levels of flavonoids, nutrients that appear to have many health benefits (Mitchell). In the meantime, however, environmental quality and, most importantly, avoiding chemicals remain convincing reasons to purchase organic food, even if the same cannot yet be claimed for nutrition.

Despite the considerable benefits for purchasing organic products, there remains each consumer's decision in the

continued >>

Garcia 6

grocery store. Are the more expensive apples ultimately worth
their extra cost to me? It's true that there are no easily
measurable one-to-one benefits, no way to ensure that
spending fifty cents more on this produce will directly improve
my quality of life by fifty cents. However, countless people are
rightly concerned these days about our personal health and the
health of the world in which we live, and I am one of them. It's
nearly impossible to put a value on a sustainable, diverse
natural environment and having the physical health to enjoy it.
The long-term benefits of buying organic, for anyone who can
reasonably afford to, far outweigh the short-term savings in the
checkout line.

continued >>

Garcia 7

Works Cited

"Dangerous Bacterial Infections Are on the Rise." *Consumer Reports on Health* 19 (Nov. 2007): 1–4. Print.

Giles, Jim. "Is Organic Food Better for Us?" *Nature* 428.6985 (22 Apr. 2004): 796–97. Print.

"Is Organic Food Really More Nutritious?" Tufts University Health and Nutrition Letter 25 (Sep. 2007): 8. Web. 25 Apr. 2008.

Gupta, Sanjay, and Shahreen Abedin. "Rethinking Organics." *Time* (20 Aug. 2007): 60. Print.

Macilwain, Colin. "Is Organic Farming Better for the Environment?" *Nature* 428.6985 (22 Apr. 2004): 797–98. Print.

Minowa, Craig. Interview by Louise Druce. "FYI on Organics: Organic Q & A." Organic Consumers Assn. 29 June 2004. Web.

Mitchell, Alyson E., Yun-Jeong Hong, Eunmi Koh, Diane M. Barrett, D. E. Bryant, R. Ford Denison, and Stephen Kaffka. "Ten-Year Comparison of the Influence of Organic and Conventional Crop Management Practices on the Content of Flavonoids in Tomatoes." *Journal of Agricultural Food Chemistry* 55.15 (2007): 6154–59. Web. 30 Apr. 2008.

National Organic Program. "Organic Food Labels and Standards: The Facts." Washington, DC: US Department of Agriculture. Jan. 2007. Web. 26 Apr 2008.

continued >>

Garcia 8

Sanborn, Margaret, Donald Cole, Kathleen Kerr, Cathy Vakil,

   Luz Helena Sanin, Kate Bassil. *Pesticides Literature*

   *Review: Systematic Review of Pesticide Human Health*

   *Effects.* Toronto: Ontario College of Family Physicians,

   2004. Web. 28 Apr. 2008.

**TEACHING TIP: COLLABORATION**

The concept underlying collaboration is that the whole is greater than the sum of its parts. Providing opportunities for students to work together allows them to see other points of view, to capitalize on one another's strengths, to develop concepts more extensively than they could on their own, and to learn from others. When you assign groups, allow students a little time to introduce themselves and get to know one another. Personalizing learning can be an important part of collaboration.

Collaborative groups work best when they comprise two or three students whose schedules allow them to work together outside class, if practical. When groups meet in class only, students can work toward the group's goals by completing individual responsibilities outside class and then merging all their work during class time. Collaborative papers, like single-authored texts, go through a series of drafts. But unlike single-authored texts, collaborative papers will actively integrate concepts of audience, tone, planning, and purpose into the writing process because at every step students must articulate to one another what they think the paper needs and why.

For an introduction to the history of collaborative writing in the Composition classroom, please see "Writing as Collaboration" by James A. Reither and Douglas Vipond (*College English* 51.8 (1989): 855–867).

**TEACHING TIP: COLLABORATION**

In both workplace and college settings, writers often team up to develop a single document. When two or three students write a paper together, they usually see the need to articulate the how and why of every dimension of the writing task, from topic selection to word choice. This ongoing discussion within collaborative groups about their writing encourages

# 6

# Writing with Others

## 6a What is writing with others?

Although it may often seem like a lonely act, a surprising amount of writing depends on two or more people working together. Anytime you ask someone else to read your draft and give you feedback for revision, you're working with others. The other person could be a friend, a classmate, a co-worker, a writing tutor (in a campus writing center), or an instructor—after all, your instructor's comments on a draft are designed to guide your revision. In the professional world, a project manager or supervisor will frequently read your reports and proposals and ask you to make changes. Of course, you'll be making suggestions about other people's writings, too. Sections 6c and 6d explain how to give and receive help effectively.

A more direct kind of writing with others happens when two or more people **collaborate** (work together) to complete a single project. This handbook is a prime example. Lynn wrote some sections, then Doug revised them—and vice versa. We planned the book over e-mail, in telephone calls, and in person. Drafts flew back and forth over the Internet. We also worked with editors who suggested—and sometimes required—revisions. Each of us brought different knowledge, experience, and talents.

Collaborative writing projects are extremely common in the business and professional world. Marketing managers, for example, lead teams who conduct consumer research and then—as a group—write up their findings. Often, the size or complexity of a project means that only a team of people can accomplish it in the given amount of time. Different team members bring different skills and expertise. In these professional settings, group members must reach general agreement on how to proceed and contribute equally to a written report.

Collaborative writing assignments are increasingly popular in college courses across the curriculum, especially in business, the sciences, and the social sciences. Even if they aren't required to write full papers, small groups are

**Figure 6.1** A collaborative group at work

commonly asked to brainstorm a topic together before individual writing tasks, to discuss various sides of a debatable topic, or to share reactions to an essay or piece of literature the class reads, and so on.

Writing collaboratively enhances confidence when writers support one another. Experience in collaborative writing has benefits beyond your college years because working well with others is a skill that employers value.

**Alert:** Some instructors and students use the terms *peer-response group* and *collaborative writing* to mean the same thing. In this handbook, we assign the terms to two different situations. We use *collaborative writing* (6b) for students writing an essay, a research paper, or a report together in a group. We use *peer-response group* (6c) for students getting together in small groups to help one another write and revise. ●

## 6b How can I collaborate with other writers?

Three qualities are essential to collaborative writing. The first is careful planning. Your group needs to decide when and how it will meet (in person, in a telephone call, in an online discussion); what steps it will follow and what the

students to view effective writing as a process under each individual's conscious control.

**BACKGROUND**
In his article "Teamwork and Feedback: Broadening the Base of Collaborative Writing," Richard Gebhardt advocates for the use of collaborative writing at every stage of the writing process: not just toward the middle and end, where instructors tend to use them. Early collaboration can help students, among other things, "locate promising topics," "generate details," "[clarify] the focus of subjects," and "develop a clearer sense of audience" (*College English* 42.1 (1980): 69–74 [qtd. 73–74]).

**QUOTATION: ON COLLABORATION**
I not only use all of the brains I have, but all I can borrow.
—Woodrow Wilson

**TEACHING TIP**
Sometimes, talented and academically adept students, who otherwise perform well in your class, may balk at the idea of working collaboratively with others. They may cite different reasons: they may see themselves as creative, high-performing students who would only be "slowed-down" by having to work with other students; they may worry that, since they are the "smart kids in class," other classmates may expect them to do most of the work on the project; they may feel that they must pick less ambitious and/or less sophisticated topics in order to complete a project with other students whom they feel are not as devoted to their educations as they are. It is important to remind these students that, in the workplace and in other areas in their lives, they will be required to work with others. As instructor, you can also try to group these students with members of the class with whom they may be more likely to work effectively; to monitor groups to make sure no one is taking on the lion's share of the work, perhaps by requiring students to submit logs of the work they have performed on the project. Conversely, make sure your more vocal students are not drowning out dissent nor prematurely limiting brainstorming sessions, and provide

feedback to students several times throughout the writing process, so that they know that their work is meeting your expectations at each stage.

## QUOTATION: ON COLLABORATION

If you have an apple and I have an apple and we exchange these apples then you and I will still each have one apple. But if you have an idea and I have an idea and we exchange these ideas, then each of us will have two ideas.

— George Bernard Shaw

## TEACHING TIP

Experts in educational group dynamics point out that instructors can facilitate student collaborations by ensuring that each student in a group takes a specific role each time the group gets together each day or each time it starts a new project. For example, you can ask the students to number off—1, 2, 3, and so on—and then say, "Number 4, you're the discussion leader today; Number 2, you're the recorder; Number 1, you're the timekeeper; Number 3, you're the 'on-point' person, responsible for ensuring that your group stays on-topic and on-task." Assigning these roles randomly and changing them from one session to another or from one activity to another keeps students focused, energized, and responsible.

## BACKGROUND

In "Asynchronous Electronic Peer Response in a Hybrid Basic Writing Classroom" (*Teaching English in the Two-Year College* 30.2 (2002): 145–155), Virginia Crank shows how basic writers can benefit from peer response.

## TEACHING TIP

If you choose to have students work in particular peer-response groups over time, you can help them build cohesiveness in their groups from the outset by asking them to share important information about themselves with others in the group. After initial get-acquainted remarks (names, where students are from, etc.), students can complete these statements: "I will

due dates will be; what software you'll use; and who will be responsible for what. Everyone in the group needs to commit to the plan, making changes only after deliberation by everyone.

The second essential quality is a fair division of labor. Almost nothing causes bad feelings more quickly than when some group members feeling like they're doing more than their share. During early planning meetings, the group should figure out the tasks involved in the project and estimate how much time and effort each will take. (You can rebalance things during later meetings, if necessary.)

One basic way a group can divide tasks is according to the different steps in the writing process. One or more people can be in charge of generating ideas or conducting research; one or more can be in charge of writing the first draft; one or more can be in charge of revising; and one or more may be in charge of editing, proofreading, and formatting the final draft. It's hard to separate these tasks cleanly, however, and we warn that writing the first draft often requires more effort than any other element. This approach also means that some group members will be waiting for others to complete their parts.

A second way to divide tasks is to assign part of the project to each person. Many projects can be broken into sections, and using an outline (2f) can help you see what those sections are. Each person can then plan, write, revise, and edit a section, and the other members can serve as a built-in peer-response group to make suggestions for revision. This approach can have the advantage of distributing the work more cleanly at the outset, but it often takes a lot of work at the end to stitch the parts together. It can be difficult when several people try to complete the final editing and compilation.

In reality, you'll probably find your group using a combination of these two approaches. You'll also probably find it useful to assign people basic roles such as leader (or facilitator) and recorder (or secretary). These roles can change during the project, but in our experience, groups find it efficient when someone takes responsibility for calling and leading meetings.

The third essential element of collaborative projects is clear communication. Open and honest communication is vital, and people need to put aside their own egos to build a productive and trusting atmosphere. Keep notes for every meeting so that the group has a clear record of what was decided; one way to do this is to have someone send an e-mail summarizing each meeting. If people disagree over the group's decisions, the group should resolve that disagreement before moving on. You'll also find it effective to ask for regular reports from each group member. These don't have to be long—a few sentences will do it—but they keep everyone informed about others' progress, and they keep you on track, too.

## Quick Reference 6.1

### Guidelines for collaborative writing

■ ■ ■ ■ ■ ■

#### STARTING

1. Learn each other's names and exchange e-mail addresses and phone numbers so that everyone can stay in touch outside of class.

2. Participate actively in the group process. During discussions, help set a tone that encourages everyone to participate by including people who don't like to interrupt, who want time to think before they talk, or who are shy. Conversely, help the group set limits if someone dominates the discussions or makes all the decisions. If you lack experience contributing in a group setting, think about some ways you can try to take an active role.

3. As a group, assign everyone work to be done between meetings. Distribute the responsibilities as fairly as possible. Also, decide whether to choose one discussion leader or to rotate leadership, unless your instructor assigns a particular procedure.

4. Make decisions regarding the technology you'll use. If everyone can use the same word-processing program, for example, that will make sharing drafts or parts of drafts much easier. If not, you can use the "Save As" function in major word processing programs like Microsoft Word to save in a common format. Decide if you'll share materials via e-mail attachments, CDs, flash drives, space on a server, or even through a WIKI (see 46e). If any group members are unfamiliar with these processes, others need to help them learn. (Different areas and levels of expertise are an advantage of working in groups.)

5. Set a timeline and deadlines for the project. Agree on what to do in the event that someone misses a deadline.

#### PLANNING

6. After discussing the project, brainstorm as a group or use structured techniques for discovering and compiling ideas.

7. Together, agree on the ideas that seem best and allow for a period of INCUBATION, if time permits. Then, discuss your group choices again.

8. As a group, divide the project into parts and distribute assignments fairly. For example, if the project requires research, decide who will do it and how they'll share their findings with others. If one person is going to be responsible for preparing drafts from pieces that others have written, make sure his or her other responsibilities are balanced.

9. As a group, OUTLINE or otherwise sketch an overview of the project to get a preliminary idea of how best to use material contributed by individuals.

continued >>

do my best in this group if you _____"; "A particular ability/resource I can contribute to the success of this group is _____"; "If you are displeased with me or my contribution at any point in our process, I will appreciate your (doing/saying) _____"; "If we need to meet outside of class (or outside of class time), please know that _____." The information presented helps individuals feel more accountable to the group, and it allows all to understand the special strengths and limitations of others. *Note:* Most multilingual students new to US classrooms are likely to be reticent about filling in honest answers or even any answers (being confessional is antithetical to most cultures outside the United States). If your class has a large number of such students, you will find it better not to use this technique or you may elect to work with each student privately to fill in the form.

#### BACKGROUND

Joseph Janangelo warns in "Intricate Inscriptions: Negotiating Conflict Between Collaborative Writers" (ERIC EJ 544 163) that collaborators don't always treat each other with reciprocal integrity and compassion. Janangelo suggests several precautions that writing instructors can take to help ensure more responsible collaboration.

## Quick Reference 6.1    (continued)

10. As you work on your part of the project, take notes in preparation for giving your group a progress report.

### DRAFTING

11. Draft a THESIS STATEMENT. The thesis statement sets the direction for the rest of the paper. Each member of the group can draft a thesis statement and the group can discuss the advantages of each, but the group needs to agree on one version before getting too far into the rest of the draft. Your group might revise the thesis statement after the whole paper has been drafted, but using a preliminary version gets everyone started in the same direction.

12. Draft the rest of the paper. Decide whether each member of the group should write a complete draft or one part of the whole. For example, each group member might take one main idea and be responsible for drafting that section. Share draft materials among the group members using disks or e-mail attachments (see step 4). If this is impossible, make photocopies. For most group meetings, it will be important to have a paper copy of group materials, so print (or photocopy) copies for everyone.

### REVISING

13. Read over the drafts. Are all the important points included?

14. Use the revision checklist (Quick Reference 2.9) and work either as a group or by assigning portions to subgroups. If different people have drafted different sections, COHERENCE and UNITY should receive special attention in revision, as should the introduction and the conclusion.

15. Agree on a final version. Either work as a group, or assign someone to prepare the final draft and make sure every group member has a copy.

### EDITING AND PROOFREADING THE WRITING

16. Use the editing checklist (Quick Reference 2.10) to double-check for errors. If you find errors, correct them and print out the page or the whole draft again. No matter how well the group has worked collaboratively, or how well the group has written the paper, a sloppy final version reflects negatively on the entire group.

17. As a group, review printouts or photocopies of the final draft. Don't leave the last stages to a subgroup. Draw on everyone's knowledge of grammar, spelling, and punctuation. Use everyone's eyes for proofreading.

18. If your instructor asks, be prepared to describe your personal contribution to the project and to describe or evaluate the contributions of others.

**EXERCISE 6-1**    Working in a small group, plan how your group would proceed on one or more of the following collaborative projects, satisfying each of the three essential criteria for group work. (*Note*: You don't actually have to complete the project; the purpose of this exercise is to develop your planning skills.)

- A report for a public audience in which you evaluate new car models.
- A research project in which you analyze the political views of students on your campus.
- A persuasive paper in which you argue whether the United States should pass laws to make it harder for American companies to move jobs to other countries.

Be prepared to explain your planning to your instructor or to class members in a way that shows your group has been thoughtful and thorough.

## 6c   How can I give useful feedback to others?

There are two main ways to give feedback to other writers. One is in a small group, usually three to five people, who together discuss each group member's draft out loud. Another way is to work in pairs, providing oral or, more often, written comments for each other.

### 6c.1   Working in peer-response groups

In some writing classes, instructors divide students into PEER-RESPONSE GROUPS. A peer is an "equal": another writer like you. Participating in a peer-response group makes you part of a respected tradition of colleagues helping colleagues. Professional writers often seek comments from other writers to improve their rough drafts. As a member of a peer-response group, you're not expected to be a writing expert. Rather, you're expected to offer responses as a practiced reader and as a fellow student writer who understands what writers go through.

⏺ **Alert:** Some instructors use the term "workshopping" for peer response. The term comes from creative-writing programs, sometimes called "Writers' Workshops," where the main learning strategy is to have students discuss each others' work in progress. ●

The role of peer-response group members is to react and discuss, not to do the work for someone. Hearing or reading comments from your peers might be a new experience, one you may find surprising, as well as informative and helpful. Also, when peers share their writing with your group, you and the other members get the added advantage of learning other students' approaches to writing the same assignment.

**ANSWERS: EXERCISE 6-1**
Answers will vary. You may wish to use this assignment several times, switching the groups and the project each time. Doing so will not only give students more practice at planning collaborative writing projects, but it may give them a sense of which class members they might wish to work with once they have an actual assignment to complete.

Peer-response groups are set up in different ways. One arrangement calls for students to pass around and read one another's drafts silently, writing down reactions or questions in the margins or on a response form created by the instructor. Figure 6.2 shows an example of a response form. In another arrangement, students read their drafts aloud, and then each peer responds either orally or in writing on a response form. Yet another arrangement asks for focused responses to

---

**Peer Response Questions and Directions**

Reviewer's name: _____

Writer's name: _____

*Directions to **Writer**: Please choose three questions you'd like the reviewer to address. Circle them.*

*Directions to **Reviewer**: Please read the work and provide clear and detailed answers to each of the THREE questions to which the writer has asked you to respond. Continue on the back, if needed. After you've completed this, talk about your answers with the writer. Then write up a half-page synthesis and suggested plan for further action.*

1.  **How can this writer make the central argument of this essay stronger, clearer, or more easily accessible to readers?**

2.  **Identify any paragraphs whose purpose is unclear or that seem to be working at cross purposes, and explain how the writer can revise them to make the purpose clear.**

3. **Does the sequence of the argument build successfully? If not, suggest a way to reorder it and identify transitions that may need clarifying.**

4. Writers can offer their readers guidance in a number of ways, such as clearly defining their terms, explaining exactly how the evidence supports their claims, etc. **Identify places in this essay where these forms of guidance could be stronger, and explain specifically how the writer can strengthen them.**

5.  **Are there places in which you feel the textures or structures of language are serving the writer's purpose effectively? Are there places in which the language could be modified?**

**Figure 6.2** A peer-response group form

only one or two features of each draft (perhaps each member's thesis statement, or topic sentences and supporting details, or use of transitional words, for example).

Whatever the arrangement of your group, you want to be clear about exactly what you are expected to do, both as a peer-responder and as a writer. If your instructor gives you guidelines for working in a group, follow them carefully. If you've never before participated in a peer-response group, or in the particular kind of group that your instructor forms, consult the guidelines in Quick Reference 6.2; watch what experienced peers do; and ask your instructor questions (your interest shows a positive, cooperative attitude). Otherwise, just dive in knowing that you'll learn as you go.

---

### Quick Reference 6.2 ■ ■ ■ ■ ■ ■ ■

#### Guidelines for participating in peer-response groups

One major principle needs to guide your participation in a peer-response group: Always take an upbeat, constructive attitude, whether you're responding to someone else's writing or receiving responses from others.

- Think of yourself as a coach, not a judge.

- Consider all writing by your peers as "works in progress."

- After hearing or reading a peer's writing, briefly summarize it to check that you and your peer are clear about what the peer said or meant to say.

- Start with what you think is well done. No one likes to hear only negative comments.

- Be honest in your suggestions for improvement.

- Base your responses on an understanding of the writing process, and remember that you're reading drafts, not finished products. All writing can be revised.

- Give concrete and specific responses. General comments such as "This is good" or "This is weak" don't offer much help. Describe specifically what is good or weak.

- Follow your instructor's system for putting your comments in writing so that your fellow writer can recall what you said. If one member of your group is supposed to take notes, speak clearly so that the person's notes can be accurate. If you're the note taker, be accurate and ask the speaker to repeat what he or she said if the comment went by too quickly.

---

## 6c.2  Giving peer response as an individual

Often an instructor will have two people exchange drafts and provide responses and suggestions to each other. All of the general guidelines for peer response in groups apply to situations when you're the only person giving feedback, especially being helpful, specific, and polite.

You might find it useful to play a role if you feel awkward about giving reactions or suggestions to a classmate—especially if you think that some critical comments will help revision. (Instructors sometimes even assign such roles.) For example, instead of responding as yourself, pretend that you're a skeptical member of the writer's target audience. Respond as that person would, even in his or her voice. Separating your own personality from your responses can provide some useful distance. However, you should still aim to be constructive. Of course, you could also take the opposite role, responding as a friendly audience member who agrees with the writer; assuming that role can be particularly helpful if you personally disagree with a draft's position. If you're playing a role as you respond, you should make that clear to the writer by explaining, for example, that you're "playing devil's advocate," a person who is disagreeing on purpose. (The term *devil's advocate* comes from old church debates where one priest was charged with making the "devil's" case, making an argument against the church's position, which would be made stronger as a result of others needing to address challenges.)

As with peer response, your instructor may have you use a response form or follow a set of questions. (See Figure 6.2.) Here are some other questions you might find useful:

- What part of the paper was most interesting or effective?
- If you had to remove one paragraph, which would you sacrifice and why?
- If you had to rearrange two parts of the paper, which would you change and why?
- What is one additional fact, argument, or piece of information that might improve the paper?

Another good strategy is for the writer to generate a couple of questions that he or she would particularly like the reviewer to answer. Avoid questions that require only a *yes* or *no* response. For example:

| | |
|---|---|
| **NOT EFFECTIVE** | Is paragraph two on page three effective? |
| **EFFECTIVE** | How can I improve paragraph two on page three? |
| **NOT EFFECTIVE** | Do you like my tone in the paper? |
| **EFFECTIVE** | How would you describe my tone in this paper? |

Instead of answering specific questions, the instructor might ask you simply to write to the author about the strengths and weaknesses of the draft. Such responses can take the form of a letter to the author. Peer response can take practice to do well. Our students have found that if they're thoughtful while writing open responses to others, they get useful responses in return. Figure 6.3 shows an example of one student's peer response to another.

**Directions.** I'll pair you up with another student. Your task is to write a letter in which you play the role of someone who disagrees with the author of the paper; explain as carefully as you can why you disagree. State your own arguments and explain why they lead to a different conclusion. Now, I want you to be polite about this; don't indulge in the extreme language we looked at earlier in the course. However, to be helpful to the author you should be as persuasive as possible—even if you're playing a role that you actually disagree with. Send this letter by e-mail, with a copy to me (dhesse@du.edu).

---------------------------------------------

Dear Leslie,

     To begin with I thought your paper was very thorough and well thought out. It was lengthy and covered all the important things you needed to. But as I've been asked to take the role of someone who disagrees, then offer constructive criticism, there are some things that I think would help clarify and convince your readers who are on the fence about your position.

     Your argument is that sex education in schools needs to be complete and that "abstinence only" education is inadequate. You use a lot of statistics and surveys. This is good, it added credibility and "scientific reasoning," but when I see these, I wonder where you found these studies and whether they are themselves factual? You reiterated multiple times that abstinence-only educators use statistics that are untrue or slanted to favor their position. How does the reader know that you haven't made your own facts up or slanted them in your favor? My suggestion would be to label your studies and discuss where they came from and why they're credible. If one of them is from a government agency, you can include the address so if the reader wanted to they could verify the facts. I'm not accusing you of doing this, but it would only make your paper more believable.

     Because I am a strong believer in no sex before marriage, I worry about giving students too much information. I think that sex before marriage causes more problems than it solves. I do believe that giving out specific advice about contraception can encourage people to engage in sex before they are ready. Instead we should encourage students to wait. Can you prove to me that having information doesn't lead to early sexual activity?

     You stated on page two that a study found that consensual sex between two teenagers had no mental health effects on them. I disagree with this finding. Regardless of age and relationship status of the two parties involved, someone often gets hurt by casual sex. If there was a relationship before, it has the potential to be destroyed due to the new baggage. If one of the parties involved uses it as a one night stand and the other person really liked the other, he or she suffers emotional distress that could be extreme. Actually, I'm not sure this point belongs in your paper; because it's controversial, I wonder if your paper would be stronger without it.

                                Sincerely,
                                  Stephen

**Figure 6.3** An example of one student's peer response.

## EXERCISE 6-2

1. Choose a paper that you're writing (or have written). Create a set of questions that you would ask a peer reviewer to answer.

2. Show your questions to someone else in your class. Ask them to comment on how effective those questions would be for generating constructive comments; let them know that they may also suggest additional questions.

**ANSWERS: EXERCISE 6-2**
Answers will vary.

## 6d   How can I benefit from others' help?

Turning to the sometimes sticky issue of how to accept criticism of your writing, we offer you two pieces of personal advice from our own experience.

    First, keep in mind that most students don't like to criticize their peers. They worry about being impolite or inaccurate, or losing someone's friendship. Try, therefore, to cultivate an attitude that encourages your peers to respond as freely and as helpfully as possible. It's particularly important to show that you can listen without getting angry or feeling intruded on.

Second, realize that most people tend to be at least a little defensive about even the best-intentioned and most tactful criticism. Of course, if a comment is purposely mean or sarcastic, you and all the others in your peer-response group have every right to say so, and to not tolerate such comments.

---

**Quick Reference 6.3**

### Making good use of peers' comments

Adopt an attitude that encourages your peers to respond freely. Listen and resist any urge to interrupt during a comment or to jump in to react. A common rule in many writing workshops is that the paper's author must remain silent until the group has finished its discussion. (It's actually useful to hear people misinterpreting what you thought you said or meant.)

Remain open-minded. Your peers' comments can help you see your writing in a fresh way, which, in turn, can help you produce a better-revised draft.

Ask for clarification if a comment isn't clear. If a comment is too general, ask for specifics.

Finally, no matter what anyone says about your writing, it remains yours alone. You retain "ownership" of your writing always, and you don't have to make every suggested change. Use only the comments that you think can move you closer to reaching your intended audience and purpose. Of course, if a comment from your instructor points out a definite problem, and you choose to ignore it, that could have an impact on your grade—though many instructors are open to an explanation of your rationale for deciding to ignore what they said.

---

**ESOL Tip:** Students from cultures other than those in the United States or Canada might feel uncomfortable in the role of critic or questioner of other people's writing. Please know, however, that peer-response groups are fairly common in schools and at jobs because people usually think that "two heads are better than one." Sharing and questioning others' ideas—as well as how they are expressed in writing—is an honorable tradition in the United States and Canada. Peer-response groups help writers politely but firmly explore concepts and language, so please feel free to participate fully. In fact, some instructors grade you on your open participation in such activities.

## 6e  How can I participate effectively in online discussions?

You might take a course that happens entirely online, where discussion happens through typed remarks via e-mail or a program like Blackboard. However, even courses that meet in traditional classrooms often have an online written component. Contributing to the discussion between class meetings makes you an active learner, allows the instructor to gauge the level of your understanding, and enriches the class by circulating a diversity of opinions.

**WHAT ELSE?**
The field of digital rhetoric is still emerging. For more information about effectively using digital discussion in your composition classroom, you may wish to refer to *Virtual Peer Review: Teaching and Learning About Writing in Online Environments* by Lee-Ann Kastman Breuch (New York: SUNY Press, 2004).

There are two kinds of online discussions. In **synchronous** discussions, all the participants are online at the same time. The discussions are scheduled in advance and everyone meets online in "real time" for a specific amount of time. Instant messaging is an example of synchronous discussion. In **asynchronous** discussions, participants are online at different times. The discussion is usually open for hours or days, and there may be long periods of time between individual messages.

Whether you're in a completely online course environment or in an enhanced traditional classroom, being prepared for a few key things will help you participate effectively. First, your instructor may post a question and require everyone to respond to it, at least once. Also, your instructor may provide additional directions about the length or content of your posting or about its timing. (For example, he or she might require, "By midnight on Tuesday, post your answer to the discussion question.") Finally, your instructor might give directions about responding to something that others have posted in the discussion. Quick Reference 6.4 contains some additional guidelines about online discussions.

---

### Quick Reference 6.4

#### Guidelines for online discussions

- Unless specifically instructed to do otherwise, write in complete sentences and paragraphs. Academic discussions are more formal than e-mails or text messages between friends, so don't use the kind of shorthand you might use in those situations.

- Provide a context for your remarks. You might begin your message by summarizing a point from a reading before giving your opinion. Your contribution should be able to stand on its own, or it should clearly connect to the rest of the conversation.

- Respond to other writers. If someone makes a particularly good point, say so—and explain why. If you disagree with someone, politely explain why you disagree and be sure to support your reasoning. Discussions work better when people are actually discussing, and not just speaking while ignoring their audience.

- Be polite and work for the good of the discussion. When people aren't meeting face to face, they can be rude—sometimes even when they don't mean to be. You have to work extra hard to make sure that your TONE is constructive and helpful.

---

For more help with your writing, grammar, and research,
go to **www.mycomplab.com**

# 7

# Strategies for Writing Typical Kinds of College Papers

## 7a  What are typical kinds of papers I'll write in college?

Arguments and research papers are two of the most common types of college writing. In a written argument you try to persuade readers to take an action, adopt a position, or see a viewpoint as legitimate even if they ultimately disagree with it. Research papers (sometimes called term papers or seminar papers) involve gathering information from several sources, which you then summarize, analyze, and synthesize. Because arguments are such a vital part of college writing, we devote all of Chapter 5 to them. In addition, since there are many elements in writing a research paper, we devote Chapters 31–36 to this kind of writing.

College students face many types of writing, and expecting one set of guidelines to be perfect for every single variety would be unrealistic. Analyzing the WRITING SITUATION (Chapter 1) and understanding the WRITING PROCESS (Chapter 2) are important and useful for all writing. But we've found that general advice is even more helpful when combined with strategies for writing particular types of papers. Explaining the most common ones is our purpose in this chapter. Your instructor may use the term **genre** instead of "type" when describing kinds of papers; the two words basically refer to the same thing.

Consider the following writing assignments you might get in college:

- A lengthy library research paper
- A summary of a reading
- A report on a laboratory experiment
- A proposal
- A personal essay
- An essay exam
- A critical response to a reading

These types of writing obviously differ in terms of length, PURPOSE, CONTEXT, and SPECIAL CONSIDERATIONS. But notice how each type also uses different

SOURCES (readings vs. experiences vs. observations, for example), how the writer's ROLE changes (for example, from an impartial observer who keeps in the background to a center of attention whose experience and personality are foregrounded), and how format and style can vary. Knowing a few strategies will help you with different kinds of writing.

🛑 **Alert:** Terms that describe different types of writing are often used interchangeably. Most instructors attach specific meanings to each one; we've listed several terms above. Listen closely so you can sort out what terms your instructor uses. If your instructor's use of terms isn't clear, ask for clarification. For example, the words *essay, theme,* and *composition* usually—but not always—refer to written works of about 500 to 1,500 words. *Essay* is probably the most common. Similarly, the word *paper* can mean anything from a few paragraphs to a complex research project; it often refers to longer works. Finally, the general term *piece of writing* can refer to all types of writing. ●

## 7b What sources will I use in college writing?

A **source** is any form of information that provides ideas, examples, information, or evidence. Commonly, people think of readings (books, articles, Web sites, and so on) when they think of sources, and clearly readings are crucial. In fact, they're so important that we devote most of Chapter 32 to finding and using written sources, and we spend all of Chapters 36 through 38 explaining how to document them. Section 7f provides strategies for writings that make thorough use of readings.

There are other kinds of sources, too. Your own memories and experiences are a source, even though you may not think of them that way. Some academic situations allow or even require personal experiences, while others would definitely exclude them. As with every assignment, check with your instructor. You'll find more about writing from experiences in section 7c.

A second kind of source is direct observation. For example, you might be asked to observe people in a particular setting (let's say standing in line for a concert), take notes on their behaviors, and write a paper that explains what you've seen. You might be asked to attend a lecture and summarize what the speaker had to say or, additionally, to write a reaction to it. You might be asked to gather instances of a particular social or cultural phenomenon and, using analysis, inference, or synthesis, explore the meaning of that phenomenon. For example, an assignment that asks you to analyze how adolescents are portrayed in current television programs would require you carefully to observe several television shows, take notes, and explain your findings. We explain some types of writing about observations in section 7d.

writing assignments that balance pedagogical and curricular goals (Urbana, IL: NCTE, 2008).

**TEACHING TIP**
Think of this chapter as an introduction to material you will explore in more detail later. For example, when you teach students about the three different types of sources—personal experience, direct observation, and statistical/quantitative information—remember that later chapters will discuss appropriate sources for academic papers. This introduction is meant to help students expand their current framework for understanding the use of sources. You can bring in several short sources—articles, newspaper editorials, blogs, and other material—and ask students to identify the type of source.

**BACKGROUND**
Wendy Bishop's "Suddenly Sexy: Creative Nonfiction Rear-Ends Composition (*College English* 65.3 (2003): 257–275) offers a model for using personal essay assignments in composition courses.

**TEACHING TIP**
You might want to differentiate between the memoir and the autobiography to help students understand how a smaller part of a person's life might take on a particular significance. In approaching the memoir and personal essay, you might also want to challenge students to think about the role of truth in personal writing. Using newspaper articles about the controversy over "truth" in James Frey's *A Million Little Pieces* should provide interesting and provocative classroom discussion.

**TEACHING TIP**
In this chapter, each type of writing is introduced with a series of "elements" and a "process" that can be used to experiment with each type of writing. The exercises in this chapter are all assignments for students so that they may try the different forms of writing discussed here. You might ask students to make a chart comparing the different elements of each form of

writing in order to help them in understanding the differences among the types of writing.

**TEACHING TIP**

Each type of writing is broken into a three-part process: generating, shaping and revising. Help students to think about the timeline for each assignment by suggesting firm deadlines in your syllabus.

**BACKGROUND**

J. Blake Scott's "The Literacy Narrative as Production Pedagogy in the Composition Classroom" (*Teaching English in the Two-Year College* 24.2 (1997): 108–117) reviews strategies for approaching literacy narrative assignments in the composition classroom. Beth Daniell's "Narratives of Literacy: Connecting Composition to Culture" (*College Composition and Communication* 50.3 (1999): 393–410) provides an overview of the evolution of literacy narratives and a caution about relying on the literacy narrative too heavily.

**ANSWER: EXERCISE 7-1**

Answers will vary. Emphasize the notion that each example would be strengthened by a combination of sources.

**QUOTATION: ON WRITING**

Stories create our first memories. From the stories we hear as children we inherit the way we talk about how we feel, the values which we hold to be important, and what we regard as the truth.

—Margaret Meek, from *On Being Literate*

**TEACHING TIP**

Memoirs can be a nice inclusion in your syllabus. The explosion of memoir writing since the mid-1990s has created a rich period in the genre from which to draw for your teaching; a well-written memoir can set the tone for polished personal writing. The National Resource Center for the First-Year Experience and Students in Transition has an online list of books used in common reading programs, many of which are memoirs, all of which are

A third kind of source is statistical or quantitative information. Statistical or quantitative information comes to us in the form of numbers ("217 people liked mushroom pizza"), as percentages ("14 percent liked mushroom pizza"), or other statistics. Of course, you might find this information in a published written source: a table of information that reports results from a survey or measurements from a laboratory study. Alternatively, you may be collecting the data yourself. Laboratory courses typically have students perform experiments, make careful measurements, and report their findings. Business, education, or social science courses often have students conduct surveys or interviews. We discuss writing about statistical or quantitative information in section 7e.

Finally, we note that many assignments mix sources. You might be asked to asked to relate one of your experiences to a reading in which someone else reports their own. You might do a study (for example, of public displays of affection or of crowd behaviors at sporting events) that combines direct observations with a survey. We've explained these types separately just to make them clearer.

**EXERCISE 7-1**    Working alone or in a group, discuss the kinds of sources you might use in each of the following writing questions.

1. Scholar Kyung Kim offers three suggestions for improving American high schools. Would her suggestions have worked at the high school you attended?

2. Are most students at your college liberal or conservative? What about students around the country?

3. What qualities generally seem true of romantic comedy movies that have been released in the past year?

# 7c    How can I write about experiences?

Some writing assignments may ask you to write about your memories or experiences. Generally, such writings will involve effectively telling a story, often accompanied by some reflection on or analysis of that story.

## 7c.1    Memoirs and personal essays

In *memoirs,* writers tell what they remember about something that happened to them. While memoirs, like autobiographies, can cover most of a person's life, they often focus on smaller slices, such as a particular incident or a related set of incidents.

Students often think that, unless they're famous or something important or exciting has happened to them, their lives aren't worth writing about. Nothing could be further from the truth. Sure, a juicy story with famous people or dramatic events can be fun to read. But what makes a memoir good is less *what* it's about than *how* the writer writes about it. Consider the following short example.

> I can remember my father driving our car into a filling station at the edge of Birmingham. Two miles after we passed a particular motel, he would turn onto Callahan drive, which was a gravel road.

There's nothing very interesting here, really just some facts and a bare description. But consider this version, in which the author writes about driving from Tennessee to Alabama in the 1950s:

> After lunch, our father would fold up his map and tuck it in the felt visor until we pulled into the filling station on the outskirts of Birmingham. *Are we there yet?* We had arrived when we saw the Moon Winx Motel sign—a heart-stopping piece of American road art, a double-sided neon extravaganza; a big taxicab-yellow crescent with a man-in-the-moon on each side, a sly smile, a blue eye that winked, and that blatant misspelling, that *X* that made us so happy. Two miles beyond the winking moon, the Chrysler's tires would crunch the bed of river pebbles on the Callahan drive. In morning light the pebbles were salmon, ochre, a calcium white—and the water-worn stones, from the one-time bed of the Tombiggee River, closed around our bare feet like cool pockets.

> —Emily Hiestand, *Angela the Upside-Down Girl*

The basic information is no more dramatic than the first version we shared. However, the careful description makes it interesting. The main purpose of a memoir is to create a vivid sense of the experience for its readers. Memoirs have an expressive or literary purpose.

Personal essays are closely related to memoirs (in fact, your instructor may use the terms interchangeably). Once again, you'll want to tell about an experience. Personal essays tend to contain more reflection and to make their points more explicitly. They answer the question "What does this experience mean?" or "How does my experience illustrate a particular idea?"

## Important Elements of Memoirs and Personal Essays

- A well-told story. Your readers will want to know what happened. They will also want to know enough background information and context so they can fully understand and appreciate what happened and why it made an impression.
- Lively details. Help your readers see and hear, perhaps even smell, taste, and feel what you were experiencing. Recreate the place and time, the people who were involved. Give readers reason to like (or dislike, as the case may be) the places or people involved by the way you characterize them.

appropriate for inclusion in a first-year writing course; see <http://nrc.fye.sc.edu/resources/reading/read.php>. You can also allow students to choose from a group of memoirs and break them into reading groups at the beginning of the semester.

**BACKGROUND**
Literacy narratives are a popular writing activity for first-year students. University of Wisconsin-Stevens Point Professor Sue Slick has published examples of her students' literacy narratives online at <http://www.uwsp.edu/education/sslick/autobio/index.htm>. Cathlena Martin, a PhD student at the University of Florida, has posted an excellent literacy narrative assignment at <http://www.clas.ufl.edu/users/cmartin/ENC3254/literacynarrative.htm>.

**BACKGROUND**
Helen Collins Sitler explores what skills students are able transfer to other writing situations after first-year composition in the article "Works in Progress: First-Year College Students After EN 101" (*The Quarterly* 23.2 (2001), available online at <http://www.nwp.org/cs/public/print/resource/145>).

**TEACHING TIP**
When working with students on observation, a nice activity is to take students outside of the classroom. Choose a large setting where students can work in individually or in pairs to describe a scene on your campus. You might choose the library, the cafeteria, or a particularly picturesque spot outside. Students can read their observations aloud and compare what they focused on in their writing to what their classmates' writing emphasized. To add in a visual element, you might ask students to take photographs of their settings—or to create dioramas—and then to compare the visual and written texts. These comparisons may reveal places where students can expand their descriptive writing skills.

## QUOTATION: ON WRITING

An ox at the roadside, when it is dying of hunger and thirst, does not lie down; it walks up and down—up and down, seeking it knows not what—but it does not lie down.

—Olive Schreiner, *From Man to Man*

## TEACHING TIP

If your campus has a play or musical performance during the semester, you may wish to assign students to write a "real" review, asking them to attend the event and review it based on guidelines you create as a class. Once revised, students might opt to submit their reviews to the campus paper. If your class is keeping a blog or blogs, you might also ask students to publish their reviews on the Internet (for more information on blogs, see Chapter 46).

## BACKGROUND

Elizabeth Chiseri-Strater's *Academic Literacies: The Public and Private Discourse of University Students* is an excellent resource for thinking about college-level writing skills and the ways in which the composition classroom prepares students to be successful writers (Portsmouth, NH: Boynton/Cook, 1991).

## QUOTATION: ON WRITING

A work has form insofar as one part of it leads a reader to anticipate another part, to be gratified by the sequence.

–Kenneth Burke

## TEACHING TIP

Although Chapter 5 focuses on argumentative writing, interpretations are an excellent place to begin to help students understand the importance of evidence. You might bring in a series of Rorschach-like inkblots and ask students to "interpret" what they see, offering evidence based on how they see the blots. You can ask students to use the "doubting game" as a way to strengthen their interpretations. Break students into pairs and have them exchange interpretations. Have students take an opposing view of the interpretation, raising questions and inconsistencies in the interpretation.

- Reflective or analytic paragraphs or passages. In addition to telling readers what happened, also tell them what you were thinking during the experience (take us inside your head at the time) or what you make of it now, looking backward.

- An effective use of STYLE and TONE (Chapter 8).

### Advice on Process

1. Generating

   - In your first draft, concentrate on getting the basic story down. Pretend you're writing to a friend who is interested in what you're saying.

   - Try creating some detailed scenes, describing the physical setting and including some dialogue so readers will get a close sense of being there.

   - Do some FREEWRITING or use other invention strategies about the significance of your story. What did you learn at the time? How about looking back now? How does the experience connect to other experiences, readings, or things you've noticed in the world around you (in movies or on television, for example, or at work, in school, or in family life).

2. Shaping

   - Your basic shape is to tell a story; however, you will also likely have some commentary or reflection (when you "step back" and explain what it all means). You can put that reflection at the beginning, in the middle, or at the end, or you can scatter it in a few places. Choose the strategy that seems most effective.

   - You can begin at the beginning of the story, of course. But you can also begin with some exciting or interesting part from the middle or the end, then go back to the beginning to tell how it all started. You've probably seen movies that have flashbacks, which are examples of this technique.

   - Try to have places in your story where you "slow down," creating a scene in detail, as well as where you "speed up," covering events quickly so you can get to the interesting stuff.

3. Revising

   - Do your story and its details convey your impression of the experience? A common piece of advice is to "show, not tell." Try this experiment. Temporarily leave out any explicit statements about the story and what it means, and show the draft to a friend or peer. Let them tell you what they see as the point or meaning. If they can't—or if their interpretation differs significantly from yours—you need to revise. Put the explicit statements back in for your final draft.

- Are there places where you need more specific detail?
- Are there places where the writing drags too much and needs to be cut?
- Are the reflective or analytic parts thoughtful and interesting, or are they formulaic or obvious?

## 7c.2 Literacy narratives

A literacy narrative is a specific kind of memoir in which you tell the story of how you developed as a reader and writer. Generally, these stories stretch from your earliest memories to the present day, and we find that students are often surprised at the memories they dig up while writing. First year writing instructors sometimes assign literacy narratives, as do some education or social sciences instructors.

### Important Elements of Literacy Narratives

- The elements important to memoirs and personal essays also matter for literacy narratives: a good story, lively details, and reflection.
- Examples of your previous reading, writing, or other language experiences. This may take the form of book titles, papers you remember writing, specific people important in your development as a reader and writer, scenes from school or home, and so on.

### Advice on Process

1. **Generating and drafting.** Several questions can help you generate ideas.
   - What are the earliest books or stories you can remember someone reading to you? The earliest you can remember reading yourself? Can you tell us about more than the titles? Why do you think you remember them?
   - If anyone read to you (a parent, a sibling, a relative, a teacher, etc.), what do you remember about them? Can you create a word picture of that person (or those people)?
   - Where do you remember reading or writing at different points in your life? Was there a particular room in your house or apartment, a particular classroom? Can you describe the setting vividly?
   - What were your favorite books? What topics did you like to read about? What particular writings do you remember?
   - What were your worst experiences reading or writing? What made them bad?

**TEACHING TIP**

A number of ethicists and medical schools have case studies readily available online for problem-based inquiry activities. You can use these case studies in class as real life examples for students to examine. Emory University's Science Net has a variety of problem-based learning links at <http://www.cse.emory.edu/sciencenet/coll_curr/pbl_links.html>.

**BACKGROUND**

Ethnographies are a popular assignment in first-year writing classes. *Becoming American, Becoming Ethnic: College Students Explore Their Roots* is a wonderful collection of student ethnographies written at Binghamton University (ed. Thomas Dublin. Philadelphia: Temple UP, 1996). The Utah State University Ethnographic Field School in Huanchaco, Perú, has student-authored ethnographies available online at <http://www.usu.edu/anthro/peru/2003/ethno_2003.html>.

**BACKGROUND**

Quantitative reasoning is increasingly being added to undergraduate general education requirements. Helping students to write about quantitative materials is an essential skill. Carleton College has an interesting curriculum and materials available online at <http://serc.carleton.edu/quirk/index.html>.

**TEACHING TIP**

Have students use "Advice on Process" at the end of section 3e.1 to peer review Marcus's paper and his use of quantitative information.

Another useful exercise is to ask students to write a reaction to a controversial topic such as "should the college cafeteria serve only organic food?" or "censoring the college radio station." After students write their reactions, ask them to read the pieces aloud. As a class, brainstorm how the arguments could be strengthened with quantitative data.

**TEACHING TIP**

You might consider collaborating with another faculty member from the science department to talk about lab reports. Ask a fellow faculty member to share his/her requirements for writing lab reports. If there's time, you might even invite him/her to speak about lab reports briefly in class and to address the ways in which writing in the sciences is different from writing in the humanities.

**TEACHING TIP**

Writing in response to text is a major skill that students need to master in the first year of their college studies. In this section of the chapter, you might want to take extra time to emphasize the importance of summaries, critical responses, interpretations, and syntheses. You can use common texts—articles, books, films, plays, etc.—as a basis for all four response activities. If your students are keeping writing portfolios, you can encourage them to include all four types of writing at the end of the semester. Equally important is for students to understand how these four types of writing are different. Ask students to reflect on the purpose of each type of writing and the difference in skills that each one requires. As with other examples in this chapter, you can ask students to use the "Advice on Process" as a checklist in reviewing their own work or peer responses to the assignments you give.

**ANSWER: EXERCISE 7-2**

Answers will vary. At the beginning of a course, personal writing can help students to feel comfortable and to gain a sense of accomplishment in completing writing assignments. You might ask students to save this assignment and come back to it at the end of the term as part of a portfolio reflection assignment. For more information on portfolio writing, see Chapter 47. Sometimes, a nice end of term activity is to create an anthology of student writing for students in the course. This assignment would make for a nice collection of student work.

- Who or what were your strongest influences on reading or writing—either for good or ill?
- How did reading and writing "fit in" (or not) with other activities in your life?
- Why do you think you became the type of reader and writer you are today—whatever kind that is?

2. Shaping. The strategies for shaping literacy narratives are the same as those for shaping memoirs and personal essays.

3. Revising and editing. Here are some questions to ask yourself, or to have a peer-response group ask (6c.1), when revising:

- Do all the incidents contribute effectively to the whole narrative? Are there any that need to be cut or shortened?
- Are there places that would be stronger if you created a more vivid scene?
- Are there smooth connections and transitions between the different elements?
- Have you reflected on the meaning of the experiences? Have you included some general observations on what your experiences "add up to" and tell about yourself as a reader and writer?

**EXERCISE 7-2**

1. Write a memoir about a trip you took, whether it was across town or across the country. The quality of your writing is more important than how unusual the trip was.

2. Write a section of a literacy narrative focusing on one of three periods in your life: birth to age 9; age 10 to 15; age 16 to the present.

# 7d How can I write about observations?

Writing about observations means writing about things you directly and intentionally see or experience. *Intentionally* is the important word. Sometimes you write about things that you just happened to notice or experience. However, in academic writing situations, observations are almost purposeful and deliberate. You observe as a writer with a specific goal.

## 7d.1 Reports of observations

Sometimes your assignment is to report about an event. You're asked to attend a presentation or lecture and summarize the talk. You go to a concert, play, or sporting event with the goal of explaining what happened. In these writing situations, your purpose is to inform, and your role is to be an objective reporter, much like a journalist. Other times you may be asked to describe a scene (a landscape, theatre set, classroom), a person, a process, an object (a sculpture, building, machine), or an image. We devote an entire separate section (4j) to viewing and analyzing images.

## Important Elements of a Report

* A clear description of what you observed, which is complete and appropriately detailed—but not excessively detailed.
* Objectivity.
* The proper format that your instructor requires.

## Advice on Process

1. Generating and drafting
   * Take careful notes. The quality of your report will depend on the clarity and fullness of the details you generate.
   * If you're writing about an event, gather information needed to answer the JOURNALIST'S QUESTIONS (see 2c.4), which are particularly useful for this kind of writing. Write your first draft as soon after the event as possible, while your notes are still fresh.
   * Ask questions, if possible, not only of speakers or performers but also of other people attending the event. Ask what they observed.
   * Be precise with descriptions, noting both major and seemingly minor details.

2. Shaping
   * Orient your readers in the first paragraph. Provide all of the general information (who, what, when, where, how, and why) in your opening.
   * Provide details in body paragraphs. You can organize events or processes either by chronological order (the sequence in which things happened) or by categories or topics.
   * Organize reports about objects by giving a big picture, then moving either spatially (left to right, top to bottom, center to edge) or by features to enhance the description.

3. Revising (questions to ask yourself or to have peers answer)
   * Have you maintained objectivity throughout? Would your report agree with the report of someone else writing about the same thing?

**TEACHING TIP**

Essays of application can be very abstract for students. While many first-year writing students are familiar with the fundamentals of college-level writing, the application of theory can be daunting. Consider offering a small theoretical piece and discussing it as a class. Then, ask students to apply that theory to another piece of writing. Many students will need extra practice with this skill, so the more opportunities you have to provide structured practice, the more confident they will be in writing this kind of assignment.

**TEACHING TIP**

Other chapters in this book will provide students with information, examples, and exercises on argument, proposal writing, annotated bibliographies, and research papers. Writing essay exams, however, is not addressed in detail. You may want to spend some time on this type of writing in class, emphasizing how the work you do in this course can be applied to timed-writing situations. You may also want to cover some of the basics of test-taking skills. Many college and university Web sites offer extensive tips on essay exams, so you will want to explore the resources your campus provides. An excellent overall resource is Purdue University's Online Writing Lab at <http://owl.english.purdue.edu/handouts/general/gl_essay.html>.

**QUOTATION: ON WRITING**

To write is to write is to write is to write is to write is to write is to write.

—Gertrude Stein

- Did you write an introduction that gives readers a good overall picture?
- Would everything be clear to an audience who hadn't observed what you did?
- Are there any places where you either need more detail or where you need to try to make the report more concise?
- Have you fulfilled all of the assignment's special considerations?

## 7d.2  Reviews or evaluations

A *review* is a report plus an evaluation: a "reasoned judgment" of whether something is good or bad, fair or unfair, true or false, effective or useless. You're familiar with movie, music, and product reviews, which are designed to help you decide whether to invest your time, attention, or money. Reviews in academic situations show how thoughtfully you can evaluate a presentation, performance, product, event, art work, or some other object.

### Elements of Reviews

- Your review needs to contain both a summary or description and one or more evaluations of the source's quality or significance. Your thesis needs to take the form of an evaluation.
- You need to provide reasons for your evaluation, and you need to provide evidence for those reasons.
- Be sure to answer any specific questions your instructor asks and to follow any special considerations of the assignment.

### Advice on Process

1. Generating and drafting
   - The advice for reporting applies. In addition, you need to generate an assessment. This involves critical thinking (Chapter 4).
   - Analyze the source, using strategies in section 4d. Pay attention to both content and style.
   - Synthesize, if appropriate. How does the source relate to other ones like it?
2. Shaping
   - Your opening paragraph needs to provide an overview of the event and your thesis.
   - Summarize the source in the early part of the paper (a paragraph or two after your opening) so your audience understands it. Depending

on the type of source you're writing about, this could include a summary of the plot, a description of the setting, a list of songs performed, a physical description of an image or object, or so on.

- Your remaining body paragraphs generally need to begin with a topic sentence that makes an assertion about some feature, followed by an explanation or evidence. You may want to save details from your summary/description, to include when you discuss particular features.

3. Revising and editing
   - Is basic information clear?
   - Have you included judgments?
   - Have you provided enough details and evidence to make your judgments convincing?

## 7d.3  Interpretations

An interpretation makes an argument about what something means or why it's significant. You might be familiar with interpretations from studying fiction or poetry, and we will talk more about that kind of writing in section 7f and in Chapter 40. However, interpretation is hardly restricted to readings. Consider the following different assignment questions:

- In the painting *Guernica,* what do you think Picasso wants his viewers to feel and understand?
- What is the atmosphere of a particular place (a coffee shop, a shopping mall, a club, and so forth)?
- How are doctors and nurses portrayed on television?

Each of these examples involves both description and interpretation. When you're doing an interpretation, don't feel like you have to "guess the right answer," as if there's one and only one right meaning. Instead, the quality of your work will depend on generating interesting insights that you then support with reasons. Analysis (section 4d) and inference (4e) are especially important for interpretation.

### Important Elements of an Interpretation

- A clear explanation of the event, phenomenon, or object that you're interpreting.
- Statements about what the subject of your interpretation means or why it's significant.

- Convincing support, including reasoning, to show why your interpretive statements are convincing.

**Advice on Process**

1. Generating

   - Summarize and describe very carefully; the act of paying close attention can generate insights.

   - Use strategies of analysis. In particular, see the strategies in Section 4d for looking at elements of the process.

   - Use strategies of inference. In particular, see the strategies in section 4e.

   - Don't be afraid to explore. Brainstorm as many possible interpretations as you can; many of them might be outlandish, but it's better to choose from several possible interpretations than to be stuck with the first thing that comes to mind.

   - Play "the believing game." Believe that you have the authority and expertise to generate an interpretation and boldly put it on paper.

2. Shaping

   - Good interpretations have a thesis that states the meaning or significance that your paper will then go on to explain.

   - Body paragraphs will each offer an explanation for your interpretation, with support and reasoning showing readers why it is plausible.

3. Revising

   - Play "the doubting game." Assume (for the purpose of thinking critically) that your interpretation is flawed. State the flaws. Then revise to address them.

   - Is the balance of summary and interpretation effective? Are there places where you need more reasoning or support?

## 7d.4   Case Studies

Some **case studies** are careful descriptions and interpretations of individuals, usually focusing on some set of features in relation to a specific situation or issue (for example, "students who work in fast food" or "parents coping with divorce" or "people involved in extreme sports"). The word *case* might suggest a hospital case to be solved, and indeed medical journals publish these kinds of cases; however, *case* also has a more neutral sense of an "instance," and people in case studies usually don't have anything wrong with them, physically or otherwise.

Case studies are important in psychology, social work, education, medicine, and similar fields in which it's useful to form a comprehensive portrait of people in order to understand them and, in some cases, to help them. In some fields, such as education, people do case studies in order to understand or test theories and practices. For example, if you learn that a certain teaching style is effective, you might do a case study of a student in order to understand how it works in a particular instance.

Case studies can also lead to theories or other kinds of research. For example, if you wondered about what factors make people happy at their jobs, you might do a case study (or two or three) of individual workers to generate possible criteria. People about whom you write case studies are called **subjects**. A kind of writing related to a case study is a **profile**, in which you create a portrait in words of a person.

## Important Elements of Case Studies of Individuals

- A combination of observation, interview, and discussion of any artifacts you might have from your subject (writings, test results, creative works, and so on).
- A focus on particular traits important to the purpose of the study.
- A combination of report and interpretation or analysis.
- Depending on the type of case study and its purpose, it may include recommendations for a course of action, a discussion of implications, or a commentary on a theory. (For this last, also see section 7f.5.)

## Advice on Process

1. Generating
   - Arrange to meet or observe the subject of your case study or profile. Take notes about the meeting, focusing on characteristics, mannerisms, and perhaps interactions with others.
   - Conduct one or more interviews, following our guidelines in Quick Reference 32.1.
   - Look for patterns in your notes. Use clustering to group similar ideas (see section 2c.5). Make each idea a paragraph or two, stating the idea in the form of a topic sentence, then using details from your notes to support your observations.

2. Shaping
   - Learn whether you're to follow a standard report format, for example, one similar to lab reports (section 7e.3).
   - Your opening needs to introduce your subject, explain your purpose for studying him or her, and include a thesis that states your main finding, interpretation, or impression.

- Organize your following paragraphs by qualities you recognized in your subject, for example, by aspects of her or his personality, behavior, attitudes, or interactions. In each case try as best you can to explain "why" your subject has those qualities or aspects.

3. Revising

- Will your readers get a complete and accurate sense of this person?

- Are there any places where your information is "thin," places where you made an interpretation but didn't really back it up?

- Have you included interpretation, trying to explain "why?" If so, have you fully justified your conclusions?

- Is your tone respectful and fair?

## 7d.5 Ethnographies

The term *case studies* also refers to a kind of research about a particular group of people or situation (consider studies of online video game players, of college basketball players and their study habits, of a store's marketing strategy, of homeless life in Seattle, and so forth). They are closely related to **ethnographies**, another form of FIELD RESEARCH (32c), in that both generally are comprehensive studies of people interacting in a particular situation. Situational case studies and ethnographies commonly occur in courses in business, education, or the social sciences, with anthropology and sociology being prime examples of disciplines that use these studies. Someone might do an ethnography of a classroom in order to understand the interactions and relationships among students. Or they might do a situational case study of an office, a club or social organization, a church, or so on.

### Important Elements of Situational Case Studies or Ethnographies

- Thick description. The anthropologist Clifford Geertz coined the term *thick description* to explain the kinds of details needed in ethnographies. Pay attention to everything, from the setting, to observed interactions, to what people say.

- Interpretation. The purpose of an ethnography is to offer an explanation of what the situation means in context.

### Advice on Process

1. Generating

- Schedule ample time to observe the situation you're writing about; visit more than once if at all possible.

- Follow the strategies for field research (section 32c).
- Take extensive notes. Double column field research notes (Figure 32.1 on page 520) are particularly effective.
- Interview people who are involved (Quick Reference 32.1), if possible, or have them complete questionnaires that you can analyze.
- Look for patterns in your notes. Group similar information or ideas together and draft sentences that say what each group means; this forms the basis for paragraphs.

2. Shaping
- Some formal case studies and ethnographies take forms similar to lab reports and other empirical studies (7e.3) and have the following sections: Introduction (explaining the issue and perhaps reviewing other literature); Procedures (describing how you chose the setting or people to study, how you gathered information, and so on); Findings (the longest part of the paper, usually, in which you relate what you learned; and Discussion or Conclusions (in which you explain what is significant about what you learned).
- Other case studies put less emphasis on the structure above; instead, they are more narrative, letting the finding unfold like a story, or they are organized according to topics and support materials.

3. Revising
- The questions for revising case studies of individuals (see above) also apply to these writings.
- Would a participant in the scene you're describing share your interpretation? Ethnographers frequently let their subjects read a draft and comment on it.
- What alternative interpretations are available? What conclusions could someone else draw from your notes?

## EXERCISE 7-3

1. Write a short report that explains a concert, lecture, or other event to an audience of people who didn't attend it.

2. Write a review of one of the following: a new electronic device, a current movie, a class that you attended, a place where you worked. Your audience is other people who are deciding whether to purchase the device, attend the movie or class, or accept a job at that place.

3. Write a case study of one of your classmates, focusing on their educational experiences, their hobbies or entertainment interests, and their career hopes.

**ANSWER: EXERCISE 7-3**
Answers will vary. As students attempt different types of writing, encourage them to read strong models of this kind of writing first.

4. Working either alone or with others, write a case study of one of the following situations: people with an activity in common (a team, a musical group, a gathering of video game players); a workplace; a class; a coffee shop.

5. Write an interpretation for a general educated audience of a representation of certain types of people on a particular type of television show. Choose one of the following types of people: adolescents; college students; single parents; white-collar professionals; working-class laborers; gays or lesbians. Then choose one of the following types of shows: sitcoms, crime dramas, medical dramas, reality shows, game shows.

# 7e    How can I write about quantitative data or information?

Quantitative information or data comes in the form of numbers. Of course, such information can be an important source of detail and evidence in almost any kind of writing. However, some writings especially require writers to translate numbers into words and to explain what they mean.

## 7e.1    Reports of data

Reporting data is parallel to summarizing. You need to present information clearly and objectively, translating numbers into words. The challenge with these types of assignments is that the numbers seem to "speak for themselves." In other words, if you have a table of information it might seem pointless to write about it. A table is an efficient way to present information, and converting absolutely everything into words would be a waste of time; as a result, reports usually combine words and numbers. To illustrate how this kind of writing works, we've included part of a student paper below. In it, Marcus Kapuranis reports information from the National Survey of Student Engagement, which each year questions first-year college students and college seniors in order to learn about their experiences in a number of areas.

## Sample Student Report of Quantitative Data

Kapuranis 1

Marcus Kapuranis

English 1122

Professor Bateman

24 May 2008

Diversity of Student Experiences Reported in the National
Survey of Student Engagement

Part of the 2007 National Survey of Student Engagement (NSSE) asked college freshmen and seniors to report on their experiences with people different from themselves. These differences included racial and ethnic backgrounds as well as attitudes and beliefs, and the final report provides not only totals for each group of students but also a breakdown of responses according to types of college. Responses to three questions, shown in Figure 1, provide a clear picture of the national situation.

When asked how often they had serious conversations with students whose religious beliefs, personal opinions, or values differed from their own, 12% of first year students reported "never," 34% said "sometimes," 29% said "often," and 25% said "very often." In response to the same question, seniors reported similarly. 10% said "never," 35% said "sometimes," 30% said "often," and 26% said "very often."

| First-Year Students  Seniors (in percentages) | | DRU-VH | | DRU-H | | DRU | | Master's-L | | Master's-M | | Master's-S | | Bac-AS | | Bac-DIV | | Top 10% | | NSSE 2007 | |
|---|---|---|---|---|---|---|---|---|---|---|---|---|---|---|---|---|---|---|---|---|---|
| Had serious conversations with students who are very different from you in terms of their religious beliefs, political opinions, or personal values | Never | 10 | 8 | 12 | 10 | 12 | 10 | 13 | 11 | 16 | 12 | 13 | 10 | 8 | 6 | 15 | 11 | 8 | 6 | 12 | 10 |
| | Sometimes | 33 | 33 | 33 | 35 | 34 | 35 | 34 | 35 | 35 | 37 | 34 | 37 | 32 | 34 | 37 | 38 | 29 | 30 | 34 | 35 |
| | Often | 31 | 31 | 30 | 30 | 29 | 28 | 29 | 29 | 27 | 27 | 29 | 29 | 30 | 31 | 28 | 28 | 30 | 33 | 29 | 30 |
| | Very often | 27 | 27 | 26 | 26 | 25 | 27 | 24 | 25 | 22 | 23 | 24 | 24 | 30 | 29 | 21 | 23 | 33 | 32 | 25 | 26 |
| Had serious conversations with students of a different race or ethnicity than your own | Never | 14 | 11 | 15 | 12 | 15 | 12 | 18 | 14 | 20 | 16 | 16 | 14 | 14 | 11 | 19 | 15 | 11 | 8 | 16 | 12 |
| | Sometimes | 34 | 34 | 34 | 35 | 35 | 33 | 34 | 34 | 35 | 37 | 34 | 36 | 34 | 37 | 37 | 38 | 31 | 32 | 34 | 35 |
| | Often | 28 | 29 | 27 | 28 | 27 | 28 | 26 | 27 | 25 | 25 | 27 | 26 | 27 | 26 | 24 | 26 | 28 | 28 | 27 | 28 |
| | Very often | 24 | 27 | 24 | 26 | 23 | 26 | 22 | 25 | 20 | 23 | 23 | 24 | 25 | 26 | 20 | 21 | 31 | 32 | 23 | 25 |
| Institutional emphasis: Encouraging contact among students from different economic, social, and racial or ethnic backgrounds | Very little | 12 | 21 | 14 | 20 | 14 | 18 | 14 | 18 | 13 | 17 | 12 | 17 | 11 | 16 | 15 | 19 | 11 | 17 | 13 | 19 |
| | Some | 33 | 36 | 34 | 36 | 32 | 34 | 32 | 35 | 33 | 34 | 31 | 34 | 31 | 35 | 33 | 36 | 29 | 35 | 33 | 35 |
| | Quite a bit | 33 | 27 | 32 | 28 | 32 | 29 | 33 | 29 | 33 | 30 | 32 | 30 | 32 | 29 | 32 | 27 | 33 | 28 | 32 | 28 |
| | Very much | 22 | 16 | 21 | 16 | 22 | 19 | 21 | 18 | 22 | 19 | 24 | 20 | 26 | 19 | 21 | 18 | 27 | 20 | 22 | 17 |

Fig. 1. Student experiences with difference.

continued >>

Kapuranis 2

The NSSE study also broke the responses down according to type of institution. There are three categories of "Doctoral Research University" (DRU): those that have "very high" (VH) research levels, those that have "high" (H), and others. There are three categories of "Master's Universities," Large, Medium, and Small (L, M, S), and two categories of "Baccalaureate Colleges," traditional liberal arts and sciences colleges (AS) and those that have a broader range of course and programs (DIV). (This particular study didn't survey two-year colleges, although the *Two-Year College Survey of Student Engagement* does.) The findings across the institutional types were fairly comparable, with the largest differences between traditional liberal arts colleges and medium-size master's universities. The liberal arts colleges had the fewest students (8%) reporting "never" talking to diverse students and most students (30%) reporting "very often" doing so. In contrast the medium-sized master's colleges had the most students (16%) reporting "never" talking to diverse students and the second fewest (22%) reporting "very often."

A second question asked students to report how frequently they had serious conversations with someone of a different race or ethnicity . . .

Kapuranis 5

Work Cited

NSSE: National Survey of Student Engagement. *Experiences That Matter: Enhancing Student Learning and Success Annual Report 2007*. Bloomington: Center for Postsecondary Research, Indiana University, 2007. Web. 14 May 2008.

In his report, Marcus opens with a brief overview of the study and then chooses to include the report itself. When he starts summarizing its findings, he moves from the big picture to the more detailed, and he takes care to explain information (such as the institutional types) that would be unclear to his audience. He selects the most important information, which takes some judgment. After all, you don't want to bore your readers with sentence after sentence telling every single finding, especially because they can read the original itself. Most important for this type of writing, he remains objective, adding nothing to the information that anyone else wouldn't.

### Important Elements of Reporting Data

- Clear and accurate translations of numbers into language.
- Judicious selection and summary of data to report.
- Objective reporting, unless your task is to go a step further to analyze or interpret (7e.2).

### Advice on Process

1. Generating

   - Ask yourself what is the key information? What do readers most need to see or recognize in this data?
   - If you're stuck, begin by trying to put everything into sentences. You probably won't want to keep all of these sentences in your final draft, because it would get boring; however, you should start writing rather than stare at a blank page.

2. Shaping

   - In the first paragraph, provide a summary or overview of the data you're reporting. Tell its source, how it was gathered, and its purpose. Your thesis will generally forecast the kind of information that follows (as in the case of Marcus Kapuranis's paper above).
   - Group pieces of related information. Each grouping will potentially become a paragraph.
   - Create or reproduce any charts or tables that would be too wordy to translate into language.

3. Revising

   - Do your words accurately report the main information?
   - Will your readers better understand the information through your language, or has your language actually contributed little?

- Have you made the writing as interesting as you can, given the limitations of maintaining objectivity that is faithful to the nature of the task?
- Have you documented the source(s) accurately?

## 7e.2   Analyses of data

Most papers that emphasize quantitative information go beyond reporting and into analysis or synthesis: drawing conclusions about what the information means or connecting it to other pieces of information or ideas. When you analyze data, you interpret it, going beyond translating numbers into language.

Marcus Kapuranis's paper in section 7e.1 reports how frequently first year students and seniors had serious conversations with people different from them. Here is what a paragraph analyzing that data might say:

> In terms of how often they had serious conversations with students whose religious beliefs, personal opinions, or values differ from their own, first-year students and seniors were disappointingly similar. For example, 34% of first years said "sometimes," almost identical to the 35% of seniors, and 25% of first years said "very often," almost identical to 26% of seniors. The reason this is disappointing is that four years in college seem to have had little effect on students in this dimension. If one of the purposes of college is to have students learn from new knowledge and experiences, one would expect an increase in the frequency of serious encounters with different types of people. Apparently, this isn't happening.

Notice that the analysis reports findings, but it does so in the context of what they might mean. This paragraph emphasizes why the results are disappointing and provides reasons for that interpretation.

### Important Elements of Analyses

- A clear report of the data, as explained in section 7e.1.
- Statements that make interpretations, inferences, or evaluations of the data.
- Reasoning and support that convince readers that your statements are justified.

### Advice on Process

1. Generating
   - Follow strategies for generating reports of data.
   - Use techniques for analysis (4d) and making inference (4e).

- Brainstorm. For example, try to write ten different statements about what the information means or what its implications might be. Many of them will be silly or invalid, but don't let that stop you. At least one or two will probably be worthwhile.

2. Shaping

- Your basic organization will be a summary of the data (report) followed by analysis. However, you don't want to summarize everything up front—just the most important materials. The reason is that during your analysis, you'll want to quote or cite some of the data. It becomes boring to see the information twice.

3. Revising

- Have you been fair and accurate in the way you've represented the information?

- Have you considered alternative interpretations?

- Have you provided clear and convincing explanations for any analytic, interpretive, or evaluative comments?

- Have you documented your paper appropriately?

## 7e.3 Lab reports and empirical studies

A **lab report** is a specific and formal way of presenting and discussing the results of experiments or laboratory measurements, in fields such as chemistry, biology, physics, engineering, and other sciences. Lab experiments are one kind of **empirical research**, a name that generally refers to attempts to measure something (from physical substances to behaviors) in order to prove or disprove a theory or hypothesis. Disciplines other than the sciences use experiments, too; among them are psychology and other social sciences, some areas of education (for example, "Does this teaching strategy work better than that teaching strategy?"), economics, and so on. However, those disciplines also use sources like surveys or very specific observations to collect data. Both lab reports and other kinds of empirical research studies tend to have the same standard elements.

### Important Sections of Lab Reports and Similar Empirical Studies

- **Introduction.** State your purpose, present background materials (for example, a review of previous studies), and your hypothesis.
- **Methods and materials.** Describe the equipment and procedures.
- **Results.** Accurately and objectively provide information that you acquired through your study.

- **Discussion.** Interpret and evaluate your results, including whether they supported your hypothesis and why or why not.
- **Conclusion.** Discuss the implications of your work, along with any limitations. Suggest further studies.

Take care to keep clear distinctions among each of these sections. Lab reports and empirical studies frequently include two other parts. One is an ABSTRACT, a short overview of the entire report, which appears directly after your title. The other is a list of REFERENCES, which is crucial if you discuss other published research. We provide more information about writing lab reports, as well as an example, in Chapter 41.

**ANSWER: EXERCISE 7-4**
Answers will vary. Encourage students to share their work in small, peer-review groups.

**EXERCISE 7-4** Following are two tables of data from the General Social Survey. Table A reports responses from the 1970s, and Table B from the 2000s. Write a 100–300 word analysis of the findings.

**"Men are better suited for politics than are women"**

| A. 1970's results, by two age groups, by percent | 18-40 | 41-89 | TOTAL | B. 2000's results, by two age groups, by percent | 18-40 | 41-89 | TOTAL |
|---|---|---|---|---|---|---|---|
| AGREE | 38.3 | 55.9 | 47.5 | AGREE | 20.7 | 25.5 | 23.4 |
| DISAGREE | 61.7 | 44.1 | 52.5 | DISAGREE | 79.3 | 74.5 | 76.6 |
| Total Percent | 100.0 | 100.0 | 100.0 | Total Percent | 100.0 | 100.0 | 100.0 |
| (Total N) | (2,418) | (2,612) | (5,030) | (Total N) | (1,480) | (1,915) | (3,395) |

SDA: Survey Documentation and Analysis. "General Social Survey Quick Tables." <http://sda.berkeley.edu/archive.htm>

Figure 7.2 Data tables from the General Social Survey

# 7f How can I write about readings?

Nearly all types of writing about observations have counterparts in writing about reading. You may be asked to write summaries, critical responses, analyses or interpretations, and syntheses. To illustrate some of these types and strategies for doing them, we'll refer to the following part of an essay by Barry Schwartz, titled "The Tyranny of Choice."

> Does increased affluence and increased choice mean we have more happy people? Not at all. Three recently published books—by the psychologist David Myers, the political scientist Robert E. Lane, and the journalist Gregg Easterbrook—point out how the growth of material affluence has not brought with it an increase in subjective well-being. Indeed, they argue that we are actually

experiencing a *decrease* in well-being. In the last 30 years, the number of Americans describing themselves as "very happy" declined by 5 percent, which means that about 14 million fewer people report being very happy today than in 1974. And, as a recent study published in *The Journal of the American Medical Association* indicates, the rate of serious clinical depression has more than tripled over the last two generations, and increased by perhaps a factor of 10 from 1900 to 2000. Suicide rates are also up, not only in the United States, but in almost every developed country. And both serious depression and suicide are occurring among people younger than ever before. Deans at virtually every college and university in the United States can testify to this malaise, as they witness a demand for psychological services that they are unable to meet.

Why are people increasingly unhappy even as they experience greater material abundance and freedom of choice? Recent psychological research suggests that increased choice may itself be part of the problem.

It may seem implausible that there can be too much choice. As a matter of logic, it would appear that adding options will make no one worse off and is bound to make someone better off. If you're content choosing among three different kinds of breakfast cereal, or six television stations, you can simply ignore the dozens or hundreds that get added to your supermarket shelves or cable provider's menu. Meanwhile, one of those new cereals or TV stations may be just what some other person was hoping for. Given the indisputable fact that choice is good for human well-being, it seems only logical that if some choice is good, more choice is better.

Logically true, yes. Psychologically true, no. My colleagues and I, along with other researchers, have begun amassing evidence—both in the laboratory and in the field—that increased choice can lead to *decreased* well-being. This is especially true for people we have termed "maximizers," people whose goal is to get the best possible result when they make decisions. Choice overload is also a problem for people we call "satisficers," people who seek only "good enough" results from their choices, but the problem is greatly magnified for maximizers. Much of the relevant research is summarized in my book, *The Paradox of Choice: Why More Is Less.* Here are some examples:

- Shoppers who confront a display of 30 jams or varieties of gourmet chocolate are less likely to purchase *any* than when they encounter a display of six.

- Students given 30 topics from which to choose to write an extra-credit essay are less likely to write one than those given six. And if they do write one, it tends to be of lower quality.

- The majority of medical patients do not want the decision authority that the canons of medical ethics have thrust upon them. Responsibility for medical decisions looks better to people in prospect than in actuality: Sixty-five percent of respondents say that if they were to get cancer, they would want to be in charge of treatment decisions, but among those who actually have cancer, only 12 percent want that control and responsibility.

- Maximizing college seniors send out more résumés, investigate more different fields, go on more job interviews, and get better, higher-paying jobs than satisficers. But they are less satisfied with the jobs, and are much more stressed, anxious, frustrated, and unhappy with the process.

These examples paint a common picture: Increasing options does not increase well-being, especially for maximizers, even when it enables choosers to do better by some objective standard. We have identified several processes that help explain why increased choice decreases satisfaction. Greater choice:

- Increases the burden of gathering information to make a wise decision.
- Increases the likelihood that people will regret the decisions they make.
- Increases the likelihood that people will *anticipate* regretting the decision they make, with the result that they can't make a decision at all.
- Increases the feeling of missed opportunities, as people encounter the attractive features of one option after another that they are rejecting.

## 7f.1  Summaries

To *summarize* is to extract the main messages or central points of a reading and restate them in a much briefer fashion. A summary doesn't include supporting evidence or details. It's the gist, the hub, the seed of what the author is saying. Also, it isn't your personal reaction to what the author says. How you summarize depends on your situation and assignment. For example, you can summarize an entire 500-page book in a single sentence, in a single page, or in five or six pages. Most of the time when you get an assignment to write a summary, your instructor will tell you how long it needs to be; if he or she doesn't, it's reasonable for you to ask.

Following are examples of two different levels of summary based on "The Tyranny of Choice" passage above.

### SUMMARY IN A SINGLE SENTENCE

Research finds that people with large numbers of choices are actually less happy than people with fewer choices (Schwartz).

**SUMMARY IN 50 TO 100 WORDS**

Boshoven 1

Kristin Boshoven

English 101

Professor Lequire

5 April 2008

Summary of "The Tyranny of Choice"

Research finds that people with large numbers of choices are actually less happy than people with fewer choices. Although the amount of wealth and choice has increased during the past thirty years, fewer Americans report themselves as being happy, and depression, suicide, and mental health problems have increased. While some choice is good, too many choices hinder decision making, especially among "maximizers," who try to make the best possible choices. Research in shopping, education, and medical settings shows that even when people eventually decide, they experience regret, worrying that the options they didn't choose might have been better (Schwartz).

Boshoven 2

Work Cited

Schwartz, Barry. "The Tyranny of Choice." *Chronicle of Higher Education* (23 Jan. 2004): B6. Print.

Notice that the longer summary begins with the same sentence as the short one, because leading a summary with the reading's main idea is effective. Notice that both summaries put ideas in the author's own words and capture only the main idea.

One decision to make is whether to refer to the author during your summary or to leave him or her out, as in the examples above. Check if your instructor has a preference. The second example above could be rewritten (the four dots are ELLIPSES, showing material left out):

> In "The Tyranny of Research," Barry Schwartz summarizes research that finds. . . . while some choice is good, too many choices. . . .

### Important Elements of Summaries

- Inclusion of only the source's main ideas.
- Proportional summary of the source. This means that longer and more important aspects of the original need to get more space and attention in your summary.
- Use of your own words. If there are particular key terms or phrases, include them in quotation marks, but otherwise put everything into your own words.
- Accurate DOCUMENTATION of the original source.

### Advice on Process

Note: For more help in writing a summary, see section 35j.

1. Generating
   - Identify TOPIC SENTENCES or main ideas, separating them from examples or illustrations. You want to focus on the main ideas.
   - Take notes in your own words, then put the source away. Write from your notes, going back to check the original only after you've written a first draft.

2. Shaping
   - Begin with a sentence that summarizes the entire reading, unless you're writing a particularly long summary.
   - Follow the order of the original.
   - Include a Works Cited page (Chapter 36) or References (Chapter 37), depending on the required style.

3. Revising
   - Have you maintained objectivity throughout?
   - Have you put things into your own words?
   - Have you been proportional?
   - Have you accurately documented?
   - Is there an even more CONCISE (see Chapter 11) way to state certain things?

## 7f.2  Critical responses

A **critical response** essay has two missions: to provide a SUMMARY of a source's main idea and to respond to that idea.

A well-written critical response accomplishes these two missions with style and grace. That is, it doesn't say, "My summary is . . ." or "Now, here's what I think. . . ." Instead, you want the two missions to blend together as seamlessly as possible. A critical response essay may be short or somewhat long, depending on whether you're asked to respond to a single passage or to an entire work.

Here's student Kristin Boshoven's short critical response to Barry Schwartz's essay, "The Tyranny of Choice," which we reprinted above. Note that it incorporates the summary she wrote for a previous assignment.

---

Boshoven 1

Kristin Boshoven

English 101

Professor Lequire

7 April 2008

Too Much Choice: Disturbing but not Destructive

Barry Schwartz argues that people with large numbers of choices are actually less happy than people with fewer choices. Although the amount of wealth and choice has increased during the past thirty years, studies show that fewer Americans report themselves as being happy. Depression, suicide, and mental health problems have increased. While some choice is good, too many choices hinder decision making, especially among people who Schwartz calls "maximizers," people who try to make the best possible choices. Research in shopping, education, and medical settings shows that even when people eventually decide, they experience regret, worrying that the options they didn't choose might have been better.

continued >>

Boshoven 2

Although Schwartz cites convincing evidence for his claims, he ultimately goes too far in his conclusions. Excessive choice does seem to make life harder, not easier, but it alone can't be blamed for whatever unhappiness exists in our society.

My own experience supports Schwartz's finding that that people who have thirty choices of jam as opposed to six (B6) often don't purchase any. About a month ago my husband and I decided to buy an inexpensive global positioning (GPS) device to use in our car. When we went to the store, we were confronted with twenty different models, and even though a helpful salesperson explained the various features to me, we couldn't make up our minds. We decided to do more research, which was a mistake. After weeks of reading reviews in everything from *Consumer Reports* to the *New York Times*, we are close to making a decision. However, I have a sinking feeling that as soon as we buy something, we'll learn that another choice would have been better, or ours will drop $50 in price. In the meantime, we could have been enjoying the use of a GPS for the past month, if we had not worried so much. I could relate similar experiences trying to choose which movie to see, which dentist to visit, and so on. I suspect others could, too, which is why I find Schwartz's argument convincing at this level.

However, when he suggests that the increase of choice is a source of things like depression and suicide, he goes too far. Our society has undergone tremendous changes in the past forty or fifty years, and many of those changes are more likely to cause problems than the existence of too much choice. For example, workers in the 1950s through the 1970s could generally count on holding jobs with one company as long as

continued >>

Boshoven 3

they wanted, even through retirement. A 1950s autoworker, for example, might not have been thrilled in his job (and these were jobs held almost exclusively by men), but at least he could count on it, and it paid enough to buy a house and education for his family. The economic uncertainties of the past twenty years, and especially since 2001, have meant that workers—and now women as well as men—do not have the same job stability as decades ago.

Although I agree that too many choices can lead to anxiety and even unhappiness, there are larger factors. If Americans report more depression and suicide than they once did, a more likely candidate is economic and social uncertainty, not having too many kinds of cereal on the grocery store shelves.

---

Boshoven 4

Work Cited

Schwartz, Barry. "The Tyranny of Choice." *Chronicle of Higher Education* (23 Jan. 2004): B6. Print.

---

## Important Elements of Critical Responses

- A clear and concise representation of the source.
- Statements of agreement, disagreement, or qualified agreement (you accept some points but not others), accompanied by reasons and evidence for your statements.

## Advice on Process

1. Generating
   - Use ACTIVE READING and CRITICAL READING to identify the main points and generate reactions to the article.

- Use techniques for ANALYZING (4d), drawing INFERENCES (4e), and ASSESSING REASONING PROCESSES (4h).

2. Shaping
   - Write a summary of the main idea or central point of the material you're responding to.
   - Write a smooth TRANSITION between the summary and what comes next: your response. This transitional statement, which bridges the two parts, need not be a formal THESIS STATEMENT, but it needs to signal clearly the beginning of your response.
   - Respond to the source based on your prior knowledge and experience.

3. Revising
   - Have you combined summary and response? Have you explained your response in a way that readers will find thoughtful and convincing?
   - Have you fulfilled all documentation requirements? See Chapters 36–38 for coverage of four DOCUMENTATION STYLES (MLA, APA, CM, and CSE). Ask your instructor which style to use.

## 7f.3   Interpretations and analyses

Interpretations and analyses resemble critical response in that both make claims about a reading. Critical responses ask whether a source is "good," but interpretations and analyses ask what a source "means." You might be most familiar with this kind of writing from previous English or literature courses in which a teacher asked you to interpret a poem, play, or story. In fact, we've devoted much of an entire chapter, along with examples, to writing about literature, Chapter 40.

## 7f.4   Syntheses

To *synthesize* is to weave together material from several sources. Unsynthesized ideas and information are like separate spools of thread, neatly lined up, possibly coordinated but not integrated. Synthesized ideas and information are threads woven into a tapestry. By synthesizing, you show evidence of your ability to bring ideas together. Synthesis goes beyond summary and comes after it in the critical thinking process (section 4b).

One common synthesizing task is to connect two or more readings or source materials into a single piece of writing. You complete this synthesis after you have summarized, analyzed, and evaluated each of the source materials. Another common type of synthesis is to connect material to what you already know, creating a new final product that is your own.

## SYNTHESIZING MULTIPLE SOURCES

Your goal in synthesizing multiple sources is to join two or more texts together into a single writing. The resulting text needs to be more than just a succession of summaries. That is, avoid merely listing who said what about a topic. Such a list isn't a synthesis. It does not create new connections among ideas.

The following example shows how student Tom Mentzer synthesized two sources. Read Source 1 and Source 2 to get familiar with the information he read. Then, read Tom's synthesis that follows.

### Source 1

In Shishmaref, calamity has already arrived. The village of 600 Inupiaq lies on the fragile barrier island of Sarichef, where sea ice forms later each year, exposing the land to autumn storms that carve away 50 feet or more of shoreline a season. Two houses have slipped into the sea; 18 others have been moved back from the encroaching ocean; others buckle from the melting permafrost. Ten million dollars has been spent on seawalls, to no avail. Residents have concluded permanent resettlement is their only option.

—Julia Whitty and Robert Knoth, "Sea Change"

### Source 2

Global temperatures have risen by about 0.6 degrees Celsius since the nineteenth century. Other measures of climate bolster the theory that the world is getting warmer: satellite measurements suggest that spring arrives about a week earlier now than in the late 1970s, for example, and records show that migratory birds fly to higher latitudes earlier in the season and stay later.

—John Browne, "Beyond Kyoto"

Now read Tom's synthesis. Notice how he used SUMMARY and PARAPHRASE to synthesize the two sources. Also notice how the first sentence in his synthesis weaves the sources together with a new concept.

### Example of a Synthesis of Two Sources

Global warming is affecting both the natural and artificial worlds. Rising temperatures have accelerated spring's arrival and changed the migration patterns of birds (Browne 20). They have also changed life for residents of Arctic regions. For example, eighteen families in Shishmaref, Alaska, had to move their houses away from the coast because the permafrost under the beaches had thawed (Whitty and Knoth).

—Tom Mentzer, student

Notice how Tom's synthesis uses in-text citations (MLA style) to signal to the reader which information he has borrowed from the two sources. In the Works

Cited list at the end of his paper, Tom listed full source information for both sources. To learn how to document your sources, see Chapters 36 (MLA), 37 (APA), or 38 (CM, CSE).

**SOURCES LISTED IN TOM'S WORKS CITED PAGE**

Browne, John. "Beyond Kyoto." *Foreign Affairs* 83.4 (2004): 20–32. Print.

Whitty, Julia, Robert Knoth. "Sea Change." *Mother Jones*. Foundation for National Progress, Sept./Oct. 2007. Web. 2 Jan. 2008.

### Process Advice

- Make comparisons with—or contrasts between—concepts, ideas, and information. Do the sources generally agree or generally disagree? What are the bases of their agreement or disagreement? Are there subtle differences or shades of meaning or emphasis?
- Create definitions that combine and extend definitions you encounter in the separate sources.
- Use examples or descriptions from one source to illustrate ideas in another. See the related discussion in section 7f.5.
- Use processes described in one source to explain those in others.
- In revising, ask, "Have I truly synthesized the sources, or have I just written about one and then the other?"

**ANSWER: EXERCISE 7-5**
Answers will vary. Ask students to read their work aloud. As a class, critique each sample against the criteria offered in this section.

**EXERCISE 7-5** Write a one-paragraph synthesis of the passage by Barry Schwartz (printed on pp. 196–198) and the following opening to a short article by Ronni Sandroff, editor of *Consumer Reports on Health:*

> Last time I dropped by my pharmacy in search of a decongestant, I was stopped cold by the wall-sized display of remedies. The brands I had used in the past had multiplied into extended families of products. Yes, I saw *Contac, Excedrin, Tylenol,* and *Vicks,* but each brand came in multiple versions. Products for severe colds, coughs and colds, and headache and flu abounded, and there were further choices: gels, tablets, capsules, extended release, extra strength. I was eager to just grab a product and go, but to find the right one I had to dig out my reading glasses and examine the fine print.
>
> —Ronni Sandroff, "Too Many Choices"

### SYNTHESIZING WITH ONE SOURCE

If you're working with only one source, you need to make connections between the source and your prior knowledge, whether from experience, films or television, classes or conversations, or previous readings. Don't be afraid to synthesize. We're always surprised when we find that some students assume that what they think has no value. Nothing could be further from the truth.

In the following example of a synthesis with one source (Source 2 above), student Mikayla Stoller connected her reading to her previous knowledge, in this case a movie she had seen. Her first sentence links the two with a new idea.

### Example of a Synthesis with One Source

Even if the existence of global warming is well established, the consequences of it may not be. A 0.6 degrees Celsius rise in temperature over the past century has caused spring to arrive earlier and migrating birds to change their habits (Browne 20). However, some believe that global warming could have the unexpected effect of causing a new ice age. The 2004 movie *The Day after Tomorrow* portrayed New York City as suddenly frozen over with ice because of climate changes. Although most scientists criticized the science in that movie, it seems clear that global warming will alter the world as we know it.

—Mikayla Stoller, student

Mikayla used parenthetical citations in the body of her paragraph and included the full citation in her Works Cited list at the end of her paper.

### SOURCE AS LISTED IN MIKAYLA'S WORKS CITED PAGE

Browne, John. "Beyond Kyoto." *Foreign Affairs* 83.4 (2004): 20–32. Print.

### Advice on Process

- Use your powers of play. Mentally toss ideas around, even if you make connections that seem outrageous. Try opposites (for example, read about athletes and think about the most nonathletic person you know). Try turning an idea upside down (for example, if you have read about the value of being a good sport, list the benefits of being a bad sport).

- Use the technique of clustering (2c.5) to lay out visually the relationships among elements in your source and other ideas that come to mind.

- Discuss the source with another person. Summarize its content and elicit the other person's opinion or ideas. Deliberately debate that opinion or challenge those ideas.

- Write your personal response to the material. Explain whether you agree or disagree and also the reasons why you respond as you do.

## 7f.5 Essays that apply theories or concepts (essays of application)

Essays that apply theories or concepts (or **essays of application**) take general information from one source (usually a reading but perhaps from a lecture) and apply it to another, usually for the purpose of interpretation or evaluation. Four example assignments will make this clearer.

1. How does Smith's theory of social deviance explain the behaviors of the criminals who are portrayed in Jones's book?

2. Based on your own experiences, are Beaudoin's categories of high school cliques accurate and sufficient?

3. Which symptoms of depression, as explained by Kho, does the narrator of *The Bell Jar* seem to display? Which does she not?

4. Kevin Sarkis argues that baseball pitchers have progressed further than batters in the past fifty years. Analyze statistics in *The Baseball Abstract* to either confirm or disprove his claim.

Assignments like these require a form of synthesis, in that they combine two or more sources into a single piece of writing. However, the sources have characteristics that distinguish essays of application from other syntheses, which is why we explain them separately. One source explains a theory, concept, or definition; even if it's based on details from formal research or study, its purpose is to offer a generalization about something. The other source is more specific, consisting of stories, experiences, scenarios, observations, quantitative data, or reports of events (perhaps even fictional situations, as in example 3 above), with little or no analysis or interpretation.

Instructors sometime assign essays of application to test how well you grasp concepts; being able to apply an idea to a new situation demonstrates your deeper understanding of it. They may also assign such essays to help you analyze or interpret a situation or body of information in ways you might not have considered. For example, suppose you're asked to read an article that claims that, from a very early age, gender determines the roles assumed by children playing in mixed groups, and then to apply the article to your own observations of children at play. You would pay attention to that situation differently if you were asked to apply a different theory (for example, that physical size determines play roles). Finally, you might apply a theory to a situation in order to test it. Suppose, in the previous example, you observe lots of play situations and find that boys and girls all play the same kinds of roles. A paper resulting from this application will explain why the theory may be invalid.

### Important Elements of Essays of Application

- A clear and accurate summary of the theory or concept you're applying.

### Advice on Process

1. Generating
   - Use strategies for summary or report (whichever is appropriate) to explain each source.
   - Brainstorm a list of all the possible ways the specific source illustrates the concept or theory. Use analysis and inference.

- Brainstorm a list of all the possible ways the specific source disproves or complicates the concept or theory. Use analysis and inference.
- Use other generating strategies.

2. Shaping

- Begin your essay in one of two ways. A. Start with a brief summary of the theory or concept, leading to a thesis that states how it applies to the specific source (situation, reading, or information) you're discussing. B. Start with a brief summary of the specific source (situation, reading, or information), leading to a thesis that states how it demonstrates, disproves, or complicates the theory or concept.
- If you follow opening strategy A, your next paragraph(s) will need to summarize the specific source. If you follow strategy B, your next paragraph(s) will need to summarize the theory or concept.
- Your next paragraphs will support your thesis, giving reasons (and support) for your assertion.
- (Optional). Discuss any facts or observations that seem not to fit your thesis. Explain why they, nonetheless, don't mean you're wrong.

3. Revising

- Have you explained both sources accurately and efficiently, using summary, QUOTATION, or paraphrase?
- Have you written a strong thesis that applies one source to the other?
- Have you provided reasons to support your thesis and developed your paragraphs to provide details that show those reasons are solid?
- Have you used complete and accurate documentation of sources, using the style required by your instructor?

## 7f.6 Annotated bibliographies

An annotated bibliography is a list of sources that includes, for each one, publishing information, a brief summary, and usually your commentary on the content. Such commentary often addresses how a particular source relates to the other sources in the bibliography (33j).

## 7f.7 Essay exams

"Essay exam" is a broadly-used term for questions that require you to answer in sentences, usually in a timed situation. Prepare for essay exams by re-reading your class material and by actually doing some writing. Making up a few possible questions is an excellent way of studying, and having yourself answer those practice questions under pressure is good preparation for the real thing. When you receive an essay question, resist the urge to dive right in to writing. Use a margin or scratch paper to jot an informal outline or series of points you want to make. Especially take care to understand the question and respond directly to it. For example, if the question asks you to RESPOND, ANALYZE, SYNTHESIZE, or APPLY, you don't just want to SUMMARIZE. While an essay exam may, rarely, simply invite you to dump information, most of the time it will ask you to perform a very specific task. After you've drafted your answer, save some time to proofread. It's easy to introduce errors when you're writing under pressure.

For more help with your writing, grammar, and research, go to **www.mycomplab.com**

# Writing Effectively, Writing with Style

# 8

# Style and Tone in Writing

## 8a What do style and tone in writing involve?

**Style** and tone both refer to *how* you say something, in contrast with *what* you're saying. Neither style nor tone are rule bound, the way that grammar is. The sentence structures you shape, from the simple to more complex, contribute to the style of your writing. The words you choose for your sentences create the tone in your sentences. They work in concert. After we discuss how they operate together, we address style and tone separately in this chapter (see 8c and 8d) to differentiate the larger elements of crafting sentences from the smaller elements of skillful word choice.

## 8b How do style and tone operate in writing?

Style and tone operate together through a combination of the varying levels of formality and personality that you employ. The level of **formality** in writing can be roughly divided into three categories. Formal writing belongs in the structures and language of ceremonies, contracts, policies, or some literary writing. "Formal writing," by the way, doesn't mean dull and drab material. Indeed, lively language always enhances such material. **Informal writing** is casual, colloquial, and sometimes playful, usually found in e-mails, text messages on cell phones, Facebook postings, and certain BLOGS.* Semiformal writing, which sits between these poles, is the style and tone found in academic writing, as well as in much business and public writing. For an audience expecting such communication, its style is clear and efficient, and its tone is reasonable and evenhanded.

Generally, when you write for an audience about whom you know little, a somewhat more formal style and tone is appropriate, though an entirely formal presentation isn't desirable. If informal writings are t-shirts and jeans, and formal writings are tuxedos and evening gowns, then semiformal writings are business-casual attire. Here are examples of writing in the three levels of formality.

| | |
|---|---|
| INFORMAL | It's totally sweet how gas makes stars. |
| SEMIFORMAL | Gas clouds slowly transform into stars. |

*Words printed in SMALL CAPITAL LETTERS are discussed elsewhere in the text and are defined in the Terms Glossary at the back of this book.

FORMAL
> The condensations of gas spun their slow gravitational pirouettes, slowly transmogrifying gas cloud into star.
> —Carl Sagan, "Starfolk: A Fable"

**Personality** refers to how much the writer reveals about him- or herself with patterns of sentence structure and choice of words. An intimate style and tone, which treats the reader as a close friend, includes specific personal experiences and opinions. A familiar or polite style and tone includes some experiences or personal thoughts, but only of a kind you might share in a professional relationship with an instructor, supervisor, or colleague. In such writing, the reader can glimpse the writer behind the language, but not as fully as in intimate writing because the emphasis is on the ideas or subject matter. An impersonal style reveals nothing about the writer, so that the content is all that the reader is aware of.

INTIMATE
> When our eighth grade teacher assigned Huckleberry Finn by Mark Twain, I got cranky and angry after the first chapter. Why did he lay something so hard on us? I couldn't catch the story or figure out what the dialect was saying.

FAMILIAR/ POLITE
> The next day in class, I was greatly relieved to discover that most other students had run into the same problems as I had reading Huckleberry Finn by Mark Twain.

IMPERSONAL
> Our teacher explicated the story line and clarified how to decode the dialect, which enabled the class to appreciate the narrative and its underlying message.

Quick Reference 8.1 lays out the levels of formality and of personality as conveyed by the style and tone you insert into your writing.

## Quick Reference 8.1

### Major elements that create style and tone in writing

| Elements | Levels | | |
|---|---|---|---|
| Formality | Informal | Semiformal | Formal |
| Personality | Intimate | Familiar/Polite | Impersonal |

**EXERCISE 8.1** Working individually or in a group, describe the style of each of the following paragraphs in terms of formality and personality.

1. I would be willing to bet serious money that right now in your kitchen you have olive oil, garlic, pasta, parmesan cheese, and dried basil (maybe

Personality—Intimate
Creativity—Artistic

2. Formality—Semiformal
   Personality—Impersonal
   Creativity—Translucent (the ironic aside draws attention to itself)

3. Formality—Informal
   Personality—Intimate (use of second person)
   Creativity—Artistic, though an argument could be made for Translucent

4. Formality—Formal
   Personality—Impersonal
   Creativity—Transparent

5. Formality—Formal
   Personality—Impersonal
   Creativity—Transparent

6. Formality—Formal
   Personality—Familiar or Polite (though some might argue for Impersonal)
   Creativity—Artistic

**QUOTATION: ON STYLE**
Style and structure are the essence of a book; great ideas are hogwash.
                    —Vladimir Nabokov

even fresh basil!). Nothing exotic there, right? They're ingredients we take for granted. But their appearance in our kitchens is a relatively recent phenomenon. Believe me, those big-flavor items did not come over on the Mayflower. It took generations, even centuries, for Americans to expand their culinary horizons to the point where just about everybody cooks Italian and orders Chinese take-out. Heck, the supermarket in my little Connecticut hometown even has a sushi bar.
                    —Thomas J. Craughwell, "If Only the Pilgrims Had Been Italian"

2. Google has yet to hit upon a strategy that combines the innovation it is known for with an appeal to the self-interest that is the currency of the capital's power brokers. One reason AT&T and Microsoft have succeeded in stoking antitrust interest against Google—quite ironic, given that both companies have been subject to large government antitrust actions—is that they're better versed in the fine points of lobbying. Both companies, for example, hold sway over many lawmakers by frequently reminding them how many employees live in their districts ("jobs" is a metric lawmakers respond to).
                    —Joshua Green, "Google's Tar Pit"

3. Prices are rising for the black sludge that helps make the world's gears turn. If you think we're talking about oil, think again. Petroleum prices have tumbled from their record highs. No sooner was there relief at the pump, however, than came a squeeze at the pot. That jolt of coffee that a majority of American adults enjoy on a daily basis has gotten more expensive and could go even higher this year. . . .
                    —*New York Times*, "Joe Economics"

4. Use Form W-9 only if you are a U.S. person (including a resident alien), to provide your correct TIN to the person requesting it (the requester) and, when applicable, to:
   1. Certify that the TIN you are giving is correct (or you are waiting for a number to be issued),
   2. Certify that you are not subject to backup withholding, or
   3. Claim exemption from backup withholding if you are a U.S. exempt payee.
                    —Internal Revenue Service, Directions for Form W-9

5. Studies of home-based telework by women yield mixed results regarding the usefulness of telework in facilitating work–life balance. Most research on the social impacts of home-based telework focuses on workers—employees or self-employed—who deliberately choose that alternative work arrangement. Labour force analysts, however, predict an increase in employer-initiated teleworking. As a case study of the workforce of one large, financial-sector firm in Canada, this article considers the conditions of employment of involuntary teleworkers, those required by their employer to work full-time from a home office. In-depth interviews were con-

ducted with a sample of 18 female teleworkers working for the case study firm in a professional occupation.

—Laura C. Johnson, Jean Andrey, and Susan M. Shaw,
"Mr. Dithers Comes to Dinner"

6. I remember vividly the moment that I entered the world of literacy, education, institutional "correctness," and, consequently, identity. I was demonstrating to my older sister how I wrote my name. The memory comes after I had been literally taught how to do it—which strokes of the pencil to use to create the symbols that equate to my name.

—Elise Geraghty, "In the Name of the Father"

# 8c   How do I write with style?

A well-respected style manual states,

> Style, with a capital S, achieves what a rule book never can: it lights the page, draws in readers, earns their delight, makes them gasp or weep, and sometimes captures a place in memory.

—*The New York Times Manual of Style and Usage*

As authors of this handbook, we can report that after seeking to inject the type of style described above into our passages, we always try to distance ourselves from our attempts, so that we can come back another day with a bit less severity or euphoria. Showing our work to each other helps, too.

Writing with style comes more naturally with lots of practice. It rarely shows up on most first drafts. The pleasure of creating a graceful, engaging style in your writing results from experimenting with different structures. And every so often, writers surprise themselves with sentences and passages of enormous power and impact that emerge almost unbidden on the page. Those are magical moments. To write with style, refer to Quick Reference 8.2; as you do, add your own personal hints so that you can make the material your own.

## Quick Reference 8.2

### How to create good writing style

- Try out different sentence types to maintain readers' interest (see 9a, 9n, 9r).
- Use sentence coordination and subordination to vary the pace (see 9d–9m).
- Vary sentence length to keep your readers' attention (see 9c).
- Experiment with diction or word choice (see 12d, 12e, 12h)

continued >>

**QUOTATION: ON VOICE**

We often refuse to accept an idea merely because the tone of voice in which it has been expressed is unsympathetic to us.

—Friedrich Nietzsche

**TEACHING TIP**

While students may not know offhand what the term "tone" means in the context of essay writing, they almost certainly will know what the phrase "tone of voice" means. You might want to build on section 8d by discussing with students just how much they already know about "tone" that they have learned from their friends and family (e.g., "Don't take that tone of voice with me!").

**BACKGROUND**

As an object lesson of how to write to a specific type of audience, you might use the "Tone in Business Writing" page at the Purdue OWL at <http://owl.english.purdue.edu/owl/resource/652/01/>.

**QUOTATION: ON TONE**

The quietness of his tone italicized the malice of his reply.

—Truman Capote

**QUOTATION: ON TONE**

We are not won by arguments that we can analyze but by the tone and temper, by the manner which is the man himself.

—Samuel Butler

---

**Quick Reference 8.2**　　　(continued)

- Use figurative language (see 12c)
- Employ the gracefulness of parallelism in sentences and larger sections for the pleasure of your readers (see Chapter 10).
- Be consistent in your level of formality and personality (see 8b)

## 8d　How do I write with appropriate tone?

Tone in writing involves choosing the right words to deliver your meaning. Tone operates like tone of voice, except that you can't rely on facial expressions and voice intonations to communicate your written message. The language you choose in your writing creates the tone you relay to your readers.

Your choice of words determines the degree to which your readers notice the language itself along with the content that the language is conveying. Well written figurative language (see 12c) can create pleasant surprises for readers. However, if you draw too much attention to your language without communicating a clear message, your writing suffers. Conversely, if you use only simple, one syllable words that create a dull drone, your writing suffers.

Your word choice can result in a wide range of possible tones, some desirable and some not. We list several in Quick Reference 8.3.

**Quick Reference 8.3**　　　■ ■ ■ ■ ■ ■

### Some examples of desirable and undesirable tone

| | |
|---|---|
| SERIOUS | The advent of space travel supported the predictions of science fiction, especially that of Jules Verne, who wrote in the nineteenth century. |
| LIGHT OR BREEZY | What a trip to flip through Verne's *From the Earth to the Moon* and find space ships taking off from Tampa, Florida, only 130 miles from today's Cape Canaveral. |
| SARCASTIC | Some poor slobs probably think Verne is worth worshiping like a god. |
| MEAN | Verne also made some dumb forecasts. |
| CONDESCENDING | Although most people struggle to read Jules Verne's sometimes complex books, those who succeed can consider themselves at least reasonably competent readers. |
| WHINING | Why should Jules Verne be the third most translated writer in the world? He's no big deal. If I put my mind to it, I could write as well as he did. |

Achieving the tone you want in each piece of your writing calls for experimenting with different words with similar meanings. If you consult a thesaurus (which can be a very productive activity), be sure to check the definition of any synonym that's new to you. Lynn once had an excellent student who used the word "profound" instead of "deep," without looking it up in a dictionary. The result was this sentence: "The trenches beneath some parts of that sea were dangerously profound." That misuse ruined an otherwise intelligent passage.

As with style in writing, appropriate tone results from your private trials, rejections, and explorations. Good tone rarely shows up on most first drafts. Quick Reference 8.4 offers you some suggestions for achieving an appropriate tone in your writing. Add your own advice to the list to personalize it.

---

**Quick Reference 8.4**  ■ ■ ■ ■ ■ ■ ■

### How to use appropriate tone in writing

- Reserve a highly informal tone for conversational writing.
- Use a semiformal level of formality in your academic writing and when you write for supervisors, professionals, and other people you know only from a distance.
- Avoid an overly formal, ceremonious tone.
- Choose a tone that suits your topic and your readers.
- Whatever tone you choose, be consistent in each piece of your writing.

---

**EXERCISE 8-2**  Revise each of the sentences to create a very different tone. The sentences in Quick Reference 8.3 provide some examples. For a further challenge, see how many different tones you can create.

1. Many Americans spend much of their leisure time watching professional sports.
2. If you want to waste your money buying organic foods, who am I to stop you?
3. When considering the purchase of clothing in order to possess a serviceable wardrobe, it is imperative to select items in which the color combinations are harmonious and pleasing.

For more help with your writing, grammar, and research, go to **www.mycomplab.com**

**ANSWERS TO EXERCISE 8.2**

Answers will vary. Here is one way the sentences may be rewritten:

**1.** Many Americans waste their precious free time watching—not participating in, but passively watching—sporting events.

**2.** Though I disagree with your decision to buy organic comestibles, I recognize that the decision is yours to make.

**3.** When building a wardrobe that's both functional and flattering, color should be one of your primary concerns: what looks good on you, and what looks good with everything else you own.

# 9

# Sentence Variety and Style

## 9a How do sentences affect style?

Sentences affect style through their length (9c), structures like COORDINATION and SUBORDINATION (9k), and types. The main sentence types in English are SIMPLE, COMPOUND, COMPLEX, and COMPOUND-COMPLEX (14q). When any one type dominates a piece of writing, it affects the style, especially if the sentences are also generally the same length. A flurry of short, simple sentences creates a blunt, direct style. Such a style often gains in clarity but loses in interest. A series of long complex or compound-complex sentences creates a lofty, sometimes even stuffy, style. It may achieve sophistication but sacrifice clarity. You can see the difference in the following example, which has two versions of the same piece.

1. Short, simple sentences

> The most worshipped and praised of all ancient sewers was Rome's Cloaca Maxima. It resided within the shrine of the goddess Cloacina. Warriors came here to purge themselves after battle. Young couples purified themselves here before marriage. The lovely Cloacina was an emanation of Venus. Her statue overlooked the imperial city's sewer pipes. The pipes transported 100,000 pounds of ancient *excrementum* [human waste] a day. It was built in the sixth century B.C. by the two Tarquins. It was hailed as one of the three marvels of Rome. The Cloaca became one of the city's great tourist traps. Agrippa rode a boat through it. Nero washed his hands in it.

2. Longer, compound and complex sentences

> The most worshipped and praised of all ancient sewers was Rome's Cloaca Maxima, whose spirit resided within the shrine of the goddess Cloacina, where warriors came to purge themselves after battle and young couples purified themselves before marriage. The lovely Cloacina was an emanation of Venus, and her statue overlooked the imperial city's sewer pipes as they transported 100,000 pounds of ancient *excrementum* [human waste] a day. Built in the sixth century B.C. by the two Tarquins, hailed as one of the three marvels of Rome, the Cloaca became one of the city's great tourist traps. Agrippa rode a boat through it. Nero washed his hands in it.

—Frederick Kaufman, "Wasteland"

The second version was published in *Harper's Magazine,* which is aimed at a well-educated general AUDIENCE. Notice that even that version ends with two simple sentences. Coming after the longer earlier ones, they offer a refreshing break. In fact, effective and stylistically interesting writing often contains a VARIETY of styles.

## 9b What are variety and emphasis in writing?

When you write sentences of different lengths and types within a piece of writing, you create **sentence variety**. Working in concert with sentence variety, **emphasis** allows you to add weight to ideas of special importance.

Using techniques of variety and emphasis adds style and clarity to your writing. When readers see variety in your writing, they see you as versatile and in control of language. Usually, the best time to apply the principles of variety and emphasis is while you are REVISING.

## 9c How do different sentence lengths create variety and emphasis?

To emphasize one idea among many others, you can express it in a sentence noticeably different in length from the sentences surrounding it. In the following example, a four-word sentence between two longer sentences carries the key message of the passage (**boldface** added).

> Today is one of those excellent January partly cloudies in which light chooses an unexpected landscape to trick out in gilt, and then shadow sweeps it away. **You know you're alive.** You take huge steps, trying to feel the planet's roundness arc between your feet.
>
> —Annie Dillard, *Pilgrim at Tinker Creek*

Sometimes a string of short sentences creates impact and emphasis. Yet, at other times, a string of short sentences can be dull to read.

**EXERCISE 9-1**   The following paragraph is dull because it has only short sentences. Combine some of the sentences to make a paragraph that has a variety of sentence lengths.

> There is a problem. It is widely known as sick-building syndrome. It comes from indoor air pollution. It causes office workers to suffer. They have trouble breathing. They have painful rashes. Their heads ache. Their eyes burn.

Similarly, a string of COMPOUND SENTENCES can be monotonous to read and may fail to communicate relationships among ideas.

method is to make a transparency copy and ask the students to decide which sentences are long and which are short—and then underline them.

**TEACHING TIP**
In class, read the following passage by Truman Capote aloud, using a single breath for each sentence. In a second reading, you might pause after each sentence for students to guess how many words are in it. After the number of words in each has been announced, students can try drawing a graph of the paragraph based on the length of the sentences. (The word count appears in brackets after each sentence.)

> Morning. [1] Frozen rime lusters the grass; the sun, round as an orange and orange as hot-weather moons, balances on the horizon, burnishes the silvered winter woods. [25] A wild turkey calls. [4] A renegade hog grunts in the undergrowth. [7] Soon, by the edge of knee-deep, rapid-running water, we have to abandon the buggy. [14] Queenie wades the stream first, paddles across barking complaints at the swiftness of the current, the pneumonia-making coldness of it. [20] We follow, holding our shoes and equipment (a hatchet, a burlap sack) above our heads. [15] A mile more: of chastising horns, burs and briers that catch at our clothes; of rusty pine needles brilliant with gaudy fungus and molted feathers. [25] Here, there, a flash, a flutter, an ecstasy of shrilling remind us that not all the birds have flown south. [20]
>
> —Truman Capote, "A Christmas Memory"

**ANSWERS: EXERCISE 9-1**
Responses will vary greatly. Here is one way of combining the sentences to make the writing more interesting. Words or phrases that were added are capitalized.

> A SERIOUS problem AFFECTING AMERICAN WORKERS TODAY is widely known as Sick Building Syndrome. It comes from indoor air pollution AND MAY cause office workers to suffer FROM A NUMBER OF AILMENTS: BREATHING TROUBLE, painful rashes, headaches, AND BURNING EYES.

**EXERCISE 9-2** The following paragraph is dull because it has only compound sentences. Revise it to provide more variety.

Science fiction writers are often thinkers, **and** they are often dreamers, **and** they let their imaginations wander. Jules Verne was such a writer, **and** he predicted spaceships, **and** he forecast atomic submarines, **but** most people did not believe airplanes were possible.

## 9d What are coordination and subordination?

Two important sentence structuring methods are **coordination** and **subordination,** which reflect relationships between ideas that you seek to express. Coordination shows the equality of ideas, while subordination shows one idea is more important than others. Using these structures effectively creates variety and emphasis. We explain each of them in sections 9e and 9h, below, but an example will help you see the basic principle:

| | |
|---|---|
| TWO SENTENCES | The sky turned dark gray. The wind died down. |
| USING COORDINATION | The sky turned dark gray, **and** the wind died down. |
| USING SUBORDINATION 1 | **As** the sky turned dark gray, the wind died down. [Here, the wind is the focus.] |
| USING SUBORDINATION 2 | **As** the wind died down, the sky turned dark gray. [Here, the sky is the focus.] |

## 9e What is coordination of sentences?

**Coordination** of sentences is a grammatical strategy to communicate that the ideas in two or more INDEPENDENT CLAUSES are equivalent or balanced. Coordination can produce harmony by bringing related elements together. Whenever you use the technique of coordination of sentences, make sure that it works well with the meaning you want to communicate.

The sky turned **brighter, and** people emerged happily from buildings.

The sky turned **brighter;** people emerged happily from buildings.

## 9f What is the structure of a coordinate sentence?

A **coordinate sentence**, also known as a *compound sentence* (14q), consists of two or more INDEPENDENT CLAUSES joined either by a semicolon or by a comma working in concert with a COORDINATING CONJUNCTION (*and, but, for, or, nor, yet, so*). Here, you can see the pattern for coordination of sentences.

$$\text{Independent clause} \begin{cases} \text{, and} \\ \text{, but} \\ \text{, for} \\ \text{, or} \\ \text{, nor} \\ \text{, yet} \\ \text{, so} \\ \text{;} \end{cases} \text{independent clause.}$$

## 9g What meaning does each coordinating conjunction convey?

Each COORDINATING CONJUNCTION has its own meaning. When you choose one, be sure that its meaning accurately expresses the relationship between the equivalent ideas that you want to convey.

- **and** means addition
- **but** and **yet** mean contrast
- **for** means reason or choice
- **or** means choice
- **nor** means negative choice
- **so** means result or effect

⓵ Alert: Always use a comma before a coordinating conjunction that joins two INDEPENDENT CLAUSES (24b). ●

## 9h How can I use coordination effectively?

COORDINATION is effective when each INDEPENDENT CLAUSE is related or equivalent. If they aren't, the result looks like a coordinated sentence, but the ideas are unrelated.

**NO** Computers came into common use in the 1970s, and they sometimes make costly errors. [The statement in each independent clause is true, but the ideas are not related or equivalent.]

**YES** Computers came into common use in the 1970s, and now they are indispensable business tools.

Coordination is also most effective when it's not overused. Simply stringing sentences together with COORDINATING CONJUNCTIONS makes relationships among ideas unclear—and the resulting sentence lacks style.

Americans value it most as a good-luck symbol for newlyweds.

Here, the independent clause stresses the connection of rice with weddings, and the food value of rice is mentioned as a less central point.

**QUOTATION: ON WRITING**

Coordination is simply a way to show ideas that are equal in importance, but subordination indicates what's powerful and what isn't.

—Betty Jean Goodwin

**QUOTATION: ON WRITING**

Blot out, correct, insert, refine,
Enlarge, diminish, interline;
Be mindful, when invention fails,
To scratch your head, and bite your nails.

—Jonathan Swift

**QUOTATION: ON WRITING**

Anything is better than not to write clearly.

—W. Somerset Maugham

**BACKGROUND**

In "On Language: Breaking the Rules," Patricia T. O'Conner rejects popular opinion that the conjunctions *and* and *but* "should only be used to join elements" (*New York Times*, 28 July 1996, late ed., sec. 6:12). She asserts that they also should be used to begin sentences: "But it has been common practice to begin sentences this way at least as far back as the 10th century. And don't let anyone tell you otherwise."

**QUOTATION: ON WRITING**

In stating as fully as I could how things really were, it was often very difficult and I wrote awkwardly and the awkwardness is what they called my style. All mistakes and awkwardness are easy to see, and they called it style.

—Ernest Hemingway

**BACKGROUND**

Adding modifiers to basic sentences is the central feature of the "generative rhetoric" developed by Francis Christensen in his classic work

*Notes Toward a New Rhetoric.* The Christensen program teaches students various ways to expand a sentence by showing them model sentences, giving students a basic sentence and having them expand it following the pattern of the models, and then having students compose their own sentences according to that pattern. These exercises not only develop the writing style of students but also teach them ways of elaborating their ideas.

### ANSWERS: EXERCISE 9-3

Answers will vary somewhat. Here is one set of possibilities.

**1.** As depicted in movies, fencing sometimes appears to be reckless swordplay, but fencing requires precision, coordination, and strategy. [9g, incorrect coordinating conjunction]

**2.** In the 1800s, fencing became very popular, and it was one of the few sports included in the first modern Olympic Games in 1896. Fencing has been part of the Olympics ever since. [9h, misuse]

**3.** Fencing equipment includes a mask, a padded jacket, a glove, and one of three weapons—a foil, épée, or saber. A fencer's technique and targets differ depending on the weapon used and the fencer's experience. [9h, misuse]

**4.** Correct

**5.** The object of fencing is to be the first to touch the opponent five times. A "president," who is sometimes assisted by a number of judges, officiates at competitions. [9h, misuse]

### QUOTATION: ON WRITING

Bain saw a hierarchical structural relationship between words, sentences, paragraphs, and entire compositions.
—Ned A. Shearer, "Alexander Bain and the Genesis of Paragraph Theory"

### BACKGROUND

The balanced sentence presents two equally weighted pieces of meaning. Usually, a punctuation mark or a coordinating conjunction (or both) acts as a centerpoint on which the

**NO**  Dinosaurs could have disappeared for many reasons, **and** one theory holds that a sudden shower of meteors and asteroids hit the earth, **so** the impact created a huge dust cloud that caused a false winter. The winter lasted for years, **and** the dinosaurs died.

**YES**  Dinosaurs could have disappeared for many reasons. One theory holds that a sudden shower of meteors and asteroids hit the earth. The impact created a huge dust cloud that caused a false winter. The winter lasted for years, killing the dinosaurs.

**EXERCISE 9-3**  Working individually or with a group, revise these sentences to eliminate illogical or overused coordination. If you think a sentence needs no revision, explain why. For help, consult sections 9e through 9h.

**EXAMPLE**  Fencing, once a form of combat, has become a competitive sport worldwide, and today's fencers disapprove of those who identify fencing with fighting.

Fencing, once a form of combat, has become a competitive sport worldwide, *but* today's fencers disapprove of those who identify fencing with fighting.

1. As depicted in movies, fencing sometimes appears to be reckless swordplay, and fencing requires precision, coordination, and strategy.

2. In the 1800s, fencing became very popular, and it was one of the few sports included in the first modern Olympic Games in 1896, and fencing has been part of the Olympics ever since.

3. Fencing equipment includes a mask, a padded jacket, a glove, and one of three weapons—a foil, épée, or saber—and a fencer's technique and targets differ depending on the weapon used and the fencer's experience.

4. Generally, a fencer specializes in one of the three weapons, but some competitors are equally skilled with all three.

5. The object of fencing is to be the first to touch the opponent five times, and a "president," who is sometimes assisted by a number of judges, officiates at competitions.

## 9i  What is subordination in sentences?

**Subordination** is a grammatical strategy to communicate that one idea in a sentence is more important than another idea in the same sentence. To use subordination, you place the more important idea in an INDEPENDENT CLAUSE and the less important—the subordinate—idea in a DEPENDENT CLAUSE. The information you choose to subordinate depends on the meaning you want to deliver.

INDEPENDENT CLAUSE ┐ ┌ DEPENDENT

Two cowboys fought a dangerous Colorado snowstorm **while they**

CLAUSE ┐ ┌ DEPENDENT CLAUSE

**were looking for cattle. When they came to a canyon,**

INDEPENDENT CLAUSE

they saw outlines of buildings through the blizzard.

To illustrate the difference in writing style when you use subordination, here's a passage with the same message as the example above, but without subordination.

Two cowboys fought a dangerous Colorado snowstorm. They were looking for cattle. They came to a canyon. They saw outlines of buildings through the blizzard.

## 9j What is the structure of a subordinate sentence?

A subordinate sentence starts the DEPENDENT CLAUSE with either a SUBORDINATING CONJUNCTION or a RELATIVE PRONOUN.

**If** they are very lucky, the passengers may glimpse dolphins breaking water playfully near the ship.

—Elizabeth Gray, student

Pandas are solitary animals, **which** means they are difficult to protect from extinction.

—Jose Santos, student

For patterns of subordination with dependent clauses, see 9f. Dependent clauses are of two types: ADVERB CLAUSES and ADJECTIVE CLAUSES. An adverb clause starts with a subordinating conjunction. An adjective clause starts with a relative pronoun.

### Quick Reference 9.1  ■ ■ ■ ■ ■ ■ ■

#### Subordination

**SENTENCES WITH ADVERB CLAUSES**

- **Adverb clause,** independent clause.

    **After the sky grew dark,** the wind died suddenly.

- Independent clause, **adverb clause.**

    Birds stopped singing, **as they do during an eclipse.**

continued >>

---

meaning balances, much like a seesaw on its base, as in this example:

Freedom is the right to be wrong, not the right to do wrong.

—John Diefenbaker

**QUOTATION: ON WRITING**

There is such an animal as a nonstylist, only they're not writers—they're typists.

—Truman Capote

**QUOTATION: ON WRITING**

I think the single most important factor in any writing is its rhythm. A badly balanced sentence jars on me with something like physical pain!

—Helen Cresswell

**QUOTATION: ON WRITING**

The ability to write clear, crisp sentences that never go beyond twenty words is a considerable achievement. You'll never confuse a reader with sprawl, wordiness, or muddy abstraction. But if you never write sentences longer than twenty words, you'll be like a pianist who uses only the middle octave: You can carry the tune, but without much variety or range.

—Joseph M. Williams

**TEACHING TIP**

Ask students to read two versions of the same passage from the opening of the twenty-second chapter of Genesis (one of five books in the Old Testament of the Bible). Then, mark the instances of coordination and subordination with them and consider the differences in style and meaning that result. The first, from the King James translation of 1611, uses coordination heavily; the second, from the Revised Standard Version of 1971, uses much less.

*King James Version*

And it came to pass after these things, that God did tempt Abraham, and said unto him, Abraham: and he said, Behold, here I am. And he said, Take now thy son, thine only son Isaac, whom thou lovest, and get thee into the land of Moriah; and offer him there for a burnt offering upon one of the mountains which I will tell thee of. And Abraham rose up early in the morning, and saddled his ass, and took two of his young men with him, and Isaac his son, and clave the wood for the burnt offering, and rose up, and went unto the place of which God had told him. Then on the third day Abraham lifted up his eyes, and saw the place afar off. And Abraham said unto his young men, Abide ye here with the ass; and I and the lad will go yonder and worship, and come again to you. And Abraham took the wood for the burnt offering, and laid it upon Isaac his son; and he took the fire in his hand, and a knife; and they went both of them together.

*Revised Standard Version*

After these things God tested Abraham, and said to him, "Abraham!" And he said, "Here am I." He said, "Take your son, your only son Isaac, whom you love, and go to the land of Moriah, and offer him there as a burnt offering upon one of the mountains of which I shall tell you." So Abraham rose early in the morning, saddled his ass, and took two of his young men with him, and his son Isaac; and he cut the wood for the burnt offering, and arose and went to the place of which God had told him. On the third day Abraham lifted up his eyes, and saw the place afar off. Then Abraham said to his young men, "Stay here with the ass; I and the lad will go yonder and worship, and come again to you." And Abraham took the wood of the burnt offering, and laid it on Isaac his son; and he took in his hand the fire and the knife. So they went both of them together.

**TEACHING TIP**

You might choose to have students read the following examples to see how sentences that seem disconnected can be improved through subordination.

**NO**  We went shopping for new winter boots. We ate ice cream despite the cold.

**YES**  After we went shopping for new winter boots, we ate ice cream despite the cold.

---

## Quick Reference 9.1  (continued)

- Independent clause **adverb clause.**

  The stores closed **before the storm began.**

### SENTENCES WITH ADJECTIVE CLAUSES

- Independent clause **restrictive (essential)\* adjective clause.**

  Weather forecasts warned of a storm **that might bring a thirty-inch snowfall.**

- Independent clause, **nonrestrictive (nonessential)\* adjective clause.**

  Spring is the season for tornadoes, **which may have wind speeds over 220 miles an hour.**

- Beginning of independent clause **restrictive (essential)\* adjective clause** end of independent clause.

  Anyone **who lives through a tornado** remembers its power.

- Beginning of independent clause, **nonrestrictive (nonessential)\* adjective clause,** end of independent clause.

  The sky, **which had been clear,** turned greenish black.

\*For an explanation of RESTRICTIVE and NONRESTRICTIVE ELEMENTS, see section 24f.

---

## 9k  What meaning does each subordinating conjunction convey?

Each SUBORDINATING CONJUNCTION has its own meaning. When you choose one, be sure that its meaning accurately expresses the relationship between the ideas that you want to convey. Quick Reference 9.2 lists subordinating conjunctions according to their different meanings.

## Quick Reference 9.2

### Subordinating conjunctions and their meanings

**TIME**
*after, before, once, since, until, when, whenever, while*

  **After** you have handed in your report, you cannot revise it.

**REASON OR CAUSE**
*as, because, since*

  **Because** you have handed in your report, you cannot revise it.

continued >>

## Quick Reference 9.2 (continued)

**PURPOSE OR RESULT**
*in order that, so that, that*

> I want to read your report **so that** I can evaluate it.

**CONDITION**
*even if, if, provided that, unless*

> **Unless** you have handed in your report, you can revise it.

**CONTRAST**
*although, even though, though, whereas, while*

> **Although** you have handed in your report, you can ask to revise it.

**CHOICE**
*than, whether*

> You took more time to revise **than** I did before the lab report deadline.

**PLACE OR LOCATION**
*where, wherever*

> **Wherever** you say, I'll come to hand in my report.

**EXERCISE 9-4**  Working individually or with a group, combine each pair of sentences, using an adverb clause to subordinate one idea. Then, revise each sentence so that the adverb clause becomes the independent clause. For help, see sections 9f through 9h, especially Quick Reference 9.1.

**EXAMPLE**  The US Mint produces new coins. The US Bureau of Engraving and Printing makes $1, $5, $10, $20, $50, and $100 bills.

> a. While the US Mint produces new coins, the US Bureau of Engraving and Printing makes $1, $5, $10, $20, $50, and $100 bills.
>
> b. While the US Bureau of Engraving and Printing makes $1, $5, $10, $20, $50, and $100 bills, the US Mint produces new coins.

1. The US Mint can produce more than 50 million coins a day. The US Bureau of Engraving and Printing can produce 20 million notes a day.

2. The Federal Reserve Banks are responsible for both destroying old money and ordering new coins and notes. They must keep the right amount of money in circulation.

3. Coins can stay in circulation for decades. People let them accumulate in jars and drawers in their homes.

**NO**  I must budget carefully. I hope to buy a new car next year.

**YES**  Since I hope to buy a new car next year, I must budget carefully.

**QUOTATION: ON WRITING**

Advice to young writers? Always the same advice: learn to trust your own judgment, learn inner independence, learn to trust that time will sort the good from the bad—including your own bad.

—Doris Lessing

**ANSWERS: EXERCISE 9-4**

Students' answers will vary. Here is one set of possibilities.

**1. a.** Although the US Mint can produce more than 50 million coins a day, the US Bureau of Engraving and Printing can produce only 20 million notes a day.

**b.** Although the US Bureau of Engraving and Printing can produce only 20 million notes a day, the US Mint can produce more than 50 million coins a day.

**2. a.** Even though the Federal Reserve Banks are responsible for both destroying old money and ordering new coins and notes, they must keep the right amount of money in circulation.

**b.** Because the Federal Reserve Banks must keep the right amount of money in circulation, they are responsible for both destroying old money and ordering new coins and notes.

**3. a.** Coins can stay in circulation for decades unless people let them accumulate in jars and drawers in their homes.

**b.** While coins can stay in circulation for decades, people sometimes let them accumulate in jars and drawers in their homes.

**4. a.** Whenever a $1 bill lasts fifteen to eighteen months, it reaches its average life span.

**b.** If it reaches its average life span, a $1 bill lasts about fifteen to eighteen months.

**5. a.** When the US Federal Reserve Banks destroy dirty, worn, and torn bills, they are destroying more than $40 billion worth of money a year.

**b.** When they destroy more than $40 billion worth of money a year, the US Federal Reserve Banks are destroying dirty, worn, and torn bills.

**ANSWERS: EXERCISE 9-5**

Having students compare and discuss the differences in emphasis between the answers to each item may help them clarify their understanding of these differences.

**1. a.** An ancient Greek law that allowed voters to banish politicians from their city asked citizens to write the name of an unpopular politician on their ballots.

**b.** An ancient Greek law that asked citizens to write the name of an unpopular politician on their ballots allowed voters to banish politicians from their city.

**2. a.** A voter who was filling out a ballot when Aristides the Just walked by needed help in spelling Aristides.

**b.** A voter who needed help in spelling Aristides was filling out a ballot when Aristides the Just walked by.

**3. a.** Aristides, who knew the voter did not recognize him, asked why the voter wanted to banish that particular politician.

**b.** Aristides, who asked why the voter wanted to banish that particular politician, knew the voter did not recognize him.

**4. a.** The voter, who said he resented hearing someone called "the Just" all the time, handed Aristides his ballot.

**b.** The voter, who handed Aristides his ballot, said he resented hearing someone called "the Just" all the time.

**5. a.** Aristides' reaction, which demonstrated that the nickname "the Just" was well deserved, was to write his own name on the voter's ballot even though that person's vote helped banish Aristides.

4. A $1 bill lasts about fifteen to eighteen months. It reaches its average life span.

5. The US Federal Reserve Banks destroy dirty, worn, and torn bills. The Federal Reserve Banks are destroying more than $40 billion worth of money a year.

**EXERCISE 9-5**   Working individually or with a group, combine each pair of sentences, using an adjective clause to subordinate one idea to the other. Then, revise each sentence so that the adjective clause becomes the independent clause. Use the relative pronoun given in parentheses. For help, consult sections 9i through 9k, especially Quick Reference 9.1.

**EXAMPLE**   Aristides was an ancient Greek politician famous for his honesty and judgment. He was known as Aristides the Just. (who)

   a. Aristides, *who* was an ancient Greek politician famous for his honesty and judgment, was known as Aristides the Just.

   b. Aristides, *who* was known as Aristides the Just, was an ancient Greek politician famous for his honesty and judgment.

1. An ancient Greek law allowed voters to banish politicians from their city. It asked citizens to write the name of an unpopular politician on their ballots. (that)

2. A voter was filling out a ballot when Aristides the Just walked by. The voter needed help in spelling *Aristides*. (who)

3. Aristides knew the voter did not recognize him. He asked why the voter wanted to banish that particular politician. (who)

4. The voter said he resented hearing someone called "the Just" all the time. He handed Aristides his ballot. (who)

5. Aristides' reaction demonstrated that the nickname "the Just" was well deserved. His reaction was to write his own name on the voter's ballot even though that person's vote helped banish Aristides. (which)

## 91   How can I use subordination effectively?

To be effective, a SUBORDINATING CONJUNCTION must communicate a sensible relationship between the INDEPENDENT CLAUSE and the DEPENDENT CLAUSE. See Quick Reference 9.2 for a list of subordinating conjunctions and their different meanings.

**NO**   **Because** Beethoven was deaf when he wrote them, his final symphonies were masterpieces. [*Because* is illogical here; it says the masterpieces resulted from the deafness.]

**YES** **Although** Beethoven was deaf when he wrote them, his final symphonies were masterpieces. [*Although* is logical here; it says Beethoven wrote masterpieces in spite of his being deaf.]

Subordination is also most effective when you avoid overusing it and crowding too many ideas together in one sentence. This causes readers to lose track of the message. Whenever you write a sentence with two or more dependent clauses, check that your message is clear. If it isn't, you've probably overused subordination.

**NO** A new technique for eye surgery, **which is supposed to correct nearsightedness, which previously could be corrected only by glasses,** has been developed, **although many eye doctors do not approve of the new technique because it can create unstable vision, which includes intense glare from headlights on cars and many other light sources.** [The base sentence *A new technique for eye surgery has been developed* is crowded with five dependent clauses attached to it.]

**YES** A new technique for eye surgery, **which is supposed to correct nearsightedness,** has been developed. Previously, only glasses could correct nearsightedness. Many doctors do not approve of the new technique **because it can create unstable vision.** The problems include intense glare from car headlights and many other sources of light. [In this revision, one long sentence has been broken into four sentences, which makes the material easier to read and the relationships among ideas clearer. Two dependent clauses remain, which balance well with the other sentence constructions. Some words have been moved to new positions.]

**ESOL Tip:** If your instructor, manager, or peer reviewers advise that your sentences are too long and complex, limit the number of words in each sentence. Many ESOL instructors recommend that you revise any sentence that contains more than three independent and dependent clauses in any combination. ●

**EXERCISE 9-6** Working individually or with a group, correct illogical or excessive subordination in this paragraph. As you revise according to the message you want to deliver, use some dependent clauses as well as some short sentences. (Also, if you wish, apply the principles of coordination discussed in sections 9d through 9g.) For help, consult 9k.

Although many people in the United States consider the hot dog an American invention, it actually originated in Germany in 1852 when butchers in Frankfurt, Germany, stuffed meat into a long casing,

**b.** Aristides' reaction, which was to write his own name on the voter's ballot even though that person's vote helped banish Aristides, demonstrated that the nickname "the Just" was well deserved.

**QUOTATION: ON WRITING**

**1.** Never use a metaphor, simile or other figure of speech which you are used to seeing in print.

**2.** Never use a long word where a short one will do.

**3.** If it is possible to cut a word out, always cut it out.

**4.** Never use the passive where you can use the active.

**5.** Never use a foreign phrase, a scientific word or jargon word if you can think of an everyday English equivalent.

**6.** Break any of these rules sooner than say anything barbarous.

—George Orwell

**QUOTATION: ON WRITING**
My first draft is unorganized thoughts about what I have to write. . . . In revising, I reorganize first by checking chronology. Then I rearrange material as I would in making a collage.
—Hana Wehle

**ANSWERS: EXERCISE 9-6**
Each sentence contains misused subordination. Answers will vary considerably. Here is one possibility.

Although many people in the United States consider the hot dog an American invention, it actually originated in Germany in 1852. Butchers in Frankfurt, Germany, stuffed meat into a long casing, and in honor of the town they called their creation a "frankfurter." Because one butcher noticed that the frankfurter resembled the shape of his dog, a dachshund, he decided to name the meat roll a "dachshund sausage." Soon, the new name caught on in Germany. Germans brought dachshund sausages to the United States, and peddlers sold them on the streets. The dachshund sausages were so hot that people often burned their fingers and had trouble holding the meat. When one clever peddler put the sausage in a bun, a *New York Times* cartoonist decided to draw a picture of hot dachshund sausages in buns. He didn't know how to spell dachshund, so he called them "hot dogs."

**QUOTATION: ON WRITING**

I revise the manuscript till I can't read it any longer, then I get somebody to type it. Then I revise the typing. Then it's retyped again. Then there's a third typing, which is the final one. Nothing should then remain that offends the eye.

—Robert Graves

**QUOTATION: ON WRITING**

I always write a thing first and think about it afterward, which is not a bad procedure because the easiest way to have consequential thoughts is to start putting them down.

—E. B. White

which, in honor of the town, they called a "frankfurter." Because one butcher noticed that the frankfurter resembled the shape of his dog, a dachshund, he decided to name the meat roll a "dachshund sausage," a name which caught on in Germany. When Germans brought dachshund sausages to the United States, peddlers sold them on the streets, although the dachshund sausages were so hot that people often burned their fingers because they had trouble holding the meat. When one clever peddler put the sausage in a bun, a *New York Times* cartoonist decided to draw a picture of hot dachshund sausages in buns, although he called them "hot dogs" because he didn't know how to spell *dachshund*.

# 9m How can I effectively use coordination and subordination together?

Your writing style improves when you use a logical and pleasing variety of SENTENCE TYPES, utilizing COORDINATION and SUBORDINATION to improve the flow of ideas. Here's a paragraph that demonstrates a good balance in the use of coordination and subordination.

> When I was growing up, I lived on a farm just across the field from my grandmother. My parents were busy trying to raise six children and to establish their struggling dairy farm. It was nice to have Grandma so close. While my parents were providing the necessities of life, my patient grandmother gave her time to her shy, young granddaughter. I always enjoyed going with Grandma and collecting the eggs that her chickens had just laid. Usually, she knew which chickens would peck, and she was careful to let me gather the eggs from the less hostile ones.
>
> —Patricia Mapes, student

When you use both coordination and subordination, never use both a COORDINATE CONJUNCTION and a SUBORDINATE CONJUNCTION to express one relationship in one sentence.

NO  **Although** the story was well written, **but** it was too illogical. [The subordinating conjunction *although* expresses the contrast, so also using *but* is incorrect.]

YES  **Although** the story was well written, it was too illogical.

YES  The story was well written, **but** it was too illogical.

● **EXERCISE 9-7**  Working individually or in a group, use subordination and coordination to combine these sets of short, choppy sentences. For help, consult all sections of this chapter.

EXAMPLE  Owls cannot digest the bones and fur of the mice and birds they eat. They cough up a furry pellet every day.

*Because* owls cannot digest the bones and fur of the mice and birds they *eat, they* cough up a furry pellet every day.

1. Owl pellets are a rich teaching tool in biology classrooms around the country. The pellets provide an alternative to dissecting frogs and other animals.

2. Inside the pellet are the remains of the owl's nightly meal. They include beautifully cleaned hummingbird skulls, rat skeletons, and lots of bird feathers.

3. The owl-pellet market has been cornered by companies in New York, California, and Washington. These companies distribute pellets to thousands of biology classrooms all over the world.

4. Company workers scour barns and the ground under trees where owls nest to pick up the pellets. The pellets sell for $1 each.

5. The owl-pellet business may have a short future. The rural areas of the United States are vanishing. Old barns are being bulldozed. All the barns are torn down. The owls will be gone, too.

# 9n How do occasional questions, commands, or exclamations create variety and emphasis?

The majority of sentences in English are DECLARATIVE—they tell something by making a statement. Declarative sentences offer an almost infinite variety of structures and patterns. For variety and emphasis, you might want to use three alternative types of sentences occasionally.

A sentence that asks a question is called INTERROGATIVE. Occasional questions, placed appropriately, tend to involve readers. A sentence that issues a mild or strong command is called IMPERATIVE. Occasional mild commands, appropriately used, gently urge a reader to think along with you. A sentence that makes an exclamation is called EXCLAMATORY. An occasional exclamatory sentence, appropriate to the context, can enliven writing, but you should use this sentence type only rarely in ACADEMIC WRITING.

🛈 Alert: A declarative statement ends with a period (Chapter 23)—or semicolon (Chapter 25) or colon (Chapter 26). A mild command ends with a period. A strong command and an exclamation end with an exclamation point (Chapter 23). ●

Here's a paragraph with declarative, interrogative, and imperative sentences.

Imagine what people ate during the winter as little as seventy-five years ago. They ate food that was local, long-lasting, and dull, like acorn squash, turnips, and cabbage. Walk into an American supermarket in February and the world lies before you: grapes, melons, artichokes, fennel, lettuce, peppers, pistachios, dates, even strawberries, to say nothing of ice cream. Have you ever considered what a triumph of civilization it is to be able to buy a pound of chicken livers? If you lived on a farm and had to kill a chicken when you wanted to eat one, you wouldn't ever accumulate a pound of chicken livers.

—Phyllis Rose, "Shopping and Other Spiritual Adventures in America Today"

**ANOTHER VIEW**
In his article "Periodicity or Structural Delay" (*American Speech* 31.1 (1956): 25–34) Henry Wilson argues that periodic sentences, rather than being a sentence structure to be used sparingly to create a powerful effect, is a specific type of a more general kind of syntax he terms, as per his title, "structural delay." He posits that structural delays, of which the periodic sentence is the most extreme example, "are ingredients of an effective style even when the writer is striving for simplicity" (33) since writers often seek to enhance their points by "obtain[ing] suspense" (31).

## 90 What are cumulative and periodic sentences?

The **cumulative sentence** is the most common sentence structure in English. Its name reflects the way information accumulates in the sentence until it reaches a period. Its structure starts with a SUBJECT and VERB and continues with modifiers. Another term for a cumulative sentence is *loose sentence* because it lacks a tightly planned structure.

For greater impact, you might occasionally use a **periodic sentence**, also called a *climactic sentence,* which reserves the main idea for the end of the sentence. This structure tends to draw in the reader as it moves toward the period. If overused, however, periodic sentences lose their punch.

CUMULATIVE   A car hit a shoulder and turned over at midnight last night on the road from Las Vegas to Death Valley Junction.

PERIODIC   At midnight last night, on the road from Las Vegas to Death Valley Junction, a car hit a shoulder and turned over.

—Joan Didion, "On Morality"

You can build both cumulative and periodic sentences to dramatic—and sometimes excessive—lengths.

EXAMPLE:
How cumulative sentences can grow
  1. The downtown bustled with new construction.
  2. **The downtown bustled with new construction,** as buildings shot up everywhere, transforming the skyline.
  3. **The downtown bustled with new constructio**n, as buildings shot up everywhere, each a mixture of glass and steel, in colors from rust red to ice blue, transforming the skyline from a shy set of bumps to a bold display of mountains

EXAMPLE:
How periodic sentences can grow
  1. Marla accepted the job offer.

2. With some reservations about the salary offer and location, **Marla accepted the job offer.**

3. After a day of agonizing and a night without sleep, still having some reservations about the salary offer and location, especially with the company being in an unappealing city more than 400 miles from her fiancé, **Marla accepted the job offer.**

# 9p How can modifiers create variety and emphasis?

MODIFIERS can expand sentences to add richness to your writing and create a pleasing mixture of variety and emphasis. The longer cumulative and periodic sentence examples in section 9o illustrate the use of modifiers. Your choice of where to place modifiers to expand your sentences depends on the focus you want each sentence to communicate, either on its own or in concert with its surrounding sentences. Be careful where you place modifiers because you don't want to introduce the error known as a MISPLACED MODIFIER.

| | |
|---|---|
| **NO (MISPLACED MODIFIER)** | A huge, hairy, grunting thing, I agreed that the bull was scary. |
| **YES** | A huge, hairy, grunting thing, the bull was scary, I agreed. |

In the No example, it sounds like the writer, I, was huge, hairy, and grunting!

| | |
|---|---|
| **BASIC SENTENCE** | The river rose. |
| **ADJECTIVE** | The **swollen** river rose. |
| **ADVERB** | The river rose **dangerously.** |
| **PREPOSITIONAL PHRASE** | The river rose **above its banks.** |
| **PARTICIPIAL PHRASE** | **Swelled by melting snow,** the river rose. |
| **ABSOLUTE PHRASE** | **Uprooted trees swirling away in the current,** the river rose. |
| **ADVERB CLAUSE** | **Because the snows had been heavy that winter,** the river rose. |
| **ADJECTIVE CLAUSE** | The river, **which runs through vital farmland,** rose. |

**EXERCISE 9-8** Working individually or with a group, expand each sentence by adding each kind of modifier illustrated in section 9p.

1. We bought a house.
2. The roof leaked.
3. I remodeled the kitchen.
4. Neighbors brought food.
5. Everyone enjoyed the barbeque.

**ANSWERS: EXERCISE 9-8**

Students are to expand each sentence by adding (a) an adjective, (b) an adverb, (c) a prepositional phrase, (d) a participial phrase, (e) an absolute phrase, (f) an adverb clause, and (g) an adjective clause. They can refer for guidance to the expansion techniques listed in section 9d. Here is a possible set of answers for item 1:

**a.** We bought a *two-story* house.

**b.** *Recently,* we bought a house.

**c.** We bought a house *near the train station.*

**d.** *Excited by low interest rates,* we bought a house costing more than we could afford.

**e.** *Space being too cramped in the apartment,* we bought a house.

**f.** *Because we saved enough for a down payment,* we bought a house.

**g.** We bought a house *that overlooks the river.*

Apply techniques of variety and emphasis to revise the following paragraph. Use different kinds of modifiers (9d). You can reduce or increase the number of words and sentences. Try to include at least one question or exclamation. Also, try to vary the word order.

Huge caves known collectively as the Carlsbad Caverns are hidden beneath the sands of New Mexico. The caverns contain a mysterious underground world. More than 20 miles of caves have been discovered. Miles more are found each year. The caves echo with watery noises and glimmer with reflected light. Some of the caves contain mysterious underground lakes. Others are huge chambers, and their ceilings rise 200 feet. Electric lights illuminate the caves for visitors. The lights create an effect that is dramatic. The lights reveal unusual rock formations. Spikes of rock hang from the ceiling. Tall, pointy rocks rise from the floor. Delicate sheets of thin rock are hanging like drapery. The slow drip of minerals through the caves' limestone roof formed them all. The desert is above. In the desert, the sun shines, and winds blow, and birds sing, and coyotes howl. Below in the caverns, no daylight penetrates. The air is cold and still. There are no winds or animal sounds. Such sounds do not disturb the silence. It is amazing to see the contrast between the desert and the caves. Not many people would have guessed that these caves beneath the desert originated as a coral reef in an ancient sea.

**Answers: Extra Exercise**
This is a summary exercise, so it should reflect many of the techniques of variety and emphasis discussed in this chapter. Here is one answer; many others are possible.

Hidden beneath the sands of New Mexico, [9p, modifiers] the huge caves known as the Carlsbad Caverns contain a mysterious underground world. [9c, sentence lengths] More than 20 miles of caves have been discovered, and miles more are found each year. [9c, revise for suitable mix by combining two sentences] Some of the caves, which echo with

# 9q How does repetition affect style?

You can repeat one or more words that express a main idea when your message is suitable. This technique creates a rhythm that focuses attention on the main idea. PARALLELISM (Chapter 10) is another kind of repetition that focuses on grammatical structures as well as words. Here's an example that uses deliberate repetition along with a variety of sentence lengths to deliver its meaning.

Coal is **black** and it warms your house and cooks your food. The night is **black,** which has a moon, and a million stars, and is beautiful. Sleep is **black,** which gives you rest, so you wake up feeling **good.** I am **black.** I feel very **good** this evening.

—Langston Hughes, "That Word *Black*"

At the same time, don't confuse deliberate repetition with a lack of vocabulary variety.

**NO**  An insurance agent can be an excellent adviser when you want to buy a car. An insurance agent has complete records on most cars. An insurance agent knows which car models are prone to have accidents. An insurance agent can tell you which car models are the most expensive to repair if they are in a collision. An insurance agent can tell you which models are most likely to be stolen. [Although only a few synonyms exist for *insurance agent, car,* and *model,* some do and should be used. Also, the sentence structure here lacks variety.]

**YES**  If you are thinking of buying a new car, an insurance agent, who usually has complete records on most cars, can be an excellent adviser. Any professional insurance broker knows which automobile models are prone to have accidents. Did you know that some cars suffer more damage than others in a collision? If you want to know which vehicles crumple more than others and which are the most expensive to repair, ask an insurance agent. Similarly, some car models are more likely to be stolen, so find out from the person who specializes in dealing with car insurance claims.

# 9r How else can I create variety and emphasis?

## CHANGING WORD ORDER
**Standard word order** in English places the SUBJECT before the VERB.

The **mayor** *walked* into the room. [*Mayor,* the subject, comes before the verb *walked.*]

Any variation from standard word order creates emphasis. For example, **inverted word order** places the verb before the subject.

> Into the room **walked** the **mayor.** [*Mayor, the subject, comes after the verb walked.*]

## CHANGING A SENTENCE'S SUBJECT

The subject of a sentence establishes the focus for that sentence. To create the emphasis you want, you can vary each sentence's subject. All of the sample sentences below express the same information, but the focus changes in each according to the subject (and its corresponding verb).

> **Our study *showed*** that 25 percent of college students' time is spent eating or sleeping. [Focus is on the study.]

> **College students *eat or sleep*** 25 percent of the time, according to our study. [Focus is on the students.]

> **Eating or sleeping *occupies*** 25 percent of college students' time, according to our study. [Focus is on eating and sleeping.]

> **Twenty-five percent of college students' time *is spent*** eating or sleeping, according to our study. [Focus is on the percentage of time.]

**EXERCISE 9-9** Working individually or with a group, revise the sentences in each paragraph to change the passage's style. For help, consult the advice in all sections of this chapter.

1. Thirst is the body's way of surviving. Every cell in the body needs water. People can die by losing as little as 15 to 20 percent of their water requirements. Blood contains 83 percent water. Blood provides indispensable nutrients for the cells. Blood carries water to the cells. Blood carries waste away from the cells. Insufficient water means cells cannot be fueled or cleaned. The body becomes sluggish. The body can survive eleven days without water. Bodily functions are seriously disrupted by a lack of water for more than one day. The body loses water. The blood thickens. The heart must pump harder. Thickened blood is harder to pump through the heart. Some drinks replace the body's need for fluids. Alcohol or caffeine in drinks leads to dehydration. People know they should drink water often. They can become moderately dehydrated before they even begin to develop a thirst.

2. June is the wet season in Ghana. Here in Accra, the capital, the morning rain has ceased. The sun heats the humid air. Pillars of black smoke begin to rise above the vast Agbobgloshie Market. I follow one plume toward its source. I pass lettuce and plantain vendors. I pass stalls

watery noises and glimmer with reflected light, contain mysterious underground lakes. [9o, periodic sentence] Others are huge chambers whose ceilings rise 200 feet. [9p, modifiers] Electric lights, which illuminate the caves for visitors, are placed for dramatic effect [9r, word order] to reveal unusual rock formations. Spikes of rock hang from the ceiling, and tall, pointy rocks rise from the floor. [9c, sentence lengths] Hanging like drapery are delicate sheets of thin rock. [9r, word order] All were formed by the slow drip of minerals through the caves' limestone roof. [9r, word order] In the desert above, the sun shines, winds blow, birds sing, and coyotes howl. [9c, sentence lengths] Below in the caverns, where no daylight penetrates, [9d, modifiers] the air is cold and still. No winds or animal sounds disturb the silence. [9c, sentence lengths] How amazing the contrast is between the desert and the caves! [9n, exclamation for variety] Who would have guessed that these caves beneath the desert originated as a coral reef in an ancient sea? [9n, question for variety]

## ANSWERS: EXERCISE 9-9
Answers will vary. Here is one possibility.

Thirst is the body's way of surviving. Because every cell in the body needs water, people can die by losing as little as 15 to 20 percent of their water requirements. Blood, which contains 83 percent water, provides indispensable nutrients for the cells. Blood carries water to the cells, and blood carries waste away from the cells. Insufficient water means cells cannot be fueled or cleaned, so the body becomes sluggish. Although the body can survive eleven days without water, bodily functions are seriously disrupted by a lack of water for more than one day. When the body loses water, the blood thickens. The heart must pump harder, for thickened blood is harder to pump through the heart. Some drinks replace the body's need for fluids, but alcohol or caffeine in drinks leads to dehydration. Unless people know they should drink water often, they can become moderately dehydrated before they even begin to develop a thirst.

of used tires. I walk through a clanging scrap market. In the market hunched men bash on old alternators and engine blocks.

—Based on a paragraph by Chris Carroll in "High Tech Trash"

3.    Because of the development of new economies around the world, with resulting demands for new construction and goods, especially in places like China, there is a high demand for steel, and a new breed of American entrepreneurs is making money in meeting this opportunity. For much of industrial history, steel was made from iron ore and coke, a process that resulted in what might be called "new steel." However, it has now become even more profitable to make recycled steel, melting down junk and recasting it, a process made possible because steel, unlike paper and plastic, can be recycled indefinitely. Because the process saves energy and helps the environment by saving on the amount of ore that has to be mined, manufacturing recycled steel has benefits beyond profitability.

For more help with your writing, grammar, and research, go to **www.mycomplab.com**

**10**

# Parallelism

## 10a    What is parallelism?

When you write words, PHRASES, or CLAUSES within a sentence to match in their grammatical forms, the result is **parallelism**. Parallelism serves to emphasize information or ideas in writing. The technique relates to the concept of parallel lines in geometry, lines that run alongside each other and never meet.

> The deer often come to eat their grain, the wolves to destroy their sheep, the bears to kill their hogs, and the foxes to catch their poultry. [The message of the multiple, accumulating assaults is echoed by the parallel structures.]
> —J. Hector St. Jean de Crèvecoeur, *Letters from an American Farmer*

You gain several advantages in using parallel structures:

- You can express ideas of equal weight in your writing.
- You can emphasize important information or ideas.
- You can add rhythm and grace to your writing style.

Many writers attend to parallelism when they are REVISING. If you think while you're DRAFTING that your parallelism is faulty or that you can enhance your writing style by using parallelism, underline or highlight the material and keep moving forward. When you revise, you can return to the places you've marked.

A **balanced sentence** is a type of parallelism in which contrasting content is delivered. The two parallel structures are usually, but not always, INDEPENDENT CLAUSES. A balanced sentence uses COORDINATION. The two coordinate structures are characterized by opposites in meaning, sometimes with one structure cast in the negative.

> By night, the litter and desperation disappeared as the city's glittering lights came on; by day, the filth and despair reappeared as the sun rose.
>
> —Jennifer Kirk, student

🛈 **Alert:** Authorities differ about using a comma, a semicolon, or nothing between the parts of a short balanced sentence. In ACADEMIC WRITING, to avoid appearing to make the error of a COMMA SPLICE, use a semicolon (or revise in some other way), as in the following sentence.

> Mosquitoes don't bite; they stab. ●

## 10b How do words, phrases, and clauses work in parallel form?

When you put words, PHRASES, and CLAUSES into parallel form, you enhance your writing style with balance and grace.

| | |
|---|---|
| **PARALLEL WORDS** | Recommended exercise includes running, swimming, and cycling. |
| **PARALLEL PHRASES** | Exercise helps people maintain healthy bodies and handle mental pressures. |

one before it." Second, writers can enhance parallel elements if they "consciously balance parts of phrases and clauses against one another."

**BACKGROUND**

The site <http://owl.english.purdue.edu/handouts/grammar/g_parallel.html> offered by Purdue University gives examples of faulty parallel structures, including proofreading strategies for recognizing parallelism errors.

**BACKGROUND**

Classical rhetoric teaches that successful speaking or writing comes, in part, from the imitation of good examples. This imitation can take the form of copying passages verbatim or of imitating particular sentence patterns. Classical rhetoricians are not the only ones who have written about the benefits of imitation. Benjamin Franklin writes in his *Autobiography* (1771) of using essays in *The Spectator* as models for organization, sentence structure, and vocabulary. Malcolm X writes in his autobiography of the benefits he gained from simply copying the dictionary in longhand. Winston Churchill and W. Somerset Maugham also write of the lessons they learned by imitating written models.

**BACKGROUND**

Martin Luther King Jr. (1929–1968) was a powerful and eloquent speaker and writer for the civil rights movement in the United States. His works include *Stride Toward Freedom* (1958), *Strength to Love* (1963), *Why We Can't Wait* (1964), and *Where Do We Go from Here: Chaos or Community* (1967), as well as his famous "I Have a Dream" speech, which he delivered to a crowd of over 250,000 people in 1963 at a massive civil rights demonstration in Washington, DC.

Among his best-known writings is his "Letter from Birmingham Jail," which he wrote from prison in 1963 in response to a published statement by eight Alabama clergymen who called his activities "unwise and untimely." In "The *Other* Beauty of Martin Luther King, Jr.'s 'Letter from Birmingham Jail'" (*College Composition and Communication* 32.1 (1981): 30–37),

Mia Klein Anderson describes the musical, rhythmical effect of parallelism in King's powerful letter. King parallels clauses, nouns, verbs, adverbs, adjectives, and adjective-noun pairs throughout the letter. Using antithesis and parallelism, he juxtaposes contrasting ideas with an engaging rhythm. King often combines parallelism with deliberate repetition of a word or group of words at the start of successive clauses, a rhetorical figure called *anaphora.* "Martin Luther King, Jr., knew that his effectiveness in reaching his wider audience would come both from what he said and from how he said it," Anderson writes. "The words can reach the mind, but the music and imagination can reach the heart and soul" (36).

Bob J. Frye's "A Habit of Being: Some Uses of Personal Letters in Freshman Composition" suggests using King's letter, along with other famous examples, as the basis for a first-year composition writing assignment (*Rhetoric Review* 1.2 (1983): 89–119).

**TEACHING TIP**

You might choose to write examples of parallelism errors on the board and have students correct them. Here are two real examples from old advertisements on fashion.

**1.** In an ad about women's robes by *Vanity Fair:* "Total Luxury . . . Total Washable"

**2.** In an ad about evening gowns: "Give her this gown to sleep or going out"

**QUOTATION: ON WRITING**

The likeness of form enables the reader to recognize more readily the likeness of content and function. The unskillful writer often violates this principle, from a mistaken belief that he should constantly vary the form of his expressions.

—William Strunk Jr., *Elements of Style*

**PARALLEL CLAUSES** Many people exercise because they want to look healthy, because they need to increase stamina, and because they hope to live longer.

## 10c How does parallelism deliver impact?

Parallel structures serve to emphasize the meaning that sentences deliver. Deliberate, rhythmic repetition of parallel forms creates an effect of balance, reinforcing the impact of a message.

> Go back to Mississippi, go back to Alabama, go back to South Carolina, go back to Georgia, go back to Louisiana, go back to the slums and ghettos of our northern cities, knowing that somehow this situation can and will be changed.
>
> —Martin Luther King Jr., "I Have a Dream"

If King had not used PARALLELISM, his message would have made less of an impact on his listeners. His structures reinforce the power of his message. A sentence without parallelism could have carried his message, but with far less effect: *Return to your homes in Mississippi, Alabama, South Carolina, Georgia, Louisiana, or the northern cities, and know that the situation will be changed.*

Here's a longer passage in which parallel structures, concepts, and rhythms operate. Together, they echo the intensity of the writer's message.

> You ask me what is **poverty?** Listen to me. Here I am, dirty, **smelly,** and with no "proper" underwear on and with the stench of my rotting teeth near you. I will tell you. Listen to me. Listen without pity. I cannot use your pity. Listen with understanding. Put yourself in my dirty, worn-out, ill-fitting shoes, and hear me.
>
> **Poverty** is getting up every morning from a dirt- and illness-stained mattress. The sheets have long since been used for diapers. **Poverty** is living in a **smell** that never leaves. This is a **smell** of urine, sour milk, and spoiling food sometimes joined with the strong **smell** of long-cooked onions. Onions are cheap. If you have **smelled** this **smell,** you did not know how it came. It is **the smell** of the outdoor privy. It is **the smell** of young children who cannot walk the long dark way in the night. It is **the smell** of the mattresses where years of "accidents" have happened. It is **the smell** of the milk that has gone sour because the refrigerator long has not worked, and it costs money to get it fixed. It is **the smell** of rotting garbage. I could bury it, but where is the shovel? Shovels cost money.
>
> —Jo Goodwin Parker, "What Is Poverty?"

**EXERCISE 10-1**    Working individually or with a group, highlight all parallel elements of the Jo Goodwin Parker passage above in addition to those shown in boldface.

# 10d How can I avoid faulty parallelism?

**Faulty parallelism** usually results when you join nonmatching grammatical forms.

## PARALLELISM WITH COORDINATING CONJUNCTIONS

The coordinating conjunctions are *and, but, for, or, nor, yet,* and *so.* To avoid faulty parallelism, write the words that accompany coordinating conjunctions in matching grammatical forms.

> **NO**    Love *and* **being married** go together.
>
> **YES**    Love *and* **marriage** go together.
>
> **YES**    **Being in love** *and* **being married** go together.

## PARALLELISM WITH CORRELATIVE CONJUNCTIONS

Correlative conjunctions are paired words such as *not only . . . but (also), either . . . or,* and *both . . . and.* To avoid faulty parallelism, write the words joined by correlative conjunctions in matching grammatical forms.

> **NO**    Differing expectations for marriage *not only* **can lead to disappointment** *but also* **makes the couple angry.**
>
> **YES**    Differing expectations for marriage *not only* **can lead to disappointment** *but also* **can make the couple angry.**

## PARALLELISM WITH *THAN* AND *AS*

To avoid faulty parallelism when you use *than* and *as* for comparisons, write the elements of comparison in matching grammatical forms.

> **NO**    **Having a solid marriage** can be more satisfying *than* **the acquisition of wealth.**
>
> **YES**    **Having a solid marriage** can be more satisfying *than* **acquiring wealth.**
>
> **YES**    **A solid marriage** can be more satisfying *than* **wealth.**

## PARALLELISM WITH FUNCTION WORDS

**Function words** include ARTICLES (*the, a, an*); the *to* of the INFINITIVE (*to* love); PREPOSITIONS (for example, *of, in, about*); and sometimes RELATIVE PRONOUNS.

---

**ANSWERS: EXERCISE 10-1**
Elements of parallelism in Parker's passage not shown in boldface include *Repetitions:* you, me, I, dirty (dirt), pity, onions, mattress(es), cost(s) money, this, urine (privy, "accidents"), long, it is, sour, rotting, shovel(s); *Paired words:* with/and with; *Imperatives* (mild commands): Listen, Put, hear; *Contrasts:* pity/understanding, without/with; *Words in a series:* my dirty, worn-out, ill-fitting shoes; smell of urine, sour milk, and spoiling food.

**ANSWERS: EXERCISE 10-2**
Answers will vary. Here is one set of possible answers.

**1.** According to the psychologist Harry Levinson, the five main types of bad boss are *the workaholic, the bully, the bad communicator, the jellyfish,* and *the perfectionist.* [10c, parallel words]

**2.** *To get* ahead, *to keep* their self-respect, and *to survive,* wise employees handle problem bosses with a variety of strategies. [10c, parallel phrases]

**3.** To cope with a bad-tempered employer, workers can *both stand up* for themselves *and reason* with a bullying boss. [10e, correlative conjunctions]

**4.** Often, *bad bosses communicate poorly or fail to calculate* the impact of their personality on others; *good bosses listen carefully and are sensitive* to others' responses. [10d, parallel sentence structures]

**5.** Employees *who* take the trouble to understand what makes their bosses tick, *who engage* in some self-analysis, and *who stay* flexible [10e, repeating parallel function words] are better prepared to cope with a difficult job environment *than employees who suffer* in silence. [10e, parallel form with *than*]

When you write a series of parallel structures, be consistent in the second and successive structures about either repeating or omitting a function word. Generally, repeat function words only if you think that the repetition clarifies your meaning or highlights the parallelism that you intend.

> **NO** **To assign** unanswered letters their proper weight, **free** us from the expectations of others, **to give** us back to ourselves—here lies the great, the singular power of self-respect.

> **YES** **To assign** unanswered letters their proper weight, **to free** us from the expectations of others, **to give** us back to ourselves—here lies the great, the singular power of self-respect.
>
> —Joan Didion, "On Self-Respect"

I have in my own life a precious friend, a woman of 65 **who has** lived very hard, **who is** wise, **who listens** well, **who has been** where I am and can help me understand it, and **who represents** not only an ultimate ideal mother to me but also the person I'd like to be when I grow up.

—Judith Viorst, "Friends, Good Friends—and Such Good Friends"

We looked into the bus, which **was** painted blue with orange daisies, **had** picnic benches instead of seats, and **showed** yellow curtains billowing out its windows.

—Kerrie Falk, student

**EXERCISE 10-2** Working individually or with a group, revise these sentences by putting appropriate information in parallel structures. For help, consult sections 10a through 10e.

EXAMPLE Difficult bosses affect not only their employees' performances but their private lives are affected as well.

Difficult bosses affect not only their employees' performances *but their private lives as well.*

1. According to the psychologist Harry Levinson, the five main types of bad boss are the workaholic, the kind of person you would describe as bullying, a person who communicates badly, the jellyfish type, and someone who insists on perfection.

2. As a way of getting ahead, to keep their self-respect, and for survival purposes, wise employees handle problem bosses with a variety of strategies.

3. To cope with a bad-tempered employer, workers can both stand up for themselves and reasoning with a bullying boss.

4. Often, bad bosses communicate poorly or fail to calculate the impact of their personality on others; being a careful listener and sensitivity to others' responses are qualities that good bosses possess.

5. Employees who take the trouble to understand what makes their bosses tick, engage in some self-analysis, and staying flexible are better prepared to cope with a difficult job environment than suffering in silence like some employees.

**EXERCISE 10-3** Working individually or with a group, combine the sentences in each numbered item, using techniques of parallelism. For help, consult sections 10a through 10e.

**EXAMPLE** College scholarships are awarded not only for academic and athletic ability, but there are also scholarships that recognize unusual talents. Other scholarships even award accidents of birth, like left-handedness.

College scholarships are awarded not only for academic and athletic ability *but also for unusual talents and even for accidents of birth, like left-handedness.*

1. A married couple met at Juniata College in Huntingdon, Pennsylvania. They are both left-handed, and they have set up a scholarship for needy left-handed students attending Juniata.

2. Writers who specialize in humor bankroll a student humor writer at the University of Southern California in Los Angeles. A horse-racing association sponsors a student sportswriter. The student must attend Vanderbilt University in Nashville, Tennessee.

3. The Rochester Institute of Technology in New York State chose 150 students born on June 12, 1979. Each one received a grant of $1,500 per year. These awards were given to select students to honor the school's 150th anniversary, which was celebrated on June 12, 1979.

4. The College of Wooster in Ohio grants generous scholarships to students if they play the bagpipes, a musical instrument native to Scotland. Students playing the traditional Scottish drums and those who excel in Scottish folk dancing also qualify.

5. In return for their scholarships, Wooster's bagpipers must pipe for the school's football team. The terms of the scholarships also require the drummers to drum for the team. The dancers have to cheer the athletes from the sidelines.

**EXERCISE 10-4** Working individually or with a group, underline the parallel elements in these three passages. Next, imitate the parallelism in the examples, using a different topic of your choice for each.

A. Our earth is but a small star in a great universe. Yet of it we can make, if we choose, a planet unvexed by war, untroubled by hunger or fear, undivided by senseless distinctions of race, color, or theory.

—Stephen Vincent Benét

**ANSWERS: EXERCISE 10-3**
Answers may vary. Here is one set of possible answers.

**1.** A married couple *who* met at Juniata College in Huntingdon, Pennsylvania, and *who* are both left-handed have set up a scholarship for needy left-handed students attending Juniata. [10e, repeating parallel function words]

**2.** Writers who specialize in humor bankroll a student humor writer at the University of Southern California in Los Angeles; a horse-racing association sponsors a student sportswriter at Vanderbilt University in Nashville, Tennessee. [10b, balanced sentence]

**3.** The Rochester Institute of Technology in New York State is choosing 150 students born on June 12, 1979. *It is granting each one $1,500 per year. It is awarding these grants to select students to honor the school's 150th anniversary,* which it celebrated on June 12, 1979. [10d, parallelism among sentences]

**4.** The College of Wooster in Ohio grants generous scholarships to students if they *play the Scottish bagpipes, play the traditional Scottish drums,* or *excel in Scottish folk dancing.* [10c, parallel phrases]

**5.** In return for their scholarships, Wooster's *bagpipers must pipe for the school's football team,* the *drummers must drum for the team,* and the *dancers must cheer the athletes from the sidelines.* [10c, parallelism among clauses]

**ANSWERS: EXERCISE 10-4**
The answers here list the examples' parallel elements.

**A.** The description "a planet *unvexed* by war, *untroubled* by hunger or fear, *undivided* by senseless distinctions of race, color, or theory" has parallel structure based on parallel words (in italics). [Some students may also list the parallel words *race, color, theory*.]

**B.** The clauses beginning with the word *some* are parallel.

**C.** The two clauses *I am lonely* are parallel, as are all the clauses beginning with *when.*

## TEACHING TIP

You may want to ask your students to identify the various techniques by which parallelism is set up in the following sentences.

**1.** Standing on a concrete jetty at seven-thirty of a drizzly morning, looking across the gray Hudson at the shore softened by fog, one can just make out an endless miniature procession of Manhattan-bound cars going down the ramp to the Lincoln Tunnel.
— "Gray Manhattan," *The New Yorker*

**2.** There is a crazy restaurant in the south of France where you are expected to eat well and copiously, to drink to excess, to listen to music and perhaps to spin to it—and also to break up the joint before you leave.
— Richard Atcheson, *Le Pirate*

**3.** On one side of this line are They: the bribers, the cheaters, the chiselers, the swindlers, the extortioners. On the other side are We. . . .
— Marya Mannes, "The Thin Grey Line"

## BACKGROUND

In *Style: Ten Lessons in Clarity and Grace,* 7th ed. (Boston: Longman, 2002), Joseph M. Williams points out that a nonparallel construction, at times, is acceptable. Skilled writers often join a noun phrase with a *how* clause ("The debater knew the facts and how to use them to her best advantage") or an adjective or adverb with a prepositional phrase ("The young team played aggressively, intelligently, and with surprising poise"). Many editors and instructors, however, do not accept these constructions.

B.     Some would recover [from polio] almost entirely. Some would die. Some would come through unable to move their legs, or unable to move arms and legs; some could move nothing but an arm, or nothing but a few fingers and their eyes. Some would leave the hospital with a cane, some with crutches, crutches and steel leg braces, or in wheelchairs—white-faced, shrunken, with frightened eyes, light blankets over their legs. Some would remain in an iron lung—a great, eighteen-hundred-pound, casket-like contraption, like the one in which the woman in the magic show (her head and feet sticking out of either end) is sawed in half.

— Charles L. Mee Jr., "The Summer Before Salk"

C.     But we always knew that hope is not blind optimism. It's not ignoring the enormity of the task ahead or the roadblocks that stand in our path. It's not sitting on the sidelines or shirking from a fight. Hope is that thing inside us that insists, despite all evidence to the contrary, that something better awaits us if we have the courage to reach for it, and to work for it, and to fight for it. . . .

Hope is what led a band of colonists to rise up against an empire; what led the greatest of generations to free a continent and heal a nation; what led young women and young men to sit at lunch counters and brave fire hoses and march through Selma and Montgomery for freedom's cause.

Hope is what led me here today—with a father from Kenya; a mother from Kansas; and a story that could only happen in the United States of America. Hope is the bedrock of this nation; the belief that our destiny will not be written for us, but by us; by all those men and women who are not content to settle for the world as it is; who have the courage to remake the world as it should be.

— Barack Obama

## 10e   How does parallelism work in outlines and lists?

All items in formal OUTLINES and lists must be parallel in grammar and structure. (For more about outline format and outline development, see section 2f.)

**OUTLINES**

    **NO**     Reducing Traffic Fatalities

        I.  Stricter laws
            A.  Top speed should be 55 mph on highways.
            B.  Higher fines
            C.  Requiring jail sentences for repeat offenders
        II.  The use of safety devices should be mandated by law.

**YES**   Reducing Traffic Fatalities

  I. Passing stricter speed laws
    A. Making 55 mph the top speed on highways
    B. Raising fines for speeding
    C. Requiring jail sentences for repeat offenders
  II. Mandating by law the use of safety devices

## LISTS

**NO**   Workaholics share these characteristics:
  1. They are intense and driven.
  2. Strong self-doubters
  3. Labor is preferred to leisure by workaholics.

**YES**   Workaholics share these characteristics:
  1. They are intense and driven.
  2. They have strong self-doubts.
  3. They prefer labor to leisure.

**EXERCISE 10-5**   Working individually or with a group, revise this outline so that all lines are complete sentences in parallel form. For help, consult sections 2f and 10e.

Improving Health

  I. Exercise
    A. Aerobics
    B. Stretching and strength training
    C. Vary routine
  II. Better Eating Habits
    A. Healthy food
    B. Eat less
    C. Eat more often

For more help with your writing, grammar, and research, go to **www.mycomplab.com**

mycomplab

**ANSWERS: EXERCISE 10-5**
Answers will vary. Here is one possibility.

*Improving Health*

  I. Exercise regularly
    A. Do aerobic exercises for 30 minutes five times per week.
    B. Do stretching and strengthening exercises five times per week.
    C. Vary your exercise routine to make it interesting.

  II. Improve your eating habits
    A. Eat healthy foods.
    B. Eat smaller portions.
    C. Eat something healthy approximately every three hours during the day.

# 11

# Conciseness

## 11a   What is conciseness?

**Conciseness** requires you to craft sentences that are direct and to the point. Its opposite, **wordiness**, means you are filling sentences with empty words and phrases that increase the word count but contribute nothing to meaning. Wordy writing is padded with deadwood, forcing readers to clear away the branches and overgrowth—an annoying waste of time that implies the writer isn't skilled. Usually, the best time to work on making your writing more concise is while you're REVISING.

WORDY   As a matter of fact, the television station which is situated in the local area wins a great many awards in the final analysis because of its type of coverage of all kinds of controversial issues.

CONCISE   The local television station wins many awards for its coverage of controversial issues.

## 11b   What common expressions are not concise?

Many common expressions we use in informal speech are not concise. Quick Reference 11.1 lists some and shows you how to eliminate them.

### Quick Reference 11.1

#### Cutting unnecessary words and phrases

| Empty Word or Phrase | Wordy Example Revised |
|---|---|
| as a matter of fact | Many marriages, as a matter of fact, end in divorce. |

continued >>

## Quick Reference 11.1 (continued)

| Empty Word or Phrase | Wordy Example Revised |
|---|---|
| at the present time | The revised proposal for outdoor lighting angers many villagers ~~at the present time.~~ *now* |
| because of the fact that, in light of the fact that, due to the fact that | Because ~~of the fact that~~ the museum has a special exhibit, it stays open late. |
| by means of | We traveled by ~~means of a~~ car. |
| factor | The project's final cost was ~~the~~ essential ~~factor~~ to consider. |
| for the purpose of | Work crews arrived ~~for the purpose of~~ *to* fixing the potholes. |
| have a tendency to | The team ~~has a tendency~~ *tends* to lose home games. |
| in a very real sense | ~~In a very real sense,~~ All firefighters are heroes. |
| in the case of | ~~In the case of~~ The election, ~~it~~ will be close. |
| in the event that | ~~In the event that~~ *If* you're late, I will buy our tickets. |
| in the final analysis | ~~In the final analysis,~~ No two eyewitnesses agreed on what they saw. |
| in the process of | We are ~~in the process of~~ reviewing the proposal. |
| it seems that | ~~It seems that~~ The union went on strike over health benefits. |
| manner | The child spoke ~~in a reluctant manner~~ *reluctantly.* |
| nature | The movie review was ~~of a~~ sarcastic ~~nature.~~ |
| that exists | The crime rate ~~that exists~~ is unacceptable. |
| the point I am trying to make | ~~The point I am trying to make is~~ Television reporters invade our privacy. |
| type of, kind of | Gordon took a relaxing ~~type of~~ vacation. |
| What I mean to say is | ~~What I mean to say is~~ I love you. |

imprecision, and other problems, but the writer must decide whether and how to revise a flagged sentence.

**TEACHING TIP**
Brenda S. Sloane's "Say It Straight: Teaching Conciseness" (*Teaching English in the Two-Year College* 30.4 (2003): 429–443) describes a series of exercises designed to help students revise their writing for clarity and conciseness. Her students report that this lesson was one of their favorites during the semester.

**QUOTATION: ON WRITING**
The language must be careful and must appear effortless. It must not sweat. It must suggest and be provocative at the same time.
—Toni Morrison

**HUMOROUS NOTE**
The *Guinness Book of World Records* accords the prize for the longest sentence in prose to William Faulkner for a 1,287 word sentence in *Absalom, Absalom.* Music critic Bernard Levin held the prize for the longest sentence published in a newspaper, 1,667 words. While these records are debatable, challenge students to join in on the fun by finding the longest sentence in one of their textbooks and rewriting that sentence concisely.

**TEACHING TIP**
Truman Capote, known for a prose style marked by clarity and lucidity, never relented in his efforts to delete everything that marred the lean simplicity of his work. In a book of essays published toward the end of his life, he included a description of an experience he had had in a Moscow subway. To Capote's surprise, he recognized a man who had lived in Capote's apartment building in New York ten years earlier. Blind, crippled, and dignified, Mr. Jones never left his apartment but received a steady stream of visitors and telephone calls. Suddenly, he disappeared. Using the following excerpt from Capote's remembrance, you might ask students if they can delete any words, reduce any phrases, or otherwise revise the passage to be more concise.

Ten years pass.

Now it is a zero-cold December afternoon, and I am in Moscow. I am riding in a subway car. There are only a few other passengers. One of them is a man sitting opposite me, a man wearing boots, a thick long coat and a Russian-style fur cap. He has bright eyes, blue as a peacock's.

After a doubtful instant, I simply stared, for even without the black glasses, there was no mistaking that lean distinctive face, those high cheekbones with a single scarlet star-shaped birthmark.

I was just about to cross the aisle and speak to him when the train pulled into a station, and Mr. Jones, on a pair of fine sturdy legs, stood up and strode out of the car. Swiftly, the train door closed behind him.

—Truman Capote, *Music for Chameleons*

**ANSWERS: EXERCISE 11-1**

First, students underline wordy material. Second, they revise each sentence (these answers will vary somewhat).

*Underlined*

1. As a matter of fact, in the popular imagination, motor scooters are the very essence of European style.

2. Today, over one million scooters are purchased by people in Europe each year, compared with a number that amounts to only 70,000 buyers in the United States.

3. In fact, Europeans have long used fuel-efficient, clean-running scooters for the purpose of getting around in a manner that is relatively easy in congested cities.

4. The use of these brightly colored, maneuverable scooters allows city dwellers to zip through traffic jams and thereby to save time and to save gas.

5. However, sales of scooters, it might interest you to know, are in the process of increasing in North America.

6. What I am trying to say is that motor scooters use much less gasoline than cars, and that as a matter of fact the cost factor

**EXERCISE 11-1**  Working individually or with a group, revise this paragraph in two steps. First, underline all words that interfere with conciseness. Second, revise each sentence to make it more concise. (You'll need to drop words and replace or rearrange others.)

**EXAMPLE**  It seems that most North Americans think of motor scooters as vehicles that exist only in European countries.

1. It seems that most North Americans think of motor scooters as vehicles that exist only in European countries.

2. Most North Americans think of motor scooters as only European vehicles.

1. As a matter of fact, in the popular imagination, motor scooters are the very essence of European style.

2. Today, over one million scooters are purchased by people in Europe each year, compared with a number that amounts to only 70,000 buyers in the United States.

3. In fact, Europeans have long used fuel-efficient, clean-running scooters for the purpose of getting around in a manner that is relatively easy in congested cities.

4. The use of these brightly colored, maneuverable scooters allows city dwellers to zip through traffic jams and thereby to save time and to save gas.

5. However, sales of scooters, it might interest you to know, are in the process of increasing in North America.

6. What I am trying to say is that motor scooters use much less gasoline than cars, and that as a matter of fact the cost factor is about one-fourth that of an inexpensive new car.

7. In addition, many motor scooters, it is pleasing to note, run on electricity, which in fact makes them noise and emission free.

8. A scooter running by means of electrical power amounts to a cost in the neighborhood of 25 cents to travel 50 miles at 30 miles per hour.

9. Members of many different population groups, from college students to retired persons, have begun to be finding this type of vehicle to be of a useful nature in a very real sense.

10. Traveling by means of an agile, snappy scooter makes getting around a college campus or doing errands in a city neighborhood quick and easy.

# 11c What sentence structures usually work against conciseness?

Two sentence structures, although appropriate in some contexts, often work against CONCISENESS because they can lead to WORDINESS: writing EXPLETIVE constructions and writing in the PASSIVE VOICE.

## AVOIDING EXPLETIVE CONSTRUCTIONS

An expletive construction starts with *it* or *there* followed by a form of the VERB *be*. When you cut the expletive construction and revise, the sentence becomes more direct.

~~It is necessary for~~ students ^S^ ~~to~~ ^must^ fill in both questionnaires.

~~There are~~ eight instructors ^E^ ~~who teach~~ in the Computer Science Department.

🌐 **ESOL Tips:** (1) *It* in an expletive construction is not a PRONOUN referring to a specific ANTECEDENT. *It* is an "empty" word that fills the SUBJECT position in the sentence but does not function as the subject. The actual subject appears after the expletive construction: *It was the teacher who answered the question.* If concise, the sentence would be *The teacher answered the question.* (2) *There* in an expletive construction does not indicate a place. Rather, *there* is an "empty" word that fills the subject position in the sentence but does not function as the subject. The actual subject appears after the expletive construction: *There are many teachers who can answer the question.* If concise, the sentence would be *Many teachers can answer the question.* ⬤

## AVOIDING THE PASSIVE VOICE

In general, the passive voice is less concise—as well as less lively—than the ACTIVE VOICE. In the active voice, the subject of a sentence does the action named by the verb.

**ACTIVE** Professor Higgins teaches public speaking. [*Professor Higgins* is the subject, and he does the action: He *teaches.*]

In the passive voice, the subject of a sentence receives the action named by the verb.

**PASSIVE** Public speaking is taught by Professor Higgins. [*Public speaking* is the subject, and it receives the action *taught.*]

Unless your meaning justifies using the passive voice, choose the active voice. (For more information, see sections 15n through 15p.)

**PASSIVE** Volunteer work was done by students for credit in sociology. [The passive phrase *was done by students* is unnecessary for the intended meaning. *Students,* not *volunteer work,* are doing the action and should get the action of the verb.]

**ACTIVE** **The students did** volunteer work for credit in sociology.

**ACTIVE** **Volunteer work earned** students credit in sociology. [Since the verb has changed to *earned, volunteer work* performs the action of the verb.]

is about one-fourth that of an inexpensive new car.

7. In addition, some motor scooters, <u>it is pleasing to note</u>, now run on electricity, which <u>in fact</u> makes them noise and emission free.

8. A scooter running by <u>means of</u> electrical power <u>amounts to a cost</u> <u>in the neighborhood of</u> 25 cents to travel 50 miles at 30 miles per hour.

9. <u>Members of</u> many different population groups, from college students to retired persons, <u>have begun to be finding</u> this type of vehicle <u>to be of a</u> useful <u>nature in a very real sense.</u>

10. <u>Traveling by means of</u> an agile, snappy scooter makes getting around a college campus or doing errands in a city neighborhood quick and easy.

*Rewritten*

1. In the popular imagination, motor scooters are the essence of European style.

2. Today, over one million scooters are purchased each year in Europe, compared with only 70,000 in the United States. [The use of the passive voice is justified here because the focus is on the scooters being purchased.]

3. Europeans have long used fuel-efficient, clean-running scooters for getting around relatively easily in congested cities.

4. These brightly colored, maneuverable scooters allow city dwellers to zip through traffic jams and thereby save time and gas.

5. However, sales of scooters are increasing in North America.

6. Motor scooters use much less gasoline than cars, and the cost is about one-fourth that of an inexpensive new car.

7. In addition, some motor scooters now run on electricity, which makes them noise and emission free.

8. A scooter running by electrical power costs about 25 cents to travel 50 miles at 30 miles per hour.

9. Many different population groups, from college students to retired persons, are finding this type of vehicle useful.

10. An agile, snappy scooter makes getting around a college campus or doing errands in a city neighborhood quick and easy.

**QUOTATION: ON WRITING**

What is written without effort is in general read without pleasure.

—Samuel Johnson

**TEACHING TIP**

Ask students to compose an excuse for missing work (either real or hypothetical!). Ask them to write it out in three forms: a text message, an e-mail, and a formal written letter. Use the three forms to talk about concise language and appropriate academic discourse.

**QUOTATION: ON WRITING**

In composing, as a general rule, run your pen through every other word you have written; you have no idea what vigor it will give your style.

—Sydney Smith

**QUOTATION: ON WRITING**

There is no artifice as good and desirable as simplicity.

—Francis de Sales

**QUOTATION: ON WRITING**

We stand now, in linguistic awe, before the mysterious word *there*. It can be an adverb ("*There* you go again"), a noun ("Let Newt take it from *there*"), an interjection ("*There, there* our day will come"), and a pronoun replacing a name ("Hi, *there*").

—William Safire

**QUOTATION: ON WRITING**

What I like in a good author is not what he says, but what he whispers.

—Logan Pearsall Smith

In mistakenly believing the passive voice sounds "mature" or "academic," student writers sometimes deliberately use it. Wordy, overblown sentences suggest that a writer hasn't carefully revised.

> **NO** One very important quality that can be developed during a first job is self-reliance. This strength was gained by me when I was allowed by my supervisor to set up and conduct a survey project on my own.
>
> **YES** Many individuals develop the important quality of self-reliance during their first job. I gained this strength when my supervisor allowed me to set up and conduct my own survey project.
>
> **YES** During their first job, many people develop self-reliance, as I did when my supervisor let me set up and conduct my own survey project.

If you are writing on a computer, you may find it helpful to use the word processing application's "Search" or "Find" feature to locate the words "was, is, be, were, and been" in your document as part of your revision. This little trick can help you find possible uses of passive voice and judge whether they are effective or need revision.

## 11d How else can I revise for conciseness?

Four other techniques can help you achieve CONCISENESS: eliminating unplanned repetition (11d.1); combining sentences (11d.2); shortening CLAUSES (11d.3); and shortening PHRASES and cutting words (11d.4). These techniques involve matters of judgment.

### 11d.1 Eliminating unplanned repetition

Unplanned repetition lacks conciseness because it delivers the same message more than once, usually in slightly different words. Unplanned repetition, or redundancy, implies that the writer lacks focus and judgment. The opposite—planned repetition—reflects both focus and judgment, as it creates a powerful rhythmic effect (see section 10e). As you revise, check that every word is necessary for delivering your message.

> **NO** Bringing **the project** to **final completion** three weeks early, the supervisor of **the project** earned our **respectful regard**.
>
> [*Completion* implies *bringing to final*; *project* is used twice in one sentence; and *regard* implies *respect*.]

YES    Completing the project three weeks early, the supervisor earned our respect. [Eighteen words reduced to eleven by cutting all redundancies.]

NO    **Astonished,** the architect **circled around** the building **in amazement.** [*Circled* means "went around," and *astonished* and *in amazement* have the same meaning.]

YES    **Astonished,** the architect **circled** the building. [Nine words reduced to six.]

YES    The architect **circled** the building **in amazement.** [Nine words reduced to seven.]

🌐 **ESOL Tip:** In all languages, words often carry an unspoken message, and native speakers understand the implied meanings of those words. In English, some implied meanings can cause redundancy in writing. For example, *I wrote my blog by computer* is redundant. In American English, *to write a blog* implies *by computer.* As you become more familiar with American English, you'll begin to notice such redundancies. ●

## 11d.2    Combining sentences

Look at sets of sentences in your writing to see if you can fit information contained in one sentence into another sentence. (For more about combining sentences, see Chapter 9, particularly sections 9c, 9e, 9j, and 9m.)

TWO SENTENCES    The *Titanic* hit an iceberg and sank. Seventy-three years later, a team of French and American scientists located the ship's resting site.

SENTENCES COMBINED    Seventy-three years after the *Titanic* hit an iceberg and sank, a team of French and American scientists located the ship's resting site.

TWO SENTENCES    Cameras revealed that the stern of the ship was missing and showed external damage to the ship's hull. Otherwise, the *Titanic* was in excellent condition.

SENTENCES COMBINED    Aside from a missing stern and external damage to the ship's hull, the *Titanic* was in excellent condition.

## 11d.3    Shortening clauses

Look at clauses in your writing to see if you can more concisely convey the same information. For example, sometimes you can cut a RELATIVE PRONOUN and its verb.

**TEACHING TIP**

You might find it effective to take a passage of good prose (professional or student writing) and clutter it with wordy language. Distribute copies and ask students to delete all unnecessary words, phrases, and clauses. Discuss their cuts. End by distributing copies of the original for students to compare with their versions. The discussion can become particularly lively if students question the conciseness of the original or champion the value of your padding.

**BACKGROUND**

In *Style: Ten Lessons in Clarity and Grace,* 7th ed. (Boston: Longman, 2002), Joseph M. Williams writes that "the first principle of clear writing" can be stated in two parts:

**1.** In the subjects of your sentences, name your cast of characters.

**2.** In the verbs of your sentences, name the crucial actions in which you involve those characters. (9)

**TEACHING TIP**

Mel Silberman in *Active Learning: 101 Strategies to Teach Any Subject* offers a variety of writing activities (Boston: Allyn and Bacon, 1996). One invites students to write a television commercial "that advertises the subject of the class." You might choose to divide the class into pairs or teams and ask students to write a commercial about their school for a free local cable-access channel. A partial list of selling points could be collaborative exercises, friendly students, and the writing lab. You may want to end the activity with a discussion about the value of pithy writing for modern communication mediums. The premise is that people are being bombarded by so many messages that they need writers to present information as concisely as possible.

| WORDY | The *Titanic,* **which was** a huge ocean liner, sank in 1912. |
| CONCISE | The Titanic, a huge ocean liner, sank in 1912. |

Sometimes you can reduce a clause to a word.

| WORDY | The scientists held a memorial service for the passengers and crew **who had drowned.** |
| CONCISE | The scientists held a memorial service for the **drowned** passengers and crew. |

Sometimes an ELLIPTICAL CONSTRUCTION (sections 14p and 22h) can shorten a clause. If you use this technique, be sure that any omitted word is implied clearly.

| WORDY | **When they were** confronted with disaster, some passengers behaved heroically, **while** others **behaved** selfishly. |
| CONCISE | Confronted with disaster, some passengers behaved heroically, others selfishly. |

## 11d.4   Shortening phrases and cutting words

Sometimes you can reduce a phrase or redundant word pair to a single word. Redundant word pairs and phrases include *each and every, one and only, forever and ever, final and conclusive, perfectly clear, few* (or *many*) *in number, consensus of opinion,* and *reason . . . is because.*

| NO | **Each and every** person was hungry after the movie. |
| YES | **Every** person was hungry after the movie. |
| YES | **Each** person was hungry after the movie. |
| NO | The **consensus of opinion** was that the movie was disappointing. |
| YES | The **consensus** was that the movie was disappointing. |
| YES | **Everyone agreed** that the movie was disappointing. |
| WORDY | More than fifteen hundred **travelers on that voyage** died in the shipwreck. |
| CONCISE | More than fifteen hundred **passengers** died in the shipwreck. |

Sometimes you can rearrange words so that others can be deleted.

| WORDY | Objects **found** inside the ship included **unbroken** bottles of wine and expensive **undamaged** china. |

CONCISE    **Undamaged** objects inside the ship included bottles of wine and expensive china.

# 11e  How do verbs affect conciseness?

ACTION VERBS are strong verbs. *Be* and *have* are weak verbs that often lead to wordy sentences. When you revise weak verbs to strong ones, you can both increase the impact of your writing and reduce the number of words in your sentences. Strong verbs come into play when you revise your writing to reduce PHRASES and to change NOUNS to verbs.

WEAK VERB    The plan before the city council **has to do with** tax rebates.

STRONG VERB    The plan before the city council **proposes** tax rebates.

WEAK VERBS    The board members **were of the opinion** that the changes in the rules **were changes they would not accept.**

STRONG VERBS    The board members **said** that **they would not accept** the changes in the rules.

## REPLACING A PHRASE WITH A VERB

Phrases such as *be aware of, be capable of, be supportive of* can often be replaced with one-word verbs.

I **envy** [not *am envious of*] your mathematical ability.

I **appreciate** [not *am appreciative of*] your modesty.

Your skill **illustrates** [not *is illustrative of*] how hard you studied.

## REVISING NOUNS INTO VERBS

Many nouns are derived from verbs. Such nouns usually end with *-ance, -ment,* and *-tion* (*tolerance, enforcement, narration*). When you turn such wordy nouns back into verbs, your writing is more concise.

NO    The **accumulation of** paper lasted thirty years.

YES    The paper **accumulated** for thirty years.

NO    We **arranged for the establishment of** a student advisory committee.

YES    We **established** a student advisory committee.

NO    The building **had the appearance of** having been neglected.

YES    The building **appeared** to have been neglected.

works. Instead, you might try one of two approaches:

**1.** Distribute copies of a first, messy draft and a final version of one of your current projects. Invite students to trace the changes you made as you took out unnecessary words and passages, wavered between synonyms, adjusted verb tenses, and so forth. If you are using an anthology of essays that includes facsimile pages from writers' early drafts, students can also look for changes there. Students are likely to take the process more seriously, however, if they see your work. A page from Keats or Faulkner is not as immediate as one from their own instructor's current project.

**2.** Distribute three or four versions of a piece (each successively more concise) without noting their order of composition. Ask the students to guess which came earlier or later and explain how they know. This activity helps prove that revising for conciseness produces noticeable results.

### BACKGROUND

In *Style: Ten Lessons in Clarity and Grace,* 7th ed. (Boston: Longman, 2002), Joseph M. Williams describes several sources of wordiness that students can look for in their writing. These sources include redundant pairs ("each and every," "hopes and desires"), redundant modifiers ("completely finish," "terrible tragedy"), irrelevant detail, and unnecessary negatives ("not many" instead of "few," "did not remember" instead of "forgot").

### ANSWERS: EXERCISE 11-2, PAGE 250

Answers will vary considerably. Here is one set of possibilities, containing only a selection of conciseness techniques. All answers demonstrate revision by combining sentences (11d.2).

**1.** Each attempt to raise exotic animals like emu, ostrich, and bison for the commercial value of their meat follows a similar pattern that begins when a few people claim that some exotic animal tastes better than beef and is more nutritious. [11c, avoiding expletive constructions; 11d.1, eliminating unplanned repetition; 11d.4, cutting words]

**2.** Ranchers discovered that emus, birds that look like small ostriches, quickly became unprofitable to raise because few consumers found the meat tasty. [11c, avoiding passive voice; 11d.1, eliminating unplanned repetition; 11d.4, cutting words]

3. Although ranchers found an early, strong demand for the meat of ostriches, consumers' interest soon fizzled out. [11c, avoiding expletive constructions and passive voice; 11d.1, eliminating unplanned repetition; 11d.4, cutting words]

4. The American Ostrich Association once had 3,000 members, but today it has only 500. [11c, avoiding expletive constructions; 11d.4, shortening phrases and cutting words]

5. Bison, also known as buffalo, were a longer-lasting craze because ranchers had a strong desire to own the mighty animals; however, demand greatly increased the price of bison, and ranchers found that purchasing young animals became uneconomical. [11c, avoiding expletive constructions and passive voice; 11d.4, cutting words; 11e, replacing weak verb with strong verb]

6. Also, bison are difficult to raise because they need strong fences to hold them in and they cannot find enough food by grazing on poor pasture land or in mountainous terrain. [11d.3, shortening clauses]

7. Ranchers recently discovered the yak, an animal from Central Asia that thrives in rugged mountainous areas and has supported the people of the Himalayan region for centuries. [11c, avoiding passive voice; 11e, choosing strong verbs]

8. Compared with bison or cows, yaks can forage more efficiently, are easier to care for, and resist many diseases better. [11d.1, eliminating unplanned repetition; 11e, choosing strong verbs, replacing nouns with verbs and phrases with verbs]

9. Chefs in gourmet restaurants have begun to devise fancy recipes for yak meat and to feature the low-fat, mild-tasting, succulent meat on their menus. [11d.1, eliminating unplanned repetition; 11d.4, cutting words]

10. Even though yaks are easy to raise and environmentally friendly, ranchers must overcome consumers' lack of familiarity with

**EXERCISE 11-2** Working individually or with a group, combine each set of sentences to eliminate wordy constructions. For help, consult sections 11c through 11e.

**EXAMPLE** In recent years, ranchers have tried to raise and market many exotic meats. These meats have included emu, ostrich, and bison. These attempts have failed.

In recent years, ranchers have failed to raise and market many exotic meats, such as emu, ostrich, and bison.

1. Each new attempt of ranchers to raise exotic animals like emu, ostrich, and bison for the commercial value of their meat follows a pattern. There is a similar pattern to each new attempt. Each new attempt begins when a few people make the claim that some exotic animal tastes better than beef and is more nutritious.

2. Emus were discovered by ranchers. Emus are birds that look like small ostriches. Emus quickly became unprofitable to raise. Only a few consumers found emu meat tasty.

3. It was found by ostrich ranchers that there was an early, strong demand for the meat of ostriches. That strong demand soon fizzled out quite a bit, the ranchers found.

4. There is the American Ostrich Association. The membership of the American Ostrich Association once used to be 3,000. Today, the membership of the American Ostrich Association now has only 500 people belonging to it.

5. Bison, also known as buffalo, were a longer-lasting craze. Ranchers had a strong desire to own the mighty animals; however, the price of bison was increased greatly by the demand. It became uneconomical for ranchers to purchase young animals.

6. Also, bison are difficult to raise. They tend to need strong fences to hold them in. They cannot find enough food to eat. They eat by grazing. The land of some buffalo ranches consists of poor pasture land or is in mountainous terrain.

7. Recently, the yak has been discovered by ranchers. The yak is an animal from Central Asia. It is from rugged mountainous areas. For centuries, the yak has supported the people of the Himalayan region.

8. Yaks have the ability to forage more efficiently compared with bison or cows. Yaks are easier to care for than bison or cows. Yaks possess a better resistance to many diseases.

9. Chefs in a few gourmet restaurants are beginning to serve yak meat. They are devising fancy recipes for it. They are featuring it on their menus. The meat is mild-tasting and succulent. The meat is also low in fat.

10. Even though yaks are easy to raise and even are environmentally friendly, there is a problem. The ranchers must overcome that problem before they can raise yaks profitably. That problem is the fact that consumers lack familiarity with yaks. Consumers have a reluctance to try yak meat.

## EXERCISE 11-3

Working individually or with a group, revise this paragraph in two steps. First, underline all words that interfere with conciseness. Second, revise the paragraph to make it more concise. (You'll need to drop words and replace or rearrange others.)

**EXAMPLE**
1. Within a matter of minutes after the completion of a championship game, the winning team's players are enabled to put on caps that have been embroidered with their team's name, the year, as well as the word "champions."
2. Minutes after completing a championship game, the winning team's players receive caps embroidered with their team's name, the year, and the word "champions."

(1) At the present time, caps for sports teams are manufactured in factories located primarily in Asian countries such as China, Korea, and Taiwan. (2) Championship caps are quickly produced and shipped by factories wherever they are needed for both of the two teams playing in a final game or series. (3) The very moment the game ends, a trucking company delivers the caps to the winning team's locker room, and it then immediately and instantly burns the losing team's caps so as to prevent embarrassing anyone. (4) Companies that produce all types of sports apparel know that in most cases there is only a short period of time available for making and earning high profits from merchandise connected to a winning team. (5) Within barely a day or two, they flood the market with all sorts of every kind of t-shirts, jackets, caps, coffee mugs, in addition to banners showing and presenting the winning team's championship information.

For more help with your writing, grammar, and research, go to **www.mycomplab.com**

 mycomplab

and reluctance to try yak meat. [11c, avoiding expletive constructions; 11d.4, shortening phrases]

**ANSWERS: EXERCISE 11-3**
First, students underline wordy material. Second, they revise each sentence. (These answers may vary considerably.)

*Underlined (Note: students will need to rewrite for passive voice as well.)*
(1) At the present time, caps for sports teams are manufactured in factories located primarily in Asian countries such as China, Korea, and Taiwan. (2) Championship caps are quickly produced and shipped by factories wherever they are needed for both of the two teams playing in a final game or series. (3) The very moment the game ends, a trucking company delivers the caps to the winning team's locker room, and it then immediately and instantly burns the losing team's caps so as to prevent embarrassing anyone. (4) Companies that produce all types of sports apparel know that in most cases there is only a short period of time available for making and earning high profits from merchandise connected to a winning team. (5) Within barely a day or two, they flood the market with all sorts of every kind of t-shirts, jackets, caps, coffee mugs, in addition to banners showing and presenting the winning team's championship information.

*Revised*
(1) Manufacturers of caps for sports teams are located primarily in China, Korea, and Taiwan. (2) The factories quickly ship championship caps wherever two teams are playing in a final game. (3) The moment the game ends, a trucking company delivers the caps to the winning team's locker room and then immediately burns the losing team's caps to prevent embarrassing anyone. (4) Sports apparel companies know that they have only a short time to make high profits from merchandise connected to a winning team. (5) Within a day or two, these companies flood the market with t-shirts, jackets, caps, coffee mugs, and banners showing the winning team's championship.

# 12

# The Impact of Words

## 12a   What is American English?

Evolving over centuries into a rich language, **American English** is the variation of English spoken in the United States. It demonstrates that many cultures have created the US "melting pot" society. Food names are good examples: Africans brought the words *okra, gumbo,* and *goober* (peanut); Spanish and Latin American peoples contributed *tortilla, taco, burrito,* and *enchilada;* Greek speakers gave us *pita,* Cantonese speakers *chow,* Japanese speakers *sushi,* and so on.

In all languages, the meanings of some words change with time. For example, W. Nelson Francis points out in *The English Language* (New York: Norton, 1965) that the word *nice* "has been used at one time or another in its 700-year history to mean: *foolish, wanton, strange, lazy, coy, modest, fastidious, refined, precise, subtle, slender, critical, attentive, minutely accurate, dainty, appetizing, agreeable.*"

## 12b   What is edited American English?

**Edited American English**, also known as STANDARD ENGLISH, reflects the standards of the written language expected of a textbook. These standards apply in magazines such as *U.S. News & World Report* and *National Geographic;* in newspapers such as the *Washington Post* and the *Wall Street Journal;* and in most nonfiction books. With edited American English, you can achieve the medium or semiformal language level required in ACADEMIC WRITING.

Edited American English isn't a special or fancy dialect for elite groups. Rather, it's a form of the language used by educated people to standardize communication in the larger world. Edited American English conforms to widely established rules of grammar, sentence structure, punctuation, and spelling—as covered in this handbook.

**Nonstandard English** is legitimately spoken by some groups in our society. With its own grammar and usage customs, it communicates clearly to other speakers of nonstandard English. Yet, one thing is certain: Speakers of nonstandard English often benefit when they can switch, as an academic, business, or public WRITING SITUATION requires, to the medium or semiformal level of language. This means that speakers of nonstandard English never need to reject their preferred or home language. Indeed, it's the right of all individuals to decide what works for them in various situations in their lives, and the ability to "code switch" gives them options.

It's true that advertising language and some trendy writings intended for mass audiences frequently ignore the conventions of edited American English. However, such departures from edited American English are not appropriate in academic writing.

## 12c What is figurative language?

**Figurative language** uses words for more than their literal meanings. Such words aren't merely decorative or pretentious (12g). Figurative language greatly enhances meaning. It makes comparisons and connections that draw on one idea or image to explain another. Quick Reference 12.1 explains the different types of figurative language and describes one type you should avoid, the **mixed metaphor**.

---

### Quick Reference 12.1  ∎ ∎ ∎ ∎ ∎ ∎

#### Types of figurative language

- **Analogy:** Comparing similar traits shared by dissimilar things or ideas. Its length can vary from one sentence (which often takes the form of a simile or metaphor) to a paragraph.

    A **cheetah sprinting across the dry plains** after its prey, the **base runner dashed** for home plate, cleats kicking up dust.

- **Irony:** Using words to suggest the opposite of their usual sense.

    Told that a minor repair on her home would cost $2,000 and take two weeks, she said, **"Oh, how nice!"**

- **Metaphor:** Comparing otherwise dissimilar things. A metaphor doesn't use the word *like* or *as* to make a comparison. (See below about not using mixed metaphors.)

    Rush-hour **traffic** in the city **bled out through major arteries** to the suburbs.

- **Personification:** Assigning a human trait to something not human.

    The **book begged** to be read.

- **Overstatement** (also called *hyperbole*): Exaggerating deliberately for emphasis.

    If this paper is late, the professor will **kill** me.

continued >>

---

**EXTRA EXERCISE A**

After analyzing the sentences that follow, decide if they are in formal, medium, or informal language. Which words are particularly effective in establishing the level of usage in the sentence?

1. Weather forecasting is a pretty good field to be in.

2. My old man watches the TV weather news every morning.

3. It takes a whole lot of work to put a forecast together.

4. The Weather Bureau collects data from reporting stations that, after analysis, are reported to the public as forecasts, weather maps, and storm warnings.

5. The bureau conducts research on a variety of topics, from solar radiation and the ozone layer to snowfall patterns.

6. My father just wants to know if it's going to rain.

7. I can't get into all that stuff either.

8. You gotta admit that the bureau has done plenty of good things.

9. In 1942, Dr. F. W. Reichelderfer was the recipient of a prestigious award for his pioneering work in advancing the practice of meteorology as it is applied to aeronautics.

10. I want to give you guys a shout out for helping me.

11. Do you want me to IM or text you the homework from today's class?

**Answers to Extra Exercise A**

1. Informal: *pretty good, be in*

2. Informal: *old man, TV*

3. Informal: *a whole lot of*

4. Formal: *collects data*

5. Medium: familiar words, but no slang, throughout

6. Medium: *just wants to know, it's, going to*

7. Informal: *get into, all that stuff*

8. Informal: *gotta, plenty, good things*

9. Formal: *recipient, prestigious award, practice of meteorology, applied to aeronautics*

10. Informal: *guys, shout out*

11. Informal: *IM, text*

## BACKGROUND

Victor Villanueva Jr. (Washington State University), a major voice in composition and rhetorical studies, argues for the terms *standardized* and *non-standardized* English (or *Englishes*) in preference to "Standard English" and "Non-Standard English." The traditional terminology, according to Villanueva, connotes a fixed rightness and wrongness (almost as moral absolutes), while the newer phrasing emphasizes both the evolution of linguistic forms and practices and the politics of power in defining cultural norms. Villanueva's memoir, *Bootstraps: From an American Academic of Color*, provides a compelling discussion of his own learning history (Urbana, IL: NCTE, 1993).

## ANSWERS: EXERCISE 12-1

1. metaphor
2. overstatement
3. simile
4. irony
5. metaphor
6. overstatement
7. personification
8. mixed metaphor; *playing with fire* or *getting in over your head* [Answers will vary.]
9. simile
10. analogy

## QUOTATION: ON LANGUAGE

Mastery of language affords remarkable power.
—Frantz Fanon

## WORD DERIVATIONS

*Metaphor* comes from *metapherein* (Greek for "to transfer"), a combination of *pherein* ("to

---

## Quick Reference 12.1   (continued)

- **Simile:** Comparing dissimilar things. A simile uses the word *like* or *as*.

  Langston Hughes observes that a deferred **dream dries up** "**like a raisin in the sun.**"

- **Understatement:** Emphasizing by using deliberate restraint.

  It feels **warm** when the temperature reaches **105 degrees.**

- **Mixed metaphor:** Combining two or more inconsistent images in one sentence or expression. Never use a mixed metaphor.

  **NO**   The violence of the hurricane reminded me of a train ride. [A train ride is not violent, stormy, or destructive.]

  **YES**   The violence of the hurricane reminded me of a train's crashing into a huge tractor trailer.

---

**EXERCISE 12-1**   Working individually or with a group, identify each type of figurative language or figure of speech. Also revise any mixed metaphors. For help, consult section 12c.

1. Good manners are the grease for the wheels of human interaction.
2. Without manners, people would be meaner than junkyard dogs.
3. Being rude is like tracking mud on a freshly mopped floor.
4. If you can't mind your business, at least mind your manners.
5. Good manners are the icing on the cake of human behavior.
6. Being rude should be a criminal offense.
7. Compliments are magicians wielding great power.
8. When you're rude to people, you're playing with fire and getting in over your head.
9. Being polite when you're frustrated is as difficult as driving at night when you're dead tired.
10. He's so tactless that if speech were a weapon, his would be a blunt instrument.

# 12d   How can using exact diction enhance my writing?

**Diction,** the term for choice of words, affects the clarity and impact of any writing you do. Your best chance of delivering your intended message to your readers is to choose words that fit exactly with each piece of writing. To choose words correctly—that is, to have good diction—you need to understand the concepts of *denotation* and *connotation* in words.

## 12d.1   What is denotation in words?

The **denotation** of a word is its exact, literal meaning. It's the meaning you find when you look up the word in a dictionary. A dictionary is your ultimate authority for a word's denotation.

- An **unabridged dictionary** contains the most extensive, complete, and scholarly entries. *Unabridged* means "not shortened." Such dictionaries include all infrequently used words that abridged dictionaries often omit. The most comprehensive, authoritative unabridged dictionary of English is the *Oxford English Dictionary* (OED), which traces each word's history and gives quotations to illustrate changes in meaning and spelling over the life of the word.

- An **abridged dictionary** contains most commonly used words. *Abridged* means "shortened." When an abridged dictionary serves the needs of most college students, the dictionaries are referred to as "college editions." Typical of these is *Merriam-Webster's Collegiate Dictionary* (available online and also in print) and *The New American Webster Handy College Dictionary.*

- A **specialized dictionary** focuses on a single area of language. You can find dictionaries of slang (for example, *Dictionary of Slang and Unconventional English,* ed. Eric Partridge); word origins (for example, *Dictionary of Word and Phrase Origins,* ed. William Morris and Mary Morris); synonyms (for example, *Roget's 21st Century Thesaurus*); usage (for example, *Modern American Usage: A Guide,* ed. Jacques Barzun); idioms (for example, *A Dictionary of American Idioms,* by Adam Makkai); regionalisms (for example, *Dictionary of American Regional English,* ed. Frederic Cassidy); and many others.

**ESOL Tip:** *The Oxford Dictionary of American English* (Cambridge: Oxford UP, 2005) is particularly useful for students who speak English as a second (or third) language.

## 12d.2   What is connotation in words?

**Connotation** refers to ideas implied by a word. Connotations are never completely fixed, for they can vary in differing contexts. Connotations involve associations and emotional overtones that go beyond a word's definition. For example, *home* usually evokes more emotion than its denotation "a dwelling place" or its synonym *house. Home* carries the connotation, for some, of the pleasures of warmth, security, and love of family. For others, however, *home* may carry unpleasant connotations, such as abusive experiences or the impersonal atmosphere of an institution to house the elderly.

carry") and *meta* ("over"). A metaphor carries the meaning from one thing over to another.

*Simile* comes from *similis* (Latin for "like"). Similes always contain *like* or *as,* making the comparison explicit. The term *simile* was first used in 1393 in *Piers Plowman,* William Langland's allegorical poem.

**TEACHING TIP**

Your students may find it interesting to discover how expressions originating in highly particular contexts have made their way into popular English usage, sometimes with fresh results, sometimes to become clichéd. Sports, for example, have given us some of these expressions: "get the ball rolling" (soccer); "right off the bat" and "off base" (baseball); "let's huddle" (football); and "a low blow" and "on the ropes" (boxing). In looking more closely at metaphor, students may discover that an expression common in oral parlance may not be so clear in writing: does one write "*toe* the line" or "*tow* the line"? A useful pre-revision activity is to have students identify such metaphors in each other's writing and decide whether the figurative language in each case enhances or dulls a sentence.

**BACKGROUND**

H. L. Mencken's classic, *The American Language: An Inquiry into the Development of English in the United States,* 2nd edition (1921), is available on-line through Bartleby at <http://www.bartleby.com/185>.

**WORD DERIVATION**

The etymology of *Rhode Island* is a mystery. There are two theories. According to one, Italian explorer Giovanni da Verrazano saw a resemblance between the island on which the city of Newport is now located and the Greek island of Rhodes. According to the second, Dutch explorers named the area *Roode Eylandt* ("red island") because of its red clay soil.

**TEACHING TIP**

Many students have little familiarity with reading a dictionary. A short exercise in how to read the etymology, pronunciation, and definitions of words might prove useful. If you have time, you might also compare two or three different dictionaries to demonstrate differences between them.

## WORD DERIVATION

*Nevada* is a shortening of the Spanish *Sierra Nevada* ("snowy range"), a mountain range in eastern California.

## EXTRA EXERCISE B

Ask students to look up the definitions of the following words. Then, ask them to discuss differences in the connotations of the following pairs of words.

1. passive, shy
2. giggle, snicker
3. buddy, cohort
4. brave, foolhardy
5. wise, intelligent

## ANSWERS: EXERCISE 12-2

The response to this exercise is likely to elicit much debate, given that shades of connotative meaning are often fairly personal. The following are some possible answers.

1. *Positive:* harmony, melody; *Neutral:* sound, music, pitch, voice; *Negative:* racket, shriek, noise

2. *Positive:* articulate, eloquent, fluent; *Neutral:* vocal, talkative, verbose; *Negative:* chattering, gossipy, gabby

3. *Positive:* beautiful, dazzling, elegant, sparkling; *Neutral:* decorative, modern, ornate; *Negative:* overelaborate, flashy

4. *Positive:* enduring, unbreakable; *Neutral:* long, continued, stretched; *Negative:* lingering, drawn-out, never-ending, incessant

5. *Positive:* ingenious, keen, sensible; *Neutral:* shrewd, crafty, smooth; *Negative:* calculating, sly, underhanded

## USING A THESAURUS

Sometimes a good college dictionary explains the small differences among synonyms, but a thesaurus is devoted entirely to providing synonyms for words. In distinguishing among **synonyms**—the other words close in meaning to a word—a thesaurus demonstrates connotation in operation. As you use a thesaurus, remain very alert to the subtle shades of meaning that create distinctions among words. For instance, using *notorious* to describe a person famous for praiseworthy achievements in public life is wrong. Although *notorious* means "well-known" and "publicly discussed"—which is true of famous people—the connotation of the word is "unfavorably known or talked about." George Washington is famous, not notorious. Jeffrey Dahmer, by contrast, is notorious.

Here's another example, with the word *obdurate,* which means "not easily moved to pity or sympathy." Its synonyms include *inflexible, obstinate, stubborn,* and *hardened.*

> **NO**  Footprints showed in the **obdurate** concrete.
>
> **YES**  The supervisor remained **obdurate** in refusing to accept excuses.
>
> **YES**  My **obdurate** roommates won't let my pet boa constrictor live in the bathtub.

🛈 Alert: Most word-processing programs include a thesaurus. But be cautious in using it. Unless you know the exact meaning of an offered synonym, as well as its part of speech, you may choose a wrong word or introduce a grammatical error into your writing. For example, one word-processing program's thesaurus offers these synonyms for *deep* in the sense of "low (down, inside)": *low, below, beneath,* and *subterranean.* None of these words could replace *deep* in a sentence such as *The crater is too deep* [not *too low, too below, too beneath,* or *too subterranean*] *to be filled with sand or rocks.* ●

**EXERCISE 12-2**   Working individually or with a group, look at each list of words and divide the words among three headings: "Positive" (good connotations); "Negative" (bad connotations); and "Neutral" (no connotations). If you think that a word belongs under more than one heading, you can assign it more than once, but be ready to explain your thinking. For help, consult a good dictionary and 12d.2.

**EXAMPLE**   grand, big, bulky, significant, oversized

> *Positive:* grand, significant; *Negative:* bulky, oversized; *Neutral:* big

1. harmony, sound, racket, shriek, melody, music, noise, pitch, voice

2. talkative, articulate, chattering, eloquent, vocal, verbose, gossipy, fluent, gabby

3. decorative, beautiful, modern, ornate, overelaborate, dazzling, flashy, elegant, sparkling

4. long, lingering, enduring, continued, drawn-out, stretched, never-ending, unbreakable, incessant

5. calculating, shrewd, crafty, ingenious, keen, sensible, sly, smooth, underhanded

## 12e How can using specific words enhance my writing?

**Specific words** identify individual items in a group (*Ford, Honda*). **General words** relate to an overall group (*car*). **Concrete words** identify what can be perceived by the senses, by being seen, heard, tasted, felt, smelled (*padded black leather dashboard*), and convey specific images and details. **Abstract words** denote qualities (*kind*), concepts (*speed*), relationships (*friends*), acts (*cooking*), conditions (*bad weather*), and ideas (*transportation*) and are more general.

Usually, specific and concrete words bring life to general and abstract words. Therefore, whenever you use general and abstract words, try to supply enough specific, concrete details and examples to illustrate them. Here are sentences with general words that come to life when revised with specific words.

GENERAL His car gets good gas mileage.

SPECIFIC His Miser gets about 35 mpg on the highway and 30 mpg in the city.

GENERAL Her car is comfortable and easy to drive.

SPECIFIC When she drives her new Cushia on a five-hour trip, she arrives refreshed and does not need a long nap to recover, as she did when she drove her ten-year-old Upushme.

What separates most good writing from bad is the writer's ability to move back and forth between the general and abstract and the specific and concrete. Consider these sentences that effectively use a combination of general and specific words to compare cars:

GENERAL    CONCRETE    ┌──── SPECIFIC ────┐    ABSTRACT
My car, a midnight-black Corvette LSI convertible, has a powerful

┌──── SPECIFIC ────┐    GENERAL    SPECIFIC    GENERAL
5.7-liter V8 engine with ride controls, the Tour for regular driving and

SPECIFIC    ┌──── CONCRETE ────┐    GENERAL
the Sport for a close-to-the-road feel. In contrast, Harvey's automobile,

## ANSWERS: EXERCISE 12-3

Because of the many possibilities for rewording posed by this exercise, answers are likely to vary widely. Students may enjoy comparing the different choices they have made. The important principle for revision is that the new versions should have a high degree of specificity and concreteness. Here is an example of an acceptable response.

> I hope to get a job as an administrative assistant in the textbook division of a major publishing company. At the interview, the supervisor of my position was easy to relate to and supportive. We seemed to be able to talk to each other easily, and she even laughed at my jokes. The other assistants in the division appeared to be friendly, interesting people. My college courses in writing, Web design, and communications have clearly prepared me to perform the tasks required for the position, such as composing memos, reviewing brochures, and working with authors. I think the job would teach me a great deal about the process of book publishing. The salary is $100 per month less than I had hoped for, but the Human Resources interviewer promised me moderate raises every six months if my work is well liked by my boss. Also, my daily drive to work would take about 20 minutes, which is quite reasonable for me. If my interviewer calls to offer me the job, I will happily accept it without hesitation.

## TEACHING TIP

To underscore the importance of subtle shades of meaning and connotation, you might ask your students how they would react to each of the following statements. Once their egos are involved, students quickly see that not all synonyms are equivalent.

> You are wrong.
> You are incorrect.
> What you say is false.
> You are inaccurate.
> You are imprecise.
> You are evil.
> You are improper.
> You are unethical.

|  CONCRETE | SPECIFIC | ABSTRACT |
| --- | --- | --- |

a bright red Dodge Viper SRT-10 convertible, has a mighty

|  | SPECIFIC |  |
| --- | --- | --- |

8.3-liter V10 engine with 6-speed manual transmission.

**EXERCISE 12-3**    Revise this paragraph by providing specific and concrete words and phrases to explain and enliven the ideas presented here in general and abstract language. You may revise the sentences to accommodate your changes in language. For help, consult 12e.

> I hope to get a job as an administrative assistant in the company. At the interview, the person who would be my supervisor was pleasant. We seemed to get along well. The other assistants in the division appeared to be nice. My college courses clearly have prepared me for the position. I think the job would teach me a great deal more. The salary is a bit less than I had hoped for, but the Human Resources representative promised me raises at regular intervals if my work is good. Also, my trip to work would not take too much time for me. If my interviewer calls to offer me the job, I will accept it.

## 12f    What is gender-neutral language?

**Gender-neutral language**, also referred to as *gender-free* or *nonsexist language,* relies on terms that don't communicate whether the person is male or female (for example, in replacing *policeman* with *police officer* or *doctors' wives* with *doctors' spouses*).

**Sexist language** assigns roles or characteristics to people based on their sex and gender. Most people recognize that sexist language discriminates against both men and women. For example, it inaccurately assumes that every nurse and homemaker is female (and therefore referred to as "she"), and that every physician and stockbroker is male (and therefore referred to as "he"). One common instance of sexist language occurs when the pronoun *he* is used to refer to someone whose sex is unknown or irrelevant. Although tradition holds that *he* is correct in such situations, most people believe that using masculine pronouns to represent all humans excludes women and thereby distorts reality.

Nearly all businesses and professional organizations require gender-neutral language in written communications. Their policies exist not only for reasons of accuracy and fairness but also for sound business practice, as they want to be inclusive of potential clients and customers.

Gender-neutral language rejects demeaning STEREOTYPES or outdated assumptions, such as "women are bad drivers" and "men can't cook." In your writing, never describe women's looks, clothes, or age unless you do the same for men or doing so is important to the context. Never use a title for one spouse and the first name for the other spouse: *Phil Miller* (not *Mr. Miller*) and *his wife, Jeannette,* travel on separate planes; or *Jeannette and Phil Miller* live in Idaho. Quick Reference 12.2 gives you guidelines for using gender-neutral language.

**EXERCISE 12-4**   Working individually or with a group, revise these sentences by changing sexist language to gender-neutral language. For help, consult 12g.

1. Dogs were one of the first animals to be domesticated by mankind.
2. Traditionally, certain breeds of dogs have helped men in their work.
3. On their long shifts, firemen often kept Dalmatians as mascots and companions, whereas policemen preferred highly intelligent and easily trained German shepherds.
4. Another breed, the Newfoundland, accompanied many fishermen on their ocean voyages, and the Newfoundland has been credited with rescuing many a man overboard.
5. Breeds known as hunting dogs have served as the helpers and companions of sportsmen.
6. Maids and cleaning women didn't need dogs, so no breed of dog is associated with women's work.
7. Another group that dogs have not helped is postmen.
8. Everyone who owns a dog should be sure to spend some time exercising his dog and making sure his dog is in good health.
9. No man-made inventions, such as televisions or computers, can take the place of having a dog.
10. Now even though most dogs do not work, they are still man's best friend.

## Quick Reference 12.2

### How to avoid sexist language

• Avoid using only the masculine pronoun to refer to males and females together. The *he or she* and *his or hers* constructions act as singular PRONOUNS, and they therefore call for singular VERBS. Try to avoid using *he or she* constructions, especially more than once in a sentence or in consecutive sentences. A better solution is revising to the plural. You can also revise to omit the gender-specific pronoun.

> **NO**   A **doctor** has little time to read outside **his** specialty.
> **YES**   A **doctor** has little time to read outside **his or her** specialty.
> **NO**   A successful **stockbroker** knows **he** has to work long hours.
> **YES**   Successful **stockbrokers** know **they** have to work long hours.

continued >>

You are unrighteous.
You are bad.
You are willfully misleading.

**ANSWERS: EXERCISE 12-4**
Answers will vary. Here are some possible gender-neutral versions.

1. Dogs were one of the first animals domesticated by humans. (or) Dogs were one of the first animals to be domesticated.
2. Traditionally, certain breeds of dogs have helped people with their work.
3. On their long shifts, firefighters often kept Dalmatians as mascots and companions, whereas police officers preferred highly intelligent and easily trained German shepherds.
4. Another breed, the Newfoundland, often went to sea on fishing expeditions, and the Newfoundland has been credited with saving many drowning people.
5. Breeds known as hunting dogs have served as the helpers and companions of hunters.
6. Domestic workers didn't need dogs, so no breed of dog is associated with housework.
7. Another group that dogs have not helped is mail carriers.
8. People who own dogs should be sure to spend some time exercising their dogs and making sure their dogs are in good health.
9. No inventions, such as televisions or computers, can take the place of having a dog.
10. Now even though most dogs do not work, they are still people's best friends.

**BACKGROUND**
In "A Brief Writing Assignment for Introducing Non-Sexist Pronoun Usage" (*Teaching English in the Two-Year College* 28.1 (2000): 74–77), Christopher G. Hayes describes how he convinces students of "the connection between language and constructions of reality" from their own writing. Hayes follows this assignment with a lively—and sometimes "warmly heated"—discussion.

## TEACHING TIP

A host of new words has been added to the English language in the past few decades. Modern science and technology, in particular, have been responsible for enriching our vocabularies both by creating new terms and by making many old words new by using them in surprising ways. The names of various experiments in space, for example, were drawn from classical mythology. Students can become aware of the evolving history of the language by collecting terms and phrases in current usage that their parents would not have known when they were children or terms that would have carried a different meaning back then. For example, in their lifetime, verbs such as "to xerox," "to google," and nouns such as "AIDS" and "Internet" have been added to dictionaries, demonstrating the evolution of the English language.

## TEACHING TIP

In addition to the techniques given in Quick Reference 12.2, here are a few more tactics for avoiding sexist language.

**1.** When appropriate, use the first person or the second person.

NO   *A person should always keep an eye on his luggage in airports.*

YES   *I should always keep my eye on my luggage in airports.*

YES   *We should always keep an eye on our luggage in airports.*

YES   *Keep an eye on your luggage in airports.*

**2.** Repeat a noun or use a synonym in place of the troublesome pronoun.

NO   *A preoccupied traveler is an easy target for thieves, who can pick his pocket in a second.*

YES   *A preoccupied traveler is an easy target for thieves, who can pick a traveler's pocket in a second.*

YES   *A preoccupied traveler is an easy target for thieves, who can pick a tourist's pocket in a second.*

---

### Quick Reference 12.2  (continued)

NO   **Everyone** hopes that **he or she** will win the scholarship.
YES   **Everyone** hopes to win the scholarship.

• Avoid using *man* when referring to both men and women.

NO   **Man** is a social animal.
YES   **People** are social animals.

NO   The history of **mankind** is predominately violent.
YES   **Human** history is predominately violent.

NO   Dogs are **men's** best friends.
YES   Dogs are **people's** best friends.

• Avoid stereotyping jobs and roles by gender when referring to both men and women.

| NO | YES |
|---|---|
| chairman | chair, chairperson |
| policeman | police officer |
| businessman | businessperson, business executive |
| statesman | statesperson, diplomat |
| teacher . . . she | teachers . . . they |
| principal . . . he | principals . . . they |

• Avoid expressions that seem to exclude one sex.

| NO | YES |
|---|---|
| the common man | the average person |
| man-sized sandwich | huge sandwich |
| old wives' tale | superstition |

• Avoid using demeaning and patronizing labels.

| NO | YES |
|---|---|
| male nurse | nurse |
| gal Friday | assistant |
| coed | student |
| My girl can help. | My secretary can help. (*Or, better still:* Ida Morea can help.) |

---

🛑 **Alert:** Increasingly, you see "they" or "their" used as a singular pronoun, as in "If someone puts in the effort, they should be rewarded." The English language continually changes, and perhaps in a few years this growing usage will become perfectly acceptable because it fills a need: English lacks a gender-neutral singular pronoun. Today, however, it is still nonstandard in almost all academic and professional settings. ●

# 12g What other types of language do I want to avoid?

Language that distorts or tries to manipulate a reader needs to be avoided in ACADEMIC WRITING. These and other types of language to avoid in an academic LEVEL OF FORMALITY are listed, with examples, in Quick Reference 12.3.

## Quick Reference 12.3 ▪▪▪▪▪▪▪

### Language to avoid in academic writing

• Never use **slanted language**, also called *loaded language;* readers feel manipulated by the overly emotional TONE and DICTION.

**NO** Our senator is a deceitful, crooked thug.
**YES** Our senator lies to the public and demands bribes.

**NO** Why do labs employ Frankensteins to maim helpless kittens and puppies?
**YES** Why do labs employ uncaring technicians who harm kittens and puppies?

• Never use **pretentious language**; readers realize you're showing off.

**NO** As I alighted from my vehicle, my clothing became besmirched with filth.
**YES** My coat got muddy as I got out of my car.

**NO** He has a penchant for ostentatiously flaunting recently acquired haberdashery accoutrements.
**YES** He tends to show off his new clothes shamelessly.

• Never use **sarcastic language**; readers realize you're being nasty.

**NO** He was a regular Albert Einstein with my questions. [This is sarcastic if you mean the opposite.]
**YES** He had trouble understanding my questions.

• Never use **colloquial language**; readers sense you're being overly casual and conversational.

**NO** Christina tanked chemistry.
**YES** Christina failed chemistry.

• Never use **euphemisms**, also called *doublespeak;* readers realize you're hiding the truth (more in 12k).

**NO** Our company will **downsize** to meet efficiency standards.
**YES** Our company has to cut jobs to maintain our profits.

**NO** We consider our hostages as **foreign guests** being guarded by **hosts**.
**YES** We consider our hostages as enemies to be guarded closely.

continued >>

**3.** Use *who.*

**NO** A traveler has little to worry about, if he stays alert.
**YES** A traveler who stays alert has little to worry about.

## BACKGROUND

The Web site <http://grammar.ccc.commnet.edu/GRAMMAR/quizzes/nova/nova6.htm> offered by Capital Community College features an interactive quiz on gender-neutral language.

## TEACHING TIP

If you have any doubts about whether encouraging nonsexist language is worth the effort, consider this passage from the introduction to the 2002 "Guidelines for Gender-Fair Use of Language" in NCTE (National Council of Teachers of English) Publications at <http://www.ncte.org/about/over/positions/category/gram/107647.htm>:

Language plays a central role in the way human beings behave and think. The National Council of Teachers of English (NCTE) is concerned about the critical role language plays in promoting fair treatment of women and girls, men and boys. Through careful selection of gender-fair language, NCTE members have the opportunity to influence thought and behavior both directly and indirectly. These guidelines offer suggestions for language use that will open rather than close possibilities and that speakers and writers should consider when engaged in communication activities that include

• writing papers and publications
• preparing handouts and materials
• designing and delivering oral presentations
• speaking with students, parents, and community members
• working with students
• developing curriculum
• selecting texts and media
• exploring language use in classrooms

• serving on local, regional, and national committees

In addition to providing instruction for gender-fair use of language, the guidelines also offer detailed examples.

**TEACHING TIP**
Because language varies from one geographical area to another, students who have lived in several different parts of the country often know expressions that are used in one region but not in another. Other members of a class may find it interesting to hear some of those regionalisms, afterward compiling a list of words and phrases peculiar to their own area.

**TEACHING TIP**
Discussions about slanted language make students more aware of biased writing. A logical follow-up assignment is to ask them to be alert to loaded diction in news articles and television broadcasts. Examples are particularly abundant during an election year. The words and phrases students collect can be the basis of another lesson, this one specific and close to home.

**TEACHING TIP**
You may want to ask students to work in groups to research the origins of a slang expression, a commonly used phrase, or a regional expression of their own choice. The results can take the form of an oral report to the rest of the class.

**WORD DERIVATION**
Florida was named by the explorer Ponce de León. *Florida* is Spanish for "abounding in flowers."

**QUOTATION: ON WRITING**
Why shouldn't we quarrel about a word? What is the good of words if they aren't important enough to quarrel over? Why do we choose one word more than another if there isn't any difference between them?
—G. K. Chesterton

**WORD DERIVATION**
*Kentucky* comes from the Iroquoian words for "level land."

---

**Quick Reference 12.3**     (continued)

• Never use NONSTANDARD ENGLISH (see 12b).
• Never use MIXED METAPHORS (see 12c).
• Never use SEXIST LANGUAGE or STEREOTYPES (see 12f).
• Never use REGIONAL LANGUAGE (see 12h).
• Never use CLICHÉS (see 12i).
• Never use unnecessary JARGON (see 12j).
• Never use BUREAUCRATIC LANGUAGE (see 12l).

## 12h  What is regional language?

**Regional language**, also called *dialectal language,* is specific to certain geographical areas. For example, a *dragonfly* is a *snake feeder* in parts of Delaware, a *darning needle* in parts of Michigan, and a *snake doctor* or an *ear sewer* in parts of the southern United States. Depending on where you live, soft drinks are known as "soda," "pop," or "coke." Using a dialect in writing for the general reading public tends to shut some people out of the communication. Except when dialect is the topic of the writing, ACADEMIC WRITING rarely accommodates dialect well. Avoid it in academic assignments.

## 12i  What are clichés?

A **cliché** is a worn-out expression that has lost its capacity to communicate effectively because of overuse. Many clichés are SIMILES or METAPHORS, once clever but now flat. For example, these are clichés: *dead as a doornail, gentle as a lamb,* and *straight as an arrow.*

If you've heard certain expressions repeatedly, so has your reader. Instead of a cliché, use descriptive language that isn't worn out. If you can't think of a way to rephrase a cliché, drop the words entirely.

Interestingly, however, English is full of frequently used word groups that aren't clichés: for example, *up and down* and *from place to place.* These common word groups aren't considered clichés, so you can use them freely. If you're not sure of how to tell the difference between a cliché and a common word group, remember that a cliché often—but not always—contains an image (*busy as a bee* and *strong as an ox*).

**EXERCISE 12-5**    Working individually or with a group, revise these clichés. Use the idea in each cliché to write a sentence of your own in plain, clear English. For help, consult 12i.

1. The bottom line is that Carl either raises his grade point average or finds himself in hot water.
2. He needs to understand that "When the going gets tough, the tough get going."
3. Carl may not be the most brilliant engineering major who ever came down the pike, but he has plenty of get-up-and-go.
4. When they were handing out persistence, Carl was first in line.
5. The $64,000 question: Will Carl make it safe and sound, or will the college drop him like a hot potato?

# 12j When is jargon unnecessary?

**Jargon** is the specialized vocabulary of a particular group. Jargon uses words that people outside that group might not understand. Specialized language exists in every field: professions, academic disciplines, business, various industries, government departments, hobbies, and so on.

Reserve jargon for a specialist AUDIENCE. As you write, keep your audience in mind as you decide whether a word is jargon in the context of your material. For example, a football fan easily understands a sportswriter's use of words such as *punt* and *safety,* but they are jargon words to people unfamiliar with American-style football. Avoid using jargon unnecessarily. When you must use jargon for a nonspecialist audience, be sure to explain any special meanings.

The example below shows specialized language used appropriately; it's taken from a college textbook. The authors can assume that students know the meaning of *eutrophicates, terrestrial,* and *eutrophic.*

> As the lake eutrophicates, it gradually fills until the entire lake will be converted into a terrestrial community. Eutrophic changes (or eutrophication) are the nutritional enrichment of the water, promoting the growth of aquatic plants.
>
> —Davis and Solomon, *The World of Biology*

# 12k What are euphemisms?

**Euphemisms** attempt to avoid the harsh reality of truth by using more pleasant, "tactful" words. Good manners dictate that euphemisms sometimes be used in social situations: For example, in US culture, *passed away* is, in some situations, thought to be gentler than *died.* Such uses of euphemisms are acceptable.

In other situations, however, euphemisms drain meaning from truthful writing. Unnecessary euphemisms might describe socially unacceptable behavior (for example, *Johnny has a wonderfully vivid imagination* instead of *Johnny lies*). They also might try to hide unpleasant facts (for example, *She is between assignments* instead of *She's lost her job*). Avoid unnecessary euphemisms.

---

**ANSWERS: EXERCISE 12-5**
Answers will vary. One set of possibilities is shown here.

**1.** Carl either raises his grade point average or risks probation.

**2.** Carl's grandfather says that difficult problems inspire strong people to come up with solutions.

**3.** Carl's abundant energy makes up for any lack of intelligence.

**4.** Persistence is one of Carl's most notable traits.

**5.** The central question is, Will Carl pass or fail college?

**BACKGROUND**
In "On Language: Let a Simile Be Your Umbrella," William Safire notes that English speakers have "about a dozen words for types of snow," including "*sleet, slush, hardpack, powder, dusting, blizzard, avalanche, flurry,* and the latest from pompous weatherpersons, *freezing precipitation activity*" (*New York Times,* 11 Feb. 1996, late ed., sec. 6:20). By contrast, the Inupiat (Eskimos of northern Alaska) have more than thirty different words for snow, according to research by one of Safire's colleagues. The research included a letter from a native Inupiat, which reads: "In the Arctic, the specific conditions of snow and ice are critical to hunting and survival; two or three words would hardly cover our needs."

**QUOTATION: ON WRITING**
As commonly used, clichés are like deflated tires—potentially useful but functionally flat.
—Daven M. Kari

**QUOTATION: ON WRITING**
Those of us who enjoy living in synonymy know that an *adage* is not quite as graven in collective wisdom as a *proverb* or a *maxim;* it is not as legalistic as a *dictum* or as scientific as an *axiom* or as sentimental as a *homily* or as corny as a *saw,* nor as formalized as a *motto,* but it is more rooted in tradition than an *observation.*
—William Safire

## BACKGROUND

In English, we say we "didn't sleep a wink." The equivalent phrase in the African language Xhosa translates: "When dawn broke, we were looking through yesterday's eyes."

—Programmed Language Courses,
Johannesburg, South Africa

## TEACHING TIP

Because every professional discipline has its own jargon, your students may find it interesting to investigate the language used by people in a particular field of work. They can do so by interviewing individuals active in that profession, talking to those who teach courses preparing people to enter a field, reading professional literature, or observing someone at work.

## BACKGROUND

The Web site <http://owl.english.purdue.edu/owl/resource/560/01/> offers suggestions and links to specialized fields of writing such as engineering and the social sciences.

## ANSWERS: EXERCISE 12-6

Answers will vary. Following is one set of possible answers.

**1.** Thank you, Mr. and Mrs. Jones, for generously sponsoring the Bowling for Youth activities of the Bay City Boys and Girls Club.

**2.** Only employees who have worked for more than six months should apply for a lateral transfer.

**3.** She died shortly after her husband.

**4.** Making a verb into a noun makes a person appear to be a wordy showoff who's saying nothing meaningful.

**5.** After his operation, he would lean to the left when he stood up and lean to the right when he sat down.

**6.** The boys and girls were driving recklessly in the stolen vehicle.

**7.** Check with your administrator before forwarding an e-mail.

**8.** Breaking up is hard to do.

## 12l   What is bureaucratic language?

**Bureaucratic language** uses words that are stuffy and overblown. Bureaucratic language (or *bureaucratese,* a word created to describe this style) is marked by unnecessary complexity. This kind of language can take on a formality that complicates the message and makes readers feel left out.

> **NO**   In reference to situations delineated above, corporate associates shall determine the existence of extraneous circumstances sufficient to preclude substantive action by management. In the event the evaluation of said circumstances results in an affirmative finding, the associate is directed to enact the policy mandated in section 4.b.7 of the procedures manual, unless said implementation would enact legal pursuits or other actions injurious to the company. Should extraneous circumstances not obtain, the unit supervisor shall be contacted through official communication means in order to pursue a mutually satisfactory conclusion to the occasioning situation.
>
> —from a corporate human resources manual

We would like to give a YES alternative for this example but regret that we can't understand enough of it to do so. If you, gentle reader, can, please contact us at doug.hesse@gmail.com or troykalq@nyc.rr.com.

**EXERCISE 12-6**   Working individually or with a group, revise these examples of pretentious language, jargon, euphemisms, and bureaucratic language. For help, consult 12g and 12j through 12l.

1. Allow me to express my humble gratitude to you two benefactors for your generous pledge of indispensable support on behalf of the activities of our Bay City's youngsters.
2. No lateral transfer applications will be processed before an employee's six-month probation period terminates.
3. She gave up the ghost shortly after her husband kicked the bucket.
4. Creating nouns in positions meant for verbs is to utter ostentatious verbalizations that will lead inexorably to further obfuscations of meaning.
5. After his operation, he would list to port when he stood up and list to starboard when he sat down.
6. The precious youths were joy riding in a temporarily displaced vehicle.
7. The forwarding of all electronic communiqués must be approved by a staff member in the upper echelon.
8. Coming to a parting of the ways is not as easy as pie.

# 13

## Usage Glossary

A usage glossary presents the customary manner of using particular words and phrases. "Customary manner," however, is not as firm in practice as the term implies. Usage standards change. If you think a word's usage might differ from what you read here, consult a dictionary published more recently than the current edition of this handbook.

The meaning of *informal* or *colloquial* in the definition of a word or phrase is that it's found in everyday or conversational speech, but it needs to be avoided in ACADEMIC WRITING. Another term, *nonstandard,* indicates that the word or phrase, although widely understood in speech and dialect writing, isn't suitable in standard spoken or written English.

Terms of grammar and writing in this Usage Glossary are defined in the Terms Glossary, which begins after the last chapter.

**a, an**   Use *a* before words that begin with a consonant (*a dog, a grade, a hole*) or a consonant sound (*a one-day sale, a European*). Use *an* before words or acronyms that begin with a vowel sound or a silent *h* (*an owl; an hour; an MRI,* because the *M* is sounded "em"). American English uses *a,* not *an,* before words starting with a pronounced *h: a* (not *an*) *historical event.*

**accept, except**   The verb *accept* means "agree to; receive." As a preposition, *except* means "leaving out." As a verb, *except* means "exclude; leave out."

> The workers wanted to **accept** [verb] management's offer **except** [preposition] for one detail: They wanted the limit on overtime **excepted** [verb] from the contract.

**advice, advise**   *Advice,* a noun, means "recommendation." *Advise,* a verb, means "recommend; give advice."

> I **advise** [verb] you to follow your car mechanic's **advice** [noun].

**affect, effect**   As a verb, *affect* means "cause a change in; influence." (*Affect* is a noun in psychology.) As a noun, *effect* means "result or conclusion"; as a verb, *effect* means "bring about."

> Loud music **affects** people's hearing for life, so some bands have **effected** changes to lower the volume. Many fans, however, don't care about the harmful **effects** of high decibel levels.

**aggravate, irritate**　*Aggravate* is used colloquially to mean "irritate." In academic writing, use *aggravate* only to mean "intensify; make worse." Use *irritate* to mean "annoy; make impatient."

> The coach was **irritated** by reduced time for practice, which **aggravated** the team's difficulties with concentration.

**ain't**　*Ain't* is a nonstandard contraction. Use *am not, is not,* or *are not* for standard spoken and written English.

**all ready, already**　*All ready* means "completely prepared." *Already* means "before; by this time."

> The team was **all ready** to play, but it had **already** begun to rain.

**all right**　*All right* is always written as two words, never one (never *alright*).

**all together, altogether**　*All together* means "in a group; in unison." *Altogether* means "entirely; thoroughly."

> The twelve jurors told the judge that it was **altogether** absurd for them to stay **all together** in a single hotel room.

**allude, elude**　*Allude* means "refer to indirectly." *Elude* means "escape notice."

> The detectives **alluded** to budget cuts by saying, "Conditions beyond our control allowed the suspect to **elude** us."

**allusion, illusion**　An *allusion* is an indirect reference to something. An *illusion* is a false impression or idea.

> The couple's casual **allusions** to European tourist sites created the **illusion** that they had visited them.

**a lot**　*A lot* is informal for *a great deal* or *a great many.* Avoid using it in academic writing. If you must use it, write it as two words (never *alot*).

**a.m., p.m.**　Use these abbreviations only with numbers, not as substitutes for the words *morning, afternoon,* and *evening.* Some editors consider capital letters wrong for these abbreviations, yet many editors and dictionaries allow both. Whichever you choose, be consistent in each piece of writing.

> We will arrive in the **evening** [not *p.m.*], and we must leave by **8:00 a.m.**

**among, amongst, between**　Use *among* for three or more items. Use *between* for two items. American English prefers *among* to *amongst.*

> My three housemates discussed **among** [not *between* or *amongst*] themselves the choice **between** staying in college and getting full-time jobs.

**amoral, immoral**  *Amoral* means "neither moral (conforming to standards of rightness) nor immoral (the opposite of *moral*)." *Amoral* also means "without any sense of what's moral or immoral." *Immoral* means "morally wrong."

Although many people consider birth control an **amoral** issue, some religions consider using birth control **immoral.**

**amount, number**  Use *amount* for noncountable things (wealth, work, happiness). Use *number* for countable items.

The **amount** of rice to cook depends on the **number** of guests.

**an**  See *a, an.*

**and/or**  This term is appropriate in business and legal writing when either or both of the two items can apply: *We are planning to open additional offices in California **and/or** New York.* In the humanities, writers usually express the alternatives in words: *We are planning to open additional offices in California, New York, or both.*

**anymore**  Use *anymore* with the meaning "now, any longer" only in negations or questions. In positive statements, instead of *anymore*, use an adverb such as *now.*

No one wants to live without air conditioning **anymore.** Summers are so hot **now** [not *anymore*] that more people than ever suffer from heatstroke.

**anyone, any one**  *Anyone* is a singular indefinite pronoun meaning "any person at all." *Any one* (two words), an adjective that modifies a pronoun, means "a member of a group."

**Anyone** could test-drive **any one** of the display vehicles.

**anyplace**  *Anyplace* is informal. Use *any place* or *anywhere* instead.

**anyways, anywheres**  *Anyways* and *anywheres* are nonstandard for *anyway* and *anywhere.*

**apt, likely, liable**  *Apt* and *likely* are used interchangeably. Strictly, *apt* indicates a tendency or inclination. *Likely* indicates a reasonable expectation or greater certainty than *apt* does. *Liable* usually denotes legal responsibility or implies unpleasant consequences but usage today allows it to mean *likely.*

Evander is **apt** to run stop signs, so he is **likely** to get a ticket. That means he's **liable** for any consequences.

**as, as if, as though, like**  Use *as, as if,* or *as though,* but not *like,* when the words coming after include a verb.

This hamburger tastes good, **as** [not *like*] a hamburger should. It tastes **as if** [or *as though*, not *like*] it were barbequed over charcoal, not gas.

Both *as* and *like* can function as prepositions in comparisons. However, use *as* to indicate equivalence between two nouns or pronouns, and use *like* to indicate similarity but not equivalence.

My friend Roger served **as** [not *like*] mediator in a dispute about my neighbor's tree that dripped sap on my driveway **like** [not *as*] a leaky water faucet.

**assure, ensure, insure**  *Assure* means "promise; convince." *Ensure* and *insure* both mean "make certain or secure," but *insure* is reserved for financial or legal matters.

The insurance agent **assured** me that he could **insure** my car, but only I could **ensure** that I would drive safely.

**as to**  *As to* is nonstandard for *about.*

**awful, awfully**  *Awful* is an adjective meaning "inspiring awe" and "creating fear." *Awfully* is an adverb meaning "in a way to inspire awe" and "terrifying." Only colloquially are *awful* and *awfully* used to mean "very" or "extremely."

I was **extremely** [not *awfully*] tired yesterday.

**a while, awhile**  As two words, *a while* (an article and a noun) can function as a subject or object. As one word, *awhile* is an adverb. In a prepositional phrase, the correct form is *for a while, in a while,* or *after a while.*

It took **a while** [article and noun] to drive to the zoo, where we saw the seals bask **awhile** [adverb modifying verb *bask*] in the sun after romping **for a while** [prepositional phrase] in the water.

**backup, back up**  As a noun, *backup* means "a replacement, fill-in, surrogate; a copy of computer files." As an adjective, *backup* means "alternate; alternative." As a verb, *back up* (two words) means "to serve as a substitute or support"; "to accumulate, as from a stoppage"; and "to make a backup copy of a computer disk or hard drive."

I'll need a **backup** [noun] of your hard drive if I'm going to serve as your **backup** [adjective] computer consultant. I **back up** [verb] all computer disks and drives when I work with them.

**bad, badly**  *Bad* is an adjective only after linking verbs (*look, feel, smell, taste, sound;* these verbs can function as either linking verbs or action verbs depending on the context). *Badly* is an adverb; it's nonstandard after linking verbs.

Farmers feel **bad** [*feel* is a linking verb, so *bad* is the adjective] because a **bad** [adjective] drought is **badly** [adverb] damaging their crops.

**been, being**   *Been* and *being* cannot stand alone as main verbs. They work only with auxiliary verbs.

You **are being** [not *being*] honest to admit that you **have been** [not *been*] tempted to eat the whole pie.

**being as, being that**   *Being as* and *being that* are nonstandard for *because* or *since.*

We had to forfeit the game **because** [not *being as* or *being that*] our goalie was badly injured.

**beside, besides**   As prepositions, *beside* means "next to, by the side of," and *besides* means "other than, in addition to." As an adverb, *besides* means "also, moreover."

She stood **beside** the new car, insisting that she would drive. No one **besides** her had a driver's license. **Besides,** she owned the car.

**better, had better**   *Better* is informal for *had better.*

We **had better** [not *better* alone] be careful of the ice.

**between**   See *among, amongst, between.*

**bias, biased**   As a noun, *bias* means "a mental leaning for or against something or someone." As an adjective, *biased* means "prejudiced." As a verb, *bias* means "create prejudice." The past tense of this verb is *biased.*

Horace's **bias** [noun] against federal-level politicians grew from his disapproval of their **biased** [adjective] attitudes toward certain foreign countries. Eventually, Horace **biased** [verb] his wife's beliefs about politicians as well.

**breath, breathe**   *Breath* is a noun; *breathe* is a verb.

Take a deep **breath** [noun] before you start so that you can **breathe** [verb] normally afterward.

**bring, take**   *Bring* indicates movement from a distant place to a near place. *Take* indicates movement from a near to a distant place.

If you **bring** over sandwiches, we'll have time to **take** [not *bring*] the dog to the vet.

**but, however, yet**   Use *but, however,* or *yet* alone, not in combination with each other.

The economy is strong, **but** [not *but yet* or *but however*] unemployment is high.

**calculate, figure**    These are colloquial terms for *estimate, imagine, expect, think,* and the like.

**can, may**    *Can* signifies ability or capacity. *May* requests or grants permission. In negative expressions, *can* is acceptable for *may.*

When you **can** [not *may*] get here on time, you **may** [not *can*] be excused early. However, if you are *not* on time, you **cannot** [or *may not*] expect privileges.

**can't hardly, can't scarcely**    These double negatives are nonstandard for *can hardly* and *can scarcely.*

**capitol, capital**    *Capitol* means "a building in which legislators meet." *Capital* means a city (Denver, the *capital* of Colorado), wealth, or "most important" (a *capital* offense).

If the governor can find enough **capital**, the state legislature will agree to build a new **capitol** for our state.

**censor, censure**    The verb *censor* means "delete objectionable material; judge." The verb *censure* means "condemn or reprimand officially."

The town council **censured** the mayor for trying to **censor** a report.

**chairman, chairperson, chair**    Many writers and speakers prefer the gender-neutral terms *chairperson* and *chair* to *chairman.* In general, *chair* is used more than *chairperson.*

**choose, chose**    *Choose* is the simple form of the verb. *Chose* is the past-tense form of the verb.

I **chose** a movie last week, so you **choose** one tonight.

**cite, site**    The verb *cite* means "quote by way of example, authority, or proof." The noun *site* means "a particular place or location."

The private investigator **cited** evidence from the crime **site** and the defendant's Web **site**.

**cloth, clothe**    *Cloth* is a noun meaning "fabric." *Clothe* is a verb meaning "dress with garments or fabric."

"**Clothe** me in red velvet," proclaimed the king, and the royal tailors ran to gather samples of **cloth** to show him.

**complement, compliment**   As a noun, *complement* means "something that goes well with or completes." As a noun, *compliment* means "praise, flattery." As a verb, *complement* means "brings to perfection; goes well with, completes." As a verb, *compliment* means "praise, flatter."

The dean's **compliment** was a perfect **complement** to the thrill of my graduating. My parents felt proud when she **complimented** me publicly, an honor that **complemented** their joy.

**comprise, include**   See *include, comprise.*

**conscience, conscious**   The noun *conscience* means "a sense of right and wrong." The adjective *conscious* means "being aware or awake."

Always be **conscious** of what your **conscience** is telling you.

**consensus of opinion**   This phrase is redundant; use *consensus* only.

The legislature reached **consensus** on the issue of campaign reform.

**continual(ly), continuous(ly)**   *Continual* means "occurring repeatedly." *Continuous* means "going on without interruption."

Larry needed intravenous fluids **continuously** for days, so the nurses **continually** monitored him.

**could care less**   *Could care less* is nonstandard for *could not care less.*

**could of**   *Could of* is nonstandard for *could have.*

**couple, a couple of**   *Couple* means "two," but it can also be nonstandard for *a few* or *several.*

Rest here for **a few** [not *a couple* or *a couple of*] minutes.

**criteria, criterion**   A *criterion* is "a standard of judgment." *Criteria* is the plural of *criterion.*

A sense of history is an important **criterion** for judging political candidates, but voters must consider other **criteria** as well.

**data**   *Data* is the plural of *datum,* a word rarely used today. Informally, *data* is used as a singular noun that takes a singular verb. In academic or professional writing, *data* is considered plural and takes a plural verb (although this usage is currently viewed as overly formal by some).

The **data** suggest [not *suggests*] some people are addicted to e-mail.

**different from, different than**   In academic and professional writing, use *different from* even though *different than* is common in informal speech.

Please advise us if your research yields data **different from** past results.

**disinterested, uninterested**   The preferred use of *disinterested* means "impartial, unbiased." Colloquially, *disinterested* can mean "not interested, indifferent," but in more formal contexts, *uninterested* is preferred for "not interested, indifferent."

Jurors need to be **disinterested** in hearing evidence, but never **uninterested.**

**don't**   *Don't* is a contraction for *do not,* never for *does not* (its contraction is *doesn't*).

She **doesn't** [not *don't*] like crowds.

**effect**   See *affect, effect.*

**elicit, illicit**   The verb *elicit* means "draw forth or bring out." The adjective *illicit* means "illegal."

The senator's **illicit** conduct **elicited** a mass outcry from her constituents.

**elude**   See *allude, elude.*

**emigrate (from), immigrate (to)**   *Emigrate* means "leave one country to live in another." *Immigrate* means "enter a country to live there."

My great-grandmother **emigrated** from Kiev, Russia, to London, England, in 1890. Then, she **immigrated** to Toronto, Canada, in 1892.

**enclose, inclose; enclosure, inclosure**   In American English, *enclose* and *enclosure* are the preferred spellings.

**ensure**   See *assure, ensure, insure.*

**enthused**   *Enthused* is nonstandard for *enthusiastic.*

Adam was **enthusiastic** [not *enthused*] about the college he chose.

**etc.**   *Etc.* is the abbreviation for the Latin *et cetera,* meaning "and the rest." For writing in the humanities, avoid using *etc.* Acceptable substitutes are *and the like, and so on,* or *and so forth.*

**everyday, every day**   The adjective *everyday* means "daily." *Every day* (two words) is an adjective with a noun.

Being late for work has become an **everyday** [adjective] occurrence for me. **Every day** [subject] brings me closer to being fired. I worry about it **every day** [object].

**everyone, every one**   *Everyone* is a singular, indefinite pronoun. *Every one* (two words) is an adjective and a pronoun, meaning "each member in a group."

**Everyone** enjoyed **every one** of the comedy skits.

**everywheres**   *Everywheres* is nonstandard for *everywhere.*

**except**   See *accept, except.*

**explicit, implicit**   *Explicit* means "directly stated or expressed." *Implicit* means "implied, suggested."

The warning on cigarette packs is **explicit:** "Smoking is dangerous to health." The **implicit** message is "Don't smoke."

**farther, further**   Although many writers reserve *farther* for geographical distances and *further* for all other cases, current usage treats them as interchangeable.

**fewer, less**   Use *fewer* for anything that can be counted (that is, with count nouns): *fewer* dollars, *fewer* fleas, *fewer* haircuts. Use *less* with collective nouns (or other noncount nouns): *less* money, *less* scratching, *less* hair.

**firstly, secondly, thirdly**   The terms *firstly, secondly,* and *thirdly* are from British English. In American English, use *first, second,* and *third.*

**former, latter**   When two items are referred to, *former* signifies the first item and *latter* signifies the second item. Never use *former* and *latter* when referring to more than two items.

Brazil and Ecuador are South American countries. Portuguese is the official language in the **former,** Spanish in the **latter.**

**go, say**   All forms of *go* are nonstandard when used in place of all forms of *say.*

While stepping on my hand, Frank **says** [not goes], "Your hand is in my way."

**gone, went**   *Gone* is the past participle of *go; went* is the past tense of *go.*

They **went** [not gone] to the concert after Ira **had gone** [not had went] home.

**good, well**   *Good* is an adjective. As an adverb, *good* is nonstandard. Instead, use *well.*

**Good** [adjective] maintenance helps cars run **well** [adverb; not good].

**good and**   *Good and* is a nonstandard intensifier. Instead, use more precise words.

They were **exhausted** [not good and tired].

**got, have**   *Got* is nonstandard for *have.*

>What do we **have** [not got] for supper?

**hardly**   Use *hardly* with *can,* never with *can't.*

**have, of**   Use *have,* not *of,* after such verbs as *could, should, would, might,* and *must.*

>You ***should* have** [not should of] called first.

**have got, have to, have got to**   Avoid using *have got* when *have* alone delivers your meaning. Also, avoid using *have to* or *have got to* for *must.*

>I **have** [not have got] several more sources to read. I **must** [not have got to] finish my reading today.

**he/she, s/he, his/her**   When using gender-neutral language, write out *he or she* or *his or her* instead of using and/or constructions. To be more concise, switch to plural pronouns and antecedents. (For more about gender-neutral language, see 12f.)

>**Everyone** bowed ***his or her*** head. [**Everyone** bowed **his** head is considered sexist language if women were present when the heads were bowed.]

>The **people** bowed **their** heads.

**historic, historical**   The adjective *historic* means "important in history" or "highly memorable." The adjective *historical* means "relating to history." Use *a,* not *an,* before these words because they start with the consonant *h.*

**hopefully**   *Hopefully* is an adverb meaning "with hope, in a hopeful manner," so as an adverb, it can modify a verb, an adjective, or another adverb. However, *hopefully* is nonstandard as a sentence modifier meaning "we hope"; therefore, in academic writing, avoid this usage.

>They waited **hopefully** [adverb] for the crippled airplane to land. **We hope** [not Hopefully,] it will land safely.

**humanity, humankind, humans, mankind**   To use gender-neutral language, choose *humanity, humankind,* or *humans* instead of *mankind.*

>Some think that the computer has helped **humanity** more than any other twentieth-century invention.

**i.e.**   This abbreviation refers to the Latin term *id est.* In academic writing, use the English translation "that is."

**if, whether**   At the start of a noun clause that expresses speculation or unknown conditions, you can use either *if* or *whether.* However, in such conditional clauses use only *whether* (or *whether or not*) when alternatives are expressed or implied. In a conditional clause that does not express or imply alternatives, use only *if*.

> **If** [not *whether*] you promise not to step on my feet, I might dance with you. Still, I'm not sure **if** [or *whether*] I want to dance with you. Once I decide, I'll dance with you **whether** [not *if*] I like the music or **whether** [not *if*] the next song is fast or slow.

**illicit**  See *elicit, illicit.*

**illusion**  See *allusion, illusion.*

**immigrate**  See *emigrate, immigrate.*

**immoral**  See *amoral, immoral.*

**imply, infer**  *Imply* means "hint at or suggest." *Infer* means "draw a conclusion." A writer or speaker *implies;* a reader or listener *infers.*

> When the governor **implied** that she wouldn't seek reelection, reporters **inferred** that she was planning to run for vice president.

**include, comprise**  The verb *include* means "contain or regard as part of a whole." The verb *comprise* means "consist of or be composed of."

**incredible, incredulous**  *Incredible* means "extraordinary; not believable." *Incredulous* means "unable or unwilling to believe."

> Listeners were **incredulous** as the freed hostages described the **incredible** hardships they had experienced.

**in lieu of**  *In lieu of* always means "instead of" or "in the place of." It never means "in light of," "in view of," or "because of."

> **In lieu of** a driver's license for identification, you can present a passport or birth certificate instead.

**in regard to, with regard to, as regards, regarding**  Use *about, concerning,* and *for* in place of these wordy phrases. Also, avoid the nonstandard *as regards to.*

> **Concerning** [not *in regard to, with regard to, as regards,* or *regarding*] your question, we can now confirm that your payment was received.

**inside of, outside of**  These phrases are nonstandard when used to mean *inside* or *outside.* When writing about time, never use *inside of* to mean "in less than."

> She waited **outside** [not *outside of*] the apartment house. He changed to clothes that were more informal in **less than** [not *inside of*] ten minutes.

**insure**  See *assure, ensure, insure.*

**irregardless**  *Irregardless* is nonstandard for *regardless.*

**is when, is where**  Never use these constructions when you define something. Instead, use active verbs.

Defensive driving **involves staying** [not *is when you stay*] alert.

**its, it's**  *Its* is a personal pronoun in the possessive case. *It's* is a contraction of *it is.*

The dog buried **its** bone today. **It's** hot today, which makes the dog restless.

**kind, sort**  Combine *kind* and *sort* with *this* or *that* when referring to singular nouns. Combine *kinds* and *sorts* with *these* or *those* when referring to plural nouns. Also, never use *a* or *an* after *kind of* or *sort of.*

To stay cool, drink **these kinds** of fluids [not *this kind*] for **this sort of** day [not *this sort of a*].

**kind of, sort of**  These phrases are colloquial adverbs. In academic writing, use *somewhat.*

The campers were **somewhat** [not *kind of*] dehydrated after the hike.

**later, latter**  *Later* means "after some time; subsequently." *Latter* refers to the second of two items.

The college library stays open **later** than the town library; also, the **latter** is closed on weekends.

**lay, lie**  The verb *lay* (**lay,** *laid, laid, laying*) means "place or put something, usually on something else" and needs a direct object. The verb *lie* (**lie,** *lay, lain, lying*), meaning "recline," doesn't need a direct object. Substituting *lay* for *lie,* or the opposite, is nonstandard. *Layed* is not a word.

**Lay** [not *lie*] down the blanket [direct object], and then place the baby to **lie** [not *lay*] in the shade.

**leave, let**  *Leave* means "depart." *Leave* is nonstandard for *let.* *Let* means "allow, permit."

Could you **let** [not *leave*] me use your car tonight?

**less**  See *fewer, less.*

**lie**  See *lay, lie.*

**like**  See *as, as if, as though, like.*

**likely**   See *apt, likely, liable.*

**lots, lots of, a lot of**   These are colloquial constructions. Instead, use *many, much,* or *a great deal.*

**mankind**   See *humanity, humankind, humans, mankind.*

**may**   See *can, may.*

**maybe, may be**   *Maybe* is an adverb; *may be* (two words) is a verb phrase.

> **Maybe** [adverb] we can win, but our team **may be** [verb phrase] too tired.

**may of, might of**   *May of* and *might of* are nonstandard for *may have* and *might have.*

**media**   *Media* is the plural of *medium,* yet colloquial usage now pairs it with a singular verb (for example, *The **media saturates** us with information about every fire*).

**morale, moral**   *Morale* is a noun meaning "a mental state relating to courage, confidence, or enthusiasm." As a noun, *moral* means an "ethical lesson implied or taught by a story or event." As an adjective, *moral* means "ethical."

> One **moral** [noun] of the story is that many people who suffer from low **morale** [noun] still abide by high **moral** [adjective] standards.

**most**   *Most* is nonstandard for *almost.* Also, *most* is the superlative form of an adjective (*some* words, *more* words, ***most*** words) and of adverbs (***most*** suddenly).

> **Almost** [not Most] all writers agree that Shakespeare penned the **most** [adjective] brilliant plays ever written.

**Ms.**   *Ms.* is a woman's title free of reference to marital status, equivalent to *Mr.* for men. Generally, use *Ms.* unless a woman requests *Miss* or *Mrs.*

**must of**   *Must of* is nonstandard for *must have.*

**nowheres**   *Nowheres* is nonstandard for *nowhere.*

**number**   See *amount, number.*

**of**   Use *have,* not *of,* after modal auxiliary verbs (*could, may, might, must, should, would*). See also *could of; may of; might of; must of; should of; would of.*

**off of**   *Off of* is nonstandard for *off.*

> Don't fall **off** [not off of] the stage.

**OK, O.K., okay**    These three forms are informal. In academic writing, choose words that express more specific meanings. If you must use the term, choose the full word *okay*.

The weather was **suitable** [not *okay*] for a picnic.

**on account of, owing to the fact that**    Use *because* or *because of* in place of these wordy phrases.

**Because of the rain** [not *On account of the rain* or *Owing to the fact that it rained*], the picnic was cancelled.

**oral, verbal**    The adjective *oral* means "spoken or being done by the mouth." The adjective *verbal* means "relating to language" (*verbal* skill) or to words rather than actions, facts, or ideas.

**outside of**    See *inside of, outside of.*

**percent, percentage**    Use *percent* with specific numbers: two *percent*, 95 *percent*. Use *percentage* to refer to portions of a whole in general terms.

Of the eligible US population, **35 percent** votes regularly in national elections. In local elections, **the percentage** [not *the percent*] is much lower.

**pixel, pixelation, pixilated**    *Pixel,* a relatively new word created from "picture/pix" and "element," is the name for a small dot on a video screen. *Pixelation* (with an *e,* as in *pixel*) is a noun meaning "a film technique that makes people appear to move faster than they are." *Pixilated* (with an *i*), a verb unrelated to *pixels,* derives from *pixie,* meaning "a mischievous elf," and now describes someone who is slightly drunk.

**plus**    *Plus* is nonstandard for *and, also, in addition,* and *moreover.*

The band booked three concerts in Hungary, **and** [not *plus*] it will tour Poland for a month. **In addition,** [not *Plus,*] it may perform once in Austria.

**precede, proceed**    *Precede* is a verb that means "go before." *Proceed* is a verb that means "to advance, go on, undertake, carry on."

**Preceded** by elephants and music, the ringmaster **proceeded** into the main tent.

**pretty**    *Pretty* is informal for *rather, quite, somewhat,* or *very.*

The flu epidemic was **quite** [not *pretty*] severe.

**principal, principle**    As a noun, *principal* means "chief person; main or original amount." As an adjective, *principal* means "most important." *Principle* is a noun that means "a basic truth or rule."

During the assembly, the **principal** [noun] said, "A **principal** [adjective] value in our democracy is the **principle** [noun] of free speech."

**proceed**   See *precede, proceed.*

**quotation, quote**   *Quotation* is a noun, and *quote* is a verb. Don't use *quote* as a noun.

One newspaper reporter **quoted** [verb] the US president, and soon the **quotations** [noun—not *quotes*, which is a verb] were widely broadcast.

**raise, rise**   *Raise* is a verb (***raise, raised, raised, raising***) that means "lift" or "construct" and needs a direct object. *Rise* (***rise, rose, risen, rising***) means "go upward" and doesn't need a direct object. Substituting *rise* for *raise,* or the opposite, is nonstandard.

When workers **rise** [not *raise*] early, they **raise** [not *rise* or *rise up*] more new walls in a day.

**real, really**   These words are nonstandard for *very* and *extremely.*

**reason is because**   This phrase is redundant. To be concise and correct, use *reason is that.*

One **reason** we moved **is that** [not *is because*] our factory was relocated.

**reason why**   This phrase is redundant. To be concise and correct, use *reason* or *why.*

I don't know **why** [not *the reason why*] they left home.

**regarding**   See *in regard to, with regard to, as regards, regarding.*

**regardless**   See *irregardless.*

**respectful, respectfully**   As an adjective, *respectful* means "marked by respect, showing regard for, or giving honor to." *Respectfully* is the adverb form of *respectful.* Be careful not to confuse these words with *respective* and *respectively* (see next entry).

The child listened **respectfully** [adverb] to the lecture about **respectful** [adjective] behavior.

**respective, respectively**   *Respective,* a noun, refers to two or more individual persons or things. *Respectively,* an adverb, refers back to two or more individuals or things in the same sequence in which they were originally mentioned.

After the fire drill, Dr. Daniel Eagle and Dr. Jessica Chess returned to their **respective** offices [that is, he returned to his office, and she returned to her office] on the second and third floors, **respectively** [his office is on the second floor, and her office is on the third floor].

**right**    *Right* is sometimes used colloquially for *quite, very, extremely,* or similar intensifiers.

You did **very** [not *right*] well on the quiz.

**rise**    See *raise, rise.*

**scarcely**    Use *scarcely* with *can,* never with *can't.*

**secondly**    See *firstly, secondly, thirdly.*

**seen**    *Seen* is the past participle of the verb *see* (*see, saw, seen, seeing*). *Seen* is nonstandard for *saw,* a verb in the past tense. Always use *seen* with an auxiliary verb.

Last night, I **saw** [not *seen*] the movie that you **had** seen [not *seen*] last week.

**set, sit**    The verb *set* (*set, set, setting*) means "put in place, position, put down" and needs a direct object. The verb *sit* (*sit, sat, sitting*) means "be seated" and doesn't need a direct object. Substituting *set* for *sit,* or the opposite, is nonstandard.

Susan **set** [not *sat*] the sandwiches beside the salad, made Spot **sit** [not *set*] down, and then **sat** [not *set*] on the sofa.

**shall, will, should**    *Shall* was once used with *I* and *we* for future-tense verbs, and *will* was used for all other persons. Today, *shall* is considered highly formal, and *will* is more widely used. Similarly, distinctions were once made between *shall* and *should,* but today *should* is preferred. However, in questions, *should* is used about as often as *shall.*

We **will** [or *shall*] depart on Monday, but he **will** [never *shall*] wait until Thursday to depart. **Should** [or *Shall*] I telephone ahead to reserve a suite at the hotel?

**should of**    *Should of* is nonstandard for *should have.*

**sit**    See *set, sit.*

**site**    See *cite, site.*

**sometime, sometimes, some time**    The adverb *sometime* means "at an unspecified time." The adverb *sometimes* means "now and then." *Some time* (two words) is an adjective with a noun that means "an amount or span of time."

**Sometime** [adverb for "at an unspecified time"] next year, I must take my qualifying exams. I **sometimes** [adverb for "now and then"] worry whether I'll find **some time** [adjective with a noun] to study for them.

**sort of**   See *kind of, sort of.*

**stationary, stationery**   *Stationary* means "not moving; unchanging." *Stationery* refers to paper and related writing products.

Using our firm's **stationery**, I wrote to city officials about a **stationary** light pole that had been knocked over in a car accident.

**such**   *Such* is informal for intensifiers such as *very* and *extremely.* However, *such* is acceptable to mean "of the same or similar kind."

The play got **very** [not *such*] bad reviews. The playwright was embarrassed by **such** strong criticism.

**supposed to, used to**   The final *-d* is essential in both phrases.

We were **suppose*d*** to [not *suppose to*] leave early. I **use*d* to** [not *use to*] wake up before the alarm rang.

**sure**   *Sure* is nonstandard for *surely* or *certainly.*

I was **certainly** [not *sure*] surprised at the results.

**sure and, try and**   Both phrases are nonstandard for *sure to* and *try to.*

Please **try to** [not *try and*] reach my doctor.

**than, then**   *Than* indicates comparison; *then* relates to time.

Please put on your gloves, and **then** your hat. It's colder outside **than** you think.

**that, which**   Use *that* with restrictive (essential) clauses only. You can use *which* with both restrictive and nonrestrictive (nonessential) clauses; however, many people reserve *which* to use only with nonrestrictive clauses.

The house **that** [or *which*] Jack built is on Beanstalk Street, **which** [not *that*] runs past the reservoir.

**that there, them there, this here, these here**   These phrases are nonstandard for *that, them, this, these,* respectively.

**their, there, they're**   *Their* is a possessive pronoun. *There* means "in that place" or is part of an expletive construction. *They're* is a contraction of *they are.*

**They're** going to **their** accounting class in the building over **there** near the library. Do you know that **there** are twelve sections of Accounting 101?

**theirself, theirselves, themself**    These words are nonstandard for *themselves.*

**them**    Use *them* as an object pronoun only. Do not use *them* in place of the adjectives *these* and *those.*

> Let's buy **those** [not them] delicious looking strawberries.

**then**    See *than, then.*

**thirdly**    See *firstly, secondly, thirdly.*

**thusly**    *Thusly* is nonstandard for *thus.*

**till, until**    Both are acceptable, although *until* is preferred for academic writing.

**to, too, two**    *To* is a preposition; it also is part of an infinitive verb. *Too* is an adverb meaning "also; more than enough." *Two* is a number.

> When you go **to** Chicago, visit the Art Institute. Try **to** visit Harry Caray's for dinner, **too.** It won't be **too** expensive because **two** people can share a meal.

**toward, towards**    Although both are acceptable, writers of American English generally prefer *toward.*

**try and, sure and**    See *sure and, try and.*

**type**    *Type* is nonstandard when used to mean *type of.*

> I recommend that you use only that **type of** [not type] glue on plastic.

**unique**    Never combine *unique* with *more, most,* or other qualifiers.

> Solar heating is **unique** [not somewhat unique] in the Northeast. One **unique** [not very unique] heating system in a Vermont house uses hydrogen for fuel.

**uninterested**    See *disinterested, uninterested.*

**used to**    See *supposed to, used to.*

**utilize**    *Utilize* is considered an overblown word for *use* in academic writing.

> The team **used** [not utilized] all its players to win the game.

**verbal, oral**    See *oral, verbal.*

**wait on**    *Wait on* is an informal substitute for *wait for. Wait on* is appropriate only when people give service to others.

> I had to **wait for** [not wait on] half an hour for the hotel desk clerk to **wait on** me.

**way, ways**   When referring to distance, use *way* rather than *ways*.

He is a long **way** [not ways] from home.

**Web site, website**   Usage at the time of this book's publication calls for two words and a capital *W*. Increasingly, the informal *website* is being used.

**well**   See *good, well*.

**where**   *Where* is nonstandard for *that* when *where* is used as a subordinating conjunction.

I read **that** [not where] salt raises blood pressure.

**where . . . at**   This phrase is redundant; use only *where*.

**Where** is your house? [not Where is your house at?]

**whether**   See *if, whether*.

**which**   See *that, which*.

**who, whom**   Use *who* as a subject or a subject complement; use *whom* as an object (see 16g).

**who's, whose**   *Who's* is the contraction of *who is*. *Whose* is a possessive pronoun.

**Who's** willing to drive? **Whose** truck should we take?

**will**   See *shall, will*.

**-wise**   The suffix *-wise* means "in a manner, direction, or position." Never attach *-wise* indiscriminately to create new words. Instead, choose words that already exist; when in doubt, consult a dictionary to see if the *-wise* word you have in mind is acceptable.

**World Wide Web**   Written out, the three words start with a capital *W*. Its abbreviation only in URLs is *www*. When you use only the word *Web,* start it with a capital *W*.

**would of**   *Would of* is nonstandard for *would have*.

**your, you're**   *Your* is a possessive pronoun. *You're* is the contraction of *you are*.

**You're** kind to volunteer **your** time at the senior center.

# 14

# Parts of Speech and Sentence Structures

## QUOTATION: ON WRITING
Grammar is the prism through which all writing is refracted.

—Patricia Robertson

## BACKGROUND
Grammar is one of the oldest fields of study in Western education. Greek and Roman boys were enrolled in grammar schools to study language and literature in preparation for the study of rhetoric in their adolescence. The *praelectio* was the central exercise of these schools. After reading a model of good or bad writing, the teacher dissected it meticulously and systematically, one word and sometimes one syllable at a time. During the *praelectio,* the teacher identified parts of speech, inflections, gender, meter, figures of speech, and other grammatical and stylistic concerns in the model; provided background about the work; discussed its meaning; noted errors and ineffective passages; and praised eloquent passages. As students advanced, they analyzed the works themselves, answering the teacher's questions. In turn, each student's composition was also subject to the same microanalysis.

## QUOTATION: ON WRITING
The grammar is an attempt to make explicit what the speaker of English does intuitively and unconsciously.

—Mark Lester

## BACKGROUND
In a September 20, 2005, entry for his blog, *Caveat: Venter,* adjunct college educator Andrew Purvis (Los Angeles–based) responds to an article entitled "The Future of Higher Ed" (from *Inside Higher Ed: News*) by reiterating a classic Essentialist philosophy: "Let's get back to education for a change. I would like to see a return to teaching, from the ground up, the basics. I want to see one college class in which every student can correctly identify the parts of speech in every sentence on one page of text before I start my first day." Purvis's position is one that continues to be debated by compositionists, a significant number of whom argue that students' skill in manipulating parts of speech in sentence

## PARTS OF SPEECH

# 14a  Why learn the parts of speech?

Knowing the names and definitions of parts of speech gives you a vocabulary for identifying words and understanding how language works to create meaning. No part of speech exists in a vacuum. To identify a word's part of speech correctly, you need to see how the word functions in a sentence. Sometimes the same word functions differently in different sentences, so check the part of speech used in each instance.

> We ate **fish.** [*Fish* is a noun. It names a thing.]
>
> We **fish** on weekends. [*Fish* is a verb. It names an action.]

# 14b  What is a noun?

A **noun** names a person, place, thing, or idea: *student, college, textbook, education.* Quick Reference 14.1 lists different kinds of nouns.

🌐 **ESOL Tips:** Here are some useful tips for working with nouns.

- Nouns often appear with words that tell how much or how many, whose, which one, and similar information. These words include ARTICLES* (*a, an, the*) and other determiners or limiting adjectives; see section 14f and Chapter 51.
- Nouns sometimes serve as ADJECTIVES. For example, in the term *police officer,* the word *police* serves as an adjective to describe *officer.*
- Nouns in many languages other than English are *inflected.* This means they change form, usually with a special ending, to communicate gender (male, female, neuter); number (singular, plural); and case (see 16a through 16k).
- Words with these suffixes (word endings) are usually nouns: *-ness, -ence, -ance, -ty,* and *-ment.* ●

---

*Words printed in SMALL CAPITAL LETTERS are discussed elsewhere in the text and are defined in the Terms Glossary at the back of this book.

## Quick Reference 14.1 ■ ■ ■ ■ ■ ■ ■

### Nouns

| | | |
|---|---|---|
| PROPER | names specific people, places, or things (first letter is always capitalized) | *Dave Matthews, Paris, Toyota* |
| COMMON | names general groups, places, people, or things | *singer, city, automobile* |
| CONCRETE | names things experienced through the senses: sight, hearing, taste, smell, and touch | *landscape, pizza, thunder* |
| ABSTRACT | names things not knowable through the senses | *freedom, shyness* |
| COLLECTIVE | names groups | *family, team* |
| NONCOUNT OR MASS | names "uncountable" things | *water, time* |
| COUNT | names countable items | *lake, minute* |

## 14c  What is a pronoun?

A **pronoun** takes the place of a NOUN. The words or word that a pronoun replaces is called the pronoun's ANTECEDENT. See Quick Reference 14.2 for a list of different kinds of pronouns. For information on how to use pronouns correctly, see Chapters 16 and 17.

**David** is an accountant. [The noun *David* names a person.]

**He** is an accountant. [The pronoun *he* refers to its antecedent, *David*.]

The finance committee needs to consult **him**. [The pronoun *him* refers to its antecedent, *David*.]

## Quick Reference 14.2 ■ ■ ■ ■ ■ ■ ■

### Pronouns

| | | |
|---|---|---|
| PERSONAL *I, you, its, her, they, ours,* and others | refers to people or things | *I saw **her** take a book to **them**.* |
| RELATIVE *who, which, that* | introduces certain NOUN CLAUSES and ADJECTIVE CLAUSES | *The book **that** I lost was valuable.* |

continued >>

construction does not necessarily stem from the ability to name and label these parts of speech.

**QUOTATION: ON WRITING**
Grammarians are not necessarily writers, but writers must always be grammarians, whether they are conscious of what they are doing or not.
—William F. Irmscher

**QUOTATION: ON WRITING**
Like everything metaphysical the harmony between thought and reality is to be found in the grammar of the language.
—Ludwig Wittgenstein

**QUOTATION: ON WRITING**
The Middle Ages envisioned the goddess of grammar, Grammatica, as an old woman. In one later incarnation, she is depicted as severe, with a scalpel and a large pair of pincers. Her right hand, which is by her side, grasps a bird by its neck, its mouth open as if in a gasp or a squawk. All this was emblematic, meant as a memory aid for the budding grammarian. But, Lord, how fitting the choices of emblem were— the living thing being strangled, beak open but silent, muted by the goddess Grammatica. And the scalpel, the pincers, are reminders to the teacher to be vigilant for error, to cut it out with the coldest tool.
—Mike Rose

## QUOTATION: ON WRITING

Just as verbs and actions go together, so do subjects and characters. There are different kinds of characters. Usually—but not always—the most important characters are the agents of actions, the source of action, or the condition that the writer is describing.

—Joseph M. Williams, *Style: Toward Clarity and Grace*

## TEACHING TIP

Ask students to explain the differences in meanings (and to compose a sentence for each meaning) of these verbs that deal with the same subjects.

1. stride, march, glide, strut

2. gobble, nibble, devour, eat

3. giggle, guffaw, chuckle, snicker

## TEACHING TIP

A fun group activity to help students review the parts of speech is to use Mad Libs. You can find free, printable Mad Libs at <http://www.madglibs.com/>.

## ANSWERS: EXERCISE 14-1

1. More and more people$^N$ live into their$^P$ eighties$^N$ and nineties$^N$ because they$^P$ get better health$^N$ benefits$^N$ and they$^P$ take better care$^N$ of themselves.$^P$

2. Many elderly people$^N$ now live busy lives,$^N$ continuing in businesses$^N$ or volunteering at various agencies.$^N$

3. My$^P$ mother,$^N$ Elizabeth,$^N$ for example,$^N$ spends four hours$^N$ each morning$^N$ as a volunteer$^N$ for the Red Cross,$^N$ where she$^P$ takes histories$^N$ from blood donors.$^N$

4. My$^P$ neighbors,$^N$ George$^N$ and Sandra,$^N$ who are eighty-six years old, still own and run a card$^N$ and candy shop.$^N$

5. Age$^N$ has become no obstacle$^N$ for active seniors,$^N$ as evidenced by the activities$^N$ they$^P$ pursue today.$^N$

---

| Quick Reference 14.2 | (continued) | |
|---|---|---|
| **INTERROGATIVE** *which, who, whose,* and others | introduces a question | ***Who** called?* |
| **DEMONSTRATIVE** *this, that, these, those* | points out the antecedent | *Whose books are **these**?* |
| **REFLEXIVE OR INTENSIVE** *myself, themselves,* and other *-self* or *-selves* words | reflects back to the antecedent; intensifies the antecedent | *They claim to support **themselves**. **I myself** doubt it.* |
| **RECIPROCAL** *each other, one another* | refers to individual parts of a plural antecedent | *We respect **each other**.* |
| **INDEFINITE** *all, anyone, each,* and others | refers to nonspecific persons or things | ***Everyone** is welcome here.* |

**EXERCISE 14-1**   Underline and label all nouns (N) and pronouns (P). Refer to 14a through 14c for help.

EXAMPLE   My$^P$ mother$^N$ celebrated her$^P$ eightieth birthday$^N$ this summer$^N$ with her$^P$ family$^N$ and friends$^N$; she$^P$ greatly enjoyed the festivities$^N$.

1. More and more people live into their eighties and nineties because they get better health benefits and they take better care of themselves.

2. Many elderly people now live busy lives, continuing in businesses or volunteering at various agencies.

3. My mother, Elizabeth, for example, spends four hours each morning as a volunteer for the Red Cross, where she takes histories from blood donors.

4. My neighbors, George and Sandra, who are eighty-six years old, still own and run a card and candy shop.

5. Age has become no obstacle for active seniors as evidenced by the activities they pursue today.

## 14d   What is a verb?

**Main verbs** express action, occurrence, or state of being. For information on how to use verbs correctly, see Chapter 15.

I **dance**. [action]

The audience **became** silent. [occurrence]

Your dancing **was** excellent. [state of being]

🛑 **Alert:** If you're not sure whether a word is a verb, try substituting a different TENSE for the word. If the sentence still makes sense, the word is a verb.

**NO**   He is a **changed** man. He is a **will change** man. [*Changed* isn't a verb because the sentence doesn't make sense when *will change* is substituted.]

**YES**   The man **changed** his profession. The man **will change** his profession. [*Changed* is a verb because the sentence makes sense when the verb *will change* is substituted.] ●

**EXERCISE 14-2**   Underline all main verbs. Refer to 14d for help.

**EXAMPLE**   The study of bats <u>produces</u> some surprising information.

1. Most bats developed many years ago from a shrewlike mammal.
2. One thousand different types of bats exist.
3. Bats comprise almost one quarter of all mammal species.
4. The smallest bat in the world measures only one inch long, while the biggest is sixteen inches long.
5. Bats survive in widely varied surroundings, from deserts to cities.

# 14e   What is a verbal?

**Verbals** are verb parts functioning as NOUNS, ADJECTIVES, or ADVERBS. Quick Reference 14.3 lists the three different kinds of verbals.

---

**Quick Reference 14.3**   ■ ■ ■ ■ ■ ■ ■

### Verbals and their functions

| | | |
|---|---|---|
| **INFINITIVE** *to* + verb | 1. noun 2. adjective or adverb | *To eat now is inconvenient.* *Still, we have far to go.* |
| **PAST PARTICIPLE** *-ed* form of REGULAR VERB or equivalent in IRREGULAR VERB | adjective | *Boiled, filtered water is safe.* |
| **PRESENT PARTICIPLE** *-ing* form of verb | 1. noun (called a GERUND) 2. adjective | *Eating in diners on the road is an adventure.* *Running water may not be safe.* |

---

So now I think of the fire; the steady film of yellow light upon the page of my book; the three chrysanthemums in the round glass bowl on the mantelpiece. Yes, it must have been the wintertime, and we had just finished our tea, for I remember that I was smoking a cigarette when I looked up and saw the mark on the wall for the first time. I looked up through the smoke of my cigarette and my eye lodged for a moment upon the burning coals, and that old fancy of the crimson flag flapping from the castle tower came into my mind, and I thought of the cavalcade of red knights riding up the side of the black rock. Rather to my relief the sight of the mark interrupted the fancy, for it is an old fancy, an automatic fancy, made as a child perhaps. The mark was a small round mark, black upon the white wall, about six or seven inches above the mantelpiece.

—Virginia Woolf, "The Mark
on the Wall"

## BACKGROUND

Knowing whether to use the article *a* or *an* before words that start with the consonant *h* can be a vexing problem for writers. In "Jericho, Trumpets, Walls, Etc.," William Safire solves this problem by using the words *history, historian,* and *historic* as examples. He proposes that article discrimination depends on which syllable, the first or the second, is emphasized. For instance, phonetic emphasis of the noun *history* falls on the first syllable, so we write "*a* history." By contrast, in the adjective *historic,* emphasis falls on the second syllable, "turning the initial *h* into a wimp, requiring a consonant to firm it up: *an* historian covering *an* historic event." (This contradicts the more modern view presented in 7f.)

## QUOTATION: ON WRITING

Grammar is more a way of thinking, a style of inquiry, than a way of being right.
—Mina P. Shaughnessy,
*Errors and Expectations*

⊕ **ESOL Tip:** For information about correctly using the verbals called *infinitives* and *gerunds* as objects, see Chapter 54. ●

## 14f What is an adjective?

**Adjectives** modify—that is, they describe or limit—NOUNS, PRONOUNS, and word groups that function as nouns. For information on how to use adjectives correctly, see Chapter 18.

> I saw a **green** tree. [*Green* modifies the noun *tree.*]
>
> It was **leafy.** [*Leafy* modifies the pronoun *it.*]
>
> The flowering trees were **beautiful.** [*Beautiful* modifies the noun phrase *the flowering trees.*]

⊕ **ESOL Tip:** You can identify some kinds of adjectives by looking at their endings. Usually, words with the SUFFIXES *-ful, -ish, -less,* and *-like* are adjectives. ●

**Determiners,** frequently called **limiting adjectives,** tell whether a noun is general (*a* tree) or specific (*the* tree). Determiners also tell which one (*this* tree), how many (*twelve* trees), whose (*our* tree), and similar information.

The determiners *a, an,* and *the* are almost always called **articles.** *The* is a **definite article.** Before a noun, *the* conveys that the noun refers to a specific item (*the* plan). *A* and *an* are **indefinite articles.** They convey that a noun refers to an item in a nonspecific or general way (*a* plan).

❗ **Alert:** Use *a* when the word following it starts with a consonant: *a carrot, a broken egg, a hip.* Also, use *a* when the word following starts with an *h* that is sounded: *a historical event, a home.* Use *an* when the word following starts with a vowel sound: *an honor, an old bag, an egg.* ●

⊕ **ESOL Tip:** For information about using articles with COUNT and NONCOUNT NOUNS, and about articles with PROPER NOUNS and GERUNDS, see Chapter 54. ●

Quick Reference 14.4 lists kinds of determiners. Notice, however, that some words in Quick Reference 14.4 function also as pronouns. To identify a word's part of speech, always check to see how it functions in each particular sentence.

**That** car belongs to Harold. [*That* is a limiting adjective.]

**That** is Harold's car. [*That* is a demonstrative pronoun.]

## Quick Reference 14.4

■ ■ ■ ■ ■ ■ ■

### Determiners (or limiting adjectives)

ARTICLES
*a, an, the*

*The news reporter used a cell phone to report an assignment.*

DEMONSTRATIVE
*this, these, that, those*

*Those students rent that house.*

INDEFINITE
*any, each, few, other, some,* and others

*Few films today have complex plots.*

INTERROGATIVE
*what, which, whose*

*What answer did you give?*

NUMERICAL
*one, first, two, second,* and others

*The fifth question was tricky.*

POSSESSIVE
*my, your, their,* and others

*My violin is older than your cello.*

RELATIVE
*what, which, whose, whatever,* and others

*We do not know which road to take.*

## 14g What is an adverb?

**Adverbs** modify—that is, adverbs describe or limit—VERBS, ADJECTIVES, other adverbs, and CLAUSES. For information on how to use adverbs correctly, see Chapter 18.

> Chefs plan meals **carefully.** [*Carefully* modifies the verb *plan.*]
>
> Vegetables provide **very** important vitamins. [*Very* modifies the adjective *important.*]
>
> Those potato chips are **too** heavily salted. [*Too* modifies the adverb *heavily.*]
>
> **Fortunately,** people are learning that overuse of salt is harmful. [*Fortunately* modifies the rest of the sentence, an independent clause.]

**Descriptive adverbs** show levels of intensity, usually by adding *more* (or *less*) and *most* (or *least*): *more* happily, *least* clearly (18e). Many descriptive adverbs are formed by adding *-ly* to adjectives: *sadly, loudly, normally.* But many adverbs do not end in *-ly: very, always, not, yesterday,* and *well* are a few. Some adjectives look like adverbs but are not: *brotherly, lonely, lovely.*

**Relative adverbs** are words such as *where, why,* and *when.* They are used to introduce ADJECTIVE CLAUSES.

### BACKGROUND

William Safire makes the point that understanding grammar helps us perceive emphasis and meaning. For example, if at a wine tasting someone says, "They taste good," we know that the reference is to the wines, but if we hear "They taste well," we know that someone has made a comment about the tasters.

### TEACHING TIP

To help students become aware of adverbs and how they function, you may want to provide a series of sentences that have blanks to be filled in with appropriate adverbs. Here is an example:

> The cat sat _____ under the kitchen table, _____ watching the mouse scampering _____ly, _____ly, almost _____ly.

### TEACHING TIP

To find out how grammar is best taught and most easily learned (whether as an isolated study, as a final step in the proofreading or sentence revision phase of writing, through sentence exercises or holistic paragraphs, etc.), you may want to check out the latest NCTE position and research in progress on the teaching of grammar at <http://www.ncte.org>. Most studies today support the viewpoint that grammar exercises apart from writing context seldom bring lasting results or transfer to actual writing.

### HUMOROUS NOTE

Misplaced prepositions and prepositional phrases can sometimes turn the serious into the comical, as Richard Lederer demonstrates in sentences he has collected and published in *Anguished English.*

- The patient was referred to a psychiatrist with a severe emotional problem.
- The judge sentenced a killer to die in the electric chair for the second time.
- Two cars were reported stolen by the Groveton police yesterday.
- Please take time to look over the brochure that is enclosed with your family.
- Berra had driven over with his wife, Carmen, from their home in a Mercedes for the softball game.

**TEACHING TIP**
Grammar Girl hosts a series of podcasts on grammar-related topics. You can play the podcasts in class or assign students to listen to them at home. Grammar Girl's podcasts also have a transcript for each episode, found at <http://grammar.quickanddirtytips.com>.

**ANSWERS: EXERCISE 14-3**
Students will provide complete sentences with the following words underlined and labeled:

**1.** Rats are clean<sup>ADJ</sup> animals that easily<sup>ADV</sup> bond to their human<sup>ADJ</sup> companions.

**2.** Two<sup>ADJ</sup> rats are better than one<sup>ADJ</sup> because they are gregarious<sup>ADJ</sup> animals who desperately<sup>ADV</sup> need social<sup>ADJ</sup> interaction.

**3.** As intelligent<sup>ADJ</sup> animals, rats can be quickly<sup>ADV</sup> trained to perform many<sup>ADJ</sup> tricks.

**4.** Humans consistently<sup>ADV</sup> have been keeping rats as household<sup>ADJ</sup> pets for over<sup>ADV</sup> 100<sup>ADJ</sup> years.

**5.** Finally<sup>ADV</sup>, they pose no<sup>ADV</sup> more<sup>ADJ</sup> health risks than other<sup>ADJ</sup> pets.

**TEACHING TIP**
To help students become aware of what conjunctions do, you might want to distribute the following passage by Langston Hughes. Omit all conjunctions and ask students to supply them. When the passage is complete, ask students to discuss the function and the effect of each word they supplied. Then distribute the original, complete passage.

> I was saved from sin *when* I was going on thirteen. *But* not really saved. It happened like this. There was a big revival at my Auntie Reed's church. Every night for weeks there had been much preaching, singing, praying *and* shouting, *and* some very hardened sinners had been brought to Christ, *and* the membership of the church had grown by leaps *and* bounds. Then just *before* the revival ended, they held a special meeting for children, "to bring the young lambs to the fold." My aunt spoke of it for days ahead. That night I was escorted to the front *and* placed on the mourners' bench with the other young sinners, who had not yet been

**Conjunctive adverbs** modify—that is, conjunctive adverbs describe or limit—by creating logical connections to give words meaning. Conjunctive adverbs can appear anywhere in a sentence: at the start, in the middle, or at the end.

> **However,** we consider Isaac Newton an even more important scientist.

> We consider Isaac Newton, **however,** an even more important scientist.

> We consider Isaac Newton an even more important scientist, **however.**

Quick Reference 14.5 lists the kinds of relationships that conjunctive adverbs can show.

**Quick Reference 14.5**

**Conjunctive adverbs and relationships they express**

| Relationship | Words |
|---|---|
| ADDITION | *also, furthermore, moreover, besides* |
| CONTRAST | *however, still, nevertheless, conversely, nonetheless, instead, otherwise* |
| COMPARISON | *similarly, likewise* |
| RESULT OR SUMMARY | *therefore, thus, consequently, accordingly, hence, then* |
| TIME | *next, then, meanwhile, finally, subsequently* |
| EMPHASIS | *indeed, certainly* |

**EXERCISE 14-3** Underline and label all adjectives (ADJ) and adverbs (ADV). For help, consult 14e through 14g.

EXAMPLE  Young<sup>ADJ</sup> families carefully<sup>ADV</sup> looking for a good<sup>ADJ</sup> pet should consider domesticated<sup>ADV</sup> rats.

1. Rats are clean animals that easily bond to their human companions.
2. Two rats are better than one because they are gregarious animals who desperately need social interaction.
3. As intelligent animals, rats can be quickly trained to perform many tricks.
4. Humans consistently have been keeping rats as household pets for over 100 years.
5. Finally, they pose no more health risks than other pets.

# 14h  What is a preposition?

**Prepositions** are words that convey relationships, usually in time or space. Common prepositions include *in, under, by, after, to, on, over,* and *since.* A

PREPOSITIONAL PHRASE consists of a preposition and the words it modifies. For information about prepositions and commas, see 24k.2.

> **In the fall,** we will hear a concert **by our favorite tenor.**

> **After the concert,** he will fly **to San Francisco.**

🌐 **ESOL Tip:** For a list of prepositions and the IDIOMS they create, see Chapter 53. ●

## 14i  What is a conjunction?

A **conjunction** connects words, PHRASES, or CLAUSES. **Coordinating conjunctions** join two or more grammatically equal words, phrases, or clauses. Quick Reference 14.6 lists the coordinating conjunctions and the relationships they express.

> We hike **and** camp every summer. [*And* joins two words.]

> We hike along scenic trails **or** in the wilderness. [*Or* joins two phrases.]

> I love the outdoors, **but** my family does not. [*But* joins two independent clauses.]

| Quick Reference 14.6 | ■ ■ ■ ■ ■ ■ ■ |
|---|---|

### Coordinating conjunctions and relationships they express

| Relationship | Words |
|---|---|
| ADDITION | *and* |
| CONTRAST | *but, yet* |
| RESULT OR EFFECT | *so* |
| REASON OR CAUSE | *for* |
| CHOICE | *or* |
| NEGATIVE CHOICE | *nor* |

**Correlative conjunctions** are two conjunctions that work as a pair: *both . . . and; either . . . or; neither . . . nor; not only . . . but (also); whether . . . or;* and *not . . . so much as.*

> **Both** English **and** Spanish are spoken in many homes in the United States.

> **Not only** students **but also** businesspeople should study a second language.

**Subordinating conjunctions** introduce DEPENDENT CLAUSES. Subordinating conjunctions express relationships making the dependent clause in a sentence grammatically less important than the INDEPENDENT CLAUSE in the sentence. Quick Reference 14.7 lists the most common subordinating conjunctions. For information about how to use them correctly, see 9d through 9m.

brought to Jesus. . . . Then I was left all alone on the mourners' bench. My aunt came *and* knelt at my knees *and* cried, *while* prayers *and* songs swirled all around me in the little church. The whole congregation prayed for me alone, in a mighty wail of moans *and* voices. *And* I kept waiting serenely for Jesus, waiting, waiting—*but* he didn't come. I wanted to see him, *but* nothing happened to me. Nothing! I wanted something to happen to me, *but* nothing happened.

—Langston Hughes, "Salvation"

### BACKGROUND
In his article "Weather Report: Yucky," William Safire defines the word *yuck* as an "onomatopoeic" interjection: He says *yuck* means what it sounds like.

### QUOTATION: ON WRITING
If you want to write, and I hope you do, the sentence is your point of departure. Part of the art of creating a sentence is knowing the substance and elements of which it is composed. We all know, or let us assume, that sentences are made of words. But words come in various guises, whatever they are intended to hide or reveal, and so we must begin with them—seeing just what they think they are, as grammarians have defined them, and bringing them together into the realm of sense.

—Karen Elizabeth Gordon

### QUOTATION: ON WRITING
When it comes to language, nothing is more satisfying than to write a good sentence.

—Barbara Tuchman

### QUOTATION: ON WRITING
I work on each sentence until I'm satisfied with it and go on. I may rewrite one sentence nineteen times, and the next sentence eight times, and the next sentence three times. When I'm lucky, one sentence just once.

—Larry L. King

**QUOTATION: ON WRITING**

Language, like the body, is so comfortable and familiar that we hardly notice its presence or complexity. Yet once examined closely, the accomplishment of any ordinary speaker is rather astonishing. He can produce and understand an indefinite number of new sentences—sentences he has never encountered previously.

—Richard Ohmann

**QUOTATION: ON WRITING**

In a significant way, a predicate is more intensely a word than a subject of a sentence is. . . . A word is an event; it is a happening.

—Walter J. Ong

**QUOTATION: ON WRITING**

A story can be wrecked by a faulty rhythm in a sentence—especially if it occurs toward the end—or a mistake in paragraphing, even punctuation.

—Truman Capote

**QUOTATION: ON WRITING**

When you write, you lay out a line of words. The line of words is a miner's pick, a woodcarver's gouge, a surgeon's probe. You wield it, and it digs a path you follow. Soon you find yourself deep in new territory. Is it a dead end, or have you located the real subject? You will know tomorrow, or this time next year.

—Annie Dillard

**ANSWERS: EXERCISE 14-4**

Instructors can require students to identify the part of speech of any word in this paragraph, in addition to those with number labels.

1. primarily: adverb (14g)
2. boundary: noun (14b)
3. eighteenth: adjective (14f)
4. previously: adverb (14g)
5. scientific: adjective (14f)
6. hired: verb (14d)
7. boundary: adjective (14f)
8. of: preposition (14h)

## Quick Reference 14.7

### Subordinating conjunctions and relationships they express

| Relationship | Words |
|---|---|
| TIME | *after, before, once, since, until, when, whenever, while* |
| REASON OR CAUSE | *as, because, since* |
| RESULT OR EFFECT | *in order that, so, so that, that* |
| CONDITION | *if, even if, provided that, unless* |
| CONTRAST | *although, even though, though, whereas* |
| LOCATION | *where, wherever* |
| CHOICE | *than, whether* |

**Because** it snowed, school was canceled.

Many people were happy **after** they heard the news.

## 14j  What is an interjection?

An **interjection** is a word or expression that conveys surprise or a strong emotion. Alone, an interjection is usually punctuated with an exclamation point (!). As part of a sentence, an interjection is usually set off by one or more commas.

**Hooray!** I won the race.

**Oh,** my friends missed seeing the finish.

**EXERCISE 14-4**  Identify the part of speech of each numbered and underlined word. Choose from noun, pronoun, verb, adjective, adverb, preposition, coordinating conjunction, correlative conjunction, and subordinating conjunction. For help, consult 14b through 14i.

The Mason-Dixon line <u>primarily</u>[1] marks the <u>boundary</u>[2] between Pennsylvania and Maryland. It was surveyed in the <u>eighteenth</u>[3] century by Charles Mason and Jeremiah Dixon, who had <u>previously</u>[4] worked together on a <u>scientific</u>[5] expedition to South Africa.

In 1760, the Calverts of Maryland and the Penns of Pennsylvania <u>hired</u>[6] Mason and Dixon to settle a <u>boundary</u>[7] dispute between their parcels <u>of</u>[8] land.

        9                   10                 11

Mason and Dixon <u>marked</u> their line every <u>five</u> miles using <u>stones</u> shipped from England, which are called crownstones. These markers were decorated with

                                       12

two coats-of-arms and can still be found scattered <u>throughout</u> this part of the country.

         13            14              15

    <u>Even though</u> Mason <u>and</u> Dixon were British, <u>they</u> had very different backgrounds. Mason was the son of a baker and trained in astronomy. Dixon was a

         16

Quaker, and <u>he</u> specialized in surveying.

                                     17        18

    The line they drew in America eventually <u>became</u> a <u>symbolic</u> division

    19                          20                       21

<u>between</u> free states and slave states <u>until</u> the end of the Civil War. <u>Because</u> of

                         22                           23

the line's importance, <u>it</u> has been the focus of <u>both</u> literature <u>and</u> music, such

         24

as the <u>song</u> "Sailing to Philadelphia" by Mark Knopfler.

9. marked: verb (14d)
10. five: adjective (14f)
11. stones: noun (14b)
12. throughout: preposition (14h)
13. Even though: subordinating conjunction (14i)
14. and: coordinating conjunction (14i)
15. they: pronoun (14c)
16. he: pronoun (14c)
17. became: verb (14d)
18. symbolic: adjective (14f)
19. between: preposition (14h)
20. until: preposition (14h)
21. Because: subordinating conjunction (14i)
22. it: pronoun (14c)
23. both . . . and: correlative conjunction (14i)
24. song: noun (14b)

## SENTENCE STRUCTURES

## 14k  How is a sentence defined?

A **sentence** is defined in several ways: On a strictly mechanical level, a sentence starts with a capital letter and finishes with a period, question mark, or exclamation point. Grammatically, a sentence consists of an INDEPENDENT CLAUSE: *Skydiving is dangerous.* You might hear a sentence described as a "complete thought," but that definition is too vague to help much. From the perspective of its purpose, a sentence is defined as listed in Quick Reference 14.8 on page 296.

## 14l  What are a subject and a predicate in a sentence?

The **subject** and **predicate** of a sentence are its two essential parts. Without both, a group of words isn't a sentence. Quick Reference 14.9 shows the sentence pattern with both. Terms used in the Quick Reference are defined after it.

**QUOTATION: ON WRITING**

Incidentally, the word *me* is not always an indirect object; it can also serve as a direct object. Bless *me!* Contact *me* if you have questions.
    —<http://grammar.ccc.commnet.edu/ GRAMMAR/objects.htm>

**QUOTATION: ON WRITING**

English usage is sometimes more than mere taste, judgment, and education—sometimes it's sheer luck, like getting across the street.
    —E. B. White

**QUOTATION: ON WRITING**

People who don't understand linguistic principles generally confuse the terms *grammar* and *usage.* . . . *Grammar* has several meanings. First, it denotes that intuitive knowledge of language human beings gain by about age five. In this sense, *grammar 1* means "a capacity for language," a native ability to create and comprehend English utterances. The term also refers to various formal systems (*grammar 2*) scholars developed to explain our capacity for language. Traditional grammar, for example, represents an accumulation of terms, rules, and methods for analyzing what we do when we use language. *Grammar 2,* the field of study, generates theories about *grammar 1,* an unconscious process or behavior. *Usage,* on the other hand, refers to linguistic etiquette, to socially sanctioned styles of language appropriate to given situations and audiences.

—Erika Lindemann

**BACKGROUND**

According to the helpful Web site <http://www .grammarlady.com>, inquiries are fielded each day by the Grammar Hotline. Here is one question that was received:

> Dear Grammar Lady: If we have the word "elsewhere," as in "We'll have to look elsewhere for the answer," why don't we have words such as "elsewhen" or "elsewhy"?

> Response: If we look in a dictionary that has historical records of words, such as the multivolume *Oxford English Dictionary* (OED), available in most libraries, we find that at one time these were viable parts of the English language. We can't know exactly why "elsewhere" survived when the others did not, but it is a good lesson in language change—a living language changes over time in ways we cannot predict.

> —Mary Newton Bruder, <http://www.grammarlady.com>

**QUOTATION: ON WRITING**

Grammar is a piano I play by ear.

—Joan Didion

**TEACHING TIP**

You might help students expand short, choppy sentences by asking them to add modifiers that describe and tell *where, when,* and *how.* For example: *Sigmund Freud was a doctor. Sigmund Freud was a Viennese doctor who influenced twentieth-century thinking about mental illness.*

**BACKGROUND**

[Dangling modifiers] most frequently occur at the beginning of sentences but can also appear at the end. Example: The experiment was a

---

**Quick Reference 14.8** ■ ■ ■ ■ ■ ■ ■

### Sentences and their purposes

- A **declarative sentence** makes a statement:   *Skydiving is dangerous.*
- An **interrogative sentence** asks a question:   *Is skydiving dangerous?*
- An **imperative sentence** gives a command:   *Be careful when you skydive.*
- An **exclamatory sentence** expresses strong feeling:   *How I love skydiving!*

---

**Quick Reference 14.9** ■ ■ ■ ■ ■ ■ ■

### Sentence pattern I: Subjects and predicates

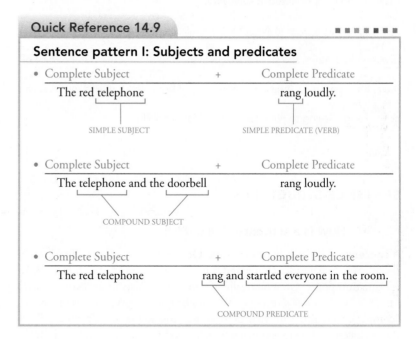

The **simple subject** is the word or group of words that acts, is described, or is acted upon.

The **telephone** rang. [Simple subject, *telephone,* acts.]

The **telephone** is red. [Simple subject, *telephone,* is described.]

The **telephone** was being connected. [Simple subject, *telephone,* is acted upon.]

The **complete subject** is the simple subject and its MODIFIERS.

**The red telephone** rang.

A **complete compound subject** consists of two or more NOUNS or PRONOUNS and their modifiers.

**The telephone and the doorbell** rang.

The **predicate** contains the VERB in the sentence. The predicate tells what the subject is doing or experiencing or what is being done to the subject.

The telephone **rang**. [*Rang* tells what the subject, *telephone*, did.]

The telephone **is** red. [*Is* tells what the subject, *telephone*, experiences.]

The telephone **was being connected**. [*Was being connected* tells what was being done to the subject, *telephone*.]

A **simple predicate** contains only the verb.

The lawyer **listened**.

A **complete predicate** contains the verb and its modifiers.

The lawyer **listened carefully**.

A **compound predicate** contains two or more verbs.

The lawyer **listened and waited**.

🌐 **ESOL Tips:** (1) The subject of a declarative sentence usually comes before the predicate, but there are exceptions (9o). In sentences that ask a question, part of the predicate usually comes before the subject. For more information about word order in English sentences, see Chapter 52. (2) In English, don't add a PERSONAL PRONOUN to repeat the stated noun.

| | |
|---|---|
| **NO** | My **grandfather he** lived to be eighty-seven. [The personal pronoun, *he*, mistakenly repeats the stated noun, *grandfather*.] |
| **YES** | My **grandfather** lived to be eighty-seven. |
| **NO** | **Winter storms** that bring ice, sleet, and snow **they** can cause traffic problems. [The personal pronoun, *they*, mistakenly repeats the stated noun, *winter storms*.] |
| **YES** | **Winter storms** that bring ice, sleet, and snow can cause traffic problems. ● |

failure, having not studied the lab manual carefully. (The experiment—the subject of the main clause—did not study the lab manual.)
—<http://owl.english.purdue.edu>

**TEACHING TIP**
Combining sentences by using modifiers and appositives can not only reduce repetition but also create more graceful statements. Students are sometimes surprised by what they produce when they are asked to combine several choppy sentences into a single effective one.

**A HUMOROUS NOTE**
Dangling participial phrases can produce some unintended meanings, such as these:

- Plunging 1,000 feet into the gorge, we saw Yosemite Falls.
- He rode his horse across Highway 12 and up and down the sidewalk in front of the saloon a good half hour before deputies arrived, shouting obscenities and being obnoxious.
- Locked in a vault for 50 years, the owner of the jewels has decided to sell them.

—Richard Lederer, *Anguished English*

**QUOTATION: ON WRITING**
One thing you want to watch out for with noun phrases is the long compound noun phrase. This is sometimes called the "stacked noun phrase" or "packed noun phrase." It is common to find one noun modifying another: student body, book cover, water commission. But when we create a long string of such attributive nouns or modifiers, we create difficulties: People who author Web pages have become aware of what is now known as the *uniform resource locator protocol problem*.

—<http://grammar.ccc.commnet.edu/grammar/phrases.htm>

**ANSWERS: EXERCISE 14-5**

**1.** Wise consumers / use the Internet to compare prices to discover the best values available.

**2.** Smart clothing shoppers / keep their eyes on the sale racks.

**3.** They / buy summer clothes in the winter and winter clothes in the summer.

**4.** The financial savings / make them content to wait a few months to wear their new clothes.

**5.** Another good way to earn money for clothing / is for people to sell their good used clothing to a resale store.

**TEACHING TIP**

Because students sometimes feel that phrases are peculiar constructions of grammar books, you might find it useful to reproduce and distribute copies of a newspaper article on a popular subject. Ask students to identify any noun phrases, verb phrases, and prepositional phrases. Students will be amazed at how often phrases appear in "real" writing. Class discussion might next cover the functions of the noun phrases and prepositional phrases (subject, object, complement, adjective, adverb).

**BACKGROUND**

At <http://owl.english.purdue.edu/>, the On-line Writing Lab (OWL) of Purdue University provides a wealth of information on grammar. Here is a sampling of facts on gerunds:

**A.** A gerund is a verbal used as a noun. Therefore, it may be used in any place that a noun would fit: subject, object, indirect object, subject complement, or object of the preposition.

**B.** The gerund always ends in *-ing.*

**C.** The gerund may be written as a phrase with its own modifiers, complements, and prepositional phrases.

**D.** The gerund usually does not require any punctuation.

**TEACHING TIP**

To determine whether a clause is independent or dependent, students can make up a yes-or-no question about the clause's statement. An

**EXERCISE 14-5**   Use a slash to separate the complete subject from the complete predicate. For help, consult 14l.

**EXAMPLE**   A smart shopper / is an intelligent, well-informed consumer.

1. Wise consumers use the Internet to compare prices to discover the best values available.
2. Smart clothing shoppers keep their eyes on the sale racks.
3. They buy summer clothes in the winter and winter clothes in the summer.
4. The financial savings make them content to wait a few months to wear their new clothes.
5. Another good way to earn money for clothing is for people to sell their good used clothing to a resale store.

## 14m   What are direct and indirect objects?

A **direct object** is a noun, pronoun, or group of words acting as a noun that receives the action of a TRANSITIVE VERB. To check for a direct object, make up a *whom?* or *what?* question about the verb.

An **indirect object** is a noun, pronoun, or group of words acting as a noun that tells *to whom* or *for whom* the action expressed by a transitive verb

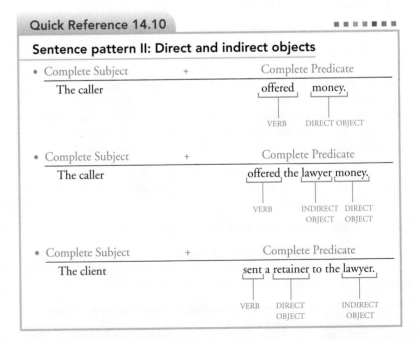

Quick Reference 14.10

**Sentence pattern II: Direct and indirect objects**

- Complete Subject     +     Complete Predicate

  The caller     offered   money.

  VERB    DIRECT OBJECT

- Complete Subject     +     Complete Predicate

  The caller     offered the lawyer money.

  VERB    INDIRECT OBJECT   DIRECT OBJECT

- Complete Subject     +     Complete Predicate

  The client     sent a retainer to the lawyer.

  VERB   DIRECT OBJECT   INDIRECT OBJECT

was done. To check for an indirect object, make up a *to whom? for whom? to what?* or *for what?* question about the verb.

Direct objects and indirect objects always fall in the PREDICATE of a sentence. Quick Reference 14.10 shows how direct and indirect objects function in sentences.

🌐 **ESOL Tips:** (1) In sentences with indirect objects that follow the word *to* or *for*, always put the direct object before the indirect object.

> **NO**    Will you please give **to John** this letter?
>
> **YES**   Will you please give this letter **to John?**

(2) When a PRONOUN is used as an indirect object, some verbs require *to* or *for* before the pronoun, and others do not. Consult the *Dictionary of American English* (Heinle and Heinle) about each verb when you're unsure.

> **NO**    Please explain **me** the rule. [*Explain* requires *to* before an indirect object.]
>
> **YES**   Please explain the rule **to me.**
>
> **YES**   Please give **me** that book. Please give that book **to me.**
>            [*Give* uses both patterns.]

(3) When both the direct object and the indirect object are pronouns, put the direct object first and use *to* with the indirect object.

> **NO**    He gave **me it.**
>
> **YES**   He gave **it to me.**
>
> **YES**   Please give **me the letter.** [*Give* does not require *to* before an indirect object.]

(4) Even if a verb does not require *to* before an indirect object, you may use *to* if you prefer. If you do use *to*, be sure to put the direct object before the indirect object.

> **YES**   Our daughter sent **our son** a gift.
>
> **YES**   Our daughter sent a gift **to our son.** ●

**EXERCISE 14-6**    Draw a single line under all direct objects and a double line under all indirect objects. For help, consult 14m.

**EXAMPLE**    Toni Morrison's award-winning novels give <u>readers</u> the <u>gifts</u> of wisdom, inspiration, and pleasure.

independent clause leads to a sensible question; a dependent clause does not.

> The knave stole the tarts.
>
> Did the knave steal the tarts?
> [a sensible question]
>
> Because he was very hungry.
>
> Because was he very hungry?
> [not a sensible question]

**TEACHING TIP**

To improve students' recognition of adjective and adverb clauses, as well as to increase their powers of concentration, you may want to read aloud the following passage by Katherine Anne Porter. Ask students to note every use of an adverb or adjective clause by listening for key words such as relative pronouns and subordinating conjunctions. After you read the passage, you may want to distribute and discuss it.

> In my grandmother's day, in Texas, everybody seemed to remember that man *who* had a way of showing up with a dozen grains of real coffee in his hand, *which* he exchanged for a month's supply of corn meal. My grandmother parched a mixture of sweet potato and dried corn *until* it was black, ground it up and boiled it, *because* her family couldn't get over its yearning for a dark hot drink in the mornings, but she would never allow them to call it coffee. It was known as That Brew. . . . The woman *who* made That Brew and the soldier *who* ate the bacon rind had been bride and groom in a Kentucky wedding somewhere around 1850. Only a few years ago a cousin of mine showed me a letter from a lady then rising ninety-five *who* remembered that wedding as if it had been only yesterday.
>
> —Katherine Anne Porter,
> "Memories of the Old South"

**ANSWERS: EXERCISE 14-6**

**1.** praise (direct object); Toni Morrison (indirect object); novel (indirect object); interest (direct object)

**2.** Morrison (indirect object); National Book Critics Circle Award (direct object); her (indirect object); Pulitzer Prize (direct object)

**3.** Toni Morrison (indirect object); Nobel Prize in Literature (direct object)

**4.** readers (indirect object); lives (direct object)

**5.** it (direct object); list (indirect object) [Note: "bestseller" acts as a subject complement here.]

**QUOTATION: ON WRITING**

A *dependent clause* is like a dependent child: incapable of standing on its own but able to cause a lot of trouble.
—William Safire

**A HUMOROUS NOTE**

Each year, the number of children coming to the mall to see Santa Claus grew larger, so the store owners decided to hire additional Santas and stationed them around the mall. The most experienced Santa was in charge. He referred to the trainees as his "subordinate Clauses."

**QUOTATION: ON WRITING**

In all speech, words and sense are as the body and the soul.
—Ben Jonson

**BACKGROUND**

At the Web site <http://www.protrainco.com/essays/grammarterms.htm>, students can find published articles on grammar usage, including examples of noun clauses.

**TEACHING TIP**

Imitation can be an effective means of expanding students' sentence-writing strategies. You can provide some samples, asking students to write a sentence on another topic, following the pattern of clauses and phrases in the model. Here are some varied possibilities for imitation, though you may want to choose your own.

1. Literary critics gave high praise to Toni Morrison for her first novel, *The Bluest Eye*, but the general public showed little interest.

2. *Song of Solomon* won Morrison the National Book Critics Circle Award in 1977, and *Beloved* won her the Pulitzer Prize in 1988.

3. A literary panel awarded Toni Morrison the 1993 Nobel Prize in Literature, the highest honor a writer can receive.

4. Her 1998 novel, *Paradise,* traces for readers the tragic lives of a rejected group of former slaves.

5. Twenty-five years after *The Bluest Eye* was published, Oprah Winfrey selected it for her reader's list, and it immediately became a bestseller.

## 14n  What are complements, modifiers, and appositives?

**COMPLEMENTS**

A **complement** renames or describes a subject or an object. It appears in the predicate of a sentence.

A **subject complement** is a NOUN, PRONOUN, or ADJECTIVE that follows a LINKING VERB. **Predicate nominative** is another term for a noun used as a subject complement, and **predicate adjective** is another term for an adjective used as a subject complement.

An **object complement** follows a DIRECT OBJECT and either describes or renames the direct object. Quick Reference 14.11 shows how subject and object complements function in a sentence.

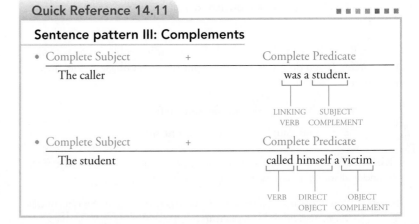

Quick Reference 14.11 ■ ■ ■ ■ ■ ■ ■

**Sentence pattern III: Complements**

- Complete Subject  +  Complete Predicate

  The caller                    was a student.

                                LINKING   SUBJECT
                                VERB      COMPLEMENT

- Complete Subject  +  Complete Predicate

  The student                   called himself a victim.

                                VERB   DIRECT   OBJECT
                                       OBJECT   COMPLEMENT

**EXERCISE 14-7**   Underline all complements and identify each as a subject complement (SUB) or an object complement (OB).

EXAMPLE   Many of the most familiar North American wildflowers are actually

SUB

nonnative <u>plants</u>.

1. The dainty Queen Anne's lace is a native of Europe.

2. The daisies and cornflowers that decorate our roadsides all summer were originally inhabitants of Europe as well.

3. The common purple loosestrife, originally from Asia, came to the North American continent as a garden plant.

4. Many scientists call these plants "alien invasives."

5. Many ecologists consider them threats to the forests, meadows, and wetlands of North America.

## MODIFIERS

A **modifier** is a word or group of words that describes or limits other words. Modifiers appear in the subject or the predicate of a sentence.

> The **large red** telephone rang. [The adjectives *large* and *red* modify the noun *telephone*.]

> The lawyer answered **quickly**. [The adverb *quickly* modifies the verb *answered*.]

> The person **on the telephone** was **extremely** upset. [The prepositional phrase *on the telephone* modifies the noun *person*; the adverb *extremely* modifies the adjective *upset*.]

> **Therefore,** the lawyer spoke **gently**. [The adverb *therefore* modifies the independent clause *the lawyer spoke gently*; the adverb *gently* modifies the verb *spoke*.]

> **Because the lawyer's voice was calm,** the caller felt reassured. [The adverb clause *because the lawyer's voice was calm* modifies the independent clause *the caller felt reassured*.]

## APPOSITIVES

An **appositive** is a word or group of words that renames the noun or pronoun preceding it.

> The student's story, **a tale of broken promises,** was complicated. [The appositive *a tale of broken promises* renames the noun *story*.]

> The lawyer consulted an expert, **her law professor.** [The appositive *her law professor* renames the noun *expert*.]

**A.** The sea, which looks so near and so tempting, is often difficult to reach.
> —Henry Miller, "The Big Sur"

**B.** Hearing the rising tide, I think how it is pressing also against other shores I know—rising on a southern beach where there is no fog, but a moon edging all the waves with silver and touching the wet sands with lambent sheen, and on a still more distant shore sending its streaming currents against the moonlit pinnacles and the dark caves of the coral rock.
> —Rachel Carson, "The Enduring Sea"

**ANSWERS: EXERCISE 14-7**

**1.** native (SUB)

**2.** inhabitants (SUB)

**3.** plant (SUB)

**4.** invasives (OB)

**5.** threats (OB)

**TEACHING TIP**
Elliptical clauses: To enhance students' appreciation of their options, you might ask them whether they prefer the elliptical or full forms of the text's sentences—and why. Here are alternate examples to use.

• Living in Spain was one of the best experiences [that] Carol had during college. When [she was] living with a family in Spain, Carol started to feel like a native.

• James Naismith, [who was] a Presbyterian minister, believed that through athletics he could teach lessons in Christian ideals. After [he had graduated from] divinity school, Naismith enrolled in the School for Christian Workers, [which] later [became] known as the International YMCA Training School. Naismith, [who was] a young man full of ideas, was given the job of devising a game that had less running and tackling than other ball games [had]. Limited indoor space and the hard surface of a wooden floor were two of the biggest problems [that] he faced. The game [that] he devised is known today as basketball.

The student, **Joe Jones,** asked to speak to his lawyer. [The appositive *Joe Jones* renames the noun *student.*]

**❗ Alert:** When an appositive is not essential for identifying what it renames (that is, when it is NONRESTRICTIVE), use a comma or commas to set off the appositive from the rest of the sentence; see 24f. ●

# 14o  What is a phrase?

A **phrase** is a group of words that does not contain both a SUBJECT and a PREDICATE and therefore cannot stand alone as an independent unit.

**NOUN PHRASE**

A **noun phrase** functions as a noun in a sentence.

The **modern census** dates back to the seventeenth century.

**VERB PHRASE**

A **verb phrase** functions as a verb in a sentence.

Two military censuses **are mentioned** in the Bible.

**PREPOSITIONAL PHRASE**

A **prepositional phrase** always starts with a preposition and functions as a modifier.

William the Conqueror conducted a census **of landowners in newly conquered England in 1086.** [three prepositional phrases in a row, beginning with *of, in, in*]

**ABSOLUTE PHRASE**

An **absolute phrase** usually contains a noun or pronoun and a present or past participle. An absolute phrase modifies the entire sentence that it's in.

**Censuses being the fashion,** Quebec and Nova Scotia took sixteen counts between 1665 and 1754.

Eighteenth-century Sweden and Denmark had complete records of their populations, **each adult and child having been counted.**

**VERBAL PHRASE**

A **verbal phrase** contains a verb part that functions not as a verb, but as a noun or an adjective. Such cases are infinitives, present participles, and past participles.

In 1624, Virginia began **to count its citizens** in a census. [*To count its citizens* is an infinitive phrase.]

**Going from door to door,** census takers interview millions of people. [*Going from door to door* is a present participial phrase.]

**Amazed by some people's answers,** census takers always listen carefully. [*Amazed by some people's answers* is a past participial phrase.]

## GERUND PHRASE

A **gerund phrase** functions as a noun. Telling the difference between a gerund phrase and a present participial phrase can be tricky because both use the *-ing* verb form. The key is to determine how the phrase functions in the sentence: A gerund phrase functions only as a noun, and a participial phrase functions only as a modifier.

**Including each person in the census** was important. [This is a gerund phrase because it functions as a noun, which is the subject of the sentence.]

**Including each person in the census,** Abby spent many hours on the crowded city block. [This is a present participial phrase because it functions as a modifier, namely, an adjective describing Abby.]

**EXERCISE 14-8**  Combine each set of sentences into a single sentence by converting one sentence into a phrase—a noun phrase, verb phrase, prepositional phrase, absolute phrase, verbal phrase, or gerund phrase. You can omit, add, or change words. Identify which type of phrase you created.

You can combine most sets in several correct ways, but make sure the meaning of your finished sentence is clear. For help, consult 14o.

**EXAMPLE**  Large chain stores often pose threats to local independent retailers. Smaller store owners must find innovative ways to stay in business.

*With large chains posing threats to local independent retailers,* smaller store owners must find innovative ways to stay in business. (prepositional phrase)

1. Independent stores develop creative marketing strategies to compete with chain stores. Independent stores figure out ways to offer special features.
2. One independent children's bookstore attracted new customers. It did that by bringing live animals into the store.
3. Animals are popular with children. The store purchased two pet chickens, plus tarantulas, rats, cats, and fish.
4. This children's bookstore did not need to lower prices to draw customers. The store could survive by owning animals that appeal to youngsters.

*experience* would seem to reflect what the best writers do.

—Arthur N. Applebee

**ANSWERS: EXERCISE 14-8**
Answers will vary. Here is one set of possible responses.

**1.** Independent stores develop creative marketing strategies *and figure out ways to offer* special features to compete with chain stores. (verb phrase)

**2.** One independent children's bookstore attracted new customers *by bringing live animals into the store.* (prepositional phrases)

**3.** *Animals being popular with children,* the store purchased two pet chickens, plus tarantulas, rats, cats, and fish. (absolute phrase)

**4.** *To draw customers without lowering prices,* this children's bookstore could survive by owning animals that appeal to youngsters. (verbal [infinitive] phrase)

**5.** *In a slightly different approach,* other independent stores compete by offering better service than the large chain stores can. (prepositional phrase)

**6.** *Independent service-oriented and customer-friendly hardware and housewares stores,* for example, sometimes can thrive financially. (noun phrase)

**7.** *To attract and hold customers,* many independent hardware and housewares store owners have begun to offer home-repair and decorating advice as well as to recommend house calls from staff members. (verbal [infinitive] phrase)

**8.** These store owners also *feature in-store displays and advertise heavily* about their high-end items that the chains do not carry. (verb phrase)

**9.** *Stocking fine items such as expensive lawn ornaments, costly brand-name paints, and rare Italian tiles,* independent hardware and housewares stores tend to attract wealthier customers. (verbal [participial] phrase)

5. Other sorts of independent stores sometimes take a slightly different approach. They compete by offering better service than the large chain stores can.

6. For example, independent hardware and housewares stores can be service-oriented and customer friendly. They sometimes can thrive financially doing this.

7. Many independent hardware and housewares store owners have begun to offer home-repair and decorating advice as well as to recommend house calls from staff members. They do this to attract and hold customers.

8. These store owners also feature high-end items that chains do not carry. They feature in-store displays and advertise heavily about their high-end items.

9. Independent hardware and housewares stores often stock fine items such as expensive lawn ornaments, costly brand-name paints, and rare Italian tiles. These stores tend to attract wealthier customers.

## 14p What is a clause?

A **clause** is a group of words with both a SUBJECT and a PREDICATE. Clauses can be either *independent clauses,* also called *main clauses,* or *dependent clauses,* also called *subordinate clauses.*

### INDEPENDENT CLAUSES

An **independent clause** contains a subject and a predicate and can stand alone as a sentence. Quick Reference 14.12 shows the basic pattern.

| Quick Reference 14.12 | | |
|---|---|---|
| **Sentence pattern IV: Independent clauses** | | |
| | Independent Clause | |
| • Complete Subject | + | Complete Predicate |
| The telephone | | rang. |

### DEPENDENT CLAUSES

A **dependent clause** contains a subject and a predicate but can't stand alone as a sentence. To be part of a complete sentence, a dependent clause must be joined to an independent clause. Dependent clauses are either adverb clauses or adjective clauses.

### ADVERB CLAUSES

An **adverb clause**, also called a subordinate clause, starts with a subordinating conjunction, such as although, because, when, or until. A subordinating conjunction expresses a relationship between a dependent clause and an independent clause; see Quick Reference 14.7 in section 14i. Adverb clauses usually answer some question about the independent clause: How? Why? When? Under what circumstances?

> **If the bond issue passes,** the city will install sewers. [The adverb clause modifies the verb phrase *will install;* it explains under what circumstances.]

> They are drawing up plans **as quickly as they can.** [The adverb clause modifies the verb phrase *drawing up;* it explains how.]

> The homeowners feel happier **because they know the flooding will soon be better controlled.** [The adverb clause modifies the entire independent clause; it explains why.]

**Alert:** When you write an adverb clause before an independent clause, separate the clauses with a comma; see 24c. ●

### ADJECTIVE CLAUSES

An **adjective clause**, also called a *relative clause,* starts with a relative pronoun, such as *who, which,* or *that.* Or an adjective clause can start with a relative adverb, such as *when* or *where.* An adjective clause modifies the noun or pronoun that it follows. Quick Reference 14.13 shows how adverb and adjective clauses function in sentences.

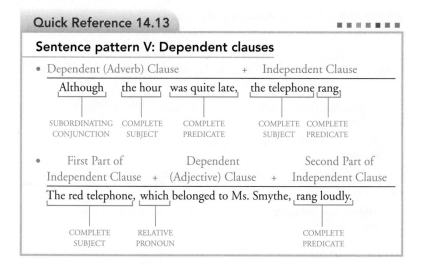

**Quick Reference 14.13**

**Sentence pattern V: Dependent clauses**

- Dependent (Adverb) Clause + Independent Clause

| Although | the hour | was quite late, | the telephone | rang. |
|---|---|---|---|---|
| SUBORDINATING CONJUNCTION | COMPLETE SUBJECT | COMPLETE PREDICATE | COMPLETE SUBJECT | COMPLETE PREDICATE |

- First Part of Independent Clause + Dependent (Adjective) Clause + Second Part of Independent Clause

| The red telephone, | which | belonged to Ms. Smythe, | rang loudly. |
|---|---|---|---|
| COMPLETE SUBJECT | RELATIVE PRONOUN | | COMPLETE PREDICATE |

The car **that Jack bought** is practical. [The adjective clause describes the noun *car; that* is a relative pronoun referring to *car.*]

The day **when I can buy my own car** is getting closer. [The adjective clause modifies the noun *day*; *when* is a relative adverb referring to *day*.]

Use *who, whom, whoever, whomever,* and *whose* when an adjective clause refers to a person or to an animal with a name.

The Smythes, **who collect cars,** are wealthy.

Their dog Bowser, **who is large and loud,** has been spoiled.

Use *which* or *that* when an adjective clause refers to a thing or to an animal that isn't a pet. Sometimes, writers omit *that* from an adjective clause. For grammatical analysis, however, consider the omitted *that* to be implied and, therefore, present.

For help in deciding whether to use *that* or *which,* see Quick Reference 16.4 in section 16s.

⚠ Alert: When an adjective clause is NONRESTRICTIVE, use *which* and set it off from the independent clause with commas. Don't use commas with *that* in a RESTRICTIVE CLAUSE.

My car, **which** I bought used, needs major repairs. [The adjective clause is nonrestrictive, so it begins with *which* and is set off with commas.]

The car **that** I want to buy has a CD player. [The adjective clause uses *that* and is restrictive, so it is not set off with commas.] ●

**ANSWERS: EXERCISE 14-9**

**1.** because it inspired Stephen King's novel *The Shining* (adv)

**2.** Although based on King's book (adv)

**3.** when he was diagnosed with tuberculosis (adv)

**4.** that now bears his name (adj)

**5.** who believe the hotel is haunted (adj)

**EXERCISE 14-9** Underline the dependent clause in each sentence, and label it an adjectival (ADJ) or an adverbial (ADV) clause. For help, consult 14p.

ADV
EXAMPLE The Stanley Hotel, <u>which is located in Estes Park, Colorado,</u> was built in 1909.

1. The Stanley Hotel is famous because it inspired Stephen King's novel *The Shining*.

2. Although based on King's book, the movie *The Shining* was filmed in England.

3. F. O. Stanley moved to Estes Park when he was diagnosed with tuberculosis.

4. He then built the hotel that now bears his name.

5. Visitors who believe the hotel is haunted claim to see Stanley's ghost in the lobby.

### NOUN CLAUSES

**Noun clauses** function as nouns. Noun clauses can begin with many of the same words that begin adjective clauses: *that, who, which,* and their derivatives, as well as *when, where, whether, why,* and *how.*

**Promises** are not always dependable. [noun]

**What politicians promise** is not always dependable. [noun clause]

The electorate often cannot figure out the **truth.** [noun]

The electorate often cannot know **that the truth is being manipulated.**
[noun clause]

Because they start with similar words, noun clauses and adjective clauses are sometimes confused with each other. The way to tell them apart is that the word starting an adjective clause has an ANTECEDENT, while the word starting a noun clause doesn't.

Good politicians understand **whom they must please.** [Noun clause; *whom* does not have an antecedent.]

Good politicians **who make promises** know all cannot be kept. [Adjective clause modifies *politicians,* which is the antecedent of *who.*]

**ESOL Tip:** Noun clauses in INDIRECT QUESTIONS are phrased as statements, not questions: *Kara asked why we needed the purple dye.* Don't phrase a noun clause this way: *Kara asked why **did** [or **do**] we need the purple dye?* If you prefer to change to a DIRECT QUESTION, usually VERB TENSE, PRONOUN, and other changes are necessary; see 22e. ●

## ELLIPTICAL CLAUSES

In an **elliptical clause**, one or more words are deliberately left out for conciseness. For an elliptical clause to be correct, the one or more words you leave out need to be identical to those already appearing in the clause.

Engineering is one of the majors [**that**] **she considered.** [*that,* functioning as a relative pronoun, omitted from adjective clause]

She decided [**that**] **she would rather major in management.** [*that,* functioning as a conjunction, omitted between clauses]

**After [he takes] a refresher course,** he will be eligible for a raise. [subject and verb omitted from adverb clause]

Broiled fish tastes better **than boiled fish [tastes].** [second half of the comparison omitted]

**EXERCISE 14-10** Use subordinate conjunctions and relative pronouns from the list below to combine each pair of sentences. You may use words more than once, but try to use as many different ones as possible. Some sentence pairs may be combined in several ways. Create at least one elliptical construction.

| since | which | if | after | when | as |
|---|---|---|---|---|---|
| although | so that | unless | because | even though | that |

**ANSWERS: EXERCISE 14-10**

Answers my vary, but one set of possibilities follow:

**1.** It seems that certain aspects of jazz have influenced bluegrass *because it involves players of an instrumental ensemble improvising around a standard melody.*

**2.** Yet, the instruments used in jazz are very different than those played in bluegrass, *which usually uses a banjo, fiddle, mandolin, and a dobro.*

**3.** *If people listen closely to the vocal arrangements,* they can hear that singing in bluegrass involves tight harmonies and a tenor lead singer.

**4.** *So that he could produce a fuller sound,* Bill Monroe, the founder of bluegrass, added banjo player Earl Scruggs to his band, the Blue Grass Boys.

**5.** *After going into the studio in 1945 to record some songs for Columbia Records,* the Blue Grass Boys hit the charts with "Kentucky Waltz" and "Footprints in the Snow."

**6.** *As they began touring America with their own large circus tent,* they became one of the most popular acts in country music.

**7.** *When Lester Flatt and Earl Scruggs left Bill Monroe's band,* they formed their own group called the Foggy Mountain Boys.

**8.** A famous Flatt & Scruggs song *that is called "Foggy Mountain Breakdown"* is considered one of the most popular and difficult to play on the banjo.

**9.** *Although most banjo players cannot play "Foggy Mountain Breakdown" at the same speed that Earl Scruggs plays it,* very skilled players can.

**10.** *Unless bluegrass continues to attract new and young fans,* it will fade into obscurity.

**EXAMPLE**  Bluegrass music is associated with American South. It has roots in Irish and Scottish folk music.

*Even though it has roots in Irish and Scottish folk music,* bluegrass is associated with the American South.

1. Certain aspects of jazz seem to have influenced bluegrass. It involves players of an instrumental ensemble improvising around a standard melody.

2. However, the instruments used in jazz are very different than those played in bluegrass. This style of music usually uses a banjo, fiddle, mandolin, and a dobro.

3. The singing in bluegrass involves tight harmonies and a tenor lead singer. People who listen closely to the vocal arrangements can hear this.

4. Bill Monroe, the founder of bluegrass, added banjo player Earl Scruggs to his band, the Blue Grass Boys. This allowed him to produce a fuller sound.

5. The Blue Grass Boys went into the studio in 1945 to record some songs for Columbia Records. They hit the charts with "Kentucky Waltz" and "Footprints in the Snow."

6. They began touring America with their own large circus tent. They then became one of the most popular acts in country music.

7. Lester Flatt and Earl Scruggs left Bill Monroe's band. They formed their own group called the Foggy Mountain Boys.

8. A famous Flatt & Scruggs song is considered one of the most popular and difficult to play on the banjo. This song is called "Foggy Mountain Breakdown."

9. Most banjo players cannot play "Foggy Mountain Breakdown" at the same speed that Earl Scruggs plays it. Very skilled players can.

10. Bluegrass must continue to attract new and young fans. Otherwise, it will fade into obscurity.

## 14q  What are the four sentence types?

English uses four **sentence types**: simple, compound, complex, and compound complex. A **simple sentence** is composed of a single INDEPENDENT CLAUSE and no DEPENDENT CLAUSES.

Charlie Chaplin was born in London on April 16, 1889.

A **compound sentence** is composed of two or more independent clauses. These clauses may be connected by a COORDINATING CONJUNCTION (*and, but, for, or, nor, yet, so*), a semicolon alone, or a semicolon and a CONJUNCTIVE ADVERB.

His father died early, **and** his mother spent time in mental hospitals.

Many people enjoy Chaplin films; others do not.

Many people enjoy Chaplin films; **however,** others do not.

A **complex sentence** is composed of one independent clause and one or more dependent clauses.

**When times were bad,** Chaplin lived in the streets. [dependent clause starting *when*; independent clause starting *Chaplin*]

**When Chaplin was performing with a troupe that was touring the United States,** he was hired by Mack Sennett, **who owned the Keystone Company.** [dependent clause starting *when*; dependent clause starting *that*; independent clause starting *he*; dependent clause starting *who*]

A **compound-complex sentence** integrates a compound sentence and a complex sentence. It contains two or more independent clauses and one or more dependent clauses.

Chaplin's comedies were immediately successful, and he became rich **because he was enormously popular for playing the Little Tramp, who was loved for his tiny mustache, baggy trousers, big shoes, and trick derby.** [independent clause starting *Chaplin's*; independent clause starting *he*; dependent clause starting *because*; dependent clause starting *who*]

**When studios could no longer afford him,** Chaplin co-founded United Artists, and then he produced and distributed his own films. [dependent clause starting *when*; independent clause starting *Chaplin*; independent clause starting *then*]

⬤**Alerts:** (1) Use a comma before a coordinating conjunction connecting two independent clauses; see 24b. (2) When independent clauses are long or contain commas, use a subordinating conjunction—or use a semicolon to connect the sentences; see 25d. ●

## EXERCISE 14-11

Decide whether each of the following sentences is simple, compound, complex, or compound-complex. For help, consult 14q.

**EXAMPLE** Many people would love to eat a healthy meal at a fast-food restaurant or a food concession at the movies. (*simple*)

1. Fast-food restaurants and healthy meals rarely go together.
2. A fried-chicken sandwich packs an enormous number of calories and fat, and a fried-fish sandwich is no better.

**ANSWERS: EXERCISE 14-11**
1. simple
2. compound
3. compound
4. complex
5. compound-complex
6. simple

7. simple
8. compound-complex
9. compound
10. simple

3. A double cheeseburger with bacon at a fast-food restaurant can contain over 1,000 calories and 80 grams of fat, but a plain burger reduces the unhealthy overload considerably.

4. You can purchase other relatively healthy meals at a fast-food restaurant, if you first get to know the chart of nutritional values provided for customers.

5. Even though US government regulations require that nutritional charts be posted on the wall in the public areas of every fast-food restaurant, consumers often ignore the information, and they choose main meals and side dishes with the most flavor, calories, and fat.

6. A healthy meal available at many fast-food restaurants is a salad with low-fat dressing, along with bottled water.

7. The temptations of high fat and calories also entice people at the food concessions in movie theaters.

8. Because calories from sugar have zero nutritional value, health experts use the expression "empty calories" for all sugar products, yet sales of colossal sugar-laden sodas at the movies continue to increase yearly.

9. The silent ingredient in a serving of chips with melted cheese, or nachos, is artery-clogging fat, and the culprits in extra-large candy bars are not only fat but also "empty calories."

10. In truth, many people need to stay away from fast-food restaurants and food concessions at the movies and thereby avoid the tasty temptations of high-calorie foods.

For more help with your writing, grammar, and research,
go to **www.mycomplab.com**

# 15

# Verbs

## 15a What do verbs do?

A **verb** expresses an action, an occurrence, or a state of being.

Many people **overeat** on Thanksgiving. [action]

Mother's Day **fell** early this year. [occurrence]

Memorial Day **is** tomorrow. [state of being]

Verbs also reveal when something occurs—in the present, the past, or the future. Verbs convey other information as well; see Quick Reference 15.1. For types of verbs, see Quick Reference 15.2 on page 312.

### Quick Reference 15.1

#### Information that verbs convey

| | |
|---|---|
| PERSON | First person (the speaker: *I dance*), second person (the one spoken to: *you dance*), or third person (the one spoken about: *the man dances*). |
| NUMBER | Singular (one) or plural (more than one). |
| TENSE | Past (*we danced*), present (*we dance*), or future (*we will dance*); see 15g through 15k. |
| MOOD | Moods are indicative (*we dance*), imperative (commands and polite requests: *Dance*), or conditional (speculation, wishes: *if we were dancing . . .*); see 15l and 15m. |
| VOICE | Active voice or passive voice; see 15n through 15p. |

### LINKING VERBS

**Linking verbs** are main verbs that indicate a state of being or a condition. They link a SUBJECT with one or more words that rename or describe the subject, called a SUBJECT COMPLEMENT. A linking verb is like an equal sign between a subject and its complement. Quick Reference 15.3 on page 312 shows how linking verbs function in sentences.

**TEACHING TIP**

Some students may feel overwhelmed by verb tenses—which they may perceive to be infinite in number—with the result that they refuse to face the fearsome verb and thus pick a form at random (or so it seems to us). It may be helpful to show them the basic distinction between tense and aspect.

Time can be divided into past, present, and future. *Tense* refers to the reflection of one of these times in a verb. Therefore, there are three basic tenses: past, present, future. *Aspect* says something about the way the action is experienced. The progressive aspect (*to be* + *-ing*) shows an action still in progress, and the perfect aspect (*has, have,* or *had* + past participle) shows a completed action or one being continued into the present from a specific point in the past. *Mood,* which describes conditions such as certainty, necessity, and possibility, is a separate issue, and so is *voice.* A verb can show all four qualities, but you might want to focus on the interplay of tense and aspect first.

**QUOTATION: ON WRITING**

Suit the action to the word, the word to the action.

—William Shakespeare

**WORD HISTORY**

*Verb* shares the same Latin root as *word*—*verbum,* meaning "word." *Verbum* is related to the Greek verb *eirein,* "to say" or "to speak."

**BACKGROUND**

Rod Ellis's "Teaching and Research: Options in Grammar Teaching" (*TESOL Quarterly* 32.1 (1998): 39–60) reviews four theoretical approaches to teaching grammar and evaluates them to determine the best way to teach grammar.

**TEACHING TIP**

Students who speak two or more dialects can adapt to changes in vocabulary with comparative ease. Their verbs, however, may need closer attention in their academic writing. You might consider reviewing the following chart to help students create and visualize the differences.

**Dialectical**     **Standardized**
(Nonstandardized
for formal writing)

*Present Tense*

I
you    *loves*    I you *love*
we           we
they         they
he, she, it *love*    he, she, it *loves*

*Past Tense*

I
you    *love*    I you *loved*
we           we
they         they
he, she, it *love*    he, she, it *loved*

Your students may find it helpful for you to point out that while nouns normally form their plurals by adding *-s* (or *-es*), verbs associated with plural nouns and pronouns do just the opposite! *Musicians play* (not *plays*) *their instruments.* Conversely, singular nouns rarely end in *-s:* Hardy (*he*); Yolanda (*she*); a Web site (*it*). Yet a singular verb associated with one of these nouns (or its third-person pronoun substitute) does exactly the opposite: *Yolanda reads* (not *read*). *A Web site stimulates* (not *stimulate*). Thus an *-s* attached to a verb "says *singular.*"

**TEACHING TIP**
The discussion of the linking verbs that deal with the senses (*look, smell, taste, sound, feel*) provides an opportunity to discuss the issues of *bad* versus *badly* and *good* versus *well.* These adjective and adverb forms are covered in 11d, but you may wish to introduce their use within the context of verbs.

**BACKGROUND**
The Grammar Hotline Archives at <http://www2.ncsu.edu/ncsu/grammar/Verbs3.html> stores student questions by category. Following is a question-answer sample from the Web site's archives on verbs: Which verb is correct? "The majority of the fairgoers *was/were* Americans." *Was* seems to work since *was* relates to one majority—or should it be *were* since it relates to many Americans? Answer: It should be *were* because *majority* is a collective noun, which can be either singular or plural. Also, because this

## Quick Reference 15.2

### Types of verbs

| | |
|---|---|
| **MAIN VERB** | The word in a PREDICATE that says something about the SUBJECT: *She **danced** for the group.* |
| **AUXILIARY VERB** | A verb that combines with a main verb to convey information about TENSE, MOOD, or VOICE (15e). The verbs *be, do,* and *have* can be auxiliary verbs or main verbs. The verbs *can, could, may, might, should, would, must,* and others are MODAL AUXILIARY VERBS. They add shades of meaning such as ability or possibility to verbs: *She **might dance** again.* |
| **LINKING VERB** | The verb that links a subject to a COMPLEMENT, a word or words that rename or describe the subject: *She **was** happy dancing. Be* is the most common linking verb; sometimes sense verbs (*smell, taste*) or verbs of perception (*seem, feel*) function as linking verbs. See also Quick Reference 15.3. |
| **TRANSITIVE VERB** | The verb followed by a DIRECT OBJECT that completes the verb's message: *They **sent** her a fan letter.* |
| **INTRANSITIVE VERB** | A verb that does not require a direct object: *Yesterday she **danced.*** |

## Quick Reference 15.3

### Linking verbs

- Linking verbs may be forms of the verb *be* (*am, is, was, were;* see 9e for a complete list).

| George Washington | *was* | president. |
|---|---|---|
| SUBJECT | LINKING VERB | COMPLEMENT (PREDICATE NOMINATIVE: RENAMES SUBJECT) |

- Linking verbs may deal with the senses (*look, smell, taste, sound, feel*).

| George Washington | *sounded* | confident. |
|---|---|---|
| SUBJECT | LINKING VERB | COMPLEMENT (PREDICATE ADJECTIVE DESCRIBES SUBJECT) |

- Linking verbs can be verbs that convey a sense of existing or becoming— *appear, seem, become, get, grow, turn, remain, stay,* and *prove,* for example.

| George Washington | *grew* | old. |
|---|---|---|
| SUBJECT | LINKING VERB | COMPLEMENT (PREDICATE ADJECTIVE DESCRIBES SUBJECT) |

continued >>

## Quick Reference 15.3 (continued)

- To test whether a verb other than a form of *be* is functioning as a linking verb, substitute *was* (for a singular subject) or *were* (for a plural subject) for the original verb. If the sentence makes sense, the original verb is functioning as a linking verb.

  **NO** George Washington *grew* a beard → George Washington *was* a beard. [*Grew* is not functioning as a linking verb.]

  **YES** George Washington *grew* old → George Washington *was* old. [*Grew* is functioning as a linking verb.]

## VERB FORMS

# 15b What are the forms of main verbs?

A **main verb** names an action (*People **dance***), an occurrence (*Christmas **comes** once a year*), or a state of being (*It **will be** warm tomorrow*). Every main verb has five forms.

- The **simple form** conveys an action, occurrence, or state of being taking place in the present (*I **laugh***) or, with an AUXILIARY VERB, in the future (*I **will laugh***).

- The **past-tense form** conveys an action, occurrence, or state completed in the past (*I **laughed***). REGULAR VERBS add *-ed* or *-d* to the simple form. IRREGULAR VERBS vary (see Quick Reference 15.4 for a list of common irregular verbs).

- The **past participle form** in regular verbs uses the same form as the past tense. Irregular verbs vary; see Quick Reference 15.4. To function as a verb, a past participle must combine with a SUBJECT and one or more auxiliary verbs (*I **have laughed***). Otherwise, past participles function as ADJECTIVES (***crumbled** cookies*).

- The **present participle form** adds *-ing* to the simple form (***laughing***). To function as a verb, a present participle combines with a subject and one or more auxiliary verbs (*I **was laughing***). Otherwise, present participles function as adjectives (*my **laughing** friends*) or as NOUNS (***Laughing** is healthy*).

- The **infinitive** usually consists of *to* and the simple form following *to* (*I started **to laugh** at his joke*); see 16i. The infinitive functions as a noun or an adjective, not a verb.

---

sentence contains overt grammatical markers (fairgoer*s*, American*s*), in this context *majority* is plural.

### TEACHING TIP

Leaving the *-s* off verbs is a common error, even among students who can quote the rule for its use. Many of these students speak or have studied second languages that have more complex systems of verb endings than English does. A discussion of the English *-s* in the context of other languages the students know may reduce the number of carelessly omitted *-s* endings.

Here is a comparison of the verb *speak* (present tense) in four languages, with endings shown in **boldface**. When no pronouns appear, the pronoun is communicated by the verb's ending.

| **Singular** | **Plural** |
|---|---|
| *English* | |
| I speak | we speak |
| you speak | you speak |
| he, she, it speak**s** | they speak |
| *Spanish* | |
| habl**o** | habl**amos** |
| habl**as** | habl**áis** |
| habl**a** | habl**an** |
| *Italian* | |
| parl**o** | parl**iamo** |
| parl**i** | parl**ate** |
| parl**a** | parl**ano** |
| *French* | |
| je parl**e** | nous parl**ons** |
| tu parl**es** | vous parl**ez** |
| il, elle, on parl**e** | ils, elles parl**ent** |

### WORD HISTORY

*Infinitive* comes from the Latin *infinitivus,* meaning "unlimited" or "indefinite." This is appropriate, since the infinitive shows no person or number. Coming from the same Latin verb, *finire* ("to limit"), the term *finite verb* refers to a verb that is limited by person and number. In contrast, a *nonfinite verb* (also known as a *verbal*) is not limited in these ways.

## LANGUAGE HISTORY

Bas Aarts and Charles F. Meyer have written a fascinating history of the verb, *The Verb in Contemporary English: Theory and Description* (New York: Cambridge University Press, 1995). In their introduction, they explain:

> Verbs are found in virtually all the languages of the world (Lyons 1977:429, Allerton 1982:1), and throughout history their semantic and syntactic properties have interested philosophers and grammarians alike. As early as c. 100 BC Dionysius Thrax stressed the importance of the verb (*rhema*) which he defined in his *Téchne grammatiké* as "a part of speech without case inflection, but inflected for tense, person, and number, signifying an activity or process performed or undergone." This definition brings out that the very earliest grammarians were interested in both formal and semantic, or "notional," characterizations of world classes. Later grammarians, such as Apolloniun Syscolus in the second century AD, became more interested in the distributional (i.e., syntactic) properties of the world classes. (1)

## WORD HISTORY

The word *conjugation* has been used since the early sixteenth century to refer to all the forms of a particular verb. *Conjugation* and *conjugate* both come from the Latin *conjugare*, basically meaning "to join together." In Latin, a list of the forms of a verb was called a *conjugatio*, and *conjugata verba* (literally "joined words") referred to words that were etymologically related.

## ANSWERS: EXERCISE 15-1

**1.** Before declaring Oregon giant earthworms a protected species, a US government agency *requires* concrete proof that they *are* not extinct.

**2.** Scientists who *find* one alive will demonstrate that the Oregon giant earthworm *does* still exist, in spite of no one's having seen any for over twenty years.

**3.** Last seen in the Willamette Valley near Portland, Oregon, the earthworm *is* white, and it *smells* like lilies.

🌐 **ESOL Tip:** When verbs function as other parts of speech, they're called VERBALS. Verbals are INFINITIVES, PRESENT PARTICIPLES, and PAST PARTICIPLES. When present participles function as nouns, they're called GERUNDS. For information about using gerunds and infinitives as OBJECTS after certain verbs, see Chapter 54. ●

## 15c What is the -s, or -es, form of a verb?

The -s **form of a verb** is the third-person singular in the PRESENT TENSE. The ending -*s* (or -*es*) is added to the verb's SIMPLE FORM (*smell* becomes *smells,* as in *The bread **smells** delicious*).

*Be* and *have* are irregular verbs. For the third-person singular, present tense, *be* uses *is* and *have* uses *has.*

> The cheesecake **is** popular.
>
> The éclair **has** chocolate icing.

Even if you tend to drop the -*s* or -*es* ending when you speak, always use it when you write. Proofread carefully to make sure you haven't omitted any -*s* forms.

❗ **Alert:** In informal speech, the LINKING, or *copula,* VERB *to be* sometimes doesn't change forms in the present tense. However, ACADEMIC WRITING requires you to use standard third-person singular forms in the present tense.

> He **is** [not *be*] hungry.
> The bakery **has** [not *have*] fresh bread. ●

**EXERCISE 15-1** Rewrite each sentence, changing the subjects to the word or words given in parentheses. Change the form of the verbs shown in italics to match the new subject. Keep all sentences in the present tense. For help, consult 15c.

**EXAMPLE** The Oregon giant earthworm *escapes* all attempts at detection. (Oregon giant earthworms)

*Oregon giant earthworms escape* all attempts at detection.

1. Before declaring the Oregon giant earthworm a protected species, US government agencies *require* concrete proof that it *is* not extinct. (a government agency) (they)

2. A scientist who *finds* one alive will demonstrate that Oregon giant earthworms *do* still exist, in spite of no one's having seen any for over twenty years. (Scientists) (the Oregon giant earthworm)

3. Last seen in the Willamette Valley near Portland, Oregon, the earthworms *are* white, and they *smell* like lilies. (the earthworm) (it)

4. Oregon giant earthworms *grow* up to three feet long. (The Oregon giant earthworm)

5. A clump of soil with a strange shape *indicates* that the giant creatures *continue* to live, but to demonstrate that they *are* not extinct, only a real specimen will do. (clumps of soil) (creature) (it)

## 15d What is the difference between regular and irregular verbs?

A **regular verb** forms its PAST TENSE and PAST PARTICIPLE by adding *-ed* or *-d* to the SIMPLE FORM: *type, typed; cook, cooked; work, worked.* Most verbs in English are regular.

In informal speech, some people skip over the *-ed* sound, pronouncing it softly or not at all. In ACADEMIC WRITING, however, you're required to use it. If you're not used to hearing or pronouncing this sound, proofread carefully to see that you have all the needed *-ed* endings in your writing.

| | |
|---|---|
| **NO** | The cake was **suppose** to be tasty. |
| **YES** | The cake was **supposed** to be tasty. |

**Irregular verbs,** in contrast, don't consistently add *-ed* or *-d* to form the past tense and past participle. Some irregular verbs change an internal vowel to make the past tense and past participle: *sing, sang, sung.* Some change an internal vowel and add an ending other than *-ed* or *-d: grow, grew, grown.* Some use the simple form throughout: *cost, cost, cost.* Unfortunately, a verb's simple form doesn't provide a clue about whether the verb is irregular or regular. Quick Reference 15.4 lists frequently used irregular verbs.

Although you can always look up the principal parts of any verb, memorizing any you don't know solidly is much more efficient in the long run. About two hundred verbs in English are irregular.

**Alert:** For information about changing *y* to *i*, or doubling a final consonant before adding the *-ed* ending, see 31d. ●

4. The Oregon giant earthworm *grows* up to three feet long.

5. Clumps of soil with a strange shape *indicate* that the giant creature *continues* to live, but to demonstrate that it *is* not extinct, only a real specimen will do.

### BACKGROUND

Old English, ancestor of our language as we know it today, used only two tenses—present and past. All other information, such as number, person, mood, and voice, was indicated by inflectional endings. All that remains of the personal endings is the *-es* or *-s* of the third person singular, which comes from the Middle English and Early Modern English *-eth* used by Chaucer, translators of the King James Bible, and Shakespeare. English verbs, like all their Germanic cognates, are distinguished by their division into weak and strong classes. In Old English, the strong classes indicated tense by changing the medial vowels; the weak ones did so by changing their endings. After the Norman Conquest, when French and Latin became the languages of power (the court and the church), many strong English verbs became weak, adopting the *-ed* ending to indicate tense changes. New verbs admitted to the language were all placed in the weak category. Today, the mixture of strong and weak forms makes it necessary for English speakers to memorize the principal parts of irregular verbs.

### QUOTATION: ON WRITING

I started off with the desire to use language experimentally. Then I saw that the right way was the way of simplicity. Straight sentences, no involutions, no ambiguities. Not much description, description isn't my line. Get on with the story. Present the outside world economically and exactly.

—Graham Greene

### QUOTATION: ON WRITING

True ease in writing comes from art, not chance,
As those move easiest who have learned to dance.

'Tis not enough no harshness gives offense,
The sound must seem an echo to the sense.

—Alexander Pope

## BACKGROUND

The site <http://www.chompchomp.com> features interactive exercises on a variety of writing topics. The following is a sample exercise on irregular verbs:

Rachel *would have wrote* a better essay for Mr. Parker, but she *had drunk* a double espresso and found that she had too much energy to sit still at a computer. Response: The first verb, *would have wrote,* is incorrect. This verb requires the past participle *written* because of the auxiliary verbs *would* and *have. Write* is an irregular verb.

—Robin L. Simmons,
at <http://www.chompchomp.com>

## BACKGROUND

The site <http://grammar.ccc.commnet.edu/ grammar/quizzes/irregular_verbsIIb.htm> features an interactive quiz on irregular verbs. The quiz takes only a few minutes, and students can receive immediate feedback on their answers. The larger site, "Guide to Grammar and Writing" at <http://grammar.ccc.commnet.edu/ grammar> has many useful exercises for students targeting problems with sentence and paragraph writing.

## BACKGROUND

In late antiquity and the Middle Ages, grammar, rhetoric, and logic were organized into the *trivium,* the three language arts of education. The trivium and *quadrivium* (geometry, arithmetic, astronomy, and music) together formed the seven liberal arts. *Grammar* meant the study of Latin until the eighteenth and nineteenth centuries, when English and other vernacular languages began to displace Latin as the language of education.

## QUOTATION: ON WRITING

Nice writing isn't enough. It isn't enough to have smooth and pretty language. You have to surprise the reader frequently, you can't just be

## Quick Reference 15.4

### Common irregular verbs

| Simple Form | Past Tense | Past Participle |
|---|---|---|
| arise | arose | arisen |
| awake | awoke *or* awaked | awaked *or* awoken |
| be (is, am, are) | was, were | been |
| beat | beat | beaten |
| become | became | become |
| begin | began | begun |
| bend | bent | bent |
| bite | bit | bitten *or* bit |
| blow | blew | blown |
| break | broke | broken |
| bring | brought | brought |
| build | built | built |
| burst | burst | burst |
| buy | bought | bought |
| catch | caught | caught |
| choose | chose | chosen |
| cling | clung | clung |
| come | came | come |
| cost | cost | cost |
| cut | cut | cut |
| deal | dealt | dealt |
| dig | dug | dug |
| dive | dived *or* dove | dived |
| do | did | done |
| draw | drew | drawn |
| drink | drank | drunk |
| drive | drove | driven |
| eat | ate | eaten |
| fall | fell | fallen |
| fight | fought | fought |
| find | found | found |
| fly | flew | flown |
| forget | forgot | forgotten *or* forgot |
| freeze | froze | frozen |
| get | got | got *or* gotten |
| give | gave | given |
| go | went | gone |
| grow | grew | grown |
| hang ("to suspend")* | hung | hung |
| have | had | had |

continued >>

## Quick Reference 15.4 (continued)

| Simple Form | Past Tense | Past Participle |
|---|---|---|
| hear | heard | heard |
| hide | hid | hidden |
| hurt | hurt | hurt |
| keep | kept | kept |
| know | knew | known |
| lay | laid | laid |
| lead | led | led |
| lend | lent | lent |
| let | let | let |
| lie | lay | lain |
| light | lighted *or* lit | lighted *or* lit |
| lose | lost | lost |
| make | made | made |
| mean | meant | meant |
| prove | proved | proved *or* proven |
| read | read | read |
| ride | rode | ridden |
| ring | rang | rung |
| rise | rose | risen |
| run | ran | run |
| say | said | said |
| see | saw | seen |
| seek | sought | sought |
| send | sent | sent |
| set | set | set |
| shake | shook | shaken |
| shoot | shot | shot |
| show | showed | shown *or* showed |
| shrink | shrank | shrunk |
| sing | sang | sung |
| sink | sank *or* sunk | sunk |
| sit | sat | sat |
| slay | slew | slain |
| sleep | slept | slept |
| speak | spoke | spoken |
| spin | spun | spun |
| spring | sprang *or* sprung | sprung |
| stand | stood | stood |
| steal | stole | stolen |
| sting | stung | stung |
| stink | stank *or* stunk | stunk |
| strike | struck | struck |

continued >>

nice all the time. Provoke the reader. Astonish the reader. Writing that has no surprises is as bland as oatmeal. Surprise the reader with the unexpected verb or adjective. Use one startling adjective per page.

—Anne Bernays

**BACKGROUND**

In "Grammar and Power" (*The English Journal* 17.10 (1928): 800–810), H. Y. Moffett recounts the difficulties of teaching grammar to students in the eighth grade. Many of the anecdotes and examples will seem familiar. However, the speech is an address to the National Council of Teachers of English in 1928.

**QUOTATION: ON WRITING**

You don't know what it is to stay a whole day with your head in your hands trying to squeeze your unfortunate brain so as to find a word. Ah! I know the agonies of style.

—Gustave Flaubert

**QUOTATION: ON WRITING**

Erasure is quite as important a function of the pen as actual writing. . . . For we have to condemn what had previously satisfied us and discover what had escaped our notice.

—Quintilian

**QUOTATION: ON WRITING**

[I]t is the invention on the page of connections in language which denote, describe and relate events (verbal occurrences that we call "word time"); and, within which, the only lapse that can count as a crime is a lapse of grammar.

—William H. Gass

**QUOTATION: ON WRITING**

Most verbs carry somewhere in their imagery or in their sound a suggestion of what they mean: *flail, poke, dazzle, squash, beguile, pamper, swagger, wheedle, vex.*

—William Zinsser, *On Writing Well*

## WORD HISTORY

An auxiliary verb is also called a helping verb, and, not surprisingly, *auxiliary* comes from *auxiliarius,* a Latin word for "help." Linking verbs were, until recently, often called copulative verbs. This usage dates back to the seventeenth century and comes from the Latin *copulativus,* meaning "connective."

## ANSWERS: EXERCISE 15-2

1. involved; lasted
2. played; created
3. served; trained; resolved
4. named; used
5. resembled; arrived; helped

## ANSWERS: EXERCISE 15-3

1. was
2. drew; stood
3. had; forbade/forbad
4. came; sang
5. lent
6. cast; stuck
7. gave
8. saw
9. strove; shot
10. led
11. became; made
12. tried; lost

## EXTRA EXERCISE A

Identify all modal auxiliaries in the following passage. (Answers appear in *italics*.)

Most professionals in the field of medicine agree that the public *ought to* be better informed about recent developments in medical science. One of the tools that patients frequently experience but *may* know little about is the X-ray. Its discoverer, Professor Wilhelm Roentgen, thought he *might* have a powerful new means of examining the body when, in 1895, he saw the glimmer of a fluorescent screen. His discovery meant

| Quick Reference 15.4 | | (continued) |
|---|---|---|
| **Simple Form** | **Past Tense** | **Past Participle** |
| swear | swore | sworn |
| swim | swam | swum |
| swing | swung | swung |
| take | took | taken |
| teach | taught | taught |
| throw | threw | thrown |
| wake | woke *or* waked | waked *or* woken |
| wear | wore | worn |
| wring | wrung | wrung |
| write | wrote | written |

*When it means "to execute by hanging," *hang* is a regular verb: *In wartime, some armies routinely **hanged** deserters.*

**EXERCISE 15-2**   Write the correct past-tense form of the regular verbs given in parentheses. For help, consult 15d.

**EXAMPLE**   Native North Americans (invent) invented the game of lacrosse.

(1) Ancient lacrosse games (involve) _____ up to 1,000 men and (last) _____ the entire day. (2) Native Americans (play) _____ the game using balls they (create) _____ out of deerskin and wood. (3) Lacrosse (serve) _____ many purposes in tribal life as warriors (train) _____ for battle and (resolve) _____ conflicts. (4) French missionaries eventually (name) _____ the game "la crosse," perhaps referring to the staffs Jesuit bishops (use) _____. (5) Lacrosse (resemble) _____ the Irish sport hurling, so when Irish immigrants (arrive) _____ in America in the 19th century, they (help) _____ to make the game more popular.

**EXERCISE 15-3**   Write the correct past-tense form of the irregular verbs given in parentheses. For help, consult Quick Reference 15.4 in 15d.

**EXAMPLE**   In August, 1969, the Woodstock music festival (begin) began as thousands of fans (drive) drove to upstate New York for three days of music.

(1) The official name of the festival (is) _____ the Woodstock Music and Art Fair. (2) It (draw) _____ nearly half a million people to Max Yasgur's farm, which (stand) _____ in the small town of Bethel, New

York. (3) The concert (have) _____ to move to Bethel at the last minute after residents of the town of Woodstock (forbid) _____ organizers to hold the festival in their town. (4) Those who (come) _____ to hear music were not disappointed, since several well known artists (sing) _____ to the large crowd. (5) Performers such as Jimi Hendrix, Santana, and Janis Joplin (lend) _____ their talents to the festival. (6) Even though rain clouds occasionally (cast) _____ a shadow on the events, most people (stick) _____ it out the entire three days. (7) According to some reports, two women (give) _____ birth during the festival. (8) Because of the relatively peaceful atmosphere, many people (see) _____ the event as a symbol of countercultural ideals. (9) Filmmaker Michael Wadleigh (strive) _____ to capture that atmosphere in the film *Woodstock,* which he (shoot) _____ and edited with the help of a young Martin Scorsese. (10) The festival also (lead) _____ to a song written by Joni Mitchell called "Woodstock." (11) That song (become) _____ a hit for Crosby, Stills, Nash, and Young, which (make) _____ its debut as a group at Woodstock. (12) Although organizers (try) _____ to turn a profit with the event, they (lose) _____ money because many attendees did not purchase tickets.

# 15e What are auxiliary verbs?

**Auxiliary verbs,** also called *helping verbs,* combine with MAIN VERBS to make VERB PHRASES. Quick Reference 15.5 shows how auxiliary verbs work.

## Quick Reference 15.5

### Auxiliary verbs

• I am shopping for new shoes.

VERB PHRASE | AUXILIARY VERB (am) | MAIN VERB (shopping)

• Clothing prices have soared recently.

VERB PHRASE | AUXILIARY VERB (have) | MAIN VERB (soared)

continued >>

that medical professionals *could* peer into the innermost recesses of the body without surgery. For example, Dr. William B. Cannon realized that fluoroscopy *could* be used to examine the alimentary canal or digestive system. Today X-ray means that doctors *can* carry diagnostic methods to previously inaccessible areas of the human body by painless techniques. A list of all of the diagnostic uses of X-ray films *would* be too lengthy to include here, but it is safe to say that they *can* be used on all parts of the body. Of course, because improper use of X-rays *may* be harmful, technologists *should* have adequate training. They *must* complete a rigorous course of study before being allowed to operate X-ray machines.

—Emily Gordon

**QUOTATION: ON WRITING**

In the lexicon of *iffiness, may* and *might* mark ranges of possibility from the probable to the unlikely.

—William Safire

**QUOTATION: ON WRITING**

What happened to *may*? Quite often these days, I find *might* used where *may* is correct. Obviously the distinction is becoming blurred in the public mind.

—Timothy B. Blodgett

**QUOTATION: ON WRITING**

*Shoulda,* short for *should have . . .* carries a sense of correctness or obligation; *coulda* implies a possibility, and *woulda* denotes conditional certainty, an oxymoron: the stated intent to have taken an action if only something had not intervened.

—William Safire

**BACKGROUND**

Many second language learners often have trouble with modal auxiliaries. Eli Hinkel's "The Use of Modal Verbs as a Reflection of Cultural Values" (*TESOL Quarterly* 29.2 (1995): 325–343) provides some good background on the cultural assumptions native speakers make when using modals.

## EXTRA EXERCISE B

Circle all transitive verbs and underline all intransitive verbs in the following sentences.

**1.** Yellowstone National Park is the oldest and largest park in the national system.

**2.** It lies in the northwestern corner of Wyoming, slightly overlapping the boundaries of Montana on the north and Idaho on the west and south.

**3.** The planners originally designed the park to run 62 miles from east to west and 54 miles from north to south.

**4.** Yellowstone has several lofty plateaus, and the Continental Divide crosses it.

**5.** The Yellowstone River flows north into Yellowstone Lake and then through its canyon across Montana to join the Missouri.

**6.** The most famous sights in Yellowstone Park are the geysers.

**7.** The park has more than three thousand springs, pools, and geysers.

**8.** Old Faithful is the most famous of the geysers, but in the same basin with it are a number of other impressive water jets.

**9.** Wildlife in the park, which includes bear, deer, elk, antelope, and mountain sheep, is protected.

### Answers to Extra Exercise B

**1.** is (intransitive)

**2.** lies (intransitive)

**3.** designed (transitive)

**4.** has (transitive); crosses (transitive)

**5.** flows (intransitive)

**6.** are (intransitive)

**7.** has (transitive)

**8.** is (intransitive); are (intransitive)

**9.** includes (transitive); is (intransitive)

## Quick Reference 15.5 (continued)

## USING *BE, DO, HAVE*

The three most common auxiliary verbs are *be, do,* and *have.* These three verbs can also be main verbs. Their forms vary more than most irregular verbs, as Quick References 15.6 and 15.7 show.

## Quick Reference 15.6

### Forms of the verb *be*

| | |
|---|---|
| SIMPLE FORM | be |
| -S FORM | is |
| PAST TENSE | was, were |
| PRESENT PARTICIPLE | being |
| PAST PARTICIPLE | been |

| Person | Present Tense | Past Tense |
|---|---|---|
| I | am | Was |
| you (singular) | are | Were |
| he, she, it | is | Was |
| we | are | Were |
| you (plural) | are | Were |
| they | are | Were |

## Quick Reference 15.7

### Forms of the verbs *do* and *have*

| | | |
|---|---|---|
| SIMPLE FORM | do | have |
| -S FORM | does | has |
| PAST TENSE | did | had |
| PRESENT PARTICIPLE | doing | having |
| PAST PARTICIPLE | done | had |

⚠️ **Alert:** In ACADEMIC WRITING, always use the standard forms for *be, do,* and *have,* as shown in Quick References 15.6 and 15.7.

The gym **is** [not *be*] a busy place.

The gym **is** [not *be*] filling with spectators. ●

🌐 **ESOL Tip:** When *be, do,* and *have* function as auxiliary verbs, change their form to agree with a third-person singular subject—and don't add *-s* to the main verb.

| | |
|---|---|
| **NO** | **Does** the library **closes** at 6:00? |
| **YES** | **Does** the library **close** at 6:00? ● |

### MODAL AUXILIARY VERBS

*Can, could, shall, should, will, would, may, might,* and *must* are the nine modal auxiliary verbs. **Modal auxiliary verbs** communicate ability, permission, obligation, advisability, necessity, or possibility. They never change form.

Exercise **can lengthen** lives. [possibility]

She **can jog** for five miles. [ability]

The exercise **must occur** regularly. [necessity, obligation]

People **should protect** their bodies. [advisability]

**May I exercise?** [permission]

🌐 **ESOL Tip:** For more about modal auxiliary verbs and the meanings they communicate, see Chapter 55. ●

**EXERCISE 15-4**   Using the auxiliary verbs in the list below, fill in the blanks in the following passage. Use each auxiliary word only once, even if a listed word can fit into more than one blank. For help, consult 15e.

> are     have     may     will     might     can     has

**EXAMPLE**   Completing a marathon <u>can</u> be the highlight of a runner's life.

(1) The marathon _____ been a challenging and important athletic event since the 19th century. (2) Athletes who _____ training for a marathon _____ use one of the many online training guides. (3) Running with a partner or friend _____ boost confidence and motivation. (4) Beginning runners _____ find the first few weeks difficult but _____ soon see dramatic improvement in their performance. (5) Those who _____ successfully finished the race often want to repeat the experience.

### A HUMOROUS NOTE

The English major was working for the summer as morning shift manager at a fast-food restaurant. One day, her least reliable worker was missing again. She called over a friend of the boy and asked, "Where's Bill?"

"He decided to lay on the beach," replied the friend.

Not wishing to embarrass the worker but unable to overcome the urge to correct him, the manager whispered, "Lie."

"All right," he said with a shrug. "Bill had to take his cat to the vet for an emergency appendectomy."

### ANSWERS: EXERCISE 15-4

1. has
2. are, might/can
3. might/can
4. might, will
5. have

### EXTRA EXERCISE C

To give students practice in identifying verbs and forming past-tense verbs, ask them to rewrite the following paragraph, changing the present-tense verbs to past tense. (Answers appear in italics within parentheses.)

Recuperation is (*was*) like spring: dormancy and vitality collide (*collided*). In any year I'm (*I was*) like a bear, a partial hibernator. During January thaws I stick (*stuck*) my nose out and peruse (*perused*) the frozen desolation as if reading a book whose language I don't (*didn't*) know. In March I'm (*I was*) ramshackle, weak in the knees, giddy, dazzled by broken-backed clouds, the passing of Halley's comet, the on-and-off strobe of sun. Like a sheepherder I X (*Xed*) out each calendar day as if time were (*no change, subjunctive voice*) a forest through which I could clear-cut (*no change, subjunctive voice*) a way to the future. My physicist friend straightens (*straightened*) me out on this point too. The notion of "time passing," like a train through a landscape, is (*was*) an illusion, he says (*said*). I hold (*held*) the Big

Ben clock taken from a dead sheepherder's wagon and look (*looked*) at it. The clock measures (*measured*) intervals of time, not the speed of time, and the calendar is (*was*) a scaffolding we hang (*hung*) as if time were (*no change, subjunctive voice*) rushing water we could harness (*no change, subjunctive voice*). Time-bound, I hinge (*hinged*) myself to a linear bias—cause and effect all laid out in a neat row—and in this we learn (*learned*) two things: blame and shame.

—Gretel Ehrlich, "Spring"

**HUMOROUS NOTE**

"What is, was. What was, will be. What will be, is."

—Horshack, *Welcome Back Kotter*

**EXTRA EXERCISE D**

Supply the progressive form of an appropriate verb in the blanks in the following sentences. (Answers will vary.)

**1.** Don't bother me now; I am _____.

**2.** My brother is _____ to apply for a job in France.

**3.** The committee is _____ at 5 p.m.

**4.** The professor was _____ on the topic of the European Union.

**5.** The doctor was _____ in the hospital.

**6.** My dog was _____ in the yard.

**7.** I can't go swimming because I am _____.

**8.** The garden is _____ more beautiful every day.

**9.** Whose car is _____ in the driveway?

**10.** The telephone has been _____ all day.

**TEACHING TIP: ESOL**

The term *present* can be confusing for ESOL students because in English, the simple present tense does not describe the present moment. Rather, our simple present is "timeless" (The sun *rises* in the east and *sets* in the west) or general (Democracy *means* "rule by the people"). In English, the present moment is expressed in the present progressive. ESOL students might

## 15f What are intransitive and transitive verbs?

A verb is **intransitive** when an OBJECT isn't required to complete the verb's meaning: *I sing.* A verb is **transitive** when an object is necessary to complete the verb's meaning: *I need a guitar.* Many verbs have both transitive and intransitive meanings. Some verbs are only transitive: *need, have, like, owe, remember.* Only transitive verbs function in the PASSIVE VOICE. Dictionaries label verbs as transitive (*vt*) or intransitive (*vi*).

### Quick Reference 15.8

**Using *lie* and *lay***

|  | lie | lay |
|---|---|---|
| SIMPLE FORM | lie | lay |
| -S FORM | lies | lays |
| PAST TENSE | lay | laid |
| PRESENT PARTICIPLE | lying | laying |
| PAST PARTICIPLE | lain | laid |

**INTRANSITIVE FORMS**

| PRESENT TENSE | The hikers **lie** down to rest. |
|---|---|
| PAST TENSE | The hikers **lay** down to rest. |

**TRANSITIVE FORMS**

| PRESENT TENSE | The hikers **lay** their backpacks on a rock. [*Backpacks* is a direct object.] |
|---|---|
| PAST TENSE | The hikers **laid** their backpacks on a rock. [*Backpacks* is a direct object.] |

The verbs *lie* and *lay* are particularly confusing. *Lie* means "to recline, to place oneself down, or to remain." *Lie* is intransitive (it cannot be followed by an object). *Lay* means "to put something down." *Lay* is transitive (it must be followed by an object). As you can see in Quick Reference 15.8, the word *lay* is both the past tense of *lie* and the present-tense simple form of *lay.* That makes things difficult. Our best advice is memorize them. Yet truthfully, each time we use *lie* and *lay,* we need to pause, think, and recite the list to ourselves.

Two other verb pairs tend to confuse people because of their intransitive and transitive forms: *raise* and *rise* and *set* and *sit.*

*Raise* and *set* are transitive (they must be followed by an object). *Rise* and *sit* are intransitive (they cannot be followed by an object). Fortunately, although each word has a meaning different from the other words, they don't share forms: *raise, raised, raised; rise, rose, risen;* and *set, set, set; sit, sat, sat.*

**EXERCISE 15-5** Underline the correct word of each pair in parentheses. For help, consult 15f.

**EXAMPLE** During the summer, Caroline enjoys (lying/laying) on the beach.

(1) One day, after (setting/sitting) her chair on the sand, Caroline (lay/laid) her blanket near her umbrella. (2) Worried about getting a sunburn, she (raised/rose) her umbrella and (lay/laid) under it. (3) After a brief nap, Caroline began (rising/raising) to her feet when she realized she had forgotten where she had (lain/laid) her cooler. (4) She soon found it (lying/laying) near her car, just where she had (sat/set) it earlier. (5) She decided to pick it up and (lie/lay) it down near where her blanket (lies/lays).

## VERB TENSE

# 15g   What is verb tense?

**Verb tense** conveys time. Verbs show tense (time) by changing form. English has six verb tenses, divided into simple and perfect groups. The three **simple tenses** divide time into present, past, and future. The simple **present tense** describes what happens regularly, what takes place in the present, and what is consistently or generally true. The simple **past tense** tells of an action completed or a condition ended. The simple **future tense** indicates action yet to be taken or a condition not yet experienced.

Rick **wants** to speak Spanish fluently. [simple present tense]

Rick **wanted** to improve rapidly. [simple past tense]

Rick **will want** to progress even further next year. [simple future tense]

The three **perfect tenses** also divide time into present, past, and future. They show more complex time relationships than the simple tenses. For information on using the perfect tenses, see section 15i.

The three simple tenses and the three perfect tenses also have **progressive forms**. These forms indicate that the verb describes what is ongoing or continuing. For information on using progressive forms, see section 9j. Quick Reference 15.9 summarizes verb tenses and progressive forms.

need many examples and much practice to grasp the confusing labels. For example: *I work in an office.* [simple present tense]; *I am working on a report.* [present progressive]

### ANSWERS: EXERCISE 15-5

**1.** setting, laid [past tense of *lay*]
**2.** raised, lay [past tense of *lie*]
**3.** rising, laid [past tense of *lay*]
**4.** lying [present participle of *lie*], set
**5.** lay [simple form of *lay*], lies [-s form of *lie*]

### EXTRA EXERCISE E
Circle the verbs in the following sentences; then, name their tenses and explain what meaning is expressed.

**1.** Dolphins, porpoises, and whales belong to the order *Cetacea*, which means that they are not fish but mammals.

**2.** They give birth to their young, nourish them with milk, and are warm-blooded.

**3.** Once whales probably lived on the land and walked on four legs, but now they are completely aquatic.

**4.** After they had left the land and had moved to the water, their body structure changed radically.

**5.** Because they are land mammals that have become adapted to an aquatic existence, if water enters their lungs, they will die.

**6.** Consequently, when a whale is diving beneath the surface, it literally holds its breath by closing its nostrils.

**7.** Whales dive for different periods of time to various depths.

**8.** The humpback whale has been known to remain submerged for twenty minutes and the blue whale for fifty, though both could probably remain longer if necessary.

**9.** For years, scientists have been researching the depths to which the various types of whale can dive.

**10.** The sperm whale has been known to dive to a depth of over 3,000 feet, which subjects it to a pressure of around 1,400 pounds per square inch.

**Answers to Extra Exercise E**

**1.** belong; means; are [all present tense; express general truths]

**2.** give; nourish; are [all present tense; express general truths]

**3.** lived; walked [both past tense; express past events]; are [present tense; expresses current fact]

**4.** had left; had moved [both past perfect tense; express an act completed in the past before another one took place]; changed [past tense; expresses an act completed in the past]

**5.** are [present tense; expresses current truth]; have become adapted [present perfect tense; act begun and completed in the past but continuing into the present]; enters [present tense; expresses general truth]; will die [future tense; expresses future action]

**6.** is diving [present progressive tense; expresses an action taking place at the moment]; holds [present tense; expresses regularly occurring action]

**7.** dive [present tense; expresses habitual action]

**8.** has been known [present perfect tense; expresses action in the past that continues into the present]; could remain [present tense with modal auxiliary; expresses possible action]

**9.** have been researching [present perfect progressive; expresses action ongoing in the past and likely to continue into the future]; can dive [present tense with modal auxiliary; expresses possible action]

**10.** has been known [present perfect tense; expresses action in the past that continues into the present]

**EXTRA EXERCISE F**

Identify the tenses of the verbs in the following sentences.

**1.** My neighbor walks to work every morning.

**2.** Jill is studying for her math test.

**3.** I will take my lunch with me to the park.

---

## Quick Reference 15.9

### Simple, perfect, and progressive tenses

**SIMPLE TENSES**

|  | Regular Verb | Irregular Verb | Progressive Form |
|---|---|---|---|
| **PRESENT** | I talk | I eat | I am talking; I am eating |
| **PAST** | I talked | I ate | I was talking; I was eating |
| **FUTURE** | I will talk | I will eat | I will be talking; I will be eating |

**PERFECT TENSES**

|  | Regular Verb | Irregular Verb | Progressive Form |
|---|---|---|---|
| **PRESENT PERFECT** | I have talked | I have eaten | I have been talking; I have been eating |
| **PAST PERFECT** | I had talked | I had eaten | I had been talking; I had been eating |
| **FUTURE PERFECT** | I will have talked | I will have eaten | I will have been talking; I will have been eating |

**ESOL Tip:** Quick Reference 15.9 shows that most verb tenses are formed by combining one or more AUXILIARY VERBS with the SIMPLE FORM, the PRESENT PARTICIPLE, or the PAST PARTICIPLE of a MAIN VERB. Auxiliary verbs are necessary in the formation of most tenses, so never omit them.

> **NO** I **talking** to you.
>
> **YES** I **am talking** to you. ●

## 15h How do I use the simple present tense?

The **simple present tense** uses the SIMPLE FORM of the verb (15b). It describes what happens regularly, what takes place in the present, and what is generally or consistently true. Also, it can convey a future occurrence with verbs like *start, stop, begin, end, arrive,* and *depart*.

> Calculus class **meets** every morning. [regularly occurring action]
>
> Mastering calculus **takes** time. [general truth]
>
> The course **ends** in eight weeks. [specific future event]

**!Alert:** For a work of literature, always describe or discuss the action in the present tense. This holds true no matter how old the work.

In Shakespeare's *Romeo and Juliet,* Juliet's father **wants** her to marry Paris, but Juliet **loves** Romeo. ●

## 15i How do I form and use the perfect tenses?

The **perfect tenses** generally describe actions or occurrences that are still having an effect at the present time or are having an effect until a specified time. The perfect tenses are composed of an AUXILIARY VERB and a main verb's PAST PARTICIPLE (15b).

For the **present perfect tense** (see Quick Reference 15.9), use *has* only for the third-person singular subjects and *have* for all other subjects. For the **past perfect**, use *had* with the past participle. For the **future perfect**, use *will have* with the past participle.

| | |
|---|---|
| **PRESENT PERFECT** | Our government **has offered** to help. [having effect now] |
| **PRESENT PERFECT** | The drought **has created** terrible hardship. [having effect until a specified time—when the rains come] |
| **PAST PERFECT** | As soon as the tornado **had passed,** the heavy rain started. [Both events occurred in the past; the tornado occurred before the rain, so the earlier event uses *had.*] |
| **FUTURE PERFECT** | Our chickens' egg production **will have reached** five hundred per day by next year. [The event will occur before a specified time.] |

## 15j How do I form and use progressive forms?

**Progressive forms** describe an ongoing event, action, or condition. They also express habitual or recurring actions or conditions. The **present progressive** uses the present-tense form of *be* that agrees with the subject in PERSON and NUMBER, plus the *-ing* form (PRESENT PARTICIPLE) of the main verb. The **past progressive** uses *was* or *were* to agree with the subject in person and number, and it uses the present participle of the main verb. The **future progressive** uses *will be* and the present participle. The **present perfect progressive** uses *have been* or *has been* to agree with the subject, plus the *-ing* form of the main verb. The **past perfect progressive** uses *had been* and the *-ing* form of the main verb. The **future perfect progressive** uses *will have been* plus the PRESENT PARTICIPLE.

**4.** The secretary has been typing the manuscript for days.

**5.** Her mother will be speaking with the supervisor in the morning.

**6.** Ms. Conrad had been planning to change jobs when she sold her company.

**7.** I closed my bank account yesterday.

**8.** We will have discussed the topic by the time you get to the meeting.

**9.** The program has generated little interest among the attendees.

**10.** The babies in the nursery were crying when I went in.

### Answers to Extra Exercise F

1. present
2. present progressive
3. future
4. present perfect progressive
5. future progressive
6. past perfect progressive; past
7. past
8. future perfect; present
9. present perfect
10. past progressive; past

### BACKGROUND

Mood in verb inflection is the form of a verb that indicates its manner of doing or being. In English, the forms are called *indicative* (for direct statement or question, or to express an uncertain condition), *imperative* (for commands), and *subjunctive* (for sentences suggesting doubt, condition, or a situation contrary to fact). The infinitive is sometimes considered an example of mood, as are phrases formed with *may, might, can, could, should, would, must,* and *ought.*
—<http://www.Encyclopedia.com>

### QUOTATION: ON WRITING

If it were not for the subjunctive, we would be less able to express desire, supposition, doubt; more important, we would find it hard to set up a situation contrary to fact—a shocker, something ridiculous—to see how we would deal with it.

—William Safire

## ANSWERS: EXERCISE 15–6

**1.** are ruining [15j, present progressive for on-going event]

**2.** typify [15h, simple present for general truth]

**3.** describe [15h, simple present for general truth]

**4.** live [15h, simple present for general truth]

**5.** are planting [15j, present progressive for on-going event]

**6.** founded [15g, past tense for completed action]; was [15g, past tense for completed action]

**7.** chose [15g, past tense for completed action]; wanted [15g, past tense for completed action]

**8.** contends [15h, simple present for general truth]; fills [15h, simple present for general truth]

**9.** indicates [15h, simple present for general truth]

**10.** has provided [15i, present perfect for condition still prevailing]

**11.** is [15h, simple present for general truth]; has encountered [15i, present perfect for condition still prevailing]

**12.** reveals [15h, simple present for general truth]; has [15h, simple present for general truth]; holds [15h, simple present for general truth]

**13.** remains [15h, simple present for general truth] or has remained [15i, present perfect for condition still prevailing]

**14.** says [15h, simple present for general truth]; wonders [15h, simple present for general truth]; motivates [15h, simple present for general truth]

**15.** exclaims [15h, simple present for general truth]; make [15h, simple present for general truth]

## OTHER EXAMPLES OF SUBJUNCTIVE MOOD

People find it interesting to speculate about how the future *could be* affected if a single aspect of our world *were* different today. For example, if the average yearly temperature *were* only a few degrees higher, the oceans *would rise* because of

| | |
|---|---|
| PRESENT PROGRESSIVE | The smog **is stinging** everyone's eyes. [event taking place now] |
| PAST PROGRESSIVE | Eye drops **were selling** well last week. [event ongoing in the past within stated limits] |
| FUTURE PROGRESSIVE | We **will be ordering** more eye drops than usual this month. [recurring event that will take place in the future] |
| PRESENT PERFECT PROGRESSIVE | Scientists **have been warning** us about air pollution for years. [recurring event that took place in the past and may still take place] |
| PAST PERFECT PROGRESSIVE | We **had been ordering** three cases of eye drops a month until the smog worsened. [recurring past event that has now ended] |
| FUTURE PERFECT PROGRESSIVE | By May, we **will have been selling** eye drops for eight months. [ongoing condition to be completed at a specific time in the future] |

● **EXERCISE 15-6** Underline the correct verb in each pair of parentheses. If more than one answer is possible, be prepared to explain the differences in meaning between the two choices. For help, consult 15g through 15j.

**EXAMPLE** According to an article in *National Geographic News*, weird plants (are taking root, would have taken root) in ordinary backyards.

1. Some, smelling like spoiled meat, (will have ruined, are ruining) people's appetites.

2. Stalks similar to male anatomy (typify, are typifying) other examples.

3. *Shockingly large, black, carnivorous*, and *volatile* (describe, is describing) additional unusual plants.

4. Indeed, many unusual plants (live, lived) in places the world over today.

5. Many people now (are planting, planted) these weird items in their backyards.

6. In 1999, in East Lothian, Scotland, Diane Halligan (founded, had founded) The Weird and Wonderful Plant Company because she (was, is) disappointed with the plant selection at her local garden centers.

7. Halligan (chose, is choosing) to open an extraordinary plant store because she (wanted, is wanting) to provide a source of unusual plants for others as well as herself.

8. Marty Harper in Staunton, Virginia, like Halligan in Scotland, (contends, are contending) that his company (fills, would have filled) a niche for himself and others.

9. Harper, after much study on the subject of strange plants, (is indicating, indicates) that Madagascar holds the record for the most weird plants on the planet.

10. Isolated from the rest of the world, Madagascar (has provided, will have provided) a haven for unusual plants to develop undisturbed.

11. *Rafflesia arnoldii* (is, are) the oddest plant Harper (has encountered, will have encountered).

12. Harper, in an interview with *National Geographic*'s John Roach, (reveals, is revealing) that *Rafflesia arnoldii,* a parasitic plant, (has, have) the world's largest bloom, stinks, and (held, holds) in its center six or seven quarts of water.

13. According to Harper, procreation (remains, has remained) the primary reason for the development of the ostensibly outlandish shapes, sizes, odors, and actions of these unusual plants the world over.

14. Douglas Justice, another weird-plant aficionado like Halligan and Harper, (says, is saying) he (wonders, is wondering) what (motivates, motivated) people to choose the odd plants.

15. Harper, however, (exclaims, is exclaiming), "Such plants (make, were making) me smile."

# 15k How do I use tense sequences accurately?

Verb **tense sequences** communicate time relationships. They help deliver messages about actions, occurrences, or states that take place at different times. Quick Reference 15.10 shows how tenses in the same sentence can vary depending on the timing of actions (or occurrences or states).

## Quick Reference 15.10

### Tense sequences

If your independent clause contains a simple-present-tense verb, then in your dependent clause you can

- use PRESENT TENSE to show same-time action:

    I **avoid** shellfish because I **am** allergic to it.

- use PAST TENSE to show earlier action:

    I **am** sure that I **deposited** the check.

- use the PRESENT PERFECT TENSE to show (1) a period of time extending from some point in the past to the present or (2) an indefinite past time:

    They **claim** that they **have visited** the planet Venus.

    I **believe** that I **have seen** that movie before.

continued >>

the melting of the polar icecaps. If serious worldwide droughts *were* to occur in several successive summers, the food supply *would dwindle.* Unless science *were* able to divert the swelling oceans or grow crops without the use of water, civilization as we know it *would be* radically *changed.* It is, consequently, important that everyone *recognize* the importance of environmental decisions. The world *should* not *act* as though the future *were* inevitably bad. If, in the early part of the twentieth century, the industrialized world *had considered* the effects of water and air pollution, our world *would be* a healthier one today.

**TEACHING TIP: ESOL**

For ESOL students, conditions and wishes are often difficult to master because to indicate hypothetical or unreal states requires changes in verb forms that usually indicate *time* shifts. For example, the form for a wish or an unreal condition in the present (*I wish I **had** a car* or *If I **were** you . . .*) uses the *past* form of the verb. Similarly, unreality in the past calls for the *past perfect* form (*I wish he **had told** me his problem*). Students can better understand these tricky structures when they can be seen and analyzed, preferably in essays the class is reading.

**QUOTATION: ON WRITING**

Verbs are the most important of all your tools. They push the sentence forward and give it momentum. Active verbs push hard; passive verbs tug fitfully.

—William Zinsser, *On Writing Well*

**QUOTATION: ON WRITING**

Use direct rather than indirect statements, the active rather than the passive voice, and make every sentence an organic whole.

—Samuel Eliot Morison

**ANOTHER EXAMPLE: NECESSARY PASSIVE VOICE**

In the days of Aristotle, air was believed to be one of four fundamental substances that could not be further subdivided into constituent components.

—Frederick K. Lutgens
and Edward J. Tarbuck, *The Atmosphere*

## EXTRA EXERCISE G

Identify each verb in the following sentences; then decide if it is in the active or the passive voice.

**1.** Windsor Castle is an official residence of the monarchs of Great Britain.

**2.** In the year 1070, William the Conqueror built a fortress on the site it now occupies.

**3.** It was improved by succeeding rulers until the reign of Edward III (1327–1377).

**4.** Edward III demolished the old castle and built a new one.

**5.** Additions were made by later kings of England.

**6.** Sir Christopher Wren was asked by Charles II to design several important additions.

**7.** The state apartments are open to the public when the royal family is not in residence.

**8.** The state apartments include the grand staircase, state bedrooms, and reception rooms.

**9.** Many rulers were buried at Windsor Castle, including Henry VIII.

### Answers to Extra Exercise G

**1.** is (active)

**2.** built (active); occupies (active)

**3.** was improved (passive)

**4.** demolished (active); built (active)

**5.** were made (passive)

**6.** was asked (passive)

**7.** are (active); is (active)

**8.** include (active)

**9.** were buried (passive)

## BACKGROUND

Using passive verbs does not usually create sharp prose. *Nominalization,* the grammatical process of transforming verbs and adjectives into nouns, is another dulling grammatical choice. In *Style:*

---

**Quick Reference 15.10**     (continued)

- use the FUTURE TENSE for action to come:

  The book **is** open because I **will be reading** it later.

If your independent clause contains a past-tense verb, then in your dependent clause you can

- use the past tense to show another completed past action:

  I **closed** the door because you **told** me to.

- use the PAST PERFECT TENSE to show earlier action:

  The sprinter **knew** that she **had broken** the record.

- use the present tense to state a general truth:

  Christopher Columbus **determined** that the world **is** round.

If your independent clause contains a present-perfect-tense or past-perfect-tense verb, then in your dependent clause you can

- use the past tense:

  The bread **has become** moldy since I **purchased** it.

  Sugar prices **had** already **declined** when artificial sweeteners first appeared.

If your independent clause contains a future-tense verb, then in your dependent clause you can

- use the present tense to show action happening at the same time:

  You **will be** rich if you **win** the prize.

- use the past tense to show earlier action:

  You **will** surely **win** the prize if you **remembered** to mail the entry form.

### TENSE SEQUENCES

- use the present perfect tense to show future action earlier than the action of the independent-clause verb:

  The river **will flood** again next year unless we **have built** a better dam by then.

If your independent clause contains a future-perfect-tense verb, then in your dependent clause you can

- use either the present tense or the present perfect tense:

  Dr. Chang **will have delivered** five thousand babies by the time she **retires**.

  Dr. Chang **will have delivered** five thousand babies by the time she **has retired**.

**Alert:** Never use a future-tense verb in a dependent clause when the verb in the independent clause is in the future tense. Instead, use a present-tense verb or present-perfect-tense verb in the dependent clause.

> **NO**   The river **will flood** us unless we **will prepare** our defense.
>
> **YES**   The river **will flood** us unless we **prepare** our defense. [*Prepare is a present-tense verb.*]
>
> **YES**   The river **will flood** us unless we **have prepared** our defense. [*Have prepared is a present-perfect-tense verb.*]●

Tense sequences may include INFINITIVES and PARTICIPLES. To name or describe an activity or occurrence coming either at the same time as the time expressed in the MAIN VERB or after, use the **present infinitive**.

> I **hope to buy** a used car. [*To buy comes at a future time. Hope is the main verb, and its action is now.*]
>
> I **hoped to buy** a used car. [*Hoped is the main verb, and its action is over.*]
>
> I **had hoped to buy** a used car. [*Had hoped is the main verb, and its action is over.*]

The PRESENT PARTICIPLE (a verb's *-ing* form) can describe action happening at the same time.

> **Driving** his new car, the man **smiled.** [*The driving and the smiling happened at the same time.*]

To describe an action that occurs before the action in the main verb, use the **perfect infinitive** (*to have gone, to have smiled*), the PAST PARTICIPLE, or the **present perfect participle** (*having gone, having smiled*).

> Candida **claimed to have written** fifty short stories in college. [*Claimed is the main verb, and to have written happened first.*]
>
> **Pleased** with the short story, Candida **mailed** it to several magazines. [*Mailed is the main verb, and pleased happened first.*]
>
> **Having sold** one short story, Candida **invested** in a computer. [*Invested is the main verb, and having sold happened first.*]

**EXERCISE 15-7**   Underline the correct verb in each pair of parentheses that best suits the sequence of tenses. Be ready to explain your choices. For help, consult 15k.

**EXAMPLE**   When he (is, was) seven years old, Yo-Yo Ma, possibly the world's greatest living cellist, (moves, moved) to the United States with his family.

*Toward Clarity and Grace,* Joseph Williams warns writers to avoid nominalizing verbs. Here are a few examples. *Dull:* We conducted an investigation of the accident. *Sharper:* We investigated the accident. *Dull:* The class held a discussion about crime prevention. *Sharper:* The class discussed crime prevention. *Dull:* The college students have no expectation of getting great coffee from the school cafeteria. *Sharper:* The college students don't expect to get great coffee from the school cafeteria.

**ANSWERS: EXERCISE 15–7**

**1.** was born [dependent clause in past tense for completed action]; lives [independent clause in present tense for current action]; tours [present tense for regularly occurring action]

**2.** will treasure [independent clause in future tense for situation continuing beyond action of dependent clause]

**3.** began [dependent clause in past tense]

**4.** became [dependent clause in simple past for a completed action]; plays [independent clause in simple present for regularly occurring action]

**5.** continues [independent clause in simple present]; take [dependent clause in simple present for same-time action]

**6.** know [dependent clause in simple present for general truth]; has made [independent clause in present perfect for action completed but condition still in effect]

**7.** was traveling [dependent clause in past progressive for ongoing action completed in the past]; filmed [independent clause in simple past for action completed in the past]

**8.** became; studied [independent and dependent clauses in simple past for actions completed in the past]

**9.** fell asleep; was [dependent clauses in simple past for completed past action]

**10.** failed [dependent clause in simple past for completed past action]

1. Yo-Yo Ma, who (had been born, was born) in France to Chinese parents, (lived, lives) in Boston, Massachusetts, today and (toured, tours) as one of the world's greatest cellists.

2. Years from now, after Mr. Ma has given his last concert, music lovers still (treasure, will treasure) his many fine recordings.

3. Mr. Ma's older sister, Dr. Yeou-Cheng Ma, was nearly the person with the concert career. She had been training to become a concert violinist when her brother's musical genius (began, had begun) to be noticed.

4. Even though Dr. Ma eventually (becomes, became) a physician, she still (had been playing, plays) the violin.

5. The family interest in music (continues, was continuing), for Mr. Ma's children (take, had taken) piano lessons.

6. Although most people today (knew, know) Mr. Ma as a brilliant cellist, he (was making, has made) films as well.

7. One year, while he (had been traveling, was traveling) in the Kalahari Desert, he (films, filmed) dances of southern Africa's Bush people.

8. Mr. Ma first (becomes, became) interested in the Kalahari people when he (had studied, studied) anthropology as an undergraduate at Harvard University.

9. When he shows visitors around Boston now, Mr. Ma has been known to point out the Harvard University library where, he claims, he (fell asleep, was falling asleep) in the stacks when he (had been, was) a student.

10. Indicating another building, Mr. Ma admits that in one of its classrooms he almost (failed, had failed) German.

## MOOD

# 151 What is "mood" in verbs?

**Mood** in verbs conveys an attitude toward the action in a sentence. English has three moods: *indicative, imperative,* and *subjunctive.* Use the **indicative mood** to make statements about real things, about highly likely things, and for questions about fact.

INDICATIVE   The door to the tutoring center opened. [real]

She seemed to be looking for someone. [highly likely]

Do you want to see a tutor? [question about a fact]

The **imperative mood** expresses commands and direct requests. Often, the subject is omitted in an imperative sentence, but nevertheless the subject is implied to be either *you* or one of the indefinite pronouns such as *anybody, somebody,* or *everybody.*

**Alert:** Use an exclamation point after a strong command; use a period after a mild command or a request (23e, 23a). ●

IMPERATIVE     Please shut the door.

Watch out! That screw is loose.

The **subjunctive mood** expresses speculation, other unreal conditions, conjectures, wishes, recommendations, indirect requests, and demands. Often, the words that signal the subjunctive mood are *if, as if, as though,* and *unless.* In speaking, subjunctive verb forms were once used frequently in English, but they're heard far less today. Nevertheless, in ACADEMIC WRITING, you need to use the subjunctive mood.

SUBJUNCTIVE     If I **were** you, I would ask for a tutor.

## 15m   What are subjunctive forms?

For the **present subjunctive**, always use the SIMPLE FORM of the verb for all PERSONS and NUMBERS.

The prosecutor asks that she **testify** [not *testifies*] again.

It is important that they **be** [not *are*] allowed to testify.

For the **past subjunctive**, use the simple past tense: *I wish that I **had** a car.* The one exception is for the past subjunctive of *be:* Use *were* for all forms.

I wish that I **were** [not *was*] leaving on vacation today.

They asked if she **were** [not *was*] leaving on vacation today.

### USING THE SUBJUNCTIVE IN *IF, AS IF, AS THOUGH,* AND *UNLESS* CLAUSES

In dependent clauses introduced by *if, as if, as though,* and sometimes *unless,* the subjunctive describes speculations or conditions contrary to fact.

If it **were** [not *was*] to rain, attendance at the race would be disappointing. [speculation]

The runner looked as if he **were** [not *was*] winded, but he said he wasn't. [a condition contrary to fact]

In an *unless* clause, the subjunctive signals that what the clause says is highly unlikely.

Unless rain **were** [not *was*] to create floods, the race will be held this Sunday. [Floods are highly unlikely.]

Not every clause introduced by *if, unless, as if, or as though* requires the subjunctive. Use the subjunctive only when the dependent clause describes speculation or a condition contrary to fact.

INDICATIVE  If she **is** going to leave late, I will drive her to the race. [Her leaving late is highly likely.]

SUBJUNCTIVE  If she **were** going to leave late, I would drive her to the race. [Her leaving late is a speculation.]

## USING THE SUBJUNCTIVE IN *THAT* CLAUSES

When *that* clauses describe wishes, requests, demands, or recommendations, the subjunctive can convey the message.

I wish that this race **were** [not *was*] over. [a wish about something happening now]

He wishes that he **had seen** [not *saw*] the race. [a wish about something that is past]

The judges are demanding that the doctor **examine** [not *examines*] the runners. [a demand for something to happen in the future]

Also, MODAL AUXILIARY VERBS *would, could, might,* and *should* can convey speculations and conditions contrary to fact.

If the runner **were** [not *was*] faster, we **would** see a better race. [*Would* is a modal auxiliary verb.]

The issue here is that when an INDEPENDENT CLAUSE expresses a conditional statement using a modal auxiliary verb, you want to be sure that in the DEPENDENT CLAUSE you don't use another modal auxiliary verb.

NO  If I **would have trained** for the race, I **might have** won.

YES  If I **had trained** for the race, I **might have** won.

**ANSWERS: EXERCISE 15–8**

**1.** were

**2.** were

**3.** suspend; be

**4.** be

**5.** continue; were

**EXERCISE 15-8**  Fill in each blank with the correct form of the verb given in parentheses. For help, consult 15l and 15m.

EXAMPLE  Imagining the possibility of brain transplants requires that we (to be) be open-minded.

(1) If almost any organ other than the brain (to be) _____ the candidate for a swap, we would probably give our consent. (2) If the brain (to be) _____ to hold whatever impulses form our personalities, few people would want to risk a transplant. (3) Many popular movies have asked that we (to suspend) _____ disbelief and imagine the consequences should a

personality actually (to be) _____ transferred to another body. (4) In real life, however, the complexities of a successful brain transplant require that not-yet-developed surgical techniques (to be) _____ used. (5) For example, it would be essential that during the actual transplant each one of the 500 trillion nerve connections within the brain (to continue) _____ to function as though the brain (to be) _____ lying undisturbed in a living human body.

## VOICE

## 15n What is "voice" in verbs?

**Voice** in a verb tells whether a SUBJECT acts or is acted upon. English has two voices, *active* and *passive*. A subject in the **active voice** performs the action.

> Most clams **live** in salt water. [The subject *clams* does the acting: Clams *live*.]
>
> They **burrow** into the sandy bottoms of shallow waters. [The subject *they* does the acting: They *burrow*.]

A subject in the **passive voice** is acted upon. The person or thing doing the acting often appears in a PHRASE that starts with *by*. Verbs in the passive voice use forms of *be, have,* and *will* as AUXILIARY VERBS with the PAST PARTICIPLE of the MAIN VERB.

> Clams **are considered** a delicacy by many people. [The subject *clams* is acted upon *by many people*.]
>
> Some types of clams **are** highly **valued** by seashell collectors. [The subject *types* is acted upon *by seashell collectors*.]

## 15o How do I write in the active, not passive, voice?

Because the ACTIVE VOICE emphasizes the doer of an action, active constructions are more direct and dramatic. Active constructions usually require fewer words than passive constructions, which makes for greater conciseness (11c). Most sentences in the PASSIVE VOICE can be converted to active voice.

> PASSIVE   African tribal masks are often imitated by Western sculptors.
>
> ACTIVE   Western sculptors often imitate African tribal masks.

## 15p What are proper uses of the passive voice?

Although the active voice is usually best, in special circumstances you need to use the passive voice.

When no one knows who or what did something or when the doer of an action isn't important, writers use the passive voice.

The lock **was broken** sometime after four o'clock. [Who broke the lock is unknown.]

In 1899, the year I was born, a peace conference **was held** at The Hague. [The doers of the action—holders of the conference—aren't important.]

—E. B. White, "Unity"

Sometimes the action in the sentence is more important than the doer of the action. For example, if you want to focus on historical discoveries in a narrative, use the passive voice. Conversely, if you want to emphasize the people making the discoveries, use the active voice.

ACTIVE    Joseph Priestley **discovered** oxygen in 1774. [*Joseph Priestley* is the subject.]

PASSIVE    Oxygen **was discovered** in 1774 by Joseph Priestley. [*Oxygen* is the subject.]

ACTIVE    The postal clerk **sent** the unsigned letter before I **could retrieve** it from the mailroom. [The emphasis is on the doers of the action, *the postal clerk* and *I*, rather than on the events, *sent* and *could retrieve.*]

PASSIVE    The unsigned letter **was sent** before it **could be retrieved** from the postal clerk. [The emphasis is on the events, *was sent* and *could be retrieved,* not on the doers of the action, the unknown sender and *the postal clerk.*]

In former years, the social sciences and natural sciences preferred the passive voice. Recently, style manuals for these disciplines have been advising writers to use the active voice whenever possible. "Verbs are vigorous, direct communicators," point out the editors of the *Publication Manual of the American Psychological Association.* "Use the active rather than the passive voice," they say.*

## ANSWERS: EXERCISE 15–9

Rewrites may vary somewhat from the possibilities shown here. Coverage is three passive to active sentences; two active to passive sentences.

**1.** *Passive, change to active:* A farmer chose a coffin in the shape of a green onion.

**2.** *Active, change to passive:* A hunter was buried by his family in a wooden coffin shaped like a leopard.

**EXERCISE 15-9**    First, determine which sentences are in the active voice and which the passive voice. Second, rewrite each sentence in the other voice, and then decide which voice better suits the meaning. Be ready to explain your choice. For help, consult 15n through 15p.

EXAMPLE    In the West African country of Ghana, a few woodcarvers are creating coffins that reflect their occupants' special interests. (*active; change to passive*)

*American Psychological Association, *Publication Manual of the American Psychological Association,* 5th ed. (Washington: APA, 2001) 41.

In the West African country of Ghana, *coffins that reflect their occupants' special interests are being created by a few woodcarvers.*

1. A coffin in the shape of a green onion was chosen by a farmer.
2. A hunter's family buried him in a wooden coffin shaped like a leopard.
3. A dead chief was carried through his fishing village by friends and relatives bearing his body in a large pink wooden replica of a fish.
4. The family of a wealthy man who greatly admired cars buried him in a coffin shaped like a Mercedes car.
5. Although a few of these fantasy coffins have been displayed in museums, most of them end up buried in the ground.

For more help with your writing, grammar, and research, go to **www.mycomplab.com**

3. *Passive, change to active:* The friends and relatives of a dead chief carried his body through his fishing village in a large pink wooden replica of a fish.

4. *Active, change to passive:* A wealthy man who greatly admired cars was buried by his family in a coffin shaped like a Mercedes car.

5. *Passive, change to active:* Museums have displayed a few of these fantasy coffins, although most of them end up buried in the ground.

# 16

# Pronouns: Case and Reference

## PRONOUN CASE

## 16a What does "case" mean?

**Case** applies in different ways to PRONOUNS and to NOUNS. For pronouns, case refers to three pronoun forms: the **subjective** (pronoun as a SUBJECT), the **objective** (pronoun as an OBJECT), and the **possessive** (pronouns used in possessive constructions). For nouns, case refers to only one noun form: the possessive. (For help in using apostrophes in the possessive case, see Chapter 27.)

## 16b What are personal pronouns?

**Personal pronouns** refer to persons or things. Quick Reference 16.1 shows the case forms of personal pronouns (subjective, objective, and possessive), in both the singular and the plural.

**QUOTATION: ON WRITING**
A sentence is more than its subject, verb, and object. It is more than the sum of its words and parts. It is a system of systems whose parts we can fit together in very delicate ways to achieve very delicate ends—if we know how.

—Joseph M. Williams,
*Style: Toward Clarity and Grace*

**LANGUAGE FACTS**
Many languages have noun and/or pronoun case systems. The smallest number of cases is two, as in the language of the Masai people in East Africa. In contrast, Sanskrit has eight cases, Latin has six, and Greek has five. The prize, however, goes to Finnish, which has fifteen noun cases.

**LANGUAGE HISTORY**
The pronoun *you* indicates little more than that the second person is being used. Unlike the first- and third-person personal pronouns, it tells the reader nothing about gender or number. Until the thirteenth century, however, *th-* forms, such as *thee, thy,* and *thou,* indicated use of the singular, and *y-* forms, such as *ye, you,* and *your,* indicated the plural. Later, the *th-*

forms came to suggest a close relationship between the speaker and listener, the *y-* forms to suggest a formal one. Today, the pronouns *thou* and *thee* linger only among some religious sects.

**TEACHING TIP**

If your classes include students who know other languages, they may enjoy explaining the noun and pronoun case systems of those other tongues to the native English speakers in the class. Their examples will demonstrate that case is not nearly as important an aspect of English as it often is in other languages.

**TEACHING TIP**

English once distinguished between the personal and impersonal relationships in the second-person pronoun *you.* Some modern languages continue to do so. French, for example, makes a distinction between *tu* and *vous;* Spanish does so between *tu* (singular), *vosotros* (plural), informally, and *usted* (singular), *ustedes* (plural), formally. You might wish to have your bilingual students explain the difference in such forms.

**LANGUAGE HISTORY**

Changes in the second-person singular pronouns (subjective and objective cases) are rooted in the Roman Empire of the fourth century. At that time, there were two emperors, one in Rome and one in Constantinople. People speaking to either emperor were required to use the plural form of address. The practice of using the plural as a sign of respect slowly spread to France, where *tu* is the second-person singular pronoun (*toi* in the objective case) and *vous* the plural. During the thirteenth century, in imitation of the French nobles who occupied their country, the English began using *thou* (*thee* in the objective case) and *you* the same way. *You* became a mark of mutual respect in conversations among the elite and a sign of deference when a person spoke to a social superior. In contrast, *thou* became a sign of intimacy among members of the same family or among those who believed in the same things.

Many of the most difficult questions about pronoun case concern *who/whom* and *whoever/whomever.* For a full discussion of how to choose between them, see 16g.

**Quick Reference 16.1**

**Case forms of personal pronouns**

| | Subjective | Objective | Possessive |
|---|---|---|---|
| SINGULAR | I, you, he, she, it | me, you, him, her, it | my, mine, your, yours, his, her, hers, its |
| PLURAL | we, you, they | us, you, them | our, ours, your, yours, their, theirs |

## 16c  How do pronouns work in case?

In the subjective case, pronouns function as SUBJECTS.

**We** were going to get married. [*We* is the subject.]

John and **I** wanted an inexpensive band for our wedding. [*I* is part of the compound subject *John and I.*]

**He and I** found an affordable one-person band. [*He and I* is the compound subject.]

In the objective case, pronouns function as OBJECTS.

We saw **him** perform in a public park. [*Him* is the direct object.]

We showed **him** our budget. [*Him* is the indirect object.]

He wrote down what we wanted and shook hands with **us**. [*Us* is the object of the preposition *with.*]

In the possessive case, nouns and pronouns usually indicate ownership or imply a relationship.

The **musician's contract** was very fair. [The possessive noun *musician's* implies a type of ownership.]

**His contract** was very fair. [The possessive pronoun *his* implies a type of ownership.]

The **musicians' problems** stem from playing cheap instruments. [The possessive noun *musicians'* implies a type of relationship.]

**Their problems** stem from playing with cheap instruments. [The possessive pronoun *their* implies a type of relationship.]

Sometimes, however, the notion of ownership or relationship calls for a major stretch of the imagination in possessive constructions. In such cases, look for the following pattern: noun + the *s* sound + noun. This means that two nouns work together, one of which does the possessing and the other of which is possessed.

The **musician's arrival** was eagerly anticipated. [The musician neither owns the arrival nor has a relationship with the arrival. Instead, the pattern noun + the *s* sound + noun is operating.]

🛑 Alert: Never use an apostrophe in personal pronouns: *ours, yours, its, his, hers, theirs* (27c). ●

## 16d  Which case is correct when *and* connects pronouns?

When *and* connects pronouns, or nouns and pronouns, the result is a **compound construction**. Compounding, which means "putting parts together in a whole," has no effect on case. Always use pronouns in the subjective case when they serve as the subjects of a sentence; also, always use pronouns in the objective case when they serve as objects in a sentence. Never mix cases.

| | |
|---|---|
| COMPOUND PRONOUN SUBJECT | **He and I** saw the solar eclipse. [*He and I* is a compound subject.] |
| COMPOUND PRONOUN OBJECT | That eclipse astonished **him and me**. [*Him and me* is a compound object.] |

When you're unsure of the case of a pronoun, use the "Troyka test for case" in Quick Reference 16.2. In this four-step test, you drop some of the words from your sentence so that you can tell which case sounds correct.

When pronouns are in a PREPOSITIONAL PHRASE, they are always in the objective case. (That is, a pronoun is always the OBJECT of the preposition.) This rule holds whether the pronouns are singular or plural.

---

### Quick Reference 16.2    ■ ■ ■ ■ ■ ■

#### Troyka test for case

**SUBJECTIVE CASE**

STEP 1:  Write the sentence twice, once using the subjective case, and once using the objective case.

continued >>

---

**QUOTATION: ON WRITING**

Form the possessive singular of nouns with *'s*. Follow this rule whatever the final consonant. Thus write, Charles's friend; Burns's poems; the witch's malice.

—William Strunk Jr., *The Elements of Style*

**TEACHING TIP**

The problem of pronoun *shifts* is covered in detail in Chapter 16 of this handbook.

**QUOTATION: ON WRITING**

If you are writing in the "first person" (*I*), don't confuse your reader by switching to the "second person" (*you*) or "third person" (*he, she, they, it*, etc.). Similarly, if you are using the "second person," don't switch to "first" or "third": *When a person comes to class, he or she should have his or her homework ready.* Not: *When a person comes to class, you should have your homework ready.*

—<http://owl.english.purdue.edu/ handouts/grammar/g_pronuse.html>

**TEACHING TIP**

The "Troyka test for case" can be more effective if students are given both oral and written activities in which they are asked not only to select correct pronouns from prepared sentences but also to generate their own sentences using pronouns as parts of compounds.

**BACKGROUND**

The site <http://www.grammarlady.com> posts questions and answers on grammar. Following is a question-answer sample: *Question:* Dear Grammar Lady: Why is "*I*" a capital (ex: Jack and I went to the store.) when "*me*" is not a capital (ex: The dog belongs to Jack and me.)? *Answer:* In the early days of printing, the printers were German. Remember Gutenberg who invented the printing press? The small *i* looked like a *j* and it was feared the pronoun would be lost, so it was capitalized to make it more visible.

—<http://www.grammarlady.com>

**QUOTATION: ON WRITING**

The discipline of the writer is to learn to be still and listen to what his subject has to tell him.

—Rachel Carson

**Quick Reference 16.2** (continued)

**STEP 2:** Cross out enough words to isolate the element you are questioning.

~~Janet and~~ me

~~Janet and~~ I

learned about the moon.

**STEP 3:** Omit the crossed-out words and read each sentence aloud to determine which one sounds right.

**NO** Me learned about the moon. [This doesn't sound right.]

**YES** I learned about the moon. [This sounds right, so the subjective case is correct.]

**STEP 4:** Select the correct version and restore the words you crossed out.

**Janet and I** learned about the moon.

**OBJECTIVE CASE**

**STEP 1:** Write the sentence twice, once using the subjective case, and once using the objective case.

**STEP 2:** Cross out enough words to isolate the element you are questioning.

The astronomer taught ~~Janet and~~ I

The astronomer taught ~~Janet and~~ me

about the moon.

**STEP 3:** Omit the crossed-out words and read each sentence aloud to determine which one sounds right.

**NO** The astronomer taught I about the moon. [This doesn't sound right.]

**YES** The astronomer taught me about the moon. [This sounds right, so the objective case is correct.]

**STEP 4:** Select the correct version and restore the words you crossed out.

The astronomer taught **Janet and me** about the moon.

| NO | Ms. Lester gave an assignment *to* **Sam and I**. [The prepositional phrase, which starts with the preposition *to*, cannot use the subjective-case pronoun *I*.] |
|---|---|
| YES | Ms. Lester gave an assignment *to* **Sam and me**. [The prepositional phrase, which starts with the preposition *to*, calls for the objective-case pronoun *me*.] |

Be especially careful when one or more pronouns follow the preposition *between*.

| NO | The dispute is *between* **Thomas and I**. [The prepositional phrase, which starts with the preposition *between*, cannot use the subjective-case pronoun *I*.] |
|---|---|
| YES | The dispute is *between* **Thomas and me**. [The prepositional phrase, which starts with the preposition *between*, calls for the objective-case pronoun *me*.] |

**EXERCISE 16-1** Underline the correct pronoun of each pair in parentheses. For help, consult 16c and 16d.

EXAMPLE  Bill and (I, me) noticed two young swimmers being pulled out to sea.

(1) The two teenagers caught in the rip current waved and hollered at Bill and (I, me). (2) The harder (they, them) both swam toward shore, the further away the undercurrent pulled them from the beach. (3) The yellow banners had warned Bill and (I, me) that a dangerous rip current ran beneath the water. (4) I yelled at Bill, "Between you and (I, me), (we, us) have to save them!" (5) (He and I, Him and me) both ran and dove into the crashing waves. (6) As former lifeguards, Bill and (I, me) knew what to do. (7) (We, Us) two remembered that the rule for surviving a rip current is to swim across the current. (8) Only when swimmers are safely away from the current should (they, them) swim toward shore. (9) I reached the teenage girl, who cried, "My boyfriend and (I, me) are drowning." (10) Bill rescued the frightened teenage boy, and when they were safely on shore, the boy looked at (he and I, him and me) and gasped, "Thanks. The two of (we, us) know you saved our lives."

# 16e  How do I match cases with appositives?

You can match cases with APPOSITIVES by putting pronouns and nouns in the same case as the word or words the appositive is renaming. Whenever you're unsure about whether to use the subjective or objective case, use the "Troyka test for case" in Quick Reference 16.2 to get the answer.

they get in the way—of meaning, of style, of the natural flow of language. . . .

Whom is unnatural in everyday speech.

For whom are you looking? Well, well, whom have we here? It's not what you know but whom you know. I forgot whom I was going to see. All these constructions are right, but that is about all they have going for them.

Real English doesn't take this guff. It laughs off a stiff, labored sentence like "For whom are you looking?" and says instead, "Who're you looking for?" There is no confusion here about who is who.

—John Allemang

**BACKGROUND**
The site <http://englishplus.com/grammar/00000021.htm> offers comprehensive explanations, examples, and links on pronoun case.

**ANSWERS: EXERCISE 16–1**

1. me [16d, objective case after preposition *at*]
2. they [16c, subjective case]
3. me [16d, objective case, compound direct object]
4. me [16d, objective case after preposition *between*]; we [9c, subjective case]
5. He and I [16c and 16d, subjective case, compound subject]
6. I [16c, subjective case]
7. We [16c, subjective case]
8. they [16c, subjective case]
9. I [16c, subjective case]
10. him and me [16d, objective case after preposition *at*, compound object]; us [16d, objective case after preposition *of*]

**QUOTATION: ON LANGUAGE**
Let us resolve to follow Safire's Rule on *Who-Whom*: whenever *whom* sounds correct recast the sentence.

—William Safire

**TEACHING TIP**
If your students have trouble choosing the appropriate relative pronoun in dependent clauses,

they can do the "Troyka test for case" using these additional sentences.

### Subjective Case

**1.** I enjoy playing volleyball with anyone (who, whom) has time to play. [who]

**2.** (Whoever, whomever) wins is obligated to buy lunch for the rest. [Whoever]

**3.** I wonder (who, whom) will show up for today's game. [who]

### Objective Case

**1.** The volleyball players (who, whom) I met yesterday were too skillful for me. [whom]

**2.** I reserve the right to play with (whoever, whomever) I choose. [whomever]

**3.** The opponent (who, whom) I want is honest as well as skillful. [whom]

### EXTRA EXERCISE A

If your students have trouble choosing the appropriate pronoun in questions, you might offer them practice with these questions:

**1.** (Who, Whom) was initially responsible for the making of silk? [Who]

**2.** (Who, Whom) developed the first method of weaving silk? [Who]

**3.** In the nineteenth century, (who, whom) claimed to produce the best silk? [who]

**4.** Theories about early fabrics come from (who, whom)? [whom]

**5.** Silkworm eggs were carried out of China by (who, whom)? [whom]

**6.** The French silk industry was developed for (who, whom)? [whom]

### ANSWERS: EXERCISE 16–2

**1.** I [16c and 16d, subjective case, compound subject]; we [16c, subjective case]

**2.** We [16c, subjective case]

**3.** her and me [16c and 16d, objective case after preposition *between*]; we [16c, subjective case]

**4.** we [16c, subjective case]

**5.** she and I [16c and 16d, subjective case, compound subject]

**We** [not *Us*] tennis players practice hard. [Here, the subjective-case pronoun *we* matches the noun phrase *tennis players*, which is the subject of this sentence.]

The winners, **she and I** [not *her and me*], advanced to the finals. [The subjective-case pronoun phrase *she and I* matches the noun *winners*, which is the subject of this sentence.]

The coach tells **us** [not *we*] tennis players to practice hard. [The objective-case pronoun *us* matches the noun phrase *tennis players*, which is the object in this sentence.]

The crowd cheered the winners, **her and me** [not *she and I*]. [The objective-case pronoun phrase *her and me* matches the noun *winners*, which is the object in this sentence.]

## 16f  How does case work after linking verbs?

A pronoun that comes after a LINKING VERB either renames the SUBJECT or shows possession. In both constructions, always use a pronoun in the subjective case. If you're unsure about how to identify a pronoun's case, use the "Troyka test for case" in Quick Reference 16.2.

The contest winner was **I** [not *me*]. [*Was* is a linking verb. *I* renames the subject, which is the noun phrase *contest winner*, so the subjective-case pronoun *I* is correct.]

The prize is **mine**. [*Is* is a linking verb. *Mine* shows possession, so the possessive-case pronoun *mine* is correct.]

**EXERCISE 16-2**  Underline the correct pronoun of each pair in parentheses. For help, consult 16c through 16f.

EXAMPLE  My college roommate and (I, me) have been interested in the Harlem Renaissance since (we, us) took an American literature survey course as sophomores.

(1) My roommate and (I, me) discovered (we, us) did not know much about the Harlem Renaissance. (2) (We, Us) two began reading the history and literature of the movement and wanted to know more about it. (3) Between (her and me, she and I), (we, us) divided the authors of the Harlem Renaissance into two groups. (4) However, learning about the movement meant more than reading works by the authors, (we, us) found. (5). It also meant (her and me, she and I) needed to study the background that created the movement. (6) (We, Us) learned that many African Americans moved from the South to large industrial cities in the North, a fact that directed (we, us) to other matters. (7) For example, a black middle class arose because (they, them) had industrial jobs, which earned (they, them) more opportunities for

education. (8) (They, them) had a thirst for reading magazines and books by other African Americans. (9) Slowly, a radical group developed a "new consciousness," with the educated writers of the Harlem Renaissance being the most outspoken among (they, them). (10) (We, us), my roommate and (I, me), became even more interested in the Harlem Renaissance then because (she and I, her and me) remembered our parents talking about their participation in the civil rights movement of the 1960s.

## 16g When should I use *who, whoever, whom,* and *whomever*?

The pronouns *who* and *whoever* are in the SUBJECTIVE CASE. The pronouns *whom* and *whomever* are in the OBJECTIVE CASE.

Informal spoken English tends to blur distinctions between *who* and *whom,* so with these words some people can't rely entirely on what "sounds right." Whenever you're unsure of whether to use *who* or *whoever* or to use *whom* or *whomever,* apply the "Troyka test for case" in Quick Reference 16.2. If you see *who* or *whoever,* test by temporarily substituting *he, she,* or *they.* If you see *whom* or *whomever,* test by temporarily substituting *him, her,* or *them.*

My father tells the same story to **whoever/whomever** he meets.

My father tells the same story to **she/her.** [*Note:* When substituting, stop at *she/her.* The objective case *whomever* is correct because the sentence works when you substitute *her* for *whoever/whomever.* In contrast, the subjective case *whoever* is wrong because the sentence doesn't work when you substitute *she* for *whoever/whomever.*]

My father tells the same story to **whomever** he meets.

The most reliable variation of the test for *who, whom, whoever, whomever* calls for you to add a word before the substituted word set. In this example, the word *if* is added:

I wondered **who/whom** would vote for Ms. Wallace.

I wondered **if he/if him** would vote for Ms. Wallace. [The subjective case *who* is correct because the sentence works when you substitute *if he* for *who/whom.* In contrast, the objective case *whom* is wrong because the sentence doesn't work when you substitute *if him* for *who/whom.*]

I wondered **who** would vote for Ms. Wallace.

Another variation of the test for *who, whom, whoever, whomever* calls for you to invert the word order in the test sentence.

---

**6.** We [16c, subjective case]; us [16c, objective case]

**7.** they [16c, subjective case]; them [16c, objective case]

**8.** They [16c, subjective case]

**9.** them [16c, objective case]

**10.** We [16c, subjective case]; I [16c and 16e, subjective case, appositive]; she and I [16c and 16d, subjective case, compound subject]

### BACKGROUND

The Online Writing Lab (OWL) of Purdue University refers to comparisons as "shorthand sentences" because certain words are usually omitted. For example, we say: "He is shorter than I (am short)"; the words in parentheses are dropped. We don't say: "He is shorter than I am short."

—<http://owl.english.purdue.edu/handouts/grammar/g_proncase.html>

### QUOTATION: ON LANGUAGE

Words are like leaves, and where they most abound,
Much fruit of sense beneath is rarely found.

—Alexander Pope

### TEACHING TIP

If your students have trouble choosing the appropriate pronoun after *than* or *as,* you might try expanding elliptical comparisons with them to verify the best choice. Here are a few practice sentences.

**1.** You are taller than (I, me). [*I*]

**2.** Your parents are taller than (me, mine). [*mine*]

**3.** My brother is as thin as (I, me). [*I*]

**4.** Your sisters are as smart as (me, mine). [*mine*]

### EXTRA EXERCISE B

Underline the correct pronoun of each pair in parentheses.

**1.** Carl's resolution to study more is a result of (him, his) getting poor grades last semester. [*his*]

**2.** The dean almost required (he, him) to take a semester off. [*him*]

**3.** His parents complained about (him, his) partying too much. [*his*]

**4.** Carl thought that nobody cared more about his grades than (him, he). [*he*]

**5.** So he was surprised when his parents told (he, him) they were disappointed with his schoolwork. [*him*]

**6.** (Them, Their) expressing their concern showed how much they cared about (he, him). [*Their, him*]

**7.** After that, whenever his parents looked for (he, him), they found (his, him) studying. [*him, him*]

**QUOTATION: ON LANGUAGE**
High thoughts must have high language.
—Aristophanes

**ANSWERS: EXERCISE 16–3**

**1.** who [subjective case]

**2.** who [subjective case]

**3.** whom [objective case]

**4.** who [subjective case]; who [subjective case]

**5.** whom [objective case]

**6.** who [subjective case]

**7.** who [subjective case]; whom [objective case]

**EXTRA EXERCISE C**
From each group of pronouns in parentheses, select the correct word and underline it.

**EXAMPLE**
My softball teammates and (myself, me, I) are confident we will make the finals this year. [*I*]

**1.** I am so certain of our success that I have already bought (me, myself) a new glove to celebrate. [*myself*]

**2.** Every practice session, the coach tells the others and (me, myself) that we are getting better and better. [*me*]

**3.** The sponsor (himself, hisself), Big Al of Big Al's Used Cars, even comes to games now. [*himself*]

Babies **who/whom** mothers cuddle grow faster and feel happier.

Mothers cuddle **they/them**. [*Note:* When substituting, stop at *they/them.* By inverting the word order in the sentence—that is, by temporarily using *mothers* as the subject of the sentence—and substituting *they/them* for *who/whom*, you see that *them* is correct. Therefore, the objective case *whom* is correct.]

Babies **whom** mothers cuddle grow faster and feel happier.

At the beginning or end of a question, use *who* if the question is about the subject and *whom* if the question is about the object. To determine which case to use, recast the question into a statement, substituting *he* or *him* (or *she* or *her*).

**Who** watched the space shuttle liftoff? [*He* (not *Him*) *watched the space shuttle liftoff* uses the subjective case, so *who* is correct.]

Ted admires **whom**? [*Ted admires him* (not *he*) uses the objective case, so *whom* is correct.]

**Whom** does Ted admire? [*Ted admires him* (not *he*) uses the objective case, so *whom* is correct.]

To **whom** does Ted speak about becoming an astronaut? [*Ted speaks to them* (not *they*) uses the objective case, so *whom* is correct.]

**EXERCISE 16-3** Underline the correct pronoun of each pair in parentheses. For help, consult 16g.

**EXAMPLE** Women (who, whom) both hold jobs outside the home and are mothers serve a "double shift."

(1) Women (who, whom) raise families do as much work at home as at their jobs. (2) In North American society, it is still mainly women (who, whom) cook dinner, clean the house, check the children's homework, read to them, and put them to bed. (3) Nevertheless, self-esteem runs high, some researchers have found, in many women on (who, whom) families depend for both wage earning and child rearing. (4) Compared with women (who, whom) pursue careers but have no children, those (who, whom) handle a double shift experience less anxiety and depression, according to the research. (5) Perhaps the reason for this finding is that those for (who, whom) the extra paycheck helps pay the bills feel pride and accomplishment when they rise to the challenge. (6) However, other studies note that women (who, whom) have both jobs and children experience tremendous stress. (7) Those (who, whom) feel unable both to support and to nurture their children despite their maximum efforts are the women for (who, whom) the dual responsibility is an almost unbearable burden.

## 16h What pronoun case comes after *than* or *as*?

When *than* or *as* is part of a sentence of comparison, the sentence sometimes doesn't include words to complete the comparison outright. Rather, by omitting certain words, the sentence implies the comparison. For example, *My two-month-old Saint Bernard is larger **than** most full-grown dogs [are]* doesn't need the final word *are*.

When a pronoun follows *than* or *as,* the meaning of the sentence depends entirely on whether the pronoun is in the subjective case or the objective case. Here are two sentences that convey two very different messages, depending on whether the subjective case (*I*) or the objective case (*me*) is used.

1. My sister loved that dog more *than* I.
2. My sister loved that dog more *than* me.

In sentence 1, because *I* is in the subjective case, the sentence means *My sister loved that dog more than **I** [loved it].* In sentence 2, because *me* is in the objective case, the sentence means *My sister loved that dog more than [she loved] **me**.* In both situations, you can check whether you're using the correct case by supplying the implied words to see if they make sense.

## 16i How do pronouns work before infinitives?

Most INFINITIVES consist of the SIMPLE FORMS of verbs that follow *to:* for example, *to laugh, to sing, to jump, to dance.* (A few exceptions occur when the *to* is optional: *My aunt helped the elderly man [to] cross the street;* and when the *to* is awkward: *My aunt watched the elderly man [to] get on the bus.*) For both the SUBJECTS of infinitives and the OBJECTS of infinitives, use the objective case.

> Our tennis coach expects me *to serve*. [Because the word *me* is the subject of the infinitive *to serve*, the objective-case pronoun is correct.]
>
> Our tennis coach expects him *to beat* me. [Because the word *him* is the subject of the infinitive *to beat*, and *me* is the object of the infinitive, the objective-case pronoun is correct.]

## 16j How do pronouns work with *-ing* words?

When a verb's *-ing* form functions as a NOUN, it's called a GERUND: *Brisk **walking** is excellent exercise.* When a noun or PRONOUN comes before a gerund, the POSSESSIVE CASE is required: ***His** brisk **walking** built up his stamina.* In contrast, when a verb's *-ing* form functions as a MODIFIER, it requires the subjective case for the pronoun, not the possessive case: *He, **walking** briskly, caught up to me.*

Here are two sentences that convey different messages, depending entirely on whether a possessive comes before the *-ing* word.

4. The other women and (I, myself) are glad that our hard work has paid off. [*I*]

5. We had an exhibition game against our husbands, who tired (theirselves, themselves) out and lost by four runs. [*themselves*]

### EXTRA EXERCISE D

From the pronouns in parentheses, select the correct one and underline it.

1. My girlfriend and (I, me) agreed long ago that we would someday take a romantic ocean cruise together. [*I*]

2. (We, Us) and a few friends would sail the legendary seas and dock at exotic ports. [*We*]

3. Together, (we, us) and (they, them) would shop in the mysterious bazaars of ancient cultures and eat the spicy foods of distant lands. [*we, they*]

4. Unfortunately, an unexpected misfortune was visited on (she, her) and (I, me). [*her, me*]

5. The day we were to leave, (she, her) and (I, me) both discovered that we had chicken pox! [*she, I*]

6. Instead of visiting romantic places, the romantic places visited (she, her) and (I, me). [*her, me*]

7. Our friend Tom gave (we, us) travel books with pictures of the many places we longed to see. [*us*]

8. They were the same books someone had given (he, him) when he missed a trip to Mexico. [*him*]

9. I guess (we, us) will have to give them to (whoever, whomever) can't make the next scheduled vacation trip. [*we, whoever*]

### WORD HISTORY

*Antecedent* comes from the Latin *ante,* meaning "before," and *cedere,* meaning "to go." Thus, the antecedent is the word that "goes before" the pronoun.

### TEACHING TIP

To help students become more aware of the connections between pronouns and their antecedents, you might want to use this excerpt by Jim Bouton. Ask students to draw connecting lines between the pronoun and the antecedent in each pair. (The pronouns are italicized here.) Do the students find any misleading or vague references?

Another thing to watch during one of the little delays *that* make up such a big part of the [baseball] game is *what* the pitcher is up to. *I* don't mean when *he's* looking in to get the sign, winding up, throwing the ball. *I* mean during the time *he* steps off the mound and seems to be looking out at *his* outfielders or into the stands at girls. What *he's* really doing is rubbing up the ball and under the latest rules *he* has to walk off the mound to do so.

*This* gives *him* some marvelous opportunities. *He* can, for one thing, stick a finger between *his* belt and trousers and come up with a gob of previously concealed vaseline. *This* while *he* has *his* back to the plate umpire. And what good is vaseline? Well, *it's* slippery like spit. *This* means *you* can throw the ball exactly as hard as *you* would a fastball and have *it* come off *your* hand behaving like a curve. *This* is very confusing for the hitter.

—Jim Bouton, "A Few World Series Sinkers"

**ANSWERS: EXERCISE 16–4**

**1.** he [16h, subjective case in elliptical *better . . . than he is*]

**2.** them [16i, objective case before infinitive]

**3.** his [16j, possessive case before gerund]

**4.** him [16i, objective case before infinitive]

**5.** his [16j, possessive case before gerund]

**6.** he [16h, subjective case in elliptical *as well as he could*]

**7.** his [16j, possessive case before gerund]

**8.** he [16h, subjective case in elliptical *as he has*]

**QUOTATION: ON WRITING**
We are all apprentices in a craft where no one ever becomes a master.
—Ernest Hemingway

1. The detective noticed the **man** *staggering*.

2. The detective noticed the **man's** *staggering*.

Sentence 1 means that the detective noticed the *man;* sentence 2 means that the detective noticed the *staggering.* The same distinction applies to pronouns: When *the man* is replaced by *him* or *the man's* by *his,* the meaning is the same as in sentences 1 and 2.

1. The detective noticed **him** *staggering*.

2. The detective noticed **his** *staggering*.

In conversation, such distinctions are often ignored, but use them in ACADEMIC WRITING.

● **EXERCISE 16-4**  Underline the correct pronoun of each pair in parentheses. For help, consult 16h through 16j.

**EXAMPLE**  Ricky Jay holds the world's record for card throwing; no one can throw a playing card faster than (he/him).

(1) Many magicians agree that no one is better at sleight-of-hand magic than (he/him). (2) Younger magicians often say that Ricky Jay influenced (their/them) to become professional performers. (3) In addition to (him/his) being a respected sleight-of-hand artist, Jay is also a scholar and historian. (4) His interest in strange performers led (him/he) to write *Learned Pigs and Fireproof Women,* which discusses unusual acts and begins with (him/his) explaining their appeal to audiences. (5) Jay's acting career has involved (his/him) performing in several different movies and TV shows. (6) In the James Bond film *Tomorrow Never Dies,* few could have played a villain as well as (he/him). (7) Other roles include (him/his) narrating the introduction to the movie *Magnolia.* (8) Overall, few performers have had such as varied and interesting career as (him/he).

# 16k  What case should I use for *-self* pronouns?

Two types of pronouns end in *-self:* reflexive pronouns and intensive pronouns.

A **reflexive pronoun** reflects back on the subject, so it needs a subject in the sentence to be reflected back on. Without a subject, the reflexive pronoun cannot operate correctly.

The **detective** disguised *himself.* [The reflexive pronoun *himself* reflects back on the subject *detective.*]

Never use a reflexive pronoun to replace a personal pronoun in the subjective case.

| NO | My teammates and **myself** will vote for a team captain. |
|---|---|
| YES | My teammates and **I** will vote for a team captain. |

Also, never use a reflexive pronoun to replace a personal pronoun in the objective case. The only exception is when the object restates the subject.

| NO | That decision is up to my teammates and **myself**. |
|---|---|
| YES | That decision is up to my teammates and **me**. |

**Intensive pronouns**, which reflect back in the same way as reflexive pronouns, provide emphasis by making the message of the sentence more intense in meaning.

The detective felt that **his career** *itself* was at risk. [*Itself* intensifies the idea that the detective's career was at risk.]

## PRONOUN REFERENCE

# 16l What is pronoun reference?

The word or group of words that a pronoun replaces is called its **antecedent**. In order for your writing to communicate its message clearly, each pronoun must relate precisely to an antecedent.

I knew a **woman**, lovely in **her** bones / When small **birds** sighed, **she** would sigh back at **them**.

—Theodore Roethke, "I Knew a Woman"

# 16m What makes pronoun reference clear?

**Pronoun reference** is clear when your readers know immediately to whom or what each pronoun refers. Quick Reference 16.3 lists guidelines for using pronouns clearly, and the section in parentheses is where each is explained.

### Quick Reference 16.3

#### Guidelines for clear pronoun reference

- Place pronouns close to their ANTECEDENTS (16n).
- Make a pronoun refer to a specific antecedent (16n).
- Do not overuse *it* (16q).
- Reserve *you* only for DIRECT ADDRESS (16r).
- Use *that, which,* and *who* correctly (16s).

**QUOTATION: ON WRITING**
I do not choose the right word. I get rid of the wrong one.
—A. E. Housman

**QUOTATION: ON WRITING**
You can be a little ungrammatical if you come from the right part of the country.
—Robert Frost

**QUOTATION: ON WRITING**
It's not wise to violate the rules until you know how to observe them.
—T. S. Eliot

**QUOTATION: ON WRITING**
For your born writer, nothing is so healing as the realization that he has come upon the right word.
—Catherine Drinker Bowen

**HUMOROUS NOTE**
Carelessly placed pronouns can result in some unintentionally funny statements, as Richard Lederer demonstrates in *Anguished English*. Consider the difference between what the writers of the following sentences meant to say and what they really said.

- Antinuclear protestors released live cockroaches inside the White House Friday, and these were arrested when they left and blocked a security gate.
- My mother wants to have the dog's tail operated on again, and if it doesn't heal this time, she'll have to be put away.
- About two years ago, a wart appeared on my left hand, which I wanted removed.
- Guilt, vengeance, and bitterness can be emotionally destructive to you and your children. You must get rid of them.

**TEACHING TIP**
You may want to point out that errors in pronoun reference sometimes occur when a student writes as she or he might speak conversationally. In casual conversation, for example,

we might say, "You just sat spellbound through that movie," when we really mean, "*I* sat spellbound." When we have heard or read a "fact" that captures our interest, we may pass along the information by reporting, "They say that drivers of red cars are twice as likely as drivers of brown cars to get stopped for speeding," allowing the imprecise "they" to carry the weight of an authority we cannot recall. Remind students that academic writing requires precision in language not required in our everyday conversation. As an extra but valuable step in the proofreading process, students who have repeated errors with pronoun reference may find it helpful to highlight and examine all their pronouns.

**TEACHING TIP**

The issue of *its* and *it's* often comes up during the study of section 16q. If this happens, you might grab the teaching moment and refer students to 27d in the apostrophe chapter; the Usage Glossary (Chapter 13); and the list of homonyms in 31f.

**QUOTATION: ON WRITING**

It is not unusual words that count but unusual combinations of usual words.

—Hart Day Leavitt

**QUOTATION: ON WRITING**

The editorial "we" has often been fatal to rising genius; though all the world knows that it is only a form of speech, very often employed by a single needy blockhead.

—Thomas Babington Macaulay

**ANOTHER EXAMPLE**

You might want to ask your students to work in groups to identify the missing antecedents of the pronouns underlined in the following sentences and then to discuss how changes could give the paragraph greater clarity and more formal style.

In India, they have cultivated cotton for centuries. You could wear cotton garments there as far back as 1500 BC. It was logical that it should become an important crop

# 16n  How can I avoid unclear pronoun reference?

Every pronoun needs to refer to a specific, nearby ANTECEDENT. If the same pronoun in your writing has to refer to more than one antecedent, replace some pronouns with nouns.

> **NO** In 1911, **Roald Amundsen** reached the South Pole just thirty-five days before **Robert F. Scott** arrived. **He** [who? Amundsen or Scott?] had told people that **he** [who? Amundsen or Scott?] was going to sail for the Arctic, but **he** [who? Amundsen or Scott?] was concealing **his** [whose? Amundsen's or Scott's?] plan. Soon, **he** [who? Amundsen or Scott?] turned south for the Antarctic. On the journey home, **he** [who? Amundsen or Scott?] and **his** [whose? Amundsen's or Scott's?] party froze to death just a few miles from safety.

> **YES** In 1911, **Roald Amundsen** reached the South Pole just thirty-five days before **Robert F. Scott** arrived. **Amundsen** had told people that **he** was going to sail for the Arctic, but **he** was concealing **his** plan. Soon, **Amundsen** turned south for the Antarctic. Meanwhile, on **their** journey home, **Scott** and **his party** froze to death just a few miles from safety.

🛑 **Alert:** Be careful with the VERBS *said* and *told* in sentences that contain pronoun reference. To maintain clarity, use quotation marks and slightly reword each sentence to make the meaning clear. ●

> **NO** **Her** mother told **her she** was going to visit **her** grandmother.

> **YES** **Her** mother told **her**, "**You** are going to visit your grandmother."

> **YES** **Her** mother told **her**, "**I** am going to visit your grandmother."

Further, if too much material comes between a pronoun and its antecedent, readers can lose track of the meaning.

Alfred Wegener, a German meteorologist and professor of geophysics at the University of Graz in Austria, was the first to suggest that all the continents on earth were originally part of one large landmass. According to this theory, the supercontinent broke up long ago and the fragments drifted apart.

*Wegener*
~~He~~ named this supercontinent Pangaea.
‸

[*He* can refer only to Wegener, but material about Wegener's theory intervenes, so using *Wegener* again instead of *he* jogs the reader's memory and makes reading easier.]

When you start a new paragraph, be cautious about beginning it with a pronoun whose antecedent is in a prior paragraph. You're better off repeating the word.

🌐 **ESOL Tip:** Many languages omit a pronoun as a subject because the verb delivers the needed information. English requires the use of the pronoun as a subject. For example, never omit *it* in the following: *Political science is an important academic subject. **It** is studied all over the world.* ●

**EXERCISE 16-5**    Revise so that each pronoun refers clearly to its antecedent. Either replace pronouns with nouns or restructure the material to clarify pronoun reference. For help, consult 16n.

EXAMPLE    People who return to work after years away from the corporate world often discover that business practices have changed. They may find fiercer competition in the workplace, but they may also discover that they are more flexible than before.

Here is one possible revision: *People who return to work after years away from the corporate world often discover that business practices have changed. Those people may find fiercer competition in the workplace, but they may also discover that business practices are more flexible than before.*

Most companies used to frown on employees who became involved in office romances. They often considered them to be using company time for their own enjoyment. Now, however, managers realize that happy employees are productive employees. With more women than ever before in the workforce and with people working longer hours, they have begun to see that male and female employees want and need to socialize. They are also dropping their opposition to having married couples on the payroll. They no longer automatically believe that they will bring family matters into the workplace or stick up for each other at the company's expense.

One departmental manager had doubts when a systems analyst for research named Laura announced that she had become engaged to Peter, who worked as a technician in the same department. She told her that either one or the other might have to transfer out of the research department. After listening to her plea that they be allowed to work together on a trial basis, the manager reconsidered. She decided to give Laura and Peter a chance to prove that their relationship would not affect their work. The decision paid off. They demonstrated that they could work as an effective research team, right through their engagement and subsequent marriage. Two years later, when Laura was promoted to assistant manager for product development and after he asked to move also, she enthusiastically recommended that Peter follow Laura to her new department.

because you have few winter frosts there. They are also free of excessive humidity. In eighteenth-century England the invention of machines that could make cotton cloth brought them a worldwide market. It was a time of great prosperity. Today you can buy cotton products from many countries.

—Emily Gordon

**QUOTATION: ON LANGUAGE**

*It's* is a contraction for *it is,* and is not and should never be confused with the neuter possessive pronoun *its*.

—William Safire

**ANSWERS: EXERCISE 16-5**

Answers may vary somewhat. Some students may think that some of the pronouns replaced here are acceptable, but clarity is the issue—avoiding intervening information that distracts the reader, ambiguous references, and so on. Here is one possible answer.

Most companies used to frown on employees who became involved in office romances. Companies often considered these employees to be using company time for their own enjoyment. Now, however, managers realize that happy employees are productive employees. With more women than ever before in the workforce and with people working longer hours, managers have begun to see that male and female employees want and need to socialize. Managers are also dropping their opposition to having married couples on the payroll, because managers no longer automatically believe that such couples will bring family matters into the workplace or stick up for each other at the company's expense.

One departmental manager had doubts when a systems analyst for research named Laura announced that she had become engaged to Peter, who worked as a technician in the same department. The departmental manager told Laura, "Either Peter or you might have to transfer out of the research department." After listening to Laura's plea that the couple be allowed to work together on a trial basis, the manager reconsidered. She decided to give Laura and Peter a chance to prove that their relationship would not affect their work. The decision paid off. Laura and Peter demonstrated that they could work as an effective research team, right through their engagement and subsequent marriage. Two years later, when Laura was promoted to assistant manager for product development and after Peter asked to move also, the research manager enthusiastically recommended that Peter follow Laura to her new department.

**TEACHING TIP**

Some instructors dislike the use of *you* in formal writing, preferring the third person *one* instead. More popular usage, however, encourages students to use *you* when they speak to their readers directly in their writing. You may want to read a couple of examples so that your students can hear the differences in tone:

Have you ever waked during the night to find yourself trapped in a nightmarish dream whose effects seem all too real? When this event happens, do you then drift once more into sleep only to repeat the nightmare from which extrication seems impossible? And, if so, are you wrestling with demons of guilt or fear that, in waking moments, you refuse to confront?

Psychologists who study the dream life of humans offer a number of interesting theories about the causes and effects of nightmares. When one becomes trapped in a terrible dream that recurs multiple times during the night, is the nightmare a projection of some guilt or fear? Or is there another, less sinister explanation? And is there any way that one can prevent such nightmares from occurring in the first place?

**QUOTATION: ON WRITING**

I still read everything aloud. I have a fundamental conviction that if a sentence cannot be read aloud with sincerity, conviction, and communicable emphasis, it is not a good sentence. Good writing requires good rhythm and good words.

# 16o How do pronouns work with *it, that, this,* and *which*?

When you use *it, that, this,* and *which,* be sure that your readers can easily understand what each word refers to.

**NO** Comets usually fly by the earth at 100,000 mph, whereas asteroids sometimes collide with the earth. **This** interests scientists. [Does *this* refer to the speed of the comets, to comets flying by the earth, or to asteroids colliding with the earth?]

**YES** Comets usually fly by the earth at 100,000 mph, whereas asteroids sometimes collide with the earth. **This difference** interests scientists. [Adding a noun after *this* or *that* clarifies the meaning.]

**NO** I told my friends that I was going to major in geology, **which** made my parents happy. [Does *which* refer to telling your friends or to majoring in geology?]

**YES** My parents were happy **because I discussed my major with my friends.**

**YES** My parents were happy **because I chose to major in geology.**

Also, the title of any piece of writing stands on its own. Therefore, in your introductory paragraph, never refer to your title with *this* or *that.* For example, if an essay's title is "Geophysics as a Major," the following holds for the first sentence:

**NO** **This subject** unites the sciences of physics, biology, and paleontology.

**YES** **Geophysics** unites the sciences of physics, biology, and paleontology.

# 16p How do I use *they* and *it* precisely?

The expression *they say* can't take the place of stating precisely who is doing the saying. Your credibility as a writer depends on your mentioning a source precisely.

**NO** **They say** that earthquakes are becoming more frequent. [*They* doesn't identify the authority who made the statement.]

**YES** **Seismologists** say that earthquakes are becoming more frequent.

The expressions *it said* and *it is said that* reflect imprecise thinking. Also, they're wordy. Revising such expressions improves your writing.

| NO | **It said** in the newspaper that California has minor earthquakes almost daily. [*It said in the newspaper that* is wordy.] |

**NO** **It said** in the newspaper that California has minor earthquakes almost daily. [*It said in the newspaper that* is wordy.]

**YES** **The newspaper reported** that California has minor earthquakes almost daily.

## 16q How do I use *it* to suit the situation?

The word *it* has three different uses in English. Here are examples of correct uses of *it*.

1. PERSONAL PRONOUN: Ryan wants to visit the 18-inch Schmidt telescope, but **it** is on Mount Palomar.

2. EXPLETIVE (sometimes called a *subject filler*, it delays the subject): **It is** interesting to observe the stars.

3. IDIOMATIC EXPRESSION (words that depart from normal use, such as using *it* as the sentence subject when writing about weather, time, distance, and environmental conditions): **It** is sunny. **It** is midnight. **It** is not far to the hotel. **It** is very hilly.

All three uses listed above are correct, but avoid combining them in the same sentence. The result can be an unclear and confusing sentence.

**NO** Because our car was overheating, **it** came as no surprise that **it** broke down just as **it** began to rain. [*It* is overused here, even though all three uses—2, 1, and 3 on the above list, respectively—are acceptable.]

**YES** **It** came as no surprise that our overheating car broke down just as the rain began. [The word order is revised so that *it* is used once.]

🌐 **ESOL Tip:** In some languages, *it* is not used as an expletive. In English, it is. ●

**NO** Is a lovely day.
**YES** **It** is a lovely day.

## 16r When should I use *you* for direct address?

Reserve *you* for **direct address**, writing that addresses the reader directly. For example, we use *you* in this handbook to address you, the student. *You* is not a suitable substitute for specific words that refer to people, situations, or occurrences.

You . . . cannot know unless you read them aloud.

—Richard Marcus

| | |
|---|---|
| **NO** | Prison uprisings often happen **when you allow** overcrowding. [The reader, *you,* did not allow the overcrowding.] |
| **YES** | Prison uprisings often happen **when prisons are** overcrowded. |
| **NO** | In Russia, **you** usually have to stand in long lines to buy groceries. [Are *you,* the reader, planning to do your grocery shopping in Russia?] |
| **YES** | **Russian consumers** usually have to stand in long lines to buy groceries. |

**ANSWERS: EXERCISE 16-6**

Answers will vary somewhat. Here is one set of possibilities.

**1.** Climbing Mount Everest is more expensive than people/the public might realize. [16r, revision changes person from *you* not used for direct address to third person]

**2.** In addition to training, climbers need to raise as much as $60,000 for the expedition. [16p, revision eliminates imprecise use of *they*]

**3.** By contacting the Nepalese embassy in Washington, DC, climbers can secure the help of Sherpa guides. [Revision changes person from *you* not used for direct address to third person, the noun *climbers*]

**4.** Correct sentence.

**5.** Climbers will need to pack oxygen bottles, a first aid kit, medications, a satellite phone, walkie-talkies, and a laptop computer. These necessities will ensure a climber's safety. [16o, revision eliminates imprecise use of *this*]

**6.** Climbers often use yaks because they are stronger than humans and can carry more equipment. [16r, revision changes person from *you* not used for direct address to third person]

**7.** Airlines do not offer direct flights, so climbers from America usually need a couple of days to get to Katmandu, Nepal. [16p, revision eliminates imprecise use of *they*]

**8.** Once atop the mountain, climbers should prepare for the descent, which is just as dangerous as the ascent. [16r, revision changes person from *you* not used for direct address to the third person]

**EXERCISE 16-6** Revise these sentences so that all pronoun references are clear. If a sentence is correct, circle its number. For help, consult 16o through 16r.

**EXAMPLE** They say that reaching the summit of Mount Everest is easiest in the month of May.

*Experienced climbers say that reaching the summit of Mount Everest is easiest in the month of May.* [Revision eliminates imprecise use of *they,* see section 16p.]

1. Climbing Mount Everest is more expensive than you realize.
2. In addition to training, they need to raise as much as $60,000 for the expedition.
3. By contacting the Nepalese embassy in Washington, DC, you can secure the help of Sherpa guides.
4. The government of Nepal requires permits, copies of passports, and letters of recommendation for each climbing team.
5. Climbers will need to pack oxygen bottles, a first aid kit, medications, a satellite phone, walkie-talkies, and a laptop computer. This will ensure a climber's safety.
6. Climbers often use yaks because they are stronger than you and can carry more equipment.
7. They do not offer direct flights, so climbers from America usually need a couple of days to get to Katmandu, Nepal.
8. Once atop the mountain, you should prepare for the descent, which is just as dangerous as the ascent.

# 16s When should I use *that, which,* and *who*?

To use the pronouns *that* and *which* correctly, you want to check the context of the sentence you're writing. *Which* and *that* refer to animals and things. Only sometimes do they refer to anonymous or collective groups of people. Quick Reference 16.4 shows how to choose between *that* and *which*. For information about the role of commas with *that* and *which*, see 24f.

*Who* refers to people and to animals mentioned by name.

**John Polanyi, who** was awarded the Nobel Prize in Chemistry, speaks passionately in favor of nuclear disarmament. [*John Polanyi* is a person.]

**Lassie, who** was known for her intelligence and courage, was actually played by a series of male collies. [*Lassie* is the name of an animal.]

Many professional writers reserve *which* for nonrestrictive clauses and *that* for restrictive clauses. Other writers use *that* and *which* interchangeably for restrictive clauses. Current practice allows the use of either as long as you're consistent in each piece of writing. However, for ACADEMIC WRITING, your instructor might expect you to maintain the distinction.

---

**Quick Reference 16.4** ■ ■ ■ ■ ■ ■ ■

### Choosing between *that* and *which*

**Choice:** Some instructors and style guides use either *that* or *which* to introduce a RESTRICTIVE CLAUSE (a DEPENDENT CLAUSE that is essential to the meaning of the sentence or part of the sentence). Others may advise you to use only *that* so that your writing distinguishes clearly between restrictive and NONRESTRICTIVE CLAUSES. Whichever style you use, be consistent in each piece of writing:

* The zoos ***that*** (or ***which***) **most children like** display newborn and baby animals. [The point in this sentence concerns children's preferences. Therefore, the words *most children like* are essential for delivering the meaning and make up a restrictive clause.]

**No choice:** You are required to use *which* to introduce a nonrestrictive clause (a dependent clause that isn't essential to the meaning of the sentence or part of the sentence).

* Zoos, **which most children like**, attract more visitors if they display newborn and baby animals. [The point in this sentence concerns attracting more visitors to zoos. Therefore, the words *most children like* are not essential to the meaning of the sentence and make up a nonrestrictive clause.]

---

**!** **Alert:** Use commas before and after a nonrestrictive clause. Don't use commas before and after a restrictive clause; see 24k.4. ●

**EXERCISE 16-7**    Fill in the blanks with *that*, *which*, or *who*. For help, consult 16s.

**EXAMPLE**    Antigua, which is an island in the West Indies, is a popular destination for European and American tourists.

1. Those _____ like to travel to Antigua may enjoy online gambling, _____ is legal on the island.

2. The sport _____ is most popular in Antigua is cricket.

3. Celebrities _____ own homes on the island include Oprah Winfrey, Eric Clapton, and Jamaica Kincaid.

4. The main airport, _____ is named after Prime Minister V. C. Bird, is located in the capital, St. John's.

5. The cruise ships _____ travel to Antigua often stop at St. John's, _____ became the seat of government in 1981.

For more help with your writing, grammar, and research, go to **www.mycomplab.com**

# 17

# Agreement

## 17a What is agreement?

In everyday speech, agreement indicates that people hold the same ideas. Grammatical **agreement** is also based on sameness. Specifically, you need to match SUBJECTS and VERBS; see 17b through 17n. You also need to match PRONOUNS and ANTECEDENTS; see 17o through 17t.

## SUBJECT-VERB AGREEMENT

## 17b What is subject-verb agreement?

Subject-verb agreement means that a SUBJECT and its VERB match in NUMBER (singular or plural) and PERSON (first, second, or third person). Quick Reference 17.1 presents these major concepts in grammatical agreement.

The **firefly glows.** [*Firefly* is a singular subject in the third person; *glows* is a singular verb in the third person.]

**Fireflies glow.** [*Fireflies* is a plural subject in the third person; *glow* is a plural verb in the third person.]

---

### Quick Reference 17.1 ■ ■ ■ ■ ■ ■ ■

## Grammatical agreement: first, second and third person

- **Number**, as a concept in grammar, refers to *singular* (one) and *plural* (more than one).
- The **first person** is the speaker or writer. *I* (singular) and *we* (plural) are the only subjects that occur in the first person.

  SINGULAR    **I see** a field of fireflies.

  PLURAL    **We see** a field of fireflies.

- The **second person** is the person spoken or written to. *You* (for both singular and plural) is the only subject that occurs in the second person.

  SINGULAR    **You see** a shower of sparks.

  PLURAL    **You see** a shower of sparks.

- The **third person** is the person or thing being spoken or written about. *He, she, it* (singular) and *they* (plural) are the third-person subject forms. Most rules for subject-verb agreement involve the third person.

  SINGULAR    The **scientist sees** a cloud of cosmic dust.

  PLURAL    The **scientists see** a cloud of cosmic dust.

---

## 17c Why is a final -s or -es in a subject or verb so important?

SUBJECT-VERB AGREEMENT often involves one letter: *s* (or *es* for words that end in *-s*). For verbs in the present tense, you form the SIMPLE FORM of third-person singular by adding *-s* or *-es: laugh, laughs; kiss, kisses.* Major exceptions are the verbs *be* (*is*), *have* (*has*), and *do* (*does*), see 9c.

> That **student agrees** that **young teenagers watch** too much television.
>
> Those **young teenagers are** taking valuable time away from studying.
>
> That **student has** a part-time job for ten hours a week.
>
> Still, that **student does** well in college.

For a subject to become plural, you add *-s* or *-es* to its end: *lip, lips; princess, princesses.* Major exceptions include most pronouns (*they, it*) and a few nouns that for singular and plural either don't change (*deer, deer*) or change internally (*mouse, mice*). Quick Reference 17.2 shows you how to visualize the basic pattern for agreement using *-s* or *-es.*

### ANOTHER EXAMPLE

Notice how many subject-verb pairs are in the following passage.

> *It is* common to refer to the sky as blue. Actually, the *sky is* black and our *atmosphere is* blue. *That is* because the tiny particles of *dust* and little moisture *droplets* in the air *are* small enough to interfere with and scatter the shorter wavelengths of the sun's light, the blue and violet colors, to produce an illusion of a blue sky. *Astronauts,* circling our planet at heights of hundreds of miles, *report* that the sky is black and that the *sun, moon, stars,* and *planets can be seen* in the daytime hours.

—Phillip D. Stern, *Our Space Environment*

### QUOTATION: ON WRITING

Style has no fixed laws; it is changed by the usage of the people, never the same for any length of time.

—Seneca

### BACKGROUND

Although English requires agreement between subject and verb, it is unlike some other modern languages in that it does not extend agreement to the gender and number of adjectives. Chinese language experts point out that although the diminished number of endings used to indicate number and gender is thought to represent a great economy of time, space, and thought, it is probably as natural for a Spanish speaker to indicate that information by the article, adjective, and noun—for example, *las muchachas bonitas*—as it is for the English speaker not to do so. Another situation is found in the Chinese languages, which use word order instead of agreement to establish relationships among words.

### TEACHING TIP

Controlled composition exercises are easy to construct and are often useful for helping students with subject-verb agreement and other grammatical and stylistic concerns. A controlled composition exercise asks the student to copy a passage several sentences long—but to make one change in the passage that addresses an area in which the student needs to improve. For example, to work on subject-verb agreement, a student might rewrite a passage changing the verbs from past tense to present tense. For help with past-tense verb forms, a student might rewrite a different passage, converting the verbs from present tense to past tense. Although the exercise focuses the efforts of the student on one particular area—copying passages—it, like other imitation exercises, helps students develop syntactic fluency in other ways at the same time.

## ANSWERS: EXERCISE 17-1

Answers will vary. Each set of sentences must use the subject once as a singular and once as a plural, and the verbs must agree accordingly.

## EXTRA EXERCISE A

Fill in the blank with the correct present-tense form of the verb in parentheses.

### EXAMPLE

Psychologists often (to use) _____ projective tests to investigate clients' unconscious memories and drives. [*use*]

**1.** Psychologists sometimes (to present) _____ their clients with questions to which there are no correct answers.

**2.** The client then (to tell) _____ what he or she (to see) _____, thus showing the psychologist some of his or her inner self.

**3.** The popular Rorschach Psycho-diagnostic Inkblot Test (to require) _____ that the client examine ten cards containing symmetrical inkblots and say what he or she (to think) _____ each means.

**4.** Next, the client (to point) _____ out where in the blot he or she (to find) _____ each image or idea.

**5.** Several scoring systems (to exist) _____ to guide psychologists in interpreting clients' responses.

## Answers to Extra Exercise A

**1.** present

**2.** tells; sees

**3.** requires; thinks

---

### Basic subject-verb agreement

- The student works long hours.   The students work long hours.

  SINGULAR SINGULAR     PLURAL PLURAL
  SUBJECT VERB          SUBJECT VERB

Here's a device for remembering how agreement works for most subject-verb constructions. Note that the final *-s* or *-es* can take only one path at a time—to the end of the verb or to the end of the subject.

## MODEL

*-s* or *-es* ⟨ subject / verb

## SINGULAR

*-s* ⟨ student / work*s*

*-s* ⟨ raindrop / dance*s*

*-es* ⟨ bus / pass*es*

## PLURAL

*-s* ⟨ student*s* / work

*-s* ⟨ raindrop*s* / dance

*-es* ⟨ bus*es* / pass

⚠ **Alert:** When you use an AUXILIARY VERB with a main verb, never add *-s* or *-es* to the main verb: *The coach **can walk*** [not can walks] *to campus. The coach **does like*** [not does likes] *his job.* ●

**EXERCISE 17-1**    Use the subject and verb in each set to write two complete sentences—one with a singular subject and one with a plural subject. Keep all verbs in the present tense. For help, consult 17c.

EXAMPLE  bird, sing

> **Singular subject:** When a *bird sings*, you will know spring is here.
>
> **Plural subject:**    When *birds sing*, you will know spring is here.

1. chair, rock
2. leaf, fall
3. river, flow
4. clock, tick
5. singer, sing
6. girl, laugh
7. hand, grab
8. loaf, rise

# 17d Can I ignore words between a subject and its verb?

You can ignore all words between a subject and its verb. Focus strictly on the subject and its verb. Quick Reference 17.3 shows you this pattern.

**NO** **Winners** of the state contest **goes** to the national finals. [*Winners* is the subject; the verb must agree with it. Ignore the words *of the state contest*.]

**YES** **Winners** of the state contest **go** to the national finals.

The words *one of the . . .* often require a second look. Use a singular verb to agree with the word *one*. Don't be distracted by the plural noun that comes after *of the*. (For information on the phrase *one of the . . . who,* see 17l.)

**NO** **One** of the problems **are** the funds needed for traveling to the national finals.

**YES** **One** of the problems **is** the funds needed for traveling to the national finals.

## Quick Reference 17.3

### When words separate subject and verb

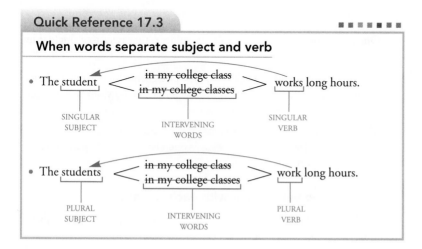

Similarly, eliminate all word groups between the subject and the verb, starting with *including, together with, along with, accompanied by, in addition to, except,* and *as well as.*

4. points; finds
5. exist

**EXTRA EXERCISE B**
Fill in the blank with the correct present-tense form of the verb in parentheses.

EXAMPLE

In the eyes of many people, the Rorschach inkblots (to be) _____ the psychologists' standard tool for getting at clients' hidden thoughts and feelings. [*are*]

**1.** Either the Holtzman Inkblot Technique or the Thematic Apperception Test (TAT) (to be) _____ given by psychologists who feel the Rorschach is unreliable.

**2.** Not only does the Holtzman series have more inkblots than the Rorschach, but the Holtzman also (to have) _____ a more standardized system of administration.

**3.** The TAT (to use) _____ a series of pictures showing people engaged in a wide range of activities.

**4.** Although the pictures show people in realistic situations, there (to be) _____ many possible acceptable answers.

**5.** It (to be) _____ the task of the person interpreting the picture to make up a story, deciding what has occurred and what the characters are thinking and feeling.

**Answers to Extra Exercise B**
**1.** is
**2.** has
**3.** uses
**4.** are
**5.** is

**QUOTATION: ON WRITING**
I have rewritten—often several times—every word I have ever published. My pencils outlast their erasers.

—Vladimir Nabokov

## EXTRA EXERCISE C

Rewrite the following passage, making the following changes: For *children,* substitute *a child.* For *adults,* substitute *an adult.* For *unicorns,* substitute *a unicorn.* For *books,* substitute *a book.* For *they,* substitute *he, she,* or *it,* considering the antecedent. For *a dragon,* substitute *dragons.* Make sure that the verbs agree with the new subjects.

So I believe that we should trust our children. Normal children do not confuse reality and fantasy—they confuse them much less often than we adults do (as a great fantasist pointed out in a story called "The Emperor's New Clothes"). Children know perfectly well that unicorns aren't real, but they also know that books about unicorns, if they are good books, are true books. All too often, that's more than Mummy and Daddy know; for, in denying . . . childhood, the adults have denied half their knowledge, and are left with the sad, sterile little fact: "Unicorns aren't real." And that fact is one that never got anybody anywhere (except in the story "The Unicorn in the Garden," by another great fantasist, in which it is shown that a devotion to the unreality of unicorns may get you straight into the loony bin). It is by such statements as, "Once upon a time there was a dragon," or "In a hole in the ground there lived a hobbit"—it is by such beautiful non-facts that we fantastic human beings may arrive, in our peculiar fashion, at the truth.

—Ursula K. Le Guin,
"Why Are Americans Afraid of Dragons?"

## Answers to Extra Exercise C

So I believe that we should trust a child. A normal child does not confuse reality and fantasy—he or she confuses them much less often than an adult does (as a great fantasist pointed out in a story called "The Emperor's New Clothes"). A child knows perfectly well that a unicorn isn't real, but he or she also knows that a book about a unicorn, if it is a good book, is a true book. All too often, that's more than Mummy and Daddy know; for, in denying . . . childhood, an adult has denied half his or her knowledge, and is left with the sad, sterile little fact: "A unicorn isn't

| | |
|---|---|
| **NO** | The **moon,** *as well as* the planet Venus, **are** visible in the night sky. [*Moon* is the subject. The verb must agree with it. Ignore the words *as well as the planet Venus*.] |
| **YES** | The **moon,** as well as the planet Venus, **is** visible in the night sky. |

## 17e How do verbs work when subjects are connected by *and*?

When two SUBJECTS are connected by *and*, they create a single COMPOUND SUBJECT. A compound subject calls for a plural verb. Quick Reference 17.4 shows you this pattern. (For related material on PRONOUNS and ANTECEDENTS, see 17p.)

The Cascade Diner *and* the Wayside Diner *have* [not *has*] fried catfish today. [These are two different diners.]

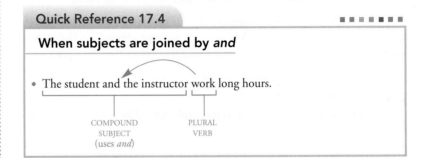

**Quick Reference 17.4**

### When subjects are joined by *and*

• The student and the instructor work long hours.

COMPOUND SUBJECT (uses *and*)    PLURAL VERB

One exception occurs when *and* joins subjects that refer to a single thing or person.

**My friend** *and* **neighbor** *makes* [not *make*] excellent chili. [In this sentence, the friend is the same person as the neighbor. If they were two different people, *makes* would become *make*.]

**Macaroni** *and* **cheese** *contains* [not *contain*] carbohydrates, protein, and many calories. [*Macaroni and cheese* is one dish, not two separate dishes, so it requires a singular verb.]

## 17f How do verbs work with *each* and *every*?

The words *each* and *every* are singular even if they refer to a compound subject. Therefore, they take a singular verb.

*Each* **human hand and foot** *makes* [not *make*] a distinctive print.

To identify lawbreakers, *every* **police chief, sheriff, and federal marshal** *depends* [not *depend*] on such prints.

**❶ Alert:** Use one word, either *each* or *every,* not both at the same time: ***Each*** [not *Each and every*] *robber has been caught.* (For more information about pronoun agreement for *each* and *every,* see 17i, 17p, and 17r.) ●

## 17g How do verbs work when subjects are connected by *or*?

As Quick Reference 17.5 shows, when SUBJECTS are joined by *or*—or by the sets *either . . . or, neither . . . nor, not only . . . but (also)*—the verb agrees with the subject closest to it. Ignore everything before the last-mentioned noun or pronoun. Quick Reference 17.5 shows this pattern with *either . . . or.* (For related material on pronouns and antecedents, see 17q.)

*Neither* ~~spiders~~ *nor* **flies upset** *me.*

*Not only* ~~spiders~~ *but also* ~~all other~~ **arachnids have** four pairs of legs.

~~A dinner of six clam fritters, four blue crabs,~~ *or* ~~one steamed~~ **lobster sounds** good.

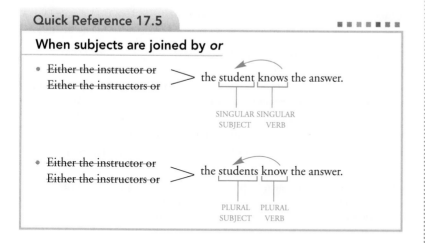

### Quick Reference 17.5

**When subjects are joined by *or***

- ~~Either the instructor or~~
  ~~Either the instructors or~~
  > the student knows the answer.

  SINGULAR SUBJECT  SINGULAR VERB

- ~~Either the instructor or~~
  ~~Either the instructors or~~
  > the students know the answer.

  PLURAL SUBJECT  PLURAL VERB

## 17h How do verbs work with inverted word order?

In English sentences, the SUBJECT normally comes before its VERB: *Astronomy is interesting.* **Inverted word order** reverses the typical subject-verb pattern by putting the verb first. Most questions use inverted word order: *Is astronomy interesting?* In inverted word order, find the subject first and then check whether the verb agrees with it.

real." And that fact is one that never got anybody anywhere (except in the story "The Unicorn in the Garden," by another great fantasist, in which it is shown that a devotion to the unreality of a unicorn may get you straight into the loony bin). It is by such statements as, "Once upon a time there were dragons," or "In a hole in the ground there lived a hobbit"—it is by such beautiful non-facts that we fantastic human beings may arrive, in our peculiar fashion, at the truth.

**BACKGROUND**
In "On Language; Oh Fudge," William Safire pledges allegiance to the *Rule of Proximity* for subject-verb agreement. However, he also recognizes that grammatical ambiguity can still occur, as in the following example: "Neither Mr. Baker nor I am young." In such cases, Safire offers sage advice passed down from other grammarians: "When it looks funny, don't argue the grammar; recast the sentence: Mr. Baker is no spring chicken, nor am I." (*New York Times,* 1 February 1987, late ed., sec. 6:8.)

**QUOTATION: ON WRITING**
After college, I sat all day in a captain's chair up on 84th Street trying to write plays for live television. Each morning I would thread my bathrobe sash through the spokes of the chair and tie myself in.

—John McPhee

**QUOTATION: ON WRITING**
The author does not only write when he's at his desk, he writes all day long, when he is thinking, when he is reading, when he is experiencing; everything he sees and feels is significant to his purpose and, consciously or unconsciously, he is forever storing and making over his impressions.

—W. Somerset Maugham

**QUOTATION: ON WRITING**
I prefer to get up very early in the morning and work. I don't want to speak to anybody or see anybody. Perfect silence. I work until the vein is out.

—Katherine Anne Porter

**QUOTATION: ON WRITING**
When a student makes a particular type of error in mechanics, it may be part of a larger set of related errors. For example, one error in verb agreement is generally accompanied by other errors in verb agreement.

—Arthur N. Applebee

**BACKGROUND**
At the site <http://www.wisc.edu/writing/Handbook/GramPunct.html>, the Online Writing Center of the University of Wisconsin at Madison features an extensive, well-organized collection of material on grammar. The following is a sample from one of its Web pages: "Other words such as *none, any, all, more, most,* and *some* may take either singular or plural verbs, depending on the context. *Some of the dollar was spent. Some of the dollars were spent.* Note: Here, the prepositional phrase does affect the subject. It tells you whether you are talking about a part of one thing (singular) or of a number of things (plural)."

**ANSWERS: EXERCISE 17-2**

**1.** wish [17e, compound subject]

**2.** knows [17g, agreement with nearest subject]; show [17e, compound subject]

**3.** reveals [17d, ignoring words between subject and verb]

**4.** are [17h, inverted subject *movements*]

**5.** is [17d, ignoring words between subject and verb]

**BACKGROUND**
In "On Language; Breaking the Rules," Patricia T. O'Conner addresses the following myth: *None is always singular.* "Not so," she says. "Many people seem to have been taught (mistakenly) that *none* always means *not one.*" However, "*none* is closer in meaning to *not any.* Though it can be singular, *none* is more likely to be plural, as Fowler and others have pointed out. For example: *None of the windows are broken*" (*New York Times*, 28 July 1996, late ed., sec. 6:12).

Into deep space **shoot** probing **satellites.** [The plural verb *shoot* agrees with the inverted plural subject *satellites.*]

On the television screen **appears** an **image** of Saturn. [The singular verb *appears* agrees with the inverted singular subject *image.*]

⓿ **Alert:** When you start a sentence with *there,* check whether the subject is singular or plural, and then choose the right form of *be* to agree with the subject. If your sentence begins with *it,* always use the singular form of *be* (*is, was*) no matter whether the subject is singular or plural.

There *are* nine **planets** in our solar system. [The verb *are* agrees with the subject *planets.*]

There *is* probably no **life** on eight of them. [The verb *is* agrees with the subject *life.*]

It *is* astronomers who explore this theory daily. [The verb *is* agrees with *it,* not with *astronomers.*]●

● **EXERCISE 17-2**    Supply the correct present-tense form of the verb in parentheses. For help, consult 17c through 17h.

**EXAMPLE**   Detectives and teachers (to know) <u>know</u> experienced liars can fool almost anybody, but a new computer can tell who is telling the truth.

1. Police officers and teachers often (to wish) _____ they could "read" people's facial expressions.

2. Trained police officers or a smart teacher (to know) _____ facial tics and nervous mannerisms (to show) _____ someone is lying.

3. However, a truly gifted liar, along with well-coached eyewitnesses, (to reveal) _____ very little through expressions or behavior.

4. There (to be) _____ forty-six muscle movements that create all facial expressions in the human face.

5. Neuroscientist Terrence Seinowski, accompanied by a team of researchers, (to be) _____ developing a computer program to recognize even slight facial movements made by the most expert liars.

# **17i**   How do verbs work with indefinite pronouns?

**Indefinite pronouns** usually refer to nonspecific persons, things, quantities, or ideas. The nonspecific aspect is the reason these pronouns are labeled "indefinite." As part of a sentence, however, the indefinite pronoun is usually clear from the meaning.

Most indefinite pronouns are singular and require a singular verb for agreement. Yet, others are always plural, and a few can be singular *or* plural. Quick

Reference 17.6 clarifies this situation by listing indefinite pronouns according to what verb form they require. (For related material on pronouns and antecedents, see 17o–17r.)

## Quick Reference 17.6

### Common indefinite pronouns

**ALWAYS PLURAL**

| | |
|---|---|
| both | many |

**ALWAYS SINGULAR**

| | | |
|---|---|---|
| another | every | no one |
| anybody | everybody | nothing |
| anyone | everyone | one |
| anything | everything | somebody |
| each | neither | someone |
| either | nobody | something |

**SINGULAR OR PLURAL, DEPENDING ON CONTEXT**

| | | |
|---|---|---|
| all | more | none |
| any | most | some |

Here are sample sentences:

### SINGULAR INDEFINITE PRONOUNS

**Everything** about that intersection **is** dangerous.

But whenever **anyone says** anything, **nothing is** done.

**Each** of us **has** [not *have*] to shovel snow; **each is** [not *are*] expected to help.

**Every** snowstorm of the past two years **has** [not *have*] been severe.

**Every** one of them **has** [not *have*] caused massive traffic jams.

### SINGULAR OR PLURAL INDEFINITE PRONOUNS (DEPENDING ON MEANING)

**Some** of our streams **are** polluted. [*Some* refers to the plural noun *streams*, so the plural verb *are* is correct.]

**Some** pollution **is** reversible, but **all** pollution **threatens** the balance of nature. [*Some* and *all* refer to the singular noun *pollution*, so the singular verbs *is* and *threatens* are correct.]

**All** that environmentalists ask **is** to give nature a chance. [*All* has the meaning here of "everything" or "the only thing," so the singular verb *is* is correct.]

**BACKGROUND**

In "On Language; O Solecism Mio," William Safire says that intention dictates whether to use a singular or plural verb form with the pronoun *one*, as in the following example: "Ms. Mitchell is *one* of the reporters who *were*—not *was*—denied permission to stay. . . . In this case, the reporter is not seeking to separate herself from the crowd to assert her singularity; on the contrary, she is expressing solidarity with her fellow female journalists, stressing the collective" (*New York Times*, July 8, 1990, late ed. sec. 6:8).

**QUOTATION: ON WRITING**

When regarded as a unit, collective nouns, as well as noun phrases denoting quantity, take singular verbs. *The whole family is active.* (*Family* is a collective noun regarded as a unit.)
—<http://www.wisc.edu/writing/Handbook/SubjectVerb.html#collective>

**EXTRA EXERCISE D**

In writing groups, students can work together to edit the following sentences for subject-verb agreement.

**1.** The couple who move into a new apartment face many decisions.

**2.** One of the biggest choices have to do with how to decorate it.

**3.** Probably the most important decision of all are the color choices.

**4.** Green is one of the colors that looks good in any room.

**Answers to Extra Exercise D**

**1.** The couple who *moves* into a new apartment *faces* many decisions.

**2.** One of the biggest choices *has* to do with how to decorate it.

**3.** Probably the most important decision of all *is* the color choices.

**4.** Green is one of the colors that *look* good in any room.

**EXTRA EXERCISE E**
Complete the following sentences by supplying an appropriate verb.

1. Physics _____ a demanding subject.

2. Do you think physics or economics _____ harder?

3. Sports _____ my favorite pastime.

4. Three-quarters of an hour of exercise several times a week _____ enough to keep a person in reasonably good shape.

5. Statistics _____ that exercise of the body as well as the mind _____ important for good health.

**Answers to Extra Exercise E**

1. is

2. is

Winter has driven the birds south; **all have** left. [*All* refers to the plural noun *birds*, so the plural verb *have* is correct.]

⚠ Alerts: (1) Don't mix singular and plural with *this, that, these,* and *those* used with *kind* and *type. This* and *that* are singular, as are *kind* and *type; these* and *those* are plural, as are *kinds* and *types:* **This** [not *These*] **kind** of rainwear is waterproof. **These** [not *This*] **kinds** of sweaters keep me warm. (2) The rules for indefinite pronouns often collide with practices of avoiding SEXIST LANGUAGE. For suggestions, see 17s and 12f. ●

## 17j How do verbs work with collective nouns?

A **collective noun** names a group of people or things: *family, audience, class, number, committee, team, group,* and the like. When the group of people or things is acting as one unit, use a singular verb. When members of the group are acting individually, use a plural verb. As you're writing, be careful not to shift back and forth between a singular and a plural verb for the same noun.

The senior **class** nervously *awaits* final exams. [The *class* is acting as a single unit, so the verb is singular.]

The senior **class** *were fitted* for their graduation robes today. [The members (of the class) were fitted as individuals, so the verb is plural.]

## 17k Why does the linking verb agree with the subject, not the subject complement?

Even though a LINKING VERB connects a sentence's SUBJECT to its SUBJECT COMPLEMENT, the linking verb agrees with the subject. It does not agree with the subject complement.

**NO**    The worst **part** of owning a car *are* the bills. [The subject is the singular *part*, so the plural verb *are* is wrong. The subject complement is the plural *bills* and doesn't affect agreement.]

**YES**    The worst **part** of owning a car *is* the bills. [The singular subject *part* agrees with the singular verb *is*. The subject complement doesn't affect agreement.]

## 17l What verbs agree with *who, which,* and *that*?

If the ANTECEDENT of *who, which,* or *that* is singular, use a singular verb. If the antecedent is plural, use a plural verb.

The scientist will share the prize with the **researchers** *who* **work** with her. [*Who* refers to *researchers*, so the plural verb *work* is used.]

George Jones is the **student** *who* **works** in the science lab. [*Who* refers to *student*, so the singular verb *works* is used.]

If you use phrases including *one of the* or *the only one of the* immediately before *who, which,* or *that* in a sentence, be careful about the verb you use. *Who, which,* or *that* always refers to the plural word immediately following *one of the,* so the verb must be plural. Although *the only one of* is also always followed by a plural word, *who, which,* or *that* must be singular to agree with the singular *one.*

Tracy is *one of the* students *who* **talk** in class. [*Who* refers to *students*, so the verb *talk* is plural. *Tracy* is pointed out, but the talking is still done by all of the students.]

Jim is *the only one of the* students *who* **talks** in class. [*Who* refers to *one*, so the verb *talks* is singular. *Jim* is the single person who is talking.]

## EXERCISE 17-3
Supply the correct present-tense form of the verb in parentheses. For help, consult 17i through 17l.

**EXAMPLE** Everybody on a class trip to the coastal waters of the Pacific Ocean (to enjoy) <u>enjoys</u> an opportunity to study dolphins in their natural habitat.

1. A class of college students in marine biology (to take) _____ notes individually while watching dolphins feed off the California coast.

2. Everyone in the class (to listen) _____ as a team of dolphin experts (to explain) _____ some of the mammals' characteristics.

3. A group of dolphins, called a pod, usually (to consist) _____ of 10,000 to 30,000 members.

4. One unique characteristic of dolphins' brains (to be) _____ the sleep patterns that (to keep) _____ one-half of the brain awake at all times.

5. All (to need) _____ to stay awake to breathe, or else they would drown.

## 17m How do verbs work with amounts, fields of study, and other special nouns?

### AMOUNTS

SUBJECTS that refer to time, sums of money, distance, or measurement are singular. They take singular verbs.

3. is

4. is

5. show (indicate); is

### BACKGROUND
At the site <http://webster.commnet.edu/sensen/part2/thirteen/pronouns_fun.html>, exercises on pronoun agreement are available.

### QUOTATION: ON WRITING
When used as a grammatical term, *antecedent* means the word or group of words referred to by a pronoun. It does not necessarily come before the pronoun, and it may not be mentioned at all.
—Cornelia Evans and Bergen Evans

### ANSWERS: EXERCISE 17-3
1. take [17j, *class* here refers to students acting individually]

2. listens [17i, *everyone* requires a singular verb]; explains [17j, *team* refers to experts speaking as a group]

3. consists [17j, *group* here refers to a single unit]

4. is [17k, verb agrees with subject *characteristic*]; keep [17l, antecedent of *that* is *patterns* and verb agrees with antecedent]

5. need [17i, *all* here requires a plural verb]

### EXTRA EXERCISE F
In writing groups, students can work together to edit the inaccurate agreement of pronouns and antecedents in the following paragraph.

Plaids have been a favorite fabric design for many centuries. It consists of bars of color crossing each other at right angles. Scotland is the home of the plaid, where they are called a tartan, or, in song, story, and legend, *plaidies.* The tartan, which distinguish the clan of their wearers, is ancient, but their origin is unknown. In its earliest forms they were pieces of cloth about two yards broad and four yards long, which was drawn round the waist in folds that was tightly buckled with a belt. The lower part came down to the knees, and the upper part fell over the left shoulder so that they left the right arm free. Early in the eighteenth century, the "belted plaid" disappeared. They were replaced by the kilt. The particular pattern of tartans which distinguish each clan must have been fixed before 1645, probably before 1600. Later, in 1746, trying to end the clan system, the British Parliament prohibited the Scots from wearing tartans. The action against it was taken following the Battle of Culloden, where Prince Charles Edward Stuart, grandson of James II, was defeated by the Duke of Cumberland. To be caught wearing them carried a penalty of six months' imprisonment. The kilt is worn today so that when the wearer is standing erect, their edges should reach the center of the kneecap. They should be made of a tartan associated with the name of the wearer. In the absence of a family claim to wear them, the Scots allow the wearing of the Royal Stuart tartan.

—Emily Gordon

**Answers to Extra Exercise F**
Plaids have been favorite fabric *designs* for many centuries. *They consist* of bars of color crossing each other at right angles. Scotland is the home of the plaid, where *it is* called a tartan, or, in song, story, and legend, *a plaidie*. The tartan, which *distinguishes* the clan of *its wearer,* is ancient, but *its* origin is unknown. In its earliest *form it was a piece* of cloth about two yards broad and four yards long, which was drawn round the waist in folds that *were* tightly buckled with a belt. The lower part came down to the knees, and the upper part fell over the left shoulder so that *it* left the right arm free. Early in the eighteenth century, the "belted plaid" disappeared. *It was* replaced by the kilt. The particular pattern of *tartan* which *distinguishes* each clan must have been fixed before 1645, probably before 1600. Later, in 1746, trying to end the clan system, the British Parliament prohibited the Scots from wearing *the tartan.* The action against it was taken following the Battle of Culloden, where Prince Charles Edward Stuart, grandson of James II, was defeated by the Duke of Cumberland. To be caught wearing *it* carried a penalty of six months' imprisonment.

**Two hours** *is* not enough time to finish. [time]

**Three hundred dollars** *is* what we must pay. [sum of money]

**Two miles** *is* a short sprint for some serious joggers. [distance]

**Three-quarters of an inch** *is* needed for a perfect fit. [measurement]

## FIELDS OF STUDY

The name for a field of study is singular even if it appears to be plural: *economics, mathematics, physics,* and *statistics.*

> *Statistics* **is** required of science majors. [*Statistics* is a course of study, so the singular verb *is* is correct.]

> *Statistics* **show** that a teacher shortage is coming. [*Statistics* isn't used here as a field of study, so the plural verb *show* is correct.]

## SPECIAL NOUNS

*Athletics, news, ethics,* and *measles* are singular despite their plural appearance. Also, *United States of America* is singular: It is one nation. However, *politics* and *sports* take singular or plural verbs, depending on the meaning of the sentence.

> The *news* **gets** better each day. [*News* is a singular noun, so the singular verb *gets* is correct.]

> *Sports* **is** a good way to build physical stamina. [*Sports* is one general activity, so the singular verb *is* is correct.]

> Three *sports* **are** offered at the recreation center. [*Sports* are separate activities, so the plural verb *are* is correct.]

*Jeans, pants, scissors, clippers, tweezers, eyeglasses, thanks,* and *riches* are some of the words that require a plural verb, even though they refer to one thing. However, if you use *pair* with *jeans, pants, scissors, clippers, tweezers,* or *eyeglasses,* use a singular verb for agreement.

> Those *slacks* **need** pressing. [plural]

> That *pair* of slacks **needs** pressing. [singular]

*Series* and *means* can be singular or plural, according to the meaning you intend.

> Two new TV *series* **are** big hits. [*Series* refers to individual items (two different series), so the plural verb *are* is correct.]

> A *series* of disasters **is** plaguing our production. [*Series* refers to a whole group (the whole series of disasters), so the singular verb *is* is correct.]

# 17n How do verbs work with titles, company names, and words as themselves?

## TITLES

A title itself refers to one work or entity (even when plural and compound NOUNS are in the title), so a singular verb is correct.

> *Breathing Lessons* by Anne Tyler **is** a prize-winning novel.

## COMPANY NAMES

Many companies have plural words in their names. However, a company should always be treated as a singular unit, requiring a singular verb.

> *Cohn Brothers* **boxes** and **delivers** fine art.

## WORDS AS THEMSELVES

Whenever you write about words as themselves to call attention to those words, use a singular verb, even if more than one word is involved.

> *We* **implies** that everyone is included.

> During the Vietnam War, *protective reaction strikes* **was** a euphemism for *bombing*.

**EXERCISE 17-4**   Supply the correct present-tense form of the verb in parentheses. For help, consult 17i through 17n.

**EXAMPLE**   The movie *Wordplay* is about those who (to enjoy) <u>enjoy</u> solving crossword puzzles.

1. When the movie plays at theaters, the audience often (to consist) _____ of different ages and types of people.
2. For fans of crossword puzzles, the major attraction (to be) _____ the challenges they present.
3. Every creator of puzzles (to know) _____ that in the most successful puzzles all of the clues (to be) _____ interesting.
4. *Setters* (to be) _____ is a term used by crossword puzzle fans to describe someone who creates puzzles.
5. These fans, which (to include) _____ celebrities like Jon Stewart, consider the Sunday puzzle in the *New York Times* one of the most difficult.

**EXERCISE 17-5**   This exercise covers all of subject-verb agreement (17b through 17n). Supply the correct form of the verb in parentheses.

**EXAMPLE**   Of the thirty thousand plant species on earth, the rose (to be) <u>is</u> the most universally known.

The kilt is worn today so that when the wearer is standing erect, *its* edges should reach the center of the kneecap. *It* should be made of a tartan associated with the name of the wearer. In the absence of a family claim to wear *one*, the Scots allow the wearing of the Royal Stuart tartan.

## BACKGROUND

Major theorists in language have pointed out that treating the pronouns *everybody* and *everyone* as plurals can be found in the works of such illustrious English writers as Shakespeare, Swift, and Cardinal Newman. Despite such evidence, however, the rule that most indefinite pronouns are singular continues to stand—at least on record. Nonetheless, you and your students may enjoy a debate on this issue. A good catalyst for this discussion is a 1986 essay by language theorist Martha Kolln (Penn State University), who argued in "Everyone's Right to Their Own Language" (*College Composition and Communication* 37.1 (1986): 100–102) that indefinite pronouns should be treated as collective nouns (taking singular or plural form according to meaning) and that the plural possessive pronoun (*their*) after collective indefinite pronouns should be accepted. You may consider assigning a short research project in which students trace the language debate on this subject.

## ANSWERS: EXERCISE 17-4

**1.** consists [17j, singular verb with collective noun *audience*]

**2.** is [17k, verb agrees with the singular subject *attraction*, not the plural complement *challenges*]

**3.** knows [17i, *every* is always singular]; are [17i, *all is* plural in this case because it refers to *clues*]

**4.** is [17n, singular verb with term or words as themselves]

**5.** includes [17l, *which* refers to the plural *fans*]

**1.** invites [17f, singular verb with subject modified by *each*]

**2.** are [17h, words in inverted order]; remain [17c, plural subject *roses*]

**3.** symbolizes [17f, singular verb with *each*]

**4.** are [17h, words in inverted order]; flourish [17c, plural subject *thirty-five*]

**5.** was [17b, singular subject *rose*]

**6.** suggests [17d, singular verb with *one*]

**7.** says [17d, ignoring intervening words]

**8.** explain [17c, plural subject *theories*]

**9.** demonstrates [17j, singular-context collective noun]

**10.** remains [17k, agreeing with subject *best seller*]

### EXTRA EXERCISE G

Rewrite this paragraph so that pronoun-antecedent agreement in person and number is maintained. It may also be necessary to change verbs or other words.

> Buying stock involves many steps. Once a stockbroker receives an order, they call their firm's telephone clerk, who is located near the edge of the trading area. The telephone clerk summons his firm's floor broker by flashing their code number on a large electronic board posted in the trading area. Seeing their number, the floor broker goes to the telephone clerk and picks up the buy order. You then go to the small area set aside for trading in that company's stock. An employee of the Stock Exchange keeps track of all bids to buy and sell that particular stock. The floor broker makes an offer. If they are accepted by the selling broker, the stock is his. If you have bid too low, he must make another bid before someone else gets the stock. Then a reporter enters the deal into the Exchange computer, and they become part of the official record in seconds. After all this, the floor broker returns to the telephone clerk, who reports the deal to the original stockbroker, who bills the client.
>
> —Emily Gordon

1. Each plant species (to invite) _____ much discussion about origins and meanings, and when talk turns to flowers, the rose is usually the first mentioned.

2. More fragrant and colorful (to be) _____ other types of flowers, yet roses (to remain) _____ the most popular worldwide.

3. Each of the types of roses (to symbolize) _____ beauty, love, romance, and secrecy.

4. There (to be) _____ more than two hundred pure species of roses and thousands of mixed species, thirty-five of which (to flourish) _____ in the soil of North America.

5. It's impossible to determine exactly where or when the first rose (to be) _____ domesticated, because roses have existed for so many centuries; one of the earliest references dates back to 3000 BC.

6. One myth from Greek mythology (to suggest) _____ that the rose first appeared with the birth of the goddess Aphrodite.

7. Another myth, which focuses on the rose's thorns, (to say) _____ that an angry god shot arrows into the stem to curse the rose forever with arrow-shaped thorns.

8. While theories of this kind (to explain) _____ the significance and evolution of the rose, few people can explain the flower's enduring popularity.

9. Even today, a couple (to demonstrate) _____ love by purchasing red roses.

10. Of all flowers, the best seller (to remain) _____ the rose.

## PRONOUN-ANTECEDENT AGREEMENT

## 17o What is pronoun-antecedent agreement?

**Pronoun-antecedent agreement** means that a PRONOUN matches its ANTECEDENT in NUMBER (singular or plural) and PERSON (first, second, or third person). Quick Reference 17.7 shows you how to visualize this pattern of grammatical agreement. You might also want to consult Quick Reference 17.1 in 17b for explanations and examples of the concepts *number* and *person*.

> The **firefly** glows when **it** emerges from **its** nest at night. [The singular pronouns *it* and *its* match their singular antecedent, *firefly*.]
>
> **Fireflies** glow when **they** emerge from **their** nests at night. [The plural pronouns *they* and *their* match their plural antecedent, *fireflies*.]

## Quick Reference 17.7

### Pronoun-antecedent agreement

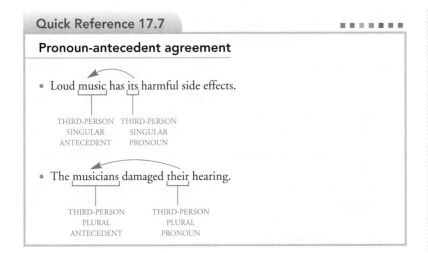

- Loud music has its harmful side effects.

  THIRD-PERSON SINGULAR ANTECEDENT — THIRD-PERSON SINGULAR PRONOUN

- The musicians damaged their hearing.

  THIRD-PERSON PLURAL ANTECEDENT — THIRD-PERSON PLURAL PRONOUN

## 17p How do pronouns work when *and* connects antecedents?

When *and* connects two or more ANTECEDENTS, they require a plural pronoun. This rule applies even if each separate antecedent is singular. (For related material on subjects and verbs, see 17e.)

> **The Cascade Diner *and* the Wayside Diner** closed for New Year's Eve to give **their** [not *its*] employees the night off. [Two separate diners require a plural pronoun.]

When *and* joins singular nouns that nevertheless refer to a single person or thing, use a singular pronoun.

> **My friend *and* neighbor** makes **his** [not *their*] excellent chili every Saturday. [The friend is the same person as the neighbor, so the singular *his* (or *her*) is correct. If two different people were involved, the correct pronoun would be *their*, and *make* would be the correct verb.]

### EACH, EVERY

The words *each* and *every* are singular, even when they refer to two or more antecedents joined by *and*. The same rule applies when *each* or *every* is used alone (17i). (For related material on subjects and verbs, see 17f.)

> *Each* **human hand *and* foot** leaves **its** [not *their*] distinctive print.

The rule still applies when the construction *one of the* follows *each* or *every*.

> *Each one of the* **robbers** left **her** [not *their*] fingerprints at the scene.

## 17q How do pronouns work when *or* connects antecedents?

When ANTECEDENTS are joined by *or*—or by CORRELATIVE CONJUNCTIONS such as *either . . . or, neither . . . nor,* or *not only . . . but (also)*—the antecedents might mix singulars and plurals. For the purposes of agreement, ignore everything before the final antecedent. Quick Reference 17.8 shows you how to visualize this pattern. (For related material on subjects and verbs, see 17g.)

> ~~After the restaurant closes,~~ *either* ~~the resident mice~~ *or* **the owner's cat** gets **itself** a meal.

> ~~After the restaurant closes,~~ *either* ~~the owner's cat~~ *or* **the resident mice** get **themselves** a meal.

---

### Quick Reference 17.8  ■ ■ ■ ■ ■ ■ ■

**When antecedents are joined by *or***

- ~~Either the loudspeakers or~~ the microphone needs its electric cord repaired.

  SINGULAR ANTECEDENT        SINGULAR PRONOUN

- ~~Either the microphone or~~ the loudspeakers needs their electric cords repaired.

  PLURAL ANTECEDENT        PLURAL PRONOUN

---

## 17r How do pronouns work when antecedents are indefinite pronouns?

INDEFINITE PRONOUNS usually refer to unknown persons, things, quantities, or ideas. The unknown aspect is the reason these pronouns are labeled "indefinite." But in a sentence, context gives an indefinite pronoun a clear meaning, even if the pronoun doesn't have a specific antecedent. Most indefinite pronouns are singular. Two indefinite pronouns, *both* and *many,* are plural. A few indefinite pronouns can be singular or plural, depending on the meaning of the sentence.

For a list of indefinite pronouns, grouped as singular or plural, see Quick Reference 17.6 in 17i. For more information about avoiding sexist language, especially when using indefinite pronouns, see 17s and 12f. (For related material on subjects and verbs, see 17i.)

## SINGULAR INDEFINITE PRONOUNS

**Everyone** taking this course hopes to get **his or her** [not *their*] college degree within a year.

**Anybody** wanting to wear a cap and gown at graduation must have **his or her** [not *their*] measurements taken.

**Each** of the students handed in **his or her** [not *their*] final term paper.

**!** Alert: The use of *their* as a singular indefinite pronoun is becoming more common, even in many respectable publications. Although this usage may become universally accepted in the future, we recommend that you avoid it. ●

## SINGULAR *OR* PLURAL INDEFINITE PRONOUNS

When winter break arrives for students, **most** leave **their** dormitories for home. [*Most* refers to *students,* so the plural pronoun *their* is correct.]

As for the luggage, **most** is already on **its** way to the airport. [*Most* refers to *luggage,* so the singular pronoun *its* is correct.]

**None** thinks that **he or she** will miss graduation. [*None* is singular as used in this sentence, so the singular pronoun phrase *he or she* is correct.]

**None** of the students has paid **his or her** [not *their*] graduation fee yet. [*None* is singular as used in this sentence, so the singular pronoun phrase *his or her* is correct.]

**None** are so proud as **they** who graduate. [*None* is plural as used in this sentence, so the plural pronoun *they* is correct.]

## 17s  How do I use nonsexist pronouns?

A word is **nonsexist** when it carries neither male nor female gender. Each PRONOUN in English carries one of three genders: male (*he, him, his*); female (*she, her, hers*); or neutral (*you, your, yours, we, our, ours, them, they, their, theirs, it, its*). Usage today favors nonsexist terms in all word choices. You therefore want to use gender-free pronouns whenever possible. In the past, it was grammatically correct to use only masculine pronouns to refer to INDEFINITE PRONOUNS: "*Everyone open his book.*" Today, however, people feel that the pronouns *he, his, him,* and *himself* exclude women, who make up over half the population. Quick Reference 17.9 shows three ways to avoid using masculine pronouns when referring to males and females together. For more information on gender-neutral language, see 12f.

Questions often arise concerning the use of *he or she* and *his or her.* In general, writers find these gender-free pronoun constructions awkward. To avoid

> ### Quick Reference 17.9
> ■ ■ ■ ■ ■ ■ ■
>
> ## Avoiding the masculine pronoun when referring to males and females together
>
> - **Solution 1:** Use a pair of pronouns—as in the phrase *he or she.* However, avoid using a pair more than once in a sentence or in many sentences in a row. A *he or she* construction acts as a singular pronoun.
>
>   **Everyone** hopes that **he or she** will win a scholarship.
>
>   A **doctor** usually has time to keep up to date only in **his or her** specialty.
>
> - **Solution 2:** Revise into the plural.
>
>   **Many students** hope that **they** will win a scholarship.
>
>   **Most doctors** have time to keep up to date only in **their** specialties.
>
> - **Solution 3:** Recast the sentence.
>
>   Everyone hopes to win a scholarship.
>
>   Few specialists have time for general reading.

them, many writers make the antecedents plural. Doing this becomes problematic when the subject is a SINGULAR INDEFINITE PRONOUN (Quick Reference 17.6 in section 17i). In the popular press (such as newspapers and magazines), the use of the plural pronoun *they* or *them* with a singular antecedent has been gaining favor. Indeed, some experts find that the history of English supports this use. In ACADEMIC WRITING, however, it is better for you not to follow the practice of the popular press. Language practice changes, however, so what we say here is our best advice as we write this book.

## 17t How do pronouns work when antecedents are collective nouns?

A COLLECTIVE NOUN names a group of people or things, such as *family, group, audience, class, number, committee,* and *team.* When the group acts as one unit, use a singular pronoun to refer to it. When the members of the group act individually, use a plural pronoun. In the latter case, if the sentence is awkward, substitute a plural noun for the collective noun. (For related material on subjects and verbs, see 17j.)

The **audience** was cheering as **it** stood to applaud the performers. [The *audience* was acting as one unit, so the singular pronoun *it* is correct.]

The **audience** put on **their** coats and walked out. [The members of the audience were acting as individuals, so all actions become plural; therefore, the plural pronoun *their* is correct.]

The **family** is spending **its** vacation in Rockport, Maine. [All the family members went to one place together.]

The parallel sentence to the last example above would be *The **family** are spending **their** vacations in Maine, Hawaii, and Rome,* which might mean that each family member is going to a different place. But such a sentence is awkward. Therefore, revise the sentence.

The **family members** are spending **their** vacations in Maine, Hawaii, and Rome. [Substituting a plural noun phrase *family members* for the collective noun *family* sounds more natural.]

**EXERCISE 17-6**     Underline the correct pronoun in parentheses. For help, consult 17o through 17t.

**EXAMPLE**    Many wonder where inventors like Benjamin Franklin get (his or her, <u>their</u>) creative energy.

1. Many so-called Founding Fathers are famous one or two of (his, his or her, their) accomplishments, but anyone who knows (his, her, his or her, their) history knows that Franklin is known for many things, including (his, her, his or her, their) inventions.

2. The armonica is not one of his well known inventions, but (its, their) design is ingenious.

3. Also called the glass harmonica, the armonica required a person to place (himself, herself, himself or herself) in front of the instrument and to rotate (its, their) glass bowls.

4. The lightning rod and the Franklin stove established his reputation as an inventor, but (it, they) remained in public domain because Franklin refused to secure patents for his inventions.

5. An inventor like Franklin does not limit (his, her, his or her, their) imagination to one field of science.

6. (He, She, He or she, They) can instead pursue many questions and the challenges (they, it) pose.

7. All scientists who study electricity should know that Ben Franklin provided the names (he, she, he or she, they) still use today for positive and negative electrons.

8. Franklin also named the Gulf Stream and mapped (their, its) current

9. Franklin formed the first public lending library in America, which allowed people to borrow (its, their) books and read them at (his, her, his or her, their) leisure.

10. His public service record also includes the reform of the postal system and the establishment of The Academy and College of Philadelphia, which later merged (their, its) students with those of the State of Pennsylvania to become the University of Pennsylvania.

**ANSWERS: EXERCISE 17-6**

1. their [17o]; his or her [17r and 17s]; his [17o]
2. its [17o]
3. himself or herself [17s]; its [17o]
4. they [17p]
5. his or her [17s]
6. He or she [17s]; they [17o]
7. they [17o]
8. its [17o]
9. its [17o], their [17o]
10. its [17o]

# 18

# Adjectives and Adverbs

## 18a What are the differences between adjectives and adverbs?

The differences between adjectives and adverbs relate to how they function. **Adjectives** modify NOUNS and PRONOUNS. **Adverbs** modify VERBS, adjectives, and other adverbs. What's the same about adjectives and adverbs is that they're both MODIFIERS—that is, words or groups of words that describe other words.

| | |
|---|---|
| ADJECTIVE | The **brisk** *wind* blew. [Adjective *brisk* modifies noun *wind.*] |
| ADVERB | The wind *blew* **briskly.** [Adverb *briskly* modifies verb *blew.*] |

Some people think that all adverbs end in *-ly.* But this isn't correct. While many adverbs do end in *-ly* (eat *swiftly,* eat *frequently,* eat *hungrily*), some do not (eat *fast,* eat *often,* eat *seldom*). To complicate matters further, some adjectives end in *-ly* (*lovely* flower, *friendly* dog). Use meaning, not an *-ly* ending, to identify adverbs.

🌐 **ESOL Tips:** (1) In English, the adjective is always singular, even if its noun is plural: *The **hot** [not *hots*] drinks warmed us up.* (2) Word order in English calls for special attention to the placement of adjectives and adverbs. Here is an example using the adverb *carefully: Thomas closed* [don't place *carefully* here] *the window **carefully*** (see 52b and 52c). ●

**EXERCISE 18-1** Underline and label all adjectives (ADJ) and adverbs (ADV). Then, draw an arrow from each adjective and adverb to the word or words it modifies. Ignore *a, an,* and *the* as adjectives. For help, consult 18a.

1. Today's singles carefully look for possible mates at discount home improvement stores across the country.

2. Understandably, many people find these stores a healthy alternative to dark bars and blind dates.

3. Recently, an employee in the flooring department quietly confided that the best nights for singles are Wednesdays and Thursdays, while weekends generally attract families.

4. A young single mom returns home excitedly because a quick trip to the lumber department for a new door resulted in a date for Saturday night.

5. A lonely widower in his fifties jokingly says he wishes he had developed earlier an interest in wallpapering and gardening.

## 18b When should I use adverbs—not adjectives— as modifiers?

Adverbs MODIFY verbs, adjectives, and other adverbs. Don't use adjectives as adverbs.

**NO** The candidate inspired us **great**. [Adjective *great* cannot modify verb *inspired*.]

**YES** The candidate inspired us **greatly**. [Adverb *greatly* can modify verb *inspired*.]

**NO** The candidate felt **unusual** energetic. [Adjective *unusual* cannot modify adjective *energetic*.]

**YES** The candidate felt **unusually** energetic. [Adverb *unusually* can modify adjective *energetic*.]

**NO** The candidate spoke **exceptional** forcefully. [Adjective *exceptional* cannot modify adverb *forcefully*.]

**YES** The candidate spoke **exceptionally** forcefully. [Adverb *exceptionally* modifies adverb *forcefully*.]

## 18c What is wrong with double negatives?

A **double negative** is a nonstandard form. It is a statement with two negative MODIFIERS, the second of which repeats the message of the first. Negative modifiers include *no, never, not, none, nothing, hardly, scarcely,* and *barely.*

**NO** The factory workers will **never** vote for **no** strike.

**YES** The factory workers will **never** vote for **a** strike.

**NO** The union members did **not** have **no** money in reserve.

**YES** The union members did **not** have **any** money in reserve.

**YES** The union members had **no** money in reserve.

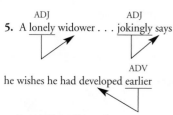

ADJ          ADJ
5. A lonely widower . . . jokingly says

                              ADV
he wishes he had developed earlier

an interest in wallpapering . . .

## BACKGROUND

The Web sites <http://grammar.ccc.commnet .edu/grammar/cgi-shl/quiz.pl/adjectives_quiz .htm> and <http://grammar.ccc.commnet.edu/ grammar/cgi-shl/quiz.pl/adverbs_quiz.htm> provide multiple-choice quizzes on adjectives and adverbs, with answer keys.

## QUOTATION: ON WRITING

I don't think in any language. I think in images. I don't believe that people think in languages.
—Vladimir Nabokov

## LANGUAGE HISTORY

The rule banning double negatives in English is a relatively new one. Double, triple, and even quadruple negatives were acceptable in Old English and Middle English. They are also acceptable in many modern languages. The first attempts to regularize English were made in the eighteenth century. It was then that the first English dictionaries and usage books were written. One of these was Robert Lowth's 1762 *Short Introduction to English Grammar,* in which he stated that "two Negatives in English destroy one another, or are equivalent to an affirmative." The new rich of the merchant class, eager to fit in by speaking and writing correctly, accepted Lowth's rule, and it became the standard.

## BACKGROUND

A Web site that cites basic rules to help students distinguish adjectives from adverbs is <http:// owl.english.purdue.edu/handouts/esl/esladjadv .html>. It also suggests how to avoid common errors. For example: *Good* is an adjective, so you do not *do good* or *live good,* but you *do well* and *live well.*

Take special care to avoid double negatives with contractions of *not: isn't, don't, didn't, haven't,* and the like (27d). The contraction containing *not* serves as the only negative in a sentence. Don't add a second negative.

| NO | He **didn't** hear **nothing**. |
| YES | He **didn't** hear **anything**. |
| NO | They **haven't** had **no** meetings. |
| YES | They **haven't** had **any** meetings. |

Similarly, be careful to avoid double negatives when you use *nor.* The word *nor* is correct only after *neither* (14i). Use the word *or* after any other negative.

| NO | Stewart **didn't** eat dinner **nor** watch television last night. |
| YES | Stewart **didn't** eat dinner **or** watch television last night. |
| YES | Stewart **neither** ate dinner **nor** watched television last night. |

## 18d Do adjectives or adverbs come after linking verbs?

LINKING VERBS connect a SUBJECT to a COMPLEMENT. Always use an adjective, not an adverb, as the complement.

The *guests looked* **happy.** [Verb *looked* links subject *guests* to adjective *happy.*]

The words *look, feel, smell, taste, sound,* and *grow* are usually linking verbs, but sometimes they're simply verbs. Check how any of these verbs is functioning in a sentence.

Zora *looks* **happy.** [*Looks* functions as a linking verb, so the adjective *happy* is correct.]

Zora *looks* **happily** at the sunset. [*Looks* doesn't function as a linking verb, so the adverb *happily* is correct.]

## BAD, BADLY

The words *bad* (adjective) and *badly* (adverb) are particularly prone to misuse with linking verbs.

| NO | The students felt **badly**. [This means the students used their sense of touch badly.] |
| YES | The student felt **bad**. [This means the student had a bad feeling about something.] |

**NO** The food smelled **badly**. [This means the food had a bad ability to smell.]

**YES** The food smelled **bad**. [This means the food had a bad smell to it.]

## GOOD, WELL

When the word *well* refers to health, it is an adjective; at all other times, *well* is an adverb. The word *good* is always an adjective.

Evander looks **well**. [This means that Evander seems to be in good health, so the adjective *well* is correct.]

Evander writes **well**. [This means that Evander writes skillfully, so the adverb *well* is correct.]

Use *good* as an adjective, except when you refer to health.

**NO** She sings **good**. [*Sings* isn't a linking verb, so it calls for an adverb, not the adjective *good*.]

**YES** She sings **well**. [*Sings* isn't a linking verb, so the adverb *well* is correct.]

## EXERCISE 18-2
Underline the correct uses of negatives, adjectives, and adverbs by selecting between the choices in parentheses. For help, consult 18a through 18d.

**EXAMPLE** Because she was only five when her father died, Bernice King, Martin Luther King's youngest child, (<u>barely</u>, bare) remembers the details of her father's (solemnly, <u>solemn</u>) funeral, yet her father's image lives (strong, <u>strongly</u>) within her.

1. Although she did feel (badly, bad) about her father's death when she was younger, King's daughter has managed to put his influence on her to good use by speaking (passionately, passionate) about issues her father first introduced.

2. In her (widely, wide) acclaimed book of sermons and speeches, titled *Hard Questions, Hard Answers,* Bernice King strives to deal with the (intensely, intense) topic of race relations.

3. Bernice King believes, as did her father, that all people must connect (genuinely, genuine), or they won't (never, ever) manage to coexist.

4. Bernice King decided to enter the ministry after she heard a (deeply, deep) voice within her directing her to this (extremely, extreme) (spiritually, spiritual) profession.

5. Bernice King entered the public eye in 1993, when she gave a (locally, local) televised Martin Luther King Day sermon at her father's church, and since then she has lived (happily, happy) in her home in Atlanta with memories of her father that are (peacefully, peaceful) recollections.

**QUOTATION: ON WRITING**

In advertising there is a direct, inverse proportion between the number of adjectives and the number of facts.

—Paul Stevens

**QUOTATION: ON WRITING**

Adverbs are words used to describe actions. They give additional information about *when, how,* and *where* something is happening. Use adverbs to make your writing more precise and interesting.

She spoke *yesterday.* (when)
She spoke *quickly.* (how)
She spoke *here.* (where)

—<http://www2.actden.com/ writ_den/tips/sentence/adverbs.htm>.

**BACKGROUND**

Students can find examples and interactive exercises on correct adjective and adverb use at the Web site <http://www.grammarbook.com/>.

**TEACHING TIP**

The Web site "Fast Hangman" features interactive exercises on adjectives and adverbs using the game Hangman, see <http://www .manythings.org/hmjs/voa-adjadv.html>.

**QUOTATION: ON LANGUAGE**

Adjectives are used so freely these days that we feel almost naked, robbed, if we don't get at least a couple.

—Paul Stevens

**ANSWERS: EXERCISE 18-2**

**1.** bad [18d, adjective modifies noun *feel*]; passionately [18b, adverb modifies verb *speaking*]

**2.** widely [18b, adverb modifies adjective *acclaimed*]; intense [18a, adjective modifies noun *topic*]

**3.** genuinely [18b, adverb modifies verb *connect*]; ever [18c, avoid double negative with *won't*]

**4.** deep [18a, adjective modifies noun *voice*]; extremely [18b, adverb modifies adjective *spiritual*]; spiritual [18a, adjective modifies noun *profession*]

**5.** locally [18b, adverb modifies adjective *televised*]; happily [18b, adverb modifies verb *lived*]; peaceful [18a, adjective modifies noun *recollections*]

**LANGUAGE HISTORY**
Adverbs in Old English and Middle English were formed differently than they are today. To make an adverb, an *-e* was simply added to an adjective. The modern *-ly* ending for adverbs comes from an adjective ending, *-lice* (meaning "like"), which became softened to *-ly* and was reinterpreted as an adverb signal. Some modern adjectives ending in *-ly* (such as *friendly* and *heavenly*) are descendants of those old *-lice* adjectives.

**BACKGROUND**
An adjective can be made from a noun by the addition of a different ending that can color the meaning of the word. For example, the *-ish* ending and the *-y* ending mean "similar to" or "characteristic of." A *yellowish substance* suggests a substance that is not exactly yellow, but close, and a *flowery paragraph* is so ornate and beautiful that it is reminiscent of a flower. Words often take an *-en* ending when they turn from nouns into adjectives (as in *wooden* and *silken*), and adjectives that had a Latin origin frequently end in *-al, -ar,* or *-ory* (as in *beneficial, oracular,* and *promissory*).

**EXTRA EXERCISE**
Underline the adjectives and adverbs. If any adjective or adverb is in an incorrect form, write the correct form above it.

**EXAMPLE**
                    more loudly
The music played <u>loud</u> in the disco than in the restaurant.

**1.** The Joneses have the bigger tree on the block.

**2.** Colorado has some of the most prettiest scenery in the country.

**3.** Which of the twins has the highest fever?

**4.** Juan is friendlier than his cousin.

**5.** The more faster runner of the two received a ribbon.

## 18e What are comparative and superlative forms?

When you write about comparisons, ADJECTIVES and ADVERBS often carry the message. The adjectives and adverbs also communicate degrees of intensity. When a comparison is made between two things, a **comparative** form is used. When a comparison is made about three or more things, a **superlative** form is used.

**REGULAR FORMS OF COMPARISON**
Most adjectives and adverbs are regular. They communicate degrees of intensity in one of two ways: either by adding *-er* and *-est* endings or by adding the words *more, most, less,* and *least* (see Quick Reference 18.1).

The number of syllables in the adjective or adverb usually determines whether to use *-er, -est* or *more, most* and *less, least.*

- **One-syllable words** usually take *-er* and *-est* endings: *large, larger, largest* (adjectives); *far, farther, farthest* (adverbs).
- **Adjectives of two syllables** vary. If the word ends in *-y*, change the *y* to *i* and add *-er, -est* endings: *pretty, prettier, prettiest.* Otherwise, some two-syllable adjectives take *-er, -est* endings: *yellow, yellower, yellowest.* Others take *more, most* and *less, least*: *tangled, more tangled, most tangled; less tangled, least tangled.*
- **Adverbs of two syllables** take *more, most* and *less, least*: *quickly, more quickly, most quickly; less quickly, least quickly.*
- **Three-syllable words** take *more, most* and *less, least*: *dignified, more/most dignified, less/least dignified* (adjective); *carefully, more/most carefully, less/least carefully* (adverb).

### Quick Reference 18.1

**Regular forms of comparison for adjectives and adverbs**

| POSITIVE | Use when nothing is being compared. |
| COMPARATIVE | Use when two things are being compared. Add the ending *-er* or the word *more* or *less*. |
| SUPERLATIVE | Use to compare three or more things. Add the ending *-est* or the word *most* or *least*. |

| Positive [1] | Comparative [2] | Superlative [3+] |
| --- | --- | --- |
| green | greener | greenest |
| happy | happier | happiest |
| selfish | less selfish | least selfish |
| beautiful | more beautiful | most beautiful |

🛑 **Alert:** Be careful not to use a double comparative or double superlative. Use either the *-er* and *-est* endings or *more, most* or *less, least.*

He was **younger** [not *more younger*] than his brother.

Her music was the **loudest** [not *most loudest*] on the stereo. ●

### IRREGULAR FORMS OF COMPARISON

A few comparative and superlative forms are irregular. Quick Reference 18.2 gives you the list. We suggest that you memorize them so they come to mind easily.

🛑 **Alerts:** (1) Be aware of the difference between *less* and *fewer.* They aren't interchangeable. Use *less* with NONCOUNT NOUNS, either items or values: *The sugar substitute has less aftertaste.* Use *fewer* with numbers or COUNT NOUNS: *The sugar substitute has fewer calories.* (2) Don't use *more, most* or *less, least* with **absolute adjectives**, that is, adjectives that communicate a noncomparable quality or state, such as *unique* or *perfect.* Something either *is,* or *is not,* one of a kind. No degrees of intensity are involved: *This teapot is **unique*** [not *the most unique*]; *The artisanship is **perfect*** [not *the most perfect*]. ●

---

### Quick Reference 18.2 ■ ■ ■ ■ ■ ■ ■

#### Irregular forms of comparison for adjectives and adverbs

| Positive [1] | Comparative [2] | Superlative [3+] |
| --- | --- | --- |
| good (*adjective*) | better | best |
| well (*adjective* and *adverb*) | better | best |
| bad (*adjective*) | worse | worst |
| badly (*adverb*) | worse | worst |
| many | more | most |
| much | more | most |
| some | more | most |
| little* | less | least |

*When you're using *little* for items that can be counted (e.g., pickles), use the regular forms *little, littler, littlest.*

---

**EXERCISE 18-3** Complete the chart that follows. Then, write a sentence for each word in the completed chart. For help, consult 18e.

**EXAMPLE** *funny, funnier, funniest:* My brother has a *funny* laugh; he thinks Mom has a *funnier* laugh; the person who has the *funniest* laugh in our family is Uncle Dominic.

**6.** The red blouse is the most attractive in the store.

**7.** Leontyne Price sings good.

**8.** That is the worse diner in town.

**9.** Spain is near to Africa than I realized.

**10.** Marc Chagall is the more famous modern artist from Russia.

### Answers to Extra Exercise

1. biggest
2. prettiest [drop *most*]
3. higher
4. Correct
5. faster [drop *more*]
6. Correct
7. well
8. worst
9. nearer
10. most famous

### WORD HISTORIES

Common irregular adjectives (and adverbs) can be confusing to students because the comparative and superlative forms seem unconnected to the positive form. The realization that these irregularities are only accidents of history rather than the product of difficult rules can make them less intimidating to students.

For example, *good* comes from the Old English *god,* related to the German *gut,* both of which come from the Indo-European word meaning "to be suitable." *Better* and *best* come from the Old English *betera* and *betst,* respectively, based on the Indo-European word meaning "good."

Another example is *worse* and *worst,* which come from their Old English synonyms, *wiersa* and *wyrsta.* However, *bad* does not come from *yfel,* the Old English word for "bad" or "evil," but from the Old English *baeddel,* meaning "hermaphrodite."

### QUOTATION: ON WRITING

As to the adjective: when in doubt, strike it out.
—Mark Twain

**ANSWERS: EXERCISE 18-3**

Sentences called for in the second part of the instructions will vary. Here is the chart filled in.

| Positive | Comparative | Superlative |
| --- | --- | --- |
| small | smaller | smallest |
| greedy | greedier | greediest |
| complete | more complete | most complete |
| gladly | more gladly | most gladly |
| few | fewer | fewest |
| thick | thicker | thickest |
| some | more | most |

**QUOTATION: ON WRITING**

I love writing. I love the swirl and swing of words as they tangle with human emotions.

—James Michener

**TEACHING TIP**

Some students have the idea that verbosity is a sign of "better writing," perhaps because they have fooled hasty readers with unnecessary padding. To help students discover for themselves how vague adjectives and adverbs, like *many, very,* and *a lot,* actually weaken a sentence, have them read aloud a sentence from their own writing, first with and then without, these modifiers. As a starter, you might ask them to tell you which of the following two sentences is more forceful:

**1.** Many of my English instructors become very excited when I enliven narration with a lot of descriptive language.

**2.** My English instructors become excited when I enliven narration with descriptive language.

It may help students to know that such noted writers as Ernest Hemingway and Flannery O'Connor have practiced the art of paring, paring, paring to strong, essential elements.

**ANSWERS: EXERCISE 18-4**

**1.** specially [18b, adverb modifies adjective *designed*]; dense [18e, positive form—nothing is being compared]; closely [18b, adverb modifies verb *imitates*]

**2.** many [18e, positive form—nothing is being compared]; most authentic [18e, superlative

| POSITIVE | COMPARATIVE | SUPERLATIVE |
| --- | --- | --- |
| small | _____ | _____ |
| _____ | greedier | _____ |
| _____ | _____ | most complete |
| gladly | _____ | _____ |
| _____ | _____ | fewest |
| _____ | thicker | _____ |
| some | _____ | _____ |

## 18f Why avoid a long string of nouns as modifiers?

NOUNS sometimes MODIFY other nouns: *truck driver, train track, security system.* Usually, these terms create no problems. However, avoid using several nouns in a row as modifiers. A string of too many nouns makes it difficult for your reader to figure out which nouns are being modified and which nouns are doing the modifying. You can revise such sentences in several ways.

**REWRITE THE SENTENCE**

**NO** I asked my adviser to write **two college recommendation letters** for me.

**YES** I asked my adviser to write *letters of recommendation to two colleges* for me.

**CHANGE ONE NOUN TO A POSSESSIVE AND ANOTHER TO AN ADJECTIVE**

**NO** He will take the **United States Navy examination** for **navy engineer training**.

**YES** He will take the *United States Navy's examination* for *naval engineer training*.

**CHANGE ONE NOUN TO A PREPOSITIONAL PHRASE**

**NO** Our **student adviser training program** has won many awards.

**YES** Our *training program for student advisers* has won many awards. [This change requires a change from the singular *adviser* to the plural *advisers*.]

**EXERCISE 18-4** Underline the better choice in parentheses. For help, consult this entire chapter.

**EXAMPLE** Alexis, a huge and powerful six-year-old Siberian tiger, (curious, curiously) explores her new zoo home together with five other tigers.

1. The new tiger home at the world-famous Bronx Zoo is a (special, specially) designed habitat, planted with (dense, denser) undergrowth so that it (close, closely) imitates the tigers' natural wilderness.

2. Like tigers in the wild, the six tigers in this habitat, which (more, many) experts consider the (more authentic, most authentic) of all artificial tiger environments in the world, will face some of the physical challenges and sensory experiences that keep them happy and (healthy, healthier).

3. Research shows that tigers feel (bad, badly) and fail to thrive in zoos without enrichment features placed in (good, well) locations to inspire tigers to stalk (stealthy, stealthily) through underbrush, loll (lazy, lazily) on heated rocks, or tug (vigorous, vigorously) on massive pull toys.

4. Wildlife zoologists think that the new Tiger Mountain exhibit will also serve zoo visitors (good, well) by allowing them to observe and admire the amazing strength, agility, and intelligence of a (rapid, rapidly) dwindling species.

5. Today, (fewer, less) than 5,000 Siberian tigers remain in the wild, which makes it imperative for zoos to raise people's awareness of the (great, greatest) need to prevent the extinction of these big cats that are considered among the (more, most) powerful, beautiful animals in the world.

For more help with your writing, grammar, and research,
go to **www.mycomplab.com**

form]; healthy [18e, positive form—nothing is being compared]

**3.** bad [18d, adjective with the linking verb *feel*]; good [18d, adjective modifies noun *locations*]; stealthily, lazily, vigorously [18b, adverbs modify verbs *stalk, loll,* and *tug*]

**4.** well [18d, adverb modifies verb *serve*]; rapidly [18b, adverb modifies adjective *dwindling*]

**5.** fewer [18e, countable items use *fewer*]; great [18e, positive form—nothing is being compared]; most [18e, superlative form]

# Sentence Fragments

## 19a What is a sentence fragment?

A **sentence fragment** looks like a sentence, but it's actually only part of a sentence. That is, even though a sentence fragment begins with a capital letter and ends with a period (or question mark or exclamation point), it doesn't contain an INDEPENDENT CLAUSE. Fragments are merely unattached PHRASES or DEPENDENT CLAUSES.

**BACKGROUND**
The site <http://www.aliscot.com/bigdog/fragments.htm> includes suggestions for identifying and correcting sentence fragments and an online quiz.

**QUOTATION: ON WRITING**
Fragments, or incomplete sentences, occur quite frequently when we speak, so it's no wonder sentence fragments are often found in formal writing.
—<http://writing2.richmond.edu/writing/wweb/fragment.html>

**TEACHING TIP**
Some students have trouble understanding that structures rather than meanings (or sense-making) determine whether or not a clause

"stands alone" or is dependent. When such students encounter a structure such as *Yet its color suggests otherwise,* they may confuse the independent clause with a fragment because, they reason, this clause does not express a complete thought and cannot stand alone. When pressed for an explanation, they may say that a reader has no idea what *it* is or to what concept the word *otherwise* signals some point of contrast. Here the analogy of a lone chimney standing oddly in a rural landscape may be instructive. The chimney as a structure stands alone even though we know that it makes no real sense apart from the house or building to which it once belonged. You may want to point out that the independent clause *It squeaks* has fewer words than the dependent clause *Because it squeaks.* To help students separate structure from meaning, use nonsense words to let them discern the difference between a fragment and an independent clause that may stand alone as a structure even while making little sense. Here are some examples: *the biglio zoosed the umstead; the biglio zoosing an umstead; until the biglio zoosed the umstead; an umstead was zoosed by the biglio; at the biglio zoosing; the umpstead zoosed by the biglio; nonetheless, it zoosed the umpstead; although it zoosed the umstead; the umstead, however, was totally zoosed by it.*

## BACKGROUND

In "The Patterns of Language: Perspective on Teaching Writing" (*Teaching English in the Two-Year College* 24.2 (1997): 136–144), Pamela Dykstra argues that when students examine syntactic units, they come to understand the concept of *sentence boundaries.* She offers three detailed ways of teaching the concept.

## QUOTATION: ON WRITING

With sixty staring me in the face, I have developed inflammation of the sentence structure and a definite hardening of the paragraphs.
—James Thurber

## TEACHING TIP: COLLABORATION

You might find it useful to have students work in groups to identify and correct fragments found in paragraphs taken from their own

| FRAGMENT | The telephone with redial capacity. [no verb] |
| CORRECT | The telephone has redial capacity. |
| FRAGMENT | Rang loudly for ten minutes. [no subject] |
| CORRECT | The telephone rang loudly for ten minutes. |
| FRAGMENT | At midnight. [a phrase without a verb or subject] |
| CORRECT | The telephone rang at midnight. |
| FRAGMENT | Because the telephone rang loudly. [dependent clause starting with subordinating conjunction *because*] |
| CORRECT | Because the telephone rang loudly, the family was awakened in the middle of the night. |
| FRAGMENT | Which really annoyed me. [dependent clause starting with relative pronoun *which*] |
| CORRECT | The telephone call was a wrong number, which really annoyed me. |

Sentence fragments can ruin the clarity of your writing. Moreover, in ACADEMIC WRITING and BUSINESS WRITING, sentence fragments imply that you don't know basic sentence structure or that you're a careless proofreader.

| NO | The lawyer was angry. When she returned from court. She found the key witness waiting in her office. [Was the lawyer angry when she returned from court, or when she found the witness in her office?] |
| YES | The lawyer was angry when she returned from court. She found the key witness waiting in her office. |
| YES | The lawyer was angry. When she returned from court, she found the key witness waiting in her office. |

Let's go beyond the grammatical terms to a more practical approach to recognizing sentence fragments, so that you can avoid them in your writing. To learn to recognize sentence fragments, see 19b; to learn several ways to correct sentence fragments, see 19c and 19d.

Many writers wait until the REVISING and EDITING stages of the WRITING PROCESS to check for sentence fragments. During DRAFTING, the goal is to get ideas down on paper or disk. As you draft, if you suspect that you've written a sentence fragment, simply underline or highlight it in boldface or italics and move on. Later, you can easily find it to check and correct.

## 19b How can I recognize a sentence fragment?

If you tend to write SENTENCE FRAGMENTS, you want a system for recognizing them. Quick Reference 19.1 shows you a Sentence Test for checking that you haven't written a sentence fragment. Following this Quick Reference, we discuss each question in more detail in 19b.1 through 19b.3.

---

### Quick Reference 19.1 ■ ■ ■ ■ ■ ■ ■

#### Sentence test to identify sentence fragments

**QUESTION 1: IS THE WORD GROUP A DEPENDENT CLAUSE?**

A DEPENDENT CLAUSE is a word group that has a subject and a verb but starts with a word that creates dependence—either a SUBORDINATING CONJUNCTION or a RELATIVE PRONOUN.

| | |
|---|---|
| FRAGMENT | **When** winter comes early. [starts with *when*, a word that creates dependence] |
| CORRECT | **When** winter comes early, **ships often rescue the stranded whales.** [adds an independent clause to create a sentence] |
| FRAGMENT | **Which** can happen quickly. [starts with *which*, a word that creates dependence] |
| CORRECT | **Whales cannot breathe through the ice and will drown, which** can happen quickly. [adds an independent clause to create a sentence] |

**QUESTION 2: IS THERE A VERB?**

| | |
|---|---|
| FRAGMENT | Thousands of whales in the Arctic Ocean. [Because a verb is missing, this is a phrase, not a sentence.] |
| CORRECT | Thousands of whales **live** in the Arctic Ocean. [adds a verb to create a sentence] |

**QUESTION 3: IS THERE A SUBJECT?**

| | |
|---|---|
| FRAGMENT | Stranded in the Arctic Ocean. [Because a subject is missing, this is a phrase, not a sentence.] |
| CORRECT | **Many whales** *were* stranded in the Arctic Ocean. [adds a subject (and the verb *were* to *stranded*) to create a sentence] |

---

writing or those that occur in the following paragraph. Each group can present to the class a revision of a paragraph, pointing out the merits of the new version. In the paragraph shown here, fragments are often signaled by the words *just, only, for example, also, mainly,* and *such as.*

> In their early history, the people of Asia followed the seasons through the valleys until they found no more land. Only the sea and sky and a sheet of ice stretching across the Bering Strait. They did not think about the past. Just the present. For example, making weapons. Such as tree limbs used for bows. Also knives made from sharpened stones. Just like their forefathers. Moving south, they eventually reached the Rio Grande. Mainly known today as the river that separates Mexico and the United States.

**BACKGROUND**

*The Internet TESL Journal: For Teachers of English as a Second Language,* a monthly Web journal, provides articles and other teaching resources at <http://iteslj.org>. The link at <http://a4esl.org/q/j> offers a large collection of interactive quizzes on grammar, including sentence fragments, for ESOL students.

**BACKGROUND**

Purdue University's Online Writing Lab (OWL) features several informative Web pages on sentence fragments. Also, the page at <http://owl.english.purdue.edu/handouts/grammar/g_frag.html> contains links to its fragment exercises for editing practice.

**TEACHING TIP**

Students sometimes create fragments as they attempt to write longer or more complicated sentences and experiment with their style. Without a range of syntactic structures available to them, students may try to vary the rhythm of their sentences, suggest pauses for emphasis, and establish sentence variety with the placement of periods. Fragments often appear because students begin using dependent clauses, participial phrases, elliptical constructions, and absolute phrases in their writing before they have enough knowledge and control of these structures.

Students benefit when they learn new sentence patterns that also help them avoid fragments. Students who use periods to suggest a long pause may benefit from instruction on the dash (Chapter 29). Students creating fragments from dependent clauses, absolute phrases, and participial phrases may benefit from studying coordination and subordination (Chapter 9), parallelism (Chapter 10), and techniques for achieving sentence variety and emphasis (Chapter 9).

**TEACHING TIP**
Group editing, as a class, can be a useful exercise to reinforce basic editing techniques. Choose a passage that has several fragments or other grammar errors. If you teach in a smart classroom, project the passage on the screen. Edit the passage on screen, taking suggestions from the class. Using "track changes," annotate why you are changing a particular word or phrase. After you have finished, e-mail the revised and annotated document to the students as a study guide.

**BACKGROUND**
The Web site <http://grammar.ccc.commnet .edu/grammar/fragments.htm> offered by Capital Community College includes quizzes, suggestions, and links for repairing sentence fragments.

**QUOTATION: ON WRITING**
I am unlikely to trust a sentence that comes easily.

—William Gass

**TEACHING TIP**
Students who regularly create fragments by omitting subjects from their sentences are likely to "hear" the subject of a preceding sentence and unconsciously allow that subject to stand as an "understood" subject for the fragment. (Example: "Students want to use complete sentences in their academic writing. Avoid fragments.") They may even create such fragments in order to avoid repetitious wording, as in "*Students also want* to avoid fragments." You may want to encourage students who have this

**19b.1**  **Question 1: Is the word group a dependent clause?**

If you answer yes to question 1, you're looking at a sentence fragment. A DEPENDENT CLAUSE is a word group that has a subject and a verb but starts with a word that creates dependence. The only words that create dependence are SUBORDINATING CONJUNCTIONS and RELATIVE PRONOUNS. Such a word before an INDEPENDENT CLAUSE creates a dependent clause, which can't stand alone as a sentence and is therefore a sentence fragment. To become a complete sentence, the fragment needs either to be joined to an independent clause or to be rewritten.

**FRAGMENTS WITH SUBORDINATING CONJUNCTIONS**

A complete list of subordinating conjunctions appears in Quick Reference 14.7 in 14i. Some frequently used ones are *after, although, because, before, if, unless,* and *when.*

| | |
|---|---|
| FRAGMENT | **Because** she returned my books. [*Because,* a subordinating conjunction, creates a dependent clause.] |
| CORRECT | **Because** she returned my books, ***I can study.*** [A comma and the independent clause *I can study* are added, and the sentence becomes complete.] |
| FRAGMENT | **Unless** I study. [*Unless,* a subordinating conjunction, creates a dependent clause.] |
| CORRECT | ***I won't pass the test*** **unless** I study. [The independent clause *I won't pass the test* is added, and the sentence becomes complete.] |

🛑 **Alert:** When a dependent clause starts with a subordinating conjunction and comes before its independent clause, use a comma to separate the clauses (24c). ●

**FRAGMENTS WITH RELATIVE PRONOUNS**

Relative pronouns are *that, which, who, whom,* and *whose.*

| | |
|---|---|
| FRAGMENT | **That** we had studied for all week. [*That,* a relative pronoun, creates a dependent clause here.] |
| CORRECT | ***We passed the exam*** **that** we had studied for all week. [The independent clause *We passed the exam* is added, and the sentence becomes complete.] |

When *which, who,* and *whose* begin questions, they function as INTERROGATIVE PRONOUNS, not relative pronouns. Questions are complete sentences, not fragments: *Which* class are you taking? *Who* is your professor? *Whose* book is that?

## 19b.2   Question 2: Is there a verb?

If you answer no to question 2, you're looking at a sentence fragment. When a VERB is missing from a word group, the result is a PHRASE, not a sentence. You can figure out if a word is a verb by seeing if it can change in TENSE. Verbs have tenses to tell what *is* happening, what *has* happened, or what *will* happen.

> Now the telephone **rings.** [present tense]
>
> Yesterday, the telephone **rang.** [past tense]

When you check for verbs, remember that VERBALS (14e) are not verbs. Verbals might look like verbs, but they don't function as verbs.

| | |
|---|---|
| FRAGMENT | Yesterday, the students **registering** for classes. [*Registering* is a verbal called a present participle, not a verb.] |
| CORRECT | Yesterday, the students **were registering** for classes. [Adding the auxiliary verb *were* to the present participle *registering* creates a verb.] |
| FRAGMENT | Now the students **to register** for classes. [*To register* is a verbal called an infinitive, not a verb.] |
| CORRECT | Now the students **want to register** for classes. [Adding the verb *want* to the infinitive *to register* creates a verb.] |

## 19b.3   Question 3: Is there a subject?

If you answer no to question 3, you're looking at a sentence fragment. When a SUBJECT is missing from a word group, the result is a PHRASE, not a sentence. To see if a word is a subject, ask, "Who (*or* What) performs the action?"

| | |
|---|---|
| FRAGMENT | Studied hard for class. [*Who* studied hard for class? unknown] |
| CORRECT | The students studied hard for class. [*Who* studied hard for class? *The students* is the answer, so a subject makes the sentence complete.] |
| FRAGMENT | Contained some difficult questions. [*What* contained some difficult questions? unknown] |
| CORRECT | The test contained some difficult questions. [*What* contained some difficult questions? *The test* is the answer, so a subject makes the sentence complete.] |

particular problem to proofread their paragraphs by reading their sentences aloud and in reverse order. This process is nearly always successful in calling attention to a fragment. When students experiment with sentence-combining techniques (both coordination and subordination), they not only create more sophisticated sentences, but also solve the problem of undue repetition.

**ANOTHER EXAMPLE**

If your students have trouble recognizing dependent clauses as fragments, you may want to give them practice. Ask them to identify the fragments in the following mixture of complete and incomplete sentences. You might also ask them to combine the sentences so that each one is complete, being careful to separate with a comma each opening dependent clause from the independent one that follows.

> Many elderly people have pets as companions. Because the elderly are often lonely. Nevertheless, pets make demands on their energy. For example, if a cat is sick, and when a dog must be bathed. Unless the owner has the strength and funds to care for the pet's needs. Then the pet is better off with a younger owner. Since the pet deserves a good home too. Before getting a cat or dog, people should be certain that they can provide adequate care.

**BACKGROUND**

The Lynchburg College Web site at <http://www.lynchburg.edu/x2383.xml> suggests likely causes of sentence fragments.

**TEACHING TIP**

To demonstrate how phrases can be turned into complete sentences, you might ask two students to read the following dialogue aloud in class and then improvise each comment as a sentence.

*A:* When are you coming?

*B:* In a minute.

*A:* Really?

*B:* Really.

*A:* Hurry up!

*B:* OK, OK. Just a second. How about Mother?

*A:* Who?

*B:* Mother.

*A:* Sure. Ready hours ago.

## TEACHING TIP

Dictating a passage like the one here for students to copy and punctuate can be a helpful exercise in identifying sentence boundaries. Students can compare their versions and discuss any differences.

> We have a nine-acre lake on our ranch and a warm spring that feeds it all winter. By mid-March the lake ice begins to melt where the spring feeds in, and every year the same pair of mallards come ahead of the others and wait. Though there is very little open water they seem content. They glide back and forth through a thin estuary, brushing watercress with their elegant folded wings, then tip end-up to eat and, after, clamber onto the lip of ice that retreats, hardens forward, and retreats again.
>
> —Gretel Ehrlich

## ANSWERS: EXERCISE 19-1

The number in brackets refers to the question in Quick Reference 19.1 that identifies what has caused the fragment.

 **1.** Fragment: starts with a subordinating conjunction (*because*), which creates dependence, and lacks an independent clause to complete the thought. [1]

 **2.** Fragment: no verb [2]

 **3.** Complete sentence

 **4.** Fragment: no subject [3]

 **5.** Fragment: no subject [3]

 **6.** Complete sentence

 **7.** Fragment: no verb [2]

 **8.** Complete sentence

 **9.** Fragment: starts with a subordinating conjunction (*although*), which creates dependence, and lacks an independent clause to complete the thought. [1]

 **10.** Fragment: no verb [2]

Be especially careful with COMPOUND PREDICATES—for example, *We **took** the bus to the movie **and walked** home.* If you were to place a period after *movie,* the second part of the compound predicate would be a sentence fragment. Every sentence needs its own subject. To check for this kind of sentence fragment, ask the question "Who?" or "What?" of each verb.

**NO**  A few students organized a study group to prepare for midterm exams. **Decided to study together for the rest of the course.** [*Who* decided to study together? The answer is *The students* (who formed the group), but this subject is missing.]

**YES**  A few students organized a study group to prepare for midterm exams. ***The students* decided to study together for the rest of the course.**

IMPERATIVE SENTENCES—commands and some requests—may appear at first glance to be fragments caused by missing subjects. They're not fragments, however. Imperative sentences are complete sentences because their subjects are implied. An implied subject can be *you, anybody, somebody, everybody,* or another INDEFINITE PRONOUN.

Run! [This sentence implies the pronoun *you.* The complete sentence would be *You run!*]

Return all library books to the front desk. [This sentence implies the indefinite pronoun *everyone.* The complete sentence would be *Everyone (should) return all library books to the front desk.*]

**EXERCISE 19-1**  Identify each word group as either a complete sentence or a fragment. If the word group is a sentence, circle its number. If it's a fragment, tell why it's incomplete. For help, see Quick Reference 19.1 in 19b and sections 19b.1 through 19b.3.

**EXAMPLE**  Although antibacterial soaps have become popular. [Starts with a subordinating conjunction (*although*), which creates dependence, and lacks an independent clause to complete the thought; see Quick Reference 19.1 and section 19c.1]

1. Because antibacterial soaps do not provide protection against viruses.
2. Viruses responsible for a variety of common health problems.
3. Regular soap often successfully eliminates bacteria, viruses, and dirt.
4. Indicate that antibacterial soaps may wash away useful bacteria.
5. Eliminates most of the harmful bacteria as effectively as regular soap.
6. Careful hand washing cannot be stressed enough.
7. To work efficiently, antibacterial soaps, even those purchased in health food stores.

8. Most studies show that antibacterial soaps do not lead to resistant bacteria.
9. Although many people still believe they should not use antibacterial soaps.
10. Bacteria from overuse of antibiotics.

## 19c What are major ways of correcting fragments?

Once you've identified a SENTENCE FRAGMENT (19b), you're ready to correct it. You can do this in one of two ways: by joining it to an independent clause (19c.1) or by rewriting it (19c.2).

### 19c.1 Correcting a sentence fragment by joining it to an independent clause

One way you can correct a sentence fragment is by joining it to an INDEPENDENT CLAUSE—that is, to a complete sentence. The first two examples that follow deal with dependent-clause fragments; the examples following the ALERT examine fragments with missing subjects and/or verbs.

**FRAGMENT** **Because** the ice was thick. [Although this word group has a subject (*ice*) and verb (*was*), it starts with the subordinating conjunction *because*.]

**CORRECT** **Because** the ice was thick, ***icebreakers were required to serve as rescue ships.*** [Adding a comma and joining the fragment to the independent clause *icebreakers were required to serve as rescue ships* creates a complete sentence.]

**CORRECT** ***Icebreakers were required to serve as rescue ships*** **because** the ice was thick. [Joining the fragment to the independent clause *Icebreakers were required to serve as rescue ships* creates a complete sentence.]

**FRAGMENT** **Who** feared the whales would panic. [This fragment starts with the relative pronoun *who*.]

**CORRECT** ***The noisy motors of the ships worried the crews,*** **who** feared the whales would panic. [Joining the fragment to the independent clause *The noisy motors of the ships worried the crews* creates a complete sentence.]

⓵ Alert: Be careful with all words that indicate time, such as *after, before, since,* and *until.* They aren't always subordinating conjunctions. Sometimes they function as ADVERBS—especially if they begin a complete sentence. At other times, they function as PREPOSITIONS. When you see one of these words that indicate time, realize that you aren't necessarily looking at a dependent-clause fragment.

> **Before,** the whales had responded to classical music. [This is a complete sentence in which *Before* is an adverb that modifies the independent clause *the whales had responded to classical music.*]

> **Before the whales had responded to classical music,** some crew members tried rock and roll music. [If the word group before the comma stood on its own, it would be a sentence fragment because it starts with *Before* functioning as a subordinating conjunction.] ●

| | |
|---|---|
| FRAGMENT | **To announce new programs for crime prevention.** [*To announce* starts an infinitive phrase, not a sentence.] |
| CORRECT | *The mayor called a news conference last week* **to announce** new programs for crime prevention. [The infinitive phrase starting with *to announce* is joined with an independent clause.] |
| FRAGMENT | **Hoping for strong public support.** [*Hoping* starts a present-participle phrase, not a sentence.] |
| CORRECT | **Hoping** for strong public support, *she gave examples of problems throughout the city.* [The present-participle phrase starting with *Hoping* is joined with an independent clause.] |
| FRAGMENT | **Introduced by her assistant.** [*Introduced* starts a past-participle phrase, not a sentence.] |
| CORRECT | **Introduced** by her assistant, *the mayor began with an opening statement.* [The past-participle phrase starting with *Introduced* is joined with an independent clause.] |
| FRAGMENT | **During the long news conference.** [*During* functions as a preposition—starting a prepositional phrase, not a sentence.] |
| CORRECT | *Cigarette smoke made the conference room seem airless* **during** the long news conference. [The prepositional phrase starting with *during* is joined with an independent clause.] |
| FRAGMENT | **A politician with fresh ideas.** [*A politician* starts an appositive phrase, not a sentence.] |

CORRECT   *Most people respected the mayor,* **a politician** with fresh ideas. [The appositive phrase starting with *a politician* is joined with an independent clause.]

## EXERCISE 19-2   Find and correct any sentence fragments. If a sentence is correct, circle its number. For help, consult 19a through 19c.

EXAMPLE   Even though lice are a common problem for young children.

Correct: Lice are a common problem for young children.

1. Even though lice are not dangerous and do not spread disease, parents tend to worry about their children. Who have been infected with this parasite.
2. Although good hygiene is important, it does not prevent lice infestation. Which can occur on clean, healthy scalps.
3. Spread only through direct contact. Lice are unable to fly or jump.
4. Evidence of lice has been found on ancient Egyptian mummies, which suggests that lice have been annoying humans for a long time.
5. While lice can spread among humans who share combs or pillows or hats. Lice cannot be spread from pets to humans.
6. Doctors may prescribe special shampoos and soaps. To help get rid of the lice on a child's head.
7. Because lice do not like heat, experts recommend putting infected sheets and stuffed animals and pillows in a dryer for thirty minutes.
8. Just one is called a *louse,* and a louse egg is called a *nit.* Which is where we get the words *lousy* and *nit-pick.*
9. Using a hair dryer after applying a scalp treatment can be dangerous. Because some treatments contain flammable ingredients.
10. Although lice cannot live for more than twenty-four hours without human contact.

## 19c.2   Correcting a sentence fragment by rewriting it

A second way you can correct a sentence fragment is by rewriting it as an INDEPENDENT CLAUSE—that is, as a complete sentence. The first two examples below deal with dependent-clause fragments; the others examine fragments with missing subjects and/or verbs.

FRAGMENT   **Because** the ice was thick. [Although this word group has a subject (*ice*) and verb (*was*), it starts with the subordinating conjunction *because.*]

CORRECT   The ice was thick. [The fragment starting with *Because* is rewritten to become a complete sentence.]

### ANSWERS: EXERCISE 19-2

1. Even though lice are not dangerous and do not spread disease, parents tend to worry about their children who have been infected with this parasite. [dependent clause attached to independent clause]

2. Although good hygiene is important, it does not prevent lice infestation, which can occur on clean, healthy scalps. [dependent clause attached to independent clause]

3. Spread only through direct contact, lice are unable to fly or jump. [past participle phrase attached to independent clause]

4. [correct sentence]

5. While lice can spread among humans who share combs or pillows or hats, lice cannot be spread from pets to humans. [dependent clause attached to independent clause]

6. Doctors may prescribe special shampoos and soaps to help get rid of the lice on a child's head. [infinitive phrase joined to independent clause]

7. [correct sentence]

8. Just one is called a louse, and a louse egg is called a nit, which is where we get the words lousy and *nit-pick.* [dependent clause attached to independent clause]

9. Using a hair dryer after applying a scalp treatment can be dangerous because some treatments contain flammable ingredients. [dependent clause attached to independent clause]

10. Lice cannot live for more than twenty-four hours without human contact. [subordinating conjunction dropped from dependent clause]

| FRAGMENT | **Who** feared the whales would panic. [This fragment starts with the relative pronoun *who*.] |
|---|---|
| CORRECT | ***The crew*** feared the whales would panic. [The fragment starting with *Who* is rewritten to become a complete sentence.] |
| FRAGMENT | **To announce** new programs for crime prevention. [*To announce* starts an infinitive phrase, not a sentence.] |
| CORRECT | ***The mayor called a news conference last week because she wanted*** **to announce** new programs for crime prevention. [The infinitive phrase starting with *To announce* is rewritten to become a complete sentence.] |
| FRAGMENT | **Hoping** for strong public support. [*Hoping* starts a present-participle phrase, not a sentence.] |
| CORRECT | ***She was*** **hoping** for strong public support. [The present-participle phrase starting with *Hoping* is rewritten to become a complete sentence.] |
| FRAGMENT | **Introduced** by her assistant. [*Introduced* starts a past-participle phrase, not a sentence.] |
| CORRECT | **Introduced** by her assistant, ***the mayor began with an opening statement.*** [The past-participle phrase starting with *Introduced* is rewritten to become a complete sentence.] |
| FRAGMENT | **During** the long news conference. [*During* functions as a preposition that starts a prepositional phrase, not a sentence.] |
| CORRECT | ***It was hard to breathe*** **during** the long news conference. [The prepositional phrase starting with *During* is rewritten to become a complete sentence.] |
| FRAGMENT | **A politician** with fresh ideas. [*A politician* starts an appositive phrase, not a sentence.] |
| CORRECT | ***She seemed to be*** **a politician** with fresh ideas. [The appositive phrase is rewritten to become a complete sentence.] |

## 19d How can I fix a fragment that is part of a compound predicate?

A COMPOUND PREDICATE contains two or more VERBS. When the second part of a compound predicate is punctuated as a separate sentence, it becomes a sentence fragment.

| | |
|---|---|
| FRAGMENT | The reporters asked the mayor many questions about the new program. **And then discussed her answers among themselves.** [*And then discussed* starts a compound predicate fragment, not a sentence.] |
| CORRECT | The reporters asked the mayor many questions about the new program and then discussed her answers among themselves. [The compound predicate fragment starting with *And then discussed* is joined to the independent clause.] |
| CORRECT | The reporters asked the mayor many questions about the new program. ***Then the reporters*** **discussed** her answers among themselves. [The compound predicate fragment starting with *And then discussed* is rewritten as a complete sentence.] |

**EXERCISE 19-3**  Go back to Exercise 19-1 and revise the sentence fragments into complete sentences. In some cases, you may be able to combine two fragments into one complete sentence.

## 19e  What are the two special fragment problems?

Two special fragment problems sometimes involve lists and examples. Lists and examples must be part of a complete sentence, unless they are formatted as a column.

You can connect a list fragment by attaching it to the preceding independent clause using a colon or a dash. You can correct an example fragment by attaching it to an independent clause (with or without punctuation, depending on the meaning) or by rewriting it as a complete sentence.

| | |
|---|---|
| FRAGMENT | You have a choice of desserts. **Carrot cake, chocolate silk pie, apple pie, or peppermint ice cream.** [The list cannot stand on its own as a sentence.] |
| CORRECT | You have a choice of desserts: carrot cake, chocolate silk pie, apple pie, or peppermint ice cream. [A colon joins the sentence and the list.] |
| CORRECT | You have a choice of desserts—carrot cake, chocolate silk pie, apple pie, or peppermint ice cream. [A dash joins the sentence and the list.] |
| FRAGMENT | Several good places offer brunch. **For example, the restaurants Sign of the Dove and Blue Yonder.** [Examples can't stand on their own as a sentence.] |

**ANSWERS: EXERCISE 19-3**
Answers will vary greatly because students can write complete sentences in many ways from the fragments in Exercise 19-1. Often students need to make up information to complete the fragments. Here's one set of possible answers.

**1.** Antibacterial soaps do not provide protection against viruses.

**2.** Viruses are responsible for a variety of common health problems.

**3. & 4.** Although regular soap often successfully eliminates bacteria, viruses, and dirt, studies indicate that antibacterial soaps may wash away useful bacteria.

**5.** Antibacterial soap eliminates most of the harmful bacteria as effectively as regular soap.

**6. & 7.** Careful hand washing cannot be stressed enough, but to work efficiently, antibacterial soaps, even those purchased in health food stores, must be used regularly.

**8.** Most studies show that antibacterial soaps do not lead to resistant bacteria.

**9. & 10.** Although many people still believe they should not use antibacterial soaps, there is a much greater danger of becoming vulnerable to bacteria from the overuse of antibiotics.

| CORRECT | Several good places offer brunch—**for example,** the restaurants Sign of the Dove and Blue Yonder. |
|---|---|
| CORRECT | Several good places offer brunch. **For example,** *there are* the restaurants Sign of the Dove and Blue Yonder. |

## 19f How can I recognize intentional fragments?

Professional writers sometimes intentionally use fragments for emphasis and effect.

> But in the main, I feel like a brown bag of miscellany propped against a wall. Pour out the contents, and there is discovered a jumble of small things priceless and worthless. **A first-water diamond, an empty spool, bits of broken glass, lengths of string, a key to a door long since crumbled away, a rusty knife-blade, old shoes saved for a road that never was and never will be, a nail bent under the weight of things too heavy for any nail, a dried flower or two still a little fragrant.**
>
> —Zora Neale Hurston, *How It Feels to Be Colored Me*

Being able to judge the difference between an acceptable and unacceptable sentence fragment comes from years of reading the work of skilled writers. For ACADEMIC WRITING, most instructors don't accept sentence fragments in student writing until a student demonstrates a consistent ability to write well-constructed, complete sentences. As a rule, avoid sentence fragments in academic writing.

**EXERCISE 19-4** Revise this paragraph to eliminate all sentence fragments. In some cases, you can combine word groups to create complete sentences; in other cases, you must supply missing elements to rewrite. Some sentences may not require revision. In your final version, check not only the individual sentences but also the clarity of the whole paragraph. For help, consult 19a through 19d.

**EXAMPLE** Although the subject of many amusing anecdotes. Diogenes remains an influential figure in Greek philosophy.

Correct: Although the subject of many amusing anecdotes, Diogenes remains an influential figure in Greek philosophy.

(1) Throughout his career as a philosopher and Cynic, Diogenes cultivated a following. That included the likes of Aristotle and Alexander the Great. (2) Diogenes was an important member of the Cynics, a group of people who rejected conventional life. The word *Cynic* comes from the Greek word for dog. (3) Diogenes lived like a beggar and slept in a tub. Which he carried around with him wherever he went. (4) He rejected the pursuit of wealth and once destroyed his wooden bowl. Because he saw a peasant boy

---

**ANSWERS: EXERCISE 19-4**
Answers may vary. One set of possibilities is shown here.

**1.** Throughout his career as a philosopher and cynic, Diogenes cultivated a following that included the likes of Aristotle and Alexander the Great. [*that* dependent clause with relative pronoun, attached to independent clause]

**2.** Correct complete sentence.

**3.** Diogenes lived like a beggar and slept in a tub, which he carried around with him wherever he went. [*which* dependent clause with relative pronoun, attached to independent clause]

**4.** He rejected the pursuit of wealth and once destroyed his wooden bowl because he saw a peasant boy drinking water with his hands. [*because* dependent clause with subordinating conjunction, attached to independent clause]

**5.** Although none of his writings have survived, Diogenes produced dialogues and a play that allegedly describes a social utopia in which people live unconventional lives. [*that* dependent clause with relative pronoun, attached to independent clause]

**6.** He often walked around Athens in broad daylight with a lamp looking for an honest man. [*since*, which starts a dependent clause with subordinating conjunction, is dropped]

**7.** When Plato defined man as a featherless biped, Diogenes plucked a chicken and said, "Here is Plato's man." [Correct complete sentence]

**8.** According to legend, Diogenes was once sunbathing when he was approached by Alexander the Great, who was a fan of the eccentric cynic. [*who* dependent clause with relative pronoun, attached to independent clause]

**9.** Alexander asked if he could do anything for Diogenes, which the philosopher answered by saying, "Don't block my sunlight." [*which* dependent clause with relative pronoun, attached to independent clause]

drinking water with his hands. (5) Although none of his writings have survived, Diogenes produced dialogues and a play. That allegedly describes a social utopia in which people live unconventional lives. (6) Since he often walked around Athens in broad daylight with a lamp looking for an honest man. (7) When Plato defined *man* as a featherless biped, Diogenes plucked a chicken and said, "Here is Plato's man." (8) According to legend, Diogenes was once sunbathing when he was approached by Alexander the Great. Who was a fan of the eccentric Cynic. (9) Alexander asked if he could do anything for Diogenes. Which the philosopher answered by saying, "Don't block my sunlight." (10) Because Diogenes is a strange and interesting character. He has inspired works by such writers and artists as William Blake, Anton Chekhov, and Rabelais.

**EXERCISE 19-5**    Revise this paragraph to eliminate all sentence fragments. In some cases, you can combine word groups to create complete sentences; in other cases, you must supply missing elements to revise word groups. Some sentences may not require revision. In your final version, check not only the individual sentences but also the clarity of the whole paragraph. Refer to 19a through 19e for help.

(1) The English games cricket and rounders. (2) Are the forerunners of the American game baseball. (3) Which became popular in America in the nineteenth century. (4) According to the *New York Morning News,* in an article from 1845. (5) Members of the New York Knickerbockers Club played the first reported baseball game. (6) Taking place at Elysian Fields in Hoboken, New Jersey. (7) Creating one of baseball's first teams, and writing "20 Original Rules of Baseball." (8) Alexander Cartwright is often called The Father of Baseball. (9) By scholars and historians of the game. (10) His new rules, which became known as Knickerbocker Rules. (11) Changed baseball in a number of ways. (12) Such as giving each batter three strikes and each inning three outs. (13) The first game, therefore. (14) That used the Knickerbocker Rules was played on June 19, 1846, in New Jersey. (15) Acting as umpire for this game. (16) Cartwright charged six-cent fines for swearing. (17) The Knickerbockers lost this game by 22 points to a team. (18) That was known as "The New York Nine."

For more help with your writing, grammar, and research, go to **www.mycomplab.com**

**ANSWERS: EXERCISE 19-5**
Answers may vary. Here is one set of possibilities.

The English games cricket and rounders are the forerunners of the American game baseball, which became popular in America in the nineteenth century. According to the New York *Morning News,* in an article from 1845, members of the New York Knickerbockers Club played the first reported baseball game, taking place at Elysian Fields in Hoboken, New Jersey. Creating one of baseball's first teams and writing "20 Original Rules of Baseball," Alexander Cartwright is often called The Father of Baseball by scholars and historians of the game. His new rules, which became known as Knickerbocker Rules, changed baseball in a number of ways, such as giving each batter three strikes and each inning three outs. The first game, therefore, that used the Knickerbocker Rules was played on June 19, 1846, in New Jersey. Acting as umpire for this game, Cartwright charged six-cent fines for swearing. The Knickerbockers lost this game by 22 points to a team that was known as "The New York Nine."

390

# 20

# Comma Splices and Run-On Sentences

## 20a What are comma splices and run-on sentences?

Comma splices and run-on sentences are somewhat similar errors: One has a comma by itself between two complete sentences, and one has no punctuation at all between two complete sentences.

A **comma splice**, also called a *comma fault,* occurs when a comma, rather than a period, is used incorrectly between complete sentences. The word *splice* means "to fasten ends together," which is a handy procedure, except when splicing has anything to do with sentences.

A **run-on sentence**, also called a *fused sentence* and a *run-together sentence,* occurs when two complete sentences run into each other without any punctuation. Comma splices and run-on sentences create confusion because readers can't tell where one thought ends and another begins.

| COMMA SPLICE | The icebergs broke off from the **glacier, they** drifted into the sea. |
| RUN-ON SENTENCE | The icebergs broke off from the **glacier they** drifted into the sea. |
| CORRECT | The icebergs broke off from the **glacier. They** drifted into the sea. |

There is one exception. You can use a comma between two independent clauses, but only if the comma is followed by one of the seven coordinating conjunctions: *and, but, for, or, nor, yet, so.* A comma in such a construction is correct; see Chapter 24.

| CORRECT | The icebergs broke off from the glacier**, and** they drifted into the sea. |

**Alert:** Occasionally, when your meaning allows it, you can use a colon or a dash to join two independent clauses. ●

Many writers wait until the REVISING and EDITING stages of the WRITING PROCESS to check for comma splices and run-on sentences. During DRAFTING, the goal is to put ideas down on paper or disk. As you draft, if you suspect that you've written a comma splice or a run-on sentence, simply underline or highlight it in boldface or italics, and move on. Later, you can easily find it to check and correct.

# 20b How can I recognize comma splices and run-on sentences?

When you know how to recognize an INDEPENDENT CLAUSE, you'll know how to recognize COMMA SPLICES and RUN-ON SENTENCES. An independent clause can stand alone as a complete sentence. An independent clause contains a SUBJECT and a PREDICATE. Also, an independent clause doesn't begin with a word that creates dependence—that is, it doesn't begin with a SUBORDINATING CONJUNCTION or a RELATIVE PRONOUN.

Interestingly, almost all comma splices and run-on sentences are caused by only four patterns. If you become familiar with these four patterns, listed in Quick Reference 20.1, you'll more easily locate them in your writing.

**Alert:** To proofread for comma splices, cover all words on one side of the comma and see if the words remaining form an independent clause. If they do, next cover all words you left uncovered, on the other side of the comma. If the second side of the comma is also an independent clause, you're looking at a comma splice. (This technique doesn't work for run-on sentences because a comma isn't present.) ●

---

## Quick Reference 20.1

■ ■ ■ ■ ■ ■

### Detecting comma splices and run-on sentences

- Watch out for a PRONOUN starting the second independent clause.

    **NO**   The physicist Marie Curie discovered **radium, she** won two Nobel Prizes.

    **YES**   The physicist Marie Curie discovered **radium. She** won two Nobel Prizes.

- Watch out for a CONJUNCTIVE ADVERB (such as *furthermore, however, similarly, therefore,* and *then;* see Quick Reference 14.5, section 14g, for a complete list) starting the second independent clause.

    **NO**   Marie Curie and her husband, Pierre, worked together at **first, however**, he died tragically at age forty-seven.

    **YES**   Marie Curie and her husband, Pierre, worked together at **first. However**, he died tragically at age forty-seven.

continued >>

---

**BACKGROUND**

The Web sites <http://grammar.ccc.commnet.edu/grammar/quizzes/nova/nova4.htm> and <http://grammar.ccc.commnet.edu/grammar/cgi-shl/quiz.pl/fragments_add1.htm> respectively provide excellent exercises for repairing comma splices and run-on sentences.

**TEACHING TIP**

Students can use a simple test to determine whether a word is a conjunction or a conjunctive adverb. Conjunctive adverbs can be shifted from the beginning of a clause to another position in the middle of the clause; conjunctions cannot be shifted.

Comma splices and run-on sentences sometimes occur when students begin a sentence with *not only* but omit *but also* at the start of the second clause. Students should remember that *but* is functioning as a conjunction in this construction and that they need to separate the clauses with a period or semicolon when they omit *but*.

**BACKGROUND**

The Web site <http://owl.english.purdue.edu/owl/resource/598/02/> provides rules for punctuating compound sentences correctly, as well as suggestions for fixing run-on sentences.

**BACKGROUND**

Professional writers often intentionally separate two independent clauses with just a comma. The clauses in these comma splices never have internal commas and are normally short, balanced, and closely related in meaning. The instructor, of course, should decide whether to allow students to experiment with this form in their writing.

**QUOTATION: ON WRITING**

If my doctor told me I had only six months to live, I wouldn't brood. I'd type a little faster.

—Isaac Asimov

**BACKGROUND**

The Web site <http://webster.commnet.edu/sensen/part2/nine/index.html>        provides suggestions for how to spot and correct run-on sentences.

### QUOTATION: ON WRITING

A writer is not someone who expresses his thoughts, his passion or his imagination in sentences but someone who thinks sentences. A Sentence-Thinker.

—Roland Barthes

### BACKGROUND

The Web site <http://grammar.ccc.commnet.edu/grammar/sentences.htm> shows how to punctuate between two independent clauses and offers links to related sites.

### TEACHING TIP

You might want to enliven a class by running a "revision contest." Divide the class into an even number of teams, each composed of four students. Tell the students that in preparation for the competition, everyone is to bring to class two paragraphs containing comma splices and run-on sentences: (1) a published paragraph that the student has intentionally edited to have three such errors, and (2) an original paragraph written for the competition, containing three intentional comma splices or run-on sentences. Ask each student to supply two copies of each paragraph: one for the contest and one filled in as an answer key.

On the day of the competition, divide the students into teams and have them exchange paragraphs. Collect the answer keys. Give the teams thirty minutes to revise the paragraphs they have received. When they finish, compare their revisions with the answer keys.

### BACKGROUND

The site <http://www2.gsu.edu/~wwwesl/egw/bryson.htm> gives an acronym to help students remember the coordinating conjunctions: **F**or, **A**nd, **N**or, **B**ut, **O**r, **Y**et, **S**o—FANBOYS. In addition, colorful charts show how to use coordinating conjunctions to fix run-on sentences.

### BACKGROUND

British English often features commas between two independent clauses. In the 1993 *Columbia*

---

> **Quick Reference 20.1**  (continued)
>
> - Watch out for a TRANSITIONAL EXPRESSION (such as *in addition, for example, in contrast, of course,* and *meanwhile;* see Quick Reference 3.5, section 3g.1, for a reference list) starting the second independent clause.
>
>   **NO**  Marie Curie and her husband won a Nobel Prize for the discovery of **radium, in addition, Marie** herself won another Nobel Prize for her work on the atomic weight of radium.
>
>   **YES**  Marie Curie and her husband won a Nobel Prize for the discovery of **radium; in addition, Marie** herself won another Nobel Prize for her work on the atomic weight of radium.
>
> - Watch out for a second independent clause that explains, says more about, contrasts with, or gives an example of what's said in the first independent clause.
>
>   **NO**  Marie Curie died of leukemia in **1934, exposure** to radioactivity killed her.
>
>   **YES**  Marie Curie died of leukemia in **1934. Exposure** to radioactivity killed her.

Experienced writers sometimes use a comma to join very short independent clauses, especially if one independent clause is negative and the other is positive: *Mosquitoes don't **bite, they** stab.* In ACADEMIC WRITING, however, many instructors consider this an error, so you'll be safe if you use a period. (Another option is a semicolon, if the two independent clauses are closely related in meaning: *Mosquitoes don't **bite; they** stab.*)

## 20c  How can I correct comma splices and run-on sentences?

Once you have identified a COMMA SPLICE or a RUN-ON SENTENCE, you're ready to correct it. You can do this in one of four ways, as shown in Quick Reference 20.2 and discussed further in sections 20c.1 through 20c.4.

### 20c.1  Using a period to correct comma splices and run-on sentences

You can use a period to correct comma splices and run-on sentences by placing the period between the two sentences. For the sake of sentence variety and emphasis (Chapter 9), however, you want to choose other options as well, such as those shown in 20c.3 and 20c.4. Strings of short sentences rarely establish relationships and levels of importance among ideas.

## Quick Reference 20.2

■ ■ ■ ■ ■ ■ ■

### Ways to correct comma splices and run-on sentences

- Use a period between the INDEPENDENT CLAUSES (20c.1).
- Use a semicolon between the INDEPENDENT CLAUSES (20c.2).
- Use a comma together with a COORDINATING CONJUNCTION (20c.3).
- Revise one independent clause into a DEPENDENT CLAUSE (20c.4).

| | |
|---|---|
| COMMA SPLICE | A shark is all **cartilage, it** doesn't have a bone in its body. |
| RUN-ON SENTENCE | A shark is all **cartilage it** doesn't have a bone in its body. |
| CORRECT | A shark is all **cartilage. It** doesn't have a bone in its body. [A period separates the independent clauses.] |

| | |
|---|---|
| COMMA SPLICE | Sharks can smell blood from a quarter mile **away, they** then swim toward the source like a guided missile. |
| RUN-ON SENTENCE | Sharks can smell blood from a quarter mile **away they** then swim toward the source like a guided missile. |
| CORRECT | Sharks can smell blood from a quarter mile **away. They** then swim toward the source like a guided missile. [A period separates the independent clauses.] |

### 20c.2 Using a semicolon to correct comma splices and run-on sentences

You can use a semicolon to correct comma splices and run-on sentences by placing the semicolon between the two sentences. Use a semicolon only when the separate sentences are closely related in meaning. For the sake of sentence variety and emphasis, however, you'll want to choose other options, such as those shown in 20c.1, 20c.3, and 20c.4; for correct semicolon use, see Chapter 25.

| | |
|---|---|
| COMMA SPLICE | The great white shark supposedly eats **humans, research** shows that most white sharks spit them out after the first bite. |
| RUN-ON SENTENCE | The great white shark supposedly eats **humans research** shows that most white sharks spit them out after the first bite. |

*Guide to Standard American English*, Kenneth G. Wilson explains that some American writers have adapted this custom; see <http://www.bartleby.com/68/42/1342.html>.

**QUOTATION: ON WRITING**

Wearing down seven number two pencils is a good day's work.

—Ernest Hemingway

**BACKGROUND**

Just as writers sometimes gainfully use sentence fragments to achieve stylistic effects, they sometimes similarly employ comma splices and run-on sentences. Stream-of-consciousness writing depends upon comma splices and run-ons for its artistic effects; writers such as José Saramago use them to portray the chaos of contemporary life and contemporary thought. You may wish to bring in a passage from a writer who uses run-on sentences and/or comma splices to show students how sometimes writers knowingly break the rules of grammar (as explained in 19f regarding sentence fragments).

**QUOTATION: ON WRITING**

Word-carpentry is like any other kind of carpentry: you must join your sentences smoothly.

—Anatole France

**QUOTATION: ON WRITING**

My goal is to write only one sentence a day. I write this on the bus on my way to work. I usually find that I write more than just one sentence, but the important point is that I have accomplished the goal I set by 9:00 a.m.

—Lavinia Dobler

**TEACHING TIP: ESOL**

The site <http://members.aol.com/Jakajk/ESLLessons.html#ESLGAMES> features a page of collaborative games and projects for ESOL students. One of the games, "Sentence Auction," invites students to work in pairs or teams. You can choose to create a combined list of ten run-on sentences and ten grammatically correct ones. Students are given a few minutes to read and discuss which sentences are correct. They can then bid points on the sentences they think are right. The class instructor, or another student, can play the auctioneer. The game also suggests using a gavel for a prop.

**BACKGROUND**

The site <http://www.english.uiuc.edu/cws/wworkshop/index.htm> offered by the University of Illinois at Champaign-Urbana suggests how to distinguish between conjunctive adverbs and coordinating conjunctions.

**QUOTATION: ON WRITING**

What's so hard about the first sentence is that you're stuck with it. Everything else is going to flow out of that sentence. And by the time you've laid down the first two sentences, your options are all gone.

—Joan Didion

**ANSWERS: EXERCISE 20-1**

Choices of correcting punctuation may vary.

**1.** During the "Celebration of Books," aspiring writers can ask published authors questions about **writing; for example**, many people wish to know how to find an agent. [20c.2, comma splice corrected by using a semicolon]

**2.** Besides asking about agents, would-be writers also query published authors about writing **techniques, and** many questions deal with whether to write using a computer, a typewriter, or longhand. [20c.3, run-on corrected by using a comma and the coordinating conjunction *and*]

**3.** The "Celebration of Books" offers panel discussions on a variety of topics, including memoir writing, poetry development, and techniques of plotting short **stories. Other** panels cover writing the western novel and true crime stories. [20c.1, run-on sentence corrected by using a period]

**4.** The "Celebration of Books" appeals to readers, many of whom can see their favorite authors in person speaking on panels and in more informal settings such as receptions and book **signings; fans** of authors greatly enjoy such opportunities. [20c.2, run-on sentence corrected by using a semicolon]

| CORRECT | The great white shark supposedly eats **humans; research** shows that most white sharks spit them out after the first bite. [A semicolon separates two independent clauses that are close in meaning.] |

### 20c.3 Using a comma together with a coordinating conjunction to correct comma splices and run-on sentences

You can connect independent clauses with a comma together with a coordinating conjunction (*and, but, for, or, nor, yet, so*) to correct a comma splice. You can also correct a run-on sentence by inserting a comma followed by a coordinating conjunction.

**Alert:** Use a comma before a coordinating conjunction that links independent clauses (24b). ●

When you use a coordinating conjunction, be sure that your choice fits the meaning of the material. *And* signals addition; *but* and *yet* signal contrast; *for* and *so* signal cause; and *or* and *nor* signal alternatives.

| COMMA SPLICE | All living creatures give off weak electrical charges in the **water, special** pores on a shark's skin can detect these signals. |
| RUN-ON SENTENCE | All living creatures give off weak electrical charges in the **water special** pores on a shark's skin can detect these signals. |
| CORRECT | All living creatures give off weak electrical charges in the **water,** and **special** pores on a shark's skin can detect these signals. |

**EXERCISE 20-1**   Revise the comma splices and run-on sentences by using a period, a semicolon, or a comma and coordinating conjunction. For help, consult sections 20c.1 through 20c.3.

EXAMPLE   Every two years, a very popular "Celebration of Books" takes place at Oklahoma State University at Tulsa writers from across the United States gather along with readers to discuss the art of writing.

Revised: Every two years, a very popular "Celebration of Books" takes place at Oklahoma State University at *Tulsa. Writers* from across the United States gather along with readers to discuss the art of writing.

1. During the "Celebration of Books," aspiring writers can ask published authors questions about writing, for example, many people wish to know how to find an agent.

2. Besides asking about agents, would-be writers also query published authors about writing techniques many questions deal with whether to write using a computer or by longhand.

3. The "Celebration of Books" offers panel discussions on a variety of topics, including memoir writing, poetry development, and techniques of plotting short stories other panels cover writing the western novel and true crime stories.

4. The "Celebration of Books" appeals to readers, many of whom can see their favorite authors in person speaking on panels and in more informal settings such as receptions and book signings fans of authors greatly enjoy such opportunities.

5. In addition to writers, many well-known artists and musicians are honored at the "Celebration of Books," its Advisory Board recommended this expansion years ago to widen the conference's appeal.

**5.** In addition to writers, many well-known artists and musicians are honored at the "Celebration of **Books." Its** Advisory Board recommended this expansion years ago to widen the conference's appeal. [20c.1, comma splice corrected by using a period]

## 20c.4 Revising one independent clause into a dependent clause to correct comma splices and run-on sentences

You can correct a comma splice or run-on sentence by revising one of the two independent clauses into a dependent clause. This method is suitable only when one idea can logically be subordinated to the other. Also, be careful never to end the dependent clause with a period or semicolon. If you do, you've created the error of a SENTENCE FRAGMENT.

### CREATE DEPENDENT CLAUSES
### WITH SUBORDINATING CONJUNCTIONS

One way to create a dependent clause is to insert a SUBORDINATING CONJUNCTION (such as *because, although, when,* and *if*—see Quick Reference 14.7, section 14i, for a complete list). Always choose a subordinating conjunction that fits the meaning of each particular sentence: *because* and *since* signal cause; *although* signals contrast; *when* signals time; and *if* signals condition. Dependent clauses that begin with a subordinating conjunction are called ADVERB CLAUSES.

| | |
|---|---|
| COMMA SPLICE | Homer and Langley Collyer had packed their house from top to bottom with **junk, police** could not open the front door to investigate a reported smell. |
| RUN-ON SENTENCE | Homer and Langley Collyer had packed their house from top to bottom with **junk police** could not open the front door to investigate a reported smell. |
| CORRECT | **Because** Homer and Langley Collyer had packed their house from top to bottom with **junk, police** could not open the front door to investigate a reported smell. [*Because* starts a dependent clause that is joined by a comma with the independent clause starting with *police*.] |

| | |
|---|---|
| **COMMA SPLICE** | Old newspapers and car parts filled every room to the **ceiling, enough** space remained for fourteen pianos. |
| **RUN-ON SENTENCE** | Old newspapers and car parts filled every room to the **ceiling enough** space remained for fourteen pianos. |
| **CORRECT** | **Although** old newspapers and car parts filled every room to the **ceiling, enough** space remained for fourteen pianos. [The subordinating conjunction *although* starts a dependent clause that is joined by a comma with the independent clause starting with *enough*.] |

🔔 **Alert:** Place a comma between an introductory dependent clause and the independent clause that follows (24c). ●

### CREATE DEPENDENT CLAUSES WITH RELATIVE PRONOUNS

You can create a dependent clause with a RELATIVE PRONOUN (*who, whom, whose, which, that*). Dependent clauses with a relative pronoun are called ADJECTIVE CLAUSES.

| | |
|---|---|
| **COMMA SPLICE** | The Collyers had been crushed under a pile of **newspapers, the newspapers** had toppled onto the brothers. |
| **RUN-ON SENTENCE** | The Collyers had been crushed under a pile of **newspapers the newspapers** had toppled onto the brothers. |
| **CORRECT** | The Collyers had been crushed under a pile of **newspapers *that* had toppled** onto the brothers. [The relative pronoun *that* starts a dependent clause and is joined with the independent clause starting with *The Collyers*, after deletion of *the newspapers*.] |

🔔 **Alert:** Sometimes you need commas to set off an adjective clause from the rest of the sentence. This happens only when the adjective is NONRESTRICTIVE (nonessential), so check carefully (24f). ●

**EXERCISE 20-2**    Working individually or with your peer-response group, identify and then revise the comma splices and run-on sentences. Circle the numbers of correct sentences. For help, consult 20b through 20c.4.

**EXAMPLE**

| | |
|---|---|
| **COMMA SPLICE** | Artists occasionally need a catalyst to set them on the road to their careers, for B. B. King, a tractor acted as that catalyst. |

**ANSWERS: EXERCISE 20-2**

Choices of punctuation may vary.

1. B. B. King, the great blues guitarist and singer, born Riley B. King in Itta Bena, Mississippi, began his working life as a sharecropper and tractor driver; he earned one dollar a day at a plantation owned by Johnson Barrett in

| | |
|---|---|
| **RUN-ON SENTENCE** | Artists occasionally need a catalyst to set them on the road to their careers for B. B. King, a tractor acted as that catalyst. |
| **CORRECT** | Artists occasionally need a catalyst to set them on the road to their **careers; for** B. B. King, a tractor acted as that catalyst. |

(1) B. B. King, the great blues guitarist and singer, born Riley B. King in Itta Bena, Mississippi, began his working life as a sharecropper and tractor driver, he earned one dollar a day at a plantation owned by Johnson Barrett in Indianola, Mississippi. (2) As a side venture to his farm work, King sang with the excellent St. John's Gospel Singers he wanted the group to leave Mississippi to find riches and recognition in the music world. (3) In 1946, King left the group, he had tried very hard to urge them to go with him. (4) King was working hard all day in Mr. Barrett's fields, driving a tractor, he always returned to the barn at the end of the day, jumping off the tractor to the ground. (5) One day, the sudden movement made the tractor charge ahead and break off its exhaust stack King had already turned off the engine. (6) A terrified young King, fearing his boss's anger over the damaged tractor, ran away to Memphis with his guitar and $2.50, his fear kept him there for many months. (7) After a year of unsuccessfully pursuing a music career, King became discouraged and returned to Indianola he went back to work for Johnson Barrett. (8) By 1948, King had saved enough money as a tractor driver, sharecropper, and street musician to try his luck again making a living as a musician and singer, he returned to Memphis and finally found recognition and fortune, not only in that city but internationally. (9) By 1999, B. B. King had been nominated for twenty Grammy Awards, he won his ninth in that year for *Blues on the Bayou*, in the category of the Best Traditional Blues Recording. (10) In 1998, B. B. King was installed in the Grammy Hall of Fame, after having received the Grammy Lifetime Achievement Award in 1987, among his most dramatic honors were honorary PhDs granted by Yale University and the University of Mississippi.

## 20d How can I correctly use a conjunctive adverb or other transitional expression between independent clauses?

CONJUNCTIVE ADVERBS and other TRANSITIONAL EXPRESSIONS link ideas between sentences. When these words fall between sentences, a period or semicolon must immediately precede them—and a comma usually immediately follows them.

Conjunctive adverbs include such words as *however, therefore, also, next, then, thus, furthermore,* and *nevertheless* (see Quick Reference 14.5, section 14g, for a complete list). Be careful to remember that conjunctive adverbs are not COORDINATING CONJUNCTIONS (*and, but,* and so on; see 20c.3).

Indianola, Mississippi. [comma splice; corrected by replacing the comma with a semicolon]

**2.** As a side venture to his farm work, King sang with the excellent St. John's Gospel **Singers. He** wanted the group to leave Mississippi to find riches and recognition in the music world. [run-on; corrected by inserting a period]

**3.** In 1946, King left the **group, which** he had tried very hard to urge to take the chance to go with him. [comma splice; corrected by inserting a relative pronoun]

**4.** King was working hard all day in Mr. Barrett's fields, driving a **tractor, and** he always returned to the barn at the end of the day, jumping off the tractor to the ground. [comma splice; corrected by inserting a coordinating conjunction]

**5.** One day, the sudden movement made the tractor charge ahead and break off its exhaust **stack although King** had already turned off the engine. [run-on; corrected by inserting a subordinating conjunction]

**6.** A terrified young King, fearing his boss's anger over the damaged tractor, ran away to Memphis with his guitar and **$2.50; King's** fear kept him there for many months. [comma splice; corrected by inserting a semicolon]

**7.** After a year of unsuccessfully pursuing a music career, King became discouraged and returned to **Indianola; furthermore,** he went back to work for Johnson Barrett. [run-on; corrected by inserting a semicolon and a conjunctive adverb]

**8.** By 1948, King had saved enough money as a tractor driver, sharecropper, and street musician to try his luck again making a living as a musician and **singer, so** he returned to Memphis and finally found recognition and fortune, not only in that city but internationally. [comma splice; corrected by inserting a coordinating conjunction]

**9.** By 1999, B. B. King had been nominated for twenty Grammy **Awards. He** won his ninth in that year for *Blues on the Bayou*, in the category of the Best Traditional Blues Recording. [comma splice; corrected by replacing the comma with a period]

**10.** In 1998, B. B. King was installed in the Grammy Hall of Fame, after having received the Grammy Lifetime Achievement Award in **1987; among** his most dramatic honors were honorary PhDs granted by Yale University and the University of Mississippi. [comma splice; corrected by replacing the comma with a semicolon]

### ANSWERS: EXERCISE 20-3

Choices of punctuation may vary.

**1.** US citizens may not realize products developed by NASA directly affect their lives. For example, NASA has developed or improved a number of goods and services now available to the general public. [correct]

**2.** People may be surprised to learn that bar coding on products grew out of NASA's need to keep track of thousands of spacecraft components; indeed, bar codes allow merchants to track what they sell and to record items for re-ordering. [comma splice; corrected with a semi-colon before a conjunctive adverb]

**3.** Methods of medical imaging today are based on NASA's developing ways to process signals for sending images from space; in addition, the ear thermometer, popular for use with adults and children, developed out of NASA technology to identify the birth of stars. [run-on; corrected with a semicolon before a transitional expression]

**4.** Firefighters now wear fire-resistant suits because of space technology. Furthermore, NASA research created protective lenses that now save welders' eyes from harmful radiation. [run-on; corrected with a period before a conjunctive adverb/transitional expression]

**5.** Not all items coming from NASA's experiments result in medical advances or safety for workers; for instance, thermal gloves, ski boots, and failsafe flashlights are now available to the general public as a direct result of NASA's work. [comma splice; corrected with semicolon before a transitional expression]

| | |
|---|---|
| **COMMA SPLICE** | Buying or leasing a car is a matter of individual preference, **however,** it's wise to consider several points before making a decision. |
| **RUN-ON SENTENCE** | Buying or leasing a car is a matter of individual preference **however** it's wise to consider several points before making a decision. |
| **CORRECT** | Buying or leasing a car is a matter of individual preference**. However,** it's wise to consider several points before making a decision. |
| **CORRECT** | Buying or leasing a car is a matter of individual preference**; however,** it's wise to consider several points before making a decision. |

Transitional expressions include *for example, for instance, in addition, in fact, of course,* and *on the one hand/on the other hand* (see Quick Reference 3.5 section 3g.1, for a complete list).

| | |
|---|---|
| **COMMA SPLICE** | Car leasing requires a smaller down payment**, for example,** in many cases, you need only $1,000 or $2,000 and the first monthly payment. |
| **RUN-ON SENTENCE** | Car leasing requires a smaller down payment **for example** in many cases, you need only $1,000 or $2,000 and the first monthly payment. |
| **CORRECT** | Car leasing requires a smaller down payment**. For example,** in many cases, you need only $1,000 or $2,000 and the first monthly payment. |
| **CORRECT** | Car leasing requires a smaller down payment**; for example,** in many cases, you need only $1,000 or $2,000 and the first monthly payment. |

⚠ **Alert:** A conjunctive adverb or a transitional expression is usually followed by a comma when it starts a sentence (24c). ●

**EXERCISE 20-3** Revise comma splices or run-on sentences caused by incorrectly punctuated conjunctive adverbs or other transitional expressions. If a sentence is correct, circle its number. For help, consult 20d.

**EXAMPLE** Yearly, the US National Aeronautics and Space Administration (NASA) requests federal funding for space exploration, however, many US citizens wonder what practical value the space program offers.

Corrected: Yearly, the U.S. National Aeronautics and Space Administration (NASA) requests federal funding for space *exploration*. *However*, many US citizens wonder what practical value the space program offers. [comma splice; corrected by inserting a period before a conjunctive adverb]

1. US citizens may not realize products developed by NASA directly affect their lives. For example, NASA has developed or improved a number of goods and services now available to the general public.

2. People may be surprised to learn that bar coding on products grew out of NASA's need to keep track of thousands of spacecraft components, indeed, bar codes allow merchants to track what they sell and to record items for reordering.

3. Methods of medical imaging today are based on NASA's developing ways to process signals for sending images from space, in addition, the ear thermometer, popular for use with adults and children, developed out of NASA technology to identify the birth of stars.

4. Firefighters now wear fire-resistant suits because of space technology furthermore, NASA research created protective lenses that now save welders' eyes from harmful radiation.

5. Not all items coming from NASA's experiments result in medical advances or safety for workers, for instance, thermal gloves, ski boots, and failsafe flashlights are now available to the general public as a direct result of NASA's work.

**EXERCISE 20-4**     Revise all comma splices and run-on sentences, using as many different methods of correction as you can.

(1) Energy psychology represents fairly new methods joining Eastern lines of thought to the mind and body and Western psychology and psychotherapy, according to an article by Leonard Holmes, PhD, proponents of energy psychology contend that striking acupuncture points and at the same time recalling an anxiety-producing incident can alleviate anxiety and phobias. (2) Holmes inquires whether this idea is true in fact, he goes on to question the connection the acupuncture points have to anxiety. (3) In the early 1980s, Roger Callahan, PhD, popularized procedures utilizing energy psychology, he called the procedures "The Callahan Technique" or "Thought Field Therapy." (4) In the beginning, Callahan's training programs were costly, generally hundreds of dollars, now, on the other hand, they are moderately priced. (5) Other therapists such as clinical psychologist David Feinstein, PhD, have joined the ranks promoting energy psychology, interestingly, Feinstein sells an interactive CD-ROM that presents guidance in energy psychology/ psychotherapy. (6) A qualified therapist can use the CD-ROM laypersons should not experiment with the contents of the CD-ROM. (7) Today, proponents of energy psychology contend it results in the successful handling

**ANSWERS: EXERCISE 20-4**
Answers will vary. The following is one possible revision.

**1.** Energy psychology represents fairly new methods joining Eastern lines of thought to the mind and body and Western psychology and psychotherapy; according [semicolon] to an article by Leonard Holmes, PhD, proponents of energy psychology contend that striking acupuncture points and at the same time recalling an anxiety-producing incident can alleviate anxiety and phobias.

**2.** Holmes inquires whether this idea is true. In fact, [period] he goes on to question the connection the acupuncture points have to anxiety.

**3.** In the early 1980s, Roger Callahan, PhD, popularized procedures utilizing energy psychology, and he [coordinating conjunction *and* after comma] called the procedures "The Callahan Technique" or "Thought Field Therapy."

**4.** In the beginning, Callahan's training programs were costly, generally hundreds of dollars. Now, on the other hand, [period] they are moderately priced.

**5.** Other therapists such as clinical psychologist David Feinstein, PhD, have joined the ranks promoting energy psychology; interestingly, [semicolon] Feinstein sells an interactive CD-ROM that presents guidance in energy psychology/psychotherapy.

**6.** A qualified therapist can use the CD-ROM although [added a subordinating conjunction] laypersons should not experiment with the contents of the CD-ROM.

**7.** Today, proponents of energy psychology contend it results in the successful handling of problems such as trauma, abuse, depression, and addictive cravings. Other [period] uses for energy psychology, or "Emotional Freedom Techniques" (EFT), as Gary Craig calls them on his Web site, include treatment for medical conditions such as headaches and breathing difficulties.

**8.** Craig, not a licensed health professional, contends the "missing piece to the healing puzzle" is EFT, and [comma and coordinating conjunction *and* after comma] he quotes from supposedly scientific clinical trials indicating that patients have seen dramatic results in their conditions because of EFT.

**9.** Because [subordinating conjunction and comma after dependent clause] Holmes thinks energy psychotherapy is still too early in its development to be widely applied, he cautions the general public to avoid trying it on their own.

**10.** Holmes advises extreme caution for psychologists who need to know more from [revised to use relative pronoun] research about continuing to use EFT.

of problems such as trauma, abuse, depression, and addictive cravings, other uses for energy psychology, or "Emotional Freedom Techniques" (EFT), as Gary Craig calls them on his Web site, include treatment for medical conditions such as headaches and breathing difficulties. (8) Craig, not a licensed health professional, contends the "missing piece to the healing puzzle" is EFT he quotes from supposedly scientific clinical trials indicating that patients have seen dramatic results in their conditions because of EFT. (9) Holmes thinks energy psychotherapy is still too early in its development to be widely applied he cautions the general public to avoid trying it on their own. (10) Holmes advises extreme caution for psychologists about continuing to use EFT more needs to be known from research.

For more help with your writing, grammar, and research, go to **www.mycomplab.com**

## 21

# Misplaced and Dangling Modifiers

## MISPLACED MODIFIERS

### 21a　What is a misplaced modifier?

A **modifier** is a word or group of words that describes or limits another word or group of words. A **misplaced modifier** is positioned incorrectly in a sentence, which means, therefore, that it describes the wrong word and changes the writer's meaning. Always place a modifier as close as possible to what it describes.

### AVOIDING SQUINTING MODIFIERS

A **squinting modifier** is misplaced because it modifies both the word that comes before it and the word that follows it. Check that your modifiers are placed so that they communicate the meaning you intend.

NO    The football player being recruited **eagerly** believed each successive offer would be better. [What was *eager*? The recruitment or the player's belief?]

YES   The football player being recruited believed **eagerly** that each successive offer would be better.

YES   The football player being **eagerly** recruited believed that each successive offer would be better.

## PLACING LIMITING WORDS CAREFULLY

Words such as *only, not only, just, not just, almost, hardly, nearly, even, exactly, merely, scarcely,* and *simply* serve to limit the meaning of a word according to where they are placed. When you use such words, position them precisely. Consider how moving the placement of the word *only* changes the meaning of this sentence: *Professional coaches say that high salaries motivate players.*

**Only** professional coaches say that high salaries motivate players. [No one else says this.]

Professional coaches **only** say that high salaries motivate players. [The coaches probably do not mean what they say.]

Professional coaches say **only** that high salaries motivate players. [The coaches say nothing else.]

Professional coaches say that **only** high salaries motivate players. [Nothing except high salaries motivates players.]

Professional coaches say that high salaries **only** motivate players. [High salaries do nothing other than motivate players.]

Professional coaches say that high salaries motivate **only** players. [High salaries do motivate the players but not the coaches and managers.]

## 21b   How can I avoid split infinitives?

An INFINITIVE is a VERB form that starts with *to: to motivate, to convince, to create* are examples (14e). A **split infinitive** occurs when words are placed between the word *to* and its verb. The effect is awkward.

NO    Orson Welles's radio drama "War of the Worlds" managed ***to, in October 1938, convince*** listeners that they were hearing an invasion by Martians. [*In October 1938* is misplaced because the words come between *to* and *convince.*]

YES   **In October 1938,** Orson Welles's radio drama "War of the Worlds" managed ***to convince*** listeners that they were hearing an invasion by Martians.

**TEACHING TIP**
If your students feel that modifier placement is a slapdash business, you might ask them to look at some ludicrous sentences and have them try to draw what is written. Here are a few.

1. When people first saw whales, they were still wearing animal skins and had stone axes.

2. The man kissed the baby with a beard.

3. Walking down the street, the Eiffel Tower came into view.

4. The wildlife specialist said that most bears are dangerous on television.

5. Poison ivy is common in the forest, which gives many people an itchy rash.

**BACKGROUND**
On the evening of October 30, 1938, the actor and director Orson Welles began narrating the famous H. G. Wells story about Martians landing on planet Earth, "The War of the Worlds," over US radio. Unbeknownst to Welles, a circumstantial quirk caused listeners to tune in late, at the very climax of the story. This simple mishap led audiences to believe that they were listening to an emergency broadcast, not a piece of fiction. Consequently, people all over the United States panicked and ran about trying frantically to escape death from the aliens. That event illustrates how a little confusion can create major pandemonium in the human psyche. Project Gutenberg has an e-version of the text of "The War of the Worlds"; see <http://www.gutenberg.org/etext/36>.

**TEACHING TIP**
Melanie LaFleur's lesson "Pardon Me, Your Modifier is Dangling" leads students through an activity to illustrate dangling modifiers by drawing sentences with misplaced modifiers, correcting the original sentence on the back of the paper, and then hanging the illustration from the ceiling. See <http://home.cogeco.ca/~rayser3/Dangmismodless1.txt>.

**QUOTATION: ON WRITING**
Writing is so difficult that I often feel that writers, having had their hell on earth, will escape all punishment hereafter.

—Jessamyn West

**BACKGROUND**
Kate Burridge's *Blooming English: Observations on the Roots, Cultivation and Hybrids of the English Language* (New York: Cambridge, 2004) and its sequel *Weeds in the Garden of Words: Further Observations on the Tangled History of the English Language* (New York: Cambridge, 2005) offer a fascinating history of the development of English.

**HUMOROUS NOTE**
Dangling modifiers can sometimes create statements that are unintentionally humorous. Consider the following examples collected and published by Richard Lederer in *Anguished English* (Layton, UT: Wyrick & Co., 2006).

- Locked in a vault for fifty years, the owner of the jewels has decided to sell them.
- Do not sit in a chair without being fully assembled.
- Washed from a layer of mudstone estimated to be more than three million years old, a young American paleoanthropologist has found several leg bones and a skull fragment.

Often, the word that splits an infinitive is an ADVERB ending in *-ly*. In general, place adverbs either before or after the infinitive.

> **NO** People feared that they would no longer be able **to *happily* live** in peace.

> **YES** People feared that they would no longer be able **to live *happily*** in peace.

The rule about split infinitives has changed recently. Current usage says that when the best placement for a single adverb is actually between *to* and the verb, use that structure freely.

> Welles wanted **to *realistically* portray** a Martian invasion for the radio audience.

If you want to avoid splitting infinitives in your ACADEMIC WRITING, revise to avoid the split:

> Welles wanted his "Martian invasion" **to sound *realistic*** for the radio audience. [The adverb *realistically* was changed to the adjective *realistic*.]

# 21c How can I avoid other splits in my sentences?

When too many words split—that is, come between—a SUBJECT and its VERB or between a verb and its OBJECT, the result is a sentence that lurches rather than flows from beginning to end.

> **NO** The **announcer,** because the script, which Welles himself wrote, called for perfect imitations of emergency announcements, **opened** with a warning that included a description of the "invasion." [The subject *announcer* is placed too far away from the verb *opened*, so this split is too large.]

> **YES** Because the script, which Welles himself wrote, called for perfect imitations of emergency announcements, the **announcer opened** with a warning that included a description of the "invasion." [The subject and verb, *announcer opened*, aren't split.]

> **NO** Many churches **held** for their frightened communities **"end of the world" prayer services.** [The verb *held* is placed too far away from the object *"end of the world" prayer services*, so this split is too large.]

> **YES** Many churches **held "end of the world" prayer services** for their frightened communities. [The verb and object, *held "end of the world" prayer services*, aren't split.]

**EXERCISE 21-1** Revise these ten sentences to correct misplaced modifiers, split infinitives, and other splits. If a sentence is correct, circle its number. For help, consult 21a through 21c.

EXAMPLE  The city of Deadwood is known for its many notorious residents made popular by a TV show including Wild Bill Hickok and Calamity Jane.

Made popular by a TV show, the city of Deadwood is known for its many notorious residents, including Wild Bill Hickok and Calamity Jane.

1. Deadwood, because of its location near the Deadwood Gulch and the Black Hills of South Dakota, was named for the dead trees found in that canyon.
2. The city's founding, during a gold rush that attracted a quarter of a million miners to the area, was in 1876.
3. The main source of revenue for the city was gambling, which was outlawed in 1905 but reinstated in 1989.
4. Today, tourists who visit Deadwood often gamble and enjoy the historical reenactments of the town's famous events.
5. Deadwood nearly was the home to a dozen of famous characters from the Old West.
6. Serving as the sheriff of Hays City and Abilene, Wild Bill Hickok worked to with an iron fist tame the lawless towns of the frontier.
7. Hickok moved to Deadwood after he without much success performed in a Wild West show.
8. During a poker game at Nuttall & Mann's saloon, Jack McCall shot for unknown reasons Will Bill.
9. The cards Hickok was holding included a pair of black aces, a pair of black eights, and an unknown fifth card now known as the dead man's hand.
10. The legends of Deadwood and Wild Bill in the stories of fiction writers and TV shows continue to grow.

**EXERCISE 21-2** Using each list of words and phrases, create all the possible logical sentences. Insert commas as needed. Explain differences in meaning among the alternatives you create. For help, consult 21a through 21c.

EXAMPLE  exchange students
learned to speak French
while in Paris
last summer

A. Last summer,/exchange students/learned to speak French/while in Paris.
B. While in Paris,/exchange students/learned to speak French/last summer.

**ANSWERS: EXERCISE 21-1**
Answers may vary somewhat. The final result must avoid all incorrect placements.

**1.** Because of its location near the Deadwood Gulch and the Black Hills of South Dakota, Deadwood was named for the dead trees found in that canyon. [21c, interruption of subject and verb]

**2.** The city's founding was in 1876, during a gold rush that attracted a quarter of a million miners to the area. [21c, interruption of subject and verb]

**3.** Correct sentence.

**4.** Today, tourists who visit Deadwood gamble often and enjoy the historical reenactments of the town's famous events. [21a, squinting modifier]

**5.** Deadwood was the home to nearly a dozen of famous characters from the Old West. [21a, ambiguous placement]

**6.** Serving as the sheriff of Hays City and Abilene, Wild Bill Hickok worked to tame the lawless towns of the frontier with an iron fist. [21b, split infinitive]

**7.** Hickok moved to Deadwood after he performed in a Wild West show without much success. [21c, interruption of subject and verb]

**8.** During a poker game at Nuttall & Mann's saloon, Jack McCall shot Will Bill for unknown reasons. [21c, awkward interruption of verb and object]

**9.** The cards Hickok was holding, now known as the dead man's hand, included a pair of black aces, a pair of black eights, and an unknown fifth card. [21c, awkward placement]

**10.** The legends of Deadwood and Wild Bill continue to grow in the stories of fiction writers and TV shows. [21c, awkward interruption of subject and verb]

**ANSWERS: EXERCISE 21-2**

**1. a.** Chicken soup, / according to folklore, / helps / cure colds.

**b.** According to folklore, / chicken soup / helps / cure colds.

**c.** Chicken soup / helps / cure colds, / according to folklore.

**2. a.** Instinctively, / tadpoles / swim / toward / their genetic relatives.

**b.** Tadpoles / instinctively / swim / toward / their genetic relatives.

**c.** Tadpoles / swim / toward / their genetic relatives / instinctively.

**d.** Tadpoles / swim / instinctively / toward / their genetic relatives.

**3. a.** While driving / carelessly, / the young driver / skidded / in the snow.

**b.** The young driver / carelessly / skidded / in the snow / while driving.

**c.** While driving, / the young driver / skidded / carelessly / in the snow.

**d.** While driving / in the snow, / the young driver / skidded / carelessly.

**e.** In the snow, / the young driver / skidded / carelessly / while driving.

**f.** Carelessly, / the young driver / skidded / while diving / in the snow.

**4. a.** The limber teenager, / quickly / climbed / a tall palm tree / to pick a ripe coconut.

**b.** The limber teenager / climbed / a tall palm tree / quickly / to pick a ripe coconut.

**c.** To pick a ripe coconut, / the limber teenager / quickly / climbed / a tall palm tree.

**d.** Quickly, / the limber teenager / climbed / a tall palm tree / to pick a ripe coconut.

**5. a.** To prevent big avalanches, / ski patrollers / often / set explosives / and cause mini-avalanches.

**b.** Ski patrollers / often / set explosives / and cause mini-avalanches / to prevent big avalanches.

**c.** Often, / ski patrollers / set explosives / and cause mini-avalanches / to prevent big avalanches.

**d.** Ski patrollers / set explosives / and cause mini-avalanches / often / to prevent big avalanches.

**C.** Exchange students/learned to speak French/while in Paris/last summer.

**D.** Exchange students/learned to speak French/last summer/while in Paris.

1. chicken soup
   according to folklore
   helps
   cure colds

2. tadpoles
   instinctively
   swim
   toward
   their genetic relatives

3. the young driver
   while driving
   in the snow
   skidded carelessly

4. climbed
   the limber teenager
   a tall palm tree
   to pick a ripe coconut
   quickly

5. and cause mini-avalanches
   ski patrollers
   set explosives
   often
   to prevent
   big avalanches

## DANGLING MODIFIERS

## 21d How can I avoid dangling modifiers?

A **dangling modifier** describes or limits a word or words that never actually appear in the sentence. Aware of the intended meaning, the writer unconsciously supplies the missing words, but the reader gets confused. To correct a dangling modifier, state clearly your intended SUBJECT in the sentence.

**NO** **Having read Faulkner's short story "A Rose for Emily," *the ending*** surprised us. [This sentence says *the ending* was reading the story, which is impossible.]

**YES** Having read Faulkner's short story "A Rose for Emily," **we were surprised by the ending.** [Second half of sentence is rewritten to include the subject *we*.]

**YES** **We** read Faulkner's short story "A Rose for Emily" **and were surprised by the ending.** [Sentence is rewritten to include the subject *We*.]

**NO** **When courting Emily, *the townspeople*** gossiped about her. [This sentence says *the townspeople* were courting Emily, which isn't true.]

**YES** **When Emily was being courted *by Homer Barron,*** the townspeople gossiped about her. [First half of sentence is rewritten to include the name of the person doing the courting: *Homer Barron*.]

A major cause of dangling modifiers is the unnecessary use of the PASSIVE VOICE. Whenever possible, use the ACTIVE VOICE.

**NO** **To earn money, china painting lessons** were offered by Emily to wealthy young women. [*China painting lessons* cannot *earn money. Were offered by Emily* is in the passive voice.]

**YES** **To earn money, Emily** offered china painting lessons to wealthy young women. [Change to the active voice; *Emily offered* corrects the problem.]

**EXERCISE 21-3** Identify and correct any dangling modifiers in these sentences. If a sentence is correct, circle its number. For help, consult 21d.

**EXAMPLE** To understand what happened to Krakatoa, the volcano and its history must be studied.

Corrected: To understand what happened to Krakatoa, one must study the volcano and its history.

1. In 1883, massive destruction was caused by the eruption of the volcano Krakatoa, an event recently examined in the book *Krakatoa: The Day the World Exploded.*
2. Exploding with a force 13,000 times stronger than the bomb dropped on Hiroshima, people thousands of miles away heard the eruption.
3. The loudest sound historically reported was generated by the explosion, with devastating tsunamis soon following.
4. Ejecting tons of debris into the air, the volcano destroyed or damaged hundreds of nearby villages.
5. Beginning to erupt around late July, larger eruptions didn't start until the middle of August.
6. Reaching over 100 feet in height and traveling at devastating speeds, major destruction was caused on the coastlines of Sumatra.
7. Lasting much longer than expected, people in nearby areas felt aftershocks until February of 1884.
8. To understand the magnitude of this volcanic eruption, changes in weather patterns were studied by scientists.
9. Darkening the sky for days afterwards and producing unusual sunsets, the ash and gases from the volcano temporarily lowered the average temperature of the earth.
10. Affecting the art of its time, the background of Edvard Munch's famous painting *The Scream* was inspired by Krakatoan sunsets.

**ANSWERS: EXERCISE 21-3**
Answers may differ somewhat. Here is one set of possibilities.

1. The eruption of the volcano Krakatoa caused massive destruction in 1883, an event recently examined in the book *Krakatoa: The Day the World Exploded.* [unnecessary passive]
2. Exploding with a force 13,000 times stronger than the bomb dropped on Hiroshima, the eruption was heard by people thousands of miles away. [dangling participle]
3. The explosion generated the loudest sound historically reported, with devastating tsunamis soon following. [unnecessary passive]
4. Correct sentence.
5. Although the volcano began erupting in late July, larger eruptions didn't start until the middle of August. [unexpressed subject]
6. Reaching over 100 feet in height and traveling at devastating speeds, tsunamis caused destruction to the coastlines of Sumatra. [unexpressed subject]
7. Lasting much longer than expected, aftershocks were felt by people in nearby areas until February of 1884. [dangling participle]
8. To understand the magnitude of this volcanic eruption, scientists studied the changes in weather patterns. [dangling infinitive phrase]
9. Correct sentence.
10. Affecting the art of its time, Krakatoan sunsets inspired the background of Edvard Munch's famous painting *The Scream.* [dangling participle]

## 21e   How can I proofread successfully for misplaced and dangling modifiers?

Sentence errors like MISPLACED MODIFIERS and DANGLING MODIFIERS are hard to spot because of the way the human brain works. Writers know what they mean to say when they write. When they PROOFREAD, however, they often misread what they've written for what they intended to write. The mind unconsciously adjusts for the error. In contrast, readers see only what's on the paper or screen. We suggest that you read your writing aloud, or have someone else read it to you, to proofread it for these kinds of problems.

For more help with your writing, grammar, and research, go to **www.mycomplab.com**

# 22

# Shifting and Mixed Sentences

## SHIFTING SENTENCES

## 22a   What is a shifting sentence?

A **shift** within a sentence is an unnecessary, abrupt change in PERSON, NUMBER, SUBJECT, VOICE, TENSE, MOOD, or DIRECT or INDIRECT DISCOURSE. These shifts blur meaning. Sometimes a shift occurs between two or more sentences in a paragraph. If you set out on one track (writing in FIRST PERSON, for example), your readers expect you to stay on that same track (and not unnecessarily shift to THIRD PERSON, for example). When you go off track, you have written a shifting sentence or paragraph.

## 22b   How can I avoid shifts in person and number?

Who or what performs or receives an action is defined by the term *person*. FIRST PERSON (*I, we*) is the speaker or writer; SECOND PERSON (*you*) is the one being spoken or written *to;* and THIRD PERSON (*he, she, it, they*) is the person or thing being spoken or written *about.*

The essential point is that shifts are incorrect unless the meaning in a particular context makes them necessary.

**NO** I enjoy reading financial forecasts of the future, but **you** wonder which will turn out to be correct. [The first person *I* shifts to the second person *you.*]

**YES** I enjoy reading financial forecasts of the future, but **I** wonder which will turn out to be correct.

NUMBER refers to whether words are *singular* (one) or *plural* (more than one) in meaning. Do not start to write in one number and then shift for no reason to the other number.

**NO** Because **people** are living longer, **an employee** now retires later. [The plural *people* shifts to the singular *employee.*]

**YES** Because **people** are living longer, **employees** now retire later.

In ACADEMIC WRITING, reserve *you* for addressing the reader directly. Use the third person for general statements.

**NO** I like my job in customer service because **you** get to solve people's problems. [*I* is in the first person, so a shift to the second person *you* is incorrect.]

**YES** I like my job in customer service because **I** get to solve people's problems.

**NO** **People** enjoy feeling productive, so when a job is unsatisfying, **you** usually become depressed. [*People* is in the third person, so a shift to the second person *you* is incorrect.]

**YES** **People** enjoy feeling productive, so when a job is unsatisfying, **they** usually become depressed.

Be careful with words in the singular (usually NOUNS) used in a general sense, such as *employee, student, consumer, neighbor,* and *someone.* These words are always third-person singular. The only pronouns for these ANTECEDENTS in the third-person singular are *he, she,* and *it.* Remember that *they* is plural, so the word *they* can't be used with singular nouns.

**NO** When **an employee** is treated with respect, **they** are more motivated to do a good job. [*Employee* is third-person singular, so the shift to the third-person plural *they* is incorrect.]

singular] will hold my hand when *I* [first; singular] get scared if *I* [first; singular] ask him. *He* [third; singular] puts my hand firmly on his knee and covers it completely with his own hand. His *knee* [third; singular] never twitches. After a while, when the scary *part* [third; singular] is past, *he* [third; singular] loosens his hand slightly and *I* [first; singular] know *that* [third; singular] is a signal to take mine away. *He* [third; singular] sits companionably close, letting his *jacket* [third; singular] just touch my sweater, but *he* [third; singular] does not infringe. *He* [third; singular] thinks *I* [first; singular] ought to know *he* [third; singular] is there if *I* [first; singular] need him.

—Susan Allen Toth, "Cinematypes"

**BACKGROUND**

English emphasizes the number of every noun or pronoun in a sentence. In fact, it is impossible to talk or write about anything in English without signaling its number. English speakers take such information for granted, but the system is not universal. In Chinese, for example, the speaker decides if it is necessary to mention whether an item is singular or plural. Usually, number is considered irrelevant, and few sentences make any reference to it.

**QUOTATION: ON WRITING**

I'm a bit like a sponge. When I'm not writing I absorb life like water. When I write I squeeze the sponge a little—and out it comes, not water but ink.

—Georges Simenon

**QUOTATION: ON WRITING**

Good writers are those who keep the language efficient. That is to say, keep it accurate, keep it clear.

—Ezra Pound

**WORD HISTORY**

According to the *Oxford English Dictionary,* the word *voice* comes from the Latin word *vox,* meaning "voice" or "sound." The earliest recorded statement in English using *voice* as a grammatical term is from 1382 by John Wyclif:

"A participle of a present tens, either preterit, or actif vois, eithir passif."

**ANSWERS: EXERCISE 22-1**
Answers may vary somewhat because of the various ways to eliminate shifts in person and number.

**1.** First-time visitors to the Mall of America in Minnesota may be overwhelmed by its size, but they will also see its helpful design. [reserve *you* for direct address and avoid shift in person and number]

**2.** Shoppers will notice that the mall is divided into architecturally distinct areas so they won't get lost. [shift in number]

**3.** The four sides of the mall have different themes and matching décor, so they are easy to navigate. [shift in number]

**4.** Sentence is correct.

**5.** They also called the fourth floor's collection of nightclubs the Upper East Side to reflect an urban environment. [shift in number from the last sentence]

**6.** Sentence is correct.

**7.** The amusement park in the middle of the mall remains an important draw for families and children, and it has roller coasters and water rides. [shift in number]

**8.** Couples can enjoy fine dining and high-end shopping, and they can even get married in the mall's wedding chapel. [reserve *you* for direct address and avoid shift in person and number]

**ANOTHER EXAMPLE**
To improve your students' skill in identifying subject and voice, you might ask them to work in groups to locate the subject and name the voice in each of the clauses in the following passage by Jack London. (The subjects and verbs appear in italics.)

The *earthquake* [subject] *shook* [active] down in San Francisco hundreds of thousands of dollars' worth of walls and chimneys. But the *conflagration* [subject] *that* [subject] *followed* [active] *burned* [active] up hundreds of millions of dollars' worth of property. *There* ["dummy" subject] *is* [active] no

| YES | When **an employee** is treated with respect, **he or she** is more motivated to do a good job. |
|---|---|
| YES | When **employees** are treated with respect, **they** are more motivated to do a good job. |
| YES | **An employee** who is treated with respect is more motivated to do a good job. |
| YES | **Employees** who are treated with respect are more motivated to do a good job. |

⚠ **Alert:** When you use INDEFINITE PRONOUNS (such as *someone, everyone,* or *anyone*), you want to use GENDER-NEUTRAL LANGUAGE. For advice, see 17s and 12f. ●

**EXERCISE 22-1**  Eliminate shifts in person and number between, as well as within, sentences. Some sentences may not need revision. For help, consult 22b.

(1) First-time visitors to the Mall of America may be overwhelmed by its size, but you will also see its helpful design. (2) A shopper will notice that the mall is divided into architecturally distinct areas so they won't get lost. (3) The four sides of the mall have different themes and matching décor, so it is easy to navigate. (4) The architects named the four sides the North Garden, South Avenue, East Broadway, and West Market. (5) He or she also called the fourth floor's collection of nightclubs the Upper East Side to reflect an urban environment. (6) In spite of skeptics who thought the mall would never make money, it has been consistently successful in renting its retail space and attracting shoppers. (7) The amusement park in the middle of the mall remains an important draw for families and children, and they have roller coasters and water rides. (8) Couples can enjoy fine dining and high-end shopping, and you can even get married in the mall's wedding chapel.

## 22c How can I avoid shifts in subject and voice?

A SHIFT in SUBJECT is rarely justified when it is accompanied by a shift in VOICE. The voice of a sentence is either *active* (*People expect changes*) or *passive* (*Changes are expected*). Some subject shifts, however, are justified by the meaning of a passage: for example, *People look forward to the future, but the future holds many secrets.*

| NO | Most **people expect** major improvements in the future, but some **hardships are** also **anticipated.** [The subject shifts from *people* to *hardships,* and the voice shifts from active to passive.] |
|---|---|
| YES | Most **people expect** major improvements in the future, but **they** also **anticipate** some hardships. |

YES  Most **people expect** major improvements in the future but also **anticipate** some hardships.

## 22d  How can I avoid shifts in tense and mood?

TENSE refers to the time in which the action of a VERB takes place—past, present, or future: *We **will go** to the movies after we **finish** dinner.* An unnecessary tense SHIFT within or between sentences can make the statement confusing or illogical.

NO  A campaign to clean up movies in the United States **began** in the 1920s as civic and religious groups **try** to ban sex and violence from the screen. [The tense incorrectly shifts from the past *began* to the present *try*.]

YES  A campaign to clean up movies in the United States **began** in the 1920s as civic and religious groups **tried** to ban sex and violence from the screen.

NO  Film producers and distributors **created** the Production Code in the 1930s. At first, violating its guidelines **carried** no penalty. Eventually, however, films that **fail** to get the board's seal of approval **do not receive** wide distribution. [This shift occurs between sentences—the past tense *created* and *carried* shift to the present tense *fail* and *do not receive*.]

YES  Film producers and distributors **created** the Production Code in the 1930s. At first, violating its guidelines **carried** no penalty. Eventually, however, films that **failed** to get the board's seal of approval **did not receive** wide distribution.

MOOD indicates whether a sentence is a statement or a question (INDICATIVE MOOD), a command or request (IMPERATIVE MOOD), or a conditional or other-than-real statement (SUBJUNCTIVE MOOD). A shift in mood creates an awkward construction and can cause confusion.

NO  The Production Code included two guidelines on violence: **Do not show** the details of brutal killings, and movies **should not be** explicit about how to commit crimes. [The verbs shift from the imperative mood *do not show* to the indicative mood *movies should not be*.]

YES  The Production Code included two guidelines on violence: **Do not show** the details of brutal killings, and **do not show** explicitly how to commit crimes. [This revision uses the imperative mood for both guidelines.]

*estimating* [subject] within hundreds of millions the actual damage *that* [subject] *was wrought* [passive].

Not in history *has* a modern imperial *city* [subject] *been* so completely *destroyed* [passive]. *San Francisco* [subject] *is* [active] gone. *Nothing* [subject] *remains* [active] of it but memories and a fringe of dwelling houses on its outskirts. Its industrial *section* [subject] *is* [active] wiped out. Its social and residential *section* [subject] *is* [active] wiped out. The *factories* [subject] and *warehouses* [subject], the great *stores* [subject] and newspaper *buildings* [subject], the *hotels* [subject] and *palaces* [subject] of the nabobs, *all* [subject] *are* [active] gone. *There* ["dummy" subject] *remains* [active] only the *fringe* [subject] of dwelling houses on the outskirts of *what* [subject] *was* [active] once San Francisco.

—Jack London

### WORD HISTORY

According to the *Oxford English Dictionary,* the term *mood* has been used since the sixteenth century to refer to verb forms that indicate commands or wishes. The earliest recorded use of the word in this way dates back to 1573, when a scholar named Golding asked a question that still concerns our students: "How shall men directly fynde the Coniugation, Nomber, Person, Tence and Moode of Verbes togither in their Kynde?"

When we speak of the *mood* of a verb, we are not discussing its emotional state. *Mood* when it refers to a mental state is related to the Latin *mos,* meaning "custom." In contrast, *mood* used to discuss verbs is an alteration of *mode,* which comes from the Latin *modus,* meaning "measure," "moderation," or (most relevant here) "manner." The earliest use of *mode* to refer to verbs dates back to 1520: "Sometyme of the infinytyve mode folowynge." Other early references make it clear that *mood/mode* was originally used for discussions of Greek and Latin rather than of English.

| | |
|---|---|
| **YES** | The Production Code included two guidelines on violence: Movies **were not to show** the details of brutal killings or explicit ways to commit crimes. |
| **NO** | The code's writers worried that **if a crime were to be** accurately **depicted** in a movie, **copycat crimes will follow.** [The sentence shifts from the subjunctive mood *if a crime were to be depicted* to the indicative mood *copycat crimes will follow*.] |
| **YES** | The code's writers worried that **if a crime were to be** accurately **depicted** in a movie, **copycat crimes would follow.** |

## 22e  How can I avoid shifts between indirect and direct discourse?

**Indirect discourse** is not enclosed in quotation marks because it reports, rather than quotes, something that someone said. In contrast, **direct discourse** is enclosed in quotation marks because it quotes exactly the words that someone said. It's incorrect to write direct discourse and omit the quotation marks. Also, it's incorrect to write sentences that mix indirect and direct discourse. Such SHIFT errors confuse readers, who can't tell what was said and what is being merely reported.

| | |
|---|---|
| **NO** | A critic said that board members were acting as censors and **what you are doing is unconstitutional.** [*Said that* sets up indirect discourse, but *what you are doing is unconstitutional* is direct discourse; it also lacks quotation marks and the changes in language that distinguish spoken words from reported words.] |
| **YES** | A critic said that board members were acting as censors and **that what they were doing was unconstitutional.** [This revision uses indirect discourse consistently.] |
| **YES** | A critic, in stating that board members were acting as censors, added, **"What you are doing is unconstitutional."** [This revision uses discourse correctly, with quotation marks and other changes in language to distinguish spoken words from reported words.] |

Whenever you change your writing from direct discourse to indirect discourse (when you decide to paraphrase rather than quote someone directly, for example), you need to make changes in VERB TENSE and other grammatical features for your writing to make sense. Simply removing the quotation marks is not enough.

**NO**    He asked **did we enjoy the movie?** [This version has the verb form needed for direct discourse, but the pronoun *we* is wrong and quotation punctuation is missing.]

**YES**    He asked **whether we enjoyed the movie.** [This version is entirely indirect discourse, and the verb has changed from *enjoy* to *enjoyed.*]

**YES**    He asked, **"Did you enjoy the movie?"** [This version is direct discourse. It repeats the original speech exactly, with correct quotation punctuation.]

**EXERCISE 22-2**    Revise these sentences to eliminate incorrect shifts within sentences. Some sentences can be revised in several ways. For help, consult 22b through 22e.

**EXAMPLE**    In 1942, the US government is faced with arresting five million people for not paying their federal income taxes.

In 1942, the US government *was faced* with arresting five million people for not paying their federal income taxes.

1. Congress needed money to pay for US participation in World War II, so a new tax system was proposed.
2. Tax payments were due on March 15, not April 15 as it is today.
3. For the first time, Congress taxed millions of lower-income citizens. Most people do not save enough to pay the amount of taxes due.
4. When a scientific poll showed lawmakers that only one in seven Americans had saved enough money, he became worried.

**EXERCISE 22-3**    Revise this paragraph to eliminate incorrect shifts between sentences and within sentences. For help, consult 22b through 22e.

(1) According to sociologists, people experience role conflict when we find ourselves trying to juggle too many different social roles. (2) When people reach overload, he or she decided, "to cut back somewhere." (3) For example, a well-known politician might decide not to run for reelection because family life would be interfered with by the demands of the campaign. (4) In other cases, you may delay having children so they can achieve early career success. (5) A person might say to themselves that I can't do this right now and focus instead on career goals. (6) In yet another example, a plant manager might enjoy social interaction with employees but consequently find themselves unable to evaluate him or her objectively. (7) In short, sociologists find that although not all role conflicts cause problems, great hardships are suffered by some individuals faced with handling difficult balancing acts.

sentences when they read aloud without noticing a problem on the page, it is often useful to ask students in pairs to exchange papers and listen to their partners read the papers aloud.

**ANSWERS: EXERCISE 22-2**
Answers will vary. Here is one set of possible answers.

**1.** Congress needed money to pay for US participation in World War II, *so members proposed a new tax system.* [22c, shift in subject and voice]

**2.** Tax payments were due on March 15, not April 15 as *they are* today. [22b, shift in number]

**3.** For the first time, Congress taxed millions of lower-income citizens. Most people *had not saved* enough to pay the amount of taxes due. [22d, shift in tense]

**4.** When a scientific poll showed lawmakers that only one in seven Americans had saved enough money, *they* became worried. [22b, shift in number]

**ANSWERS: EXERCISE 22-3**
Answers may vary. Here is one set of possibilities.

**1.** According to sociologists, people experience role conflict when *they* find *themselves* trying to juggle too many different social roles. [22b, person and number]

**2.** When people reach overload, *they may decide to cut back somewhere.* [22b, person and number; 22d, tense; 22e, indirect/direct discourse]

**3.** For example, a well-known politician might decide not to run for reelection because *the demands of the campaign would interfere with* family life. [22c, voice]

**4.** In other cases, *people might* delay having children so they can achieve early career success. [22b, reserve *you* for direct address and avoid shift in person and number]

**5.** *People* might say to themselves, *"I can't start a family right now,"* and focus instead on career goals. [22b, number; 22e, indirect/direct discourse]

**6.** In yet another example, a plant manager might enjoy social interaction with employees but consequently find *himself* (or *herself,* or *himself or herself*) unable to evaluate *them* objectively. [22b, person and number—twice]

**7.** In short, sociologists find that although not all role conflicts cause problems, *some individuals faced with handling difficult balancing acts suffer great hardships.* [22c, voice]

**8.** People can minimize role conflicts, however, if *they* learn to compartmentalize *their* lives. [22b, person]

**9.** A good example of this is people saying, *"I'm going to stop thinking about my job before I head home to my family."* [22e, indirect/direct discourse]

### MORE EXAMPLES

What is inconsistent in the following mixed constructions? You might want to ask students to work in groups to revise these four sentences so that the parts make sense together.

**1.** Because you want to visit the great art museums of the world is why you should go to the Louvre in Paris.

**2.** Paris, the capital of France, one of the great museums of the world is located there.

**3.** Tourists from all over the world, the Louvre draws them.

**4.** The collection is composed of works of art from many cultures is what distinguishes the Louvre.

### QUOTATION: ON WRITING

Have something to say, and say it as clearly as you can. That is the only secret of style.
—Matthew Arnold

### BACKGROUND

At the site <http://www.uccs.edu/~wrtgcntr/>, you will find a practice exercise on correcting predication problems.

### TEACHING TIP

Besides reading aloud, another way students can become aware of trickier grammar points is through having them make grammatically correct sentences incorrect. Assign each student in class a grammatically correct sentence and a common grammar error. Then, have the

(8) People can minimize role conflicts, however, if we learn to compartmentalize our lives. (9) A good example of this is people saying that I'm going to stop thinking about my job before I head home to my family.

## MIXED SENTENCES

## 22f  What is a mixed sentence?

A mixed sentence has two or more parts, with the first part starting in one direction and the rest of the parts going off in another. This mixing of sentence parts leads to unclear meaning. To avoid this error, as you write each sentence, remember how you started it and make sure that whatever comes next in the sentence relates grammatically and logically to that beginning.

> **NO**  Because our side lost the contest eventually motivated us to do better. [*Because our side lost the contest* starts the sentence in one direction, but *eventually motivated us to do better* goes off in another direction.]

> **YES**  Because our side lost the contest, **we** eventually became motivated to do better.

> **YES**  Our side lost the contest, **which** eventually motivated us to do better.

> **NO**  Because television's first transmissions in the 1920s included news programs became popular with the public. [The opening dependent clause starts off on one track (and is not correctly punctuated), but the independent clause goes off in another direction. What does the writer want to emphasize, the first transmissions or the popularity of news programs?]

> **NO**  Because television's first transmissions in the 1920s included news, programs became popular with the public. [The revision helps but is partial: the dependent clause talks about the news, but the independent clause goes off in another direction by talking about the popularity of the programs in general.]

> **YES**  Television's first transmissions in the 1920s included news programs, **which were** popular with the public. [Dropping *because* and adding *which were* solves the problem by keeping the focus on news programs throughout.]

> **NO**  By increasing the time for network news to thirty minutes increased the prestige of network news programs. [A prepositional phrase, such as *by increasing,* can't be the subject of a sentence.]

**YES** Increasing the time for network news to thirty minutes increased the prestige of network news programs. [Dropping the preposition *by* clears up the problem.]

**YES** By increasing the time for network news to thirty minutes, **the network executives** increased the prestige of network news programs. [Inserting a logical subject, *the network executives*, clears up the problem.]

The phrase *the fact that* lacks CONCISENESS, and it also tends to cause a mixed sentence.

**NO** The fact that quiz show scandals in the 1950s prompted the networks to produce even more news shows.

**YES** The fact **is** that quiz show scandals in the 1950s prompted the networks to produce even more news shows. [Adding *is* clarifies the meaning.]

**YES** Quiz show scandals in the 1950s prompted the networks to produce even more news shows. [Dropping *the fact that* clarifies the meaning.]

## 22g How can I correct a mixed sentence due to faulty predication?

**Faulty predication**, sometimes called *illogical predication,* occurs when a SUBJECT and its PREDICATE don't make sense together.

**NO** The purpose of television was invented to entertain people. [A *purpose* cannot be *invented.*]

**YES** The purpose of television was to entertain people.

**YES** Television was invented to entertain people.

Faulty predication often results from a lost connection between a subject and its SUBJECT COMPLEMENT.

**NO** Walter Cronkite's outstanding **characteristic** as a newscaster **was credible.** [The subject complement *credible* could logically describe *Walter Cronkite,* but *Walter Cronkite* is not the sentence's subject. Rather, the sentence's subject is his *characteristic.* Therefore, the sentence lacks a subject complement that would name a *characteristic* of *Walter Cronkite* as a newscaster.]

**YES** Walter Cronkite's outstanding **characteristic** as a newscaster **was credibility.** [When *credibility* is substituted for *credible,* the sentence is correct.]

students rewrite the sentence, including the assigned grammar error, Finally, have the students exchange papers, and assign them the job of identifying the grammar error on the sheet of paper they have received and correcting it.

Your students are likely to enjoy this exercise: The student who originally authored the sentence will verify whether his or her partner fixed the grammar error, while the student's partner will verify whether the original author wrote a "correct" incorrect sentence!

**QUOTATION: ON WRITING**
Everything that can be thought at all can be thought clearly. Everything that can be said can be said clearly.
—Ludwig Wittgenstein

**BACKGROUND**
The Web site <http://grammar.ccc.commnet.edu/grammar/clauses.htm> provides a definition, as well as examples, of elliptical clauses.

**QUOTATION: ON WRITING**
The secret of good writing is to say an old thing a new way or to say a new thing an old way.
—Richard Harding Davis

**QUOTATION: ON WRITING**
I love being a writer. What I can't stand is the paperwork.
—Peter De Vries

**TEACHING TIP**
Because conversation frequently includes incomplete comparisons, you might want to ask students to turn the following spoken dialogue into a paragraph written in the third person.

*A:* I'm so glad we came here. This restaurant is so much better.

*B:* You're right. A place that has fresh flowers on the tables is more appealing.

*A:* I always think linen napkins are nicer.

*B:* This place has a fine reputation for good service, but it's a shame that it's so much less spacious.

**ANSWERS: EXERCISE 22-4**

1. Showing babies plain, black-and-white images will help them learn to recognize shapes and focus their vision. [22f, mixed sentence]

2. Even though babies can see their parents' faces, they will not respond with a smile until they are a few weeks old. [22f, mixed sentence]

3. Correct sentence.

4. Eye coordination develops while a baby follows an object with her eyes. [22g, faulty predication with *is when*]

5. A newborn's limited ability to see color forces him to focus only on bright colors. [22f, mixed sentence]

6. Babies occasionally cross their eyes because they are perfecting their tracking skills. [22g, fault predication with *the reason . . . is because*]

7. Correct sentence

8. Newborns can vary dramatically in their sensitivity to sounds and ability to sleep in noisy environments. [22f, mixed sentence with *the fact that*]

9. A two-month-old baby turns her head toward her parents' voice because she is beginning to recognize familiar sounds. [22g, faulty predication with *the reason . . . is because*]

10. Changing his facial expression indicates he may find a particular sound soothing or comforting. [22f, mixed sentence]

**YES** Walter Cronkite was credible as a newscaster. [When *Walter Cronkite* becomes the sentence's subject, *credible* is correct,]

In ACADEMIC WRITING, avoid nonstandard constructions such as *is when* and *is where*. They should be avoided not only because they are nonstandard, but also because they usually lead to faulty predication.

**NO** A disaster **is when** TV news shows get some of their highest ratings.

**YES** TV news shows get some of their highest ratings during a disaster.

In academic writing, avoid constructions such as *the reason . . . is because*. Using both *reason* and *because* makes the construction redundant (it says the same thing twice). Instead, use either *the reason . . . is that* or *because* alone.

**NO** One **reason** that TV news captured national attention in the 1960s **is because** it covered the Vietnam War thoroughly.

**YES** One **reason** TV news captured national attention in the 1960s **is that** it covered the Vietnam War thoroughly.

**YES** TV news captured national attention in the 1960s **because** it covered the Vietnam War thoroughly.

**EXERCISE 22-4** Revise the mixed sentences so that the beginning of each sentence fits logically with its end. If a sentence is correct, circle its number. For help, consult 22f and 22g.

**EXAMPLE** The reason a newborn baby may stare at her hands or feet is because she can only focus on nearby objects.

*A newborn baby may stare at her hands or feet* because she can only focus on nearby objects.

1. By showing babies plain, black-and-white images will help them learn to recognize shapes and focus their vision.

2. Even though babies can see their parents' faces will not respond with a smile until they are a few weeks old.

3. Babies may gaze intently into a small, unbreakable mirror attached to the inside of their cribs.

4. While following an object with her eyes is when eye coordination develops.

5. Because of a newborn's limited ability to see color forces him to focus only on bright colors.

6. The reason babies occasionally cross their eyes is because they are perfecting their tracking skills.

7. Whether a light sleeper or a heavy sleeper, a typical baby does not need complete silence in order to rest well.

8. The fact that newborns can vary dramatically in their sensitivity to sounds and ability to sleep in noisy environments.

9. The reason that a two-month-old baby turns her head toward her parents' voice is because she is beginning to recognize familiar sounds.

10. Through changing his facial expression indicates he may find a particular sound soothing or comforting.

## 22h What are correct elliptical constructions?

An **elliptical construction** deliberately leaves out one or more words in a sentence for CONCISENESS.

> Victor has his book and Joan's. [This means *Victor has his book and Joan's book.* The second *book* is left out deliberately.]

For an elliptical construction to be correct, the one or more words you leave out need to be identical to those already appearing in the sentence. For instance, the sample sentence above about Victor and Joan would have an incorrect elliptical construction if the writer's intended meaning were *Victor has his book, and Joan has her own book.*

> **NO** During the 1920s in Chicago, the cornetist Manuel Perez **was leading** one outstanding jazz group, and Tommy and Jimmy Dorsey another. [The words *was leading* cannot take the place of *were leading*, which is required after *Tommy and Jimmy Dorsey.*]
>
> **YES** During the 1920s in Chicago, the cornetist Manuel Perez **was leading** one outstanding jazz group, and Tommy and Jimmy Dorsey **were leading** another.
>
> **YES** During the 1920s in Chicago, the cornetist Manuel Perez **led** one outstanding jazz group, and Tommy and Jimmy Dorsey another. [*Led* is correct with both *Manuel Perez* and *Tommy and Jimmy Dorsey*, so *led* can be omitted after *Dorsey.*]

## 22i What are correct comparisons?

When you write a sentence in which you want to compare two or more things, make sure that no important words are omitted.

> **NO** Individuals driven to achieve make **better** business executives. [*Better* is a word of comparison (18e), but no comparison is stated.]
>
> **YES** Individuals driven to achieve make **better** business executives **than do people not interested in personal accomplishments.**
>
> **NO** Most personnel officers value high achievers **more than risk takers.** [*More* is a word of comparison, but it's unclear whether the

sentence says *personnel officers value high achievers over risk takers* or *personnel officers value high achievers more than risk takers value them.*]

YES  Most personnel officers value high achievers **more than they value** risk takers.

YES  Most personnel officers value high achievers **more than** risk takers **do.**

## 22j  How can I proofread successfully for little words I forget to use?

If you're rushing or distracted as you write, you might unintentionally omit little words, such as ARTICLES, PRONOUNS, CONJUNCTIONS, and PREPOSITIONS. Lynn does, unfortunately. She solves this by reading her writing aloud, word by word; or, better still, she asks someone else to read it aloud because she tends to fill in mentally any missing words in her own work.

NO  On May 2, 1808, citizens Madrid rioted against French soldiers and were shot.

YES  On May 2, 1808, citizens **of** Madrid rioted against French soldiers and were shot.

NO  The Spanish painter Francisco Goya recorded both the riot the execution in a pair of pictures painted 1814.

YES  The Spanish painter Francisco Goya recorded both the riot **and** the execution in a pair of pictures painted **in** 1814.

**ANSWERS: EXERCISE 22-5**
Answers may vary somewhat. One set of possibilities is shown here.

**1.** A giant tsunami is as destructive *as* [22i, incomplete comparison] and even larger than a tidal wave.

**2.** The word *tsunami* is Japanese for "harbor wave," for this kind *of* wave appears suddenly in *a* [22j, small words omitted] harbor or bay.

**3.** A tsunami begins with *a* rapid shift in *the* [22j, small words omitted] ocean floor caused by an undersea earthquake or volcano.

**4.** The wave this produces in the open sea is less than three feet high, but it can grow to a height of a hundred feet as it rushes *toward* [22h, incorrect elliptical] and strikes against the shore.

**5.** For this reason, tsunamis are much more dangerous to seaside towns than *they are to* [22i, ambiguous comparison] ships on the open sea.

**6.** In 1960, a huge tsunami that struck *the* coasts of Chile, Hawaii, and Japan killed *a* [22j, small words omitted] total of 590 people.

**7.** In 2004, a huge tsunami that struck *the* coasts of Indonesia, Thailand, Malaysia, and other countries killed *a* total *of* [22j, small words omitted] 275,000 people.

**EXERCISE 22-5**  Revise this paragraph to create correct elliptical constructions, to complete comparisons, and to insert any missing words. For help, see 22h through 22j.

(1) A giant tsunami is as destructive and even larger than a tidal wave. (2) The word *tsunami* is Japanese for "harbor wave," for this kind wave appears suddenly in harbor or bay. (3) A tsunami begins with rapid shift in ocean floor caused by an undersea earthquake or volcano. (4) The wave this produces in the open sea is less than three feet high, but it can grow to a height of a hundred feet as it rushes and strikes against the shore. (5) For this reason, tsunamis are much more dangerous to seaside towns than ships on the open sea. (6) In 1960, a huge tsunami that struck coasts of Chile, Hawaii, and Japan killed total of 590 people. (7) In 2004, a huge tsunami that struck coasts of Indonesia, Thailand, Malaysia, and other countries killed total 275,000 people.

PART

# 4

# Using Punctuation and Mechanics

# 23

# Periods, Question Marks, and Exclamation Points

**Periods, question marks**, and **exclamation points** are collectively called *end punctuation* because they occur at the ends of sentences.

I love you**.** Do you love me**?** I love you**!**

## PERIODS

## 23a  When does a period end a sentence?

A **period** ends a statement, a mild command, or an INDIRECT QUESTION.*
Never use a period to end a DIRECT QUESTION, a strong command, or an emphatic declaration.

### END OF A STATEMENT

A journey of a thousand miles must begin with a single step.

—Lao-tsu, *The Way of Lao-tsu*

### MILD COMMAND

Put a gram of boldness into everything you do.

—Baltasar Gracian

### INDIRECT QUESTION

I asked if they wanted to climb Mt. Everest. [As an indirect question, this sentence reports that a question was asked. If it were a direct question, it would end with a question mark: *I asked, "Do you want to climb Mt. Everest?"*]

## 23b  How do I use periods with abbreviations?

Most **abbreviations**, though not all, call for periods. Typical abbreviations with periods include *Mt., St., Dr., Mr., Ms., Mrs., Jr., Fri., Feb., a.m.,* and *p.m.* (For more about *a.m.* and *p.m.,* see Chapter 22, "Usage Glossary," and section 30j; for more about abbreviations in general, see 30i through 30l.)

---

*Words printed in SMALL CAPITAL LETTERS are discussed elsewhere in the text and are defined in the Terms Glossary at the back of this book.

**❶Alert:** Spell out the word *professor* in ACADEMIC WRITING; never abbreviate it.●

Abbreviations without periods include the postal codes for states (for example, IL, CO) and the names of some organizations and government agencies (for example, CBS and NASA).

> **Ms.** Yuan, who works at **NASA,** lectured to **Dr.** Garcia's physics class at 9:30 **a.m.**

**❶Alert:** When the period of an abbreviation falls at the end of a sentence that calls for a period, the period of the abbreviation serves also to end the sentence. If, however, your sentence ends in a question mark or an exclamation point, put it after the period of the abbreviation.

> The phone rang at 4:00 **a.m.**
>
> It's upsetting to answer a wrong-number call at 4:00 **a.m.!**
>
> Who would call at 4:00 **a.m.?** ●

## QUESTION MARKS

## 23c  When do I use a question mark?

A **question mark** ends a **direct question**, one that quotes the exact words the speaker used. (In contrast, an **indirect question** reports a question and ends with a period.)

> How many attempts have been made to climb Mt. Everest? [An indirect question would end with a period: *She wants to know how many attempts have been made to climb Mt. Everest.*]

**❶Alert:** Never use a question mark with a period, comma, semicolon, or colon.

> **NO**   She asked, "How are you**?**."
>
> **YES**   She asked, "How are you**?**" ●

Questions in a series are each followed by a question mark, whether or not each question is a complete sentence.

> After the fierce storm, the mountain climbers debated what to do next. Turn back**?** Move on**?** Rest for a while**?**

**❶Alert:** When questions in a series are not complete sentences (as in the preceding example), you can choose whether to capitalize the first letter, but be consistent within each piece of writing. ●

**QUOTATION: ON WRITING**

A question mark should stay at the end of an interrogative sentence that is part of another sentence: How had this dreadful suspicion arisen? was everyone's question in that tense saloon.

—Karen Elizabeth Gordon

**BACKGROUND**

Nancy Mann argues that punctuation is either not taught or not taught well at every educational level. In her article "Point Counterpoint: Teaching Punctuation as Information Management" (*College Composition and Communication* 54.3 (2003): 359–393), she offers a model of punctuation pedagogy based on a punctuation system.

**QUOTATION: ON WRITING**

A kiss can be a comma, a question mark, or an exclamation mark.

—Mistinguett

**TEACHING TIP**

Encourage students to look for punctuation mistakes in flyers on campus, in take-out menus, and on signs. They can bring these examples (or photographs of them) into class for discussion.

### QUOTATION: ON WRITING

Without some convention for showing the groupings and relationships of words, for suggesting pace and intonation, the written sentence becomes a puzzle to the modern reader, and the writer, with freedom to do *anything* in the way of charting his reader's course through lines of words, must set about doing something, selecting some kind of systematic spacing or marking arrangement that will clarify his meaning.

—Mina P. Shaughnessy

### BACKGROUND

Bergen Evans and Cornelia Evans in *A Dictionary of Contemporary American Usage* define an exclamation as a spontaneous expression of strong emotion, shown in speech by pitch and in writing by the exclamation point. Advising that exclamation points should be reserved for true exclamations "and not wasted on sentences where commas would serve as well," they list several forms in which exclamations commonly appear. They may take the form of a sentence that begins with *how, what,* or *why,* in which the subject precedes the verb, as in *What a surprise this is!* They may appear as a declarative sentence, as in *The tree blew down!* They are often incomplete expressions, sometimes having a verb but no written subject, as in *Bless your heart!*

### QUOTATION: ON WRITING

Punctuation: what is it, after all, but another way of cutting up time, creating or negating relationships, telling words when to take a rest, when to get on with their relentless stories, when to catch their breath?

—Karen Elizabeth Gordon

### BACKGROUND

In today's world of digital communication, the exclamation point seems to proliferate. Jacob Rubin explains:

Indeed the "wonderful" is what the exclamation point was originally devised to

Sometimes a statement or mild command is phrased as a question to be polite. In such cases, a question mark is optional, but be consistent in each piece of writing.

Would you please send me a copy**.**

or

Would you please send me a copy**?**

## 23d    When can I use a question mark in parentheses?

The only time to use a question mark in parentheses (?) is if a date or other number is unknown or doubtful. Never use (?) to communicate that you're unsure of information.

Mary Astell, a British writer of pamphlets on women's rights, was born in 1666 **(?)** and died in 1731.

The word *about* is often a more graceful substitute for (?): *Mary Astell was born* **about** *1666.*

Also, never use (?) to communicate IRONY or sarcasm. Choose words to deliver your message.

| | |
|---|---|
| **NO** | Having altitude sickness is a pleasant **(?)** experience. |
| **YES** | Having altitude sickness is **as** pleasant **as having a bad case of the flu.** |

## EXCLAMATION POINTS

## 23e    When do I use an exclamation point?

An **exclamation point** ends a strong command or an emphatic declaration. A strong command is a firm and direct order: *Look out behind you!* An emphatic declaration is a shocking or surprising statement: *There's been an accident!*

🛈 **Alert:** Never combine an exclamation point with a period, comma, semicolon, or colon.

| | |
|---|---|
| **NO** | "There's been an accident**!,**" she shouted. |
| **YES** | "There's been an accident**!**" she shouted. |
| **YES** | "There's been an accident," she shouted. [Use this form if you prefer not to use an exclamation point.] ● |

## 23f What is considered overuse of exclamation points?

In ACADEMIC WRITING, words, not exclamation points, need to communicate the intensity of your message. Reserve exclamation points for an emphatic declaration within a longer passage.

> When we were in Nepal, we tried each day to see Mt. Everest. But each day we failed. **Clouds defeated us!** The summit never emerged from a heavy overcast.

Also, using exclamation points too frequently suggests an exaggerated sense of urgency.

**NO** Mountain climbing can be dangerous. You must know correct procedures! You must have the proper equipment! Otherwise, you could die!

**YES** Mountain climbing can be dangerous. You must know correct procedures. You must have the proper equipment. Otherwise, you could die!

Never use (!) to communicate amazement or sarcasm. Choose words to deliver your message.

**NO** At 29,035 feet (!), Mt. Everest is the world's highest mountain. Yet, Chris (!) wants to climb it.

**YES** At **a majestic** 29,035 feet, Mt. Everest is the world's highest mountain. Yet, Chris, **amazingly,** wants to climb it.

**EXERCISE 23-1** Insert any needed periods, question marks, and exclamation points and delete any unneeded ones. For help, consult all sections of this chapter.

**EXAMPLE** Dr Madan Kataria, who calls himself the Giggling Guru (!), established the world's first laughter club in 1995.

Dr. Madan Kataria, who calls himself the Giggling Guru, established the world's first laughter club in 1995.

1. More than 1,000 (?) laughter clubs exist throughout the world, each seeking to promote health by reducing stress and strengthening the immune system!

2. Dr Madan Kataria, a physician in Bombay, India, developed a yoga-like (!) strategy based on group (!) laughter and then set up laughter clubs.

3. Laughter clubs say, "Yes!" when asked, "Is laughter the best medicine."

4. The clubs' activities include breathing and stretching exercises and playful (?) behaviors, such as performing the opera laugh (!), the chicken laugh (!), and the "Ho-Ho, Ha-Ha" (?) exercise.

connote. A relatively recent addition to the punctuation clan, it first appeared in print around 1400 and was known until 1700 as a "mark of admiration," though admiration in this case meant something like "wonderment" (of a religious variety). Some scholars believe it derives from the Latin *Io* (meaning joy). *Io*, the theory goes, might have been rendered with its second letter under the first, thus producing an exclamation mark.

As Shipley and Schwalbe would have it, the advent of electronic communication creates a greater need for pre-modern wonderment. In their view, the exclamation is no mere crutch for the lazy writer but an essential tonic against the grayness of electronic communication: "Because email is without affect, it has a dulling quality that almost necessitates kicking everything up a notch just to bring it to where it would normally be."

—"So Many Exclamation Points! A New Style Guide Says We Should Pepper Our E-mail With Them. Really?" Slate.com 30 August 2007 <http://www.slate.com/id/2173076>

**ANSWERS: EXERCISE 23-1**

**1.** More than 1,000 laughter clubs exist throughout the world, each seeking to promote health by reducing stress and strengthening the immune system.

**2.** Dr. Madan Kataria, a physician in Bombay, India, developed a yogalike strategy based on group laughter and then set up laughter clubs.

**3.** Laughter clubs say, "Yes!" when asked, "Is laughter the best medicine?"

**4.** The clubs' activities include breathing and stretching exercises and playful behaviors, such as performing the opera laugh, the chicken laugh, and the "Ho-Ho, Ha-Ha" exercise.

**5.** According to the German psychologist Dr. Michael Titze, "In the 1950s people used to laugh eighteen minutes a day, but today we laugh not more than six minutes per day, despite huge rises in the standard of living."

## ANSWERS: EXERCISE 23-2

Weather experts refer to a rise in surface temperature of the Pacific Ocean as El Niño, but La Niña refers to a drop in ocean temperature. What effects can these changes cause? In the spring of 1998, the cold water of La Niña surfaced quickly and produced chaotic and destructive weather. In the American Northeast, rainfall amounts for June were three times above normal. But no one expected the strangest consequence: snow in June! Can you imagine waking up on an early summer morning in New England and seeing snow? Throughout the summer, most New England states failed to experience a single heat wave, which requires more than three days of 90 degree weather. During that winter, the Great Lakes experienced record warmth, but California suffered from disastrously cold air. A citrus freeze caused $600 million of damage. That's more than half a million dollars!

### QUOTATION: ON WRITING

Next in importance to the longest pause of all, the period or full stop, comes the shortest, the comma. The practice does not seriously differ from the theory implied by the etymology: *comma,* the Latin transliteration of Greek *komma,* related to *keptein,* to cut, means literally "a cutting," hence "a cutting-off," hence a clause, which after all, is nothing but a part, especially a (comparatively) short part, cut off from the rest of the sentence; hence the sign that indicates the division. In modern practice, the comma serves to separate not only clauses but phrases and words; more precisely, certain kinds of clauses and certain kinds of phrases and certain groupings of words.

—Eric Partridge

### BACKGROUND

In "The Pauses -, ; . : ?! - That Refresh" (*New York Times,* 23 March 1988, late ed.: C17),

5. According to the German psychologist Dr Michael Titze, "In the 1950s people used to laugh eighteen minutes a day (!), but today we laugh not more than six (?) minutes per day, despite huge rises in the standard of living."

● **EXERCISE 23-2**    Insert needed periods, question marks, and exclamation points. For help, consult all sections of this chapter.

Weather experts refer to a rise in surface temperature of the Pacific Ocean as El Niño, but La Niña refers to a drop in ocean temperature What effects can these changes cause In the spring of 1998, the cold water of La Niña surfaced quickly and produced chaotic and destructive weather In the American Northeast, rainfall amounts for June were three times above normal But no one expected the strangest consequence: snow in June Can you imagine waking up on an early summer morning in New England to snow Throughout the summer, most New England states failed to experience a single heat wave, which requires more than three days of 90 degree weather During that winter, the Great Lakes experienced record warmth, but California suffered from disastrously cold air A citrus freeze caused $600 million of damage That's more than half a billion dollars

For more help with your writing, grammar, and research, go to **www.mycomplab.com**

# 24

# Commas

## 24a    What is the role of the comma?

Commas are the most frequently used marks of punctuation, occurring twice as often as all other punctuation marks combined. A comma must be used in certain places, it must not be used in other places, and it's optional in still other places. This chapter helps you sort through the various rules.

For quick access to most answers when you have a comma question, consult Quick Reference 24.1. The sections in parentheses indicate where you can find fuller explanations.

**Quick Reference 24.1**

**Key uses of commas**

**COMMAS WITH COORDINATING CONJUNCTIONS LINKING INDEPENDENT CLAUSES (24b)**

Postcards are ideal for brief greetings**, and** they can also be miniature works of art. [*and* is a coordinating conjunction]

**COMMAS AFTER INTRODUCTORY ELEMENTS (24c)**

**Although most postcards cost only a quarter,** one recently sold for thousands of dollars. [clause]

**On postcard racks,** several designs are usually available. [phrase]

**For example,** animals are timeless favorites. [transitional expression]

**However,** most cards show local landmarks. [word]

**COMMAS WITH ITEMS IN A SERIES (24d)**

**Places, paintings, and people** appear on postcards. [*and* between last two items]

**Places, paintings, people, animals** occupy dozens of display racks. [no *and* between last two items]

**COMMAS WITH COORDINATE ADJECTIVES (24e)**

Some postcards feature **appealing, dramatic** scenes.

**NO COMMAS WITH CUMULATIVE ADJECTIVES (24e)**

Other postcards feature **famous historical** scenes.

**COMMAS WITH NONRESTRICTIVE ELEMENTS (24f)**

**Four years after the first postcard appeared,** the US government began to issue prestamped postcards. [nonrestrictive element introduces independent clause]

The Golden Age of postcards**, which lasted from about 1900 to 1929,** yielded many especially valuable cards. [nonrestrictive element interrupts independent clause]

Collectors attend postcard shows**, which are similar to baseball-card shows.** [nonrestrictive element ends independent clause]

**NO COMMAS WITH RESTRICTIVE ELEMENTS (24f)**

Collectors **who attend these shows** may specialize in a particular kind of postcard. [restrictive clause]

continued >>

Richard F. Shepard explains that although the comma was devised around 260 BC, it was not widely used in writing until "a Latin grammarian named Donatus revived it and applied the marks to the points where he felt breathing cues were needed while reading aloud."

**QUOTATION: ON WRITING**
The gods, they say, give breath, and they take it away. But the same could be said—could it not?—of the humble comma.
—Pico Iyer

**QUOTATION: ON WRITING**
There are hard and fast rules about commas, but within those rules there is plenty of room for nuance and interpretation.
—Bill Walsh, *Lapsing into a Comma*

**QUOTATION: ON WRITING**
All morning I worked on the proof of one of my poems, and I took out a comma; in the afternoon I put it back.
—Oscar Wilde

**EXTRA EXERCISE A**
Insert commas before coordinating conjunctions that link independent clauses. Some sentences may be correct.

**1.** England, Scotland, and Wales are located on the same island.

**2.** Wales is located on the western peninsula of the island and England and Scotland occupy the rest of it.

**3.** It is bounded on the east by the North Sea and on the south by the English Channel.

**4.** The Teutonic invaders of the fifth century had to struggle with native Britons for possession of the island for the Romans had virtually abandoned the island by that time.

**5.** Britain is the proper name of the whole island but England is the political name of the part conquered by the Angles.

**6.** Neither the Jutes nor the Saxons moved north for they chose to settle in what is today Kent or moved on to Sussex, Wessex, and Essex.

**7.** The Scots were actually the people of Ireland yet a small colony they established in the northern part of the island eventually gave Scotland its name.

**8.** The Norman Conquest of Britain was begun under William the Conqueror and was continued by his sons.

**9.** With few exceptions, all the existing shires of England had been established at the time of the Norman Conquest but the boundaries were not always exactly the same as they are now.

**10.** Since the eleventh century, the map of Britain has remained little changed yet the reins of power have shifted many times.

**Answers to Extra Exercise A**

**1.** Correct
**2.** Comma before *and England*
**3.** Correct
**4.** Comma before *for the Romans*
**5.** Comma before *but England*
**6.** Comma before *for they chose*
**7.** Comma before *yet a small colony*
**8.** Correct
**9.** Comma before *but the boundaries*
**10.** Comma before *yet the reins*

**BACKGROUND**

In *Pause and Effect: Punctuation in the West,* M. B. Parkes explains the origin of the word *comma (Los Angeles: University of California Press, 1993).* Fifteenth-century writers called the comma a *title,* from the Latin word *titulus* ("label" or "title"). In early medieval manuscripts, commas appeared as a full slash mark called a *solidus (/).*

**BACKGROUND**

The site <http://owl.english.purdue.edu/handouts/grammar/g_commaproof.html> offers students a proofreading strategy for using commas.

**BACKGROUND**

We use *of course* in two ways, one with the comma and one without, according to Bill

**Quick Reference 24.1** (continued)

**COMMAS WITH QUOTED WORDS (24h)**

One collector told me, "Attending a show is like digging for buried treasure." [quoted words at end of sentence]

"I always expect to find a priceless postcard," he said. [quoted words at start of sentence]

"Everyone there," he joked, "believes a million-dollar card is hidden in the next stack." [quoted words interrupted mid-sentence]

## 24b How do commas work with coordinating conjunctions?

Never use a comma when a coordinating conjunction links only two words, two PHRASES, or two DEPENDENT CLAUSES.

**NO** Habitat for Humanity depends on volunteers for **labor, and donations** to help with its construction projects. [*Labor* and *donations* are two words; the conjunction explains their relationship. No comma is needed.]

**YES** Habitat for Humanity depends on volunteers for **labor and donations** to help with its construction projects.

**NO** Each language has **a beauty of its own, and forms of expression** that are duplicated nowhere else. [A *beauty of its own* and *forms of expression* are only two phrases.]

**YES** Each language has **a beauty of its own and forms of expression** that are duplicated nowhere else.

—Margaret Mead, "Unispeak"

Do use a comma when a coordinating conjunction links two or more INDEPENDENT CLAUSES. Place the comma before the coordinating conjunction.

The sky turned dark gray, **and** the wind died suddenly.

The November morning had just begun, **but** it looked like dusk.

Shopkeepers closed their stores early, **for** they wanted to get home.

Soon high winds would start, **or** thick snow would begin silently.

Farmers could not continue harvesting, **nor** could they round up their animals in distant fields.

People on the road tried to reach safety, **yet** a few unlucky ones were stranded.

The firehouse whistle blew four times**, so** everyone knew a blizzard was closing in.

## Exceptions

- When two independent clauses are very short and they contrast with each other, you can link them with a comma without using a coordinating conjunction: *Mosquitoes don't bite, they stab.* Some instructors consider this an error, so in ACADEMIC WRITING, you'll never be wrong if you use a period or semicolon (Chapter 25) instead of a comma.
- When one or both independent clauses linked by a coordinating conjunction happen to contain other commas, dropping the coordinating conjunction and using a semicolon instead of the comma can help clarify meaning.

  With temperatures below freezing**,** the snow did not melt**; and people** wondered, gazing at the white landscape**,** when they would see grass again.

❗ **Alerts:** (1) Never put a comma *after* a coordinating conjunction that joins independent clauses.

**NO**  A house is renovated in two weeks **but,** an apartment takes a week.

**YES**  A house is renovated in two weeks**, but** an apartment takes a week.

(2) Never use a comma alone between independent clauses, or you'll create the error known as a COMMA SPLICE (see Chapter 20).

**NO**  Five inches of snow fell in two hours**,** driving was hazardous.

**YES**  Five inches of snow fell in two hours**, and** driving was hazardous. ●

**EXERCISE 24-1**  Working individually or in a group, combine each pair of sentences using the coordinating conjunction shown in parentheses. Rearrange words when necessary. For help, consult 24b.

**EXAMPLE**  Children spend less time playing outdoors than ever before. That has been found to be a significant problem. (and)

  Children spend less time playing outdoors than ever before**, and** that has been found to be a significant problem.

1. If your parents ever said to you, "Go outside and burn off some energy," you should thank them. They did you a big favor. (for)

---

Walsh, copy desk chief at the *Washington Post,* in his book *Lapsing Into a Comma.* With the comma, *of course* means "by the way": *I can attend your meeting on Friday.* Of course, *that will postpone by a few hours my finishing the report.* Without the comma, *of course* emphasizes a point: *Will I be there? Of course I will.*

### BACKGROUND
The site <http://www.wisc.edu/writing> offered by the University of Wisconsin at Madison features an interactive quiz on comma use under the heading "The Writer's Handbook" in the section titled "Grammar and Punctuation."

### QUOTATION: ON WRITING
Anyone who can improve a sentence of mine by the omission or placing of a comma is looked upon as my dearest friend.
—George Moore

### ANSWERS: EXERCISE 24-1
1. If your parents ever said to you, "Go outside and burn off some energy," you should thank them, for they did you a big favor.

2. Spending time outside as children is good for people, and now there is scientific proof.

3. As children play outside, their senses are stimulated, and that helps them learn in numerous ways.

4. For example, children's vision is fully stimulated by being outside, so they should spend more time playing outdoors than reading or watching TV, which stimulates only a narrow part of their vision.

5. When children spend time playing outside, they may engage in intense physical activity, or they may be less active but still discover the magic of the natural world.

6. The outdoors can be a child's greatest source of stimulation, yet many parents don't realize this.

7. Sadly enough, recess at many schools has been reduced, so children miss out on an opportunity for what scientists now know is another form of education.

**8.** But as people learn more about the many benefits of outdoor play for children, parents will not allow children to spend so much time on indoor activities, nor will schools continue to reduce recess time.

**9.** Instead, school leaders may heed renowned educators such as Maria Montessori, Rudolf Steiner, and Howard Gardner, who understood the close connection between movement and learning, and children will once again enjoy the benefits of a longer recess.

**10.** Enjoying the natural world may be part of our genetic makeup, so it only makes sense that children should be encouraged to get their vitamin D from sunlight and to use up some energy.

**TEACHING TIP**

A surprising number of students, especially those inexperienced with academic writing, tend to equate writing ability with knowledge of spelling and rules for the comma. (Not all students who have these ideas admit them freely, but often such notions emerge on anonymous questionnaires or in teacher-student conferences.) You might deal with this misperception about comma rules in two ways. First, you can put commas in their place by referring to the writing process, especially the different concerns that occupy a writer during drafting, revision, and editing—students can reread Chapter 2 to refresh their memories about these activities. Second, you can invite students to circle any comma in their writing about which they have a question—or any spot where they have not written a comma and have a question—and to jot the question in the margin. This helps students avoid getting snagged on commas while at the same time allowing them to get answers to their questions when you return their work. You will probably find that students have used most commas correctly (a fact that when pointed out enhances students' confidence) and that you can categorize the areas of confusion and thus clarify them for the students. Finally, after students have studied topics such as coordination, subordination, parallelism, and variety and emphasis, you can offer a tutorial review of commas—and students

**2.** Spending time outside as children is good for people. Now there is scientific proof. (and)

**3.** As children play outside, their senses are stimulated. That helps them learn in numerous ways. (and)

**4.** For example, children's vision is fully stimulated by being outside. They should spend more time playing outdoors than reading or watching TV, which stimulates only a narrow part of their vision. (so)

**5.** When children spend time playing outside, they may engage in intense physical activity. They may be less active but still discover the magic of the natural world. (or)

**6.** The outdoors can be a child's greatest source of stimulation. Many parents don't realize this. (yet)

**7.** Sadly enough, recess at many schools has been reduced. Children miss out on an opportunity for what scientists now know is another form of education. (so)

**8.** But as people learn more about the many benefits of outdoor play for children, parents will not allow children to spend so much time on indoor activities. Schools will not continue to reduce recess time. (nor)

**9.** Instead, school leaders may heed renowned educators such as Maria Montessori, Rudolf Steiner, and Howard Gardner, who understood the close connection between movement and learning. Children will once again enjoy the benefits of a longer recess. (and)

**10.** Enjoying the natural world may be part of our genetic makeup. It only makes sense that children should be encouraged to get their vitamin D from sunlight and to use up some energy. (so)

## 24c    How do commas work with introductory clauses, phrases, and words?

A comma follows any introductory element that comes before an INDEPENDENT CLAUSE. An introductory element can be a CLAUSE, PHRASE, or words. Because these elements are not sentences by themselves, you need to join them to independent clauses.

> **When the topic is dieting,** many people say sugar craving is their worst problem. [introductory dependent clause]
>
> **Between 1544 and 1689,** sugar refineries appeared in London and New York. [introductory prepositional phrase]
>
> **Beginning in infancy,** we develop lifelong tastes for sweet foods. [introductory participial phrase]
>
> **Sweets being a temptation for many adults,** most parents avoid commercial baby foods that contain sugar. [introductory absolute phrase]

**For example,** fructose comes from fruit, but it's still sugar. [introductory transitional expression]

**Nevertheless,** many people think fructose isn't harmful. [introductory conjunctive adverb]

**To satisfy a craving for ice cream,** even timid people sometimes brave midnight streets. [introductory infinitive phrase]

## EXCEPTION

When an introductory element is short, and the sentence can be understood easily, some writers omit the comma. However, in ACADEMIC WRITING, you'll never be wrong if you use the comma.

> **YES** In 1992, the Americans with Disabilities Act was passed. [preferred]
>
> **YES** In 1992 the Americans with Disabilities Act was passed.

An **interjection** is an introductory word that conveys surprise or other emotions. Use a comma after an interjection at the beginning of a sentence: *Oh, we didn't realize that you're allergic to cats. Yes, your sneezing worries me.*

**Alert:** Use a comma before and after a transitional expression that falls in the middle of a sentence. When the transitional expression starts a sentence, follow it with a comma. When the transitional expression ends a sentence, put a comma before it.

> **By the way,** the parade begins at noon. [introductory transitional expression with comma after it]
>
> The parade, **by the way,** begins at noon. [transitional expression with comma before and after it, in middle of sentence]
>
> The parade begins at noon, **by the way.** [transitional expression with comma before it, at end of sentence]
>
> **However,** our float isn't finished. [introductory conjunctive adverb with comma after it]
>
> Our float, **however,** isn't finished. [conjunctive adverb with comma before and after it, in middle of sentence]
>
> Our float isn't finished, **however.** [conjunctive adverb with comma before it, at end of sentence] ●

**EXERCISE 24-2** Working individually or with a group, combine each set of sentences into one sentence according to the direction in parentheses. Use a comma after the introductory element. You can add, delete, and rearrange words as needed. For help, consult 24c.

will be happy to discover how much they already know.

## TEACHING TIP

Unless they are set off by commas, some adverbs that double as prepositions are likely to cause confusion when placed before the subject of a sentence. You can advise students to apply common sense to avoid confusion.

> **NO** Below the submarine checked the water for mines. [What is below the submarine?]
>
> **YES** Below, the submarine checked the water for mines.
>
> **NO** After the crew expected to escort the president's ship. [Then what?]
>
> **YES** After, the crew expected to escort the president's ship.

## QUOTATION: ON WRITING

[Punctuation] scores the music in our minds, gets our thoughts moving to the rhythm of our hearts. Punctuation is the notation in the sheet music of our words, telling us when to rest, or when to raise our voices; it acknowledges that the meaning of our discourse, as of any symphonic composition, lies not in the units but in the pauses, the pacing and the phrasing.

—Pico Iyer

## ANSWERS: EXERCISE 24-2

**1.** When people laugh, scientists study them to find out what actually happens. [introductory adverb clause]

**2.** In fact, scientists track our physiological reactions to discover the chemicals we produce while we are laughing. [introductory transitional expression]

**3.** Produced in our bodies, dopamine is a chemical that makes us feel good and that our brain uses when we laugh. [introductory past-participial phrase]

**4.** Interestingly, we sometimes activate our tear ducts by laughing, which may reduce stress. [introductory word]

**5.** Immediately after people laughed, scientists tested their saliva and concluded that immune systems may benefit from laughter. [introductory adverb clause]

**6.** Although blood pressure and heart rates tend to go below baseline after we laugh, people should be happy about this effect because that's what happens after we exercise well. [introductory adverb clause]

**7.** In addition, laughter causes the lining of our blood vessels to expand and produce good chemicals in our bodies. [introductory transitional expression]

**8.** In the human body, one of these good chemicals, nitric oxide, reduces inflammation and clotting. [introductory prepositional phrase]

**9.** Seeming to have an analgesic effect, laughter may even help with pain management. [introductory present-participial phrase]

**10.** Because humor has so many physical benefits and makes us feel better, try to enjoy a few laughs every day. [introductory adverb clause]

## BACKGROUND

The placement of a comma can have important consequences. Consider these examples:

**1.** A comma once saved a man's life. Czar Alexander III had signed a death warrant reading: "Pardon impossible, to be sent to Siberia." Being sent to Siberia inevitably led to death. However, Czarina Maria Fyodorovna saved the

**EXAMPLE**  People have known that humor is good for them. They have known this for a long time. (Begin with *for a long time*.)

**For a long time,** people have known that humor is good for them.

1. People laugh. Scientists study them to find out what actually happens. (Begin with *when*.)

2. Scientists track our physiological reactions. They discover the chemicals we produce while we are laughing. (Begin with *in fact*.)

3. Our brains use dopamine when we laugh. Dopamine is a chemical we produce that makes us feel good. (Begin with *produced*.)

4. We sometimes activate our tear ducts by laughing. That reduces stress. (Begin with *interestingly*.)

5. Scientists tested people's saliva immediately after they laughed. Scientists concluded that immune systems may benefit from laughter. (Begin with *immediately*.)

6. Blood pressure and heart rates tend to go below baseline after we laugh. People should be happy about this effect because that's what happens after we exercise well. (Begin with *although*.)

7. Laughter causes the inner lining of our blood vessels to expand. This expansion produces good chemicals in our bodies. (Begin with *in addition*.)

8. One of these good chemicals is nitric oxide. It reduces inflammation and clotting. (Begin with *in the human body*.)

9. Laughter may even help with pain management. Laughter seems to have an analgesic effect. (Begin with *seeming*.)

10. Humor has so many physical benefits, and it makes us feel better. Try to enjoy a few laughs every day. (Begin with *because*.)

## 24d   How do commas work with items in a series?

A **series** is a group of three or more elements—words, PHRASES, or CLAUSES—that match in grammatical form and are of equal importance in a sentence.

Marriage requires **sexual, financial, and emotional** discipline.

—Anne Roiphe, "Why Marriages Fail"

Culture is a way of **thinking, feeling, believing.**

—Clyde Kluckhohn, *Mirror for Man*

My love of flying goes back to those early days **of roller skates, of swings, and of bicycles.**

—Tresa Wiggins, student

We have been taught **that children develop by ages and stages, that the steps are pretty much the same for everybody, and that to grow out of the limited behavior of childhood, we must climb them all.**

—Gail Sheehy, *Passages*

Many general publications omit the comma between the next to last item of a series and the coordinating conjunction. Recently, practice is changing even in ACADEMIC WRITING, which means that some instructors require the use of a comma here and others consider it an error. Check with your instructor.

**NO**   The sweater comes in **blue, green, pink and black.** [Do the sweaters come in three or four colors?]

**YES**   The sweater comes in **blue, green, pink, and black.** [The comma before *and* clarifies that the sweaters come in four colors.]

At all times, however, follow the "toast, juice, and ham and eggs" rule. That is, when one of the items in a series contains *and,* don't use a comma in that item.

When items in a series contain commas or other punctuation, separate them with SEMICOLONS instead of commas (25e).

If it's a bakery, they have to sell cake; if it's a photography shop, they have to develop film; and if it's a dry-goods store, they have to sell warm underwear.

—Art Buchwald, "Birth Control for Banks"

Numbered or lettered lists within a sentence are considered items in a series. With three or more items, use commas (or semicolons if the items themselves contain commas) to separate them.

To file your insurance claim, please enclose (1) a letter requesting payment, (2) a police report about the robbery, and (3) proof of purchase of the items you say are missing.

**Alert:** In a series, never use a comma before the first item or after the last item, unless a different rule makes it necessary.

**NO**   Many **artists, writers, and composers, have indulged** in day-dreaming.

**YES**   Many artists, writers, and composers have indulged in day-dreaming.

**NO**   Such dreamers include, Miró, Debussy, Dostoevsky, and Dickinson.

**YES**   Such dreamers include Miró, Debussy, Dostoevsky, and Dickinson.

man by altering the message to read: "Pardon, impossible to be sent to Siberia."

**2.** Elizabeth Langmore (Letters, *Time,* July 4, 1988) points out how very different it is to ask "Have you seen the elephant eating Tom?" and "Have you seen the elephant eating, Tom?"

**3.** In another letter to *Time,* Leslie Bryant asks readers to decipher "That that is is that that is not is not is that it it is." With commas and periods, it reads: "That that is, is. That that is not, is not. Is that it? It is."

**QUOTATION: ON WRITING**
In music, the punctuation is absolutely strict; the bars and rests are absolutely defined. But our prose cannot be quite strict, because we have to relate it to the audience. In other words, we are continually changing the score.
—Sir Ralph Richardson

**QUOTATION: ON WRITING**
A world that has only periods is a world without inflections. It is a world without shade. It has a music without sharps and flats. It is a martial music. It has a jackboot rhythm. Words cannot bend and curve. A comma, by comparison, catches the gentle drift of the mind in thought, turning in on itself and back on itself, reversing, re-doubling and returning along the course of its own sweet river music; while the semicolon brings clauses and thoughts together with all the silent discretion of a hostess arranging guests around her dinner table.
—Pico Iyer

**QUOTATION: ON WRITING**
In conversation you can use timing, a look, inflection, pauses. But on the page all you have is commas, dashes, the amount of syllables in a word. When I write, I read everything out loud to get the right rhythm.
—Fran Lebowitz

**QUOTATION: ON WRITING**
When I stepped from hard manual work to writing, I just stepped from one kind of hard work to another.
—Sean O'Casey

**ANSWERS: EXERCISE 24-3**

**1.** To socialize future Seeing Eye dogs, families with children ages 9 to 14 care for specially bred German shepherds, retrievers, and mixed-breed puppies for up to 16 months.

**2.** One youngster in each family becomes the pup's primary caretaker and is responsible for feeding, training, and grooming the future Seeing Eye dog.

**3.** While living with their families, the pups learn basic obedience commands, such as *sit, stay, come,* and *down.*

**4.** Groups of families get together frequently to take their Seeing Eye dogs-in-training on outings, so that the puppies become familiar with things that frighten some dogs, such as riding in cars, being in crowds, walking on slippery floors, and hearing loud noises.

**5.** Correct; no series of items.

**TEACHING TIP**
The words *restrictive* and *nonrestrictive* are being replaced in many classrooms with the words *essential* and *nonessential.* For this reason, this chapter uses the more grammatically descriptive terms and then gives in parentheses the terms more accessible to nongrammarians. No matter what words you use in your teaching,

---

**YES** Such dreamers include**,** **of course,** Miró, Debussy, Dostoevsky, and Dickinson. [As a transitional expression, *of course* is set off from the rest of the sentence by commas before and after it (24c).]●

● **EXERCISE 24-3** Insert commas to separate the items in a series. If a sentence needs no commas, explain why. For help, consult 24d.

EXAMPLE   Families from New York New Jersey and Pennsylvania raise the puppies that become Seeing Eye dogs.

Families from *New York***,** *New Jersey,* and *Pennsylvania* raise the puppies that become Seeing Eye dogs.

1. To socialize future Seeing Eye dogs, families with children ages 9 to 14 care for specially bred German shepherds retrievers and mixed-breed puppies for up to 16 months.

2. One youngster in each family becomes the pup's primary caretaker and is responsible for feeding training and grooming the future Seeing Eye dog.

3. While living with their families, the pups learn basic obedience commands, such as sit stay come and down.

4. Groups of families get together frequently to take their Seeing Eye dogs-in-training on outings, so that the puppies become familiar with things that frighten some dogs, such as riding in cars being in crowds walking on slippery floors and hearing loud noises.

5. When the puppies grow up, the families have the pain of giving them up but the satisfaction of knowing that their dogs will lead happy and productive lives while improving the quality of life for their future owners.

## 24e   How do commas work with coordinate adjectives?

**Coordinate adjectives** are two or more ADJECTIVES of equal weight that describe—that is, modify—a NOUN. In contrast, **cumulative adjectives** build meaning from word to word, as they move toward the noun. The key to applying this rule is recognizing when adjectives are coordinate and when they aren't. Quick Reference 24.2 tells you how.

The audience cheered when the **pulsating, rhythmic** music filled the stadium. [*Pulsating* and *rhythmic* are coordinate adjectives.]

Each band had a **distinctive musical** style. [*Distinctive* and *musical* aren't coordinate adjectives.]

## Quick Reference 24.2

### Tests for coordinate and cumulative adjectives

If either one of these tests works, the adjectives are coordinate and require a comma between them.

- Can the order of the adjectives be reversed without changing the meaning or creating nonsense? If yes, use a comma.

   **NO** The concert featured **new several** bands. [*New several* makes no sense.]

   **YES** The **huge, restless** crowd waited for the concert to begin. [*Restless, huge* still carries the same meaning, so these are coordinate adjectives.]

- Can *and* be sensibly inserted between the adjectives? If yes, use a comma.

   **NO** The concert featured **several and new** bands. [*Several and new* makes no sense.]

   **YES** The **huge and restless** crowd waited. [Modifier *huge and restless* makes sense, so these are coordinate adjectives.]

**Alert:** Don't put a comma between a final coordinate adjective and the noun it modifies.

   **NO** Hundreds of **roaring, cheering, yelling, fans** filled the stadium.

   **YES** Hundreds of **roaring, cheering, yelling fans** filled the stadium. ●

**EXERCISE 24-4**    Insert commas to separate coordinate adjectives. If a sentence needs no commas, explain why. For help, consult 24e.

**EXAMPLE**    Only corn grown for popcorn pops consistently because all other kinds of corn lack tough enamel-like shells.

Only corn grown for popcorn pops consistently because all other kinds of corn lack *tough, enamel-like* shells.

1. The outside of an unpopped popcorn kernel is a hard plastic-like coating.
2. Inside an unpopped kernel is a soft starchy substance combined with water.
3. Applying heat causes the water molecules to expand until the pressure pops the dark yellow kernel.
4. The popped kernel turns itself inside out and absorbs air into its white pulpy matter.
5. The thinner softer shells of nonpopcorn corn don't allow water to heat to the high popping temperature.

the concept of *restriction* is a helpful one for students to understand. To illustrate this concept, you might focus on how the words *the* and *a* in these sentences affect restriction and the role of the commas:

   I took the bus, which made many stops, to get here.

   I took a bus that made many stops to get here.

### ANSWERS: EXERCISE 24-4

1. hard, plasticlike
2. soft, starchy
3. Correct; adjectives *dark* and *yellow* are not coordinate
4. white, pulpy
5. thinner, softer

### ADDITIONAL EXAMPLES

*Restrictive clauses and phrases*

1. People *who travel abroad* should be willing to alter their eating habits.
2. Tours *that make dining decisions for travelers* sometimes provide surprises.
3. Diners *with conservative tastes* are sometimes offended.
4. For example, the evening meal *in Spain* is usually served after 9 p.m.
5. The restaurant *where I often had dinner in Madrid* was never filled until after 10 p.m.

*Nonrestrictive clauses and phrases*

1. My aunt, *who often travels abroad*, enjoys experimenting with unusual foods.
2. Holiday Tours, *which makes all the dining decisions for its travelers*, provides too few surprises for her.
3. Her tastes, *after her many excursions to exotic places*, are still adventuresome.
4. For example, eating in Spain, *which is always a late-evening affair*, is one of her favorite excursions.

5. Las Tres Encinas, *where she often dines when she is in Madrid,* is never filled until after 10 p.m.

## EXTRA EXERCISE B

Circle unnecessary commas and add needed commas where restrictive and nonrestrictive phrases, clauses, and appositives appear in the following sentences.

**1.** Elizabeth II, who is queen of the United Kingdom, was born in London in 1926.

**2.** She is the elder daughter of King George VI and Queen Consort Elizabeth who was known as the Queen Mother.

**3.** Her education administered at home by private tutors included many subjects.

**4.** She was married, at Westminster Abbey to Philip Mountbatten, who was formerly Prince Philip of Greece.

**5.** He was created Duke of Edinburgh, with all the rights and privileges of the title, on the eve of the marriage.

**6.** Prince Charles Elizabeth's first child was born on November 14, 1948.

**7.** Princess Anne the second child was born on August 15, 1950.

**8.** Elizabeth's father George VI died in 1952.

**9.** Elizabeth was crowned, queen of England, in Westminster Abbey a historic site on June 2, 1953.

**10.** Prince Charles, now himself a parent, thus became, the heir apparent.

## Answers to Extra Exercise B

**1.** Correct

**2.** Elizabeth, who

**3.** education, administered . . . tutors, included

**4.** married at

**5.** Correct

**6.** Charles, Elizabeth's first child, was

**7.** Anne, the second child, was

**8.** father, George VI, died

## 24f How do commas work with nonrestrictive elements?

A **restrictive element** contains information (a descriptive word, clause, or phrase) that's essential for a sentence to deliver its message; thus, it is often called an *essential element.* A **nonrestrictive element** contains information that's not essential for a sentence to deliver its meaning, and therefore, it is often called a *nonessential element.* The key is in recognizing what's essential (restrictive) and what's nonessential (nonrestrictive) in a sentence. Quick Reference 24.3 defines and explains the differences in the meanings of these terms.

### Quick Reference 24.3 ▪ ▪ ▪ ▪ ▪ ▪ ▪ ▪

#### Restrictive and nonrestrictive defined

**RESTRICTIVE**

A restrictive element contains information essential for the sentence to deliver its message. By being essential, the words in the element limit—that is, "restrict"—the meaning in some way. Don't use commas with restrictive elements.

> Many US states retest drivers **who are over sixty-five** to check their driving competency.

The information *who are over sixty-five* is essential to understanding the sentence because it limits or restricts the meaning of *drivers* to only those over the age of sixty-five. Drivers *under* sixty-five are not included. To check whether an element is essential, drop it and read the sentence. If the meaning of the sentence changes, then the information element is essential in delivering the message intended in the sentence. This means the element is restrictive (essential), and commas are not used.

**NONRESTRICTIVE**

A nonrestrictive element contains information that's *not* essential for the sentence to deliver its message. By being nonessential, the words in the element don't limit—or "restrict"—the meaning. Use commas with nonrestrictive (nonessential) elements.

> My parents**, who are both over sixty-five,** took a defensive-driving course.

The information *who are both over sixty-five* is not essential because the words *my parents* carry the sentence's message so that we know who took a defensive driving course. (Information about their age is "extra" to this message, so commas are required.)

Quick Reference 24.4 shows the pattern for comma use with nonrestrictive elements. The pattern for restrictive elements calls for no commas.

## Quick Reference 24.4

■ ■ ■ ■ ■ ■ ■

### Commas with nonrestrictive elements

Nonrestrictive element, independent clause.

Beginning of independent clause, **nonrestrictive element,** end of independent clause.

Independent clause, **nonrestrictive element.**

Restrictive and nonrestrictive elements can fall at the beginning, in the middle, or at the end of a sentence. To test whether an element is nonrestrictive, read the sentence without the element. If the meaning of the sentence does not change, the element is nonrestrictive.

#### MORE EXAMPLES OF RESTRICTIVE ELEMENTS

Some people **in my neighborhood** enjoy jogging. [The reader needs the information *in my neighborhood* to know which people enjoy jogging. The information is essential, so no commas are used.]

Some people **who are in excellent physical condition** enjoy jogging. [The reader needs the information *who are in excellent physical condition* to know which people enjoy jogging. The information is essential, so no commas are used.]

The agricultural scientist **Wendy Singh** has developed a new fertilization technique. [*Wendy Singh* is essential to identify exactly which agricultural scientist developed the new technique, so no commas are used.]

#### MORE EXAMPLES OF NONRESTRICTIVE ELEMENTS

**An energetic person,** Anna Hom enjoys jogging. [Without knowing that Anna Hom is *an energetic person*, the reader can understand that she enjoys jogging. The information is nonessential, so a comma is used.]

Anna Hom, **who is in excellent physical condition,** enjoys jogging. [Without knowing Anna Hom's *physical condition*, the reader can understand that Anna Hom enjoys jogging. The information is nonessential, so commas are used.]

Anna Hom enjoys jogging, **which is also Adam's favorite pastime.** [Without knowing about *Adam's favorite pastime*, the reader can understand that Anna Hom enjoys jogging. The information is nonessential, so commas are used.]

The agricultural scientist, **a new breed of farmer,** explains how to control a farming environment. [Without knowing that the scientist is *a new breed of farmer*, the reader can understand that the agricultural scientist explains how to control a farming environment. The information is nonessential, so commas are used.]

9. crowned queen of England in Westminster Abbey, a historic site, on

10. became the

#### QUOTATION: ON WRITING

The use of commas is not simply a matter of following rules. It requires a sensitivity to the rhythms of the language, to the pace of the line, to the sense of what is being said.
—Margaret Babcock

#### QUOTATION: ON WRITING

It is frequently hard to decide whether a single word, such as *however,* or a brief phrase, is or is not parenthetic. If the interruption to the flow of the sentence is but slight, the writer may safely omit the commas. But whether the interruption be slight or considerable, he must never omit one comma and leave the other.
—William Strunk Jr., *Elements of Style*

#### QUOTATION: ON WRITING

The comma tells the reader to pause, just as the blinking yellow light tells a driver to slow down and proceed with caution.
—Gary A. Olson

#### QUOTATION: ON WRITING

The earliest grammar books defined punctuation marks as cues for oral reading. From the Middle Ages to the twentieth century, however, grammarians in Europe and England slowly dissociated punctuation from speech, defining language as a spatial *structure* rather than a spoken linear stream. As stated in the classic grammar book *The King's English,* 1906 [H. W. Fowler and F. G. Fowler]: "The old stopping was frankly to guide the voice in reading aloud, while the modern is mainly to guide the mind in *seeing* through the construction."
—*Period Styles: A History of Punctuation,* catalog, The Cooper Union for the Advancement of Science and Art

#### QUOTATION: ON WRITING

By clearing up any errors you may be making in using commas, you will probably clear up a high percentage of your total mistakes in punctuation.

—Charles W. Dawe

**ANSWERS: EXERCISE 24-5**

**1.** In spring, as birds and bees look for water and food, certain plants and trees provide those needs and thus attract the greatest amount of airborne visitors. [nonrestrictive prepositional phrase]

**2.** Correct: no commas with restrictive relative clause.

**3.** During suburban sprawl, when cities eat up more and more land, birds have to adapt by putting their nests in buildings. [nonrestrictive dependent clause]

**4.** Birds are attracted to pines and evergreens, where they can find food and shelter. [nonrestrictive relative clause]

**5.** Hungry birds, who are not picky, will enjoy a feeder stocked with black oil sunflower seeds. [nonrestrictive relative clause]

**6.** Birds also need to eat insects, which provide a higher protein content than seeds. [nonrestrictive relative clause]

**7.** Some common plants, such as butterfly weed and lantana, are ideal for attracting butterflies. [nonrestrictive adjectival phrase]

**8.** Because they have the nectar that butterflies want, these plants enhance any butterfly garden. [nonrestrictive dependent clause, and no comma with the restrictive relative clause]

**9.** As butterflies pass by a garden, looking for bright colors and strong fragrances, they will notice flowers planted in large clumps. [nonrestrictive participial phrase]

**10.** Correct: no commas with restrictive relative clauses

**QUOTATION: ON WRITING**

I can't turn out slews of stuff each day. I wish I could. I seem to have some neurotic need to perfect each paragraph—each sentence, even—as I go along.

—William Styron

**EXERCISE 24-5** Using your knowledge of restrictive and nonrestrictive elements, insert commas as needed. If a sentence is correct, explain why. For help, consult 24f.

EXAMPLE During the summer when butterflies are most active gardeners can attract them by planting the right flowers.

During the summer, when butterflies are most active, gardeners can attract them by planting the right flowers.

1. In spring as birds and bees look for water and food certain plants and trees provide those needs and thus attract the greatest number of airborne visitors.

2. Gardeners who learn to attract birds may find they have fewer problems with insects and other unwelcome pests.

3. During suburban sprawl when cities eat up more and more land birds have to adapt by putting their nests in buildings.

4. Birds are attracted to pines and evergreens where they can find food and shelter.

5. Hungry birds who are not picky will enjoy a feeder stocked with black oil sunflower seeds.

6. Birds also need to eat insects which provide a higher protein content than seeds.

7. Some common plants such as butterfly weed and lantana are ideal for attracting butterflies.

8. Because they have the nectar that butterflies want these plants enhance any butterfly garden.

9. As butterflies pass by a garden looking for bright colors and strong fragrances they will notice flowers planted in large clumps.

10. Gardens that are favorable to birds and butterflies will also invite honeybees and other pollinators.

## 24g How do commas set off parenthetical expressions, contrasts, words of direct address, and tag sentences?

**Parenthetical expressions** are "asides." They add information but aren't necessary for understanding the message of a sentence. Set them off with parentheses or commas.

American farmers **(according to US government figures)** export more wheat than they sell at home.

A major drought, **sad to say,** wiped out this year's wheat crop.

Expressions of **contrast** state what is *not* the case. Set them off with commas.

Feeding the world's population is a serious, **though not impossible,** problem.

We must work against world hunger continuously, **not only when famines strike.**

Words of **direct address** name the person or group being spoken to (addressed). Set them off with commas.

Join me, **brothers and sisters,** to end hunger.

Your contribution to the Relief Fund, **Steve,** will help us greatly.

A **tag sentence** is a normal sentence that ends with a "tag," an attached phrase or question. Set off a tag with a comma. When the tag is a question, the sentence ends with a question mark. This holds whether or not the **tag question** is formed with a CONTRACTION.

People will give blood regularly, **I hope.**

The response to the blood drive was impressive, **wasn't it?**

**EXERCISE 24-6**   Add commas to set off any parenthetical or contrasting elements, words of direct address, and tag sentences. Adjust end punctuation as necessary. For help, consult 24g.

**EXAMPLE**   Writer's block it seems to me is a misunderstood phenomenon.

Writer's block, *it seems to me,* is a misunderstood phenomenon.

1. An inability to write some say stems from lack of discipline and a tendency to procrastinate.

2. In other words the only way to overcome writer's block is to exert more willpower.

3. But writer's block is a complex psychological event that happens to conscientious people not just procrastinators.

4. Such people strangely enough are often unconsciously rebelling against their own self-tyranny and rigid standards of perfection.

5. If I told you my fellow writer that all it takes to start writing again is to quit punishing yourself, you would think I was crazy wouldn't you?

## 24h   How do commas work with quoted words?

**Explanatory words** are *said, stated, declared,* and other words that introduce DIRECT DISCOURSE. When they fall in the same sentence, quoted words are set off from explanatory words.

**ANSWERS: EXERCISE 24-6**

Answers may vary slightly. Here is one set of possibilities.

**1.** An inability to write, some say, [parenthetical expression] stems from lack of discipline and a tendency to procrastinate.

**2.** In other words, [parenthetical expression] the only way to overcome writer's block is to exert more willpower.

**3.** But writer's block is a complex psychological event that happens to conscientious people, not just procrastinators. [expression of contrast]

**4.** Such people, strangely enough, [parenthetical expression] are often unconsciously rebelling against their own self-tyranny and rigid standards of perfection.

**5.** If I told you, my fellow writer, [direct address] that all it takes to start writing again is to quit punishing yourself, you would think I was crazy, wouldn't you? [tag sentence]

She stole my playthings first, the jealous thief,
   And left me there forlorn.

The birds that in my garden would have sung,
   She scared away with her unending moan;
She slew my lovers too when I was young,
   And left me there alone.

Grief, I have cursed thee often—now at last
   To hate thy name I am no longer free;
Caught in thy bony arms and prisoned fast,
   I love no love but thee.

### ANSWERS: EXERCISE 24-7

**1.** "I'm happy to answer any questions you have," said the rancher to the tourist. [explanatory words at the end of a quotation]

**2.** "Well, then," said the tourist, "I'd like to know how you make ends meet on such a tiny ranch." [explanatory words in the middle of a quotation]

**3.** Correct: no comma should follow a question mark.

**4.** The rancher continued, "He works for me, but I don't pay him any money. Instead, I have promised him that after two years of work, he will own the ranch." [explanatory words at the beginning of a quotation]

**5.** "Then, I'll work for him, and in two more years, the ranch will be mine again!" said the rancher with a smile. [no comma should follow an exclamation point]

### QUOTATION: ON WRITING

During the rise of printing, punctuation was left to the compositor's discretion: in English, as in other vernacular languages, there were not yet any strict conventions to follow. The *Mechanick Exercises of the Whole Art of Printing*, 1683 [Joseph Moxon], outlines the haphazard method of an English shop:

> *As he Sets on, he considers how to Point his Work, viz. when to Set, where; where, where to make ( ) where [ ] and when to make a Break . . . When he meets with proper Names*

Speaking of ideal love, the poet William Blake wrote**,** "Love seeketh not itself to please."

"My love is a fever**,**" said William Shakespeare about love's passion.

"I love no love**,**" proclaimed the poet Mary Coleridge**,** "but thee."

### EXCEPTION

When the quoted words are blended into the grammatical structure of your sentence, don't use commas to set them off. These are instances of INDIRECT DISCOURSE, usually occurring with *as* and *that*.

The duke describes the duchess **as** "too soon made glad."

The duchess insists **that** "appearing glad often is but a deception."

**Alert:** When the quoted words end with an exclamation point or a question mark, retain that original punctuation, even if explanatory words follow.

| QUOTED WORDS | *"O Romeo! Romeo!"* |
|---|---|
| NO | "O Romeo! Romeo**!,**" whispered Juliet from her window. |
| NO | "O Romeo! Romeo**,**" whispered Juliet from her window. |
| YES | "O Romeo! Romeo**!**" whispered Juliet from her window. |
| QUOTED WORDS | *"Wherefore art thou Romeo?"* |
| NO | "Wherefore art thou Romeo**?,**" Juliet urgently asked. |
| NO | "Wherefore art thou Romeo**,**" Juliet urgently asked. |
| YES | "Wherefore art thou Romeo**?**" Juliet urgently asked. ● |

**EXERCISE 24-7** Punctuate the following dialogue correctly. If a sentence is correct, explain why. For help, consult 24h.

EXAMPLE  "Can you tell me just one thing?," asked the tourist.

    "Can you tell me just one thing**?**" asked the tourist.

1. "I'm happy to answer any questions you have" said the rancher to the tourist.

2. "Well, then" said the tourist "I'd like to know how you make ends meet on such a tiny ranch."

3. "Do you see that man leaning against the shed over there?" asked the rancher.

4. The rancher continued "He works for me, but I don't pay him any money. Instead, I have promised him that after two years of work, he will own the ranch."

5. "Then, I'll work for him, and in two more years, the ranch will be mine again!," said the rancher with a smile.

## 24i  How do commas work in dates, names, addresses, correspondence, and numbers?

When you write dates, names, addresses, correspondence, and numbers, use commas according to accepted practice. Quick References 24.5 through 24.8 provide some guidelines.

### Quick Reference 24.5

**Commas with dates**

- Use a comma between the date and the year: *July 20, 1969.*
- Use a comma between the day and the date: *Sunday, July 20.*
- Within a sentence, use a comma on both sides of the year in a full date: *Everyone planned to be near a TV set on July 20, 1969, to watch the lunar landing.*
- Never use a comma when only the month and year, or the month and day, are given. Also, never use a comma between the season and year.

  **YES**  People knew that one day in **July 1969** would change the world.

  **YES**  News coverage was especially heavy on **July 21.**

  **YES**  In **summer 1969** a man walked on the moon.
- Never use a comma in an inverted date, a form used in the US military and throughout the world except in the United States.

  **YES**  People stayed near their televisions on **20 July 1969** to watch the lunar landing.

### Quick Reference 24.6

**Commas with names, places, and addresses**

- When an abbreviated academic degree (*MD, PhD*) comes after a person's name, use a comma between the name and the title (*Angie Eng, MD*), and also after the title if other words follow in the sentence: *The jury listened closely to the expert testimony of **Angie Eng, MD, last week.***

continued >>

*of Persons or Places he Sets them in* Italick . . . *and Sets the first Letter with a* Capital. . . .
—*Period Styles: A History of Punctuation,* catalog, The Cooper Union for the Advancement of Science and Art

**QUOTATION: ON WRITING**
Punctuation serves to govern the interior of a text as well as its format The librarian at Alexandria who was named Aristophanes designed a Greek punctuation system circa 260 BC His system marked the shortest segments of discourse with a centered dot • called a comma • and marked the longer sections with a low dot called a colon. All the letters were the same height • providing a consistent frame of reference for the dots.
—*Period Styles: A History of Punctuation,* catalog, The Cooper Union for the Advancement of Science and Art

**QUOTATION: ON WRITING**
In language, clearness is everything.
—Confucius

**QUOTATION: ON WRITING**
Usage is the only test. I prefer a phrase that is easy and unaffected to a phrase that is grammatical.
—W. Somerset Maugham

**QUOTATION: ON WRITING**
Students who have learned to be careful about commas understandably "write around" the problem. Sentence-combining exercises not only illustrate how punctuation organizes sentence elements for a reader but also how to solve punctuation problems which for years have limited a student's range of syntactic options. Furthermore, the exercises sometimes expose misunderstood punctuation rules discussed in previous English classes . . . [and] grammatical labels [that] sometimes create punctuation problems. Sentence combining allows teachers to dispense with terminology altogether or, if they wish, to name constructions *after* students have practiced them.
—Erica Lindemann

**QUOTATION: ON WRITING**

Anyone who undervalues the use of the comma in creating meaning should compare the statement "God rest you, merry gentlemen" with its older form, "God rest you merry, gentlemen."

—Carolyn Good

**QUOTATION: ON WRITING**

Unlike the period, question mark, exclamation [point], colon, dash, and parentheses, the comma has no clear special quality. . . . It is not a terminal marking like the period, a specialized coordinating mark like the semicolon, or an anticipatory mark like the colon. Even the dash, which comes nearest the comma in a variety of uses, has a characteristic quality, and all the points except the dash have a much more limited number of uses. The comma may be used alone or in pairs; it may stand between coordinate expressions or may separate expressions of different grammatical rank; it may set off a group for emphasis or clearness even when the grammatical relation is close.

—George Summey Jr.

**QUOTATION: ON WRITING**

I have performed the necessary butchery. Here is the bleeding corpse.

—Henry James, comment following a request to cut three lines from a 5,000-word article

**BACKGROUND**

At a Republican National Convention late last century, a single comma actually reshaped meaning in the party platform. An item proposed for the platform read, "The Convention opposes any form of tax increase which would hurt the economy." Someone called for the addition of a comma, so that the item would read, "The Convention opposes any form of tax increase, which would hurt the economy."

That comma was a reflection of the conservative economic position of its proposer. In the first version of the sentence, *which* begins a restrictive clause. The author of the proposal was talking only of harmful tax increases and

---

**Quick Reference 24.6** (continued)

- When an indicator of birth order or succession ( *Jr., Sr., III, IV* ) follows a name, never use a comma: *Martin Luther **King Jr.*** or *Henry **Ford II***

- When you invert a person's name, use a comma to separate the last name from the first: ***Troyka, David***

- When city and state names are written together, use a comma to separate them: ***Philadelphia, Pennsylvania.*** If the city and state fall within a sentence, use a comma after the state as well: *My family settled in **Philadelphia, Pennsylvania,** before I was born.*

- When a complete address is part of a sentence, use a comma to separate all the items, except the state and ZIP code: *I wrote to **Shelly Kupperman, 1001 Rule Road, Upper Saddle River, NJ 07458,** for more information about the comma.*

---

**Quick Reference 24.7**

**Commas in correspondence**

- For the opening of an informal letter, use a comma: **Dear Betty,**

- For the opening of a business or formal letter, use a colon:

  **Dear Ms. Kiviat:**

- For the close of a letter, use a comma:

  **Sincerely yours,**    **Best regards,**    **Love,**

---

**Quick Reference 24.8**

**Commas with numbers**

- Counting from right to left, put a comma after every three digits in numbers with more than four digits.

  72,867                156,567,066

- A comma is optional in most four-digit numbers. Be consistent within each piece of writing.

  $1776            $1,776

  1776 miles        1,776 miles

  1776 potatoes      1,776 potatoes

continued >>

## Quick Reference 24.8    (continued)

- Never use a comma in a four-digit year: **1990** (*Note:* If the year has five digits or more, do use a comma: **25,000 BC.**)
- Never use a comma in an address of four digits or more: *12161 Dean Drive*
- Never use a comma in a page number of four digits or more: *see page 1338*
- Use a comma to separate related measurements written as words: *five feet, four inches*
- Use a comma to separate a scene from an act in a play: *act II, scene iv* (or *act 2, scene 4*)
- Use a comma to separate references to a page and a line: *page 10, line 6*

**EXERCISE 24-8**    Insert commas where they are needed. For help, consult 24i.

**EXAMPLE**    On June 1 1984 the small German-French production company released a feature film called *Paris Texas.*

On June 1, 1984, the small German-French production company released a feature film called *Paris, Texas.*

1. Made by the noted German director Wim Wenders, *Paris Texas* was set in an actual town in Lamar County Texas with a population of 24699.
2. The movie's title was clearly intended to play off the slightly more famous Paris in France.
3. The custom of naming little towns in the United States after cosmopolitan urban centers in the Old World has resulted in such places as Athens Georgia and St. Petersburg Florida.
4. As of December 1 2005 the American St. Petersburg was estimated to have nearly 250000 citizens and the American Athens nearly 109000.
5. By comparison, St. Petersburg Russia and Athens Greece were estimated to have populations of 4 million and 1 million, respectively.

## 24j  How do commas clarify meaning?

A comma is sometimes needed to clarify the meaning of a sentence, even though no rule calls for one. The best solution is to revise the sentence.

**NO**    Of the gymnastic team's twenty five were injured.

**YES**    Of the gymnastic team's **twenty, five** were injured.

**YES**    Of **twenty on** the gymnastic team, five were injured. [preferred]

implying that nonharmful increases would be acceptable. In the second version, *which* begins a nonrestrictive clause. This author saw all tax increases as harmful.

**QUOTATION: ON WRITING**

Commas separate adjectives in a series [a]. When the noun and the adjective directly preceding it are a conceptual unit, do not separate them [b].

**A.** Jane is a little, radiant, polite girl.

**B.** Jane is a radiant, polite little girl.

—*Period Styles: A History of Punctuation,* catalog, The Cooper Union for the Advancement of Science and Art

**ANSWERS: EXERCISE 24-8**

**1.** Made by the noted German director Wim Wenders, *Paris, Texas* [comma after city in title] was set in an actual town in Lamar County, Texas, [commas after county and state] with a population of 24,699. [comma with numbers]

**2.** Correct

**3.** The custom of naming little towns in the United States after cosmopolitan urban centers in the Old World has resulted in such places as Athens, Georgia, and St. Petersburg, Florida. [commas after cities and after state within sentence]

**4.** As of December 1, 2005, [commas with dates] the American St. Petersburg was estimated to have nearly 250,000 [comma with numbers] citizens and the American Athens nearly 109,000. [comma with numbers]

**5.** By comparison, St. Petersburg, Russia, and Athens, Greece, [commas after cities and countries within sentences] were estimated to have populations of 4 million and 1 million, respectively.

## BACKGROUND

*Period Styles: A History of Punctuation,* a catalog from The Cooper Union for the Advancement of Science and Art, offers these examples of when commas are and are not needed with appositives: *Dick, a boy, chased Jane, a girl* [commas needed; nonrestrictive]; *The boy Dick chased the girl Jane* [no commas needed; restrictive] .

## ANSWERS: EXERCISE 24-9

**1.** Lasting for thirteen days in August 1992, Hurricane Andrew, after 2005's Katrina, was the second most expensive hurricane.

**2.** Andrew was rated a category four, smaller than 2005's Katrina, when it made landfall in south Florida.

**3.** The highest gust officially recorded, 164 miles per hour at 130 feet above the ground, occurred before Andrew shut down the National Hurricane Center's measuring devices.

**4.** The thousands of vortexes within Andrew, as with many high-intensity storms, are what caused the worst damage.

**5.** Andrew, difficult to measure accurately, was upgraded from a category four to a category five hurricane ten years after it occurred.

## QUOTATION: ON WRITING

The most important fact about a comma is that there are places where it must not be used. That is, there are places where a comma alters the meaning of a statement. Max Beerbohm was being witty when he used a comma in writing about *Frank Harris, and many good writers.* There are also a few places where a comma must be used in order to protect the meaning.

—Bergen Evans and Cornelia Evans

## QUOTATION: ON WRITING

Avoid commas, that are not necessary.

—William Safire, *Fumblerules*

| | |
|---|---|
| **NO** | Those who can practice many hours a day. |
| **YES** | **Those who can,** practice many hours a day. |
| **YES** | **They** practice many hours a day **when they can.** [preferred] |
| **NO** | George dressed and performed for the sellout crowd. |
| **YES** | **George dressed,** and performed for the sellout crowd. |
| **YES** | **After** George dressed, **he** performed for the sellout crowd. [preferred] |

**EXERCISE 24-9**  Working individually or with a group, insert commas to prevent misreading. For help, consult 24j.

**EXAMPLE**  For scientists tracking and measuring hurricanes is still an inexact science.

For scientists, tracking and measuring hurricanes is still an inexact science.

1. Lasting for thirteen days in August 1992 Hurricane Andrew after 2005's Katrina was the second most expensive hurricane.

2. Andrew was rated a category four smaller than 2005's Katrina when it made landfall in south Florida.

3. The highest gust officially recorded 164 miles per hour at 130 feet above the ground occurred before Andrew shut down the National Hurricane Center's measuring devices.

4. The thousands of vortexes within Andrew as with many high-intensity storms are what caused the worst damage.

5. Andrew difficult to measure accurately was upgraded from a category four to a category five hurricane ten years after it occurred.

## 24k  How can I avoid misusing commas?

Throughout this chapter, Alert notes remind you about comma misuses as they relate to each comma rule. Most of these misuses are overuses—inserting a comma where one is unnecessary. This section summarizes the Alert notes and lists other frequent misuses of the comma.

When advice against overusing a comma clashes with a rule requiring one, follow the rule that requires the comma.

The town of Kitty Hawk, North Carolina, attracts thousands of tourists each year. [Even though the comma after *North Carolina* separates the subject and its verb (which it normally shouldn't), the comma is required here because of the rule that calls for a comma when the name of a state follows the name of a city within a sentence (24i).]

## 24k.1 Commas with coordinating conjunctions

Never use a comma after a COORDINATING CONJUNCTION that joins two INDEPENDENT CLAUSES, unless another rule makes it necessary (24b). Also, don't use a comma to separate two items joined with a coordinating conjunction—there must be at least three (24d).

| | |
|---|---|
| **NO** | The sky was dark gray **and,** it looked like dusk. |
| **YES** | The sky was dark gray**, and** it looked like dusk. |

| | |
|---|---|
| **NO** | **The moon, and the stars** were shining last night. |
| **YES** | **The moon and the stars** were shining last night. |

## 24k.2 Commas with subordinating conjunctions and prepositions

Never put a comma after a SUBORDINATING CONJUNCTION or a PREPOSITION, unless another rule makes it necessary.

| | |
|---|---|
| **NO** | **Although,** the storm brought high winds, it did no damage. |
| **YES** | **Although the storm brought high winds,** it did no damage. [comma follows full subordinated dependent clause, not the subordinate conjunction that begins it] |

| | |
|---|---|
| **NO** | The storm did no damage **although,** it brought high winds. |
| **YES** | The storm did no damage **although it brought high winds.** [no comma after a subordinating conjunction] |

| | |
|---|---|
| **NO** | People expected worse **between,** the high winds and the heavy downpour. |
| **YES** | People expected worse **between the high winds and the heavy downpour.** [preposition begins sentence element that needs no comma before or after] |

## 24k.3 Commas in a series

Never use a comma before the first, or after the last, item in a series, unless another rule makes it necessary (24d).

| | |
|---|---|
| **NO** | The gymnasium was decorated **with, red, white, and blue** ribbons for the Fourth of July. |
| **NO** | The gymnasium was decorated with **red, white, and blue, ribbons** for the Fourth of July. |
| **YES** | The gymnasium was decorated with **red, white, and blue** ribbons for the Fourth of July. |

**QUOTATION: ON WRITING**

The commas are the most useful and usable of all the stops. It is highly important to put them in place as you go along. If you try to come back after doing a paragraph and stick them in the various spots that tempt you you will discover that they tend to swarm like minnows into all sorts of crevices whose existence you hadn't realized and before you know it the whole long sentence becomes immobilized and lashed up squirming in commas. Better to use them sparingly, and with affection, precisely when the need for each one arises, nicely, by itself.

—Lewis Thomas

Never put a comma between a final COORDINATE ADJECTIVE and the NOUN that the adjectives modify. Also, don't use a comma between adjectives that are not coordinate (24e).

| NO | He wore an **old, baggy, sweater.** |
|---|---|
| YES | He wore an **old, baggy sweater.** [coordinate adjectives] |
| NO | He has **several, new sweaters.** |
| YES | He has **several new sweaters.** [noncoordinate, or cumulative, adjectives] |

## 24k.4 Commas with restrictive elements

Never use a comma to set off a RESTRICTIVE (essential) element from the rest of a sentence (24f).

| NO | **Vegetables, stir-fried in a wok,** are crisp and flavorful. [The words *stir-fried in a wok* are essential, so they are not set off with commas.] |
|---|---|
| YES | **Vegetables stir-fried in a wok** are crisp and flavorful. |

## 24k.5 Commas with quotations

Never use a comma to set off INDIRECT DISCOURSE; use a comma only with DIRECT DISCOURSE (24h).

| NO | Jon said **that, he likes** stir-fried vegetables. |
|---|---|
| YES | Jon said **that he likes** stir-fried vegetables. |
| YES | **Jon said,** "I like stir-fried vegetables." |

## 24k.6 Commas that separate a subject from its verb, a verb from its object, or a preposition from its object

A comma does not make sense between these elements, though in some cases another comma rule might supersede this guideline (as in the first example in section 24k).

| NO | **The brothers Wright, made** their first successful airplane flights on December 17, 1903. [As a rule, a comma doesn't separate a subject from its verb.] |
|---|---|
| YES | **The brothers Wright made** their first successful airplane flights on December 17, 1903. |
| NO | These inventors enthusiastically **tackled, the problems** of powered flight and aerodynamics. [As a rule, a comma doesn't separate a verb from its object.] |
| YES | These inventors enthusiastically **tackled the problems** of powered flight and aerodynamics. |

| | |
|---|---|

NO    Airplane hobbyists **from, all over the world** visit Kitty Hawk's flight museum. [As a rule, a comma doesn't separate a preposition from its object.]

YES    Airplane hobbyists **from all over the world** visit Kitty Hawk's flight museum.

**EXERCISE 24-10**    Some commas have been deliberately misused in these sentences. Delete misused commas. If a sentence is correct, explain why. For help, consult all parts of this chapter, especially 24j and 24k.

EXAMPLE    The Harlem Renaissance was a cultural and artistic movement, that began around 1919 and lasted until the early 1930s.

The Harlem Renaissance was a cultural and artistic movement that began around 1919 and lasted until the early 1930s.

1. Although, this movement is named for Harlem, its impact spread to urban areas throughout the country, and the world.
2. During the Harlem Renaissance, artists in many fields found new ways to express the different facets, of black life in America.
3. The migration of millions of African Americans from the rural South to the urban North in the early twentieth century, helped make the Harlem Renaissance possible.
4. W. E. B. Du Bois played an important role in the Harlem Renaissance, for he edited the magazine, that became the official publication of the NAACP.
5. Furthermore, Du Bois rose to prominence by becoming, the first African American to receive a PhD. from Harvard University.
6. The music, of the Harlem Renaissance, became a vital tool for expressing and celebrating, the culture of those who lived there.
7. In particular, many people listened to jazz after, musicians from the South moved north and began playing it in clubs, theaters, and private homes.
8. The Harlem Renaissance produced diverse, original, writers, and they created everything from plays to poems.
9. For example, Claude McKay wrote novels that those in, literary studies, still study today.
10. The political and cultural gains achieved by African Americans during this time paved, the way for future generations.

# 24l  How can I avoid comma errors?

You can avoid most comma errors with these two bits of advice:

- As you write or reread what you've written, never insert a comma simply because you happen to pause to think or take a breath before moving on.

**ANSWERS: EXERCISE 24-10**

**1.** Although [omit: no comma after subordinating conjunction, 24k.2] this movement is named for Harlem, [keep: comma after introductory dependent clause, 24c] its impact spread to urban areas throughout the country [omit: no comma with coordinating conjunction between two items, 24b] and the world.

**2.** During the Harlem Renaissance, [keep: introductory phrase, 24c] artists in many fields found new ways to express the different facets [omit: no comma between preposition and its object. 24k.6] of black life in America.

**3.** The migration of millions of African Americans from the rural South to the urban North [omit: no comma between a subject and its verb, 24k.6] helped make the Harlem Renaissance possible.

**4.** W. E. B. Du Bois played an important role in the Harlem Renaissance, [keep: comma before coordinating conjunction that separates two independent clauses, 24b] for he edited the magazine [omit: restrictive clause, 24k.4] that became the official publication of the NAACP.

**5.** Furthermore, [keep: comma after introductory element, 24c] Du Bois rose to prominence by becoming [omit: no comma between verb and its object] the first African American to receive a PhD from Harvard University.

**6.** The music [omit: no commas for restrictive prepositional phrase, 24k.4] of the Harlem Renaissance [omit: no commas for restrictive prepositional phrase, 24k.4] became a vital tool for expressing and celebrating [omit: no comma with restrictive element, 24k.4] the culture of those who lived there.

**7.** In particular, [keep: comma after introductory element, 24c] many people listened to jazz after [omit: no comma between preposition and its object, 24k.6] musicians from the South moved north and began playing it in clubs, [keep: items in a series, 24d] theatres, [keep: items in a series, 24d] and private homes.

**8.** The Harlem Renaissance produced diverse, original [omit: no comma between final of two coordinate adjectives and noun, 24k.3] writers, [keep: comma before coordinating conjunction that separates two independent clauses, 24b] and they created everything from plays to poems.

**9.** For example, [keep: comma after introductory element (transitional expression), 24c] Claude McKay wrote novels that those in [omit: no comma between preposition and its object, 24k.6] literary studies [omit: no comma between subject and verb, 24k.6] still study today.

**10.** The political and cultural gains achieved by African Americans during this time paved [omit: no comma between verb and its object, 24k.6] the way for future generations.

**QUOTATION: ON WRITING**

For what is Punctuation, and what its aim? It is the art of dividing a literary composition into sentences, and parts of sentences, by means of points, for the purpose of exhibiting the various combinations, connections, and dependencies of words. And what is this process but a means of facilitating that analysis and combination which must be made, consciously or unconsciously, before we can penetrate to the very core of an author's thoughts, and appropriate them as food for the life and growth of our own minds?

—John Wilson

**HUMOROUS NOTE**

Erin McKean's blog, "Dictionary Evangelist" at <http://www.dictionaryevangelist.com>, follows the contemporary travails of the English language in print. McKean created amusing t-shirts for the "Semi-Colon Appreciation Society" that say "The semi-colon is not used enough; the comma is used too often."

**QUOTATION: ON WRITING**

I have grown fond of semicolons in recent years. The semicolon tells you that there is still some question about the preceding full sentence; something needs to be added; it reminds you sometimes of the Greek usage. It is almost always a greater pleasure to come across a semicolon than a period. The period tells you that is that; if you didn't get all the meaning you

Pausing isn't a reliable guide for writers, although that myth continues to thrive. Throughout the United States, and indeed the world, people's breathing rhythms, accents, and thinking patterns vary greatly.

- As you're writing, if you're unsure about a comma, insert it and circle the spot. Later, when you're EDITING, check this handbook for the rule that applies.

For more help with your writing, grammar, and research, go to **www.mycomplab.com**

## 25

## Semicolons

### 25a What are the uses of a semicolon?

While a period signals the complete separation of INDEPENDENT CLAUSES, a **semicolon** indicates only a partial ("semi") separation. Use a semicolon in only two situations. A semicolon can replace a period between sentences that are closely related in meaning (25b and 25c). Also, a semicolon belongs between sentence structures that already contain one or more commas (25d) and with certain lists (25e). Quick Reference 25.1 shows different patterns for using semicolons.

### 25b When can I use a semicolon, instead of a period, between independent clauses?

The choice between a period and a semicolon for separating independent clauses depends on whether your meaning is better communicated by a complete separation (period) or a partial separation (semicolon).

> The desert known as Death Valley became a US National Park in 1994; it used to be a US National Monument.

> This is my husband's second marriage; it's the first for me.

> —Ruth Sidel, "Marion Deluca"

## Quick Reference 25.1

■ ■ ■ ■ ■ ■ ■ ■

### Semicolon patterns

- Independent clause; independent clause. [25b]
- Independent clause; conjunctive adverb, independent clause. [25c]
- Independent clause; transitional expression, independent clause. [25c]
- Independent clause, one that contains a comma; coordinating conjunction followed by independent clause. [25d]
- Independent clause; coordinating conjunction followed by independent clause, one that contains a comma. [25d]
- Independent clause, one that contains a comma; coordinating conjunction followed by independent clause, one that contains a comma. [25d]
- Independent clause containing a series of items, any of which contains a comma; another item in the series; and another item in the series. [25e]

**Alert:** Never use a comma alone between independent clauses—this rule will prevent you from creating the error known as a COMMA SPLICE (Chapter 20). ●

## 25c When else can I use a semicolon between independent clauses?

When the second of a set of independent clauses closely related in meaning starts with a CONJUNCTIVE ADVERB or with a TRANSITIONAL EXPRESSION, you can choose to separate the clauses with a semicolon instead of a period. Also, insert a comma following a conjunctive adverb or transitional expression that starts an independent clause. Although some professional writers today omit the comma after short words (*then, next, soon*), the rule remains for most ACADEMIC WRITING. Quick Reference 25.1 shows this pattern for using semicolons.

> The average annual rainfall in Death Valley is about two inches; **nevertheless,** hundreds of plant and animal species survive and even thrive there. [conjunctive adverb]

> Photographers have spent years recording desert life cycles; **as a result,** we can watch bare sand flower after a spring storm. [transitional expression]

wanted or expected, anyway you got all the writer intended to parcel out and now you have to move along. But with a semicolon there you get a pleasant little feeling of expectancy; there is more to come; to read on; it will get clearer.
—Lewis Thomas

### BACKGROUND

Students will find two practice exercises on the use of commas and semicolons at the Web site <http://owl.english.purdue.edu/handouts/interact/g_commacompEX1.html>, which also links to the answers.

### ADDITIONAL EXAMPLES OF SEMICOLON PATTERNS

**1.** Each year, people from all over the world visit the Tower of London; for centuries, it served as a prison for famous persons who were deemed to be enemies of the crown.

**2.** The tower is located in the borough of Stepney; it covers about eighteen acres.

**3.** The central portion, called the White Tower, was begun in 1078; it was modernized by the architect Christopher Wren.

**4.** The Beauchamp Tower has ninety-one inscriptions of prisoners in it; the Bloody Tower served as the prison of Sir Walter Raleigh, who wrote an incomplete history of the world during his stay there in 1614.

**5.** The place of execution within the walls was Tower Green; Anne Boleyn was beheaded there in 1536.

**6.** Black varieties of the leopard are common in humid parts of India; however, they are rare in Africa.

**7.** Leopards prey on monkeys, birds, and reptiles; consequently, they must hunt both in trees and on the ground.

**8.** A leopard begins its meal by tearing at the forequarters of its prey; in contrast, the tiger starts with the hindquarters of its victim.

**9.** One Indian leopard was alleged to have killed two hundred human beings in two years before it was shot; similarly, a leopard in Ceylon used to lie in wait for passersby on a main road.

**10.** The leopard's roar of belligerence is different from its mating call; nevertheless, both sound fierce to the human ear.

**BACKGROUND**

Beginning in the eighth century, the inverted semicolon served as a pause somewhere between a comma and a colon. After about seven hundred years of use, it was discarded. The semicolon as it is known today dates from the seventeenth century.

**QUOTATION: ON WRITING**

I think of myself as a stylist, and stylists can become notoriously obsessed with the placing of a comma, the weight of a semicolon.

—Truman Capote

**BACKGROUND**

Angela Petit's "The Stylish Semicolon: Teaching Punctuation as Rhetorical Choice" (*English Journal* 92.3 (2003): 66–72) gives advice on creating a workshop on semicolon usage to improve student writing style.

**QUOTATION: ON WRITING**

Punctuation contributes to art as well as to correctness, to style as well as to styling. Make it work for you, not just to develop prose that is "clear enough"—not just to prevent confusion—but to help you express yourself, or your characters express themselves. Don't lean on it; don't shy away from it; just use it—and in doing so, let it help you convey nuances too subtle for words alone to convey; let it help you evoke effects so delicate that talk would shatter them. And remember that if you frequently use more marks than usual—or fewer than usual—you will call attention to your craft, with the results possibly seeming artful rather than artistic, posturing rather than expressive. Nor do I for a moment suggest that punctuation can, or should, be charged with sole responsibility for effectiveness: descriptive detail, diction, sentence length, sentence rhythm, paragraph structure, timing—these and other elements of style can and must share the load.

—Robert M. Pierson

**! Alert:** Never use only a comma between independent clauses that are connected by a conjunctive adverb or word of transition—this rule will prevent you from creating the error known as a COMMA SPLICE. ●

## 25d How do semicolons work with coordinating conjunctions?

As a general rule, when INDEPENDENT CLAUSES are linked by a COORDINATING CONJUNCTION, good practice calls for a comma, not a period or semicolon, before the coordinating conjunction (24b). However, when one or more of the independent clauses already contain a comma, link the independent clauses by substituting a semicolon for the period. This can help your reader see the relationship between the ideas more clearly. Quick Reference 25.1 shows the various combinations of this pattern.

> When the peacock has presented his back, the spectator will usually begin to walk around him to get a front view**; but** the peacock will continue to turn so that no front view is possible.
>
> —Flannery O'Connor, "The King of the Birds"

> Our Constitution is in actual operation; everything appears to promise that it will last**; but** in this world, nothing is certain but death and taxes.
>
> —Benjamin Franklin, in a 1789 letter

> For anything worth having, one must pay the price**; and** the price is always work, patience, love, self-sacrifice.
>
> —John Burroughs

## 25e When should I use semicolons between items in a series?

When a sentence contains a series of items that are long or that already contain one or more commas, separate the items with semicolons. Punctuating this way groups the elements so that your reader can see where one item ends and the next begins. Quick Reference 25.1 shows this pattern.

> The assistant chefs chopped onions, green peppers, and parsley**;** sliced chicken and duck breasts into strips**;** started a broth simmering**; and** filled a large, shallow copper pan with oil.

## 25f How do I avoid misusing the semicolon?

**NOT USING A SEMICOLON AFTER AN INTRODUCTORY PHRASE**

If you use a semicolon after an introductory phrase, you create the error known as a sentence fragment (Chapter 19).

**NO** **Open until midnight;** the computer lab is well used. [Using a semicolon turns an introductory phrase into a sentence fragment.]

**YES** **Open until midnight,** the computer lab is well used.

## NOT USING A SEMICOLON WITH A DEPENDENT CLAUSE

If you use a semicolon with a DEPENDENT CLAUSE, you create the error known as a sentence fragment.

**NO** **Although the new dorms have computer facilities;** many students still prefer to go to the computer lab. [Using a semicolon turns a dependent clause into a sentence fragment.]

**YES** **Although the new dorms have computer facilities,** many students still prefer to go to the computer lab.

## NOT USING A SEMICOLON TO INTRODUCE A LIST

When the words that introduce a list form an independent clause, use a colon, never a semicolon (26b).

**NO** **The newscast featured three major stories;** the latest pictures of Uranus, a speech by the president, and dangerous brush fires in Nevada. [*The newscast featured three major stories* is an independent clause, so the punctuation before the list should be a colon, not a semicolon.]

**YES** **The newscast featured three major stories:** the latest pictures of Uranus, a speech by the president, and dangerous brush fires in Nevada.

**EXERCISE 25-1** Insert semicolons as needed in these items. Also, fix any incorrectly used semicolons. If a sentence is correct, explain why. For help, consult all sections of this chapter.

**EXAMPLE** Bicycle racing is as popular in Europe as baseball or basketball is in the United States, it is even more heavily commercialized.

Bicycle racing is as popular in Europe as baseball or basketball is in the United States; it is even more heavily commercialized.

1. The Tour de France is the world's best-known bicycle race, the 94-year-old Giro d'Italia runs a close second.

2. Both are grueling, three-week-long events that require cyclists to cover over 2,000 miles of difficult, mountainous terrain, and both are eagerly anticipated, draw enormous crowds along their routes, and receive extensive media coverage.

3. That media attention leads to marketing opportunities for the events' sponsors; which place ads along the race's route, in the nearby towns, and on the cyclists themselves.

---

**QUOTATION: ON WRITING**
From the reader's point of view, punctuation provides a map for one who must otherwise drive blindly past the by-ways, intersections, and detours of a writer's thought.
—Mina P. Shaughnessy

**BACKGROUND**
In "Celebrating the Semicolon in a Most Unlikely Location," Sam Roberts chronicles the unexpected (and correct!) usage of the semicolon in a New York City transit agency service announcement, "Please put it in a trash can; that's good news for everyone." (*New York Times*, 18 Feb. 2008, late ed., sec. B:3).

**ANSWERS: EXERCISE 25-1**

**1.** The Tour de France is the world's best-known bicycle race; the 94-year-old Giro d'Italia runs a close second. [25b, closely related independent clauses]

**2.** Both are grueling, three-week-long events that require cyclists to cover over 2,000 miles of difficult, mountainous terrain; and both are eagerly anticipated, draw enormous crowds along their routes, and receive extensive media coverage. [25d, two closely related independent clauses containing commas and connected by a coordinating conjunction]

**3.** That media attention leads to marketing opportunities for the events' sponsors, which place ads along the race's route, in the nearby towns, and on the cyclists themselves. [25f, no semicolon with dependent clause]

**4.** Martin Hvastija, a participant in the 2003 Giro d'Italia, had no chance of winning the race; nevertheless, he drew extensive media attention for his sponsors. [25c, second closely related independent clause starts with conjunctive adverb]

**5.** Correct sentence; semicolon separates closely related independent clauses.

**6.** Although he had no chance of winning the race, newscasters beamed his image around the world during the short time he was a front-runner, during the same period showing the world the brightly colored advertising logos on his jersey. [25f, no semicolon after dependent clause; also, 25f, no semicolon after introductory phrase]

**7.** In addition to sponsoring individual athletes, corporations plaster ads all over the towns that the race goes through; they toss samples, coupons, and gadgets to spectators from promotional vehicles that ride the route an hour ahead of the cyclists; and they run ads during TV and radio coverage of the race. [25e, items in a series that contain commas; also, 25b, closely related independent clauses]

**8.** In 2003, the organizers of the Giro took in over $8 million in fees from advertisers and $12 million in broadcast rights from the Italian state-owned TV network, RAI; however, these figures were down a bit from the previous year. [25c, second closely related independent clause starts with conjunctive adverb]

**9.** An additional source of revenues for race organizers is fees from the towns where the race starts and ends each day; as a result, organizers determine the actual course according to which cities are willing to pay the $120,000 charge. [25c, second closely related independent clause starts with transitional expression]

**10.** Media watchers think the Giro d'Italia could become even more profitable and popular, especially among young adults, but only if it took a cue from the Tour de France by encouraging more international press coverage, more star riders, and even heavier corporate sponsorship. [25f, no semicolon to introduce a list]

**QUOTATION: ON WRITING**
Used sparingly, the semicolon emphasizes your crucial contrasts; used recklessly, it merely clutters your page.

—Sheridan Baker

**ANSWERS: EXERCISE 25-2**

**1.** Tesla was born in what is now Croatia and studied at the Technical University at Graz, Austria; he excelled in physics, mechanical engineering, and electrical engineering. [25d, semicolons between independent clauses already containing commas]

**2.** Tesla's accomplishments include inventing alternating current; contributing to the fields of robotics, computer science, and wireless

4. Martin Hvastija, a participant in the 2003 Giro d'Italia, had no chance of winning the race, nevertheless, he drew extensive media attention for his sponsors.

5. His method was simple; he managed to ride out in front of the field for a few brief miles.

6. Although he had no chance of winning the race; newscasters beamed his image around the world during the short time he was a front-runner, during the same period; showing the world the brightly colored advertising logos on his jersey.

7. In addition to sponsoring individual athletes, corporations plaster ads all over the towns that the race goes through, they toss samples, coupons, and gadgets to spectators from promotional vehicles that ride the route an hour ahead of the cyclists, and they run ads during TV and radio coverage of the race.

8. In 2003, the organizers of the Giro took in over $8 million in fees from advertisers and $12 million in broadcast rights from the Italian state-owned TV network, RAI, however, these figures were down a bit from the previous year.

9. An additional source of revenues for race organizers is fees from the towns where the race starts and ends each day, as a result, organizers determine the actual course according to which cities are willing to pay the $120,000 charge.

10. Media watchers think the Giro d'Italia could become even more profitable and popular, especially among young adults, but only if it took a cue from the Tour de France by encouraging; more international press coverage, more star riders, and even heavier corporate sponsorship.

**EXERCISE 25-2** Combine each set of sentences into one sentence so that it contains two independent clauses. Use a semicolon correctly between the two clauses. You may add, omit, revise, and rearrange words. Try to use all the patterns in this chapter, and explain the reasoning behind your decisions. More than one revision may be correct. For help, consult all sections of this chapter.

**EXAMPLE** Although not as well known as Thomas Edison, the inventor Nikola Tesla was a revolutionary and important scientist. One biographer calls him "the man who invented the twentieth century."

Although not as well known as Thomas Edison, the inventor Nikola Tesla was a revolutionary scientist; one biographer calls him "the man who invented the twentieth century."

1. Tesla was born in what is now Croatia and studied at the Technical University at Graz, Austria. He excelled in physics, mechanical engineering, and electrical engineering.

2. Tesla's accomplishments include inventing alternating current. He also contributed to the fields of robotics, computer science, and wireless

technology. And he helped increase knowledge of nuclear physics, ballistics, and electromagnetism.

3. The Italian inventor Guglielmo Marconi and Tesla both claimed to have invented the radio. However, the US Supreme Court, in 1943, upheld Tesla's radio patent and officially credited him as the device's inventor.

4. In 1901, Tesla began construction of a tower that he claimed would create a global network of wireless communication and be able to control the weather. Unfortunately, Tesla soon lost funding and never finished the project.

5. At his lab in Colorado Springs, he was able to produce artificial lightning. This scene was vividly portrayed in the 2006 film *The Prestige*.

For more help with your writing, grammar, and research, go to **www.mycomplab.com**

# 26

# Colons

## 26a What are the uses of a colon?

A **colon** is a full stop that draws attention to the words that follow. It can be placed only at the end of an INDEPENDENT CLAUSE. A colon introduces a list, an APPOSITIVE, or a QUOTATION. Quick Reference 26.1 shows different patterns for using a colon.

### Quick Reference 26.1

**Colon patterns**

- Independent clause: list. [26b]
- Independent clause: appositive. [26b]
- Independent clause: "Quoted words." [26b]
- Independent clause: Independent clause that explains or summarizes the prior independent clause. [26c]

technology; and helping increase knowledge of nuclear physics, ballistics, and electromagnetism. [25e, semicolons between items in a series already containing commas]

**3.** The Italian inventor Guglielmo Marconi and Tesla both claimed to have invented the radio; however, the US Supreme Court, in 1943, upheld Tesla's radio patent and officially credited him as the device's inventor. [25c, second closely related independent clause starts with a conjunctive adverb]

**4.** In 1901, Tesla began construction of a tower that he claimed would create a global network of wireless communication and be able to control the weather; unfortunately, Tesla soon lost funding and never finished the project. [25c, second closely related independent clause starts with a transitional expression]

**5.** At his lab in Colorado Springs, he was able to produce artificial lightning; this scene was vividly portrayed in the 2006 film *The Prestige*. [25b, closely related independent clauses]

**BACKGROUND**

A *colon* (in Greek, *ko⁻lon*) was originally a person's or an animal's limb. As such, it came to be used to refer to a portion of a strophe in choral dancing, then to a division in prosody, and later to a principal clause in a sentence. Finally, it became the sign marking the breathing space at the end of a clause.

Historically, the colon as a mark of punctuation was preceded by the semicolon; but in English, the colon had more use than the semicolon until the nineteenth century, when it began to be employed almost solely as a mark of anticipation. It regained prestige with the publication of H. W. Fowler's *Dictionary of Modern English Usage* in 1926 and has experienced increased usage since that time.

**BACKGROUND**

*Emoticons* are clusters of punctuation, such as :-) for a smile and :-( for a frown, that are used in electronic messages to set the tone for the sentence that precedes them. The knack for interpreting them starts with tilting your head sideways to the left and looking for a facial expression or symbol. Here are a few other examples:

:-D or :D    a laughing smile
*<:)         happy birthday
;-) or ;)    a wink
@–>–>-       a long-stemmed rose

Some e-mail programs have now changed emoticons to characters that show the emotions described by the emoticon. For example, in Yahoo mail, if you type in :-), the program changes the emoticon to a smiley face (☺) automatically.

**QUOTATION: ON WRITING**

The colon is usually a mark of addition or expectation, with emphasis on a following explanation, list, table, or quotation. With formal words (*as follows* or the like) it raps for attention; with easy wording it is a little more formal than the somewhat lighter semicolon. It is not a series or balancing point like the semicolon; it seems to say "Watch carefully what comes next."

—George Summey Jr.

**QUOTATION: ON WRITING**

Remember that colons—perhaps the mark we exploit least—generally mean that what is to come will explain what has just gone by. They imply identity, whereas semicolons imply "separate but equal" status. "I have just learned three facts: that St. Paul is the capital of Minnesota; that Helena is the capital of Montana; and that Lincoln is the capital of Nebraska." Everything after the colon adds up to "three facts"—whereas the three statements of fact, though they have much in common, are not identical.

Colons can also save words and create special effects. Compare:

• I admire her poetry. Its imagery is magnificent.

• I admire her poetry for its magnificent imagery.

• I admire her poetry: its imagery is magnificent.

## 26b When can a colon introduce a list, an appositive, or a quotation?

When a complete sentence—that is, an INDEPENDENT CLAUSE—introduces a list, an APPOSITIVE, or a QUOTATION, place a colon before the words being introduced. These words don't have to form an independent clause themselves, but a complete sentence before the colon is essential.

**INTRODUCING LISTED ITEMS**

When a complete sentence introduces a list, a colon is required, as demonstrated in the following example.

> **If you really want to lose weight, you must do three things:** eat smaller portions, exercise, and drink lots of water. [The required independent clause comes before the listed items, so a colon is correct.]

When the lead-in words at the end of an independent clause are *such as, including, like,* or *consists of,* never use a colon. In contrast, if the lead-in words at the end of an independent clause are *the following* or *as follows,* do use a colon.

> **The students demanded improvements *such as*** an expanded menu in the cafeteria, improved janitorial services, and more up-to-date textbooks.

> **The students demanded *the following*:** an expanded menu in the cafeteria, improved janitorial services, and more up-to-date textbooks.

**INTRODUCING APPOSITIVES**

An APPOSITIVE is a word or words that rename a NOUN or PRONOUN. When an appositive is introduced by an independent clause, use a colon.

> **Only cats are likely to approve of one old-fashioned remedy for cuts:** a lotion of catnip, butter, and sugar. [The required independent clause comes before the appositive: *a lotion of catnip, butter, and sugar* renames *old-fashioned remedy.*]

**INTRODUCING QUOTATIONS**

When an independent clause introduces a quotation, use a colon after it. (If the words introducing a quotation don't form an independent clause, use a comma.)

> **The little boy in *E.T.* did say something neat:** "How do you explain school to a higher intelligence?" [The required independent clause comes before the quotation.]

—George F. Will, "Well, I Don't Love You, E.T."

## 26c When can I use a colon between two independent clauses?

When a second SMALL CAPS INDEPENDENT CLAUSE explains or summarizes a first independent clause, you can use a colon to separate them. Quick Reference 26.1 shows this pattern for using a colon.

⚠️ **Alert:** You can choose to use a capital letter or a lowercase letter for the first word of an independent clause that follows a colon. Whichever you choose, be consistent within a piece of writing. We use a capital letter in this handbook.

> We will never forget the first time we made dinner together**:** **H**e got stomach poisoning and was too sick to go to work for four days.
>
> —Lisa Baladendrum, student ●

## 26d What standard formats require a colon?

A variety of standard formats in American English require a colon. Also, colons are used in many DOCUMENTATION STYLES, as shown in Chapters 36, 37, and 38.

**TITLE AND SUBTITLE**

*A Brief History of Time***:** *From the Big Bang to Black Holes*

**HOURS, MINUTES, AND SECONDS**

The plane took off at 7**:**15 p.m.

The runner passed the halfway point at 1**:**23**:**02.

⚠️ **Alert:** In the military, hours and minutes are written without colons and with four digits on a 24-hour clock: *The staff meeting originally scheduled for Tuesday at* **0930** *will be held Tuesday at* **1430** *instead.* ●

**REFERENCES TO BIBLE CHAPTERS AND VERSES**

Psalms 23**:**1–3

Luke 3**:**13

**MEMOS**

Date**:**     January 9, 2009
To**:**       Dean Kristen Olivero
From**:**     Professor Daniel Black
Re**:**       Student Work-Study Program

**SALUTATION IN A BUSINESS LETTER**

Dear Dr. Jewell**:**

All three versions are "correct." The first is emphatic and probably clear—or clear enough: Probably your reader will realize that the second sentence explains the first. The second version is clearer, and it flows along smoothly. The third is clearer than the first and just as clear as the second, and it gives us a unique kind of silence—not just a break (the period did that) but mild suspense. Your job is to decide which way of punctuating best expresses what you want to express.

—Robert M. Pierson

**QUOTATION: ON WRITING**

Punctuation is like an engine: it pulls the sentence along.

—Anonymous

**QUOTATION: ON WRITING**

When we are very young, we tend to regard the ability to use a colon much as a budding pianist regards the ability to play with crossed hands: many of us, when we are older, regard it as a proof of literary skill, maturity, even of sophistication: and many, whether young, not so young, or old, employ it gauchely, haphazardly, or at best inconsistently.

—Eric Partridge

**ADDITIONAL EXAMPLES**

To introduce quotations, summaries, and lists:

**1.** Alice Roosevelt Longworth's colorful reputation is exemplified by this remark: "I have a simple philosophy. Fill what's empty. Empty what's full. And scratch where it itches."

**2.** Greek mythology comprises the descriptions of the gods and the various stories told about them: It is a series of narratives depicting their personalities, functions, and relationships.

**3.** Zeus, the supreme god of the Greeks, served in a number of capacities: weather god, sender of rain and lightning, and ruler over the other gods.

To separate material:

**1.** Eric Partridge is the author of *You Have a Point There: A Guide to Punctuation and Its Allies* as well as *Usage and Abusage: A Guide to Good English.*

**2.** I will cite the work in the bibliography as follows:

O'Connor, Flannery. "The Life You Save May Be Your Own." *The Realm of Fiction: Seventy-Four Stories.* Ed. James B. Hall and Elizabeth Hall. 3rd ed. New York: McGraw, 1977. 479–88.

**3.** Date:   January 15, 2006
    To:     Professor Jill Alexander
    From: Professor Max Gregorian
    Re:    Selection of textbooks

### ALTERNATE EXERCISE

You might ask your students to rewrite the following sentences, *omitting the colons.* The students will probably have to divide each into several sentences.

**1.** The institution of marriage is generally divided by sociologists into four main types: monogamy, polygyny, polyandry, and group marriage.

**2.** An early reference to group marriage was made by Julius Caesar concerning the early Britons: "Ten and even twelve have wives common to them, and particularly brothers among brothers, and parents among their children."

**3.** Monogamy, the marriage of one man with one woman, is the most widely approved form in contemporary society: It is the basis of the modern family.

**4.** Polygyny is practiced by some religious sects: It is acceptable, for example, in some Arab countries.

**5.** Most modern women do not generally favor such an arrangement: They have no desire to be one of several wives.

### QUOTATION: ON WRITING

An unnecessary [punctuation] mark is worse than useless. It is an interruption.
—George Summey Jr.

## 26e   When is a colon wrong?

### INDEPENDENT CLAUSES

A colon can introduce a list, an APPOSITIVE, or a QUOTATION, but only when an INDEPENDENT CLAUSE does the introducing. Similarly, a colon can be used between two independent clauses when the second summarizes or explains the first. In following these rules, be sure that you're dealing with independent clauses, not other word groups.

> **NO**   The cook bought: eggs, milk, cheese, and bread. [*The cook bought* isn't an independent clause.]
>
> **YES**   The cook bought eggs, milk, cheese, and bread.

Never use a colon to separate a PHRASE or DEPENDENT CLAUSE from an independent clause. Otherwise, you'll create the error known as a SENTENCE FRAGMENT.

> **NO**   Day after day: the drought dragged on. [*Day after day* is a phrase, not an independent clause.]
>
> **YES**   Day after day, the drought dragged on.
>
> **NO**   After the drought ended: the farmers celebrated. [*After the drought ended* is a dependent clause, not an independent clause.]
>
> **YES**   After the drought ended, the farmers celebrated.

### LEAD-IN WORDS

Never use a colon after the lead-in words *such as, including, like,* and *consists of.*

> **NO**   The health board discussed many problems **such as:** poor water quality, aging sewage treatment systems, and the lack of alternative water supplies. [A colon is incorrect after *such as.*]
>
> **YES**   The health board discussed poor water quality, aging sewage treatment systems, and the lack of alternative water supplies. [*Such as* is dropped and the sentence slightly revised so that the colon is not needed.]
>
> **YES**   The health board discussed many problems, **such as** poor water quality, an aging sewage treatment system, and the lack of alternative water supplies. [Comma before *such as* tells the reader that the list coming up is nonrestrictive (nonessential)—it illustrates *problems.*]
>
> **YES**   The health board discussed many problems: poor water quality, aging sewage treatment systems, and the lack of alternative water supplies. [If *such as* is dropped, a colon after the independent clause is correct.]

**EXERCISE 26-1**    Insert colons where needed and delete any not needed. If a sentence is correct, explain why. For help, consult all sections of this chapter.

EXAMPLE    The twentieth century saw a flowering of Irish literature, W. B. Yeats, G. B. Shaw, Samuel Beckett, and Seamus Heaney all won the Nobel Prize for Literature.

The twentieth century saw a flowering of Irish literature: W. B. Yeats, G. B. Shaw, Samuel Beckett, and Seamus Heaney all won the Nobel Prize for Literature.

1. People who work the night shift are typically deprived of essential sleep, an average of nine hours a week.

2. The Iroquois of the Great Lakes region lived in fortified villages and cultivated: corn, beans, and squash.

3. Five nations originally formed the Iroquois Confederacy: the Mohawk, the Oneida, the Onondaga, the Cayuga, and the Seneca.

4. Later, these five Iroquois nations were joined by: the Tuscarora.

5. Shouting: "Come back!" Adam watched the vehicle speed down the highway.

6. When a runner breaks through that unavoidable wall of exhaustion, a very different feeling sets in; an intense sense of well-being known as the "runner's high."

7. However: the "runner's high" soon disappears.

8. Two new nations were born on the same day in 1947, India and Pakistan achieved their independence from Britain at midnight on August 15.

9. Date       December 8, 2008
   To         English 101 Instructors
   From       Dean of Instruction
   Re         Classroom Assignments

10. Only a hurricane could have kept Lisa from meeting Nathaniel at 800 p.m.; unfortunately, that night a hurricane hit.

11. George's interests were typical of a sixteen-year-old's, cars, music, and dating.

12. Like many people who have never learned to read or write, the woman who told her life story in *Aman; The Story of a Somali Girl* was able to remember an astonishing number of events in precise detail.

For more help with your writing, grammar, and research, go to **www.mycomplab.com**

mycomplab

**ANSWERS: EXERCISE 26-1**

**1.** (change comma to colon) essential sleep: an [26b, introducing appositives]

**2.** (delete colon) cultivated corn, beans, and squash [26e, no colon when listed items are not introduced by an independent clause]

**3.** Correct; colon introduces listed items after an independent clause

**4.** (delete colon) joined by the Tuscarora [26e, no colon to separate a phrase from the rest of its independent clause]

**5.** (delete colon) Shouting "Come [26b, no colon when introduction to quotation is not an independent clause]

**6.** (change semicolon to colon) sets in: an intense [26b, introducing appositives]

**7.** (change colon to comma) However, the [26e, no colon to separate an introductory word from the rest of its independent clause]

**8.** (change comma to colon) in 1947: India and Pakistan [26c, separating two complete independent clauses]

**9.** (insert colons)
   Date:   December 8, 2005
   To:     English
   From:   Dean
   Re:     Classroom [26d, memos]

**10.** (insert colon) 8:00 p.m. [26d, hours, minutes, and seconds]

**11.** (change comma to colon) sixteen-year-old's: cars [26b, introducing listed items]

**12.** (change semicolon to colon) *Aman: The Story* [26d, title and subtitle]

# 27

# Apostrophes

## 27a What is the role of the apostrophe?

The **apostrophe** plays four roles in writing: It creates the POSSESSIVE CASE of NOUNS, forms the possessive case of INDEFINITE PRONOUNS, stands for one or more omitted letters in a word (a CONTRACTION), and can help form plurals of letters and numerals.

In contrast, here are two roles the apostrophe doesn't play: It doesn't belong with plurals of nouns, and it doesn't form the plural of PERSONAL PRONOUNS in the possessive case.

## 27b How do I use an apostrophe to show a possessive noun?

An apostrophe works with a NOUN to form the POSSESSIVE CASE, which shows ownership or a close relationship.

OWNERSHIP    The **writer's** pen ran out of ink.

CLOSE RELATIONSHIP    The **novel's** plot is complicated.

Possession in nouns can be communicated in two ways: by a PHRASE starting with *of* (*comments of the instructor; comments of Professor Furman*) or by an apostrophe and the letter *s* (*the instructor's comments; Professor Furman's comments*). Here's a list of specific rules governing the usage of *'s*.

- **Add *'s* to nouns not ending in -*s*:**

  She felt a **parent's** joy. [*Parent* is a singular noun not ending in -s.]

  They care about their **children's** education. [*Children* is a plural noun not ending in -s.]

- **Add *'s* to singular nouns ending in -*s*:**  You can add *'s* or the apostrophe alone to show possession when a singular noun ends in -*s*. In this handbook, we use *'s* to clearly mark singular-noun possessives, no matter what letter ends the noun. Whichever rule variation you choose, be consistent within each piece of writing.

The **bus's** (or **bus'**) air conditioning is out of order.

**Chris's** (or **Chris'**) ordeal ended.

If you encounter a tongue-twisting pronunciation (*Charles **Dickens's** novel*), you may decide not to add the additional *-s* (*Charles **Dickens'** novel*). You must, however, be consistent in each piece of writing.

- **Add only an apostrophe to a plural noun ending in *-s*:**

  The **boys'** statements were taken seriously.

  Three **months'** maternity leave is in the **workers'** contract.

- **Add *'s* to the last word in compound words and phrases:**

  His **mother-in-law's** corporation has bought out a competitor.

  The **tennis player's** strategy was brilliant.

  We want to hear the **caseworker's** recommendation.

- **Add *'s* to each noun in individual possession:**

  **Shirley's** and **Kayla's** houses are next to each other. [Shirley and Kayla each own a house; they don't own the houses jointly.]

- **Add *'s* to only the last noun in joint or group possession:**

  **Kareem and Brina's** house has a screened porch. [Kareem and Brina own one house.]

  **Avram and Justin's** houses always have nice lawns. [Avram and Justin jointly own more than one house.]

## 27c How do I use an apostrophe with possessive pronouns?

When a POSSESSIVE PRONOUN ends with *-s* (*hers, his, its, ours, yours,* and *theirs),* never add an apostrophe. Below is a list of PERSONAL PRONOUNS and their possessive forms.

| Personal Pronouns | Possessive Forms |
|---|---|
| I | my, mine |
| you | your, yours |
| he | his |
| she | her, hers |
| it | its |
| we | our, ours |
| they | their, theirs |
| who | whose |

female person's lurch in any direction can be called a *woman's movement,* but the apostrophe always goes before the *s.*" (*New York Times,* 8 May 1988, late ed.: sec. 6:14).

**TEACHING TIP**
You may want to point out that while pronouns do take the place of nouns, they form their possessives in an altogether different way from the nouns they represent: pronouns through their own possessive spellings, *never* with apostrophes; nouns, of course, with apostrophes. Apostrophes are used with pronouns *only* in their contracted pronoun-verb forms. When students see these grammatical forms represented side by side, they can more readily recognize the differences: "That *student's* studies" (possessive noun with apostrophe); "*His* studies" (possessive pronoun without apostrophe); "*He's* studying" (pronoun-verb contraction for "He is studying"); the *machine's* characteristics (possessive noun with apostrophe); *its* chief characteristics (possessive pronoun without apostrophe); "*It's* chiefly a gas-driven machine" (contraction for "It is . . .").

**TEACHING TIP**
Grammar Girl's "Apostrophe Catastrophe" podcast features a history of the apostrophe, an original song about the apostrophe, and commentary on correct apostrophe usage; see <http://grammar.quickanddirtytips.com/apostrophe-1.aspx>. (Make sure to listen to both Parts One and Two.)

**EXTRA EXERCISE A**
The questions that follow this brief paragraph are designed to point out how much information about the situation has been provided by the apostrophes. You may want to use the questions in a class discussion of apostrophe usage.

The jury's deliberations were over. Charles's trial had at last come to an end. The defendants' lawyers seemed calm as they waited, but the prosecuting attorney's hands twitched with nervousness. Charles's and his family's lives would be either ruined or saved by the verdict of the court. The judge's face was impassive as he addressed the jury about its verdict. The jury foreman's voice trembled as he began to speak.

**1.** Does the writer think of the jury as a single body or as individuals?

**2.** Is there one defendant or more than one?

**3.** Is there one prosecuting attorney or more than one?

**4.** Whose lives are affected?

**5.** Why is there no apostrophe in *its verdict* (next to last sentence)?

**6.** Why do the words *jury's* (first sentence), *judge's* (next to last sentence), and *foreman's* (last sentence) end in *'s*?

### Answers to Extra Exercise A

**1.** as a single body

**2.** more than one

**3.** one

**4.** those of Charles and his family

**5.** The personal pronoun *its* is possessive without an apostrophe.

**6.** Each word is a singular noun that does not end in -*s*.

### QUOTATION: ON WRITING

Such forms as *Achilles' heel, Moses' laws, Isis' temple* are commonly replaced by *the heel of Achilles, the laws of Moses, the temple of Isis.*
—William Strunk Jr., *Elements of Style*

### QUOTATION: ON WRITING

It is perhaps appropriate that the plural possessive *s'*, which struggled so long to attain acceptance, should be among the primary victims of confusion regarding the apostrophe. One of the commonest errors in student writing is the treatment of the genitive [possessive] plural as if it were a genitive singular construction: "These player's money demands are going to kill pro basketball."
—Elizabeth S. Sklar

### TEACHING TIP

Some instructors despair of ever having students remember the differences between certain

## 27d  How do I use an apostrophe with contractions?

In a **contraction**, an apostrophe takes the place of one or more omitted letters. Be careful not to confuse a contraction with a POSSESSIVE PRONOUN. Doing so is a common spelling error, one that many people—including employers—consider evidence of a poor education. Whether or not that's fair, it's usually true.

**it's** (contraction for *it is*)    **its** (possessive pronoun)
**they're** (contraction for *they are*)    **their** (possessive pronoun)
**who's** (contraction for *who is*)    **whose** (possessive form of *who*)
**you're** (contraction for *you are*)    **your** (possessive pronoun)

**NO** The government has to balance **it's** budget.
**YES** The government has to balance **its** budget.
**NO** The professor **who's** class was canceled is ill.
**YES** The professor **whose** class was canceled is ill.

In choosing whether or not to use a contraction, consider that many instructors think contractions aren't appropriate in ACADEMIC WRITING. Nevertheless, the *MLA Handbook* accepts contractions, including *'90s* for *the 1990s*. In this handbook, we use contractions because we're addressing you, the student. We suggest, however, that before you use contractions in your academic writing, you check with your instructor. Here's a list of common contractions.

### Common Contractions

aren't = *are not*    she's = *she is*
can't = *cannot*    there's = *there is*
didn't = *did not*    they're = *they are*
don't = *do not*    wasn't = *was not*
he's = *he is*    we're = *we are*
I'd = *I would, I had*    weren't = *were not*
I'm = *I am*    we've = *we have*
isn't = *is not*    who's = *who is*
it's = *it is*    won't = *will not*
let's = *let us*    you're = *you are*

⚠ **Alert:** One contraction required in all writing is *o'clock* (which stands for *of the clock,* an expression used long ago). ●

## 27e How do I use an apostrophe with possessive indefinite pronouns?

An apostrophe works with an INDEFINITE PRONOUN (see list in Quick Reference 17.6 in 17i) to form the POSSESSIVE CASE, which shows ownership or a close relationship.

OWNERSHIP **Everyone's** dinner is ready.
CLOSE RELATIONSHIP **Something's** aroma is appealing.

Possession in indefinite pronouns can be communicated in two ways: by a PHRASE starting with *of* (*comments of everyone*) or by an apostrophe and the letter *s* (*everyone's comments*).

## 27f How do I form the plural of miscellaneous elements?

Until recently, the plural of elements such as letters meant as letters, words meant as words, numerals, and symbols could be formed by adding either *'s* or *s*. The most current MLA guidelines endorse the use of *s* only, with the exception of adding *'s* to letters meant as letters. MLA recommends using italics for letters meant as letters and words meant as words. The examples below reflect MLA practices.

| | |
|---|---|
| PLURAL OF LETTERS MEANT AS LETTERS | Printing *M's* and *N's* confuses young children.<br>Printing *m's* and *n's* confuses young children. |
| PLURAL OF LETTERS MEANT AS WORDS | He was surprised to get all **B**s in his courses. |
| PLURAL OF WORDS MEANT AS WORDS | Too many *ifs* in a contract make me suspicious. |
| PLURAL OF NUMBERS | Her e-mail address contains many 7**s**. |
| PLURAL OF YEARS | I remember the **1990**s well. |
| PLURAL OF SYMBOLS | What do those **&**s mean? |

## 27g When is an apostrophe wrong?

If you're a writer who makes the same apostrophe errors repeatedly, memorize the rules you need (some you're likely to know almost without thought). Then you won't be annoyed by "that crooked little mark," a nickname popular with

common contractions and their homonyms (*their, they're; its, it's*). You might find it helpful to let students know how experienced writers recognize the differences. Many writers pronounce the two-word form of each possibility. If the two-word form makes no sense in that context, then the other word (usually a possessive pronoun) is needed. If the two-word form makes sense, experienced writers ask themselves if the informal contraction is appropriate. Of course, experienced writers do this in a microsecond, but some of our students need to do it slowly, consciously, and methodically.

I need to know if *their/they're* home. [I need to know if they are home.]

I need to know if *their/they're* gas meter is working. [I need to know if they are gas meter is working = nonsense; therefore, *their* is correct.]

**BACKGROUND**
In "On Language; High Jinks and Low Bogeys," William Safire discusses the habit of retail manufacturers to replace the conjunction *and* with *'n'* in the names of their products. Following are just a few of Safire's many examples: *Spray 'n' Wash, Shake 'n' Bake,* and *Brown 'n' Serve* (*New York Times*, 29 January 1989, late ed.: sec. 6:14).

**QUOTATION: ON WRITING**
Punctuation marks are one means of helping us get our exact meaning on the page. They do more than mark such obvious facts of language as "This is a sentence." "This is a question." They help us separate words (and thoughts) and so present them distinctly to a reader; they help group and keep together related ideas; they set off certain words for emphasis. Their use affects the tempo of writing.
—Porter Perrin

**BACKGROUND**
Students can practice their understanding of apostrophe use by taking the interactive quiz at The Blue Book of Grammar and Punctuation Web site at <http://www.grammarbook.com/grammar_quiz/apostrophes_1.asp>.

**TEACHING TIP**

One need not look far in popular culture to find apostrophe errors in abundance. Billboards, restaurant menus, names of businesses, and instructional signs are particularly predictable places to find these errors. You may want to heighten students' awareness of apostrophe errors by offering a little extra credit when they produce evidence of apostrophes placed incorrectly in possessive nouns (Womens' Rest Room); added inappropriately to nonpossessive plurals (Rest Room's); used in error with possessive pronouns ("Dining at It's Finest"); and/or omitted from a contraction ("Its Bike Week!").

**ANSWERS: EXERCISE 27-1**

1. product's; consumers'
2. people's; product's
3. box's; product user's; shopper's
4. Arm & Hammer's; Tide's
5. Heinz's; Coca-Cola's
6. company's; adult female's; adult males'; children's; teenagers'
7. marketing business's; consumers'; companies'
8. test takers'; Gross's; Sylvester Stallone's; Oprah Winfrey's; someone else's
9. companies'; Gross's; image makers'
10. Sports teams'; teams'

students who wish the apostrophe would go away. Quick Reference 27.1 lists the major apostrophe errors.

**Quick Reference 27.1**

**Leading apostrophe errors**

- Never use an apostrophe with the PRESENT-TENSE VERB.
  Cholesterol **plays** [not **play's**] an important role in how long we live.
- Always use an apostrophe after the -s in a POSSESSIVE plural of a noun.
  **Patients'** [not **Patients**] questions seek detailed answers.
- Never add an apostrophe at the end of a nonpossessive noun ending in -s.
  Medical **studies** [not **studies'** or **study's**] show this to be true.
- Never use an apostrophe to form a nonpossessive plural.
  **Teams** [not **Team's**] of doctors have studied the effects of cholesterol.

**EXERCISE 27-1**   Rewrite these sentences to insert 's or an apostrophe alone to make the words in parentheses show possession. (Delete the parentheses.) For help, consult 27b and 27e.

EXAMPLE   All boxes, cans, and bottles on a (supermarket) shelves are designed to appeal to (people) emotions.

All boxes, cans, and bottles on a *supermarket's* shelves are designed to appeal to *people's* emotions.

1. A (product) manufacturer designs packaging to appeal to (consumers) emotions through color and design.
2. Marketing specialists know that (people) beliefs about a (product) quality are influenced by their emotional response to the design of its package.
3. Circles and ovals appearing on a (box) design supposedly increase a (product user) feelings of comfort, while bold patterns and colors attract a (shopper) attention.
4. Using both circles and bold designs in (Arm & Hammer) and (Tide) packaging produces both effects in consumers.
5. (Heinz) ketchup bottle and (Coca-Cola) famous logo achieve the same effects by combining a bright color with an old-fashioned, "comfortable" design.
6. Often, a (company) marketing consultants will custom-design products to appeal to the supposedly "typical" (adult female) emotions or to (adult males), (children), or (teenagers) feelings.

7. One of the (marketing business) leading consultants, Stan Gross, tests (consumers) emotional reactions to (companies) products and their packages by asking consumers to associate products with well-known personalities.

8. Thus, (test takers) responses to (Gross) questions might reveal that a particular brand of laundry detergent has (Russell Crowe) toughness, (Oprah Winfrey) determination, or (someone else) sparkling personality.

9. Manufacturing (companies) products are not the only ones relying on (Gross) and other corporate (image makers) advice.

10. (Sports teams) owners also use marketing specialists to design their (teams) images, as anyone who has seen the angry bull logo of the Chicago Bulls basketball team will agree.

**EXERCISE 27-2**     Rewrite these sentences so that each contains a possessive noun. For help, consult 27b and 27e.

**EXAMPLE**     The light of a firefly gives off no heat.

A *firefly's* light gives off no heat.

1. The scientific name of a firefly is *lampyridae,* but the nicknames of the bug include *glowworm* and *lightning bug.*

2. More than two thousand species of fireflies can be found throughout the temperate climates of the world.

3. The light of a firefly is caused by a chemical reaction in the organs of the abdomen.

4. Fireflies played a role in the mythology of ancient Mayans and were often compared to the light of a star.

5. Although it may be in the interest of nobody to know, fireflies are not flies at all; they are, according to the classifications of scientists, beetles.

For more help with your writing, grammar, and research,
go to **www.mycomplab.com**

Mine says: "PLEASE, do *not* knock, do *not* say hello or goodbye, do *not* ask what's for dinner, do *not* disturb me unless the police or firemen have to be called."

—Judith Krantz

**ANSWERS: EXERCISE 27-2**

If students revise this material to include all possible uses of the apostrophe, you might point out that good style usually calls for a balance of possessive and nonpossessive structures in a single passage. Then you might ask them to restore some nonpossessive structures to achieve a suitable balance in the material. All possible possessives are included in the answers below.

**1.** The firefly's scientific name is *lampyridae,* but the bug's nicknames include glowworm and lightning bug.

**2.** More than two thousand species of fireflies can be found throughout the world's temperate climates.

**3.** The firefly's light is caused by a chemical reaction in the abdomen's organs.

**4.** Fireflies played a role in ancient Mayans' mythology and were often compared to a star's light.

**5.** Although it may be in nobody's interest to know, fireflies are not flies at all; they are, according to scientists' classifications, beetles.

# 28

# Quotation Marks

## 28a  What is the role of quotation marks?

**Quotation marks** are used most often to enclose **direct quotations**—the exact spoken or written words of a speaker or writer. Quotation marks also set off some titles, and quotation marks can call attention to words used in a special sense.

Double quotation marks (" ") are standard. In most computer fonts, the opening marks differ slightly in appearance from the closing marks. The opening marks look like tiny 6s, the closing marks like tiny 9s. In some computer fonts, the opening and closing marks look the same (" " or " "). Single quotation marks (' or ') are used for quotations within quotations: *Gregory said, "I heard the man shout 'Help me' but could not reach him in time."* Quotation marks operate only in pairs: to open and to close. When you proofread your writing, check carefully that you've inserted the closing mark.

Please note, before you continue reading this chapter, that we use MLA STYLE to format the examples here and in other chapters. This affects the documentation features and the lengths of "short" and "long" quotations. These factors vary with different documentation styles. For MLA style, used in most English courses, see Chapter 36. For APA STYLE, see Chapter 37.

## 28b  How do I use quotation marks with short direct quotations?

DIRECT QUOTATIONS are exact words from print or nonprint sources. In MLA STYLE, a quotation is considered *short* if it occupies no more than four typed lines. Use double quotation marks at the start and finish of a short quotation. Give DOCUMENTATION information after a short quotation, before the sentence's ending period.

### SHORT QUOTATIONS

Gardner has suggested the possibility of a ninth intelligence: existential, "the proclivity to pose (and ponder) questions about life, death, and ultimate realities" (72).

Susana Urbina, who surveyed many studies about intelligence, found that intelligence "is such a multifaceted concept that no single quality can define it . . ." (1130).

# 28c   Are quotation marks used with long quotations?

No. With a long DIRECT QUOTATION, don't use quotation marks. In MLA STYLE, a quotation is *long* if it occupies more than four typed lines. Instead of using quotation marks with a long quotation, indent all its lines as a block (that is, the quotation is "set off" or "displayed"). This format makes quotation marks unnecessary. Give DOCUMENTATION information after the period that ends the quotation.

### LONG QUOTATIONS

Gardner uses criteria by which to judge whether an ability deserves to be categorized as an "intelligence." Each must confer

> a set of skills of problem solving--enabling the individual to resolve genuine problems or difficulties [author's emphasis] that he or she encounters and laying the groundwork for the acquisition of new knowledge. (*Frames* 60-61)

In the Gardner example above, note that a capital letter is *not* used to start the quotation. The lead-in words (*Each must confer*) are an incomplete sentence, so they need the quotation to complete the sentence.

Goleman also emphasizes a close interaction of the emotional and rational states with the other intelligences that Gardner has identified:

> These two minds, the emotional and the rational, operate in tight harmony for the most part, intertwining their very different ways of knowing to guide us through the world. Ordinarily there is a balance between emotional and rational minds, with emotion feeding into and informing the operations of the rational mind, and the rational mind refining and sometimes vetoing the inputs of the emotions. (9)

In the Goleman example above, note that a capital letter starts the quotation because the lead-in words are a complete sentence. (A colon can—but isn't required to—end the lead-in sentence because it's an independent clause; see 26b.)

**Alert:** Whether a quotation is one word or occupies many lines, always document its SOURCE. Also, when you quote material, be very careful to record the words exactly as they appear in the original. ●

use of quotation marks is an indicator of original student voice.

**TEACHING TIP**

Many students think that they are not plagiarizing as long as they use quotation marks to indicate material taken from an outside source. These students do not realize that they must also document the source. You might find it useful, therefore, to take some time to explain documentation and the use of parenthetical citations, which may be unfamiliar to students inexperienced in writing research papers. Explain further that the placement of the parenthetical citation depends on the length of the quotation. If the quotation is "run in," the citation comes before the period; if the quotation is displayed, the citation comes after the period.

You may also want to discuss, for students who are writing blogs and other on-line material, how to hyperlink to original sources as well as citing them in their text.

**TEACHING TIP**

You may want to divide the class into groups of three or four, asking two members of each group to assume the role of a particular person or type of person. Giving one of them an opening statement that is likely to generate a dialogue, you can ask the two to engage in a conversation with each other. When they have finished, the group can write what they heard, first as direct discourse and then as indirect discourse. The first writing can take the form of a short play; the second, a short story.

**TEACHING TIP**

One pleasant way to review the use of quotation marks is to have students "translate" passages of indirect discourse found in short stories into dialogues. An alternative is to give students a short scene from a play they enjoy and ask them to rewrite it as if it were a chapter in a short story. Their first task is to set the scene and present the dialogue as conversation, following the conventions of the short story rather than those of the play. Then, they can rewrite the scene using indirect discourse in all the conversations.

**BACKGROUND**
The Web site <http://grammar.ccc.commnet
.edu/GRAMMAR/quizzes/quotes_quiz.htm>
features an interactive quiz on using quotation
marks.

**TEACHING TIP**
Since 2005, *The "Blog" of "Unnecessary" Quotation Marks* at <http://quotation-marks
.blogspot.com> keeps a running photo-log of
misused quotation marks.

**QUOTATION: ON WRITING**
When punctuation was first employed, it was in
the role of the handmaid of prose; later the
handmaid was transformed by the pedants into
a harsh-faced chaperone, pervertedly ingenious
in the contriving of stiff regulations and
starched rules of decorum; now, happily, she is
content to act as an auxiliary to the writer and
as a guide to the reader.

—Harold Herd

**BACKGROUND**
Classical Greek and Latin manuscripts usually
had no word separation, but in both inscriptions and nonliterary works, dots or apostrophes were often used to set off individual words.
The custom of separating words by spacing was
used off and on, beginning in the seventh century, becoming systematic only in the eleventh.

**ADDITIONAL EXAMPLES**
**1.** Virginia Woolf was a member of the
"Bloomsbury Group," the name taken from the
district of London in which she and her sister
lived after the death of their father.

**2.** She was the author of many short stories,
essays, and sketches, such as "The Mark on the
Wall."

**3.** She was an early user of "stream of consciousness" writing.

**4.** Have you read her long essay called "A
Room of One's Own"?

**28d** **How do I use quotation marks for quotations within quotations?**

In MLA STYLE, practice varies between short and long quotations when a quo-
tation contains internal quotation marks. In short quotations of prose, use single quotation marks for any internal quotation marks, and use double quotation
marks for the entire quotation. Give DOCUMENTATION information after the entire quotation, before the sentence's ending period. For other documentation
styles, check each style's manual.

In long quotations of prose—those that are displayed (set off in a block)
and not enclosed in quotation marks—keep the double quotation marks as
they appear in the original. Give DOCUMENTATION information after the long
quotation following any closing punctuation, and before the period that ends
a short quotation.

**SHORT QUOTATIONS: USE SINGLE WITHIN DOUBLE
QUOTATION MARKS (MLA STYLE)**

With short quotations, the double quotation marks show the beginning and end
of words taken from the source; the single quotation marks replace double
marks used in the source.

> **ORIGINAL SOURCE**
> Most scientists concede that they don't really know what "intelligence" is.
> Whatever it might be, paper and pencil tests aren't the tenth of it.
>
> —Brent Staples, "The IQ Cult," p. 293

> **STUDENT'S USE OF THE SOURCE**
> Brent Staples argues in his essay about IQ as an object of reverence:
> "Most scientists concede that they don't really know what 'intelligence'
> is. Whatever it might be, paper and pencil tests aren't the tenth of it" (293).

**LONG QUOTATIONS: USE QUOTATION MARKS AS IN SOURCE**

All long quotations must be set off (displayed) without being enclosed in quotation marks. Therefore, show any double and single quotation marks exactly
as the source does.

**28e** **How do I use quotation marks for quotations of poetry and dialogue?**

**POETRY (MLA STYLE)**

A quotation of poetry is *short* if it includes three lines or fewer of the poem.
As with prose quotations (28d), use double quotation marks to enclose the

material. If the poetry lines have internal double quotation marks, change them to single quotation marks. To show when a line of poetry breaks to the next line, use a slash (/) with one space on each side. Give DOCUMENTATION information after a short poetry quotation, before the period that ends the sentence (see also 29e).

> As Auden wittily defined personal space, "some thirty inches from my nose / The frontier of my person goes" (*Complete* 205).

A quotation of poetry is *long* if it includes more than three lines of the poem. As with prose quotations (28d), indent all lines as a block, without quotation marks to enclose the material. Start new lines exactly as they appear in your source. Give documentation information after the long quotation and after the period that ends the quotation.

**Alert:** When you quote lines of poetry, follow the capitalization of your source.

## DIALOGUE (MLA AND APA STYLES)

Dialogue, also called DIRECT DISCOURSE, presents a speaker's exact words. Enclose direct discourse in quotation marks. In contrast, INDIRECT DISCOURSE reports what a speaker said. Don't enclose indirect discourse in quotation marks. In addition to these differences in punctuation, PRONOUN use and VERB TENSES also differ for these two types of discourse.

| | |
|---|---|
| DIRECT DISCOURSE | The mayor said, **"I** intend to veto that bill.**"** |
| INDIRECT DISCOURSE | The mayor said **that he intended** to veto that bill. |

Whether you're reporting the words of a real speaker or making up dialogue in a short story, use double quotation marks at the beginning and end of a speaker's words. This tells your reader which words are the speaker's. Also, start a new paragraph each time the speaker changes.

> "I don't know how you can see to drive," she said.
> "Maybe you should put on your glasses."
> "Putting on my glasses would help you to see?"
> "Not me; you," Macon said. "You're focused on the windshield instead of the road."
>
> —Anne Tyler, *The Accidental Tourist*

In American English, if two or more paragraphs present a single speaker's words, use double opening quotation marks at the start of each paragraph, but save the closing double quotation marks until the end of the last quoted paragraph.

**QUOTATION: ON WRITING**

How to read writers on writing: With respect, amusement, and skepticism. They will contradict one another—as they should—for each writer brings an individual history to the writing task. There is no single theology here.

—Donald M. Murray

**TEACHING TIP**

Lewis Thomas objects to the misuse and overuse of quotation marks in ordinary prose. He cites advertising as a prime culprit in the practice. You might want to ask students to bring to class examples of questionable uses of quotation marks that they find in stores, in newspapers, on billboards, and in other advertising spaces. What point was the advertiser trying to make by using quotation marks? Was the advertiser successful?

**QUOTATION: ON WRITING**

If we had to say what writing is, we would have to define it essentially as an act of courage.

—Cynthia Ozick

**QUOTATION: ON QUOTATIONS**

It is a good thing for an uneducated man to read books of quotations.

—Winston Churchill

**TEACHING TIP**

Comic strips and graphic novels offer wonderful examples of dialogue. To practice quotation, have students convert the conversations of comic characters, usually displayed via speech balloons, into quoted text.

**QUOTATION: ON WRITING**

Manuscript: Something submitted in haste and returned at leisure.

—Oliver Herford

## ANSWERS: EXERCISE 28-1

**1.** The counselor asked Betty whether she would be interested in taking an introductory electronics course. [from direct to indirect discourse]

**2.** "Why would I take such a course when I'm a nursing major?" asked Betty. [from indirect to direct discourse]

**3.** The counselor looked Betty straight in the eye and said that some knowledge of electronics might not be part of her major, but it was a very important modern subject, nevertheless. [from direct to indirect discourse]

**4.** Betty wondered, "Well, maybe it would give me a greater understanding of all the electronics used in medical diagnosis and treatment today. But isn't there another elective that might do more to enhance my nursing career?" [from indirect to direct discourse]

**5.** The counselor was quiet a moment and then declared that electronics was something Betty could always fall back on and the more a person had to fall back on, the softer the landing would be. [from direct to indirect discourse]

**EXERCISE 28-1**  Working individually or with a group, decide whether each sentence below is direct or indirect discourse and then rewrite each sentence in the other form. Make any changes needed for grammatical correctness. With direct discourse, put the speaker's words wherever you think they belong in the sentence. For help, consult 28b through 28e.

**EXAMPLE**  A school counselor told Betty, a senior at Whatsamatta U, that she needed to take one more three-unit elective to graduate in May.

A school counselor told Betty, a senior at Whatsamatta U, "You need to take one more three-unit elective to graduate in May."

1. "Betty, would you be interested in taking an introductory electronics course?" asked the counselor.

2. Betty asked why she would take such a course when she was a nursing major.

3. The counselor looked Betty straight in the eye and said, "Some knowledge of electronics may not be part of your major, but it's a very important modern subject, nevertheless."

4. Betty wondered whether it might give her a greater understanding of all the electronics used in medical diagnosis and treatment today. But she also asked if there wasn't another elective that might do more to enhance her nursing career.

5. The counselor was quiet for a moment and then declared, "And don't forget, electronics is something you can always fall back on, Betty. And the more you have to fall back on, the softer the landing."

## 28f  How do I use quotation marks with titles of short works?

When you refer to certain short works by their titles, enclose the titles in quotation marks (other works, usually longer, need to be in italics; see 30g). Short works include short stories, essays, poems, articles from periodicals, pamphlets, brochures, songs, and individual episodes of a series on television or radio.

What is the rhyme scheme of Andrew Marvell's "Delight in Disorder"? [poem]

Have you read "The Lottery"? [short story]

The best source I found is "The Myth of Political Consultants." [magazine article]

"Shooting an Elephant" describes George Orwell's experiences in Burma. [essay]

Titles of some other works are neither enclosed in quotation marks nor written in italics. For guidelines, see Quick Reference 30.1 in 30e and Quick Reference 30.2 in 30g.

🛈 **Alert:** When placing the title of your own piece of writing on a title page or at the top of a page, never use quotation marks. ●

**EXERCISE 28-2**  Working individually or with a group, correct any misuses of quotation marks. For help, consult 28f.

1. The song America the Beautiful by Katharine Lee Bates celebrates the natural beauty and the ideals that many people associate with the United States.

2. Ralph Waldo Emerson's essay The American Scholar praises the ideals of independence and self-reliance in American education and was first heard as an oration delivered to the "Phi Beta Kappa Society."

3. However, not only the ideals, but also the harsh realities of life in America for Filipino immigrants form the basis of Carlos Bulosan's autobiography, America Is in the Heart.

4. A film that honestly and poignantly reveals the realities facing a family of Irish immigrants in New York City and their hopes for a better life is In America.

5. The poet Langston Hughes in his poem Let America Be America Again is fierce in his criticism of the way poor people and minorities are often treated in the United States.

## 28g  How do I use quotation marks for words used as words?

When you refer to a word as a word, you can choose to either enclose it in quotation marks or put it in italics. Whichever you choose, be consistent throughout each piece of writing.

> **NO**  Many people confuse affect and effect.
>
> **YES**  Many people confuse "affect" and "effect."
>
> **YES**  Many people confuse *affect* and *effect*.

Always put quotation marks around the English translation of a word or PHRASE. Also, use italics for the word or phrase in the other language.

> My grandfather usually ended arguments with *de gustibus non disputandum est* ("there is no disputing about tastes").

Many writers use quotation marks around words or phrases meant ironically or in other nonliteral ways.

The proposed tax "reform" is actually a tax increase.

Some writers put technical terms in quotation marks and define them—but only the first time they appear. Never reuse quotation marks after a term has been introduced and defined.

"Plagiarism"—the undocumented use of another person's words or ideas—can result in expulsion. Plagiarism is a serious offense.

Some student writers put quotation marks around words that they sense might be inappropriate for ACADEMIC WRITING, such as a SLANG term or a CLICHÉ used intentionally to make a point. However, when possible, use different language—not quotation marks. Take time to think of accurate, appropriate, and fresh words instead. If you prefer to stick with the slang or cliché, use quotation marks.

They "eat like birds" in public, but they "stuff their faces" in private.

They **eat almost nothing** in public, but they **eat hefty heaps of food** in private.

A nickname doesn't call for quotation marks, unless you use the nickname along with the full name. When a person's nickname is widely known, you don't have to give both the nickname and the full name. For example, use *Senator Ted Kennedy* or *Senator Edward Kennedy,* whichever is appropriate in context. Because he's well known, don't use *Senator Edward "Ted" Kennedy.*

**ANSWERS: EXERCISE 28-3**

**1.** Shakespeare's phrases such as "the sound and the fury" from *Macbeth* and "pale fire" from *The Tempest* have been used by authors such as William Faulkner and Vladimir Nabokov as titles for their books. [use quotation marks around quoted phrases]

**2.** Shakespeare's understanding of human nature was profound and helped him become a prolific writer. [misuse of quotation marks to call attention to words]

**3.** Correct [quotation marks around words used as words]

**4.** To understand the difference between the words "sanguinary" and "sanguine" (or *sanguinary* and *sanguine*) is important for a

**EXERCISE 28-3** Working individually or with a group, correct any misuses of quotation marks. If you think a sentence is correct, explain why. For help, consult 28g.

EXAMPLE   The word asyndeton simply means that a conjunction has been omitted, as when Shakespeare writes, A woman mov'd is like a fountain troubled, / Muddy, ill seeming, thick, bereft of beauty.

The word "asyndeton" simply means that a conjunction has been omitted, as when Shakespeare writes, "A woman mov'd is like a fountain troubled, / Muddy, ill seeming, thick, bereft of beauty."

1. Shakespeare's phrases such as the sound and the fury from *Macbeth* and pale fire from *The Tempest* have been used by authors such as William Faulkner and Vladimir Nabokov as titles for their books.

2. Shakespeare's understanding of human nature was "profound" and helped him become a "prolific" writer.

3. Many words used commonly today, such as "addiction" and "alligator," were first used in print by Shakespeare.

4. To understand the difference between the words sanguinary and *sanguine* is important for a reader of Shakespeare because the former means bloody and the latter means optimistic.

5. In the play *Romeo and Juliet,* one of Shakespeare's most famous quotations is What's in a name? That which we call a rose / By any other name would smell as sweet.

reader of Shakespeare because the former means "bloody" and the latter means "optimistic." [consistent treatment needed]

5. In the play *Romeo and Juliet,* one of Shakespeare's most famous quotations is "What's in a name? That which we call a rose / By any other name would smell as sweet." [quotation marks around quotation]

## **28h** How do I use quotation marks with other punctuation?

### COMMAS AND PERIODS WITH QUOTATION MARKS

A comma or period that is grammatically necessary is always placed inside the closing quotation mark.

> Jessica enjoyed F. Scott Fitzgerald's story "The Freshest Boy," so she was eager to read his novels. [comma before closing quotation mark]
>
> Max said, "Don't stand so far away from me." [comma before opening quotation mark (24k.5); period before closing quotation mark]
>
> Edward T. Hall coined the word "proxemia." [period before closing quotation mark]

### SEMICOLONS AND COLONS WITH QUOTATION MARKS

A semicolon or colon is placed outside the closing quotation mark, unless it is part of the quotation.

> Computers offer businesses "opportunities that never existed before"; some workers disagree. [semicolon after closing quotation mark]
>
> We have to know each culture's standard for "how close is close": No one wants to offend. [colon after closing quotation mark]

### QUESTION MARKS, EXCLAMATION POINTS, AND DASHES WITH QUOTATION MARKS

If the punctuation marks belong to the words enclosed in quotation marks, put them inside the quotation marks.

> "Did I Hear You Call My Name?" was the winning song.
>
> "I've won the lottery!" Arielle shouted.
>
> "Who's there? Why don't you ans—"

If a question mark, an exclamation point, or a dash doesn't belong to the material being quoted, put the punctuation outside the quotation marks.

> Have you read Nikki Giovanni's poem "Knoxville, Tennessee"?
>
> If only I could write a story like David Wallace's "Girl with Curious Hair"!

Weak excuses—a classic is "I have to visit my grandparents"—change little.

When you use quotation marks and want to know how they work with capital letters, see 30d; with brackets, 29c; with ellipsis points, 29d; and with the slash, 29e.

## 28i When are quotation marks wrong?

Never enclose a word in quotation marks to call attention to it, to intensify it, or to be sarcastic.

> **NO** I'm "very" happy about the news.
>
> **YES** I'm very happy about the news.

Never enclose the title of your paper in quotation marks (or underline it). However, if the title of your paper contains another title that requires quotation marks, use those marks only for the included title.

> **NO** "The Elderly in Nursing Homes: A Case Study"
>
> **YES** The Elderly in Nursing Homes: A Case Study
>
> **NO** Character Development in Shirley Jackson's Story The Lottery
>
> **YES** Character Development in Shirley Jackson's Story "The Lottery"

**EXERCISE 28-4**  Correct any errors in the use of quotation marks and other punctuation with quotation marks. If you think a sentence is correct, explain why. For help, consult 28e through 28i.

1. Dying in a shabby hotel room, the witty writer Oscar Wilde supposedly said, "Either that wallpaper goes, or I do".

2. Was it the Russian novelist Tolstoy who wrote, "All happy families resemble one another, but each unhappy family is unhappy in its own way?"

3. In his poem A Supermarket in California, Allen Ginsberg addresses the dead poet Walt Whitman, asking, Where are we going, Walt Whitman? The doors close / in an hour. Which way does your beard point tonight?

4. Toni Morrison made this reply to the claim that "art that has a political message cannot be good art:" She said that "the best art is political" and that her aim was to create art that was "unquestionably political" and beautiful at the same time.

5. Benjamin Franklin's strange question—"What is the use of a newborn child?—" was his response to someone who doubted the usefulness of new inventions.

---

**ANSWERS: EXERCISE 28-4**

**1.** Dying in a shabby hotel room, the witty writer Oscar Wilde supposedly said, "Either that wallpaper goes, or I do." [28h, period always placed inside closing quotation mark]

**2.** Was it the Russian novelist Tolstoy who wrote, "All happy families resemble one another, but each unhappy family is unhappy in its own way"? [28h, question mark not part of the quotation]

**3.** In his poem "A Supermarket in California," Allen Ginsberg addresses the dead poet Walt Whitman, asking, "Where are we going, Walt Whitman? The doors close / in an hour. Which way does your beard point tonight?" [28f, title of poem; 28e, direct quotation; 28h, question mark part of the quotation]

**4.** Toni Morrison made this reply to the claim that "art that has a political message cannot be good art": She said that "the best art is political" and that her aim was to create art that was "unquestionably political" and beautiful at the same time. [28h, colon always placed outside closing quotation mark]

**5.** Benjamin Franklin's strange question— "What is the use of a newborn child?"—was his response to someone who doubted the usefulness of new inventions. [28h, dash not part of the quotation]

# 29

# Other Punctuation Marks

This chapter explains the uses of **dashes, parentheses, brackets, ellipsis points, slashes,** and **hyphens.** These punctuation marks aren't used often, but each serves a purpose and gives you options with your writing style.

## DASH

## 29a When can I use a dash in my writing?

The **dash,** or a pair of dashes, lets you interrupt a sentence to add information. Such interruptions can fall in the middle or at the end of a sentence. To make a dash, hit the hyphen key twice (--). Do not put a space before, between, or after the hyphens. Some word processing programs automatically convert two hyphens into a dash; either form is correct. In print, the dash appears as an unbroken line approximately the length of two hyphens joined together (—). If you handwrite, make the dash at least twice as long as a hyphen.

### USING DASHES FOR SPECIAL EMPHASIS

If you want to emphasize an example, a definition, an appositive, or a contrast, you can use a dash or dashes. Some call a dash "a pregnant pause"—that is, take note, something special is coming. Use dashes sparingly so that you don't dilute their impact.

#### EXAMPLE

The caretakers—those who are helpers, nurturers, teachers, mothers—are still systematically devalued.

—Ellen Goodman, "Just Woman's Work?"

#### DEFINITION

Although the emphasis at the school was mainly language—speaking, reading, writing—the lessons always began with an exercise in politeness.

—Elizabeth Wong, *Fifth Chinese Daughter*

### QUOTATION: ON WRITING

A *dash* derives from "to *dash,*" to shatter, strike violently, to throw suddenly or violently, hence to throw carelessly in or on, hence to write carelessly or suddenly, to add or insert suddenly or carelessly to or in the page. "To *dash*" comes from Middle English *daschen,* itself probably from Scandinavian—compare Danish *daske,* to beat, to strike. Ultimately the word is—rather obviously—echoic.

—Eric Partridge

### ADDITIONAL EXAMPLES: DASH

#### Appositive
Elizabeth Barrett Browning—the wife of Robert Browning—was probably a more popular poet than her husband in the nineteenth century.

#### Example
Many students—elementary school, high school, and college students—find themselves taking required courses that they would not choose for themselves.

#### Definition
Futuristic novels with a bleak vision of the prospects for the free individual characteristically portray a society in which history—knowledge of the past—has been systematically eliminated.

—Diane Ravitch

Dinner at the Huntercombes possessed only two dramatic features—the wine was a farce and the food a tragedy.

—Anthony Powell

#### Contrast
It's not right or wrong—it's just fattening.

#### An Aside
If you choose to vote for that candidate—and I don't care whether you do or not—then you have put yourself in the conservative camp.

#### Broken-off Speech
"It's not that I don't love you, Tom, it's just that—"

469

**BACKGROUND**

In "On Language" (*New York Times*, 8 April 1984, late ed., sec. 6:12), William Safire warns against using dashes indiscriminately: "Writing is different from speaking. Organize your written thoughts so that you don't have to stud your sentences with asides, sudden additions, curses, or last-minute entries."

**QUOTATION: ON WRITING**

The dash has been described as the interruption, the mark of abruptness, the sob, the stammer, and the mark of ignorance. The last name—which might be equally well applied to the comma as crude writers use it—records the fact that the uninformed mistake the dash for an all-purpose mark for every possible occasion.

—George Summey Jr.

**BACKGROUND**

John Dawkins' delightful "Teaching Punctuation as a Rhetorical Tool" (*College Composition and Communication* 46.4 (1995): 533–548) discusses using successful writers like Annie Dillard or George Orwell as examples of using punctuation for rhetorical effect.

**QUOTATION: ON WRITING**

Surely the unnecessary profusion of straight lines, particularly on a printed page, is offensive to good taste, is an index of the *dasher's* profound ignorance of the art of punctuation, and, so far from helping to bring out the sense of an author, is better adapted for turning into nonsense some of his finest passages.

—John Wilson

**QUOTATION: ON WRITING**

In the camp, this meant committing my verse—many thousands of lines—to memory. To help me with this I improvised decimal counting beads and, in transit prisons, broke up matchsticks and used the fragments as tallies. As I approached the end of my sentence I grew more confident of my powers of memory, and began writing down and memorizing prose—dialogue at first, but then, bit by bit, whole densely written passages. My memory found room for them! It worked. But more and more of my time—in the end as much as one week every

**APPOSITIVE**

Two of the strongest animals in the jungle are vegetarians—the elephant and the gorilla.

—Dick Gregory, *The Shadow That Scares Me*

**CONTRAST**

Fire cooks food—and burns down forests.

—Smokey the Bear

Place what you emphasize with dashes next to or nearby the material it refers to so that what you want to accomplish with your emphasis is not lost.

**NO** The current **argument is**—one that faculty, students, and coaches debate fiercely—whether to hold athletes to the same academic standards as others face.

**YES** The current **argument**—one that faculty, students, and coaches debate fiercely—**is** whether to hold athletes to the same academic standards as others face.

## USING DASHES TO EMPHASIZE AN ASIDE

An **aside** is a writer's comment, often the writer's personal views, on what's been written. Generally, this technique isn't appropriate for academic writing, so before you insert an aside, carefully consider your writing purpose and your audience.

Television showed us the war. It showed us the war in a way that was—if you chose to watch television, at least—unavoidable.

—Nora Ephron, *Scribble Scribble*

🛈 Alerts: (1) If the words within a pair of dashes require a question mark or an exclamation point, place it before the second dash.

A first date—do you remember?—stays in the memory forever.

(2) Never use commas, semicolons, or periods next to dashes. If such a need arises, revise your writing.

(3) Never enclose quotation marks in dashes except when the meaning requires them. These two examples show that, when required, the dash stops before or after the quotation marks; the two punctuation marks do not overlap.

Many of George Orwell's essays—"A Hanging," for example—draw on his experiences as a civil servant.

"Shooting an Elephant"—another Orwell essay—appears in many anthologies. ●

**EXERCISE 29-1**    Write a sentence about each topic, shown in italics. Use dashes to set off what is asked for, shown in roman, in each sentence. For help, consult 29a.

**EXAMPLE**    *punctuation mark*, an aside

Sometimes I get confused—but what's new**?**—about the difference between a colon and a semicolon.

1. *ice cream flavor*, an aside
2. *a shape*, a definition
3. *sport*, an appositive
4. *public transportation*, an example
5. *occupation*, a contrast
6. *musical instrument*, a definition
7. *TV show*, an aside
8. *American president*, an example
9. *country*, an appositive
10. *animal*, a contrast

## PARENTHESES

# 29b   When can I use parentheses in my writing?

**Parentheses** let you interrupt a sentence to add various kinds of information. Parentheses are like dashes (29a) in that they set off extra or interrupting words—but unlike dashes, which emphasize material, parentheses de-emphasize what they enclose. Use parentheses sparingly because overusing them can make your writing lurch, not flow.

### USING PARENTHESES TO ENCLOSE INTERRUPTING WORDS

#### EXPLANATION
After they've finished with the pantry, the medicine cabinet, and the attic, they will throw out the red geranium (too many leaves), sell the dog (too many fleas), and send the children off to boarding school (too many scuffmarks on the hardwood floors).

—Suzanne Britt, "Neat People vs. Sloppy People"

#### EXAMPLE
Though other cities (Dresden, for instance) had been utterly destroyed in World War II, never before had a single weapon been responsible for such destruction.

—Laurence Behrens and Leonard J. Rosen, *Writing and Reading Across the Curriculum*

#### ASIDE
The older girls (non-graduates, of course) were assigned the task of making refreshments for the night's festivities.

—Maya Angelou, *I Know Why the Caged Bird Sings*

month—went into the regular repetition of all I had memorized.

—Aleksandr Solzhenitsyn

**ANSWERS: EXERCISES 29-1**
Answers will vary. When checking them, make sure the dashes are used according to the instructions. This particular exercise lends itself well to peer-review, to help students identify and check correct usage.

**BACKGROUND**
Style is ever-changing among authors. Lynne Truss, of *Eats, Shoots and Leaves* remarks, "Why is the dash the mark a la mode? Because it is so easy to use, perhaps, and because it is hard to use wrongly; but also because it is, simply, easy to see. Full stops and commas are often quite tiny in modern typefaces, whereas the horizontal dash is a lot harder to miss. ("Points of Punctuation: The Dash Has Become the Most Fashionable of Marks, Says Lynne Truss," *Daily Telegraph*, 27 December 2003: 2).

**QUOTATION: ON WRITING**
[The dash] is a comfortable punctuation mark since even the most rigorous critic can seldom claim that any particular example of it is a misuse. Its overuse is its greatest danger, and the writer who can't resist dashes may be suspected of uncoordinated thinking.

—Cornelia Evans and Bergen Evans

**ADDITIONAL EXAMPLES: PARENTHESES**

**Explanations**
Most Americans try to be honest about filing their income tax returns (no matter how much it hurts to pay).

**Examples**
Many modern zoos (such as the Santa Barbara Zoo) try to present the animals so that young children can easily see them.

**Asides**
House plants are subject to bug infestations (at least mine are) that require special treatment if the attack is to be repelled.

**Numbers and Letters**

There are five basic ingredients in a good gumbo: (1) a roux, (2) a variety of chopped vegetables, (3) water, (4) seafood or chicken, and (5) seasonings.

**Numerical Repetition**

A freshman is required to take twelve (12) hours of course work to be in regular status.

**Expression of Doubt**

She was born in 1463 (?) in Rome.

**QUOTATION: ON WRITING**

Though parentheses seem to say "here it is if you wish it; it's only an aside," such an aside may be intended for special notice—like many a remark that begins with the disarming *by the way* or *incidentally.*
—George Summey Jr.

**QUOTATION: ON WRITING**

Writing is my vacation from living.
—Eugene O'Neill

**BACKGROUND**

In "On Language; #@\/()! = Hash, At, Slash, Backslash, Open, Close, Bang," (*New York Times,* 30 June 1991, late ed., sec. 6:8.), William Safire reflects on the changes in nomenclature for computer keyboard symbols. Safire writes, "What we old-timers know as 'parentheses' are now just *open* and *close,* or more descriptively, *left banana* and *right banana.*"

**BACKGROUND**

Literally, *parenthesis* indicates "an insertion beside" the basic meaning of the sentence. (The term applies to both the insertion itself and either of the punctuation marks used to surround it.) The Greek from which it comes (by way of Medieval Latin) is composed of *para,* "beside"; *en,* "in"; and *thesis,* "placing, position," from *tithenai,* "to place or put." Hence, a parenthesis is a thought placed alongside the principal meaning.

The sheer decibel level of the noise around us is not enough to make us cranky, irritable, or aggressive. (It can, however, affect our mental and physical health, which is another matter.)
—Carol Tavris, *Anger: The Misunderstood Emotion*

## USING PARENTHESES FOR LISTED ITEMS AND ALTERNATIVE NUMBERS

When you number listed items within a sentence, enclose the numbers (or letters) in parentheses. Never use closing parentheses to set off numbers in a displayed list; use periods.

> Four items are on the agenda for tonight's meeting: (1) current treasury figures, (2) current membership figures, (3) the budget for renovations, and (4) the campaign for soliciting additional public contributions.

**Alerts:** For listed items that fall within a sentence, (1) use a colon before a list only if an INDEPENDENT CLAUSE comes before the list, and (2) use commas or semicolons to separate three or more items, but be consistent within a piece of writing. If, however, any item contains punctuation itself, use a semicolon to separate the items. ●

In legal writing and in some BUSINESS WRITING, you can use parentheses to enclose a numeral that repeats a spelled-out number.

> The monthly rent is three hundred fifty dollars ($350).

> Your order of fifteen (15) gross was shipped today.

In ACADEMIC WRITING, especially in subjects in which the use of figures or measurements is frequent, enclose alternative or comparative forms of the same number in parentheses: *2 mi (3.2 km).*

## USING OTHER PUNCTUATION WITH PARENTHESES

When a complete sentence enclosed in parentheses stands alone, start it with a capital letter and end it with a period. When a sentence in parentheses falls within another sentence, never start with a capital or end with a period.

| | |
|---|---|
| **NO** | Looking for his car keys (He had left them at my sister's house.) wasted an entire hour. |
| **YES** | Looking for his car keys (he had left them at my sister's house) wasted an entire hour. |
| **YES** | Looking for his car keys wasted an entire hour. (He had left them at my sister's house.) |

If the material before the parenthetical material requires a comma, place that comma after the closing parenthesis unless you're using commas to set off numbers in a list.

**NO**   Although clearly different from my favorite film**,** (*The Wizard of Oz*) *Gone With the Wind* is also outstanding.

**YES**   Although clearly different from my favorite film (*The Wizard of Oz*)**,** *Gone With the Wind* is also outstanding.

**YES**   Dorothy wore (1) a white blouse**,** (2) a blue pinafore**,** and (3) ruby slippers.

You can use a question mark or an exclamation point within parentheses that occur in a sentence.

Looking for clues (what did we expect to find**?**) wasted four days.

Place parentheses around quotation marks that come before or after any quoted words.

**NO**   Alberta Hunter **"**(Down Hearted Blues**)"** is known for singing jazz.

**YES**   Alberta Hunter (**"**Down Hearted Blues**"**) is known for singing jazz.

# BRACKETS

## 29c   When do I need to use brackets in my writing?

**Brackets** allow you to enclose words that you want to insert into quotations, but only in the specific cases discussed below.

### ADJUSTING A QUOTATION WITH BRACKETS

When you use a quotation, you might need to change the form of a word (a verb's tense, for example), add a brief definition, or fit the quotation into the grammatical structure of your sentence. In such cases, enclose the material you have inserted into the quotation in brackets. (These examples use MLA style for parenthetical references; see 36b.)

#### ORIGINAL SOURCE
Current research shows that successful learning takes place in an active environment.

—Deborah Moore, "Facilities and Learning Styles," p. 22

### QUOTATION: ON WRITING
The author must keep his mouth shut when his work starts to speak.

—Friedrich Nietzsche

### ADDITIONAL EXAMPLES: PARENTHESES

When eating at a formal restaurant (such as Chez Marcelle), a man is expected to wear a coat and tie.

Although the rain kept falling (and the river rising!), we decided to wait for the rescue boat instead of striking out on our own.

*Casablanca* has become a favorite film of many people too young to have seen it when it was originally released (or to have seen Bogart and Bergman in their other films).

### ADDITIONAL EXAMPLES: BRACKETS

#### Insertion of Words
Describing the end of grief, Marjorie Waters wrote, "[It] was a homecoming, a returning to myself made sweeter by the long separation."

To be reasonably comfortable for even short walks outdoors [in Moscow during the winter] it is necessary to wear coats of natural fur.

—Leona P. Schecter, "Moscow"

#### Brief Parenthetical Material Inside Parentheses
The Declaration of Independence (subtitled "The Unanimous Declaration of the Thirteen United States of America" [and published by Congress in 1776]) is an eloquent assertion of human rights.

### QUOTATION: ON WRITING
Punctuation is the art of dividing a written composition into sentences, or parts of sentences, by points or stops, for the purpose of marking the different pauses which the sense, and an accurate pronunciation require.

—Lindley Murray, 1794

### QUOTATION: ON WRITING
I blame myself for not often enough seeing the extraordinary in the ordinary. Somewhere in his

journals, Dostoyevsky remarks that a writer can begin anywhere, at the most commonplace thing, scratch around in it long enough, pry and dig away long enough, and lo! soon he will hit upon the marvelous.

—Saul Bellow

**BACKGROUND**

In *How Do You Spell,* Perry W. Buffington cites research to suggest that gifted spellers are avid readers. He also notes that "the ancient Greeks believed that a lesser god named Skripto was responsible for all errors in spelling, grammar, and diction."

**BACKGROUND**

In *It's Hyphen Time,* Carl Kane suggests inserting a hyphen "whenever a *re* prefix creates a word identical to another word," such as, *recreation* and *re-creation; resigned* and *re-signed; resolve* and *re-solve.*

**QUOTATION WITH BRACKETS**

Deborah Moore supports a student-centered curriculum and agrees with "current research [which] shows that successful learning takes place in an active environment" (22).

**ORIGINAL SOURCE**

The logic of the mind is *associative;* it takes elements that symbolize a reality, or trigger a memory of it, to be the same as that reality.

—Daniel Goleman, *Emotional Intelligence,* p. 294

**QUOTATION WITH BRACKETS**

The kinds of intelligence are based in the way the mind functions: "The logic of the mind is *associative* [one idea connects with another]; it takes elements that symbolize a reality, or trigger a memory of it, to be the same as that reality" (Goleman 294).

## USING BRACKETS TO POINT OUT AN ERROR IN A SOURCE OR TO ADD INFORMATION WITHIN PARENTHESES

In words you want to quote, sometimes page-makeup technicians or authors make a mistake without realizing it—a wrong date, a misspelled word, or an error of fact. You fix that mistake by putting your correction in brackets, without changing the words you want to quote. This tells your readers that the error was in the original work and not made by you.

### USING [SIC] TO SHOW A SOURCE'S ERROR

Insert *sic* (without italics), enclosed in brackets, in your MLA-style essays and research papers to show your readers that you've quoted an error accurately. *Sic* is a Latin word that means "so," or "thus," which says "It is so (or thus) in the original."

**USE FOR ERROR**

A journalist wrote, "The judge accepted an [sic] plea of not guilty.

**USE FOR MISSPELLING**

The building inspector wrote about the consequence of doubling the apartment's floor space: "With that much extra room per person, the tennants [sic] would sublet."

### USING BRACKETS WITHIN PARENTHESES

Use brackets to insert information within parentheses.

That expression (first used in *A Fable for Critics* [1848] by James R. Lowell) was popularized in the early twentieth century by Ella Wheeler Wilcox.

# ELLIPSIS POINTS

## 29d How do I use ellipsis points in my writing?

The word *ellipsis* means "omission." **Ellipsis points** in writing are a series of three spaced dots (use the period key on the keyboard). You're required to use ellipsis points to indicate you've intentionally omitted words—perhaps even a sentence or more—from the source you're quoting. These rules apply to both prose and poetry.

The *MLA Handbook* no longer recommends that ellipsis points you have inserted be enclosed in brackets to make it clear to your reader that the omission is yours. See Chapter 36 for more information.

### 29d.1 Using ellipsis points with prose

**ORIGINAL SOURCE**

These two minds, the emotional and the rational, operate in tight harmony for the most part, intertwining their very different ways of knowing to guide us through the world. Ordinarily, there is a balance between emotional and rational minds, with emotion feeding into and informing the operations of the rational mind, and the rational mind refining and sometimes vetoing the inputs of the emotions. Still, the emotional and rational minds are semi-independent faculties, each, as we shall see, reflecting the operation of distinct, but interconnected, circuitry in the brain.

—Daniel Goleman, *Emotional Intelligence*, p. 9

**QUOTATION OF SELECTED WORDS, NO ELLIPSIS NEEDED**

Goleman explains that the "two minds, the emotional and the rational" usually provide "a balance" in our daily observations and decision making (9).

**QUOTATION WITH ELLIPSIS MID-SENTENCE**

Goleman emphasizes the connections between parts of the mind: "Still, the emotional and rational minds are semi-independent faculties, each . . . reflecting the operation of distinct, but interconnected, circuitry in the brain (9).

**QUOTATION WITH ELLIPSIS AND PARENTHETICAL REFERENCE**

Goleman emphasizes that the "two minds, the emotional and the rational, operate in tight harmony for the most part . . ." (9). [Note: In MLA style, place a sentence-ending period after the parenthetical reference.]

**QUOTATION: ON WRITING**

Speech is highly elliptical. It would scarcely be endurable otherwise. Ellipsis is indispensable to the writer or speaker who wants to be brief and pithy, but it can easily cause confusion and obscurity and must be used with skill.

—Cornelia Evans and Bergen Evans

**ADDITIONAL EXAMPLES, MLA STYLE: ELLIPSIS POINTS**

Give me liberty or . . . death!

—Patrick Henry

As a recommendation for raising children in the future, Elizabeth Janeway urges "the establishment of enriching and exciting childcare facilities at industrial plants, commercial centers, educational establishments. . . ."

In a comment about Dashiell Hammett, Lillian Hellman says, "He had made up honor early in his life and stuck with his rules . . ." (*An Unfinished Woman*, 126), and then she cites examples of that honor from his own acts.

**TEACHING TIP**

One very good way of teaching students the art of quoting sources without overquoting is to have them experiment with inserting a portion of a quoted statement (preferably one of their own choosing) into sentences of their own. Remind them not only to use ellipsis points (to signal the omission of words from the original quotation) but also to use quotation marks and provide needed documentation as well. Teaching punctuation within the larger context of artful writing often produces astonishingly good results.

**QUOTATION WITH ELLIPSIS ENDING THE SENTENCE**

On page 9, Goleman states: "These two minds, the emotional and the rational, operate in tight harmony for the most part...."  [*Note:* In MLA style, when all needed documentation information is written into a sentence—that is, not placed in parentheses at the end of the sentence—there's no space between the sentence-ending period and an ellipsis.]

**QUOTATION WITH SENTENCE OMITTED**

Goleman explains: "These two minds, the emotional and the rational, operate in tight harmony for the most part, intertwining their very different ways of knowing to guide us through the world.... Still, the emotional and rational minds are semi-independent faculties" (9).

**QUOTATION WITH WORDS OMITTED FROM THE MIDDLE OF ONE SENTENCE TO THE MIDDLE OF ANOTHER**

Goleman states: "Ordinarily, there is a balance between emotional and rational minds ... reflecting the operation of distinct, but interconnected, circuitry in the brain" (9).

**QUOTATION WITH WORDS OMITTED FROM THE BEGINNING OF A SENTENCE AND FROM THE MIDDLE OF ONE SENTENCE TO A COMPLETE OTHER SENTENCE**

Goleman explains: "... there is a balance between emotional and rational minds.... Still, the emotional and rational minds are semi-independent faculties, each, as we shall see, reflecting the operation of distinct, but interconnected, circuitry in the brain" (9).

When you omit words from a quotation, you also omit punctuation related to those words, unless it's needed for the sentence to be correct.

Goleman explains: "These two minds ... operate in tight harmony" (9). [comma in original source omitted after *minds*]

Goleman explains that the emotional and rational minds work together while, "still, ... each, as we shall see, [reflects] the operation of distinct, but interconnected, circuitry in the brain" (9).  [comma kept after *still* because it's an introductory word; *still* changed to begin with lowercase letter because it's now in the middle of the sentence; form of *reflecting* changed to improve the sense of sentence]

## 29d.2 Using ellipsis points with poetry

When you omit one or more words from a line of poetry, follow the rules stated above for prose. However, when you omit a full line or more from poetry, use a full line of spaced dots.

ORIGINAL SOURCE

**Little Boy Blue**
Little boy blue, come blow your horn,
The sheep's in the meadow, the cow's in the corn
Where is the little boy who looks after the sheep?
He's under the haystack, fast asleep.

QUOTATION WITH LINES OMITTED

**Little Boy Blue**
Little boy blue, come blow your horn,

. . . . . . . . . . . . . . . . . . . . . . . . . . . . . . . .

Where is the little boy who looks after the sheep?
He's under the haystack, fast asleep.

## SLASH

## 29e When can I use a slash in my writing?

The **slash** (/), also called a *virgule* or *solidus,* is a diagonal line that separates or joins words in special circumstances.

### USING A SLASH TO SEPARATE QUOTED LINES OF POETRY

When you quote more than three lines of a poem, no slash is involved; you merely follow the rules in 28e. When you quote three lines or fewer, enclose them in quotation marks and run them into your sentence—and use a slash to divide one line from the next. Leave a space on each side of the slash.

> One of my mottoes comes from the beginning of Anne Sexton's poem "Words": "Be careful of words, / even the miraculous ones."

Capitalize and punctuate each line of poetry as in the original—but even if the quoted line of poetry doesn't have a period, use one to end your sentence. If your quotation ends before the line of poetry ends, use ellipsis points (29d).

BACKGROUND
The punctuation mark we call the *slash* is called a *stroke* in British English.

## ANSWERS: EXERCISE 29-2

Answers may vary somewhat, especially in usage of dashes and parentheses.

**1.** In *The Color Purple* (a successful movie as well as a novel), Alice Walker explores the relationships between women and men in traditional African American culture. [29b, parentheses for interruptive aside; dashes too distracting]

**2.** W. C. Fields offered two pieces of advice on job hunting: (1) never show up for an interview in bare feet, and (2) don't read your prospective employer's mail while he is questioning you about your qualifications. [29b, parentheses around numbers for listed items in sentence]

**3.** A series of resolutions was passed 11–0 (with one council member abstaining) calling on the mayor and the district attorney to improve safety conditions and step up law enforcement on city buses. [29b, parentheses for interruptive explanation; dashes too distracting]

**4.** All the interesting desserts—ice cream, chocolate fudge cake, pumpkin pie with whipped cream—are fattening, unfortunately. [29a, dashes for interruptive example; dashes add emphasis]

**5.** Thunder is caused when the flash of lightning heats the air around it to temperatures up to 30,000°F (16,666°C). [29b, parentheses for alternative numbers]

**6.** Christina Rossetti wonders if the end of life also means the end of love in a poem that opens with these two lines: "When I am dead, my dearest, / Sing no sad songs for me." [29e, slash between lines of quoted poetry]

**7.** Correct

**8.** In his famous letter from the Birmingham jail on April 16, 1963, Martin Luther King Jr. wrote: "You [the eight clergymen who had urged him not to hold a protest] deplore the demonstrations taking place in Birmingham." [29c, brackets for words inserted into quotation]

**9.** The world's most expensive doll house (sold for $256,000 at a London auction) [29b, parentheses for interruptive explanation because dash used later in sentence] contains sixteen

## USING A SLASH FOR NUMERICAL FRACTIONS IN MANUSCRIPTS

To type numerical fractions, use a slash (with no space before or after the slash) to separate the numerator and denominator. In mixed numbers—that is, whole numbers with fractions—leave a space between the whole number and its fraction: 1 2/3, 3 7/8. Do not use a hyphen. (For information about using spelled-out and numerical forms of numbers, see 30m through 30o.)

## USING A SLASH FOR *AND/OR*

When writing in the humanities, try not to use word combinations connected with a slash, such as *and/or.* In academic disciplines in which such combinations are acceptable, separate the words with a slash. Leave no space before or after the slash. In the humanities, listing both alternatives in normal sentence structure is usually better than separating choices with a slash.

> **NO**  The best quality of reproduction comes from 35 mm slides**/**direct-positive films.
>
> **YES**  The best quality of reproduction comes from 35 mm slides **or** direct-positive films.

## EXERCISE 29-2    Supply needed dashes, parentheses, brackets, ellipsis points, and slashes. If a sentence is correct as written, circle its number. In some sentences, when you can use either dashes or parentheses, explain your choice. For help, consult all sections of this chapter.

**EXAMPLE**    Two tiny islands in the English Channel Jersey and Guernsey have breeds of cows named after them.

Two tiny islands in the English Channel—Jersey and Guernsey—have breeds of cows named after them.

1. In *The Color Purple* a successful movie as well as a novel, Alice Walker explores the relationships between women and men in traditional African American culture.

2. W. C. Fields offered two pieces of advice on job hunting: 1 never show up for an interview in bare feet, and 2 don't read your prospective employer's mail while he is questioning you about your qualifications.

3. A series of resolutions was passed 11–0 with one council member abstaining calling on the mayor and the district attorney to improve safety conditions and step up law enforcement on city buses.

4. All the interesting desserts ice cream, chocolate fudge cake, pumpkin pie with whipped cream are fattening, unfortunately.

5. Thunder is caused when the flash of lightning heats the air around it to temperatures up to 30,000°F 16,666°C.

6. Christina Rossetti wonders if the end of a life also means the end of love in a poem that opens with these two lines: "When I am dead, my dearest, Sing no sad songs for me."

7. After the internationally famous racehorse Dan Patch died suddenly from a weak heart, his devoted owner, Will Savage, died of the same condition a mere 32 1/2 hours later.

8. In his famous letter from the Birmingham jail on April 16, 1963, Martin Luther King Jr. wrote: "You the eight clergymen who had urged him not to hold a protest deplore the demonstrations taking place in Birmingham."

9. The world's most expensive doll house sold for $256,000 at a London auction contains sixteen rooms, a working chamber organ, and a silver clothes press but no toilet.

10. The person renting this apartment agrees to pay seven hundred fifty dollars $750 per month in rent.

11. Railroad entrepreneur George Francis Train his real name! dreamed of creating a chain of great cities across the United States, all connected by his Union Pacific Railroad.

12. Patients who pretend to have ailments are known to doctors as "Munchausens" after Baron Karl Friedrich Hieronymus von Münchhausen he was a German army officer who had a reputation for wild and unbelievable tales.

**EXERCISE 29-3**  Follow the directions for each item. For help, consult all sections of this chapter.

**EXAMPLE**  Write a sentence about getting something right using a dash.

*I tried and failed, I tried and failed again—and then I did it.*

1. Write a sentence that quotes only three lines of the following sonnet by William Shakespeare:

Let me not to the marriage of true minds
Admit impediments. Love is not love
Which alters when it alteration finds,
Or bends with the remover to remove.
O, no! it is an ever-fixèd mark
That looks on tempests and is never shaken;
It is the star to every wand'ring bark,
Whose worth's unknown, although his height be taken.
Love's not Time's fool, though rosy lips and cheeks
Within his bending sickle's compass come;
Love alters not with his brief hours and weeks,
But bears it out even to the edge of doom.
    If this be error, and upon me proved,
    I never writ, nor no man ever loved.

---

rooms, a working chamber organ, and a silver clothes press—but no toilet. [29a, dash for contrast]

**10.** The person renting this apartment agrees to pay seven hundred fifty dollars ($750) per month in rent. [29b, parentheses for repetition of a spelled-out number]

**11.** Railroad entrepreneur George Francis Train (his real name!) dreamed of creating a chain of great cities across the United States, all connected by his Union Pacific Railroad. [29b, parentheses for interruptive aside; dashes too distracting]

**12.** Patients who pretend to have ailments are known to doctors as "Munchausens" after Baron Karl Friedrich Hieronymus von Münchhausen. (He was a German army officer who had a reputation for wild and unbelievable tales.) [29b, parentheses for interruptive explanation because explanation is separate sentence]

**ANSWERS: EXERCISE 29-3**
Answers will vary greatly. As with Exercise 29-1, peer review is a useful strategy to assist students in identifying correct usage of punctuation marks.

2. Write a sentence using parentheses to enclose a brief example.
3. Write a sentence using dashes to set off a definition.
4. Write a sentence that includes four numbered items in a list.
5. Quote a few sentences from any source you choose. Omit words without losing meaning or use brackets to insert words to maintain meaning or grammatical structure. Use ellipsis points to indicate the omission, and place the parenthetical reference where it belongs.

## HYPHEN

### 29f When do I need a hyphen in my writing?

A **hyphen** serves to divide words at the end of a line, to combine words into compounds, and to communicate numbers.

### 29g When do I use a hyphen at the end of a line?

Generally, try not to divide a word with a hyphen at the end of a line. (In printed books, hyphens are acceptable because of the limits on line length.) Word processing programs can be set either to space the words in a line (in order to avoid dividing words at the end of a line) or to hyphenate words automatically. If you must divide a word, or if the computer divides one automatically, try hard not to divide the last word on the first line of a paper, the last word in a paragraph, or the last word on a page.

When you can't avoid using a hyphen at the end of a line, break the word only between syllables. If you aren't sure about the syllables in a word, consult a dictionary. Never divide words that are short, contain only one syllable, or are pronounced as one syllable.

wealth envy screamed

Divide words between two consonants according to pronunciation.

full-ness omit-ting punc-ture

Never divide a word when only one or two letters would be left or carried over to another line.

alive touchy helicop-ter

### 29h How do I use a hyphen with prefixes and suffixes?

**Prefixes** are syllables in front of a **root**—a word's core, which carries the origin or meaning. Prefixes modify meanings. **Suffixes** also have modifying power, but they follow roots. Some prefixes and suffixes are attached to root words with hyphens, but others are not. Quick Reference 29.1 shows you how to decide.

---

**Quick Reference 29.1** ■ ■ ■ ■ ■ ■ ■ ■

### Hyphens with prefixes and suffixes

- Use hyphens after the prefixes *all-, ex-, quasi-,* and *self-.*

  **YES**    all-inclusive    self-reliant

- Never use a hyphen when *self* is a root word, not a prefix.

  **NO**    self-ishness       self-less

  **YES**    selfishness        selfless

- Use a hyphen to avoid a distracting string of letters.

  **NO**    ant**ii**ntellectual     bel**ll**ike     pr**oo**utsourcing

  **YES**    ant**i-i**ntellectual     bel**l-l**ike     pr**o-o**utsourcing

- Use a hyphen to add a prefix or suffix to a numeral or a word that starts with a capital letter.

  **NO**    post1950      proAmerican     Rembrandtlike

  **YES**    post-1950     pro-American    Rembrandt-like

- Use a hyphen before the suffix *-elect.*

  **NO**    presidentelect

  **YES**    president-elect

- Use a hyphen to prevent confusion in meaning or pronunciation.

  **YES**    re-dress (means *dress again*)        redress (means *set right*)

  **YES**    un-ionize (means *remove the ions*)    unionize (means *form a union*)

- Use a hyphen when two or more prefixes apply to one root word.

  **YES**    pre- and post-Renaissance

---

## 29i    How do I use hyphens with compound words?

A **compound word** puts two or more words together to express one concept. Compound words come in three forms: an open-compound word, as in *night shift;* hyphenated words, as in *tractor-trailer;* and a closed-compound word, as in *handbook.* Quick Reference 29.2 lists basic guidelines for positioning hyphens in compound words.

## Quick Reference 29.2

### Hyphens with compound words

- Divide a compound word already containing a hyphen only after that hyphen, if possible. Also, divide a closed-compound word only between the two complete words, if possible.

  **NO**   self-con-scious   sis-ter-in-law   mas-terpiece

  **YES**   self-conscious   sister-in-law   master-piece

- Use a hyphen between a prefix and an open-compound word.

  **NO**   antigun control [*gun control* is an open-compound word]

  **YES**   anti-gun control

- Use a hyphen for most compound words that precede a noun but not for most compound words that follow a noun.

  **YES**   well-researched report   report is well researched

- Use hyphens when a compound modifier includes a series.

  **YES**   two-, three-, or four-year program

- Never use a hyphen when a compound modifier starts with an *-ly* adverb.

  **NO**   happily-married couple   loosely-tied package

  **YES**   happily married couple   loosely tied package

- Use a hyphen with most COMPARATIVE (*-er*) and SUPERLATIVE (*-est*) compound forms, but not when the compound modifier includes *more/most* or *less/least.*

  **NO**   better fitting shoe

  **YES**   better-fitting shoe

  **NO**   least-significant factors

  **YES**   least significant factors

- Never use a hyphen when a compound modifier is a foreign phrase.

  **YES**   *post hoc* fallacies

- Never use a hyphen with a possessive compound.

  **NO**   a full-week's work   eight-hours' pay

  **YES**   a full week's work   eight hours' pay

**EXERCISE 29-4** Provide the correct form of the words in parentheses, according to the rules in 29f through 29i. Explain your reasoning for each.

1. The tiger is (all powerful) _____ in the cat family.

2. (Comparison and contrast) _____ studies of tigers and lions show that the tiger is the (more agile) _____ and powerful.

3. Male tigers and lions look similar except for their hair length: Tigers have (ultra short) _____ hair and male lions have (extra long) _____ hair in their manes.

4. The tiger's body is a (boldly striped) _____ yellow, with a white (under body) _____.

5. The Bengal tiger, the largest of the family, is aggressive and (self confident) _____.

6. In India, where the Bengal tiger is called a (village destroyer) _____, it goes (in to) _____ villages to hunt for food.

7. Entire villages have been temporarily abandoned by (terror stricken) _____ people who have seen a Bengal tiger nearby.

8. Villagers seek to protect their homes by destroying tigers with traps, (spring loaded) _____ guns, and (poisoned arrows) _____.

9. Bengal tigers are also called (cattle killers) _____, although they attack domestic animals only when they cannot find wild ones.

10. Many people who do not live near a zoo get to see tigers only in (animal shows) _____, although (pro animal) _____ activists try to prevent tigers from being used this way.

For more help with your writing, grammar, and research, go to **www.mycomplab.com**

**ANSWERS: EXERCISE 29-4**

**1.** all-powerful [*all-* prefix hyphenated]

**2.** Comparison-and-contrast [hyphenate open compound preceding noun it modifies]; **more agile** [no hyphen with *more*]

**3.** ultra-short; extra-long [in both cases, hyphenate compound before the noun]

**4.** boldly striped [no hyphen after *-ly* adverb in a compound modifier]; underbody [*under-* prefix spelled closed]

**5.** self-confident [*self-* prefix hyphenated]

**6.** village destroyer [open compound]; **into** [closed compound]

**7.** terror-stricken [hyphenate compound before the noun]

**8.** spring-loaded [hyphenate compound before the noun]; poisoned arrows [not a compound]

**9.** cattle killers [open compound]

**10.** animal shows [not a compound]; pro-animal [*pro-* prefix hyphenated before vowel]

# 30

# Capitals, Italics, Abbreviations, and Numbers

## CAPITALS

## BACKGROUND

The terms *uppercase* and *lowercase* originally referred to the drawers, or cases, that held the fonts in a print shop. Although the use of capital letters is still not fully standardized, by the seventeenth century, the spread of printing had made it regular practice to place capital letters at the beginnings of sentences and of proper names and titles. Before the advent of printing, lowercase characters, a full set of which existed by the sixth century, were generally mixed with uppercase ones, and large letters, though not necessarily uppercase letters, were used to mark the beginning of a sentence.

## TEACHING TIP

Because capitalization practice sometimes varies from one publisher to another, and even from one instructor to another, writers must be aware of the basic rules that are in general use but should stand prepared to adjust minor matters, depending on the guidelines under which they are working at the time. Students should also be aware that capitalization (as well as research documentation and other conventions of the mechanics of writing) varies from one discipline to another, which makes it necessary for students to be alert to the requirements of the situation in which they are writing.

ESOL students may need special attention when they are learning capitalization conventions in English, since practices are not the same in all languages. German, for instance, capitalizes all nouns, whereas English does not. Many Asian and Middle Eastern languages have no capital letters at all.

## BACKGROUND

Some readers of *Time* have wondered why the magazine does not capitalize the name of the planet earth, since the editors do capitalize other planets, such as Venus and Pluto. Here is the magazine's editorial reply (June 12, 1989): "Following grammatical rules for capitalizing proper names, we uppercase those celestial bodies named after mythological gods. Inasmuch as the earth, the moon, and the sun have no mythical forebears, they remain lowercase."

## 30a  When do I capitalize a "first" word?

### FIRST WORD IN A SENTENCE

Always capitalize the first letter of the first word in a sentence.

> Four inches of snow fell last winter.

### A SERIES OF QUESTIONS

If questions in a series are complete sentences, start each with a capital letter. If, however, the questions aren't complete sentences, you can choose to capitalize or not. Whatever your choice, be consistent in each piece of writing. In this handbook, we use capitals for a series of questions.

> What facial feature would most people like to change? Eyes? Ears? Nose?

> What facial feature would most people like to change? eyes? ears? nose?

### SMALL WORDS IN TITLES OR HEADINGS

Capitalize small words (*the, a, an,* and short PREPOSITIONS such as *of, to*) in a title or heading only when they begin the title or when the source capitalizes these small words.

Always capitalize *I*, no matter where it falls in a sentence or group of words: *I love you now, although I didn't use to.* The same holds for *O*, the INTERJECTION: *You are, O my fair love, a burning fever; O my gentle love, embrace me.* In contrast, never capitalize the interjection *oh,* unless it starts a sentence or is capitalized in words you're quoting.

### AFTER A COLON

When a complete sentence follows a colon, you can choose to start that sentence with either a capital or a lowercase letter, but be consistent in each piece of writing. When the words after a colon are not a complete sentence, do not capitalize.

> She reacted instantly: She picked up the ice cream and pushed it back into her cone.

> She reacted instantly: she picked up the ice cream and pushed it back into her cone.

> She bought four pints of ice cream: vanilla, chocolate, strawberry, and butter pecan.

**Alert:** A colon can follow only a complete sentence (an INDEPENDENT CLAUSE; see 26a). ●

### FORMAL OUTLINE

In a formal outline, start each item with a capital letter. Use a period only when the item is a complete sentence.

## 30b When do I use capitals with listed items?

### A LIST RUN INTO A SENTENCE

If run-in listed items are complete sentences, start each with a capital and end each with a period (or question mark or exclamation point). If the run-in listed items are incomplete sentences, start each with a lowercase letter and end each with a comma—unless the items already contain commas, in which case use semicolons. If you list three or more items that are incomplete sentences, use *and* before the last item.

> **YES** We found three reasons for the delay: (1) Bad weather held up delivery of materials. (2) Poor scheduling created confusion. (3) Improper machine maintenance caused an equipment failure.

> **YES** The reasons for the delay were (1) bad weather, (2) poor scheduling, and (3) equipment failure.

> **YES** The reasons for the delay were (1) bad weather, which had been predicted; (2) poor scheduling, which is the airline's responsibility; and (3) equipment failure, which no one can predict.

### A DISPLAYED LIST

In a displayed list, each item starts on a new line. If the items are sentences, capitalize the first letter and end with a period (or question mark or exclamation point). If the items are not sentences, you can use a capital letter or not. Whichever you choose, be consistent in each piece of writing. Punctuate a displayed list as you would a run-in list.

in the 1930s, he was not aware that it had been used in some cultures for up to 4,000 years. *the* technique of applying electrical eels to the head of a patient is referred to in the writings of *aristotle, pliny,* and *plutarch. what* kinds of results do therapists in other cultures—witch doctors—achieve? a *canadian* psychiatrist, *dr. raymond prince,* spent 17 months studying 46 *nigerian* witch doctors and judged that the therapeutic results were about equal to those obtained in *north american* clinics and hospitals.

—Edwin Fuller Torrey, *The Mind Game*

**TEACHING TIP**

You might find that students overcapitalize in their writing. Comparison can be a useful tool in encouraging them to distinguish between common and proper nouns. First, review the basic rule: Proper (capitalized) nouns are the official names of specific people, places, or things; common (uncapitalized) nouns refer more generally to people, places, or things. Then, give students pairs of noun phrases, one of which contains a proper noun and one a common noun. Omit all capitals. Ask students to identify and capitalize the proper noun: *president washington, the president of the country; hunter high school, the high school band; a new car, a cadillac seville; psychological testing, psychology 101.* Augment this list with pairs representing your students' most common errors.

Your students will probably find this rather easy because contrast highlights the specific nouns. The next step can be to make up or edit a paragraph to eliminate all capital letters except those that begin sentences. Ask students to capitalize the first letters of all proper nouns.

You might also ask students to bring in some examples of their own informal writing—text messages and e-mails—to discuss how they use capitalization (or don't) in their informal writing. You might also discuss with students some of the differences between using capitalization for emphasis in an e-mail (sometimes known as "shouting") versus using the formal rules of capitalization.

YES  We found three reasons for the delay:
1. Bad weather held up delivery of materials.
2. Poor scheduling created confusion.
3. Improper machine maintenance caused an equipment failure.

YES  The reasons for the delay were
1. bad weather,
2. poor scheduling, and
3. equipment failure.

**Alerts:** (1) If a complete sentence leads into a displayed list, you can end the sentence with a colon. However, if an incomplete sentence leads into a displayed list, use no punctuation. (2) Use PARALLELISM for items in a list. For example, if one item is a sentence, use sentences for all the items (10e); or if one item starts with a VERB, start all items with a verb in the same TENSE; and so on. ●

## 30c  When do I use capitals with sentences in parentheses?

When you write a complete sentence within parentheses that falls within another sentence, don't start with a capital or end with a period—but do use a question mark or exclamation point, if needed. When you write a sentence within parentheses that doesn't fall within another sentence, capitalize the first word and end with a period (or question mark or exclamation point).

I did not know till years later that they called it the Cuban Missile Crisis. But I remember Castro. (We called him Castor Oil and were awed by his beard.) We might not have worried so much (what would the communists want with our small New Hampshire town?) except we lived 10 miles from a U.S. air base.

—Joyce Maynard, "An 18-Year-Old Looks Back on Life"

## 30d  When do I use capitals with quotations?

If a quotation within your sentence is itself less than a complete sentence, never capitalize the first quoted word. If the quotation you have used in your sentence is itself a complete sentence, capitalize the first word.

Mrs. Enriquez says that students who are learning a new language should visit that country and "absorb a good accent with the food."

Talking about students who live in a new country Mrs. Enriquez says, "They'll absorb a good accent with the food."

When you write DIRECT DISCOURSE—which you introduce with verbs such as *said, stated, reported,* and others (see 35k) followed by a comma, capitalize the first letter of the quoted words. However, never capitalize a partial quotation, and never capitalize the continuation of a one-sentence quotation within your sentence.

Mrs. Enriquez said, "Students who are learning a new language should visit that country. They'll absorb a good accent with the food." [complete sentence]

Mrs. Enriquez told me that the best way to "absorb a good accent" in a language is to visit the country and eat its food. [part of a quotation integrated in a sentence]

"Of course," she continued with a smile, "the accent lasts longer than the food." [continuation of a one-sentence quotation]

## 30e  When do I capitalize nouns and adjectives?

Capitalize PROPER NOUNS (nouns that name specific people, places, and things): *Abraham Lincoln, Mexico, World Wide Web.* Also, capitalize **proper adjectives** (adjectives formed from proper nouns): *a Mexican entrepreneur, a Web address.* Don't capitalize ARTICLES (*the, a, an*) that accompany proper nouns and proper adjectives, unless they start a sentence.

When a proper noun or adjective loses its very specific "proper" association, it also loses its capital letter: *french fries, pasteurized.* When you turn a common noun (*lake*) into a proper noun (*Lake Mead*), capitalize all words.

Expect sometimes that you'll see capitalized words that this handbook says not to capitalize. For example, a corporation's written communications usually capitalize its own entities (*our Board of Directors or this Company*), even though the rule calls for lowercase (*the board of directors, the company*). Similarly, the administrators of your school might write *the Faculty* and *the College* (or *the University*), even though the rule calls for a lowercase *f, c,* and *u.* How writers capitalize can depend on AUDIENCE and PURPOSE in each specific context.

Quick Reference 30.1 is a capitalization guide. If you don't find what you need, locate an item in it (or in Quick Reference 30.2 on page 492) that's close to what you want, and use it as a model.

**TEACHING TIP**
The interactive quiz on capitalization at the Capital Community College site is an engaging way for students to review this material; see <http://www.grammar.ccc.commnet.edu/grammar/cgi-shl/par_numberless_quiz.pl/caps_quiz.htm>.

**TEACHING TIP**
The variety of computer fonts available today, together with increasing emphasis on visual presentation of print and nonprint media from business documents to Web sites, results in many departures from conventional rules of capitalization. An article online may well be titled "capital lessons for the capital letter," all words in lowercase type. A business document may use SMALL CAPS or even ALL CAPS to bring emphasis to a concept or to signal a new topic. You may want to have students collect several such examples and show how they would appear under conventional rules of capitalization. Ask your students to observe how MLA, APA, and other style manuals ask writers to "translate" titles from one style of capitalization to another.

**QUOTATION: ON WRITING**
Some readers think my writing is a capital offense. Others think it is capital fun. I hope it converts into capital.
—Diana Davis

**ESOL TEACHING TIP**
Some students write in languages that have very different rules for capitalization than American English. Students with a second language background will find detailed rules about capitalization and an emphasis on standardization particularly useful.

**Quick Reference 30.1**  ■ ■ ■ ■ ■ ■ ■

## Capitalization

|  | Capitals | Lowercase Letters |
|---|---|---|
| NAMES | Mother Teresa (*also, used as names:* Mother, Dad, Mom, Pa) | my mother [relationship] |
|  | Doc Holliday | the doctor [role] |
| TITLES | President Truman | the president |
|  | Democrat [party member] | a democrat [believer in democracy] |
|  | Representative Harold Ford | the congressional representative |
|  | Senator Edward M. Kennedy | a senator |
|  | Queen Elizabeth II | the queen |
| GROUPS OF PEOPLE | Caucasian [race] | white, black [*also* White, Black] |
|  | African American, Hispanic [ethnic group] | |
|  | Irish, Korean, Canadian [nationality] | |
|  | Jewish, Catholic, Protestant, Buddhist [religious affiliation] | |
| ORGANIZATIONS | Congress | the legislative branch of the US government |
|  | the Ohio State Supreme Court | the state supreme court |
|  | the Republican Party | the party |
|  | National Gypsum Company | the company |
|  | Chicago Cubs | a baseball team |
|  | American Medical Association | a professional group |
|  | Sigma Chi | a fraternity |
|  | Alcoholics Anonymous | a self-help group |
| PLACES | Los Angeles | the city |
|  | the South [region] | turn south [direction] |
|  | the West Coast | the US states along the western seaboard |
|  | Main Street | the street |
|  | Atlantic Ocean | the ocean |
|  | the Black Hills | the hills |

continued >>

## Quick Reference 30.1 (continued)

|  | **Capitals** | **Lowercase Letters** |
|---|---|---|
| BUILDINGS | the Capitol [in Washington, DC] | the state capitol |
|  | Ace High School | a high school |
|  | Front Road Café | a restaurant |
|  | Highland Hospital | a hospital |
| SCIENTIFIC TERMS | Earth [as one of nine planets] | the earth [otherwise] |
|  | the Milky Way, the Galaxy [as name] | our galaxy, the moon, the sun |
|  | *Streptococcus aureus* | a streptococcal infection |
|  | Gresham's law | the theory of relativity |
| LANGUAGES, SCHOOL COURSES | Spanish, Chinese | |
|  | Chemistry 342 | a chemistry course |
|  | History 111 | my history class |
|  | Introduction to Photography | a photography course |
| NAMES OF SPECIFIC THINGS | Black Parrot tulip | a climbing rose |
|  | Purdue University | the university |
|  | Heinz ketchup | ketchup, sauce |
|  | a Toyota Camry | a car |
|  | Twelfth Dynasty | the dynasty |
|  | the *Boston Globe* | a newspaper |
| TIMES, SEASONS, HOLIDAYS | Monday, Fri. | today |
|  | September, February | a month |
|  | the Roaring Twenties | the decade |
|  | the Christmas season | spring, summer, autumn, winter, the fall semester |
|  | Kwanzaa, New Year's Day | a feast day, the holiday |
|  | Passover, Ramadan | a religious holiday or observance |
| HISTORICAL EVENTS AND DOCUMENTS | World War II | the war |
|  | Battle of the Bulge | the battle |
|  | the Great Depression (of the 1930s) | the depression [any serious economic downturn] |
|  | the Reformation | the eighteenth century |
|  | Paleozoic | an era or age, prehistory |
|  | the Bill of Rights | fifth-century manuscripts |

continued >>

**QUOTATION: ON WRITING**

Mechanics are a necessary part of the writing process. Without them the most profound statements would be misunderstood, but with them, sentences take on clarity. Mechanics tell us when new sentences begin, when they end, and when we should pause in our reading. Mechanics signal us when different ideas will be presented. They indicate when the words of another have been used and when people and places have been named. In short, they make an essay a finished product ready to be displayed in public.

—Andrew Hirt

**ANSWERS: EXERCISE 30-1**

If a word needs to start with a capital letter, the *whole word* is italicized here to be clearly seen.

**1.** The state of *California* is best known as *The Golden State,* but other nicknames include *The Land of Milk* and *Honey, The El Dorado State,* and *The Grape State.*

**2.** Most people think of *San* Francisco as northern *California,* but the city of Eureka, from the *Greek* word meaning "I have found it," is 280 miles north of *San* Francisco, and the state line is another 90 miles north of *Eureka.*

**3.** South of *San* Francisco on the *California* coast is *Santa* Barbara, which hosts the annual Dickens Universe, a weeklong series of studies and celebrations of the works of the famous writer *Charles Dickens.*

**4.** The highest point in the continental United States is *Mt.* Whitney at 14,495 feet high, and the lowest place in the continental United States is *Bad* Water in *Death Valley* at 282 feet below sea level, both located in *California.*

**5.** Having approximately 500,000 detectable seismic tremors per year, *California* rocks, literally.

**Quick Reference 30.1**     (continued)

| | Capitals | Lowercase Letters |
|---|---|---|
| **RELIGIOUS TERMS** | Athena, God | a goddess, a god |
| | Islam | a religion |
| | the Torah, the Koran (or Qur'an) | a holy book |
| | the Bible | biblical |
| **LETTER PARTS** | Dear Ms. Schultz: Sincerely, Yours truly, | |
| **PUBLISHED AND RELEASED MATERIAL** | "The Lottery" | [Capitalize first letter of first word and all other major words] |
| | *A History of the United States to 1877* | |
| | *Jazz on Ice* | the show, a performance |
| | Nixon Papers | the archives |
| | Mass in B Minor | the B minor mass |
| **ACRONYMS AND INITIALISMS** | NASA, NATO, UCLA, AFL-CIO, DNA | |
| **COMPUTER TERMS** | Gateway, Dell | a computer company |
| | Microsoft Word, WordPerfect | computer software |
| | Netscape Navigator | a browser |
| | the Internet | a computer network |
| | World Wide Web, the Web | www |
| | Web site, Web page | a home page, a link |
| **PROPER ADJECTIVES** | Victorian | southern |
| | Midwestern | transatlantic |
| | Indo-European | alpine |

● **EXERCISE 30-1**    Individually or with a group, add capital letters as needed. See 30a through 30e for help.

1. The state of california is best known as the golden state, but other nicknames include the land of milk and honey, the el dorado state, and the grape state.

2. Most people think of san Francisco as northern california, but the city of Eureka, from the greek word meaning "I have found it," is 280 miles north of san Francisco, and the state line is another 90 miles north of eureka.

3. South of san Francisco on the california coast is santa Barbara, which hosts the annual Dickens Universe, a weeklong series of studies and celebrations of the famous writer charles dickens.

4. The highest point in the contiguous United States is mt. Whitney at 14,495 feet high, and the lowest place in the contiguous United States is bad Water in death valley at 282 feet below sea level, both located in california.

5. Having approximately 500,000 detectable seismic tremors per year, california rocks, literally.

6. Because the tehema county fairgrounds are located in red bluff, california hosts the largest three-day rodeo in the united States.

7. Numerous songs have been written about california, including "california girls" by the beach boys and the theme of the tv show *the beverly hillbillies.*

8. san Bernardino county with almost three million acres is the largest county in the united states.

9. Hollywood and movie stars are what many people associate california with, and well they might because two of California's governors, ronald reagan and arnold schwarzenegger, were actors before they became governors.

10. When told all these fantastic facts about california, a stereotypical valley girl would respond, "whatever."

**6.** Because the *Tehema County Fairgrounds* are located in *Red Bluff, California* hosts the largest three-day rodeo in the *United* States.

**7.** Numerous songs have been written about *California,* including "*California Girls*" by the *Beach Boys* and the theme of the *TV* show *The Beverly Hillbillies.*

**8.** *San Bernardino County* with almost three million acres is the largest county in the *United States.*

**9.** Hollywood and movie stars are what many people associate *California* with, and well they might because two of California's governors, *Ronald Reagan* and *Arnold Schwarzenegger,* were actors before they became governors.

**10.** When told all these fantastic facts about *California,* a typical *Valley* girl would respond, "*Whatever.*"

## ITALICS

## 30f What are italics?

**Italic typeface** slants to the right (*like this*); **roman typeface** does not (like this). MLA STYLE requires italics, not underlining, in all documents.

|  |  |
|---|---|
| **ROMAN** | your writing |
| **ITALICS** | *your writing* |

## 30g How do I choose between using italics and quotation marks?

As a rule, use italics for titles of long works ( *Juno,* a movie) or for works that contain subsections (*Masterpiece Theater,* a television show). Generally, use quotation marks for titles of shorter works ("Smells like Teen Spirit," a song) and for titles of subsections within longer works such as books (Chapter 1, "Loomings").

Quick Reference 30.2 is a guide for using italics, quotation marks, or nothing. If you don't find what you need, locate an item that is as much like what you want as possible and use it as a model.

**BACKGROUND**

The three basic type forms are gothic, old-style roman, and modern roman. (There are many variations of these basic ones.) Italic type is a companion form of modern roman, one that is lighter and slopes to the right. The earliest type forms were based on contemporary manuscript hands, for the printer was replacing the scribe. The old-style roman form reached its zenith in the fifteenth century, and in 1501, Aldus Manutius of Venice produced and used the first italic form in the printing of a series of Latin texts, the first volume of which was called *Aldine Virgil.* The "modern" roman form, the kind of type most used in Western publishing today, originated about 1693 with Philippe Grandjean. Benjamin Franklin was responsible for introducing a variety of roman type, designed by William Caslon, to the American colonies. The Declaration of Independence was printed using it. The early type founders were artists who were concerned about the aesthetics of their typefaces. In the nineteenth century, however, emphasis shifted from artistry to quantity, and attention to the beauty of printed letters suffered a decline.

## EXTRA EXERCISE B

What is the difference in meaning suggested by the following changes in the italicized words? (Answers will vary.)

**1. a.** Six *different* bodies compose the United Nations.

**b.** Six different bodies compose the *United Nations.*

**2. a.** All members of the UN can send *five* representatives to the General Assembly.

**b.** All members of the UN can send five representatives to the *General Assembly.*

**3. a.** The *primary* responsibility of the Security Council is to maintain international peace and security.

**b.** The primary responsibility of the Security Council is to maintain *international* peace and security.

## TEACHING TIP

In more informal writing, italics are often used to indicate irony and humor. Consider using examples from blogs and newspaper editorials to demonstrate how italics can be a stylistic choice in informal writing.

## ADDITIONAL EXAMPLES: ITALICS

Can your students cite the rule governing the following italicized words?

**1.** *Hamlet* is still one of the world's most frequently produced plays.

**2.** Several magazines, such as *TV Guide* and *U.S. News & World Report,* have significantly changed their format in recent years.

**3.** Some people prefer to keep up with current events by watching the *CBS Evening News* instead of reading *USA Today.*

**4.** The reruns of *Star Trek* continue to attract viewers.

**5.** The *Challenger* and *Columbia* disasters will be long remembered.

**6.** My grandfather always told me, "Mind your *p*'s and *q*'s, young man!"

**7.** The literary works of the *fin de siècle* were shocking to many readers.

---

### Quick Reference 30.2

#### Italics, quotation marks, or nothing

| Italics | Quotation Marks or Nothing |
|---|---|
| **TITLES AND NAMES** | |
| *Sense and Sensibility* [a novel] | title of student essay |
| *Death of a Salesman* [a play] | act 2 [part of a play] |
| *A Beautiful Mind* [a film] | the Epilogue [a part of a film or book] |
| *Collected Works of O. Henry* [a book] | "The Last Leaf" [a story in a book] |
| *Simon & Schuster Handbook for Writers* [a textbook] | "Agreement" [a chapter in a book] |
| *The Prose Reader* [a collection of essays] | "Putting in a Good Word for Guilt" [an essay] |
| *Iliad* [a book-length poem] | "Nothing Gold Can Stay" [a short poem] |
| *Scientific American* [a magazine] | "The Molecules of Life" [an article in a magazine] |
| *Symphonie Fantastique* [a long musical work] | Violin Concerto No. 2 in B-flat Minor [a musical work identified by form, number, and key—neither quotation marks nor italics] |
| *U2 18 Singles* [an album] | "With or Without You" [a song] |
| *Lost* [a television series] | "Something Nice Back Home" [an episode of a television series] |
| *Kids Count* [a Web site title] the *Los Angeles Times* [a newspaper]* | Excel [a software program] |
| **OTHER WORDS** | |
| *semper fidelis* [words in a language other than English] | burrito, chutzpah [widely understood non-English words] |
| What does *our* imply? [a word meant as a word] | |
| the *abc*'s; the letter *x* [letters meant as letters] | 6s and 7s; & [numerals and symbols] |

*When *The* is part of a newspaper's title, don't capitalize or italicize it in MLA-style or CM-style documentation. In APA-style and CSE-style documentation, capitalize and italicize *The.*

## 30h Can I use italics for special emphasis?

Some professional writers, especially writers of nonfiction and self-help material, occasionally use italics to clarify a meaning or stress a point. In ACADEMIC WRITING, however, you're expected to convey special emphasis through your choice of words and sentence structure, not with italics (or underlining). If your message absolutely calls for it, use italics sparingly—and only after you're sure nothing else will do.

> Many people we *think* are powerful turn out on closer examination to be merely frightened and anxious.
>
> —Michael Korda, *Power!*

**EXERCISE 30-2** Edit these sentences for correct use of italics (or underlining), quotation marks, and capitals. For help, consult 30a through 30h.

1. The article "the Banjo" in the Encyclopaedia Britannica calls the Banjo "America's only national instrument" because it combines the traditional mbanza (an instrument native to certain southern areas of africa) and some European stringed instruments.

2. The writer of a humor column at a newspaper called The "Globe and Mail" has described an imaginary newspaper called The mop and pail, where things are more ridiculous than in Real Life.

3. "Porgy and Bess," a Folk Opera by George and ira Gershwin and Du Bose Heyward, introduced the beautiful, haunting song *Summertime*.

4. Marlon Brando persuaded the Director of *The Godfather* to cast him as the Elderly don Corleone by auditioning with cotton-stuffed cheeks and mumbling hoarsely.

5. When the name of a Small Business begins with the letter a repeated many times, as in AAAAAbc "Auto Body," we know its marketing plan includes being listed First in the telephone directory.

## ABBREVIATIONS

## 30i What are standard practices for using abbreviations?

Some abbreviations are standard in all writing circumstances (*Mr.*, not *Mister,* in a name; *St.* Louis, the city, not *Saint* Louis). In some situations, you may have a choice whether to abbreviate or spell out a word. Choose what seems suited to your PURPOSE for writing and your AUDIENCE, and be consistent within each piece of writing.

8. English has borrowed many words from other languages, including *chauffeur, taco,* and *moccasin.*

9. *The Red Badge of Courage* is a modern epic.

10. The *Titanic* was originally thought to be invulnerable.

**ANSWERS: EXERCISE 30-2**
Corrected words appear underlined here. Corrections to capitals are in boldface.

**1.** The article "**T**he Banjo" in the *Encyclopaedia Britannica* calls the banjo "America's only national instrument" because it combines the traditional *mbanza* (an instrument native to certain southern areas of **A**frica) and some European stringed instruments.

**2.** The writer of a humor column at a newspaper called the *Globe and Mail* has described an imaginary newspaper called the *Mop and Pail,* where things are more ridiculous than in real life.

**3.** *Porgy and Bess,* a folk opera by George and Ira Gershwin and Du Bose Heyward, introduced the beautiful, haunting song "Summertime."

**4.** Marlon Brando persuaded the director of *The Godfather* to cast him as the elderly Don Corleone by auditioning with cotton-stuffed cheeks and mumbling hoarsely.

**5.** When the name of a small business begins with the letter *a* repeated many times, as in AAAAAbc Auto Body, we know its marketing plan includes being listed first in the telephone directory.

| NO | The great painter Vincent Van Gogh was **b.** in Holland in 1853, but he lived most of his life and died in **Fr.** |
|---|---|
| YES | The great painter Vincent Van Gogh was **born** in Holland in 1853, but he lived most of his life and died in **France.** |
| NO | Our field hockey team left after Casey's **psych** class on **Tues., Oct.** 10, but the flight had to make an unexpected stop (in **Chi.**) before reaching **L.A.** |
| YES | Our field hockey team left after Casey's **psychology** class on **Tuesday, October** 10, but the flight had to make an unexpected stop (in **Chicago**) before reaching **Los Angeles.** |
| NO | Please confirm in writing your order for one **doz.** helmets in **lg** and **x-lg.** |
| YES | Please confirm in writing your order for one **dozen** helmets in **large** and **extra large.** |

**Alerts:** (1) Many abbreviations call for periods (*Mrs., Ms., Dr.*), but the practice is changing. The trend today is to drop the periods (*PS,* not *P.S.; MD,* not *M.D.; US,* not *U.S.*), yet firm rules are still evolving.

(2) **Acronyms** (pronounceable words formed from the initials of a name) generally have no periods: *NASA* (National Aeronautics and Space Administration) and *AIDS* (*a*cquired *i*mmune *d*eficiency *s*yndrome).

(3) **Initialisms** (names spoken as separate letters) usually have no periods (*IBM, ASPCA, UN*).

(4) US Postal abbreviations for states have no periods (30k).

(5) When the final period of an abbreviation falls at the end of a sentence, that period serves also to end the sentence. ●

## 30j How do I use abbreviations with months, time, eras, and symbols?

**MONTHS**

According to MLA STYLE, abbreviations for months belong only in "Works Cited" lists, tables, charts, and the like. Write out the full spelling, never the abbreviation, in your ACADEMIC WRITING.

**TIMES**

Use the abbreviations *a.m.* and *p.m.* only with exact times: *7:15 a.m.; 3:47 p.m.* Although some publication styles use the capitalized versions, *A.M.* and *P.M.,* MLA style calls for the use of lowercase letters.

**!** Alert: Never use *a.m.* and *p.m.* in place of the words *morning, evening,* and *night.*

NO  My hardest final exam is in the **a.m.** tomorrow, but by early **p.m.**, I'll be ready to study for the rest of my finals.

YES  My hardest final exam is in the **morning** tomorrow, but by early **evening**, I'll be ready to study for the rest of my finals. ●

### ERAS

In MLA style, use capital letters, without periods, in abbreviations for eras. Some writers prefer using *CE* ("common era") in place of *AD* (Latin for *anno Domini,* "in the year of our Lord") as the more inclusive term. In addition, many writers prefer using *BCE* ("before the common era") in place of *BC* ("before Christ").

When writing the abbreviations for eras, place *AD* before the year (*AD 476*) and all the others after the year (*29 BC; 165 BCE; 1100 CE*).

### SYMBOLS

In MLA style, decide whether to use symbols or spelled-out words according to your topic and the focus of your document (see also 30m). However, never use a freestanding symbol, such as *$, %,* or *¢* in your sentences; always use it with a numeral. With many exceptions, spell out both the symbol and the numeral accompanying it (*twenty centimeters*), unless the number is more than one or two words (*345 centimeters,* not *three hundred forty-five centimeters*).

The exceptions include *$18; 7 lbs.; 24 KB; 6:34 a.m., 5″; 32°*; and numbers in addresses, dates, page references, and decimal fractions (*8.3*). In writing about money, the form *$25 million* is an acceptable combination of symbol, numeral, and spelled-out word.

In confined spaces, such as charts and tables, use symbols with numerals (*20¢*). In documents that focus on technical matters, use numerals but spell out the unit of measurement (*2,500 pounds*)—in MLA style. In other documentation styles, such as APA, CM, and CSE, the guidelines differ somewhat, so you need to check each style's manual.

## 30k  How do I use abbreviations for other elements?

### TITLES

Use either a title of address before a name (**Dr.** *Daniel Klausner*) or an academic degree after a name (*Daniel Klausner,* **PhD**), not both. However, because *Jr., Sr., II, III,* and so forth are part of a given name, you can use both titles of address and academic degree abbreviations: *Dr. Martin Luther King Jr.; Gavin Alexander II, MD.*

🛇 **Alerts:** (1) Insert a comma both before and after an academic degree that follows a person's name, unless it falls at the end of a sentence: *Joshua Coleman, LLD, is our guest speaker,* or *Our guest speaker is Joshua Coleman, LLD.* (2) Never put a comma before an abbreviation that is part of a given name: *Steven Elliott Sr., Douglas Young III.* ●

## NAMES AND TERMS

If you use a term frequently in a piece of writing, follow these guidelines: The first time you use the term, spell it out completely and then put its abbreviation in parentheses immediately after. In later references, use the abbreviation alone.

Spain voted to continue as a member of the **North Atlantic Treaty Organization (NATO)**, to the surprise of other **NATO** members.

When referring to the United States, use the abbreviation *US* as a modifier before a noun (*the US ski team*), but spell out *United States* when you use it as a noun (*the ski team from the **United States***).

## ADDRESSES

If you include a full address in a piece of writing, use the two-letter postal abbreviation for the state name. For any other combination of a city and a state, or a state by itself, spell out the state name; never abbreviate it.

🛇 **Alert:** When you write the names of a US city and state within a sentence, use a comma before and after the state.

NO    Portland, Oregon is much larger than Portland, Maine.

YES    Portland, Oregon, is much larger than Portland, Maine.

If you include a ZIP code, however, don't use a comma after the state. Do place the comma after the ZIP code. ●

## SCHOLARLY WRITING (MLA STYLE)

MLA style permits abbreviations for a selection of scholarly terms. These are listed in Quick Reference 30.3. Never use them in the body of your ACADEMIC WRITING. Reserve them for your "Works Cited" lists and for any notes you might write in a separate list at the end of your research paper.

## Quick Reference 30.3

■ ■ ■ ■ ■ ■ ■

### Major scholarly abbreviations—MLA style

| | | | |
|---|---|---|---|
| **anon.** | anonymous | **i.e.** | that is |
| **b.** | born | **ms., mss.** | manuscript, |
| **c.** *or* © | copyright | | manuscripts |
| **c.** *or* **ca.** | circa *or* about | **NB** | note well (*nota bene*) |
| | [with dates] | **n.d.** | no date (of |
| **cf.** | compare | | publication) |
| **col., cols.** | column, columns | **p., pp.** | page, pages |
| **d.** | died | **par.** | paragraph |
| **ed., eds.** | edition, edited by, | **pref.** | preface, preface by |
| | editor(s) | **rept.** | report, reported by |
| **e.g.** | for example | **rev.** | review, reviewed by; |
| **esp.** | especially | | revised, revised by |
| **et al.** | and others | **sec., secs.** | section, sections |
| **ff.** | following pages, | **v.** *or* **vs.** | versus [*v.* in legal |
| | following lines, | | cases] |
| | folios | **vol., vols.** | volume, volumes |

## 30l When can I use *etc.?*

The abbreviation *etc.* comes from the Latin *et cetera,* meaning "and the rest." In ACADEMIC WRITING, don't use *etc.* Accepted substitutes include *and the like, and so on, and so forth,* among others. Even better is a more concrete description. An acceptable use of *etc.* is in tables and charts.

> **NO** We took paper plates, plastic forks, **etc.,** to the picnic.
>
> **YES** We took paper plates, plastic forks, **and other disposable items** to the picnic.

🔔 **Alert:** If you do write *etc.,* always put a comma after the period if the abbreviation falls in the middle of a sentence. ●

**EXERCISE 30-3** Working individually or with a group, revise these sentences for correct use of abbreviations. For help, consult 30i through 30l.

1. Originally named the Geo. S. Parker Company, located in Salem, Mass., the toy co. changed its name to Parker Bros. when Chas. joined the business in 1888.

2. Sev. of their games have become quite famous, esp. Monopoly and Clue, both of which were released in the 20th cent.

**ANSWERS: EXERCISE 30-3**
The corrected abbreviations are shown here in italics.

**1.** Originally named the *George* S. Parker Company, located in Salem, *Massachusetts,* the toy *company* changed its name to Parker *Brothers* when *Charles* joined the business in 1888.

**2.** *Several* of their games have become quite famous, *especially* Monopoly and Clue, both of which were released in the *twentieth century.*

**3.** The *object* of the game Monopoly (meaning "dominating the *market*") is to get the most *money* by purchasing, renting, *and* selling real estate.

4. Clue, another *popular board* game, is a murder *mystery* in which players move from *one room* to another, making accusations to reveal the *identity* of the murderer, the weapon used, and the room where the crime took place.

5. On a cold day in *January,* when the snow is *three feet deep* and it's dark by *five,* passing the *hours* with your *family* and friends playing a board game is great fun.

### BACKGROUND

Conventions for written numbers differ from place to place and from one institution to another. Where Americans use a decimal point to separate numbers, for example, Europeans use a comma; in Britain, an earlier practice called for a raised dot in that position. The traveler should also be aware that dates are cited in a different way in some other countries. The American who invites a British friend to a spring picnic on 6/1/04, the first day of June, will cause some confusion, because the invited person will assume the event is to take place in the snow, planned, as it seems, for January 6. The American military follows the European practice, even in letters, using as a heading, for instance, 2 July 2004 instead of July 2, 2004.

3. The obj. of the game Monopoly (meaning "dominating the mkt.") is to get the most $ by purchasing, renting, & selling real est.

4. Clue, another pop. brd. game, is a murder mys. in which players move from 1 rm. to another, making accusations to reveal the i.d. of the murderer, the weapon used, and the room where the crime took place.

5. On a cold day in Jan., when the snow is 3 ft. deep and it's dark by early eve., passing the hrs. with your fam. and friends playing a board game is great fun.

## NUMBERS

### 30m When do I use spelled-out numbers?

Your decision to write a number as a word or as a figure depends on what you're referring to and how often numbers occur in your piece of writing. The guidelines we give in this handbook are for MLA STYLE, which focuses on writing in the humanities. For other disciplines, follow the guidelines in their style manuals.

When you write numbers for more than one category in a piece of writing, reserve figures for some categories of numbers and spelled-out words for other categories. Never mix spelled-out numbers and figures for a particular category.

**NO** In **four** days, our volunteers increased from **five** to **eight** to **17** to **233**.

**YES** In **four** days, our volunteers increased from **5** to **8** to **17** to **233**. [Numbers referring to volunteers are in numerals, while *four* is spelled out because it refers to a different category: days.]

**Alert:** When you write a two-word number, use a hyphen between the spelled-out words, starting with *twenty-one* and continuing through *ninety-nine.*

If you use numbers infrequently in a document, spell out all numbers that call for no more than two words: *fifty-two cards, twelve hundred students.* If you use specific numbers often in a document (temperatures when writing about climate, percentages in an economics essay, or other specific measurements of time, distance, and other quantities), use figures: *36 inches, 11 nanoseconds.* If you give only an approximation, spell out the numbers: *About twelve inches of snow fell.*

In the humanities, the names of centuries are always spelled out: *the eighteenth century.*

When you write for courses in the humanities, never start a sentence with a figure. Spell out the number—or better still, revise the sentence so that the number doesn't need to fall at the beginning. For practices in other disciplines, consult their manuals.

**NO**    $375 **dollars** for each credit is the tuition rate for nonresidents.

**YES**    **Three hundred seventy-five dollars** for each credit is the tuition rate for nonresidents.

**YES**    The tuition rate for nonresidents is $375 for each credit.

## 30n   What are standard practices for writing numbers?

Quick Reference 30.4 shows standard practices for writing numbers. Consider it a basic guide, and rely on the manual of each documentation style for answers to other questions you may have.

| Quick Reference 30.4 | |
| --- | --- |
| **Specific numbers in writing** | |
| **DATES** | August 6, 1941 |
| | 1732–1845 |
| | from 34 BC to AD 230 (*or* 34 BCE to 230 CE) |
| **ADDRESSES** | 10 Downing Street |
| | 237 North 8th Street |
| | Export Falls, MN 92025 |
| **TIMES** | 8:09 a.m., 6:00 p.m. |
| | six o'clock (*not* 6 o'clock) |
| | four in the afternoon *or* 4 p.m. (*not* four p.m.) |
| **DECIMALS** | 0.01 |
| **AND FRACTIONS** | 98.6 |
| | 3.1416 |
| | 7/8 |
| | 12 1/4 |
| | a sixth |
| | three-quarters (*not* 3-quarters) |
| | one-half |
| **CHAPTERS** | Chapter 27, page 2 |
| **AND PAGES** | p. 1023 *or* pp. 660–62 (MLA style) |
| **SCORES** | a 6–0 score |
| **AND STATISTICS** | 29% (or twenty-nine percent) |
| | a 5 to 1 ratio (*and* a ratio of 5:1) |
| | a one percent change (*and* at the 1 percent level) |

continued >>

**Quick Reference 30.4** (continued)

| | |
|---|---|
| IDENTIFICATION NUMBERS | 94.4 on the FM dial |
| | please call (012) 345–6789 |
| MEASUREMENTS | 67.8 miles per hour |
| | 2 level teaspoons |
| | a 700-word essay |
| | 8-by-10-inch photograph |
| | 2 feet |
| | 1.5 gallons |
| | 14 liters |
| ACT, SCENE, AND LINE | act 2, scene 2 (*or* act II, scene ii) |
| | lines 75–79 |
| TEMPERATURES | 40°F *or* −5°F |
| | 20° Celsius |
| MONEY | $1.2 billion |
| | $3.41 |
| | 25¢ (*or* twenty-five cents) |
| | $10,000 |

**ANSWERS: EXERCISE 30-4**

The corrected numbers are in italics.

**1.** At *5:15 p.m.*, the nearly empty city streets filled with *thousands* of commuters.

**2.** A tarantula spider can survive without food for about two years and *three* months.

**3.** By the end of *act 1, scene 5* [or act I, scene v], Romeo and Juliet are in love and at the mercy of their unhappy fate.

**4.** Sound travels through air at a speed of 1,089 feet per second, but in water it travels *450%* faster, at *4,859* feet per second.

**5.** *Twenty-one* years old and unhappily married, Cleopatra met middle-aged Julius Caesar in *48* BCE.

**6.** An adult blue whale, which can weigh one hundred tons—the combined weight of *thirty* elephants—has gained over *seven and a half* pounds an hour since infancy. [*However, in more technical writing:* An adult blue whale, which can weigh *100* tons—the combined weight of *30* elephants—has gained over *7.5* pounds an hour since infancy.]

**EXERCISE 30-4** Revise these sentences so that the numbers are in correct form, either spelled out or as figures. For help, consult 30m and 30n.

1. At five fifteen p.m., the nearly empty city streets filled with 1000's of commuters.

2. A tarantula spider can survive without food for about two years and 3 months.

3. By the end of act one, scene five, Romeo and Juliet are in love and at the mercy of their unhappy fate.

4. Sound travels through air at a speed of 1,089 feet per second, but in water it travels four hundred and fifty percent faster, at four thousand, eight hundred fifty-nine feet per second.

5. 21 years old and unhappily married, Cleopatra met middle-aged Julius Caesar in forty-eight BCE.

6. An adult blue whale, which can weigh one hundred tons—the combined weight of 30 elephants—has gained over seven-point-five pounds an hour since infancy.

7. On the morning of August thirteen, nineteen hundred thirty, 3 huge meteorites smashed into the Amazon jungle.

8. 2 out of every 5 people who have ever lived on earth are alive today, according to 1 estimate.

9. The house at six hundred and fifty-three Oak Street—the 1 that children think is haunted—has been empty for 8 years, waiting for a buyer willing to pay its price of $ six million, forty-nine thousand dollars.

10. The 1912 sinking of the *Titanic,* in which one thousand five hundred and three people drowned, is widely known, but few people remember that more than three thousand people lost their lives aboard the ferryboat *Doña Paz* when it hit an oil tanker in the Philippines in nineteen eighty-seven.

# 30o How do I use hyphens with spelled-out numbers?

A **spelled-out number** uses words, not figures. Quick Reference 30.5 gives you guidelines.

**! Alert:** Use figures rather than words for a fraction written in more than two words. If your context calls for figures, use hyphens only between the words of the numerator and only between the words of the denominator—but never between the numerator and the denominator: two one-hundredths (*2/100*), thirty-three ten-thousandths (*33/10,000*). ●

---

**Quick Reference 30.5**    ■ ■ ■ ■ ■ ■ ■

## Hyphens with spelled-out numbers

* Use a hyphen between two-word numbers from *twenty-one* through *ninety-nine,* whether they stand alone or are part of a larger number.

  **YES**    thirty-five    two hundred thirty-five

* Use a hyphen in a COMPOUND-WORD modifier formed from a number and a word, whether the number is in words or figures.

  **YES**    fifty-minute class [*also* 50-minute class]

  **YES**    three-to-one odds [*also* 3-to-1 odds]

* Use a hyphen between the numerator and the denominator of two-word fractions.

  **YES**    one-half    two-fifths    seven-tenths

* Use a hyphen between compound nouns joining two units of measure.

  **YES**    light-years    kilowatt-hours

---

7. On the morning of August *13, 1930, three* huge meteorites smashed into the Amazon jungle.

8. *Two* out of every *five* people who have ever lived on earth are alive today, according to *one* estimate.

9. The house at *653* Oak Street—the *one* that children think is haunted—has been empty for *eight* years, waiting for a buyer willing to pay its price of $6,049,000.

10. The 1912 sinking of the *Titanic,* in which *1,503* people drowned, is widely known, but few people remember that more than *3,000* people lost their lives aboard the ferryboat *Doña Paz* when it hit an oil tanker in the Philippines in *1987.*

**TEACHING TIP**

Some students may need a review of roman numerals. The major ones are: I = 1; V = 5; X = 10; L = 50; C = 100; D = 500; M = 1,000.

In academic writing, roman numerals have few uses. They designate the major divisions in outlines. They are used as parts of names and titles: *Peter Brown III, Queen Elizabeth II, Rocky IV.* You might remind students that roman numerals are not interchangeable with arabic (regular) numerals in addresses, dates, or measurements.

# 31

# Spelling

## 31a What makes a good speller?

You might be surprised to hear that good spellers don't know how to spell and hyphenate every word they write. What they do know, however, is to check if they're not sure of a word's spelling. If your inner voice questions a spelling, do what good spellers do—consult a dictionary.

What do you do if even the first few letters of a word seem mysterious? Our best advice is that you think of an easy-to-spell SYNONYM for the word you need; look up that synonym in a thesaurus; and among the synonyms, find the word you need to spell.

Many people incorrectly believe that only naturally skilled spellers can write well. The truth is that correct spelling matters a great deal in final drafts, but not in earlier drafts. The best time to check spellings you doubt is when you're EDITING.

The various origins and ways that English-speaking people around the world pronounce words make it almost impossible to rely solely on pronunciation to spell a word. What you can rely on, however, are the proofreading hints and spelling rules explained in this chapter.

**❶ Alert:** Word-processing software usually includes a spell-check program, which claims to spot spelling errors because the words typed in don't match the spellings in the software's dictionary. Such programs have one major drawback. The programs can't detect that you've spelled a word incorrectly if what you've typed is a legitimate spelling of a legitimate word. For example, if you mean *top* but type *too,* or if you mean *from* and type *form,* no spell-check program will "see" that mistake. In these and similar cases, only the human eye (that is, a reader) can discover the errors. ●

## 31b How can I proofread for errors in spelling and hyphen use?

Many spelling errors are the result of illegible handwriting, slips of the pen, or typographical mistakes. Catching these "typos" requires especially careful proofreading, using the techniques in Quick Reference 31.1.

## 31c  How are plurals spelled?

In American English, plurals take many forms. The most common form adds -s or -es at the end of the word. The following list covers all variations of creating plurals.

- **Adding -s or -es:** Plurals of most words are formed by adding -s, including words that end in "hard" -ch (sounding like k): *leg, legs; shoe, shoes; stomach, stomachs.* Words ending in -s, -sh, -x, -z, or "soft" -ch (as in *beach*) are formed by adding -es to the singular: *lens, lenses; tax, taxes; beach, beaches.*

- **Words ending in -o:** Add -s if the -o is preceded by a vowel: *radio, radios; cameo, cameos.* Add -es if the -o is preceded by a consonant: *potato, potatoes.* With a few words, you can choose the -s or -es plural form, but current practice generally supports adding -es: *cargo, cargoes; tornado, tornadoes; zero, zeros or zeroes.*

- **Words ending in -f or -fe:** Some words ending in -f and -fe are made plural by adding -s: *belief, beliefs.* Others require changing -f or -fe to -ves: *life, lives; leaf, leaves.* Words ending in -ff or -ffe simply add -s: *staff, staffs; giraffe, giraffes.*

- **Compound words:** For most compound words, add -s or -es at the end of the last word: *checkbooks, player-coaches.* In a few cases, the first word is made plural: *sister-in-law, sisters-in-law; miles per hour.* (For information about hyphens in compound words, see 31g.)

- **Internal changes and endings other than -s:** A few words change internally or add endings other than -s to become plural: *foot, feet; man, men; crisis, crises; child, children.*

commonly misspelled words. It's a good idea to assign words for study in groups of twenty-five at a time.

**TEACHING TIP**
While spelling is best handled during the editing process in writing, you might want to talk with students about the fact that in the age of digital communication, something as simple as an e-mail should probably be drafted, revised, and edited. Students often forget to check their spelling before hitting "send" on e-mails.

**LANGUAGE HISTORY**
During the period of colonization, English continued to expand. From Native American words, we took *tomahawk, wigwam, squash, hominy,* among many other familiar terms, and place names such as *Nebraska, Allegheny, Kentucky, Seattle,* and *Dakota.* From spoken Spanish in the New World, we have *mustang, ranch, patio, bonanza, rodeo, vigilante, sombrero,* and others. From words arrived from India, we have *thug, loot, pajamas, bandana.* From German words, we have *kindergarten, semester, delicatessen, frankfurter, hamburger.*

Borrowing continues unabated. Recent borrowings have come from Italian (*casino, malaria, studio*); Spanish (*cigar, canyon, cafeteria*); German (*pumpernickel, iceberg, protein*); Slavic (*pogrom, soviet, robot*); Arabic (*genie, candy, safari*); Hebrew (*hallelujah, kosher*); Persian (*spinach, lilac, bazaar*); Tibeto-Chinese (*tea, ketchup*); and Japanese (*zen, karate*).

Over the centuries, the Anglo-Saxons' vocabulary of 50,000 words has expanded to more than 600,000 words. Irregular spelling is the price we pay for this acquired richness and flexibility.

## ANSWERS: EXERCISE 31-1

1. yourselves
2. sheep
3. photos
4. women
5. appendixes (*or* appendices)
6. millennia
7. lamps
8. runners-up
9. criteria
10. lunches
11. echoes
12. syllabi
13. wives
14. get-togethers
15. crises

## WORDS OFTEN MISSPELLED

### ie/ei

| | | |
|---|---|---|
| achievement | conceive | niece |
| apiece | conscientious | receive |
| atheist | eighth | relief |
| belief | foreign | relieve |
| believed | forfeit | review |
| ceiling | height | seize |
| chief | leisure | view |
| conceited | lenient | weird |

### Unstressed Syllables (including syllables frequently not pronounced)

| | | |
|---|---|---|
| adolescent | cemetery | despair |
| alcohol | census | destroy |
| amateur | certain | develop |
| analysis | challenge | disease |
| angel | channel | dispel |
| apology | children | divide |
| article | chocolate | divine |
| aspirin | chosen | ecstasy |
| average | coarsely | embarrass |
| bargain | concentrate | enemy |
| boundary | controversial | escape |
| cafeteria | curious | everything |
| calendar | decorate | exercise |
| category | delicate | family |

- **Foreign words:** The best advice is to check your dictionary. In general, many Latin words ending in *-um* form the plural by changing *-um* to *-a*: *curriculum, curricula; datum, data; medium, media.* Also, Latin words that end in *-us* usually form the plural by changing *-us* to *-i: alumnus, alumni; syllabus, syllabi.* Additionally, Greek words that end in *-on* usually form the plural by changing *-on* to *-a: criterion, criteria; phenomenon, phenomena.*

- **One-form words:** Some words have the same form in both the singular and the plural: *deer, elk, fish.* You need to use modifiers, as necessary, to indicate which form you mean: **one** *deer,* **nine** *deer.*

**EXERCISE 31-1** Write the correct plural form of these words. For help, consult 31c.

1. yourself
2. sheep
3. photo
4. woman
5. appendix
6. millennium
7. lamp
8. runner-up
9. criterion
10. lunch
11. echo
12. syllabus
13. wife
14. get-together
15. crisis

## 31d How are suffixes spelled?

A **suffix** is an ending added to a word that changes the word's meaning or its grammatical function. For example, adding the suffix *-able* to the VERB *depend* creates the ADJECTIVE *dependable.*

- **-y words:** If the letter before a final *-y* is a consonant, change the *-y* to *-i* and add the suffix: *try, tries, tried.* In the case of *trying* and similar words, the following rule applies: Keep the *-y* when the suffix begins with *-i* (*apply, applying*). If the letter before the final *-y* is a vowel, keep the final *-y: employ, employed, employing.* These rules don't apply to IRREGULAR VERBS (see Quick Reference 15.4 in section 15d).

- **-e words:** Drop a final *-e* when the suffix begins with a vowel, unless doing this would cause confusion: for example, *be + ing* can't be written *bing,* but *require* does become *requiring; like* does become *liking.* Keep the final *-e* when the suffix begins with a consonant: *require, requirement; like, likely.* Exceptions include *argue, argument; judge, judgment; true, truly.*

- **Words that double a final letter:** If the final letter is a consonant, double it *only* if it passes three tests: (1) Its last two letters are a vowel followed by a consonant; (2) it has one syllable or is accented on the last syllable;

(3) the suffix begins with a vowel: *drop, drop**ped**; begin, begin**ning**; forget, forget**table**.*

- **-cede, -ceed, -sede words:** Only one word in the English language ends in *-sede:* super**sede**. Only three words end in *-ceed:* ex**ceed**, pro**ceed**, suc**ceed**. All other words with endings that sound like "seed" end in *-cede:* con**cede**, inter**cede**, pre**cede**.

- **-ally and -ly words:** The suffixes *-ally* and *-ly* turn words into adverbs. For words ending in *-ic*, add *-ally:* logic**ally**, statistic**ally**. Otherwise, add *-ly:* quick**ly**, sharp**ly**.

- **-ance, -ence, and -ible, -able:** No consistent rules govern words with these suffixes. When in doubt, look up the word.

# 31e   What is the *ie, ei* rule?

The famous rhymed rule for using *ie* and *ei* is usually true:

*I* before *e* [bel**ie**ve, f**ie**ld, gr**ie**f],
Except after *c* [c**ei**ling, conc**ei**t],
Or when sounded like "ay"—
As in n**ei**ghbor and w**ei**gh [**ei**ght, v**ei**n].

There are major exceptions (sorry!) to the *ie, ei* rule, listed here. Our best advice is that you memorize them.

- ***ie:*** consc**ie**nce, financ**ie**r, sc**ie**nce, spec**ie**s

- ***ei:*** **ei**ther, n**ei**ther, l**ei**sure, s**ei**ze, counterf**ei**t, for**ei**gn, forf**ei**t, sl**ei**ght (as in *sl**ei**ght of hand*), w**ei**rd

**EXERCISE 31-2**   Follow the directions for each group of words. For help, consult 31d and 31e.

1. Add *-able* or *-ible:* (a) profit; (b) reproduce; (c) control; (d) coerce; (e) recognize.

2. Add *-ance* or *-ence:* (a) luxuri____; (b) prud____; (c) devi____; (d) resist____; (e) independ____.

3. Drop the final *-e* as needed: (a) true + ly; (b) joke + ing; (c) fortunate + ly; (d) appease + ing; (e) appease + ment.

4. Change the final *-y* to *-i* as needed: (a) happy + ness; (b) pry + ed; (c) pry + ing; (d) dry + ly; (e) beautify + ing.

5. Double the final consonant as needed: (a) commit + ed; (b) commit + ment; (c) drop + ed; (d) occur + ed; (e) regret + ful.

6. Insert *ie* or *ei* correctly: (a) rel____f; (b) ach____ve; (c) w____rd; (d) n____ce; (e) dec____ve.

| | | |
|---|---|---|
| favorite | pigeon | sentence |
| grammar | pitiful | separate |
| heroes | pleasant | several |
| holiday | poison | sheriff |
| hundred | practical | similar |
| imagine | prepare | sophomore |
| imitate | privilege | specimen |
| integrate | propaganda | sponsor |
| interest | pumpkin | statistics |
| introduce | purpose | strategy |
| laboratory | pursue | surprise |
| liable | pursuit | temperature |
| luxury | quandary | therefore |
| magazine | rebel | thorough |
| manual | recognize | tobacco |
| mathematics | regular | together |
| medicine | remember | tomorrow |
| miniature | reproduce | typical |
| participle | resources | vitamins |
| perhaps | restaurant | Wednesday |
| persuade | sacrifice | woman |
| physical | saxophone | women |

**ANSWERS: EXERCISE 31-2**

1. **a.** profitable
   **b.** reproducible
   **c.** controllable
   **d.** coercible
   **e.** recognizable
2. **a.** luxuriance
   **b.** prudence
   **c.** deviance
   **d.** resistance
   **e.** independence
3. **a.** truly
   **b.** joking
   **c.** fortunately
   **d.** appeasing
   **e.** appeasement

4. **a.** happiness
   **b.** pried
   **c.** prying
   **d.** dryly
   **e.** beautifying
5. **a.** committed
   **b.** commitment
   **c.** dropped
   **d.** occurred
   **e.** regretful
6. **a.** relief
   **b.** achieve
   **c.** weird
   **d.** niece
   **e.** deceive

## BACKGROUND

A survey of problems found in student writing at the University of Michigan reports the following most frequent spelling errors: "Words that contain unstressed vowels: Is it *seperate* or *separate*, *indispensible* or *indispensable*? Metathesis, the name we give that wrong ordering of cart and horse that makes us write *calvary* for *cavalry*. Problems in handling an unstressed *i*, as in *efficient*."

## WORDS OFTEN MISSPELLED

### Double Consonants

| | | |
|---|---|---|
| accommodate | committee | missile |
| accompanied | controlled | occasion |
| accomplish | different | occurred |
| accordion | disappear | parallel |
| accustomed | disappoint | processes |
| address | disapprove | quizzes |
| annihilate | efficient | satellite |
| appoint | equipped | stepped |
| appreciate | fulfill | succeed |
| appropriate | happened | suppose |
| arrest | harass | surround |
| bulletin | interrupt | tyranny |
| commercial | mirror | villain |

# 31f How are homonyms and other frequently confused words spelled?

**Homonyms** are words that sound exactly like other words: *to, too, two; no, know*. The different spellings of homonyms tend to confuse many writers. The same holds for words that sound almost alike (*accept, except; conscience, conscious*).

Another reason for spelling problems is so-called swallowed pronunciation, which means one or more letters at the end of a word aren't pronounced clearly. For example, the *-d* ending in *used to* or *prejudiced* or the *-ten* ending in *written* are often swallowed rather than pronounced. When writers spell as they mispronounce, spelling errors result.

For more information about word usage that affects spelling, see Chapter 13, "Usage Glossary." Quick Reference 31.2 lists homonyms and other words that can be confused and lead to misspellings.

### Quick Reference 31.2

#### Homonyms and other frequently confused words

| | | |
|---|---|---|
| • | ACCEPT | to receive |
| | EXCEPT | with the exclusion of |
| • | ADVICE | recommendation |
| | ADVISE | to recommend |
| • | AFFECT | to influence [verb]; emotion [noun] |
| | EFFECT | result [noun]; to bring about or cause [verb] |
| • | AISLE | space between rows |
| | ISLE | island |
| • | ALLUDE | to make indirect reference to |
| | ELUDE | to avoid |
| • | ALLUSION | indirect reference |
| | ILLUSION | false idea, misleading appearance |
| • | ALREADY | by this time |
| | ALL READY | fully prepared |
| • | ALTAR | sacred platform or place |
| | ALTER | to change |
| • | ALTOGETHER | thoroughly |
| | ALL TOGETHER | everyone or everything in one place |
| • | ARE | PLURAL form of *to be* |
| | HOUR | sixty minutes |
| | OUR | plural form of *my* |

continued >>

## Quick Reference 31.2     (continued)

- ASCENT     the act of rising or climbing
  ASSENT     consent [noun]; to consent [verb]

- ASSISTANCE     help
  ASSISTANTS     helpers

- BARE     nude, unadorned
  BEAR     to carry; an animal

- BOARD     piece of wood
  BORED     uninterested

- BRAKE     device for stopping
  BREAK     to destroy, make into pieces

- BREATH     air taken in
  BREATHE     to take in air

- BUY     to purchase
  BY     next to, through the agency of

- CAPITAL     major city; money
  CAPITOL     government building

- CHOOSE     to pick
  CHOSE     PAST TENSE of *choose*

- CITE     to point out
  SIGHT     vision
  SITE     a place

- CLOTHES     garments
  CLOTHS     pieces of fabric

- COARSE     rough
  COURSE     path; series of lectures

- COMPLEMENT     something that completes
  COMPLIMENT     praise, flattery

- CONSCIENCE     sense of morality
  CONSCIOUS     awake, aware

- COUNCIL     governing body
  COUNSEL     advice [noun]; to advise [verb]

- DAIRY     place associated with milk production
  DIARY     personal journal

- DESCENT     downward movement
  DISSENT     disagreement

continued >>

## Word Ending (Suffixes)

| | |
|---|---|
| acceptable | despicable |
| accessible | disastrous |
| accidentally | discussion |
| accuracy | dormitory |
| acreage | easily |
| actually | elaborately |
| admission | entirely |
| affectionately | environment |
| aggression | equipment |
| announcement | especially |
| apparent | evidently |
| appearance | existence |
| approximately | experiment |
| arguing | explanation |
| argument | extremely |
| assassination | finally |
| attendance | financially |
| barbarous | generally |
| basically | government |
| beautiful | governor |
| beginning | guidance |
| beneficial | happily |
| biggest | hindrance |
| bureaucracy | hoping |
| business | humorous |
| calculator | hungry |
| carrying | hurriedly |
| changeable | hypocrisy |
| changing | ideally |
| characteristic | idiosyncrasy |
| Christianity | ignorant |
| commitment | illogical |
| competent | imaginary |
| competition | immediately |
| completely | immensely |
| confident | incalculable |
| consistent | incidentally |
| continuous | incredible |
| convenient | independent |
| coolly | indispensable |
| criticism | individually |
| criticize | influential |
| cruelty | innocuous |
| curiosity | insurance |
| decision | intelligent |
| definitely | interference |
| description | irrelevant |
| desirable | irresistible |
| desperate | irritated |

likelihood
listening
liveliest
livelihood
lying
magnificent
maintenance
manageable
management
marriage
meanness
mischievous
mysterious
narrative
naturally
necessary
noticeable
noticing
nuisance
numerous
occasionally
occurrence
occurring
official
omission
omitting
opponent
opportunity
opposite
oppression
optimism
ordinarily
originally
particularly
peaceable
peculiar
performance
permanence
permissible
politician
possession
practicality
predominant
preparation
prevalent
prisoner
probably
professor
prominent
pronunciation

publicly
pursuing
questionnaire
rarity
reality
realize
really
recession
recommend
referring
regulate
rehearsal
religious
remembrance
repetition
representative
resemblance
ridiculous
scarcity
scenery
secretary
senseless
shining
shrubbery
significant
simply
sincerely
skiing
strenuous
stubbornness
studying
suburban
succession
sufficient
summary
superintendent
supersede
suppress
surely
susceptible
suspicious
swimming
technical
temporary
tendency
tragedy
tremendous
truce
unanimous
unconscious

## Quick Reference 31.2     (continued)

- DESERT    to abandon [verb]; dry, usually sandy area [noun]
  DESSERT    final, sweet course in a meal

- DEVICE    a plan; an implement
  DEVISE    to create

- DIE    to lose life (dying) [verb]; one of a pair of dice [noun]
  DYE    to change the color of something (dyeing)

- DOMINANT    commanding, controlling
  DOMINATE    to control

- ELICIT    to draw out
  ILLICIT    illegal

- EMINENT    prominent
  IMMANENT    living within; inherent
  IMMINENT    about to happen

- ENVELOP    to surround
  ENVELOPE    container for a letter or other papers

- FAIR    light-skinned; just, honest
  FARE    money for transportation; food

- FORMALLY    conventionally, with ceremony
  FORMERLY    previously

- FORTH    forward
  FOURTH    number four in a series

- GORILLA    animal in ape family
  GUERRILLA    fighter conducting surprise attacks

- HEAR    to sense sound by ear
  HERE    in this place

- HOLE    opening
  WHOLE    complete; an entire thing

- HUMAN    relating to the species *Homo sapiens*
  HUMANE    compassionate

- INSURE    to buy or give insurance
  ENSURE    to guarantee, protect

- ITS    POSSESSIVE form of *it*
  IT'S    CONTRACTION for *it is*

- KNOW    to comprehend
  NO    negative

continued >>

## Quick Reference 31.2 (continued)

| | |
|---|---|
| • LATER | after a time |
| LATTER | second one of two things |
| • LEAD | a heavy metal [noun]; to guide [verb] |
| LED | past tense of *lead* |
| • LIGHTNING | storm-related electricity |
| LIGHTENING | making lighter |
| • LOOSE | unbound, not tightly fastened |
| LOSE | to misplace |
| • MAYBE | perhaps [adverb] |
| MAY BE | might be [verb] |
| • MEAT | animal flesh |
| MEET | to encounter |
| • MINER | a person who works in a mine |
| MINOR | underage; less important |
| • MORAL | distinguishing right from wrong; the lesson of a fable, story, or event |
| MORALE | attitude or outlook, usually of a group |
| • OF | PREPOSITION indicating origin |
| OFF | away from; not on |
| • PASSED | past tense of *pass* |
| PAST | at a previous time |
| • PATIENCE | forbearance |
| PATIENTS | people under medical care |
| • PEACE | absence of fighting |
| PIECE | part of a whole; musical arrangement |
| • PERSONAL | intimate |
| PERSONNEL | employees |
| • PLAIN | simple, unadorned |
| PLANE | to shave wood; aircraft |
| • PRECEDE | to come before |
| PROCEED | to continue |
| • PRESENCE | being at hand; attendance at a place or in something |
| PRESENTS | gifts |
| • PRINCIPAL | foremost [adjective]; school head [noun] |
| PRINCIPLE | moral conviction, basic truth |

continued >>

| | |
|---|---|
| undoubtedly | vegetable |
| usage | vengeance |
| using | violence |
| usually | visible |
| valuable | writing |
| various | written |

### TEACHING TIP

Much of the recent research on spelling improvements stresses the importance of using as many of the senses as possible during word study. You may want to suggest to students that they try to improve their visual memory by writing a word in the air, using a finger to make the troublesome letters especially large. Ask them to try to imagine a word as if it were on an outdoor movie screen. Then, they can try to write the word mentally in "longhand." The auditory sense can be invoked by making exaggerated pronunciations. That is, the speaker emphasizes the problem portion of a word when saying it. For example, the person who habitually leaves off the final *-d* of *used* should practice pronouncing the word as "you said." The kinesthetic and tactile senses are combined when a writer records a problem word on paper using a different kind of medium to write the difficult spots, changing from a ballpoint pen, for instance, to a crayon. This technique can include a visual element if the student puts the problem letters in red or some other bright color.

### QUOTATION: ON WRITING

English orthography satisfies all the requirements of the canons of reputability under the law of conspicuous waste. It is archaic, cumbrous, and ineffective; its acquisition consumes much time and effort; failure to acquire it is easy of detection.

—Thorstein Veblen

### TEACHING TIP

For fun, you might want to host an old-fashioned spelling bee with your students for a quick exercise in emphasizing the importance of spelling. You can create a list of words as a class and give students time to memorize the spelling.

An alternative activity is working on crossword puzzles with your students, which reinforces both vocabulary and spelling.

Two recent documentaries highlight our cultural fascination with words. You might show students clips from Patrick Creadon's 2006 film *Wordplay* about the popularity of the *New York Times* crossword puzzle or Director Jeffrey Blitz's 2002 documentary, *Spellbound*, on the Scripps-Howard National Spelling Bee.

## BACKGROUND

In *Back to Front*, Chauncey Mabe reflects on the "quirky inventiveness" of palindromes: "words or phrases that spell the same frontwards and backwards." According to Mabe, "A man, a plan, a canal: Panama," is a perfect example of a palindrome: "It not only makes sense, it tells the story of the Panama Canal in miniature." Following are briefer examples: *civic, madam, pull-up, race car,* and *radar.*

## TEACHING TIP

A sophisticated relative of the spelling test is the dictation exercise. Passages can be created to test students' ability to spell, punctuate, or capitalize. Here is a sample dictation passage aimed at testing whether students can distinguish among homonyms and commonly confused words. The context gives students clues about which word is intended (much as the sentences normally given as part of a spelling test do); at the same time, the paragraph format is more interesting than random illustrative sentences.

The institution of marriage has received its share of public attention over the past few years. Rising divorce rates, seen as a symptom of a troubled society, have led people to question why some marriages break up and others succeed. One reason may be that the effect of courtship is to cause the bride and groom to lose sight of reality. Researchers cite evidence that some couples are too unrealistic. They proceed to the altar carrying romantic illusions about themselves, each other, and marriage itself. Having grown accustomed to compliments and presents, they find themselves walking down the aisle expecting a lifetime of romantic

## Quick Reference 31.2    (continued)

| | | |
|---|---|---|
| • | QUIET | silent, calm |
| | QUITE | very |
| • | RAIN | water that falls to earth [noun]; to fall like rain [verb] |
| | REIGN | to rule |
| | REIN | strap to guide or control an animal [noun]; to guide or control [verb] |
| • | RAISE | to lift up |
| | RAZE | to tear down |
| • | RESPECTFULLY | with respect |
| | RESPECTIVELY | in that order |
| • | RIGHT | correct; opposite of *left* |
| | RITE | ritual |
| | WRITE | to put words on paper |
| • | ROAD | path |
| | RODE | past tense of *ride* |
| • | SCENE | place of an action; segment of a play |
| | SEEN | viewed |
| • | SENSE | perception, understanding |
| | SINCE | measurement of past time; because |
| • | STATIONARY | standing still |
| | STATIONERY | writing paper |
| • | THAN | in comparison with; besides |
| | THEN | at that time; next; therefore |
| • | THEIR | possessive form of *they* |
| | THERE | in that place |
| | THEY'RE | contraction of *they are* |
| • | THROUGH | finished; into and out of |
| | THREW | past tense of *throw* |
| | THOROUGH | complete |
| • | TO | toward |
| | TOO | also; indicates degree (*too much*) |
| | TWO | number following *one* |
| • | WAIST | midsection of the body |
| | WASTE | discarded material [noun]; to squander, to fail to use up [verb] |

continued >>

## Quick Reference 31.2     (continued)

| | | |
|---|---|---|
| • | WEAK | not strong |
| | WEEK | seven days |
| • | WEATHER | climatic condition |
| | WHETHER | if, when alternatives are expressed or implied |
| • | WHERE | in which place |
| | WERE | past tense of *be* |
| • | WHICH | one of a group |
| | WITCH | female sorcerer |
| • | WHOSE | possessive form of *who* |
| | WHO'S | contraction for *who is* |
| • | YOUR | possessive form of *you* |
| | YOU'RE | contraction for *you are* |
| | YORE | long past |

bliss to follow. The groom may assume that his bride is an angel, and she may choose to think of him as a knight on a white horse. They may fail to realize that one expects to dominate rather than complement the other or that he lacks patience and she is not as quiet as she seems. They're reluctant to look at the whole situation until later, when they are called on to accept the serious responsibilities of marriage. The best advice, of course, is for husbands and wives to live by principles that lead them to treat each other respectfully, lightening each other's troubles and acknowledging each other's rights.

**EXERCISE 31-3**    Circle the correct homonym or commonly confused word of each group in parentheses.

Imagine that you (are, our) standing in the middle of a busy sidewalk, with a worried look on (your, you're, yore) face. In your hand (your, you're, yore) holding a map, (which, witch) you are puzzling over. If that happened in (real, reel) life, (its, it's) almost certain that within (to, too, two) or three minutes a passerby would ask if you (where, were) lost and would offer you (assistance, assistants). That helpful passerby, (buy, by) taking a (personal, personnel) interest in your problem, is displaying a quality known as empathy—the ability (to, too, two) put oneself in another person's place. Some researchers claim that empathy is an instinct that (human, humane) beings share with many other animals. Other scientists wonder (weather, whether) empathy is instead a (conscience, conscious) (moral, morale) choice that people make. Whatever explanation for the origin (of, off) empathy is (right, rite, write), such empathy generally has a positive (affect, effect)—especially if (your, you're, yore) a person who (maybe, may be) (to, too, two) lost to (know, no) (where, were) (to, too, two) turn.

**ANSWERS: EXERCISE 31-3**
Imagine that you *are* standing in the middle of a busy sidewalk, with a worried look on *your* face. In your hand *you're* holding a map, *which* you are puzzling over. If that happened in *real* life, *it's* almost certain that within *two* or three minutes a passerby would ask if you *were* lost and would offer you *assistance*. That helpful passerby, *by* taking a *personal* interest in your problem, is displaying a quality known as empathy—the ability *to* put oneself in another person's place. Some researchers claim that empathy is an instinct that *human* beings share with many other animals. Other scientists wonder *whether* empathy is instead a *conscious moral* choice that people make. Whatever explanation for the origin *of* empathy is *right*, such empathy generally has a positive *effect*—especially if *you're* a person who *may be too* lost to *know where to* turn.

## 31g    What are compound words?

A **compound word** puts together two or more words to express one concept.

> **Open compound words** remain as separate words, such as *decision making*, *problem solving*, and *editor in chief*.

**Hyphenated compound words** use a hyphen between the words, such as *trade-in, fuel-efficient,* and *tax-sheltered.* For punctuation advice about hyphens, see 29i.

**Closed compound words** appear as one word, such as *proofread, citywide,* and *workweek.*

Single-word compounds usually start as open (two-word) compounds and then become hyphenated compounds before ending up as closed compounds. To check whether a compound term consists of closed, hyphenated, or open words, consult an up-to-date dictionary.

For more help with your writing, grammar, and research, go to **www.mycomplab.com**

# 32

# Types and Uses of Research in Writing

## 32a What is the role of research in writing?

**Research** is a systematic process of gathering information to answer a question. You're doing research when you're trying to decide which college to attend, which MP3 player to buy, or which summer job to accept. Perhaps you find facts or information, in print or online. You analyze and evaluate what you learn and then make a decision.

Other kinds of research are more formal. People wanting to start small businesses usually have to research the local business climate and present their findings to lenders to get a loan. Citizens wanting to oppose a new construction project have to research its impact and present their findings in a careful way to elected officials.

The amount of research in a piece of writing can vary, depending on your audience, purpose, and type of writing (see 1b; 7a). You might be familiar with RESEARCH PAPERS* or TERM PAPERS, which are dense with sources, synthesizing information to support a thesis. Chapter 33 will help you with extended formal research projects.

However, any essay might potentially benefit from even a little research. Finding a crucial fact might improve an argument. Consider the original and revised paragraphs below:

ORIGINAL     The homeless situation is even more serious when we understand the variety of people who lack a place to sleep every night. It's not just a problem that afflicts single men or individuals with physical or mental problems. Many families are homeless.

RESEARCHED     The homeless situation is even more serious when we understand the variety of people who lack a place to sleep every night. It's not just a problem that afflicts single men or individuals with physical or mental problems. According to the U.S. Department of

---

*Words printed in SMALL CAPITAL LETTERS are discussed elsewhere in the text and are defined in the Terms Glossary at the back of this book.

Housing and Urban Development, of the 750,000 homeless people in America, nearly 40% are families (Eaton-Robb).

### WORK CITED

Eaton-Robb, Pat. "Number of Homeless Families Rises." *USA Today* 10 Oct. 2007. Web. 15 Oct. 2007.

In the second version, the writer specifically answers the research question, "How many families are homeless?" Whenever writing has a vague term like "a lot" or "many" or "some," research can improve it with more precise information. Of course, you might also find facts that complicate your argument. For example, trying to persuade people to oppose "the death tax" (taxes paid by a deceased person's estate) may become more difficult when you learn that it affects only the wealthiest two percent of Americans who leave heirs over $2 million.

**EXERCISE 32-1**    The following paragraph has a number of general statements. Generate a list of all the possible research questions you might pursue to strengthen the paragraph.

**EXAMPLE**    "If we fail to act on global warming, our coastal cities will be damaged by rising ocean levels."

**POSSIBLE QUESTIONS**    How will global warming affect oceans? How much will oceans rise? Which cities will be affected?

In a troubling reversal of roles, boys are now considerably more at risk in school than are girls. Girls used to be denied many opportunities in schools and colleges, as boys enjoyed several unfair advantages. Now, however, girls are graduating from high schools at much higher rates. They are performing better on standardized tests and entering colleges and universities at much higher levels, to the extent that several colleges now have programs specifically targeted to attract and admit more male students. Women substantially outnumber men in admission to medical and law schools. A number of factors is responsible, but unless we take actions to ensure academic quality and success for both boys and girls, we will need to create affirmative action programs for men.

## 32b    What are reasons for doing research?

Writers do research for several reasons and at different points in the writing process, from generating and planning to revising.

1. **To find a fact or piece of information.** Sometimes you simply need to answer a direct question of "how much?" or "when?" or "where?" or "who?" In each case, you need to find a credible source and extract only

complete advanced research as part of the requirements for your degree. Share with your students some of your stories around the research you had to conduct, including both the frustrations and difficulties you encountered as well as the sense of accomplishment you felt at the end of your work. Telling your own story may help students understand that research is considered to be an intrinsic part of education, no matter what the discipline.

As a means of introducing the research paper to students, you may want to give them a mini-research assignment in your field of study. Base it around some interesting or surprising fact. For instance, if your expertise is in seventeenth-century Women Writers, you might give your students the homework assignment of answering the seemingly simple question "Who is George Sand?" Even a cursory amount of research will reveal a very interesting literary personality, and you can supplement their research with some of the interesting findings you made during your own investigations.

**HISTORY**

In 2003, Margaret Moulton and Vicki Holmes reviewed over 350 articles about the process of having students write research papers, tracing the history of these assignments since the 1870s ("The Research Paper: A Historical Perspective," *Teaching English in the Two-Year College* 30.4 (2003): 365–373). They show that research papers have long been controversial, with critics of the practice as well as with advocates. Among their findings: (1) Originally, the purpose of a research paper was to create new universal knowledge, but later the emphasis shifted to teaching the process of researching; (2) teachers have tended to value relevance and interest to students when assigning research-paper topics—or allowing students to choose their own; (3) the use of primary sources—interviews, surveys, work with primary documents—creates interest and also helps lessen the possibility of plagiarism; (4) multiple media have begun to play an important role in research papers, although as early as the 1940s, media had a place in the curriculum; and (5) many instructors have begun to use multiple, shorter, source-based papers, rather than a single long research

the specific information necessary to answer the question. Example: How does the cost of college today compare to the cost twenty years ago?

2. **To understand an issue or situation more fully.** Sometimes you need to learn basic information about a topic, even before writing. You're trying to learn not only information new to you but also the range of viewpoints or opinions on a particular topic. Rather than identifying a single fact from a source, you're reading many sources, sometimes with a goal of synthesizing them, sometimes with the goal of generating more specific research questions. Example: What are the effects of globalization?

3. **To synthesize current information.** Even if you know a good deal about a topic, you may need to bring together the most current information. A **review of the literature** is a synthesis of the latest knowledge on a particular topic. It may be part of a longer project, as in the case of SCIENCE REPORTS (41i.1), or it may be the project itself as in the case of SCIENCE REVIEWS (41i.2). Example: What treatments are now possible for Alzheimer's disease?

4. **To identify a specific opinion or point of view.** A good strategy in argumentative writing is to state and refute counter arguments. You might research in order to find out what people who disagree with you believe and, more important, why. You can then explain the shortcomings of their views or explain why your position is better. You might also look for expert viewpoints that support your own. Example: What are the main arguments in favor of censoring cable television programs? For more information on writing arguments, see Chapter 5.

5. **To create new knowledge.** Writers often do kinds of research that make new knowledge rather than find knowledge others have already created. This is the kind of research that chemists and biologists do, but so do psychologists, sociologists, journalists and so on. This kind of research includes experiments, surveys, interviews, ethnographies, and observations. For example, if you were writing a guide to coffee houses in a certain area, you'd need to visit all of them, take notes, and present your findings to readers. Field research (32e) is a general name for this kind of research.

## 32c What is the process of doing research?

Although the research process varies according to the specific reason you're doing research (32b) and to your writing situation (1a), a few general steps are common to most projects involving research.

1. **Develop a research question.** What is the question that you need to answer by conducting research? Some questions might be very specific, such as when you're looking for a piece of data; consider, for example, "What was the population of Canada in 1880?" or "How much methane is produced by dairy cattle in the United States?" With substantial projects, however, your research question involves more than looking for a single fact. Consider, for example, "What is the most practical way to reduce global warming caused by automobile emissions?" or "How might the depiction of college students on television influence general attitudes about higher education?" Section 33e has more advice about developing effective research questions.

2. **Decide what kinds of sources will best answer your question.** Some research questions are best answered by finding appropriate PUBLISHED SOURCES, generally through the library (Chapter 34). Others might require **field research**, gathering data firsthand through surveying, interviewing, or observing (32e). We talk about kinds of sources in 32d.

3. **Develop a search strategy.** Once you determine the sources you need, develop a plan for finding them. How will you search the library, for example (34b)? Whom will you contact to interview? When will you visit a location for direct observations, and how will you take notes once you're there? Be purposeful in designing your strategy so you'll be effective and efficient.

4. **Gather your sources.** This is the stage where you not only find appropriate books and articles, for example, but also take notes (33k). Your goal is to accumulate more than enough materials so that you feel confident you can answer your research question.

5. **Interpret your source materials.** Having a bunch of reading notes, a lot of survey answers, a transcript of an interview, or a list of direct observations is only part of the process. Organizing and interpreting them to understand how they answer your research question is just as vital. This stage can also tell you whether your search strategy has been successful or whether you need to gather even more sources. Look for themes or patterns. Look not only for information and ideas that seem to fit together but also for conflicts or tensions.

6. **Draft, revise, edit, and proofread your paper.** The general writing processes that we explained in Chapter 2 also apply to researched writing. In sections 33l–33n, we explain how to apply specifically those processes to writing research papers.

paper, to teach text analysis and documentation skills.

**QUOTATION: ON WRITING**
Writing is a process of dealing with not-knowing. . . . At best there's a slender intuition, not much greater than an itch.
—Donald Barthelme

**TEACHING TIP**
Ask students to list the kinds of "research" they might do as part of their normal lives. For instance, they might comparison shop for .mp3 players (which might include reading reviews, going to company Web sites, and getting opinions from [i.e., interviewing] friends and family); try to lose weight, stay healthy, or build muscle (which would involve reading about proper diet and exercise, interviewing people they know, and perhaps soliciting the advice of a doctor, nutritionist, or other health expert); or write a review about one of their favorite music artists on a Web site (which would involve the primary research of listening to the artist's work and the secondary research of seeing what other people have written about the artist).

As a tie-in to Chapter 34, "Finding and Evaluating Published Sources," you can further ask students about which methods of research have yielded good results for them, and which they found lacking. Would their decision-making process for some of the research they mentioned have benefited from finding more authoritative sources?

**QUOTATION: ON RESEARCH**
Research is formalized curiosity. It is poking and prying with a purpose.
—Zora Neale Hurston

**TEACHING TIP**
To make an interview valuable, the interviewer must approach the expert with questions that will produce answers that supply the information needed for the project at hand. Simply holding an open-ended conversation with a knowledgeable person may be interesting, but

it won't necessarily be helpful for the researcher. You may want to ask students to work in groups to formulate a series of "ice-breaker" questions to use as they begin an interview, some general questions that can be applied to any topic. Then ask the students to list specific questions designed especially for the person being interviewed.

**TEACHING TIP: TERTIARY SOURCES?**
Some of us learned that *tertiary sources* are those sources that distill a body of knowledge in order to provide people who may be new to the subject access to general information about that subject. Encyclopedias, almanacs, and dictionaries are all classic examples of tertiary sources. All of these sources, however, fit the definition of secondary sources we provide in 32e. For the sake of simplicity, therefore, we have chosen to collapse secondary and tertiary sources into one inclusive category.

# 32d  What kinds of sources do writers use?

A **source** is any form of information that provides ideas, examples, information, or evidence, and different kinds of college writing require different kinds of sources (7b). You're probably most familiar with PUBLISHED SOURCES: books, magazine or journal articles, sources from organizational Web sites, and so on. Being able to use published sources effectively is so fundamental, especially to academic writing, that we've devoted two chapters entirely to them. Chapter 34 talks about finding and evaluating published sources and Chapter 35 talks about using them and avoiding plagiarism.

However, writers use other sources, too. As we discussed in Chapter 7, these include interviews; surveys; direct observations of situations, places, or people; performances or lectures; museums; and so on.

**ESOL Tip:** In the United States, PLAGIARISM is a major offense in academic writing. In some cultures, it's customary to take material from scholarly authorities on your topic. However, this practice is forbidden in the United States unless you use quotation marks around the exact words and then state the place where you found those words. For detailed information about how to avoid plagiarism, see Chapter 35.

A source is either primary or secondary. **Primary sources** are firsthand evidence based on your own or someone else's original work or direct observation. Primary sources can take the form of experiments, surveys, interviews, memoirs, FIELD RESEARCH (32e), or original creative works (for example, poems, novels, paintings and other art, plays, films, or musical compositions). **Secondary sources** report, describe, comment on, or analyze the experiences or work of others. Quick Reference 4.4 on page 114 illustrates the difference.

Suppose you're researching student attitudes toward marriage. Surveying several students would be primary research. Consulting scholars' books and articles about students and marriage would be secondary research. Your decision to use primary or secondary sources depends on your RESEARCH QUESTION or the nature of your assignment.

# 32e  What is field research?

**Field research** involves going into real-life situations to observe, survey, interview, or join some activity firsthand. A field researcher might, for example, go to a factory, a lecture, a day-care center, or a mall— anywhere that people engage in everyday activities. A field researcher might also interview experts and other identified individuals. Because field research yields original data, it's a PRIMARY SOURCE.

Conducting field research takes careful planning. Be sure to allow time to gather the data you want, ANALYZE it, and then SYNTHESIZE it with other sources and with your own knowledge and experience. Field research often involves events that can't be revisited. Therefore, record as much information as possible during your research and decide later what information you can use. Afterwards, while your memory is fresh, go over your notes and highlight major types of information. Also, fill in any details you might not have written down.

## 32e.1 Surveying

Surveys use several questions to gather information from a number of people, asking about experiences, situations, opinions, or attitudes. Responses to multiple choice or true/false questions are easy for people to complete and for researchers to summarize and report, as totals or averages. Open-ended questions, in which people are asked to respond in writing to a question, require more effort on the part of researchers and people completing the survey. However, they sometimes have the advantage of providing more complete or accurate information.

If you want to survey a group of people, allow time to write, reflect on, and revise a questionnaire. Test the questionnaire on a few people. Revise any questions that don't work well. For advice, see Quick Reference 32.1.

---

### Quick Reference 32.1

#### Guidelines for developing a questionnaire

1. Define what you want to learn.
2. Identify the appropriate type and numbers of people to answer your survey so that you get the information you need.
3. Write questions to elicit the information.
4. Use appropriate language when phrasing questions so that they are easy to understand.
5. Make sure that your wording does not imply what you want to hear.
6. Decide whether to include open-ended questions that allow people to write their own answers.
7. Test a draft of the questionnaire on a small group of people. If any question is misinterpreted or difficult to understand, revise and retest it.

---

When you report findings from a survey, keep within your limitations. For example, if the only people who answer your survey are students at a particular college or people at a particular shopping mall, you can't claim your results represent "all college students" or "all Americans and Canadians." For further advice on writing about quantitative information, see section 3e.

## 32e.2 Observing people and situations

CASE STUDIES (7d.4) and ETHNOGRAPHIES (7d.5) are examples of researching people in specific situations. For observations of behavior (for example, the audience at a sporting event or elementary school children at play during recess), you can take notes during the activity. Permission to videotape instead of taking notes is hard to get because of privacy concerns. Try to remain objective so that you can see things clearly. One strategy is to take notes in a two-column format. On the left, record only objective observations; on the right, record comments or possible interpretations. Figure 32.1 is an example of a double-column note strategy.

## 32e.3 Interviewing

An expert can offer valuable information, a new point of view, and firsthand facts, statistics, and examples. Probably the best place to start is with the faculty at your college. Your instructors are also scholars and researchers with expertise in many areas. They may suggest good additional sources, as well as other experts to contact. Indeed, your family and friends might qualify as

| Notes | Comment/Analyses |
|---|---|
| Small conference room; round table covered with papers | |
| JP suggests fundraising plan | JP seems nervous. Her normal behavior, or is it this situation? |
| AR and CT lean forward; SM leans back | |
| SM interrupts JP's plan, asks for more; CT silent | The fact that JP and AR are women might explain SM's response. Or is it that he's more senior? |
| JP continues proposal | |
| SM looks out window, taps pencil | Seems to have made up his mind. A power move? |

**Figure 32.1** A double-column field research note

experts, if they've been involved with an issue you're researching. Corporations, institutions, and professional organizations often have public relations offices that can answer questions or put you in contact with experts.

Make every attempt to conduct interviews in person so that you can observe body language and facial expressions as you talk. However, if distance is a problem, you can conduct interviews over the phone or online. Quick Reference 32.2 provides specific suggestions for conducting interviews.

---

| Quick Reference 32.2 | ■ ■ ■ ■ ■ ■ ■ |
| --- | --- |

### Conducting research interviews

- Arrange the interview well in advance, conduct background research, prepare specific questions, and show up on time.
- Rehearse how to ask your questions without reading them (perhaps highlight the key word in colored ink). Looking your interviewee in the eye as you ask questions establishes ease and trust. If you're interviewing on the telephone, be organized and precise.
- Create a shortcut symbol or letter for key terms you expect to hear during the interview. This cuts down on your time needed to look away from your interviewee.
- Take careful notes, listening especially for key names, books, and other print materials, or online sources.
- Use standard 8 1/2-by-11-inch paper so that you have room to write.
- Bring extra pens or pencils.
- Never depend on recording an interview. People have become very reluctant to permit anyone to record them, and many will cancel appointments on the spot if recording is even mentioned.

---

## 32e.4 Gathering data about things or practices

Some kinds of primary research involve looking at objects, artifacts, or practices, describing or counting what you observe, and reporting what you find. Consider three research questions:

1. How are women portrayed on the covers of national magazines?

2. What are the most popular colors to paint houses in middle-class neighborhoods and in wealthy neighborhoods?

3. Are characters with foreign-sounding names or accents in current movies more likely to be heroes or villains?

**QUOTATION: ON INTERVIEWING**
The most upsetting thing about taking the chance to be interviewed is that you can only be as smart and as clever as the person that's interviewing you.

—Susan Sarandon

that readers would not disturb other people in the library with their noise.

## EXTRA EXERCISE A

For an assigned research paper, form a group to study and implement the principles given in Quick Reference 33.1, "Sample schedule for a research project." Work together to clarify the various steps listed on the schedule by referring to later sections of this chapter and to your own experience. Then, make a simplified schedule that the whole group can use, leaving space for each student to add specific steps when needed. Base the schedule on the actual deadlines given by your instructor. Include at least these four steps: (1) topic firmly chosen, (2) research substantially completed and writing begun, (3) full draft completed, and (4) final paper due. Keep in mind that the writing process is always recursive. For example, you may find that even a topic you have committed to firmly might need to change if you discover insufficient information is available.

Advice to instructor: Most students find it useful when instructors specify more than a final deadline. Having a deadline for at least the first full draft will help eliminate last-minute work—as well as plagiarism—by panicked students. It also allows you to check whether students understand the proper format before they hand in the final draft. Better still, establishing a series of deadlines or "check-points" (topic selection, working bibliography, content notes, early drafts) will give you a sense of how well the research-writing process is going—and whether you need to explain or review the parts of the process that students seem to be unable to put into practice.

## QUOTATION: ON RESEARCH

While place might determine what research methods are possible, the research question determines what research methods are necessary.
—Cindy Johanek

## TEACHING TIP

Students might feel overwhelmed if they had to do a research paper on, say, the role of the media in shaping public attitudes toward

---

## Quick Reference 33.1

■ ■ ■ ■ ■ ■ ■

### Sample schedule for a research project

Assignment received _____

Assignment due date _____

**PLANNING**  **FINISH BY (DATE)**

1. Start my research log (33c). _____
2. Choose a topic suitable for research (33d). _____
3. Draft my research question (33e). _____
4. Understand my writing situation (33f). _____
5. Take practical steps (33g):
   a. Gather materials and supplies. _____
   b. Learn how to use my college library. _____
6. Determine what documentation style I need to use (33h). _____

**RESEARCHING**

7. Plan my "search strategy," but modify as necessary (34b). _____
8. Decide the kinds of research I need to do:
   a. Field research (32d). If yes, schedule tasks. _____
   b. Published sources (34). _____
9. Locate and evaluate sources (34d, 34j). _____
10. Compile a working bibliography (33i) or annotated bibliography (33j). _____
11. Take content notes from sources I find useful (33k). _____

**WRITING**

12. Draft my thesis statement (33l). _____
13. Outline, as required or useful (33m). _____
14. Draft my paper (33n). _____
15. Use correct parenthetical citations (34b–34c; 35b–35c; 36a, 36c). _____
16. Revise my paper (33o). _____
17. Compile my final bibliography (Works Cited or References), using the documentation style required (Chapters 36–38). _____

## 33c  What is a research log?

A **research log** is your diary of your research process. Use a separate notebook for the log, or create a new folder or file on the computer. Whichever format you rely on, make your research schedule one of the first entries.

Although much of your research log will never find its way into your research paper itself, what you write in it greatly increases your efficiency. A well-kept log traces your line of reasoning as your project evolves, tells where you've ended each work session, and suggests what your next steps might be. It can also provide information about your process in a way that helps your instructor note your effort and determine how best to help you. In your log, always record the date as well as the following elements:

* Your **current step** in your search for information.
* The **search strategy** you used to find that information.
* The **name, location,** and other details of exactly where you found the information.
* The **main point** of the information you found.
* The exact **file or folder name** in which you've stored your detailed content notes.
* Your suggested **next step** for when you return to your research.
* Your evolving **overall thoughts** and insights as you move through the research and writing processes; particularly pay attention to the movements away from gathering material to organizing it, from organizing to drafting, and from drafting to revising.

Figure 33.1 (page 526) shows a selection from the research log of Andrei Gurov, who wrote the MLA-style research paper shown in section 36e.

## 33d  How do I choose and narrow a research topic?

Sometimes, of course, you don't get to choose a research topic. Research in the workplace and many public arenas often emerges from specific situations. A doctor needs to decide the best way to treat a patient. An office manager needs to make a decision about purchasing new computers. An actor needs to research a time period to better portray an historical character.

Some instructors assign a specific topic for research (for example, "What are the most compelling scientific theories to explain false memory?"). Others leave more choice to you, assigning a general subject area appropriate to a specific course (for example, "memory" in a psychology course) and expecting you to narrow it to a manageable topic. Still other instructors expect you to choose

politics or the implications of cloning mammals. The problem has more to do with students' fears than the actual complexity of such assignments. You can build students' confidence with research skills if you assign "accessible" topics—especially for preliminary exercises in research skills and notetaking. Here are a few possibilities.

1. Write a biography of someone you would like to know more about: a sports figure, a cartoonist, a movie director, a state legislator, a dictator.

2. Write an essay recommending a particular type or model of some expensive consumer item that you are interested in buying, such as a car, a computer, or a home gym.

3. Write an essay recommending and explaining an eating regimen that can help someone lose weight, train for a sport, or control a health problem (such as diabetes or high blood pressure).

4. Imagine you're a US travel agent hired to plan a tour of Asia or Africa. Money is no object. You have been instructed to arrange stops in all countries with which the United States has friendly relations. For each country they'll visit, advise your clients of (1) entry requirements, such as a visa and the limitations on what they may bring into each country; (2) health precautions needed, including inoculations; and (3) local laws or customs that they must not violate, such as those dealing with alcohol and drugs.

5. If you haven't chosen a career or major, write an essay exploring the pros and cons of a particular career or major you're considering. If you have chosen your field, write an essay exploring a particular job in that field or arguing a position about an ethical or political problem in the field.

**TEACHING TIP**

Too often students view research writing as a knowledge-telling exercise rather than an inquiry-based assignment. As a result, their papers can become a string of disconnected paragraphs and citations as they try to include relevant sources but fail to integrate sources and to synthesize information; falter in providing appropriate documentation; and neglect to speak in their own voices. One approach to research that helps reduce the pain of writing (and reading!) stream-of-information papers is to help your students select a topic that originates in wonder. An "I wonder about/if _____" brainstorming activity helps awaken curiosity. From the subjects that surface from this activity, students can choose a topic that lends itself to research (of both primary and secondary sources). If you guide them through the types of resources that are available (reference works, scholarly journals, popular magazines, newspapers, personal interviews, Web sites in addition to online postings of print materials, etc.), your students can move from an inquiry-based topic to an inquiry-based investigation of sources. For instance, if the topic question is "Are gender distinctions 'hard-wired' or socialized?" further questions for exploration may include the following: (1) Are there cases of identical twins being raised as boy and girl? (2) What do transgendered men and women say on this subject? (3) What biological tests, if any, can shed light on this topic? (4) What do reputable social scientists and psychologists say? (5) Do present conjectures about gender apply across cultures? As students experience the pleasure of inquiry, they can see that a research paper seeks to solve a problem or answer a question for a particular audience. While this process does not guarantee smooth integration of sources, it certainly helps students see how source material needs to be used to help build a case or debate a point. As a result, this approach encourages students to speak in their own voices as they integrate source material to support an argument rather than merely to show off how many citations, however unrelated to one another, they may have gleaned in their research process.

**TEACHING TIP**
You may find it helpful to ask students to bring to class research assignments made in other classes. Working in groups, they can analyze the assignments in terms of audience, purpose, and scope of topic. Also, they might discuss a search strategy for carrying out the assignment,

> October 20: Because I'm not sure where online to start searching for sources about déjà vu, I've decided to use the "Research Navigator" our professor told us is available at <prenhall.com/troyka>. [Pause] Done—sure enough, when I clicked on the cover of this book, then on "research," and finally on the EBSCO database, I could navigate my way to a number of sources. I filed them in the folder offered and printed out what looked like the best ones. One problem I noted immediately: because the topic of déjà vu seems largely to be studied by psychologists and neuroscientists, the researchers use only the first initial of their first names. That's okay for APA style, but MLA requires the full first name. That's a problem I'll have to tackle.

**Figure 33.1** A selection from the research log of Andrei Gurov, who wrote the MLA-style research paper shown in section 36e

a topic on your own (for example, "Write a research paper on a topic of current interest or importance"). This last example happens most often in composition courses, where instructors often emphasize learning research skills more than mastering a particular content area.

## 33d.1 Choosing a topic on your own

The freedom to choose any topic you want can sometimes be overwhelming. Don't panic. Instead, use some of the strategies for generating ideas in Quick Reference 33.2.

## 33d.2 Narrowing a general topic into a workable one

Whether you're working with a topic of your choice or an assigned one, you want to check that it's sufficiently narrow for the time frame and other requirements of your research paper. Also, you want to be sure that the narrowed topic is worthy of a college research project.

- **Expect to consider various topics before making your final choice.** Give yourself time to think. Keep your mind open to flashes of insight and to alternative ideas. At the same time, be careful not to let indecision paralyze you.

## Quick Reference 33.2

### Finding general ideas for research

- **Talk with others.** Ask instructors or other experts in your area of interest what issues currently seem "hot" to them. Ask them to recommend readings or the names of authorities on those issues.

- **Browse some textbooks.** Read the table of contents and major headings of textbooks for subjects that interest you. As you narrow your focus, note the names of important books and experts, often mentioned in reference lists at the end of chapters or in the final pages of the book.

- **Browse the library or a well-stocked bookstore.** Stroll through the **stacks** (the rows of bookshelves) to find subjects that interest you. Look at books as well as periodicals. Thumb through popular magazines, and browse academic journals in fields that interest you.

- **Browse the Internet.** Many search engines provide topic directories. Click on some general categories and review subcategories until you locate specific topics that interest you. Then try further subject searches or KEYWORD searches (34d) to see where they lead.

- **Read encyclopedia articles about your interests.** General encyclopedias survey a wide range of topics, while specialized encyclopedias concentrate on a specific area. Never, however, stop with encyclopedias—they are too basic for college-level research.

- **Get ready.** Carry a small notebook and a pen, a laptop, or a PDA. Ideas have a way of popping into your mind when you least expect them. Jot down your thoughts on the spot so that they don't slip away.

---

- **Select a topic that interests you.** Your topic will be a companion for a while, sometimes for most of a semester. Select a topic that arouses your interest and allows you the pleasure of satisfying your intellectual curiosity.

- **Choose a sufficiently narrow topic.** You want to be successful within the time and length given by the assignment. Avoid topics that are too broad, such as "emotions." A better choice would be "how people perceive and respond to anger in others."

- **Choose a topic worth researching.** Avoid trivial topics that prevent you from doing what instructors and others expect of a student researcher.

  **NO**   The colors of MP3 players.

  **YES**  The legal issues of sharing downloaded music.

---

something that the student charged with doing the work would find quite helpful.

### BACKGROUND

In "'Building a Mystery': Alternative Research Writing and the Academic Act of Seeking" (*College Composition and Communication* 51.3 (2000): 417–446), Robert Davis and Mark Shadle suggest that "the research paper as we now teach it, like many things modern, scarcely lives up to" its promise as a means of constructing knowledge within the academy. Davis and Shadle offer "alternative research writing strategies" that ask students to move past the habit of reporting sources and toward more personal, academic, and social purposes for research. These authors discuss one research model currently endorsed in composition classes, the research argument, but they add three additional models for research paper assignments: "the personal research paper," "the research essay," and "the multi-genre/media/disciplinary/cultural research paper."

### QUOTATION: ON RESEARCH

One of the skills of research is knowing when you have enough information; in considering too many side issues or too many perspectives, you may lose the main thread of your subject.

—Charles Bazerman

### TEACHING TIP

For composition courses that have a service-learning component or that seek to offer students "real world" applications of their learning, many instructors speak glowingly of research projects from an organization, agency, or business in which their students participate. Local journalists, government officials, business leaders, and even faculty in other disciplines can also offer (and sometimes help direct) research projects for composition students. Positive benefits from such projects include the mentoring relationships that develop and the opportunity students have to be credited in print (scholarly articles, business and organization brochures, government reports, etc.) for the contributions they have made.

- **Choose a topic that has a sufficient number of appropriate sources available.** If you can't find useful sources—ones that relate directly to your topic and ones that are credible, not simply plentiful—drop the topic.
- **Talk with a professor in your field of interest, if possible.** Before the meeting, read a little about your topic so that you can ask informed questions. Ask whether you've narrowed your topic sufficiently and productively. Also, ask for the titles of major books and the names of major authorities on your topic.

A good academic topic allows you to demonstrate your critical thinking abilities. There are two broad ways of doing this. First, you might choose a topic on which intelligent people have formed different opinions. Then, you might analyze your sources and draw on your own experiences to decide which position appears best. The purpose of such a paper would be to attempt to PERSUADE readers that you've considered the various positions and reached a reasonable conclusion.

Alternatively, you might choose to INFORM readers in a paper that synthesizes several sources related to a complex subject. Writing a SYNTHESIS means pulling together extensive information from varied sources to examine essential points that relate to a topic. For example, imagine you've been assigned to write the sample research paper about déjà vu in section 36e. After you've read a dozen articles on the topic of déjà vu, you might try to identify three or four key points and then organize information from your reading around those points. Your goal is to clarify complicated or scattered information for your readers.

For a more detailed narrative of Andrei Gurov's research process and the final draft of his research paper, see 36e.1 and 36e.2.

# 33e What is a research question?

A **research question** about your topic is the controlling question that drives your research. Few research paper assignments are phrased as questions. Therefore, most research writing calls on you to ask a thought-provoking, underlying question and then to search for answers to it. Regarding research as a quest for an answer gives your work a specific focus: You can't know whether you've found useful source material unless you know what you're looking for.

Research questions, whether stated or implied, and the strategies needed to answer them vary widely. Your purpose might be to present and explain information: "How does penicillin destroy bacteria?" Or your purpose might be to argue one side of an issue: "Is Congress more important than the Supreme Court in setting social policy?" You can then consult various sources in an attempt to work toward an answer.

*Attempt* is an important word in relation to research. Some research questions lead to a final, definitive answer, but some do not. The previous question about penicillin leads to a reasonably definitive answer (you describe how the antibiotic penicillin destroys the cell walls of some bacteria); this means your writing has an informative purpose. The other question about social policy has no definitive answer, so you're asked to offer an informed opinion based on facts and authoritative viewpoints gathered from your research; this means your writing has a persuasive purpose.

To formulate a research question, begin by BRAINSTORMING a list of questions that come to mind about your topic. Write your list of ideas in your research log (33c).

Suppose, for example, the topic you want to write about is "homelessness." Here are some typical questions you might ask.

- Why can't a rich country like the United States eliminate homelessness?
- Who is homeless?
- How do people become homeless?
- Is it true that many families—not just adults—are homeless?
- Is the homelessness problem getting better or worse?
- What are we doing to solve the problem of homelessness?
- What is it like to be homeless?

Some questions will interest you more than others, so begin with one of those. If a question leads to a dead end, pursue another. Only when you find yourself accumulating answers—or in the case of questions without definitive answers, accumulating viewpoints—is it likely you're dealing with a usable research question. Once you have an explicitly stated research question, you can streamline your research by taking notes from those sources that help you answer your research question. If your research paper requires you to state an informed opinion, keep in mind that dealing with opposing positions is crucial to writing an effective argument (see section 5l).

Stay flexible as you work. The results of your research may lead you to modify the research question slightly. Actually, such modifying is part of the "moving ahead and circling back" that characterizes research writing. When you've finished researching and notetaking in response to your final research question, you have a starting place for formulating your preliminary THESIS STATEMENT (see 2d).

# 33f How does the writing situation shape my research paper?

Your TOPIC, PURPOSE, AUDIENCE, ROLE, and SPECIAL CONSIDERATIONS (1b) all influence your research paper. If you receive an assignment to argue for a position but instead you inform readers about possible positions, your paper will

that is selected for notes and the information that is rejected. You may want to ask students to bring their notes to class for comparison with those taken by their fellow students. The comparison will be even more interesting if the student-researchers keep a complete record of their research in their logs, recording the title and precise location (call number, URL, etc.) of any source not used, with a note as to why it was rejected.

**QUOTATION: ON WRITING**
I almost always urge people to write in the first person. . . . Writing is an act of ego and you might as well admit it.
—William Zinsser

**TEACHING TIP**
As students today rely on computers not only for final stage writing but also for notetaking and drafting as well, the need for safeguarding files becomes increasingly important. To prevent the "I lost my file" scenario, you may want to caution students to create backup files for which they must be responsible: on hard drive, CD or other portable disk/flashkey, and even through e-mail or other online storage services. Remind them to save their work often, using several of the methods listed in the previous sentence, in order to give them the best chance of maintaining the integrity of the files. Creating separate files for each section of a project can assist students in organizing as well as in safeguarding their work.

If you are teaching using a content management system that features a forum for class discussion, you might encourage students to post their notes and process-based writing as part of their public class work. This opens up greater possibilities for peer review of all stages of the research process, ensures that students have a ready back up for all of their files, and also ensures that students are meeting the course research schedule in a timely fashion.

**QUOTATION: ON RESEARCH**
By asking students to stick to researching the known, we teach them to fear the unknown.
—Robert Davis and Mark Shadle

fall short. The same would happen if you were assigned to write a ten-page paper, in MLA style, for an audience of people knowledgeable on a certain topic and instead you wrote fifteen pages in APA style, for a very general audience. When you receive a research paper assignment, make sure to understand if you're being asked to write for a specific situation. Maybe the assignment will specify only a few elements of the situation but not all; follow, then, the ones required.

Even if you receive a very open assignment, you'll find it useful to create a writing situation for that paper, especially a purpose and audience. Doing so will give you a guidepost to see if you're on the right track. To decide whether your paper will have an informative purpose or a persuasive purpose, see what your research question asks. If the answer to it involves giving facts, information, and explanation, your purpose is to inform. For example, "How have computers changed over time?" calls for INFORMATIVE WRITING. Conversely, if the answer involves offering an educated opinion based on contrasting views and supporting evidence, your purpose is to persuade. For example, "Why should people be aware of current developments in computers?" calls for PERSUASIVE WRITING. You may find that during your research or writing process, a different purpose would make more sense. Usually, it makes sense to change to the new purpose, adjusting your thesis in the process. However, if your instructor has asked for a proposal or otherwise approved your research project, you'll want to check to make sure the new direction is OK.

AUDIENCES for research papers can vary. Your instructor, of course, is always an audience. However, in some cases he or she will read as a representative of other, larger audiences, and you'll want to meet their expectations. For example, if you're writing about the topic of déjà vu for a specialized audience (1d.2) that knows psychology and expects your paper to have the characteristics of writing in that field, your research paper will differ slightly from one on the very same topic but for a general educated audience (1d.1). Your sense of audience can guide your decisions about content, prior knowledge, assumptions, level of detail and explanations needed, STYLE, TONE, and so on. Section 1d provides advice for analyzing audience.

## 33g What practical steps can help me work efficiently?

To conduct your research with greatest efficiency, you need to do some footwork before you start researching. First, gather the materials listed in Quick Reference 33.3 so that they're organized and ready for use at a moment's notice. Second, become familiar with your college library, especially its catalogs and databases (34d). Third, be sure to become skilled with finding and evaluating appropriate resources on the Internet (34k–34m).

---

**Quick Reference 33.3**  ▪ ▪ ▪ ▪ ▪ ▪ ▪

## Materials you might need for research

1. A copy of your assignment.

2. This handbook, especially Part Five, or access to the Internet so that you can read the book online and use its guidelines.

3. Your research log (33c).

4. Index cards for taking notes (unless you use a laptop). If you use different colors of index cards, you might color-code the different categories of information you find. Also, you might use one size for bibliography cards and the other for content note cards. Another coding strategy is to use pens of different ink colors or self-sticking dots of various colors.

5. Money or a debit card for copy machines or printers.

6. A flash drive or other means for storing downloaded source materials, if you're not exclusively using your own computer.

7. If you use index cards and other paper, a small stapler, paper clips, and rubber bands.

8. A separate bag or backpack with wheels to carry research-project materials and books you check out from the library. (Librarians joke about researchers with wheelbarrows.)

---

## 33g.1  Learning how to use library resources

When you learn how your college library functions, your research efficiency increases. Though almost all libraries in the United States and Canada are organized around the same principles for organizing information, physical layouts and procedures differ considerably. If you visit your college library for the sole purpose of figuring out what's located where, you'll feel comfortable and confident when you work there.

Some college libraries provide orientations through English courses; some offer individual training sessions; and most offer informative Web sites or handouts about their resources. Quick Reference 33.4 provides a checklist for familiarizing yourself with your library.

## 33g.2  Deciding how you'll use the computer

How you use the computer in the research process is largely a matter of personal preference. Some students use a computer only for finding sources and for DRAFTING and REVISING the paper itself. These students do the rest of their research steps by hand on index cards and sheets of paper: keeping their

some research goes against the prescribed methodology. In that case, you might ask students to imagine what a thesis statement would look like if, hypothetically, the research leaned one way or the other. For instance, if a student had chosen number 1, "Fishing," narrowed down to the topic of "overfishing and the world's food supply," and then followed with the research question, "Are we overfishing and threatening the world's food supply?" you might ask the student to write three different thesis statements: one that argues that we are overfishing the world's oceans, one that argues we are not, and one for which the evidence is inconclusive.

**QUOTATION: ON WRITING**
To me, the greatest pleasure of writing is not what it's about, but the inner music that words make.
—Truman Capote

**QUOTATION: ON WRITING**
The longer I write, the more important I believe it is to write the first draft as fast as possible. In drafting, I push myself so I am at the edge of discomfort. . . . Later, it will be time for consideration and reconsideration, slow, careful revision and editing. But on the first draft I have to achieve velocity, just as you do if you want the bike to balance.
—Donald M. Murray

**TEACHING TIP**
You may want to point out to students that the revision checklist in this section contains questions about content, organization, paragraph style, and documentation. Questions about grammar and punctuation are absent, not because these elements are unimportant in the final presentation of a paper, but because they do not need attention until absolutely all concerns about content, organization, audience, and voice have been addressed. If you help students focus on these fundamental issues in the notetaking and drafting stages of their work (by giving feedback and raising questions), they will soon realize that sentence-polishing and paper-formatting concerns are best left until last.

Indeed, correcting errors at the sentence level becomes moot if sentences (even whole paragraphs) must be deleted or changed altogether to satisfy a content or organizational matter of clear, focused communication.

**QUOTATION: ON TRUTH**

When you want to fool the world, tell the truth.

—Otto von Bismarck

**QUOTATION: ON WRITING**

All I needed was a steady table and a typewriter. . . . A marble-topped bedroom washstand table made a good place; the dining-room table between meals was also suitable.

—Agatha Christie

---

**Quick Reference 33.4** ■ ■ ■ ■ ■ ■ ■

## Learning your library's resources

- How do you get access to the library's catalog and databases, both from inside the library and through the Internet? What are the log-in procedures?

- How does the library's catalog work?

- What periodical indexes or databases does your library have, online or in print? (*Indexes* and *databases* are lists of articles in journals and magazines, grouped by subject areas.)

- Where is the general reference collection? (You can't check out reference books, so when you need to use them, build extra time into your schedule to spend at the library.)

- Where is the special reference collection? (Same rules apply as for general reference books.)

- Are the book and journal stacks open (fully accessible shelves) or closed (request each item by filling out a form to hand to library personnel)? If the latter, become familiar with the required procedures not only for asking for a book or journal but also for picking it up when it's ready.

- Where are the library's physical collections of periodicals (journals, magazines, and newspapers) stored? Libraries are increasingly moving from paper to digital storage, but some publications might still exist only in print. Most libraries place periodicals published recently in open areas, and they place older ones in bound volumes, on microfilm or microfiche, or online. Learn to use whatever system is in place at your library.

- How do you identify when periodical articles exist digitally, in versions that you can read completely online rather than only from a paper copy? When you find that an article has a digital version, how do you access it?

- What, if anything, is stored on microfilm or microfiche? If you think you'll use that material, take the time to learn how to use the machines. (We find that each library's machines work differently—and many of them have stumped us on occasion.)

- Does the library have special collections, such as local historical works or the writings of persons worthy of such an exclusive honor?

---

research log (33c), compiling their WORKING BIBLIOGRAPHY (33i), taking content notes (33k), and so forth.

Other students carry out their entire research process on computer. They set up folders for every phase of their project. To accumulate print sources for their working bibliography, these students download them onto a computer hard drive or a flash drive—always carefully recording the origin of the source in the documentation style they've selected (33h). They type their research log, working bibliography, and content notes directly into computer files.

# 33h What documentation style should I use?

A **documentation style** is a system for providing information about each source you've used in your research paper. Documentation styles vary from one academic discipline to another. The humanities often use MLA (Modern Language Association) style (Chapter 36). The social sciences frequently use APA (American Psychological Association) style (Chapter 37). Biology and other natural sciences often use CSE (Council of Science Editors) style (Chapter 38). CM (*Chicago Manual*) style is used in various disciplines, generally in the humanities (Chapter 38). Instructors almost always have precise expectations about which style they want you to use. Find it out, and follow it to the letter! Using the wrong documentation style—or using the right one badly—is like showing up to a formal wedding wearing flip-flops and a ripped shirt. You don't want an instructor to minimize your research and writing effort because he or she is so distracted by careless documentation.

Determining the required documentation style at the start of the process helps to guarantee that you'll write down the exact details you need to document your sources. You'll need to document all secondary sources. If you're doing primary research, decide what you must document before you begin. Your instructor may have special requirements, such as asking you to submit your research notes or results from observations, questionnaires, surveys, interviews, or anything else that produces primary data.

# 33i What is a working bibliography?

A **working bibliography** is a preliminary list of the PRIMARY and SECONDARY SOURCES you gather in your research. It contains information about the source and where others might find it. The following is a list of basic elements to include (see more detailed information about documenting specific types of sources in Chapters 36–38).

| **Books** | **Periodical Articles** | **Online Sources** |
|---|---|---|
| Author(s) | Author(s) | Author (if available); editor or sponsor of site |
| Title | Title | Title of document and title of site |

| Books | Periodical Articles | Online Sources |
|---|---|---|
| **Books** | **Periodical Articles** | **Online Sources** |
| Publisher and place of publication | Name of periodical, volume number, issue number | Name of database or sponsor of online source |
| Year of publication | Date of issue | Date of electronic publication |
| Call number | Page numbers of article | Electronic address (URL) Date you accessed the source |

Begin your working bibliography as soon as you start identifying sources. Compiling a working bibliography will help you find out what is available on a particular subject before you do extensive reading and notetaking. If your search turns up very few sources, you may want to change your topic. If it reveals a vast number of sources, you definitely want to narrow your topic or even choose a different one. At the outset, don't leave anything out; even an unpromising source may later prove useful. Expect to add and drop sources throughout the research writing process. As a rough estimate, your working bibliography needs to be about twice as long as the list of sources you end up using. You can record your working bibliography on note cards or on a computer.

On the one hand, note cards have the advantage of being easy to sift through and rearrange. You can also carry them with you when you do library research. At the end of your writing process, you can easily sort and alphabetize them to prepare your final bibliography. Write only one source on each card. Figure 33.2 displays a handwritten bibliography note card by Andrei Gurov for his MLA-style research paper in section 36e.

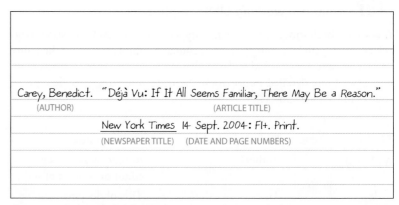

**Figure 33.2** Sample bibliography note card in MLA style

On the other hand, putting your working bibliography on a computer saves you from having to type your list of sources later. If you use a computer for this purpose, clearly separate one entry from another. You can organize the list alphabetically, by author, or according to your subtopics.

Your library may even have a program like RefWorks or EndNote that allows you to download bibliographic information directly onto your computer, and then easily reformat it to the appropriate documentation style.

Whichever method you use, when you come across a potential source, immediately record the information exactly as you need it to fulfill the requirements of the DOCUMENTATION STYLE you need to use for your assignment (33h). Spending a few extra moments at this stage can save you hours of work and frustration later on.

## 33j What is an annotated bibliography?

An **annotated bibliography** includes not only publishing information about your sources but also your brief summary of each one, and perhaps a commentary. Figure 33.3 shows part of an annotated bibliography for sources used in the APA-style student paper in Chapter 37.

McKenna, K. Y., Green, A. S., & Gleason, M. E. (2003). Relationship formation
on the Internet: What's the big attraction? *Journal of Social Issues,*
*58,* 9–31.

> Two studies show that people who share "true selves" over
> the Internet often form closer relationships than when they meet
> face to face. One study surveyed Internet users. A second study
> found that students who meet first on the Internet tend to like
> each other better than students who meet first in person.

Miyake, K., & Zuckerman, M. (1993). Beyond personality impressions.
*Journal of Personality, 61*(3), 411–436.

> This research study examines how both physical and vocal
> attractiveness affect judges' responses to individuals. The
> researchers found that, for five different personality measures,
> judges rate more attractive people more highly.

**Figure 33.3** Section from an annotated bibliography in APA style

# 33k How do I take content notes?

When you write **content notes,** you record information from your sources. As with your working bibliography, you can make content notes either in a computer file or on index cards.

- If you're using index cards, put a heading on each card that gives a precise link to one of your bibliography items. Include the source's title and the numbers of the pages from which you're taking notes.

- On the computer, keep careful track of the source of each idea. One strategy is to open a new file for each. Later, after you've taken notes on many of your sources, you can determine what subtopics are important for your paper. You can then open a new file for each topic and use the "Cut" and "Paste" functions to gather notes from all of your sources under each topic.

- On every note card or every file in your computer, do one of three things: (1) Copy exact words from a source in a quotation, enclosing it in quotation marks; (2) write a paraphrase of the source; or (3) write a summary of the source. Keeping track of the kind of note you're taking will help you avoid PLAGIARISM. You might use the codes *Q* for QUOTATION, *P* for PARAPHRASE, and *S* for SUMMARY. Or you might use a different typeface or ink color.

- As you're taking notes, separately record your own reactions and ideas, but take care to differentiate your ideas from those found in your sources. You might write your own thoughts in a different colored ink (note card) or font (computer); you might use the back of your note cards or a computer's "Comment" feature. You can also record your thinking in your RESEARCH LOG.

Figure 33.4 shows one of Andrei Gurov's note cards for his paper in section 36e.2.

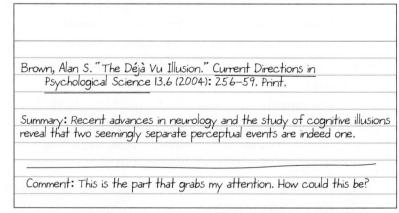

Brown, Alan S. "The Déjà Vu Illusion." *Current Directions in Psychological Science* 13.6 (2004): 256–59. Print.

Summary: Recent advances in neurology and the study of cognitive illusions reveal that two seemingly separate perceptual events are indeed one.

Comment: This is the part that grabs my attention. How could this be?

**Figure 33.4** A handwritten content note card in MLA style

## 331 How do I draft a thesis statement for a research paper?

Drafting a THESIS STATEMENT for a research paper marks the transition from the research process to the writing process. A thesis statement in a research paper sets out the central theme, which you need to sustain throughout the paper (see section 2d, especially Box 2.3). As with any piece of writing, your research paper must fulfill the promise of its thesis statement.

You might begin thinking of a preliminary thesis statement at some middle point in the research process, although it's perfectly acceptable to wait until you've completely finished researching. To start your thesis statement, you might try to convert your RESEARCH QUESTION into a preliminary thesis statement. Remember that a good thesis statement makes an assertion that conveys your point of view about your topic and foreshadows the content of your paper (see Quick Reference 2.3 in 2d). And not least, remember that your research needs to support your thesis statement. Ask yourself whether the material you've gathered from sources can effectively give support. If not, revise your thesis statement, conduct further research, or do both.

Here are examples of subjects narrowed to topics, focused into research questions, and then cast as thesis statements.

| | |
|---|---|
| SUBJECT | *nonverbal communication* |
| TOPIC | Personal space |
| RESEARCH QUESTION | How do standards for personal space differ among cultures? |
| INFORMATIVE THESIS STATEMENT | Everyone has expectations concerning the use of personal space, but accepted distances for that space are determined by each person's culture. |
| PERSUASIVE THESIS STATEMENT | To prevent intercultural misunderstandings, people must be aware of cultural differences in standards for personal space. |
| SUBJECT | *computers* |
| TOPIC | artificial intelligence |
| RESEARCH QUESTION | How close are researchers to developing artificial intelligence in computers? |
| INFORMATIVE THESIS STATEMENT | Scientists disagree about whether computers need emotions to have artificial intelligence. |
| PERSUASIVE THESIS STATEMENT | Because emotions play a strong role in human intelligence, computers must have emotions before they can truly have artificial intelligence. |

Andrei Gurov (whose research paper appears in section 36e) revised his preliminary thesis statement twice before he felt that it expressed the point he wanted to make. Andrei also took the key step of checking that he would be able to support it sufficiently with sources throughout the paper.

**FIRST PRELIMINARY THESIS STATEMENT**

Déjà vu can be explained by a variety of scientific theories. [Andrei realized that this draft thesis would lead to a paper that would merely list, paragraph by paragraph, each theory, and that the paper would lack synthesis.]

**SECOND PRELIMINARY THESIS STATEMENT**

Many people believe feelings of déjà vu have mysterious origins, but science has shown this is not true. [Andrei liked this statement better because it began to get at the complexity of the topic, but he wanted to work on it more because he felt the second part was too general.]

**FINAL THESIS STATEMENT**

Although a few people today still prefer to believe that feelings of déjà vu have mysterious or supernatural origins, recent research in cognitive psychology and the neurosciences has shed much rational light on the phenomenon.

## 33m How do I outline a research paper?

Some instructors require an OUTLINE of your research paper, either before you hand in the paper or along with the paper. In such cases, your instructor is probably expecting you to be working from an outline as you write your drafts. Your research log often comes in handy when you group ideas, especially for a first draft of your paper—and as you make an *informal outline* for it. An outline can serve as a guide as you plan and write your paper. For directions on composing a *formal outline,* see section 2f. To see a topic outline of Andrei Gurov's research paper, turn to section 36e.

## 33n How do I draft a research paper?

DRAFTING and REVISING a research paper is like drafting and revising any other piece of writing (Chapter 2). Yet to write a research paper, you need extra time for planning, drafting, thinking, redrafting, rethinking, and creating a final draft because you need to demonstrate all of the following:

- You've followed the steps of the research processes presented in Chapters 32–35.

- You understand the information that you've located during your research.
- You've evaluated the SOURCES you've used in your research.
- You haven't PLAGIARIZED your material from someone else (35b).
- You've used sources well in your writing, correctly employing QUOTATIONS, PARAPHRASES, and SUMMARIES (35f–35k).
- You've moved beyond SUMMARY to SYNTHESIS so that your sources are interwoven with each other and with your own thinking, not merely listed one by one (4f).
- You've used DOCUMENTATION accurately. (For MLA STYLE, see Chapter 36; for APA STYLE, see Chapter 37; for other documentation styles, see Chapter 38)

Expect to write a number of drafts of your research paper. The first draft is your chance to discover new insights and connections. Successive drafts help you master the information you've learned and add it authoritatively to the knowledge you already had about the topic. In the first draft, organize the broad categories of your paper. Quick Reference 33.5 suggests some ways to write your first draft.

# 33o How do I revise a research paper?

Before you write each new draft, read your previous draft with a sharp eye. For best results, take a break of a few days (or at least a few hours) before beginning this process. This gives you distance from your material, and a clearer vision of what you need to revise. For a more objective point of view, consider asking a few people you respect to read and react to your first, or perhaps your second, draft.

One key to REVISING any research paper is to examine carefully the evidence you have included. **Evidence** consists of facts, statistics, expert studies and opinions, examples, and stories. As a reader, you expect writers to provide solid evidence to back up their claims and conclusions. Similarly, when you write, readers expect you to provide evidence that clearly supports your claims and conclusions. Use RENNS (3f) to see if you can develop paragraphs more fully. Identify each of the points you have made in your paper, including your thesis and all your subpoints. Then ask the questions in Quick Reference 33.6.

Experienced writers know that writing is really *rewriting*. Research papers are among the most demanding composing assignments, and most writers revise several times. Once you've produced a *final draft,* you're ready to edit (2j), proofread (2k), and format (2c.5) your work. Check for correct grammar,

> ## Quick Reference 33.5
>
> ### Suggestions for drafting a research paper
>
> - Some writers categorize their notes and write a section at a time. They organize the notes into broad categories by making a separate group for each topic. As patterns begin to emerge, these writers might move material from one category to another. Each category becomes a section of the first draft. This method not only assures writers that their first draft will include all of the material from their research, but reveals any gaps in information that call for additional research. Of course, you may discover that some of your research doesn't fit your topic and thesis. Put it aside; it might be useful in a later draft.
>
> - Some writers generate a list of questions that their paper needs to address, then answer each question, one at a time, looking for the content notes that will help them. For example, writing on the topic of organic foods, some possible questions might be, "What are organic foods? What benefits do people see for eating them? Why do they cost more than regular foods? Does everyone agree that they are beneficial?" Generating and answering questions can be a way of turning a mass of information into manageable groupings.
>
> - Some writers finish their research and then slowly review half of the information they've gathered. Next, setting aside that information, they write a partial first draft by drawing on the information they remember from their reading. Then, they use the same process with the second half of the information that they've gathered. Finally, with their two partial drafts and all of their research notes in front of them, they write a complete first draft. Writers who use this method say it gives them a broad overview of their material quickly and identifies any gaps in information that they need to fill in with further research.
>
> - Some writers stop at various points during their research and use FREEWRITING to get their ideas into words. Writers who use this method say that it helps them recognize when they need to adjust their RESEARCH QUESTION or change the emphasis of their search. After a number of rounds of researching and freewriting, these writers find that they can complete their first draft relatively easily.
>
> - Some writers review their sources and create an OUTLINE before drafting (2f). Some find a formal outline helpful, while others use a less formal approach.

## Quick Reference 33.6

■ ■ ■ ■ ■ ■ ■

### Questions for evaluating your evidence

- **Is the evidence sufficient?** To be sufficient, evidence can't be thin or trivial. As a rule, the more evidence you present, the more convincing your thesis will be to readers.

- **Is the evidence representative?** Representative evidence is customary and normal, not based on exceptions. When evidence is representative, it provides a view of the issue that reflects the usual circumstances rather than rare ones.

- **Is the evidence relevant?** Relevant evidence relates directly to your thesis or topic sentences. It illustrates your reasons straightforwardly and never introduces unrelated material.

- **Is the evidence accurate?** Accurate evidence is correct, complete, and up to date. It comes from a reliable SOURCE. Equally important, you present it honestly, without distorting or misrepresenting it.

- **Is the evidence reasonable?** Reasonable evidence is not phrased in extreme language, such as *all, never,* or *certainly.* Reasonable evidence is well thought out and free of logical fallacies (4i).

punctuation, capitalization, and spelling. (No amount of careful research and good writing can make up for an incorrectly presented, sloppy, error-laden document.)

Consult Quick References 2.8 and 2.9 to remind yourself of the general principles of revising, and consult the research paper revision checklist in Quick Reference 33.7. One of the best things you might do is apply the strategies of critical thinking (Chapter 4) to your own writing. Read your own paper as if you were an outside critical reader. Additionally, have a classmate or trusted friend provide peer response (6c).

To see one example of the research writing process in action, turn to section 36e. There you'll see the final draft of an MLA-style research paper; a narrative of decisions that the student made during his research process; and commentary (on the text page facing each page of the student's paper) that gives you insight into specific aspects of his paper.

For an APA-style research paper, turn to section 37h. There you'll see the final draft of a student's paper and a narrative of the decisions that the student made during his research process.

## Quick Reference 33.7

■ ■ ■ ■ ■ ■ ■

### Revising a research paper

If the answer to any of the following questions is no, you need to revise. The section numbers in parentheses tell you where to find useful information.

**WRITING**

- Does your introductory paragraph lead effectively into the material? (3b)
- Have you met the basic requirements for a written thesis statement? (2d)
- Do your thesis statement and the content of your paper address your research question(s)? (33e)
- Have you developed effective body paragraphs? (3d; 3f, Quick Reference 3.3)
- Does the concluding paragraph end your paper effectively? (3k)
- Does your paper satisfy a critical thinker? (Chapter 4)

**RESEARCH**

- Have you included appropriate and effective evidence? (3d and Quick Reference 33.6)
- Have you deleted irrelevant or insignificant information? (3g)
- Have you used quotations, paraphrases, and summaries well? (35f–35k)
- Have you integrated your source material well without plagiarizing? (35c)

**FORMAT AND DOCUMENTATION**

- Have you used the correct format for your parenthetical citations or other documentation style? (Chapters 36–38)
- Does each citation tie into an item in your WORKS CITED (MLA style) or REFERENCES (APA style) list of sources at the end of your paper? (36d and 37f)
- Does the paper exactly match the format you've been assigned to follow? Check margins, spacing, title, headings, page number, font, and so on (Chapter 45).

# 34

# Finding and Evaluating Published Sources

## 34a   What is a published source?

A **published source** is a book, article, Web page, or other type of writing that appears in print or in electronic format. While the kinds of field research we discuss in section 32e require you to gather information and turn it into words, in published sources other writers have already done that work. However, it's up to you to decide whether they have done it accurately, fairly, and well. Your goal is to find sources needed to answer your research question, evaluate their quality, and SYNTHESIZE them into your own writing, using QUOTATION, SUMMARY, or PARAPHRASE. Published sources are PRIMARY if they are firsthand reports of experiments, observations, and so on, or if they are creative works like poems, letters, or stories. A SECONDARY published source is one that reports, describes, or comments on someone else's work. Section 4d explains the differences.

## 34b   What is a search strategy?

A **search strategy** is an organized procedure for locating and gathering information to answer your specific RESEARCH QUESTION. Some research, such as finding one particular fact or piece of information, doesn't require an extensive strategy (34b). Others, such as fully understanding an issue or synthesizing current knowledge, require care and planning. Using a search strategy means working systematically rather than haphazardly.

Following are three frequently used search strategies. If no single one meets your requirements, create your own.

The **expert method** is useful when you know your topic well enough to begin "at the top," with the best current thinking by experts on that subject. You'll begin by reading their books and articles to identify the main subtopics, positions, or issues. You'll ask yourself: What is in agreement? What is in dispute? What are the main questions under investigation?

Of course, the expert method means that you have to know who the experts are, and sometimes that's difficult. Talk with people who are generally knowledgeable about your topic, learn what you can from them, and ask them to refer you to work by experts on the topic. Your professors are an obvious place to start.

**TEACHING TIP: ONLINE RESEARCH**
To provide students with the clearest, most up-to-date information on how to do library research, we have included throughout this chapter many examples of real screens accessed through real URLs. All are correct at the time of writing this book. However, because the Internet changes quickly, and access to databases and search engines depends on the Internet service provider you or your institution uses, we advise that you alert students that they might not be able to access the URLs shown in many of the sample screens in this chapter. Instead, they need to check with a librarian at your institution's library for information on how to access particular resources. (You might ask students to bring access information to class to share with everyone.)

**TEACHING TIP**
This chapter builds on the introductory information in Chapters 32 and 33. When you are ready to begin teaching the research paper in your course, schedule a library orientation with your library's reference librarian. The librarian should be able to give your students an in-depth tour of all of the resources in the library. In general, creating structured activities—such as a library scavenger hunt and hands-on searches—will help your students to become quickly familiar with the wide range of sources available.

To make a library session go smoothly, distribute paper maps of the college library before you go. Also, if your students have to activate their student ID in order to use the library and access its services, ask your students to do that prior to the library session.

You may also want to distribute the library's hours and a list of the databases that students can access off campus. Many libraries have this information easily available on the library homepage. If you are using a course management system like BlackBoard or Angel, you can put a link to the relevant information on your course site.

**TEACHING TIP**
Quoting, Summarizing, Paraphrasing, and Synthesizing are covered in Chapter 35.

For example, if you're researching Internet dating, a psychology instructor may be able to tell you who are the leading experts on that topic. In some cases, you might be able to interview an expert in person, on the phone, or through e-mail. Turn to section 32e.3 for detailed advice about conducting effective interviews.

The **chaining method** is useful when you know only general things about your topic or can't tell who the experts are. Start by reading or skimming reference books or some current articles in scholarly journals, popular magazines, or newspapers. As you do, pay close attention to people who are cited in those readings or in any bibliographies at the end. Then search for works by those people or look for the specific books or articles mentioned.

For example, suppose you read an article on Internet dating in *Time* magazine, and that article quotes a scholar named Monica Whitty, who seems to be an expert. You use your library's catalog or databases to see if Whitty has published anything, and you discover she has co-authored a book *Cyberspace Romances: The Psychology of Online Relationships.* You then find and browse that book both to see how it contributes to your research question and also to find the names of other scholars, publications, and key terms. You keep following the links in this chain until you're confident you've identified expert sources and you have gathered the breadth and depth of information you'll need.

The **questioning method** means breaking your overall research question into several smaller questions, then finding sources to answer each of them. This method has the advantage of allowing you to see if your sources cover all the areas important to your research question. Suppose your research question is, "How successful are relationships that begin on the Internet?" The list of questions you brainstorm might include, "Who participates in Internet dating? Are there typical ways Internet relationships develop? How may Internet contacts result in actual meetings?" Generating a list of questions like this can give your search a direction and purpose.

You may find yourself switching or combining methods. That's fine. "Flexibility with focus" is the guiding principle for experienced researchers. Discovering early in the process what sources are available allows you time to find those that are harder to locate; to use interlibrary loan if an item isn't available in your library or online; to wait for someone to return checked-out books you need; or to schedule interviews, arrange visits, or conduct surveys.

As you locate, assemble, and evaluate sources, expect to accumulate much more information than you'll actually use. Indeed, the quality of a research paper depends partly on your ability to eliminate inadequate or repetitive sources and to recognize what is valuable material. Turn to section 34j for detailed guidelines for evaluating sources.

One more piece of advice: Avoid getting too far along in your search until you're reasonably certain you're going in a useful direction. Rather than spend endless hours simply gathering sources, read and analyze some of your materials to make sure your topic is a good one. Your RESEARCH LOG can be useful for this purpose.

## 34c What are library-based sources?

In an age when the Internet contains billions of pages of information, it might seem almost prehistoric to talk about libraries. After all, the **library** is where generations of college students have traditionally gone to find sources: books and periodicals organized by catalogs and indexes. However, notice that we've referred to "library-based" sources and not necessarily to the library itself. In many respects, the function that a library performs is even more important than its physical building. Librarians and scholars have systematically gathered and organized sources so that students and researchers can find the best ones efficiently and reliably. Many libraries give you online access to their holdings, so you might use library-based sources without ever setting foot in the building itself.

Still, the building itself continues to be a vital place for all research. One key advantage of going to the library is your chance to consult face-to-face with librarians. They train for their profession by learning how to advise students and other researchers about using library resources to the greatest advantage. Never hesitate to ask questions about how to proceed or where to find a resource.

**Catalogs** list sources—usually books, but also films, recordings, and documents—that the library owns (34d). **Databases** contain extensive lists of articles, reports, and books, organized and searchable in many ways (34d). Your library will own or provide access to many sources included in a database, but it almost certainly won't have all of them. Catalogs and databases exist in electronic formats that you can access and search from computers in the library or, often, by connecting to the library online. Both college and public libraries subscribe to database services, although they may be limited depending on the library's size. Many businesses and corporations also subscribe to databases, making them available to people associated with the company. A law firm, for example, likely subscribes to LexisNexis, which provides searchable access to legal cases and decisions.

If you're accessing a database by connecting to the library online, you need to use a **browser** (such as Firefox or Internet Explorer), a software program that gives you access to the Web.

## 34d How do I use catalogs and databases?

Sources that you identify through catalogs and scholarly databases are almost always more reliable and appropriate than sources you find by simply browsing the Web. The reliability of scholarly databases stems from their origins: Only experts and professionals who judge works to have merit compile them.

### USING COLLABORATION

Working together, students can undertake more extensive primary research than they can working alone. A group of students can draw up a list of interview questions to ask in individually conducted interviews. The identical question set ensures that students can compare the information from each interview. Conversely, some projects may benefit from having members of the group ask different questions so that each gathers information on a different aspect of the topic. Indeed, you could decide to tell students that the person they interview might sometimes mention new and intriguing subjects. In such cases, even though questions about these new areas don't appear on the prepared list, students can choose to explore the new subjects during the interview. Interviewer flexibility usually pays off in such situations.

### HISTORY

Benjamin Franklin organized the Library Company of Philadelphia in 1731, the first American subscription library. Its original purpose was to provide ready access to books for members of the Junto Club, a public service group to which Franklin belonged. Franklin himself said that he spent time at the library almost daily, learning foreign languages or reading for general knowledge.

Until the founding of the Library Company, there were few public libraries in the American colonies. The earliest one was the library of Harvard College, which was founded in 1638 with nearly four hundred volumes bequeathed by John Harvard. Libraries were established at Yale and at William and Mary around 1700. In the southern colonies, the Reverend Thomas Bray (1656–1730), working by appointment of the Bishop of London as commissary of the Anglican Church, established parochial libraries. In 1876, a report titled *Public Libraries in the United States* read: "So far as is known, there were, in 1776, twenty-nine public libraries in the thirteen American colonies, and they numbered altogether 45,623 volumes; in the year 1800 the number of libraries had increased to forty-nine, and the number of volumes to about 80,000." The Library of Congress, which contains over 72 million pieces of material (among them 16.5 million books and 31 million manuscripts), was begun by Congress in 1800 with a budget of $5,000.

**TEACHING TIP**

What is available on campus and in your area? Do you have a local historical society? On-campus archives? If so, helping students to work with primary historical documents can be an exciting way to frame a research assignment.

**ANSWERS: EXERCISE 34-1**

Answers will vary. Depending on the variety of sources available through your library, you may want to help students categorize databases into "general knowledge" and "specialized" databases. You can also expand this exercise by asking students to explore what additional databases are available through the local public library.

**HISTORY**

"The very idea of a public library—that is to say, of a library to be used by the people, not theoretically, but practically, and the success or failure of which should be estimated not by the number or the variety of the books it contains, but by the number of its readers and the quality of the books it circulates—is peculiarly a product of the modern era, and though the United States can not perhaps lay claim to having originated it, yet, from the evidence afforded by this report, it has met with such a hearty reception in this country, and has been so apt an aid to our system of popular education, that certainly it is here we may expect to find the best results arising from its practical realization."
—Edward Howland ("The Public Libraries of the United States," *Harper's New Monthly Magazine* 54.323 (1877): 722–730)

**BACKGROUND: THE NEXT GENERATION IN LIBRARIES**

Second Life, the popular 3-D virtual world (free), hosts a lively library population. The next generation in thinking about making knowledge publicly accessible, libraries in Second Life are actively experimenting with new ways to distribute text and information to the residents

The best way to access a database at your library is to go to your college library's Web site, whether you're online in the library, at home, or in a dormitory.

Each home page of a library shows the resources available through that Web site, although more might be available in the library itself. Most college libraries subscribe to one or more database services, such as EBSCO, ProQuest, or FirstSearch. Because your tuition pays for these services, you can take advantage of them without further expense, but you'll need an ID or password to gain access.

Each entry in a database contains bibliographic information, including a title, author, date of publication, and publisher (in the case of books or reports) or periodical (in the case of articles). The entry might also provide an abstract, or summary, of the material. Once you locate an entry that seems promising, you need to find the actual book or complete article itself, and we explain how to do that below in sections 34e (for books) and 34f (for periodicals).

**EXERCISE 34-1** Working either individually or as part of a group, access your library's Web site. List all of the types of information available. In particular, list the indexes and databases you can search and the subject areas each one covers. Note whether any of the databases have full-text versions of articles.

**USING KEYWORDS**

When you search library databases, **keywords**, also called *descriptors* or *identifiers,* are your lifeline to success. Keywords are the main words in a source's title or the words that the author or editor has identified as central. Without keywords, you'd have great difficulty accessing sources listed in electronic databases.

When you search using keywords, chances are you'll come up with a large or even overwhelming number of sources. Much of what turns up won't be relevant to your topic. Two main ways to make keyword searches more efficient are using guided searches (answers to prompts) and using Boolean expressions (keyword combinations).

**USING GUIDED SEARCHES**

**Guided searches**, also called *advanced searches,* allow you to look through a database or search engine by answering prompts provided in an onscreen form. A typical search involves selecting a range of dates of publication (for example, after 2006 or between 1990 and 1995) and specifying only a certain language (such as English) or a certain format (such as books). Figure 34.1 is an example of a search for sources that have the words *déjà vu* in their titles and sources that use *false memory* as another keyword but are not about *crime.*

**USING BOOLEAN EXPRESSIONS**

Using **Boolean expressions** means that you search a database or search engine by typing keyword combinations that narrow and refine your search. To combine keywords, use the words *AND, OR,* and *NOT,* or the symbols that represent those words. Boolean expressions, generally placed between keywords,

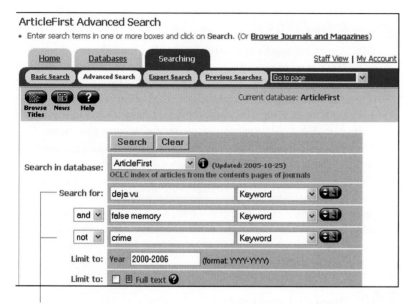

ArticleFirst Advanced Search

• Enter search terms in one or more boxes and click on **Search**. (Or **Browse Journals and Magazines**)

Users can list the keywords
they want to search for or
not to search for

**Figure 34.1** A guided or advanced search

instruct the search engine to list only those Web sites in which your keywords
appear in certain combinations and to ignore others. Quick Reference 34.1
explains a few ways to search with keywords more effectively, using the subject
"relationships" as an example.

## Quick Reference 34.1

■ ■ ■ ■ ■ ■ ■

### Refining keyword searches with Boolean expressions

**AND or the + ("plus") symbol:** Narrows the focus of your search because
both keywords must be found. For example, if you were researching the
topic of the APA paper in section 37h (the role of physical attractiveness in
new relationships over the Internet) you would search for *relationships AND
attractiveness AND Internet*. Many search engines, such as Google.com, don't
require the word *AND* between terms. Figure 34.2 illustrates the results.

**NOT or the − ("minus") symbol:** Narrows a search by excluding texts containing the specified word or phrase. If you want to eliminate instant messaging from your search, type *relationships AND attractiveness AND Internet
NOT instant messaging*.

continued >>

of the Second Life world. Many libraries have
a virtual equivalent in Second Life, such as the
libraries at Tufts University and Texas State University, the State Library of Kansas, and the very
popular main Second Life libraries on Info Islands 1 and 2. You can read more about libraries
in Second Life at the Info Island blog at <http://
infoisland.org/about/>. You can learn more
about Second Life at <http://secondlife.com>.

**TEACHING TIP**

By exposing students to the library and encouraging them to find out more about the expert
sources available, you will help students to understand the world of research beyond Internet
searches. Because of the proliferation of poor
sources and plagiarism, writing instructors are
loathe to allow students to use the Internet in
their research papers. As more and more sources
move to a digital environment, however, students will be expected in their future work and
academic lives to be able to integrate Internet
research with library-based, peer-reviewed
sources. Helping students to understand this
combination will give them an edge in their
writing, research, and critical thinking ability.

**BACKGROUND**

Some very famous people have been librarians.
A few of them may even have helped students
with research papers.

• The German diplomat and philosopher-
  mathematician Gottfried Wilhelm Leibniz
  (1646–1716) served two terms as a university librarian.

• The Scottish philosopher, economist, and
  historian David Hume (1711–1776) spent
  five years as a librarian at the Library of the
  Faculty of the Advocates at Edinburgh while
  writing his *History of England*.

• The infamous Casanova (1725–1798)
  served as a private librarian to royalty for
  thirteen years at the end of his life.

• Pope Pius XI (1857–1939) spent nineteen
  years at the Ambrosian Library in Milan,
  where he served as chief librarian. In 1911,
  he began updating and reorganizing the

Vatican Library and four years later was named its prefect. He became pope in 1922.

- Archibald MacLeish (1892–1982), poet, playwright, assistant secretary of state, and three-time winner of the Pulitzer Prize, served as Librarian of Congress under Franklin D. Roosevelt.

- Mao Zedong (1893–1976) was at one time assistant to the chief librarian of the University of Beijing.

- The longtime Federal Bureau of Investigation chief J. Edgar Hoover (1895–1972) was a messenger and cataloger at the Library of Congress as a young man.

**TEACHING TIP**

Many students are good at basic, online searches. They are familiar and comfortable with retrieving information digitally. Fewer students know how to look up and retrieve books in the library. You might want to create an assignment for students to become familiar with the call number system and how to use it to find books.

**HISTORY**

Libraries are as old as recorded history. In fact, they were the repository of the records of past civilizations. In what was ancient Mesopotamia, for example, temples and princely houses have been excavated that held thousands of clay tablets inscribed with epic poems, liturgic and magic texts, and commercial records. The palace of Ashurbanipal, who reigned 668–633 BCE in Nineveh, has provided tablets bearing stamps of ownership, catchwords, and sometimes source and place indications, thereby testifying to the existence of a well-developed cataloging system. In Egypt, every temple had its library and school. Although the Egyptian collections were made on papyrus (and thus have been found mostly in graves and tombs rather than in temples), the content was similar. Much has been lost, but records often remain. In the temple at Edfu, for instance, a full catalog of all the hieratical works the library contained was incised on the walls, bearing witness to what was once there.

**Quick Reference 34.1**   (continued)

**OR:**   Expands a search's boundaries by including more than one keyword. If you want to expand your search to include sources about relationships begun through either instant messaging or chat rooms, try the expression *relationships AND attractiveness AND Internet AND instant messaging OR chat rooms.* You'll get pages mentioning relationships and attractiveness only if they also mention instant messaging or chat rooms.

**" ":**   Quotation marks direct a search engine to match your exact word order on a Web page. For example, a search for "online relationships" will find pages that contain the exact phrase *online relationships.* However, it won't return pages with the phrase *relationships online.* If you search for *James Joyce* without using quotation marks, most engines will return all pages containing the words *James* and *Joyce* anywhere in the document; however, a search using "James Joyce" brings you closer to finding Web sites about the Irish writer.

# 34e   How do I find books?

A library's **book catalog**, which lists its entire collection, exists as a computer database in almost every modern library. You can find a book by searching by **author**, by **title**, by **subject**, and by KEYWORD. Figure 34.3 shows the home page for a typical type of catalog, this one at the Library of Congress. Note

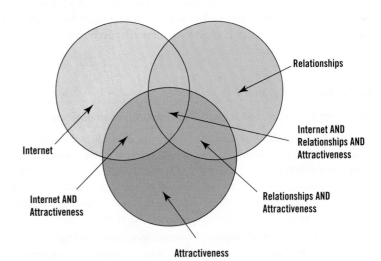

**Figure 34.2** A Venn diagram showing overlaps among *relationships, attractiveness,* and *Internet* (see Quick Reference 34.1)

URL for Library of Congress Catalog

Begin here for new search

Advanced search

General help areas

Links

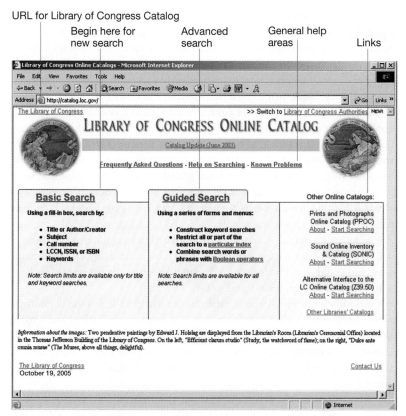

**Figure 34.3** Library of Congress Online Catalog

that it allows you to search by title, author, subject, call number, or keyword; to search particular indexes; or to search using BOOLEAN EXPRESSIONS.

Suppose you're using the EXPERT SEARCH STRATEGY and a source recommends that you find a book by the **author** Thomas L. Friedman, but you don't know its title. You can search the catalog for books by this author. A screen on your library's computer will have a place for you to type "Friedman, Thomas" in a space for "author." (Usually, you enter last name, then first name, but check which system your library uses.) If your library owns any books by Thomas Friedman, the computer will display their titles and other bibliographic information, such as the library call number. Then you can use the call number to request the book or to find it yourself.

Among the books you might find when searching for "Friedman, Thomas" is *The World Is Flat: A Brief History of the Twenty-first Century* (New York: Farrar, Straus and Giroux, 2005). Suppose you know that book's **title**, but not its author, director of libraries (1904–1906). He remade the state library into one of the most efficient in the country, and he set up traveling libraries and picture collections. His innovations were widely copied throughout the United States and abroad.

**QUOTATION: ON WRITING**

The presence of humans, in a system containing high-speed electronic computers and high-speed, accurate communications, is quite inhibiting.

—Stuart Luman Seaton

**QUOTATION: ON RESEARCH**

You should always collect more material than you will eventually use. Every article is strong in proportion to the surplus of details from which you can choose the few that will serve you best—if you don't go on gathering facts forever. At some point you must decide to stop researching and start writing.

—William Zinsser

**QUOTATION: ON RESEARCH**

Research is the ability to investigate systematically and truly all that comes under your observation in life.

—Marcus Aurelius

**BACKGROUND**

According to Donnelyn Curtis and Stephen A. Bernhardt, computers and the information explosion are changing the nature of indexing ("Keywords, Titles, Abstracts, and Online Searches: Implications for Indexing," *The Technical Writing Teacher* 18.2: 142–161). Books and articles increasingly are indexed by title and search keywords instead of by subject. Subject indexing requires readers to scan and classify each item for the index and is a slower, more expensive process than indexing by title and keywords, which can be done by computers. The process of having readers scan and classify makes it difficult and more expensive for indexes to adjust to the present rapid increase in journals and the development of new subject areas. Curtis and Bernhardt argue that the new

and want to see if your library owns a copy. Your library's online catalog will have a place for you to type in the title; some systems omit words like *the* or *a,* so that in this case, you would type in only "World Flat Brief History Twenty-first Century."

Suppose, however, you don't know an author's name or a book title. You have only a research topic, and you need to find sources. In this case, you need to search by **subject**, using the terms listed in the *Library of Congress Subject Headings (LCSH)*. The *LCSH* is a multivolume catalog available, primarily in book form, in the reference section of every library. A version of the information in the *LCSH* is online at http://authorities.loc.gov. The *LCSH* lists only **subject headings**, which are organized from most general to most narrow. Suppose you're researching the topic of "globalization." If you enter that term into a space for subject searches in your own library's "Search" screen, *The World Is Flat: A Brief History of the Twenty-first Century* by Thomas Friedman will be listed if the book is available.

Finally, you may wish to search by **keyword** in your library's holdings. If you were researching a paper on the future of jobs in the changing world economy, you could find Friedman's book using the keywords *economy, globalization, outsourcing, employment,* and so on.

An entry in the library's book catalog contains a great deal of useful information: a book's title, author, publisher, date and place of publication, and length, along with its location in the library. A full-record catalog entry (a complete set of information about the source rather than a brief listing that may have only author, title, and call number) lists additional subjects covered in that book. The list of additional subjects can provide valuable clues for further searching.

Many libraries allow you to print out this information, send it to your e-mail account, or download and save it. Whether you choose one of these options or copy the information yourself directly into your WORKING BIBLIOGRAPHY, it's crucial to record the **call number** exactly as it appears, with all numbers, letters, and decimal points. The call number tells where the book is located in the library's stacks (storage shelves). If you're researching in a library with *open stacks* (that is, you're permitted to go where books are shelved), the call number leads you to the area in the library where you can find all books on the same subject. Simply looking at what's on the shelves may yield useful sources. Keep in mind that in physically browsing the stacks, however, you're missing sources that other students have checked out or that are "on hold" at the library's reserve desk. The book catalog generally will contain information about whether a book is checked out or on reserve.

A call number is especially crucial in a library or special collection with *closed stacks* (that is, a library where you fill in a call slip, hand it in at the call desk, and wait for the book to arrive). Such libraries don't permit you to browse the stacks, so you have to rely entirely on the book catalog. If you fill in the wrong number or an incomplete number, your wait will be in vain.

# 34f How do I find periodicals?

**Periodicals** are newspapers, magazines, and journals published at set intervals. Different kinds of periodicals will meet different research purposes. Quick Reference 34.2 describes several important types.

## Quick Reference 34.2

### Types of periodicals

| Type | Characteristics | Useful for |
|---|---|---|
| JOURNALS | Scholarly articles written by experts for other experts; usually focus on one academic discipline or field; published relatively infrequently (often 3–6 times per year, generally not more than once per month); examples are *College Composition and Communication* and *American Journal of Public Health*. | The most reliable expert research on a particular subject; detailed articles and extensive bibliographies that can point to other sources or experts; may also have book reviews |
| NEWS MAGAZINES | Short to modest length articles on current events or topics that are of interest to a broad readership; have lots of photographs and graphics; may have opinions or editorials, as well as reviews; generally are published weekly; examples are *Time* and *U.S. News and World Report*. | Easily understandable and timely introductions to current topics; often can point to more expert sources, topics, and keywords |
| SPECIAL INTEREST OR "LIFESTYLE" MAGAZINES | Written for audiences (including fans and hobbyists) interested in a particular topic; include news and features on that topic; generally published monthly, with entertainment as an important goal; examples include *Outside, Rolling Stone, Wired*. | Providing "how to" information on their topics of focus, as well as technical information or in-depth profiles of individuals, products, or events; many include reviews related to emphasis; the more serious examples are well-written and reliable |

continued >>

emphasis on titles and keywords in indexes and computer searches means that writing teachers and students need to give more attention to composing titles.

### HISTORY

The first general index of magazine articles was *Poole's Index of Periodical Literature,* which lists articles from the years 1802 through 1906 and is still a valuable reference tool. The idea for *Poole's Index* originated in the 1840s when a college student from Yale, William Frederick Poole, noticed that the many periodicals in the Yale library were going unused because people could not find the articles they wanted except by going through the journals one by one. Poole decided to scan the periodicals himself, compile a list of articles, and organize the list under subject headings. At first, he wrote out a single copy, which he shared with others, but the demand for the list was so great that Poole published it in 1848. For many years, Poole updated and expanded the index himself, until 1876, when he asked the American Library Association to sponsor the index and assign fifty librarians from across the United States to the project. Receiving no pay, each librarian went through a list of assigned magazines to record and classify the articles and then sent this information to Poole for the next volume of the index.

### HISTORY

One of the most famous libraries of antiquity was the one at Alexandria, founded by Ptolemy I (c. 323–285 BCE) and greatly augmented by his son and heir, Ptolemy II Philadelphus (c. 285–247 BCE), and his grandson Ptolemy III Euergetes (c. 247–221 BCE). Manuscripts were imported from all parts of Greece and Asia; the holdings are estimated to have been as high as 700,000 papyrus rolls during the time of Julius Caesar (100–44 BCE). Because of its riches, leading scholars of the Hellenistic world were drawn to it. The result was a flurry of scholarly activity. Books were edited to a standard format, and systems of punctuation and accents were introduced. Textual scholarship, revisions of books to incorporate new knowledge, and the writing of new books went on constantly. Most of the books have been lost. Only works that were widely copied and distributed have managed to survive. As the political importance of Alexandria waned, the library suffered from neglect. Finally, in 270 CE, much of it was razed, and a good part of the rest was destroyed by fire a century later.

### HISTORY

Denis Diderot spent over twenty years writing and editing his *Encyclopédie*. In twenty-eight volumes, he and famous contributors, such as Rousseau and Voltaire, collected all the scientific thinking of the Age of Reason. The project began as a commission from a French publisher to translate a one-volume British encyclopedia into French. Diderot earned about $12 a week while working on the encyclopedia. When the project was completed, he was forced to sell his library to provide his daughter with a dowry. Catherine II, Empress of Russia, paid him $5,000—and also allowed him access to the books for the rest of his life.

### BACKGROUND

The *Nuremberg Chronicle* (1493) was the world's first encyclopedia. Its three volumes were written by one man, Hartmann Schedel, who used his extensive personal library for most of the research such a work requires.

### HISTORY

Under the strong influence of the Renaissance, Italy became the center of book collecting in the Western world. Florence was one of the major trading cities because of the support of the princes, who served as patrons to scholars who searched for the lost treasures of Greek and Latin literature. The scholars' efforts were in large measure responsible for transmitting classical learning to a new age through the works they found, translated, recopied, and sold. Among the princes of that time, Cosimo de Medici (1389–1464) is especially notable for building the Medici Library, the first public library in Europe to have been opened since the Romans. The Medicis invested $15 million from 1434 to 1469, collecting and commissioning copies of manuscripts. The collection

---

**Quick Reference 34.2** (continued)

| Type | Characteristics | Useful for |
|---|---|---|
| "INTELLECTUAL" OR LITERARY MAGAZINES | Publish relatively longer articles that provide in-depth analysis of issues, events, or people; may include creative work as well as nonfiction; aimed at a general well-educated audience; usually published monthly (though sometimes more or less often); examples include *The Atlantic, Harper's, The New Yorker.* | Learning about a topic in depth but in way more accessible than scholarly journals; becoming aware of major controversies and positions; learning who experts are and what books or other sources have been published; reading arguments on topics |
| TRADE MAGAZINES | Focus on particular businesses, industries and trade groups; discuss new products, legislation, or events that will influence individuals or businesses in that area; examples include *National Hog Farmer, Sound and Video Contractor.* | Specialized information focusing on applying information or research in particular settings; seeing how specific audiences or interest groups may respond to a particular position |
| NEWSPAPERS | Publish articles about news, sports, and cultural events soon after they happen; contain several sections, including opinions and editorials, lifestyle (home, food, movies, etc.), sports and so on; most appear daily, though some smaller ones are weekly or twice-weekly; examples are *The Washington Post; The Rocky Mountain News; The DeWitt, Iowa, Observer.* | Very current information on things as they happen; national newspapers (such as the *New York Times*) cover world events and frequently have analysis and commentary; local newspapers cover small happenings you likely won't find elsewhere; opinion sections and reviews are stimulating sources of ideas and positions |

To use periodicals efficiently, consult databases or **indexes** to periodicals, which allow you to search by subject, title, keyword, or author. Most exist as online databases that are updated frequently. Your library very likely subscribes to several of the ones that you'll need, and you can access them through the library's Web site.

**Alert:** The terms DATABASE and INDEX are often used interchangeably, but there are differences between the two. Before electronic means of storing information in databases became common, periodical information was organized in lists of references called indexes, which existed only in print. A very few still do, but most are now electronic. An index only had bibliographic information. A database, however, often includes not only that information but also connections to the articles themselves. A database is more comprehensive than an index. Generally, if you're referring to online lists of sources, you can't go wrong simply using the broader term database. ●

## 34f.1 Using databases to find periodicals

Your library's home page generally provides different ways to access various databases. Figure 34.4 shows an example. Users who know the name of a database can go directly to it. However, users who know only a general field can "Search by Category" and see an alphabetical list of subject areas. When you choose a category, you'll see a list of all the databases for that area. For example, Figure 34.4 shows the subject databases for anthropology. It's important to choose the right database for your search because the wrong one may miss some of the best sources for your paper.

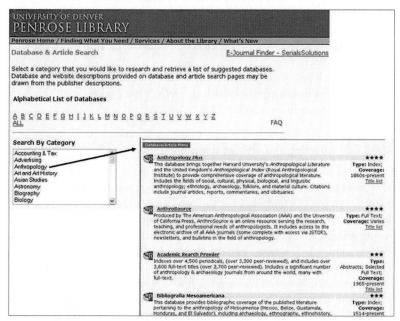

**Figure 34.4** Listing of indexes that include relevant articles

acquired under their patronage, especially that of Cosimo and his successor, Lorenzo the Magnificent (1449–1492), are now housed in the Laurentian and National Libraries of Florence.

**TEACHING TIP**

To help students understand generalized knowledge, such as that found in reference books, choose a common entry from an encyclopedia. Have each student in the class read the entry and then create a list of additional questions that they would like answered on the topic to demonstrate the need to move beyond general knowledge.

**QUOTATION: ON WRITING**

It's not a bad idea to get in the habit of writing down one's thoughts. It saves one having to bother anyone else with them.

—Isabel Colegate

**TEACHING TIP**

Encourage students to use some periodicals that are in the stacks or on microfilm. Many times students rely on only the full-text articles easily available. Encouraging students to understand the full range of materials available in your library will greatly strengthen their research skills.

**QUOTATION: ON RESEARCH**

Research means to give each and every element its final value by grouping it in the unity of an organized whole.

—Pierre Teilhard de Chardin

**TEACHING TIP**

If your students are researching similar or related topics, encourage them to create a shared file of basic background information (with proper citations!) that everyone in the class can draw upon.

**BACKGROUND**

*The Guinness Book of Records* was founded as a result of the curiosity of Sir Hugh Beaver, the managing director of the Arthur Guinness, Son and Co. brewery. One day in 1954, Sir Hugh went bird hunting. He shot at some plovers—

and missed. He started wondering if plovers were the fastest game birds, and he tried to satisfy his curiosity in an encyclopedia. Neither it nor any other reference work had the answer.

As a result, Sir Hugh decided that people needed a book that would accurately list record sizes, speeds, and durations. His plan was to have a copy of the book in every pub that sold Guinness stout, as an aid in settling bets. He set about finding someone to compile such a book, and one of his executives recommended the McWhirter brothers. Trivia history was made.

Norris and Ross McWhirter, identical twin sons of a newspaper writer, had grown up around newspapers, magazines, and reference books. Their childhood hobby had been to collect information of the very type Sir Hugh was seeking. They had frequently found contradictions in their sources, so as adults they had founded a company to verify these statistics and to "supply facts and figures to newspapers, yearbooks, encyclopedias, and advertisers."

Four months after Sir Hugh interviewed them, the McWhirters published the first book in the series. The 198-page "bet-settler" became England's all-time nonfiction bestseller in only four months. Immediately, readers began submitting their own fantastic facts. The McWhirters collected and checked these submissions, and soon an updated volume was on the way. Norris and Ross McWhirter served as coeditors until 1975.

## USING COLLABORATION

Student collaboration on a research project has both benefits and pitfalls. Chief among the benefits is a "real-world" application of teamwork skills along with the usually positive result of students' developing supportive, academic relationships. When students collaborate in searching for sources, they feel less awkward about asking for assistance and less intimidated by exploring a library, interviewing an expert, or using an unfamiliar technology (such as microfilm). To help address pitfalls that may arise from unequal student contributions, you may want to include peer evaluation to differentiate students' individual contributions to their projects and/or to have students take individual

**General databases** index articles in journals, magazines, and newspapers. Large libraries have many general databases. Among common ones are the following:

- *Academic Search Premier* covers thousands of general and scholarly publications in the social sciences, humanities, education, computer sciences, engineering, language and linguistics, arts and literature, medical sciences, and ethnic studies. Most of the sources in this database are available in full text. This database is suitable for academic research projects, as long as you take care to focus on journal articles and well-regarded general publications.
- *General Reference Center Gold* covers current events, popular culture, business and industry, the arts and sciences, and sports published in newspapers, reference books, and periodicals; it focuses on general interest periodicals.
- *LexisNexis Academic* provides abstracts of news, business, and legal information. Sources include foreign news publications; regional US news services; radio and television transcripts; federal and state case law; medical, legislative and industry news; and so on.

**Specialized databases** are more appropriate than general ones for much college-level research. They list articles in journals published by and for expert, academic, or professional readers. Many specialized databases include the abstract, or summary, that is printed at the beginning of each scholarly article. Examples of specialized databases include *General Science Abstracts, Business Abstracts, Humanities Index, Social Sciences Abstracts, MLA International Bibliography,* and *PsycINFO*.

You search periodical indexes by using KEYWORDS. Shown in Figure 34.5 are three screens from a keyword search of *PsycINFO* for Andrei Gurov's research paper that appears in section 36e.2.

## 34f.2 Locating the articles themselves

Periodical indexes help you locate the titles of specific articles on your topic. Once you have the listing, though, how do you get your hands on the article itself? Often you can find a full-text online version of the article to read, download, or print. A full-text version may be either in HTML format or PDF. The listing will tell you which one; if you have a choice, we recommend using the PDF version, which is easier to cite because it has the layout of a common article. Figure 34.6 shows location information in a typical database entry.

Sometimes, however, you need to find a printed copy of the periodical. Often the listing in the database will tell you whether your library owns a print copy and what its call number is. Otherwise, you'll need to check if the periodical is listed in the library's catalog. Search for the periodical name you want

Keyword search

Partial
search
result

One article selected from database

**Figure 34.5** Keyword search of *PsycINFO*

responsibility for various sections of the final presentation.

**BACKGROUND**

The retention and pass rates of underprepared writers may increase in classes where students learn and compose on computers, according to Smokey Wilson ("When Computers Come to English Class," *TETYC,* May 2000: 387–399). Wilson compares the retention and pass rates of two discussion-based and two computer-based classes and concludes that moving composition instruction to an online format in a workshop-style class has a measurably positive effect on student performance.

**TEACHING TIP**

Using the information in Quick Reference 34.3, ask students to add this information to their research log. As they consider each source for their paper, they should also be constantly evaluating sources. You might even set aside a day to ask the class to vet one another's sources. Have students present several of their sources to the rest of the class. In a presentation, students need to be able to answer the five questions in Quick Reference 34.3. If they cannot authenticate a source, then they need to gather additional information on the source and its potential usefulness in the paper.

**QUOTATION: ON RESEARCH**

I have come to believe that a scholar can be scholarly and still be ethically and pathetically connected to the subject.

—Jacqueline Jones Royster

**TEACHING TIP**

Modeling Internet search for students through inquiry activities helps students to learn to critically examine web sources. For example, if you ask students to search "Martin Luther King," many sites come up. Among the first ten hits on Google are The Nobel Prize's Biography of King at <http://nobelprize.org/nobel_prizes/peace/laureates/1964/king-bio.html>; The King Center in Atlanta, Georgia at <http://www.thekingcenter.org>; and <http://www.martinlutherking.org>, a site which promises a

"True Historical Examination" of Dr. King and his work. When students have the opportunity to carefully explore each site, they discover that sites one and two are sponsored by legitimate organizations, while the third is hosted by Stormfront, a white supremacist organization. Creating directed inquiry activities such as this allows students to begin to learn how to critically engage both the wonderful possibilities and the problematic nature of doing Web-based research.

## QUOTATION: ON READING
You know, children, I don't read such small stuff as letters, I read men and nations.
—Sojourner Truth

## QUOTATION: ON WRITING
If you copy from one author, it's plagiarism. If you copy from two, it's research.
—Wilson Mizner

## ANSWERS: EXERCISE 34-2
Answers will vary. This exercise is intended to demonstrate that different databases have different information so that students become accustomed to looking in more than one place for research material. If you have more time, you might expand this exercise to include an Internet search using Google or another search engine and a book search. This will allow students to see results from four different types of sources.

## BACKGROUND
Many library Web sites contain suggestions for evaluating sources. You can find them by entering a search phrase like "evaluating sources" (or "resources") in a search engine. Examples of such suggestions are available at the following Web sites, active at the time this handbook went to press:

- Thinking Critically About World Wide Web Resources <http://www.library.ucla.edu/libraries/college/help/critical/index.htm>
- Thinking Critically About Discipline-Based World Wide Web Resources <http://www

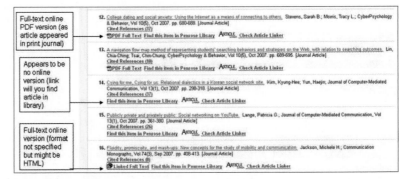

**Figure 34.6** Location information in a database

(for example, *American Literature* or *The Economist*), not for the article's author or title. If your library subscribes to that periodical, you can use its call number to find its location. You then need to find the specific article you want by looking for the issue in which the article you're looking for is printed.

Few libraries subscribe to all of the periodicals listed in specialized databases. For advice on locating sources that your college doesn't own, see 34i.

**EXERCISE 34-2**   Use two databases that are available through your library to conduct two searches for one or more of the terms below. (Alternatively, your instructor may suggest a different term or have you pursue a topic of your own choosing.)

If possible, choose one general and one specialized database. Compile a brief report that compares the sources you generate. You might address questions like these: How many sources did each search turn up? Is there any overlap? What kinds of periodicals are represented in each database? What access does your library provide to the several sources you find most interesting in each search? Note: If you're generating lots of hits, restrict your search to the past year or two.

Suggested terms for searching (with type of specialized database to consult in parentheses): *memory* (psychology); *globalization* (business, economics, sociology); *cloning* (biology); *global warming* (geology, geography, political science); *obesity* (medicine, psychology).

## 34g   How do I use reference works?

**Reference works** include encyclopedias, almanacs, yearbooks, fact books, atlases, dictionaries, biographical reference works, and bibliographies. Some references are *general,* providing information on a vast number of subjects, but without any depth. Others are *specialized,* providing information on selected topics, often for more expert or professional audiences.

## 34g.1   General reference works

Reference works are the starting point for many college and other advanced researchers—but they're no more than a starting point. **General reference works** by themselves are insufficient for academic research. Still, they help researchers identify useful KEYWORDS, find examples, and verify facts. Most widely used reference works are available in electronic versions, usually online. Check your library's Web site to see if the reference work you want is available online through a subscription or license the library has purchased. For example, your library may have a subscription to the *Gale Virtual Reference Library,* which allows libraries to choose up to 1000 reference books available to users online. You can also check your library's catalog. Finally, you can search the World Wide Web by entering the work's name to see if it's available there. (For example, *Encyclopaedia Britannica* is at http://www.britannica.com.) Be aware that often you have to pay a fee for works you don't access through the library.

### GENERAL ENCYCLOPEDIAS

Articles in multivolume general encyclopedias, such as the *Encyclopaedia Britannica,* summarize information on a wide variety of subjects. The articles can give you helpful background information and the names of major figures and experts in the field. Best of all, many articles end with a brief bibliography of major works on the subject. General encyclopedias aren't the place to look for information on recent events or current research, although sometimes they cover a field's ongoing controversies up until the date that the reference was published.

### ALMANACS, YEARBOOKS, FACT BOOKS

Almanacs, yearbooks, and fact books are huge compilations of facts in many subject areas. They're often available both in print and online. They're excellent for verifying information from other sources and, in some cases, for finding supporting facts and figures. Almanacs, such as *The World Almanac,* present capsule accounts of a year's events and data about government, politics, economics, science and technology, sports, and many other categories. *Facts on File,* which is indexed online by LexisNexis, covers world events in a weekly digest and in an annual one-volume yearbook. The annual *Statistical Abstract of the United States* (accessed online through http://www.census.gov) contains a wealth of data on the United States. *Demographic Yearbook* and the *United Nations Statistical Yearbook* carry worldwide data.

### ATLASES AND GAZETTEERS

Atlases (such as *The Times Atlas of the World*) contain maps of our planet's continents, seas, and skies. Gazetteers (such as *The Columbia Gazetteer of the World,* available online for a fee at http://www.columbiagazetteer.org) provide

.library.ucla.edu/libraries/college/help/critical/discipline.htm>
- Evaluating Web Resources <http://www3.widener.edu/Academics/Libraries/Wolfgram_Memorial_Library/Evaluate_Web_Pages/659>

**TEACHING TIP**
The Web site above, "Evaluating Web Resources" from Widener University's Wolfgram Memorial Library, gives several separate checklists to identify and evaluate five of the most common types of Web pages: advocacy, business/marketing, news, informational, and personal. This site is written by librarians experienced in using and teaching about the Web and is on the home page of Widener University in Chester, Pennsylvania.

**BACKGROUND**
Writing for the Spring 2005 issue of the online journal *Computers and Composition,* Shawn Apostel and Moe Folk (Michigan Tech University) argue in their essay "First Phase Information Literacy on a Fourth Generation Website: An Argument for a New Approach to Website Evaluation Criteria" (<http://www.bgsu.edu/cconline/apostelfolk/c_and_c_online_apostel_folk/index.htm>) that as Web sites become more visually based and as Web sites evolve from their text-only beginnings, the book-derived criteria for evaluating credible sources are becoming increasingly archaic. Comparing sources both to verify information and to find the "original", considering site design and its citation ethos, and using the algorithms of Google to consider which sites to visit are elements of a newer approach suggested by Apostel and Folk to locate credible information on the Web and incorporate it into academic discourse.

**BACKGROUND**
James Strickland's "Just the FAQs: An Alternative to Teaching the Research Paper" (*The English Journal* 94.1 (2004): 23–28) suggests a new approach to the research paper that follows inquiry-based activities, rather than the thesis-driven research paper.

comprehensive geographical information on topography, climates, populations, migrations, natural resources, crops, and so on.

### DICTIONARIES

Dictionaries define words and terms. In addition to general dictionaries, specialized dictionaries exist in many academic disciplines to define words and phrases specific to a field.

### BIOGRAPHICAL REFERENCE WORKS

Biographical reference books give brief factual information about famous people—their accomplishments along with pertinent events and dates in their lives. Biographical references include the *Who's Who* series, *The Dictionary of American Biography,* and many others. Specialized biographical references in various fields are also available.

### BIBLIOGRAPHIES

Bibliographies list books, articles, documents, films, and other resources and provide publication information so that you can find those sources. Some bibliographies are comprehensive and list sources on a wide range of topics. Others list only sources on a particular subject. Specialized bibliographies can be very helpful in your research process. Annotated or critical bibliographies describe and evaluate the works that they list. These resources are increasingly available online but require you either to access them through a library's paid subscription service or to pay a fee each time you use them.

## 34g.2 Specialized reference works

**Specialized reference works** provide more authoritative and specific information than do general reference works. Specialized reference works are usually appropriate for college-level research because the information is more advanced and detailed. They can be invaluable for introducing you to the controversies and KEYWORDS in a subject area. In particular, finding authors' names in such books can help you begin to accumulate a list of credible authors.

There are hundreds of specialized references. Some examples include the *Encyclopedia of Banking and Finance,* the *Oxford Companion to American Literature,* the *Encyclopedia of Chemistry,* the *Dictionary of American Biography,* and the *International Encyclopedia of Film.*

Because hundreds of one-volume works are highly specific, we haven't listed them here. Check what specialized reference books your college library has available that might help you in your search. They may be listed in the library's catalog or in a references database, such as the *Gale Virtual Reference Library.*

## 34h How do I find government publications?

Government publications are available in astounding variety. You can find information on laws and legal decisions, regulations, population, weather patterns, agriculture, national parks, education, and health, to name just a few topics. Since the middle 1990s, most government documents have been available through the World Wide Web. The Government Printing Office maintains the *Catalog of U.S. Government Publications* at http://www.gpoaccess.gov.

The GPO site has a searchable database. Information about legislation is also available at the Web site THOMAS, a service of the Library of Congress, which you can access at http://thomas.loc.gov. A directory of all federal government sites that provide statistical information is at http://www.fedstats.gov.

The LexisNexis database service provides access to a huge number of other governmental reports and documents. For example, it includes the *Congressional Information Service (CIS),* which indexes all papers produced by US congressional panels and committees. These documents include the texts of hearings (for example, testimony about homelessness) and reports (for example, a comparative study of temporary shelters for homeless people).

## 34i What if my library doesn't have a source I need?

Almost no library owns every book or subscribes to every periodical. However, many libraries are connected electronically to other libraries' book catalogs and can give you access to additional holdings. Often you or a librarian can request materials from other libraries through interlibrary loan (generally free of charge). Alternatively, your college may have a different document delivery system (perhaps at a cost to you).

## 34j How do I evaluate sources?

Finding a source is only part of your effort. Your next step is to evaluate the quality of each source. Your critical thinking skills (Chapter 4) will be important in this effort. First, decide whether the information in the source relates to your topic in more than a vague, general sense. Then, ask how a source might help you answer your research question (33e). Finally, using the criteria in Quick Reference 34.3, evaluate each source with a cold, critical eye.

**ESOL Tip:** The definition of *authority* can differ across cultures. However, in the United States, a source must meet specific criteria to be considered authoritative. A source is not reliable simply because the author or speaker is an important member of the community, claims to have knowledge about a topic, or publishes material in print or online. When considering whether to use a source for your research, ask yourself the questions in Quick Reference 34.3. ●

---

### Quick Reference 34.3

#### Evaluating sources

1. **Is the source authoritative?** Generally, encyclopedias, textbooks, and academic journals (*The American Scholar, Journal of Counseling and Development*) are authoritative. Books published by university presses (Indiana University Press) and by publishers that specialize in scholarly books are also trustworthy. Material published in newspapers, in general-readership magazines (*Newsweek, U.S. News & World Report*), and by established commercial publishers (Prentice Hall) are usually reliable, but you want to apply the other criteria in this list with special care, cross-checking names and facts whenever possible. Web sites maintained by professional organizations, such as the National Council of Teachers of English at http://www.ncte.org, are authoritative.

2. **Is the author an expert?** Biographical material in the article or book may tell you if the author is an expert on the topic. Look up the author in a reputable, up-to-date biographical dictionary. Alternatively, enter the author's name in an Internet search engine. Look to see if the author has a degree in this field and whether he or she is affiliated with a reliable institution. Also, if an author is often cited by professionals in the field and published in journals, he or she is probably considered an expert.

3. **Is the source current?** Check the publication date. Research is ongoing in most fields, and information is often modified or replaced by new findings. Check databases and online subject directories to see if newer sources are available.

4. **Does the source support its information sufficiently?** Are its assertions or claims supported with sufficient evidence? Separate facts from opinions (4d.1) and see if the writer relies too much on opinion. If the author expresses a point of view, check what kind of evidence he or she offers to back up that position (4d.2). If there are claims of cause and effect, ask yourself if they're justified (4d.3). If the writer resorts to logical fallacies, reject the source (4i). Use wise judgment and don't take chances.

5. **Is the author's tone balanced?** If the TONE is unbiased and the reasoning is logical, the source is probably useful (4d.4, 4e.2). Some warning signs of biased tone are name calling, sarcasm, stereotyping, or absolute assertions about matters that are open to interpretation (using *always, everyone,* and similar words).

## 34k What should I know about searching the Web?

Sources from the library or from library databases have the advantage of being selected by experts. While you still have to evaluate them, they have passed a screening process. On the other hand, anyone can put anything on the Web. This makes the Web a rich source of information, but it also makes finding what you need difficult, and it opens the possibility of encountering inaccurate or biased materials. Therefore, searching library databases remains a crucial method of finding many scholarly sources.

## 34l How do I search the Web?

Finding information on the Web has become so common that "google" has become a verb. The principles for searching the Web are much like those for searching databases (34d). Once you use a browser to get on the Web, you can search for sites by using a SEARCH ENGINE or by typing an address (called a **URL**, for "universal resource locator" or "uniform resource locator") into the search box. **Search engines** are programs designed to hunt the Internet for sources on specific topics that you identify by using keywords (34l.1) or through subject directories (34l.2). Some commonly used search engines include Google (http://www.google.com) or Yahoo (http://www.yahoo.com).

As the Internet matures, search engines are constantly acquiring new features. A special page on the Google search engine, Google Scholar (http://scholar.google.com) and its Advanced Scholar Search Function permit scholarly searches that have features in common with the searches of library databases.

**⓵ Alert:** When you cite a URL as a source, such as the Web site for MyCompLab, the Modern Language Association (MLA) tells you to surround it with angle brackets, such as <www.MyCompLab.com>. However, don't use angle brackets when you type a URL in the locator box at the top of a Web page'. ●

As you know, the Internet contains many types of sources. We've listed a few of the main ones in Quick Reference 34.4.

### 34l.1 Using keywords

In the same way you use KEYWORDS to find materials in library databases (34d), you can use them to find information on the Internet. Type a word or group of words in the search box on the opening page of the search engine, and click on the "Search" or "Enter" button. The engine scans for your word(s) in Web pages, and then lists sites that contain them.

## Quick Reference 34.4

■ ■ ■ ■ ■ ■ ■

### Types of sources on the Internet

**Periodicals and news sites.** Many newspapers and magazines put content online, although some of them give access to all of their material only to subscribers. Some periodicals put only print content online, while others have extra content that appears only on the Web. Finally, there are periodicals that exist only online. Examples include *Salon.com* and *Kairos* (http://english.ttu.edu/Kairos/).

   Mainstream news organizations (for example, CNN or MSNBC) frequently have sites, too, in which they publish video and sound clips as well as articles.

**Organizational Web sites.** Interest groups, clubs, businesses, museums, universities, and similar organizations frequently have Web sites. They often provide basic facts and information about the organization, but they may include articles, reports, research findings, position papers, policy statements, and so on. Some of them can be very authoritative and useful; others require more evaluation and care, especially when the organization is promoting itself, as is reasonable.

**Government Web sites.** Federal, state, and local governments maintain Web sites to provide all sorts of information to their citizens. This frequently includes not only news about laws or events, but often research or articles. (In his argument paper about organic food in Chapter 5, Alex Garcia found the US Department of Agriculture's Web site very helpful.) A number of GOVERNMENT DOCUMENTS can also help researchers (34h). The Library of Congress is a powerful source for many kinds of digital information and its Web site includes many useful and usable public access materials, like images and recordings, that are not available on commercial sites.

**Blogs.** Much of what appears now on the Web is in the form of blogs, regular short articles published by people ranging from experts to amateurs. Blogs tend to be highly opinionated, so evaluate them carefully, but several well-regarded scholars and other experts do keep blogs.

**Images, sounds, and videos.** Both as parts of other sites and in sites of their own, images, sounds, and videos appear on the Web. A podcast or a documentary may offer expert information on a particular topic. There may be a video of a press conference or a recording of a speech. The On-line Speech Bank at http://www.americanrhetoric.com, for example, has over 5,000 recordings and videos.

## 341.2  Using subject directories

**Subject directories** provide an alternative to keyword searches. These directories list topics (education, computing, entertainment, and so on) or resources and services (shopping, travel, and so on), with links to Web sites on those topics and resources. Most search engines' home pages have one or more subject directories. In addition, there are some independent subject directories. Some examples are *Educator's Reference Desk* (http://www.eduref.org), *Internet Public Library* (http://www.ipl.org), and *Refdesk.com* (http://www.refdesk.com).

Clicking on a general category within a subject directory will take you to lists of increasingly specific categories. Eventually, you'll get a list of Web pages on the most specific subtopic you select. These search engines also allow you to click on a category and enter keywords for a search. For example, suppose that you are using Google to search for information on organic food. As Figure 34.7 shows, you'll first go to Google's general category of "Health." Under "Health" you'll find the category of "Nutrition," and within "Nutrition," you'll find a link to "Organic Food," a page that lists dozens of additional categories and sources.

Quick Reference 34.5 summarizes the information in this section by providing some general guidelines for using search engines and directories with keywords.

**Figure 34.7** A Google subject directory for "Organic Food"

---

### Quick Reference 34.5

■ ■ ■ ■ ■ ■ ■ ■

**Tips on using search engines and directories**

- Use keyword combinations or BOOLEAN EXPRESSIONS (Quick Reference 34.1) unless you have a very specific, narrow topic with unique keywords. A search for even a moderately common topic may produce thousands of hits, many of which won't be relevant to your topic. You might also switch to a subject directory.

- Most search engines attempt to search as much of the World Wide Web as possible. But because the Web is vast and unorganized, different search engines will give different results for the same search. Try using more than one search engine, or use a **metasearch engine** that searches several search engines at once, such as Dogpile (http://dogpile.com).

- Use the "Advanced Search" page, if one is available. It allows you to search or sort by date, language, file format, and domain type, as well as by various combinations of keywords.

- When you find a useful site, go to the toolbar at the top of the screen and click on "Bookmark" or "Favorites" and then click on "Add." This will make it easy for you to return to a good source.

- Use the "History" or "Go" function to track the sites you visit, in case you want to revisit one you previously thought was not helpful.

- Sources on the Web may come in various formats. Most common are Web pages in html (Hypertext Markup Language) format. However, you may also encounter Word or Excel documents, PowerPoint slides, or PDF (portable document format) files, each of which requires specific software. PDF files, which require the free Adobe Acrobat Reader that you can download from http://www.adobe.com, allow people to preserve documents in their original formats.

---

**EXERCISE 34-3**    Use a search engine of your choice to search for sources on "déjà vu." (To make the search easier, you may omit the accents.) For each option below, record how many hits occur.

1. Enter the phrase *"deja vu"*
2. Enter the word *"memory"*
3. Enter the phrase *"memory" AND "deja vu"*
4. Enter the phrase *"deja vu" AND "consciousness"*
5. To any of the searches above, add the word *"research"*
6. Repeat this exercise by searching another topic that interests you.

# 34m How do I evaluate Web sources?

The same strategies for evaluating library sources, discussed in 34c, apply to evaluating Web sources. Ask yourself if the Web source is well supported with evidence and free from fallacies or bias. Use strategies for critical thinking and analysis in Chapter 4.

However, you need to evaluate Web sources with additional care for two reasons. First, because anyone can post anything on the Web, some sources may very well be plagiarized. Second, many sources on the Web have been written by individuals posing as experts and, as a result, may offer false or misleading information.

You're always accountable for the sources you choose. Most sites also contain material that will help you assess their credibility, such as a bibliography, links to the author or editor, or a description of the sponsoring organization. You want to discard sites that do not contain such verifying information, however useful they may seem. Err on the side of caution.

An important question to ask about any Web site is why the information exists and why it was put on the Internet. What motives might the site's authors have? Are you asked to take action of any kind? If yes, take special care to judge the source's bias. For example, the World Wildlife Fund can ask for contributions and still maintain a Web site that contains reliable information. Conversely, a hate group or extreme political organization can't be trusted to be objective. Quick Reference 34.6 summarizes the questions to ask about Web sites.

---

## Quick Reference 34.6

### Judging the reliability of Web sources

**Reliable sources are . . .**

**From educational, not-for-profit, or government organizations.** One sign is an Internet address ending in *.edu, .org, .gov,* or a country abbreviation such as *.us* or *.uk.* However, if any of these organizations fail to list their sources, don't use them. After all, many colleges and universities now host student Web sites, which also end in *.edu.*

**Questionable sources are . . .**

**From commercial organizations advertising to sell a product (*.com*); Web sites that are advertisements or personal pages; junk mail.** These sites may or may not list sources. If they fail to, don't use them. If they do, check that the sources are legitimate, not a front for some commercial enterprise.

continued >>

**Quick Reference 34.6** (continued)

**From expert authors.** Experts have degrees or credentials in their fields that you can check. See if their names appear in other reliable sources, in bibliographies on your topic, or in reference books in your college's library. Check whether the site's author gives an e-mail address for questions or comments.

**From anonymous authors or authors without identifiable credentials.** Chat rooms, discussion groups, bulletin boards, and similar networks are questionable when they don't give credentials or other qualifying information.

**From reliable print sources.** Online versions of the *New York Times, Time* magazine, and other publications that are produced by the publisher are just as reliable as the print versions.

**Secondhand excerpts and quotations.** Materials that appear on a site that is not the official site of the publisher (such as a quotation taken from the *New York Times*) may be edited in a biased or inaccurate manner. Such sources may be incomplete and inaccurate.

**Well supported with evidence.** The information is presented in a balanced, unbiased fashion.

**Unsupported or biased.** These sites carry declarations and assertions that have little or no supporting evidence.

**Current.** The site's information is regularly updated.

**Outdated.** The site's information hasn't been updated in a year or more.

For more help with your writing, grammar, and research, go to **www.mycomplab.com**

mycomplab

# Using Sources and Avoiding Plagiarism

## 35a  How do I use sources well?

Using sources well means using QUOTATIONS (35h), PARAPHRASES (35i), and SUMMARIES (35j) to create a synthesis of those materials and your own thoughts. It also means documenting your sources and avoiding PLAGIARISM. Generally, you'll begin this process after you've located most of your sources and evaluated them (Chapter 34), written a WORKING BIBLIOGRAPHY (33i), and taken content notes (33k). Of course, during the process of DRAFTING, you might discover the need to do some additional research, and that's fine. Be careful, though, to avoid a trap into which we see some writers fall—endlessly researching to put off the challenging work of drafting.

Pulling together a SYNTHESIS of your sources and your own thinking about the topic means:

* Mastering the information from each source
* Finding relationships among the pieces of information from various sources
* Adding your own thinking to the mix

To write effectively, organize your paper around a logical sequence based on the main points in your synthesis. Further, support each main point and important subpoint with specific evidence, explanations, ideas, or facts drawn from your sources. You'll also want to support your points with ideas generated through your own CRITICAL THINKING (Chapter 4), especially through ANALYSIS (4d), INFERENCE (4e), SYNTHESIS (4f), EVALUATION (4g), and assessment of authors' reasoning processes (4h). If your PURPOSE is persuasive rather than informative, remember to present opposing viewpoints evenhandedly and then refute them reasonably (5e, 5l).

All SOURCE-BASED WRITING needs to be:

* Accurate
* Effective
* Honest (the only way to avoid plagiarism)

**BACKGROUND**
Technology now makes possible the digitizing of whole libraries. (In 2005, a Google project to digitize holdings of major collections, including those at the University of Michigan, Harvard, Stanford, and Oxford, was a major initiative.) Daniel B. Wood's discussion of this project in "Copyright Lawsuit Challenges Google's Vision of Digital 'Library'" (*Christian Science Monitor*, 26 September 2005) calls attention to issues of copyright that such projects must consider. A key spokesperson for the American Library Association has expressed fear that the capabilities of electronic technology will lead to considerable violations at the expense of authors. This issue presents not only a good topic for research and argumentation but also an intellectual and ethical question to stimulate class discussion and awareness.

**BACKGROUND**
In "The Long and Short of It," Robert F. Hogan, the late former executive director of the National Council of Teachers of English, gives the etymology of the word *plagiarism*. Hogan writes, "The word stems from *plaga*, the Latin word for hunting net. One particular use for such a net was *plagium*—the snaring and capturing of another's slave or child." In the sixteenth century, the meaning evolved in English "to include stealing another person's words or ideas."

In 2003, the National Council of Writing Program Administrators (WPA) adopted a position paper, "Defining and Avoiding Plagiarism: The WPA Statement on Best Practices." The document is available at <http://wpacouncil.org/positions/plagiarism.html>. Authored by a blue-ribbon panel, it defines plagiarism in instructional contexts as occurring "when a writer deliberately uses someone else's language, ideas, or other original (not common-knowledge) material without acknowledging its source." WPA advises faculty not to label as plagiarizers the student "who attempts (even if clumsily) to identify and credit his or her source, but who misuses a specific citation format or incorrectly uses quotation marks or other forms of identifying materials taken from other sources." Certainly, such a student has produced writing that doesn't follow proper conventions, and in the same way that writing with excessive grammatical errors would warrant a lower grade, so too would poor citation practices.

The WPA Statement notes that students plagiarize for a number of reasons. Students often fear failure and risk-taking in a culture that emphasizes grades; they often have poor time-management skills and therefore rush writing projects; some may view the assignment or the consequences of cheating as unimportant; some may come from cultural backgrounds where students incorporate other writers' language very differently, and so on.

The WPA Statement offers ways for educators to prevent plagiarism. In addition to having a clear policy that students understand and can follow, and in addition to providing students with ample opportunities to learn about citation practices, this document suggests that instructors not use "recycled or formulaic assignments that may invite stock or plagiarized responses." Asking that students generate process assignments toward the final paper, including early drafts, peer responses, and analyses of their own work, will also help students write documents that are difficult to plagiarize.

**TEACHING TIP**

Some colleges and universities have begun to use plagiarism detection services. If you are interested in using such a service, inquire at the reference desk of your library to find out if your institution has already enrolled in one. If your school does not offer this service, you can learn more about them from a bibliography created by the Intellectual Property Caucus of the Conference on College Composition and Communication at <http://ccccip.org/pds>. While such services can be useful, also remember that the classroom is the first place to stop plagiarism from happening. In "Beyond 'Gotcha!': Situating Plagiarism in Policy and Pedagogy" (*CCC*, September 2002: 85–115), Margaret Price examines current scholarship about this academic issue and calls for a contextual approach to plagiarism. This article provides a useful counterbalance to the "Gotcha!" approach of plagiarism detection services. Price includes practices she

A crucial part of honesty is using correct documentation (Chapters 36–38). **Documentation** means making two types of entries in your research paper each time you use a source:

1. Writing a parenthetical citation for each quotation, paraphrase, and summary you take from sources (for examples in MLA STYLE, see 36c; for APA, see 37c).

2. Composing a BIBLIOGRAPHY for the end of your paper. MLA calls this list of sources WORKS CITED, while APA calls it REFERENCES. This list needs to include full bibliographic information on each source from which you have quoted, paraphrased, and summarized in your paper (for examples, see 36d for MLA style, 37f for APA, or 38 for CMS or CSE).

Today's bibliographies differ from those of the past. The root word *biblio-* means "book," so traditionally, the bibliographic information referred to a book's title, author, publisher, and place and year of publication. In the age of digital technology, researchers include in their bibliographies not only print sources but also electronic sources.

Documentation is vital for three reasons. It tells readers where to find your sources in case they want to consult those sources in greater depth or verify that you've used them properly. It lends credibility and weight to your writing, strengthening your ethos as someone who has done the careful work needed to develop well-supported papers. It also gives credit to others for their work. A **documentation style** refers to a specific system for providing information on sources used in a research paper. Documentation styles vary among the disciplines. This handbook presents four documentation styles in Chapters 36–38. Refer to the directory on the first page of each documentation chapter for a detailed index of where to find MLA, APA, CM, and CSE style information.

## 35b What is plagiarism?

**Plagiarism** is presenting another person's words, ideas, or visual images as if they were your own. Plagiarizing is like stealing: It is a form of academic dishonesty or cheating. Plagiarism is a serious offense that can be grounds for a failing grade or expulsion from a college. Beyond that, you're hurting yourself. If you're plagiarizing, you're not learning.

Plagiarism isn't something that just college instructors get fussy about. In the workplace, it can get you fired and hinder your being hired elsewhere. Plagiarism at work also has legal implications; words, ideas, and images, especially those that describe or influence business practices and decisions, are *intellectual property*. Using someone else's intellectual property without permission or credit is a form of theft that may land you in court. Furthermore, plagiarism in any setting—academic, business, or civic—hurts your credibility and reputation. Quick Reference 35.1 lists the major types of plagiarism.

**Quick Reference 35.1**

**Types of plagiarism**

You're plagiarizing if you . . .

- Buy a paper from an Internet site, another student or writer, or any other source and pass it off as your own.
- Turn in any paper that someone else has written, whether the person has given it to you, you've downloaded it from the Internet, or you've copied it from any other source.
- Change selected parts of an existing paper and claim the paper as your own.
- Neglect to put quotation marks around words that you quote directly from a source, even if you document the source.
- Copy or paste into your paper any *key terms, phrases, sentences,* or *longer passages* from another source without using documentation to tell precisely where the material came from. This is equally true for both library-based sources and sources you find on the Internet.
- Use *ideas* from another source without correctly citing and documenting that source, even if you put the ideas into your own words.
- Combine ideas from many sources and pass them off as your own without correctly citing and documenting the sources.
- Take language, ideas, or visual images from anyone (colleagues, companies, organizations, and so on) without obtaining permission or crediting them.

**ESOL Tip:** Perhaps you come from a country or culture that considers it acceptable for students to copy the writing of experts and authorities. Some cultures, in fact, believe that using another's words, even without citing them, is a sign of respect or learning. However, this practice is considered unacceptable in American and most Western settings. It is plagiarism, and you need to avoid it by using the strategies we discuss in this chapter.

## 35c How do I avoid plagiarism?

You can avoid plagiarism two ways. First, be very systematic and careful when you take content notes and when you quote, paraphrase, or summarize materials. Second, become comfortable with the concept of DOCUMENTATION, which you need each time you use a source. Quick Reference 35.2 describes the main strategies you can use to avoid plagiarism.

uses to help her students understand instances of plagiarism as "context-specific phenomena."

**QUOTATION: ON WRITING**
The purpose of the research paper is not coverage of material, but critical assessment. Stated another way, your research should help you create an effective judgment of recent thought on a problem. It involves a lengthy process and assumes the evolution of thought. You are educating yourself, coming to see what you think, presenting yourself as a fellow investigator of a particular research problem, and learning the various steps in performing research. You are not merely summarizing what others have concluded or showing your instructor that you have covered the course material.

—Diane B. Durkin

**TEACHING TIP**
Believing that most students who plagiarize from their sources do so because they don't know how to avoid the problem, Kathleen Mouton has devised a technique that can be demonstrated in class to help students avoid taking notes that are too close to the words of the source. She suggests that instructors ask students to read a short, informative passage of material and then put it away and make notes from memory. Students can check afterward to make sure that facts (such as dates and names) are correct. With larger amounts of material, students can stop frequently to make their notes, still being careful not to look at the source while recording each note.

**BACKGROUND**
Jonathan Hall (Rutgers University) considers the challenge of preventing plagiarism rather than "catching" those who plagiarize, in his essay "Plagiarism Across the Curriculum: How Academic Communities Can Meet the Challenge of the Undocumented Writer" (*Across the Disciplines: Interdisciplinary Perspectives on Language, Learning, and Academic Writing*, February 2005, at <http://wac.colostate.edu/atd/articles/hall2005.cfm>). Hall suggests a variety of pedagogical strategies, including subtle but important linguistic changes ("insufficient

documentation" rather than "theft") to eliminate moralizing and focus more descriptively on documentation, and integrative techniques that address writing and documentation skills holistically rather than individually and sequentially.

**BACKGROUND**

The November 2005 *Council Chronicle* from NCTE suggests that "Students listen when teachers discuss the issues" in an article entitled "Teaching About Plagiarism in a Digital Age" (<http://www.ncte.org/pubs/chron/highlights/122871.htm>).

**TEACHING TIP**

To give your students practice in notetaking before they are assigned research paper topics, you might distribute copies of a newspaper or magazine article on a popular subject and ask your students to take notes in support of a particular thesis.

Once they (and you) are sure of their skills, the students can move on to more complex issues with confidence, but at first they should keep to popular subjects that interest them.

Encourage students to paraphrase, summarize, and quote as they feel necessary and to take as many (or as few) notes as they feel would be useful in supporting a thesis. Then, collect their notes and distribute copies of all or some sets of notes. As a class (or in groups), discuss the notes one set at a time, using the following questions:

**1.** Do all the notes support the thesis?

**2.** Are paraphrases accurate?

**3.** Are summaries accurate?

**4.** Are quotations appropriate and accurate?

**5.** Are quoted words within paraphrases and summaries placed in quotation marks?

**6.** Would any material be better presented in a different kind of note?

**BACKGROUND**

The University of Alberta Library has a direct set of practices aimed at preventing plagiarism. Read the full list at <http://www.library.ualberta.ca/guides/plagiarism/preventing/

Another important way to avoid plagiarism is to dive willingly into any interim tasks your instructors build into research assignments. For example, many instructors set interim deadlines such as a date for handing in a WORKING BIBLIOGRAPHY (33i) or an ANNOTATED BIBLIOGRAPHY (33j). Further, some instructors want to read and coach you about how to improve one or more of your research paper drafts. In some cases, they might want to look over a research log (33c), content notes (33k), and/or photocopies of your sources.

---

### Quick Reference 35.2

■ ■ ■ ■ ■ ■ ■ ■

#### Strategies for avoiding plagiarism

- Use DOCUMENTATION to acknowledge your use of the ideas or phrasings of others, taken from the sources you've compiled on your topic.

- Become thoroughly familiar with the documentation style that your instructor tells you to use for your research paper (Chapters 36–38). To work efficiently, make a master list of the information required to document all sources that you quote, paraphrase, or summarize according to your required documentation style.

- Write down absolutely all the documentation facts that you'll need for your paper, keeping careful records as you search for sources. Otherwise, you'll waste much time trying to retrace your steps to get a documentation detail you missed.

- Use a consistent system for taking CONTENT NOTES, making sure to maintain the distinction between your own thinking and the ideas that come directly from a source. Perhaps use different colors of ink or another coding system to keep these three uses of sources separate:
  1. Quotations from a source (documentation required)
  2. Material paraphrased or summarized from a source (documentation required)
  3. Thoughts of your own triggered by what you've read or experienced in life (no documentation required)

- Write clear, perhaps oversized, quotation marks when you're directly quoting a passage. Make them so distinct that you can't miss seeing them later.

- Consult with your instructor if you're unsure about any phase of the documentation process.

---

Never assume that your instructor can't detect plagiarism. Instructors have keen eyes for writing styles that are different from the ones students generally produce and from your own style in particular. They recognize professionally drawn visuals and charts. Instructors can access Web sites that electronically check your submitted work against all material available online. Further, services such as http://www.turnitin.com allow instructors to check your writing against hundreds of thousands of papers for free or for sale on the World Wide Web and the Internet. (Also, that site adds your paper to its huge database of student papers so that no one can plagiarize your work.) Moreover, when instructors receive papers that they suspect contain plagiarized passages, they can check with other professors to see whether a student paper looks familiar.

## 35d How do I work with Internet sources to avoid plagiarism?

Online sources can both greatly help researchers and create new possible problems. Because it's so easy to download source materials, it's potentially easy to misrepresent someone else's work as your own, even if you don't intend to be dishonest.

You might be tempted to download a completed research paper from the Internet. *Don't.* That's intellectual dishonesty, which can get you into real trouble. Or you might be tempted to borrow wording from what you wrongly consider an "obscure" Internet source. *Don't.* Not only is this intellectual dishonesty, but instructors will easily detect it. Even if you have absolutely no intention of plagiarizing, being careless, especially with cutting and pasting, can easily lead to trouble. Quick Reference 35.3 suggests ways to avoid plagiarism when you're working with digital or online sources.

## 35e What don't I have to document?

You don't have to document common knowledge or your own thinking. **Common knowledge** is information that most educated people know, although they may need to remind themselves of certain facts by looking up information in a reference book. For example, here are a few facts of common knowledge that you don't need to document.

- Bill Clinton was the US president before George W. Bush.
- Mercury is the planet closest to the sun.
- Normal human body temperature is 98.6 degrees Fahrenheit.
- All the oceans on our planet contain salt water.

Sometimes, of course, a research paper doesn't contain common knowledge. For example, Andrei Gurov, whose research paper appears in 36e.2, had only very general common knowledge about the topic of déjà vu. Most of his

index.cfm>. One of the tips includes downloading one of the free essays available from a paper mill and critiquing it in class.

**TEACHING TIP: PLAGIARISM**
ESOL students may have more problems than native speakers in understanding the concept of plagiarism. In many cultures, copying and memorizing are respected forms of learning. Originality and creativity are not always valued as they are in the United States and Canada, where uniqueness in many forms (fashion, language, behavior) is often prized. ESOL students may say that they understand the concept of plagiarism rather than question anything the instructor says. Therefore, difficult, culture-bound concepts like plagiarism may have to be explained and demonstrated repeatedly for ESOL students.

Copyright and the "ownership" of ideas and texts are not concepts recognized worldwide. Additionally, in many cultures, using the exact words or ideas of past scholars is a form of expected respect. The boundaries of intellectual property in the United States and other Western nations need to be clarified more than once for ESOL students.

**BACKGROUND**
In "Copyrights and Conversations: Intellectual Property in the Classroom" (*Computers & Composition* 15.2: 243–251), Janice R. Walker claims that writing instructors can help students arrive at an enhanced understanding of the nature of scholarship in the digital age by focusing on copyright issues when approaching rules of citation and prohibitions against plagiarism.

**TEACHING TIP: STOPPING PLAGIARISM BEFORE IT HAPPENS**
Techniques for plagiarism-proofing assignments are plentiful: requiring submission, in the student's own handwriting, of working bibliographies, note cards, outlines, and rough drafts; assigning unusual topics and changing them every semester; replacing the semester-long research project with several shorter ones to prevent students from having time to contact research-paper mills; limiting research to the

use of a particular casebook. All of these efforts work to some degree, but at the price of turning us into thought police, ever on the alert for the student who might find a way around our system. We take on extra stress and extra paperwork—and students continue to think of us as fussy creatures who demand they follow rituals peculiar to English classes. If we are to stop wasting energy tracking down plagiarized passages in the library stacks and on the Internet, we need to take steps to counter the mixed signals about plagiarism that our students have received over the years—and continue to receive.

In a survey of fourteen first-year composition classes at Brigham Young University, Doris R. Dant found that 17 percent of the students reported being advised by their high school teachers to copy "the information word for word from other sources." Dant also found that there was a correlation between the number of teachers who taught when to document sources and the students' avoidance of plagiarism. Students who reported that all their teachers explained how to credit sources were far more likely to understand the concept of plagiarism and to avoid copying reports than those students who received such instruction from just a few of their teachers.

Only 47 percent of the students questioned understood, when they were seniors in high school, how to write an unplagiarized report. Among the untrained students, some felt that putting ideas into their own words and providing a bibliography (no parenthetical references or footnotes) was sufficient. Others felt that copying was fine without using quotation marks, provided that they supplied footnotes, parenthetical references, or a bibliography. Almost 6 percent had no idea what the word *plagiarism* meant. Not surprisingly, over 60 percent of the students in these groups reported having copied high school reports.

Some students, however, consciously plagiarize to receive higher grades, and you may want to devote class time to a discussion of the ethics of plagiarism. To start the discussion, you might report that in a survey of 150 first-year Indiana University students, Barry M. Kroll found that most respondents regarded plagiarism as a violation of one's responsibility to do one's own

---

### Quick Reference 35.3

■ ■ ■ ■ ■ ■ ■ ■

#### Guidelines for avoiding plagiarizing online sources

- Never cut material from an online source and paste it directly in your paper. You can too easily lose track of which language is your own and which comes from a source.

- Keep material that you downloaded or printed from the Internet separate from your own writing, whether you intend to QUOTE, SUMMARIZE, or PARAPHRASE the material. Be careful how you manage copied files. Use another color or a much larger font as a visual reminder that this isn't your work. Just as important, make sure that you type in all of the information you need to identify each source, according to the documentation style you need to use.

- Copy or paste downloaded or printed material into your paper only when you intend to use it as a direct quotation or visual. Immediately place quotation marks around the material, or set off a long passage as a block quotation. Be sure to document the source at the same time as you copy or paste the quotation into your paper. Don't put off documenting the passage until later because you may forget to do it or do it incorrectly.

- Summarize or paraphrase materials *before* you include them in your paper. If you have printed or downloaded Internet sources to separate files, don't copy directly from those files into your paper. Summarize or paraphrase the sources in a different file, and then paste the summaries or paraphrases into your paper. Document the source of each passage at the same time as you insert it in your paper. If you put off this task until later, you may forget to do it or get it wrong.

- Use an Internet service to check a passage you're not sure about. If you're concerned that you may have plagiarized material by mistake, try submitting one or two sentences that concern you to http://www.google.com. To make this work, always place quotation marks around the sentences you want to check when you type them into the search window.

---

paper consists of ideas and information that he quotes, paraphrases, and summarizes from sources.

A very important component of a research paper that doesn't need documentation is **your own thinking,** which is based on what you've learned as you built on what you already knew about your topic. Sara Cardini, whose paper appears in section 2l, knew an extensive amount about anime from years of personal experience and reading, so her own thinking is evident throughout her paper. Still, even that paper might have been stronger had she included some research to add more specific support for her observations.

Your own thinking consists of your ANALYSIS, SYNTHESIS, and interpretation of new material as you read or observe it. You don't have to document your own thinking. Your own thinking helps you formulate a THESIS STATEMENT and organize your research paper by composing TOPIC SENTENCES that carry along your presentation of information. For example, suppose that you're drawing on an article about the connections between emotions and logic in people. While reading the article, you come to a personal conclusion that computers can't have emotions. This idea is not stated anywhere in the article you are reading or in any other source you use. Certainly, you need to cite the ideas from the article that led to your conclusion, but you don't need to cite your own thinking. On the other hand, if you find a source that states this very idea, you should cite it. Among other things, doing so will add force to your paper and strengthen your credibility.

## 35f What must I document?

You must document everything that you learn from a source. This includes ideas as well as specific language. Expressing the ideas of others in your own words doesn't release you from the obligation to tell exactly where you got those ideas—you need to use complete, correct documentation. Here's an example in action.

**SOURCE**

Park, Robert L. "Welcome to Planet Earth." *The Best American Science Writing 2001*. Ed. Jesse Cohen. New York: Ecco-Harper, 2001. 302–08. Print. [This source information is arranged in MLA documentation style.]

**ORIGINAL (PARK'S EXACT WORDS)**

The widespread belief in alien abductions is just one example of the growing influence of pseudoscience. Two hundred years ago, educated people imagined that the greatest contribution of science would be to free the world from superstition and humbug. It has not happened. (304)

**PLAGIARISM EXAMPLE**

Belief in alien kidnappings illustrates the influence of pseudoscience. In the nineteenth century, educated people imagined that science would free the world from superstition, but they were wrong.

Even though the student changed some wording in the example above, the ideas aren't original to her. To avoid plagiarism she's required to document the

work, as a failure to give authors just credit for their work, or as theft of someone's ideas. Few students identified deliberate plagiarism as lying, fraud, or a betrayal of trust, which are issues, Kroll believes, that students need to consider in a class discussion.

**BACKGROUND**

Laura Hennessey DeSena's *Preventing Plagiarism: Tips and Techniques* (Urbana, IL: NCTE Press, 2007) offers concrete tips for preventing plagiarism in your class.

**EXTRA EXERCISE A**

Which of the following statements should be documented, and which need not be documented?

1. The Declaration of Independence was issued in 1776.

2. The sediments on the ocean floor are the accumulation of silt carried by rivers to the sea, volcanic dust, coastal sands, and discarded shells of living creatures.

3. Levi Strauss, the inventor of blue jeans, came to the United States from Germany in 1848.

4. Coca-Cola is a popular soft drink all around the world.

5. According to Germaine Greer, the reason few women artists have achieved greatness is that they have historically internalized their oppression, thereby draining the energy required for creative work.

6. The United States is a substantially less secure society today than it was forty years ago.

7. The Olympic Games are held every four years.

8. The initials *GDP* stand for the term *gross domestic product*.

9. As a society, we should read poetry because it makes us live more fully and live more deeply.

10. Henry David Thoreau lived at Walden Pond for two years.

**Answers to Extra Exercise A**

1. No. Common knowledge.

**2.** Yes. Not common knowledge.

**3.** Not necessary. Can be found in a general encyclopedia.

**4.** No. Common knowledge.

**5.** Yes. Opinion of someone besides the writer.

**6.** No, if opinion of the writer. Yes, if opinion of someone besides the writer.

**7.** No. Common knowledge.

**8.** No. Common knowledge.

**9.** No, if opinion of the writer. Yes, if opinion of someone besides the writer.

**10.** Not necessary. Can be found in a general encyclopedia.

**BACKGROUND**

Current technology is capable of reading student texts for both stylistic elements and content, and educators and administrators are beginning to test software that grades papers. In their essay "What Happens When Machines Read Our Students' Writing?" (*College English,* March 2001: 480–499), Anne Herrington and Charles Moran survey the history of this type of technology and evaluate two grading programs, WritePlacer Plus and Intelligent Essay Assessor. Their conclusions are highly critical: "We have serious concerns about the potential effects of machine reading of student writing on our teaching, on our students' learning, and therefore on the profession of English" (495).

**QUOTATION: ON WRITING**

I often quote myself. It adds spice to my conversation.

—George Bernard Shaw

**EXTRA EXERCISE B**

Practice working quotations smoothly into your own writing by devising introductions to the following statements. (Answers will vary.)

**1.** Boys and girls grow up in different worlds, but we think we're in the same one, so we judge each other's behavior by the standards of our own.

—Deborah Tannen, *You Just Don't Understand: Men and Women in Conversation*

source. The underlined phrases are especially problematic examples of plagiarism because they're Park's exact wording.

**CORRECT EXAMPLE (USING QUOTATION, PARAPHRASE, AND DOCUMENTATION)**

Robert Park calls people's beliefs in alien kidnapping proof of "the growing influence of pseudoscience" (304). Centuries of expectation that science would conquer "superstition and humbug" are still unfulfilled (304).

[This citation is arranged in MLA documentation style.]

The writer of the correct example above has used Park's ideas properly through a combination of quotation and paraphrase and documentation. For example, she correctly quotes the phrase "the growing influence of pseudoscience," and she paraphrases the statement "Two hundred years ago, educated people imagined that the greatest contribution of science would be to free the world," rephrasing it as "Centuries of expectation that science would conquer." She also gives the author's name in the sentence and twice includes parenthetical citations, which would lead the reader to find the source on the WORKS CITED page. Sections 35g through 35j explain exactly how to use sources effectively and document correctly.

# 35g How can I effectively integrate sources into my writing?

**Integrating sources** means blending information and ideas from others with your own writing. Before trying to integrate sources into your writing, you need to ANALYZE and SYNTHESIZE your material. Analysis requires you to break ideas down into their component parts so that you can think them through separately. Do this while reading your sources and reviewing your notes. Synthesis requires you to make connections among different ideas, seeking relationships and links that tie them together.

# 35h How can I use quotations effectively?

A **quotation** is the exact words of a source enclosed in quotation marks. Well-chosen quotations can lend a note of authority and enliven a document with someone else's voice. Think, for example, of a good marketing campaign. A company can incorporate real-life quotes to help support its claim that a product or service works effectively. In academic writing, you achieve some of the same benefits by supporting your work with quotations.

You face conflicting demands when you use quotations in your writing. Although quotations provide support, you can lose coherence in your paper if you use too many of them. If more than a quarter of your paper consists of quotations, you've probably written what some people call a "cut and paste special"—

merely stringing together a bunch of someone else's words. Doing so gives your readers—including instructors—the impression that you've not bothered to develop your own thinking and you're letting other people do your talking.

In addition to avoiding too many quotations, you also want to avoid using quotations that are too long. Readers tend to skip over long quotations and lose the drift of the paper. Also, your instructor might assume that you just didn't take the time required to PARAPHRASE or SUMMARIZE the material. Generally, paraphrases and summaries are more effective for reconstructing someone else's argument. If you do need to quote a long passage, make absolutely sure every word in the quotation counts. Edit out irrelevant parts, using ellipsis points to indicate deleted material (29d and 35h.1). Quick Reference 35.4 provides guidelines for using quotations. Sections 35h.1 and 35h.2 give examples of acceptable and unacceptable quotations.

---

### Quick Reference 35.4　■ ■ ■ ■ ■ ■ ■

#### Guidelines for using quotations

1. Use quotations from authorities on your subject to support or refute what you write in your paper.

2. Never use a quotation to present your THESIS STATEMENT or a TOPIC SENTENCE.

3. Select quotations that fit your message. Choose a quotation for these reasons:
   - Its language is particularly appropriate or distinctive.
   - Its idea is particularly hard to paraphrase accurately.
   - The source's authority is especially important to support your thesis or main point.
   - The source's words are open to interpretation.

4. Never allow quotations to make up more than a quarter of your paper. Instead, rely on paraphrases (35i) and summaries (35j).

5. Quote accurately. Always check each quotation against the original source—and then recheck it.

6. Integrate quotations smoothly into your writing.

7. Avoid PLAGIARISM (35b–35d).

8. Document quotations carefully.

---

## 35h.1　Making quotations fit smoothly with your sentences

When you use quotations, the greatest risk you take is that you'll end up with incoherent, choppy sentences. You can avoid this problem by making the words you quote fit smoothly with three aspects of your writing: grammar, style, and

**2.** Science does not aim at establishing immutable truths and eternal dogmas: its aim is to approach the truth by successive approximations, without claiming that at any stage final and complete accuracy has been achieved.
　　　　　—Bertrand Russell, *The ABC of Relativity*

**3.** Femininity, in essence, is a romantic sentiment, a nostalgic tradition of imposed limitations.
　　　　　—Susan Brownmiller, "Femininity"

**4.** In books I've read since I was young I've searched for heroines who could serve as ideals, as models, as possibilities.
　　　　　—Judith Viorst, "How Books Helped Shape My Life"

**5.** Every gift we give carries with it our idea of what a present is. Perhaps it expresses our personality; perhaps, on the contrary, it is what we believe the recipient really wants, a choice based on careful listening for the slightest hint of what he longs for or needs or should have, even though he may not realize it.
　　　　　—Margaret Mead and Rhoda Metraux, "The Gift of Autonomy"

**QUOTATION: ON WRITING**
I quote others only the better to express myself.
　　　　　—Montaigne

**QUOTATION: ON WRITING**
Be sure you go to the author to get at his meaning, not to find yours.
　　　　　—John Ruskin

**QUOTATION: ON WRITING**
I've never discussed my writing with others much, but I don't believe it can do any harm. I don't think that there's any risk that ideas or materials will evaporate.
　　　　　—Aldous Huxley

**QUOTATION: ON WRITING**
Why can't somebody give us a list of things that everybody thinks and nobody says, and another list of things that everybody says and nobody thinks?
　　　　　—Oliver Wendell Holmes

logic. Here are some examples of sentences that don't mesh well with quotations, followed by revised versions.

**SOURCE**

Goleman, Daniel. *Emotional Intelligence.* New York: Bantam, 1995. 9. Print. [This source information is arranged in MLA documentation style.]

**ORIGINAL (GOLEMAN'S EXACT WORDS)**

These two minds, the emotional and the rational, operate in tight harmony for the most part, intertwining their very different ways of knowing to guide us through the world.

**INCOHERENT GRAMMAR PROBLEM**

Goleman explains how the emotional and rational <u>minds "intertwining</u> their very different ways of knowing to guide us through the world" (9). [Corrected: Goleman explains how emotional and rational minds mix "their very different ways of knowing to guide us through the world" (9).]

**INCOHERENT STYLE PROBLEM**

Goleman explains how the <u>emotional minds based on reason</u> work together by "intertwining their very different ways of knowing to guide us through the world" (9). [Corrected: Goleman explains how the emotional and rational minds work together by "intertwining their very different ways of knowing to guide us through the world" (9).]

**INCOHERENT LOGIC PROBLEM**

Goleman explains how the emotional and rational minds <u>work together</u> by "their very different ways of knowing to guide us through the world" (9). [Corrected: Coleman explains how the emotional and rational minds work together by combining "their very different ways of knowing to guide us through the world" (9).]

**CORRECT USE OF THE QUOTATION**

Goleman explains how the emotional and rational minds work together by "intertwining their very different ways of knowing to guide us through the world" (9). [This citation is arranged in MLA documentation style.]

After writing sentences that contain quotations, read the material aloud and listen to whether the language flows smoothly and gracefully. Perhaps you need to add a word or two placed in brackets (29c) within the quotation so that the wording works grammatically and effortlessly with the rest of your sentence. Of course, make sure your bracketed additions don't distort the meaning of the quotation. For example, the following quotation comes from the same page of the source quoted above. The bracketed material explains what the phrase *these minds* refers to in the original quotation—this helps the reader understand what was clear in the context of the original source but isn't clear when quoted in isolation.

**ORIGINAL (GOLEMAN'S EXACT WORDS)**

In many or most moments, these minds are exquisitely coordinated; feelings are essential to thought, thought to feeling.

**QUOTATION WITH EXPLANATORY BRACKETS**

"In many or most moments, these minds [emotional and rational] are exquisitely coordinated; feelings are essential to thought, thought to feeling" (Goleman 9). [This citation is arranged in MLA documentation style.]

Another way to create a smooth integration of a quotation into your sentence is to delete some words, always using an ellipsis where the deletion occurs (29d). You also might delete any part of the quotation that interferes with conciseness and the focus you intend in your sentence. When you use an ellipsis, make sure that the remaining words accurately reflect the source's meaning and that your sentence structure still flows smoothly.

**ORIGINAL (GOLEMAN'S EXACT WORDS)**

These two minds, the emotional and the rational, operate in tight harmony for the most part, intertwining their very different ways of knowing to guide us through the world (9).

**QUOTATION WITH ELLIPSIS**

Goleman contends that, generally, "these two minds, the emotional and the rational, operate in tight harmony . . . to guide us through the world" (9). [This citation is arranged in MLA documentation style.]

In the preceding example, the words "for the most part, intertwining their very different ways of knowing" have been deleted from the original material so that the quotation is more concise and focused.

## 35h.2  Using quotations to enhance meaning

Perhaps the biggest complaint instructors have about student research papers is that sometimes quotations are simply stuck in, for no apparent reason. Whenever you place words between quotation marks, they take on special significance for your message as well as your language. Without context-setting information in the paper, the reader can't know exactly what logic leads the writer to use a particular quotation.

- with your Office of Student Conduct, for preliminary advice
- with your college's policies and procedures manual

**B.** Address
- inform the student promptly and in private
- always keep the original of suspected work of academic dishonesty (you can return a copy to student)
- meet with the student and let him/her know your specific concerns; ask an open-ended question of student, e.g., what do you have to say about it?
- if appropriate, try to determine how justified your concerns are by
  - checking student's familiarity with vocabulary or concepts used
  - asking about sources
  - requesting to see sources/research notes, etc.

**C.** Decide what to do next
- do nothing if you have become convinced that there has been no academic dishonesty
- consider whether this is poor academic work or academic dishonesty
- consider academic support resources for a student who is struggling to do it right but needs help
- know and follow university procedures
- even if you are convinced a student has cheated or lied, treat him/her respectfully, professionally, and candidly
- tell him/her what you intend to do

**QUOTATION: ON WRITING**
You could compile the worst book in the world entirely out of selected passages from the best writers in the world.
—G. K. Chesterton

**QUOTATION: ON WRITING**
Originality consists in thinking for yourself, and not in thinking unlike other people.
—J. Fitzjames Stephen

**EXTRA EXERCISE C**

Working in small groups or in pairs, students can learn good techniques of paraphrasing by trying to find acceptable synonyms for key words in a passage. The italicized words and phrases in the following excerpts can be used for the exercise.

**1.** It is clear that between what a man calls (a) "*me*" and what he simply calls (b) "*mine*," the line is difficult to draw. We (c) *feel and act about* certain things that are ours very much as we (d) *feel and act about* ourselves. . . . In its widest possible sense, a man's Self is the sum total of all that he can call his, not only his (e) *body* and his (f) *psychic powers*, but his (g) *clothes* and his (h) *house*, his (i) *wife and his children*, his (j) *ancestors* and his (k) *friends*, his (l) *reputation* and his (m) *works*, his (n) *land and horses and yacht and bank account*. If they (o) *wax and prosper*, he feels triumphant, if they (p) *dwindle and die away*, he feels (q) *cast down*—not necessarily in the same degree for each thing, but in much the same way for all.

—William James, *Principles of Psychology*

**2.** Subject to (a) *infinite variables* of winds and currents, of (b) *supply and demand*, of crops and markets, trade has a way of (c) *carving its own paths* not always obedient to (d) *the mercantilist faith*. The faith was (e) *embodied* in Britain's Navigation Act, enacted under Oliver Cromwell in 1651 in the interests of the (f) *rising middle class* and the industrial towns and major trading ports—the so-called Cinque Ports, so long (g) *influential* in British history. Aimed specifically at the Dutch to protect British trade against its (h) *most dangerous rival*, the Act raised (i) *a wall of customs duties*, and permitted (j) *transshipment of goods* only in British (k) *bottoms* calling at British ports. The natural result had been (l) *maritime war* with Holland and (m) *bitter resentment* of customs duties in the Colonies, feeding the (n) *spirit of rebellion* which led to the American war. For Britain, the expense of fighting the Dutch and trying to (o) *suppress the American revolt* was more costly than anything that could be gained by the trade laws, causing (p) *higher taxes* at home and their natural consequence, a rise in (q) *domestic disaffection*. That

Furthermore, always make sure your readers know who said each group of quoted words. Otherwise, you've used a *disembodied quotation* (some instructors call them "ghost quotations"), which reflects poorly on your writing.

**SOURCE**

Wright, Karen. "Times of Our Lives." *Scientific American* Sept. 2002: 58-66. Print. [This source information is arranged in MLA documentation style.]

**ORIGINAL (WRIGHT'S EXACT WORDS)**

In human bodies, biological clocks keep track of seconds, minutes, days, months and years. (66)

**INCORRECT (DISEMBODIED QUOTATION)**

The human body has many subconscious processes. People don't have to make their hearts beat or remind themselves to breathe. "In human bodies, biological clocks keep track of seconds, minutes, days, months and years" (Wright 66).

**CORRECT**

The human body has many subconscious processes. People don't have to make their hearts beat or remind themselves to breathe. However, other processes are less obvious and perhaps more surprising. Karen Wright observes, for example, "In human bodies, biological clocks keep track of seconds, minutes, days, months and years" (66).

Rarely can a quotation begin a paragraph effectively. Start your paragraph by relying on your TOPIC SENTENCE, based on your own thinking. Then, you can fit in a relevant quotation somewhere in the paragraph, if it supports or extends what you have said.

Another strategy for working quotations smoothly into your paper is to integrate the name(s) of the author(s), the source title, or other information into your paper. You can prepare your reader for a quotation using one of these methods:

- Mention in your sentence directly before or after the quotation the name(s) of the author(s) you're quoting.

- Mention in your sentence the title of the work you're quoting from.

- Give additional authority to your material. If the author of a source is a noteworthy figure, you gain credibility when you refer to his or her credentials.

- Mention the name(s) of the author(s), with or without the name of the source and any author credentials, along with your personal introductory lead-in to the material.

Here are some examples, using the original source material from Karen Wright on page 578, of effective integration of an author's name, source title, and credentials, along with an introductory analysis.

### AUTHOR'S NAME

**Karen Wright explains that** "in human bodies, biological clocks keep track of seconds, minutes, days, months and years" (66).

### AUTHOR'S NAME AND SOURCE TITLE

**Karen Wright explains in "Times of Our Lives" that** "in human bodies, biological clocks keep track of seconds, minutes, days, months and years" (66).

### AUTHOR'S NAME AND CREDENTIALS

**Karen Wright, an award-winning science journalist, explains that** "in human bodies, biological clocks keep track of seconds, minutes, days, months and years" (66).

### AUTHOR'S NAME WITH STUDENT'S INTRODUCTORY ANALYSIS

**Karen Wright reviews evidence of surprising subconscious natural processes, explaining that** "in human bodies, biological clocks keep track of seconds, minutes, days, months and years" (66).

**Alert:** After using an author's full name in the first reference, you can decide to use only the author's last name in subsequent references. This holds unless another source has that same last name. ●

## EXERCISE 35-1

Working individually or with a group, read the following original material, from page 60 of "What Makes You Who You Are" by Matt Ridley in *Time* (2 June 2003). Then, read items 1 through 5 and explain why each is an incorrect use of a quotation. Next, revise each numbered sentence so that it correctly uses a quotation. End each quotation with this MLA-style parenthetical reference: (Ridley 60).

### ORIGINAL (RIDLEY'S EXACT WORDS)

Human beings differ from chimpanzees in having complex, grammatical language. But language does not spring fully formed from the brain; it must be learned from other language-speaking human beings. This capacity to learn is written into the human brain by genes that open and close a critical window during which learning takes place. One of those genes, FoxP2, has recently been discovered on human chromosome 7 by Anthony Monaco and his colleagues at the Wellcome Trust Centre for Human Genetics in Oxford. Just having the FoxP2 gene, though, is not enough. If a child is not exposed to a lot of spoken language during the critical learning period, he or she will always struggle with speech.

---

was not the least of Britain's (r) *afflictions* in her (s) *embattled time.*
—Barbara W. Tuchman, *The First Salute*

**Answers to Extra Exercise C**
Answers will vary, but here are possible responses.

1. (a) myself, (b) my people and my things, (c) respond to, (d) behave, (e) physical substance, (f) spiritual capacities, (g) dress, (h) home, (i) family, (j) lineage, (k) favored companions, (l) general character estimation by others, (m) accomplishments, (n) possessions, (o) increase and thrive, (p) decrease and disappear, (q) undone.

2. (a) unlimited possibilities, (b) resources and desires, (c) going its own way, (d) commercial assumptions, (e) contained, (f) growing bourgeois class, (g) a force, (h) greatest enemy, (i) tariff barriers, (j) transfer of merchandise, (k) ships, (l) naval battles, (m) animosity, (n) defiant temper, (o) put down the American Revolution, (p) greater levies, (q) discontent among the people, (r) ills, (s) period of struggle.

**ANSWERS: EXERCISE 35-1**
Here are possible analyses:

1. Analysis: Quotation does not relate clearly to the sentence it follows. A traditional introduction to the quotation is needed. According to MLA style, brackets must be used around any change in the capitalization of the source (see also answers 2 and 5). Acceptable version (answers will vary): Scientists are learning more about how people learn languages, which is an ability unique in all the animal kingdom. For example, "[h]uman beings differ from chimpanzees in having complex, grammatical language" (Ridley 60).

2. Analysis: Quotation omits several words but does not indicate where material has been deleted. Acceptable version (answers will vary): People might assume that individuals can acquire speaking abilities through hard individual work, "[b]ut language . . . must be learned from other language-speaking human beings" (Ridley 60).

**3.** Analysis: Sentence is grammatically incorrect. The quotation does not fit with the rest of the sentence. The first part of the sentence should be revised so that the information flows smoothly. Acceptable version (answers will vary): The language learning process is enabled "by genes that open and close a critical window during which language takes place" (Ridley 60).

**4.** Analysis: Tense of the verb in the quotation is incorrect. Brackets can be used to change the tense of the verb in the quotation so that it is grammatically correct, or the quotation might begin later. Acceptable version (answers will vary): In 2002, one gene important for language development was "discovered on human chromosome 7 by Anthony Monaco and his colleagues" (Ridley 60).

**5.** Analysis: Quotation is inaccurate. The writer substitutes "children" and "they" for "a child" and "he or she." Acceptable version (answers will vary): Parents should continually read to and speak with young children, because "[i]f a child is not exposed to a lot of spoken language during the critical learning period, he or she will always struggle with speech" (Ridley 60).

**ANSWERS: EXERCISE 35-2**

**1.** Answers will vary; here is one possibility: Several generations ago, parents or matchmakers arranged most marriages, and the practice still continues in many cultures. However, in America today, people choose their own spouses, usually on the basis of "love instead of social or economic gain" (Razdan 70).

**2.** Answers will vary; here is one possibility: Biologists are a long way from classifying all of the earth's living creatures. In fact, "biologists estimate that as few as 10% of the different kinds of insects, nematode worms, and fungi have been discovered" (Wilson 29–30).

**3.** Answers will vary because students write on the topics of their research papers.

**QUOTATION: ON WRITING**
The student who masters paraphrasing is capable of learning everything.
—Quintilian

UNACCEPTABLE USES OF QUOTATIONS
1. Scientists are learning more about how people learn languages. "Human beings differ from chimpanzees in having complex, grammatical language" (Ridley 60).

2. People might assume that individuals can acquire speaking abilities through hard individual work, "but language must be learned from other language-speaking human beings" (Ridley 60).

3. Helping the language learning process "by genes that open and close a critical window during which learning takes place" (Ridley 60).

4. In 2002, one gene important for language development "has recently been discovered on human chromosome 7 by Anthony Monaco and his colleagues" (Ridley 60).

5. Parents should continually read to and speak with young children, because "if children are not exposed to a lot of spoken language during the critical learning period of childhood, they will always struggle with speech" (Ridley 60).

**EXERCISE 35-2** Working individually or with your peer-response group, do the following:

1. For a paper that argues how a person should choose a spouse, write a two- to three-sentence passage that includes your own words and a quotation from the following paragraph, from page 70 of "What's Love Got to Do with It?" by Anjula Razdan in *Utne* (May-June 2003). After the quoted words, use this parenthetical reference: (Razdan 70).

**ORIGINAL (RAZDAN'S EXACT WORDS)**
Fast forward a couple hundred years to a 21st-century America, and you see a modern, progressive society where people are free to choose their mates, for the most part, based on love instead of social or economic gain. But for many people, a quiet voice from within wonders: Are we really better off? Who hasn't at some point in their life—at the end of an ill-fated relationship or midway through dinner with the third "date-from-hell" this month—longed for a matchmaker to find the right partner? No hassles. No effort. No personal ads or blind dates.

2. For a paper arguing that biologists need more funding to speed up our understanding of the earth's living creatures before many more of them become extinct, quote from the Wilson material in Exercise 35-6 (section 35j). Be sure to include at least one numerical statistic in your quotation. (For documentation purposes, keep in mind that Wilson's article appears on pages 29–30 in the original source.)

3. Write a two- to three-sentence passage that includes your own words and a quotation from a source you're currently using for a paper assigned in one of your courses. If you have no such assignment, choose any material suitable for a college-level research paper. Your instructor might request a

photocopy of the material from which you're quoting, so make a copy to have on hand.

# 35i   How can I write good paraphrases?

A **paraphrase** precisely restates in your own words and your own writing style the written or spoken words of someone else. Select for paraphrase only the passages that carry ideas you need to reproduce in detail. Because paraphrasing calls for a very close approximation of a source, avoid trying to paraphrase more than a paragraph or two; for longer passages, use SUMMARY instead. Expect to write a number of drafts of your paraphrases, each time getting closer to effectively rewording and revising the writing style so that you avoid PLAGIARISM. Quick Reference 35.5 provides guidelines for writing paraphrases.

---

**Quick Reference 35.5**    ■ ■ ■ ■ ■ ■ ■

## Guidelines for writing paraphrases

1. Decide to paraphrase authorities on your subject to support or counter what you write in your paper.

2. Never use a paraphrase to present your THESIS STATEMENT or a TOPIC SENTENCE.

3. Say what the source says, but no more.

4. Reproduce the source's sequence of ideas and emphases.

5. Use your own words and writing style to restate the material. If some technical words in the original have no or awkward synonyms, you may quote the original's words—but do so very sparingly. For example, you can use the term *human chromosome 7* if you're paraphrasing the original source by Matt Ridley in Exercise 35-1.

6. Never distort the source's meaning as you reword and change the writing style.

7. Expect your material to be as long as, and often longer than, the original.

8. Integrate your paraphrases smoothly into your writing.

9. Avoid plagiarism (35b–35d).

10. Enter all DOCUMENTATION precisely and carefully.

---

Here's an example of an unacceptable paraphrase and an acceptable one.

**SOURCE**

Hulburt, Ann. "Post-Teenage Wasteland?" *New York Times Magazine* 9 Oct. 2005: 11-12. Print. [This source information is arranged in MLA documentation style.]

---

neither intellectual nor heroic and her plots are not elaborate, her skill at telling stories and drawing characters continues to please her readers.

**3.** On the map, Mexico resembles a great funnel, or rather, a cornucopia, with its widest part towards the north and its smallest end twisting to the south and east, meeting there the sudden expansion of the Maya area. There are few regions in the world with such a diverse geography as we find within this area—Mexico is not one, but many countries. All the climatic extremes of our globe are found, from arctic cold near the summits of the highest volcanoes to the Turkish-bath atmosphere of the coastal jungle. Merely to pass from one valley to another is to enter a markedly different ecological zone.

—Michael D. Coe, *Mexico*, p. 12

**4.** In 1773 we know that [Francisco] Goya was in Madrid, where he married Josefa Bayeau, the sister of the painter who had introduced him into Madrid society. His first important chance was a commission for a series of cartoons [preparatory sketches] for tapestries, which Mengs (possibly advised by Bayeau, who had acquired a certain reputation and had become part of a group of young academic painters, which included his brothers) commissioned for the Royal Tapestry Factory at Santa Barbara. It was an important opportunity because it meant that Goya was admitted to court circles; in addition this kind of work allowed him great freedom in his choice of subject matter and of technique. Perhaps most important of all, the sketchy nature of the cartoon medium spared Goya the necessity of "finishing" his work. His style was slow to mature; until now he had displayed a dexterous hand but had shown no signs of genius.

—Margherita Abbaruzzese, *Goya*, p. 5

**ORIGINAL (HULBURT'S EXACT WORDS)**

[T]he available data suggest that the road to maturity hasn't become as drastically different as people think—or as drawn out, either. It's true that the median age of marriage rose to 25 for women and almost 27 for men in 2000, from 20 and 23, respectively, in 1960. Yet those mid-century figures were record lows (earnestly analyzed in their time). Moreover, Americans of all ages have ceased to view starting a family as the major benchmark of grown-up status. When asked to rank the importance of traditional milestones in defining the arrival of adulthood, poll respondents place completing school, finding full-time employment, achieving financial independence and being able to support a family far above actually wedding a spouse or having kids. The new perspective isn't merely an immature swerve into selfishness; postponing those last two steps is good for the future of the whole family (11).

**UNACCEPTABLE PARAPHRASE (UNDERLINED WORDS ARE PLAGIARIZED)**

Data suggest that the road to maturity hasn't changed as much as people think. True, the median age of marriage was 25 for women and 27 for men in 2000, up from 20 and 23 in 1960. Yet those 1960 figures were record lows. Furthermore, Americans have stopped regarding beginning a family as the signpost of grown-up status. When they were asked to rank the importance of traditional benchmarks for deciding the arrival of adulthood, people rated graduating from school, finding a full-time job, gaining financial status, and being a breadwinner far above marrying or having kids. This new belief isn't merely immature selfishness; delaying those last two steps is good for the future of the whole family (Hulburt 11).

**ACCEPTABLE PARAPHRASE**

According to Ann Hulburt, statistics show that people are wrong when they believe our society is delaying maturity. She acknowledges that between 1960 and 2000, the median age at which women married rose from 20 to 25 (for men it went from 23 to 27), but points out that the early figures were extreme lows. Hulburt finds that Americans no longer equate adulthood with starting a family. Polls show that people rank several other "milestones" above marriage and children as signaling adulthood. These include finishing school, securing a full-time job, and earning enough to be independent and to support a family. Hulburt concludes that we should regard postponing marriage and children not as being selfish or immature but as investing in the family's future (11).

[This citation is arranged in MLA documentation style.]

The first attempt to paraphrase is not acceptable. The writer simply changed a few words. What remains is plagiarized because the passage keeps most of the original's language, has the same sentence structure as the original, and uses no quotation marks. The documentation is correct, but its accuracy doesn't make up for the unacceptable paraphrasing. The second paraphrase is acceptable. It captures the meaning of the original in the student's own words.

**EXERCISE 35-3**  Working individually or with your peer-response group, read the original material, a paragraph from page 49 of *Uniforms: Why We Are What We Wear* by Paul Fussell (Boston: Houghton, 2002). Then, read the unacceptable paraphrase, and point out each example of plagiarism. Finally, write your own paraphrase, starting it with a phrase naming Fussell and ending it with this parenthetical reference: (49).

### ORIGINAL (FUSSELL'S EXACT WORDS)
Until around 1963, part of the routine for Levi's wearers was shrinking the trousers to fit, and the best way to do that was to put them on wet and let them dry on your body. This gave the wearer the impression that he or she was actually creating the garment, or at least emphasizing one's precious individuality, and that conviction did nothing to oppose the illusion of uniqueness precious to all American young people (49).

### UNACCEPTABLE PARAPHRASE
Paul Fussell says that until around 1963 Levi's wearers used to shrink new trousers to fit. The best way to do that was to put them on wet and let them dry while wearing them. Doing this created the impression that wearers were actually creating the garment or emphasizing their precious individuality. It reinforced the illusion of uniqueness precious to all American teens (49).

**EXERCISE 35-4**  Working individually or with your peer-response group, do the following:

1. For a paper on the place of censorship in the coverage of military conflicts, paraphrase the following paragraph from page 65 of *Regarding the Pain of Others* by Susan Sontag (New York: Farrar, 2003). Start with words mentioning Sontag, and end with this parenthetical reference: (65).

### ORIGINAL (SONTAG'S EXACT WORDS)
There had always been censorship, but for a long time it remained desultory, at the pleasure of generals and heads of state. The first organized ban on press photography at the front came during the First World War; both the German and French high commands allowed only a few selected military photographers near

**ANSWERS: EXERCISE 35-3**
Analysis: Paraphrase is unacceptable because it uses many words and phrases from the original. Acceptable paraphrase (answers will vary): Paul Fussell explains that people used to shrink new pairs of Levi's jeans to fit their own bodies by putting them on wet and wearing them until they dried. This created the important illusion for young Americans that each pair of jeans was unique to them (49).

**ANSWERS: EXERCISE 35-4**

1. Answers will vary; here is one acceptable paraphrase:

Years ago, only generals and leaders practiced censorship, and then in a random fashion. World War I witnessed the first organized censorship, when German and French commanders restricted battle photography to a few individuals. Television and photographic coverage of the Vietnam War was fairly unrestricted, and the images, which implicitly criticized the war, shocked the public. The mainstream media had not previously served to upset citizens, let alone convey antiwar sentiments.

2. Answers will vary.

Following the guidelines for writing a summary, summarize one of the following paragraphs.

**1.** The Elizabethan Age takes its name from the queen who reigned over England and Ireland from 1558 to 1603. Elizabeth I was an intelligent and gifted ruler, managing for decades to escape political disasters at home and abroad. Always an insightful judge of character, she achieved her success in large part because of her tendency to make use of the shrewdest people around her. However, her clear awareness of what she wanted and why she wanted it sometimes led her to go her own way. She used a variety of means to reach the ends she desired. And, on occasion, she was devious, even false, but she managed to outwit her opposition time after time. As a result, it was a glorious time in the history of Britain, for under her rule, the nation rose from a relatively weak position among the nations of Europe to the highest rank. England's power and success grew rapidly in the sixteenth century, leaving it, at Elizabeth's death, a leader in navigation and exploration, in literary productivity—particularly in drama—and in colonization of the New World.

**2.** When she died in 1986, Georgia O'Keeffe the person generated almost as much interest among the public as Georgia O'Keeffe the artist. Sometimes, she was thought of as the wife and often-photographed model of Alfred Stieglitz, but more often, she was pictured as a romantic recluse who, when she grew older, moved increasingly away from the world of art critics and historians and closer to the rugged but exotic New Mexico countryside and culture. In the long run, however, it is for her art that she will be best remembered. Some viewers admire her abstractions; others, her figurative works. Even those who disagree about the relative quality of her paintings agree that her art is memorable, clear, and strong. She painted with a distinctive, powerful, personal vision, one that continues to speak strongly to viewers today. Her red poppies, purple hills, and bleached skulls fix themselves in the mind's eye, not to be easily erased.

the fighting. (Censorship of the press by the British General Staff was less inflexible.) And it took another fifty years, and the relaxation of censorship with the first televised war coverage, to understand what impact shocking photographs could have on the domestic public. During the Vietnam era, war photography became, normatively, a criticism of war. This was bound to have consequences: Mainstream media are not in the business of making people feel queasy about the struggles for which they are being mobilized, much less of disseminating propaganda against waging war.

2. In one of your sources for a current research assignment, locate a paragraph that is at least 150 words in length and write a paraphrase of it. If you have no such assignment, choose any material suitable for a college-level paper. Your instructor may request that you submit a photocopy of the original material, so make a copy to have on hand.

# 35j  How can I write good summaries?

A **summary** differs from a PARAPHRASE (35i) in one important way: A paraphrase restates the original material completely, but a summary provides only the main point of the original source. A summary is much shorter than a paraphrase. Summarizing is the technique you'll probably use most frequently in writing your research paper, both for taking notes and for integrating what you have learned from sources into your own writing.

As you summarize, you trace a line of thought. This involves deleting less central ideas and sometimes transposing certain points into an order more suited to summary. In summarizing a longer original—say, ten pages or more—you may find it helpful first to divide the original into subsections and summarize each. Then, group your subsection summaries and use them as the basis for further condensing the material into a final summary. You'll probably have to revise a summary more than once. Always make sure that a summary accurately reflects the source and its emphases.

When you're summarizing a source in your CONTENT NOTES, resist the temptation to include your personal interpretation along with something the author says. Similarly, never include in your summary your own judgment about the point made in the source. Your own opinions and ideas, although they have value, don't belong in a summary. Instead, jot them down immediately when they come to mind, but separate them clearly from your summary. Write your notes so that when you go back to them you can be sure to distinguish your opinions or ideas from your summary. On a computer, highlight your personal writing with a screen of yellow or some other color, or use an entirely different font for it. Quick Reference 35.6 provides guidelines for writing good summaries.

## Quick Reference 35.6

### Guidelines for writing summaries

1. Use summaries from authorities on your subject to support or refute what you write in your paper.
2. Identify the main points you want to summarize and condense them using your own words without losing the meaning of the original source.
3. Never use a summary to present your THESIS STATEMENT or a TOPIC SENTENCE.
4. Keep your summary short.
5. Integrate your summaries smoothly into your writing.
6. Avoid PLAGIARISM (35b–35d).
7. Enter all DOCUMENTATION precisely and carefully.

Here's an example of an unacceptable summary and an acceptable one.

**SOURCE**

Tanenbaum, Leora. *Catfight: Women and Competition.* New York: Seven Stories, 2002. 117-18. Print. [This source information is arranged in MLA documentation style.]

**ORIGINAL (TANENBAUM'S EXACT WORDS)**

Until recently, most Americans disapproved of cosmetic surgery, but today the stigma is disappearing. Average Americans are lining up for procedures—two-thirds of patients report family incomes of less than $50,000 a year—and many of them return for more. Younger women undergo "maintenance" surgeries in a futile attempt to halt time. The latest fad is Botox, a purified and diluted form of botulinum toxin that is injected between the eyebrows to eliminate frown lines. Although the procedure costs between $300 and $1000 and must be repeated every few months, roughly 850,000 patients have had it performed on them. That number will undoubtedly shoot up now that the FDA has approved Botox for cosmetic use. Even teenagers are making appointments with plastic surgeons. More than 14,000 adolescents had plastic surgery in 1996, and many of them are choosing controversial procedures such as breast implants, liposuction, and tummy tucks, rather than the rhinoplasties of previous generations.

**UNACCEPTABLE SUMMARY (UNDERLINED WORDS ARE PLAGIARIZED)**

Average Americans are lining up for surgical procedures. The latest fad is Botox, a toxin injected to eliminate frown lines. This is an insanely foolish waste of money. <u>Even teenagers are making appointments with plastic surgeons, many of them</u> for <u>controversial procedures such as breast implants, liposuction, and tummy tucks</u> (Tanenbaum 117-18).

**ACCEPTABLE SUMMARY**

Tanenbaum explains that plastic surgery is becoming widely acceptable, even for Americans with modest incomes and for younger women. Most popular is injecting the toxin Botox to smooth wrinkles. She notes that thousands of adolescents are even requesting controversial surgeries (117-18). [This citation is arranged in MLA documentation style.]

The unacceptable summary above has several major problems: It doesn't isolate the main point. It plagiarizes by taking much of its language directly from the source. Examples of plagiarized language include all the underlined phrases. Finally, the unacceptable summary includes the writer's interpretation ("This is an insanely foolish waste of money") rather than objectively representing the original. The acceptable summary concisely isolates the main point, puts the source into the writer's own words, calls attention to the author by including her name in the summary, and remains objective throughout.

**EXERCISE 35-5**   Working individually or with your peer-response group, read the original material from pages 23–24 of *Diversity: The Invention of a Concept* by Peter Wood (San Francisco: Encounter, 2003). Then, read the unacceptable summary. Point out each example of plagiarism. Finally, write your own summary, starting it with a phrase mentioning Wood and ending it with this parenthetical reference: (23-24).

**ORIGINAL (WOOD'S EXACT WORDS)**
Among the many meanings of diversity, let's for the moment distinguish two: the actual racial and ethnic condition of America, which I will call *diversity I,* and the diversiphile ideal of how American society should recognize and respond to its racial and ethnic composition, which I will call *diversity II*. In principle, it ought to be easy to distinguish between these two meanings. One refers to the facts, the other to hopes or wishes. *Diversity I* is the sort of thing that we might expect could be counted, or at least approximated, with wide agreement. We know with reasonable certainty, for example, that about 13 percent of the U.S. population considers itself of African descent. We can and do argue with one another over the significance of this fact, but the fact itself is not seriously in dispute.
*Diversity II,* by contrast, is an ideal. It expresses a vision of society in which people divide themselves into separate groups, each with profound traditions of its own, but held together by mutual esteem, respect and tolerance. It would be futile, however, to look for general agreement about the exact details of this ideal.

**UNACCEPTABLE, PLAGIARIZED SUMMARY**

Peter Wood distinguishes between *diversity I,* the actual racial and ethnic condition of America, and *diversity II,* the diversiphile ideal of how American society should recognize and respond to its racial and ethnic composition. *Diversity I* could be counted or approximated with wide agreement. *Diversity II* is an ideal vision of society, but there can be no general agreement about the exact nature of this ideal (23-24).

**EXERCISE 35-6**   Working individually or with your peer-response group, do the following:

1. Summarize the following paragraph from pages 29–30 of "Vanishing Before Our Eyes" by Edward O. Wilson in *Time* (24 Apr. 2000). Start your summary with a phrase mentioning the author, and end with this parenthetical reference: (29-30).

   **ORIGINAL (WILSON'S EXACT WORDS)**
   By repeated sampling, biologists estimate that as few as 10% of the different kinds of insects, nematode worms, and fungi have been discovered. For bacteria and other microorganisms, the number could be well below 1%. Even the largest and most intensively studied organisms are incompletely cataloged. Four species of mammals, for example, have recently been discovered in the remote Annamite Mountains along the Vietnam-Laos border. One of them, the saola or spindlehorn, is a large cowlike animal distinct enough to be classified in a genus of its own. Earth, as far as life is concerned, is still a little-known planet.

2. Write a summary of your paraphrase of the Sontag material in Exercise 35-4. Use the parenthetical reference given there.

3. Write a summary of a passage from a source you're currently using for a paper assigned in one of your courses. If you have no such assignment, choose any material suitable for a college-level research paper. Your instructor might request a photocopy of the material you're summarizing, so make a copy to have on hand.

**ANSWERS: EXERCISE 35-6**

1. Answers will vary; here is one possible summary:

   According to Wilson, biologists have classified only a small percentage of earth's living creatures. Biologists are constantly discovering new kinds of life, from microorganisms to large mammals, on our planet (29–30).

2. Answers will vary; here is one possible summary:

   Sontag observes that military leaders first consistently censored photography in World War I. The relaxation of censorship during the Vietnam War resulted in images that shocked the public and served to criticize the war, something the media previously had not intended (65).

3. Answers will vary.

# 35k   Which verbs can help me weave source material into my sentences?

The verbs listed in Quick Reference 35.7 can help you work quotations, paraphrases, and summaries smoothly into your writing. Some of these verbs imply your position toward the source material (for example, *argue, complain, concede, deny, grant, insist,* and *reveal*). Other verbs imply a more neutral stance (for example, *comment, describe, explain, note, say,* and *write*). For many examples of effective use of such verbs, see the student research papers presented in sections 36e.2 and 37h.2.

## Quick Reference 35.7

### Verbs useful for integrating quotations, paraphrases, and summaries

| | | |
|---|---|---|
| acknowledges | discusses | organizes |
| agrees | distinguishes | points out |
| analyzes | between/among | prepares |
| argues | emphasizes | promises |
| asks | endeavors to | proves |
| asserts | establishes | questions |
| balances | estimates | recognizes |
| begins | explains | recommends |
| believes | expresses | refutes |
| claims | finds | rejects |
| comments | focuses on | remarks |
| compares | grants | reports |
| complains | illuminates | reveals |
| concedes | illustrates | says |
| concludes | implies | sees |
| confirms | indicates | shows |
| connects | informs | signals |
| considers | insists | specifies |
| contends | introduces | speculates |
| contradicts | maintains | states |
| contrasts | means | suggests |
| declares | negates | supports |
| demonstrates | notes | supposes |
| denies | notices | thinks |
| describes | observes | wishes |
| develops | offers | writes |

For more help with your writing, grammar, and research, go to **www.mycomplab.com**

# MLA Documentation with Case Study

Following are two directories that point you to guidance you'll find in this chapter. The first lists examples of MLA in-text parenthetical citations. The second lists examples of MLA Works Cited entries.

## MLA-STYLE DIRECTORY

MLA

MLA

**TEACHING TIP**

Many of the approaches to teaching MLA, APA, CM, and CSE citation styles are similar. If you are only teaching MLA style, be sure to look at the teaching tips and background information in the Instructor's Annotations in the APA (Chapter 37) and the CM and CSE (Chapter 38) chapters for additional ideas.

**READING-WRITING CONNECTION**

Place the responsibility for learning on the student by reiterating the reading-writing connection. The technical aspects of the research format and the density of the instructional material (e.g., the reading) strain the abilities of many students. Well-guided reflection can teach reading strategies such as previewing, skimming, and questioning. If you are using a portfolio method, students can date these reflections and include them as part of a process portfolio.

Provide five to ten minutes of class time for the students to skim this entire chapter and to record impressionistic responses to the following questions/prompts:

**1.** What seems clear to you?

**2.** What confuses you?

**3.** Which sections seem most important and why?

**4.** Write out five questions and rank them from "dumb" to "important." How much time do you need to study this chapter to understand the material and why? When will you do this studying?

**TEACHING TIP**

Consider how important MLA style and documentation is in the course you are teaching. You will want to teach this chapter, and the other chapters on citation styles, in accordance with the student learning objectives for your course. Strict adherence to MLA style might be less appropriate for a first-year composition class and more appropriate in a research- or writing-intensive class, or in a course in the major. Be guided by your program's and your classroom's goals.

# 36a What is MLA style?

A DOCUMENTATION STYLE is a standard format that writers follow to tell readers what SOURCES they used in conducting their research and how to find those sources. Different disciplines follow different documentation styles. The one most frequently used in the humanities (Chapter 40) is from the Modern Language Association (MLA).

MLA style requires you to document your sources in two connected, equally important ways.

1. Within the text of the paper, use parenthetical documentation, as described in section 36b. Section 36c shows twenty models of in-text parenthetical documentation, each for a different type of source.

2. At the end of the paper, provide a WORKS CITED list of the sources you used in your paper. Title this list "Works Cited." It should include only the sources you've actually used in your research paper, not any

---

**Important MLA Style Changes**

As part of our continuing efforts to ensure that this book provides the most current information on documentation styles, the guidelines and examples in this chapter have been adapted from the Third Edition of *The MLA Style Manual and Guide to Scholarly Publishing* (2008). According to the MLA's Web site, this edition of the *MLA Style Manual* provides documentation style guidelines that will be used in MLA publications beginning in 2009. Thus, the guidelines in the sixth edition of the *MLA Handbook for Writers of Research Papers* should only be followed until the seventh edition is released in spring 2009. If you need more information regarding MLA style updates, check http://www.mla.org.

Although MLA citations should include the minimum amount of information necessary to allow readers to locate the original source, there are several new requirements for entries in works cited lists:

- Include the **medium of publication** for each entry, such as "Print" or "Web."
- Include the URL *only* when the reader probably could not locate the source without it.
- Include both an issue and volume number for scholarly journals.
- Use italics for titles instead of underlining for all works cited entries.

See Quick Reference 36.1 on page 600 for more guidance on these requirements.

you've consulted but haven't used. Section 36d gives instructions for composing a Works Cited list, followed by ninety-six models, each based on different kinds of sources (book, article, Web site, and so on) that you might use.

For an example of a research paper that uses MLA-style parenthetical documentation and a Works Cited list, see section 36e.2. As you read the research paper, notice how the two requirements for crediting sources work together so that readers can learn the precise origin of QUOTATIONS, PARAPHRASES, and SUMMARIES.

# 36b What is MLA in-text parenthetical documentation?

MLA-style **parenthetical documentation** places SOURCE information in parentheses within the sentences of your research papers. Also called an *in-text citation,* this information is given each time that you quote, summarize, or paraphrase source materials. It signals materials used from outside sources and enables readers to find the originals.

If you include an author's name (or, if none, a shortened title of the work) in the sentence to introduce the source material, you include in parentheses only the page number where you found the material:

> According to Brent Staples, IQ tests give scientists little insight into intelligence (293). [Author name cited in text; page number cited in parentheses.]

For readability and good writing technique, try to introduce names of authors (or titles of sources) in your own sentences. If you don't include this information in your sentence, you need to insert it before the page number, in parentheses. There is no punctuation between the author's name and the page number:

> IQ tests give scientists little insight into intelligence (Staples 293).
>
> [Author name and page number cited in parentheses.]

When possible, position a parenthetical reference at the end of the quote, summary, or paraphrase it refers to—preferably at the end of a sentence, unless that would place it too far from the source's material. When you place the parenthetical reference at the end of a sentence, insert it before the sentence-ending period.

If you're citing a quotation enclosed in quotation marks, place the parenthetical information after the closing quotation mark but before sentence-ending punctuation.

> Coleman summarizes research that shows that "the number, rate, and direction of time-zone changes are the critical factors in determining the

**TEACHING TIP: COLLABORATION**
Documentation can be tedious even for seasoned scholars. Students inexperienced with documentation style may simply not "see" the fine points of punctuation and arrangement of bibliographical data so apparent to an English instructor. Asking students to function as reviewers and editors by working in pairs or small groups to proofread documentation in one another's work is a particularly effective strategy. As students take responsibility for proofreading carefully, knowing that the favor is being reciprocated, they often observe details formerly unnoticed. As they explain to one another what is needed where and why, they become teachers themselves and, in the process, commit to memory what they learn.

**BACKGROUND**
While some professors may ask for different style guides, students should know that, in general, art history, classics, English, history, modern languages, music, philosophy, religion, and theater courses ask for MLA style documentation in papers.

**QUOTATION: ON WRITING**
An original writer is not one who imitates no one but one whom no one can imitate.
—François-René de Chateaubriand

**BACKGROUND**
Robert J. Connors "The Rhetoric of Citation Systems, Part II: Competing Epistemic Values in Citation" (*Rhetoric Review* 17.2 (1999): 219–245) traces the history of modern documentation systems in scholarly practice. Of the origins of MLA style, he writes,

> The MLA asked William Riley Parker in 1951 to convene a committee to formalize MLA style, and the first MLA Style Sheet was published that year in *PMLA*. It was a relaxed reflection in most ways of Turabian forms, dictating consecutively numbered citation footnotes providing author, title, place of publication, and date. The MLA style was little more than a codification of the scholarly practice that had existed since Gibbon, but it largely mirrored the *Chicago*

*Manual,* and most literary journals adopted it. The little booklet printed under the title *The MLA Style Sheet* sold over a million copies in the next two decades. (232)

An earlier article, "The Rhetoric of Citation Systems, Part I: The Development of Annotation Structures from the Renaissance to 1900" (*Rhetoric Review* 17.1 (1998): 6–48) explores earlier annotation systems.

**QUOTATION: ON WRITING**

Your audience is one single reader. I have found that sometimes it helps to pick out one person—a real person you know, or an imagined person—and write to that one.

—John Steinbeck

**QUOTATION: ON WRITING**

Beginning to write, you discover what you have to write about.

—Kit Reed

**QUOTATION: ON WRITING**

The greatest part of a writer's time is spent in reading, in order to write; a man will turn over half a library to make one book.

—Samuel Johnson

**EXTRA EXERCISE A**

Devise parenthetical references for the following quotation and paraphrase. The source is provided at the end of each selection.

**1.** "If indeed we note in [Thomas Carlyle's] writings those passages in which the words and rhythms are most resonant, and the accent falls with the strongest emphasis, we shall find they are the expression of the cosmic wonder and terror which formed the darkly flaming background of all his thoughts." (Logan Pearsall Smith, "Thomas Carlyle: The Rembrandt of English Prose," *Reperusals and Re-Collections,* Harcourt, 1936, 115.)

**2.** "Ethologists study the traits that distinguish a group—a group of people or a group of animals. They try to discover how the group usually acts by observing its members in their natural surroundings, and to understand their

extent and degree of jet lag symptoms" (67). [Author name cited in text; page number cited in parentheses.]

The one exception to this rule concerns quotations that you set off in BLOCK STYLE, meaning one inch from the left margin. (MLA style requires that quotations longer than four typed lines be handled this way.) For block quotations, put the parenthetical reference after the period.

> Bruce Sterling worries that people are pursuing less conventional medical treatments, and not always for good reasons:
>
>> Medical tourism is already in full swing. Thailand is the golden shore for wealthy, sickly Asians and Australians. Fashionable Europeans head to South Africa for embarrassing plastic surgery. Crowds of scrip-waving Americans buy prescription drugs in Canada and Mexico. (92)

## 36c What are MLA guidelines for parenthetical documentation?

This section shows examples of how to handle parenthetical documentation in the text of your papers. The directory at the beginning of this chapter corresponds to the numbered examples in the following pages. Most of these examples show the author's name or the title included in the parenthetical citation, but remember that it's usually more effective to include that information in your sentences in the paper itself.

### 1. Paraphrased or Summarized Source—MLA

According to Brent Staples, IQ tests give scientists little insight into intelligence (293). [Author name cited in text; page number cited in parentheses.]

In "The IQ Cult," the journalist Brent Staples states that IQ tests give scientists little insight into intelligence (293). [Title of source, author name, and author credentials cited in text; page number cited in parentheses.]

IQ tests give scientists little insight into intelligence (Staples 293). [Author name and page number cited in parentheses.]

### 2. Source of a Short Quotation—MLA

Given that "thoughts, emotions, imagination and predispositions occur concurrently . . . [and] interact with other brain processes" (Caine and Caine 66), it is easy to understand why "whatever [intelligence] might be, paper and pencil tests aren't the tenth of it" (Staples 293).

MLA

Coles asks, "What binds together a Mormon banker in Utah with his brother, or other coreligionists in Illinois or Massachusetts?" (2).

### 3. Source of a Long Quotation—MLA

A long quotation in MLA style consists of more than four typed lines. It's set off block style, indented one inch or ten spaces from the left margin. Never put quotation marks around a set-off quotation because the indentation and block style communicate that the material is quoted. At the end of an indented quotation, place the parenthetical reference after the end punctuation mark.

> Gray and Viens explain how, by tapping into a student's highly developed spatial-mechanical intelligence, one teacher can bolster a student's poor writing skills:
>
> > The teacher asked that during "journal time" Jacob create a tool dictionary to be used as a resource in the mechanical learning center. After several entries in which he drew and described tools and other materials, Jacob confidently moved on to writing about other things of import to him, such as his brothers and a recent birthday party. Rather than shy away from all things linguistic--he previously had refused any task requiring a pencil--Jacob became invested in journal writing. (23-24)

### 4. One Author—MLA

Give an author's name as it appears on the source: for a book, on the title page; for an article, directly below the title or at the end of the article.

> One test asks four-year-olds to choose between one marshmallow now or two marshmallows later (Gibbs 60).

Many nonprint sources also name an author; for CDs or DVDs, for example, check the printed sleeve or cover. For an online source, look at the beginning or end of the file for a link to the author, or at the site's home page. (For more information about citing electronic sources, see items 18 through 20.)

### 5. Two or Three Authors—MLA

Give the names in the same order as in the source. Spell out *and*. For three authors, use commas to separate the authors' names.

> As children get older, they begin to express several different kinds of intelligence (Todd and Taylor 23).

> Another measure of emotional intelligence is the success of inter- and intrapersonal relationships (Voigt, Dees, and Prigoff 14).

behavior by testing it, when possible, in the laboratory." (Sally Carrighar, "Ethology," from *Wild Heritage*, Houghton, 1965, 174–175.)

**Answers to Extra Exercise A**

1. (Smith 115).
2. (Carrighar 174–75).

**QUOTATION: ON WRITING**
There is no way to write unless you read, and read a lot.
　　　　　　　　　　　　—Walter J. Ong

**TEACHING TIP**
Write a quick paragraph making an argument about a text you are using in class. Use direct quotations from the material, but do not cite it. Give this paragraph to students and ask them to create parenthetical citations in the paragraph and a Works Cited page at the end.

**QUOTATION: ON WRITING**
I am profoundly uncertain about how to write. I know what I love and what I like, because it's a direct, passionate response. But when I write, I'm very uncertain whether it's good enough. That is, of course, the writer's agony.
　　　　　　　　　　　　—Susan Sontag

**TEACHING TIP**
If you teach in a "smart" (i.e., technology-enhanced) classroom, or if you put documents online for your students, consider color coding an MLA Works Cited page, making items that are the same in the same color to demonstrate a visual pattern of citation style to the students (e.g., all author names appear in blue, all titles in red, etc.).

**QUOTATION: ON WRITING**
When I sit at my table to write, I never know what it's going to be till I'm under way. I trust in inspiration, which sometimes comes and sometimes doesn't. But I don't sit back waiting for it. I work every day.
　　　　　　　　　　　　—Alberto Moravia

MLA

**TEACHING TIP**

Many libraries and writing centers offer citation clinics, online chats, and other resources to assist students in the process of proper citations. Make a list of available resources on your campus and share those resources with your students.

**QUOTATION: ON WRITING**

When you first start writing—and I think it's true for a lot of beginning writers—you're scared to death that if you don't get that sentence right that minute it's never going to show up again. And it isn't. But it doesn't matter—another one will, and it'll probably be better. And I don't mind writing badly for a couple of days because I know I can fix it—and fix it again and again and again, and it will be better.
—Toni Morrison

**TEACHING TIP**

Many students can find MLA and other style guides very daunting. They do not understand the rationale or importance of what they consider to be small issues: matters of punctuation and organization of information. Whenever possible, point to real life examples of documentation style in the material you bring to class. You might also show students samples of your own scholarly work and talk about your approach to tackling MLA documentation in your articles and books.

**QUOTATION: ON WRITING**

I write the first draft quickly. This is most often done in longhand. I simply fill up the pages as rapidly as I can. In some cases, there's a kind of personal shorthand, notes to myself for what I will do later when I come back to it.
—Raymond Carver

**TEACHING TIP**

While many students understand that they need to cite their work, they do not always understand why it is important to have the relevant publication information. Take your students to the library and break them into groups. Give each group 2–3 items from a longer Works

## 6. More Than Three Authors—MLA

If your source has more than three authors, you can name them all or use the first author's name only, followed by *et al.,* either in a parenthetical reference or in your sentence. In MLA citations, do not underline or italicize *et al.*

> Emotional security varies, depending on the circumstances of the social interaction (Carter et al. 158).

**Alerts:** (1) The abbreviation *et al.* stands for "and others." The Latin term *et* means "and" and requires no period. The term *al* is an abbreviation of *alii,* so it requires a period. (2) When an author's name followed by *et al.* is a subject, use a plural verb.

> Carter et al. have found that emotional security varies, depending on the circumstances of the social interaction (158). ●

## 7. More Than One Source by an Author—MLA

When you use two or more sources by an author, include the relevant title in each citation. In parenthetical citations, use a shortened version of the title. For example, in a paper using two of Howard Gardner's works, *Frames of Mind: The Theory of Multiple Intelligences* and "Reflections on Multiple Intelligences: Myths and Messages," use *Frames* and "Reflections." Shorten the titles as much as possible, keeping them unambiguous to readers and starting them with the word by which you alphabetize each work in your Works Cited list. Separate the author's name and the title with a comma, but do not use punctuation between the title and the page number. When you incorporate the title into your own sentences, you can omit a subtitle, but never shorten the main title.

> Although it seems straightforward to think of multiple intelligences as multiple approaches to learning (Gardner, *Frames* 60-61), an intelligence is not a learning style (Gardner, "Reflections" 202-03).

## 8. Two or More Authors with the Same Last Name—MLA

Use each author's first initial and full last name in each parenthetical citation. This is the only instance in MLA style where you use an initial in a parenthetical reference. If both authors have the same first initial, use the full name in all instances.

> According to Anne Cates, psychologists can predict how empathetic an adult will be from his or her behavior at age two (41), but other researchers disagree (T. Cates 171).

## 9. Work with a Group or Corporate Author—MLA

When a corporation or other group is named as the author of a source you want to cite, use the corporate name just as you would an individual's name.

In a five-year study, the Boston Women's Health Collective reported that these tests are usually unreliable (11).

A five-year study shows that these tests are usually unreliable (Boston Women's Health Collective 11).

## 10. Work Listed by Title—MLA

If no author is named, use the title in citations. In your own sentences, use the full main title and omit a subtitle, if any. For parenthetical citations, shorten the title as much as possible (making sure that the shortened version refers unambiguously to the correct source), and always make the first word the one by which you alphabetize it. "Are You a Day or Night Person?" is the full title of the article in the following citation.

The "morning lark" and "night owl" connotations are typically used to categorize the human extremes ("Are You" 11).

## 11. Multivolume Work—MLA

When you cite more than one volume of a multivolume work, include the relevant volume number in each citation. Give the volume number first, followed by a colon and one space, and then the page number(s).

By 1900, the Amazon forest dwellers had been exposed to these viruses (Rand 3: 202).

Rand believes that forest dwellers in Borneo escaped illness from retroviruses until the 1960s (4: 518-19).

## 12. Material from a Novel, Play, Poem, or Short Story—MLA

Literary works frequently appear in different editions. When you cite material from literary works, providing the part, chapter, act, scene, canto, stanza, or line numbers usually helps readers locate what you are referring to more than page numbers alone. Unless your instructor tells you not to, use Arabic numerals for these references, even if the literary work uses Roman numerals. For novels that use them, give part and/or chapter numbers after page numbers. Use a semicolon after the page number but a comma to separate a part from a chapter.

Flannery O'Connor describes one character in *The Violent Bear It Away* as "divided in two—a violent and a rational self" (139; pt. 2, ch. 6).

For plays that use them, give act, scene, and line numbers. Use periods between these numbers. For short stories, use page numbers.

Among the most quoted of Shakespeare's lines is Hamlet's soliloquy beginning "To be, or not to be: that is the question" (3.1.56).

Cited list. Have them find the texts. Later, discuss how having all of the information, such as publication dates and issue numbers and page numbers, was useful in retrieving the text. You can use this exercise to emphasize the communal knowledge-building component of citations—to help others who want to do additional research on a related topic. If it proves relevant, you might even suggest that in writing a research paper for your class that students follow up on one of their source's citations.

**QUOTATION: ON READING**
In a very real sense, people who have read good literature have lived more than people who cannot or will not read. . . . It is not true that we have only one life to live; if we can read, we can live as many more lives and as many kinds of lives as we wish.

—S. I. Hayakawa

**QUOTATION: ON WRITING**
My writing is a process of rewriting, of going back and changing and filling in. In the rewriting process you discover what's going on, and you go back and bring it up to that point.

—Joan Didion

**QUOTATION: ON WRITING**
Writer's block is a natural affliction. Writers who have never experienced it have something wrong with them. It means there isn't enough friction—that they aren't making enough of an effort to reconcile the contradictions of life. All you get is a sweet monotonous flow. Writer's block is nothing to commit suicide over. It simply indicates some imbalance between your experience and your art, and I think that's constructive.

—Stanley Kunitz

**TEACHING TIP**
Depending on how much time you have allotted for teaching MLA citation, you might consider any of the following additional exercises as ways to reinforce citation information.

- Bring a variety of textual materials to class—DVDs, cassette tapes, books, articles, journals, newspaper clippings, photographs, etc.—and ask the class to work in groups to use the MLA guidelines to create a class-generated Works Cited list. Have students put the Works Cited lists on the board, and as a group edit each list. If you teach in a smart classroom, you might consider annotating this list, using the comment function in Microsoft Word, to explain where students made mistakes and how to correct the mistake.

- Host a citation clinic day in class where students can participate in a workshop for MLA citations for their papers, both in-text and Works Cited.

- Divide the class into groups of two or three students. Assign each group a date by which the students will be responsible for preparing three MLA citations. Ask students to come to class five minutes early on their assigned day and put the citations on the board. Spend the first 10 minutes of class critiquing the citations until each group has had an opportunity to put material on the board.

- Removing all personal information (student name, section number), photocopy 2–3 old Works Cited pages from a previous class and ask students to critique it.

- Try a puzzle exercise. Prior to class, prepare envelopes for a predetermined number of groups. For each group, choose a single citation from a book. Cut the citation up into parts. Put the parts in an envelope. In class, distribute the envelopes and ask students to reassemble the citations.

**QUOTATION: ON WRITING**

A lot of young writers wait for inspiration. The inspiration only hits you at the desk.

—Robert Anderson

**QUOTATION: ON WRITING**

I don't care to talk about a novel I'm doing because if I communicate the magic spell, even in an abbreviated form, it loses its force for me.

The old man in John Collier's short story "The Chaser" says about his potions, "I don't deal in laxatives and teething mixtures . . ." (79).

For poems and plays that use them, give canto, stanza, and line numbers. Use periods between these numbers.

In "To Autumn," Keats's most melancholy image occurs in the lines "Then in a wailful choir the small gnats mourn / Among the river swallows" (3.27-28).

### 13. Bible or Sacred Text—MLA

Give the title of the edition you're using, the book (in the case of the Bible), and the chapter and verse. Spell out the names of books in sentences, but use abbreviations in parenthetical references.

He would certainly benefit from the advice in Ephesians to "get rid of all bitterness, rage, and anger" (*New International Version Bible*, 4.31).

He would certainly benefit from the advice to "get rid of all bitterness, rage, and anger" (*New International Version Bible*, Eph. 4.31).

### 14. Work in an Anthology or Other Collection—MLA

You may want to cite a work you have read in a book that contains many works by various authors and that was compiled or edited by someone other than the person you're citing. Your in-text citation should include the author of the selection you're citing and the page number. For example, suppose you want to cite the poem "Several Things" by Martha Collins, in a literature text edited by Pamela Annas and Robert Rosen. Use Collins's name and the title of her work in the sentence and the line numbers (see item 12) in a parenthetical citation.

In "Several Things," Martha Collins enumerates what could take place in the lines of her poem: "Plums could appear, on a pewter plate / A dead red hare, hung by one foot. / A vase of flowers. Three shallots" (2-4).

### 15. Indirect Source—MLA

When you want to quote words that you found quoted in someone else's work, put the name of the person whose words you're quoting into your own sentence. Give the work where you found the quotation either in your sentence or in a parenthetical citation beginning with *qtd. in.*

Martin Scorsese acknowledges the link between himself and his films: "I realize that all my life, I've been an outsider. I splatter bits of myself all over the screen" (qtd. in Giannetti and Eyman 397).

Giannetti and Eyman quote Martin Scorsese as acknowledging the link between himself and his films: "I realize that all my life, I've been an outsider. I splatter bits of myself all over the screen" (397).

## 16. Two or More Sources in One Reference—MLA

If more than one source has contributed to an idea, opinion, or fact in your paper, cite them all. Suppose, as in the following example, that three sources all make the same point. An efficient way to credit all is to include them in a single parenthetical citation, with a semicolon separating each block of information.

> Once researchers agreed that multiple intelligences existed, their next step was to try to measure or define them (West 17; Arturi 477; Gibbs 68).

## 17. Entire Work—MLA

References to an entire work usually fit best into your own sentences.

> In *Convergence Culture,* Henry Jenkins explores how new digital media create a culture of active participation rather than of passive reception.

## 18. Electronic Source with Page Numbers—MLA

The principles that govern in-text parenthetical citations of electronic sources are exactly the same as the ones that apply to books, articles, or other sources. When an electronically accessed source identifies its author, use the author's name for parenthetical references. If no author is named, use the title of the source. When an electronic source has page numbers, use them exactly as you would the page numbers of a print source.

> Learning happens best when teachers truly care about their students' complete well-being (Anderson 7).

## 19. Electronic Source with Paragraph Numbers—MLA

When an electronic source has numbered paragraphs (instead of page numbers), use them for parenthetical references, with two differences: (1) Use a comma followed by one space after the name (or title); and (2) use the abbreviation *par.* for a reference to one paragraph or *pars.* for a reference to more than one paragraph, followed by the number(s) of the paragraph(s) you are citing. Note that the practice of numbering paragraphs is rare.

> Artists seem to be haunted by the fear that psychoanalysis might destroy creativity while it reconstructs personality (Francis, pars. 22-25).

## 20. Electronic Source Without Page or Paragraph Numbers—MLA

Many online or digital sources don't number pages or paragraphs. Simply refer to those works in their entirety. Here are two examples referring to "What Is Artificial Intelligence?" by John McCarthy; this Web site does not use page numbers or paragraph numbers. Include the name of the author in your sentence; it is also helpful to include the title.

Once you have talked, the act of communication has been made.

—Angus Wilson

**TEACHING TIP**

One useful way to merge communications skills with research paper writing is to ask students to prepare research presentations. In addition to sharing their thesis and relevant findings with the class, students can prepare a visual presentation, such as a PowerPoint, to show their research. When MLA style is used in these presentations, it reinforces citation skills.

**QUOTATION: ON WRITING**

I don't think that writer's block exists really. I think that when you're trying to do something prematurely, it just won't come. Certain subjects just need time, as I've learned over and over again. You've got to wait before you write about them.

—Joyce Carol Oates

**EXTRA EXERCISE B**

Using the following information, compile a Works Cited list in MLA style.

**1.** *Abraham Lincoln: The Man behind the Myths,* by Stephen B. Oates. Harper & Row, Publishers, New York, Cambridge, Philadelphia, San Francisco, London, Mexico City, São Paulo, and Sydney, 1984.

**2.** Barbara W. Tuchman. *Practicing History.* Alfred A. Knopf, Inc. Copyright 1936, 1959, 1966, 1974, 1981. New York.

**3.** *Time's Arrow, Time's Cycle: Myth and Metaphor in the Discovery of Geological Time.* Stephen Jay Gould. Harvard University Press, Cambridge, Massachusetts. 1987.

**4.** T. C. Smout. *A Century of the Scottish People, 1830–1950.* New Haven and London, 1986, Yale University Press.

**5.** Thomas J. Peters and Robert H. Waterman Jr. *In Search of Excellence.* Harper & Row, Publishers, New York, 1982.

**6.** *The Rise and Fall of the House of Medici.* 1974. Penguin Books. New York. By Christopher Hibbert.

MLA

7. *Capote: A Biography.* 1988. Simon & Schuster. New York. Gerald Clarke.

**Answers to Extra Exercise B**

**Works Cited**

Clarke, Gerald. *Capote: A Biography.* New York: Simon, 1988. Print.

Gould, Stephen Jay. *Time's Arrow, Time's Cycle: Myth and Metaphor in the Discovery of Geological Time.* Cambridge: Harvard UP, 1987. Print.

Hibbert, Christopher. *The Rise and Fall of the House of Medici.* New York: Penguin, 1974. Print.

Oates, Stephen B. *Abraham Lincoln: The Man behind the Myths.* New York: Harper, 1984. Print.

Peters, Thomas J., and Robert H. Waterman Jr. *In Search of Excellence.* New York: Harper, 1982. Print.

Smout, T. C. *A Century of the Scottish People, 1830–1950.* New Haven: Yale UP, 1986. Print.

Tuchman, Barbara W. *Practicing History.* New York: Knopf, 1981. Print.

**TEACHING TIP**

In professional writing, students will have to learn to follow exact formats. For example, when entrepreneurs write business plans, they have to follow an exact format. Working with MLA format is a good way to anticipate other writing that must follow strict guidelines.

**TEACHING TIP**

Encourage students to use a variety of sources when writing research papers. Often students rely on Internet, full-text articles and books. Challenge them to use audio, visual, and primary source documents, where appropriate.

**BACKGROUND**

In "'Building a Mystery': Alternative Research Writing and the Academic Act of Seeking," Robert Davis and Mark Shadle suggest that this new era of information calls for a different approach to the traditional research paper, one that encourages research as honoring mystery

According to McCarthy, the science of artificial intelligence includes efforts beyond trying to simulate human intelligence.

In "What Is Artificial Intelligence?" John McCarthy notes that the science of artificial intelligence includes efforts beyond trying to simulate human intelligence.

# 36d What are MLA guidelines for a Works Cited list?

In MLA-STYLE DOCUMENTATION, the Works Cited list gives complete bibliographic information for each SOURCE used in your paper. Include only the sources from which you quote, paraphrase, or summarize. Never include sources that you consulted but don't refer to in the paper. Quick Reference 36.1 gives general information about the Works Cited list. The rest of this chapter gives models of many specific kinds of Works Cited entries.

---

**Quick Reference 36.1**    ■ ■ ■ ■ ■ ■ ■

## Guidelines for an MLA-style Works Cited list

**TITLE**
Use "Works Cited" (without quotation marks) as the title.

**PLACEMENT OF LIST**
Start a new page numbered sequentially with the rest of the paper, following the Notes pages, if any.

**CONTENT AND FORMAT**
Include all sources quoted from, paraphrased, or summarized in your paper. Start each entry on a new line and at the regular left margin. If the entry uses more than one line, indent the second and all following lines one-half inch (or five spaces) from the left margin. Double-space all lines.

**SPACING AFTER PUNCTUATION**
When typewriters were common, it improved readability to leave two spaces after punctuation at the end of a sentence. Computers have made this practice no longer necessary. The *MLA Handbook* uses one space, as does this book. Either style is acceptable. However, you should use two spaces if that's the style your instructor prefers. Always put only one space after a comma or a colon.

**ARRANGEMENT OF ENTRIES**
Alphabetize by author's last name. If no author is named, alphabetize by the title's first significant word (ignore *A, An,* or *The*).

continued >>

## Quick Reference 36.1    (continued)

### AUTHORS' NAMES
Use first names and middle names or middle initials, if any, as given in the source. Don't reduce to initials any name that is given in full. For one author or the first-named author in multiauthor works, give the last name first. Use the word *and* with two or more authors. List multiple authors in the order given in the source. Use a comma between the first author's last and first names and after each complete author name except the last. After the last author's name, use a period: **Fein, Ethel Andrea, Bert Griggs, and Delaware Rogash.**

Include *Jr., Sr., II,* or *III* but no other titles and degrees before or after a name. For example, an entry for a work by Edward Meep III, MD, and Sir Richard Bolton would start like this: **Meep, Edward, III, and Richard Bolton.**

### CAPITALIZATION OF TITLES
Capitalize all major words and the first and last words of all titles and subtitles. Don't capitalize ARTICLES (*a, an, the*), PREPOSITIONS, COORDINATING CONJUNCTIONS (*and, but, for, nor, or, so, yet*), or *to* in INFINITIVES in the middle of a title.

### SPECIAL TREATMENT OF TITLES
Use quotation marks around titles of shorter works (poems, short stories, essays, articles). Italicize titles of longer works (books, periodicals, plays).

When a book title includes the title of another work that is usually italicized (as with a novel, play, or long poem), the preferred MLA style is not to italicize the incorporated title: *Decoding* Jane Eyre. For an alternative that MLA accepts, see item 20 in 36d.1.

If the incorporated title is usually enclosed in quotation marks (such as a short story or short poem), keep the quotation marks and italicize the complete title of the book: *Theme and Form in "I Shall Laugh Purely": A Brief Study.*

Drop *A, An,* or *The* as the first word of a periodical title.

### PLACE OF PUBLICATION
If several cities are listed for the place of publication, give only the first. MLA doesn't require US state names no matter how obscure or confusing the city names might be. For an unfamiliar city outside the United States, include an abbreviated name of the country or Canadian province.

### PUBLISHER
Use shortened names as long as they are clear: *Random* for *Random House.* For companies named for more than one person, name only the first: *Prentice* for *Prentice Hall.* For university presses, use the capital letters *U* and *P* (without periods): **Oxford UP; U of Chicago P**

continued >>

(*College Composition and Communication,* 51.3 (2000): 417–446).

### TEACHING TIP
Make citation real for your students. There have been several highly publicized plagiarism cases lately. Historian Stephen E. Ambrose was accused of plagiarizing Thomas Childers' *The Wings of Morning* in his book *The Wild Blue.* Dan Brown faced a lawsuit over historical information he used in *The DaVinci Code.*

Take passages from *The DaVinci Code* and ask students how they could cite the material. This promises to raise interesting and lively class discussion since *The DaVinci Code* is fiction. You might also take passages from *The Wings of Morning* and *The Wild Blue* and ask students to undertake a similar exercise in suggesting proper citation information. Alternatively, you might ask students to research recent high profile plagiarism cases in music and film.

### TEACHING TIP
Professor J. P. Lesko of Saginaw Valley State University, runs the Famous Plagiarists Web site which examines both historic and recent cases of alleged plagiarism; see <http://www.famousplagiarists.com/index.html>.

### RESEARCH: PORTFOLIO APPROACHES AND ACTIVITIES
The research project offers a sound opportunity for a task-oriented, self-contained portfolio or a rich selection for a program or class portfolio. Obviously, the research process requires the student to synthesize multiple correlated skills and concepts. By carefully dating, labeling, and reflecting on this sophisticated reading and writing task, students can see, refine, and deepen learning before, during, and after various strategic stages of the process. The pivotal component of portfolio assessment that separates it from traditional assessments is student reflection about the process. Students must assume the responsibility of creating and defending the meaning and quality of the learning taking place.

## USING THE REPORTER'S QUESTIONS IN REFLECTING AND RESEARCHING

Keep the instructional responsibility on the student by using the material summarized in the Quick References throughout this handbook as the basis of reflective informal journals. For example, certain items in Quick Reference 33.1, "Sample schedule for a research project," in section 33b, combined with the exemplified research log in section 33c, provide excellent roots for reflective questions and answers.

Item 2 in Quick Reference 33.1, "Choose a topic suitable for research," could be presented as a two- to three-minute class opener to establish prior knowledge and preview the lesson in the following manner: What would be a suitable topic for research and why? What topics would you like to learn and read about? Does this topic have two sides? Which side do you presently support and why?

Item 9 in Quick Reference 33.1, "Locate and evaluate sources," could yield a subsequent set of questions: Where would information on this topic probably be found? Who would be best qualified to offer an opinion and why? How many different types of sources might be available? Where and how could you locate these sources?

This procedural model yields as many questions for lively class discussion and quiet written reflection as you have time for in your curriculum. Choose your own focus and create questions that help students connect the function, form, and processes of learning activities to knowledge.

## RESEARCH PORTFOLIO: TASK-ORIENTED, SELF-CONTAINED PROFILE OF A STUDENT RESEARCHER

Portfolios are discussed in detail in Chapter 47. Portfolios are an excellent way to help students organize all of the stages of research writing. If you decide to teach the research paper using a portfolio method, you will want to determine how much of the process you want students to showcase. This can include anything from a research log to notes to outlines to drafts to final reflections. The following is a brief overview of the research portfolio. For more information,

---

### Quick Reference 36.1 (continued)

#### PUBLICATION MONTH ABBREVIATIONS

Abbreviate all publication months except *May, June,* and *July.* Use the first three letters followed by a period (*Dec., Feb.*) except for September (*Sept.*).

#### PAGE RANGES

Give the page range—the starting page number and the ending page number, connected by a hyphen—of any paginated electronic source and any paginated print source that is part of a longer work (for example, a chapter in a book, an article in a journal). A range indicates that the cited work is on those pages and all pages in between. If that isn't the case, use the style shown next for discontinuous pages. In either case, use numerals only, without the word *page* or *pages* or the abbreviation *p.* or *pp.*

Use the full second number through *99.* Above that, use only the last two digits for the second number unless to do so would be unclear: 113-14 is clear, but 567-602 requires full numbers.

#### DISCONTINUOUS PAGES

A source has discontinuous pages when the source is interrupted by material that's not part of the source (for example, an article beginning on page 32 but continued on page 54). Use the starting page number followed by a plus sign (+): 32+.

#### MEDIUM OF PUBLICATION

Include the MEDIUM OF PUBLICATION for each Works Cited entry. For example, every entry for a print source must include "Print" at the end, followed by a period (if required, certain supplementary bibliographic information like translation information, name of a book series, or the total number of volumes in a set should follow the medium of publication). Every source from the World Wide Web must include "Web" at the end, followed by a period and the date of access. The medium of publication also needs to be included for broadcast sources ("Television", "Radio"), sound recordings ("CD", "LP", "Audiocassette"), as well as films, DVDs, videocassettes, live performances, musical scores and works of visual arts, and so on. (See examples 34–96.)

#### ISSUE AND VOLUME NUMBERS FOR SCHOLARLY JOURNALS

Include both an issue and volume number for each Works Cited entry for scholarly journals. This applies both to journals that are continuously paginated and those that are not.

#### WORKS CITED INFORMATION REQUIRED FOR ONLINE SOURCES

The following publication information should be listed for all online sources:

1. Name of the author, director, narrator, performer, editor, compiler, or producer of the work. If no author is given, begin the entry with the title of the work.

continued >>

## Quick Reference 36.1 (continued)

2. Title of the work. Italicize the title, unless it is part of a larger work. Titles that are part of a larger work should be enclosed in quotation marks.

3. Title of the overall Web site (in italics) if this is distinct from the title of the work.

4. Version or edition of the site.

5. Publisher or sponsor of the site. If this information is not available, use n.p. (for no publisher).

6. Date of publication (day, month, and year, if available). If no date is given, use n.d.

7. Medium of publication. For all online sources, the medium of publication is "Web."

8. Date of access (day, month, and year).

### URLs IN ELECTRONIC SOURCES

Entries for online citations should include the URL only when the reader probably could not locate the source without it.

If the entry requires a URL, enclose it in angle brackets <like this>. Put the URL before the access date and end it with a period. If your computer automatically creates a hyperlink when you type a URL (the text changes color, the URL is underlined, or both) format the URL to look the same as the rest of the entry by changing the font color to black, removing the underline, and making any other changes. In some applications, like Microsoft Word, you can use the command "remove hyperlink," which you can find on the "Insert" menu or by right-clicking on the hyperlink.

If a URL must be divided between two lines, only break the URL after a slash and do not use a hyphen.

## 36d.1 Following MLA guidelines for specific sources in a Works Cited list

The Works Cited directory above corresponds to the numbered entries in this section. Not every possible documentation model is shown in this chapter. You may find that you have to combine features of models to document a particular source. You'll also find more information in the *MLA Handbook for Writers of Research Papers*. Figure 36.1 provides another tool to help you find the Works Cited model you need: a decision-making flowchart.

### BOOKS

Citations for books have three main parts: author, title, and publication information (place of publication, publisher, and date of publication). Figure 36.2 (p. 605) illustrates where to find this information and the proper citation format.

please see the student and instructor information in Chapter 47.

The following information can be quickly and easily translated into an overview handout for a research portfolio. Such a handout provides the student with a reference document throughout the learning and assessment process. However, many of the question, reflection, and writing activities may be assigned in an ongoing fashion through daily, informal journals that can, by design, preview, reinforce, or review specific steps in the research process. To reinforce the relationships among reading, listening, speaking, and writing, try scheduling some time for small-group and whole-class discussion as talk-aloud reflections. Sponsor a "hallway bull session" in class; just remind students to record their questions and insights.

*Before research begins,* establish prior knowledge and stimulate learning readiness by asking students to record reflections in any or all of the following ways: Briefly describe your research history—how many times have you researched? How will information already learned in this class help in the research process? What are the purposes of research? What was the required documentation style? Describe your success with the process. Describe your struggles with the process. Describe your preferred method of research.

*As research proceeds,* encourage students to track and document every minute spent on research by dating and recording reflections on any or all of the following topics (you may want to reword these prompts in language appropriate for your student audience):

- *Concepts:* What is the value of your topic—who cares or needs to know about it? What is its value to the audience? What are the inherent biases for or against the topic? What propaganda techniques are used by opposing sides of this topic, if any, and how are they employed? Record and describe new insights or changed views as you research. What action, if any, do you want from your reader?

- *Procedures:* Date and record questions that occur to you as you listen to instruction and lectures, hunt for proper formats in the

MLA

textbook, create bibliography and note cards, and then apply the style rules to your paper. Date, record, and label answers to your questions as you learn them. Using the model in Quick Reference 33.1 in section 33b, present your own step-by-step research process. Discuss why you might implement your own adaptations of textbook- or lecture-given procedures. This method can be quickly refined into an additional five minutes of quickly written reflections that create a daily record of the attention you are giving to your studies.

- *Technology:* Date, record, and label the ways in which technology enhances or complicates your work. Do you have access to a computer or word processor? How often and in what ways do you use the library's or learning center's computerized databases? How often and in what ways do you use the Internet? Discuss the ease or frustration of your experiences. What are the greatest benefits of computers in the research-writing process?

*Once research concludes,* ask students to determine the value of their work by assigning themselves a grade and then defending that grade through a formal reflective summary and synthesis of learning activities, growth, and mastery. Remember, the following questions serve only as models; experiment and create your own questions that mirror your instructional emphasis.

- *Concepts:* Re-address relevant questions asked before research began with the intent to demonstrate dynamic understanding. Also, include a discussion about things you still need to learn, as evidenced in the portfolio. In what ways would you improve your use of the research process? This paper? What still confuses you? Based on feedback and grades, what do you still need to learn? How would you do so, if given the chance? Record and reflect on the connections between research and writing strategies learned earlier in the term. For example, discuss the way in which the use of verbs helped you integrate source material into your prose (see 35k).

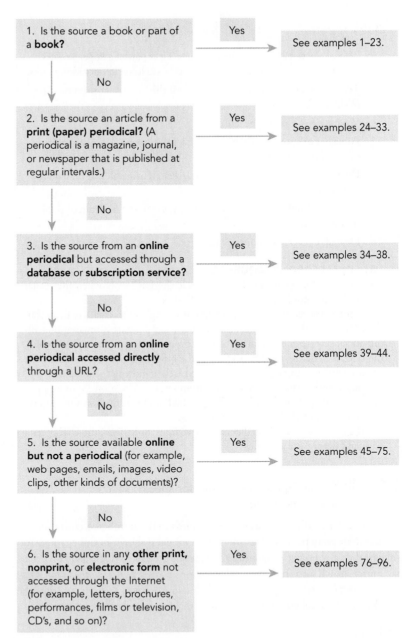

**Figure 36.1** MLA Works Cited visual directory

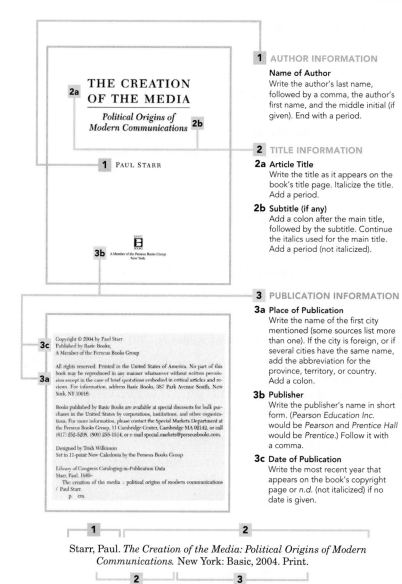

**1 AUTHOR INFORMATION**

**Name of Author**
Write the author's last name, followed by a comma, the author's first name, and the middle initial (if given). End with a period.

**2 TITLE INFORMATION**

**2a Article Title**
Write the title as it appears on the book's title page. Italicize the title. Add a period.

**2b Subtitle (if any)**
Add a colon after the main title, followed by the subtitle. Continue the italics used for the main title. Add a period (not italicized).

**3 PUBLICATION INFORMATION**

**3a Place of Publication**
Write the name of the first city mentioned (some sources list more than one). If the city is foreign, or if several cities have the same name, add the abbreviation for the province, territory, or country. Add a colon.

**3b Publisher**
Write the publisher's name in short form. (*Pearson Education Inc.* would be *Pearson* and *Prentice Hall* would be *Prentice*.) Follow it with a comma.

**3c Date of Publication**
Write the most recent year that appears on the book's copyright page or *n.d.* (not italicized) if no date is given.

Starr, Paul. *The Creation of the Media: Political Origins of Modern Communications.* New York: Basic, 2004. Print.

**Figure 36.2** Locating and citing source information in a book

- *Procedures:* Discuss the effectiveness of bibliography and note cards (see 33i and 33k). In what way does your portfolio reflect the use and value of your various sources (34j and 34m)? Describe your search strategy and its success (34b). Discuss why you implemented your own adaptations of textbook- or lecture-given procedures. How have research skills developed study skills? How are these skills relevant to other courses, life, or career?

- *Technology:* What new technological knowledge or skills did you gain from the research process? What are the pitfalls or limitations of technology?

**CREATING A RESEARCH PROCESS PROFILE**
This approach allows students to showcase their growing understanding and mastery of the research process. Encourage students to chronicle the research process through a show-and-tell technical report that demonstrates skills and applications and discusses procedural decisions and the impact of those decisions. Consider, for example, the following series of steps and journal reflections:

**1.** Create a registry that logs and tracks sources (33i).

**2.** Create and catalog bibliography cards or note card files on the computer (33k).

**3.** Provide sample photocopies or printouts of sources.

**4.** Use these to identify and highlight possible ideas for note cards.

**5.** Create and label note cards (33k).

**6.** Reclassify cards into outline order (33m).

**7.** Write a draft from the note cards rearranged into outline order (33n).

**8.** Complete the writing process.

**9.** Write an informal research summary reflection. It should describe your individual adaptations or variations from the expected procedures; describe the relationship between steps in the procedure; discuss challenges, insights, and rewards met through this process; and

MLA

discuss any specific, new knowledge and fact-versus-opinion, authoritative sources, notetaking, and synthesis skills you learned or used. In what way does this profile prove your mastery and the grade you seek? (See Quick References 33.5 and 33.6 for points that can be adapted. A sample sentence may read, "This researcher worked with her notes in front of her.")

**10.** Write a formal draft of the research reflection.

## CREATING A RESEARCH SKILL PROFILE

This variation of the show-and-tell technical approach allows students to showcase and illustrate the relationship between building individual skills and creating the final product. Encourage students to target independent and individual needs and demonstrate goal setting, time on task, growing understanding, and, ultimately, mastery. Once the need is targeted, chronicle growth by creating a series of reflections based on the following steps:

**1.** Create a self-monitoring log or registry for daily work.

**2.** Survey instruction and feedback (scores and comments), and write a list of things you need to know to earn the desired grade (needs will run the gamut from time management to grammar to computer skills).

**3.** Locate print resources that address each item on the need-to-know list (take note of textbooks, libraries, learning centers), and set up a study system.

**4.** Locate nonprint resources that address each need-to-know item (take note of computer software, tutors, peers, instructor conferences, etc.).

**5.** Set up a study schedule timeline.

**6.** Create and organize print copies of each study session.

**7.** Label each study session with date, time spent on task, and purpose of task.

**8.** After each study session (or periodically), write an application reflection discussing how the information studied will improve research

### 1. Book by One Author—MLA

Bradway, Becky. *Pink Houses and Family Taverns*. Bloomington: Indiana UP, 2002. Print.

### 2. Book by Two or Three Authors—MLA

Edin, Kathryn, and Maria Kefalas. *Promises I Can Keep: Why Poor Women Put Motherhood before Marriage*. Berkeley: U of California P, 2005. Print.

Lynam, John K., Cyrus G. Ndiritu, and Adiel N. Mbabu. *Transformation of Agricultural Research Systems in Africa: Lessons from Andreiya*. East Lansing: Michigan State UP, 2004. Print.

### 3. Book by More Than Three Authors—MLA

Give only the first author's name, followed by a comma and the phrase *et al.* (abbreviated from the Latin *et alii*, meaning "and others"), or list all names in full and in the order in which they appear on the title page.

Saul, Wendy, et al. *Beyond the Science Fair: Creating a Kids' Inquiry Conference*. Portsmouth: Heinemann, 2005. Print.

### 4. Two or More Works by the Same Author(s)—MLA

Give author name(s) in the first entry only. In the second and subsequent entries, use three hyphens and a period to stand for exactly the same name(s). If the person served as editor or translator, put a comma and the appropriate abbreviation (*ed.* or *trans.*) following the three hyphens. Arrange the works in alphabetical (not chronological) order according to book title, ignoring labels such as *ed.* or *trans.*

Jenkins, Henry. *Convergence Culture: Where Old and New Media Collide*. New York: New York UP, 2006. Print.

---. *Fans, Bloggers, and Gamers: Exploring Participatory Culture*. New York: New York UP, 2006. Print.

### 5. Book by Group or Corporate Author—MLA

Cite the full name of the corporate author first, omitting the first articles *A, An,* or *The*. When a corporate author is also the publisher, use a shortened form of the corporate name in the publication information.

American Psychological Association. *Publication Manual of the American Psychological Association*. 5th ed. Washington: APA, 2001. Print.

Boston Women's Health Collective. *Our Bodies, Ourselves for the New Century*. New York: Simon, 1998. Print.

### 6. Book with No Author Named—MLA

If there is no author's name on the title page, begin the citation with the title. Alphabetize the entry according to the first significant word of the title ignoring *A, An* or *The.*

*The Chicago Manual of Style.* 15th ed. Chicago: U of Chicago P, 2003. Print.

### 7. Book with an Author and an Editor—MLA

If your paper refers to the work of the book's author, put the author's name first; if your paper refers to the work of the editor, put the editor's name first.

Brontë, Emily. *Wuthering Heights.* Ed. Richard J. Dunn. New York: Norton, 2002. Print.

Dunn, Richard J., ed. *Wuthering Heights.* By Emily Brontë. New York: Norton, 2002. Print.

### 8. Translation—MLA

Kundera, Milan. *The Unbearable Lightness of Being.* Trans. Michael Henry Heim. New York: Harper, 1999. Print.

### 9. Work in Several Volumes or Parts—MLA

If you're citing only one volume, put the volume number before the publication information. If you wish, you can give the total number of volumes at the end of the entry. MLA recommends using Arabic numerals, even if the source uses Roman numerals (*Vol. 6* rather than *Vol. VI*).

Chrisley, Ronald, ed. *Artificial Intelligence: Critical Concepts.* Vol. 1. London: Routledge, 2000. Print. 4 vols.

### 10. Anthology or Edited Book—MLA

In the following example, *ed.* stands for "editor," so use *eds.* when more than one editor is named; also see items 9, 11, and 12.

Purdy, John L., and James Ruppert, eds. *Nothing but the Truth: An Anthology of Native American Literature.* Upper Saddle River: Prentice, 2001. Print.

### 11. One Selection from an Anthology or an Edited Book—MLA

Give the author and title of the selection first and then the full title of the anthology. Information about the editor starts with *Ed.* (for "Edited by"), so don't use *Eds.* when there is more than one editor. Give the name(s) of the editor(s) in normal order rather than reversing first and last names. Give the page range at the end.

Trujillo, Laura. "Balancing Act." *Border-Line Personalities: A New Generation of Latinas Dish on Sex, Sass, and Cultural Shifting.* Ed. Robyn Moreno and Michelle Herrera Mulligan. New York: Harper, 2004. 61-72. Print.

writing. Remember, voluminous practice produces skill, so reflect and write often.

**9.** As mastery of an individual skill is achieved, make a significant registry entry as proof or evidence of growth and reward.

**10.** Upon completion of the research project, write a final informal self-assessment defending the value of your studies and the worth of your new information. Assign yourself a grade, and give evidence to support the worth of that judgment.

**11.** Write a final, formal draft to submit with the registry.

**QUOTATION: ON WRITING**

Since long before the invention of universities, not to mention university programs in creative writing, authors have acquired their authority in four main ways—first, by paying a certain sort of attention to the experience of life as well as merely undergoing it; second, by paying a certain sort of attention to the works of their great and less great predecessors in the medium of written language, as well as merely reading them; third, by practicing that medium themselves, usually a lot (Charles Newman, the writer and critic, declares that the first prerequisite for aspiring writers is sufficient motor control to keep their pens moving left to right, line after line, hour after hour, day after day, and I would add year after year, decade after decade); and fourth, by offering their apprentice work for discussion and criticism by one or several of their impassioned peers, or by some more experienced hand or by both.

—John Barth

**QUOTATION: ON WRITING**

Of making many books there is no end; and much study is a weariness of the flesh.

—Ecclesiastes 12:12

**QUOTATION: ON WRITING**

The wastepaper basket is the writer's best friend.

—Isaac Bashevis Singer

**QUOTATION: ON WRITING**

You must learn to write rather than be a writer. Write as well as you can. Don't think of what is wanted, what is popular, what will sell. Write what you want, and write as well as you can.
— Margery Sharp

**TEACHING TIP**

Are your students especially nervous about their research work? To reduce the stress that sometimes accompanies research projects (especially if end-of-term deadlines loom), try incorporating music into classroom workshop activities. You may want to refer to Howard Gardner's eight multiple intelligences to see how music can be used also to enhance learning.

**TEACHING TIP**

Explain that formats are of major importance in many disciplines other than English composition. The formats constitute "genres" that readers expect. The formats ease communication because readers know where to look for specific information: background, data, conclusions.

**TEACHING TIP**

Point out to students that symbols, such as # and ¢, should not be used in the body of a paper, although they can appear in graphs and tables. The dollar sign ($) can be used anywhere when accompanied by figures.

**QUOTATION: ON WRITING**

There are no dull subjects. There are only dull writers.
— H. L. Mencken

**TEACHING TIP**

People are increasingly interested in experimenting with automated MLA citation services and software. Web sites like *BibMe: Fast & Easy Bibliography Maker,* designed originally as a student project, can automate Works Cited pages. If you are interested in exploring sites like these with your students, start with the free service BibMe at <http://www.bibme.org>. Other services and software include EasyBib, NoodleBib, EndNote, Zotero, and RefWorks. When using

### 12. More Than One Selection from the Same Anthology or Edited Book—MLA

If you cite more than one selection from the same anthology, you can list the anthology as a separate entry with all the publication information. Also, list each selection from the anthology by author and title of the selection, but give only the name(s) of the editor(s) of the anthology and the page number(s) for each selection. List selections separately in alphabetical order by author's last name.

Bond, Ruskin. "The Night Train at Deoli." Chaudhuri 415-18.

Chaudhuri, Amit, ed. *The Vintage Book of Modern Indian Literature.* New York: Vintage, 2004. Print.

Vijayan, O.V. "The Rocks." Chaudhuri 291-96.

### 13. Signed Article in a Reference Book—MLA

A "signed article" means that the author of the article is identified. If the articles in the book are alphabetically arranged, you don't need to give volume and page numbers.

Burnbam, John C. "Freud, Sigmund." *The Encyclopedia of Psychiatry, Psychology, and Psychoanalysis.* Ed. Benjamin B. Wolman. New York: Holt, 1996. Print.

### 14. Unsigned Article in a Reference Book—MLA

Begin with the title of the article. If you're citing a widely used reference work, don't give full publication information. Instead, give only the edition and year of publication.

"Ireland." *The New Encyclopaedia Britannica: Macropaedia.* 15th ed. 2002. Print.

### 15. Second or Later Edition—MLA

If a book isn't a first edition, the edition number appears on the title page. Place the abbreviated information (*2nd ed., 3rd ed.,* etc.) between the title and the publication information. Give only the latest copyright date for the edition you're using.

Gibaldi, Joseph. *MLA Handbook for Writers of Research Papers.* 6th ed. New York: MLA, 2003. Print.

### 16. Introduction, Preface, Foreword, or Afterword—MLA

Give first the name of the writer of the part you're citing and then the name of the cited part, capitalized but not underlined or in quotation marks. After the book title, write *By* or *Ed.* and the full name(s) of the book's author(s) or editor(s), if different from the writer of the cited material. If the writer of the cited material is the same as the book author, include only the last name after

MLA

*By.* Following the publication information, give inclusive page numbers for the cited part, using Roman or Arabic numerals as the source does.

Hesse, Doug. Foreword. *The End of Composition Studies.* By David W. Smit.
Carbondale: Southern Illinois UP, 2004. ix-xiii. Print.

When the introduction, preface, foreword, or afterword has a title (as in the next example), include it in the citation before the section name.

Fox-Genovese, Elizabeth. "Mothers and Daughters: The Ties That Bind."
Foreword. *Southern Mothers.* Ed. Nagueyalti Warren and Sally Wolff.
Baton Rouge: Louisiana State UP, 1999. iv-xviii. Print.

### 17. Unpublished Dissertation or Essay—MLA

State the author's name first, then the title in quotation marks (not italicized), then a descriptive label (such as *Diss.* or *Unpublished essay*), followed by the degree-granting institution (for dissertations), and, finally, the date. Treat published dissertations as books.

Stuart, Gina Anne. "Exploring the Harry Potter Book Series: A Study of
Adolescent Reading Motivation." Diss. Utah State U, 2006. Print.

### 18. Reprint of an Older Book—MLA

Republishing information can be found on the copyright page. Give the date of the original version before the publication information for the version you're citing.

O'Brien, Flann. *At Swim-Two-Birds.* 1939. Normal: Dalkey Archive, 1998. Print.

### 19. Book in a Series—MLA

Goldman, Dorothy J. *Women Writers and World War I.* New York: Macmillan,
1995. Print. Lit. and Soc. Ser.

Mukherjee, Meenakshi. *Jane Austen.* New York: St. Martin's, 1991. Print. Women
Writers Ser.

### 20. Book with a Title Within a Title—MLA

The MLA recognizes two distinct styles for handling normally independent titles when they appear within an italicized title. (Use whichever style your instructor prefers.) When using the MLA's preferred style, do not italicize the embedded title or set it within quotation marks.

Lumiansky, Robert M., and Herschel Baker, eds. *Critical Approaches to Six
Major English Works:* Beowulf *Through* Paradise Lost. Philadelphia: U of
Pennsylvania P, 1968. Print.

**BACKGROUND**
A direct title tells exactly what the essay will be about. An indirect title hints at the essay's topic. In either case, it stands alone, not as part of the body of the essay.

**TEACHING TIP**
A number of instructors have reported good results when they invite two classes to exchange papers. The class members then read, comment upon, and suggest grades for one another's work. Students in each class identify their work by a code name or number, not by name. Through this process, students in both classes learn the importance of writing for a reader other than their instructor, and they tend to give and to take peer comments quite seriously. If this strategy is applied to the penultimate draft of a paper, you and your students may discover that final revisions are even more polished than they might be apart from the feedback.

**TEACHING TIP**
If your students are posting their papers online, in addition to supplying the MLA citations, encourage them to hyperlink their Works Cited page to the original source.

**QUOTATION: ON WRITING**
The desire to write grows with writing.
—Erasmus

**QUOTATION: ON WRITING**
A writer who waits for ideal conditions under which to work will die without putting a word on paper.
—E. B. White

**QUOTATION: ON WRITING**
Each paragraph almost discovers the paragraph it precedes. When I end one paragraph I know it must lead to another.
—Roger Rosenblatt

However, because MLA also accepts a second style for handling such embedded titles, you can set the normally independent titles within quotation marks and italicize them.

Lumiansky, Robert M., and Herschel Baker, eds. *Critical Approaches to Six Major English Works: "Beowulf" Through "Paradise Lost."* Philadelphia: U of Pennsylvania P, 1968. Print.

### 21. Bible or Sacred Text—MLA

*Bhagavad-Gita.* Trans. Juan Mascaro. Rev. ed. New York: Penguin, 2003. Print.

*The Holy Bible: New International Version.* New York: Harper, 1983. Print.

*The Qur'an.* Trans. Abdullah Yusuf Ali. 13th ed. Elmhurst: Tahrike Tarsile Qur'an, 1999. Print.

### 22. Government Publication—MLA

For government publications that name no author, start with the name of the government or government body. Then name the government agency. *GPO* is a standard abbreviation for *Government Printing Office,* the publisher of most US government publications.

United States. Cong. House. Committee on Resources. *Coastal Heritage Trail Route in New Jersey.* 106th Cong., 1st sess. H. Rept. 16. Washington: GPO, 1999. Print.

---. ---. Senate. Select Committee on Intelligence. *Report on the U.S. Intelligence Community's Prewar Intelligence Assessment of Iraq.* 108th Cong., 1st sess. Washington: GPO, 2004. Print.

### 23. Published Proceedings of a Conference—MLA

Rocha, Luis Mateus, et al., eds. *Artificial Life X: Proceedings of the Tenth International Conference on the Simulation and Synthesis of Living Systems.* Bloomington, IN. 3-7 June 2006. Cambridge: MIT P, 2006. Print.

### PERIODICAL PUBLICATIONS—PRINT VERSIONS

Citations for periodical articles contain three major parts: author information, title information, and publication information. Figure 36.3 shows a citation for an article in a scholarly journal (see item 27).

### 24. Signed Article in a Weekly or Biweekly Periodical—MLA

Brink, Susan. "Eat This Now!" *US News and World Report* 28 Mar. 2005: 56-58. Print.

MLA

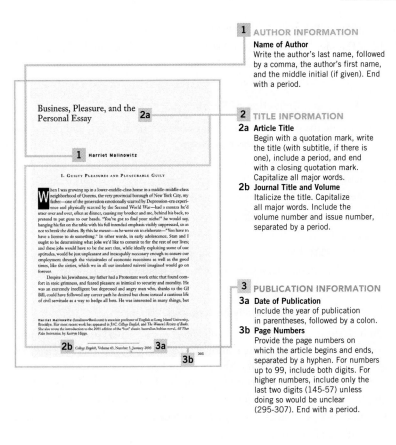

**1 AUTHOR INFORMATION**
**Name of Author**
Write the author's last name, followed by a comma, the author's first name, and the middle initial (if given). End with a period.

**2 TITLE INFORMATION**
**2a Article Title**
Begin with a quotation mark, write the title (with subtitle, if there is one), include a period, and end with a closing quotation mark. Capitalize all major words.
**2b Journal Title and Volume**
Italicize the title. Capitalize all major words. Include the volume number and issue number, separated by a period.

**3 PUBLICATION INFORMATION**
**3a Date of Publication**
Include the year of publication in parentheses, followed by a colon.
**3b Page Numbers**
Provide the page numbers on which the article begins and ends, separated by a hyphen. For numbers up to 99, include both digits. For higher numbers, include only the last two digits (145-57) unless doing so would be unclear (295-307). End with a period.

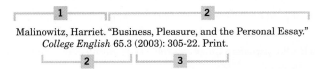

Malinowitz, Harriet. "Business, Pleasure, and the Personal Essay." *College English* 65.3 (2003): 305-22. Print.

**Figure 36.3** Locating and citing sources from a journal article

## 25. Signed Article in a Monthly or Bimonthly Periodical—MLA

Fallows, James. "The $1.4 Trillion Question." *The Atlantic* Jan.-Feb. 2008: 36-48. Print.

## 26. Unsigned Article in a Weekly or Monthly Periodical—MLA

"The Price Is Wrong." *Economist* 2 Aug. 2003: 58-59. Print.

example of student writing should dispel some of the myths and fears associated with research paper writing. As Andrei shows, taking the research paper one step at a time yields excellent results.

**QUOTATION: ON WRITING**

Vigorous writing is concise. A sentence should contain no unnecessary words, a paragraph no unnecessary sentences, for the same reason that a drawing should have no unnecessary lines and a machine no unnecessary parts. This requires not that the writer make all his sentences short, or that he avoid all detail and treat his subjects only in outline, but that every word tell.

—William Strunk Jr., *The Elements of Style*

**QUOTATION: ON WRITING**

Writing is an odd thing to do. You turn your back on the real world and favor an invisible world you invent. You have to search deep in your inner life. I hear things in a kinesthetic way. I tap into a rhythm of language to portray what I feel.

—Mary Gordon

**QUOTATION: ON WRITING**

It's as hard to get from almost finished to finished as to get from beginning to almost done.

—Elinor Fuchs

**QUOTATION: ON WRITING**

Sometimes I organize a piece so carefully that I will not only know the general thought I want to end with, I will write the last sentence before having written anything else. This sentence will contain all of the feeling of a piece unwritten, but I know it will be there and almost always I'm right.

—Roger Rosenblatt

**QUOTATION: ON WRITING**

In every real sense, the writer writes in order to teach himself, to understand himself, to satisfy himself; the publishing of the ideas is a curious anticlimax.

—Alfred Kazin

### 27. Article in a Scholarly Journal

Adler-Kassner, Linda, and Heidi Estrem. "Rethinking Research Writing: Public Literacy in the Composition Classroom." *WPA: Writing Program Administration* 26.3 (2003): 119-31. Print.

### 28. Article in a Collection of Reprinted Articles—MLA

First include the original publication information, then *Rpt.* and information about the place the article was republished.

Brumberg, Abraham. "Russia after Perestroika." *New York Review of Books* 27 June 1991: 53-62. Rpt. in *Russian and Soviet History*. Ed. Alexander Dallin. Vol. 14 of *The Gorbachev Era*. New York: Garland, 1992. 300-20. Print.

Textbooks used in college writing courses often collect previously printed articles.

Rothstein, Richard. "When Mothers on Welfare Go to Work." *New York Times* 5 June 2002: A20. Rpt. in *Writing Arguments: A Rhetoric with Readings*. Ed. John D. Ramage, John C. Bean, and June Johnson. New York: Longman, 2004. 263. Print.

### 29. Signed Article in a Daily Newspaper—MLA

Omit *A, An,* or *The* as the first word in a newspaper title. Give the day, month, and year of the issue (and the edition, if applicable). If sections are designated, give the section letter as well as the page number. If an article runs on nonconsecutive pages, give the starting page number followed by a plus sign (for example, *23+* for an article that starts on page 23 and continues on a later page).

Green, Penelope. "The Slow Life Picks Up Speed." *New York Times* 31 Jan. 2008, natl. ed.: D1+. Print.

### 30. Unsigned Article in a Daily Newspaper—MLA

"Oscars Ready Plans to Deal with Strike." *Denver Post* 31 Jan. 2008: B3. Print.

If the city of publication is not part of the title, put it in square brackets after the title, not italicized.

"Hackers Hit Northwestern Computer Net." *Pantagraph* [Bloomington] 26 Mar. 2005: A5. Print.

### 31. Editorial, Letter to the Editor, or Review—MLA

After the author's name or title, provide information about the type of publication.

"Primary Considerations." Editorial. *Washington Post* 27 Jan. 2008: B6. Print.

Finanger, Emily. Letter. *Outside* Feb. 2008: 14. Print.

Shenk, David. "Toolmaker, Brain Builder." Rev. of *Beyond Big Blue: Building the Computer That Defeated the World Chess Champion*, by Feng-Hsiung Hsu. *American Scholar* 72 (Spring 2003): 150-52. Print.

## 32. Article in a Looseleaf Collection of Reprinted Articles—MLA

Give the citation for the original publication first, followed by the citation for the collection.

Hayden, Thomas. "The Age of Robots." *US News and World Report* 23 Apr. 2001:
44+. Print. *Applied Science* 2002. Ed. Eleanor Goldstein. Boca Raton: SIRS,
2002. Art. 66.

## 33. Abstract in a Collection of Abstracts—MLA

To cite an abstract, first give information for the full work: the author's name, the title of the article, and publication information about the full article. If a reader could not know that the cited material is an abstract, write the word *Abstract,* not italicized, followed by a period. Give publication information about the collection of abstracts. For abstracts identified by item numbers rather than page numbers, use the word *item* before the item number.

Marcus, Hazel R., and Shinobu Kitayamo. "Culture and the Self: Implications
for Cognition, Emotion, and Motivation." *Psychological Review* 88 (1991):
224-53. *Psychological Abstracts* 78 (1991): item 23878. Print.

### PERIODICALS—ONLINE VERSIONS FROM SUBSCRIPTION SERVICES

A large (and increasing) number of periodicals are available in digital versions online, as well as in print; some periodicals are available only online. Online periodicals fall into two categories: (1) periodicals you access through a DATABASE or **subscription service** paid for by your library or company, such as EBSCO or FirstSearch, or through an online service to which you personally subscribe (examples 34–38); and (2) periodicals you directly access by entering a specific URL (examples 39–44). Articles you access through a subscription service are the most important for academic research. Of course, many other online sources are not from periodicals; we explain them in examples 45–75.

🛈 **ALERT:** Online periodical articles are frequently available in both "HTML" (hypertext mark-up language) and "PDF" (portable document format) versions. The PDF versions are almost always preferable for research because they present an image of articles exactly as they appear in print. This means the PDF version of an article has page numbers, images and graphics, side-bar stories, headings, and so on. As a result, PDFs are easier to cite. The HTML version of an article does include all of the text; however, because it has been formatted to work efficiently in databases, it contains no page numbers or graphics. HTML versions load more quickly on your computer, but citing them is less precise. If you have a choice, always use the PDF version. ●

**QUOTATION: ON WRITING**

Whatever machine you use, however sophisticated your technology, it's ideas that count. In the beginning was the idea. No machine will give you the ability to spot an opening, take a new idea, and see it through to profitable fruition.

—Tom Crabtree

**QUOTATION: ON WRITING**

The ink of the scholar is more sacred than the blood of the martyr.

—Muhammad

**QUOTATION: ON WRITING**

For me, writing is the only thing that passes the three tests of métier: (1) when I'm doing it, I don't feel that I should be doing something else instead; (2) it produces a sense of accomplishment and, once in a while, pride; and (3) it's frightening.

—Gloria Steinem

**QUOTATION: ON WRITING**

My task—which I am trying to achieve—is by the power of the written word to make you hear, to make you feel. It is, before all, to make you see.

—Joseph Conrad

### 34. Subscription Service: Article with a Print Version—MLA

Jackson, Gabriel. "Multiple Historic Meanings of the Spanish Civil War."
    *Science and Society* 68.3 (2004): 272-76. *Academic Search Elite.* Web.
    7 Mar. 2005.

VandeHei, Jim. "Two Years after White House Exit, Clinton Shaping Democratic
    Party." *Washington Post* 21 June 2003, final ed.: A1. *Academic Universe.*
    Web. 5 May 2005.

Figure 36.4 illustrates citing an article that has a print version but has been accessed through a subscription service.

### 35. Subscription Service: Material with No Print Version—MLA

Siemens, Raymond G. "A New Computer-Assisted Literary Criticism?"
    *Computers and the Humanities* 36.3 (2002). *America Online.* Web.
    12 Nov. 2002.

### 36. Subscription Service: Abstract—MLA

The example below is for the same abstract shown in item 33, but here it is accessed from an online database (*PsycINFO*) by means of a library subscription service. The name of the library shows where the source was accessed, and *10 Apr. 2004* is the date it was accessed.

Marcus, Hazel R., and Shinobu Kitayamo. "Culture and the Self: Implications
    for Cognition, Emotion, and Motivation." *Psychological Abstracts* 78 (1991).
    *PsycINFO.* Web. 10 Apr. 2004.

### 37. Subscription Service Access with a Keyword: Article in a Periodical with a Print Version—MLA

Electronic versions of sources that also appear in print start with information about the print version. Here's an entry for a journal article accessed through a computer service; it also has a print version.

Wynne, Clive D. L. " 'Willy' Didn't Yearn to Be Free." Editorial. *New York Times*
    27 Dec. 2003: *New York Times Online. America Online.* Web. 29 Dec. 2003.
    Keyword: nytimes.

Information applying to the print version of this article in the *New York Times* ends with the publication date and information about the online version starts with the title of the database, *New York Times Online. America Online* is the service through which the database was accessed, and *29 Dec. 2003* is the access date. The keyword *nytimes* was used to access *New York Times Online.*

**1** AUTHOR INFORMATION

**Name of Author**
Write the author's last name, followed by a comma, the author's first name, and the middle initial (if given). End with a period.

**2** TITLE INFORMATION

**Article Title**
State the full title of the article, enclosed in quotation marks. Use a period before the closing quotation mark.

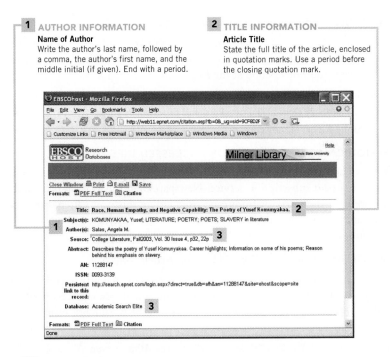

**3** PUBLICATION INFORMATION

**3a Name of Periodical**
Provide the journal title (italicized).

**3b Volume and Issue Numbers**
Leave one space after the journal title and provide the volume and issue numbers, separated by a period.

**3c Date of Publication**
Provide the year of publication, in parentheses, followed by a colon.

**3d Page Numbers**
Provide the inclusive page numbers for the complete article, not just the portion you used. End with a period.

**3e Title of Database**
Italicize the name of the database. End with a period.

**3f Medium of Publication**
Provide the medium of publication consulted (*Web*), followed by a period.

**3g Date of Access**
Provide the day, month, and year that you accessed the article online. End with a period.

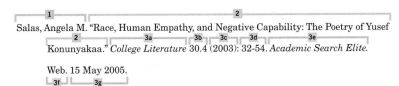

**Figure 36.4** Locating and citing source information for a journal found in an online database

### 38. Subscription Service Access Showing a Path—MLA

When you access a source by choosing a series of keywords, menus, or topics, end the entry with the "path" of words you used. Use semicolons between items in the path, and put a period at the end.

Futrelle, David. "A Smashing Success." *Money.com* 23 Dec. 1999. America Online. Web. 26 Dec. 1999. Path: Personal Finance; Business News; Business
Publications; Money.com.

### PERIODICALS—ONLINE VERSIONS ACCESSED DIRECTLY

You can access some online versions of periodicals directly, without going through a paid subscription service. Newspapers and magazines often publish some of their articles from each issue online this way. Often, however, you can't access every single article—or any older articles—without being a subscriber.

### 39. Online Version of a Print Magazine Article—MLA

The example below is for the online version of the same article cited in 25, above. In addition to the print information, include the date you accessed the online version. (If the page numbers from the print version are available, include them, too, before the access date.)

Fallows, James. "The $1.4 Trillion Question." *The Atlantic.com.* Atlantic
Monthly Group, Jan.-Feb. 2008. Web. 2 May 2008.

If the article is unsigned, begin with the title.

"Too Smart to Marry." *The Atlantic.com.* Atlantic Monthly Group, 14 Apr. 2005.
Web. 7 Mar. 2005.

### 40. Online Version of a Print Journal Article—MLA

Hoge, Charles W., et al. "Mild Traumatic Brain Injury in U.S. Soldiers
Returning from Iraq." *New England Journal of Medicine* 358.5 (2008):
453-63. Web. 10 Sept. 2008.

### 41. Periodical Article Published Only Online—MLA

Many periodicals are published only online; others have "extra" online content that doesn't appear in print. Figure 36.5 illustrates how to cite an article that appears only online.

Ramirez, Eddy. "Comparing American Students with Those in China and
India." *U.S. News and World Report.* U.S. News and World Report, 30 Jan.
2008. Web. 4 Mar. 2008.

Shipka, Jody. "This Was (Not!!) an Easy Assignment." *Computers and
Composition Online.* Computers and Composition Online, Fall 2007.
Web. 2 May 2008.

MLA

**1 AUTHOR INFORMATION**

**Name of Author**
Write the author's last name, followed by a comma, the author's first name, and the middle initial (if given). End with a period.

**2 TITLE INFORMATION**

**Article Title**
State the full title of the article, enclosed in quotation marks. Unless the title contains its own closing punctuation (question mark), use a period before the closing quotation mark.

**3 PUBLICATION INFORMATION**

**3a Title of the Overall Web Site**
Provide the title of the Web site (italicized), followed by a period.

**3b Publisher or Sponsor of the Web Site**
Leave one space after the title of the overall Web site and provide the publisher or sponsor of the Web site. If this information is not available, use "n.p." End with a comma.

**3c Date of Publication**
Provide the day, month, and year of publication, followed by a period. If no date is available, use "n.d."

**3d Medium of Publication**
Provide the medium of publication consulted (Web), followed by a period.

**3e Date of Access**
Provide the day, month, and year that you accessed the article online. End with a period.

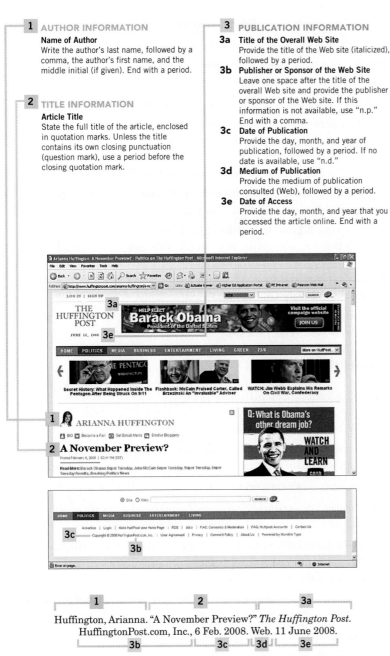

| 1 | 2 | 3a |

Huffington, Arianna. "A November Preview?" *The Huffington Post.*
HuffingtonPost.com, Inc., 6 Feb. 2008. Web. 11 June 2008.

| 3b | 3c | 3d | 3e |

**Figure 36.5** Locating and citing source information for an article published only online

### 42. Online Version of a Print Newspaper Article—MLA

If the article is signed, begin with the author's name, last name first.

Wilson, Janet. "EPA Fights Waste Site near River." *Los Angeles Times*. Los
Angeles Times, 5 Mar. 2005. Web. 7 Mar. 2005.

If the article is unsigned, begin with the article title.

"Remnant of Revolutionary War Washes Ashore." *CNN.com*. Cable News
Network, 28 Mar. 2005. Web. 29 Mar. 2005.

### 43. Online Editorial or Letter to the Editor—MLA

"Garbage In, Garbage Out." Editorial. *Los Angeles Times*. Los Angeles
Times, 2 Feb. 2008. Web. 22 Mar. 2008.

Ennis, Heather B. Letter to the Editor. *U.S. News and World Report*. U.S. News
and World Report, 20 Dec. 2007. Web. 22 Dec. 2007.

### 44. Online Material from a Newspaper or News Site Published Only Online—MLA

Harris, Edward. "Rain Forests Fall at 'Alarming' Rate." *denverpost.com*.
Denver Post, 3 Feb. 2008. Web. 3 Feb. 2008.

### OTHER INTERNET SOURCES

This section shows models for online sources. For such sources, provide as
much of the following information as you can.

- The author's name, if given.
- In quotation marks, the title of a short work (Web page, brief document,
  essay, article, message, and so on); or italicized, the title of a book.
- Publication information for any print version, if it exists.
- The name of an editor, translator, or compiler, if any, with an abbreviation
  such as *Ed., Trans.,* or *Comp.* before the name.
- The italicized title of the Internet site (scholarly project, database, online
  periodical, professional or personal Web site). If the site has no title, de-
  scribe it: for example, *Home page.*
- The date of electronic publication (including a version number, if any) or
  posting or the most recent update.
- The name of a sponsoring organization, if any.
- The medium of publication.
- The date you accessed the material.

MLA

- The URL in angle brackets (< >), only when the reader probably could not locate the source without it. If you must break a URL at the end of a line, break only after a slash and do not use a hyphen.

### 45. Online Book—MLA

Chopin, Kate. *The Awakening*. 1899. *PBS Electronic Library*. 10 Dec. 1998. PBS.
Web. 13 Nov. 2008.

### 46. Online Book in a Scholarly Project—MLA

Herodotus. *The History of Herodotus*. Trans. George Rawlinson. 1947. *Internet
Classics Archive*. Ed. Daniel C. Stevenson. 11 Jan. 1998. MIT. Web. 15 May
2006.

### 47. Online Government-Published Book—MLA

Start with the name of the government or government body, and then name the government agency, the title, the work's author (if known), the publication date, the access date, and the URL, if the reader needs it.

United States. Cong. Research Service. *Space Stations*. By Marcia S. Smith. 12
Dec. 1996. Web. 4 Dec. 2007.

MLA also permits an alternative format, with the author's name first, then title, then government body.

Huff, C. Ronald. *Comparing the Criminal Behavior of Youth Gangs and At-Risk
Youths*. United States. Dept. of Justice. Natl. Inst. of Justice. Oct. 1998. Web.
5 Aug. 2008.

### 48. Professional Home Page—MLA

Provide as much of the following information as you can find.

- If available, include the name of the person who created or put up the home page. If first and last names are given, reverse the order of the first author's name.
- For a professional home page, include the name of the sponsoring organization.
- Include the date you accessed the material.

*Association for the Advancement of Artificial Intelligence*. Web. 17 Mar. 2008.

### 49. Personal Home Page—MLA

Follow guidelines for professional home pages, with the following changes. Give the name of the person who created the page, last name first. Include the page's title, if there is one, italicized; if there is no title, add the description *Home page,* not italicized, followed by a period.

Hesse, Doug. Home page. Web. 1 Nov. 2007. <http://portfolio.du.edu/dhesse>.

**1  TITLE**

**Title of the Work**
State the full title of the work cited, enclosed in quotation marks. Use a period before the closing quotation mark.

**2  PUBLICATION INFORMATION**

**2a  Title of the Overall Web Site**
Provide the title of the Web site (italicized), followed by a period.

**2b  Publisher or Sponsor of the Web Site**
Leave one space after the title of the overall Web site and provide the publisher or sponsor of the Web site. If this information is not available, use "n.p." End with a comma.

**2c  Date of Publication**
Provide the available date (day, month, and year) of publication, followed by a period. If no date is available, use "n.d."

**2d  Medium of Publication**
Provide the medium of publication consulted (Web), followed by a period.

**2e  Date of Access**
Provide the day, month, and year that you accessed the article online. End with a period.

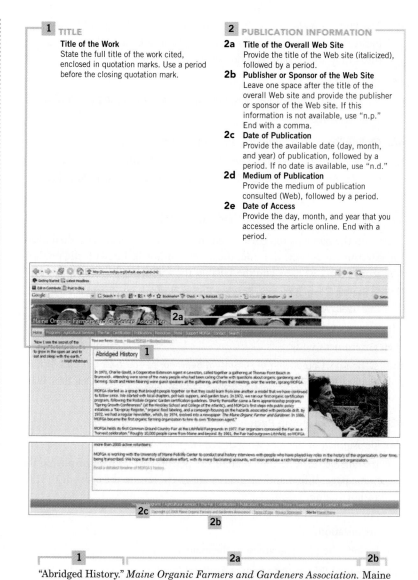

"Abridged History." *Maine Organic Farmers and Gardeners Association.* Maine Organic Farmers and Gardeners Assn., 2008. Web. 13 Feb. 2008.

**Figure 36.6** Locating and citing source information for a Web page with no author

### 50. Page from a Web Site—MLA

Provide as much information as you can (see Figure 36.6).

"Protecting Whales from Dangerous Sonar." *National Resources Defense
    Council.* NRDC, 9 Nov. 2005. Web. 12 Dec. 2005.

"Abridged History." *Maine Organic Farmers and Gardeners Association.*
    Maine Organic Farmers and Gardeners Assn., 2007. Web. 13 Dec. 2007.

### 51. Entire Internet Site—MLA

*WebdelSol.Com.* Ed. Michael Neff. 2008. Web. 11 Nov. 2008.

### 52. Academic Department Home Page—MLA

Write the name of the academic department, followed by the words *Dept. home
page.* (Do not put any words in quotations or in italics.) Also include the name
of the institution and the date you accessed the page.

Writing. Dept. home page. Grand Valley State U. Web. 26 Feb. 2008.

### 53. Course Home Page—MLA

St. Germain, Sheryl. Myths and Fairytales: From *Inanna* to *Edward Scissorhands.*
    Course home page. Summer 2003. Dept. of English, Iowa State U. Web. 20
    Feb. 2005. <http://www.public.iastate.edu/~sgermain/531.homepage.html>.

### 54. Government or Institutional Web Site—MLA

Home Education and Private Tutoring. Pennsylvania Department of Education,
    2005. Web. 15 Dec. 2005.

### 55. Online Poem—MLA

Browning, Elizabeth Barrett. "Past and Future." *Women's Studies Database
    Reading Room.* U of Maryland. Web. 9 June 2003.

### 56. Online Work of Art—MLA

Provide artist, title of work, creation date (optional), the museum or individual who owns it, the place and the access date.

van Gogh, Vincent. *The Starry Night.* 1889. Museum of Mod. Art, New York.
    Web. 5 Dec. 2003. Keyword: Starry Night.

In this example, the keyword "Starry Night" is what a researcher types into a
search box on the museum's Web site.

**MLA**

**Title of the Work**
State the full title of the work cited, enclosed in quotation marks. Use a period before the closing quotation mark.

**2a Title of the Overall Web Site**
Provide the title of the Web site (italicized), followed by a period.

**2b Publisher or Sponsor of the Web Site**
Leave one space after the title of the overall Web site and provide the publisher or sponsor of the Web site. If this information is not available, use "N.p." End with a comma.

**2c Date of Publication**
Provide the day, month, and year of publication, followed by a period. If no date is available, use "n.d."

**2d Medium of Publication**
Provide the medium of publication consulted (*Web*), followed by a period.

**2e Date of Access**
Provide the day, month, and year that you accessed the article online. End with a period.

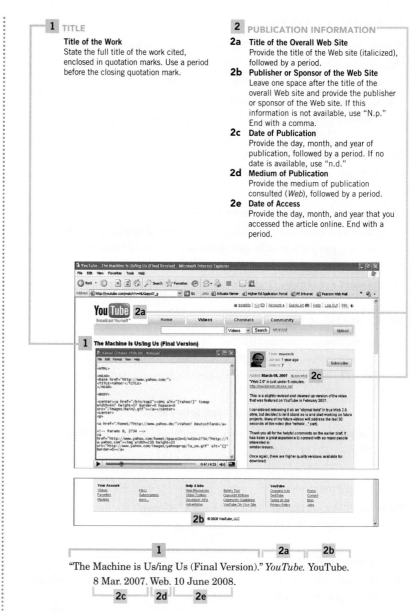

"The Machine is Us/ing Us (Final Version)." *YouTube*. YouTube. 8 Mar. 2007. Web. 10 June 2008.

**Figure 36.7** Locating and citing source information for an online video

### 57. Online Image or Photograph—MLA

As with images from print publications (see item 88), include information about the photographer and title, if known. Otherwise, describe the photograph briefly and give information about the Web site and the access date.

Bourke-White, Margaret. "Fort Peck Dam, Montana." 1936. Gelatin silver print.
Metropolitan Museum of Art, New York. Web. 5 Aug. 2008.

### 58. Online Interview—MLA

Pope, Carl. Interview by Amy Standen. *Salon.com*. Salon Media Group, 29 Apr.
2002. Web. 27 Jan. 2005.

### 59. Online Video or Film Clip—MLA

See Figure 36.7.

Reeves, Matt, dir. *Cloverfield*. Trailer. Bad Robot, 2008. Web. 18 Jan. 2008.

### 60. Online Cartoon—MLA

Harris, Sidney. "We have lots of information technology." Cartoon. *New Yorker*
27 May 2002. Web. 9 Feb. 2007.

### 61. Online Television or Radio Program—MLA

Chayes, Sarah. "Concorde." *All Things Considered*. Natl. Public Radio. 26 July
2000. Web. 7 Dec. 2001.

"The Beginning of the End." *Lost*. ABC. 30 Jan. 2008. Web. 1 Feb. 2008.

### 62. Online Discussion Posting—MLA

To cite an online message, give the author's name (if any), the title of the message in quotation marks, and then *Online posting*. Give the date of the posting and the name of the bulletin board, if any. Then give the access date and, in angle brackets, the URL if needed.

Firrantello, Larry. "Van Gogh on Prozac." Online posting. 23 May 2005. *Salon
Table Talk*. Web. 7 June 2005. <http://tabletalk.salon.com/
webx?50@931.xC34anLmwOq.1@.773b2ad1>.

Be cautious about using online postings as sources. Some postings contain cutting-edge information from experts, but some contain trash. Unfortunately, it is nearly impossible to find out whether people online are who they claim to be.

### 63. Real-Time Communication—MLA

Give the name of the speaker or writer, a title for the event (if any), the forum, date, and access date.

Berzsenyi, Christyne. Online discussion of "Writing to Meet Your Match:
Rhetoric, Perceptions, and Self-Presentation for Four Online Daters."
*Computers and Writing Online*. 13 May 2007. AcadianaMoo. Web. 13 May
2007.

### 64. E-Mail Message—MLA

Start with the name of the person who wrote the e-mail message. Give the title or subject line in quotation marks. Then describe the source (*e-mail*) and identify the recipient. End with the date.

Pessin, Eliana. "Scottish Writers." Message to Georgia Dobyns. 11 Nov. 2007.
　　Email.

### 65. Part of an Online Book—MLA

Teasdale, Sara. "Driftwood." *Flame and Shadow*. Ed. A. Light. N.p., 1920.
　　*Project Gutenberg*. 1 July 1996. Web. 18 Aug. 2008.

### 66. Online Review—MLA

Travers, Peter. Rev. of *No Country for Old Men*, dir. Joel Coen and Ethan Coen.
　　*Rollingstone.com*. Rolling Stone, 1 Nov. 2007. Web. 25 Nov. 2007.

### 67. Online Abstract—MLA

Avery, Christopher, et al. "A Revealed Preference Ranking of U.S. Colleges and
　　Universities." NBER Working Paper No. W10803. Abstract. Web. 11 Oct. 2004.

### 68. Posting on a Blog—MLA

McLemee, Scott. "To Whom It May Concern." *Quick Study*. 1 Jan. 2008. Web.
　　14 May 2008.

### 69. Online Sound Recording or Clip—MLA

Komunyakaa, Yusef. "My Father's Love Letters." Poets.org Listening Booth.
　　Academy of American Poets, 5 May 1993. Web. 27 Apr. 2005.

### 70. Online Advertisement—MLA

Samsung. Advertisement. *RollingStone*. 8 Nov. 2005. Web.

### 71. Online Manuscript or Working Paper—MLA

deGrandpre, Andrew. "Baseball Destined to Die in Hockey Town." 2002.
　　Unpublished article. Web. 7 Mar. 2005.

### 72. Podcast—MLA

A podcast is an audio recording that is posted online. Include as much of the following information as you can identify: author, title, sponsoring organization or Web site, date posted, and date accessed.

"Business Marketing with Podcast: What Marketing Professionals Should
　　Know." *Podblaze.com*. The Info Gurus, 13 Oct. 2005. Web. 19 Oct. 2005.

### 73. Online Slide Show—MLA

Erickson, Britta, narr. *Visionaries from the New China.* July 2007. Web. 11 Sept.
    2008.

### 74. Online Photo Essay—MLA

Nachtwey, James. "Crime in Middle America." *Time* 2 Dec. 2006. Web. 5 May 2007.

### 75. Online Map, Chart, or Other Graphic—MLA

"Hurricane Rita." Graphic. *New York Times Online.* New York Times. 24 Sept.
    2005. Web. 24 Sept. 2005.

## OTHER PRINT, NONPRINT, AND ELECTRONIC SOURCES

### 76. Published or Unpublished Letter—MLA

Begin the entry with the author of the letter. Note the recipient, too.

Irvin, William. Letter to Lesley Osburn. 7 Dec. 2007. Print.

Williams, William Carlos. Letter to his son. 13 Mar. 1935. *Letters of the Century:*
    *America 1900-1999.* Ed. Lisa Grunwald and Stephen J. Adler. New York:
    Dial, 1999. 225-26. Print.

### 77. Microfiche Collection of Articles—MLA

A microfiche is a transparent sheet of film (a *fiche*) with microscopic printing
that needs to be read through a special magnifier. Each fiche holds several pages,
with each page designated by a grid position. A long document may appear on
more than one fiche.

Wenzell, Ron. "Businesses Prepare for a More Diverse Work Force." *St. Louis*
    *Post Dispatch* 3 Feb. 1990: 17. Microform. *NewsBank: Employment* 27 (1990):
    fiche 2, grid D12.

### 78. Map or Chart—MLA

*Colorado Front Range Mountain Bike Topo Map.* Map. Nederland: Latitude 40,
    2001. Print.

### 79. Report or Pamphlet—MLA

Use the format for books, to the extent possible.

National Commission on Writing in America's Schools and Colleges. *The*
    *Neglected "R": The Need for a Writing Revolution.* New York: College
    Board, 2003. Print.

### 80. Legal Source—MLA

Include the name of the case, the number of the case (preceded by *No.*), the
name of the court deciding the case, and the date of the decision.

Brown v. Board of Ed. No. 8. Supreme Ct. of the US. 8 Oct. 1952. Print.

### 81. Interview—MLA

Note the type of interview—for example, "Telephone," "Personal" (face-to-face), or "E-mail."

Friedman, Randi. Telephone interview. 30 Aug. 2008.

For a published interview, give the name of the interviewed person first, identify the source as an interview, and then give details as for any published source: title; author, preceded by the word *By;* and publication details.

Winfrey, Oprah. "Ten Questions for Oprah Winfrey." By Richard Zoglin. *Time*
15 Dec. 2003: 8. Print.

### 82. Lecture, Speech, or Address—MLA

Kennedy, John Fitzgerald. Greater Houston Ministerial Assn. Rice Hotel,
Houston. 12 Sept. 1960. Address.

### 83. Film, Videotape, or DVD—MLA

Give the title first, and include the director, the distributor, and the year. For older films that were subsequently released on tape or DVD, provide the original release date of the movie *before* the type of medium. For video downloads, include the download date and the source. Other information (writer, producer, major actors) is optional but helpful. Put first names first.

*Shakespeare in Love.* Screenplay by Marc Norman and Tom Stoppard. Dir.
John Maddon. Prod. David Parfitt, Donna Gigliotti, Harvey Weinstein,
Edward Zwick, and Mark Norman. Perf. Gwyneth Paltrow, Joseph
Fiennes, and Judi Dench. Miramax, 1998. Film.

*It Happened One Night.* Screenplay by Robert Riskin. Dir. and Prod. Frank Capra.
Perf. Clark Gable and Claudette Colbert. 1934. Sony Pictures, 1999. DVD.

*It Happened One Night.* Screenplay by Robert Riskin. Dir. and Prod. Frank
Capra. Perf. Clark Gable and Claudette Colbert. Columbia 1934. 2007.
4 Mar. 2008. MPEG file.

### 84. Musical Recording—MLA

Put first the name most relevant to what you discuss in your paper (performer, conductor, the work performed). Include the recording's title, the medium for any recording other than a CD (*LP, audiocassette*), the name of the issuer (*Vanguard*), and the year the work was issued.

Smetana, Bedrich. *My Country.* Czech Philharmonic Orch. Cond. Karel Anserl.
LP. Vanguard, 1975. CD.

Springsteen, Bruce. "Lonesome Day." *The Rising.* Sony, 2002. CD.

Radiohead. "Jigsaw Falling into Place." *In Rainbows.* Radiohead, 2007. MP3 file.

### 85. Live Performance (Play, Concert, etc.)—MLA

*All My Sons*. By Arthur Miller. Dir. Calvin McLean. Center for the Performing
　　Arts, Normal, IL. 27 Sept. 2005. Performance.

### 86. Work of Art, Photograph, or Musical Composition—MLA

Cassatt, Mary. *La Toilette*. 1890. Oil on canvas. Art Institute of Chicago.

Mydans, Carl. *General Douglas MacArthur Landing at Luzon*, 1945. Gelatin sil-
　　ver print. Soho Triad Fine Art Gallery, New York. 21 Oct.-28 Nov. 1999.

Don't underline or put in quotation marks music identified only by form, number, and key.

Schubert, Franz. Symphony no. 8 in B minor. Print.

Italicize any work that has a title, such as an opera or ballet or a named symphony.

Schubert, Franz. *Unfinished Symphony*. Print.

To cite a published score, use the following format.

Schubert, Franz. *Symphony in B Minor (Unfinished)*. Ed. Martin Cusid. New
　　York: Norton, 1971. Print.

### 87. Television or Radio Program—MLA

Include at least the title of the program or series (underlined), the network,
the local station and its city, and the date of the broadcast.

*Not for Ourselves Alone: The Story of Elizabeth Cady Stanton and Susan B.*
　　*Anthony*. Writ. Andrei Burns. Perf. Julie Harris, Ronnie Gilbert, and Sally
　　Kellerman. Prod. Paul Barnes and Andrei Burns. PBS. WNET, New York.
　　8 Nov. 1999. Television.

Supply the title of a specific episode (if any) in quotation marks before the title
of the program (italicized) and the title of the series (if any) neither italicized
nor in quotation marks.

"The Middle of Nowhere." *This American Life*. Prod. Ira Glass. Chicago Public
　　Radio. KCFR-AM, Denver. 7 Dec. 2007. Radio.

Note that many radio programs also exist as podcasts (see item 72).

### 88. Image or Photograph in a Print Publication—MLA

To cite an image or a photograph that appears as part of a print publication (perhaps as an illustration for an article), give the photographer (if known), the
title or caption of the image, and complete publication information, as for an
article. If the image has no title, provide a brief description.

Greene, Herb. "Grace Slick." *Rolling Stone* 30 Sept. 2004: 102. Print.

### 89. Advertisement—MLA

American Airlines. Advertisement. ABC. 24 Aug. 2003. Television.

Canon Digital Cameras. Advertisement. *Time* 2 June 2003: 77. Print.

### 90. Video Game or Software—MLA

*Guitar Hero III: Legends of Rock.* Santa Monica: Activision, 2007.

### 91. Nonperiodical Publications on CD, DVD, or Magnetic Tape—MLA

Citations for publications on DVD, CD-ROM, or other recording formats follow guidelines for print publications, with two additions: list the publication medium (for example, *CD*), and give the vendor's name.

Perl, Sondra. *Felt Sense: Guidelines for Composing.* Portsmouth: Boynton, 2004. CD.

### 92. Materials on CD or DVD with a Print Version—MLA

Before the maturity of the Internet, many print materials were previously stored on CD-ROMs.

"The Price Is Right." *Time* 20 Jan. 1992: 38. *Time Man of the Year.* CD-ROM. New York: Compact, 1993.

Information for the print version ends with the article's page number, 38. The title of the CD-ROM is *Time Man of the Year,* its producer is the publisher Compact, and its copyright year is 1993. Both the title of the print publication and the title of the CD-ROM are italicized.

### 93. Materials on CD or DVD with No Print Version—MLA

"Artificial Intelligence." *Encarta 2003.* CD-ROM. Redmond: Microsoft, 2003.

*Encarta 2003* is a CD-ROM encyclopedia with no print version. "Artificial Intelligence" is the title of an article in *Encarta 2003.*

### 94. Book in Digital Format—MLA

Many books are now available for downloading from the Internet in digital format, to be read on special players.

Gilbert, Elizabeth. *Eat, Pray, Love.* New York: Viking, 2007. Kindle Edition.

### 95. PowerPoint or Similar Presentation—MLA

Delyser, Ariel. "Political Movements in the Philippines." University of Denver. 7 Apr. 2006. PowerPoint.

### 96. Work in More Than One Publication Medium—MLA

Shamoon, Linda, et al., eds. *Coming of Age: The Advanced Writing Curriculum.*
   *Coming of Age Course Descriptions.* Portsmouth: Boynton, 2000. CD-ROM,
   print.

This book and CD-ROM come together. Each has its own title, but the publication information—*Portsmouth: Boynton, 2000*—applies to both.

## 36d.2  Using content or bibliographic notes in MLA style

In MLA style, footnotes or endnotes serve two specific purposes: (1) You can use
them for content (ideas and information) that does not fit into your paper but is
still worth relating; and (2) you can use them for bibliographic information that
would intrude if you were to include it in your text. Place a note number at the
end of a sentence, if possible. Put it after any punctuation mark except the dash.
Do not put any space before a note number, and put one space after it. Raise the
note number a little above the line of words, as shown in the following examples.

#### TEXT OF PAPER

Eudora Welty's literary biography, *One Writer's Beginnings,* shows us
how both the inner world of self and the outer world of family and place
form a writer's imagination.[1]

#### CONTENT NOTE—MLA

[1]Welty, who valued her privacy, always resisted investigation of her
life. However, at the age of seventy-four, she chose to present her own
autobiographical reflections in a series of lectures at Harvard University.

#### TEXT OF PAPER

Barbara Randolph believes that enthusiasm is contagious (65).[1] Many
psychologists have found that panic, fear, and rage spread more quickly
in crowds than positive emotions do, however.

#### BIBLIOGRAPHIC NOTE—MLA

[1]Others who agree with Randolph include Thurman 21, 84, 155; Kelley
421-25; and Brookes 65-76.

## 36e  A student's MLA-style research paper

## 36e.1  Researching and writing the paper

The following is student writer Andrei Gurov's assignment for an MLA-style
research paper.

MLA

> Write an MLA-style research paper on the general subject of "memory."
> You are required to write 1,800 to 2,000 words, using a variety of sources.
> Your final paper is due in six weeks. Interim deadlines for parts of the work
> will be announced. To complete this assignment, you need to engage in
> three interrelated processes: conducting research, understanding the re-
> sults of that research, and writing a paper based on the first two processes.
> Consult the *Simon & Schuster Handbook for Writers,* especially Chapters
> 33–35 for guidance on how to complete this assignment, and Chapter 36
> for guidance on MLA-style parenthetical citations and Works Cited en-
> tries. You may also consult the MLA Web site at http://www.mla.org.

Andrei's instructor also assigned a bonus exercise asking students to chronicle their research processes in a brief informal narrative. This exercise could help
students see what worked well for them and what didn't, and then they could
apply that knowledge when researching future papers. The following is from
Andrei's narrative about how he researched his topic and sources for his MLA-
style paper about déjà vu.

> I started by immediately filling in the research schedule
> suggested in section 33b of our handbook. I also looked for
> ideas in Box 33.2: Finding General Ideas for Research. In the
> past, brainstorming has worked well for me, so I just started
> listing anything that came to mind about the assigned topic of
> "memory" (e.g., how much memory is on my iPod, past
> vacations, my sister's wedding, relatives, when I broke my
> collarbone, forgetfulness, flashbacks). I had a lot of personal
> memories to write about, but those wouldn't have worked
> because I couldn't have done formal research on them.
>
> So, I turned to the Web and searched Google using the
> keyword "memory." The computer screen practically exploded

continued >>

with 326 million hits, and they generally pointed to four large categories: brain memory, computer memory, entertainment venues, and music. I didn't expect so many directions. In an attempt to narrow this down, I tried some Boolean NOT instructions, but even eliminating "computer + music + entertainment + girls" made little difference. Then I realized I hadn't used Google Scholar, which has been recommended for academic research. So, I tried again, and although I reduced the number of hits, I still would've spent a lifetime trying to sort through all of these resources.

I knew I needed something else to spark ideas. As advised by Box 33.2 in my handbook, I decided to flip through other textbooks. My anthropology book came with a study skills guide that offered some tips about memory retention. That could've been a topic, but it really didn't interest me enough to want to learn more about it. My intro sociology textbook had some information about eyewitness testimony and false memory--both pretty interesting, so I kept those topics in reserve. Then, a chapter in my intro psychology textbook (Saul Kassin's *Psychology,* 4th ed.) turned up a topic that I'd always been curious about: déjà vu. I'd experienced that weird feeling of being somewhere before--even though I'd never been there in my life--and was really curious to know what caused it. So, I decided to narrow my formal research question to "What is known today about the experience of déjà vu?"

Back in front of the computer, I did online searches using "déjà vu." Google Scholar brought up 14 million hits. AltaVista brought up only music DVDs. I went to good old Yahoo and got

continued >>

mostly music DVDs along with a few popular press articles. Searching with Mozilla Firefox, I typed in "memory + deja vu" and got 726,000 hits, which, under the circumstances, seemed relatively small. But very few of the resources seemed as relevant as the ones on the first few pages of Google Scholar. To help me determine how scholarly many of the online resources were, I went to the library and skimmed Alan S. Brown's 2004 scholarly book *The Déjà Vu Experience* and Weiten's *Psychology: Themes and Variations*. I found I'd been fooled three times out of eleven. When I read the printouts, I knew almost immediately that two of the three unreliable sources were bad, but figuring out the third one took me a while longer.

In my research, I took notes and carefully recorded my sources. (I created a lot of new documents on my computer and gave each a descriptive name that I'd understand.) Then, I organized the notes into folders. At that point, I felt ready to do some planning. I knew my audience was mainly my instructor, but because my first draft was going to be peer-edited, I wanted to make sure my paper also appealed to other students in my class. I wasn't too sure about which purpose I wanted to tackle. Originally, I had wanted to write with a persuasive purpose and argue against the concept of déjà vu having anything to do with witchcraft, reincarnation, and that stuff. But the more I read, the more I became convinced that I wanted to educate people about the scientific aspects of déjà vu experiences. Therefore, I switched to an informative purpose.

I used the note documents that I had created, making sure that I kept track of when I was quoting, summarizing,

continued >>

and paraphrasing (I hardly paraphrased at all). As much as possible, I kept revising so that I could work into my sentences the author and document title because I preferred to include only page numbers in my parenthetical citations. Having had a bad experience in high school with losing track of my sources, I kept a separate document as my working bibliography, which would make it easier to list each of my sources in my Works Cited list at the end of my paper.

At this stage, I felt ready to write my first draft. I sat on the floor and surrounded myself with all my printed notes sorted into categories. I then wrote a very rough draft with numbers where I thought notes would fit. Next, I went to the computer and strung my paper together. Unfortunately, but not too surprisingly, my first draft ran on for too many pages. It was time to cut. My major cuts had to do with (a) at least two pages about other terms related to déjà vu but not the same as déjà vu, and (b) a table reporting an unscientific survey I had taken of the déjà vu memories of each member in a family of fifteen.

I then worked through the paper and worked on conciseness of language (I found lots of repetition) and tried to draft my concluding paragraph. It was a struggle. I had to synthesize complicated material in a fairly limited space. I kept wanting to introduce new information, but I knew that would only set me off track and confuse readers. If you look at the next page of this narrative, you'll see my first try at a concluding paragraph, which I show in block format. (You can compare it with the one in my final draft at the end of my paper.) [Page 652.] I rejected it because it's closer to a conclusion

continued >>

that might work, if it were better organized, at the end of a paper about the paranormal and déjà vu. It definitely didn't work for the paper I wrote.

> We know more today than we did hundreds of years ago about the phenomenon of déjà vu. But there is more to be learned. In the last two decades, the real investigations have begun. Alan S. Brown seems to be the researcher who has led the field into an age of enlightenment, and many more mentioned in this paper are his fellow researchers. No longer can people settle for explanations that involve reincarnation and visits from the dead. No longer can we accept that spirits from the "other side" are coming back to visit us in the form of visions.

Overall, my research and writing process went well. In giving an account of it, I've simplified the details to keep the assignment brief. However, I will say that learning how to brainstorm ideas and how to do keyword searches effectively definitely saved me some anxiety, time, and effort in getting the topic and the information I needed.

## 36e.2  Formatting the MLA-style research paper

### TITLE PAGE

MLA style doesn't call for a title page for research papers or any other types of writing. Many instructors, however, do require one. If you're asked to use a title page, follow the format of the example on page 635. Never assign a page number to a title page.

Whether or not you use a title page, use the headings shown on the first page of the sample research paper on page 638. If you're required to hand in a formal outline with your paper, place the outline after the title page, unless told to do otherwise by your instructor.

**Title page of Andrei Gurov's MLA-style research paper**

MLA style doesn't call for a title page; however, many instructor's who do require one follow this format.

One-third down from top of page

Déjà Vu: At Last a Subject for Serious Study

Double-space title if more than one line

by

Andrei Gurov

Lowercase "by" and double-space

Professor Ryan

University of Middle Byrd

English 101, Section A4

12 December 2007

Instructor

Institution

Course and section

Date order: day month year

MLA

### PAGE 1 OF PAPER WITH OR WITHOUT A TITLE PAGE

On the first page of your paper, in the upper right corner, type your last name, followed by a space, and then followed by the numeral 1 placed one-half inch below the top edge of the page and one inch in from the right margin. Next, at the left margin, one inch in from the left side, type the four lines with the information shown on the first page of the sample paper on page 638. Finally, type your paper's title centered one double space below the last of the four lines that you just finished typing flush left.

Double-space after the title, and start your paper, indenting the first line of the first—and all—paragraphs five character spaces. The indent in Microsoft Word is a hanging indent of 0.5″ for "first line."

### OUTLINES

Even though MLA doesn't officially endorse using outlines, some instructors, including Andrei Gurov's, require that students submit formal outlines with their research papers. In this handbook, you'll find examples of two formal outlines in section 2f. The traditional formal outline follows long-established conventions for using numbers and letters to show relationships among ideas. A less traditional formal outline includes these elements but also includes the planned content for a research paper's introductory and concluding paragraphs. Both the traditional and the less traditional outlines can be sentence outlines (composed entirely of complete sentences) or topic outlines (composed only of words and phrases). In your outlines, however, never mix the two styles.

The outline on page 637 is for Andrei Gurov's research paper about déjà vu. To format the outline, he used the less traditional outline, which was what his instructor preferred and asked her class to use. In the name-page number line in the upper right corner of his outline, Andrei typed his last name, left one space, and then typed the lowercase Roman numeral *i* for the page number, the conventional way of indicating any page that comes before the first page of the essay itself. He placed that information one-half inch from the top of the page and made sure it ended one inch in from the right edge of the paper. He then left a half-inch space below the name-number heading and centered the word *Outline*. The thesis statement in the outline matches the last sentence of the first paragraph of his paper (see p. 638).

Even if your instructor doesn't require an outline, you'll probably find that developing one to go with a later draft of your paper will help you clarify the overall organization and logic of your research paper (or, indeed, any essay you write). Examining the paper's "skeleton" enables you to focus on the overall shape of the paper and may reveal gaps in your paper's development that you can fill in.

### PAGE NUMBERING AFTER THE FIRST PAGE OF THE PAPER

In the upper right corner, type your last name, followed by a space, and then followed by the Arabic numeral of the page in sequence (2, 3, and so on). Place

MLA

Gurov i

1"    1/2"

Outline

Double-space

I. Introduction

   A. The meaning of the term déjà vu

   B. Thesis statement: Although a few people today still prefer to believe that feelings of déjà vu have mysterious and supernatural origins, recent research in cognitive psychology and the neurosciences has shed much rational light on the phenomenon.

II. Percentage of people who report experiencing déjà vu

III. Misunderstandings of the phenomenon of déjà vu

   A. Precognition

   B. False memory

IV. New psychological and medical theories of déjà vu

   A. Human sight's two pathways

   B. Implanted memories

      1. Natural: from old memories long forgotten

      2. Manipulated: from subliminal stimulation

      3. Inattentional blindness

V. Conclusion

   A. Many years of paranormal explanations of déjà vu

   B. Scientific research after 1980

   C. Much promise for further research

this name-number heading one-half inch below the top edge of the page and one inch in from the right margin. Number the pages consecutively, including the last page of your Works Cited. Many writers use the "header and footer" word-processing function that inserts last names and sequential page numbers, updating automatically. This feature is especially convenient during revision, when your writing causes your pages to fall differently than they originally did.

MLA

1"  Use 1/2-inch top margin, 1-inch bottom and side margins; double-space throughout.  ½"  Gurov 1  1

Andrei Gurov

Put identifying information in upper left corner.

Professor Ryan

English 101, Section A4

12 December 2007

Center title.  Déjà Vu: At Last a Subject for Serious Study

"Brain hiccup" might be another name for *déjà vu*, French  2

for "already seen." During a moment of déjà vu, a person

relives an event that in reality is happening for the first time.

The hiccup metaphor seems apt because each modern

scientific explanation of the déjà vu phenomenon involves

a doubled event, as this paper will demonstrate. However,

Quotation marks around phrases show they appeared separately in the source.  such modern scientific work was long in coming. In his article

"The Déjà Vu Illusion," today's leading researcher in the field,

Alan S. Brown at Southern Methodist University, states that

"for over 170 years, this most puzzling of memory illusions

has intrigued scholars" but was hampered when "during

The ellipsis indicates words omitted from a quotation.  the behaviorist era . . . the plethora of parapsychological and

psychodynamic interpretations" multiplied rapidly (256). Thus,  3

notions of the supernatural and magic halted the scientific

study of déjà vu for almost two centuries. By the first quarter

of the twentieth century, it began again slowly. Although a  4

few people today still prefer to believe that feelings of déjà vu

have mysterious or supernatural origins, recent research in

cognitive psychology and the neurosciences has shed much

rational light on the phenomenon.

continued >>

(Proportions shown in this paper are adjusted to fit space limitations of this book. Follow actual dimensions discussed in this book and your instructor's directions.)

COMMENTARY

1 **Computer tip.** Following MLA style, Andrei uses his last name and the page number as a header (meaning "at the top" of his pages) throughout the paper. He doesn't use a footer (meaning "at the bottom" of his pages). To do this, he accesses the "header and footer" option in the "View" choice on the toolbar in his Microsoft Word word processing program and inserts the proper information so that it will appear automatically on each page.

2 **Introductory strategy.** Andrei hopes to attract his readers' interest by making up the unusual phrase "brain hiccups," which ties into the dual visual processing that he describes later in his paper. He also refers briefly to the paranormal and immediately discredits it by quoting the leading modern researcher into déjà vu, Alan S. Brown.

3 **PROCESS NOTE:** I use a quotation from Brown's journal article "The Déjà Vu Illusion," so I include the page number in parentheses.

4 **Thesis statement.** The last sentence of Andrei's introductory paragraph is his THESIS STATEMENT. He drafted two preliminary thesis statements, shown in section 33l. The thesis statement is a bridge from his introduction to the rest of his paper and helps his readers anticipate the main message of his paper. All of his topic sentences have to tie into his thesis statement.

Gurov 2

Header has student's last name and page number.

Some people report never having experienced déjà vu, and the percentages vary for the number of people who report having lived through at least one episode of it. In 2004, Brown reports that of the subjects he has interviewed, an average of 66 percent say that they have had one or more déjà vu experiences during their lives (*Experience* 33). However, in early 2005 in "Strangely Familiar," Uwe Wolfradt reports that "various studies indicate that from 50 to 90 percent of the people [studied] can recall having had at least one such déjà vu incident in their lives."

World Wide Web source has no page numbers or paragraph numbers.

Perhaps part of the reason for this variation in the range of percentages stems from a general misunderstanding of the phrase *déjà vu*, even by some of the earlier scientific researchers twenty or more years ago. Indeed, in today's society, people throw around the term *déjà vu* without much thought. For example, it is fairly common for someone to see or hear about an event and then say, "Wow. This is déjà vu. I had a dream that this exact same thing happened." However, dreaming about an event ahead of time is a different phenomenon known as *precognition*, which relates to the paranormal experience of extrasensory perception. To date, precognition has never been scientifically demonstrated. As Johnson explains about dreams, however,

Use block indent of 1-inch (or ten spaces) for a quotation longer than four typed lines.

. . . there is usually very little "data," evidence, or documentation to confirm that a Precognition has taken place. If a person learns about some disaster and THEN [author's emphasis] tells people that he/she has foreseen it the day before, that may or may not

continued >>

## COMMENTARY

5 **Summarizing and citing a source by an author of two different sources used in this paper.** Andrei summarizes the percentage information that Brown gives in his book *The Déjà Vu Experience.* Then Andrei cites his source with a shortened title and page number. He includes a title because he has been drawing on two of Brown's writings for this paper—one book and one journal article that he accesses online—and he knows that he needs to make a clear distinction between them whenever he cites them.

6 **The writer inserting words to fit a quotation into the writer's sentence.** Nothing is wrong with Uwe Wolfradt's sentence, but Andrei needs to add the word *studied* to make the meaning clear within his research paper. To do this in proper MLA form, Andrei put his added word in brackets to indicate that he is adding the word—that is, the word is not in the original text by Uwe Wolfradt.

7 **Figuring out a page number from an online source.** Andrei found the article "Strangely Familiar" by Uwe Wolfradt online through his search using http://www.googlescholar.com. Even though the citation for the article on the opening screen page says that the page spread is pages 32–37, and Andrei might feel quite safe in assuming that his information is on the first page—namely, page 32—he can't be sure, so he can't include a page number.

8 **PROCESS NOTE:** I kept being distracted about using the word *déjà vu* as a term or as the name of an experience. As I was drafting, I purposely overlooked the problem, but I circled each use so that I could tackle the issue on my final draft.

9 **PROCESS NOTE:** I'm fairly certain that my instructor will know that this quotation is not from a source, but it's rather one I made up from everyday speech.

10 **No capital letter to start block-indented quotation.** Andrei took this quotation from the middle of a sentence in the source, so he can't start it with a capital letter. The ellipsis indicates he omitted words to make the quotation fit stylistically.

11 **How "[author's emphasis]" is used.** Whenever a source uses a typographical technique of emphasis—such as italics or all capital letters—the writer who quotes that source is required to indicate that the emphasis belongs to the source, not to the writer. In MLA style, "[author's emphasis]" is required so that the reader won't think the emphasis has been made by the writer of the paper.

MLA

Gurov 3

be true, because there is usually not corroborative 12
confirmation of what the person claims.

Thus, precognition, a phenomenon talked about
frequently but one that has never held up under scientific
scrutiny, is definitely not the same as déjà vu.

False memory is another phenomenon mislabeled *déjà
vu*. It happens when people are convinced that certain events
took place in their lives, even though the events never
happened. This occurs when people have strong memories of
many unrelated occurrences that suddenly come together into
a whole that's very close to the current experience. It seems
like a déjà vu experience. This occurs from the "converging
elements of many different but related experiences. When this
abstract representation, which has emerged strictly from the
melding together of strongly associated elements, happens to
correspond to the present experience, a déjà vu may be the
outcome" (Brown, *Experience* 160). To illustrate lab-induced 13
false memory, Brown in *Experience* cites investigations in 14
which subjects are shown lists of words related to sleep;
however, the word *sleep* itself is not on the list. In recalling
the list of words, most subjects insist that the word *sleep* was
indeed on the list, which means that the memory of a word that
was never there is false memory. This is exactly what happens
when well-intentioned eyewitnesses believe they recall certain
criminal acts even though, in fact, they never saw or
experienced the events at all (159).

In the last twenty years especially, new theories
have come to the fore as a result of rigorous work from
psychological and medical points of view. In *Experience*, 15
Brown surveys the literature and concludes that this relatively

Intro-
ductory
phrase
smoothly
leads into
direct
quotation.

Put only
page
number
in paren-
theses
when
author
is named
in text.

continued >>

## COMMENTARY

12  **MLA style for a block-indent quotation.** MLA style requires that when a quotation takes up four or more lines in a research paper that it be set off in a block. A block indent calls for all lines to be indented ten spaces from the left margin. The quoted material in the block has to end with a period. Then the source information has to come after the period in parentheses. Because Andrei's online source did not provide page, paragraphs, or screen numbers, he could not include a parenthetical citation after the quotation.

13  **PROCESS NOTE:** I want to use Brown in two different ways in this paragraph because I've drawn on Brown as a major reference throughout my paper. I don't want to only use quotations or only summaries. Here I use a quotation but don't call attention to the source. I place all source information in parentheses after the end of the quotation. I include a shortened version of the title of the source because I've used two different sources by the same author to write this paper.

14  **PROCESS NOTE:** To follow up on Process Note 13, this time I summarize Brown's words and fit in his name and the shortened title of the source.

15  **PROCESS NOTE:** I now need to write a paragraph of transition from what was *not* déjà vu to what was. My plan is to write about two types of phenomena that aren't déjà vu, and then write about three types of phenomena that are. I checked my outline to make sure I was adhering to my plan.

MLA

Gurov 4

young field of investigation is dividing itself into four categories: (1) dual processing, (2) memory, (3) neurological, and (4) attentional. This paper briefly discusses the first and second as each relates to the third. Next, I discuss the fourth as it relates to the second.

Brain-based studies of the human sense of sight are one heavily researched theory of déjà vu that has been partially explained in the last two decades. Such studies focus on the dual pathways by which the sight of an event reaches the brain (Glenn; Carey F1). For example, the left hemisphere processes information from the right eye and the right hemisphere processes information from the left eye. The brain is incapable of storing data with respect to time and is only able to "see" events in relation to others. Each eye interprets data separately, at the same precise time. According to research, the human brain can perceive two visual stimuli at one instant as long as they are "seen" less than 25 milliseconds apart. Since the human brain is capable of interpreting both signals within this time, when events are perceived normally, they are seen and recognized by the brain as one single event (Weiten 69, 97-99, 211).

Occasionally, however, the neurological impulses that carry data from each eye to the brain are delayed. As Johnson explains, the person might be fatigued or have had his or her attention seriously distracted (as when crossing the street at a dangerous intersection). As a result, one signal may reach the brain in under 25 milliseconds, while the other signal is slowed and reaches the brain slightly more than 25 milliseconds later. Even a few milliseconds' delay makes the second incoming signal arrive late--and, without fail, the brain interprets the

16

17

18

19

Put author and page number in parentheses when author is not named in the sentence.

Paragraph summarizes several pages of source material, as parenthetical citation shows.

continued >>

## COMMENTARY

16 **PROCESS NOTE:** Every time I type the word *attentional* (using Microsoft Word) into my paper, a red wavy line pops up under it, which means a misspelling. However, because the word is spelled that way consistently in all my sources, I've just ignored the red wavy line and added the word, with confidence, to my personal dictionary provided by the Microsoft Word program.

17 **Two sources for one piece of information.** When two sources contain the same information, MLA style permits the citing of both sources. Each source is given with its page number; don't provide a page number if you're using a one-page source or an online source with no page numbers. A semicolon divides the sources.

18 **Words used in a nonliteral way.** The words *see* and *seen* here do not carry their literal meaning related to conscious sight. Rather, they refer to subconscious sight. Therefore, they belong in quotation marks.

19 **PROCESS NOTE:** Earlier in the paper, I devoted two paragraphs to each of two non-déjà vu topics. Now, I'm giving more attention to each of the three types of legitimate déjà vu phenomena that I've chosen to discuss (dual pathways of sight, implanted memories, and inattentional blindness). This paragraph is the second I'm writing about dual pathways of sight.

Gurov 5

stimuli as two separate events rather than one event. The person thus has the sensation of having seen the event before because the brain has recognized the milliseconds-later event as a memory.

Implanted memories is another well-researched [20] explanation for the déjà vu phenomenon. Examples of this originate in both the natural and the lab-induced experiences of people. For instance, perhaps a person walks into the kitchen of a new friend for the first time and, although the person has never been there before, the person feels certain that he or she has. With hypnosis and other techniques, researchers could uncover that the cupboards are almost exactly like those that the person had forgotten were in the kitchen of the person's grandparents' house and that the scent of baking apple pie is identical to the smell the person loved when walking into the grandparents' home during holidays (Carey F1).

Thomas McHugh, a researcher at MIT, believes he has even discovered the specific "memory circuit" in the brain that is the source of this kind of déjà vu (Lemonick). This circuit allows people to complete memories with just a single cue. For example, you can remember much about a football game you saw even if someone just mentions the two teams involved. Sometimes, however, the circuit "misfires," and it signals that a new memory is actually part of the pattern of an old one.

Wolfradt describes a lab-induced experiment in which [21] psychologist Larry L. Jacoby in 1989 manipulated a group of subjects so that he could implant a memory that would lead to a déjà vu experience for each of them. He arranged for his subjects to assemble in a room equipped with a screen in front. He flashed on the screen one word so quickly that no one was

continued >>

## COMMENTARY

20 **PROCESS NOTE:** I'm now starting to write about the second of the three types of déjà vu that I'm covering in this paper. I'm intentionally using the word *another* in my topic sentence to bridge from dual pathways of sight to implanted memories. Because there are so many concepts and examples of them in this paper, I'm trying to be very clear in my transitions.

21 **PROCESS NOTE:** Specific examples are very important to me as I write this paper. It's far too easy for me to write on and on about theory and concepts. As I'm writing this paper, I find myself often cutting generalizations to make room for details. When I've read my sophomore and junior friends' papers from when they were freshmen, I'm surprised to see how few specifics and concrete details they put in their freshman composition papers—and their grades and the comments they got reflect this fact.

MLA

Gurov 6

consciously aware they had seen the word. Jacoby was certain, however, that the visual centers of the brain of each subject had indeed "seen" the word. Later, when he flashed the word leaving it on the screen long enough for the subjects to consciously see it, everyone indicated they had seen the word somewhere before. All the subjects were firmly convinced that the first time they had seen the word, it absolutely was not on the screen at the front of the room they were in. Some became annoyed at being asked over and over. Since Jacoby's work, lab-induced memory research has become very popular in psychology. In fact, it has been given its own name: *priming*.

Inattention, or what some researchers call "inattentional blindness," is also an extensively researched explanation for the déjà vu experience. Sometimes people can see objects without any impediment right before them but still not process the objects because they're paying attention to something else (Brown, *Experience* 181). The distraction might be daydreaming, a sudden lowering of energy, or simply being drawn to another object in the environment. As David Glenn explains in "The Tease of Memory":

> Imagine that you drive through an unfamiliar town but pay little attention because you're talking on a cellphone [sic]. If you then drive back down the same streets a few moments later, this time focusing on the landscape, you might be prone to experience déjà vu. During your second pass, the visual information is consciously processed in the hippocampus [of the brain] but feels falsely "old"

22

23

continued >>

MLA

## COMMENTARY

22 **PROCESS NOTE:** When I wrote my first draft, I felt that my discussion of implanted memories was pretty weak. I did some further research and was happy to find enough information to write this additional paragraph in my second draft. It is, to me, a dramatic demonstration of laboratory-manipulated implanted memory.

23 **Using [sic].** This quotation spells "cell phone" as one word. Therefore, Andrei uses [sic] to tell his readers that he knows this is a misspelling.

MLA

Gurov 7

because the images from your earlier drive still
linger in your short term memory.                                    24

The busy lifestyle today would seem to lead to many
distractions of perception and thus to frequent experiences of
déjà vu; however, these are no more frequently reported than
any other causes reported concerning déjà vu.

One compelling laboratory experiment studying           25
inattention is described by Carey in "Déjà Vu: If It All Seems
Familiar, There May Be a Reason." He recounts a test with
many college students from Duke University in Durham, North
Carolina. The students were asked to look at a group of
photographs of the campus of Southern Methodist University in
Dallas, Texas, that were flashed before them at a very quick
speed. A small black or white cross was superimposed on each
photograph, and the students were instructed to find the cross
and focus on it (F6). Brown in *Experience* explains that the
researchers assumed that the quick speed at which the
photographs had been shown would result in no one's having
noticed the background scenes. A week's time passed, and
the same students were shown the pictures again, this time
without the crosses. Almost all insisted that they had been to
the college campus shown in the photos, which was physically
impossible for that many students since they lived in Durham,
North Carolina, and the college in the photographs was in
Dallas, Texas (182-83). This means that the scenes in the
photographs did indeed register in the visual memories of the
students in spite of the quick speed and the distraction of
looking only for the crosses.

continued >>

**COMMENTARY**

24 **PROCESS NOTE:** Here's how I wasted a day of researching for this paper. I know it's not unusual for freshmen to go off the topic and waste their time, so I am trying to stay very conscious of what I am doing so that I can learn what NOT to do in the future. What happened was that I was becoming aware that psychologists have named many phenomena that are closely related to déjà vu, each somewhat different from it and from each other. For example, Brown in *Experience* names over twenty relatives of déjà vu, while other sources name as few as eight. This captured my interest, but once I got into writing up the information, I began to realize that I was going off my topic. I'll list here some that had potential but that, in the end, I never used in my paper:

- **Déjà eprouvé:** A sense that this act has already been attempted and didn't work out.
- **Déjà senti:** A mental feeling that one is *feeling* something again. It is limited to feeling, and does not include a sense of being in a place.
- **Déjà visité:** The knowledge of a large place, such as an entire village, but knowing still that one has never been there.
- **Jamais vu:** This is the opposite of déjà vu. Even though one knows something has happened before, the experience feels completely unfamiliar.
- **Presque vu:** This is the sense of almost, but not quite, remembering something—as in "it's on the tip of my tongue."

25 **PROCESS NOTE:** To stay on the topic, I needed a third type of déjà vu—for which I used inattentional blindness—to drive home my thesis statement.

MLA

Gurov 8

The worlds of psychology and neurology have learned    26
much since the age of paranormal interpretations of déjà vu
experiences, starting around 1935. That is when rational
science energetically began its disciplined investigations of
brain-based origins of the déjà vu phenomenon. Concepts
such as dual processing of sight, implanted memories, and
inattentional blindness, among other theories, have gone far in
opening the door to the possibilities of many more inventive
theories to explain incidents of déjà vu. The leading researcher
in the field today, Alan S. Brown, is among the strongest voices
urging a vast expansion of investigations into this still
relatively unexplored phenomenon. He is optimistic this will
happen, given his whimsical remark to Carlin Flora of
*Psychology Today:* "We are always fascinated when the
brain goes haywire."

Concluding paragraph summarizes paper.

continued >>

## COMMENTARY

26 **PROCESS NOTE:** In my second draft, I decided to check whether all my topic sentences tied together with each other. I remembered that neither the introductory nor the concluding paragraphs have topic sentences. Here's a list of my thesis and topic sentences.

**THESIS STATEMENT:** Although a few people today still prefer to believe that feelings of déjà vu have mysterious or supernatural origins, recent research in cognitive psychology and the neurosciences has shed much rational light on the phenomenon.

- Some people report never having experienced déjà vu, and the percentages vary for the number of people who report having lived through at least one episode of it.

- Perhaps part of the reason for this variation in the range of percentages stems from a general misunderstanding of the phrase *déjà vu,* even by some of the earlier scientific researchers twenty or more years ago.

- False memory is another phenomenon mislabeled *déjà vu.*

- In the last twenty years especially, new theories have come to the fore as a result of rigorous work from psychological and medical points of view.

- Brain-based studies of the human sense of sight are one heavily researched theory of déjà vu that has been partially explained in the last two decades.

- Occasionally, however, the neurological impulses that carry data from each eye to the brain are delayed.

- Implanted memories is another well-researched explanation for the déjà vu phenomenon.

- Wolfradt describes a lab-induced experiment in which psychologist Larry L. Jacoby in 1989 manipulated a group of subjects so that he could implant a memory that would lead to a déjà vu experience for each of them.

- Inattention, or what some researchers call "inattentional blindness," is also an extensively researched explanation for the déjà vu experience.

- One compelling laboratory experiment studying inattention is described by Carey in "Déjà Vu: If It All Seems Familiar, There May Be a Reason."

Gurov 9

Works
Cited
begins
on a new
page.

Double-
space
throughout.

List
sources in
alphabetical
order.

Works Cited      27

Brown, Alan S. *The Déjà Vu Experience: Essays in Cognitive*   28

     *Psychology.* New York: Psychology, 2004. Print.

---. "The Déjà Vu Illusion." *Current Directions in Psychological*

     *Science* 13.6 (2004): 256-59. Print.

Carey, Benedict. "Déjà Vu: If It All Seems Familiar, There May

     Be a Reason." *New York Times* 14 Sept. 2004: F1+.

     *LexisNexis.* Web. 11 Nov. 2007.   29

Flora, Carlin. "Giving Déjà Vu Its Due." *Psychology Today*

     Mar.-Apr. 2005: 27. *Academic Search Premier.* Web.   30

     7 Nov. 2007.

Glenn, David. "The Tease of Memory." *Chronicle of Higher*

     *Education* 23 July 2004: A12. Print.

Johnson, C. "A Theory on the Déjà Vu Phenomenon." 8 Dec.

     2001. Web. 20 Nov. 2007.

Lemonick, Michael D. "Explaining Déjà Vu." *Time* 20 Aug. 2007.

     *Academic Search Premier.* Web. 5 Dec. 2007.

Thompson, Rebecca G., et al. "Persistent Déjà Vu: A Disorder of

     Memory." *International Journal of Geriatric Psychiatry*

     19.9 (2004): 906-07. Print.

Weiten, Wayne. *Psychology: Themes and Variations.* Belmont:

     Wadsworth, 2005. Print.

Wolfradt, Uwe. "Strangely Familiar." *Scientific American Mind*

     16.1 (2005): 32-37. *Academic Search Elite.* Web. 7 Nov. 2007.

MLA

## COMMENTARY

27 **Working versus final bibliography.** In keeping with MLA style, Andrei developed a working bibliography using those sources referred to in his research paper. His bibliography contained over twice the number of sources in his Works Cited. He dropped sources he considered less authoritative and ones that were not specifically targeted to the subjects that he chose to discuss related to déjà vu.

28 **Balance of source types.** Andrei's final list of Works Cited contains ten works, five from online databases and five from print sources—a proportion that is typical of today's college-level research papers.

29 **What is LexisNexis?** LexisNexis is an online database, available to students through their college library, that contains a large number of research and other scholarly collections, including the LexisNexis Academic and Library Solutions. Originally a document service for law students and lawyers, it now includes areas of study such as government, business, and environmental issues.

30 **What is Academic Search Premier?** Academic Search Premier is a widely used online database in English studies and the humanities. It's available to students through their college library and gives access to over one hundred reference databases, thousands of online journals, lists of book titles at some libraries, linking services, and much more.

For more help with your writing, grammar, and research, go to **www.mycomplab.com**

the same last name. In such cases, each separate citation must include the date to identify which work you're citing.

## 37c What are APA guidelines for in-text citations?

The following numbered examples show how to cite various kinds of sources in the body of your research paper. Remember, though, that you often can introduce source names, including titles when necessary, and sometimes even years, in your own sentences rather than in the parenthetical IN-TEXT CITATIONS.

### 1. Paraphrased or Summarized Source—APA

People from the Mediterranean prefer an elbow-to-shoulder distance from each other (Morris, 1977). [Author name and date cited in parentheses; note comma.]

Desmond Morris (1977) notes that people from the Mediterranean prefer an elbow-to-shoulder distance from each other. [Author name cited in text; date cited in parentheses.]

### 2. Source of a Short Quotation—APA

A recent report of reductions in SAD-related "depression in 87 percent of patients" (Binkley, 1990, p. 203) reverses the findings of earlier studies. [Author name, date, and page reference in parentheses immediately following the quotation.]

Binkley (1990) reports reductions in SAD-related "depression in 87 percent of patients" (p. 203). [Author name followed by the date in parentheses incorporated into the words introducing the quotation; page number in parentheses immediately following the quotation.]

### 3. Source of a Long Quotation (and Format of Quotation)—APA

Incorporate a direct quotation of fewer than forty words into your own sentence and enclose it in quotation marks. Place the parenthetical in-text citation after the closing quotation mark and, if the quotation falls at the end of the sentence, before the sentence-ending punctuation. When you use a quotation longer than forty words, set it off in block style indented one-half inch or five spaces from the left margin. Never enclose a set-off quotation in quotation marks because the placement in block style carries the message that the material is quoted. Place the parenthetical reference citation one space after the end punctuation of the last sentence.

## DISPLAYED QUOTATION (FORTY OR MORE WORDS)

Jet lag, with its characteristic fatigue and irregular sleep patterns, is a common problem among those who travel great distances by jet airplane to different time zones:

> Jet lag syndrome is the inability of the internal body rhythm to rapidly resynchronize after sudden shifts in the timing. For a variety of reasons, the system attempts to maintain stability and resist temporal change. Consequently, complete adjustment can often be delayed for several days—sometimes for a week—after arrival at one's destination. (Bonner, 1991, p. 72)

### 4. One Author—APA

In a parenthetical reference in APA style, a comma and a space separate a name from a year, and a year from a page reference. (Note: Examples 1 through 3 are also citations of works by one author.)

> One of his questions is "What binds together a Mormon banker in Utah with his brother, or other coreligionists in Illinois or Massachusetts?" (Coles, 1993, p. 2).

### 5. Two Authors—APA

If a work has two authors, give both names in each citation.

> One report describes 2,123 occurrences (Krait & Cooper, 2003).

> The results that Krait and Cooper (2003) report would not support the conclusions Davis and Sherman (1999) draw in their review of the literature.

When you write a parenthetical in-text citation naming two (or more) authors, use an ampersand (&) between the final two names, but write out the word *and* for any reference in your own sentence.

### 6. Three, Four, or Five Authors—APA

For three, four, or five authors, use the last names of all the authors in the first reference. In all subsequent references, use only the first author's last name followed by *et al.* (a Latin term meaning "and others"). Note that *et al.* is followed by a period and is not italicized.

#### FIRST REFERENCE

In one study, only 30% of the survey population could name the most commonly spoken languages in five Middle Eastern countries (Ludwig, Rodriquez, Novak, & Ehlers, 2008).

### BACKGROUND

As commonly used, the term *bibliography* sometimes refers to a science, sometimes to an art, and sometimes to the product of that art. As a science, it is an organized body of knowledge dealing with all aspects of books, both as physical objects and as the expression of ideas. Bibliography as an art consists of the techniques for finding, organizing, and presenting information about books. The bibliography that is produced by that art is a systematic listing of books that share common characteristics.

The objective of a bibliography may be analytical or systematic. Analytical bibliography tries to discover information about the authorship, publication, and derivation of a text. Systematic bibliography produces systematic lists of books. The result is many different kinds of bibliographies. For example, bibliographies may be critical (critically appraising the books they list), current or retrospective, comprehensive or selective, annotated or not, enumerative (presenting an inventory) or subject-oriented (presenting content). In all their varied forms, they provide the modern researcher with valuable assistance in finding out where to look to learn what is already known about a subject.

### TEACHING TIP

Asking students to make up a title and citation for their imaginary autobiography, perhaps published this year by Simon & Schuster, may inject a little fun into learning to cite a book. Similarly, they might enjoy making up article titles and citations for the imaginary *Journal of Fanciful Ideas.*

### BACKGROUND

*Copyright* is the term used to refer to a group of exclusive rights given for a limited time to the authors or owners of original literary, dramatic, visual, or musical works. It includes the exclusive right to copy the work and to prevent others from doing so without permission. It also allows the owner to translate a work, to dramatize or arrange it, and to change it into other versions.

To be granted a copyright, a work must be original; its merit and aesthetic quality are of

no consequence. The law specifies several classes of works that can receive copyright protection. They include books, periodicals, musical compositions, dramatic works, motion pictures, works prepared for oral delivery, maps and other scientific or technical works, photographs, works of art, works of the graphic arts, and commercial prints and labels.

TEACHING TIP

Older documentation styles often called for the use of abbreviations, many of them in Latin. Although current style manuals have dropped most of the abbreviated terms, your students may need to know what the terms mean when they appear in articles encountered in the course of doing research. Students should be cautioned not to use them in their own papers unless you, another instructor, or their style manual asks them to do so. Some of the more common scholarly abbreviations appear in Quick Reference 30.3 in section 30k.

BACKGROUND

Until the middle of the fifteenth century, the only books available to Europeans were handwritten manuscripts, which were costly and often inaccurate. The development of printing made books available to the common people for the first time.

The major breakthrough in the history of printing was the invention of movable type, the making of a stamp for each letter on a separate base so that the letters could be assembled to form a page. Although this system was already known in China and Korea (where it was little used because of the large number of Chinese characters and the lack of suitable ink), its discovery in Europe was made independently. Credit for the European development has been given to Johannes Gutenberg (c. 1400–1468), though scholars increasingly acknowledge other contributors to his work. The so-called Gutenberg Bible, printed c. 1455, was not his first printed work, but it is his most famous one.

Today, it is often remarked that the world is going through another printing revolution. With the availability of copying machines, memory typewriters, word-processing computer

SUBSEQUENT REFERENCE

Ludwig et al. (2008) found that most Americans could identify the language spoken in Saudi Arabia.

7. Six or More Authors—APA

For six or more authors, name the first author followed by *et al.* in all in-text references, including the first.

These injuries can lead to an inability to perform athletically, in addition to initiating degenerative changes at the joint level (Mandelbaum et al., 2005).

8. Author(s) with Two or More Works in the Same Year—APA

If you use more than one source written in the same year by the same author(s), alphabetize the works by their titles for the References list and assign letters in alphabetical order to the years—(2007a), (2007b), (2007c). Use the year-letter combination in parenthetical references. Note that a citation of two or more such works lists the years in alphabetical order.

Most recently, Torrevillas (2007c) draws new conclusions from the results of eight experiments conducted with experienced readers (Torrevillas, 2007a, 2007b).

9. Two or More Authors with the Same Last Name—APA

Include first initials for every in-text citation of authors who share a last name. Use the initials appearing in the References list. (In the second example, a parenthetical citation, the name order is alphabetical, as explained in item 12.)

R. A. Smith (2008) and C. Smith (1999) both confirm these results.

These results have been confirmed independently (C. Smith, 1999; R. A. Smith, 2008).

10. Work with a Group or Corporate Author—APA

If you use a source in which the "author" is a corporation, agency, or group, an in-text reference gives that name as author. Use the full name in each citation, unless an abbreviated version of the name is likely to be familiar to your audience. In that case, use the full name and give its abbreviation at the first citation; then, use the abbreviation for subsequent citations.

This exploration will continue into the 21st century (National Aeronautics and Space Administration [NASA], 2004). [In subsequent citations, use the abbreviated form, NASA, alone.]

### 11. Work Listed by Title—APA

If no author is named, use a shortened form of the title for in-text citations. Ignoring *A, An,* or *The,* make the first word the one by which you alphabetize the title in your References. The following example refers to an article fully titled "Are You a Day or Night Person?"

> Scientists group people as "larks" or "owls" on the basis of whether individuals are more efficient in the morning or at night ("Are You," 1989).

### 12. Reference to More Than One Source—APA

If more than one source has contributed to an idea or opinion in your paper, cite the sources alphabetically by author in one set of parentheses; separate each block of information with a semicolon, as in the following example.

> Conceptions of personal space vary among cultures (Morris, 1977; Worchel & Cooper, 1983).

### 13. Personal Communication, Including E-Mail and Other Nonretrievable Sources—APA

Telephone calls, personal letters, interviews, and e-mail messages are "personal communications" that your readers can't access or retrieve. Acknowledge personal communications in parenthetical references, but never include them in your References list at the end of your paper.

> Recalling his first summer at camp, one person said, "The proximity of 12 other kids made me—an only child with older, quiet parents— frantic for eight weeks" (A. Weiss, personal communication, January 12, 2005).

### 14. References to Retrievable Online Sources—APA

When you quote, paraphrase, or summarize an online source that is available to others, cite the author (if any) or title and the date as you would for a print source, and include the work in your References list.

> It's possible that similarity in personality is important in having a happy marriage (Luo & Clonen, 2005, p. 324).

### 15. Reference to an Online Source with No Pages—APA

If an online source doesn't provide page numbers, use the paragraph number, if available, preceded by the abbreviation *para.* It is rare, however, to number paragraphs. If you can't decipher a page or paragraph number, cite a heading if possible.

programs, and a variety of desktop printers, methods of producing printed material have undergone another major shift. Whereas only a few years ago having a document printed meant handing it over to a professional printer, today a document is likely to be produced on equipment readily available in most offices and many homes.

**EXTRA EXERCISE A**

Using the same sources that appeared in Extra Exercise B in Chapter 34, compile a References list, following APA style.

**Answers to Extra Exercise A**

#### References

Clarke, G. (1988). *Capote: A biography.* New York: Simon & Schuster.

Gould, S. J. (1987). *Time's arrow, time's cycle: Myth and metaphor in the discovery of geological time.* Cambridge, MA: Harvard University Press.

Hibbert, C. (1974). *The rise and fall of the House of Medici.* New York: Penguin Books.

Oates, S. B. (1984). *Abraham Lincoln: The man behind the myths.* New York: Harper & Row.

Peters, T. J., & Waterman, R. H., Jr. (1982). *In search of excellence.* New York: Harper & Row.

Smout, T. C. (1986). *A century of the Scottish people, 1830–1950.* New Haven, CT: Yale University Press.

Tuchman, B. W. (1981). *Practicing history.* New York: Knopf.

**QUOTATION: ON WRITING**

Forward motion is also carried by the sounds. When I write, I write out loud. It's very important to me how the consonants click off against one another and how the vowels move into one another and out again. I also like the sounds of a line to move in an interesting and logical way through the mouth.

—Miller Williams

**QUOTATION: ON WRITING**

Most writing is done away from the typewriter, away from the desk. I'd say it occurs in the quiet, silent moments.

—Henry Miller

**BACKGROUND**

The Committee on Disability Issues in Psychology of the APA has created "Guidelines for Non-Handicapping Language in APA Journals" at <http://apastyle.apa.org/disabilities.html>. Consider sharing these guidelines with students including, "It is recommended that the word *disability* be used to refer to an attribute of a person, and *handicap* to the *source* of limitations" and "Use of the terms *non-disabled* or *persons without disabilities* is preferable to the term *normal* when comparing persons with disabilities to others. Usage of *normal* makes the unconscious comparison of *abnormal*, thus stigmatizing those individuals with differences." The APA also provides guidelines on removing bias in language regarding sexuality and race and ethnicity.

**QUOTATION: ON WRITING**

Good writing is full of surprises and novelties, moving in a direction you don't expect.

—Iris Murdoch

**BACKGROUND: ON WRITING**

In "The Use and Overuse of Electronic Research in Freshman Composition Research Papers: Problems in Traditional and Online Universities" (Abstract, ERIC ED 459461, 2002), Suzanne Abram finds that instructors teaching purely online writing courses have to take special steps to ensure that their students use a range of sources.

**QUOTATION: ON WRITING**

They're fancy talkers about themselves, writers. If I had to give young writers advice, I would say don't listen to writers talk about writing or themselves.

—Lillian Hellman

(Anderson, 2003, para. 14)

(Migueis, 2002, Introduction)

## 16. Source Lines for Graphics and Table Data—APA

If you use a graphic from another source or create a table using data from another source, provide a note at the bottom of the table or graphic, crediting the original author and the copyright holder. Here are examples of two source lines—one for a graphic from an article, the other for a graphic from a book.

### GRAPHIC USING DATA FROM AN ARTICLE—APA

*Note.* The data in columns 1 and 2 are from "Advance Organizers in Advisory Reports: Selective Reading, Recall, and Perception" by L. Lagerwerf et al., 2008, *Written Communication, 25*(1), p. 68. Copyright 2008 by Sage Publications. Adapted with permission of the author.

### GRAPHIC FROM A BOOK—APA

*Note.* From *The Road to Reality: A Complete Guide to the Laws of the Universe* (p. 270), by R. Penrose, 2005, New York: Alfred Knopf. Copyright 2004 by R. Penrose. Reprinted with permission of the publisher.

## 37d What are APA guidelines for writing an abstract?

As the APA *Publication Manual* explains, "an abstract is a brief, comprehensive summary" (p. 12) of a longer piece of writing. The APA estimates that an abstract should be no longer than about 120 words. Your instructor may require that you include an abstract at the start of a paper; if you're not sure, ask. Make the abstract accurate, objective, and exact. Actually, as you study the social sciences, you may become familiar with effective abstracts because many disciplines have online abstracts of longer sources. See 37g for guidelines on formatting an abstract page. The student paper in 37h.2 has an abstract you can study as an example.

## 37e What are APA guidelines for content notes?

Content notes in APA-style papers add relevant information that can't be worked effectively into a text discussion. Use consecutive Arabic numerals for note numbers, both within your paper and on any separate page following the last text page of your paper. Try to arrange your sentence so that the note number falls at the end. Use a numeral raised slightly above the line of words and immediately after the final punctuation mark. See 37g for instructions on formatting the Footnotes page.

## 37f  What are APA guidelines for a References list?

The REFERENCES list at the end of your research paper provides complete bibliographic information for readers who may want to access the sources you draw on for your paper.

Include in a References list all the sources you QUOTE, PARAPHRASE, or SUMMARIZE in your paper so that readers can find the same sources with reasonable effort. Never include in your References list any source that's not generally available to others (see item 13 in 37c). Quick Reference 37.1 presents general format guidelines.

### Quick Reference 37.1

#### Guidelines for an APA-style References list

**TITLE**
The title is "References" (centered without quotation marks, italics, or underlining).

**PLACEMENT OF LIST**
Start a new page. Number it sequentially with the rest of the paper and place it immediately after the body of the paper.

**CONTENTS AND FORMAT**
Include all quoted, paraphrased, or summarized sources in your paper that are not personal communications, unless your instructor tells you to include all the references you have consulted, not just those you have to credit. Start each entry on a new line, and double-space all lines. APA recommends that student papers follow journal formatting by using a *hanging indent* style: The first line of each entry begins flush left at the margin, and all other lines are indented. The hanging indent makes source names and dates more prominent. Type the first line of each entry full width, and indent subsequent lines one-half inch. The easiest way to do this is using the word processor's ruler bar.

Shuter, R. (1977). A field study of nonverbal communication in Germany, Italy, and the United States. *Communication Monographs, 44,* 298–305.

**SPACING AFTER PUNCTUATION**
APA calls for one space after end-punctuation marks.

continued >>

APA

**APA**

## BACKGROUND: ON WRITING

In "Writing in a Psychology Classroom: Learning and Adopting the APA Epistemology" (Diss., University of North Dakota, 2000), SuEllen Shaw studies how students learn to use APA style, which includes learning the values and habits of thinking associated with that style.

## TEACHING TIP

Computers have taken much of the tedium out of formatting research papers. You may want to explain to students such now-quaint practices as having to measure pages to leave room for footnotes, creating templates to put behind papers in a typewriter, or hiring typists to produce the final draft. However, as ubiquitous as computers and word processing are, a surprising number of students still don't know how to use such labor-saving features as the ruler line to set margins, paragraph indentations, block quotations, and hanging indents, or the header feature to set running titles and page numbers. Spending a few minutes demonstrating these features in a classroom, lab, or your office can make students very appreciative.

## QUOTATION: ON READING

A man ought to read just as inclination leads him; for what he reads as a task will do him little good.

— Samuel Johnson

## QUOTATION: ON TECHNOLOGY

While a generation ago, most people assumed the relationship between man and machine would become antagonistic ("Open the pod door, HAL"), today most people are completely comfortable with technology—some to the point where technological contact is more comfortable than human contact (I used to pray I wouldn't have to talk to an answering machine; now I frequently pray I won't have to talk to a person). Even acknowledging that, however, there is still a big gap between preferring to get a credit card update on an automated system and wanting to marry my PDA.

— Maureen Fitzpatrick, "Losing Control: Writers, Readers, and Hypertext," <http://english.ttu.edu/kairos/6.1/>

---

### Quick Reference 37.1 (continued)

#### ARRANGEMENT OF ENTRIES
Alphabetize by the author's last name. If no author is named, alphabetize by the first significant word (ignore *A, An,* or *The*) in the title of the work.

#### AUTHORS' NAMES
Use last names, first initials, and middle initials, if any. Reverse the order for all authors' names, and use an ampersand (&) before the last author's name: Mills, J. F., & Holahan, R. H.

Give names in the order in which they appear on the work (on the title page of a book or under the title of an article or other printed work). Use a comma between each author's last name and first initial and after each complete name except the last. Use a period after the last author's name.

#### DATES
Date information follows the name information and is enclosed in parentheses. Place a period followed by one space after the closing parenthesis.

For books, articles in journals that have volume numbers, and many other print and nonprint sources, the year of publication or production is the date to use. For articles from most general-circulation magazines and newspapers, use the year followed by a comma and then the exact date that appears on the issue (month and day for daily and weekly publications, month alone for monthly and bimonthly publications, and season for quarterly publications). Capitalize any words and use no abbreviations. Individual entries that follow show how much information to give for various sources.

#### CAPITALIZATION OF TITLES
For book, article, and chapter titles, capitalize the first word, the first word after a colon between a title and subtitle, and any proper nouns. For names of journals and proceedings of meetings, capitalize the first word, all nouns, verbs, adverbs, and adjectives, and any other words four or more letters long.

#### SPECIAL TREATMENT OF TITLES
Use no special treatment for titles of shorter works (poems, short stories, essays, articles). Italicize titles of longer works (books, names of newspapers or journals). If an italic typeface is unavailable, draw an unbroken line beneath the title *and* beneath the punctuation.

Don't drop any words, such as *A, An,* or *The,* from the titles of periodicals (such as newspapers, magazines, and journals).

#### PUBLISHERS
Use a shortened version of the publisher's name except for an association, corporation, or university press. Drop *Co., Inc., Publishers,* and the like, but retain *Books* or *Press.*

continued >>

## Quick Reference 37.1    (continued)

### PLACE OF PUBLICATION

For US publishers, give the city and add the state (use the two-letter postal abbreviations listed in most dictionaries) for all US cities except Baltimore, Boston, Chicago, Los Angeles, New York, Philadelphia, and San Francisco. For publishers in other countries, give city and country spelled out; no country name is needed with Amsterdam, Jerusalem, London, Milan, Moscow, Paris, Rome, Stockholm, Tokyo, and Vienna. However, if the state or country is part of the publisher's name, omit it after the name of the city.

### ABBREVIATIONS OF MONTHS

Don't abbreviate the names of months in any context.

### PAGE NUMBERS

Use all digits, omitting none. For references to books or newspapers only, use *p.* and *pp.* before page numbers. List all discontinuous pages, with numbers separated by commas: pp. 32, 44–45, 47–49, 53.

### REFERENCES ENTRIES: BOOKS

Citations for books have four main parts: author, date, title, and publication information (place of publication and publisher). Each part ends with a period.

AUTHOR    DATE                TITLE

Wood, P. (2003). *Diversity: The invention of a concept.*

PUBLICATION INFORMATION

San Francisco: Encounter Books.

### REFERENCES ENTRIES: ARTICLES

Citations for periodical articles contain four major parts: author, date, title of article, and publication information (usually, the periodical title, volume number, and page numbers). Each part ends with a period.

AUTHOR        DATE        ARTICLE TITLE

Wood, W., Witt, M. G., & Tam, L. (2005). Changing circumstances, disrupting

PERIODICAL TITLE        VOLUME  PAGE
                         NUMBER  RANGE

habits. *Journal of Personality and Social Psychology, 88,* 918–933.

### REFERENCES ENTRIES: ELECTRONIC AND ONLINE SOURCES

Styles for documenting electronic and online sources continue to evolve. The *APA Style Guide to Electronic References* (Washington, D.C.: American Psychological Association, 2007) is available on the APA Web page http://www.apastyle.org/elecref.html and is the best source for current guidelines on these formats. This guide updates the *Publication Guide of the American Psychological Association* (5th ed.).

continued >>

**TEACHING TIP**

You might want to explain that formats are of major importance in many disciplines other than English composition. The formats constitute "genres" that readers expect. The formats ease communication because readers know where to look for specific information: background, data, conclusions. You might invite colleagues from a few other disciplines to serve as guest experts for part of a class period to explain how they conduct and write research. Alternatively, you may have students interview some professors to learn about their writing practices and then have them write up accounts for the class.

**QUOTATION: ON WRITING**

As late as 1806 I was waiting for genius to descend upon me so that I might write. . . . If I had spoken around 1795 of my plan to write, some sensible man would have told me "to write every day for an hour or two." Genius or no genius. That advice would have made me use ten years of my life that I spent stupidly waiting for genius.

—Stendhal

**TEACHING TIP**

Ask students to compare Shawn's research paper to their own research paper in progress. In particular, ask students to reflect on how polished Shawn's final draft appears. Encourage students to use the annotated notes to help them with their own final draft preparation. This concrete example of student writing should dispel some of the myths and fears associated with research paper writing. You may want to use the Research Portfolio handout from Chapter 36 of the Annotated Instructor's Edition. You might also ask students to do a peer-review exercise on Shawn's paper.

**QUOTATION: ON WRITING**

No one can write decently who is distrustful of the reader's intelligence, or whose attitude is patronizing.

—E. B. White

APA

---

## TEACHING TIP

Christopher L. Aberson and David P. Nalbone published an article "Refining Use of APA Style: Eliminating Common Errors" on the Psi Chi Web site, The National Honor Society in Psychology, which reviews the common errors in student usage of APA style; see <http://www.psichi.org/pubs/articles/article_578.asp>.

## QUOTATION: ON WRITING

Writing is thinking on paper. Anyone who thinks clearly should be able to write clearly—about any subject at all.

—William Zinsser

## QUOTATION: ON WRITING

I have the words already. What I am seeking is the perfect order of words in the sentence. You can see for yourself how many different ways they might be arranged.

—James Joyce

## QUOTATION: ON WRITING

Until you understand a writer's ignorance, presume yourself ignorant of his understanding.

—Samuel Taylor Coleridge

## QUOTATION: ON WRITING

If you would not be forgotten,
As soon as you are dead and rotten,
Either write things worthy reading,
Or do things worth the writing.

—Benjamin Franklin

## QUOTATION: ON READING

The readers and the hearers like my books,
But yet some writers cannot them digest;
But what care I? For when I make a feast
I would my guests should praise it, not the
    cooks.

—Sir John Harington

## QUOTATION: ON WRITING

[The writing process] is sort of like when you've got no electricity and you've gotten up in the middle of the night to find the bathroom,

---

## Quick Reference 37.1     (continued)

When citing electronic or online sources, include the name(s) of author(s) the same way as for books and journals. Always include the publication date in parentheses after the author(s) name(s), followed by a period. Titles of books, periodicals, and whole Web sites should be italicized; titles of articles or pages in a Web site should not use italics. Articles retrieved online should always list the volume and issue number; this is a change from previous APA guidelines.

You then include retrieval information for the electronic source. For articles with DOI (Digital Object Identifier) numbers, this is simply the letters "doi" followed by a colon, then the number. Figure 37.1 (page 670) shows how to find publication information in a journal article with a DOI. Figure 37.1a shows how the source is listed in a database. Figure 37.1b shows the actual page of the article itself. We illustrate this below and in example 39.

For nearly all other references, retrieval information begins with the words "Retrieved from," sometimes followed by the date you actually retrieved it, then the URL and, occasionally, additional information, such as database names. We provide more detailed information about documenting electronic resources beginning on page 676.

In the meantime, however, here are three examples of electronic source entries. The first is for an article that does not have a DOI number. Because it is for a permanent version of the article, you don't include a date in your "retrieved from" statement.

| AUTHOR | DATE | ARTICLE TITLE |
|---|---|---|

Overbye, D. (2005, June 28). Remembrance of things future: The mystery

|  | ONLINE NEWSPAPER TITLE | RETRIEVAL INFORMATION |
|---|---|---|

of time. *The New York Times.* Retrieved from http://www.nytimes.com

Notice that the only punctuation in the URL is part of the address. Don't add a period after a URL.

The second example is for an electronic article that has a DOI number. Note that this is for the article in Figure 37.1.

| AUTHOR | DATE | ARTICLE TITLE |
|---|---|---|

Agliata, A.K., Tantelff-Dunn, S., & Renk, K. (2007). Interpretation of teasing

|  | PUBLICATION INFORMATION |
|---|---|

during early adolescence. *Journal of Clinical Psychology, 63*(1), 23–30,

| DOI |
|---|

doi: 10.1002/jclp.20302

continued >>

| Quick Reference 37.1 | (continued) |
| --- | --- |

A third example is for an article from a Web site. Because Web sites may change, the retrieval statement includes the date retrieved as well as the URL. This example has no author.

ARTICLE TITLE        DATE

Think again: Men and women share cognitive skills. (2006).

PUBLICATION INFORMATION        RETRIEVAL INFORMATION

American Psychological Association. Retrieved January 18, 2006,

URL

from http://www.psychologymatters.org/thinkagain.html

The following samples of entries may appear in an APA References list. You can find others in the *Publication Manual of the American Psychological Association* or at http://www.apastyle.org. For quick help deciding which example you should follow, see the decision flowchart in Figure 37.2 (page 671).

**PRINT REFERENCES—BOOKS**

**1. Book by One Author—APA**

Note that all entries use the hanging indent style: The first line of an entry is flush to the left margin, and all other lines in the entry are indented one-half inch.

Bradway, B. (2002). *Pink houses and family taverns*. Bloomington: Indiana University Press.

**2. Book by Two Authors—APA**

Edin, K., & Kefalas, M. (2005). *Promises I can keep: Why poor women put motherhood before marriage*. Berkeley: University of California Press.

**3. Book by Three or More Authors—APA**

For a book by three to six authors, include all the authors' names. For a book by more than six authors, use only the first six names followed by *et al.*

Lynam, J. K., Ndiritu, C. G., & Mbabu, A. N. (2004). *Transformation of agricultural research systems in Africa: Lessons from Kenya*. East Lansing: Michigan State University Press.

feeling your way along in the dark. I can't hardly tell you what I do because I really don't know.
—Carolyn Chute

**QUOTATION: ON WRITING**
I have long since decided if you wait for the perfect time to write, you'll never write. There is no time that isn't flawed somehow.
—Margaret Atwood

**QUOTATION: ON WRITING**
No tears in the writer, no tears in the reader. No surprise for the writer, no surprise for the reader.
—Robert Frost

**QUOTATION: ON READING**
A book is like a garden carried in the pocket.
—Chinese proverb

**QUOTATION: ON WRITING**
Writing comes more easily if you have something to say.
—Sholem Asch

**QUOTATION: ON WRITING**
How can you sit down to write until you have stood up to live?
—Henry David Thoreau

APA

### 18. Reprint of an Older Book—APA

O'Brien, F. (1998). *At Swim-Two-Birds*. Normal, IL: Dalkey Archive Press.
(Original work published 1939)

You can find republishing information on the copyright page.

### 19. Book in a Series—APA

Give the title of the book but not of the whole series.

Goldman, D. J. (1995). *Women writers and World War I*. New York: Macmillan.

### 20. Book with a Title Within a Title—APA

Never italicize a title within a title, even though it would appear in italic typeface if it were by itself.

Lumiansky, R. M., & Baker, H. (Eds.). (1968). *Critical approaches to six major English works:* Beowulf *through* Paradise Lost. Philadelphia: University of Pennsylvania Press.

### 21. Government Publication—APA

Use the complete name of a government agency as author when no specific person is named.

U.S. Congress. House Subcommittee on Health and Environment of the Committee on Commerce. (1999). *The nursing home resident protection amendments of 1999* (99-0266-P). Washington, DC: U.S. Government Printing Office.

U.S. Senate Special Committee on Aging. (1998). *The risk of malnutrition in nursing homes* (98-0150-P). Washington, DC: U.S. Government Printing Office.

### 22. Published Proceedings of a Conference—APA

Rocha, L., Yaeger, L., Bedau, M., Floreano, D., Goldstone, R. & Vespignani, A. (Eds.). (2006, June). *Artificial life X: Proceedings of the tenth international conference on the simulation and synthesis of living systems*. Bloomington, IN. Cambridge: MIT Press.

## PRINT REFERENCES—PERIODICALS

### 23. Article in a Journal with Continuous Pagination—APA

Give the volume number, italicized after the journal title. In the 2001 edition of the APA style manual, only the volume number appears. The new (2007) APA style for electronic references directs writers also to include the issue number in parentheses, immediately after the volume number. We have followed that new practice in the example below.

Tyson, P. (1998). The psychology of women. *Journal of the American Psychoanalytic Association, 46*(3), 361–364.

### 24. Article in a Journal That Pages Each Issue Separately—APA

Give the volume number, italicized with the journal title. Give the issue number in parentheses; don't italicize it and leave no space before it. Note that the new APA practice now uses this style for journals with continuous pagination, too (see item 23).

Adler-Kassner, L., & Estrem, H. (2003). Rethinking research writing: Public
   literacy in the composition classroom. *WPA: Writing Program
   Administration, 26*(3), 119–131.

### 25. Signed Article in a Weekly or Biweekly Periodical—APA

Give year, month, and day for a periodical published every week or every two weeks. Don't use the abbreviation *p.* (or *pp.*) for magazines or journals.

Brink, S. (2005, March 28). Eat this now! *U.S. News & World Report,* 56–58.

### 26. Signed Article in a Monthly or Bimonthly Periodical—APA

Give the year and month(s) for a periodical published every month or every other month. Insert the volume number, italicized with the periodical title. Put the issue number in parentheses; don't italicize it, and don't put a space before it.

Fallows, J. (2008, January/February). The $1.4 trillion question. *The Atlantic,
   301*(1), 36–48.

### 27. Unsigned Article in a Weekly or Monthly Periodical—APA

The price is wrong. (2003, August 2). *The Economist, 368,* 58–59.

### 28. Signed Article in a Daily Newspaper—APA

Use the abbreviation *p.* (or *pp.* for more than one page) for items from newspapers.

Green, P. (2008, January 31). The slow life picks up speed. *The New York Times,*
   p. D1.

### 29. Unsigned Article in a Daily Newspaper—APA

Oscars ready plans to deal with strike. (2008, January 31). *The Denver Post,* p. B3.

### 30. Editorial, Letter to the Editor, or Review—APA

Primary considerations. (2008, January 27). [Editorial]. *The Washington Post,* p. B6.

Finanger, E. (2008, February). [Letter to the editor]. *Outside,* 14.

Shenk, D. (2003, Spring). Toolmaker, brain builder. [Review of the book *Beyond
   Big Blue: Building the computer that defeated the world chess champion*].
   *The American Scholar, 72,* 150–152.

### 31. Article in a Looseleaf Collection of Reprinted Articles—APA

Hayden, T. (2002). The age of robots. In E. Goldstein (Ed.), *Applied Science 2002. SIRS 2002*, Article 66. (Reprinted from *U.S. News & World Report*, pp. 44–50, 2001, April 23).

### OTHER PRINT REFERENCES

### 32. Published and Unpublished Letters—APA

In the APA system, unpublished letters are considered personal communication inaccessible to general readers, so they don't appear in the References list. Personal communications are cited only in the body of the paper (see also item 66).

Williams, W. C. (1935). Letter to his son. In L. Grunwald & S. J. Adler (Eds.), *Letters of the century: America 1900–1999* (pp. 225–226). New York: Dial Press.

### 33. Map or Chart—APA

*Colorado Front Range Mountain Bike Topo Map* [Map]. (2001). Nederland, CO: Latitude 40.

### 34. Report or Pamphlet—APA

National Commission on Writing in America's Schools and Colleges. (2003). *The neglected "R": The need for a writing revolution* [Report]. New York: College Board.

Student Environmental Coalition. (2005). *Reduce, reuse, recycle* [Brochure]. Normal, IL: Author.

### 35. Legal Source—APA

Include the name of the case, the citation (usually a volume number, publication title, and page) or a record number, the name of the court deciding the case (if other than the US Supreme Court), and the year of the decision. The following example shows the citation for a published case. See Appendix D of the APA *Publication Manual* for other types of legal citations.

Brown v. Board of Educ., 347 U.S. 483 (1954).

### ELECTRONIC AND ONLINE SOURCES

In general, APA recommends giving the same information, in the same order, as you would for a print source: author name(s), date of publication, title, and publication information (title, volume, issue, pages). Then you add as much retrieval information as others will need to locate the source. This retrieval information may include a DOI number (see example 39) or it may consist of a "Retrieved from" statement along with a URL. In certain cases, you may also need to include the date you retrieved the information.

APA

- DOI (Direct Object Identifier): These numerical codes are sometimes assigned to online journal articles and are typically located on the first page of the online article or included in the database. The DOI for an article will be the same even if the article appears on many different Web sites. As a result, you don't use a URL or a "retrieved from" statement if a source contains a DOI. Include the number after the publication information. Note: This is a change from earlier APA formats.

- URL: You should include the full URL for most works accessed online, including any articles that don't have a DOI. If the material is only available by search or subscription, include the URL of the home page up to the first slash. If a URL must be divided on two or more lines, only break the address before slashes or punctuation marks (except within "http://"). Don't use a hyphen, underlining, italics, angle brackets, or an end period.

- Databases: A retrieval line is not needed for materials located on widely available databases like library subscription services. If, however, the source is difficult to locate, include the name of the database in the retrieval line.

- Retrieval date: Include the date you retrieved the information only if the item does not have a publication date, is from an online reference book, or is likely to be changed in the future (such as a prepublication version of an article, a Web page, or a Wiki). Note: This is a change from the previous APA style. APA recommends citing the "archival" or permanent version of a source whenever possible. Usually, an archival version is one that either has appeared in print, has a volume and issue number, or has a specific publication date. APA has determined that retrieval dates are unnecessary for archival versions.

Treat information from an online source that your readers can't readily retrieve for themselves—for example, an e-mail message—as a personal communication. Never include it in your References list; instead, cite it in the text with a parenthetical notation saying it's a personal communication. (Also see example 66.) If you have a scholarly reason to cite a message from a newsgroup, forum, or electronic mailing list that is available in an electronic archive, then see examples 52 or 53.

## ELECTRONIC BOOKS

### 36. Entire Electronic Book—APA

Provide information about the print version, if available. The retrieval statement gives the specific URL of the work.

Adams, H. (1918). *The education of Henry Adams.* New York: Houghton Mifflin.
   Retrieved from http://www.columbia.edu/acis/bartleby/159/index/html

### 37. Chapter from Electronic Book—APA

Gembris, H. (2006). The development of musical abilities. In R. Colwell (Ed).
*MENC handbook of musical cognition and development.* New York:
Oxford University Press (pp.124–164). Retrieved from Ebrary database
at http://site.ebrary.com.bianca.penlib.du.edu/

In this example, the name of the database (Ebrary) is given, along with the initial part of the URL where the book was specifically found.

### 38. Thesis or Dissertation—APA

Stuart, G. A. (2006). *Exploring the Harry Potter book series: A study of
adolescent reading motivation.* Retrieved from ProQuest Digital
Dissertations. (AAT 3246355)

The number in parentheses at the end is the accession number.

### ELECTRONIC JOURNALS

### 39. Article with DOI Assigned—APA

Gurung, R., & Vespia, K. (2007). Looking good, teaching well? Linking liking,
looks, and learning. *Teaching of Psychology, 34*(1), 5-10. doi:
10.1207/s15328023top3401_2

### 40. Article with No DOI Assigned—APA

Pollard, R. (2002). Evidence of a reduced home field advantage when a team
moves to a new stadium. *Journal of Sports Sciences 20*(12), 969–974.
Retrieved from http://0-find.galegroup.com.bianca.penlib.du.edu:
80/itx/start.do?prodId=AONE

No retrieval date is included because the final version of the article is being referenced.

### 41. In-press Article—APA

*In-press* means that an article has been accepted for publication but has not yet been published in its final form. Therefore, there is no publication date, and the retrieved from statement includes a date.

George, S. (In press). How accurately should we estimate the anatomical
source of exhaled nitric oxide? *Journal of Applied Physiology.*
doi:10.1152/japplphysiol.00111.2008. Retrieved February, 2008 from
http://jap.physiology.org/papbyrecent.shtml

**OTHER ELECTRONIC PERIODICALS**

### 42. Newspaper Article—APA

Wilson, J. (2005, March 5). EPA fights waste site near river. *Los Angeles Times*.
Retrieved from http://www.latimes.com/news/science/environment
/la-me-moab05.html

### 43. Online Magazine Content Not Found in Print Version—APA

Shulman, M. (2008, January 23). 12 diseases that altered history. [Online
exclusive]. *U.S. News and World Report*. Retrieved January 28, 2007,
from http://health.usnews.com/articles/health/2008/01/03/12-diseases-
that-altered-history.html

### 44. Web Page or Article on Web Site—APA

Think again: Men and women share cognitive skills. (2006). *American
Psychological Association*. Retrieved January 18, 2006, from
http://www.psychologymatters.org/thinkagain.html

**ELECTRONIC REFERENCE MATERIALS**

### 45. Online Encyclopedia—APA

Turing test. (2008). In *Encyclopædia Britannica*. Retrieved February 9, 2008,
from http://www.britannica.com/bps/topic/609757/Turing-test

Because the reference is to a work that may change, a retrieval date is included.

### 46. Online Dictionary—APA

Asparagus. (n.d.). *Merriam-Webster's online dictionary*. Retrieved February 9,
2008, from http://dictionary.reference.com/browse/asparagus

### 47. Online Handbook—APA

Gembris, H. (2006). The development of musical abilities. In R. Colwell (Ed).
*MENC handbook of musical cognition and development*. New York:
Oxford University Press. 124–164. Retrieved October 8, 2007, from
http://0-site.ebrary.com.bianca.penlib.du.edu/lib/udenver
/Doc?id=10160594

### 48. Wiki—APA

Machine learning. (n.d.). Retrieved January 5, 2008, from Artificial Intelligence
Wiki: http://www.ifi.unizh.ch/ailab/aiwiki/aiw.cgi

Note that (n.d.) means "no date."

APA

**ELECTRONIC ABSTRACTS**

### 49. Abstract from Secondary Source—APA

Walther, J.B., Van Der Heide, B., Kim, S., Westerman, D., & Tong, S. (2008). The role of friends' appearance and behavior on evaluations of individuals on Facebook: Are we known by the company we keep? *Human Communication Research 34*(1), 28–49. Abstract retrieved April 20, 2008 from PsycINFO database.

### 50. Abstract Submitted for Meeting or Poster Session—APA

Wang, H. (2007). Dust storms originating in the northern hemisphere of Mars. AGU 2007 Fall Meeting. Abstract retrieved from http://www.agu.org /meetings/fm07/?content=program

**OTHER ELECTRONIC REFERENCES**

### 51. Personal or Professional Web Site—APA

Hesse, Doug. (2008, November). Home page. Retrieved November 21, 2008, from http://http://portfolio.du.edu/dhesse

Association for the Advancement of Artificial Intelligence. (2008, March). Retrieved March 17, 2008, from http://www.aaai.org

Because material on a Web site may change, use a retrieved from date.

### 52. Message on a Newsgroup, Online Forum, or Discussion Group—APA

Boyle, F. (2002, October 11). Psyche: Cemi field theory: The hard problem made easy [Msg 1]. Message posted to news://sci.psychology.consciousness

### 53. Message on an Electronic Mailing List (Listserv)—APA

Haswell, R. (2005, October 17). A new graphic/text interface. Message posted to Writing Program Administrators electronic mailing list, archived at http://lists.asu.edu/archives/wpa-l.html

APA advises using *electronic mailing list,* as Listserv is the name of a specific software.

### 54. Course Home Page—APA

St. Germain, S. (2003, Summer). Myths and fairytales: From *Inanna* to *Edward Scissorhands.* Retrieved February 20, 2005, from http://www.public.iastate. edu/~sgermain/531.homepage.html

### 55. Blog (Web Log) Post—APA

McLemee, S. (2008, January 1). To whom it may concern. Message posted to
http://www.artsjournal.com/quickstudy/

### 56. Video Web Log Post—APA

APA treats every video posted online as a Video Web log, which suggests a regular series of postings. In fact, many videos are not produced in Web log format. Still, we present the APA format. Also see 59, for online television programs or movies.

Tobias, R. (2008, February 7). *Ranching the new West*. [Video file]. Video posted
to http://www.lifeonterra.com/

Wesch, M. (2007, January 31). *Web 2.0 ... the machine is us/ing us*. [Video file].
Video posted to http://www.youtube.com/watch?v=6gmP4nk0EOE

### 57. Online Digital Recording—APA

Komunyakaa, Y. (2005). My father's love letters. Retrieved March 7, 2005, from
the Academy of American Poets Web site: http://www.poets.org
/poems/poems.cfm?prmID=2065

### 58. Audio Podcast—APA

Business marketing with podcast: What marketing professionals should know
(2005, October 13). *Podblaze*. Podcast retrieved http://business.podblaze.com/

### 59. Online Television Program—APA

If producers or directors can be identified, list them in the author position. Include the episode title, if any, and the title of the series. If it is a one-time program, list only the title.

Bender, J. (Director/Producer). (2008, January 30). The beginning of the end. *Lost*.
Video retrieved February 1, 2008, from http://dynamic.abc.go.com
/streaming/landing

### 60. Online Advertisement—APA

Samsung. (2005, November). [Advertisement]. Retrieved from
http://rollingstone.com

### 61. Computer Software or Video Game—APA

Provide an author name, if available. Standard software (Microsoft Word) and program languages (C++) don't need to be given in the References list.

*Guitar hero III: Legends of rock*. (2007). [Video game]. Santa Monica: Activision.

APA

### 62. Brochure—APA

US Department of Agriculture. (2007). *Organic foods and labels*. [Brochure].
Retrieved December 8, 2008, from http://www.ams.usda.gov/nop
/Consumers/brochure.html

### 63. Policy Brief—APA

Haskins, R., Haskins, R., Paxson, C., & Donahue, E. (2006). *Fighting obesity in
the public schools*. Retrieved from http://www.brookings.edu/~/media
/Files/rc/papers/2006/spring_childrenfamilies_haskins/20060314foc.pdf

### 64. Presentation Slides—APA

Alaska Conservation Solutions. (2006). *Montana Global Warming* [PowerPoint
slides]. Retrieved from http://www.alaskaconservationsolutions.com/acs
/presentations.html

### 65. Graphs, Maps, Other Images—APA

New York Times Online. (2005, September 24). *Hurricane Rita*. [Interactive
map]. Retrieved from http://www.nytimes.com/packages/html/national
/20050923_RITA_GRAPHIC/index.html

### OTHER NONPRINT REFERENCES
### 66. Interview—APA

In APA style, a personal interview is considered personal communication and
is not included in the References list. Cite the interview in the text with a parenthetical notation saying that it's a personal communication.

Randi Friedman (personal communication, June 30, 2007) endorses this view.

Because a published interview is recoverable by readers, treat it as you would a
journal or magazine article, depending on its place of publication.

Zoglin, R. (2003, December 15). Ten questions for Oprah Winfrey. *Time*, 8.

### 67. Lecture, Speech, or Address—APA

Kennedy, J. F. (1960, September 12). Speech to the Greater Houston Ministerial
Association, Rice Hotel, Houston, TX.

### 68. Motion Picture—APA

Capra, F. (Director/Producer). (1934). *It happened one night* [Motion picture].
United States: Columbia Pictures.

Capra, F. (Director/Producer). (1999). *It happened one night* [Videocassette].
(Original motion picture released 1934)

Madden, J. (Director), Parfitt, D., Gigliotti, D., Weinstein, H., Zwick, E., & Norman, M. (Producers). (2003). *Shakespeare in love* [DVD]. (Original motion picture released 1998)

### 69. Music Recording—APA

Smetana, B. (1975). *My country* [Recorded by the Czech Philharmonic Orchestra with K. Anserl conducting]. [Record]. London: Vanguard Records. (1975)

Springsteen, B. (2002). Lonesome day. On *The rising* [CD]. New York: Columbia Records.

Radiohead. (2007). Jigsaw falling into place. On *Rainbows* [MP3]. Radiohead.

### 70. Live Performance—APA

Miller, A. (Author), & McLean, C. (Director). (2005, September 27). *All my sons* [Theatrical performance]. Center for the Performing Arts, Normal, IL.

### 71. Work of Art, Photograph, or Musical Composition—APA

Cassatt, M. (1891). *La toilette* [Artwork]. Chicago: Art Institute of Chicago.

Mydans, C. (1999, October 21–November 28). *General Douglas MacArthur landing at Luzon, 1945* [Photograph]. New York: Soho Triad Fine Art Gallery.

Schubert, F. (1822). *Unfinished symphony* [Musical composition].

### 72. Radio or Television Broadcast—APA

Burns, K. (Writer/Producer), & Barnes, P. (Producer). (1999, November 8). *Not for ourselves alone: The story of Elizabeth Cady Stanton and Susan B. Anthony* [Television broadcast]. New York and Washington, DC: Public Broadcasting Service.

If you're citing a television series produced by and seen on only one station, cite its call letters.

### 73. Information Services—APA

Chiang, L. H. (1993). *Beyond the language: Native Americans' nonverbal communication.* (ERIC Document Reproduction Service No. ED368540)

### 74. Advertisement—APA

Swim at home. (2005). [Advertisement]. *The American Scholar 74*(2), 2.

### 75. Images—APA

If you're reproducing an image in your paper, follow the guidelines for graphics in item 16 in 37c. Include the citation in the body of your paper. If you're only referring to an image, cite the photographer or illustrator (if known), the title (or a brief description of the image), and source information.

Arthur Miller in 1961. (2005). [Photograph]. *The American Scholar 74*(2), 123.

## 37g What are APA format guidelines for research papers?

Ask whether your instructor has instructions for preparing a final draft. If not, you can use the APA guidelines here. For an illustration of these guidelines, see the student paper in 37h.2.

### GENERAL INSTRUCTIONS—APA

Use 8 1/2-by-11-inch white paper. The APA *Publication Manual* recommends double-spacing for a final manuscript of a student research paper. Set at least a one-inch margin on the left (slightly more if you submit your paper in a binder) and leave no less than one inch on the right and at the bottom.

Leave one-half inch from the top edge of the paper to the title-and-page-number line (*header*). Leave another one-half inch (or one inch from the top edge of the paper) before the next line on the page, whether that's a heading (such as "Abstract" or "Notes") or a line of your paper.

❶ **Alert:** Most word-processing programs set the top and bottom margins at one inch as their default. Also, they generally set the "header" function at a default of one-half inch. Therefore, formatting the margins for your paper is probably less troublesome than it might seem. You simply need to check the default settings. ●

Use indents of one-half inch for the first line of all paragraphs, except in an abstract, the first line of which isn't indented. Don't justify the right margin. Indent footnotes one-half inch.

### ORDER OF PARTS—APA

Number all pages consecutively. Use this order for the parts of your paper:

1. Title page
2. Abstract (if required)
3. Body of the paper
4. References
5. Appendixes, if any
6. Footnotes, if any
7. Attachments, if any (questionnaires, data sheets, or other material your instructor asks you to include)

### TITLE-AND-PAGE-NUMBER LINE FOR ALL PAGES—APA

Use a title-and-page-number line on all pages of your paper. Leaving a margin of one-half inch from the top edge of the paper, type the title (use a shortened version if necessary), leave a five-character space, and then type the page number. End the title-and-page-number line one inch from the right edge of the paper. Ask whether your instructor wants you to include your last name in this title-and-page-number line. The "header" feature on a word-processing program will help you create the title-and-page-number line easily.

### TITLE PAGE—APA

Use a separate title page. On it, begin with the title-and-page-number line described above, using the numeral *1* for this first page. Then, center the complete title vertically and horizontally on the page. Use two or more double-spaced lines if the title is long. Don't italicize or underline the title or enclose it in quotation marks. On the next line, center your name, and below that center the course title and section, your professor's name, and the date.

**⚠ Alerts:** (1) Use the following guidelines for capitalizing the title of your own paper and for capitalizing titles you mention in the body of your paper. (For capitalization of titles in the References list, see Quick Reference 37.1.)

(2) Use a capital letter for the first word of your title and for the first word of a subtitle, if any. Start every noun, pronoun, verb, adverb, and adjective with a capital letter. Capitalize each main word in a hyphenated compound word (two or more words used together to express one idea): *Father-in-Law, Self-Consciousness.*

(3) Don't capitalize articles (*a, an, the*) unless one of the other capitalization rules applies. Don't capitalize prepositions and conjunctions unless they are four or more letters long. Don't capitalize the word *to* used in an infinitive. ●

### ABSTRACT—APA

See 37d for advice about what to include in an abstract of your paper. Type the abstract on a separate page, using the numeral *2* in the title-and-page-number line. Center the word *Abstract* one inch from the top of the paper. Don't italicize or underline it or enclose it in quotation marks. Double-space below this title, and then start your abstract, double-spacing it. Don't indent the first line.

### SET-OFF QUOTATIONS—APA

Set off (display in BLOCK-STYLE form) quotations of forty words or more. Double-space to start a new line for the quoted words, indenting each line of the (double-spaced) quotation one-half inch or five spaces from the left margin. Don't enclose the quoted words in quotation marks.

If you're quoting part of a paragraph or one complete paragraph, don't indent the first line more than one-half inch. But if you quote two or more

APA

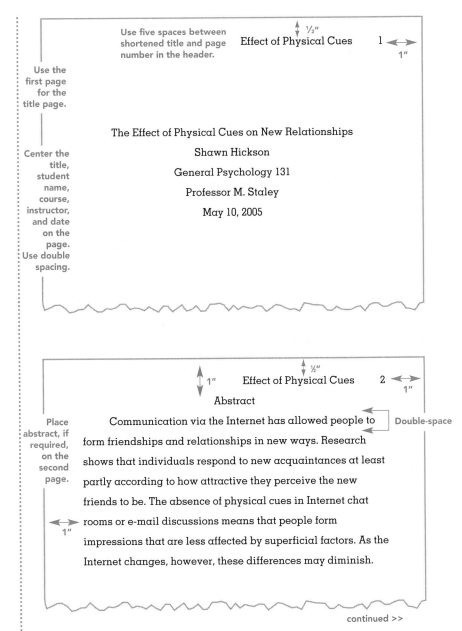

Use five spaces between shortened title and page number in the header.

½"

Effect of Physical Cues       1

1"

Use the first page for the title page.

The Effect of Physical Cues on New Relationships

Shawn Hickson

General Psychology 131

Professor M. Staley

May 10, 2005

Center the title, student name, course, instructor, and date on the page. Use double spacing.

½"

1"       Effect of Physical Cues       2

1"

Abstract

Place abstract, if required, on the second page.

Communication via the Internet has allowed people to form friendships and relationships in new ways. Research shows that individuals respond to new acquaintances at least partly according to how attractive they perceive the new friends to be. The absence of physical cues in Internet chat rooms or e-mail discussions means that people form impressions that are less affected by superficial factors. As the Internet changes, however, these differences may diminish.

Double-space

1"

continued >>

Effect of Physical Cues 3

APA STYLE:
1-inch
margins;
double-
space
throughout

The Effect of Physical Cues on New Relationships

Over the past 20 years, the Internet has enabled people to meet others from around the world with a few simple keystrokes. Occasionally, these interactions extend beyond the confines of chat rooms and e-mail discussions, so that individuals arrange to meet in person. Of course, people have learned to be cautious because others online can easily misrepresent themselves and their intentions. Nonetheless, lasting friendships, romances, and even marriages have resulted from first interactions that have happened online. Surprisingly, research shows that compared with people who meet face to face, those who meet on the Internet develop a greater liking for each other (McKenna, Green, & Gleason, 2003). This result is an example of a larger phenomenon: The presence or absence of physical characteristics during first meetings can influence how people respond to each other.

INTRODUCTION

APA-STYLE
IN-TEXT
CITATION:
Doesn't
require
page num-
bers for a
paraphrase
or summary;
check
whether
your
instructor
prefers that
you include
them

THESIS
STATE-
MENT:
Gives
paper's
focus

Judging People by Appearances

FIRST
HEADING

It can be troubling to know that something as shallow as someone's physical attractiveness can affect how people treat that person. However, the truth is that even if people do not mean to judge others based on their appearance, they tend to do so. Dion, Berscheid, and Walster (1972) showed research participants pictures of stereotypically attractive and unattractive individuals and then asked them to judge the people in the photographs according to several personality traits. The researchers found that the more attractive a person was judged to be, the more desirable traits that person was judged to have. For example, people might believe that

PARA-
GRAPH 2:
Provides
background
information

APA-STYLE
INTE-
GRATED
CITATION:
Author
name cited
in text; date
cited in par-
entheses

continued >>

(Proportions shown in this paper are adjusted to fit space limitations of this book. Follow actual dimensions discussed in this book and your instructor's directions.)

beautiful women are smarter or that handsome men are more clever. Several studies found that individuals assume that attractive people will agree with them more often than those who are unattractive; they assume that the attractive person will be more like them (Miyake & Zuckerman, 1993).

**PARAGRAPH 3: Provides further examples of thesis**

Even when people are young, appearance colors how others perceive them. Studies of preschoolers show that both peers and teachers treat children differently on the basis of their physical appearances. Both expect attractive children to be more active socially, and teachers believe that attractive children have more academic potential (Kachel, 1996). Perhaps more astounding, some controversial research shows that children's physical appearances may affect how their very own parents treat them (Bakalar, 2005).

**PARAGRAPH 4: Provides information and bridges to next paragraph**

Attractiveness has a different importance for men and women. While both sexes value physical attractiveness in brief relationships, men tend to view it as vital in long-term relationships. In contrast, women tend to regard other qualities more highly, especially financial stability and high social status (Singh, 2004).

**PARAGRAPH 5: Summarizes research findings**

However, for men and women alike, physical cues at the first meeting can shape not only impressions but also behaviors. Snyder, Tanke, and Berscheid (1977) showed male participants a picture of either an attractive or an unattractive female and then asked the men to rate her personality traits. Results of this initial rating were very similar with those obtained by Dion et al. (1972). Snyder's group next took the study one step further. Each male participant then had a phone conversation with a female participant who he thought was

continued >>

Effect of Physical Cues     5

the female from the picture. In these conversations, men treated their phone partners as if the women possessed the characteristics they believed went along with the photograph. However, the men really knew nothing about the women; they had assigned the women traits simply on the basis of a photograph. Even more interesting, women responded in a manner that was consistent with the images that were being projected onto them. Attractive women who were treated as if they were unattractive actually behaved as if they were, and vice versa. What happened was a clear example of a self-fulfilling prophecy (Snyder et al., 1977). Judgments based on appearance clouded other realities.

Meeting on the Internet

Meeting people online, especially through e-mail or in a chat room, obviously differs from meeting them face to face because there are no physical cues, only other people's words. Do people meeting in that environment engage one another differently? A study conducted by McKenna et al. (2003) suggests that they do. McKenna and colleagues divided participants into two groups: an experimental group and a control group. All participants had two separate conversations, one in person and the other online. Both conversations took place with the same person. Those in the control group knew this, but those in the experimental group believed they were talking with two different people. Participants in both groups then rated the quality of the interactions on three factors: (a) the quality of the conversations, (b) the degree to which they felt they had gotten to know the other person, and (c) how well they liked the other person in general. For the control groups,

**Replaces names with** *et al.* **because this is second reference to same work with multiple authors**

**SECOND HEADING**
**PARA-GRAPH 6: Explains research found on the Internet**

**Creates clarity by using letters in parentheses to identify factors**

continued >>

APA

Effect of Physical Cues     6

the ratings were similar in all categories, for both in-person and online conversations. However, differences emerged with the participants who thought they had been interacting with two different people, not the same person: They consistently rated the Internet partner higher in all three categories.

PARA-
GRAPH 7:
Interprets
findings
summarized
in previous
paragraph

One probable explanation for this occurrence is that Internet interactions do away with traditional physical judgments. Attractiveness, extreme shyness, speech impediments, and many other superficial factors can hinder people from expressing their true selves and accepting others who are deficient in one area or another (McKenna et al., 2003). Because early judgments determine how two people will interact, a physical meeting makes it harder for some individuals to become comfortable and disclose themselves at the same level as they would in a situation where physical cues don't matter.

PARA-
GRAPH 8:
Explains
interests of
people
meeting
online

By the time people engage in online romantic relationships, according to researcher Malin Sveningsson (2002), they have already established a written relationship based on common interests. They know each other on a basis other than that of physical characteristics. Most people who enter chat rooms do so with the hope of making "contact with people, getting into a rewarding discussion, or just small-talking and having a good time in general" (p. 49). Those who

APA-STYLE
IN-TEXT
CITATION:
Requires
page
number for
direct
quotation;
uses *p.* not
*page*

meet on Internet chat sites or electronic mailing lists nearly always come together over a shared interest. A chat room frequenter named Richard explained his reasons for taking part in online conversations: "When you enter a place like that, you just want somebody to talk to . . . so you actively [look] for

continued >>

Effect of Physical Cues        7

people who [have] something to say. And all the time you [make] comments just to find someone who [has] something to tell" (p. 50). Women and men are nearly equal in their use of the Internet for purposes of community. The Cyber Dialogue group found that about 27% of women and 31% of men first went to the Internet to "join an online community" and that 85% of women and 82% of men came to believe that "the Internet community is an important part" of their lives (Hawfield & Lyons, 1998). It appears, then, that the primary motivation for both men and women is not physical but rather communicative.

Attractiveness is hardly the only physical quality by which men and women judge others. Broad features of identity such as race, gender, and ethnicity can also trigger uninformed responses. Researcher Lisa Nakamura (2002) found that when a person's race is revealed on the Internet, he or she can be just as subject to prejudicial assumptions as if the reality had been revealed face to face. Because of this, some people online deliberately try to mask their race or sex. They want others to judge them by what they say and think rather than by how they look, especially in a first encounter.

Whether Internet communication will continue to support first meetings that occur purely in writing is uncertain. With the increased use of digital images and audio, the Internet has begun to provide more and more physical cues. Participants in chat rooms tend to request images earlier as a sign of interest. People can post false photographs or videos, of course, but deception complicates any desired face-to-face meeting later on. Further, the sound of a person's voice shapes others'

Shawn uses brackets in quotation to show that she (not the speaker) has altered wording to improve clarity

Uses statistics to illustrate example

PARA-GRAPH 9: Gives other factors that influence relationships

PARA-GRAPH 10: Explains how increased use of images and sounds changes nature of online meetings

continued >>

APA

Effect of Physical Cues          8

perceptions. When voice communication over the Internet becomes more prevalent, it is likely that our stereotypical notions will return. Dr. Clifford Nass of Stanford University has predicted that when voice becomes a part of online interaction, people will "apply gender stereotypes" (Eisenberg, 2000, para. 6). Nass says that people tend to interpret the female voice as being "less accurate," with deeper male voices projecting authority. Some voices are perceived as more attractive than others, too.

Conclusions

Research on Internet relationships suggests that communication without visual cues can increase people's acceptance of one another. In face-to-face meetings, people form impressions based solely on physical appearance, impressions that influence both the way they treat others and the way those people respond. People who are treated well, for example, tend to take on positive characteristics. Because Internet conversations rely more heavily on the quality of communication than on superficial factors, meeting online allows people to suspend judgments based on appearance. This advantage may disappear as images and sounds increasingly accompany online meetings. Perhaps society would be healthier if people judged others not by their looks but by their character as expressed in words and ideas; however, the current tendency to treat stereotypically attractive and unattractive people differently shows the remoteness of that ideal.

continued >>

Effect of Physical Cues        9

References

Bakalar, N. (2005, May 3). Ugly children may get parental short shrift. *The New York Times*, p. F7.

Dion, K., Berscheid, E., & Walster, E. (1972). What is beautiful is good. *Journal of Personality and Social Psychology, 24*(3), 285–290.

Eisenberg, A. (2000, October 12). Mars and Venus on the Net: Gender stereotypes prevail. *New York Times*. Retrieved from http://www.nytimes.com/2000/10/12/technology /12VOIC.html

Hawfield, K., & Lyons, E. (1998). Conventional wisdom about women and Internet use: Refuting traditional perceptions. Retrieved March 25, 2005, from http://elab.vanderbilt.edu/research/papers/html /studentprojects/women/conventional_wisdom.html

Kachel, J. (1996, March). Good looks count during childhood. *Brown University Child and Adolescent Newsletter, 12*(3). Retrieved April 7, 2005, from Academic Search Elite database.

McKenna, K. Y., Green, A. S., & Gleason, M. E. (2003). Relationship formation on the Internet: What's the big attraction? *Journal of Social Issues, 58*(1), 9–31.

Miyake, K., & Zuckerman, M. (1993). Beyond personality impressions. *Journal of Personality, 61*(3), 411–436. doi: 10.1111/1467-6494.ep9402021314

Nakamura, L. (2002). *Cybertypes: Race, ethnicity, and identity on the Internet.* New York: Routledge.

**Begins References on new page**

**Double-spaces throughout**

**Lists References in alphabetical order by author**

**Provides a source that appears only on the Web**

continued >>

Effect of Physical Cues    10

Singh, D. (2004). Mating strategies of young women: Role of physical attractiveness. *Journal of Sex Research, 41*(1), 43–54.

Snyder, M., Tanke, E. D., & Berscheid, E. (1977). Social perception and interpersonal behavior: On the self-fulfilling nature of social stereotypes. *Journal of Personality and Social Psychology, 35*, 656–666.

Sveningsson, M. (2002). Cyberlove: Creating romantic relationships on the Net. In J. Fornäs, K. Klein, M. Ladendorf, J. Sundén, & M. Sveningsson (Eds.), *Digital borderlands: Cultural studies of identity and interactivity on the Internet* (pp. 48–78). New York: Lang.

Provides source information for chapter in a book

APA

# 38

# Chicago Manual (CM) and Council of Science Editors (CSE) Documentation

This chapter presents two more systems of documentation (in addition to MLA STYLE in Chapter 36 and APA STYLE in Chapter 37). They are the styles of the University of Chicago Press (CM) and the Council of Science Editors (CSE). The following directory provides a list of the CM-style entries you'll find in this chapter. For the CSE directory, turn to page 714.

CM

**TEACHING TIP**

Many of the approaches to teaching MLA, APA, CM, and CSE citation styles are similar. If you are only teaching CM and/or CSE styles, be sure to look at the teaching tips and background information in the Annotated Instructor's Edition in the MLA (Chapter 36) and APA (Chapter 37) chapters for additional ideas.

**READING-WRITING CONNECTION**

Place the responsibility for learning on the student by reiterating the reading-writing connection. The technical aspects of the research format and the density of the instructional material (e.g., the reading) strain the abilities of many students. Well-guided reflection can teach reading strategies such as previewing, skimming, and questioning. If you are using a portfolio method, students can date these reflections and include them as part of a process portfolio.

Provide five to ten minutes of class time for the students to skim this entire chapter and to

## CM-STYLE DOCUMENTATION

# 38a What is CM-style documentation?

*The Chicago Manual of Style* (CM) endorses two styles of documentation. One CM style is an author-date style, similar to the APA style of IN-TEXT CITATIONS (Chapter 37), that includes a list of sources usually titled "Works Cited" or "References." The other CM style uses a **bibliographic note system**. This system gives information about each source in two places: (1) in a footnote (at the bottom of a page) or an endnote (on a separate page following your paper) and, (2) if required, in a BIBLIOGRAPHY that begins on a separate page. We present the bibliographic note system here because it's often used in courses in such humanities subjects as art, music, history, philosophy, and sometimes English. Within the bibliographic note system, there are two substyles: "full" and "abbreviated."

## 38a.1 The full bibliographic note system in CM style

The CM full bibliographic note system requires you to give complete information, in a footnote or an endnote, the first time you cite a source. Because you're giving full information, you don't need to include a bibliography page.

If you cite a source a second time, you provide shortened information that includes the last name(s) of the author(s) and the key words in the work's title. The following example uses the full bibliographic note system.

**TEXT**

Ulrich points out that both Europeans and Native Americans told war stories, but with different details and different emphases.[3]

**FULL FOOTNOTE (SAME PAGE) OR ENDNOTE**
**(SEPARATE PAGE FOLLOWING TEXT)**

3. Laurel Thatcher Ulrich, *Age of Homespun: Objects and Stories in the Creation of an American Myth* (New York: Knopf, 2001), 269.

**SECOND CITATION OF THIS SOURCE**

6. Ulrich, *Age of Homespun*, 285.

## 38a.2 The abbreviated bibliographic note system, plus bibliography, in CM style

In the abbreviated bibliographic note system, even your first endnote or footnote provides only brief information about the source. You provide complete information in a bibliography, which appears as a separate page at the end of the paper. Following is an example using the abbreviated bibliographic note system.

**TEXT**

Ulrich points out that both Europeans and Native Americans told war stories, but with different details and different emphases.[3]

**ABBREVIATED FOOTNOTE (SAME PAGE) OR ENDNOTE**
**(SEPARATE PAGE FOLLOWING TEXT)**

3. Ulrich, *Age of Homespun*, 269.

**BIBLIOGRAPHY (SEPARATE PAGE AT END OF THE PAPER)**

Ulrich, Laurel Thatcher. *Age of Homespun: Objects and Stories in the Creation of an American Myth*. New York: Knopf, 2001.

**Alert:** Use either the full or the abbreviated bibliographic note style, but don't mix them. Ask your instructor which style he or she prefers. Remember that CM style requires a separate bibliography only if you use the abbreviated notes style. ●

Quick Reference 38.1 provides guidelines for compiling CM-style bibliographic notes.

---

record impressionistic responses to the following questions/prompts:

**1.** What seems clear to you?

**2.** What confuses you?

**3.** Which sections seem most important and why?

**4.** Write out five questions and rank them from "dumb" to "important." How much time do you need to study this chapter to understand the material and why? When will you do this studying?

**BACKGROUND**
In 2003, the University of Chicago Press published a new edition of *The Chicago Manual of Style*. Its Preface begins: "In preparing this fifteenth edition of *The Chicago Manual of Style*, we have sought to address the increasing proportion of our users who work with . . . electronic publications, Web sites, and other nonbook or nonprint documents" (xi).

**BACKGROUND**
Colorado State University maintains a number of excellent resources for writing instructors, including "teaching guides" on a variety of topics at <http://writing.colostate.edu/teaching_guides.cfm>. Also, the Academic Writing site at <http://wac.colostate.edu/aw/> includes an online journal about teaching writing. The WAC Clearinghouse at <http://wac.colostate.edu/> is a national center for sources about writing across the curriculum.

**BACKGROUND**
Your students may be familiar with *The Chicago Manual of Style* because it is very similar to Kate Turabian's *A Manual for Writers of Term Papers, Theses, and Dissertations*, which is sometimes used in high schools.

**BACKGROUND**
Nicolás Antonio (1617–1684) is credited with the creation of modern bibliography and the shaping of literary history into a scholarly discipline. His *Bibliotheca Hispana* is an index in Latin of Old World and New World Spanish

writers after 1500. It also contains a history of earlier Spanish literature.

## TEACHING TIP

Many college libraries and writing centers maintain Web pages that compare different documentation styles, generally including MLA, APA, CM, CSE, and others. A search for "style guide" or "citation style" or "documentation style" will turn up plenty of links. Alternatively, use the search engine's directory to find links. At the time of our writing this tip, for example, the path "Reference, Style Guides" on Google.com led to a list of resources at <http://directory.google.com/Top/Arts/ Writers_ Resources/ Style_Guides/>. One possible assignment for students, working individually or in groups, is to browse the Internet to select "the top ten sites for providing help with documentation." Students might then write an annotation for each site, identifying what's there and telling why the site is useful for student writers. The whole collection could be published as a resource, either in paper or online. An addition to this assignment could ask students to identify some sources that are less helpful (perhaps because they are outdated or incomplete, have poor examples, or are incorrect) and to explain why these Web sites are inferior to the others.

## QUOTATION: ON WRITING

Much of the early struggle in writing is with what I call "The Censor," that voice that says "It's no good" or wants to know what the third line will be before you've written the first one. That voice is very, very untalented, and when I really get going, it just vanishes.

—David Rab

## TEACHING TIP

Sometimes students think writing papers is a purely academic exercise, between the instructor and the student. Find ways to make research "real" for your students. You might consider hosting a research paper symposium or other public event where students present their research. *The Journal of Undergraduate Research* at <http://www.clas.ufl.edu/jur/index.html> is

---

## Quick Reference 38.1

### Guidelines for compiling CM-style bibliographic notes

**TITLE AND PLACEMENT OF NOTES**

If you're using endnotes, place them all on a separate page, before your bibliography. Center the heading "Notes," without using italics, underlining, or quotation marks, an inch from the top of the page. If you're using footnotes, place them at the bottom of the page on which the source needs to be credited. Never use a title above any note(s) at the foot of the page. CM generally uses blank space (not a line) to divide the footnote(s) from the body text.

**TITLE AND PLACEMENT OF BIBLIOGRAPHY**

The abbreviated notes style requires a bibliography, which begins on a separate page at the end of the paper, following the endnotes page. An inch from the top of the page, center the heading "Bibliography" or "Works Cited" (either is acceptable in CM style). Don't underline the heading or put it in quotation marks.

**FORMAT FOR ENDNOTES AND FOOTNOTES**

Include an endnote or a footnote every time you use a source. Number notes sequentially throughout your paper whether you're using endnotes or footnotes. Use superscript (raised) arabic numerals for the footnote or endnote numbers in your paper. Position note numbers after any punctuation mark except the dash. The number comes best at the end of a sentence, unless that position would be so far from the source material that the citation would be confusing. Don't use raised numbers in the endnote or footnote itself. Place the number followed by a period, on the same line as the content of the note. Single-space both within each note and between notes. Indent each note's first line about three-tenths of an inch (0.3-inch tab), which equals about three characters, but place subsequent lines flush left at the margin.

**SPACING AFTER PUNCTUATION**

A single space follows all punctuation, including the period.

**AUTHORS' NAMES**

In endnotes and footnotes, give the name in standard (first-name-first) order, with names and initials as given in the original source. Use the word *and* before the last author's name if your source has two or three authors. For more than three authors, list only the first followed by *and others*. In the bibliography, invert the name: last name, first name. If a work has two or more authors, invert only the first author's name. If your source has up to ten authors, give all the authors' names. If your source has eleven or more authors, list only the first seven and use *et al.* for the rest.

continued >>

## Quick Reference 38.1    (continued)

### CAPITALIZATION OF SOURCE TITLES
Capitalize the first and last words and all major words.

### SPECIAL TREATMENT OF TITLES
Use italics for titles of long works, and use quotation marks around the titles of shorter works. Omit *A, An,* and *The* from the titles of newspapers and periodicals. For an unfamiliar newspaper title, list the city (and state, in parentheses, if the city isn't well known): *Newark (NJ) Star-Ledger,* for example. Use postal abbreviations for states.

### PUBLICATION INFORMATION
Enclose publication information in parentheses. Use a colon and one space after the city of publication. Give complete publishers' names or abbreviate them according to standard abbreviations in *Books in Print.* Omit *The* before and *Co., Inc.,* and so on after a name. Spell out *University* or abbreviate to *Univ.* Never use *U* alone. Also spell out *Press.* Never use *P* alone. Don't abbreviate publication months.

### PAGE NUMBERS
For inclusive page numbers, give the full second number for 2 through 99. For 100 and beyond, give the full second number only if a shortened version would be ambiguous: 243–47, 202–6, 300–404. List all discontinuous page numbers. (See "First Endnote or Footnote: Book" toward the end of this box.) Use a comma to separate parenthetical publication information from the page numbers that follow it. Use the abbreviations *p.* and *pp.* with page numbers only for material from newspapers, for material from journals that do not use volume numbers, and to avoid ambiguity.

### CONTENT NOTES
Try to avoid using CONTENT NOTES. If you must use them, use footnotes, not endnotes, with symbols rather than numbers: an asterisk (*) for the first note on that page and a dagger (†) for a second note on that page.

### FIRST ENDNOTE OR FOOTNOTE: BOOK
For books, include the author, title, publication information, and page numbers when applicable.

   1. Eudora Welty, *One Writer's Beginnings* (Cambridge, MA: Harvard University Press, 1984), 25–26, 30, 43–51, 208.

continued >>

an excellent online resource to expose students to a wide range of well-written papers by University of Florida undergraduates.

**QUOTATION: ON WRITING**
To write you have to set up a routine, to promise yourself that you will write. Just state in a loud voice that you will write so many pages a day, or write for so many hours a day. Keep the number of pages or hours within reason, and don't be upset if a day slips by. Start again; pick up the routine. Don't look for results. Just write, easily, quietly.

—Janwillem van de Wetering

**QUOTATION: ON WRITING**
An author arrives at a good style when his language performs what is required of it without shyness.

—Cyril Connolly

**QUOTATION: ON WRITING**
I have tried simply to write the best I can; sometimes I have good luck and write better than I can.

—Ernest Hemingway

CM

CM

> **Quick Reference 38.1** (continued)
>
> **FIRST ENDNOTE OR FOOTNOTE: ARTICLE**
> For articles, include the author, article title, journal title, volume number, year, and page numbers.
>
> 1. D. D. Cochran, W. Daniel Hale, and Christine P. Hissam, "Personal Space Requirements in Indoor versus Outdoor Locations," *Journal of Psychology* 117 (1984): 132–33.
>
> **SECOND MENTION IN ENDNOTES OR FOOTNOTES**
> Second (or later) citations of the same source can be brief. See 38b for an explanation.

## 38a.3 Citing graphics in CM style

Place the credit line for a table or illustration from another source next to or directly below the reproduced material. (If you intend to publish your paper, you must obtain permission to reprint copyrighted material from its source.) Spell out the terms *map*, *plate*, and *table*, but abbreviate *figure* as *fig.*

> Reprinted by permission from Dennis Remington, A. Garth Fisher, and Edward Parent, *How to Lower Your Fat Thermostat: The No-Diet Reprogramming Plan for Lifelong Weight Control* (Provo, UT: Vitality House International, 1983), 74, fig. A2–1.

## 38b What are CM guidelines for bibliographic notes?

The CM directory that appears at the beginning of this chapter corresponds to the sample bibliographic note forms that follow. In a few cases, we give sample bibliography forms as well. If you need a model that isn't here, consult *The Chicago Manual of Style*, Fifteenth Edition (Chicago: University of Chicago Press, 2003), which gives footnote, endnote, and bibliography forms for a multitude of sources.

**BOOKS AND PARTS OF BOOKS—PRINT**

### 1. Book by One Author—CM
*Footnote or Endnote*

1. Becky Bradway, *Pink Houses and Family Taverns* (Bloomington, IN: Indiana University Press, 2001).

*Bibliography*

Bradway, Becky. *Pink Houses and Family Taverns*. Bloomington, IN: Indiana University Press, 2001.

The format for the bibliography is the reverse of the format for the note, in which first lines indent. In bibliographic form, the first line is placed flush left to the margin and the second and other lines are indented three-tenths to one half inch (0.3-inch–0.5-inch tab). Notice also where periods replace commas and where parentheses are omitted.

## 2. Book by Two or Three Authors—CM

*Footnote or Endnote*

    1. Edward E. Gordon and Elaine H. Gordon, *Literacy in America: Historic Journey and Contemporary Solutions* (Westport, CT: Praeger, 2003).

    2. John K. Lynam, Cyrus G. Ndiritu, and Adiel N. Mbabu, *Transformation of Agricultural Research Systems in Africa: Lessons from Kenya* (East Lansing: Michigan State University Press, 2004), 41.

*Bibliography*

Gordon, Edward E. and Elaine H. Gordon. *Literacy in America: Historic Journey and Contemporary Solutions.* Westport, CT: Praeger, 2003.

Lynam, John K., Cyrus G. Ndiritu, and Adiel N. Mbabu. *Transformation of Agricultural Research Systems in Africa: Lessons from Kenya.* East Lansing: Michigan State University Press, 2004.

In a bibliography entry, invert only the name of the first author listed.

## 3. Book by More Than Three Authors—CM

    1. Wendy Saul and others, *Beyond the Science Fair: Creating a Kids' Inquiry Conference* (Portsmouth, NH: Heinemann, 2005), 72.

## 4. Multiple Citations of a Single Source—CM

For subsequent references to a work you've already named, use a shortened citation. Give the last name of the author, the title of the work, and the page number, all separated by commas. Shorten the title if it's longer than four words. This example shows the form for a subsequent reference to the work fully described in item 1.

    1. Bradway, *Pink Houses,* 25.

If there are more than three authors for a source, use only the name of the first author, followed by *and others* or *et al.* The following example shows the shortened citation for the work in item 3.

    2. Saul et al., *Beyond the Science Fair,* 72.

If you cite two or more authors with the same last name, include first names or initials in each note.

3. Eudora Welty, *One Writer's Beginnings*, 25.

4. Paul Welty, *Human Expression*, 129.

If you cite the same source as the source immediately preceding, you may use *ibid.* (capitalized at the beginning of a note), followed by a comma and the page number, instead of repeating the author's name and the title.

5. Ibid., 152.

### 5. Book by a Group or Corporate Author—CM

1. American Psychological Association, *Publication Manual of the American Psychological Association*, 5th ed. (Washington, DC: American Psychological Association, 2001).

2. Boston Women's Health Collective, *Our Bodies, Ourselves for the New Century* (New York: Simon & Schuster, 1998).

If a work issued by an organization has no author listed on the title page, give the name of the organization as the author of the work. The organization may also be the publisher of the work.

### 6. Book with No Author Named—CM

1. *The Chicago Manual of Style*, 15th ed. (Chicago: University of Chicago Press, 2003).

Begin the citation with the name of the book.

### 7. Book with an Author and an Editor—CM

1. Emily Brontë, *Wuthering Heights*, ed. Richard J. Dunn (New York: Norton, 2002).

In this position, the abbreviation *ed.* stands for "edited by," not "editor." Therefore, *ed.* is correct whether a work has one or more than one editor. (Also see items 10 and 16.)

### 8. Translation—CM

1. Milan Kundera, *The Unbearable Lightness of Being*, trans. Michael Henry Heim (New York: HarperPerennial Library, 1999).

The abbreviation *trans.* stands for "translated by," not "translator."

### 9. Work in Several Volumes or Parts—CM

The following notes show ways to give bibliographic information for a specific place in one volume of a multivolume work. Use whichever you prefer, staying consistent throughout a paper.

1. Ernest Jones, *The Last Phase*, vol. 3 of *The Life and Work of Sigmund Freud* (New York: Basic Books, 1957), 97.

1. Ernest Jones, *The Life and Work of Sigmund Freud*, vol. 3, *The Last Phase* (New York: Basic Books, 1957), 97.

If you're citing an entire work in two or more volumes, use the form shown below.

2. Ronald Chrisley, ed., *Artificial Intelligence: Critical Concepts*, 4 vols. (London: Routledge, 2000).

### 10. One Selection from an Anthology or an Edited Book—CM

1. Laura Trujillo, "Balancing Act," in *Border-Line Personalities: A New Generation of Latinas Dish on Sex, Sass, and Cultural Shifting*, ed. Robyn Moreno and Michelle Herrera Mulligan. (New York: Harper, 2004), 61–72.

### 11. More Than One Selection from an Anthology or an Edited Book—CM

If you cite more than one selection from the same anthology or edited book, give complete bibliographical information in each citation.

### 12. Signed Article in a Reference Book—CM

1. John C. Burnbam, "Freud, Sigmund," in *The Encyclopedia of Psychiatry, Psychology, and Psychoanalysis*, ed. Benjamin B. Wolman (New York: Henry Holt, 1996), 220.

### 13. Unsigned Article in a Reference Book—CM

1. *Encyclopaedia Britannica*, 15th ed., s.v. "Ireland."

The abbreviation *s.v.* stands for *sub verbo*, meaning "under the word." Capitalize the heading of the entry only if it's a proper noun. Omit publication information except for the edition number.

### 14. Second or Later Edition—CM

1. Anthony F. Janson, *History of Art*, 6th ed. (New York: Abrams, 2001).

Here the abbreviation *ed.* stands for "edition." Give the copyright date for the edition you're citing.

### 15. Anthology or Edited Book—CM

1. Eduardo del Rio, ed., *The Prentice Hall Anthology of Latino Literature* (Upper Saddle River, NJ: Prentice Hall, 2002).

2. Emily Finanger, letter to the editor, *Outside*, February 2008, 14.

3. David Shenk, "Toolmaker, Brain Builder," review of *Beyond Big Blue: Building the Computer That Defeated the World Chess Champion*, by Feng-Hsiung Hsu, *American Scholar* 72 (Spring 2003): 150–52.

Before page numbers, use a comma for popular magazines and a colon for journals.

### 26. Unsigned Article in a Daily Newspaper—CM

1. "Oscars Ready Plans to Deal with Strike," *Denver Post*, sec. B, January 31, 2008.

### 27. Signed Article in a Weekly or Biweekly Magazine or Newspaper—CM

1. Christine Gorman, "How to Age Gracefully," *Time*, June 6, 2005, 73–74.

For general-readership weekly and biweekly magazines and newspapers, give the month, day, and year of publication. Separate page numbers from the year with a comma.

### 28. Signed Article in a Monthly or Bimonthly Periodical—CM

1. James Fallows, "The $1.4 Trillion Question," *The Atlantic*, January/February 2008, 36–48.

For general-readership monthly and bimonthly magazines, give the month and year of publication. Separate page numbers from the year with a comma.

### 29. Unsigned Article in a Weekly or Monthly Periodical—CM

1. "The Price Is Wrong," *Economist*, August 2, 2003, 58–59.

### 30. Article in a Collection of Reprinted Articles—CM

1. Thomas Hayden, "The Age of Robots," in *Applied Science*, Social Issues Resources Series (Boca Raton, FL: Social Issues Resources, 2002).

Cite only the publication actually consulted, not the original source. If you use a bibliography, cite its location in both the reprinted publication you consulted and the publication where the article first appeared.

### 31. Article in a Journal with Continuous Pagination—CM

1. Phyllis Tyson, "The Psychology of Women Continued," *Journal of the American Psychoanalytic Association* 46, no. 2 (1998): 361–64.

### 32. Article in a Journal That Pages Each Issue Separately—CM

1. Linda Adler-Kassner and Heidi Estrem, "Rethinking Research Writing: Public Literacy in the Composition Classroom," *WPA: Writing Program Administration* 26, no. 3 (2003): 119–31.

The issue number of a journal is required if each issue of the journal starts with page 1. In this example, the volume number is 26 and the issue number, abbreviated *no.,* is 3.

### INTERNET SOURCES

If there is a print version of the source (as in item 35), provide information about that source. Also include information about how to find the electronic version. Unlike some other documentation styles (such as MLA), CM style doesn't generally recommend including access dates, nor does it use angle brackets around URLs. Following are examples in CM style of a few common types of electronic sources. For additional types, consult *The Chicago Manual of Style.*

### 33. Online Book—CM

Include the author's name, the title, and access information—in this case, the name of the organization that sponsors the site, and the URL.

1. Kate Chopin, *The Awakening* (Washington, DC: PBS, 1998), http://www.pbs.org/katechopin/library/awakening.

### 34. Article from a Periodical Available Only Online—CM

Include the author, title of the article, title of the publication, volume and issue number (if given), publication date, and URL.

1. Jody Shipka, "This Was (NOT!!) an Easy Assignment," *Computers and Composition Online,* fall 2007, http://www.bgsu.edu/cconline/not_easy/.

### 35. Article Accessed Through a Database—CM

Include the author, title of the article, title of the publication, volume and issue numbers (if given) of the original publication, the original publication date, and the URL of the database through which you accessed the article. CM style recommends that you include an access date when citing information retrieved through a database. Insert the access date in parentheses after the URL, followed by a period.

1. Gail Dutton, "Greener Pigs," *Popular Science* 255, no. 5 (November 1999): 38–39, http://proquest.umi.com (accessed September 2, 2007).

### 36. Source from an Internet Site—CM

Provide the author's name, the title of the Web page, the title or owner of the site, and the URL. When no specific author is listed, you may use the owner of the site as the author, as in the following example. Include an access date if your source is likely to be updated frequently, as is often the case with Internet sites.

1. Association for the Advancement of Artificial Intelligence, "AI Overview," Association for the Advancement of Artificial Intelligence, http://www.aaai.org/AITopics/html/overview.html (accessed January 22, 2008).

### 37. Electronic Mailing List—CM

1. T. Caruso, e-mail to Calls for Papers mailing list, June 30, 2002, http://www.cfp.english.upenn.edu/archive/2002-09/0041.html.

### 38. E-Mail Message—CM

1. Eliana Pessin, e-mail message to Georgia Dobyns, November 11, 2007.

### 39. Web Log Entry—CM

1. Scott McLemee, "To Whom It May Concern," Web log posting to *Quick Study*, January 1, 2008, http://www.artsjournal.com/quickstudy/ (accessed May 14, 2008).

### 40. Online Video or Podcast—CM

1. Michael Wesch, *Web 2.0 . . . The Machine is Us/ing Us*, video posted January 31, 2007 (accessed July 7, 2007).

Wesch is the director and producer of this video.


### OTHER SOURCES

### 41. Speech or Conference Presentation—CM

1. Peter Leslie Mortensen, "Meet the Press: Reading News Coverage of Research on Writing" (paper presented at the annual meeting of the Modern Language Association, Washington, DC, December 29, 2005).

To cite a paper read at a meeting, give the name of the meeting in parentheses, along with the location and the date.

### 42. Personal Interview—CM

1. Randi Friedman, interview by author, August 30, 2008, Austin, Texas.

For an unpublished interview, give the name of the interviewee and the interviewer, the date of the interview, and the location of the interview. CM style recommends that you incorporate this information into the text, rather than place it in a note.

### 43. Published and Unpublished Letters—CM

    1. William Carlos Williams to his son, 13 March 1935, in *Letters of the Century: America 1900–1999*, ed. Lisa Grunwald and Stephen J. Adler (New York: Dial, 1999), 225–26.

    2. Theodore Brown, letter to author, December 7, 2005.

For an unpublished letter, give the name of the writer, the name of the recipient, and the date the letter was written.

### 44. Film, Videotape, or DVD—CM

    1. Marc Norman and Tom Stoppard, *Shakespeare in Love*, DVD (1998; New York: Miramax Films/Universal Pictures, 2003).

    2. Robert Riskin, *It Happened One Night*, VHS (1934; Hollywood: Columbia Pictures, 1999).

In note 1, the first information gives the authors of the screenplay. If the point of the note was about the director or the producers, then the title would appear first and *directed by* or *produced by* would follow a comma after the title along with the relevant names.

### 45. Sound Recording—CM

    1. Bedrich Smetana, *My Country*, Czech Philharmonic, Karel Anserl, Vanguard SV-9/10.

Bedrich Smetana is the composer, and Karel Anserl is the conductor.

    2. Bruce Springsteen, "Lonesome Day," on *The Rising*, Sony CD B000069 HKH.

### 46. Computer Software—CM

    1. *Guitar Hero III: Legends of Rock*, 2007. Activision, Santa Monica.

    2. *Dreamweaver*, Ver. MX, Macromedia, San Francisco, CA.

Place the date or version (or release) number, abbreviated *Ver.* or *Rel.*, directly after the name of the software. Then, list the company that owns the rights to the software, followed by that company's location.

**QUOTATION: ON NOTES**

He listens well who takes notes.

—Dante Alighieri

**QUOTATION: ON WRITING**

Some authors type their works, but I cannot do that. Writing is tied up with the hand, almost with a special nerve.

—Graham Greene

**BACKGROUND**

Technological developments have made reproducing written work as easy as pushing a button on a photocopier or hitting the "Send," "Print," or "Download" keys on a computer. If copyright laws sometimes seem too demanding to instructors or researchers, for whom seeking permission to copy something can take time and energy, the effort is nonetheless required by law. In "Copyright: It's for the Public Good" (*Chronicle of Higher Education*, May 9, 2003: B35), Peter Givler discusses how copyright benefits teachers and scholars. He notes that "Shakespeare . . . furnishes an instructive example of the perils of authorship before copyright. Under the laws of his day, once his company had performed one of his plays, Shakespeare lost the legal ability to prevent further performance by anyone else. All he could do to control performance rights, as it were, was to keep the acting script, or prompt book, under lock and key."

**QUOTATION: ON WRITING**

Writing, I think, is not apart from living. Writing is a kind of double living. The writer experiences everything twice. Once in reality and once in that mirror which waits always before or behind.

—Catherine Drinker Bowen

**QUOTATION: ON WRITING**

Writing is a difficult trade which must be learned slowly by reading great authors; by trying at the outset to imitate them; by daring them to be original; by destroying one's first productions.

—André Maurois

2. Crowder W. Seashore life between the tides. New York: Dodd, Mead; 1931. New York: Dover Reprint; 1975. 372 p.

Thereafter, throughout your paper, follow each citation of Sybesma's *Introduction to Biophysics* by a superscript [1] and each citation of Crowder's *Seashore Life* by a superscript [2].

When you're citing more than one reference—for example, a new source and three previous sources as well as a source from your first page—list each source number, followed by a comma with no space. Use a hyphen to show the range of numbers in a continuous sequence, and put all in superscript: [2,5–7,9]

Quick Reference 38.2 gives guidelines for compiling a References list for the Citation-Sequence system. Especially pay attention to the Arrangement of Entries in a Citation-Sequence system.

---

**Quick Reference 38.2**

### Guidelines for a References list (CSE-style)

**TITLE**

Use "References" or "Cited References" as the title (no underlining, no italics, no quotations marks). (CSE also permits "Bibliography" or "Literature Cited" as acceptable titles.)

**PLACEMENT OF LIST**

Begin the list on a separate page at the end of the research paper. Number the page sequentially with the rest of the paper.

**CONTENT AND FORMAT OF CITED REFERENCES**

Include all sources that you quote, paraphrase, or summarize in your paper. Center the title one inch from the top of the page. Start each entry on a new line. If an entry takes more than one line, indent the second and all other lines under the first word, not the number. Single-space each entry and double-space between entries.

**SPACING AFTER PUNCTUATION**

CSE style specifies no space after date, issue number, or volume number of a periodical, as shown in the models in 38d.

**ARRANGEMENT OF ENTRIES—CITATION-SEQUENCE SYSTEM**

Sequence and number the entries in the precise order in which you first used them in the body of your paper. Put the number, followed by a period and a space, at the regular left margin.

continued >>

## Quick Reference 38.2 (continued)

### ARRANGEMENT OF ENTRIES—NAME-YEAR SYSTEM
Sequence the entries in alphabetical order by author, then title, etc. Do not number the entries.

### ARRANGEMENT OF ENTRIES—CITATION-NAME SYSTEM
Sequence the entries in alphabetical order by author, then title, etc. Number the entries. Put the number, followed by a period and a space, at the regular left margin.

### AUTHORS' NAMES
Reverse the order of each author's name, giving the last name first. For book citations, you can give first names or use only the initials of first and (when available) middle names; for journal citations, use only initials; however, CSE style recommends you use only initials. Don't use a period or a space between first and middle initials. Use a comma to separate the names of multiple authors identified by initials; however, if you use full first names, use a semicolon. Don't use *and* or & with authors' names. Place a period after the last author's name.

### TREATMENT OF TITLES
Never underline titles or enclose them in quotation marks. Capitalize a title's first word and any proper nouns. Don't capitalize the first word of a subtitle unless it's a proper noun. Capitalize the titles of academic journals. If the title of a periodical is one word, give it in full; otherwise, abbreviate the title according to recommendations established by the *American National Standard for Abbreviations of Titles of Periodicals.* Capitalize a newspaper title's major words, giving the full title but omitting *A, An,* or *The* at the beginning.

### PLACE OF PUBLICATION
Use a colon after the city of publication. If the city name could be unfamiliar to readers, add in parentheses the postal abbreviation for the US state or Canadian province. If the location of a foreign city will be unfamiliar to readers, add in parentheses the country name, abbreviating it according to International Organization for Standardization (ISO) standards. Find ISO abbreviations at http://un.org/Depts/cartographic/english/geoinfo/geoname.pdf.

### PUBLISHER
Give the name of the publisher, without periods after initials, and use a semicolon after the publisher's name. Omit *The* at the beginning or *Co., Inc., Ltd.,* or *Press* at the end. However, for a university press, abbreviate *University* and *Press* as *Univ* and *Pr,* respectively, without periods.

continued >>

**QUOTATION: ON WRITING**
Writing stopped being fun when I discovered the difference between good writing and bad and, even more terrifying, the difference between it and true art. And after that, the whip came down.
—Truman Capote

**BACKGROUND**
The best-established online journal devoted to the developments in writing, rhetoric, technology, and pedagogy is *Kairos,* available at <http://english.ttu.edu/kairos/>.

**QUOTATION: ON WRITING**
Writing is a dog's life, but the only life worth living.
—Gustave Flaubert

**QUOTATION: ON WRITING**
Writing is an exploration. You start from nothing and learn as you go.
—E. L. Doctorow

**QUOTATION: ON WRITING**
When I stop [working] the rest of the day is posthumous. I'm only really alive when I'm writing.
—Tennessee Williams

**QUOTATION: ON WRITING**
[Writing] has nothing to do with communication between person and person, only with communication between different parts of a person's mind.
—Rebecca West

**QUOTATION: ON WRITING**
If writing must be a precise form of communication, it should be treated like a precision instrument. It should be sharpened, and it should not be used carelessly.
—Theodore M. Bernstein

CSE

CSE

**Quick Reference 38.2**     (continued)

**PUBLICATION MONTH**
Abbreviate all month names longer than three letters to their first three letters, but do not add a period.

**INCLUSIVE PAGE NUMBERS**
Shorten the second number as much as possible, making sure that the number isn't ambiguous. For example, use 233–4 for 233 to 234; 233–44 for 233 to 244; but 233–304 (not 233–04) for 233 to 304.

**DISCONTINUOUS PAGE NUMBERS**
Give the numbers of all discontinuous pages, separating successive numbers or ranges with a comma: 54–7, 60–6.

**TOTAL PAGE NUMBERS**
In the citation for an entire book, the last information unit gives the total number of book pages, followed by the abbreviation *p* and a period.

**FORMAT FOR REFERENCES ENTRIES: BOOKS**
The basic format for the **Citation-Sequence** and **Citation-Name Systems** is

> Author(s). Title. Edition [if other than first]. Place of publication: Publisher; Date. Pages.

For "Pages," list total pages when citing an entire work or inclusive pages when citing part of a book. Note that the Author, Title, and Edition sections end with a period. Place of publication is followed by a colon, and Publisher by a semicolon. Date and Pages end with a period.

1. Primrose SB, Twyman RM, Old RW. Principles of gene manipulation.
   London: Blackwell; 2002. 390 p.

The basic format for the **Name-Date System** is

> Author(s). Date. Title. Edition [if other than first]. Place of publication: Publisher. Pages.

Primrose SB, Twyman RM, Old RW. 2002. Principles of gene manipulation.
   London: Blackwell. 390 p.

**FORMAT FOR CITED REFERENCES ENTRIES: ARTICLES**
The basic format for the **Citation-Sequence** and **Citation-Name Systems** is

> Author(s). Article title. Journal title. Date;Volume(Issue):Pages.

Each section ends with a period. Notice there is no space after the semicolon, before the parentheses, or after the colon. Abbreviate a journal's name only if it's

continued >>

| Quick Reference 38.2 | (continued) |

standard in your scientific discipline. For example, *Exp Neurol* is the abbreviated form for *Experimental Neurology.* In the following example, the volume number is 184, and the issue number, in parentheses, is 1.

1. Ginis I, Rao MS. Toward cell replacement therapy: promises and caveats. Exp Neurol. 2003;184(1):61–77.

The basic format for the **Name-Year System** is

    Author(s). Date. Article title. Journal title. Volume(Issue):Pages.

Ginis I, Rao MS. 2003. Toward cell replacement therapy: promises and caveats. Exp Neurol. 184(1):61–77.

## 38c.2 The CSE name-year system

In the Name-Year system, in-text references include the last name of the author or authors, along with the year of publication, placed in parentheses. The end references in this system are organized in alphabetical order by author. (This system resembles APA style.)

### IN-TEXT REFERENCE

This behavior occurs periodically (Sybesma 1977), although some claim never to have observed it (Crowder 1931).

or

Sybesma (1977) insists that this behavior occurs periodically, but Crowder (1931) claims never to have observed it.

### END REFERENCE

1. Crowder W. Seashore life between the tides. New York: Dodd, Mead; 1931. New York: Dover Reprint; 1975. 372 p.

2. Sybesma C. An introduction to biophysics. New York: Academic; 1977. 648 p.

If there are two authors, give both names in the in-text reference, separated by *and.* If there are more than two authors, give only the first author's name, then include *et al.* and the publication year. If no author is given, include the first word or first few words of the title, followed by an ELLIPSIS and the date.

### IN-TEXT REFERENCE

Various therapies have proven effective (Treatment . . . 2007).

Quick Reference 38.2 gives guidelines for compiling a References list. Especially pay attention to the Arrangement of Entries in a Name-Year system.

## 38c.3  The CSE citation-name system

In the Citation-Name system, the in-text references use numbers to refer to end references that are arranged alphabetically. In other words, first complete the list of end references, arranging them alphabetically by author. Then, number each reference; for example, if you were documenting references by Schmidt, Gonzalez, Adams, and Zurowski, in your end references, they would be arranged:

1. Adams . . .

2. Gonzalez . . .

3. Schmidt . . .

4. Zurowski.

Finally, your in-text references should use a superscript number corresponding to the name in your end references. The system resembles the Citation-Sequence system, except that the alphabetical order of the end references determines the number rather than the order of appearance in the text.

**IN-TEXT REFERENCES—CITATION-NAME**

Sybesma[2] insists that this behavior occurs periodically, but Crowder[1] claims never to have observed it.

**END REFERENCES—CITATION-NAME**

1. Crowder W. Seashore life between the tides. New York: Dodd, Mead; 1931. New York: Dover Reprint; 1975. 372 p.

2. Sybesma C. An introduction to biophysics. New York: Academic; 1977. 648 p.

Quick Reference 38.2 gives guidelines for compiling a References list. Especially pay attention to the arrangement of entries in a Citation-Name system.

# 38d  What are CSE guidelines for sources on a list of references?

The CSE directory on page 714 corresponds to the sample references that follow. If you need a model not included in this book, consult the seventh edition of *Scientific Style and Format*. The examples that follow are for the Citation-Sequence and Citation-Name Systems; the Name-Date system differs by the placement of the date and by not numbering the entries. See Quick Reference 38.2 for illustrations of the differences.

CSE

## BOOKS AND PARTS OF BOOKS

### 1. Book by One Author—CSE

1. Hawking SW. Black holes and baby universes and other essays. New York: Bantam; 1993. 320 p.

Use one space but no punctuation between an author's last name and the initial of the first name. Don't put punctuation or a space between first and middle initials (*Hawking SW*). Do, however, use the hyphen in a hyphenated first and middle name (for example, *Gille J-C* represents *Jean-Claude Gille* in the next item).

### 2. Book by More Than One Author—CSE

1. Wegzyn S, Gille J-C, Vidal P. Developmental systems: at the crossroads of system theory, computer science, and genetic engineering. New York: Springer-Verlag; 1990. 595 p.

### 3. Book by a Group or Corporate Author—CSE

1. Chemical Rubber Company. Handbook of laboratory safety. 3rd ed. Boca Raton (FL): CRC; 1990. 1352 p.

### 4. Anthology or Edited Book—CSE

1. Herrman B, Hummel S, editors. Ancient DNA: recovery and analysis of genetic material from paleontological, archeological, museum, medical, and forensic specimens. New York: Springer-Verlag; 1994. 1020 p.

### 5. One Selection or Chapter from an Anthology or Edited Book—CSE

1. Basov NG, Feoktistov LP, Senatsky YV. Laser driver for inertial confinement fusion. In: Bureckner KA, editor. Research trends in physics: inertial confinement fusion. New York: American Institute of Physics; 1992. p. 24–37.

### 6. Translation—CSE

1. Magris C. A different sea. Spurr MS, translator. London: Harvill; 1993. 194 p. Translation of: Un mare differente.

### 7. Reprint of an Older Book—CSE

1. Carson R. The sea around us. New York: Oxford Univ Pr; 1951. New York: Oxford Univ Pr; 1991. 288 p.

### 8. All Volumes of a Multivolume Work—CSE

1. Crane FL, Moore DJ, Low HE, editors. Oxidoreduction at the plasma membrane: relation to growth and transport. Boca Raton (FL): CRC; 1991. 2 vol.

**CSE**

### 22. Web pages—CSE

Begin with author, if available; otherwise, begin with title.

1. Think again: men and women share cognitive skills [Internet]. Washington, DC: American Psychological Association; 2006 [cited 2007 Jan 17]. Available from: http://www.psychologymatters.org/thinkagain.html

2. Welcome to AAAI [Internet]. Menlo Park (CA): Association for the Advancement of Artificial Intelligence. c2008 [cited 2008 Mar 17]. Available from: http://www.aaai.org

### 23. Videos or Podcasts—CSE

1. Wesch M. Web 2.0 . . . the machine is us/ing us [video on the Internet]. 2007 Jan 31 [cited 2007 Dec 14]. Available from: http://www.youtube.com/watch?v=6gmP4nk0EOE

### OTHER SOURCES

Include the type of medium in brackets after the title. Examples include [*map*], [*CD*], [*DVD*], [*poster*], and so on.

### 24. Map—CSE

1. Russia and post-Soviet republics [political map]. Moscow: Mapping Production Association; 1992. Conical equidistant projection; 40 × 48 in.; color, scale 1:8,000,000.

### 25. Unpublished Letter—CSE

1. Darwin C. [Letter to Mr. Clerke, 1861]. Located at: University of Iowa Library, Iowa City.

### 26. Video Recording—CSE

1. Nova—The elegant universe [DVD]. Boston: WGBH; 2004. 2 DVDs: 180 min, sound, color.

### 27. Slide Set—CSE

1. Human parasitology [slides]. Chicago: American Society of Clinical Pathologists; 1990. Color. Accompanied by: 1 guide.

### 28. Presentation Slides—CSE

1. Beaudoin E. Fruit fly larvae [PowerPoint slides]. Denver, CO: University of Denver; 2007 Oct 17. 49 slides.

# 39

# Comparing the Disciplines

## 39a  What is writing across the curriculum?

**Writing across the curriculum** refers to the writing you do in college courses beyond first-year composition. Good writing in various subject areas, such as history, biology, or psychology, has many common features. However, there are also important differences. This section will help you adapt general principles of writing so you'll be successful in writing across the curriculum.

People commonly group academic disciplines into three broad categories: the humanities, the social sciences, and the natural sciences. Each has its own knowledge, vocabulary, and perspectives on the world; its own specialized assignments and purposes; its own common types of SOURCES* (3b); and its own expected documentation styles (Chapters 36–38).

No matter what differences exist among the academic disciplines, writing processes and strategies interconnect and overlap across the curriculum. It's always important to consider the WRITING SITUATION, including your TOPIC, PURPOSE, AUDIENCE, ROLE, CONTEXT, and SPECIAL REQUIREMENTS (1b). Every paper benefits from attention to the WRITING PROCESS, including PLANNING, SHAPING, DRAFTING, REVISING, EDITING, and PROOFREADING (Chapter 2), and certain types of writing, such as reports, SUMMARIES, ANALYSES, and SYNTHESES, are common in disciplines across the curriculum. Chapter 3 provides extensive discussion of specific types of papers common in many academic situations. Quick Reference 39.1 compares elements of the academic disciplines.

To understand some of the differences among the disciplines, consider these three quite different paragraphs about a mountain.

### HUMANITIES

The mountain stands serene but troubled above the surrounding plains, like a peaceful leader threatened by a noisy crowd. Giant timber—part of a collage of evergreen and deciduous trees—conceals the expansive mountain's slope. At its base, a cool stream flows over flat and jagged rocks, gray, orange, and steel blue. Next to the outer bank of the stream stands a shingled farmhouse, desolate, yet suggesting its active past. Unfortunately, billboards, chairlifts, and trinket shops litter the scene, landmarks of unrelenting commercial life that

---

*Words printed in SMALL CAPITAL LETTERS are discussed elsewhere in the text and are defined in the Terms Glossary at the back of this book.

## Quick Reference 39.1

### Comparing the disciplines

| Discipline | Types of assignments | Primary sources | Secondary sources | Usual documentation styles |
|---|---|---|---|---|
| **HUMANITIES** e.g., history, languages, literature, philosophy, art, music, theater | essays, response statements, reviews, analyses, original works such as stories, poems, memoirs | literary works, manuscripts, paintings and sculptures, historical documents, films, plays, photographs, artifacts from popular culture, personal experiences | reviews, journal articles, research papers, books | MLA, CMS |
| **SOCIAL SCIENCES** e.g., psychology, sociology, anthropology, education | research reports, case studies, reviews of the literature, analyses, ethnographies | surveys, interviews, observations, tests and measures | journal articles, scholarly books, literature reviews | APA |
| **NATURAL SCIENCES** e.g., biology, chemistry, physics, mathematics | research or lab reports, reports of data, research proposals, science reviews | experiments, field notes and direct observations, measurements | journal articles, research papers, books | often CSE but varies by discipline |

have no patience with mere nature. Thoreau would hardly have chosen this place to escape his crowded society.

### SOCIAL SCIENCES

Among the favorite pastimes of North American city dwellers is the "return to nature." Many people plan trips to mountains even though they hardly want a purely natural experience. They know they have arrived at the

WAC incorporate computer-mediated tools and techniques, such as e-mail, asynchronous learning networks, MOOS (text-based virtual reality environments), and the World Wide Web, into their pedagogies.

**BACKGROUND**

In "Clearing the Air: WAC Myths and Realities" (*College English* 62.5 (2000): 573–583), Susan McLeod and Elaine Maimon, two pioneers in WAC theory and practice, refute common WAC myths in a "full scale corrective." They offer a comprehensive definition of WAC and refer readers to models worthy of emulation.

**BACKGROUND**

*JIME* (Journal of Interactive Media in Education) devoted its 2004 publication to a special issue editorial on the topic "Designing and Developing for the Disciplines" (available online at <http://www-jime.open.ac.uk/2004/11/>). One article, "Using Interactive Elements Between Disciplines" (V. Sieber, R. Haynes, C. Dobson, D. Holley, and D. Andrew), emphasizes how Flash programs that create interaction can be used effectively in a wide variety of specific learning contexts, both within and across disciplines; see <http://www.jime.open.ac.uk/2004/16>.

**PORTFOLIO APPROACHES AND ACTIVITIES FOR WRITING ACROSS THE CURRICULUM**

Literacy is ultimately the student's responsibility. The instructional cycle is complete only to the degree that students can translate information into a skill or tool. Portfolios allow students to transfer what they have learned in a writing course to other courses. By identifying, organizing, and reflecting on the various writing and reading activities necessary to master a course, students learn connections between curricula that exceed what can be taught.

Recent approaches to portfolios include digital or ePortfolios (see Chapter 47). *Electronic Portfolios: Emerging Practices in Student, Faculty, and Institutional Change*, edited by Barbara Cambridge, Susan Kahn, Daniel P. Tompkins, and Kathleen Blake Yancey (Washington, DC: American Association of Higher Education, 2001), provides an excellent starting place for reading more about ePortfolios.

## SCORING ISSUES

Scoring a content portfolio (an application of Writing Across the Curriculum) can be as simple as assigning a percentage as if it were an independent project. Even 10 percent of a final college grade will provide an incentive to make the process work. However, truthfully, the more the process is valued and weighted, the more the student pays attention to the process. Holistic scoring, accompanied with published rubrics and eventually even sample student portfolios, makes the process surprisingly manageable. However, checklists and point systems for individual entries work just as well. In fact, the great strength of portfolio assessment is that the instructor is free to choose weights and values. A portfolio is a means to an end, a framework to house learning, a way to connect learning to assessment.

## READING-WRITING-LISTENING CONNECTION

Understanding the interdependence of listening to lectures, reading, notetaking, test taking, and essay writing marks a mature student. Portfolios can become a system of tracking and communicating that connection, thereby nurturing this maturity. Ideally, success will demonstrate itself in measurable ways, such as in quiz and test scores, reading speed, and organizational and time management skills.

Students need to develop inferential, interpretive reading skills. These critical thinking skills, the cornerstone of portfolios, are recorded by careful student notetaking.

## NOTETAKING

Notetaking is a key portfolio activity if teachers take time to recommend notetaking strategies. Provide visual models for students. Present an outline of the daily lesson in an overhead as you present a lecture, or divide the board into vertical sections with headings such as "Questions," "Answers," and "Applications" to guide

mountain that they have traveled hundreds of miles to see because huge billboards are directing them to its base. As they look up the mountain, dozens of people are riding over the treetops in a chairlift, littering the slope with paper cups and food wrappers. At the base of the mountain stands the inevitable refreshment or souvenir stand, found at virtually all American tourist attractions. People seem to want things "natural" but not too natural. Just as chain restaurants provide travelers with comfortably familiar surroundings, so do commercial enterprises keep mountain visitors within their comfort zones.

## NATURAL SCIENCES

The mountain rises approximately 9,600 feet above sea level. The underlying rock is igneous, of volcanic origin, composed primarily of granites and feldspars. Three distinct biological communities are present on the mountain. The community at the top of the mountain is alpine, dominated by very short grasses and forbs. At middle altitudes, the community is a typical northern boreal coniferous forest community, and at the base and lower altitudes, deciduous forest is the dominant community. This community has, however, been highly affected by agricultural development along the river at its base and by recreational development.

These examples illustrate that each discipline has its own perspective and emphasis. The paragraph written for the humanities describes and interprets the mountain from the writer's personal perspective. The paragraph written for the social sciences focuses on the behavior of people as a group. The paragraph written for the natural sciences is an objective observation of natural phenomena. Of course, the lines between disciplines can blur.

## 39b What are primary research and secondary research in the disciplines?

As we discussed in section 7b, different source materials lead to different kinds of writing. In the humanities, primary sources are original creative works, including novels, stories, poems, autobiographies, plays, films, musical compositions, and works of art (Chapter 40). In the social and natural sciences, primary sources may include your own research, generated by conducting experiments, surveys, or careful observations. Or they may include books and articles in which researchers report findings from their research studies for the first time (Chapter 41).

SECONDARY SOURCES are scholarly writings that SUMMARIZE, ANALYZE, or SYNTHESIZE primary sources. In the humanities, secondary sources offer analysis and interpretation of primary works. In the social and natural sciences, secondary sources summarize, then synthesize findings, and draw parallels that offer new insights. You might review Quick Reference 4.4 on page 114 to understand the distinctions between primary and secondary sources.

## 39c What can help me write assignments in various disciplines?

A useful strategy for writing assignments in different disciplines is to analyze successful writings that match the requirements of your assignment. Instructors sometimes provide models for such papers or point you to similar published works. Following are some types of questions that will help you analyze model writings.

1. Are papers divided by subheadings or not?

2. Are specific parts required? Is there a specified format?

3. Does the paper require sources? If so, do writers tend to place most of their sources in one place (for example, near the beginning), or do they place sources throughout?

4. What kinds of sources appear in the writing? Are they primary or secondary? Which kinds of books, periodicals, or other sources does the writer tend to use?

5. Is the tone informal or very formal? Do writers use first person or third person?

6. Is the writing characterized by explanations and discussions that are full and expansive or concise and terse?

7. To what extent are writers expected to include their opinions or personal experiences, and to what extent are they expected to rely on objective analyses or source materials?

8. What is the mix of summary and analysis or interpretation?

9. What are typical introduction and conclusion strategies in model sources?

10. What documentation style does the writer use?

## 39d How do I use documentation in the disciplines?

Writers use DOCUMENTATION to credit the sources they've used and to help their readers learn more. A writer who neglects to credit a source is guilty of PLAGIARISM (35b).

DOCUMENTATION STYLES differ among the disciplines. In the humanities, most fields use the documentation style of the Modern Language Association (MLA), as explained and illustrated in Chapter 36. Occasionally, the humanities use CM (Chicago Manual) style, as explained and illustrated in Chapter

small-group work. Reward good notetakers with warm-up, open-note quizzes as a bridge between lessons. (These quizzes can form an excellent portfolio entry or series of entries.)

### CREATING A CONTENT PORTFOLIO

**1.** Establish prior knowledge and current needs: Use informal journal writing.

Preview the course: Read syllabus; mark calendar for important due dates.

Review prior experience: Identify barriers (consider everything from time management and reading and writing skills to the specialized vocabulary or jargon of the course).

Recognize your audience: Consider the instructor; record instructor's opinions and preferences.

Identify resources: Find out about the library, learning centers, tutors, instructor's office hours.

**2.** Set temporary goals and activities for study sessions: Use a formal essay.

Keep written records of all activities in and out of class (33e): Use a notetaking system for academic research (33i and 33j) and for self-study and class notes (see Chapter 4 for close reading techniques.).

Reflect frequently: What did I learn? How will this help? What is its relevance?

Label and organize everything: date, type, and purpose of assignment.

Set up sections as needed: Class notes, reading log, research project, test previews, reviews and revisions, and so on.

**3.** Adjust goals as necessary and continue reflective study process. Comment on successes and growth as they occur.

**4.** Reflect on your progress in final piece of formal writing. Prove you deserve the grade you want.

38. In the social sciences, most fields use the documentation style of the American Psychological Association (APA), as explained and illustrated in Chapter 37. In the natural sciences, documentation styles vary widely, although the Council of Science Editors (CSE) style is frequently used (see Chapter 38). Ask each of your science and technology instructors about the particular documentation style required for his or her assignments.

For more help with your writing, grammar, and research, go to **www.mycomplab.com**

# 40

# Writing About the Humanities and Literature

## 40a  What are the humanities?

The humanities consist of a set of disciplines that seek to represent and understand human experience, creativity, thought, and values. These disciplines include literature, languages, philosophy, and history, although some colleges group history with the social sciences. Also, many colleges consider the fine arts (music, art, dance, theater, and creative writing) part of the humanities, while other colleges group them separately.

## 40b  What types of sources do I use in the humanities?

In the humanities, existing documents or artifacts are PRIMARY SOURCES, and the writer's task generally is to analyze and interpret them. Some humanities papers will require SECONDARY SOURCES. These are articles and books that someone has written to explain or interpret a primary source. For example, suppose you're writing about a movie you saw. The movie is a primary source. If you consult a review of that movie, the review would be a secondary source.

## 40c   What types of papers do I write in the humanities?

Because the humanities cover an impressively broad range of knowledge, writing in the humanities covers many types and purposes.

### SUMMARIES

Occasionally your instructor will request an objective summary of a text; you might need to tell the plot of a novel or present the main points of an article. Generally, however, a summary is a means to a larger end. For example, writing an interpretation often requires you to summarize parts of the source so that your points about it are clear. See section 7f.1.

### SYNTHESES

SYNTHESIS relates several texts, ideas, or pieces of information to one another (4c). For example, you might read several accounts of the events leading up to the Civil War and then write a synthesis that explains what caused that war. See section 7f.4.

### RESPONSES

In a response, you give your personal reaction to a work, supported by explanations of your reasoning. Even though a response is a personal reaction, think of it as writing to inform or, even, to argue; provide reasons for your response so your readers understand clearly why you believe as you do and so that they're convinced your response is reasonable. Some instructors want you to justify your response with references to a text, while other instructors do not. Clarify what your instructor wants before you begin. See section 7f.2.

### NARRATIVES

When you write a NARRATIVE, you construct a coherent story out of separate facts or events. You might do the kind of work that a biographer does, gathering information about isolated events in people's lives, conducting interviews with those people or with others who knew them, or researching letters or other writings and related SOURCES—all to form a coherent story of their lives.

### INTERPRETATIONS

An interpretation explains the meaning or significance of a particular text, event, or work of art. You present your point of view and explain your reasoning, and the quality of your reasoning determines how successfully you've conveyed your point. See section 7f.3.

### CRITIQUES

In a critique (also called a CRITICAL RESPONSE or a review), you present judgments about a particular work, supported by your underlying reasoning.

genre, Laura L. Behling (Gustavus Adolphus College, MN) contends in her essay "'Generic' Multiculturalism: Hybrid Texts, Cultural Contexts" (*College English* 65.4 (2003): 411–426) that a new form of "colonialism" may develop if instructors require students to write in traditional ways about hybrid texts; conversely, that new ways of writing about generic hybrids, ways that break rules and transgress boundaries, may themselves become marginalized. Behling poses these thorny questions not to offer solutions but to raise consciousness about how instructors do (and perhaps need to) help students gain heightened understandings of multicultural identities.

### WHAT ELSE?

*Strategies and Resources* is a free 400-page book written especially for instructors who adopt this handbook. It offers a "primer for students" on reading and writing about literature and includes definitions, samples of student writing, and the complete text of "The Necklace" by Guy de Maupassant. Also, it offers specific, practical ways to "stimulate students to carry out deeper and more methodical explorations of literary works."

### TEACHING TIP

Some students have great difficulty engaging in analysis of a text and confuse plot summary for interpretation/analysis/critique. One way to help these students is to require them to include a plot summary in their writing, and then move on to more cerebral kinds of analysis. That way, if they include plot summary where critique belongs, you only need relocate the plot summary to the correct section and then ask them to use that summary as the basis for more critical analysis.

### BACKGROUND

In "Critical Analysis of Literature: Making the Connection between Reading and Writing" (*English Journal* 89.4(2000): 85–88), Michael A. Gunther describes a reading-writing course design that encourages students to actively read, think, debate, and write about literature.

methods of comparative literature, save that it also duly recognizes that "all national traditions are plural rather than singular" (18).

**QUOTATION: ON READING**

Language is the soul of intellect, and reading is the essential process by which that intellect is cultivated beyond the commonplace experiences of everyday life.

—Charles Scribner Jr.

**QUOTATION: ON WRITING**

I spent 15 years wandering about, weighed horribly with masses of paper and little else. Yet for this vocation of writing I was and am willing to die, and I consider very few other things of the slightest importance.

—Katherine Anne Porter

**QUOTATION: ON WRITING**

Form in literature is an arousing and fulfillment of desires. A work has form insofar as one part of it leads a reader to anticipate another part, to be gratified by the sequence.

—Kenneth Burke

**QUOTATION: ON WRITING**

If you are a writer you locate yourself behind a wall of silence and no matter what you are doing, driving a car or walking or doing housework . . . you can still be writing, because you have that space.

—Joyce Carol Oates

**QUOTATION: ON WRITING**

To begin with, our perception of the world is deformed, incomplete. Then, our memory is selective. Finally, writing transforms.

—Claude Simon

**QUOTATION: ON WRITING**

We are nauseated by the sight of trivial personalities decomposing in the eternity of print.

—Virginia Woolf

## 40e   What is literature and why write about it?

Literature includes fiction (novels and short stories); drama (plays, scripts, and some films); poetry (poems and lyrics); as well as nonfiction with artistic qualities (memoirs, personal essays, and the like).

Writing about literature generates insights about your reading. It helps you understand other people, ideas, times, and places. It shows you how authors use language to stir the imaginations, emotions, and intellects of their readers. Finally, writing is a way to share your own reading experiences and insights with other readers.

## 40f   What general strategies can help me write about literature?

When you write about literature, you want to read the work closely as well as actively (Chapter 4). Such reading involves asking what the work means, why the author made a particular choice, and why readers react to the work as they do. Quick References 40.2, 40.3, and 40.4 list several questions or elements that encourage active reading.

Sometimes instructors ask students to answer questions that deal with material on a literal level, that is, to tell exactly what is said on the page. If a question asks what happens in the plot or what a passage is saying, you need to answer with a SUMMARY or PARAPHRASE of the work. If a question asks about the historical context of a work, or asks for biographical or situational information about the author, you probably need to do some research and then report exactly what you find.

More often, assignments call for making INFERENCES. Making inferences means reading "between the lines" to figure out what is implied but not stated. This reading skill is especially crucial for reading literature because it tends to "show" rather than to "tell." Inferential thinking is necessary when your instructor asks you to discuss why a character does something for which the author provides no explicit reason. It's necessary when your instructor asks you to explain the effect of images in a poem, to discuss how a work implies the author's stance on a social issue, or to analyze how the author depicts the role of women, men, or specific ethnic groups.

Writing effective papers about literature involves more than summarizing the plot. It involves CRITICAL THINKING and SYNTHESIS. In such papers, you state a CLAIM (an observation or a position about the work of literature) and convince your readers that the thesis is reasonable. To be effective, your papers must be thorough and well supported. For support, you make direct references to the work, by SUMMARIZING, PARAPHRASING, and QUOTING specific passages

(35h–35j) and by explaining precisely *why* and *how* the selected passages support your interpretation.

## 40g How do I write different types of papers about literature?

When you read, look for details or passages that relate to your thesis. Mark up the text as you read by selectively underlining passages or by writing notes, comments, or questions in the margin. Alternatively, take notes separately.

### WRITING A PERSONAL RESPONSE

In a personal response paper, you explain your reaction to a literary work or some aspect of it. You might write about why you did or did not enjoy reading a particular work; discuss whether situations in the work are similar to your personal experiences; explain whether you agree or disagree with the author's point of view and why; or answer a question or explore a problem that the work raised for you.

### WRITING AN INTERPRETATION

An interpretation explains the message or viewpoint that you think the work conveys. Most works of literature are open to more than one interpretation. Your task, then, is not to discover the single right answer. Instead, your task is to determine a possible interpretation and provide an argument that supports it. The questions in Quick Reference 40.2 can help you write an effective interpretation paper.

---

**Quick Reference 40.2** ■ ■ ■ ■ ■ ■ ■

#### Questions for an interpretation paper

1. What is a central theme of the work?
2. How do particular parts of the work relate to the theme?
3. If patterns exist in the work, what might they mean? Patterns include repeated images, situations, words, and so on.
4. What meaning does the author create through the elements listed in Quick Reference 40.3?
5. Why might the work end as it does?

---

### WRITING A FORMAL ANALYSIS

A formal analysis explains how elements of a literary work function to create meaning or effect. Quick Reference 40.3 describes some of the major literary elements that you might expect to use in formal analyses.

> ## Quick Reference 40.3
>
> ### Major elements of formal analysis in literary works
>
> | | |
> |---|---|
> | **PLOT** | Events and their sequence |
> | **THEME** | Central idea or message |
> | **STRUCTURE** | Organization and relationship of parts to each other and to the whole |
> | **CHARACTERIZATION** | Traits, thoughts, and actions of the people in the plot |
> | **SETTING** | Time and place of the action |
> | **POINT OF VIEW** | Perspective or position from which the material is presented—by a narrator, a main character, or another person either in the plot or observing the plot |
> | **STYLE** | How words and sentence structures present the material |
> | **IMAGERY** | Descriptive language that creates mental pictures for the reader |
> | **TONE** | Author's attitude toward the subject of the work—and sometimes toward the reader—expressed through choice of words, imagery, and point of view (Chapter 1) |
> | **FIGURE OF SPEECH** | Unusual use or combination of words, as in metaphor and simile, for enhanced vividness or effect |
> | **SYMBOLISM** | Meaning beneath the surface of the words and images |
> | **RHYTHM** | Beat, meter |
> | **RHYME** | Repetition of similar sounds for their auditory effect |

To prepare to write a formal analysis, read the work thoroughly, looking for patterns and repetitions. Write notes as you read to help you form insights about these patterns and repetitions.

## WRITING A CULTURAL ANALYSIS

A cultural analysis relates the literary work to broader historical, social, cultural, and political situations. Instructors might ask you to explain how events or prevailing attitudes influence the writing of a work or the way readers understand it. Quick Reference 40.4 lists some common focuses for cultural analysis.

> **Quick Reference 40.4**
>
> ## Major topics for cultural analysis
>
> | | |
> |---|---|
> | GENDER | How does a work portray women or men and define— or challenge—their respective roles in society? |
> | CLASS | How does a work portray relationships among the upper, middle, and lower economic classes? How do characters' actions or perspectives result from their wealth and power—or the lack thereof? |
> | RACE AND ETHNICITY | How does a work portray the influences of race and ethnicity on the characters' actions, status, and values? |
> | HISTORY | How does a work reflect—or challenge—past events and values in a society? |
> | AUTOBIOGRAPHY | How might the writer's experiences have influenced this particular work? Similarly, how might the times in which the writer lives or lived have affected his or her work? |
> | GENRE | How is the work similar to or different from other works of its type (plays, sonnets, mysteries, comic novels, memoirs, and so on)? |

# 40h    What special rules apply to writing about literature?

When you write about literature, certain special elements come into play.

## 40h.1    Using present and past tense correctly

Always use the PRESENT TENSE when you describe or discuss a literary work or any of its elements: *George Henderson* [a character] ***takes** control of the action and **tells** the other characters when they may speak.* The present tense is also correct for discussing what the author has done in a specific work: *Because Susan Glaspell* [the author] ***excludes** Minnie and John Wright from the stage as speaking characters, she **forces** her audience to learn about them through the words of others.*

Use a PAST-TENSE VERB to discuss historical events or biographical information: *Susan Glaspell **was** a social activist who **was** strongly **influenced** by the chaotic events of the early twentieth century.*

## 40h.2    Using your own ideas and secondary sources

Some assignments call for only your own ideas about the literary work that is the subject of your essay. Other assignments require you additionally to use

Cheek 3

> For life is greater than the thousand wars
>
> Men wage for it in their insatiate lust,
>
> And will remain like the eternal stars,
>
> When all that shines to-day is drift and dust.
>
> (lines 9-12)

If this level of diction is reminiscent of Shakespeare, it is no accident. Both poems employ the English sonnet rhyme scheme (a b a b c d c d e f e f g g) and division into three quatrains and a closing couplet. McKay introduces a touch of his own, however. Although the English sonnet form calls for the "thematic turn" to fall at the closing couplet, McKay defies convention. He incorporates two turns into each sonnet instead of one. This allows him to use the first "mini-turn" to further develop the initial theme set forth in the first eight lines while dramatically bringing the poem to a conclusion with a forcefully ironic turn in the closing couplet. Specifically, in "The White City," McKay uses the additional turn to interrupt his description of his "Passion" with a vision of "the mighty city through a mist" (9). In "In Bondage," he uses the additional turn to justify his desire to escape the violent existence that society has imposed on his people.

McKay also demonstrates his poetic ability through his choice of words within his customized sonnets. Consider the opening of "In Bondage":

> I would be wandering in distant fields
>
> Where man, and bird, and beast, lives leisurely,
>
> And the old earth is kind, and ever yields
>
> Her goodly gifts to all her children free;
>
> Where life is fairer, lighter, less demanding,

continued >>

Cheek 4

> And boys and girls have time and space for play
>
> Before they come to years of understanding--
>
> Somewhere I would be singing, far away. (1-8)

The conditional power of *would* in the first line, coupled with the alliterative *wandering,* subtly charms us into a relaxed, almost dreamlike state in which the poet can lead us gently through the rest of the poem. The commas in the second line force us to check our progress to a "leisurely" crawl, mirroring the people and animals that the line describes. By the time we reach the eighth line, we are probably ready to join the poet in this land of "somewhere . . . far away."

Then this optimistic bubble is violently burst by the closing couplet:

> But I am bound with you in your mean graves,
>
> O black men, simple slaves of ruthless slaves.
>
> (13-14)

In "The White City" McKay again surprises us. This time, he does so by turning the traditional love sonnet upside down; instead of depicting a life made endurable through an overpowering love, McKay shows us a life made bearable through a sustaining hate:

> I will not toy with it nor bend an inch.
>
> Deep in the secret chambers of my heart
>
> I muse my life-long hate, and without flinch
>
> I bear it nobly as I live my part.
>
> My being would be a skeleton, a shell,
>
> If this dark Passion that fills my every mood,
>
> And makes my heaven in the white world's hell,
>
> Did not forever feed me vital blood. (1-8)

continued >>

Cheek 5

If it were not for the presence of "life-long hate" in the third line, this opening would easily pass as part of a conventional love sonnet. However, as the critic William Maxwell notes in "On 'The White City'," the first quatrain is "designed to ambush those anticipating another rehearsal of love's powers." The emotion comes from "deep in the secret chambers" of the speaker's heart (2), it allows him to transcend "the white world's hell" (7), and it is a defining "Passion." Once again, however, McKay uses the couplet to defy our expectations by making it plain that he has used the form of the love sonnet only for ironic effect: "The tides, the wharves, the dens I contemplate, / Are sweet like wanton loves because I hate" (13-14).

McKay's impressive poetic ability made him a master of the sonnet form. His language could at times rival even Shakespeare's, and his creativity allowed him to adapt the sonnet to his own ends. His ironic genius is revealed in his use of one of Western society's most elevated poetic forms to critique that same society. He held that critique so strongly that shortly after publishing these poems, McKay spent six months in the Soviet Union, where he met with Communist leaders (Hathaway 282). McKay once described himself as "a man who was bitter because he loved, who was both right and wrong because he hated the things that destroyed love, who tried to give back to others a little of what he had got from them . . ." (qtd. in Barksdale and Kinnamon 491). As these two sonnets show, McKay gave back very much indeed.

continued >>

Cheek 6

Works Cited

Barksdale, Richard, and Kenneth Kinnamon, eds. *Black Writers of America: A Comprehensive Anthology*. New York: Macmillan, 1972. Print.

Cooper, Wayne F. *Claude McKay: Rebel Sojourner in the Harlem Renaissance*. Baton Rouge: Louisiana State UP, 1987. Print.

---, ed. *The Passion of Claude McKay*. New York: Schocken, 1973. Print.

Giles, James R. *Claude McKay*. Boston: Twayne, 1976. Print.

Hathaway, Heather. "Claude McKay." *The Concise Oxford Companion to African American Literature*. Ed. William L. Andrews, Frances Smith Foster, and Trudier Harris. New York: Oxford UP, 2001. 282-83. Print.

Maxwell, William. "On 'The White City.'" *New Negro, Old Left: African American Writing and Communism Between the Wars*. New York: Columbia UP, 1999. *Modern American Poetry*. Web. 5 Mar. 2008 <http://www.english.uiuc.edu/maps/poets/m_r/mckay/whitecity.htm>.

McKay, Claude. "In Bondage." *Literature: An Introduction to Reading and Writing*. 8th ed. Ed. Edgar V. Roberts and Henry E. Jacobs. Englewood Cliffs: Prentice, 2007. 949-50. Print.

---. "The White City." *Literature: An Introduction to Reading and Writing*. 8th ed. Ed. Edgar V. Roberts and Henry E. Jacobs. Englewood Cliffs: Prentice, 2007. 1212. Print.

student interviews, in addition to traditional surveys that quantify responses.

**TEACHING TIP**
Research Papers in composition classes, depending on their subject matter, may very well use experiments and case studies from the social and natural sciences in order to support their arguments. The converse, however, is less often true: It is rare that a science professor and at least uncommon that a social science professor will require students to use materials from the humanities—save perhaps a prescriptive grammar textbook. Ask your students why they think this might be the case and what that difference tells them about how we as a society view knowledge, information, and truth.

**QUOTATION: ON RESEARCH**
If politics is the art of the possible, research is surely the art of the soluble.
—Peter Medawar

**QUOTATION: ON WRITING**
But for any writer worthy of the name . . . there are moments during the writing process when the rest of the planet might as well have gone to Venus. And those moments are not for sale.
—Maria Lenhart

**BACKGROUND**
In "Bridging the Disciplines: Interdisciplinary Discourse and Faculty Scholarship" (*The Journal of Higher Education* 74.2 (2003), 119–149) Susan Frost and Paul Jean describe Emory University's eight-year experiment to foster true communication and build meaningful interactions between academic disciplines through their "Luce Seminars."

**QUOTATION: ON SCIENCE**
Science is nothing but trained and organized common sense, differing from the latter only as a veteran may differ from a raw recruit. . . .
—T. H. Huxley

## 41d What are different types of papers in the social sciences?

Instructors will sometimes assign the same kinds of writing in the social sciences we explained for the humanities in section 40c. Four additional types of papers are case studies, research reports, research papers (or reviews of the literature), and ethnographies.

### CASE STUDIES

A case study is an intensive study of one group or individual. We discussed them in some detail in section 7d.4, but here are some additional perspectives. If you write a case study, describe situations as a neutral observer. Refrain from interpreting them unless your assignment says that you can add your interpretation to your report. Also, always differentiate between fact and opinion (4d.1).

A case study is usually presented in a relatively fixed format, but the specific parts and their order vary. Most case studies contain the following components: (1) basic identifying information about the individual or group; (2) a history of the individual or group; (3) observations of the individual's or group's behavior; and (4) conclusions as well as possible recommendations that resulted from the observations.

### RESEARCH REPORTS

**Research reports** explain your own original research based on PRIMARY SOURCES. These may result from interviews, questionnaires, observations, or experiments. Research reports in the social sciences often follow a prescribed format: (1) statement of the problem; (2) background, sometimes including a review of the literature; (3) methodology; (4) results; and (5) discussion of findings.

### RESEARCH PAPERS (OR REVIEWS OF THE LITERATURE)

More often for students, social science research requires you to summarize, analyze, and synthesize SECONDARY SOURCES. To prepare a **review of literature**, comprehensively gather and analyze the sources that have been published on a specific topic. Sometimes a review of the literature is a part of a longer paper, usually the "background" section of a research report. Other times the entire paper might be an extensive review of the literature.

### ETHNOGRAPHIES

Ethnographies are comprehensive studies of people interacting in a particular situation. Section 7d.5 provides advice on writing them.

## 41e What documentation style should I use in the social sciences?

If you use sources when writing about the social sciences, you must credit them using documentation. The American Psychological Association (APA) is the most commonly used documentation style in the social sciences. APA style uses PARENTHETICAL REFERENCES in the body of a paper and a list of REFERENCES at the end. We describe APA documentation style in detail in Chapter 37, providing a sample student research paper using APA style in section 37h.

Chicago Manual (CM) documentation style is sometimes used in the social sciences. The CM BIBLIOGRAPHIC NOTE style is described in detail in Chapter 38.

## NATURAL SCIENCES

## 41f What are the natural sciences?

The natural sciences include disciplines such as astronomy, biology, chemistry, geology, and physics. The sciences focus on natural phenomena. Scientists form and test hypotheses, which are assumptions made to prove their logical soundness and consequences in the real world. They do this to explain CAUSE AND EFFECT (4d.3) as systematically and objectively as possible.

The scientific method, commonly used in the sciences to make discoveries, is a procedure for gathering information related to a specific hypothesis. The scientific method is the cornerstone of all inquiry in the sciences. Quick Reference 41.1 gives guidelines for using the scientific method.

## 41g What are writing purposes and practices in the natural sciences?

Because scientists usually write to inform their AUDIENCE about factual information, SUMMARY and SYNTHESIS are important fundamental writing techniques. Exactness is extremely important in scientific writing. Readers expect precise descriptions of procedures and findings, free of personal bias. Scientists expect to be able to *replicate*—repeat step by step—the experiment or process the researcher carried out and obtain the same outcome.

Completeness is as important as exactness in scientific writing. Without complete information, a reader can misunderstand the writer's message and reach a wrong conclusion.

---

**Quick Reference 41.1**

### Guidelines for using the scientific method

1. Formulate a tentative explanation—known as a *hypothesis*—for a scientific phenomenon. Be as specific as possible.

2. Read and summarize previously published information related to your hypothesis.

3. Plan and outline a method of investigation to uncover the information needed to test your hypothesis.

4. Experiment, following exactly the investigative procedures you've outlined.

5. Observe closely the results of the experiment, and write notes carefully.

6. Analyze the results. If they prove the hypothesis to be false, rework the investigation and begin again. If the results confirm the hypothesis, say so.

7. Write a report of your research. At the end, you can suggest additional hypotheses that might be investigated.

---

Because science writing depends largely on objective observation rather than subjective comments, scientists generally avoid using the FIRST PERSON (*I, we, our*) in their writing.

When writing for the sciences, you're often expected to follow fixed formats, which are designed to summarize a project and present its results efficiently. Writers in the sciences sometimes use charts, graphs, tables, diagrams, and other illustrations to present material. In fact, illustrations, in many cases, can explain complex material more clearly than words can, as in Figure 41.1.

## 41h What documentation style should I use in the natural sciences?

If you use secondary sources when you write about the sciences, you are required to credit your sources by using documentation. Documentation styles in the various sciences differ somewhat from discipline to discipline and, even, from publication to publication. Ask your instructor which style to use.

The Council of Science Editors (CSE) has compiled style and documentation guidelines for the life sciences, the physical sciences, and mathematics. CSE documentation guidelines are described in sections 38c and 38d.

**COMMON DISEASES AND INFECTIONS WITH THEIR MICROBIAL CAUSES**

| | Bacteria | Fungus | Protozoa | Virus |
|---|---|---|---|---|
| Athlete's foot | | ▲ | | |
| Chickenpox | | | | ▲ |
| Common cold | | | | ▲ |
| Diarrheal disease | ▲ | | ▲ | ▲ |
| Flu | | | | ▲ |
| Genital herpes | | | | ▲ |
| Malaria | | | ▲ | |
| Meningitis | ▲ | | | ▲ |
| Pneumonia | ▲ | ▲ | | ▲ |
| Sinusitis | ▲ | ▲ | | |
| Skin diseases | ▲ | ▲ | ▲ | ▲ |
| Strep throat | ▲ | | | |
| Tuberculosis | ▲ | | | |
| Urinary tract infection | ▲ | | | |
| Vaginal infections | ▲ | ▲ | | |
| Viral hepatitis | | | | ▲ |

**Figure 41.1** A table conveying data

## 41i  How do I write different types of papers in the natural sciences?

Kinds of writing that are common in the natural sciences include REPORTS AND ANALYSES OF DATA (7e.1; 7e.2), LAB REPORTS AND EMPIRICAL STUDIES (7e.3), and RESEARCH PAPERS (7g.4).

Two additional major types of papers in the sciences are *reports* and *reviews*.

### 41i.1  Science reports

Science reports tell about observations and experiments. When they describe laboratory experiments, as is often the case in academic settings, they're usually called laboratory reports. Formal reports feature the eight elements identified in Quick Reference 41.2. Less formal reports, which are sometimes assigned in introductory college courses, might not include an abstract or a review of the literature. Ask your instructor which sections to include in your report.

**Quick Reference 41.2**

### Parts of a science report

1. **Title.** Precisely describes your report's topic. Your instructor may require a title page that lists the title, your name, the course name and section, your instructor's name, and the date. If so, there is no

---

**Quick Reference 41.2**  (continued)

recommended format in CSE style; generally, students use APA format (37g) or their instructor's.

2. **Abstract.** Provides a short overview of the report to help readers decide whether your research interests them.

3. **Introduction.** States the purpose behind your research and presents the hypothesis. Any needed background information and a review of the literature appear here.

4. **Methods and Materials.** Describes the equipment, material, and procedures used.

5. **Results.** Provides the information obtained from your efforts. Charts, graphs, and photographs help present the data in a way that is easy for readers to grasp.

6. **Discussion.** Presents your interpretation and evaluation of the results. Did your efforts support your hypothesis? If not, can you suggest why not? Use concrete evidence in discussing your results.

7. **Conclusion.** Lists conclusions about the hypothesis and the outcomes of your efforts, paying particular attention to any implications that can be drawn from your work. Be specific in suggesting further research.

8. **References.** Presents references cited in the review of the literature, if any. Its format conforms to the requirements of the documentation style preferred by your instructor.

---

### SAMPLE STUDENT SCIENCE REPORT

The sample science report presented on the following pages was written by a student in an intermediate course in biology. Like the sample report, yours would likely follow APA format for margins, page numbering, and title page. The text and references would follow CSE-style recommendations.

Effectiveness 1

Adam Furman

Biology 201, Lab

Professor Joshua Mann

November 13, 2007

Title of report → The Effectiveness of Common Antibiotics

Abstract omitted on this sample

Title of subsection → Introduction

The purpose of this experiment was to test the effectiveness of antibiotics against two common bacteria.

Antibiotics are substances that inhibit life processes of bacteria. There are two types of antibiotics. One interferes with cell wall synthesis, causing death. The other disrupts protein synthesis, thus preventing replication.

*Escherichia coli* is a gram-negative bacterium. It is found in the colon of many mammals, including humans. Commonly, it contaminates beef and chicken products. *Staphylococcus epidermidis* is a gram-positive bacterium found naturally on the skin. This bacterium is often the cause of infected burns and cuts. Both bacteria were used in this experiment.

It is hypothesized that five chemical antibiotics will be effective against both bacteria. Also hypothesized is that two natural antimicrobials, echinacea and garlic, would not work very well.

Methods and Materials

Using aseptic techniques, two petri dishes were inoculated. *Staphylococcus epidermidis* was used on one dish and *Escherichia coli* on a second dish. A sterile paper disc was saturated with Streptomycin. The disc was placed on one of the dishes. The process was repeated for the other dish. Both

continued >>

dishes were marked with identification and location of the paper discs. Each of the following was also saturated on paper discs and placed into its own zone on both dishes: sterile water (control), ampicillin, erythromycin, chloramphenicol, tetracycline, gentamycin, echinacea, and garlic.

The dishes were incubated overnight at room temperature. The zone of inhibition of growth in centimeters was measured and recorded.

### Results

Streptomycin, a protein synthesis disrupter, worked effectively to prevent growth of the *S. epidermidis* and the *E. coli*. Tetracycline inhibited the reproduction of the *S. epidermidis* and the *E. coli*. Ampicillin, a common bactericide, worked better on the *S. epidermidis* than the *E. coli*, because the *S. epidermidis* is gram positive and the *E. coli* is gram negative. Gentamycin effectively prevented the growth of *E. coli*. Erythromycin and chloramphenicol behaved similarly to the ampicillin.

The antibiotics behaved as expected in regard to effectiveness against gram-positive and gram-negative bacteria. As hypothesized, the echinacea inhibited growth only slightly, indicating that it probably would not function as an antibiotic. The garlic had a zone of inhibition greater than expected for a non-antibiotic. Zero centimeters of inhibition from the sterile water control demonstrates that there was no contamination of the experiment.

Discussion section omitted in this sample

continued >>

Effectiveness   3

Conclusion

The results imply that the ampicillin would be an effective treatment against *S. epidermidis* infection and gentamycin would prove effective in treating an infection of *E. coli*.

As with any experiment, it would be wise to repeat the tests again to check for accuracy. Other antibiotics could be tested against a larger range of bacteria for broader results.

No Cited References needed in this type of science report

## 41i.2  Science reviews

A science review is a paper discussing published information on a scientific topic or issue. The purpose of the review is SUMMARY: to assemble for readers all the current knowledge about the topic or issue. Sometimes, the purpose of a science review is SYNTHESIS: to suggest a new interpretation of the old material. In such reviews, the writer must present evidence to persuade readers that the new interpretation is valid.

If you're required to write a science review, you want to (1) choose a very limited scientific issue currently being researched; (2) use information that is current—the more recently published the articles, books, and journals you consult, the better; (3) accurately PARAPHRASE (35i) and SUMMARIZE (35j) material; and (4) DOCUMENT your sources (Chapters 36–38). If your review runs longer than two or three pages, you might want to use headings to help your reader understand the organization and idea progression of your paper. See Chapters 32–34 for advice on finding and using sources.

For more help with your writing, grammar, and research,
go to **www.mycomplab.com**

# 42

# Making Presentations and Using Multimedia

## 42a What are presentations?

Presentations, which are speeches often supported with multimedia tools, are common not only in academic disciplines across the curriculum, but also in work and public settings. Preparing a presentation and drafting a paper involve similar processes, and the information in Chapters 1 and 2 will help you. The rest of this chapter will provide additional information for preparing presentations and using multimedia tools.

## 42b How does my situation focus my presentation?

Just as you need to adjust your writing according to each SITUATION, so you need to adjust presentations to fit PURPOSES, AUDIENCES, ROLES, and any SPECIAL CONSIDERATIONS. Consider three different situations.

- You want to address a group of students to inform them about a film club you're starting.
- You need to persuade a management group at work to adopt a new set of procedures for making purchasing decisions.
- You plan to give a toast at a friend's wedding to express your feelings and to entertain the wedding guests.

Different approaches will be successful in each instance because your purpose and audience are different.

The three main purposes for presentations are to entertain, to INFORM and to PERSUADE (1b). In academic and work situations, the last two are most important. For an oral presentation, determine your purpose, and keep it in mind as you draft and revise your speech. Common INFINITIVE PHRASES for an informative presentation include: *to explain why, to clarify, to show how, to report, to define, to describe,* and *to classify.* Common phrases for a persuasive presentation include: *to convince, to argue, to agree with, to disagree with, to win over, to defend,* and *to influence.*

## 42c How do I adapt my message to my audience?

Adapting your presentation to your listening audience means holding their interest and being responsive to their viewpoints. Consult the general strategies for analyzing audiences in Quick Reference 2.1. Especially consider your listeners' prior knowledge of your topic, their desire to learn more, and whether they agree with your point of view. You'll find that your audience falls into one of three categories: *uninformed, informed,* or *mixed.*

**UNINFORMED AUDIENCE** — Start with the basics, and then move to a few new ideas. Define new terms and concepts, and avoid unnecessary technical terms. Use visual aids and give examples. Repeat key ideas—but not too often.

**INFORMED AUDIENCE** — Don't waste your audience members' time with the basics. From the beginning, reassure them that you'll be covering new ground. Devote most of your time to new ideas and concepts.

**MIXED AUDIENCE** — In your introduction, acknowledge the more informed audience members who are present. Explain that you're going to review the basic concepts briefly so that everyone can build from the same knowledge base. Move as soon as possible toward more complex concepts.

Adapting your presentation to the general needs and expectations of your audience doesn't mean saying only what they might want to hear. It means rather that you need to consider their knowledge of your topic and their interest in it. You can then make your message understandable and relevant by using appropriate language and examples.

## 42d How do I organize my presentation?

As with essays, an oral presentation has three parts: INTRODUCTION, BODY, and CONCLUSION. Within the body, you present your major points, with support for each point. Drafting a SENTENCE OUTLINE gets you close to your final form and forces you to sharpen your thinking. Quick Reference 42.1 shows you a sample outline for an oral presentation.

**QUOTATION: ON VISUAL RHETORIC**

Because the process of design is fundamentally visual and multimodal, it can be challenging, but it leads students to a new understanding of how designed spaces and artifacts impact audiences.

—Mary Hocks

**QUOTATION: ON SPEAKING**

A speech is like an airplane engine. It may sound like hell but you've got to go on.

—William Thomas Piper

**TEACHING TIP**

Here are some general pointers for making a good PowerPoint presentation:

**1.** Make sure it is easy to read, especially from a distance. Distracting backgrounds, color clashes, or too little color differentiation may make your presentation difficult to follow.

**2.** Avoid using too much clip art. Not every slide requires an image.

**3.** Avoid writing too much text. Your audience will find it difficult to read, and you will be tempted to simply read from your slides, which will inhibit your ability to deliver a powerful speech.

**4.** Avoid bulleted lists. Oftentimes, bulleted lists are used simply because the default template for a PowerPoint slide is "title/bulleted list." On the other hand, if you will spend some time explaining each of the bulleted points, you might consider creating a unique slide for each point. Doing so will emphasize those points a great deal more than a bulleted list would.

**5.** Use sound sparingly, if at all. Sound files are more difficult to package with your presentation than are images, and the quality of audio speakers at your venue may not allow the sound to be heard.

**6.** Do not feel that you must stand dutifully next to your computer to advance slides. The PowerPoint is there to help you; you are not there to tend to the PowerPoint.

**7.** Make hard copies of slides and print them out, in case the technology fails and you will not be able to use your PowerPoint presentation.

---

## Quick Reference 42.1

### Organizational outline for an oral presentation

Title: _____

Topic: _____

Specific purpose: _____

Thesis statement: _____

I. Introduction (followed by a clear transition to point 1 in the body)
II. Body
    A. Major point 1 and specific supporting examples (followed by a clear transition from point 1 to point 2, perhaps with a brief reference to the introduction)
    B. Major point 2 and specific supporting examples (followed by a clear transition from point 2 to point 3, perhaps with a brief reference to point 1 and the introduction)
    C. Major point 3 and specific supporting examples (perhaps with a brief reference to points 1 and 2)
III. Conclusion (Refer to your introduction but do not repeat it verbatim or your audience will lose interest.)

### INTRODUCING YOURSELF AND YOUR TOPIC

Your ETHOS is perhaps even more important in speaking than in writing. Your audiences needs to trust you and, even, like you. All audience members want to know three things about a speaker: Who are you? What are you going to talk about? Why should I listen? To respond effectively to these unasked questions, try these suggestions.

- Grab your audience's attention with an interesting question, quotation, or statistic; a bit of background information; a compliment; or an anecdote. If necessary to establish your credibility—even if someone has introduced you—briefly and humbly mention your qualifications as a speaker about your topic.

- Give your audience a road map of your talk: Tell where you're starting, where you're going, and how you intend to get there. Your listeners need to know that you won't waste their time.

### FOLLOWING YOUR ROAD MAP

Although much advice for writing applies to oral presentations, listening to a presentation is very different from reading an essay. When you're reading an article and lose sight of the main point, you can reread a few paragraphs. But when you're listing to a speech, you can't go back. As a result, audiences generally need help following the speaker's line of reasoning. Here are some strategies to keep your listeners' minds from wandering and to help them follow your points.

- Signal clearly where you are on your road map by using cue word transitions such as *first, second,* and *third;* or *subsequently, therefore,* and *furthermore;* or *before, then,* and *next.*
- Define unfamiliar terms and concepts, and follow up with strong, memorable examples.
- Occasionally tell the audience what you consider significant, memorable, or especially relevant, and why. Do so sparingly, at key points.
- Provide occasional summaries at points of transition. At each interval, recap what you've covered and say how it relates to what's coming next.

### WRAPPING UP YOUR PRESENTATION

Demonstrate that you haven't let key points simply float away. Try ending with these suggestions.

- Never let your voice volume fall or your clarity of pronunciation falter because the end is in sight.
- Don't introduce new ideas at the last minute.
- Signal that you're wrapping up your presentation using verbal cues, such as "In conclusion" and "Finally." When you say "finally," mean it!
- Make a dramatic, decisive statement; cite a memorable quotation; or issue a challenge. Allow a few seconds of silence, and then say "thank you." Use body language, such as stepping slightly back from the podium, and then sit down.

## 42e  How do I research and write a presentation?

Doing research for an oral presentation requires the same kind of planning as doing research for written documents. To keep yourself calm and focused, divide the preparation into manageable tasks according to a realistic time line. Set small goals and stick to them to give yourself enough time to research, organize, and practice your presentation. Review Chapters 33–35 for help on finding and evaluating sources, taking notes, planning a research strategy, and documenting sources. An oral presentation won't have a WORKS CITED or REFERENCES list to be read out, but your listeners might appreciate a handout in which you list your sources. In academic situations, your instructor might ask you to turn in your Works Cited or References.

Most of the preparation involved in an oral presentation is written work. Writing helps you take four important steps in your preparation: (1) to organize

**8.** In short, think of your PowerPoint presentation as a "speech enhancer," not a "speech maker." That way, if the technology fails—and everyone who presents with PowerPoint regularly has stories of stupendous, show-stopping technological failures—you will still be able to deliver your speech.

**TEACHING TIP**
The History Channel maintains a large Web site of famous speeches from the fields of politics, entertainment, science and technology, and war and diplomacy; go to <http://www.historychannel.com/speeches/>. Another good resource is the Online Speech Bank, at the Web site <http://www.americanrhetoric.com/speechbank.htm>. Over five thousand speeches are available.

**TEACHING TIP**
One way to help students learn how to use their voices effectively and deliver a memorized speech with passion is to have them commit a classic speech, soliloquy from a play, or other dramatic monologue to memory and deliver it to the class. As they practice, have them make "stage notes" to themselves about their use of voice, gesture, movement, eye contact, etc. Remind them to match their delivery to the tone of the speech they are reciting.

**TEACHING TIP**
Although students need to know that preparation and practice provide the best way to reduce stage fright and ensure a strong presentation, they may feel better when they hear that most performers and public speakers have learned to welcome a little anxiety as a good sign that the presentation will have energy. "Consider the worst that can happen," one expert recommends; then picture your response to that scenario. Cardiac arrest? Doubtful. But someone moving into the presenter role and imagining that "worst case scenario" could ask his or her audience to memorize the emergency number "911" and then repeat it twice to assure himself or herself they will remember. The audience will laugh, and the presenter will relax. You may also mention to your students that beginning a

presentation with a little touch of humor, if appropriate to the topic and smoothly integrated into the introductory remarks, can build in the chuckle that helps everyone relax.

**TEACHING TIP**

Like actors, students may find it helpful to "step into character" before giving their speeches. Ask them to think about who, ideally, would deliver the speeches they have written. The person each chooses could be an actor, living or dead, a person from history, or even a fictional character. When the students go to give their speeches, have them imagine that they are "playing" that person. The distance created by playing a character rather than "speaking for themselves" may prove helpful for some students' nerves. Furthermore, imagining someone else delivering their speeches may help them think about effective ways to use voice, gesture, etc.

**QUOTATION: ON WRITING**

Literature is the art of writing something that will be read twice.

—Cyril Connolly

your thoughts; (2) to distance yourself from the ideas and remain objective; (3) to pay attention to words and language; and (4) to polish for clarity and impact.

When drafting your speech, it may help you to review Chapter 8 on style and tone. In particular, see sections 8d and 8e for a discussion of a medium LEVEL OF FORMALITY in language, which is an appropriate level for most public speaking. Careful DICTION (12d) will make your speech both easy to listen to and memorable.

An oral presentation calls for the same careful language selection that you employ in your writing. Here are some tips on using language in oral presentations.

- Recognize the power of words. For example, read this statement by Winston Churchill, made after World War II: "Never in the field of human conflict was so much owed by so many to so few." Now try substituting the word *history* for "the field of human conflict." Note that while the single word *history* is more direct, using it destroys the powerful impact of the original words. Also consider this version: "Never in the field of human conflict did so many people benefit from the contributions of a relatively few others." This sentence is much less effective because it loses the PARALLELISM of the original (Chapter 10).

- Never alienate your audience by using words, phrases, or examples that could offend your listeners or people connected with them.

- Use GENDER-NEUTRAL LANGUAGE by avoiding sexist terms and inappropriate words and expressions (12f).

- Present yourself with dignity in body language, tone of voice, and dress.

## 42f How do I incorporate multimedia into my presentation?

Multimedia elements such as visual aids, sound, and video can reinforce key ideas in your speech by providing illustrations or concrete images for the audience. If done well, they can make long explanations unnecessary and add to your credibility. Still, they can never take the place of a well-prepared presentation.

### 42f.1 Using traditional visual aids

Here are various types of visual aids and their uses. For each of them, always make text and graphics large enough for others to read and grasp at a distance.

- **Posters** can dramatize a point, often with color or images. Because you need to make sure posters are large enough for everyone in your audience to see them, they tend to work best with smaller audiences of thirty or fewer.

- **Dry-erase boards** are preferable to chalkboards because you can use various colors that are visually appealing on them. Use them to roughly sketch an illustration or to emphasize a technical word. Doing this adds a dynamic element to your presentation, but take care not to turn your back on the audience for more than a few seconds.

- **Handouts** are useful when the topic calls for a longer text or when you want to give your audience something to refer to later. Short, simple handouts work best during a presentation, but longer, more detailed ones are more effective at the end; remember that listeners can pay more attention to what's on the page than to you, and you don't want to compete with yourself! Always include DOCUMENTATION information for any SOURCES on the handout. A strategic handout can be a useful backup just in case other technologies are missing or broken; remember to wait until everyone has one before you begin speaking about it.

- **Transparencies** require an overhead projector. You can prepare them in advance, either by hand or by using a computer and printer, which helps clarity and also allows you to incorporate visual materials. For emphasis during a presentation, you can write on transparencies with a marker.

## 42f.2   Using electronic media

Computers offer a range of possibilities for enhancing oral presentations, and they are by far the most common means of including images and sounds. The trick is to make sure that they add to your presentation rather than distract your audience. You need to balance the time you spend developing multimedia materials with the time you spend writing and practicing your presentation.

### POWERPOINT PRESENTATIONS

Microsoft PowerPoint® is the most widely used presentation software that creates digital slides. Another program, called "Impress" is available for free from www.openoffice.org. These slides can contain words, images, or combinations of both; they can even include sound or movie clips. To project your slides during a presentation, you need an LCD projector connected to your computer and a screen.

To design PowerPoint slides, follow the principles of unity, variety, balance, and emphasis discussed in Chapter 45. Never present so much information on each slide that your audience pays more attention to reading it than to listening to you. Also, never simply read large amounts of text from your slides; your audience will quickly—and rightfully—become bored. Remember the power of photographs, illustrations, or other visual materials for conveying information or making points (4j, 4k, 4m, and Chapter 45).

## Quick Reference 42.2

### Preparing materials for delivering a mapped presentation

- Type your key words in a large font for easier reading.
- Highlight the most important point(s) you want to make.
- Use only one side of a page or card to avoid losing your place.
- Number your pages or cards in large type in case you drop them.
- Clearly distinguish your introduction, body, and conclusion so that your audience can follow along easily.
- Mark cues to yourself on your pages for pauses, emphasis, and use of visuals.
- Include information on your sources so that you can briefly mention them (and offer to give more details after your speech).

## 42i   How do I use my voice effectively?

Your voice is the focus of any oral presentation. If you're unsure whether you can be heard in a particular setting, speak briefly and then ask your listeners whether they can hear you. When you use a microphone, speak into it without raising your voice.

Speak naturally but clearly. Articulate your words by pronouncing the end of each word. Swallowing word endings leads to poor speech delivery. Speak slowly and deliberately—but make sure that your words have rhythm and pace so that your listeners will stay engaged. Vary your tone of voice for emphasis and clarity. Pause every now and then to let your points sink in.

## 42j   How do I use nonverbal communication?

Your body language can either add to or detract from your message. Eye contact is your most important nonverbal communication tool because it communicates confidence and shows respect for your listeners. If you have to walk up to the front of a room or a podium, don't begin speaking before you get there and are looking directly at the audience. Smile or nod at your listeners as you begin. To do this smoothly, you need to memorize your first few sentences.

Use appropriate facial expressions to mirror the emotions in your message. Gestures, if not overdone, contribute to your message by adding emphasis; they are best when they appear to be natural rather than forced or timed. If you use a podium, stand squarely behind it. When gestures aren't needed, rest your hands on the podium—don't scratch your head, dust your clothing, or fidget. You may step slightly forward or backward from a microphone to indicate transitions in your message, but never sway from side to side. And, of course, dress appropriately for your audience and the type of event.

## 42k  What can I do to practice for my oral presentation?

Good delivery requires practice. In preparing to speak, figure in enough time for at least four complete run-throughs of your entire presentation, using visuals if you have them. When you practice, keep the following in mind:

- Practice conveying ideas rather than particular words so that your TONE doesn't become stilted.
- Time yourself and cut or expand material accordingly.
- Practice in front of a mirror or videotape yourself. As you watch yourself, notice your gestures. Do you look natural? Do you make nervous movements that you weren't aware of as you spoke?
- Practice in front of a friend. Ask for constructive feedback by posing these questions: What was my main point? Did the points flow? Did any information seem to come from out of nowhere or not fit in with the information around it? Did I sound natural? Did I look natural? How did the visuals add to my message?

## 42l  How can I overcome stage fright?

If you suffer from stage fright, remember that the more prepared and rehearsed you are, the less frightened you'll be. Your aim is to communicate, not to perform. If you worry that your audience will see that you're nervous, Quick Reference 42.3 suggests ways to overcome physical signs of anxiety.

## 42m  How do I make a collaborative presentation?

A common practice in many academic settings—and in business and public situations—is to present an oral report as part of a group. All members of the group are required to contribute in some way to the collaborative enterprise. The advice in section 6a will help you work together productively. Here are some additional guidelines for effective collaborative presentations:

- Make sure, when choosing a topic or a position about an issue, that most members of the group are familiar with the subject.

# 43b What are typical policies concerning business writing?

Most workplaces have policies that strictly govern their employees' use of the organization's e-mail system and stationery. As soon as you start with a new employer, speak to your supervisor about policies. Also ask for the employee manual and take time to read it carefully. If no one seems to know the official policy, always assume that the policies are strict until you're told differently. See Quick Reference 43.1 for a list of typical business writing policies for employees.

**Quick Reference 43.1**

### Typical business writing policies for employees

- Companies reserve e-mail systems and any uses of company letterhead stationery for their operations only.
- Companies own all correspondence written, sent, or received via e-mail or other means, including courier or regular mail. Furthermore, their administrators and supervisors at all levels have complete access to view and save all of this correspondence.
- Companies prohibit employees from writing, sending, or receiving correspondence (by any means) with content that is potentially harmful to the company. This includes, but is not limited to, content that makes libelous comments, enters into preliminaries to contractual agreements or into contracts themselves, contains chain letters, mentions material that degrades someone, circulates confidential or embarrassing information, or reveals other offensive material.
- Companies have the right to monitor your Internet use. If you spend time shopping online or viewing sites not related to work, you might be subject to discipline.
- Companies own the writing (and other products) you produce in their employment.

# 43c What are legal considerations concerning business writing?

Legal considerations involving business writing involve two entities at least: you as an employee and the company for which you work.

## 43c.1 Legal considerations involving you as an employee

Because employers have complete access to your business e-mail, business letters, and business memos, they can use such documents as evidence of your job performance. You might not be aware during the normal course of your workday that your supervisors have access to your written conduct of business, but they do legally. Judge your writing, therefore, as if it were being read in a formal assessment of your work.

## 43c.2 Legal considerations involving your company

For legal purposes, your business e-mail as well as your business letters and business memos written on company letterhead stationery may be used as evidence in legal disputes, in court, and by the government, regarding you or the company you work for. In some situations, e-mails sent to customers or other parties within and outside the company may be construed as legally binding on the company; therefore, they're your responsibility.

## 43d What are special considerations concerning business e-mail?

E-mail is the primary form of written business communication today. Therefore, use it with special care, even though you might use it quite informally in your personal life. Here are some overriding guidelines for business use.

- Find out whether personal e-mail is tolerated. (You can usually find e-mail policies in an employee manual.) Even if personal e-mail is permitted, realize that monitoring systems in most workplaces can quickly identify such e-mails. Therefore, you might want to avoid sending or receiving personal e-mails on your workplace computer.

- Ask your supervisor whether there are restrictions regarding the size of attachments that you can send or receive. (Large attachments can overload the computer system at work.) If there are restrictions, use NETIQUETTE and alert your recipients about the size of any large attachments before you send them. In turn, ask senders to alert you before sending large ones to you.

- Protect the ID numbers and passwords you're assigned or have created to access your organization's electronic systems. As an employee, you're accountable for all activity conducted on password-protected accounts.

Some businesses automatically insert or require employees to insert a DISCLAIMER—a statement appended to the top or bottom of e-mails designed

**BACKGROUND**

The Web site <http://jobstar.org/tools/resume/index.cfm>, which is sponsored by JobStar, offers helpful definitions on various types of resumés as well as suggestions for creating a customized resumé.

**BACKGROUND**

The OWL at Purdue has a great number of resources available to "workplace writers," including techniques, samples, guidelines, and tips for writing to Chinese and Indian business audiences; see <http://owl.english.purdue.edu/owl/resource/681/01/>.

**QUOTATION: ON WRITING**

I for one appreciate a good form letter, having worked on Capitol Hill and learned several dozen cordial ways to say nothing.
—Carrie Johnson

**BACKGROUND**

The Genesee Valley Center Writing Program of Empire State College, at <http://www.esc.edu/ESConline/Across_ESC/WritingResourceCenter.nsf/wholeshortlinks2/Business+Writing>, provides both theoretical and discussion concerning some of the most common types of business writing.

**QUOTATION: ON READING**

The more I like a book, the more slowly I read. . . . This spontaneous talking back to a book [is] one of the things that makes reading so valuable.
—Anatole Broyard

to protect the company from legal liability. The value of disclaimers is limited. Only a court of law can determine the effectiveness of such statements, but they might prove effective in limiting a company's liability in some cases.

### 43d.1 Following guidelines for content of work-related e-mail

The subject line in an e-mail tells your recipients how to sort, file, and prioritize a message. Be very specific in stating your subject so that you don't show disrespect for your recipient's time. You might have to write the same people more than one e-mail about different subjects in the same day, but at least your recipients will be able to keep their records straight.

| NO (VAGUE) | YES (SPECIFIC) |
| --- | --- |
| Travel Approval | Approval Request for Chicago Trip |
| E-mail Policy | New E-mail Retention Policy |
| Meeting | Meeting on Annual Report Schedule |
| Schedule Change | Cancellation of Chicago Trip |

In the "Cc" or "Copies" space, insert the e-mail addresses of people who need to see your message, even when they aren't expected to respond. Never send copies to people who don't really need the information; it can backfire and simply annoy someone who already has too many messages in his or her Inbox. If you use the "Bcc" (Blind Copy) space, you're sending a copy to people without your primary recipients knowing about it. Generally, people consider blind copying rude because it's akin to talking behind someone's back. However, certain rare, delicate situations might call for it. For example, in a mass mail-out, it would be good netiquette to blind copy dozens of customers because you would be protecting their privacy by not disclosing their e-mail addresses to everyone else.

For the message of your e-mail, single-space the text, and double-space between paragraphs and before your complimentary closing. Start paragraphs flush left at the margin. When you need to include a separate document of more than a paragraph or two with your e-mail, such as a report, compose it as a separate document in your word-processing program, and attach it to your e-mail using the "Attachments" function of your e-mail service. Attached documents, rather than copied and pasted documents, look better because they maintain the original formatting (margins, spacing, italics). As you compose your message, follow the principles in Quick Reference 43.2.

Figure 43.1 is an example of a professional e-mail.

### 43d.2 Using e-mail netiquette

**Netiquette,** a word coined from *net* and *etiquette,* refers to good e-mail manners. For example, unless your business recipients give you permission to loosen

| To: | sherrel.ampadu@jpltech.com |
|---|---|
| From: | Chris Malinowitz <cmalinowitz@chateauby.com> |
| Subject: | Confirming Meeting Arrangements |
| Cc: | dmclusky@chateauby.com |
| Bcc: | |
| Attached: | C:\Documents and Settings\Desktop\Chateau Menus.doc |

Dear Ms. Ampadu:

I am writing to confirm the final arrangements for your business meeting on June 17, 2009, at our conference center.

As you directed, we will set the room in ten round tables, each seating six. We will provide a podium and microphone, an LCD projector and screen, and a white board with markers. I understand that you will be bringing your own laptop. Our technician can help you set up.

You indicated that you would like to provide lunch and refreshments at two breaks. Attached please find our menus. You will need to make your lunch selections at least 48 hours in advance.

If you have any questions or wish to make any changes, I would be pleased to accommodate your needs. Thank you for choosing The Chateau at Brickyard.

Sincerely,

Chris Malinowitz
Catering Director, The Chateau at Brickyard

**Figure 43.1** A professional e-mail

your level of formality, always address them by their full names and titles, especially when your recipients are people you've never met or corresponded with before. As important, always use GENDER-NEUTRAL LANGUAGE. Finally, try to reply to e-mail messages within one or two days after receiving them. When you can't respond quickly, always acknowledge that you've received a message. Say when you'll reply, and don't forget to follow up.

## Quick Reference 43.2  ■ ■ ■ ■ ■ ■ ■

### Content of a business e-mail

- Keep the message of your business e-mail brief and your paragraphs short. Reading a screen is harder on the eyes than reading a print document.

- Restrict each business e-mail to one topic, even if you have to write the recipients about more than one topic in the same day.

continued >>

---

**Quick Reference 43.2** (continued)

- Start your business e-mail with a sentence that tells what your message is about.

- Put the details of your business e-mail message in the second paragraph. Supply any background information that your recipients aren't already aware of or might have forgotten.

- Conclude your e-mail in a short, final paragraph by asking for explicit information or specific action, if needed; or by restating your reason for writing (for example, keeping someone apprised of a situation or reporting on a meeting).

- If your e-mail runs longer than three to four paragraphs, add topic headings to help your readers speed through the material.

- Never write in all capital letters (WE NEED TO TAKE ACTION NOW) or all lowercase letters (i think we need to check with the denver office). Not only are they annoying to read, but all capital letters are considered the written equivalent of rudely shouting. All-lowercase letters suggest laziness and a lack of respect.

- At the end of your message, before your full name and position, use a commonly accepted complimentary closing, such as *Sincerely, Cordially,* or *Regards.*

- Be cautious about what you say in a business e-mail. After all, the recipient can forward any e-mail, including ones received as blind copies, to others without your permission, even though this practice is considered unethical and rude.

- Forward an e-mail message only if you've asked the original sender for permission.

---

# 43e How do I format and write memos?

**Memos** are usually exchanged internally (within an organization or business). Today e-mail takes the place of most memos, unless the correspondence requires a paper record or signature. The guidelines for writing e-mail (43d.1) also pertain to memos. The appropriate form of communication—paper memos or e-mail—depends on what's customary in your work environment.

The standard format of a memo includes two major parts: the headings and the body.

To:    [Name your audience—a specific person or group.]
From:  [Give your name and your title, if any.]
Date:  [Give the date on which you write the memo.]
Re:    [State your subject as specifically as possible in the "Subject" or "Re" line.]

The content calls for a beginning, middle, and end, with all parts holding closely to your topic. Don't ramble. If you need more than one or, at most, two pages, change your format into that of a brief report. Here are some guidelines for preparing a memo.

- **Introduction:** Briefly state your purpose for writing and why your memo is worth your readers' attention. Mention whether the recipient needs to take action, making it clear either here or at the conclusion.

- **Body:** Present the essential information on your topic, including facts the recipient needs to know. If you write more than three or four paragraphs, use headings to divide the information into subtopics so that the memo can be scanned quickly.

- **Conclusion:** End with a one- to two-sentence summary, a specific recommendation, or what action is needed and by when. Finish with a "thank you" sentence.

## 43f  How do I write business letters?

Business letters are more formal and official than business e-mails or business memos. Choose to write a business letter, rather than a business e-mail, to add appropriate weight and respect to your message, for ceremonial occasions, and to ensure that your message is placed on the record and thereby becomes part of a "paper trail." Business letters generally fall into two official categories based on their purposes.

- **Regular business letters** are business-to-business communications. These letters make up the majority of business correspondence. Always use company letterhead stationery, and follow any special guidelines for style or format that your company uses.

- **Social business letters** are letters to business colleagues on matters that serve a business-related social function, such as congratulations on an achievement, condolences in a time of loss, thank you letters, invitations to social events, and the like. Given that these letters are written in a business context, social business letters may be written on company letterhead stationery.

There are some general guidelines for addressing recipients in business letters. The old-fashioned "To Whom It May Concern" rarely reaches the right person in an organization. Use the full name of your recipient whenever possible. If you can't locate a name, either through a phone call to a central switchboard or on the Internet, use a specific category—for example, "Dear Billing Department," placing the keyword "Billing" first (not "Department of Billing"). Always use gender-neutral language. Figure 43.2 is an example of a business letter from a not-for-profit group.

Here are guidelines for the format and content of your business letters.

- **Paper:** Use 8½ × 11-inch paper. The most suitable colors are white, off-white, and light beige. Fold your business letters horizontally into thirds to fit into a standard number 10 business envelope (9½ × 4 inches). Never fold a business letterhead stationery page in half and then into thirds.

- **Letterhead stationery:** Use the official letterhead stationery (name, address, and logo, if any) of the business where you're employed. If no letterhead stationery exists, imitate the format that others have used. If no such tradition exists, center the company's full name, address, and phone number at the top of the page, and use a larger and different font than for the content of your letter.

- **Format:** Without indents, use single spacing within paragraphs and double spacing between paragraphs. All lines start flush left, which means at the left margin. This is called **block style**. An equally acceptable alternative form is called **modified block style** in which the lines for the inside address and the body begin flush left but the heading, closing, and signature begin about halfway across the page. Quick Reference 43.3 (on page 776) lists the features of block style and modified block style letter formats.

Use block or modified block formats for business correspondence of a personal nature, such as job application letters, letters of complaint concerning personal matters, or letters asking for information for you personally. Use plain white paper, and if you have personal stationery, use it.

ArtsFlamenco

3B-243 West 21st Street
New York, NY 10011
artsflamenco@msn.com
www.artsflamenco.org

January 11, 2009

Mr. Antonio Alducin
Advisor, Latino Heritage Club
George Washington High School
324 Mapleview Road
Englewood, New Jersey 07631

Dear Mr. Alducin,

We enjoyed speaking with you earlier this week regarding *ArtsFlamenco*'s arts-in-education programs. We can certainly work with you to develop an after-school workshop that ties in elements of Spanish language, culture, music, and dance.

We are enclosing three program plans and their estimated costs. For your further interest, we are also including a DVD showing clips from two of our recent arts-in-education programs. After you have reviewed these materials, please contact us to discuss any questions you might have.

We very much look forward to speaking with you again.

All the best,

*Jorge Navarro*

Jorge Navarro
President and Artistic Director

Encl: 3

*A Section 501(c)(3) New York Not-for-Profit Corporation*

**Figure 43.2** A business letter in block style

## Quick Reference 43.3

### Features of block and modified block styles

**BLOCK-STYLE FORMAT**

- Begin the dateline two inches below the top of the page or three lines below the last line of the letterhead, depending on the depth of the letterhead copy.
- Begin all elements at the left margin.
- Allow one inch for left, right, and bottom margins.
- Leave three blank lines between the dateline and the inside address.
- Leave one blank line between the inside address and the salutation.
- Leave one blank line between the salutation and the body.
- Type the body single-spaced and leave one blank line between paragraphs.
- Leave one blank line between the body and complimentary closing.
- Leave three blank lines between the complimentary closing and the signature block.

**MODIFIED BLOCK STYLE FORMAT**

- Begin the dateline two inches below the top of the page or three lines below the last line of the letterhead, depending on the depth of the letterhead copy.
- Center:
  - Dateline
  - Complimentary closing
  - Signature block
- Allow one inch for left, right, and bottom margins.
- Leave three blank lines between the dateline and the inside address.
- Leave one blank line between the inside address and the salutation.
- Leave one blank line between the salutation and the body.
- Type the body single-spaced and leave one blank line between paragraphs.
- Leave one blank line between the body and complimentary closing.
- Leave three blank lines between the complimentary closing and the signature block.

## 43g  How do I prepare a meeting agenda?

An agenda is a plan for a meeting. It lets everyone who is attending know the purpose of the meeting and the topics it will cover. The specific forms of an agenda can vary from company to company, so if you're asked to prepare one, the best way to begin is to study the agendas and minutes of prior meetings of the same group.

Agendas sent before the meeting can help everyone prepare for it, especially if some individuals are to give reports or review materials ahead of time. (In fact, preparing an agenda in advance might let you know a meeting is unnecessary, that information can be shared through an e-mail, or a decision can be made without getting everyone together; no one likes meetings that waste time.) Agendas generally provide the following information:

1. The time, date, and place of the meeting (and perhaps a list of who will attend).

2. The topics of the meeting, in the order in which the group will take them up (perhaps with the approximate amount of time to be devoted to each), and with a note about who (if anyone) is in charge of that particular topic.

3. The purpose of each topic on the agenda. For example, is the purpose simply to share or discuss information? Is the purpose, rather, to make decisions or judgments? People attending the meeting need to know what they're expected to accomplish.

4. A list of what material needs to be reviewed ahead of time or what will be available at the meeting.

Figure 43.3 shows you the agenda for an informal meeting.

## 43h  How do I write meeting minutes?

Minutes are the record of a meeting. Generally, minutes cover all important topics that were discussed, both those on the agenda and not. Exactly what is defined as "important" is hard to know when you're new to a company, so your best route is to write down just about everything that comes up. Pay special attention to any decisions the group made, any votes, and any assignments of tasks to individuals or groups. After the meeting you can ask at least two colleagues who were there to advise you about what to leave out when you write up the minutes.

On rare occasions, minutes are very detailed, recording all the points and nuances raised, in an approach that seems something like a transcript. Most times, however, the minutes are much shorter, briefly summarizing the

**FORMAT OF HEADING**
Name and title centered, single-spaced
Double space to date and time on one line and location on one line
"Agenda" two lines below

Human Resources Department
Planning Meeting for Open Enrollment Communication

Friday, July 18, 2008, 3–4 p.m.
Michigan Avenue Conference Room

Agenda

**Attendees**
Margaret Alexander, HR
Joanna Bergstrom, HR Director-Organizer
Rebecca Greenfield, Freelance HR Writer/Editor
Larry Jordan, HR Services
Bob LeGorce, Finance
Bernard Moore, HR Services
Chris Papparello, Finance

| Topics | Discussion leader (time) |
|---|---|
| • Introductions/Roles and Responsibilities | Joanna (5 minutes) |
| • Tentative enrollment dates | Joanna and Bob (5 minutes) |
| • Possible benefits plan changes | Bob (10 minutes) |
| • Goals/strategies for communication | Bob and Chris (10 minutes) |
| • Communication elements | Joanna and Beth (25 minutes) |
| • Next steps/assignments | Joanna (5 minutes) |

**REQUIRED IN INFORMAL AGENDA**
Organization or department name
List of attendees
Topics to be discussed

**OPTIONAL IN INFORMAL AGENDA**
Statement of purpose after title of meeting
Bullets for names
Name of chair or organizer
Time allotments

**Figure 43.3** Agenda for a meeting

highlights and focusing on conclusions and decisions that were reached rather than on all details. Such minutes summarize outcomes, not entire discussions. Minutes generally have several elements:

1. Date, time, and place of the meeting, including when it began and ended.

2. Who was present (and perhaps who was absent).

3. Summaries of topics, decisions, and responsibilities.

Using headings or lists can help organize the minutes.

Sometimes who takes the minutes is assigned spontaneously at the beginning of a meeting, often to new employees. Therefore, always go to meetings prepared with a laptop or a notebook, pens or pencils—and a smile. Once they're written, minutes can be distributed in paper copies or, more frequently, as e-mail attachments, or on a protected company Intranet site or blog. You'll need to follow the method your company or supervisor prefers. It goes without saying that you want to edit and proofread the minutes very carefully.

The sample set of minutes shown in Figure 43.4 is being communicated by e-mail because the minutes-taker found out this is the traditional way the minutes of this particular group are circulated.

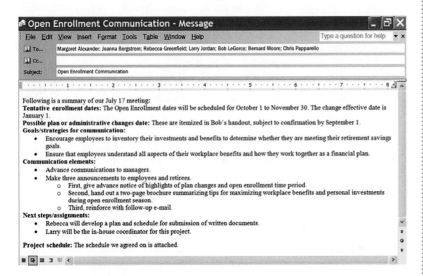

**Figure 43.4** Meeting minutes

## 43i    How do I write business reports and manuals?

Reports and manuals are documents that exist for the purpose of informing others inside or outside the workplace. Some manuals explain procedures or processes to help employees do their work consistently and effectively: how to handle specific situations (filing claims, dealing with customer concerns, processing orders, and so on). Customers often see "how-to" manuals when they buy a new product. Other manuals document policies. Among the most important of these are employee or personnel manuals, which explain things like workplace dress and behavior, benefits, use of technology, and so on.

If you're in charge of writing a manual, clarity and completeness are your most important considerations. Readers need to be able to find information easily and be able to use it accurately. As a writer, you need to anticipate the questions people will have and write the manual accordingly. Analyzing your audience is crucial. Document design is important as you lay out the information in the most effective way.

### 43i.1    Writing internal reports

Internal reports are designed to convey information to others in your workplace. They can be various lengths and serve various purposes. Consider four examples:

- You attend a professional meeting and provide a report on what you learned there for your supervisor and for colleagues who weren't there.
- You're working on a lengthy project. You report on your progress so that others can understand what you have completed, what remains, and what problems or delays you anticipate, if any.
- You conduct extensive consumer research through telephone interviews with potential customers, and you summarize and analyze your findings.
- You identify all the available solutions to a particular problem and write a report that discusses the strengths and weaknesses of each.

In each of these cases, follow the principals of reporting, analyzing, and interpreting information and data (7b–7c). Being clear and concise are especially vital.

### 43i.2    Writing external reports

External reports inform audiences beyond the workplace. Generally, they have a secondary function of creating a good impression of the company or organization. Probably the most common examples are annual reports, in which companies summarize for investors their accomplishments during the previous

**Figure 43.5** A company's external report

years, especially their profits and losses. However, other kinds of external reports are also common. For example, a school principal may write a report to parents that explains students' results on a statewide achievement test. Figure 43.5 shows a section of one company's report.

Because external reports are written for more general audiences, they require explaining many terms and concepts that would be clear to your co-workers. Document design, whether in print or on the computer screen, is also important (Chapter 45). Notice how the report in Figure 43.5 uses images and color.

## 43j  How do I write business proposals?

Proposals persuade readers to follow a plan, choose a product or service, or implement an idea. A marketing specialist might propose a new product line. A teacher might propose a change in the curriculum. A leader in a not-for-profit organization might propose a way to raise funding. Proposals generally describe a project, the steps for starting and completing the project, and how much it will cost.

Readers evaluate proposals based on how well the writers have anticipated and answered their questions. If some readers have a high level of knowledge about the subject of the proposal, and others have little, then you need to explain the basic information and offer a glossary of terms. Here are some guidelines for preparing a proposal.

| | |
|---|---|
| **INTRODUCTION** | Explain the purpose and scope of the project. Describe the problem that the project seeks to solve. Lay out the solution your project will provide. Include dates for beginning and completing the work. Project the outcomes and the costs. Be accurate and precise. |
| **BODY** | What is the product or service? What resources are needed? What are the phases of the project? What is the detailed budget? Precisely how is each phase to be completed? By what date is each phase to be completed? How will the project be evaluated? |
| **CONCLUSION** | Summarize briefly the benefits of this proposal. Thank readers for their time. Offer to provide further information. |

## 43k How do I write a resumé?

A **resumé** details your accomplishments and employment history. Its PURPOSE is to help a potential employer (the AUDIENCE) determine whether you'll be a suitable candidate for employment. To make a favorable impression, follow the guidelines for writing a resume in Quick Reference 43.4.

---

### Quick Reference 43.4

#### Guidelines for writing a resumé

- Place your name, address, e-mail address, and telephone number at the top. If you have a professional Web site or online PORTFOLIO (Chapter 47), include the URL.

- Make sure you have a professional e-mail address. No employer will be impressed by beermaster@gmail.com or daddyslittlegirl@hotmail.com.

- Make it easy to read. Label the sections clearly, and target the resumé to the position you want. Help employers see your most significant attributes as quickly and as easily as possible.

- Adjust your resumé to fit your PURPOSE. For example, if you're applying for a job as a computer programmer, you'll want to emphasize different facts than you would if you're applying for a job selling computers in an electronics store.

- Use headings to separate blocks of information. Include the following headings, as appropriate: Position Desired or Career Objective;

continued >>

## Quick Reference 43.4    (continued)

Education; Experience; Licenses and Certifications; Related Experience; Honors or Awards; Publications or Presentations; Activities and Interests; and Special Abilities, Skills, and Knowledge.

- When you list your work experience, place your most recent job first; when listing education, place your most recent degrees, certificates, or enrollments first.

- Write telegraphically. Start with verb phrases, not with the word *I,* and omit *a, an,* and *the.* For example, write "Created new computer program to organize company's spreadsheets" instead of "*I* created *a* new computer program to organize *the* company's spreadsheets."

- Include only relevant information.

- Tell the truth. Even if you get the job, an employer who discovers you lied will probably fire you.

- Include references, or state that you can provide them on request. (Be sure to have them at hand so that you can respond speedily to such a request.) Before you start the job application process, ask people who can comment on your professional qualifications if you may list them as references.

- Fit all of the information on one page. If you need a second page, make sure the most important information is on the first page.

- Use high-quality paper that is white or off-white.

- Prepare your resumé in three different formats: traditional print, digitally scannable, and plain text.

- Proofread carefully; even one spelling error or one formatting error can eliminate you from consideration.

Your resumé can take many formats, and an employer may specifically require one of them.

Traditional print resumés can take advantage of the full range of document design, including columns, different fonts, graphics, and so on. Still, you want the overall effect to be clean and clear. Figure 43.6 shows an example of a traditional print resumé.

Scannable resumés are designed to be scanned by machines that digitize their content. Sophisticated software then searches the database to match key terms to position requirements. As a result, these resumés need to be simpler: don't use columns, different fonts, lines or other graphics, bold or italics fonts, and so on. Choose a clean sans serif font such as Arial or Geneva in a 10–12

MONICA A. SCHICKEL

1817 Drevin Avenue
Denver, CO 80208
Cell phone: (303) 555-7722
E-mail: mnsschl@wordnet.com
Professional portfolio: www.schickelgraphics.net

OBJECTIVE: Entry level position as a graphic designer or publications assistant

EXPERIENCE

9/08 – present    **Publications Intern** (half-time; paid), *Westword* (Denver, CO)
                  • Design advertisements
                  • Prepare photographs for publications
                  • Lay out the "Tempo" section
                  • Fact-check, edit, and proofread articles

6/06 - 8/08       **Customer Service Representative,** Wells Fargo Bank (Aurora CO).
                  • Sold accounts to customers; made all sales goals
                  • Created promotional posters

4/03 - 8/05       Evening Assistant Manager, McDonalds Restaurant (Longmont, CO).
                  • Supervised 7 cooks and counter workers
                  • Assured food and service quality

EDUCATION

8/07 – present    Bachelor of Arts, The University of Denver, expected June 2009
                  Major: Graphic Arts; Minor: Digital Media Studies

8/05 – 5/07       AA General Education, Front Range Community College, May 2007

SKILLS AND SELECTED EXPERIENCES

                  • Expert in complete Adobe Creative Suite
                  • Expert in complete Microsoft Office Suite
                  • Excellent Spanish language skills
                  • Illustrator and photographer; have completed several commissions (see
                    portfolio, above)
                  • Vice President, Student Residence Halls Association
                  • Cartoonist and Designer, *The DU Clarion* (campus newspaper)
                  • Excellent customer service skills

REFERENCES: Available on request

**Figure 43.6** A traditional print resumé

point size. Include keywords that the computer can match to the job. Figure 43.7 on page 786 shows a scannable version of the resumé in 43.6.

Plain text resumés are simpler yet. They can be pasted directly into e-mails (for companies that won't open attachments for fear of viruses) or into application databases. If you have time to prepare only one type of resumé, we suggest you create one that's scannable.

## 43l   How do I write a job application letter?

A **job application letter** (sometimes called a *cover letter*) always needs to accompany your resumé. Avoid repeating what's already on the resumé. Instead, connect the company's expectations to your experience by emphasizing how your background has prepared you for the position. Your job application letter, more than your resumé, reflects your energy and personality. However, there are limits; this is not the place to be too cute or clever.

Each job application letter needs to be tailored to each job. While you can use basic information in multiple letters, one generic letter will not represent you effectively. Among other things, a very general letters tells prospective employers that you didn't care enough to address the specific circumstances of their organizations. Here are guidelines for writing a job application letter.

- Use one page only.
- Overall, think of your letter as a polite sales pitch about yourself and what benefits you can bring to the company. Don't be shy, but don't exaggerate.
- Use the same name, content, and format guidelines as for a business letter (43f).
- Address the letter to a specific person. If you can't discover a name, use a gender-neutral title such as *Dear Personnel Director.* Below we explain how to write gender-neutral salutations.
- Open your letter by identifying the position for which you're applying.
- Mention your qualifications, and explain how your background will meet the job requirements.
- Make clear that you're familiar with the company or organization; your research will impress the employer.
- End by being specific about what you can do for the company. If the job will be your first, give your key attributes—but make sure they're relevant. For instance, you might state that you're punctual, self-disciplined, eager to learn, and hardworking.
- State when you're available for an interview and how the potential employer can reach you.

Monica A. Schickel
1817 Drevin Avenue
Denver, CO 80208
Cell phone: (303) 555-7722
E-mail: mnsschl@wordnet.com
Professional portfolio: www.schickelgraphics.net

KEYWORDS

Publications experience, graphic design, editing, photography, supervisor, editing, customer service, digital media, excellent Spanish, Adobe creative suite, Photoshop, InDesign, Quark, CSS, Dreamweaver, Web design, illustrator, proofread, Excel, Access, Publisher, newspaper, layout, sales, willing to relocate

OBJECTIVE

Entry level position as a graphic designer or editorial assistant

EXPERIENCE

Publications Intern (half-time; paid), Westword (Denver, CO). September 2008 to present
—Design advertisements
—Prepare photographs for publications
—Lay out the "Tempo" section
—Fact-check, edit, and proofread articles

Customer Service Representative, Wells Fargo Bank (Aurora CO). April 2006-August 2008
—Sold accounts to customers; made all sales goals
—Created promotional posters

Evening Assistant Manager, McDonalds (Longmont, CO). June 2003-August 2005
—Supervised 7 cooks and counter workers
—Assured food and service quality

EDUCATION

Bachelor of Arts in Graphic Design, Minor in Digital Media Studies
The University of Denver, expected June 2009

Associate of Art in General Education, Front Range Community College, May 2007

SKILLS AND SELECTED EXPERIENCES

Expert in complete Adobe Creative Suite
Expert in complete Microsoft Office Suite
Excellent Spanish language skills
Illustrator and photographer; have completed several commissions (see portfolio, above)
Vice President, Student Residence Halls Association
Cartoonist and Designer, Clarion (newspaper)
Excellent customer service skills

REFERENCES AVAILABLE ON REQUEST

**Figure 43.7** A scannable resumé

• Edit and proofread the letter carefully. If you have to hand-correct even one error, print the letter again.

For an example of a job application letter, see Figure 43.8.

---

**Monica A. Schickel**
1817 Drevin Avenue
Denver, CO 80208

Cell phone: (303) 555-7722
E-mail: mnsschl@wordnet.com
Professional portfolio: www.schickelgraphics.net

May 3, 2009

Jaime Cisneros
Publications Director
R.L. Smith Consulting
2000 Wabash Avenue
Chicago, IL 60601

Dear Mr. Cisneros:

Please consider my application for the graphic designer position currently being advertised on your company's Web site. I believe that my professional experiences, education, and skills prepare me well for this opportunity.

I am currently completing a paid internship at Westword, a weekly features and entertainment magazine in Denver, CO, where I have worked as an effective member of a creative team. My responsibilities have included designing advertisements, laying out sections, and editing photographs. Other related experience includes commissions as an illustrator and photographer. My professional portfolio demonstrates the range and quality of my work. As the enclosed resumé notes, I have additional experience in business environments.

Next month I will earn a BA in graphic design from The University of Denver, where my course of study has included extensive work in graphic design, photography, drawing, and illustration. Simultaneously, I will complete a minor in digital media studies that has included courses in Web design, video editing, and sound editing. I have expertise in all the standard software applications that would be relevant to your position.

I would be pleased to provide further information and to interview at your convenience. The opportunities at R.L. Smith closely match my background and goals, and the prospect of joining your team in Chicago is exciting. I look forward to discussing how I can contribute to your publications department.

Sincerely,

*Monica A. Schickel*

Monica A. Schickel

---

**Figure 43.8** A job application letter

**ESOL Tip:** In some cultures, job applications may include personal information, such as an applicant's age, marital status, number of children, religion, or political beliefs. In North America, however, this is not standard practice. Such personal information does not help an employer determine how well you can perform a particular job, so avoid including it in your application.

Thinking, speaking, and writing with gender-neutral language (12f) is very important in the workplace, particularly when addressing recipients in memos, job application letters, and so on. Following are some guidelines for writing a gender-neutral salutation:

1. Telephone or send an e-mail to the company to which you're sending the letter. State your reason for contacting them, and ask for the name of the person you want to receive your letter.

2. Address men as Mr., and address women as Ms., unless you're specifically told to use Miss or Mrs. If your recipient goes by another title such as Dr. or Professor, use it.

3. If you can't identify a proper name and need to use a title alone, keep the title generic and gender-neutral.

> **NO** Dear Sir: [sexist]
> Dear Sir or Madam: [sexist for both genders]
>
> **YES** Dear Human Resources Officer:
> Dear Apple Sales Manager:

For more help with your writing, grammar, and research, go to **www.mycomplab.com**

# 44

# Writing for the Public

## 44a What is public writing?

**Public writing** is intended for people who are reading for reasons other than work, school, or professional obligations. Instead, they read it out of interest or a desire to keep informed. Some public writing is also known as CIVIC

**BACKGROUND: ON "PUBLIC WRITING" AND "CIVIC DISCOURSE"**
Writing teachers and scholars have long been vexed by what to call the huge variety of writings produced for nonexpert readers who are reading not in academic or vocational settings but, rather, as members of a diffuse and varied public. A common term, which we generally adopt here, is "public writing." Indeed, over twenty-five years ago, Janice Lauer, Gene Montague, Andrea Lunsford, and Janet Emig distinguished between "four worlds of writing: the academic, the vocational, the personal, and the

WRITING because you're writing to affect knowledge, actions, or beliefs among other citizens in a democratic society.

Examples of writing for the public include a letter or e-mail to refute a newspaper editorial, a program for a play or concert, a brochure to draw new members into a service organization, a proposal to build a town park, a fund-raising letter for a worthy cause, a script for a radio announcement, a Web site for a hobby or social cause that interests you, a blog on current events or a specific issue, or an e-mail urging your representative to vote for a certain bill.

## 44b How can I understand public writing situations?

As the examples in section 44a indicate, public writing takes a wide range of forms, depending on the situation. The familiar categories of TOPIC, PURPOSE, AUDIENCE, ROLE, and CONTEXT/SPECIAL REQUIREMENTS are especially important for understanding your options and requirements (1b).

Much public writing has the purpose of INFORMING or PERSUADING, and our earlier advice applies. One thing to keep in mind is that, unlike an instructor or someone in a work setting, public audiences aren't obligated to read your work, for the most part. This means that you have to take particular care as you write for them, especially when you're writing for an AUDIENCE that you don't know personally. Among other things, this means analyzing your readers and establishing your credibility for them.

"Establishing credibility" means convincing your readers that they need or want to listen to you. Create a strong ETHOS by being accurate and honest and by explaining your connection with the readers. What do you have in common with them?

For example, if you're writing a letter to the editor of your local newspaper, you'll gain credibility if you begin, "As a resident of Green County for twelve years," and then state your position. By establishing yourself first as a member of your audience's community, you convey that you have a sincere and long-standing interest in the welfare of that community.

Establishing credibility in public writing can also come through your style and ingenuity. After all, another common purpose of this writing is to entertain. Newspapers and magazines are full of feature stories that inform, certainly, but that are also enjoyable to read.

People also write for the public for the pleasure of expressing themselves. They share opinions on plays or on presidents; they talk about music or about moods. Social networking sites and software like Facebook or MySpace (46h) are prime examples of this purpose, as are certain blogs and the online comment sections maintained by many newspapers. However, expressing yourself doesn't give you license to be insulting, irresponsible, or inflammatory—at least if

public" (*The Four Worlds of Writing*, New York: Harper & Row, 1981). However, "public" has always been something of a fuzzy term. Defined as the opposite of "private," for example, "public" writings could include nearly anything intended for other readers. The conventional limiting distinction, then, has been between audiences that are defined by some specialized knowledge or affiliation (including different academic, professional, and vocational discourse communities, such as literary scholars, lawyers, and restaurant operators) and audiences either with no specific identities or, at most, some broader affiliation (for example, residents of a certain town or locality, people of specific genders or political beliefs, or even people who share hobbies).

Complicating definitions even further are the various reasons that people write for these public audiences. Both newspaper editorials and comic strips are public writings. So are brochures and manifestos—but also poems and memoirs and novels. A published letter to the editor is public writing, but what about a letter to a legislator? In that last instance, no one beyond the legislator and his or her staff is likely to read it. But surely the letter is not academic, personal, or vocational discourse.

In light of this situation, several rhetoricians have adopted a more precise name for the kinds of public writing most common in undergraduate composition courses: "civic discourse." The word *civic* invokes the rhetorical situations that are part and parcel of functioning as an active citizen in a democratic society. Writing in such situations aims to affect law, policy, practices, knowledge, and beliefs. It tends to have a persuasive emphasis at its core, even if that emphasis is muted. To promote the term *civic discourse* is to remind teachers and students of the roots of composition studies in ancient Greek and Roman rhetoric.

While civic discourse is generally also public writing, not all public writing is necessarily civic discourse. Plenty of nonfiction is published for personal or artistic expression and for entertainment or contemplation—not necessarily to compel fellow citizens toward a certain action or stance.

> gatorbait wrote on Mar 24, 2008 9:15 PM:
>
> i say if you don't feel like tipping the delivery guy, then you should get off your fat lazy butts and go pick it up yourself. but alas, you people are too busy sitting in front of the tv while you scratch yourself and wonder how you'll ever lose that tire that magically appeared around your midsection. ...that is until you drip ice cream all over the front of your shirt and you realize that you'd better polish off the whole container before it melts. cheap, lazy townies.

**Figure 44.1** A poor example of an online comment

you expect anyone to pay attention to you. (And what's the point of publishing your writing if you don't want readers?) The writer in Figure 44.1 posted this comment in an online discussion about how much to tip pizza deliverers: Maybe the writer enjoyed insulting his or her readers, but the tone and approach (not to mention the capitalization and punctuation) did little for the writer's position.

# 44c How do I write reports for the public?

Reports for the public vary in length, format, and content. An *action brief* from a political organization might consist of a few pages detailing recent developments on an issue of concern, such as a proposed law. Often these are published on Web sites or distributed through e-mail messages.

Write your material in an evenhanded TONE so that your credibility is supported by your fairness. If you want to criticize something, be sure your argument is well reasoned and supported—and that it lacks BIAS or malice toward any person(s) or specific idea(s). This doesn't mean that your writing needs to be limp. Indeed, you can choose writing that's spirited, enthusiastic, and even stirring.

## 44c.1 Public reports

Figure 44.2 (page 792) shows the executive summary of a report on climate changes in the American West. An executive summary is a brief overview sometimes included before a lengthy report. The report was produced by The National Resources Defense Council. The entire work was published online and as a 64-page booklet. Figure 44.3 (page 793) shows a "fact sheet," a four-page version of the longer report.

To write a public report, follow the guidelines in Quick Reference 44.1.

## Quick Reference 44.1

### Writing a public report

- Decide your purpose. Will you only inform, or will you also analyze the information you present? Or—going one step further—will you make a recommendation based on the information and your analysis?

- State your findings objectively. Though you may later bring in your opinion by recommending a course of action, your credibility depends on your first reporting accurately.

- Organize a formal report using the following sections. Depending on the purpose of your report, however, you might combine or expand any of the sections.

  - **Executive summary:** Provides a very brief summary of the entire report, including conclusions or recommendations.
  - **Introduction:** Explains the purpose of the report, describes the problem studied, and often describes or outlines the organization of the entire report.
  - **Methods or sources:** Describes the data or information that were collected for the report and how they were gathered.
  - **Results:** Presents the findings of the report.
  - **Discussion:** States the meanings and implications of your findings.
  - **Conclusion:** Makes recommendations or simply summarizes the findings.

## 44c.2 Policy briefs

A policy brief is a kind of public report in which experts put technical information into a form that nonexperts and decision makers can understand. These days, most of them are published on the Internet. "To brief" someone is to inform them in a concise way. The usual purpose of policy briefs is to persuade people with facts and analysis that support a specific decision. Your readers need to perceive you as objective and careful, basing your position on logic and evidence. On the other hand, if you want to use a policy brief in a research paper, carefully analyze the quality of the source (34m). Figure 44.4 (page 794) shows the opening of a policy brief.

**EXERCISE 44-1** Using your Internet browser, enter "policy brief" (in quotation marks so that you search for this specific phrase), and the following other terms (one at a time): food, health, energy, crime, or other terms that interest you. List the policy briefs you find for each, and evaluate their quality.

differences between each. How does this information impact the authors' ability to persuade or inform students? Why?

**EXTRA EXERCISE B**
Break students into pairs. Assign each pair a topic connected to local issues in your area. For example, are there any recent discussions over funding for public schools? Libraries? Headlines about local public institutions? Then, have each pair of students decide on a "persona" who would be able to provide a compelling argument about one of these issues. Have students write a brief character sketch describing their potential authority and what gives this person a unique ability to comment on the issue. As a class, talk about how authority is constructed in the community. What counts? What do the students value in listening to the different character sketches? How can students use ethos in their own writings about public issues?

**TEACHING TIP**
A staged research paper can focus on a community issue. If students do original research on a community issue, the final research paper can be written as a public report. In addition to providing an important community resource in written form, students might also keep a blog or host a public forum on the issue. Copies of a student research paper can be compiled in a booklet and deposited in the university and public libraries.

**ANSWERS: EXERCISE 44-1**
Answers will vary. Consider giving students a peer review sheet, based on the criteria in Quick Reference 44.1, and have them present their evaluations to the class.

## TEACHING TIP

As you work with students on the topic of public writing, many students will reference FaceBook and other social networking sites. As Figure 44.2 demonstrates, online writing can sometimes lead to derisive comments or even *ad hominem* attacks. Cornell University provides an excellent set of guidelines to help students navigate the world of social networking. You might want to discuss these guidelines in detail with your students, if your university does not have a similar document. See <http://www.cit.cornell.edu/policy/memos/facebook.html>.

There are a number of high profile cases and discussions about social networking sites. You may want to engage students in a discussion of public writing and what "public" actually means. A February 10, 2008 article in *The Independent* entitled "FaceBook Can Ruin Your Life. And So Can MySpace, Bebo" reviews a variety of recent cases about inappropriate uses of social networking sites. See <http://www.independent.co.uk/life-style/gadgets-and-tech/news/facebook-can-ruin-your-life-and-so-can-myspace-bebo780521.html>.

You will also want to point to the positive uses of social networking. So, for example, you might contrast a highly public and negative case about social networking with positive examples, such as sites that offer reviews of movies or medical information. While not a study of a social networking site, the 2006 article "Googling For a Diagnosis—Use of Google As a Diagnostic Aid: Internet Based Study" by Hangwi Tang and Jennifer Hwee Kwoon Ng examines how often physicians use Google searches as part of the diagnostic process, thus demonstrating the changing nature of public writing and public information; see *British Medical Journal* 333.7579 (2006): 1270.

## EXTRA EXERCISE C

Ask students to research how policy decisions are made on your campus. Is there one main decision-making body or several? Are the decisions of these bodies public? Published? If so, where? Have students find out if these materials are online, in the campus library, and/or archived by the school newspaper. Students can review past policy decisions that directly affect

# Executive Summary

**H**uman activities are already changing the climate of the American West. This report by the Rocky Mountain Climate Organization (RMCO) and the Natural Resources Defense Council (NRDC), drawn from 50 scientific studies, 125 other government and scientific sources, and our own new analyses, documents that the West is being affected more by a changed climate than any other part of the United States outside of Alaska. When compared to the 20th century average, the West has experienced an increase in average temperature during the last five years that is 70 percent greater than the world as a whole. Responding quickly at all levels of government by embracing the solutions that are available is critical to minimizing further disruption of this region's climate and economy.

### The West Is Getting Hotter

The planetary warming that scientists predict will result from human emissions of heat-trapping gases is already underway. In February 2007, the Intergovernmental Panel on Climate Change (IPCC) declared, "Warming of the climate system is unequivocal," and it is "very likely" that most of the warming since the middle of the 20th century is the result of human pollutants.

The American West has heated up even more than the world as a whole. For the last five years (2003 through 2007), the global climate has averaged 1.0 degrees Fahrenheit warmer than its 20th century average. For this report, RMCO found that during the 2003 through 2007 period, the 11 western states averaged 1.7 degrees Fahrenheit warmer than the region's 20th century average. That is 0.7 degrees, or 70 percent, more warming that for the world as a whole. And scientists have confirmed that most of the recent warming in the West has been caused by human emissions of heat-trapping gasses.

### Understanding the Conclusions of the IPCC

The Intergovernmental Panel on Climate Change (IPCC) recently released *Climate Change 2007*, an assessment of the current scientific understanding of climate change and its effects, prepared by hundreds of scientists and approved by the governments of countries in the United Nations. Key terms used by the IPCC (and often quoted in this report) were defined as follows:

- "Very likely" means greater than 90 percent probability of occurring.
- "Likely" means about an 80 percent probability of occurring.
- "Very high confidence" means at least 9 out of 10 chances of being correct.
- "High confidence" means about 8 out of 10 chances of being correct.
- "Medium confidence" means 5 out of 10 chances of being correct.

iv

**Figure 44.2** Executive summary of a public report

# 44d How do I write arguments for my community or decision makers?

Writers can influence public opinions or actions by decision makers by writing persuasive arguments. Perhaps you want to endorse a new public project or react to a proposal or endorse a law under consideration.

White "bathtub rings" show the pre-drought water level of Lake Powell in Arizona.

## Hotter and Drier: The West's Changed Climate

Human activities are already changing the climate of the American West. A new report by the Rocky Mountain Climate Organization (RMCO) and the Natural Resources Defense Council (NRDC), drawn from 50 scientific studies, 125 other government and scientific sources, and our own new analyses, documents that the West is being affected more by a changed climate than any other part of the United States outside of Alaska. When compared to the 20th century average, the West has experienced an increase in average temperature during the last five years that is 70 percent greater than the world as a whole. Responding quickly at all levels of government by embracing available solutions is critical to minimizing further disruption of this region's climate and economy.

To read the full report on the impacts of global warming in the West, visit **www.nrdc.org/policy**.

For more information, please contact:
**Theo Spencer** at NRDC
(212) 727-2700

**Stephen Saunders** at RMCO
(303) 880-4598

**ROCKY MOUNTAIN CLIMATE** *Organization*

**NRDC**
THE EARTH'S BEST DEFENSE
www.nrdc.org/policy
March 2008
© Natural Resources Defense Council

### The West Is Getting Hotter

The planetary warming that scientists predict will result from human emissions of heat-trapping gases is already underway. In February 2007, the Intergovernmental Panel on Climate Change (IPCC) declared, "Warming of the climate system is unequivocal," and it is "very likely" that most of the warming since the middle of the 20th century is the result of human pollutants.

The American West has heated up even more than the world as a whole. For the last five years (2003 through 2007), the global climate has averaged 1.0 degree Fahrenheit warmer than its 20th century average. RMCO found that during the 2003 through 2007 period, the 11 western states averaged 1.7 degrees Fahrenheit warmer than the region's 20th century average—which represents 70 percent more warming than for the world as a whole. The West has also experienced more frequent and severe **heat waves**, with the number of extremely hot days increasing by up to four days per decade since 1950.

**More Rapid Warming in the West**

2003 to 2007 5-Year Average Temperatures Compared to 20th Century Averages

| | |
|---|---|
| Planet | +1.0°F |
| Western United States | +1.7°F |
| Colorado River Basin | +2.2°F |
| Arizona | +2.2°F |
| California | +1.1°F |
| Colorado | +1.9°F |
| Idaho | +1.8°F |
| Montana | +2.1°F |
| Nevada | +1.7°F |
| New Mexico | +1.3°F |
| Oregon | +1.4°F |
| Utah | +2.1°F |
| Washington | +1.4°F |
| Wyoming | +2.0°F |

**Figure 44.3** A fact sheet based on a report

## 44d.1 Letters to the editor

When you respond to a previous piece of writing in a publication, always begin by referring precisely to the source, using title, section, and date, if possible.

Many letters to the editor (most often sent as e-mails) propose solutions to a community problem. These letters aim to persuade other readers that a

them and their studies. An extension of this exercise might also include having students draft a policy recommendation for the decision-making body.

**BACKGROUND**

Paula Mathieu's *Tactics of Hope: The Public Turn in English Composition* (Portsmouth: Boynton/Cook, 2005) examines the shift in composition studies towards public writing and civic engagement.

**BACKGROUND**

Floyd Ogburn and Barbara Wallace's article "Freshman Composition, the Internet, and Service-Learning" examines a first year writing course where students published profiles of local social-service agencies (*Michigan Journal of Community Service* 5 (1998): 68–74). Linda Adler-Kassner's "Digging a Groundwork for Writing: Underprepared Students and Community Service Courses" (*College Composition and Communication* 46.4 (1995): 552–555) offers another model. Bruce Herzberg's "Service Learning and Public Discourse" (*JAC: A Journal of Composition Theory* 20.2 (2000): 391–404) offers a discussion of the role of service learning in composition courses. Similarly, Jim Wilcox's "The Spirit of Volunteerism in English Composition" looks at ways that first-year composition helps to build social awareness (*The Quarterly* 25.2 (2003), available online at <http://www.nwp.org/cs/public/print/resource/579>). Rebecca Moore Howard offers an extensive bibliography of articles on "Civic Engagement, Community Engagement, Democratic Education, Service Learning: Some Sources" on her Web site at <http://wrt-howard.syr.edu/Bibs/CivicServiceDemocracyComm.htm>. Christian R. Weisser's *Moving Beyond Academic Discourse: Composition Studies and the Public Sphere* (Carbondale, IL: Southern Illinois UP, 2002) examines the place of public writing in academic institutions.

**RESOURCE**

Interested in connecting with your local K–12 schools? You might want to visit the National Writing Project to learn about collaborations between teachers of all levels and their students; see <http://www.nwp.org/cs/public/print/doc/about.csp>.

POLICY BRIEF   SPRING 2006

## Fighting Obesity in the Public Schools
*Ron Haskins, Christina Paxson, and Elisabeth Donahue*

> Childhood obesity is a growing national problem. Federal, state, and local policymakers and practitioners recognize the need to take strong action. Public schools are playing a central role in fighting childhood obesity despite both political and financial constraints. But schools should do even more to reduce the availability of junk food, make school meals more nutritious, and increase students' daily exercise.

**Figure 44.4** Opening of a policy brief

problem exists and that a particular solution isn't only feasible but also the most advantageous of all the possible alternatives. Follow the general guidelines for writing ARGUMENTS (see Chapter 5). Use the format for a business letter or e-mail, and keep the following guidelines in mind when writing to propose a solution:

- Explain briefly the specific problem you're attempting to solve.
- Tell how your solution will solve all elements of the problem.
- Address briefly the possible objections or alternatives to your proposed solution.
- State why your solution offers the most advantages of all the alternatives.

In the letter in Figure 44.5, a citizen argues for preserving a city park in its present form.

### 44d.2   Editorials, op-ed pieces, and reviews

*Editorials* are fairly short arguments that appear in newspapers and magazines. So are *"Op-Ed"* pieces (short for "opposite editorial," in reference to where they were usually published in newspapers—on the right-hand page, "opposite" the newspaper's editorials). They are also called "commentaries" or "opinion pieces." *Reviews* discuss movies, books, plays, music and so on, explaining and summarizing them for readers and commenting on their quality. All are common forms of public writing.

To the Editor:

Re "Parking Plan Threatens Green Space" (news article, May 14):

For well over a century, Lincoln Park has provided a welcome oasis in downtown Springfield. In this park, office workers eat lunches, schoolchildren play on the way home, and evening concerts and other events unite the community.

It is very shortsighted, then, that the City Council now considers converting a third of the park into additional parking.

I acknowledge that parking downtown has gotten difficult. As the manager of a small shop, I know that our customers sometimes have trouble finding a parking place. However, the park itself is one of the reasons our downtown has become more popular in the past decade.

Ironically, destroying the park's attractive green space will reduce the need for more parking, which will hurt business.

A better solution is for the city to purchase the vacant property at the corner of Main and Jefferson and build a multistory garage. No doubt this option is more expensive than using the park. However, the land would be available cheaply, a multistory garage would actually provide more parking than the park land, and a preserved park would bolster business, thereby increasing tax revenues. I'm sure most citizens would prefer to leave future generations a legacy of trees, grass, and inviting beaches rather than a debt of sterile concrete.

Joel C. Bradway
Springfield, May 17, 2009

**Figure 44.5** A letter printed from a community newspaper

## 44e What other types of public writing exist?

Many people write simply to express themselves or to entertain others. The most obvious examples are fiction, poetry, plays, film scripts, journals, and scrapbooks. In addition, many people produce newsletters, brochures, or similar documents, using not only words, but also graphic designs and images (Chapter 45).

### COLUMNS

Columns are a series of pieces written by one author, usually appearing on a regular basis. Columnists tend to focus on a particular topic: sports, relationships, politics, food, and so on.

## WEB SITES

Writing for the Internet is perhaps the broadest form of public writing, in the sense that anything you post there is available to any reader with online access. On the Internet, you might post book reviews on a bookseller's Web site or a message about an upcoming concert to a newsgroup. You might create a Web site about your talents, interests, or accomplishments, or a Web site for an organization, a social cause, or a special interest group. Chapter 46 discusses writing for the Web in detail.

## BLOGS

One form of public writing is the Web log (BLOG), an online journal that a writer updates on a fairly regular basis. Some writers focus their blogs on a single topic or a narrow range of topics. Others record the events of their lives, as in a diary open for the world to read. We explain how to write blogs in 46e.

For more help with your writing, grammar, and research, go to **www.mycomplab.com**

mycomplab

# 45

# Document and Visual Design

## 45a What is visual design?

**Visual design** refers to the appearance of a document (how it looks), as opposed to its content (what it says). We're using the term *document* to refer broadly to all kinds of texts, including papers, reports, letters, brochures, flyers, posters, PowerPoint slides, and Web pages. Designing documents includes everything from choosing typefaces, heading styles, and colors, to selecting and placing photographs, illustrations, or other graphics.

Chapter 4 explained how to analyze visual images, and the advice there can help you choose images for your own documents. However, visual design involves the relationship between words and images. A well-designed document shows that you respect your readers and have spent time formatting your work

**BACKGROUND**

*The Non-Designer's Design Book,* 2nd ed., by Robin Williams (Berkeley, CA: Peachpit Press, 2003) is an excellent introduction to design principles. Williams suggests that document design can be reduced to four basic principles: proximity, alignment, repetition, and contrast. This work takes readers through each principle, suggesting guidelines for each and providing examples from brochures, pamphlets, newsletters, posters, and flyers that use or abuse these principles.

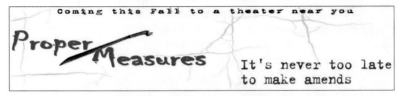

**Figure 45.1** Two Internet banner advertisements

**TEACHING TIP**

A good classroom activity is to have students gather examples of flyers and brochures to bring to class for discussion and analysis. Individually or in groups, they can critique the materials, pointing out strengths and weaknesses in their designs by using the four principles of unity, variety, balance, and emphasis. This activity can be most effective when students gather "amateur" as well as "professional" examples. An effective further question to ask is, "What was the intention of the designer?" In other words, what seemed to inform the choices that the writer/designer made?

**TEACHING TIP**

A basic review of color theory can help students avoid creating hard-to-read, distracting, or visually unappealing designs. Two Web sites where students can find information about the use of colors are <http://www.colormatters.com/colortheory.html> (for a basic overview) and <http://www.worqx.com/color/> (for a more extensive overview). If nothing else, students will want to examine the color wheel—and possibly keep one handy—to help them use colors effectively in their designs.

**BACKGROUND**

In *The Computer and the Page: The Theory, History, and Pedagogy of Publishing, Technology, and the Classroom* (Norwood, NJ: Ablex, 1996), James Kalmbach provides an overview of how technological advances have altered writing classrooms. *Reading Images: The Grammar of Visual Design,* by Gunther R. Kress and Theo Van Leeuwen (London: Routledge, 1996) explains how visual elements have specific effects on readers that writers should recognize and use to their advantage. Kress's later work, *Literacy in the New Media Age (Literacies)* (London: Routledge, 2003), takes his thinking a step further, as Kress contends that the screen and the image have replaced the book and writing as the dominant medium of communication.

**RESOURCES**

Web design software can be prohibitively expensive. The good news is that there are

so that it's attractive and helps achieve your PURPOSE. For example, imagine two movie Internet banner advertisements, both movies with the same name. Figure 45.1 shows these two movie titles designed in very different ways. What can the design tell you about the movie before you even see a preview for either one?

On larger documents, many smaller elements work together to emphasize certain points by focusing a reader's attention, portraying a complex message in an efficient manner. Note how all of the elements in the poster in Figure 45.2 work together.

Some documents follow formats that are fairly standardized, such as letters, memos, and e-mail messages (Chapter 46). Papers you write in academic settings usually follow guidelines established by the Modern Language Association (Chapter 36); the American Psychological Association (Chapter 37); the Chicago Manual of Style; or the Council of Science Editors (both in Chapter 38). Check with your instructor about which style to use. Some instructors encourage—or even require—design elements such as photos, illustrations, and diagrams. However, before spending time and effort incorporating extensive design elements into academic work, ask your instructor whether he or she appreciates design elements.

Other document types—flyers, brochures, annual reports, reports on special projects, programs for concerts or plays, and so on—invite more design creativity and originality. Consider, once again, the public service announcement in Figure 45.2. Overall, the best design is always the one appropriate to the PURPOSE and writing situation at hand.

You don't have to be a graphic artist to produce well-designed documents. Even if you only have a few tools and a little knowledge, you can still produce open-source versions that mimic more expensive photo-manipulation and desktop publishing software. For photo-manipulation, one of the most popular programs available is called The Gimp, at <www.gimp.org>, which duplicates much of the functionality of Photoshop. For a free suite of programs that includes word processing, desktop publishing, and photo manipulation, have a look at OpenOffice <www.openoffice.org>. (The Mac-native equivalent of OpenOffice is NeoOffice, available at <www.neooffice.org>; for Linux, search for "other platforms" on the OpenOffice main page).

**BACKGROUND**
Karen A. Schriver's *Dynamics in Document Design* (New York: Wiley, 1997) offers practical approaches to teaching design in the classroom. Her fourth chapter, for example, examines the ways in which poor document design may cause readers to lose confidence in their own intelligence rather than lose faith in the document's designer. Schriver's sixth chapter examines the integration of verbal and visual features in texts.

**BACKGROUND**
A comprehensive list of document design resources, indexed by topic, is available online at <http://www.wcdd.com/index.html>. Some of the topics include links to sites dealing with graphics, type, desktop publishing, journals, books, and organizations associated with document design.

**BACKGROUND**
A Web site hosted by Pennsylvania State University suggests that a "well-designed poster is eye-catching, attractive, and communicates information effectively and economically." Guidelines for constructing effective posters are offered at <http://www.pop.psu.edu/info-core/library/posters.htm>.

**BACKGROUND**
Paul Dunham's Web site "Newbie Tech Writer" contains information on writing, editing, and design skills that new technical writers will want to master as they design their documents. This information is available online at <http://www

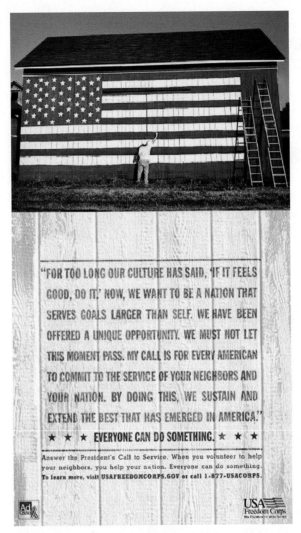

**Figure 45.2** A poster showing various design elements

visually effective documents. Word processing programs such as Microsoft Word, Corel WordPerfect, and the freely available OpenOffice are sufficient for designing most basic documents. Graphic design software such as Adobe Photoshop or freely available GIMP allows you to edit photos, create other complex images, and format them to place into your word-processed document.

## 45b   What are basic principles of design?

The basic principles of design—whether for a chair, a car, a painting, a written document, or a Web page—are unity, variety, balance, and emphasis. **Unity** results from repetition and consistency of like elements. **Variety** comes from an appropriate break from unity that adds interest or sets elements apart. **Balance** refers to a sense of harmony or equilibrium. **Emphasis** directs the reader of the design to what is most important. Quick Reference 45.1 describes how to check for these principles.

---

**Quick Reference 45.1** ■ ■ ■ ■ ■ ■ ■

### Checklist for document design

- **Unity:** Do all elements in my document work together visually, such as a consistent font for consistent content? Is there a consistent use of bitmap or vector images?

- **Variety:** Have I introduced elements, where appropriate, that break up monotony, such as headings in a different font from that used in my content? Do these elements add clarity? Do my images add to content?

- **Balance:** Are the elements of my document in proportion to each other, such as equally placed text elements countering or mirroring equally placed images?

- **Emphasis:** Does my document design draw attention to key information, such as framing important text, or placing important elements in the middle or at the top?

---

The flyer that a student produced for The Nature Club in Figure 45.3 reflects the four basic design principles. UNITY results from similar parts of the flyer sharing the same features. All of the headings in this example (except the title) use the same font and color, a color that matches colors in the photographs, and all of the body text uses the same font. In addition, dates for the speakers and events are displayed in a matching indented format. VARIETY in the flyer comes from the use of photographs to complement the text. Headings, colors, and font sizes are different from the main text. Variety is also one way to create EMPHASIS. For example, the title of the organization is the largest text on the page and is in a different font. Headings signal different types of information, and the ample use of white space allows information to stand out clearly. The contact information is emphasized through the use of a frame and white background that sets the information apart.

Finally, the page demonstrates BALANCE in many ways. The center or focal point of the flyer is split into quadrants, each side with two evenly spaced text and picture elements.

.cloudnet.com/~pdunham/techwritingtools .html>.

**TEACHING TIP**

Have students design their own personal logo! A logo is one of the ways in which organizations, businesses, and artists quickly and easily identify themselves to the world at large (the marketing concept for this falls under the rubric of "brand management"). Have students consider what kind of logo they would create to represent themselves to the outside world, and then have them create it. For inspiration, have them look at some recent trends in logo creation at <http://www.logolounge.com/ articles/default.asp?ArticleID=540>.

Once they have created a logo, have them include it on all assignments they submit for the class. This is one fun way to help them remember the importance of design elements and visual presentation.

**TEACHING TIP**

Several students will be familiar with *zines*, alternative or underground magazines with origins in fanzines and published in print or online. Having groups of students produce a zine on a particular topic or subject matter offers a good opportunity for them to try design strategies. Owing to their spirit and origins, zines typically use counterculture or retro formats, even relying on pasted and taped photocopied documents in a raw pastiche. However, some zines are becoming more polished in their design, and the freewheeling nature of these publications, designed for local or insider distribution, provides a kind of free experimentation area that more staid genres do not. A clearinghouse of information on zine publishing is available from *The Book of Zines: Readings from the Fringe,* edited by Chip Rowe (New York: Henry Holt, 1997). The online site for the clearinghouse can be found at <http://www.zinebook .com/>. Dagmar Corrigan and Chidsey Dickson published an article on electronic zines in the classroom in the online journal *Kairos* (Summer 2002). The article, found at <http://english.ttu.edu/kairos/7.2/binder.html?s ectiontwo/corrigan/description.html>, contains links to specific assignments and directions to students.

## BACKGROUND

In "Design for Reading," a site at <http://www .worsleypress.com/media/simple.txt>, Gordon Woolf recommends that document designers study successful documents, like newspapers, to determine what principles govern these publications. For example, he addresses issues of establishing effective picture placement and breaking up long blocks of text with drop quotes and sidebars.

## TEACHING TIP

Much like grammar rules, the "grammar" of design changes and evolves over time; it is not static and fixed. Be sure to inform students that sometimes the best design violates some received rule about design. For instance, there are many "grunge" fonts available now that are intentionally smeared, faded, and harder to read that traditional fonts; these fonts, however, evoke a certain counterculture mindset that may more effectively connect with some audiences. When students design documents for class, have them consider when they might violate some design principle in order to communicate more powerfully.

## QUOTATION: ON DESIGN

In matters of grave importance, style, not sincerity, is the vital thing.

—Oscar Wilde

## ANSWERS: EXERCISE 45-1

**1.** The first version of the flyer violates principles of unity, emphasis, and balance. The writer uses a distracting variety of typefaces and colors, and fails to use bulleted lists correctly or white space effectively. The clip art included in the right column doesn't match the content of the flyer; it appears to have been thrown in gratuitously.

**2.** The second version of the flyer primarily violates the principles of variety and emphasis. Because everything is centered, there is no excitement to the page. Furthermore, all the body

# The Nature Club

## Please join us!

The Nature Club is open to all members of the campus community. Our purpose is to share our common enjoyment of nature and to address environmental concerns. We meet the first Wednesday of each month, 7:00 p.m., at 114 Mercer Hall

## Spring Speakers

**James Franklin**
Biology
"Prairie Wildlife"
*January 15*

**Sarah Minkowski**
Political Science
"Alaskan Refuges and Energy Policy"
*February 12*

**Cesar Sanchez**
The Nature Conservancy
"The Last Best Places"
*March 12*

**Sherita Jones**
State Representative
"Pending Environmental Legislation"
*April 9*

## Upcoming Special Events

- **Fundraising Dance for The Nature Conservancy**
  *February 19*

- **Salt River Canoeing**
  *April 18*

- **Camping and Hiking in Grand Teton National Park**
  *June 3-10*

*For more information, contact*
**Jesse Longland, President**
**The Nature Club**
jklong@tnc.gkztg.edu

**Figure 45.3** A flyer for The Nature Club

**EXERCISE 45-1** Figures 45.4 and 45.5 (see pages 801 and 802) are two alternative versions of the flyer for The Nature Club. Each of the two has problems with unity, variety, balance, or emphasis—or a combination of all four. Work alone or in groups to identify the problems in each design.

## THE NATURE CLUB

### Spring Speakers

James Franklin
Biology
"Prairie Wildlife"
January 15

Sarah Minkowski
Political Science
"Alaskan Refuges
and Energy Policy"
February 12

### Please join us!

The Nature Club is open to all members of the campus community. Our purpose is to share our common enjoyment of nature and to address environmental concerns. We meet the first Wednesday of each month, 7:00 p.m., at 114 Mercer Hall

Cesar Sanchez
The Nature Conservancy
"The Last Best Places"
March 12

Sherita Jones
State Representative
"Pending Environmental Legislation"
April 9

### Upcoming Special Events

*Fundraising Dance for The Nature Conservancy*
*February 19*
*Salt River Canoeing*
*April 18*
*Camping and Hiking in Grand Teton National Park*
*June 3-10*

For more information, contact Jesse Longland, President, The Nature Club
jklong@tnc.gkztg.edu

**Figure 45.4** A poorly designed flyer

# 45c How do I design with text?

Text consists of letters and words. To format text, you need to decide which typeface—such as Times or Arial Schoolbook—that you'll use. Also called *fonts,* they come in two major categories. **Serif** fonts have little "feet" or finishing lines at the top and bottom of each letter; **sans serif** (*sans* is a French term

text is the same typeface and size; the headings are not large enough to draw interest. Except for the photographs, there are no colors, highlights, or graphical elements.

**QUOTATION: ON DESIGN**
Design is what you do when you don't [yet] know what you are doing.
—George Stiny

**BACKGROUND**
Students whose documents include symbols or icons should consider the guidelines offered by Stuart Mealing and Masoud Yazdani in "A Computer-based Iconic Language," found at <http://www.intellectbooks.com/iconic/com_base/icon-2.htm>. Mealing and Yazdani suggest that icons should be "graphically clear; semantically unambiguous; without cultural, racial or linguistic bias; adaptable (open to modification to express nuance); and simple."

**BACKGROUND**
Susan Hilligoss's *Visual Communication* (Boston: Longman, 2001) includes a discussion of the rhetoric of visual information. This textbook offers chapters that detail tips for planning effective documents: brochures, newsletters, Web sites, and others.

**TEACHING TIP**
Clip art that is recognizable as clip art—for instance, the clip art that comes packaged with Microsoft Word—almost always detracts from a document's design. A little effort spent on either finding less-common clip art or, even better, taking original photographs will help make documents less generic and more interesting.

**TEACHING TIP**
If anything, animation should be used even more sparingly than still images. Insofar as we can expect the Internet to become the medium of choice for documents of every variety, however, the question of using animation as part of visual design will become increasingly important. For some advice on how to best use animation to enhance design, read the blog post on

animation at The Fluid Weblog, found at <http://flog.fluid.com/2008/01/23/effective-motion-graphics-and-animation/>.

## BACKGROUND

Many design experts consider Edward R. Tufte's *The Visual Display of Quantitative Information*, 2nd ed. (Cheshire, CT: Graphics Press, 2001), the best source on how complex information can most effectively be presented graphically. Tufte presents examples of bad design as well as good, and the charts, graphs, and other visuals provide useful illustrations for teaching.

## QUOTATION: ON DESIGN

If a major project is truly innovative, you cannot possibly know its exact cost and its exact schedule at the beginning. And if in fact you do know the exact cost and the exact schedule, chances are that the technology is obsolete.

—Joseph G. Gavin Jr.

## QUOTATION: ON DESIGN

Always design a thing by considering it in its next larger context—a chair in a room, a room in a house, a house in an environment, an environment in a city plan.

—Eliel Saarinen

## QUOTATION: ON DESIGN

Less is more.

—Ludwig Mies van der Rohe

## QUOTATION: ON WRITING

Life can't ever really defeat a writer who is in love with writing, for life itself is a writer's lover until death—fascinating, cruel, lavish, warm, cold, treacherous, constant.

—Edna Ferber

## QUOTATION: ON WRITING

[My stories] run up and bite me on the leg—I respond by writing down everything that goes on during the bite. When I finish, the idea lets go and runs off.

—Ray Bradbury

## THE NATURE CLUB

### Please join us!

The Nature Club is open to all members of the campus community. Our purpose is to share our common enjoyment of nature and to address environmental concerns. We meet the first Wednesday of each month, 7:00 p.m., at 114 Mercer Hall

### Spring Speakers

James Franklin, Biology, "Prairie Wildlife", January 15
Sarah Minkowski, Political Science, "Alaskan Refuges and Energy Policy", February 12
Cesar Sanchez, The Nature Conservancy , "The Last Best Places", March 12
Sherita Jones, State Representative, "Pending Environmental Legislation", April 9

### Upcoming Special Events

Fundraising Dance for The Nature Conservancy February 19
Salt River Canoeing April 18
Camping and Hiking in Grand Teton National Park June 3-10

For more information

Jesse Longland
President
The Nature Club
jklong@tnc.gkztg.edu

**Figure 45.5** Another example of a poorly designed flyer

meaning *without*) don't. Times New Roman is serif; Arial is sans serif. When considering font use, there are two qualities to keep in mind. The first quality, *readability,* refers to the ease of reading a particular block of text. Some studies have suggested that the serifs at the bottom of each letter help guide readers' eyes through lines of text; therefore, when you're writing longer segments of text, use serif fonts. The second quality, *legibility,* refers specifically to the design of fonts and whether they are visible or not to a reader, making them easy to see.

Sans serif fonts are highly legible and are good for short, isolated lines such as headings and captions.

Remember that a font can set a tone, so avoid using a playful font (**Comic Sans MS**) or a simulated handwriting font (*Kaufmann*) in academic and business writing. Fonts come in different sizes (heights) that are measured in "points" (units smaller than .02 inch). For body text in longer documents, use 10- to 12-point serif typefaces.

8 point    12 point    16 point    24 point

### 45c.1 Highlighting text

Highlighting draws attention to key words or elements of a document. You can highlight in various ways, but in all cases, use moderation.

#### BOLDFACE, ITALICS, AND UNDERLINING

*Italics* and underlining—they serve the same purpose—have special functions in writing (for example, to indicate titles of certain works, as we discuss in 30f and Chapters 36–38), but they're also useful for emphasis and for headings. **Boldface** is reserved for heavy emphasis.

#### BULLETED AND NUMBERED LISTS

You can use bulleted and numbered lists when you discuss a series of items or steps in a complex process, or summarize key points or guidelines. A bulleted list identifies items with small dots, squares, or other shapes and symbols. Lists provide your reader with a way to think of the whole idea you're communicating. For this reason, they work particularly well as summaries.

#### COLOR

Adding color to a document can change it dramatically. In addition to including colorful visuals or BORDERS (45e), you can also change the font color or use a colored background for certain words or sections. Take time, however, to think about your reasons for adding color to your text. How does color suit the type of document? How will it help you accomplish your purpose? Use color sparingly for variety and emphasis.

#### JUSTIFYING

When you make your text lines even in relation to the left or right margin, you're **justifying** them. There are four kinds of justification, or ways to line up text lines on margins: left, right, centered, and full.

Most academic and business documents are left justified, which means that the right ends of the lines are unjustified, or *ragged*. Center, right, and full justification are useful for designing shorter documents (flyers, posters, and so on) because they can attract attention.

> **Left justified** text (text aligns on the left)

> **Right justified** text (text aligns on the right)

> **Center justified** text (text aligns in the center)

> **Full justified** text (both left and right justified to full length, or measure, of the line of type)

## INDENTATION

When you move text toward the right margin, you are **indenting**. Using the ruler line in your word-processing program to control indentations makes it easier to make global changes in your indentation. The top arrow of the bar sets the paragraph indentation, while the bottom arrow sets the indentation for everything else in the paragraph. MLA-style Works Cited pages and APA References pages use *hanging indentations* in which the first line of an entry aligns at the left margin and every following line is indented. Indent bulleted and numbered lists to make them stand out, as in the list in 45d.

## SETTING MARGINS

**Margins** are the boundaries of a page, which means the white space or blank areas at the top, bottom, and sides of a paper or screen. College essays, research papers, and most BUSINESS WRITING call for one inch of space on all sides.

Narrow margins allow you to fit more information on a page but also decrease the amount of white space available. This can make a page appear cluttered, dense, and difficult to read. Wide margins let you fit less information on a page. For ACADEMIC WRITING, margins greater than one inch make your document look thin because there's less content on a page.

## 45d How do I use headings?

Headings clarify how you've organized your material and tell your readers what to expect in each section. Longer documents, including handbooks (like ours), reports, brochures, and Web pages, use headings to break content into chunks that are easier to digest and understand. In academic writing, APA style favors headings, whereas MLA tends to discourage them. Following are some guidelines for writing and formatting headings.

- **Create headings in a slightly larger type than the type size in the body of your text.** You can use the same or a contrasting typeface, as long as it coordinates visually and is easy to read.
- **Keep headings brief and informative.** Your readers can use them as cues.
- **Change the format for headings of different levels.** Think of levels in headings the way you think of items in an outline (see 2e). Level one headings show the main divisions of a document. Level two headings divide material that appears under level one headings, and so on. Changing the format for different levels of headings creates a clear outline for the reader. You can do this in various ways: centering heads or left justifying them; using a different font or type size; highlighting using **boldface,** *italics,* or underlining; or using various combinations of capitals and lowercase letters. Always be consistent in the style you use within each document.
- **Use parallel structure.** All headings at the same level should be similar in kind. For example, you might make all first-level heads questions and all second-level heads noun phrases. Quick Reference 45.2 presents common types of headings, with examples showing parallel structure.

---

**Quick Reference 45.2** ■ ■ ■ ■ ■ ■ ■

### Style choices for headings

- NOUN PHRASES **can cover a variety of topics.**
   Executive Branch of Government

   Judicial Branch of Government
- **Questions can evoke reader interest.**
   When and How Does the President Use the Veto Power?

   How Does the Supreme Court Decide Whether to Consider a Case?
- GERUNDS **and** *-ing* **phrases can explain instructions or solve problems.**
   Submitting the Congressional Budget

   Approving the Congressional Budget
- **Imperative sentences can give advice or directions.**
   Identify a Problem

   Draft the Bill

---

# 45e   How do I use borders?

**Borders** are lines used to set apart sections of text. They can take a number of forms, from single lines of varying thickness to patterns. A single rule (a simple straight line, horizontal or vertical) can emphasize breaks between major sections of a long report. Borders around text serve to set off information, as in a table or chart.

## 45f How should I incorporate graphics?

*Graphics,* also called *images* or *visuals,* can enhance document design when used appropriately. A visual can condense, compare, and display information more effectively than words, but only if its content is suitable. A graph showing how sales increased over a period of time, for example, makes the point more quickly and clearly than an explanation.

### CHARTS, GRAPHS, AND TABLES

Business and scientific reports rely heavily on charts and graphs, as do some research papers. They're compact ways to present large amounts of information. The next four figures illustrate bar graphs (45.6), line graphs (45.7), pie charts (45.8), and tables (45.9).

**Figure 45.6 Bar graphs** compare values, such as the number of different majors at a college, as shown in this graph.

**Figure 45.7 Line graphs** indicate changes over time. For example, advertising revenue is shown over an eight-month period in this chart.

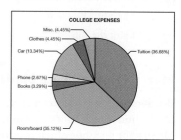

**Figure 45.8 Pie charts** show the relationship of each part to a whole, such as a typical budget for a college student, as shown in the chart.

TABLE 45.1   TOTAL NUMBER OF STUDENTS IN SERVICE PROJECTS

| Semester | Students | Percentage (%) of Student Population |
|----------|----------|--------------------------------------|
| Spring 2008 | 1,321 | 25.8 |
| Summer 2008 | 394 | 6.6 |
| Fall 2008 | 2,425 | 38.1 |

**Figure 45.9 Tables** present data in list form, as shown here, allowing readers to grasp much of the information at a glance.

In academic or business documents, especially lengthy ones, number figures and tables, if more than one, and number them sequentially. If possible, choose only one term in a relatively short piece of writing: *Table 1, Table 2;* or *Figure 1, Figure 2,* and so forth.

## CLIP ART

**Clip art** refers to pictures, sketches, and other graphics available on some word-processing programs. It can also be downloaded from the Internet, sometimes from free sites, and sometimes for a small fee. Although clip art is rarely, if ever, appropriate in academic writing and business writing, it can add interest to flyers, posters, newsletters, and brochures designed for certain audiences.

## PHOTOGRAPHS

In an age of digital cameras, not to mention an age when cell phones have the capacity to take pictures and send them around the world, **photographs** are everywhere. Because you can fairly easily download photographs from a digital camera, you can place them easily into documents. You can also scan photographs from printed photos or from books and articles. The Internet is another source of images; several Web sites (including many at libraries) offer thousands of photographs for free. Most images online, however, are copyrighted, and thus you need to gain permission to use images for any type of publication. Quick Reference 45.3 contains terms and special considerations when using images found on the Web.

Quick Reference 45.3

### Considerations when using visuals from the Web

**Always observe copyrights.** Images, just like text, are copyrighted as soon as they are fixed in any medium. In other words, most images online are owned by somebody. Searching for images using Google or Yahoo might provide

continued >>

## Quick Reference 45.3 (continued)

access to images useful for a project, but such results can hide the legal rights of the author of the image from you. Although the copyright law is fairly generous in allowing students to use found images for projects done strictly for courses, you should document the source of the image. If you're using an image in a project for a wider audience, including any Web-based project, you need to get permission from the photographer or whomever owns the rights. Here are some important terms to understand.

- Rights-Managed—when an image is rights-managed, it means that the owner of the image charges you, the user, based on how you will use the image. Many stock-photo Web sites such as http://www.images.com offer pricing options for use of photos.
- Royalty-free—this does not mean the image is free. Instead, the author of the image is selling a one-time use of the photo for a flat fee and doesn't expect royalties from your use of the image. Web sites such as http://www.istockphoto.com offer many royalty-free photos.
- Creative Commons—creative commons is a copyright alternative that allows authors to control how others may or may not use their works without the added issue of asking permissions. There are many creative commons options available at http://creativecommons.org/. A number of photos at Flickr, see http://www.flickr.com/creativecommons/, have a creative commons license.
- Public Domain—Works in the public domain are free to use in whatever fashion a user wants without gaining permission first. Government publications and images are, by law, in the public domain. Web sites such as the National Archives, http://www.archives.gov offer many public domain images that you may use.

Once a photograph is in your computer, you can place it in your document, usually with an "Insert" or "Import" command. A modest software program, such as the pictures toolbar within Microsoft Word, can help you adjust a photograph by cropping it (trimming the top, bottom, or sides), rotating it, or making it larger or smaller. A powerful program like Adobe Photoshop lets you modify colors or create special effects.

For additional help in using visuals in your documents, follow the guidelines in Quick Reference 45.4.

## 45g What is page layout?

**Layout** is the arrangement of text, visuals, color, and space on a page. You'll want to arrange these elements so that you follow the basic principles of design (45b).

## Quick Reference 45.4

■ ■ ■ ■ ■ ■

### Guidelines for using visuals

- **Design all visuals to be simple and uncluttered.**

- **Use the highest resolution and best images possible.** Small images stretched to fit an area will not look professional and can disrupt a document's design. It's always best to use large pictures and then reduce the size later. Reducing the size of a picture will not harm the resolution, while stretching a picture to make it bigger will.

- **Include a heading or title for each visual.** Doing so helps readers quickly understand what they're seeing.

- **Never use unnecessary visuals.** Make sure all visuals clearly contribute to your PURPOSE. Putting cute clip art on the pages of your writing won't make your reader think your work is well done. However, including a chart that summarizes your findings might.

- **Consider your audience and their sensibilities.** You don't want to offend your readers, nor do you want them to be confused.

- **Credit your source if a visual isn't your own.** Always avoid plagiarism by crediting your source using DOCUMENTATION. If you're using a visual (including a photograph) for a public purpose other than for a class project, you need written permission to use it in your work.

Experiment with ideas for layout by creating a variety of mock-up pages on a computer or by sketching possibilities by hand.

You might also see if any suitable **templates** are available. A template is a professionally designed form that shows you where to place visuals in relation to text; a template has predefined typefaces, heading styles, margins, and so on. Page layout software and most word-processing software have a variety of templates for brochures, flyers, newsletters, and many other types of documents; and several Web sites offer them, too.

Quick Reference 45.5 explains how to position texts and visuals.

You have many options for placing images in relation to text. Figure 45.10 shows one standard kind of placement, the image centered above the words. In contrast, Figure 45.11 shows the text wrapped around the picture, which creates a better sense of connection between the two. Finally, Figure 45.12 illustrates that words can also wrap elements other than photographs, in this case a list enclosed in borders forming a box.

## Guidelines for positioning text and visuals

- Consider the size of visuals in placing them so that they don't cluster at the top or the bottom of a page. That is, avoid creating a page that's top-heavy or bottom-heavy.

- To create balance in a document, imagine it as divided into halves, quarters, or eighths. As you position texts or images in the spaces, see which look full, which look empty, and whether the effect seems visually balanced.

- Use the "Table" feature of your word-processing program to position text and visuals exactly where you want them. Turn off the grid lines when you're done so that the printed copy shows only the text and visuals.

- Avoid splitting a chart or table between one page and the next. If possible, the entire chart or table needs to fit on a single page. If it runs slightly more than a page, look for ways to adjust spacing or reduce words. If you have no choice but to continue a chart or table, then on the second page, repeat the title and add the word *continued* at the top.

- Use the "Print Preview" feature to see what each printed version will look like, which will help you revise before completing your final document.

- Print copies of your various layouts and look at them from different distances. Ask others to look at your layouts and tell you what they like best and least about each.

### USING WHITE SPACE

**White space**, the part of your document that has neither text nor visuals, allows readers to read your document more easily and to absorb information in chunks rather than in one big block. White space indicates breaks between ideas and thereby focuses attention on the key features of your document.

Flyers, brochures, posters, reports, Web pages, and similar documents tend to make extensive and varied use of white space because they rely heavily on graphics. Styles change over time, but most current professional designers prefer an uncluttered look with lots of white space.

However, our research shows that students who are involved in a volunteer project actually achieve better grades than those who are not. One possible reason is that having too much free time actually encourages people to waste it; being busier forces them to be more organized.

**Figure 45.10** An image centered above text

However, our research shows that students who are involved in a volunteer project actually achieve better grades than those who are not. One possible reason is that having too much free time actually encourages people to waste it; being busier forces them to be more organized. A more interesting reason is that volunteering for a meaningful project gives people a sense of purpose that carries over into other phases of their lives. Students who  are concerned about the state of the environment, for example, draw energy from working with others who share their passion.

**Figure 45.11** Text wrapped around the image

However, our research shows that students who are involved in a volunteer project actually achieve better grades than those who are not. One possible reason is that having too much free time actually encourages people to waste it; being busier forces them to be more organized. A more interesting reason is that volunteering for a meaningful project gives people a sense of purpose that carries over into other phases of their lives.

**Successful volunteers:**
-Follow their passions
-Budget their time
-Have positive outlooks
-Seek likeminded others

**Figure 45.12** Text wrapped around a box

For more help with your writing, grammar, and research,
go to **www.mycomplab.com**

## BACKGROUND

In teaching multimodal composition, you will want to see what programs your university already has and uses. For example, many course management systems already support wikis and blogs. You can also use free sites on the Internet.

*Blogs:*

- Blogger <http://www.blogger.com>
- WordPress <http://www.wordpress.com>
- Drupal <http://drupal.org/about>

*Image Collages:*

- Scrapblog <http://www.scrapblog.com>
- VUVOX <http://www.vuvox.com/collage>
- Photobucket <http://photobucket.com/images/collage>
- Collagr <http://collagr.com/Default.aspx>

*Wikis:*

- Wikispaces <http://www.wikispaces.com>
- Wetpaint <http://www.wetpaint.com>
- PBWiki <http://pbwiki.com>

*Podcasting:*

- PodBean <http://www.podbean.com>
- My Podcast <http://www.mypodcast.com>
- Our Media <http://www.ourmedia.org>

*Instant Ad Creation:*

- iBloks <http://www.ibloks.com>

## BACKGROUND

The CCCC Position Statement on Teaching, Learning, and Assessing Writing in Digital Environments, adopted in 2004, argues that "the curriculum of composition is widening to include not one but two literacies: a literacy of print and a literacy of the screen"; see <http://www.ncte.org/cccc/resources/positions/123773.htm>. This statement also outlines best practices in digital environments.

## ANSWERS: EXERCISE 46-2

Answers will vary. You may want to refer students back to Chapter 2 (2b1) for a discussion of purpose in writing.

**Figure 46.2** The Nature Club's home page

As you know, Web pages are common in academic, business, and public settings. They inform, entertain, and persuade through text, images, animation, sound, and video. Because Web sites allow readers to jump from page to page to find information within a site and beyond, they provide exceptional flexibility. When you design a Web site you need to consider not only how a page looks but also how it relates to others, both ones you've created and ones already online. Writing for the Web means you can freely and easily change the content of your pages.

Figure 46.2 shows the home page of The Nature Club's Web site (the club whose flyer we discussed in Chapter 45). Some of the information is similar to the information on the flyer shown there. However, the Web page allows more personal and up-to-date news about the organization, and the addition of links helps organize the Web site into various sections, including picture albums. Visitors to this page can tell in a glance what kinds of information the site contains and go directly to the pages that interest them.

**EXERCISE 46-2**   Discuss how the Web site in Figure 46.2 differs from the flyer in Figure 45.2. How do the purposes of those two modes shape those differences?

## 46d  How do I create a Web site?

The **Web writing process** has five parts: (1) writing the content, (2) creating the structure of the content, (3) designing the layout of the material on the computer screen, (4) checking whether the Web material is usable, and (5) loading the Web site on a **server**, a computer that is always online and available to Internet users. This process has many similarities with the general processes for doing any type of writing; planning, revising, and editing are crucial, for example (Chapter 2).

### 46d.1  How do I plan content for my Web site?

The Web differs from other media in distinct ways that affect your writing.

- Web writing calls for smaller blocks of text than print writing. Web readers prefer not to scroll down long sections of information.
- Web writing highlights the connections or links between related Web sites.
- Web writing emphasizes visual elements such as color and pictures.

As you plan your writing ask yourself these questions:

- What purpose will my site fulfill? Is it to inform, to persuade, to entertain?
- Who will my readers be? What knowledge and expectations will they have? How will they need to navigate—that is, move—within my site?
- What is the size of my Web writing project? How many pages will I want and how much content will I include in each?
- Should I include links to other Web sites? Which sites will support my purpose, perhaps with an illustration, an explanation, a reference, or so on?

### 46d.2  How do I create a structure for my Web site?

**Web structure** is the organization of the content and documents that site creators include in a Web project. Almost all Web sites have a **home page** that introduces the site and provides links to the other pages that the site contains. The home page functions like a table of contents in print or, perhaps, the entryway to a building. It should be appealing and give visitors to the home page clear directions for how they can navigate your site, or move from page to page. Here are some guidelines for creating a site's structure.

- Determine all of the pages your site might contain and whether these pages should be grouped into **categories** (groups of pages all on the same topic).
- Generate a list of categories. You might use the planning techniques of BRAINSTORMING, FREEWRITING, and CLUSTERING discussed in Chapter 2.

electronic zines (underground magazines). Their essay is published in *Kairos* (Summer 2002) at <http://english.ttu.edu/kairos/7.2/binder.html?sectiontwo/corrigan/description.html>.

**BACKGROUND**

The Web site *Design & Publishing,* located at <http://www.graphic-design.com>, offers several resources, including tips on designing Web sites, using Adobe Photoshop for improving digital photographs, selecting fonts, and so on.

**QUOTATION: ON DESIGN**

When a Web site is structured well, we usually don't even notice. But when we can't find what we're looking for, when labels are misleading or confusing, when navigation doesn't work in the way we expect it to, or when it's not easy to see where we've already been, we're left feeling annoyed, incompetent, or even angry.

—Mir G. Haynes

**QUOTATION: ON DESIGN**

Architecture starts when you carefully put two bricks together. There it begins.

—Ludwig Mies van der Rohe

**BACKGROUND**

The informative Web site *3D Cafe,* found at <http://www.3dcafe.com>, offers free material for Web designers, including tutorials, three-dimensional models, Web tools, and more.

**BACKGROUND: DISABILITY CONSIDERATIONS**

The World Wide Web Consortium (W3C) has a comprehensive site devoted to exploring how people with disabilities use and experience the Web at <http://www.w3.org/wai/>. Click "Accessibility," for example. This site includes guidelines for constructing sites that are "universally" usable.

In "From Symptoms to Barrier Free Authority/Authorship: Promoting Student Agency in Writers with Learning Disabilities" (*Writing at the Center: Conference in Rhetoric and Composition,* 2004), Victoria Littman (University of

- Plan a Web structure by drawing a map of all of your separate documents and the best way they connect to one other. Figure 46.3 shows two possible structures.
- Plan **hyperlinks**, which are direct electronic connections between two pages. Combinations of hyperlinks are the glue that holds Web writings together.

## 46d.3 How do I design Web pages?

Once you've drafted a map of your Web site, you begin designing and creating your individual Web pages. Generally, all the pages within a site need to have the same basic design and similar navigation features to ensure that the site is unified and that users have an easy, pleasant experience. Most guidelines and principles that contribute to good design in printed documents apply equally to Web design. Use the basic design principles of unity, variety, balance, and emphasis discussed in Chapter 45.

Begin by planning a Web page's general appearance. Make decisions about the placement of texts and graphics, the use of color and white space, and what you want to emphasize. Early in your planning process, you might look at some Web sites that seem similar to what you have in mind. Figures 46.4 and 46.5 show two popular designs. In these figures, A is a *banner* or title of the Web site or organization, B is an onsite menu of links to the various pages of the site, C is the main section for content, and D is for offsite or additional links.

Figure 46.6 (page 819) is the home page of the National Science Foundation. Notice how the menu for onsite categories (B) appears under the heading (A) with the center section filled with the home page content (C). Figure 46.7

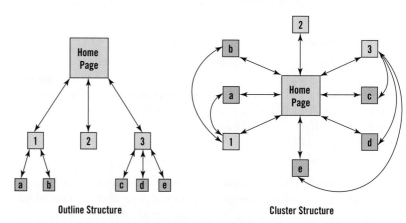

Outline Structure          Cluster Structure

**Figure 46.3** Two possible Web site structures

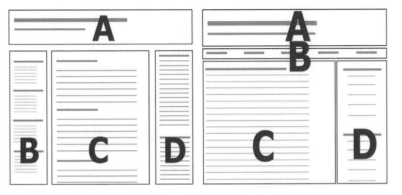

**Figure 46.4** Popular Web design 1    **Figure 46.5** Popular Web design 2

(page 820) is the home page of the National Archives, which has the menu for onsite categories (B) on the left side. In both examples, readers can tell at a glance what kinds of information the Web site contains, and then go directly to the pages that interest them. Quick Reference 46.1 contains some general advice about designing Web pages.

## 46d.4  How do I use Web writing software?

Web pages are written in a computer program language called **HTML,** for **H**yper**T**ext **M**arkup **L**anguage. Although it's possible to create Web pages directly using HTML, it's easier to use a WYSIWYG (**W**hat **Y**ou **S**ee **I**s **W**hat **Y**ou **G**et) HTML editor—a program that generates tags, or codes, in much the same way that word-processing programs generate boldface type or other formatting.

### USING STYLE SHEETS AND TABLES

Most contemporary Web designs use CSS (**C**ascading **S**tyle **S**heets). What CSS allows you to do is define what particular elements, such as headings, links, and block text will look like, and then all you have to do is define each element and apply the style sheet. For example, by applying a different style sheet to The Nature Club Web site (Figure 46.2), we changed the entire look of the site (Figure 46.8, page 821), and all we did was change one brief code.

   **Tables** allow you to use HTML editors to place text and images accurately. The word *table* here differs from the display visual shown in section 45f. Unlike designing with pen and paper or with computer drawing software, HTML editors don't allow you to position materials immediately at different points on the screen. First, you have to define specific areas, and the easiest

Toronto) advocates pedagogical methods that work to empower learning-disabled writers.

**BACKGROUND**
A database of thousands of digital texts (poetry, drama, fiction, and nonfiction) is maintained by the Electronic Literature Directory. Works that make extensive use of electronic techniques are linked from this page at <http://www.eliterature.org/dir/>. Project Gutenberg, at <http://www.gutenberg.org>, has thousands of free etexts available. Bartelby.com is an additional resource for free online texts; see <http://www.bartleby.com>.

**TEACHING TIP**
Students may be more familiar with word-processing software than with Web page software, so novice designers may wish to begin their designs in Microsoft Word. Jeffrey Branzburg addresses how to "Create a Web Page with Your Word Processor" in his *Technology and Learning* article (January 2003).

**QUOTATION: ON DESIGN**
Good design keeps the user happy, the manufacturer in the black and the aesthete unoffended.

—Raymond Loewy

**BACKGROUND: ON DESIGN**
Whereas the Web supports many Web-writing style guides, one of the most comprehensive may be found at <http://websitetips.com/design>. Additionally, the World Wide Web Consortium provides extensive information on Web site design from accessibility to style sheets at <http://www.w3.org>. New Web designers will also want to learn more about accessibility. The World Wide Web Consortium has extensive guidelines for usability at <http://www.w3.org/WAI>. A related newsletter associated with usability issues can be found at <http://www.usabilitynews.org>.

**QUOTATION: ON DESIGN**
We don't make Web sites the way our parents did. The typical welcome-to-my-homepage,

menu-driven, icon-encrusted model is fast being replaced by a model I call third-generation site architecture. Though third-generation sites rely heavily on today's browser technology, the difference is not technology per se—the difference is design.

—David Siegel

**QUOTATION: ON DESIGN**

To me, a building—if it's beautiful—is the love of one man, he's made it out of his love for space, materials, things like that.

—Martha Graham

**QUOTATION: ON WRITING**

The translation from paper to an electronic medium has a number of advantages. First and foremost, students are engaged by designing Web documents in a way they are not by a traditional print report. . . . Second, the demands of designing for the Web are high.

. . . Designing good documents for the Web forces students not only to address significant technical issues but also to hone their skills in communication in order to entice the fickle Web user. Finally, the fact that the projects are accessible to friends and family in distant places, as well as to prospective employers, definitely encourages more thoughtful and polished work than that found in text reports. Just by virtue of being "published," even if they are never looked at by anyone outside of class, these documents become more significant in the eyes of their authors.

—Carole Meyer

**BACKGROUND**

Try <http://www.andyart.com> to download free images, animated gifs, and templates, among other things. ScreamDesign sponsors the site.

**BACKGROUND**

The United States Copyright Office sponsors a site, at <http://www.copyright.gov>, that provides comprehensive information on copyrights.

---

## Quick Reference 46.1

### General advice for designing Web pages

- **Choose an appropriate title.** Make sure your page has a title that tells readers exactly what they'll find there.

- **Keep backgrounds and text simple.** Strive for a clean, uncluttered look. Dark text on a plain light background is easiest to read. In contrast to print documents, SANS SERIF fonts tend to be easier to read on computer screens than SERIF fonts. Avoid multiple typefaces, sizes, and colors, multiple images and graphics, and busy backgrounds.

- **Use images to attract attention to important elements and to please the reader.** Readers will tend to look first at pictures and graphics on a page, so choose and then position them to reinforce your page's content.

- **Unify the pages in your site.** Keep the overall appearance of pages within one site consistent in terms of typefaces, graphics, and color. Make sure pages share some features, perhaps the same basic layout, font, color scheme, and header or **navigation bar** (the set of links on every Web page that allows users to get back to the site's home page and to major parts of the site). This can be easily accomplished using the **style sheet** in your HTML editor (see 46d.4).

- **Provide identifying information.** Generally, the bottom of a page includes the date the page is updated, or added to, along with contact information for the site's creator or administrator.

---

way to do this is with tables. A table divides the screen into a grid of spaces. You can then change the size of different rows, columns, or cells in the table to place blocks of text, images, links, and so on exactly where you want them. Tables allow you to fix images in the same place in relation to the text regardless of different browsers viewers may have. Figure 46.9 (page 822) shows the basic table design underlying The Nature Club home page.

## 46d.5    How do I incorporate images into Web pages?

Web pages can include many different kinds of graphics. For example, bullets can mark off a list of items, as they do in print documents. Borders or rule lines can divide the page. You can also use photographs imported from a digital camera, scanned from print, or downloaded from the Internet, along with clip art and other graphics. Quick Reference 46.2 covers ways to use graphics most effectively.

Be careful and respectful using any images that you haven't created yourself, especially when copying images from the Internet. E-mail the site's creator to ask permission before using any image you have saved from another source.

**Figure 46.6** The home page of the National Science Foundation

**BACKGROUND**
At <http://www.bellsnwhistles.com/>, a Web site created by Charles H. Tupper, students will find the claim "everything you need to build your web site—for free!" At this URL, students can find software, Web tools, HTML codes, and other helpful resources.

**BACKGROUND**
In "Moving to the Public: Weblogs in the Writing Classroom," Charles Lowe and Terra Williams argue that public writing helps students to connect to the world outside the classroom. They offer several examples of how they incorporate blogs in their classrooms, such as reading responses, personal explorations, and research responses. See <http://blog.lib.umn.edu/blogosphere/moving_to_the_public.html>.

**TEACHING TIP**
John Udell's "Heavy Metal Umlaut," at <http://weblog.infoworld.com/udell/gems/umlaut.html>, provides a look at a Wikipedia page that changed over the course of several months. The commentary discusses the nature of wiki production, authoring by multiple users, and the impact on the final product.

**QUOTATION: ON WRITING**
Good writing comes from having something to say and saying it well. This simple fact is equally true in any medium. It was true in the time of the ancients and was true in the time of the medieval monks. It remained true through the invention of the printing press, the typewriter and the word processor. It is truer than ever in the age of on-line publishing and hypertext.
—Christopher B. Daly

**QUOTATION: ON WRITING**
By recognizing the need for altered definitions of literacy in the electronic writing classroom, we increase the understanding and importance of writing in our students' lives as well as our own scholarly lives.
—Joe Wilferth

**Quick Reference 46.2**

## Using graphics effectively on the Web

- **Only use images that enhance your message or design.** Most images require lots of digital storage space and loading time. Therefore, use only the images that enhance your page.

- **Resize or crop the image using graphic design software.** Although you should use the largest, highest resolution digital images possible, you should size the image and set the resolution at 72 ppi (pixels per inch) before you insert it into your design.

- **Save the image in a compressed format.** The two most popular formats for images on the Web are Graphic Interchange Format (GIF) and Joint

continued >>

> **Quick Reference 46.2** (continued)
>
> Photographic Experts Group (JPEG). If you have a button, small piece of clip art, or a black and white picture, GIF is an ideal format since these types of graphics only use a few colors. JPEG uses 16.7 million colors and compresses the file size of the picture by getting rid of empty space and blending like colors together. In a detailed photograph, you would never notice such a change. However, this process of blending and squeezing can leave little imperfections in solid color images. Also, each time you save a JPG image, it recompresses it so that even a good photo can turn into mud if repeatedly worked on and saved in this format.

**Figure 46.7** The home page of the National Archives

Quick Reference 45.4 explained some terms and considerations when using images in document design, and they also apply to images for Web sites. As with any source that you did not create yourself, you should document where any

**Figure 46.8** The Nature Club's home page with a different CSS

images you use came from. For the correct DOCUMENTATION format for your graphic sources, see Chapter 36 (MLA), Chapter 37 (APA), or Chapter 38 (CMS and CSE). Also see the copyright considerations in Chapter 45.

**EXERCISE 46-3**    Working alone or in a group, further analyze the use of images on the Web page in Figure 46.6. For help, consult the discussions of images in Chapter 4 and visual design in Chapter 45. Optional: Choose one or more current Web sites on the Internet for your analysis.

## 46d.6   How do I edit my page and test usability?

Before you publish your Web page (that is, before you upload it to a server), edit and proofread it as carefully as you would a print document. The key difference between editing a Web page and a print document is that you also need to check that all of the interactive parts of your Web page are working properly. Before you finalize your Web page, use the following checklist:

**ANSWERS: EXERCISE 46-3**
Answers will vary. You might want to compile a class checklist, based on the Quick References in this chapter and in Chapter 45 to create a list of compelling Web design and the use of images.

- **Are any images broken?** Broken images show up as small icons instead of the pictures you want. The usual cause of broken images is mistyping the file name or failing to upload the image.
- **Do all the links work?** For each link to a page on your own site, be sure a file with that exact name exists on the server. Mistyped or mislabeled files can cause broken links.
- **Is the Web site user-friendly?** Ask your friends, classmates, or colleagues to report any sections in which information is unclear or difficult to find. They can also provide feedback about your content.

### 46d.7 How do I display my Web page?

After you've created and tested a Web page, you're ready to display it on the Web. To do this, you need two things: First, you need space on a WEB SERVER, a centralized computer always online and primarily dedicated to storing and making Web pages available. Second, you need the ability to load all of your files to that server, including the page(s) you've made and any associated graphics that you've included.

#### FINDING SPACE ON THE WEB

If you have a commercial Internet Service Provider (ISP), you may be able to use it to post your Web site. Your college may offer Web space to its students,

**Figure 46.9** Tables used to create The Nature Club home page

so check with your computing service office. Some services on the Internet offer free Web space as well as help in building Web pages. Try searching for "free Web hosting." Note that if you use "free" Web space, the provider may insert advertising on your page.

You'll also need some kind of File Transfer Protocol (FTP) program to upload the HTML files to your Web server. The host of your space should be able to advise you on the best way to upload files and which FTP program to use.

**PUBLISHING YOUR PAGE**

Posting a Web page is a form of publishing. Like all original writings, your Web site is automatically copyrighted. If you want to make this clear to users (to discourage PLAGIARISM, for example) include a copyright notice by typing the word *copyright,* the copyright symbol ©, the year of publication, and your name. If you want feedback, include your e-mail address. If you use material from SOURCES, credit them completely by using DOCUMENTATION; you might include a link titled "Works Cited," "References," or "Sources" that takes your readers to a separate page. Always ask for permission to use someone else's work on your Web site. Plagiarism is plagiarism (35b), whether the medium is print or electronic.

## 46e  How do I write in a blog?

A Web log, or blog, is a type of Web site that displays a series of posts, or items, usually diary-like entries or observations, but also images, videos, audio files, and links. There are thousands of blogs on the Internet, with most focused on a particular topic.

Some instructors have students keep blogs as a course requirement. This follows the tradition of having students keep journals as a regular way of writing about course content. The twist is that others can easily read and comment on each person's postings. If you're assigned to produce a course blog, your instructor will provide specific directions. Figure 46.10 shows a typical blog design.

If you'd like to create your own blog, decide on a type and purpose. Some blogs collect links and ask others to comment on those links. For example, Digg (http://digg.com/) and Fark (http://www.fark.com/), two popular news blogs, collect news story links and users' brief comments on them. Other blogs, such as Reuters (http://blogs.reuters.com/us/) invite much longer response posts about current news stories or happenings around the Web. Still other blogs provide original material or refer to happenings in somebody's life (an example is Figure 1.2, on page 7). Decide, then, whether you want a blog that collects, responds, reports, or is more like a journal.

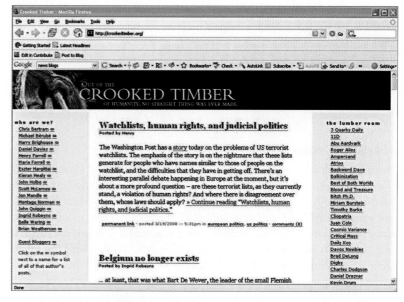

**Figure 46.10** A typical blog design

Next, you'll want to figure out how much control you want over your blog's appearance. Some software allows you to easily start blogging almost immediately with little worry or knowledge. However, if you would like to have more control, you may need to buy server space and set up the software yourself. CMS (**C**ontent **M**anagement **S**oftware) such as Movable Type and Drupal are powerful programs to design, write, and maintain your own blog.

You need to find an AUDIENCE that cares about your perspective. You might participate in blogs and network with others, eventually gaining people who are interested in what you have to say. Most important, have something interesting to say. Not all blogs have to be public, but if you want to take advantage of the technology of sharing your ideas and experiences with others, you should make these ideas and experiences entertaining, persuasive, and enlightening. Quick Reference 46.3 contains some guidelines.

# 46f How do I write in a wiki?

A wiki is a technology that allows anybody to change the content of a Web page without using special Web writing or uploading software. Wiki is a Hawaiian word meaning "fast," and the name refers to how quickly people using this technology can collaborate and revise information. One of the more popular wiki applications is the online encyclopedia, Wikipedia. (See Figure 1.7 on page 20.)

### Guidelines for writing in a blog

- **Pick a unique title for your blog.** People and Internet search engines will recognize your blog if it has a good title.

- **Decide whether to use your own name or a made-up username.** You can protect your privacy to some degree if you have a *pseudonym* (literally, a "false name") or *username*. Especially if you're writing about controversial topics or taking controversial positions, you might not want employers, instructors, or even relatives to know your identity. Of course, an anonymous username doesn't give you license to be irresponsible or unethical. On the other hand, the advantage of your real name is that you get credit (and, we suppose, blame) for your writings. Think carefully about this decision.

- **Observe netiquette.** NETIQUETTE refers to etiquette in online environments like the Web. Remember, the Internet is available around the world to many people in many cultures and of many ages. What might seem normal in your life isn't necessarily normal to someone else online. So be respectful in your posts, avoid vulgar language or SHOUTING (typing in all capital letters), and if you disagree with somebody, try to find common ground or evidence to the contrary rather than resorting to *ad hominem* (4j) attacks.

- **Link, show, and share.** Use the Web and its multimodality in your posts. Include links in your posts to other, similar posts or items from the Web. Post images, videos, or audio files, but do respect copyrights. And share your posts and blog with others through the use of a blogroll or by participating on other blogs. Blogging is about sharing your ideas and experiences with others so that they might share their ideas and experiences with you.

The technology behind wikis is similar to that in blogs; both use software that runs in the background and organizes the content. However, wikis and blogs serve different purposes. Wikis are designed to allow collaborative writing and presentation rather than individual commentary and response. A wiki entry, or node, is updated and presented immediately as the content of a Web site. Whatever was written at a particular node before it was edited is deleted, and the new content replaces it. In some ways, a wiki is more temporary than any other type of multimodal writing because many people can change it.

Wikis can be useful tools for collaborative writing projects because they keep a draft in front of all group members all the time. Individuals can easily make contributions and changes. However, as you can imagine, this can also lead to complications. If you're using a wiki for a college project, you'll want to review strategies in Chapter 6 for writing with others.

There is usually no need to create a wiki if one already exists to serve a particular purpose. Contributing to the existing wiki is usually time better spent. However, if you want to create a wiki for an unmet need, such as providing information for an upcoming election, creating a collaborative space for a business, or designing a study aid for a course, setting one up is fairly easy. Simple software like Pbwiki (http://pbwiki.com/education.wiki) will allow you quickly to start creating your own wiki without worrying about server space. However, if you need more control, you will have to install specialized software such as TikiWiki, MediaWiki, or SnipSnap on a dedicated Web server. In either case, you should observe the guidelines in Quick Reference 46.4 for writing or revising a wiki node.

---

### Quick Reference 46.4  ■ ■ ■ ■ ■ ■ ■

#### Guidelines for writing in a wiki

- **Revise with respect for others.** When revising a node, always consider ways to preserve what was originally written before deleting what another person has written. The strength of a wiki is in its ability to allow people to collaborate their expertise, so try to maintain what others have said. In some cases, you might post on a wiki and find you totally disagree with what is written. Instead of deleting what's there, you might add qualifications, for example, adding words like, "possibly" or phrases such as "in some cases" or "some have argued." However, you might also add another section to the node entitled "opposing arguments" (see 5l) and then add an alternative viewpoint to the node.

- **Cite your sources whenever possible.** Much of the controversy concerning Wikipedia in recent years has to do with the fact that some entries do not have cited references. Whenever possible, if updating or adding to a wiki, you should cite your sources, and in some cases, find corroborating sources. Any addition to a wiki node that contains reference to reputable sources is less likely to be deleted or revised later.

- **Remember a wiki is multimodal.** Just as with a blog, use the Web and its multimodality in your node edits. Include links and references from other sources on the Web. Post images, videos, or audio files, respecting copyrights in every case. The Web is suited to multimodal presentation, so take advantage of this capability when revising or writing in a wiki.

---

**ANSWERS: EXERCISE 46-4**

Answers will vary. In lectures, Marc Prensky, author of "Digital Natives, Digital Immigrants," says that there is a difference between "search" and "research." Encourage students to think about positive uses of a resource like Wikipedia while also encouraging them to consider the differences between peer-reviewed sources and user-generated sources. Prensky's groundbreaking article on digital native is available at <http://www.marcprensky.com/writing/default.asp>.

● **EXERCISE 46-4**    Considering what you know about blogs, wikis, and multimodal writing, what are the benefits of using Wikipedia? What are the drawbacks?

## 46g How do I create podcasts or videos?

**Podcasts** are short audio or video files (for example, as on YouTube) that are distributed via the Internet. People can view or listen to them directly online (called "streaming") or as downloads to their computers or a digital player such as an Apple iPod. (Not every podcast can be downloaded.) Audio podcasts are oral presentations, and serious ones need to be carefully planned and written so that listeners can easily follow them, just as they would a speech. Video podcasts often imitate formats that appear on television, although the production is usually not as elaborate. A podcast might be a useful source for a paper. Take care to evaluate and cite it as you would any source, and follow the appropriate documentation styles (Chapters 36–38).

Although you can create advanced Web designs or flyers with affordable computer software and hardware, creating a professional audio or video presentation or podcast can require more specialized and expensive equipment. However, you should still be able to produce effective podcasts if you observe the guidelines in Quick Reference 46.5. Plan, draft, revise, and edit a podcast just as you would any other writing project.

---

**Quick Reference 46.5**  ■ ■ ■ ■ ■ ■ ■

### Guidelines for producing a podcast

- **Consider the benefits of the mode.** Besides thinking about your AUDIENCE and PURPOSE, you need to also consider whether an audio or video is an effective mode for your situation. Producing audio or video requires far more time than any other type of multimodal writing, which becomes a factor when deciding whether to take on such a project. Additionally, audio and video are both linear in nature, which is to say that a good podcast has a beginning, a middle, and an end, and listeners or viewers can't easily skip around.

- **Create and practice a script.** You should write out a script that contains not only what you intend to say but also list how you will say particular passages, what might be appearing on the camera during a particular section, as well as cues for music or sound effects. Once the script is written, you should practice the script often by reading it aloud, just as you would if you were practicing a musical instrument or a part in a play.

- **Create a storyboard for video projects.** A storyboard is a series of rough sketches (you can use "stick" people, for example) that show the major scenes or elements in your video. It helps you plan the sequence and keep track of what shots you need to make.

continued >>

**Quick Reference 46.5** (continued)

- **Find an appropriate place to record.** When recording audio or video, you should always be aware that microphones and cameras record more than you might have intended. Background sounds such as your neighbor's television, the wind, or the fan in your computer might go unnoticed in your day to day life, but as soon as you record your podcast, everybody will be able to hear them. Many universities have practice rooms in the music departments that are specifically designed to dampen noise, but at least look for a quiet place with good acoustics to record any audio.

- **Use the best equipment available to you.** Although many digital cameras have record-to-video functions, you will get better footage from a dedicated video camera. Similarly, although a laptop might have a built-in microphone, a dedicated microphone will produce the best results. Some music departments have recording rooms with professional equipment that you can rent for less than a professional studio would cost. However, you might not have access to such equipment at your university. Ask faculty, friends, and neighbors if they have access to any equipment that you might borrow.

## 46h What do I need to know about writing in social networking sites?

**Social networking Web sites** like MySpace and Facebook allow you to share your experiences, interests, and writing with other people of similar interests. Designing in these sites is limited by the software that each company uses, but you can still make your Web site interesting and effective. Most of the visual design elements that have been discussed in this chapter are applicable to setting up your space on a social networking Web site. For example, many MySpace and Facebook pages suffer from complicated and dark backgrounds with dark text, making them difficult to read. Consider Quick References 46.1 and 46.3 when designing and writing on a social networking Web site.

There are some additional considerations when using any social networking Web site. Remember that even if you have made your page private, a friend of a friend or even a future employer could easily end up viewing material that you meant only close friends to see. People have lost jobs and job opportunities because of what employers have seen on their pages. Always assume that anything you post is public and permanent. Only post images, text, or music that you are confident are appropriate and that represent you well.

**Figure 46.11** Example of a social networking site

On the other hand, because of the powerful social networking capability, an effectively designed page might attract potential employers or professional contacts more easily than a traditional resumé or Web site. Make sure, then, to represent yourself well for multiple audiences. Because viewers can often link to your friends' pages as well, make sure you accept friends who also reflect well on you. Additionally, although you might think that private information such as your address or phone number is safe from others if you are listed as private, this information still can be leaked. You're not as anonymous as you might think. These concerns shouldn't scare you from creating a presence on a social networking site that you and others can enjoy. Just be cautious and only post personal information when absolutely necessary.

For more help with your writing, grammar, and research,
go to **www.mycomplab.com**

mycomplab

# 47

# Creating a Writing Portfolio

## 47a What is a writing portfolio?

A portfolio is a collection of your writings that you present to others in order to achieve some purpose. You might be familiar with artists or graphic artists who make portfolios of their work in order to show gallery owners or prospective employers. Writing portfolios are similar collections of best works. Students frequently need to submit them at the end of a course, as part or all of their final grades. Some students are required to submit a portfolio of work at the end of their major or program to demonstrate what they've accomplished in the previous two or four years. Portfolios can even be part of the hiring process for some jobs, as candidates show their skills and experiences in a sample of their best work. Figure 47.1 shows one student's online career portfolio.

As we explain in this chapter, portfolios can exist in physical, paper formats, or they can exist electronically, in digital versions. There are four key steps in making a successful portfolio: collecting all of your writings; selecting the works to include in a given portfolio; writing an introduction to, or analysis of, those works; and designing the presentation format. We explain each step below.

## 47b What do I need to collect for a portfolio?

To put it simply: Save everything you write. Save every paper and project, every exam or lab report, even every draft. You can't put together a good portfolio if you don't have plenty of works to choose from, including plenty of works to ignore. Because computer storage is so cheap and plentiful, it's easy to keep electronic copies of everything. It's a good idea to keep paper copies, too, especially when they have instructor's comments or grades; some portfolios, such as those submitted for awards or graduate school admissions, often require instructors' comments.

## 47c How do I choose works to include in a portfolio?

Selection is crucial to an effective portfolio. Rather than including everything you've written, you need to choose your best pieces that satisfy the requirements of the portfolio. One obvious thing you need to do is to meet any

**Figure 47.1** A student's career portfolio

requirements for the number of works or pages to include. If you're asked to select three pieces, don't include two or four. If you're asked to submit a total of 20–25 pages, don't turn in 17 or 29. Beyond those specific requirements, you need to pay attention to specific things requested in a particular situation.

## 47c.1 Portfolios that demonstrate your general writing ability

Consider this kind of assignment: "Present three works that best display your strengths as a writer." Clearly, you're going to choose your best writing, which sounds simple. However, you might additionally judge whether you can choose pieces that show a range of your abilities. For example, if you're choosing from six papers, and three of them are all the same kind of writing, you might not want to include all of them. Instead, you might choose at least one different kind of paper that allows you to show how versatile you are. (Of course, if the other papers are considerably weaker than the three similar ones, go with your strengths.)

## 47c.2 Portfolios that demonstrate a particular quality or set of qualities

Consider another kind of situation: "One goal in this course was to improve your ability to write for different situations. Create a portfolio of three works

selection of content, the basis for the selection, and the guidelines for evaluation, and must engage in ongoing self-reflection. This process is properly identified as authentic for performance assessment because it relies on what the student actually produces in a given situation. The power of the process lies in students' ability to see patterns of behaviors in their work, set independent goals, and monitor their own growth.

Portfolios will and should be as varied and diverse as the instructors and students creating them because they arise directly out of the needs of the class or program and the instruction delivered. This flexibility is a major strength of portfolio assessment; however, there are characteristics or guidelines that make the process distinctive. All portfolios should include work created over time, work selected by the instructor, work selected by the student, and an in-depth explanation or analysis in which the student justifies how and why the included work represents effort, progress, and achievement. In the chapter for students, we have outlined several possibilities for the different kinds of portfolios students might be asked to create for their coursework. If you decide to use a portfolio approach to your writing class, we recommend that you create a specific portfolio assignment, with a list of the items you would like included in the portfolio. The ePortfolio provides an additional way for students to create a portfolio and is especially useful when a course teaches and evaluates multimodal compositions.

**TEACHING TIP**
The portfolio mantra that students and instructors should always remember is "collect, select, reflect."

**THREE-PHASE PROGRAM: DIAGNOSTIC, WORKING, AND DISPLAY PORTFOLIOS**
Although the individuality and flexibility of portfolios are their chief benefits, sometimes the process of managing the paperwork seems overwhelming. To avoid the helter-skelter stress associated with portfolios, use a three-phase

portfolio template, which should allow for sensible implementation and yet maintain the diversity of instructional and learning needs. This is just one approach that has proved workable; feel free to design your own program.

### Diagnostic Portfolio (Weeks 1–4)

This portfolio is created during the early weeks of the term through the assembly of all early work, which could include everything from in-class and formal writing assignments to journal entries to text and class notes. The whole point of this phase is to provide a clear, written record of the student's current abilities and commitment. This means that students must reflect (in a cover essay) on the implications of their work by analyzing their grades and their instructors' comments; self-analysis allows students to set individual goals to be fulfilled throughout the remainder of the semester. This process is a modified application of the scientific method (see Chapter 41).

### Working Portfolio (Weeks 5–13)

This portfolio contains all the work produced during the semester (except, of course, for the work already housed in the Diagnostic Portfolio): all formal and informal writing assignments, all prewriting and drafts, and any independent work on individual needs identified in the Diagnostic Portfolio, such as grammar remediation. The Working Portfolio could also contain all work associated with the research project, such as bibliography and note cards and photocopies of articles. The purpose of this phase in the portfolio process is to document progress and commitment and the relationship between the two. This does, indeed, profile time on task. In fact, this is the phase that clearly illustrates the relationship between quantity and quality of work.

### Display Portfolio (Weeks 14–16)

This portfolio contains best works only. Therefore, the only pieces in this phase will be clean, polished drafts of writing produced and chronicled in the previous portfolio phases. The only new work in this section will be the student's final reflection essay that discusses in depth the student's achievement and establishes the evidence of the grade desired by the student. This

that demonstrate how you're able to write for different audiences and purposes and in different roles." In this case, you need to choose works that reflect different writing situations. Choosing becomes a little more like putting together a puzzle, as you look for the right combination of writings that allows you to meet the requirement. Occasionally, this means that a strong work gets omitted because it doesn't fit all the purposes. Often, you need to choose works that satisfy multiple requirements. For example, you might choose papers A and B to illustrate different audiences, papers A and C to show different purposes, and B and C to show different roles.

### 47c.3   Portfolios that demonstrate improvement

Consider a third kind of portfolio: "Select four examples of your writing from this semester that demonstrate how your writing has developed." In this case, your instructor wants to see your improvement. One way to do this is to choose writings from the beginning, middle, and end of the course. Another way is to choose both early and late, revised drafts from the same paper. In this kind of portfolio, as well as the others, an introductory or analytic statement will be valuable.

## 47d   How do I write a portfolio introduction, reflection, or analysis?

A statement or essay in which you introduce or explain the works you're presenting is an important part of most portfolios. This writing, which may range from a few paragraphs to several pages, depending on the situation and requirements, can go by several names: introduction, reflection, analysis, reflective introduction, reflective analysis, and so on. While there are subtle differences in each of these names, the basic elements are the same: You want to introduce yourself as a writer; you want to introduce the works that follow (perhaps with a one- or two-sentence summary of each of them); and you want to make some points about them, especially how they satisfy your purpose.

Whatever the purpose, it's helpful to think of the reflective introduction as a kind of argument. You're making claims about your work, and you're providing support for those claims. For example, if you say, "These pieces show my ability to adjust my writing for academic and popular audiences," then you need to "prove" your assertion. In this case, your evidence is one or more of the papers in the portfolio, and you'll want to summarize, paraphrase, or quote the appropriate passage. You'll need to explain how the evidence fits your claim. A helpful basic structure is the following:

1. Claim about your writing.

2. Summaries, paraphrases, or quotations from papers in the portfolio that support the claim.

3. Discussion of how the summary, paraphrase, or quotations support your claim.

Repeat this pattern for as many claims as you have about your portfolio. The following example illustrates weak and strong sections from reflective introductions.

EXAMPLE

**Weak and Strong Sections from a Reflective Introduction** [The following paragraph is common to all three examples that follow.]

During the 2008 spring semester, I completed five papers in English 101, revising each of them several times with response from my peers and feedback from my instructor. At times the process was frustrating; I came into the course feeling confident about my writing, but I learned that there's always room for improvement. As I reflect back on my experiences, I'm especially satisfied with new strategies I learned for making effective arguments and with the skills I acquired about different kinds of academic papers. This portfolio includes three papers I've chosen to represent my current strengths as a writer.

**Weak** [Same introduction as above]

One quality apparent in these papers is my ability to adjust writings for different audiences, both academic and general. For example, "Analyzing the Merits of Organic Produce" addresses an academic readership. In contrast, "Is that Organic Apple Really Worth It?" is aimed at a more general audience.

**Better** [Same introduction as above]

One quality apparent in these papers is my ability to adjust writings for different audiences, both academic and general. For example, "Analyzing the Merits of Organic Produce" addresses an academic readership. This can be seen in my consistent use of APA citation style and a scholarly tone suitable for experts, as in my opening sentence, "Research on the health values of organic produce over nonorganic reveals that this issue remains unresolved" (Johnson, 2006; Akule, 2007).

In contrast, my paper "Is that Organic Apple Really Worth It?" is aimed at a more general audience. That paper uses scenes and examples designed to engage readers with a friendly tone. This is clear in my opening sentence, "As sticker shock in the grocery checkout line continues to worsen, consumers have to judge whether everything in their carts belongs there."

discussion should include references to the work contained in both of the other portfolios.

**SHARPENING THE LISTENING–READING–WRITING CONNECTION**

Portfolios offer a structured, systematic "reading in the content course" approach. Indeed, the success of portfolio assessment rests in the comforting roots of its pedagogy, the synergistic relationships among listening, reading, and writing. Understanding this fundamental connection, as used in portfolio assessment, will make for effective and exciting results. Foster students' critical reading skills by asking them to pay attention to the purpose of each assignment, your feedback, and the textbook's information. For example, the Diagnostic Portfolio not only establishes preexisting abilities and becomes a measuring tool for future growth and reflection but also quickly establishes the ongoing connections among listening, reading, and writing.

Using a variety of early semester learning activities—such as in-class and take-home writing assignments, instructor feedback and scores, interest and behavior inventories, a diagnostic grammar test, and class notes—ask students to discuss their strengths and needs by providing a set of reflective questions. Once the student has identified an individual list of needs, require a textbook reconnaissance for the solutions for each problem, and have the student create a study plan based on the pages required to study, projected amount of time needed to study, and ways to measure mastery of each skill. Notice that the student has had to actually read instructor comments, survey the textbook, establish prior knowledge, and use inference, prediction, and time-management skills.

**INSTRUCTOR FEEDBACK IN THE USE OF PORTFOLIO ASSESSMENT**

Too often, instructors hold on to information that students really need. Portfolio assessment can be a tool to communicate this very information in a nonthreatening and motivational manner. Instructor feedback is a valuable communication opportunity. Generally speaking, feedback comes to the student in one of

What is the relationship between your performance on the grammar test and your writing scores?

What do the grammar test and instructor feedback show that you need to study?

How many pages in the handbook do these skills cover?

How long do you think you need to study each skill?

How will you measure your mastery of these skills?

Do you practice writing outside of the classroom?

What kinds of writing do you do regularly? Does this writing practice strengthen your writing for class? Why or why not?

What is your plan of study?

How will you use your textbooks?

What is your greatest strength as a writer?

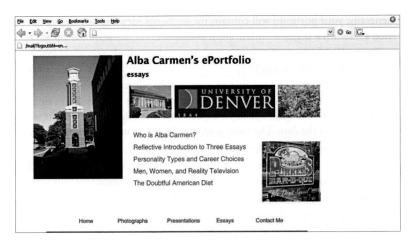

**Figure 47.2** A student's digital portfolio

can be seen in my consistent use of APA citation style and a scholarly tone suitable for . . .

The blue underlined text is a link that readers can click to take them directly to the paper. The most highly developed digital portfolios have an opening page that allows readers to understand all of the elements in the portfolio. From these pages, which combine the functions performed by the cover and contents pages of a paper portfolio, readers can link to any of the components in the portfolio. In digital portfolios, all the elements of visual design are important. Figure 47.2 shows one example.

For more help with your writing, grammar, and research, go to **www.mycomplab.com**

# Writing When English Is Not Your First Language

## A Message to Multilingual Writers

If you ever worry about your English writing, you have much in common with us and many US college students. Still, we recognize that multilingual writers face special challenges. Depending on how, when, and where you began learning English, you might feel very comfortable with spoken English but not academic, written English. Or you might understand English grammar quite well, but you might struggle with idioms and slang. Multilingual writers' different backgrounds in English will affect the kinds of writing challenges they face. For example, you might be an international student just learning the expectations of academic English, or you might be a bilingual student who went to high school in the United States. You might be an adult returning to school encountering academic language for the first time, or you might be a student who received an advanced degree in another country but must now master academic writing in English. To become a skilled writer in English, though, you will likely need to concentrate on almost every word, phrase, sentence, and paragraph in ways native speakers of English do not.

Many multilingual writers get very upset about the errors that they make in written English. We encourage you not to get frustrated about errors, but to learn from them. The good news is that errors demonstrate that you're moving normally through the stages of second-language development. As with your progress in speaking, listening, and reading in a new language, developing writing skills takes time. The process of learning to write English is like learning to play a musical instrument. Few people can play fluently without first making many errors.

What can help you advance as quickly as possible from one writing stage to another? If you attended school elsewhere before coming to the United States, we recommend that you start by thinking about school writing in your first language. Recall how you were taught to present ideas in your written native language, especially when explaining information, giving specific details, and arguing logically about a topic. Then compare it to how writing American English works. Making yourself aware of the similarities and differences will help you learn English strategies more easily.

Most college essays and research papers in the United States are direct in tone and straightforward in structure. Typically, the THESIS STATEMENT (the central message of the piece of writing) is at the end of the first paragraph or, in a longer piece of writing, in the second paragraph. Each paragraph that follows relates in content directly to the essay's thesis statement. Also, each paragraph after the thesis statement needs to begin with a TOPIC SENTENCE that contains the main point of the paragraph, and the rest of the paragraph supports the point made in the topic sentence. The final paragraph brings the content to a logical conclusion that grows out of what has come before.

As you continue writing in English, you might look for interesting ways to blend the traditions and structures of writing in your first language with the conventions of academic writing in the United States. It's important to honor your culture's writing traditions and structures; they reflect the richness of your heritage. At the same time, you can adapt to and practice the writing styles typical in the United States. The *American Heritage English as a Second Language Dictionary,* which is available in paperback and hardcover, can ease your way with English words and expressions. If your college library doesn't own a copy, ask your professor to request that the reference librarian purchase a few copies for students to consult.

The *Simon & Schuster Handbook* offers three special features that we've designed specifically for you as a multilingual learner. Chapters 8 through 31 focus on the most challenging grammar issues that you face as you learn to write English. In other chapters throughout the book, ESOL Tips offer you more helpful hints about possible cultural references and grammar issues. Finally, in Chapter 49, we've provided an "English Errors Transferred from Other Languages" chart. In this chart, you'll find information about trouble spots that commonly occur when speakers of certain first languages (Spanish, Russian, and so on) speak, read, or write in English.

Distinctive variations in school writing styles among people of different cultures and language groups have interested researchers for the past thirty years. If you have written academically in languages other than American English, you might notice similarities and differences between the writing you have done in school prior to now and the writing you are asked to do in English. As individuals, we greatly enjoy discovering the rich variations in the writing traditions of our students from many cultures of the world. As American writing teachers, however, our responsibilities call for us to explain what you need to do as writers in the United States. If you were in one of our classes, we would say "Welcome!" and ask you to teach us about writing in your native language. You bring a richness of experience in communicating in more than one language that most US students have never had, and you should be proud of that experience. Using the knowledge of writing in your first language, we could then help you learn how to approach writing effectively in the United States so that you will succeed as a writer and learner in a US college.

Lynn Quitman Troyka
Doug Hesse

Teachers of English to Speakers of Other Languages (TESOL) is, in the language of their Mission Statement, "a global association for English language teaching professionals" with the mission to "ensure excellence in English language teaching to speakers of other languages." TESOL sponsors a yearly conference and a journal to promote scholarship in the field of English language acquisition; they also serve as a public advocate around the issues pertinent to educators and ESOL/EFL (English as a Foreign Language) students. (*Note*: For a list of common acronyms used by TESOL, and the distinctions the organization draws between them, see <http://www.tesol.org/s_tesol/sec_document.asp?CID=709&DID=387>).

The TESOL Web site <www.tesol.org> is by far the most comprehensive Web site available for educators working with ESOL/EFL students. Among the many resources you will find there, you may wish to look at TESOL's many position statements on a number of issues relevant to learning English as a second/foreign language. Furthermore, these position statements might serve well as classroom readings, helping students understand what the discipline believes are the best ways to teach English to students in the process of acquiring the language in the setting of the American educational system. Some especially appropriate readings might include:

- Position Statement on the Acquisition of Academic Proficiency in English <http://www.tesol.org/s_tesol/bin.asp?CID=32&DID=378&DOC=FILE.PDF>

- Position Statement on Multilingualism <http://www.tesol.org/s_tesol/bin.asp?CID=32&DID=2933&DOC=FILE.PDF>

- Position Paper on English-only Legislation in the United States <http://www.tesol.org/s_tesol/bin.asp?CID=32&DID=4162&DOC=FILE.PDF>

- Position Statement on the Diversity of English Language Learners in the United States <http://www.tesol.org/s_tesol/bin.asp?CID=32&DID=7212&DOC=FILE.PDF>

# 48

# Multilingual Students Writing in US Colleges and Universities

## 48a How is writing taught in US colleges?

Multilingual students who went to high school outside the United States may find that teachers and students in this country behave differently from teachers and students in their home countries. If you're one of these students, you might be surprised by the seemingly informal interaction between teachers and students in the United States. No matter how you interpret what you might see, rest assured that the casual teacher-student relationship is based on respect. Instructors still expect students to pay attention, obey class rules, and meet all assignment deadlines.

In the United States, teachers usually expect students to participate in class discussions. This can be very challenging for multilingual students if they aren't used to this style of classroom interaction, especially if they don't feel confident about speaking English. If this is the case for you, do your best to make as many contributions to class discussion as you possibly can. The more you try, the easier it will become.

When your instructors assign work, they may show you model papers. It can be very helpful to examine the parts of these sample papers to see how the authors have organized information, presented main points, and supported those main points. This is especially true if the assignment is a new type of writing for you. When you look at examples, be sure you know which aspects of the papers your teacher thinks are strong, and which aspects he or she thinks need improvement. Of course, when you analyze sample papers, you're doing so only to learn which writing techniques work well. Remember: Don't copy phrases, ideas, content, or images from them. In the United States, copying someone else's work is called PLAGIARISM\*, and it's ethically and legally wrong. For a detailed discussion about plagiarism, see Chapter 35.

If your instructor asks you to analyze a sample paper, pay close attention to the features of that type of paper. For example, the characteristics that make a lab report effective are not always the same characteristics that make a

---

\*Words printed in SMALL CAPITAL LETTERS are discussed elsewhere in the text and are defined in the Terms Glossary at the back of this book.

narrative essay effective. Chapter 7 explains some types of academic writing that are common in the United States.

Just as classroom expectations and writing assignments differ from culture to culture, the way that writing is taught also varies. In writing classes in US colleges, many instructors teach a process approach to writing. This approach emphasizes the steps that writers go through as they compose assignments for themselves and for college and work. The basic steps are planning, drafting, revising, editing, and proofreading. For more specific details about the writing process, see Chapter 2 of this handbook.

Sometimes multilingual students become so concerned about making grammar mistakes that they neglect taking enough time to think about the ideas in their paper. Always remember that writing is about communicating ideas. To ensure you're conveying your own ideas and fulfilling the requirements of your assignments, spend as much time thinking about the content of your paper as you do working on your grammar. You might find it helpful to work on content and grammar separately as you draft. For help in working on thinking of ideas and expressing them, review sections 2b–2f, which describe activities to help you come up with interesting material for your writing.

## 48b   How does my past writing experience affect my writing in English?

Thinking about your own writing experiences and learning about others' can help you set goals for improving your writing. Exercise 48-1 can help you do both.

**EXERCISE 48-1**   Think about the following sentences. For each sentence, write "True," "False," or "I'm not sure." If invited, share your answers with your instructor so he or she can learn more about your previous writing experiences. Next, write your thoughts about all or some of the statements, which can give you insight into yourself as a writer in English. Outside of class, you might also discuss your answers with one or more of your multilingual classmates or friends.

1. I am better at writing in another language than I am at writing in English.
2. I have more experience writing in another language than I do in English.
3. I feel confident about writing in English.
4. I received all of my secondary (high school) education outside the United States.
5. When I write in English, I have trouble finding the appropriate vocabulary.
6. When I write in English, I use a dictionary that translates words between English and my first language.
7. When I write in English, I use an English-English dictionary.
8. When I write in English, I use a computer spell-check program.

**BACKGROUND**

"Second Language Learning and the Teaching of Grammar," by Carl Zhonggang Gao, is an excellent overview of the issues that surround teaching of ESOL/EFL students (*Education.* Winter 2001. FindArticles.com. 11 May, 2008, at <http://findarticles.com/p/articles/mi_qa3673/is_200101/ai_n8946417>).

**TEACHING TIP**

Students from some educational backgrounds may be accustomed to their instructors providing sample essays as models to imitate. It's important to let students know to what extent you want them to model their own writing after the samples you provide.

**TEACHING TIP**

Most grammar-check programs are not designed to check for the kinds of errors typically made by ESOL students (e.g., article usage). Warn ESOL students, in particular, about the limitations of such programs.

**ANSWERS: EXERCISE 48-1**

Answers will vary.

**BACKGROUND**

In "Abdullah's Blogging: A Generation 1.5 Student Enters the Blogosphere" (*Language Learning & Technology: A Refereed Journal for Second and Foreign Language Educators* 11.2 (2007): 128–141. <http://llt.msu.edu/>), Joel Bloch describes how blogs can contribute to the sense of ownership and empowerment that Generation 1.5 students (students who have received at least a partial education in the United States, but who may have also received part of their education in another country, or who may continue to use their first language in most or all of their noneducational settings) have for their writing. He gives special emphasis to teaching students about plagiarism and helping them acquire rhetorical strategies for argument making and evidence analysis.

**TEACHING TIP**

Some ESOL students may have first languages that have no written form.

9. When I write in English, I use a computer grammar-check program.
10. In the past, I have written many different kinds of papers in English.
11. When I write in English, I can write fairly quickly.
12. I think I will need to write a lot for my major.
13. I think I will need to write a lot in English for my future career.
14. When I write in English, I sometimes have trouble generating ideas.
15. A serious problem I have with writing in English is writing correct sentences.

## 48c How can I know what my instructor expects in my writing?

Your past writing experiences influence the way you approach writing assignments. In the next passage, a bilingual student illustrates how her past experiences influenced her interpretation of writing assignments in the United States. (Note: The original draft has been edited to improve readability.)

> When I studied here, I felt puzzled with different types of writing assignments. When I wrote my first term paper, I really did not know what my professor did expect from me and how to construct my paper. My previous training in my first and second language writing taught me little about how to handle writing assignments by using composing strategies. Since language teaching in my country is exam-oriented, I learned to write in Chinese and in English basically in the same way. Under the guidance of my professor, I read a sample paper, analyzed its content and structure, and tried to apply its strengths to my own writing. Writing was not a creative process to express myself but something that was to be copied for the purpose of taking exams. As a result, when I don't have a sample for my assignments, I really don't know how to start.

Like this student, you may have difficulty understanding what your instructor expects you to do when completing a specific writing assignment. Your instructor may expect you to take a clear position on your topic. He or she may want you to use examples from your personal experience to support your ideas, quotations and specific ideas from an assigned reading, outside sources, or all three. Do not hesitate to ask your instructor questions about the assignment to make sure you understand exactly what he or she expects.

**EXERCISE 48-2**    Have you ever had trouble figuring out what an instructor expected from you when he or she assigned a writing exercise? Have you ever written a paper and later found out that what you wrote was not at all what your instructor expected? Write a paragraph or two describing your experiences.

When your instructor gives you a writing assignment, you may not know how to start because you don't know much about the topic. This might be especially true if the topic that your instructor asks students to write about relates to aspects of American culture that you're not very familiar with. If you feel this is the case, you might need to talk to your instructor about the situation and try to find more information about the topic in newspapers or magazines or by discussing the topic with other students. Similarly, if you're writing about your own culture, keep in mind that your instructor and classmates may not know very much about it. This means you may need to explain information for them in more detail than you would if you were writing a paper for people who share your cultural background.

**EXERCISE 48-3**    Have you ever written or read something that didn't make sense because it didn't include the necessary cultural background information? Write a paragraph or two describing your experiences and explaining the source of miscommunication. Before you begin, read the following passage by a student who describes the importance of providing background information in writing. (Note: This excerpt has been edited for readability.)

> If I were writing in Chinese to Chinese readers and wanted to quote a story in Chinese history as evidence, I would simply have to mention the name of the people involved in the historic event or briefly introduce the story. However, when I am writing in English to tell the readers the same story, I have to tell the whole story in detail, even though I might only want to use a small part of it in my essay. Otherwise, the readers will surely get lost.

**ANSWERS: EXERCISE 48-3**
Answers will vary.

## 48d    How do I organize my writing?

As part of the writing process, many instructors ask students to write an OUTLINE and a THESIS STATEMENT for their papers (2d–2e). Some writers from other countries have observed that American readers expect papers to have a standardized organization and communicate their purpose in a clear, obvious way. In some cases, this rigid structure poses challenges. For example, one bilingual student wrote that when he writes in his first language, he can use a "flexible organization" and can place his thesis "at the beginning, middle, or end of the essay" or "simply leave the thesis out and then let the reader draw the conclusion to show respect for the reader's intelligence." He explains that he finds it challenging writing in English because he must follow a "restricted organization" that presents a thesis in the first paragraph and then supporting subtopics and detailed examples. Keep in mind, though, that you need to follow the conventions of the type of writing you're assigned (Chapter 7).

**EXERCISE 48-4**   Are there differences between how you were taught to organize your writing in the past and how your instructors expect you to organize it now? Describe the differences in a paragraph or two, and, if you can, draw a picture that illustrates the differences. Before you begin, think back to the paragraph in Exercise 48-3 and what the student wrote about the differences organizing his papers in Chinese and English. Also, consider the following descriptions of organization in writing. (Note: Both of these examples have been edited for readability.)

EXAMPLE 1   Russian composition is not about composing supportive arguments around your own personal opinion, but instead is about composing a hierarchy of others' opinions on a certain topic. The process is very much like making a chain: You pick a citation and link it to another citation and so on.

EXAMPLE 2   From my TOEFL [Test of English as a Foreign Language] preparation class, I learned the basic framework for English writing: introduction plus body paragraphs plus conclusion, with topic sentences in the body paragraphs. I was impressed by the great difference between writing in my first language and English writing. For example, in a persuasive essay, writers from my country usually prefer to explain the problem first and then come up with their opinion. But for English writing, writers may be more likely to express the opinion at the very beginning and then give reasons to support the idea.

## 48e   How can I use other writers' work to improve my writing?

If you are writing a paper based on other texts that you have read, such as a reading your teacher has given you or sources you have found for a research project, it is important to understand how directly your teacher wants you to draw on the text(s). For example, he or she may want you to read the text and simply use it as a springboard for your own ideas; however, your instructor may also expect you to read and analyze the text closely and refer to specific ideas and sentences in the source text when you write your paper. It can be especially difficult for multilingual students to analyze a text closely and write about it without relying too heavily on the author's wording and sentence structure. In US colleges and universities, however, using another author's words, sentence structure, or even ideas without giving the author credit is considered to be a serious offense called PLAGIARISM, or stealing something that belongs to someone else (Chapter 35). In contrast, in some cultures, reliance on the author's wording is not a problem, and may even be seen as a way of complimenting the author. As one bilingual student said, "When you are writing in my first language, you can always feel free to copy good sentences from other articles or writing pieces. But in the United States, it is a violation of copyright. When you are writing in English, you cannot use someone else's work without citing it."

Chapter 35 of this handbook provides detailed information about how to document sources and avoid plagiarism. Documenting sources in your writing is very important in US academic writing because it helps to develop your credibility as a writer, or what we often call your ETHOS (5g.2). Giving credit to the original authors shows that you have done the necessary background work to find out what other people have said on a topic. Documenting sources, especially those written by experts, can help develop your credibility because your sources are reliable. Chapters 36–38 provide examples of four different documentation styles that you might use in your academic writing in the United States. Always ask your instructor if you're uncertain which style to follow.

## 48f  What kind of dictionary do I use?

Although it can be helpful to use a dictionary that translates words from your native language into English, sometimes such dictionaries are not adequate. One ESOL student, who has problems with word choice, says that dictionaries "don't always work" because some terms are "translated literally." She goes on to explain that when she uses dictionaries, she doesn't accept just any definition. The student learns how to use a word in a "real English way" and whether it is "appropriate to use in a certain context."

If you realize that you need a dictionary that does more than translating words between your native language and English, you might try an English-English dictionary (also called a "Learner's Dictionary"), especially one that was written for nonnative learners of English. Using an English-English dictionary can also help you increase your vocabulary in English as you learn different ways to express the same idea.

## 48g  What should I do with my classmates' and instructor's comments?

As part of the writing process, you and your classmates may participate in peer response, sometimes called peer review or peer editing. (See Chapter 6.) You might exchange papers or sit together and read your paper to the students in your group. The purpose of peer response is to offer and receive advice about how to improve your writing from your classmates. This type of group work may be uncomfortable for you if teachers in your home country did not assign group work or expect students to critique each other's work, or if you prefer working individually. Here are some strategies to help make peer response successful for you and your classmates.

- Let your group members know you really do want them to give you advice on your paper so that you can improve its quality before you turn it in for a grade.
- Ask your group members specific questions about your writing.
- Provide other group members with specific, considerate advice about their writing. Two strategies in written English can make suggestions more tactful:

> **Ask questions about your other group members' essays.** For example, asking "How does this reason relate back to your claim?" sounds more polite than stating "This reason doesn't relate to your claim." Your question also helps the author to revise and make his or her writing better.

> **Use modals to "hedge" your suggestions.** In English, modal verbs are often used to "soften" a command. For example, if you write, "This reason does not seem to relate to your claim," the word "seem" makes the observation more polite than if you write, "This reason does not relate to your claim."

- Talk to your instructor if you don't know whether you need to follow a specific piece of advice from a classmate.
- See Chapter 6 for more information about peer response.

In addition to receiving feedback from your classmates, try to get feedback from your instructor before he or she gives your paper a grade. Instructors expect to see significant changes based on their comments. If you have questions about how to revise your writing in response to what your teacher has told you, you need to talk to your instructor or a tutor.

## 48h   Where can I find strategies for editing my work?

When you are satisfied with the content, organization, and development of the ideas in your paper, you need to focus on language-related concerns in your writing. Chapter 49 outlines strategies for proofreading your papers.

## 48i   How can I set long-term goals for my writing?

Improving your writing can take a long time, whether you are writing in your first language or in a second, third, or fourth language. Some students find it helpful to set long-term goals for writing to help them focus on what to improve. You may want to talk to a professor in your major (or in a subject you are thinking about majoring in) so that you can ask him or her what kinds of writing you might be expected to do later, both in your college courses and in the workplace (if you plan to work in an English-speaking environment or in a context where English is used to communicate with other nonnative English speakers).

**EXERCISE 48-5** Interview a professor in your major (or in a subject you are thinking about majoring in). Ask him or her the following questions, and write a report about the answers you receive. Compare your report with that of a classmate.

1. What kinds of writing do you assign to students in your classes?
2. How do students learn how to write these assignments?
3. (Choose one or two types of writing assignments that the professor mentions.) What are the important parts of this assignment? What steps do students go through to complete this kind of assignment?
4. When you grade student writing, what aspects are most important to you?
5. What kinds of writing do graduates in this major usually do in the workplace?
6. Can you show me some examples of student writing from your courses?

For more help with your writing, grammar, and research, go to **www.mycomplab.com**

**ANSWERS: EXERCISE 48-5**
Answers will vary.

# 49

# Handling Sentence-Level Issues in English

## 49a How can I improve the grammar and vocabulary in my writing?

The best way to improve your English-language writing, including your grammar and vocabulary, is by writing. Many students also find it helpful to read as much as they can in English to see how other authors organize their writing, use vocabulary, and structure their sentences. Improving your writing in a second language—or a first language, for that matter—takes time. You will

**TEACHING TIP**
It is not realistic to expect that the English-language writing of most ESOL students will sound like that of native English speakers. Just as most ESOL students speak with an accent, they will probably also always write with an "accent." Section 49b of this chapter is designed to help students make progress in addressing serious sentence structure problems; the remainder of the chapter is devoted to helping students become more aware of common ESOL errors so that they can look for them in their own writing and attempt to correct them.

Since language acquisition is a complicated, long-term process, it is not realistic to expect ESOL students to be able to avoid a certain type of error just because that type of error has been pointed out or corrected in the past. In fact, the efficacy of error correction in second-language writing is a hotly debated topic, since some research on error correction has indicated that it has no effects or, in some cases, is detrimental to writing development (See John Truscott, "The Case Against Grammar Correction in L2 Writing Classes," *Language Learning* 46 (1996):327–369.) Most ESOL specialists advocate selectively marking the location of one or two categories of students' errors (e.g., subject-verb agreement) and asking students to try to make corrections, with a teacher or tutor nearby to assist as necessary. Robert Yates and James Kenkel's "Responding to Sentence-Level Errors in Writing" addresses the importance of not misinterpreting a student's text when providing error-correction (*Journal of Second Language Writing* 11.1 (2002): 29–47).

## TEACHING TIP

One recent addition to ESOL teaching tools is the online virtual world Second Life. Many ESOL teachers have been working in Second Life to create "English Village," a virtual island where students can learn and practice essential speaking and writing skills. To learn more about this work, visit the "Second Life English Blog" at <http://www.esl-secondlife.blogspot.com>.

## RESOURCE

*TESOL Quarterly* and *Journal of Second Language Writing* regularly publish articles on the most up-to-date practices in teaching second language learners.

## ANSWERS: EXERCISE 49-1

Answers will vary. You might want to have students present or peer review paragraphs after completion. An additional way of approaching this assignment is to rewrite the paragraph as a whole class. If you choose to do this, annotate the changes students make and provide them with a copy of the old paragraph, the revised paragraph, and the revision notes.

## ANSWERS: EXERCISE 49-2

Answers will vary. You might consider breaking students into peer-review groups based on similar error patterns. Students can revise paragraphs, using their error logs as a guide.

probably find that your ability to communicate with readers improves dramatically if you work on the ideas outlined in the previous chapter, including understanding the writing assignment and improving the organization and ideas in your writing. Sometimes, though, readers may find it hard to understand your ideas because of grammar or word choice problems in your sentences. In other cases, readers may become distracted from your ideas because you have a great many technical errors. We have designed this chapter to help you improve in these areas.

## 49b How can I improve my sentence structure?

Sometimes students write sentences that are hard to understand because of problems with overall sentence structure or length. For example, one student wrote the following sentence, which contains sentence-level errors.

> When the school started, my first English class was English 1020 as a grammar class, I started learning the basics of grammar, and at the same time the basic of writing, I worked hard in that class, taking by the teacher advice, try to memorize a lot of grammar rules and at the same time memorize some words I could use them to make an essay point.

To correct the structural and length errors, the student needs to do several things to improve the sentence. She needs to break it into several shorter sentences (Chapter 20). Also, she needs to revise her sentences so that they clearly connect to each other. Additionally, she needs to work on her verb tenses in certain phrases, such as "to make an essay point." This means she needs to ask for extra help at the writing center or from her instructor. After patient study and work, her revision might look like this:

> When school started, my first English class, English 1020, was a grammar class, where I started learning the basics of grammar. At the same time, I learned the basics of writing. I worked hard in that class, taking the teacher's advice and memorizing a lot of grammar rules. In addition, I memorized some words I could use in my essays to make my points.

**EXERCISE 49-1** Many different revisions of the previous example of a student's uncorrected paragraph are possible. Write a different revision of that student's paragraph.

**EXERCISE 49-2** A student wrote the following passage in a paper he wrote about his experiences learning English. Rewrite the passage, improving the student's sentence structure and punctuation. In your revision of this passage, correct any errors that you see in grammar or spelling. Afterward, compare your revision with a classmate's. Then examine a piece of your own writing to see if you need to revise any of your sentences because of problems with sentence structure. (While you are doing this, if you have any questions about correct word order in English, see Chapter 52.)

> I went to school in my country since I was three years old, I was in Arabic and French school, and that's was my dad choice because his second language is French. So my second language at that time was French. In my elementary school I started to learn how to make an essay in French and Arabic. I learned the rules and it is too deferent from English. But later on when I was in my high school I had two choices between English class and science class so I choose the science because that's was my major. After I graduate I went to American university and I start studying English and my first class was remedial English for people doesn't know anything about this language. I went to this class about two months and then I have moved to a new place and I start from the beginning as an ESL student.

## 49c How can I improve my word choice (vocabulary)?

An important aspect of writing in a second language is having enough vocabulary to express your ideas. Many students enjoy learning more and more words to be able to communicate precise meanings. For example, one multilingual student explains that she has improved her writing and made it more "desirable" by using "words as tools." She also says that by using "different words every time" she "refreshes" her writing and "eliminates the routine" from it. You, too, can experiment in your writing with new words that you hear and read in other contexts. To help make sure you're using a new word in the right way, we recommend the *American Heritage English as a Second Language Dictionary*, which is available in paperback and hardback. It can ease your way with English words and expressions because it's intended specifically for multilingual learners of English.

## 49d How can I find and correct errors in my own writing?

Some multilingual writers find it easiest to find and correct their grammar errors by reading their writing aloud and listening for mistakes. This method is often preferred by students who feel their spoken English is better than their written English. Other writers like to ask a friend who is a native speaker of English to check their writing for grammatical mistakes. Still other multilingual writers prefer to circle each place where they think they've made an error and then use their handbook to check themselves.

Many multilingual writers like to keep a list of the types of grammar errors they make so that they can become especially sensitive to errors when proofreading their papers. The best system is to make a master list of the errors in categories so that the checking can be as efficient as possible. Section 49j provides an example of how to track your errors in English.

**BACKGROUND**

Teachers who are new to teaching second language learners will find Rebecca Oxford's "Integrated Skills in the ESOL/EFL Classroom" an excellent overview of contemporary practices in teaching <http://www.cal.org/resources/Digest/0105oxford.html>. Additionally, "Innovative Programs and Promising Practices in ESL Literacy" by Heide Spruck Wrigley offers additional ideas for teaching; see <http://www.ericdigests.org/1993/promising.htm>.

**TEACHING TIP**

Since some languages do not use verb endings to show time frame in the way that English does, some ESOL students will have difficulty with this aspect of English usage.

**TEACHING TIP**

Some languages do not add suffixes to nouns to show plural forms; for this reason, some ESOL students may have difficulty with making singular/plural distinctions in English.

**RESOURCE**

A 2005 issue of *Computers and Composition* (22.3) is devoted to the topic of "Second Language Writers in Digital Contexts."

**TEACHING TIP**

Using prepositions can be especially difficult for ESOL writers because English has so many of them. There are no rules that accurately describe which preposition to use; students must simply memorize which prepositions belong in which phrases.

## 49e How can I correct verb form (tense) errors in my writing?

Many multilingual writers consider verb-form errors the most difficult to correct. They want to be sure that their verb forms express the appropriate time frame for the event or situation they're describing. For a detailed discussion of verb forms, see 15b–15f.

**EXERCISE 49-3** Read the following passage in which a student describes her experience learning to write in English. The student's instructor has underlined errors related to time frames expressed by the verbs. Correct the underlined verbs, changing them to the correct time frames.

> I must have started writing when I was nine years old. I remember my father used to give us papers and watercolors and let us draw as much as we want. At the end, he made sure that we write comments about why we have sketched the way we did. The only written thing that I find dating to that period was a kind of comment about a picture which I have sketched of a village enveloped in water.
>
> I don't remember much about the kind of writing assignments we have at school, whether in my native language Arabic, or in my second languages, at that time, English and French. That period is a little bit hazy in my mind. However, I remember that whenever we had the chance to go to school, we made sure that we fill the playgrounds with creative farewell sentences indicating that we have been there. It is our little game against the witchcraft of war and against the will of the principal, who forgive us easily once we have recited the multiplication table or sing the national anthem.

If you struggle with errors in verb tense in your writing, try reading through your draft once and circling all of the verbs. Then check each one in isolation.

## 49f How can I correct my errors in subject-verb agreement?

Subject-verb agreement means that a subject (a noun or a pronoun) and its verb must agree in number and in person. In the following two sentences, notice the difference in the way the subjects and the verbs that describe their actions agree: *Carolina runs charity marathons. They give her a sense of accomplishment.*

For more information about subject-verb agreement, review Chapter 17. To help you put subject-verb agreement rules into practice, try the next exercise.

**EXERCISE 49-4** Examine the following student's description of his experiences learning English. The student's instructor has underlined verbs that do not agree with their subjects. Correct the underlined verb forms, changing them to agree with their subjects.

**ANSWERS: EXERCISE 49-3**

I must have started writing when I was nine years old. I remember my father used to give us papers and watercolors and let us draw as much as we **wanted.** At the end, he made sure that we **wrote** comments about why we **had** sketched the way we did. The only written thing that I **found** dating to that period was a kind of comment about a picture which I **had** sketched of a village enveloped in water.

I don't remember much about the kind of writing assignments we **had** at school, whether in my native language Arabic, or in my second languages, at that time, English and French. That period is a little bit hazy in my mind. However, I remember that whenever we had the chance to go to school, we made sure that we **filled** the playgrounds with creative farewell sentences indicating that we **had** been there. It **was** our little game against the witchcraft of war and against the will of the principal, who **forgave** us easily once we **had** recited the multiplication table or **sung** the national anthem.

**ANSWERS: EXERCISE 49-4**

I describe the way I learned English as a natural way, where one first learns how to speak and communicate with others, before

I describe the way I learned English as a natural way, where one first <u>learn</u> how to speak and communicate with others, before learning the grammar rules that <u>supports</u> a language. When I arrived in the United States, I <u>works</u> hard to improve my communications skills in English, trying to speak even when the people <u>does</u> not understand me. Also, making friends with native speakers <u>help</u> a person learn the language. One can learn from them every single minute that one <u>spend</u> with them.

Do you have similar problems with subject-verb agreement in your own writing? Examine something you've written recently to check whether your subjects and verbs agree. Try underlining the subject and verb in each sentence to isolate the words in the sentence that need to agree.

## 49g How can I correct my singular/plural errors?

In English, if you're referring to more than one noun that is a count noun, you must make that noun plural, often by adding an *-s* ending. If you would like more information on this topic, see Chapter 50. To help you recognize when necessary plural forms are missing, try the next exercise.

**EXERCISE 49-5** In the following passage, a student comments on the differences between writing in English and in Chinese. The student's instructor has underlined only the first two nouns that need to be plural. Read the passage, correct the two underlined nouns, and then find and correct the other nouns in the passage that need to be plural.

English and Chinese have many <u>similarity</u>. They both have <u>paragraph</u>, sentence, and punctuation mark, like comma, full stops, and question marks. The biggest difference is that English has an alphabet with letter, while Chinese uses symbol for writing. My mother told me that about two thousand year ago, people in China used picture to draw what they wanted to say on turtle shells. Day after day, the pictures changed and turned into the Chinese character.

Examine a piece of your own writing and make sure that you have used plural words correctly.

## 49h How can I correct my preposition errors?

Prepositions are words such as *in, on, for, over,* and *about,* which usually show where, how, or when. For example, in the sentence *She received flowers from her friend for her birthday,* the prepositions are *from* and *for.* Unlike some other languages, English has many prepositions, and knowing which one to use can be very difficult. You can find information about using prepositions in section 14h and in Chapter 53. To practice finding and correcting preposition errors in your own writing, complete the next exercise.

learning the grammar rules that support a language. When I arrived in the United States, I worked hard to improve my communications skills in English, trying to speak even when the people did not understand me. Also, making friends with native speakers helps a person learn the language. One can learn from them every single minute that one spends with them.

**ANSWERS: EXERCISE 49-5**

English and Chinese have many similarities. They both have paragraphs, sentences, and punctuation marks, like commas, full stops, and question marks. The biggest difference is that English has an alphabet with letters, while Chinese uses symbols for writing. My mother told me that about two thousand years ago, people in China used pictures to draw what they wanted to say on turtle shells. Day after day, the pictures changed and turned into the Chinese characters.

## ANSWERS: EXERCISE 49-6

I've always wanted to learn languages other than my native language. I started taking English and French lessons **at** school and I liked the idea of becoming fluent **in** at least one language. I thought English would help me a lot **in** the future because it could help me communicate **with** people from all over the world.

## TEACHING TIP

The Web site Free Rice at <http://www.freerice.com> provides fun, interactive vocabulary practice. Every correct answer donates 20 grains of rice to countries facing the threat of hunger.

**EXERCISE 49-6** In the following passage about one student's learning experiences as a second-language learner, the student's instructor has underlined problems with preposition use. Try to correct the preposition errors. In some cases, more than one answer may be correct. If you can't find the information you need from Chapter 53 or in a dictionary, you might ask a native English speaker for help.

I've always wanted to learn languages other than my native language. I started taking English and French lessons of school and I liked the idea of becoming fluent for at least one language. I thought English would help me a lot to the future because it could help me communicate to people from all over the world.

If prepositions are something you struggle with in your own writing, ask an instructor or a native speaker of English to underline the errors in preposition usage in a piece of writing that you have done. Then go through your writing and correct the errors that have been underlined.

## 49i What other kinds of errors might I make?

Depending on your language background and your prior experience with writing in English, you may make errors related to the use of articles (*a, an, the*), word order (where to place adjectives and adverbs in sentences), and various verb forms and noun forms (for example, problems with noncount nouns and helping verbs). For example, the next sentence has a problem with one article and the order of an adjective: *The New York City is a place exciting.* The corrected sentence is *New York City is an exciting place.*

Chapters 50 through 55 address grammar errors that are often made by multilingual writers. Try to keep track of your most common errors and refer to the relevant sections of this handbook for help.

## 49j How can I keep track of my most common errors?

One way of becoming more aware of the types of errors you make is to keep track of the errors you often make in the papers you write. You can ask your instructor or a tutor to help you identify such errors, and you can make a list of them that you update regularly. Remember the passage from Exercise 49-3 about a student's experiences learning to write? After the student examined the teacher's comments on her paper, she made a list of her errors and included a correction and a note about the error type for each. After making this list of her errors, the student writer realized that many of her errors related to verb form.

| Specific Error | Correction | Type of Error |
|---|---|---|
| as much as we want | wanted | verb form |
| that we write comments | wrote | verb form |
| about why we have sketched | had | verb form |
| which I have sketched | had | verb form |
| we fill the playground | filled | verb form |
| that we have been there | had | verb form |
| once we have recited | had | verb form |

**EXERCISE 49-7** Using one or more pieces of your writing, make an error list similar to the previous one. (You could make this list on a sheet of paper or in an electronic file.) Examine the list. What are the most common types of errors that you make? Once you have identified your common error types, refer to the relevant proofreading exercises in the previous sections of this chapter and to the relevant ones in Chapters 50 through 55. Also, remember to keep your common errors in mind when you proofread your future writing assignments. You might even keep a master checklist that you can return to when you proofread your writing.

## 49k How can I improve my proofreading skills?

The most effective way to improve your proofreading skills is to practice frequently. Proofread your own writing and, after you have done so, ask your instructor, a tutor, or a friend who is a native English speaker to point out the location of errors that you did not see on your own. If you know you often make a particular kind of error, such as errors with subject-verb agreement (Chapter 11), ask the person helping you to check for these problems specifically. When you know which errors you've made, try to correct the errors without help. Finally, have your instructor or tutor check your corrections.

Another effective way to improve your proofreading skills is to exchange your writing with a partner. You can check for errors in his or her writing and he or she can check for errors in yours. You might find that, at first, it is easier to find errors if you look for one kind of error at a time. Try Exercises 49-8 and 49-9 for more proofreading practice.

**EXERCISE 49-8** The following passage was written by a bilingual student about her experiences learning to write in English. After you read it, rewrite it, correcting the linguistic errors you find.

I've always faced some problem in writing in English as it took me some time to get used to it. Facing these complexities encourage me to

**ANSWERS: EXERCISE 49-7**
Answers will vary. Encourage students to share their error logs with one another. Or, as a class, come up with a format that all students would like to use in keeping track of their errors.

**ANSWERS: EXERCISE 49-8**
These are some primary errors; however, answers will vary.

I've always faced some **problems when** writing in English **because** it took me some time to get used to it. Facing these complexities **encouraged** me to **develop** my skills in English writing. My first class in English was about grammar, spelling, and writing. I **realized** later that grammar is hard to learn, so I knew I **had** to put in a lot of effort to understand it perfectly and use it properly. I also had some difficulties **in** vocabulary, as it was hard to understand the meaning of some **words**.

Another thing that helped me with my English was when my mother **enrolled** me in an English learning center that **specialized** in **teaching** writing skills. After a month of taking classes, my teacher saw some improvement in my grammar and vocabulary. To test me, she asked me to write an essay on how to be successful. I was really **excited about** it and started **to write** (or **writing**) it immediately. After I **finished** my essay and my teacher **checked** it, my teacher suggested that I take a few more classes for her. She taught me how to **organize** my ideas. After finishing these classes I **realized** that my writing was getting much better with time.

**ANSWERS: EXERCISE 49-9**

These are some primary errors; however, answers will vary.

Recently, the number of private language schools have increased in Japan. These schools put special emphasis on oral communication skills. In them, students take not only grammar and reading classes, which help them pass school examinations, but also speaking and listening classes. They can also study English for six years, which is the same period as in public schools. Some of the teachers in these schools are native speakers of English. Since these teachers do not speak Japanese in the classes, the students have to use English to participate in them. They have the opportunity to use the English in these classes more than public school students. Some people have observed that the students who took English in private schools can speak English better than those students who took English-language classes in public schools.

developed my skills in English writing. My first class in English was about grammar, spelling, and writing. I realize later that grammar is hard to learn, so I knew I have to put in a lot of effort to understand it perfectly and use it properly. I also had some difficulties for vocabulary, as it was hard to understand the meaning of some word.

Another thing that helped me with my English was when my mother enroll me in an English learning center that specialize in teach writing skills. After a month of taking classes, my teacher saw some improvement in my grammar and vocabulary. To test me, she asked me to write an essay on how to be successful. I was really excite of it and started write it immediately. After I finish my essay and my teacher check it, my teacher suggested that I take a few more classes for her. She taught me how to organized my ideas. After finishing these classes I realize that my writing was getting much better with time.

**EXERCISE 49-9**    In the following paragraph, a student describes the study of English at private schools in Japan. After you read the paragraph, rewrite it, correcting the errors that you find.

Recently, the number of private language schools are increased in Japan. These schools put special emphasize on oral communication skills. In them, student takes not only grammars and reading classes, which help them pass school examinations, but also speaking, listening classes. They can also study English for six year, which is same period as in public schools. Some of the teacher in these school are native speaker of English. Since these teachers do not use Japanese in the class, the students have to use the English to participate it. They have the opportunity to use the English in their class more than public school students. It is said that the students who took English in private schools can speak English better than those student who go to public schools.

The following chart contains information about errors that may be caused by a difference between your native language and English. The chart does not include all languages or all possible errors. Instead, it focuses on languages commonly spoken by ESOL students in the United States, and it includes errors that often cause significant difficulties for students.

**ENGLISH ERRORS TRANSFERRED FROM OTHER LANGUAGES**

| Languages | Error Topic | Sample Errors | Corrected Errors |
|---|---|---|---|
| | **Singulars and Plurals (Ch. 50)** | | |
| Chinese, Japanese, Korean, Thai | no (or optional) plural forms of nouns, including numbers | NO: She wrote many good **essay.** NO: She typed two **paper.** | YES: She wrote many good **essays.** YES: She typed two **papers.** |

continued >>

| Languages | Error Topic | Sample Errors | Corrected Errors |
|---|---|---|---|
| Hebrew, Italian, Japanese, Spanish | use of plural with embedded plurals | NO: We cared for five **childrens.** | YES: We cared for five **children.** |
| Italian, Spanish | adjectives carry plural | NO: They are **Americans** students. | YES: They are **American** students. |

### Articles (Ch. 51)

| | | | |
|---|---|---|---|
| Chinese, Japanese, Hindi, Korean, Russian, Swahili, Thai, Turkish, Urdu | no article (*a, an, the*) but can depend on whether article is definite/indefinite | NO: He ate sandwich. | YES: He ate **a** sandwich. |

### Word Order (Ch. 52)

| | | | |
|---|---|---|---|
| Arabic, Hebrew, Russian, Spanish, Tagalog | verb before subject | NO: **Questioned Avi** the teenagers. | YES: **Avi questioned** the teenagers. |
| Chinese, Japanese, Hindi, Thai | inverted word order confused in questions | NO: **The book was it** heavy? | YES: **Was the book** heavy? |
| Chinese, Japanese, Russian, Thai | sentence adverb misplaced | NO: We will go home **possibly** now. | YES: **Possibly,** we will go home now. |

### Gerunds, Infinitives, and Participles (Ch. 54)

| | | | |
|---|---|---|---|
| French, German, Greek, Hindi, Russian, Urdu | no progressive forms or overuse of progressive forms with infinitive | NO: They **talk** while she **talk.** | YES: They **are talking** while she **is talking.** |
| | | NO: They **are wanting** to talk now. | YES: They **want** to talk now. |
| Arabic, Chinese, Farsi, Russian | omit forms of *be* | NO: She happy. | YES: She **is** happy. |
| Chinese, Japanese, Korean, Russian, Thai | no verb ending changes for person & number | NO: She **talk** loudly. | YES: She **talks** loudly. |
| Arabic, Chinese, Farsi, French, Thai, Vietnamese | no or non-standard verb-tense markers | NO: He **laugh** yesterday. | YES: He **laughed** yesterday. |
| | | NO: They **has arrived** yesterday. | YES: They **arrived** yesterday. |
| Japanese, Korean, Russian, Thai, Vietnamese | nonstandard passives | NO: A car accident **was happened.** | YES: A car accident **was caused by the icy roads.** |

For more help with your writing, grammar, and research, go to **www.mycomplab.com**

# 50

# Singulars and Plurals

## 50a What are count and noncount nouns?

**Count nouns** name items that can be counted: *a radio* or *radios, a street* or *streets, an idea* or *ideas, a fingernail* or *fingernails.* Count nouns can be SINGULAR or PLURAL.

**Noncount nouns** name things that are thought of as a whole and not split into separate, countable parts: *rice, knowledge, traffic.* There are two important rules to remember about noncount nouns: (1) They're never preceded by *a* or *an,* and (2) they are never plural.

Here are several categories of noncount nouns, with examples in each category:

| | |
|---|---|
| GROUPS OF SIMILAR ITEMS | clothing, equipment, furniture, jewelry, junk, luggage, mail, money, stuff, traffic, vocabulary |
| ABSTRACTIONS | advice, equality, fun, health, ignorance, information, knowledge, news, peace, pollution, respect |
| LIQUIDS | blood, coffee, gasoline, water |
| GASES | air, helium, oxygen, smog, smoke, steam |
| MATERIALS | aluminum, cloth, cotton, ice, wood |
| FOOD | beef, bread, butter, macaroni, meat, pork |
| PARTICLES OR GRAINS | dirt, dust, hair, rice, salt, wheat |
| SPORTS, GAMES, ACTIVITIES | chess, homework, housework, reading, sailing, soccer |
| LANGUAGES | Arabic, Chinese, Japanese, Spanish |
| FIELDS OF STUDY | biology, computer science, history, literature, math |
| EVENTS IN NATURE | electricity, heat, humidity, moonlight, rain, snow, sunshine, thunder, weather |

Some nouns can be countable or uncountable, depending on their meaning in a sentence. Most of these nouns name things that can be meant either individually or as "wholes" made up of individual parts.

---

**WHAT ELSE?**

*Strategies and Resources,* a 400-page book provided free to faculty who use this handbook, offers specific, practical ways to help students whose first language is not English. This auxiliary text first examines cultural issues that make studying in the United States a challenging situation for many international students and suggests ways in which a composition teacher can integrate international students into the classroom. It also discusses some of the general concerns in cross-cultural education and provides insights into the differing perspectives of international students. The second section describes some of the difficulties new international students may have in speaking and listening. It discusses classroom activities that have proved useful in helping ESOL students improve their listening comprehension and speaking abilities. The third section looks more specifically at writing pedagogy for the ESOL student, covering such issues as understanding differences in rhetorical expectations of native and nonnative students, handling errors in ESOL students' writing, and adapting pedagogical techniques such as peer review and collaborative writing to a class that includes nonnative students.

**TEACHING TIP**

Since some languages do not add suffixes to nouns to show plural forms, some ESOL students may have difficulty with making singular/plural distinctions in English.

**TEACHING TIP**

Purdue University's OWL has an additional exercise on count and noncount nouns; see <http://owl.english.purdue.edu/handouts/esl/eslcountEX1.html>.

**QUOTATION: ON WRITING**

An original writer is not one who imitates no one but one whom no one can imitate.

—François-Auguste-René de Chateaubriand

**TEACHING TIP**

Many ESOL Web sites offer additional exercises and lesson plans. These can be very attractive when you are short on time! However,

| | |
|---|---|
| COUNT | You have **a hair** on your sleeve. [In this sentence, *hair* is meant as an individual, countable item.] |
| NONCOUNT | Kioko has black **hair.** [In this sentence, all the strands of *hair* are referred to as a whole.] |
| COUNT | The **rains** were late last year. [In this sentence, *rains* is meant as individual, countable occurrences of rain.] |
| NONCOUNT | The **rain** is soaking the garden. [In this sentence, all the particles of *rain* are referred to as a whole.] |

When you are editing your writing (see Chapter 2), be sure that you have not added a plural *-s* to any noncount nouns, for they are always singular in form.

**Alert:** Be sure to use a singular verb with any noncount noun that functions as a SUBJECT in a CLAUSE. ●

To check whether a noun is count or noncount, look it up in a dictionary such as the *Dictionary of American English* (Heinle and Heinle). In this dictionary, count nouns are indicated by [C], and noncount nouns are indicated by [U] (for "uncountable"). Nouns that have both count and noncount meanings are marked [C;U].

# 50b How do I use determiners with singular and plural nouns?

**Determiners,** also called *expressions of quantity,* are used to tell how much or how many with reference to NOUNS. Other names for determiners include *limiting adjectives, noun markers,* and ARTICLES. (For information about articles—the words *a, an,* and *the*—see Chapter 51.)

Choosing the right determiner with a noun can depend on whether the noun is NONCOUNT or COUNT (see 50a). For count nouns, you must also decide whether the noun is singular or plural. Quick Reference 50.1 lists many determiners and the kinds of nouns that they can accompany.

**Alert:** The phrases *a few* and *a little* convey the meaning "some": *I have* **a few** *rare books* means "I have *some* rare books." *They are worth* **a little** *money* means "They are worth *some* money."

Without the word *a,* the words *few* and *little* convey the meaning "almost none": *I have* **few** [or *very few*] *books* means "I have *almost no* books." *They are worth* **little** *money* means "They are worth *almost no* money." ●

make sure that you check the accuracy of these sites before using materials in class, as the sites are not peer-reviewed. One excellent site is "Activities for ESL Students," sponsored by the Internet *TESL Journal* at <http://www.iteslj.org>.

One interesting lesson plan online for count and noncount nouns is a card game by Karin M. Cintron at <http://www.eslpartyland.com/teachers/grammar/cncnouns.htm>. Ron Belisle offers several activities for teaching count and noncount noun distinctions at <http://iteslj.org/Lessons/Belisle-CountAndNoncount.html>.

**BACKGROUND**
A classic article by Betty Wallace Robinett, "The Application of Linguistics to TESOL: Once More" argues that linguistic study reveals a situational or contextual ambiguity that leads to student errors in correct count and noncount noun usage (*TESOL Quarterly* 7.4 (1973): 425–435).

## Quick Reference 50.1

▪ ▪ ▪ ▪ ▪ ▪ ▪

### Determiners to use with count and noncount nouns

#### GROUP 1: DETERMINERS FOR SINGULAR COUNT NOUNS

With every **singular count noun**, always use one of the determiners listed in Group 1.

| | | | |
|---|---|---|---|
| *a, an, the* | a house | an egg | the car |
| *one, any, some, every, each, either, neither, another, the other* | any house | each egg | another car |
| *my, our, your, his, her, its, their,* nouns with *'s* or *s',* | your house | its egg | Connie's car |
| *this, that* | this house | that egg | this car |
| *one, no, the first the second,* etc. | one house | no egg | the fifth car |

#### GROUP 2: DETERMINERS FOR PLURAL COUNT NOUNS

All the determiners listed in Group 2 can be used with **plural count nouns**. Plural count nouns can also be used without determiners, as discussed in section 50b.

| | | | |
|---|---|---|---|
| *the* | the bicycles | the rooms | the idea |
| *some, any, both, many, more, most, few, fewer, the fewest, a lot of, a number of, other, several, all, all the* | some bicycles | many rooms | all ideas |
| *my, our, your, his, her, its, their,* nouns with *'s* or *s'* | our bicycles | her rooms | student's ideas |
| *these, those* | these bicycles | those rooms | these ideas |
| *no, two, three,* etc.; *the first, the second, the third,* etc. | no bicycles | four rooms | the first ideas |

continued >>

| Quick Reference 50.1 | (continued) | | |
|---|---|---|---|

**GROUP 3: DETERMINERS FOR NONCOUNT NOUNS**

All the determiners listed in Group 3 can be used with **noncount nouns** (always singular). Noncount nouns can also be used without determiners, as discussed in section 47b.

| | | | |
|---|---|---|---|
| *the* | the rice | the rain | the pride |
| *some, any, much, more, most, other, the other, little, less, the least, enough, all, all the, a lot of* | enough rice | a lot of rain | more pride |
| *my, our, your, his, her, its, their, nouns with 's or s'* | their rice | India's rain | your pride |
| *this, that* | this rice | that rain | this pride |
| *no, the first, the second, the third, etc.* | no rice | the first rain | no pride |

# 50c  How do I use *one of*, nouns as adjectives, and *states* in names or titles?

## *ONE OF* CONSTRUCTIONS

*One of* constructions include *one of the* and a NOUN or *one of* followed by a DETERMINER-noun combination (*one of my hats, one of those ideas*). Always use a plural noun as the OBJECT when you use *one of the* with a noun or *one of* with an adjective-noun combination.

> **NO**  *One of the* **reason** to live here is the beach.
>
> **YES**  *One of the* **reasons** to live here is the beach.
>
> **NO**  *One of her best* **friend** has moved away.
>
> **YES**  *One of her best* **friends** has moved away.

The VERB in these constructions is always singular because it agrees with the singular *one*, not with the plural noun: **One** *of the most important inventions of the twentieth century* **is** [not *are*] *television*.

For advice about verb forms that go with *one of the . . . who* constructions, see 17l.

## NOUNS USED AS ADJECTIVES

ADJECTIVES in English do not have plural forms. When you use an adjective with a PLURAL NOUN, make the noun plural but not the adjective: *the* **green** [not *greens*] *leaves.* Be especially careful when you use a word as a MODIFIER that can also function as a noun.

> The bird's wingspan is ten inches. [*Inches* is functioning as a noun.]
>
> The bird has a ten-inch wingspan. [*Inch* is functioning as a modifier.]

Do not add -*s* (or -*es*) to the adjective even when it is modifying a plural noun or pronoun.

> **NO** Many **Americans** students are basketball fans.
>
> **YES** Many **American** students are basketball fans.

## NAMES OR TITLES THAT INCLUDE THE WORD *STATES*

*States* is a plural word. However, names such as *United States* or *Organization of American States* refer to singular things—one country and one organization, even though made up of many states. When *states* is part of a name or title referring to one thing, the name is a SINGULAR NOUN and therefore requires a SINGULAR VERB.

> **NO** The **United States have** a large entertainment industry.
>
> **NO** The **United State has** a large entertainment industry.
>
> **YES** The **United States has** a large entertainment industry.

# 50d How do I use nouns with irregular plurals?

Some English nouns have irregularly spelled plurals. In addition to those discussed in section 31c, here are others that often cause difficulties.

## PLURALS OF FOREIGN NOUNS AND OTHER IRREGULAR NOUNS

Whenever you are unsure whether a noun is plural, look it up in a dictionary. If no plural is given for a singular noun, add -*s* to form the plural.

Many nouns from other languages that are used unchanged in English have only one plural. If two plurals are listed in the dictionary, look carefully for differences in meaning. Some words, for example, keep the plural form from the original language for scientific usage and have another, English-form plural for nonscientific contexts: *formula, formulae, formulas; appendix, appendices, appendixes; index, indices, indexes; medium, media, mediums; cactus, cacti, cactuses; fungus, fungi, funguses.*

Words from Latin that end in *-is* in their singular form become plural by substituting *-es: parenthesis, parentheses; thesis, theses; oasis, oases.*

## OTHER WORDS

Medical terms for diseases involving an inflammation end in *-itis: tonsillitis, appendicitis.* They are always singular.

The word *news,* although it ends in *s,* is always singular: *The* **news is** *encouraging.* The words *people, police,* and *clergy* are always plural even though they do not end in *s: The* **police are** *prepared.*

**EXERCISE 50-1**  Consulting all sections of this chapter, select the correct choice from the words in parentheses and write it in the blank.

**EXAMPLE**  At the beginning of every school year, all (student, students) stu-dents can expect (homework, homeworks) homework that teaches them about the toll-free No Bully hot line.

1. One of the main (reason, reasons) _____ for such a hot line is the change in tempers and violent capacities of (American, Americans) _____ students.

2. Because students are often bullied by a fellow classmate when outside the classroom, it is important that they receive (information, informations) _____ about how to react when confronted by such a threat.

3. Many a child in the (United State, United States) _____ is in danger not only of being teased and taunted by others but also of being the victim of a crime in which (blood, bloods) _____ is spilled, such as from assault or robbery.

4. Because (many, much) _____ classrooms are unsupervised after school, this (time, times) _____ becomes especially dangerous.

5. In a moment of danger, (ignorance, ignorances) _____ can be deadly, so the No Bully hot line was set up to give students (advice, advices) _____ on how to handle bullying and other threaten-ing situations.

For more help with your writing, grammar, and research, go to **www.mycomplab.com**

**ANSWERS: EXERCISE 50-1**

**1.** reasons [50c, plural object with *one of*]; American [50c, singular for noun used as adjective]

**2.** information [50a, singular for noncount nouns]

**3.** United States [50c, *States* plural in *United States*]; blood [50a, singular for noncount nouns]

**4.** many [50b, *many* the correct determiner with the plural count noun *classrooms*]; time [50b, singular for count noun after the determiner *this*]

**5.** ignorance [50a, singular for noncount nouns]; advice [50a, singular for noncount nouns]

# Articles

## 51a How do I use *a*, *an*, or *the* with singular count nouns?

The words *a* and *an* are called **indefinite articles**. The word *the* is called the DEFINITE ARTICLE. Articles are one type of DETERMINER. (For more on determiners, see 14f; for other determiners, see Quick Reference 50.1 in 50b.) Articles signal that a NOUN will follow and that any MODIFIERS between the article and the noun refer to that noun.

| | |
|---|---|
| **a** chair | **the** computer |
| **a** brown chair | **the** teacher's computer |
| **a** cold, metal chair | **the** lightning-fast computer |

Every time you use a singular count noun, a COMMON NOUN that names one countable item, the noun requires some kind of determiner; see Group 1 in Quick Reference 50.1 (in 50b) for a list. To choose between *a* or *an* and *the*, you need to determine whether the noun is **specific** or **nonspecific**. A noun is considered *specific* when anyone who reads your writing can understand exactly and specifically to what item the noun is referring. If the noun refers to any of a number of identical items, it is *nonspecific.*

For nonspecific singular count nouns, use *a* (or *an*). When the singular noun is specific, use *the* or some other determiner. Quick Reference 51.1 can help you decide when a singular count noun is specific and therefore requires *the.*

❶ Alert: Use *an* before words that begin with a vowel sound. Use *a* before words that begin with a consonant sound. Go by the sound, not the spelling. For example, words that begin with *h* or *u* can have either a vowel or a consonant sound. Make the choice based on the sound of the first word after the article, even if that word is not the noun.

| | |
|---|---|
| **an i**dea | **a g**ood idea |
| **an u**mbrella | **a u**seless umbrella |
| **an h**onor | **a h**istory book ● |

## Quick Reference 51.1

### When a singular count noun is specific and requires *the*

- **Rule 1: A noun is specific and requires *the* when it names something unique or generally and unambiguously known.**

  **The sun** has risen above **the horizon.** [Because there is only one *sun* and only one *horizon*, these nouns are specific in the context of this sentence.]

- **Rule 2: A noun is specific and requires *the* when it names something used in a representative or abstract sense.**

  Benjamin Franklin favored **the turkey** as **the national bird** of the United States. [Because *turkey* and *national bird* are representative references rather than references to a particular turkey or bird, they are specific nouns in the context of this sentence.]

- **Rule 3: A noun is specific and requires *the* when it names something defined elsewhere in the same sentence or in an earlier sentence.**

  **The ship** *Savannah* was the first steam vessel to cross the Atlantic Ocean. [*Savannah* names a specific ship.]

  **The carpet in my bedroom** is new. [*In my bedroom* defines exactly which carpet is meant, so *carpet* is a specific noun in this context.]

  I have **a computer** in my office. **The computer** is often broken. [*Computer* is not specific in the first sentence, so it uses *a*. In the second sentence, *computer* has been made specific by the first sentence, so it uses *the*.]

- **Rule 4: A noun is specific and requires *the* when it names something that can be inferred from the context.**

  Monday, I had to call **the technician** to fix my computer again. [*A technician* would be any of a number of individuals; *the technician* implies the same person has been called before, and so it is specific in this context.]

---

One common exception affects Rule 3 in Quick Reference 51.1. A noun may still require *a* (or *an*) after the first use if more information is added between the article and the noun: *I bought **a sweater** today. It was **a** (not *the*) **red sweater.** (Your audience has been introduced to *a sweater* but not *a red sweater*, so *red sweater* is not yet specific in this context and cannot take *the*.) Other information may make the noun specific so that *the* is correct. For example, *It was **the red sweater that I saw in the store yesterday*** uses *the* because the *that* CLAUSE makes specific which red sweater the writer means.

**QUOTATION: ON GRAMMAR**
Grammar, which knows how to control even kings.

—Molière

**BACKGROUND**
Among the many exercises available at Activities for ESOL Students at <http://a4esl.org/q/h/grammar.html>, students will find several exercises of increasing difficulty on proper article usage.

# 51b How do I use articles with plural nouns and with noncount nouns?

With plural nouns and NONCOUNT NOUNS, you must decide whether to use *the* or to use no article at all. (For guidelines about using DETERMINERS other than articles with nouns, see Quick Reference 50.1 in 50b.) What you learned in 51a about NONSPECIFIC and SPECIFIC NOUNS can help you choose between using *the* or using no article. Quick Reference 51.1 in 51a explains when a singular count noun's meaning is specific and calls for *the.* Plural nouns and noncount nouns with specific meanings usually use *the* in the same circumstances. However, a plural noun or a noncount noun with a general or nonspecific meaning usually does not use *the.*

> Geraldo grows **flowers** but not **vegetables** in his garden. He is thinking about planting **corn** sometime. [three nonspecific nouns]

## PLURAL NOUNS

A plural noun's meaning may be specific because it is widely known.

> **The oceans** are being damaged by pollution. [Because there is only one possible meaning for *oceans*—the oceans on the earth—it is correct to use *the.* This example is related to Rule 1 in Quick Reference 51.1.]

A plural noun's meaning may also be made specific by a word, PHRASE, or CLAUSE in the same sentence.

> Geraldo sold **the daisies from last year's garden** to the florist. [Because the phrase *from last year's garden* makes *daisies* specific, *the* is correct. This example is related to Rule 3 in Quick Reference 51.1.]

A plural noun's meaning usually becomes specific by its use in an earlier sentence.

> Geraldo planted **tulips** this year. **The tulips** will bloom in April. [*Tulips* is used in a general sense in the first sentence, without *the.* Because the first sentence makes *tulips* specific, *the tulips* is correct in the second sentence. This example is related to Rule 3 in Quick Reference 51.1.]

A plural noun's meaning may be made specific by the context.

> Geraldo fertilized **the bulbs** when he planted them last October. [In the context of the sentences about tulips, *bulbs* is understood as a synonym for *tulips*, which makes it specific and calls for *the.* This example is related to Rule 4 in Quick Reference 51.1.]

## NONCOUNT NOUNS

Noncount nouns are always singular in form (see 50a). Like plural nouns, noncount nouns use either *the* or no article. When a noncount noun's meaning is specific, use *the* before it. If its meaning is general or nonspecific, do not use *the*.

> Kalinda served us **rice.** She flavored **the rice** with curry. [*Rice* is a noncount noun. By the second sentence, *rice* has become specific, so *the* is used. This example is related to Rule 3 in Quick Reference 51.1.]

> Kalinda served us **the rice that she had flavored with curry.** [*Rice* is a noncount noun. *Rice* is made specific by the clause *that she had flavored with curry,* so *the* is used. This example is related to Rule 3 in Quick Reference 51.1.]

## GENERALIZATIONS WITH PLURAL OR NONCOUNT NOUNS

Rule 2 in Quick Reference 51.1 tells you to use *the* with singular count nouns that carry general meaning. With GENERALIZATIONS using plural or noncount nouns, omit *the*.

> **NO**   **The tulips** are **the flowers** that grow from **the bulbs.**

> **YES**   **Tulips** are **flowers** that grow from **bulbs.**

> **NO**   **The dogs** require more care than **the cats** do.

> **YES**   **Dogs** require more care than **cats** do.

## 51c   How do I use *the* with proper nouns and with gerunds?

### PROPER NOUNS

PROPER NOUNS name specific people, places, or things (see 14b). Most proper nouns do not require ARTICLES: *We visited **Lake Mead** with **Asha** and **Larry.*** As shown in Quick Reference 51.2, however, certain types of proper nouns do require *the*.

### GERUNDS

GERUNDS are PRESENT PARTICIPLES (the *-ing* form of VERBS) used as nouns: ***Skating** is challenging.* Gerunds are usually not preceded by *the*.

> **NO**   **The constructing** new bridges is necessary to improve traffic flow.

> **YES**   **Constructing** new bridges is necessary to improve traffic flow.

Use *the* before a gerund when two conditions are met: (1) The gerund is used in a specific sense (see 51a), and (2) the gerund does not have a DIRECT OBJECT.

**She is not only** a talented artist **but also** an excellent musician.

**Not only is she** a talented artist, **but she is also** an excellent musician.

I didn't like the book, and **my husband didn't either**.

I didn't like the book, and **neither did my husband.**

⊘ Alerts: (1) With INDIRECT QUESTIONS, use standard word order.

| | |
|---|---|
| NO | She asked **how did I drop** the book. |
| YES | She asked **how I dropped** the book. |

(2) Word order deliberately inverted can be effective, when used sparingly, to create emphasis in a sentence that is neither a question nor an exclamation (also see 9e). ●

## 52b How can I understand the placement of adjectives?

ADJECTIVES modify—describe or limit—NOUNS, PRONOUNS, and word groups that function as nouns (see 14f). In English, an adjective comes directly before the noun it describes. However, when more than one adjective describes the same noun, several sequences may be possible. Quick Reference 52.1 shows the most common order for positioning several adjectives.

---

### Quick Reference 52.1  ■ ■ ■ ■ ■ ■

#### Word order: cumulative adjectives

1. **Determiners, if any:** *a, an, the, my, your, this, that, these, those,* and so on
2. **Expressions of order, including ordinal numbers, if any:** *first, second, third, next, last, final,* and so on
3. **Expressions of quantity, including cardinal (counting) numbers, if any:** *one, two, few, each, every, some,* and so on
4. **Adjectives of judgment or opinion, if any:** *pretty, happy, ugly, sad, interesting, boring,* and so on
5. **Adjectives of size or shape, if any:** *big, small, short, round, square,* and so on
6. **Adjectives of age or condition, if any:** *new, young, broken, dirty, shiny,* and so on
7. **Adjectives of color, if any:** *red, green, blue,* and so on
8. **Adjectives that can also be used as nouns, if any:** *French, Protestant, metal, cotton,* and so on

continued >>

| Quick Reference 52.1 | (continued) |
|---|---|

**9. The noun**

| 1 | 2 | 3 | 4 | 5 | 6 | 7 | 8 | 9 |
|---|---|---|---|---|---|---|---|---|
| a | | few | | tiny | | red | | ants |
| the | last | six | | | | | Thai | carvings |
| my | | | fine | | old | | oak | table |

## 52c How can I understand the placement of adverbs?

ADVERBS modify—describe or limit—VERBS, ADJECTIVES, other adverbs, or entire sentences (see 14g). Adverbs may be positioned first, in the middle, or last in CLAUSES. Quick Reference 52.2 summarizes adverb types, what they tell about the words they modify, and where each type can be placed.

**Quick Reference 52.2**  ■ ■ ■ ■ ■ ■ ■

### Word order: positioning adverbs

| ADVERBS OF MANNER | • describe *how* something is done | Nick **carefully** groomed the dog |
|---|---|---|
| | • are usually in middle or last position | Nick groomed the dog **carefully**. |
| ADVERBS OF TIME | • describe *when* or *how long* about an event | **First,** he shampooed the dog. |
| | • are usually in first or last position | He shampooed the dog **first**. |
| | • include *just, still, already,* and similar adverbs, which are usually in middle position | He had **already** brushed the dog's coat. |
| ADVERBS OF FREQUENCY | • describe *how often* an event takes place | Nick has **never** been bitten by a dog. |
| | • are usually in middle position | |
| | • are in first position when they modify an entire sentence (see "Sentence Adverbs" below) | **Occasionally,** he is scratched while shampooing a cat. |

continued >>

## Quick Reference 52.2 (continued)

| | | |
|---|---|---|
| ADVERBS OF DEGREE OR EMPHASIS | • describe *how much* or *to what extent* about other modifiers<br>• are directly before the word they modify<br>• include *only*, which is easy to misplace (see 21a) | Nick is **extremely** calm around animals. [*Extremely* modifies *calm*.] |
| SENTENCE ADVERBS | • modify the entire sentence rather than just one word or a few words<br>• include transitional words and expressions (see 7g.1), as well as such expressions as *maybe, probably, possibly, fortunately, unfortunately,* and *incredibly*<br>• are in first position | **Incredibly,** he was once asked to groom a rat. |

**!** Alert: Do not let an adverb separate a verb from its DIRECT OBJECT or INDIRECT OBJECT.●

**ANSWERS: EXERCISE 52–1**

**1.** A few beautiful flowers [52b, expressions of quantity precede adjectives of opinion]

**2.** Did you grow [52a, inverted word order for questions, form of *do* precedes subject]

**3.** my husband's favorite [52b, *husband's* as adjective that can also be a noun is positioned before the word it modifies, *favorite*]

**4.** was extremely impressed [52c, adverb of degree is positioned before the word it modifies, *impressed*]

**5.** her happily planting seeds [52c, adverb of manner is positioned before the word it modifies, *planting*]

**EXERCISE 52-1**   Consulting all sections of this chapter, find and correct any errors in word order.

1. A beautiful few flowers began to bloom in my garden this week.

2. A neighbor asked me, "You did grow all these yourself?"

3. "Yes," I replied, "the roses are my favorite husband's, but the tulips are my favorite."

4. My neighbor, who extremely was impressed with my gardening efforts, decided to grow some flowers of her own.

5. Weeks later, as I strolled by her house, I saw her planting happily seeds from her favorite type of plant—petunias.

For more help with your writing, grammar, and research, go to **www.mycomplab.com**

# 53

# Prepositions

**Prepositions** function with other words in PREPOSITIONAL PHRASES (14o). Prepositional phrases usually indicate *where* (direction or location), *how* (by what means or in what way), or *when* (at what time or how long) about the words they modify.

This chapter can help you with several uses of prepositions, which function in combination with other words in ways that are often idiomatic—that is, peculiar to the language. The meaning of an IDIOM differs from the literal meaning of each individual word. For example, the word *break* usually refers to shattering, but the sentence *Yao-Ming **broke into** a smile* means that a smile appeared on Yao-Ming's face. Knowing which preposition to use in a specific context takes much experience in reading, listening to, and speaking the language. A dictionary like the *Dictionary of American English* (Heinle and Heinle) can be especially helpful when you need to find the correct preposition to use in cases not covered by this chapter.

## 53a How can I recognize prepositions?

Quick Reference 53.1 lists many common prepositions.

### Quick Reference 53.1

#### Common prepositions

| | | | | |
|---|---|---|---|---|
| about | around | beside | down | inside |
| above | as | between | during | instead of |
| across | at | beyond | except | into |
| after | because of | but | for | like |
| against | before | by | from | near |
| along | behind | concerning | in | next |
| among | below | despite | in front of | of |

continued >>

**QUOTATION: ON WRITING**
If the writing is honest it cannot be separated from the man who wrote it.
—Tennessee Williams

**BACKGROUND**
The Web site Lanternfish has delightful flashcards to help students learn how to use prepositions correctly at <http://bogglesworldesl.com/prepositions.htm>.

**TEACHING TIP**
Using prepositions can be especially difficult for ESOL writers because English has so many of them. There are no rules that accurately describe which preposition to use; students must simply memorize which prepositions belong in which phrases.

**BACKGROUND**
The Web site <http://www.english-zone.com/grammar/1preps.html> offers quizzes of varying levels on prepositions.

**BACKGROUND**
At the Web site <http://www.wordskills.com/reception.shtml>, students can find a different phrasal verb posted each day, along with its definition.

**TEACHING TIP**
In teaching prepositions, don't be afraid to try kinesthetic exercises where you have students act out their relationships to prepositions. "On" could be standing on a chair; "by" could be standing near a chair, etc. This will help to give students a visual sense of prepositions and their relationships.

**QUOTATION: ON WRITING**
In the writing process, the more a story cooks, the better.
—Doris Lessing

**BACKGROUND**
The Web site ESLflow.com has exercises for students and lesson plans for instructors on prepositions at <http://www.eslflow.com/prepositionlessonplans.html>. The "Command Preposition Game" may appeal especially to students who are kinesthetic learners.

**QUOTATION: ON WRITING**
Writing is manual labor of the mind: a job, like laying pipe.
—John Gregory Dunne

---

### Quick Reference 53.1 (continued)

| | | | | |
|---|---|---|---|---|
| off | outside | since | under | within |
| on | over | through | underneath | without |
| onto | past | throughout | unlike | |
| on top of | plus | till | until | |
| opposite | regarding | to | up | |
| out | round | toward | with | |

## 53b How do I use prepositions with expressions of time and place?

Quick Reference 53.2 shows how to use the prepositions *in, at,* and *on* to deliver some common kinds of information about time and place. Quick Reference 53.2, however, does not cover every preposition that indicates time or place, nor does it cover all uses of *in, at,* and *on.* Also, the Quick Reference does not include expressions that operate outside the general rules. (Both these sentences are correct: *You ride **in** the car* and *You ride **on** the bus.*)

### Quick Reference 53.2

#### Using *in*, *at*, and *on* to show time and place

**TIME**

- *in* **a year or a month** (*during* is also correct but less common)

    **in** 1995        **in** May

- *in* **a period of time**

    **in** a few months (seconds, days, years)

- *in* **a period of the day**

    **in** the morning (afternoon, evening)

    **in** the daytime (morning, evening) *but* **at** night

- *at* **a specific time or period of time**

    **at** noon        **at** 2:00        **at** dawn        **at** nightfall

    **at** takeoff (the time a plane leaves)

    **at** breakfast (the time a specific meal takes place)

- *on* **a specific day**

    **on** Friday        **on** my birthday

continued >>

**Quick Reference 53.2**     (continued)

**PLACE**

- *in* a location surrounded by something else

  **in** the province of Alberta          **in** the kitchen

  **in** Utah          **in** the apartment

  **in** downtown Bombay          **in** the bathtub

- *at* a specific location

  **at** your house          **at** the bank

  **at** the corner of Third Avenue and Main Street

- *on* a surface

  **on** page 20

  **on** the second floor *but* **in** the attic *or* **in** the basement

  **on** Washington Street

  **on** the mezzanine

  **on** the highway

## 53c   How do I use prepositions in phrasal verbs?

**Phrasal verbs**, also called *two-word verbs* and *three-word verbs,* are VERBS that combine with PREPOSITIONS to deliver their meaning. In some phrasal verbs, the verb and the preposition should not be separated by other words: ***Look at** the moon* [not ***Look** the moon **at***]. In **separable phrasal verbs**, other words in the sentence can separate the verb and the preposition without interfering with meaning: ***I threw away** my homework* is as correct as ***I threw** my homework **away.***

Here is a list of some common phrasal verbs. The ones that cannot be separated are marked with an asterisk (*).

**SELECTED PHRASAL VERBS**

| | | |
|---|---|---|
| ask out | get along with* | look into |
| break down | get back | look out for* |
| bring about | get off | look over |
| call back | go over* | make up |
| drop off | hand in | run across* |
| figure out | keep up with* | speak to* |
| fill out | leave out | speak with* |
| fill up | look after* | throw away |
| find out | look around | throw out |

Position a PRONOUN OBJECT between the words of a separable phrasal verb: *I threw **it** away.* Also, you can position an object PHRASE of several words between the parts of a separable phrasal verb: *I threw **my research paper** away.* However, when the object is a CLAUSE, do not let it separate the parts of the phrasal verb: *I threw away **all the papers that I wrote last year.***

Many phrasal verbs are informal and are used more in speaking than in writing. For ACADEMIC WRITING, a more formal verb is usually more appropriate than a phrasal verb. In a research paper, for example, *propose* or *suggest* might be a better choice than *come up with.* For academic writing, acceptable phrasal verbs include *believe in, benefit from, concentrate on, consist of, depend on, dream of* (or *dream about*), *insist on, participate in, prepare for,* and *stare at.* None of these phrasal verbs can be separated.

**EXERCISE 53-1**    Consulting the preceding sections of this chapter and using the list of phrasal verbs in 53c, write a one- or two-paragraph description of a typical day at work or school in which you use at least five phrasal verbs. After checking a dictionary, revise your writing, substituting for the phrasal verbs any more formal verbs that might be more appropriate for academic writing.

## 53d    How do I use prepositions with past participles?

PAST PARTICIPLES are verb forms that function as ADJECTIVES (54f). Past participles end in either *-ed* or *-d,* or in an equivalent irregular form (15d). When past participles follow the LINKING VERB *be,* it is easy to confuse them with PASSIVE verbs (15n), which have the same endings. Passive verbs describe actions. Past participles, because they act as adjectives, modify NOUNS and PRONOUNS and often describe situations and conditions. Passive verbs follow the pattern *be* + past participle + *by: The child **was frightened by** a snake.* An expression containing a past participle, however, can use either *be* or another linking verb, and it can be followed by either *by* or a different preposition.

- The child **seemed frightened by** snakes.
- The child **is frightened of** all snakes.

Here is a list of expressions containing past participles and the prepositions that often follow them. Look in a dictionary for others. (See 54b on using GERUNDS after some of these expressions.)

**SELECTED PAST PARTICIPLE PHRASES + PREPOSITIONS**

| | |
|---|---|
| be accustomed to | be disappointed with (*or* in someone) |
| be acquainted with | be discriminated against |
| be composed of | be divorced from |
| be concerned/worried about | be excited about |

be finished/done with

be interested in

be known for

be located in

be made of (*or* from)

be married to

be pleased/satisfied with

be prepared for

be tired of (*or* from)

## 53e   How do I use prepositions in expressions?

In many common expressions, different PREPOSITIONS convey great differences in meaning. For example, four prepositions can be used with the verb *agree* to create five different meanings.

**agree to** means "to give consent": *I cannot **agree to** my buying you a new car.*

**agree about** means "to arrive at a satisfactory understanding": *We certainly **agree about** your needing a car.*

**agree on** means "to concur": *You and the seller must **agree on** a price for the car.*

**agree with** means "to have the same opinion": *I **agree with** you that you need a car.*

**agree with** also means "to be suitable or healthful": *The idea of having such a major expense does not **agree with** me.*

You can find entire books filled with English expressions that include prepositions. The following list shows a few that you're likely to use often.

**SELECTED EXPRESSIONS WITH PREPOSITIONS**

| | | |
|---|---|---|
| ability in | different from | involved with *someone* |
| access to | faith in | knowledge of |
| accustomed to | familiar with | made of |
| afraid of | famous for | married to |
| angry with *or* at | frightened by | opposed to |
| authority on | happy with | patient with |
| aware of | in charge of | proud of |
| based on | independent of | reason for |
| capable of | in favor of | related to |
| certain of | influence on *or* over | suspicious of |
| confidence in | interested in | time for |
| dependent on | involved in [*something*] | tired of |

# 54

# Gerunds, Infinitives, and Participles

PARTICIPLES are verb forms (see 15b). A verb's *-ing* form is its PRESENT PARTICIPLE. The *-ed* form of a regular verb is its PAST PARTICIPLE; IRREGULAR VERBS form their past participles in various ways (for example, *bend, bent; eat, eaten; think, thought*—for a complete list, see Quick Reference 15.4 in 15d). Participles can function as ADJECTIVES (*a smiling face, a closed book*).

A verb's *-ing* form can also function as a NOUN (*Sneezing spreads colds*), which is called a GERUND. Another verb form, the INFINITIVE, can also function as a noun. An infinitive is a verb's SIMPLE or base FORM, usually preceded by the word *to* (*We want everyone to smile*). Verb forms—participles, gerunds, and infinitives—functioning as nouns or MODIFIERS are called VERBALS, as explained in 14e. This chapter can help you make the right choices among verbals.

## 54a  How can I use gerunds and infinitives as subjects?

Gerunds are used more commonly than infinitives as subjects. Sometimes, however, either is acceptable.

> **Choosing** the right health club is important.

> **To choose** the right health club is important.

**!** **Alert:** When a gerund or an infinitive is used alone as a subject, it is SINGULAR and requires a singular verb. When two or more gerunds or infinitives create a COMPOUND SUBJECT, they require a plural verb. (See 14l and 17e.) ●

## 54b  When do I use a gerund, not an infinitive, as an object?

Some VERBS must be followed by GERUNDS used as DIRECT OBJECTS. Other verbs must be followed by INFINITIVES. Still other verbs can be followed by either a gerund or an infinitive. (A few verbs can change meaning depending on whether they are followed by a gerund or an infinitive; see 54d.) Quick Reference 54.1 lists common verbs that must be followed by gerunds, not infinitives.

Yuri **considered** *calling* [not *to call*] the mayor.

He **was having trouble** *getting* [not *to get*] a work permit.

Yuri's boss **recommended** *taking* [not *to take*] an interpreter to the permit agency.

**BACKGROUND**
The Continuing Studies page at the University of Victoria has a set of interactive exercises at <http://web2.uvcs.uvic.ca/elc/StudyZone/410/grammar/gerund1.htm> to test students' ability to form gerunds.

---

**Quick Reference 54.1** ■ ■ ■ ■ ■ ■ ■

### Verbs and expressions that must be followed by gerunds

| | | |
|---|---|---|
| admit | dislike | object to |
| anticipate | enjoy | postpone |
| appreciate | escape | practice |
| avoid | finish | put off |
| consider | give up | quit |
| consist of | imagine | recall |
| contemplate | include | resist |
| delay | mention | risk |
| deny | mind | suggest |
| discuss | miss | tolerate |

---

#### GERUND AFTER *GO*

The word *go* is usually followed by an infinitive: *We can **go to see*** [not *go seeing*] *a movie tonight.* Sometimes, however, *go* is followed by a gerund in phrases such as *go swimming, go fishing, go shopping,* and *go driving: I will **go shopping*** [not *go to shop*] *after work.*

#### GERUND AFTER *BE* + COMPLEMENT + PREPOSITION

Many common expressions use a form of the verb *be* plus a COMPLEMENT plus a PREPOSITION. In such expressions, use a gerund, not an infinitive, after the preposition. Here is a list of some of the most frequently used expressions in this pattern.

##### SELECTED EXPRESSIONS USING *BE* + COMPLEMENT + PREPOSITION

| | |
|---|---|
| be (get) accustomed to | be interested in |
| be angry about | be prepared for |
| be bored with | be responsible for |
| be capable of | be tired of |
| be committed to | be (get) used to |
| be excited about | be worried about |

We **are excited about** *voting* [not *to vote*] in the next presidential election.

Who **will be responsible for** *locating* [not *to locate*] our polling place?

**❗ Alert:** Always use a gerund, not an infinitive, as the object of a preposition. Be especially careful when the word *to* is functioning as a preposition in a PHRASAL VERB (see 53c): *We are committed* **to changing** [not *to change*] *the rules.* ●

## 54c  When do I use an infinitive, not a gerund, as an object?

Quick Reference 54.2 lists selected common verbs and expressions that must be followed by INFINITIVES, not GERUNDS, as OBJECTS.

She **wanted** *to go* [not *wanted going*] to the lecture.

Only three people **decided** *to question* [not *decided questioning*] the speaker.

### Quick Reference 54.2  ■ ■ ■ ■ ■ ■ ■

**Verbs and expressions that must be followed by infinitives**

| | | | |
|---|---|---|---|
| agree | decline | like | promise |
| arrange | demand | manage | refuse |
| ask | deserve | mean | wait |
| attempt | expect | need | want |
| beg | hesitate | offer | |
| claim | hope | plan | |
| decide | learn | pretend | |

### INFINITIVE AFTER *BE* + COMPLEMENT

Gerunds are common in constructions that use a form of the verb *be* plus a COMPLEMENT and a PREPOSITION (see 54b). However, use an infinitive, not a gerund, when *be* plus a complement is not followed by a preposition.

We **are eager** *to go* [not *going*] camping.

I **am ready** *to sleep* [not *sleeping*] in a tent.

### INFINITIVE TO INDICATE PURPOSE

Use an infinitive in expressions that indicate purpose: *I read a book* **to learn** *more about Mayan culture.* This sentence means "I read a book for the purpose of learning more about Mayan culture." *To learn* delivers the idea of purpose more concisely (see Chapter 11) than expressions such as *so that I can* or *in order to*.

### INFINITIVE WITH THE FIRST, THE LAST, THE ONE

Use an infinitive after the expressions *the first, the last,* and *the one: Nina is the first* **to arrive** [not *arriving*] *and the last* **to leave** [not *leaving*] *every day. She's always the one* **to do** *the most.*

### UNMARKED INFINITIVES

Infinitives used without the word *to* are called **unmarked infinitives**, or sometimes *bare infinitives*. An unmarked infinitive may be hard to recognize because it is not preceded by *to*. Some common verbs followed by unmarked infinitives are *feel, have, hear, let, listen to, look at, make* (meaning "compel"), *notice, see,* and *watch*.

> Please let me **take** [not *to take*] you to lunch. [unmarked infinitive]
>
> I want **to take** you to lunch. [marked infinitive]
>
> I can have Kara **drive** [not *to drive*] us. [unmarked infinitive]
>
> I will ask Kara **to drive** us. [marked infinitive]

The verb *help* can be followed by a marked or an unmarked infinitive. Either is correct: *Help me* **put** [or **to put**] *this box in the car.*

**!** **Alert:** Be careful to use parallel structure (see Chapter 10) correctly when you use two or more gerunds or infinitives after verbs. If two or more verbal objects follow one verb, put the verbals into the same form.

| | |
|---|---|
| **NO** | We went **sailing** and **to scuba dive**. |
| **YES** | We went **sailing** and **scuba diving**. |
| | |
| **NO** | We heard the wind **blow** and the waves **crashing**. |
| **YES** | We heard the wind **blow** and the waves **crash**. |
| **YES** | We heard the wind **blowing** and the waves **crashing**. |

Conversely, if you are using verbal objects with COMPOUND PREDICATES, be sure to use the kind of verbal that each verb requires.

| | |
|---|---|
| **NO** | We enjoyed **scuba diving** but do not plan **sailing** again. |
| | [*Enjoyed* requires a gerund object, and *plan* requires an infinitive object; see Quick References 54.1 and 54.2 in this chapter.] |
| **YES** | We enjoyed **scuba diving** but do not plan **to sail** again. ● |

# 54d How does meaning change when certain verbs are followed by a gerund or an infinitive?

### WITH *STOP*

The VERB *stop* followed by a GERUND means "finish, quit." *Stop* followed by an INFINITIVE means "interrupt one activity to begin another."

> We **stopped** *eating.* [We finished our meal.]
>
> We **stopped** *to eat.* [We stopped another activity, such as driving, to eat.]

### WITH *REMEMBER* AND *FORGET*

The verb *remember* followed by an infinitive means "not to forget to do something": *I must remember to talk with Isa. Remember* followed by a gerund means "recall a memory": *I remember talking in my sleep last night.*

The verb *forget* followed by an infinitive means "fail to do something": *If you forget to put a stamp on that letter, it will be returned. Forget* followed by a gerund means "do something and not recall it": *I forget having put the stamps in the refrigerator.*

### WITH *TRY*

The verb *try* followed by an infinitive means "make an effort": *I tried to find your jacket.* Followed by a gerund, *try* means "experiment with": *I tried jogging but found it too difficult.*

# 54e Why is the meaning unchanged whether a gerund or an infinitive follows sense verbs?

Sense VERBS include words such as *see, notice, hear, observe, watch, feel, listen to,* and *look at.* The meaning of these verbs is usually not affected by whether a GERUND or an INFINITIVE follows as the OBJECT. *I saw the water rise* and *I saw the water rising* both have the same meaning in American English.

**ANSWERS: EXERCISE 54-1**

1. riding [54b, gerund after preposition *about*]
2. take [54c and 59d, unmarked infinitive with *let*]
3. to bring [54c, infinitive following *force*]
4. to walk [54c, infinitive following *need*]
5. Stepping [54a, gerund as subject]

**EXERCISE 54-1**   Write the correct form of the verbal object (either a gerund or an infinitive) for each verb in parentheses. For help, consult 54b through 54e.

**EXAMPLE**   People like (think) to think that they have a good memory, but everybody shows signs of forgetfulness from time to time.

1. Think about (ride) _____ the railroad to work on a rainy Monday morning.

2. The comfortable reclining seats let passengers (take) _____ a relaxing nap on the way to work.

3. Because of the rain, commuters are forced (bring) _____ an umbrella and a raincoat, along with their usual traveling items.

4. Once they reach their destination, passengers forget that they need their umbrellas and raincoats (walk) _____ the few blocks to work.

5. (Step) _____ out into the rain makes the passengers suddenly realize that they've left their umbrellas and raincoats on the train, which has already left the station.

## 54f How do I choose between *-ing* and *-ed* forms for adjectives?

Deciding whether to use the *-ing* form (PRESENT PARTICIPLE) or the *-ed* form (PAST PARTICIPLE of a regular VERB) as an ADJECTIVE in a specific sentence can be difficult. For example, *I am amused* and *I am amusing* are both correct in English, but their meanings are very different. To make the right choice, decide whether the modified NOUN or PRONOUN is causing or experiencing what the participle describes.

Use a present participle (*-ing*) to modify a noun or pronoun that is the agent or the cause of the action.

> Micah described your **interesting** plan. [The noun *plan* causes what its modifier describes—interest; so *interesting* is correct.]
>
> I find your plan **exciting.** [The noun *plan* causes what its modifier describes—excitement; so *exciting* is correct.]

Use a past participle (*-ed* in regular verbs) to modify a noun or pronoun that experiences or receives whatever the modifier describes.

> An **interested** committee wants to hear your plan. [The noun *committee* experiences what its modifier describes—interest; so *interested* is correct.]
>
> **Excited** by your plan, they called a board meeting. [The pronoun *they* experiences what its modifier describes—excitement; so *excited* is correct.]

Here are frequently used participles that convey very different meanings, depending on whether the *-ed* or the *-ing* form is used.

| | |
|---|---|
| amused, amusing | depressed, depressing |
| annoyed, annoying | disgusted, disgusting |
| appalled, appalling | fascinated, fascinating |
| bored, boring | frightened, frightening |
| confused, confusing | insulted, insulting |

offended, offending      reassured, reassuring

overwhelmed, overwhelming      satisfied, satisfying

pleased, pleasing      shocked, shocking

## ANSWERS: EXERCISE 54-2

**1.** interesting [*life* conveys rather than experiences interest]

**2.** horrified [*observers* experience rather than convey horror]; injured [*Kahlo* experiences rather than causes injury]

**3.** disappointed [*Kahlo* experiences rather than causes disappointment]

**4.** disturbing [*images* cause rather than experience disturbance]

**5.** fascinating [*works of art* cause rather than experience fascination]; overwhelming [*paintings* overwhelm rather than experience being overwhelmed—*overwhelming* modifies the pronoun *them,* for which the referent is *paintings*]

● **EXERCISE 54-2**    Choose the correct participle from each pair in parentheses. For help, consult 54f.

**EXAMPLE**    It can be a (satisfied, satisfying) <u>satisfying</u> experience to learn about the lives of artists.

1. The artist Frida Kahlo led an (interested, interesting) _____ life.

2. When Kahlo was eighteen, (horrified, horrifying) _____ observers saw her (injured, injuring) _____ in a streetcar accident.

3. A (disappointed, disappointing) _____ Kahlo had to abandon her plan to study medicine.

4. Instead, she began to create paintings filled with (disturbed, disturbing) _____ images.

5. Some art critics consider Kahlo's paintings to be (fascinated, fascinating) _____ works of art, though many people find them (overwhelmed, overwhelming) _____.

For more help with your writing, grammar, and research, go to **www.mycomplab.com**

 mycomplab

# 55

# Modal Auxiliary Verbs

AUXILIARY VERBS are known as *helping verbs* because adding an auxiliary verb to a MAIN VERB helps the main verb convey additional information (see 15e). For example, the auxiliary verb *do* is important in turning sentences into questions. *You have to sleep* becomes a question when *do* is added: *Do you have to sleep?* The most common auxiliary verbs are forms of *be, have,* and *do.* Quick References 15.6 and 15.7 in section 15e list the forms of these three verbs.

MODAL AUXILIARY VERBS are one type of auxiliary verb. They include *can, could, may, might, should, had better, must, will, would,* and others discussed in this chapter. Modals differ from *be, have,* and *do* used as auxiliary verbs in the specific ways discussed in Quick Reference 55.1. This chapter can help you use modals to convey shades of meaning.

---

### Quick Reference 55.1 ■ ■ ■ ■ ■ ■ ■

#### Modals versus other auxiliary verbs

- Modals in the present future are always followed by the SIMPLE FORM of a main verb: *I **might go** tomorrow.*

- One-word modals have no *-s* ending in the THIRD-PERSON SINGULAR: *She **could** go with me; he **could** go with me; they **could** go with me.* (The two-word modal *have to* changes form to agree with its subject: *I **have to** leave; she **has to** leave.*) Auxiliary verbs other than modals usually change form for third-person singular: *I **do** want to go; he **does** want to go.*

- Some modals change form in the past. Others (*should, would, must,* which convey probability, and *ought to*) use *have* + a PAST PARTICIPLE. *I **can do** it* becomes *I **could do** it* in PAST-TENSE CLAUSES about ability. *I **could do** it* becomes *I **could have done** it* in clauses about possibility.

- Modals convey meaning about ability, necessity, advisability, possibility, and other conditions: For example, *I can go* means "I am able to go." Modals do not describe actual occurrences.

---

## 55a How do I convey ability, necessity, advisability, possibility, and probability with modals?

### CONVEYING ABILITY

The modal *can* conveys ability now (in the present), and *could* conveys ability before (in the past). These words deliver the meaning "able to." For the future, use *will be able to.*

> We **can** work late tonight. [*Can* conveys present ability.]
>
> I **could** work late last night, too. [*Could* conveys past ability.]
>
> I **will be able to** work late next Monday. [*Will be able* is the future tense; *will* here is not a modal.]

Adding *not* between a modal and the MAIN VERB makes the CLAUSE negative: *We **cannot** work late tonight; I **could not** work late last night; I **will not be able to** work late next Monday.*

**Alert:** You will often see negative forms of modals turned into CONTRACTIONS: *can't, couldn't, won't, wouldn't,* and others. Because contractions are considered informal usage by some instructors, you will never be wrong if you avoid them in ACADEMIC WRITING, except when you are reproducing spoken words. ●

## CONVEYING NECESSITY

The modals *must* and *have to* convey a need to do something. Both *must* and *have to* are followed by the simple form of the main verb. In the present tense, *have to* changes form to agree with its subject.

> You **must** leave before midnight.
>
> She **has to** leave when I leave.

In the past tense, *must* is never used to express necessity. Instead, use *had to*.

> **PRESENT TENSE**   We **must** study today. We **have to** study today.
>
> **PAST TENSE**   We **had to** [not *must*] take a test yesterday.

The negative forms of *must* and *have to* also have different meanings. *Must not* conveys that something is forbidden; *do not have to* conveys that something is not necessary.

> You **must not** sit there. [Sitting there is forbidden.]
>
> You **do not have to** sit there. [Sitting there is not necessary.]

## CONVEYING ADVISABILITY OR THE NOTION OF A GOOD IDEA

The modals *should* and *ought to* express the idea that doing the action of the main verb is advisable or is a good idea.

> You **should** go to class tomorrow morning.

In the past tense, *should* and *ought to* convey regret or knowing something through hindsight. They mean that good advice was not taken.

> You **should have** gone to class yesterday.
>
> I **ought to have** called my sister yesterday.

The modal *had better* delivers the meaning of good advice or warning or threat. It does not change form for tense.

> You **had better** see the doctor before your cough gets worse.

*Need to* is often used to express strong advice, too. Its past-tense form is *needed to*.

> You **need to** take better care of yourself. You **needed to** listen.

**CONVEYING POSSIBILITY**

The modals *may, might,* and *could* can be used to convey an idea of possibility or likelihood.

> We **may** become hungry before long.

> We **could** eat lunch at the diner next door.

For the past-tense form, use *may, might,* and *could,* followed by *have* and the past participle of the main verb.

> I **could have studied** French in high school, but I studied Spanish instead.

**CONVEYING PROBABILITY**

In addition to conveying the idea of necessity, the modal *must* can also convey probability or likelihood. It means that a well-informed guess is being made.

> Marisa **must** be a talented actress. She has been chosen to play the lead role in the school play.

When *must* conveys probability, the past tense is *must have* plus the past participle of the main verb.

> I did not see Boris at the party; he **must have left** early.

**EXERCISE 55-1**    Fill in each blank with the past-tense modal auxiliary that expresses the meaning given in parentheses. For help, consult 55a.

**EXAMPLE**    I (advisability) <u>should have</u> gone straight to the doctor the instant I felt a cold coming on.

1. Since I (necessity, no choice) _____ work late this past Monday, I could not get to the doctor's office before it closed.

2. I (advisability) _____ fallen asleep after dinner, but I stayed awake for a while instead.

3. Even after I finally got into bed, I (ability) _____ not relax.

4. I (making a guess) _____ not _____ heard the alarm the next morning, because I overslept nearly two hours.

5. When I finally arrived at work, my boss came into my office and said, "Julie, you (necessity) _____ stayed home and rested if you are sick."

**ANSWERS: EXERCISE 55-1**

**1.** had to *or* needed to  [either past-tense form of modal auxiliary is acceptable]

**2.** should have *or* ought to have  [either past-tense form of modal auxiliary is acceptable]

**3.** could  [past-tense form of modal auxiliary]

**4.** must/could/might/may; have  [any of the past-tense forms for conveying possibility and making a guess is acceptable]

**5.** should have *or* ought to have  [either past-tense form of modal auxiliary is acceptable]

## 55b    How do I convey preferences, plans, and past habits with modals?

**CONVEYING PREFERENCES**

The modal *would rather* expresses a preference. *Would rather,* the PRESENT TENSE, is used with the SIMPLE FORM of the MAIN VERB, and *would rather have,* the PAST TENSE, is used with the PAST PARTICIPLE of the main verb.

We **would rather see** a comedy than a mystery.

Carlos **would rather have stayed** home last night.

## CONVEYING PLAN OR OBLIGATION

A form of *be* followed by *supposed to* and the simple form of a main verb delivers a meaning of something planned or of an obligation.

I **was supposed to meet** them at the bus stop.

## CONVEYING PAST HABIT

The modals *used to* and *would* express the idea that something happened repeatedly in the past.

I **used to** hate going to the dentist.

I **would** dread every single visit.

🛑 Alert: Both *used to* and *would* can be used to express repeated actions in the past, but *would* cannot be used for a situation that lasted for a period of time in the past.

| | |
|---|---|
| NO | I **would** live in Arizona. |
| YES | I **used to** live in Arizona. ● |

## 55c How can I recognize modals in the passive voice?

Modals use the ACTIVE VOICE, as shown in sections sections 55a and 55b. In the active voice, the subject does the action expressed in the MAIN VERB (see 15n and 15o).

Modals can also use the PASSIVE VOICE (15p). In the passive voice, the doer of the main verb's action is either unexpressed or is expressed as an OBJECT in a PREPOSITIONAL PHRASE starting with the word *by*.

| | |
|---|---|
| PASSIVE | The waterfront **can be seen** from my window. |
| ACTIVE | **I can see** the waterfront from my window. |
| PASSIVE | The tax form **must be signed** by the person who fills it out. |
| ACTIVE | The person who fills out the tax form **must sign** it. |

**EXERCISE 55-2**   Select the correct choice from the words in parentheses and write it in the blank. For help, consult 55a through 55c.

**EXAMPLE**   When I was younger, I (would, used to) <u>used to</u> love to go bicycle riding.

1. You (ought to have, ought have) _____ called yesterday as you had promised you would.

2. Judging by the size of the puddles in the street outside, it (must be rained, must have rained) _____ all night long.

3. Ingrid (must not have, might not have been) _____ as early for the interview as she claims she was.

4. After all the studying he did, Pedro (should have, should have been) _____ less frightened by the exam.

5. I have to go home early today, although I really (cannot, should not) _____ leave before the end of the day because of all the work I have to do.

**EXERCISE 55-3**  Select the correct choice from the words in parentheses and write it in the blank. For help, consult 55a through 55c.

**EXAMPLE**  We (must have, must) <u>must</u> study this afternoon.

1. Unfortunately, I (should not, cannot) _____ go to the movies with you because I have to take care of my brother tonight.

2. Juan (would have, would have been) _____ nominated class valedictorian if he had not moved to another city.

3. You (ought not have, ought not to have) _____ arrived while the meeting was still in progress.

4. Louise (must be, must have been) _____ sick to miss the party last week.

5. Had you not called in advance, you (may not have, may not have been) _____ aware of the traffic on the expressway.

For more help with your writing, grammar, and research, go to **www.mycomplab.com**

**3. might not have been** [55a, correct form for past-tense modal auxiliary expressing possibility or likelihood]

**4. should have been** [55c, passive modal auxiliary with *Pedro* receiving the action of the verb]

**5. should not** [55a, correct form for modal auxiliary expressing negative advisability rather than negative ability]

**ANSWERS: EXERCISE 55-3**

**1. cannot** [55a, correct form for modal auxiliary expressing negative ability rather than negative advisability]

**2. would have been** [55c, passive modal auxiliary with *Juan* receiving the action of the verb]

**3. ought not to have** [55a, correct form for past-tense modal auxiliary expressing advisability]

**4. must have been** [55a, correct form for past-tense modal auxiliary expressing possibility or likelihood]

**5. may not have been** [55a, correct form for past-tense modal auxiliary expressing possibility or likelihood]

# TERMS GLOSSARY

This glossary defines important terms used in this handbook, including the ones that are printed in small capital letters. Many of these glossary entries end with parenthetical references to the handbook section(s) or chapter(s) where the specific term is fully discussed.

**absolute phrase** A phrase containing a subject and a participle that modifies an entire sentence. (14n) ***The semester** [subject] **being** [present participle of be] **over**, the campus looks deserted.*

**abstract** A very short summary that presents all the important ideas of a longer piece of writing. Sometimes appears before the main writing, as in APA style.

**abstract noun** A noun that names something not knowable through the five senses: *idea, respect.* (14b)

**academic writing** Writing you do for college classes, usually intended to inform or to persuade. (1d)

**action verbs** Strong verbs that increase the impact of your language and reduce wordiness. *Weak verbs,* such as *be* or *have,* increase wordiness. (11e)

**active reading** Reading for critical understanding, using such strategies as making interpretations; looking for bias or omissions; assessing evidence, reasoning processes, claims of cause and effect; applying the reading to other contexts; and so on.

**active voice** An attribute of verbs showing that the action or condition expressed in the verb is done by the subject, in contrast with the *passive voice,* which conveys that the action or condition of the verb is done to the subject. (15n, 15o)

**adjective** A word that describes or limits (modifies) a noun, a pronoun, or a word group functioning as a noun: *silly, three.* (14f, Chapter 18)

**adjective clause** A dependent clause, also known as a *relative clause.* An adjective clause modifies a preceding noun or pronoun and begins with a relative word (such as *who, which, that,* or *where*) that relates the clause to the noun or pronoun it modifies. Also see *clause.* (14p)

**adverb** A word that describes or limits (modifies) verbs, adjectives, other adverbs, phrases, or clauses: *loudly, very, nevertheless, there.* (14g, Chapter 18)

**adverb clause** A dependent clause beginning with a subordinating conjunction that establishes the relationship in meaning between the adverb clause and its independent clause. An adverb clause modifies the independent clause's verb or the entire independent clause. Also see *clause, conjunction.* (14p)

**agreement** The required match of number and person between a subject and verb or a pronoun and antecedent. A pronoun that expresses gender must match its antecedent in gender also. (Chapter 17)

**analogy** An explanation of the unfamiliar in terms of the familiar. Like a simile, an analogy compares things not normally associated with each other; but unlike a simile, an analogy does not use *like* or *as* in making the comparison. Analogy is also a rhetorical strategy for developing paragraphs. (3i, 21d, 41b)

**analysis** A process of critical thinking that divides a whole into its component parts in order to understand how the parts interrelate. Sometimes called *division,* analysis is also a rhetorical strategy for developing paragraphs. (3i, 4b, 40h, 41f)

**analytic frameworks** Systematic ways of investigating a work. (40c)

**antecedent** The noun or pronoun to which a pronoun refers. (16l–16s, 7o–7t)

**APA style** See *documentation style.*

**appeals to reason** Tools a writer uses to convince the reader that the reasoning in an argument is sound and effective; there are three types—logical, emotional, and ethical appeals. (5j)

**apply** In writing, to examine how a particular theory, interpretation, or perspective explains or fits—or doesn't—a specific situation or reading.

**appositive** A word or group of words that renames a preceding noun or noun phrase: *my favorite month,* **October**. (14n)

**argument** A rhetorical attempt to convince others to agree with a position about a topic open to debate. (1c, Chapter 5)

**argument to the person (also known as "ad hominum")** A logical fallacy that involves finding fault with an individual rather than more properly with the argument he or she has made. Example: *Don't believe Smith's views on the environment because he dresses so strangely.*

**articles** Also called *determiners* or *noun markers,* articles are the words *a, an,* and *the. A* and *an* are indefinite articles, and *the* is a definite article; also see *determiner.* (14f, Chapter 51)

**assertion** A statement. In a thesis statement, an assertion expresses a point of view about a topic; in an argument, an assertion states the position you want to argue. (2d, 5d)

**assessing reasoning processes** Judging whether the claims made in a piece of writing are justified by the evidence, reasons, explanations, and thinking presented. Often involves asking whether certain facts or statements actually lead to certain conclusions.

**audience** The readers to whom a piece of writing is directed; the three types include *general audience, peer audience,* and *specialist audience.* (1d)

**auxiliary verb** Also known as a *helping verb,* an auxiliary verb is a form of *be, do, have, can, may, will,* or certain other verbs, that combines with a main verb to help it express tense, mood, and voice. Also see *modal auxiliary verb.* (15e)

**balanced sentence** A sentence composed of two parallel structures, usually two independent clauses, that present contrasting content. (10b)

**base form** See *simple form.*

**bias** In writing, a distortion or inaccuracy caused by a dislike or hatred of individuals, groups of people, or ideas. (4c.2)

**bibliographic notes** In a note system of documentation, a *footnote* or *endnote* gives the bibliographic information the first time a source is cited. (35f, 36d.2, Chapter 38)

**bibliography** A list of sources used or consulted for research writing. (Chapters 36, 37, and 38)

**block style** Style used in writing business letters. Block style uses no indents, single spacing within paragraphs and double spacing between paragraphs. All lines start flush left, which means at the left margin. (43f)

**blog** Shortened form of "**Web log,**" a kind of online journal. (46e)

**body paragraphs** Paragraphs that provide the substance of your message in a sequence that makes sense. (3d)

**Boolean expressions** In a search engine, symbols or words such as And, Or, Not, and Near that let you create keyword combinations that narrow and refine your search. (34l)

**borders** Lines used to set apart sections of text. (45e)

**brainstorming** Listing all ideas that come to mind on a topic and then grouping the ideas by patterns that emerge.

**bureaucratic language** Sometimes called *bureaucratese;* language that is overblown or overly complex. (12l)

**business writing** Writing designed for business, including letters, memos, resumes, job application letters, and e-mail messages. (1d, 3a, Chapter 43)

**case** The form of a noun or pronoun in a specific context that shows whether it is functioning as a subject, an object, or a possessive. In modern English, nouns change form in the possessive case only (city = form for subjective and objective cases; city's = possessive-case form). Also see *pronoun case.* (16a–16k)

**cause and effect** The relationship between outcomes (effects) and the reasons for them (causes). Cause-and-effect analysis is a rhetorical strategy for developing paragraphs. (3i, 4h, 4i)

**chronological order** Also called *time order,* an arrangement of information according to time sequence; an organizing strategy for sentences, paragraphs, and longer pieces of writing. (3h)

**citation** Information that identifies a source quoted, paraphrased, summarized, or referred to in a piece of writing; *in-text citations* appear within sentences or as *parenthetical references.* Also see *documentation.* (Chapters 34 and 35)

**civic writing** Writing done to influence public opinion or to advance causes for the public good. (44d)

**claim** States an issue and then takes a position on a debatable topic related to the issue. A claim is supported with evidence and reasons, moving from broad reasons to specific data and details. (5d)

**classical argument** An argument with a six-part structure consisting of introduction, thesis statement, background, evidence and reasoning, response to opposing views, and conclusion. (5e)

**classification** A rhetorical strategy for paragraph development that organizes information by grouping items according to underlying shared characteristics. (3i)

**clause** A group of words containing a subject and a predicate. A clause that delivers full meaning is called an *independent* (or *main*) *clause.* A clause that lacks full meaning by itself is called a *dependent* (or *subordinate*) *clause.* Also see *adjective clause, adverb clause, nonrestrictive element, noun clause, restrictive element.* (14p)

**cliché** An overused, worn-out phrase that has lost its capacity to communicate effectively: *flat as Kansas, ripe old age.* (12i)

**climactic order** Sometimes called *emphatic order,* an arrangement of ideas or other kinds of information from least important to most important. (3h, 5e )

**clip art** Refers to pictures, sketches, and other graphics available on some word processing programs. (45f )

**clustering** See *mapping.*

**coherence** The clear progression from one idea to another using transitional expressions, pronouns, selective repetition, or parallelism to make connections between ideas. (3g)

**collaborative writing** Students working together to write a paper. (Chapter 6)

**collective noun** A noun that names a group of people or things: *family, committee.* Also see *noncount noun.* (14b, 17j, 17t)

**colloquial language** Casual or conversational language. Also see *slang.* (12h)

**comma fault** See *comma splice.*

**comma splice** The error that occurs when only a comma connects two independent clauses; also called a *comma fault.* (Chapter 20)

**common noun** A noun that names a general group, place, person, or thing: *dog, house.* (14b)

**comparative form** The form of a descriptive adjective or adverb that shows a different degree of intensity between two things: *bluer, less blue; more easily, less easily.* Also see *positive form, superlative form.* (18e)

**comparison and contrast** A rhetorical strategy for organizing and developing paragraphs by discussing similarities (*comparison*) and differences (*contrast*). It has two patterns: *point-by-point* and *block organization.* (3i)

**complement** An element after a verb that completes the predicate, such as a direct object after an action verb or a noun or adjective after a linking verb. Also see *object complement, predicate adjective, predicate nominative, subject complement.* (14n)

**complete predicate** See *predicate.*

**complete subject** See *subject.*

**complex sentence** See *sentence types.*

**compound-complex sentence** See *sentence types.*

**compound construction** A group of nouns or pronouns connected with a coordinating conjunction. (16d)

**compound noun** See *subject.*

**compound predicate** See *predicate.*

**compound sentence** See *coordinate sentence, sentence types.*

**compound subject** See *subject.* (14l, 17e)

**compound word** Two or more words placed together to express one concept. (31g)

**conciseness** An attribute of writing that is direct and to the point. (Chapter 11)

**concrete noun** A noun naming something that can be seen, touched, heard, smelled, or tasted: *smoke, sidewalk.* (14b)

**conjunction** A word that connects or otherwise establishes a relationship between two or more words, phrases, or clauses. Also see *coordinating conjunction, correlative conjunction, subordinating conjunction.* (14i)

**conjunctive adverb** An adverb, such as *therefore* or *meanwhile,* that communicates a logical connection in meaning. (14g)

**connotation** An idea implied by a word, involving associations and emotional overtones that go beyond the word's dictionary definition. (12d)

**contraction** A word where an apostrophe takes the place of one or more omitted letters. (27d)

**coordinate adjectives** Two or more adjectives of equal weight that modify a noun. (24e)

**coordinate sentence** Two or more independent clauses joined by either a semicolon or a comma with coordinating conjunction showing their relationship; also called a *compound sentence.* Also see *coordination.* (9d)

**coordinating conjunction** A conjunction that joins two or more grammatically equivalent structures: *and, or, for, nor, but, so, yet.* (14i, 20b)

**coordination** The use of grammatically equivalent forms to show a balance or sequence of ideas. (9d, 9e)

**correlative conjunction** A pair of words that joins equivalent grammatical structures, including *both . . . and, either . . . or, neither . . . nor, not only . . . but* (or *but also*). (14i)

**count noun** A noun that names an item or items that can be counted: *radio, streets, idea, fingernails.* (14b, 50a)

**critical reading** A parallel process to critical thinking where you think about what you're reading while you're reading it. (4d)

**critical response** Formally, an essay summarizing a source's central point or main idea. It includes a *transitional statement* that bridges this summary and the writer's synthesized reactions in response. (4f)

**critical thinking** A form of thinking where you take control of your conscious thought processes. (4a, 4b, 40g)

**cumulative adjectives** Adjectives that build meaning from word to word: *distinctive musical style.* (24e)

**cumulative sentence** The most common structure for a sentence, with the subject and verb first, followed by modifiers adding details; also called a *loose sentence.* (9q)

**dangling modifier** A modifier that attaches its meaning illogically, either because it is closer to another noun or pronoun than to its true subject or because its true subject is not expressed in the sentence. (21d)

**declarative sentence** A sentence that makes a statement: *Sky diving is exciting.* Also see *exclamatory sentence, imperative sentence, interrogative sentence.* (14k)

**deduction, deductive reasoning** The process of reasoning from general claims to a specific instance. (4i)

**definite article** See *articles.*

**definition** A rhetorical strategy in which you define or give the meaning of words or ideas. Includes *extended definition.* (3i)

**demonstrative pronoun** A pronoun that points out the antecedent: *this, these; that, those.* (14c, 14f)

**denotation** The dictionary definition of a word. (12e.1)

**dependent clause** A clause that cannot stand alone as an independent grammatical unit. Also see *adjective clause, adverb clause, noun clause.* (14p, 19b)

**description** A rhetorical strategy that appeals to a reader's senses—sight, sound, smell, taste, and touch. (3i)

**descriptive adjective** An adjective that names the condition or properties of the noun it modifies and (except for a very few, such as *dead* and *unique*) has comparative and superlative forms: *flat, flatter, flattest.*

**descriptive adverb** An adverb that names the condition or properties of whatever it modifies and that has comparative and superlative forms: *happily, more happily, most happily.* (14g)

**determiner** A word or word group, traditionally identified as an adjective, that limits a noun by telling how much or how many about it. Also called *expression of quantity, limiting adjective,* or *noun marker.* (14f, 50b, Chapter 51)

**diction** Word choice. (12d)

**digital portfolio** A collection of several texts in electronic format that you've chosen to represent the range of your skills and abilities. (1f)

**direct address**  Words naming a person or group being spoken to. Written words of direct address are set off by commas. (24g) *The answer,* **my friends,** *lies with you. Go with them,* **Gene.**

**direct discourse**  In writing, words that repeat speech or conversation exactly and so are enclosed in quotation marks. (22e, 24g, 28b)

**direct object**  A noun or pronoun or group of words functioning as a noun that receives the action (completes the meaning) of a transitive verb. (14m)

**direct question**  A sentence that asks a question and ends with a question mark: *Are you going?* (23a, 23c)

**direct quotation**  See *quotation.*

**direct title**  A title that tells exactly what the essay will be about. (2i)

**discovery draft**  A first draft developed from focused freewriting. (2g)

**disclaimer**  A statement appended to the top or bottom of e-mails designed to protect the company from legal liability. (43d)

**documentation**  The acknowledgment of someone else's words and ideas used in any piece of writing by giving full and accurate information about the person whose words were used and where those words were found. For example, for a print source, documentation usually includes names of all authors, title of the source, place and date of publication, and related information. (35a–35k, Chapters 36–38)

**documentation style**  A system for providing information about the source of words, information, and ideas quoted, paraphrased, or summarized from some source other than the writer. Documentation styles discussed in this handbook are MLA, APA, CM, CSE, and COS. (33h, Chapters 36–38)

**document design**  A term for the placement of tables, graphs, and other illustrations on printed and online material. (Chapter 45)

**double negative**  A nonstandard negation using two negative modifiers rather than one. (18c)

**drafting**  A part of the writing process in which writers compose ideas in sentences and paragraphs. *Drafts* are versions—*first* or *rough, revised,* and *final*—of one piece of writing. (2g)

**edited American English**  English language usage that conforms to established rules of grammar, sentence structure, punctuation, and spelling; also called *standard American English.* (12b)

**editing**  A part of the writing process in which writers check the technical correctness of grammar, spelling, punctuation, and mechanics. (2j)

**ellipses**  Punctuation consisting of three periods that shows material has been omitted. Example: *(1) That person playing the loud music should leave. (2) That person . . . should leave.*

**elliptical construction**  The deliberate omission of one or more words in order to achieve conciseness in a sentence. (14p, 22h, 11d.3)

**emotional appeal**  Rhetorical strategy which employs the use of descriptive language and concrete details or examples to create a mental picture for readers, leading them to feel or understand the importance of a claim. Greek name is *pathos.* (5g)

**essential element**  See *restrictive element.*

**ethical appeal**  Rhetorical strategy intended to reassure readers that the writer is authoritative, honest, fair, likable, and so on. Greek name is ethos. (5g)

**ethnography**  A research method that involves careful observation of a group of people or a setting, often over a period of time. Ethnography also refers to the written work that results from this research.

**euphemism**  Language that attempts to blunt certain realities by speaking of them in "nice" or "tactful" words. (12k)

**evaluate**  A step in the critical thinking process where you judge the quality of the material you are assessing. (4b, 4c.3, 4g)

**evidence**  Facts, data, examples, and opinions of others used to support assertions and conclusions. Also see *sources.* (4g)

**exclamatory sentence**  A sentence beginning with *What* or *How* that expresses strong feeling: *What a ridiculous statement!* (14k)

**expletive**  The phrase *there is (are), there was (were), it is,* or *it was* at the beginning of a clause, changing structure and postponing the subject: ***It is*** *Mars that we hope to reach.* [Compare: *We hope to reach Mars*]. (11c)

**expository writing** See *informative writing.*

**expressive writing** Writing that reflects your personal thoughts and feelings. (1b)

**faulty parallelism** Grammatically incorrect writing that results from nonmatching grammatical forms linked with coordinating conjunctions. (10e)

**faulty predication** A grammatically illogical combination of subject and predicate. (22g)

**field research** Primary research that involves going into real-life situations to observe, survey, interview, or be part of some activity. (32c)

**figurative language** Words that make connections and comparisons and draw on one image to explain another and enhance meaning. (12c)

**finite verb** A verb form that shows tense, mood, voice, person, and number while expressing an action, occurrence, or state of being.

**first person** See *person.*

**focused freewriting** A technique that may start with a set topic or may build on one sentence taken from earlier freewriting. (2g)

**formal outline** An outline that lays out the topic levels of generalities or hierarchies that marks them with Roman numerals, letters, numbers indented in a carefully prescribed fashion. (2f)

**frames** A part of a Web page that functions independently of the other parts of the page. (Chapter 46)

**freewriting** Writing nonstop for a period of time to generate ideas by free association of thoughts. Also see *discovery draft.* (2g)

**fused sentence** See *run-on sentence.*

**future perfect progressive tense** The form of the future perfect tense that describes an action or condition ongoing until some specific future time: *I will have been talking.* (15j)

**future perfect tense** The tense indicating that an action will have been completed or a condition will have ended by a specified point in the future: *I will have talked.* (15i)

**future progressive tense** The form of the future tense showing that a future action will continue for some time: *I will be talking.* (15j)

**future tense** The form of a verb, made with the simple form and either *shall* or *will,* expressing an action yet to be taken or a condition not yet experienced: *I will talk.* (15g)

**gender** The classification of words as masculine, feminine, or neutral. (17s, 12f)

**gender-free language** See *gender-neutral language.*

**gender-neutral language** Also called *gender-free language* or *nonsexist language,* it uses terms that do not unnecessarily say whether a person is male or female, as with *police officer* instead of *policeman.* (17s, 12f)

**generalization** A broad statement without details. (1c)

**gerund** A present participle functioning as a noun: ***Walking*** *is good exercise.* Also see *verbal.* (14e, 51c, Chapter 54)

**helping verb** See *auxiliary verb.*

**homonyms** Words spelled differently that sound alike: *to, too, two.* (31f)

**home page** The opening main page of a Web site that provides access to other pages on the site categories. (46d)

**HTML** (**H**yper **T**ext **M**arkup **L**anguage) A computer program language used for Web pages. (46c)

**hyperbole** See *overstatement.*

**hyperlink** Connection from one digital document to another online. (46d)

**idiom** A word, phrase, or other construction that has a different meaning from its literal meaning: *He lost his head. She hit the ceiling.* (Chapter 53)

**illogical predication** See *faulty predication.*

**imperative mood** The mood that expresses commands and direct requests, using the simple form of the verb and often implying but not expressing the subject, you: *Go.* (15l)

**imperative sentence** A sentence that gives a command: *Go to the corner to buy me a newspaper.* (14k, 19b.3)

**incubation** The prewriting technique of giving ideas time to develop and clarify.

**indefinite article** See *articles, determiner.*

**indefinite pronoun** A pronoun, such as *all, anyone, each,* and *others,* that refers to a non-specific person or thing. (14c, 14f, 17i)

**independent clause** A clause that can stand alone as an independent grammatical unit. (14p)

**indicative mood** The mood of verbs used for statements about real things or highly likely ones: *I think Grace is arriving today.* (15l, 22d)

**indirect discourse** Reported speech or conversation that does not use the exact structure of the original and so is not enclosed in quotation marks. (22e, 24h)

**indirect title** Hints at an essay's topic; tries to catch the reader's interest by presenting a puzzle that can be solved by reading the essay. (2i)

**indirect object** A noun or pronoun or group of words functioning as a noun that tells to whom or for whom the action expressed by a transitive verb was done. (14m)

**indirect question** A sentence that reports a question and ends with a period: *I asked if you are leaving.* (23a, 23c, 48a)

**indirect quotation** See *quotation.*

**induction** The reasoning process of arriving at general principles from particular facts or instances. (4h)

**inductive reasoning** A form of reasoning that moves from particular facts or instances to general principles. (4h)

**inference** What a reader or listener understands to be implied but not stated. (4d)

**infinitive** A verbal made of the simple form of a verb and usually, but not always, *to* that functions as a noun, adjective, or adverb. Infinitives without the word *to* are called *unmarked* (or *bare*) *infinitives.* (14e, 15k, Chapter 54)

**infinitive phrase** An infinitive, with its modifiers and object, that functions as a noun, adjective, or adverb. Also see *verbal phrase.* (14e)

**informal language** Word choice that creates a tone appropriate for casual writing or speaking. (1d, 12g)

**informal outline** Non-traditional outline that doesn't follow the rules of a *formal outline.* (2f)

**informative writing** Writing that gives information and, when necessary, explains it; also known as *expository writing.* (1b)

**intensive pronoun** A pronoun that ends in *-self* and that emphasizes its antecedent. Also called *reflexive pronoun: Vida **himself** argued against it.* (14c)

**interjection** An emotion-conveying word that is treated as a sentence, starting with a capital letter and ending with an exclamation point or a period: *Oh! Ouch!* (14j, 24j)

**interrogative pronoun** A pronoun, such as *whose* or *what,* that implies a question: ***Who** called?* (14c, 19b)

**interrogative sentence** A sentence that asks a direct question: *Did you see that?* (14k)

**in-text citation** Source information placed in parentheses within the body of a research paper. Also see *citation, parenthetical reference.* (36b, 37b)

**intransitive verb** A verb that does not take a direct object. (15f)

**invention techniques** Ways of gathering ideas for writing. Also see *planning.*

**inverted word order** In contrast to standard order, the main verb or an auxiliary verb comes before the subject in inverted word order. Most questions and some exclamations use inverted word order. (17h, 9r, Chapter 51)

**irony** Words used to imply the opposite of their usual meaning. (12c)

**irregular verb** A verb that forms the past tense and past participle in some way other than by adding *-ed* or *-d.* (15d)

**jargon** A particular field's or group's specialized vocabulary that a general reader is unlikely to understand. (12k)

**journalist's questions** Who? What? When? Where? Why? How? Traditionally, every news story should answer these questions.

**justify** When used as a design term, it refers to aligning text evenly along both the left and right margins. (45c)

**key terms** In an essay, the words central to its topic and its message. (5d)

**keywords** The main words in a source's title or the words that the author or editor has identified as central to that source. Use keywords in searching for sources online or in library databases. (34c)

**layout** The arrangement of text, visuals, color, and space on a page. (45g)

**levels of formality** Word choices and sentence structures reflecting various degrees of formality of language. A formal level is used for ceremonial and other occasions when stylistic flourishes are appropriate. A medium level, neither too formal nor too casual, is acceptable for most academic writing. (12b)

**levels of generality** Degrees of generality used to group or organize information or ideas as you write, as when moving from the most general to the most specific. Conversely, *levels of specificity* move from the most specific to the most general.

**levels of specificity** Degrees of specificity used to group or organize information or ideas as you write, as when moving from the most specific to the most general. Conversely, *levels of generality* move from the most general to the most specific.

**limiting adjective** See *determiner.*

**linking verb** A main verb that links a subject with a subject complement that renames or describes the subject. Linking verbs, sometimes called *copulative verbs,* convey a state of being, relate to the senses, or indicate a condition. (15a, 15c)

**logical appeal** Rhetorical strategy that intended to show readers that the reasoning depends on formal reasoning, including providing evidence and drawing conclusions from premises. Greek name is *logos.* (5g)

**logical fallacies** Flaws in reasoning that lead to illogical statements. (4i)

**main clause** See *independent clause.*

**main verb** A verb that expresses action, occurrence, or state of being and that shows mood, tense, voice, number, and person. (14d, 15b)

**mapping** An invention technique based on thinking about a topic and its increasingly specific subdivisions; also known as *clustering* or *webbing.*

**margins** The boundaries of a page, which means the white space or blank areas at the top, bottom, and sides of a paper or screen. (45c)

**mechanics** Conventions governing matters such as the use of capital letters, italics, abbreviations, and numbers. (Chapter 30)

**memo or memorandum** A brief form of business correspondence with a format that is headed with lines for "To," "From," and "Subject" and uses the rest of its space for its message. (43e)

**metaphor** A comparison implying similarity between two things. A metaphor does not use words such as *like* or *as,* which are used in a simile and which make a comparison explicit: *a mop of hair* (compare the simile *hair like a mop*). (12d)

**misplaced modifier** Describing or limiting words that are wrongly positioned in a sentence so that their message is either illogical or relates to the wrong word or words. Also see *squinting modifier.* (21a)

**mixed construction** A sentence that unintentionally changes from one grammatical structure to another, incompatible one, so that the meaning is garbled. (22f)

**mixed metaphors** Incongruously combined images. (12c)

**MLA style** See *documentation style, parenthetical reference.*

**modal auxiliary verb** One of a group of nine auxiliary verbs that add information such as a sense of needing, wanting, or having to do something or a sense of possibility, likelihood, obligation, permission, or ability. (15e, Chapter 55)

**modified block style** An alternative to block style, in modified block style the lines for the inside address and the body begin flush left but the heading, closing, and signature begin about halfway across the page. (43f)

**modifier, modify** A word or group of words functioning as an adjective or adverb to describe or limit another word or word group. Also see *misplaced modifier.* (14n, Chapter 18, 9d)

**mood** The attribute of verbs showing a speaker's or writer's attitude toward the action by the way verbs are used. English has three moods: imperative, indicative, and subjunctive. Also see *imperative mood, indicative mood, subjunctive mood.* (15l, 15m)

**multimodal** The use of a combination of words and images. (4l)

**narrative** A rhetorical strategy that tells a story; a narrative deals with what is or what has happened. (3i)

**navigation bar** The set of links on every Web page that allows users to get back to the site's home page and to major parts of the site. (46c)

**netiquette** Coined from the word etiquette, netiquette is good manners when using e-mail, the Internet, and online sites such as bulletin boards, chatrooms, etc. (43d)

**noncount noun** A noun that names a thing that cannot be counted: *water, time.* Also see *collective noun.* (14b, Chapters 50 and 51)

**nonessential element** See *nonrestrictive element.*

**nonrestrictive clause** See *nonrestrictive element.*

**nonrestrictive element** A descriptive word, phrase, or dependent clause that provides information not essential to understanding the basic message of the element it modifies and so is set off by commas. Also see *restrictive element.* (24f)

**nonsexist language** See *gender-neutral language.*

**nonspecific noun** A noun that refers to any of a number of identical items; it takes the indefinite articles *a, an.* (51a)

**nonstandard English** Language usage other than what is called *edited American English.* (12b)

**noun** A word that names a person, place, thing, or idea. Nouns function as subjects, objects, or complements. (14b)

**noun clause** A dependent clause that functions as a subject, object, or complement. (14p)

**noun complement** See *complement.*

**noun determiner** See *determiner.*

**noun phrase** A noun and its modifiers functioning as a subject, object, or complement. (14o)

**number** The attribute of some words indicating whether they refer to one (*singular*) or more than one (*plural*). (15a, 17b, 22b, Chapter 49)

**object** A noun, pronoun, or group of words functioning as a noun or pronoun that receives the action of a verb (*direct object*); tells to whom or for whom something is done (*indirect object*); or completes the meaning of a preposition (*object of a preposition*). (14m)

**object complement** A noun or adjective renaming or describing a direct object after verbs such as *call, consider, name, elect,* and *think: I call the most obsessive joggers **fanatics**.* (14n)

**objective case** The case of a noun or pronoun functioning as a direct or indirect object or the object of a preposition or of a verbal. A few pronouns change form to show case (*him, her, whom*). Also see *case.* (Chapter 16)

**outline** Technique for laying out ideas for writing. An outline can be formal or informal. (2f)

**overstatement** Deliberate exaggeration for emphasis; also called *hyperbole.* (12c)

**paragraph** A group of sentences that work together to develop a unit of thought. They are the structured elements of an essay, which is composed of an *introductory paragraph, body paragraphs,* and a *concluding paragraph.* Also see *shaping.* (Chapter 3)

**paragraph arrangement** Ordering sentences by specific techniques to communicate a paragraph's message. (3h)

**paragraph development** Using specific, concrete details (RENNS) to support a generalization in a paragraph; rhetorical strategies or patterns for organizing ideas in paragraphs. (3f, 3i)

**parallelism** The use of equivalent grammatical forms or matching sentence structures to express equivalent ideas and develop coherence. (Chapter 10)

**paraphrase** A restatement of someone else's ideas in language and sentence structure different from those of the original. (35i)

**parenthetical reference** Information enclosed in parentheses following quoted, paraphrased, or summarized material from a source to alert readers to the use of material from a specific source. Parenthetical references, also called *in-text citations,* function together with a list of bibliographic information about each source used in a paper to document the writer's use of sources. Also see *citation.* (36b)

**participial phrase** A phrase that contains a present participle or a past participle and any modifiers and that functions as an adjective. Also see *verbal phrase.* (14o)

**passive construction** See *passive voice.*

**passive voice** The form of a verb in which the subject is acted on; if the subject is mentioned in the sentence, it usually appears as the object of the preposition *by: **I was frightened by** the thunder.* [Compare the active voice: *The thunder **frightened me**.*] The passive voice emphasizes the action, in contrast to the *active voice,* which emphasizes the doer of the action. (15n)

**past participle** The third principal part of a verb, formed in regular verbs, like the past tense, by adding *-d* or *-ed* to the simple form. In irregular verbs, it often differs from the simple form and the past tense: *break, broke, broken.* (14e, 15b, 54f )

**past perfect progressive tense** The past perfect tense form that describes an ongoing condition in the past that has been ended by something stated in the sentence: *I had been talking.* (15j)

**past perfect tense** The tense that describes a condition or action that started in the past, continued for a while, and then ended in the past: *I had talked.* (15g, 15i)

**past progressive tense** The tense that shows the continuing nature of a past action: *I was talking.* (15j)

**past subjunctive** The simple past tense in the subjunctive mood. (15m)

**past tense** The tense that tells of an action completed or a condition ended. (15g)

**past-tense form** The second principal part of a verb, in regular verbs formed by adding *-d* or *-ed* to the simple form. In irregular verbs, the past tense may change in several ways from the simple form. (15b, 15d)

**peer-response group** A group of students formed to give each other feedback on writing. (Chapter 6)

**perfect infinitive** Also called *present perfect participle,* a tense used to describe an action that occurs before the action in the main verb. (15k)

**perfect tenses** The three tenses—the present perfect (*I have talked*), the past perfect (*I had talked*), and the future perfect (*I will have talked*)—that help show complex time relationships between two clauses. (15g, 15i)

**periodic sentence** A sentence that begins with modifiers and ends with the independent clause, thus postponing the main idea— and the emphasis—for the end; also called a *climactic sentence.* (9q)

**periodical** A publication such as a newspaper, magazine, or journal that is published at a regular interval, that is "periodically."

**person** The attribute of nouns and pronouns showing who or what acts or experiences an action. *First person* is the one speaking (*I, we*); *second person* is the one being spoken to (*you, you*); and *third person* is the person or thing being spoken about (*he, she, it, they*). All nouns are third person. (15a, 17b)

**personal pronoun** A pronoun that refers to people or things, such as *I, you, them, it.* (14c, 16n)

**personality** The sense of the writer that comes through his or her writing; for example, friendly, bossy, shy, assertive, concerned, angry, and so on.

**persuasive appeal** Rhetorical strategies which appeal to the emotions, logic, or ethics of readers. (5g)

**persuasive writing** Writing that seeks to convince the reader about a matter of opinion. It is also known as *argumentative writing.* (Chapter 5)

**phrasal verb** A verb that combines with one or more prepositions to deliver its meaning: *ask out, look into.* (53c)

**phrase** A group of related words that does not contain both a subject and a predicate and thus cannot stand alone as an independent grammatical unit. A phrase functions as a noun, verb, or modifier. (14o)

**plagiarism** A writer's presenting another person's words or ideas without giving credit to that person. Documentation systems allow writers to give proper credit to sources in ways recognized by scholarly communities. Plagiarism is a serious offense, a form of intellectual dishonesty that can lead to course failure or expulsion. (Chapter 35)

**planning** An early part of the writing process in which writers gather ideas. Along with shaping, planning is sometimes called *prewriting.* (Chapter 2)

**plural** See *number.*

**podcasts** Brief sound files that are shared over the Internet, somewhat like online radio broadcasts. (46g)

**positive form** The form of an adjective or adverb when no comparison is being expressed: *blue, easily.* Also see *comparative form, superlative form.* (18e)

**possessive case** The case of a noun or pronoun that shows ownership or possession: *my, your, their,* and so on. Also see *case, pronoun case.* (Chapter 16, 27a–27c)

**predicate** The part of a sentence that contains the verb and tells what the subject is doing or experiencing or what is being done to the subject. A *simple predicate* contains only the main verb and any auxiliary verbs. A *complete predicate* contains the verb, its modifiers, objects, and other related words. A *compound predicate* contains two or more verbs and their objects and modifiers, if any. (14l)

**predicate adjective** An adjective used as a subject complement: *That tree is **leafy**.* (14n)

**predicate nominative** A noun or pronoun used as a subject complement: *That tree is a **maple**.* (14n)

**prediction** A major activity of the *reading process,* in which the reader guesses what comes next. (4c)

**premises** In a deductive argument expressed as a syllogism, statements presenting the conditions of the argument from which the conclusion must follow. (4h)

**preposition** A word that conveys a relationship, often of space or time, between the noun or pronoun following it and other words in the sentence. The noun or pronoun following a preposition is called its *object.* (14h, Chapter 53)

**prepositional phrase** A preposition and the word it modifies. Also see *phrase, preposition.* (14h, 14o)

**presentation style** The way you deliver what you have to say. Memorization, reading, mapping and speaking with notes are different types of presentation styles. (42h)

**present infinitive** Names or describes an activity or occurrence coming together either at the same time or after the time expressed in the main verb. (15k)

**present participle** A verb's *-ing* form. Used with auxiliary verbs, present participles function as main verbs. Used without auxiliary verbs, present participles function as nouns or adjectives. (14e, 15b, 55f )

**present perfect participle** See *perfect infinitive.*

**present perfect progressive tense** The present perfect tense form that describes something ongoing in the past that is likely to continue into the future: *I have been talking.* (15j)

**present perfect tense** The tense indicating that an action or its effects, begun or perhaps completed in the past, continue into the present: *I had talked.* (15g, 15i)

**present progressive tense** The present-tense form of the verb that indicates something taking place at the time it is written or spoken about: *I am talking.* (15j)

**present subjunctive** The simple form of the verb for all persons and numbers in the subjunctive mood. (15m)

**present tense** The tense that describes what is happening, what is true at the moment, and what is consistently true. It uses the simple form (*I talk*) and the *-s* form in the third-person singular (*he, she, it talks*). (15g, 15h)

**prewriting** All activities in the writing process before drafting. Also see *planning, shaping.*

**primary sources** Firsthand work: write-ups of experiments and observations by the researchers who conducted them; taped accounts, interviews, and newspaper accounts by direct observers; autobiographies, diaries, and journals; expressive works (poems, plays, fiction, essays). Also known as *primary evidence.* Also see *secondary source.* (32a, 32d)

**process** A rhetorical strategy in writing that reports a sequence of actions by which something is done or made. (3i)

**progressive forms** Verb forms made in all tenses with the present participle and forms of the verb *be* as an auxiliary. Progressive forms show that an action, occurrence, or state of being is ongoing. (15g, 15j)

**project proposal** A piece of writing intended to persuade readers that a future project is worth doing and that the writer has the ability and resources to complete the project successfully.

**pronoun** A word that takes the place of a noun and functions in the same ways that nouns do. Types of pronouns are *demonstrative, indefinite, intensive, interrogative, personal, reciprocal, reflexive,* and *relative.* The word (or words) a pronoun replaces is called its *antecedent.* (14c, Chapter 16)

**pronoun-antecedent agreement** The match in expressing number and person—and for personal pronouns, gender as well—required between a pronoun and its antecedent. (17o–17t)

**pronoun case** The way a pronoun changes form to reflect its use as the agent of action (*subjective case*), the thing being acted upon (*objective case*), or the thing showing ownership (*possessive case*). (16a–16k)

**pronoun reference** The relationship between a pronoun and its antecedent. (16l–16s)

**proofread** The act of reading a final draft to find and correct any spelling or mechanics mistakes, typing errors, or handwriting illegibility; the final step of the writing process. (2k)

**proper adjective** An adjective formed from a proper noun: *Victorian, American.* (30e)

**proper noun** A noun that names specific people, places, or things and is always capitalized: *Dave Matthews, Buick.* (14b, 30e, 51c)

**proposal of solution** A piece of writing intended to persuade readers that a particular problem is best solved by the solution explained in that writing.

**public writing** Writing intended for readers outside of academic and work settings. (Chapter 44)

**purpose** The goal or aim of a piece of writing: to express oneself, to provide information, to persuade, or to create a literary work. (1b)

**quotation** Repeating or reporting another person's words. *Direct quotation* repeats another's words exactly and encloses them in quotation marks. *Indirect quotation* reports another's words without quotation marks except around any words repeated exactly from the source. Both *direct* and *indirect quotation* require *documentation* of the *source* to avoid *plagiarism.* Also see *direct discourse, indirect discourse.* (Chapter 28, 35h)

**readers** Readers are the audiences for writing; readers process material they read on the literal, inferential, and evaluative levels. (4c)

**reading process** Critical reading that requires the reader to read for *literal meaning,* to draw *inferences,* and to *evaluate.* (4c)

**reasons** Statements or ideas presented in order to provide support for a claim.

**reciprocal pronoun** The pronouns *each other* and *one another* referring to individual parts of a plural antecedent: *We respect **each other**.* (14c)

**References** In many documentation styles, including APA, the title of a list of sources cited in a research paper or other written work. (33h, 33i, 34c, 35f)

**reflexive pronoun** A pronoun that ends in *-self* and that refers back to its antecedent: *They claim to support **themselves**.* (14c)

**regular verb** A verb that forms its past tense and past participle by adding *-ed* or *-d* to the simple form. Most English verbs are regular. (15b, 15d)

**relative adverb** An adverb that introduces an adjective clause: *The lot **where** I usually park my car was full.* (14g)

**relative clause** See *adjective clause.*

**relative pronoun** A pronoun, such as *who, which, that, whom,* or *whoever,* that introduces an adjective clause or sometimes a noun clause. (14c)

**RENNS Test** See *paragraph development.* (3f)

**research question** The controlling question that drives research. (33c)

**research writing** Also called *source-based writing,* a process in three steps: conducting research, understanding and evaluating the results of the research, and writing the research paper with accurate documentation. (Chapter 33)

**respond** In writing, to provide your reaction to a reading or idea, with reasons and explanations for your response.

**restrictive clause** See *restrictive element.*

**restrictive element** A word, phrase, or dependent clause that contains information that is essential for a sentence to deliver its message. Do not set off with commas. (24f)

**revising, revision** A part of the writing process in which writers evaluate their rough drafts and, based on their assessments, rewrite by adding, cutting, replacing, moving, and often totally recasting material. (2i)

**rhetoric** The area of discourse that focuses on the arrangement of ideas and choice of words as a reflection of both the writer's purpose and the writer's sense of audience. (Chapter 1)

**rhetorical strategies** In writing, various techniques for presenting ideas to deliver a writer's intended message with clarity and impact. Reflecting typical patterns of human thought, rhetorical strategies include arrangements such as chronological and climactic order; stylistic techniques such as parallelism and planned repetition; and patterns for organizing and developing writing such as description and definition. (3i)

**Rogerian argument** An argument technique adapted from the principles of communication developed by the psychologist Carl Rogers. (5j)

**role** The position the writer is emphasizing for a given task; for example, student, client, taxpayer, parent, supervisor, helper, critic, or so on.

**run-on sentence** The error of running independent clauses into each other without the required punctuation that marks them as complete units; also called a *fused sentence* or *run-together sentence*. (Chapter 20)

**sans serif** Font types that do not have little "feet" or finishing lines at the top and bottom of each letter. (45c)

**search engine** An Internet-specific software program that can look through all files at Internet sites. (34l)

**secondary source** A source that reports, analyzes, discusses, reviews, or otherwise deals with the work of someone else, as opposed to a primary source, which is someone's original work or firsthand report. A reliable secondary source should be the work of a person with appropriate credentials, should appear in a respected publication or other medium, should be current, and should be well reasoned. (34a, 34i)

**second person** See *person.*

**sentence** See *sentence types.*

**sentence fragment** A portion of a sentence that is punctuated as though it were a complete sentence. (Chapter 19)

**sentence outline** Type of outline in which each element is a sentence. (2f)

**sentence types** A grammatical classification of sentences by the kinds of clauses they contain. A *simple sentence* consists of one independent clause. A *complex sentence* contains one independent clause and one or more dependent clauses. A *compound-complex sentence* contains at least two independent clauses and one or more dependent clauses. A *compound* or *coordinate sentence* contains two or more independent clauses joined by a coordinating conjunction. Sentences are also classified by their grammatical function; see *declarative sentence, exclamatory sentence, imperative sentence, interrogative sentence.* (14k, 14q, 9f)

**sentence variety** Writing sentences of various lengths and structures; see *coordinate sentence, cumulative sentence, periodic sentence, sentence types.* (9a)

**serif** Font types that are characterized by little "feet" or finishing lines at the top and bottom of each letter. (45c)

**server** A computer that is always online and available to Internet users. (46b)

**sexist language** Language that unnecessarily communicates that a person is male or female. For example, *fireman* is a sexist term that says only males fight fires, while *fire fighter* includes males and females. (17s, 12f)

**shaping** An early part of the writing process in which writers consider ways to organize their material. Along with planning, shaping is sometimes called *prewriting.*

**shift** Within a sentence, an unnecessary abrupt change in *person, number, subject, voice, tense, mood,* or *direct* or *indirect discourse.* (22a–22c)

**simile** A comparison, using *like* or *as,* of otherwise dissimilar things. (12c)

**simple form** The form of the verb that shows action, occurrence, or state of being taking place in the present. It is used in the singular for first and second person and in the plural for first, second, and third person. It is also the first principal part of a verb. The simple form is also known as the *dictionary form* or *base form.* (15b)

**simple predicate** See *predicate.*

**simple sentence** See *sentence types.*

**simple subject** See *subject.*

**simple tenses** The present, past, and future tenses, which divide time into present, past, and future. (15g, 15h)

**singular** See *number.*

**slang** A kind of colloquial language, it is coined words and new meanings for existing words, which quickly pass in and out of use; not appropriate for most academic writing. (12a)

**slanted language** Language that tries to manipulate the reader with distorted facts. (12g)

**source-based writing** See *research writing.*

**sources** Books, articles, print or Internet documents, other works, and persons providing credible information. In *research writing,* often called *outside sources.* (Chapters 34 and 35)

**spatial order** An arrangement of information according to location in space; an organizing strategy for sentences, paragraphs, and longer pieces of writing. (3h)

**specific noun** A noun understood to be exactly and specifically referred to; uses the definite article *the.* (51a)

**split infinitive** One or more words coming between the two words of an infinitive. (14b)

**squinting modifier** A modifier that is considered misplaced because it is not clear whether it describes the word that comes before it or the word that follows it. (21a)

**standard American English** See *edited American English.*

**standard word order** The most common order for words in English sentences: The subject comes before the predicate. Also see *inverted word order.* (9r, Chapter 52)

**stereotype** A kind of hasty generalization (a *logical fallacy*) in which a sweeping claim is made about all members of a particular ethnic, racial, religious, gender, age, or political group. (4i)

**subject** The word or group of words in a sentence that acts, is acted upon, or is described by the verb. A *simple subject* includes only the noun or pronoun. A *complete subject* includes the noun or pronoun and all its modifiers. A *compound subject* includes two or more nouns or pronouns and their modifiers. (14l)

**subject complement** A noun or adjective that follows a linking verb, renaming or describing the subject of the sentence; also called a *predicate nominative.* (14n)

**subjective case** The case of the noun or pronoun functioning as a subject. Also see *case, pronoun case.* (Chapter 16)

**subject tree** Shows you visually whether you have sufficient content, at varying levels of generality or specificity, to start a first draft of your writing. A subject tree also visually demonstrates whether you have a good balance of general ideas and specific details.

**subject-verb agreement** The required match between a subject and a verb in expressing number and person. (17b–17n)

**subjunctive mood** A verb mood that expresses wishes, recommendations, indirect requests, speculations, and conditional statements. *I wish you **were** here.* (15l, 15m)

**subordinate clause** See *dependent clause.*

**subordinating conjunction** A conjunction that introduces an adverb clause and expresses a relationship between the idea in it and the idea in the independent clause. (14i, 20c.4, Chapter 9)

**subordination** The use of grammatical structures to reflect the relative importance of ideas. A sentence with logically subordinated information expresses the most important information in the independent clause and less important information in dependent clauses or phrases. (Chapter 9)

**summary** A brief version of the main message or central point of a passage or other discourse; a critical thinking activity preceding synthesis. (35j)

**superlative form** The form of an adjective or adverb that expresses comparison among three or more things: *bluest, least blue; most easily, least easily.* (18e)

**syllogism** The structure of a deductive argument expressed in two *premises* and a *conclusion.* The first premise is a generalized assumption or statement of fact. The second premise is a different assumption or statement of fact based on evidence. The conclusion is also a specific instance that follows logically from the premises. (4h)

**synonym** A word that is very close in meaning to another word: *cold* and *icy.* (12d)

**synthesis** A component of critical thinking in which material that has been summarized, analyzed, and interpreted is connected to what is already known (one's prior knowledge) or to what has been learned from other authorities. (4b, 4f)

**tag question** An inverted verb-pronoun combination added to the end of a sentence, creating a question that asks the audience to agree with the assertion in the first part of the sentence. A tag question is set off from the rest of the sentence with a comma: *You know what a tag question is, **don't you?*** (24g)

**tense** The time at which the action of the verb occurs: the present, the past, or the future. Also see *perfect tenses, simple tenses.* (15g–15k)

**tense sequence** In sentences that have more than one clause, the accurate matching of verbs to reflect logical time relationships. (15k)

**thesis statement** A statement of an essay's central theme that makes clear the main idea, the writer's purpose, the focus of the topic, and perhaps the organizational pattern. (2d)

**third person** See *person.*

**title** The part of an essay that clarifies the overall point of the piece of writing. It can be *direct* or *indirect.* (2i)

**tone** The writer's attitude toward his or her material and reader, especially as reflected by word choice. (1d, Chapter 8)

**topic** The subject of discourse. (1b)

**topic sentence** The sentence that expresses the main idea of a paragraph. A topic sentence may be implied, not stated. (3e)

**Toulmin model** A model that defines the essential parts of an argument as the *claim* (or *main point*), the *support* (or *evidence*), and the *warrants* (or *assumptions behind the main point*). (5h)

**transition** The connection of one idea to another in discourse. Useful strategies within a paragraph for creating transitions include transitional expressions, parallelism, and the planned repetition of key terms and phrases. In a long piece of writing, a *transitional paragraph* is the bridge between discussion of two separate topics. Also see *critical response.* (3g.1, 3j)

**transitional expressions** Words and phrases that signal connections among ideas and create coherence. (3g.1)

**transitive verb** A verb that must be followed by a direct object. (15f )

**understatement** Figurative language in which the writer uses deliberate restraint for emphasis. (12c)

**unity** The clear and logical relationship between the main idea of a paragraph and the evidence supporting the main idea. (3d, 3e)

**unstated assumptions** Premises that are implied but not stated. (4h)

**usage** A customary way of using language. (Chapter 13)

**valid** Correctly and rationally derived; applied to a deductive argument whose conclusion follows logically from the premises. Validity applies to the structure of an argument, not its truth. (4i)

**variety** In writing, the presence of different types or lengths of sentences, a diverse vocabulary, kinds of examples or evidence, and so on.

**verb** Any word that shows action or occurrence or describes a state of being. Verbs change form to convey time (*tense*), attitude (*mood*), and role of the subject (*voice,* either *active* or *passive*). Verbs occur in the predicate of a clause and can be in verb phrases, which may consist of a main verb, auxiliary verbs, and modifiers. Verbs can be described as *transitive* or *intransitive,* depending on whether they take a direct object. Also see *voice.* (Chapter 15)

**verbal** A verb part functioning as a noun, adjective, or adverb. Verbals include *infinitives, present participles* (functioning as adjectives), *gerunds* (present participles functioning as nouns), and *past participles.* (15e, Chapter 54)

**verbal phrase** A group of words that contains a verbal (an infinitive, participle, or gerund) and its modifiers. (14o)

**verb phrase** A main verb, any auxiliary verbs, and any modifiers. (14o)

**verb tense** Verbs show tense (time) by changing form. English has six verb tenses. (15g)

**visual design** Refers to the appearance of a document (how it looks), as opposed to its content (what it says). (45a)

**voice** An attribute of verbs showing whether the subject acts (*active voice*) or is acted on (*passive voice*). Verbs are sometimes referred to as *strong* or *action verbs* or *weak verbs*. (15n–15p)

**warrants** One of three key terms in the *Toulmin model* for argument; refers to implied or inferred assumptions. They are based on *authority, substance,* and *motivation.* (5h)

**Web** See *World Wide Web.*

**webbing** See *mapping.*

**Web page** On the Internet, a file of information. Such a file is not related in length to a printed page, as it may be a paragraph or many screens long. (46c)

**Web site** One page or a home page that provides links to a collection of documents or files related to the home page. (46c)

**Web structure** The organization of the content and documents that site creators include in a Web project. (46d)

**white space** The part of a document that has neither text nor visuals. (45g)

**wiki** A Web site that allows multiple readers to change its content. (46f)

**wordiness** An attribute of writing that is full of empty words and phrases that do not contribute to meaning. The opposite of *conciseness.* (11a)

**World Wide Web** The *Web,* a user-friendly computer network allowing access to information in the form of text, graphics, and sound on the Internet. (Chapter 46)

**working bibliography** A preliminary list of useful sources in research writing. (33i)

**Works Cited** In MLA documentation style, the title of a list of all sources cited in a research paper or other written work. (36a)

**writer's block** The desire to start writing, but not doing so. (2h)

**writing process** Stages of writing in which a writer gathers and shapes ideas, organizes material, expresses those ideas in a rough draft, evaluates the draft and revises it, edits the writing for technical errors, and proofreads it for typographical accuracy and legibility. The stages often overlap; see *planning, shaping, drafting, revising, editing, proofreading.* (Chapters 1 and 2)

**writing situation** The beginning of the writing process for each writing assignment as defined by four elements: topic, purpose, audience, special requirements. (1b)

# CREDITS

■ ■ ■ ■ ■ ■ ■
NOTES

# NOTES

■ ■ ■ ■ ■ ■ ■ ■
# NOTES